Handbook of Adolescent Drug Use Prevention

Handbook of Adolescent Drug Use Prevention

Research, Intervention Strategies, and Practice

Edited by
Lawrence M. Scheier

American Psychological Association

Washington, DC

Published by
American Psychological Association
750 First Street, NE
Washington, DC 20002
www.apa.org

To order
APA Order Department
P.O. Box 92984
Washington, DC 20090-2984
Tel: (800) 374-2721; Direct: (202) 336-5510
Fax: (202) 336-5502; TDD/TTY: (202) 336-6123
Online: www.apa.org/pubs/books
E-mail: order@apa.org

In the U.K., Europe, Africa, and the Middle East, copies may be ordered from
American Psychological Association
3 Henrietta Street
Covent Garden, London
WC2E 8LU England

Typeset in Berkeley by Circle Graphics, Inc., Columbia, MD

Printer: Edwards Brothers, Inc., Lillington, NC
Cover Designer: Minker Design, Sarasota, FL

Library of Congress Cataloging-in-Publication Data

Handbook of adolescent drug use prevention : research, intervention strategies, and practice / edited by Lawrence M. Scheier. — First edition.
pages cm
Includes bibliographical references and index.
ISBN 978-1-4338-1899-8 — ISBN 1-4338-1899-X 1. Teenagers—Drug use—Prevention. I. Scheier, Lawrence M.
HV5824.Y68H364 2015
362.29′170835—dc23
2014032458

British Library Cataloguing-in-Publication Data
A CIP record is available from the British Library.

Printed in the United States of America
First Edition

http://dx.doi.org/10.1037/14550-000

This book is dedicated in loving memory to Howard B. Kaplan, a giant of a mentor, person, colleague, and friend. I have no qualms over the fact that Howard's training was in sociology whereas mine was in psychology. I say this because his theoretically rich ideas and the concepts he introduced to the field regarding deviance and the self were able to effectively span the two disciplines. I also credit his discerning and insightful writing, which inspired me to loosen my grip on the interior world and absorb the rich context of our lives. His ideas and theoretical rapture have helped to germinate numerous seedlings of thought in the minds of many scientists, myself included. We are all indebted to Howard's tireless efforts to study the roots of social deviance and his ability to walk a tightrope between generations of scientists and their social constructions.

To my two "conventional" and law-abiding daughters, Kyley and Shane: I owe you a great debt for cementing in my mind the value of parenting, and more importantly, sharing the love that transpires between father and daughter. To my now deceased parents, I am in deep awe of the monumental charge you took in raising, protecting, and supporting me over those troubled years called "adolescence." Regrettably, my initial tastes of financial and emotional freedom led me to believe I should never have left home for college. To the countless number of reviewers who plodded through my grant submissions, peer review papers, and books, I owe you a scholarly debt for helping me to refine my unbridled ideas. The gut-wrenching process has made us all better people, richer in thought and steeled against scurrilous disparagement. Finally, to my newly found gal friend from Texas, I thank you for shepherding my tongue through the capsicum world of hot peppers, and for providing fresh insight into the meaning of "love." Without your undying support, I would not have finished this opus.

De mal en bien, de bien en mieux. Pour l'achever, je deviens vieux.
[From bad to good, from good to better. To make this happen, I am getting old.]

—Jean de Laval, Seigneur de Châteaubriand
(Governor of Brittany 1531–1542)

Contents

Contributors

Eusebio M. Alvaro, MPH, PhD, Claremont Graduate University, Claremont, CA
Susan E. Barkan, PhD, Partners for Our Children, Seattle, WA
Sherry L. Barr, PsyD, Center for Supportive Schools, Princeton, NJ
Lauren Borduin, BA, Iowa State University, Ames
Gilbert J. Botvin, PhD, Weill Medical College of Cornell University, New York, NY
Caroline L. Boxmeyer, PhD, University of Alabama, Tuscaloosa
Catherine P. Bradshaw, PhD, MEd, Johns Hopkins Bloomberg School of Public Health, Baltimore, MD
Eric C. Brown, PhD, University of Washington, Seattle
William Bukoski, PhD, Independent Practice, College Park, MD
Wilson M. Compton, MD, MPE, National Institute on Drug Abuse, Bethesda, MD
William D. Crano, PhD, Claremont Graduate University, Claremont, CA
Aria D. Crump, ScD, National Institute on Drug Abuse, Bethesda, MD
James H. Derzon, PhD, Battelle Health & Analytics, Arlington, VA
Thomas J. Dishion, PhD, Arizona State University, Tempe
Joseph A. Durlak, PhD, Loyola University, Chicago, IL
J. Mark Eddy, PhD, Partners for Our Children, Seattle, WA
Abigail A. Fagan, PhD, University of Florida, Gainesville
Brian P. Flaherty, PhD, University of Washington, Seattle
Charles B. Fleming, MA, University of Washington, Seattle
Frederick X. Gibbons, PhD, University of Connecticut, Storrs
Kenneth W. Griffin, PhD, MPH, Weill Medical College of Cornell University, New York, NY
Joel W. Grube, PhD, Pacific Institute for Research and Evaluation, Oakland, CA
Kevin P. Haggerty, MSW, PhD, University of Washington, Seattle
William B. Hansen, PhD, Tanglewood Research, Greensboro, NC
Nancy Grant Harrington, PhD, University of Kentucky, Lexington
J. David Hawkins, PhD, University of Washington, Seattle
Donald W. Helme, PhD, University of Kentucky, Lexington
Viviana E. Horigian, MD, University of Miami Miller School of Medicine, Miami, FL
Jennifer K. Ibrahim, PhD, MPH, Temple University, Philadelphia, PA
Valerie L. Johnson, PhD, Rutgers, The State University of New Jersey, Piscataway
Kathryn Kavanagh, PhD, Consultant, Portland, OR

Yasemin Kisbu-Sakarya, PhD, Northwestern University, Evanston, IL
Lindsay Lanham, MSW, Office of Program Research, Olympia, WA
John E. Lochman, PhD, ABPP, University of Alabama, Tuscaloosa
Sarah D. Lynne-Landsman, PhD, University of Florida, Gainesville
David P. MacKinnon, PhD, Arizona State University, Tempe
Patrick S. Malone, PhD, University of South Carolina, Columbia
W. Alex Mason, PhD, National Research Institute for Child and Family Studies, Boys Town, NE
Seth M. Noar, PhD, University of North Carolina at Chapel Hill
Patrick M. O'Malley, PhD, University of Michigan, Ann Arbor
Holly P. O'Rourke, MA, Arizona State University, Tempe
Robert J. Pandina, PhD, Rutgers, The State University of New Jersey, Piscataway
Elise T. Pas, PhD, NCSP, Johns Hopkins Bloomberg School of Public Health, Baltimore, MD
Megan E. Patrick, PhD, University of Michigan, Ann Arbor
Harold I. Perl, PhD, National Institute on Drug Abuse, Bethesda, MD
Cameron E. Powe, MA, University of Alabama, Tuscaloosa
Nicole P. Powell, PhD, MPH, University of Alabama, Tuscaloosa
Ronald J. Prinz, PhD, University of South Carolina, Columbia
Cleve Redmond, PhD, Iowa State University, Ames
Eve E. Reider, PhD, National Institute on Drug Abuse, Bethesda, MD
Elizabeth B. Robertson, PhD, Retired, Washington Grove, MD
Robert F. Saltz, PhD, Pacific Institute for Research and Evaluations, Oakland, CA
Lisa Schainker, PhD, Iowa State University, Ames
Lawrence M. Scheier, PhD, University of Pennsylvania, Philadelphia, PA, and Research Facilitation Laboratory, Army Analytics Group, Office of the Deputy Under Secretary of the Army, Monterey, CA
Jason T. Siegel, PhD, Claremont Graduate University, Claremont, CA
Jeffrey S. Simons, PhD, University of South Dakota, Vermillion
Belinda E. Sims, PhD, National Institute on Drug Abuse, Bethesda, MD
Zili Sloboda, ScD, Applied Prevention Science, Inc., Ontario, OH
Richard Spoth, PhD, Iowa State University, Ames
Elizabeth A. Stormshak, PhD, University of Oregon, Eugene
Steven Y. Sussman, PhD, FAAHB, FAPA, University of Southern California, Los Angeles
José Szapocznik, PhD, University of Miami Miller School of Medicine, Miami, FL
Melissa K. Tibbits, PhD, University of Nebraska Medical Center, Omaha
Andrew J. Treno, PhD, Pacific Institute for Research and Evaluation, Oakland, CA
Marie-Hélène Véronneau, PhD, Université du Québec à Montréal, Canada
Alexander C. Wagenaar, PhD, University of Florida, Gainesville
Thomas A. Wills, PhD, University of Hawaii Cancer Center, Honolulu
Darren T. Woodlief, MA, University of South Carolina, Columbia

Preface

SHADES OF *WISDOM*

Yiddish is an interesting conglomeration of several languages, including Romanian, German, Polish, and Dutch. The language has an incredible history paralleling the Diaspora movement of Jews throughout Europe from 1700 onward. Yiddish is considered a very rich and effusive language marked by incredible intensity in pitch and tone. Even non-Yiddish speakers are familiar with the oft-used phrase *oy vey* ("Oh, no! This isn't happening to me") and the term *kvetch*, used to refer to a constant vocal complainer. These are only two of the many linguistic examples that have found their way into English conversations. One striking point to make about Yiddish is its versatility. In other words, it has many phrases that can be used in different situations but veritably convey the same meaning.

The term *der seykhel* (pronounced "say-khull") is a prime example of this versatility because it can be used to communicate a certain meaning in several ways. The term *der seykhel* is defined as "reason, sense, and intellect" (Galvin & Tamarkin, 1986, p. 246). One can use this Yiddish phrase to say "*Der seykhel kumt nokh di yorn*," or "Wisdom comes with the years." Technically, *wisdom* (*hokhmah* in Hebrew) is meant to convey the richness of thought that comes from experience. For instance, one can say "*Der seykhel iz a krikher*" or "Wisdom moves at a snail's pace," which can literally be stated as "Understanding (or good sense) is a creeper." In a bit, two things will be very clear to readers: First, that wisdom or reason is the backbone of this handbook and, second, that although the accumulation of wisdom moves at a snail's pace, prevention science has made great strides in the past few decades.

THE UNTOLD STORY

Despite the urgency to find a voice for drug prevention, there are reasons why wisdom moves at a snail's pace. Emery Cowen, one of the more influential minds in the field of prevention science, once suggested that most scientists make headway in their respective fields using cautious, almost guarded advances that take the form of baby steps (Cowen, 1977). This slow pace of progress arises because first and foremost scientists need time for their education to gain traction. Gaining such a foothold is most likely reflected through the arduous process of peer review, published scholarship, and procuring funded grants. At the same time, scientists should also give pause to reflect on the fact that their backgrounds and training are quite different, representing a composite of several academic and professional disciplines. Blending these academic disciplines into a cohesive whole is part of the synthesis of knowledge making up wisdom (Kitchener & Benner, 1990). Weaving a tapestry that incorporates this diversity takes considerable time, as does finding ways to secure the integration of thought and practice.

The somewhat colorful metaphor about knowledge moving at a snail's pace is really quite relevant to prevention science. For one thing, an accumulation of evidence suggests that despite laudatory scientific efforts, many schools across the United States still fail to implement evidence-based drug use prevention programs (Ringwalt et al., 2011). This leads to a different discussion involving how to address the apparent gap in the public's awareness of what prevention scientists do. For one thing, we should probably ask whether our accumulated wisdom can help shape public discourse regarding helping adolescents at risk (Resnick et al., 1997). There is also concern regarding whether we are finding appropriate outlets that can incorporate our scientific findings (Fielding et al., 2002) and, furthermore, whether we can ensure that our arduous efforts shape social and public policy (e.g., Hallfors, Pankratz, & Hartman, 2007; Pentz, 2000). Here, wisdom is formulated more as balance, reflecting the fit of a solution to its context (Sternberg, 1998).

Notwithstanding the laudable efforts of prevention science, we should also ask whether our wisdom has gained sufficient traction to make a difference in the lives of youths. For one thing, it is not enough that congressional acts mandate the use of evidence-based programs (No Child Left Behind Act of 2001). In an era of increasingly dwindling fiscal resources and demands for accountability, economists will prod us, asking whether there is any concrete monetary gain to what we do (Cohen & Piquero, 2009). Such fiscal prudence demands that we satisfy taxpayers by yielding a reasonable return on investment (Griffith & Scheier, 2013). We can probably address these legitimate concerns by pointing to favorable downturns in drug prevalence rates among youths (e.g., Johnston, O'Malley, Bachman, Schulenberg, & Miech, 2014). However, this notable decline in consumption (and incidence of new users) may be no more than a statistical blip on the radar screen with scant evidence suggesting a durable historical effect.

THE UNWAVERING SPEED OF PROGRESS

The organization of this handbook, with its emphasis on prevention of drug use, also suggests the need to recognize that the work we do is not by any stretch of the imagination "simple." In fact, the ideas herein reflect the complex nature of the scholarly pursuits that constitute drug prevention research (e.g., Lich, Ginexi, Osgood, & Mabry, 2013). The snail's pace referenced earlier is captured by the undaunted history of drug prevention (Sloboda, Cottler, Hawkins, & Pentz, 2009)—a lengthy history that has involved a tight-knit group of scientists from many academic disciplines. In just 3 decades, the field has transcended its roots in ethnographic studies of street addicts (e.g., Goode, 1974; Johnson, 1973) and now includes large-scale drug surveillance and monitoring efforts (Johnston et al., 2014). Combing through this trove of epidemiological data capturing trends in consumption, risk, and protection for U.S. youths provides a foundation to rationally guide prevention. The handbook also pays considerable homage to the plethora of information obtained from well-designed randomized trials testing interventions that have strong ties to psychosocial theory.

The design of prevention programs, the application of novel statistical methods to evaluate their efficacy, and the recent advances in implementation science are by themselves only several of the many indicators of the field's incipient growth. There are many other notable gains in the field that we should treasure. Among several recent milestones are that we have shepherded our own professional society (http://www.preventionresearch.org) and created an interdisciplinary forum for scholarship in the peer-reviewed journal *Prevention Science* (Botvin, 2000). For a while, there was a legislative mandate to influence public consciousness using social marketing and health persuasion strategies to mount a national youth anti-drug media campaign. The federal government has sponsored the development of registries intended to provide consumers with technical information about model drug prevention programs (http://www.nrepp.samhsa.gov). We should also not discount the wide readership of our work in other professional outlets that more readily court us now. All of this hard work provides a cause célèbre based on important discoveries and advances that provide a richer understanding of behavior change.

Prevention science can also lay claim to new intellectual horizons because the field is more actively blending techniques from seemingly remote disciplines. These cross-disciplinary efforts include engineering (e.g., Collins et al., 2011), computer simulation (e.g., Verduin, LaRowe, Myrick, Cannon-Bowers, & Bowers, 2013), genetics (e.g., Beach, Brody, Lei, & Philibert, 2010), and neural sciences (e.g., Bava & Tapert, 2010; Giedd, 2004). More than just tweaking our programs or repackaging our ideas, we are harnessing new ideas and concepts at many different levels to promote an important prevention agenda for decades to come. To put things succinctly, despite the earlier analogy likening the field's progress to a snail's pace, one could alternatively pose that there are real markers of burgeoning intellectual growth and, on balance, greater wisdom. Indeed, the progress within our own rank and file has allowed many investigators the luxury of seeing their own work achieve the much-desired goals of translational research (Pentz, 2010; Rohrbach, Grana, Sussman, & Valente, 2006; Sakuma, Riggs, & Pentz, 2012). All of this incipient growth comes from a field that was at one point described as being notoriously slow in making the transition from efficacy to effectiveness (e.g., Glasgow, Lichtenstein, & Marcus, 2003).

SPLITTING HAIRS

We should also be cognizant that despite clear evidence of well-managed growth in the field, some scientific concerns linger. One of more salient ones revolves around the trenchant problem of analyzing effects associated with complex, multimodal programs (e.g., Hill & Owens, 2013; Stigler, Perry, Komro, Cudeck, & Williams, 2006). Analysis of multicomponent programs can be structured to tease apart the different effects only if the components are delivered in some time-ordered fashion, with appropriately timed pre- and posttest assessments (including adherence measures). Program evaluations can also be supported with stringent design features that forcibly distinguish the delivery of program content from its effect on behavior (i.e., a crossover or Latin squares design). The latter approach represents a better way of distinguishing cumulative exposure effects on youth behavior, in which one component augments or facilitates another (i.e., the combination of refusal skills and normative education is superior to either program modality alone). Unfortunately, this type of rigorous componential analysis applying comparative or dismantling strategies is rarely done in real-world settings (West & Aiken, 1997). This makes it hard to reach unambiguous conclusions about program effects, especially when youths are active participants in a complexly layered social milieu.

If there is some concern with broad-brush multimodal programs, it arises because in the interests of saving money, economists push for streamlining programs by using only those components that work (Chatterji, Caffray, Jones, Lillie-Blanton, & Werthamer, 2001; Miller

& Hendrie, 2008). Prevention experts, however, promote an agenda consisting of broad-brush programs containing multiple program modalities (Botvin, Baker, Dusenbury, Tortu, & Botvin, 1990; Pentz et al., 1989). One argument in favor of multicomponent programs is meta-analytic findings suggesting their apparent larger effect sizes compared with single-modality programs (e.g., Tobler & Stratton, 1997).[1] The underlying current dominating the field is the *strongest form notion*; in other words, the practical among us suggest that program developers use the best parts of a program regardless of how many modalities or intervention strategies this may entail. Those adhering to the strict principles of evaluation science have suggested there is a need to pare programs down to the bare essentials (active ingredients) and eliminate any components, dormant or otherwise, that do not produce any bang for the buck.

Fractional factorial designs represent one optimal strategy to tease apart the independent contributions of different components, but because of their intensive and costly nature they are rarely applied (e.g., Chakraborty, Collins, Strecher, & Murphy, 2009). Consider that with four components (e.g., social skills, generic life skills, normative education, and information about the consequences of drug use), a full fractional design would require $2^4 = 16$ cells (with no interactions specified among the factorial effects) to dissect program efficacy. These stringent tests may be more suitable for experiments that involve web-based delivery of interventions in which mixing and matching are not so onerous or demanding (a researcher can alter message content, presentation or delivery mode, dose, and other facets of persuasive communication at little cost). School-based programs require much larger samples, greater attention to program fidelity, and costly staff or physical resources to implement. Also, factorial designs can backfire when components do not work synergistically but cancel each other out (this happens with social skills training and normative education). Hopefully, with our modest arsenal of analytic tools, we should be able to keep pace with advances in intervention theory and solve these structural problems proficiently.

RANDOMIZATION AS THE GOLD STANDARD

Despite the rigorous tools in our repertoire of experimental methods, using randomized experiments as a form of controlling threats to internal validity is not a surefire solution (Derzon, 2014). What randomization does achieve is to take any possible confounders that would potentially disrupt the pathway from treatment to outcome and to displace these "aliasing" effects equally between experimental conditions (the correlation between treatment variables and uncontrolled exogenous variables is forced to be zero). Following this assignment scheme, the treatment and control groups have in theory been equated with regard to any systematic influences that might bias treatment effects (Cook & Campbell, 1979, referred to this state as *probabilistic equivalence*). The resulting equivalent displacement of initial selection differences through randomization supports causal inferences about program effects because the two experimental groups differ only with regard to whether they received the program and not other observed covariates or unspecified measures (which is considered the ideal comparison).

[1] For the purpose of this argument, I use *multimodal, multicomponent, multifaceted*, and *multilevel* interchangeably. *Multicomponent* can refer to the various behavioral intervention strategies, the way the program is implemented, and the different delivery methods. *Multilevel* usually refers to the involvement of different social fields for intervention focus, usually involving school, community, and other instrumental agencies that can deliver prevention services. Some have used the distinction between individual-level demand and supply or environmental strategies to distinguish between different components or levels.

Consider, however, that we do not randomize youths on the basis of mediators (i.e., putative risk factors that are the targets of intervention); rather, randomization usually occurs on the basis of prior membership in an intact group, such as a school or classroom. Consider also that youths present to a study with many different preexisting skill sets, they hold many different beliefs about drug use, they engage regularly in dramatically different social networks, and their parents use radically different parenting styles. When push comes to shove, even when equipped with strong intervention theory, we have limited or no control over these relevant confounding issues as they influence program outcomes. Randomization does not reinforce treatment construct validity (McCaul & Glasgow, 1985) or elaborate the precise generative mechanisms that contribute to behavior change. Nor does randomization really address Selection × Maturation effects (risk status changing with age). As a result, despite our best methodological efforts to tease apart the efficacy of different intervention modalities, the young, impressionable minds that are the focus of psychoeducational programs often evade dissection.[2]

BRIDGING GAPS

The accumulation of wisdom has in many ways taught us to sharpen our epidemiological and etiologic tools and use them to obtain greater insight into prevention (Kellam, Koretz, & Moscicki, 1999). Preparation for a career in drug prevention requires that we know the causes of drug use, its natural course, and its consequences. We should also have some faint notion of what prevention does to youths (and families) in terms of their future experiences and whether interventions canalize or track youths into desired trajectories supporting positive youth adaptation. This emphasis reflects my own imprimatur and seeks ways to bridge disciplines as a necessary function of science and social dialogue. This handbook does little to evade this premise, encouraging several authors to recollect what has helped shape modern-day prevention. If the handbook is to be useful in this regard, it should be a constant reminder of the marriage or close alliance between etiology and prevention, a point that more than one author in this handbook has articulated at some point in his or her career (e.g., Hansen et al., 2010; Hawkins, Catalano, & Miller, 1992). The handbook should also reinforce that despite our claims, assertions, and accumulation of findings, pragmatically we are still searching for the truth. Here we should acknowledge the lack of certainty in our work. For one thing, we do not have sufficient longitudinal investigations to determine

[2] There is some truth that a standard two-group randomized controlled trial does minimize certain threats to internal validity (Brown & Liao, 1999). Added precision arises from modeling statistical controls for pretest (or base-curve) levels of a hypothesized mediator specified in a longitudinal randomized controlled trial. Inclusion of appropriate controls and potential confounders will result in some certainty as to whether differences in rates of change for targeted risk factors (mediators) between treated and control subjects can be attributed to the experimental manipulation. Alternatively, in the absence of randomization on the mediator, latent class analysis can also be used to detect discrete, homogeneous subgroups on the basis of measured response profiles of the mediator to ascertain whether program effects are specious to nonrandomized subgroups (e.g., Lanza & Rhoades, 2013). The use of finite mixture models can be extended with longitudinal data to detect program effects on heterogeneity in behavioral growth trajectories (e.g., Liu, Hedeker, Segawa, & Flay, 2010). Nevertheless, the lack of randomization based on mediators does introduce some specification error in the form of variance heterogeneity to the model. The lack of precision arises because mediator variances are pooled for both treated and control youths (between- and within-class variance is modeled as a single term). This ignores both experimental assignment (between-class) and real (within-class) differences in how youths came into the study. These differences manifest in two ways with regard to participants' standing on the mediators: (a) differential susceptibility (motivation) to drug use and (b) differential responsiveness to the benefits of the program. Examples of the former can be summarily dealt with using stratification and matching procedures or finite mixture models that stratify on the basis of levels of mediators. Examples of the latter and, perhaps more problematic, cases involving program effects moderated by nonrandomized features of participants abound in prevention science. A doubly randomized design (Kirk, 1982) that stratifies subjects to classrooms on the basis of baseline levels of target risk mechanisms (i.e., poor social skills) and then randomly assigns classrooms to condition might provide greater model precision but is quite costly and logistically prohibitive.

whether prevention programs implemented at younger ages maintain durable, lasting effects, both on drug use and on other forms of deviance. Several chapters explore this issue, but practically speaking the data are very limited (for an exception, see Reider, Robertson, & Sims, 2014, who guest-edited a recent supplemental issue of *Prevention Science* reinforcing certain unanticipated domino effects of several drug prevention programs on health-risking sexual behaviors tied to sexually transmitted diseases, including HIV).

Along these same lines, we do not have a clear picture of what facilitates a developmental cascade (e.g., Masten et al., 2005) and whether drug use prevention fosters successful youthful adaptation in multiple areas of functioning valued by society. This could be as simple as examining whether drug prevention improves academic outcomes or social and emotional learning (e.g., Greenberg et al., 2003). We also lack a credible understanding of the many factors that predict uptake of community-wide prevention programs and which intervention strategies are truly the active ingredients in these large-scale, multicomponent efforts. As one of several points to highlight, we lack instrumental knowledge about the forces limiting the effect of media-based health persuasion campaigns (Magura, 2012) or why the Office of National Drug Control Policy's national media campaign produced specious rather than the desired broad-brush effects (Hornik, Jacobsohn, Orwin, Piesse, & Kalton, 2008; Scheier & Grenard, 2010).

These and other considerations should serve as harsh reminders that even with our own devout dedication to the field, and the rich promise of our empirical treasure chest, our work still remains in front of us, not behind us. Despite a proliferation of findings and faced with the largest federally sponsored prevention budget in recorded history, we are still, in a nutshell, searching for our own paradigm. Achieving this paradigm is a sign of maturity and indicates the intellectual cohesiveness of the field (Kuhn, 1970). When we speak of science at a general level, and even more specifically prevention science, it should be patently clear that the progressive accretion of knowledge with regard to intervention success (what works, for whom, and under what conditions) has taken considerable time. This slow unfolding of knowledge is a testament to what Kuhn (1970) termed *normal science*, owing to the lengthy process that substantiates both theory and reality. The function of this handbook, then, is to tell the story of normal science and how this body of work has shaped the collective episteme of drug prevention. It is a testament to the contributors' wisdom, which guides our thinking regarding the fundamental pragmatics of life (Baltes & Staudinger, 2000). By this, I mean that the core ingredients of the handbook represent the sagacity that drives our search for truth in science. Its proper use can ensure that youths live the good life, a life without experiencing the ravages of drugs, delinquency, depression, and eventual despair.

References

Baltes, P. B., & Staudinger, U. M. (2000). Wisdom: A metaheuristic (pragmatic) to orchestrate mind and virtue toward excellence. *American Psychologist, 55*, 122–136. doi:10.1037/0003-066X.55.1.122

Bava, S., & Tapert, S. F. (2010). Adolescent brain development and the risk for alcohol and other drug problems. *Neuropsychology Review, 20*, 398–413. doi:10.1007/s11065-010-9146-6

Beach, S. R. H., Brody, G. H., Lei, M.-K., & Philibert, R. A. (2010). Differential susceptibility to parenting among African American youths: Testing the DRD4 hypothesis. *Journal of Family Psychology, 24*, 513–521. doi:10.1037/a0020835

Botvin, G. J. (2000). Inaugural editorial. *Prevention Science, 1*, 1–2. doi:10.1023/A:1010091031329

Botvin, G. J., Baker, E., Dusenbury, L., Tortu, S., & Botvin, E. M. (1990). Preventing adolescent drug abuse through a multimodal cognitive–behavioral approach: Results of a 3-year study. *Journal of Consulting and Clinical Psychology, 58*, 437–446. doi:10.1037/0022-006X.58.4.437

Brown, C. H., & Liao, J. (1999). Principles for designing randomized preventive trials in mental health: An emerging developmental epidemiology paradigm. *American Journal of Community Psychology, 27*, 673–710. doi:10.1023/A:1022142021441

Chakraborty, B., Collins, L. M., Strecher, V. J., & Murphy, S. A. (2009). Developing multicomponent interventions using fractional factorial designs. *Statistics in Medicine, 28*, 2687–2708. doi:10.1002/sim.3643

Chatterji, P., Caffray, C. M., Jones, A. S., Lillie-Blanton, M., & Werthamer, L. (2001). Applying cost analysis methods to school-based prevention programs. *Prevention Science, 2*, 45–55. doi:10.1023/A:1010086928908

Cohen, M. A., & Piquero, A. R. (2009). New evidence on the monetary value of saving a high-risk youth. *Journal of Quantitative Criminology, 25*, 25–49. doi:10.1007/s10940-008-9057-3

Collins, L. M., Baker, T. B., Mermelstein, R. J., Piper, M. E., Jorenby, D. E., Smith, S. S., . . . Fiore, M. C. (2011). The multiphase optimization strategy for engineering effective tobacco use interventions. *Annals of Behavioral Medicine, 41*, 208–226. doi:10.1007/s12160-010-9253-x

Cook, T. D., & Campbell, D. T. (1979). *Quasi-experimentation: Design and analysis issues for field settings*. Boston, MA: Houghton Mifflin.

Cowen, E. L. (1977). Baby-steps toward primary prevention. *American Journal of Community Psychology, 5*, 1–22. doi:10.1007/BF00884781

Derzon, J. H. (2014). Differences-indifferences in approaches. In G. J. N. Bruinsma & D. L. Weisburd (Eds.), *Encyclopedia of criminology and criminal justice* (pp. 1054–1064). New York, NY: Springer Science+Business Media.

Fielding, J. E., Marks, J. S., Myers, B. W., Nolan, P. A., Rawson, R. D., & Toomey, K. E. (2002). How do we translate science into public health policy and law? *Journal of Law, Medicine & Ethics, 30*, 22–32.

Galvin, H., & Tamarkin, S. (1986). *The Yiddish dictionary sourcebook: A transliterated guide to the Yiddish language*. Hoboken, NJ: Ktav Press.

Giedd, J. N. (2004). Structural magnetic resonance imaging of the adolescent brain. In R. E. Dahl & L. P. Spear (Eds.), *Adolescent brain development: Vulnerabilities and opportunities* (pp. 77–85). New York: New York Academy of Sciences. doi:10.1196/annals.1308.009

Glasgow, R. E., Lichtenstein, E., & Marcus, A. C. (2003). Why don't we see more translation of health promotion research to practice? Rethinking the efficacy-to-effectiveness transition. *American Journal of Public Health, 93*, 1261–1267. doi:10.2105/AJPH.93.8.1261

Goode, E. (1974). Marijuana use and the progression to dangerous drugs. In L. L. Miller (Ed.), *Marijuana effects on human behavior* (pp. 303–338). New York, NY: Academic Press.

Greenberg, M. T., Weissberg, R. P., O'Brien, M. U., Zins, J. E., Fredericks, L., Resnik, H., & Elias, M. J. (2003). Enhancing school-based prevention and youth development through coordinated social, emotional, and academic learning. *American Psychologist, 58*, 466–474. doi:10.1037/0003-066X.58.6-7.466

Griffith, K. N., & Scheier, L. M. (2013). Did we get our money's worth? Bridging economic and behavioral measures of success in adolescent drug prevention. *International Journal of Environmental Research and Public Health, 10*, 5908–5935. doi:10.3390/ijerph10115908

Hallfors, D. D., Pankratz, M., & Hartman, S. (2007). Does federal policy support the use of scientific evidence in school-based prevention programs? *Prevention Science, 8*, 75–81. doi:10.1007/s11121-006-0058-x

Hansen, W. B., Derzon, J., Dusenbury, L., Bishop, D., Campbell, K., & Alford, A. (2010). Operating characteristics of prevention programs: Connections to drug etiology. In L. M. Scheier (Ed.), *Handbook of drug use etiology: Theory, methods, and empirical findings* (pp. 597–616). Washington, DC: American Psychological Association.

Hawkins, J. D., Catalano, R. F., & Miller, J. Y. (1992). Risk and protective factors for alcohol and other drug problems in adolescence and early adulthood: Implications for substance abuse prevention. *Psychological Bulletin, 112*, 64–105. doi:10.1037/0033-2909.112.1.64

Hill, L. G., & Owens, R. W. (2013). Component analysis of adherence in a family intervention. *Health Education, 113*, 264–280. doi:10.1108/09654281311329222

Hornik, R., Jacobsohn, L., Orwin, R., Piesse, A., & Kalton, G. (2008). Effects of the National Youth Anti-Drug Media Campaign on youths. *American Journal of Public Health, 98*, 2229–2236. doi:10.2105/AJPH.2007.125849

Johnson, B. D. (1973). *Marihuana users and drug subcultures.* New York, NY: Wiley.

Johnston, L. D., O'Malley, P. M., Bachman, J. G., Schulenberg, J. E., & Miech, R. A. (2014). *Monitoring the future national survey results on drug use, 1975–2013: Vol. I. Secondary school students.* Ann Arbor: University of Michigan.

Kellam, S. G., Koretz, D., & Moscicki, E. K. (1999). Core elements of developmental epidemiology based prevention research. *American Journal of Community Psychology, 27*, 463–482. doi:10.1023/A:1022129127298

Kirk, R. E. (1982). *Experimental design: Principles for the behavioral sciences* (2nd ed.). Montgomery, CA: Brooks/Cole.

Kitchener, K. S., & Benner, H. G. (1990). Wisdom and reflective judgment: Knowing in the face of uncertainty. In R. J. Sternberg (Ed.), *Wisdom: Its nature, origins, and development* (pp. 212–229). doi:10.1017/CBO9781139173704.011

Kuhn, T. S. (1970). *The structure of scientific revolutions* (3rd ed.). Chicago, IL: University of Chicago Press.

Lanza, S. T., & Rhoades, B. L. (2013). Latent class analysis: An alternative perspective on subgroup analysis in prevention and treatment. *Prevention Science, 14*, 157–168. doi:10.1007/s11121-011-0201-1

Lich, K. H., Ginexi, E. M., Osgood, N. D., & Mabry, P. L. (2013). A call to address complexity in prevention science research. *Prevention Science, 14*, 279–289. doi:10.1007/s11121-012-0285-2

Liu, L. C., Hedeker, D., Segawa, E., & Flay, B. R. (2010). Evaluation of longitudinal intervention effects: An example of latent growth mixture models for ordinal drug-use outcomes. *Journal of Drug Issues, 40*, 27–43. doi:10.1177/002204261004000103

Magura, S. (2012). Failure of intervention or failure of evaluation: A meta-evaluation of the National Youth Anti-Drug Media Campaign Evaluation. *Substance Use & Misuse, 47*, 1414–1420. doi:10.3109/10826084.2012.705706

Masten, A. S., Roisman, G. I., Long, J. D., Burt, K. B., Obradovic, J., Riley, J. R., . . . Tellegen, A. (2005). Developmental cascades: Linking academic achievement and externalizing and internalizing symptoms over 20 years. *Developmental Psychology, 41*, 733–746. doi:10.1037/0012-1649.41.5.733

McCaul, K. D., & Glasgow, R. E. (1985). Preventing adolescent smoking: What have we learned about treatment construct validity? *Health Psychology, 4*, 361–387. doi:10.1037/0278-6133.4.4.361

Miller, T., & Hendrie, D. (2008). *Substance abuse prevention dollars and cents: A cost-benefit analysis* (DHHS Pub. No. (SMA) 07–4298). Rockville, MD: Substance and Mental Health Services Administration.

No Child Left Behind Act of 2001, Pub. L. No. 107–110, 20 U.S.C. §§ 6301-8962.

Pentz, M. A. (2000). Institutionalizing community-based prevention through policy change. *Journal of Community Psychology, 28*, 257–270. doi:10.1002/(SICI)1520-6629(200005)28:3<257::AID-JCOP3>3.0.CO;2-L

Pentz, M. A. (2010). Translating research into practice and practice into research for drug use prevention. In L. M. Scheier (Ed.), *Handbook of drug use etiology: Theory, methods, and empirical findings* (pp. 581–596). Washington, DC: American Psychological Association.

Pentz, M. A., Dwyer, J. H., MacKinnon, D. P., Flay, B. R., Hansen, W. B., Wang, E. Y. I., & Anderson Johnson, C. (1989). A multicommunity trial for primary prevention of adolescent drug abuse. *JAMA, 261*, 3259–3266. doi:10.1001/jama.1989.03420220073030

Reider, E. E., Robertson, E. R., & Sims, B. E. (Eds.). (2014). Does early intervention prevention health-risking sexual behaviors related to HIV/AIDS? *Prevention Science, 15*, 1–5. doi:10.1007/s11121-013-0455-x

Resnick, M. D., Bearman, P. S., Blum, R. W., Bauman, K. E., Harris, K. M., Jones, J., . . . Udry, J. R. (1997). Protecting adolescents from harm: Findings from the National Longitudinal Study on Adolescent Health. *JAMA, 278*, 823–832. doi:10.1001/jama.1997.03550100049038

Ringwalt, C., Vincus, A., Hanley, S., Ennett, S., Bowling, J., & Haws, S. (2011). The prevalence of evidence-based drug use prevention curricula in U.S. middle schools in 2008. *Prevention Science, 12*, 63–69. doi:10.1007/s11121-010-0184-3

Rohrbach, L. A., Grana, R., Sussman, S., & Valente, T. W. (2006). Type II translation: Transporting prevention interventions from research to real-world settings. *Evaluation & the Health Professions, 29*, 302–333. doi:10.1177/0163278706290408

Sakuma, K. L., Riggs, N. R., & Pentz, M. A. (2012). Translating evidence based violence and drug use prevention to obesity prevention: Development and construction of the Pathways program. *Health Education Research, 27*, 343–358. doi:10.1093/her/cyr095

Scheier, L. M., & Grenard, J. L. (2010). Influence of a nationwide social marketing campaign on adolescent drug use. *Journal of Health Communication, 15*, 240–271. doi:10.1080/10810731003686580

Sloboda, Z., Cottler, L. B., Hawkins, J. D., & Pentz, M. A. (2009). Reflections on 40 years of drug abuse prevention research. *Journal of Drug Issues, 39*, 179–195. doi:10.1177/002204260903900114

Sternberg, R. J. (1998). A balance theory of wisdom. *Review of General Psychology, 2*, 347–365. doi:10.1037/1089-2680.2.4.347

Stigler, M. H., Perry, C. L., Komro, K. A., Cudeck, R., & Williams, C. L. (2006). Teasing apart a multiple component approach to adolescent alcohol prevention: What worked in Project Northland? *Prevention Science, 7*, 269–280. doi:10.1007/s11121-006-0040-7

Tobler, N. S., & Stratton, H. H. (1997). Effectiveness of school-based drug prevention programs: A meta-analysis of the research. *Journal of Primary Prevention, 18*, 71–128. doi:10.1023/A:1024630205999

Verduin, M. L., LaRowe, S. D., Myrick, H., Cannon-Bowers, J., & Bowers, C. (2013). Computer simulation games as an adjunct for treatment in male veterans with alcohol use disorder. *Journal of Substance Abuse Treatment, 44*, 316–322. doi:10.1016/j.jsat.2012.08.006

West, S. G., & Aiken, L. S. (1997). Toward understanding individual effects in multicomponent prevention programs: Design and analysis strategies. In K. J. Bryant, M. Windle, & S. G. West (Eds.), *The science of prevention: Methodological advances from alcohol and substance abuse research* (pp. 167–209). doi:10.1037/10222-006

Acknowledgments

Gilbert J. Botvin, PhD, author of the Life Skills Training Program, taught me everything I ever learned about prevention. A very long time ago, I attended a professional conference on drug prevention and Gil was the keynote speaker. Following the opening remarks by another luminary in the field, Gil strutted to the stage and grabbed the edges of the lectern with a strong but comforting grip. He looked around at the audience with a relaxed smile, leaned over to the microphone, and stated quite simply, "Prevention works." Gil went on to describe prevention as a system, an approach to life that applies psychological principles to advance health promotion through behavior change. In his talk, he underscored several important markers of the field's success owing to greater program diffusion, national data banks providing critical information on evidence-based programs, a new scholarly prevention science journal, and the increasing amount of attention paid to prevention in all walks of life. He suggested that when prevention works, it saves lives, and he drove this point home quite richly and colorfully by showing how many lives are saved through the implementation of school-based drug abuse prevention. Gil eloquently suggested that we should all think about the ramifications of not implementing drug prevention programs and the incredible risk of morbidity or even mortality that occurs when some unsuspecting youth begins smoking cigarettes or drinking alcohol at a tender young age. Gil reinforced the economic benefits of prevention obtained through what economists term *cost avoidance*, and made it patently clear that preventing one teenager from smoking his or her first cigarette or drinking alcohol before the Friday night football game conveys tremendous value to our society. It was on that day that I became heavily vested in becoming a prevention scientist, and I guess I owe this important and valuable career decision to Gil.

Handbook of

Adolescent Drug Use Prevention

Introduction: Telling A Compelling Story About Drug Prevention

Joseph A. Durlak

Drug abuse is a serious issue in society and is associated with numerous psychological, social, and economic problems. This handbook is about drug prevention, a scientific field that attempts to delay the onset of drug use among those who have not yet begun experimenting with drugs and to prevent the misuse or abuse of drugs among those who have already starting using them to some degree. Depending on the intervention, the target might include underage drinking or tobacco use; use of one or more of the so-called illicit drugs, such as cocaine, heroin, and nonmedical marijuana; or the inappropriate use of prescription drugs. Most of the research presented in this handbook focuses on interventions for school-age youths because evidence has shown that even modest reductions in drug use or misuse among this population can have important long-term public health benefits.

Two basic questions must be answered satisfactorily to advance the field of drug prevention most effectively. The first question involves the quality of the current evidence. Do we have credible evidence that it is possible to prevent drug use? If, and only if, we can answer this first question affirmatively is the second question relevant: How can we scale up interventions to reach as many individuals as possible?

The clear and consistent message of this handbook is an affirmative answer to the first question: Yes, there is good evidence that we can prevent drug use. Moreover, many evidence-based drug prevention approaches can at the same time also prevent other serious personal and social problems. In other words, evidence-based drug prevention is often a win–win situation, sometimes even a triple win in terms of the positive benefits that accrue to its participants and to society in general. The answer to the second question is less emphatic but nevertheless positive in tone: Yes, we are learning what it takes to disseminate and implement evidence-based drug prevention on a wider scale to reach more people. A brief discussion of many of the issues related to these two questions follows.

CAN WE PREVENT DRUG USE?

Convincing evidence that drug use can be prevented involves demonstrating through careful and rigorous experimental evaluations that (a) it is possible to prevent drug use in the short term, (b) intervention effects last for some time, (c) program effects are meaningful in practical or clinical terms as opposed to merely being statistically significant, (d) programs achieve positive outcomes on other important indices of adjustment in addition to drug use, and (e) interventions are cost effective. Although it is not essential that programs achieve positive effects on multiple adjustment outcomes, doing so increases the inherent value of interventions and supports a widely applied theory in prevention that the judicious targeting of developmentally salient risk and protective factors should lead to several positive effects over the short and long term.

http://dx.doi.org/10.1037/14550-001
Handbook of Adolescent Drug Use Prevention: Research, Intervention Strategies, and Practice, L. M. Scheier (Editor)

Empirical data on each of these issues are discussed in a scholarly manner throughout this handbook. For example, many well-controlled research studies have shown that reductions in the level of drug use can be substantial and of public health importance after intervention. More than a few chapters in the handbook provide substantial evidence of this significant accomplishment. In addition, evidence is increasing that effects can last for several years, that many other problems in addition to drug use can also be reduced, and that the financial benefits associated with drug prevention considerably outweigh its costs. Furthermore, the outcomes for several different types of evidence-based programs have been successfully replicated—one of the hallmarks of credible science—and these replications have been achieved not only by the initial program developers but also by independent groups working in different settings, with different ethnic populations, and sometimes in different countries and cultures. In sum, readers should be impressed with the progress made in drug prevention research over the past 25 years or so and with its current sophistication and scientific credibility.

Surveying the evidence-based programs reviewed in this volume, one sees that they share at least four common characteristics. They are (a) theory based and often draw on theories from multiple disciplines or subdisciplines to develop the specific components of intervention; (b) carefully evaluated using strong research designs, valid and reliable assessment tools, and appropriate data-analytic strategies; (c) well implemented to provide assurance that the main ingredients of the intervention are delivered to the intended audience; and, finally, (d) capable of being modified yet still remain effective in different circumstances. The latter two characteristics are related to the second broad question, which I discuss next.

CAN WE SCALE UP INTERVENTIONS TO REACH AS MANY AS POSSIBLE?

The creation of evidence-based programs matters because such interventions demonstrate a worthwhile approach to dealing with an important public health concern such as drug use. But what really matters from a public health perspective is whether these programs can be replicated or adapted for use in multiple communities and remain effective during these new trials, so that more in the population can benefit. For example, Jonas Salk's polio vaccine was an important scientific discovery in its own right, but it assumed critical public health importance by being delivered to millions of individuals throughout the world. Because one size does not fit all, another important issue is whether different types of evidence-based programs have been developed so that those who want to mount drug prevention programs can chose among alternatives. This handbook clearly indicates that effective school-, family-, and community-based programs are available.

This handbook contains some impressive examples of how drug prevention can be effectively disseminated and implemented into new settings. For example, see the details on Life Skills Training (Chapter 10), the PROSPER model (Chapter 15), the Communities That Care approach (Chapter 19), and the Positive Parenting Program (Triple P; Chapter 13), to name only a few. Three prime features of these and several other disseminated interventions are (a) the programs can be delivered by several different types of individuals (e.g., teachers, counselors, mental health staff, health care workers, family advocates, extension agents, or various individuals involved in community coalitions); (b) the programs can be modified to suit different settings, needs, and populations and still be effective; and (c) the program developers have used successful training and consultation methods so that others with less hands-on research and evaluation experience can implement the new program with quality.

All three of these features fit nicely with findings from the multidisciplinary field of implementation science, which has expanded exponentially in breadth and depth within the past 10 to 15 years. *Implementation* has been defined as "efforts designed to get evidence-based programs or practices of known dimensions into use via effective change strategies" (Damschroder & Hagedorn, 2011, p. 195). This definition recognizes that implementation is a critical factor influencing program outcomes and that quality implementation does not occur spontaneously, but through the use of systematic methods to increase the odds that new staff will implement the program as well as possible. As a result, multiple disciplines have contributed information on how to define and measure different aspects of implementation (e.g., fidelity, adaptation, quality of delivery); on the many factors that affect implementation, one of which is delivering sound training and ongoing consultation to new program users; and on articulating the steps and actions needed to achieve quality implementation (Durlak & DuPre, 2008; Dusenbury, Brannigan, Hansen, Walsh, & Falco, 2005; Meyers, Durlak, & Wandersman, 2012)

More research and practice needs to concentrate on effective dissemination and implementation efforts, and two additional issues currently limit the widespread use of evidence-based programs: (a) In many cases, we do not know what the active ingredients of successful programs are and (b) we need to better integrate policy, research, and practice so that these components work together to foster the adoption and careful conduct of evidence-based programs.

The contents of several chapters in this handbook indicate that some program developers have sought to examine the active ingredients (sometimes called *core components*) of their intervention to determine what is responsible for their outcomes, yet this work is not definitive and needs to continue. Identifying a program's active ingredients would increase the possibility of wider adoption and use because current programs would likely become more efficient (i.e., probably briefer and simpler), which would make them more attractive to other potential users and at the same time reduce the time, effort, and cost it takes to train new staff in their implementation.

Recognizing that the large-scale use of evidence-based programs is the joint responsibility of multiple stakeholders involved with policy, funding, administration, research, and practice is also important. Members of these groups must work collaboratively. For example, both policymakers and funders must allow sufficient time and provide sufficient resources for wise program adoption and effective program implementation; researchers need to specify and test the presumed active ingredients of their programs and develop and evaluate training and consultation services for the frontline providers of new programs; administrators must provide the necessary organizational leadership; and frontline providers need to provide input to the other groups regarding what is effective and practical in their settings. In general, what would be extremely helpful is an ongoing infrastructure that can coordinate the efforts of these multiple stakeholders most efficiently. Steps in this direction are just beginning in the United States and elsewhere in the form of governmental subagencies whose prime purpose is to encourage the systematic adoption and implementation of evidence-based programs (Meyers et al., 2012). For example, an implementation training institute has been established in the United States (Proctor et al., 2013). We must support things of value and recognize that if prevention work of any kind is to reach more of the population who can benefit, we must devote more resources to the systematic adoption, implementation, and sustainability of successful interventions.

One additional issue mentioned by several contributors is the potential to use technology in the development and spread of drug prevention programs. In fact, I would predict that the next few years will provide multiple, creative examples of how several different types of technological strategies can advance the field of prevention (e.g., interactive Internet and computer programs, virtual reality simulations, mobile applications for smartphones). These types of technologies can have several uses, including training, mass marketing, and collecting real-time assessment data. There are challenges in evaluating technology-based interventions in terms of accurately monitoring participants' behaviors and dealing with the disparities that currently exist across populations in terms of availability and comfort with technology. For example, many teachers are probably much less familiar and at ease with certain technologies than their students. However, the learning challenges associated with the judicious application of technological advances can be overcome.

AN OVERVIEW OF THIS HANDBOOK

Critical information loses its impact unless it is well organized and presented to tell a compelling story. Novels have a beginning, then a middle portion, and then an end. Good science stories, however, have a past, present, and future because the work is never ending, always subject to critical reflection, refinement, and continual improvement. The editor of this handbook, Lawrence M. Scheier, has involved contributors who are clearly up to the task of telling a compelling scientific story about drug prevention. This handbook informs readers about the past, present, and future of drug prevention and is divided into nine major sections. Part I includes chapters devoted to definitions and terminology (Robertson et al., Chapter 1) and a historical overview of approaches to drug prevention (Bukoski, Chapter 2). In this same vein, the authors of other chapters on specific drug prevention programs also provide information on how their particular approaches have evolved over time. Part II discusses epidemiology (Patrick and O'Malley, Chapter 3) and which theories have been particularly useful in understanding drug use and mounting effective interventions (Scheier, Chapter 4, and Sloboda, Chapter 5).

With the chapters on history, definitions, epidemiology, and theory as a useful beginning, the next four sections focus on different types of intervention. Part III contains three chapters related to programs designed to prevent conduct disorders and other externalizing problems, and they explicate how intervention for these problems is pertinent to drug use and prevention. These chapters—Chapters 6, 7 and 8—are by Boxmeyer, Lochman, Powell, and Powe; Wills, Simons, and Gibbons; and Eddy, Barkan, and Lanham, respectively.

School-based programs, which have been the most common strategy for drug prevention, are discussed in Part IV. Four evidence-based programs are discussed: Project Towards No Drug Abuse in Chapter 9, by Sussman; Life Skills Training in Chapter 10, by Botvin and Griffin; All Stars in Chapter 11, by Hansen; and Peer Group Connection in Chapter 12, by Pandina, Johnson, and Barr. All four chapters provide slightly different angles on the role of prevention (both universal and selective) and use different program modalities to achieve the same target outcome, less drug use.

Part V discusses the value and success of family intervention to prevent drug use and includes information on why family intervention is pertinent and details on various effective programs. Prinz describes the Triple P approach in Chapter 13, Horigian and Szapocznik discuss brief strategic family therapy as an intervention to deal with adolescent behavior problems and drug use in Chapter 14, Spoth, Redmond, Mason, Schainker, and Borduin describe the development and dissemination of the PROSPER program (Chapter 15), and Dishion, Véronneau, Stormshak, and Kavanagh describe the EcoFit model (Family Check-Up) and its forerunner, the Adolescent Transition Program, in Chapter 16.

Continuing the theme that successful drug prevention can take multiple forms, the next two sections discuss approaches at the environmental and community levels. In Part VI, Chapter 17 (Saltz, Grube, & Treno) discusses large-scale environmental strategies, including social host ordinances, dram shop liability, and other policies that can affect consumption (e.g., roadside sobriety checks). The other chapters discuss issues relevant at the community level, such as policies to deter alcohol use (Chapter 18 by Lynne-Landsman & Wagenaar) and helping community-based coalitions select and implement evidence-based programs (Chapter 19 by Fagan & Hawkins). The three chapters in Part VII focus on critical components of successful media campaigns such as lessons that can be learned from the tobacco field about the importance of dealing with vested interests who may oppose prevention programs (Ibrahim, Chapter 20); considerations regarding the composition and delivery of specific messages (Harrington, Helme, & Noar, Chapter 21); and programs' general design, implementation, and evaluation (Crano, Alvaro, & Siegel, Chapter 22).

Using an appropriate design and data-analytic strategy is important, and the four chapters in Part VIII focus on several different methodological approaches. Latent variable modeling and latent class analysis are discussed by Malone and Woodlief and by Flaherty in Chapters 23 and 24, respectively. Kisbu-Sakarya, MacKinnon, and O'Rourke discuss mediational analyses in Chapter 25, and Mason, Brown, Fleming, and Haggerty discuss latent growth curve modeling in Chapter 26. All of these different approaches provide unique angles from which to examine program effects.

The last section covers issues related to the large-scale introduction and use of effective interventions (i.e., diffusion) and focuses on such topics as the adoption of evidence-based programs

(Derzon, Chapter 28) or their sustainability (Tibbits, Chapter 27) and overcoming the barriers to successful dissemination (Pas & Bradshaw, Chapter 29). The editor, Lawrence M. Scheier, concludes the volume by emphasizing some important issues discussed throughout this volume and ending with a clarion call for action. In sum, this handbook tells a compelling story about drug prevention that includes why it has always been important, where we have been, where we are now, and where we need to go to continue to make progress in reducing the prevalence and incidence of drug use.

WHO SHOULD READ THIS BOOK?

This handbook will be of benefit to a wide range of researchers, practitioners, and policymakers working in disciplines such as psychology, education, social work, health education, juvenile justice, and community organization and development. It covers an array of school-, family-, and community-based interventions for different populations and provides helpful references for those who want to further their understanding of different topics.

WHY THIS HANDBOOK IS SO VITAL AND IMPORTANT

Several features make this handbook particularly vital and important. The handbook tells a fascinating and illuminating story about the past, the present, and the future of drug prevention that includes the following eight elements:

1. The book gives due attention and importance to history, showing how past strategies of drug prevention have informed the present generation of programs and how both past and current developments provide directions for the future.
2. The book provides insight into the theoretical models that drive drug prevention efforts.
3. The book explains the scientific reasoning that program developers have consistently applied to their programs beginning from the point of initial conceptualization through subsequent implementations, evaluations, and revisions as necessary.
4. The book describes how a wide array of evaluation tools can be used to document that a program is evidence based.
5. The book offers an extensive review of the logistical, implementation, evaluation, and dissemination challenges faced and overcome by prevention scientists.
6. The book indicates how the prevention of drug use has relevance and application to other important issues such as those related to family, school, and community life and the development of other youth problems such as depression and externalizing behaviors.
7. The book is forward thinking, anticipating and outlining potentially important directions for the future of prevention science.
8. Finally, the book sheds light on the collective wisdom that has been accumulated through the activities of the contributors, who have been leaders in the field.

Although a few previous publications may include some of these features, none contains them all, making this handbook truly a unique contribution.

References

Damschroder, L. J., & Hagedorn, H. J. (2011). A guiding framework and approach for implementation research in substance use disorders treatment. *Psychology of Addictive Behaviors, 25*, 194–205. doi:10.1037/a0022284

Durlak, J. A., & DuPre, E. P. (2008). Implementation matters: A review of research on the influence of implementation on program outcomes and the factors affecting implementation. *American Journal of Community Psychology, 41*, 327–350. doi:10.1007/s10464-008-9165-0

Dusenbury, L., Brannigan, R., Hansen, W. B., Walsh, J., & Falco, M. (2005). Quality of implementation: Developing measures crucial to understanding the diffusion of preventive interventions. *Health Education Research, 20*, 308–313.

Meyers, D. C., Durlak, J. A., & Wandersman, A. (2012). The quality implementation framework: A synthesis of critical steps in the implementation process. *American Journal of Community Psychology, 50*, 462–480. doi:10.1007/s10464-012-9522-x

Proctor, E. K., Landsverk, J. L., Baumann, A. A., Mittman, B. S., Aarons, G. A., Brownson, C., . . . Chambers, D. (2013). The implementation research institute: Training mental health implementation researchers in the United States. *Implementation Science, 8*, 105. doi:10.1186/1748-5908-8-105

PART I

HISTORICAL TRENDS IN DRUG PREVENTION: WHAT GOT US HERE?

CHAPTER 1

DRUG USE PREVENTION: DEFINITIONS AND TERMINOLOGY

Elizabeth B. Robertson, Harold I. Perl, Eve E. Reider, Belinda E. Sims, Aria D. Crump, and Wilson M. Compton

Licit and illicit drugs of abuse exact a tremendous toll on individuals, families, communities, and broader society. Significant progress has been made over the past few decades in identifying and understanding effective approaches to the prevention of drug abuse and drug use disorders. Although the specific focus of this chapter is drug abuse prevention, many features of this area are common to the prevention of other health-risking behaviors, disorders, and diseases. In fact, theories of human development, encompassing physiological, genetic, psychological, behavioral, and social perspectives, inform the design of interventions that aim to reduce risk and enhance protective factors at the individual, family, peer, community, and environmental levels, including laws and policies related to health behaviors.

This chapter provides a brief introduction to the terms and concepts inherent to the science of drug abuse prevention. It starts with a widely recognized definition and describes four broad domains of drug abuse prevention research: epidemiology, etiology, intervention testing, and research methodology. The next section discusses the importance of a robust theoretical foundation for advancing the discipline of prevention science and outlines some key theoretical frameworks in developing interventions, several of which are described in greater detail in later chapters of this volume. Following this material, factors that either increase the risk of subsequent drug use and abuse (risk factors) or protect against the onset and progression of drug use (protective factors) are highlighted as critical elements for prevention science. Various aspects of both effective and ineffective prevention programs across a range of intervention settings are discussed next. The chapter concludes with three brief sections: The first section outlines unique opportunities for advancing prevention arising out of health care reform; the next section discusses goals of the National Institute on Drug Abuse (NIDA) prevention research portfolio; and the final section synthesizes the different views presented and provides some closing comments.

DEFINITION AND DOMAINS OF PREVENTION SCIENCE

A thorough understanding of any area of scientific inquiry depends on clear, concise, and commonly accepted definitions. In this section, we lay out the fundamental definitions of prevention science and its major components.

We acknowledge the assistance of Matthew S. Finger, MA, in preparing this chapter.

http://dx.doi.org/10.1037/14550-002
Handbook of Adolescent Drug Use Prevention: Research, Intervention Strategies, and Practice, L. M. Scheier (Editor)

Definition

Prevention science draws from a broad range of disciplines, including the biological, psychological, social, and other sciences. For example, the development and assessment of a particular preventive intervention may demand expertise in physiological processes, behavior change, economics, marketing, research design, and statistical techniques. The Institute of Medicine (IOM) report *Preventing Mental, Emotional, and Behavioral Disorders Among Young People* (National Research Council [NRC] & IOM, 2009) defined *prevention science* as a multidisciplinary field devoted to the scientific study of the theories, research, and practices related to the prevention of social, physical, mental health, and behavioral problems and encompassing the areas of etiology, epidemiology, intervention, and methodology.

Prevention interventions are intended to prevent the onset of drug use and its progression to abuse and thus are differentiated from treatment interventions for individuals manifesting drug abuse disorder. The IOM report (NRC & IOM, 2009) categorized prevention interventions on the basis of three levels of risk: *universal interventions* targeted to the general population, *selective interventions* for groups at risk because of a particular common vulnerability factor, or *indicated interventions* for individuals demonstrating signs and early symptoms that foreshadow disorder onset. This categorization had been proposed by Gordon (1983) and refined Caplan's (1964) earlier classifications of primary, secondary, and tertiary prevention commonly used in public health. The 2009 report added health promotion as a separate category encompassing interventions aimed at enhancing an individual's ability to achieve age-appropriate tasks (competencies); attain a positive sense of self-esteem, mastery, well-being, and social inclusion; and strengthen the ability to cope with adversity. Within the NIDA prevention research portfolio, considerable overlap exists between health promotion and other prevention interventions.

Four interrelated domains encompass the majority of the research in prevention science: epidemiology, etiology, prevention intervention development and testing, and research methodology. Each is briefly discussed next as it influences the current knowledge regarding drug prevention science.

Epidemiology

Epidemiology is the study of patterns of causal factors of health and disease conditions in defined populations (Lilienfeld & Lilienfeld, 1980). It is the cornerstone of public health and provides the foundation for prevention by promoting a richer understanding of risk and protective factors (both proximal and distal) related to health-risking behaviors, diseases, and disorders (Anthony, 2010). Drug abuse epidemiology emphasizes the nature, extent, and patterns of risk and protective factors that influence initiation and trajectories of continued drug use as well as patterns of drug use in different populations (defined on the basis of age, gender, race, geographic location, and behavioral or physical risk).

Etiology

Etiology is a specific arm of epidemiology that focuses on the causes or originations of disease or disorder and refers to the study of factors that contribute to the occurrence of disease or disorder (Scheier, 2010). Understanding the causal factors that lead to exposure, initiation, progression, and maintenance of drug abuse is fundamental to the development of effective prevention interventions. Subsequent chapters in this handbook provide greater detail on the rich scholarly connections between the causes and prevention of drug use. Drug abuse etiology research has suggested that individual, interpersonal, and environmental factors interact to increase or reduce vulnerability to drug use, abuse, dependence, and associated problem behaviors.

Etiologic analyses of population data have provided many concepts important for understanding the outcomes of prevention interventions. For example, Figure 1.1 shows how the process of multifinality helps one understand how individuals exposed to the same risk factors can develop multiple divergent outcomes. Figure 1.1 also shows how the process of equifinality operates to yield common maladaptive outcomes from divergent causes (Cicchetti & Blender, 2006; Cicchetti & Rogosch, 1996). These important concepts demonstrate

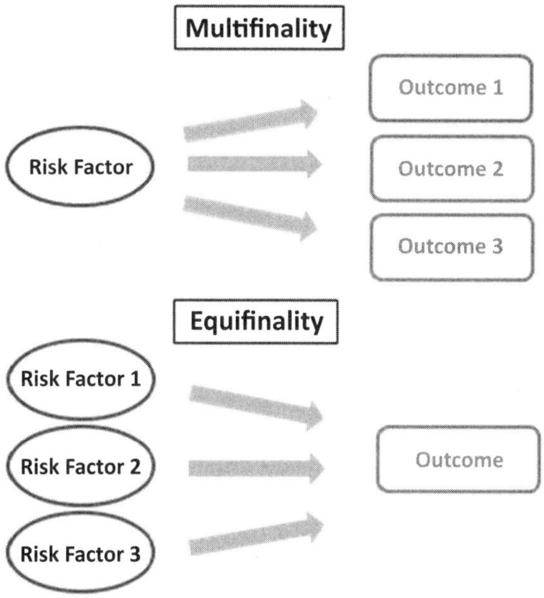

FIGURE 1.1. Multifinality and equifinality.

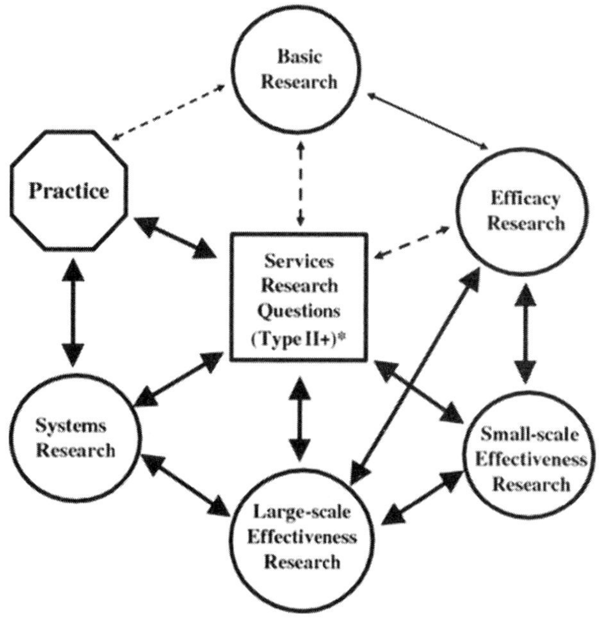

FIGURE 1.2. Schematic conceptualization of prevention science at the National Institute on Drug Abuse. *Type II translation research* refers to translation research focused on factors associated with the adoption and utilization of scientifically validated interventions by service systems under controlled, uncontrolled, and uncontrollable conditions (Robertson, Sims, & Reider, 2012). Other researchers, for example, Khoury et al. (2007), have further distinguished translational research into Types III and IV. To account for differences in definitions of translation research, this figure refers to Type II+.

the reciprocal relation among etiology, theories of human development, and behavior. Theory informs the design of etiologic studies, and the findings from those studies inform further refinement of theory.

Prevention Intervention Development and Testing

Findings from epidemiological and etiologic studies, as well as from basic physiological and behavioral research and other studies on the origins, pathways, and mechanisms of vulnerability to drug abuse disorders, inform the design of interventions intended to experimentally manipulate malleable risk factors. NIDA (2011) has supported a developmentally grounded portfolio focused on preventing or delaying the initiation of drug use, the progression to abuse and dependence, and the transmission of drug-related HIV infection. A schematic conceptualization of NIDA-supported prevention research is depicted in Figure 1.2, highlighting the interactions between various types of research. The top circle, labeled *Basic Research*, recognizes the interplay among basic science, epidemiological and etiologic research, and prevention research in the development of basic prevention research, or Type 1 translation research, which involves the incorporation of emerging scientific discovery into the development or refinement of prevention interventions. Discoveries used in basic prevention research could include findings from the biological (e.g., neurobiology, adolescent endocrinology, physical development), psychological (e.g., emotional, behavioral, cognitive, developmental), social (e.g., social learning, peer network, communications), and other related sciences.

Efficacy trials are designed to establish the impact of an intervention on targeted outcomes under rigorously controlled experimental conditions. Studies of program efficacy use randomized controlled trials or other methodologically sound research designs. One important and too often neglected aspect of efficacy studies is establishing the relevance and acceptability of the intervention for translation to real-world settings. Thus, strong quasi-experimental designs may be appropriate to use in situations in which the research question cannot be tested with a fully randomized approach.

Effectiveness trials test efficacious interventions and strategies in real-world settings that are less controlled, with larger and more diverse samples; they generally use a randomized controlled trial or equivalent research design. In addition, effectiveness studies usually incorporate prevention services research questions related to factors such as participant recruitment and retention, intervention dosage, cost analysis, fidelity of implementation, and implementer training. In other words, they examine issues that affect the transportability and sustainability of programs to real-world settings, facilitators and barriers to implementation, and whether programs can be generalized to diverse populations and geographic settings.

Systems research examines implementation features such as the availability, organization, management, financing, and sustainability of prevention interventions. Typically, these larger scale studies are conducted in the context of an existing service delivery system (e.g., school, workplace, primary health care, or social services setting). Occasionally, studies of this nature are conducted through a service delivery system that has been created for the purpose of translating a prevention intervention into practice at the community level, perhaps involving a community coalition. A major emphasis of systems trials is identifying and understanding the operation of organizational factors that affect the sustainability of the program being tested.

Central to prevention science are two types of services research questions: those at the programmatic level and those at the systems–implementation model level. Programmatic-level services questions most often occur when conducting efficacy and effectiveness research; the answers to these questions are critical for further effectiveness and systems research. Typical research questions include engagement and retention in interventions, program fidelity, and local adaptations of the model, among others. An important focus for further study is mechanisms of action (also referred to as *core components* and *essential* or *active ingredients*) of prevention interventions. Knowing what specific elements of an intervention are absolutely essential to induce behavior change is critical and would allow practitioners to understand why, how, and under what circumstances a program works, making it possible for them to make more informed decisions when considering local adaptations.

Systems and implementation model questions can address the same research areas as program-level questions (e.g., engagement, retention, fidelity, dosage) but generally do so with an emphasis on organizational structure or policy. Additional research questions, which are more likely to occur in larger effectiveness and systems trials, involve training and technical assistance, data platforms (e.g., tracking progress in addressing targeted risk factors in real time for continuous quality improvement), and long-term sustainability. Answers to these types of research questions may be most salient to community policy and funding agency decision makers. These areas of prevention science are relatively new, and research questions are evolving as interdisciplinary practitioner–researcher team combinations work to take evidence-based interventions (EBIs) to scale in service systems. A major challenge in addressing systems and implementation model research questions is the development of reliable measures to examine the processes that underlie the successful scaling up of system-level EBIs (Riemer, Kelley, Casey, & Taylor Haynes, 2012; Robertson, Sims, & Reider, 2012).

Prevention services research is a critical component of prevention science, focused on identifying and determining how features of an intervention's dissemination and implementation contribute to the uptake and sustainability of evidence-based interventions in practice (Pentz, 2010). In recent years, areas outside of drug abuse and mental health have developed research in this area under the designation of Type 2 translation research, which examines both internal and external characteristics that contribute to efficacy, effectiveness, and sustainability. Chapters 27 and 29 of this handbook examine the features of prevention services research, so we only briefly cover the main features here. Examples of internal features include intervention content; recruitment, retention, and implementation strategies; fidelity; dosage; characteristics of the delivery setting; and training of implementer personnel.

Examples of external features include exposure to other programs, media messages, enforcement of regulations and laws related to substance use, and community norms around substance abuse.

Replications of efficacious interventions with other population groups and in alternate environmental contexts can also aid in differentiating between programmatic features that are essential and those that can be adapted to meet the needs of particular groups and settings. Characteristics such as program duration, reinforcement and consistency of prevention messages over time and across settings, developmentally appropriate content and materials, interactive teaching techniques, intermittent reinforcement, client–facilitator fit, and grouping of clients need further investigation to improve the quality of programming and increase the potential for translation into real-world settings (N. S. Tobler et al., 2000).

Services research also forms an integral link between research and practice. For that reason, researchers often integrate prevention practitioners into the research process, from inception through program execution, to ensure that successful interventions meet the self-identified needs of the end user and to foster ownership and sustainability among the host community (Swisher & Clayton, 2000). Services questions are clearly central to large-scale effectiveness or practice research. However, consideration of practical implementation issues from the earliest stages is essential to maximize the likelihood of broad uptake and population impact. Finally, note that this full model is recursive; new topics for research and new questions arise through the process of examining the impact of specific interventions.

Research methodology in prevention science is critical to advancing the field of drug abuse prevention, as it is in all other scientific endeavors, yet inadequate or inappropriate research designs can thwart potential advances if they do not provide the opportunity for a true test of an intervention's effectiveness (Biglan, Ary, & Wagenaar, 2000; Brown et al., 2009; Collins et al., 2011). NIDA's interest in advances in research methodology is twofold: the development of methodologically rigorous designs appropriate to answering pressing questions and the development and validation of new and innovative approaches that advance the conduct of prevention science. Together, these may include study designs to strengthen causal inference and external validity; individual-, program-, and systems-level measurement tools and analytic approaches; adaptive designs; designs to address the problems of missing data and attrition when following intervention and control subjects over time; analytic unbundling strategies to disentangle important features of prevention interventions (i.e., core components); simulation modeling of prevention service delivery alternatives; and new measurement instruments and statistical approaches appropriate for use in complex multisite systems trials. In addition, NIDA supports the adaptation and assessment of proven scientific procedures from other disciplines, such as those from systems science and engineering, to determine their applicability to drug abuse prevention research (Chakraborty, Collins, Strecher, & Murphy, 2009; Collins et al., 2011).

THEORETICAL FRAMEWORKS

The life course developmental perspective suggests that individual, interpersonal, and environmental factors interact to increase or reduce vulnerability to drug use and abuse. Vulnerability may occur at many points along the life course but often peaks during critical life transitions. Thus, prevention researchers pay particular attention to the importance of timing interventions to coincide with important life transitions, be they biological, such as puberty; normative, such as moving from elementary to middle school; social, such as dating; or traumatic, such as the death or loss of a parent (including prolonged separation that may arise from military service).

Vulnerability to drug abuse involves dynamic intrapersonal (e.g., temperament), interpersonal (e.g., family or peer communications), and environmental (e.g., classroom management) influences; thus, prevention intervention research must target interactions between individuals and social systems across the life span. To address this complexity, intervention research needs to test strategies designed to alter specific modifiable mediators (i.e., putative risk factors) to determine which are most effective in reducing drug use initiation and escalation with varied audiences and under varied conditions. The life course perspective reflects the broad understanding that a child's stage of life, aspects of his or her social and physical environment, and life events over time all contribute to his or her physical, psychological, emotional, and cognitive development (Bronfenbrenner, 1979, 2005). For example, the life events or transitions referenced in the Life Course–Social Field concept (Kellam, 1975; Kellam et al., 2011) call attention to points from birth to death at which the individual is in a period of change, sometimes called a sensitive, critical, or vulnerable period (Bornstein, 1989). Change occurring within and around the child during these critical periods can present developmental opportunities as well as challenges. Some children and parents require help in identifying and building the skills and resources needed to successfully negotiate such changes; consequently, prevention interventions are often planned to coincide with these expected transitions.

This integrated theoretical perspective provides a broad view of the complex forces and interactions that influence development in general and problem behaviors in particular. Theory-based interventions are more likely to succeed because a coherent model guides the development of the intervention's content and duration and also highlights for whom the intervention is predicted to work. Various developmental, behavioral, cognitive, and personality theories have informed prevention science to date. Theory-based intervention development has led to research examining modification of precursors of substance use, such as sensation seeking, emotion regulation, aggressive behavior, academic problems and failure, poor social skills, misperceptions of social norms, poor parent–child attachment, and inappropriate parental expectations and responses. The broad category of learning theories, especially social learning theory, social cognitive theory, and problem behavior theory, has been particularly useful in the development of interventions. Numerous chapters in this handbook discuss the integration of these theories with the fundamental elements of prevention science in action. Chapter 4 of this handbook pays particular attention to the important role of theory in prevention science.

RISK AND PROTECTIVE FACTORS

Prevention research focuses on reducing risk factors and enhancing protective factors through a variety of developmentally and contextually appropriate strategies, introduced at the universal, selective, and indicated levels as appropriate. Hawkins, Catalano, and colleagues (Catalano, Haggerty, Hawkins, & Elgin, 2011; Catalano & Hawkins, 1996; Hawkins, Catalano, & Miller, 1992; Hawkins, Jenson, Catalano, & Lishner, 1988; Hawkins & Weis, 1985) have comprehensively reviewed the literature on risk and protective factors pertaining to drug abuse prevention. Their seminal work, spanning almost 3 decades, has emphasized a broad theoretical approach examining the origins and etiologic pathways of drug abuse and addiction. According to the social development model, children develop along a trajectory, reflecting how they adapt either positively or negatively to intrapersonal, interpersonal, and environmental factors at different developmental stages over the life course. Identifying and understanding common sets of factors associated with subsequent problem behaviors can help define major inflection points and targets of interventions along these trajectories.

Risk Factors

Risk factors associated with drug abuse and other mental, emotional, and behavioral problems can alter a child's developmental trajectory or pathway by affecting specific behaviors or, more generally, the achievement of developmental tasks at different stages of a child's life. One of the better-documented trajectories can be traced from out-of-control aggressive behavior in a very young child (Moffitt, 2003). If not successfully addressed through preventive intervention within the school and home contexts, over time these developmental risks can increase the likelihood of other risk behaviors for drug use, such as truancy, delinquency, and associating with drug-abusing peers (Bierman, Bruschi, Domitrovich, Fang, & Miller-Johnson, 2004; Farmer & Bierman, 2002; Miller-Johnson, Coie, Maumary-Gremaud, & Bierman, 2002). This example illustrates several important aspects of successful prevention. First, intervening early increases the likelihood of successful development across the life course; second, life transitions, in this case school transitions, are points of vulnerability and provide opportunities for intervention; and finally, interventions that address the problem in multiple contexts such as family, peers, and school are generally more successful than those limited to a single context. This example also suggests that factors internal to a child (e.g., temperament, learning style), the social and physical context, and the interaction between internal and contextual factors can contribute to risk for later drug abuse. For young children already exhibiting serious risk factors, delaying intervention until later childhood or adolescence makes it more difficult to overcome risks, in large part because behaviors and attitudes that fuel deviance have become well established and are less amenable to change.

Furthermore, as children grow and develop, social contexts outside the family (e.g., school and classrooms, peer groups, the community) have increasingly greater influence on the child's development. Difficulties in these contexts influence children's physical, emotional, cognitive, and social development. For example, during the preadolescent and adolescent years, associations with drug-using or otherwise deviant peers is often the most immediate risk for drug use and other problem behaviors, but other factors such as drug availability, the perception that drug use is not harmful, and inflated misperceptions about the extent to which same-age peers use drugs can influence adolescents' decision making about drug use.

Nevertheless, even during the adolescent years, parents and other caregivers can provide protection through a number of actions, such as age-appropriate monitoring of social behaviors, including establishing curfews and sharing adult supervision of activities outside the home; knowing their children's friends and their parents; enforcing rules; facilitating and valuing success in academics and involvement in extracurricular activities; and fostering strong bonds with prosocial institutions, including school, recreation activities, and religious institutions. Research has demonstrated that peers are a major force in determining immediate behaviors such as choosing clothing styles, activities, and other friends; nevertheless, parents remain the most important source of information and consultation regarding long-term life choices such as education and career (Hunter & Youniss, 1982; A. L. Tobler & Komro, 2010).

Protective Factors

Protective factors are those qualities of humans and their environments that promote successful coping with life situations and change. Thus, protective factors are not simply the absence of risk; rather, protective factors explicitly serve to reduce or mitigate the negative impact of risk factors (Cowen & Work, 1988; Hawkins et al., 1992; Rutter, 1985). An important goal of prevention is to change the balance between risk and protection so that the effects of protective factors outweigh the effects of risk factors. Protective factors may also be present at various environmental levels, including the individual, family, school, and community.

Research on protective factors among children has its origins in research on risk factors and associated problem behaviors. A major conclusion from risk factor research was that many children do not develop problem behaviors, despite the presence of a significant number of risk factors. This realization led to a strong interest in what is now called *resilience* (Masten, 2011, 2012). Resilience and protective factors both involve internal strengths or psychological assets as well as features of the family and other external contexts, including the school and community. However, resilience refers specifically to those children who, absent intervention, exhibit higher than expected adaptive functioning given the number, intensity, and duration of risk factors they experience. Intervention developers and researchers use findings from protective factor and resilience research to inform their decisions about what child, parent, and other resources and skills should be enhanced through prevention interventions.

Similar to risk factors, resilience and protective factors play a major role in the developmental trajectory or path of the child's life course (Masten, 2012). However, even when children are progressing along the normal course of physical, cognitive, social, and emotional development, improvements in critical contexts can further their development. Thus, an important goal of prevention interventions is to support the development of skills and resources among those who interact with children in various contexts, including parents, school personnel, and other community figures (Durlak et al., 2007).

CONTEXTS AND TARGETS OF PREVENTION INTERVENTIONS

Prevention interventions specify the knowledge, skills, and competencies that are targeted for change for a particular population of interest. For example, family-based programs often include both parent and child behavioral targets and outcomes. Interventions that combine contexts, as in the case of family and school, could target children, parents, and teachers. In programs in which multiple actors are involved, activities for one actor often reinforce those for another. For example, a program targeted to children entering school may aim to reduce aggressive behavior through increasing attention and self-control. These child-oriented targets can be reinforced by training teachers on effective classroom management and teaching parents and other caregivers the skills of consistent, contingent, nonabusive parenting.

Family-Based Interventions

A major emphasis of family-based preventive interventions is training parents with regard to developmentally appropriate expectations and responses to their children's behaviors, along with making appropriate interpersonal adjustments as the child matures. Interventions with parents have demonstrated long-term outcomes that extend beyond childhood to include adolescence (Spoth, Redmond, & Shin, 2001; Spoth, Redmond, et al., 2013). Thus, the effect of intervening in childhood by teaching new family relations skills and methods to monitor and supervise children is to alter the life course through adolescence by protecting youths from harm.

The majority of interventions targeting families of infants, toddlers, and preschoolers are selective interventions for groups at heightened risk because of factors such as teenage parents, low social capital and material resources (i.e., poverty), families with a child exhibiting early behavior problems, or involvement in the child welfare system. These interventions often target skills that may be lacking or that have not been a parental focus. For example, nurse visitation programs for pregnant teens begin with teaching self-care to the mother, which directly affects the health and well-being of the fetus, as well as addressing broader family issues and needs. After the child is born, the emphasis shifts to teaching parenting skills that will promote child development, beginning with responsive positive interactions.

The transition to elementary school can be difficult for many families because it can strain the flexibility of families and place additional cognitive and social demands on the child. Similarly, as children reach middle school, new challenges surface; they become involved with peers, extracurricular activities, and growing academic expectations. Family-based interventions during these developmental periods focus on warmth, support, monitoring of children's whereabouts, and communication. One universal program for parents of middle school–age children teaches the strategy of reinforcing appropriate behaviors that the child expresses naturally and ignoring inappropriate behaviors to the greatest extent possible (Hawkins, Catalano, Kosterman, Abbott, & Hill, 1999). This is what the intervention developers called "catching them being good," indicating that parents learn to spot, point out, and express approval of children's appropriate behavior despite whatever other behaviors are present. This extremely powerful parenting strategy reinforces the child's existing social skills and gives the child a sense of control over his or her environment while reinforcing socially acceptable behaviors. In addition, it provides the parents with the sense of parenting efficacy that is especially needed with a difficult child (Spoth, Guyll, & Day, 2002; Spoth, Redmond, & Shin, 2000; Spoth et al., 2001).

Another type of program offered to families of middle school–age and adolescent youths is an adaptive or tiered intervention family program. First, all families are given universal access to informational materials that cover parenting, child development, and other child-rearing resources. The selective-level component of the intervention starts with a confidential assessment of family strengths and weaknesses that offers more specific information to address their needs. Families already manifesting problem behaviors and identified as appropriate for an indicated intervention are provided more intense assistance and information tailored to their specific problems, such as individual or family therapy, intensive parent coaching, therapeutic foster care, or other family-specific interventions (Dishion & Kavanagh, 2000). The importance of the parent–child relationship continues through adolescence and beyond with parents continuing to play a key role in decision making even after youths begin to drive, date, go off to college, or move out after getting a job. Interestingly, few efficacious or effective family-based drug abuse prevention programs for young adults currently exist (Brody, Yu, Chen, Kogan, & Smith, 2012).

School-Based Interventions

Schools are an obvious context for prevention interventions because nearly all children attend school and are expected to develop cognitive competencies, increase knowledge, and behave in socially acceptable ways. Not surprisingly, a number of school-based drug abuse prevention programs have been developed and tested; many have demonstrated successful social, behavioral, and academic outcomes, as well as reductions in substance abuse problems. One important programming approach is effective classroom management, which trains teachers to build resources for rewarding positive behaviors. The goal of this intervention approach is to create an environment in which learning is the primary goal and the primary source of reward. Over time, this training has the effect of reducing the bulk of negative classroom behaviors (Ialongo, Poduska, Werthamer, & Kellam, 2001; Ialongo et al., 1999; Kellam et al., 2014). Although classroom management can be thought of as an integral part of teaching, many beginning teachers are not equipped to manage the types of classroom problem behaviors that take away from the first priority of the school—learning. Thus, training teachers to use effective, consistent, and easy-to-learn routines that are fun for students can enhance learning and bonding to school, two important protective factors. These types of approaches are considered environmental change strategies because they seek to shift the classroom context from one with a primary focus on reducing negative behaviors to one centered on promoting positive behavior skills and learning.

Another type of classroom management approach, typically used with students in kindergarten through Grade 3, is called *social–emotional learning* (Bierman, Coie, et al., 2004; Bierman et al., 2010; Farmer & Bierman, 2002; Greenberg & Kusche 1998; Miller-Johnson et al., 2002). The central goal of this approach is to help children identify feelings that are interfering with learning, such as frustration, anger, and overstimulation, and provide them the cognitive tools to manage these feelings. Developing social–emotional awareness at a young age has long-term positive effects on both academic and social performance across the school years and into adulthood. Promotion of academic competence during the early grades can have profound effects on fostering positive attitudes toward learning, furnish a sense of mastery and accomplishment, and provide an understanding of the academic basics necessary for future learning. These skills serve as protective factors, leading to a greater likelihood of a positive life trajectory. For example, the inability to read by the third or fourth grade is one very potent risk factor for subsequent substance abuse, delinquency, school dropout, and underemployment (Barrera et al., 2002). Ensuring that children get the additional support they need to achieve reading by this critical period helps to ensure ongoing academic success (Ramey & Campbell, 1991). A potentially debilitating risk factor can thus be transformed into a powerful protective factor with tremendous implications for positive adaptation.

As previously noted, transitions to elementary school and to subsequent school levels constitute major periods of vulnerability and risk. Expectations for academic and social performance escalate over the school years and can be very threatening to some children; parental support and involvement are crucial during these transitions. This underscores the need for parents to become familiar with their child's teachers, friends, and their friends' parents; monitor their school work and social opportunities; and take an active interest in their increasingly autonomous life. The transition to middle school or junior high school is typically most proximal to exposure to and experimentation with drugs. For this reason, a number of prevention interventions target this time point in particular. Social resistance skill prevention approaches stress the importance of social factors in the initiation of drug use. The intervention paradigm focuses on teaching youths the requisite social and assertiveness skills needed to handle peer pressure to experiment with drugs, often including role-play or video vignettes in which a drug offer is made and then strategies for rebuffing the offer are taught and practiced.

Social resistance (or refusal) skills programs applied in a regular classroom setting have been shown to be highly successful. For example, in one randomized controlled trial, youths in the intervention groups were 30% to 40% less likely to initiate tobacco use than those in the nonintervention group (Botvin, Griffin, Paul, & Macaulay, 2003). Interestingly, recent findings have indicated that 6 years after this drug abuse prevention intervention was completed, students who received the intervention during junior high school were significantly less likely to have driving violations and infraction points on their Department of Motor Vehicles record than those who did not receive the intervention (Griffin, Botvin, & Nichols, 2004). This illustrates the phenomenon of *crossover effects*, that is to say, positive effects on behaviors not addressed explicitly in the original intervention. Crossover effects are relatively common in long-term follow-up studies of drug prevention programs. Other examples of crossover effects—some as long as 2 decades later—include reductions in conduct disorder and suicide (Wilcox et al., 2008); reductions in later use of mental health services (Kellam et al., 2011); reductions in criminal justice involvement for girls (Eckenrode et al., 2010); reductions in internalizing behaviors and the use of cigarettes, alcohol, and marijuana, as well as higher academic achievement (Kitzman et al., 2010); reductions in family usage of government welfare benefits (Olds et al., 2010); reductions in sexual risk behaviors (Caruthers, Van Ryzin, & Dishion, 2014); and reductions in the use of drugs of abuse such as methamphetamine (Spoth, Trudeau, Shin, & Redmond, 2008) and prescription opioids (Spoth, Trudeau, et al., 2013).

Normative education is another prevention strategy that has some positive effects but only when used in conjunction with social and personal competence skills development strategies. The goal of normative education is to correct misperceived positive norms about the actual use and acceptance of drug use. In one commonly used strategy, students in a school are surveyed about their perceptions of drug use among their peers, their perceptions of their peers' acceptance of use, and their own drug use. In most cases, students' perceptions of use and acceptance of use are much higher than actual use and social acceptance by peers. These data are then reported back to students, placing the real school drug climate in perspective and allowing students to feel that they are within the norm if they do not use drugs rather than among the outliers. Normative education can also reinforce the perception of the school as a safe and nurturing environment (Botvin, Epstein, Baker, Diaz, & Ifill-Williams, 1997; Dusenbury, Brannigan, Falco, & Hansen, 2003; Hansen, Giles, & Fearnow-Kenney, 2000).

Community-Based Interventions

At the community level and beyond, prevention strategies typically involve policy and media interventions. Policy interventions include activities such as training shopkeepers in how to request identification from purchasers of tobacco and alcohol products and how to refuse sales to underage youths who do not meet the minimum age requirements. Other policy approaches include enforcing college campus rules about the underage use of licit drugs and any use of illicit drugs (Pentz, 2000). The majority of these environmental approaches address substance use problems among youths in the later high school grades and the years beyond high school.

Media strategies can be successful prevention tools for reducing the initiation and progression of drug abuse when theoretically derived, targeted, well executed, and based on sound scientific principles. For example, research has identified a personality trait called *high sensation seeking* as a risk factor for substance abuse. In a media intervention targeted to young adult marijuana users with the high sensation-seeking trait, alternative activities with high sensation value, such as rock climbing, were promoted via mass media in one community, and a second community did not receive the media spots. Identified groups of high sensation seekers were followed over time. The intervention community group had a 27% reduction in marijuana use compared with the control community group after 6 months (Palmgreen, Donohew, Lorch, Hoyle, & Stephenson, 2001, 2002). In recent years, social media interventions, particularly those taking advantage of new developments in personal electronics technologies, have become an increasing focus for developing innovative prevention programs.

INEFFECTIVE AND EFFECTIVE INTERVENTION STRATEGIES

Unfortunately, drug abuse prevention programs and strategies that have been demonstrated to be ineffective are still used too frequently. Fear arousal is one strategy that has been demonstrated to be highly ineffective (N. S. Tobler, 2000; N. S. Tobler et al., 2000). An example of this approach is the use of testimonials from former substance abusers, which has actually been demonstrated to have the unintended negative effect of making drug-using lifestyles sound exciting and desirable. Other examples include media spots that portray drugs inaccurately or parking crashed cars on the school grounds as a supposed effective deterrent. Youths tend to discount extreme examples and substitute the negative information with information that is unrealistically positive.

Other ineffective strategies do not have unintended negative effects but do not yield positive outcomes. For example, although information is an important component of most interventions, providing information alone is not effective in altering behavior. Similarly, affective education models in which children are involved only in activities intended to build self-esteem are not effective in developing positive behaviors (or adequate deterrents to drug use). Finally, providing alternative programming only, such as encouraging extracurricular activities alone, is not an effective prevention intervention. Consequently, these types of approaches should be considered as ancillary to and not replacements for other effective prevention interventions.

Implementing any intervention with fidelity to the model is crucial for obtaining the expected prevention outcomes (Fixsen, Naoom, Blase, Friedman, & Wallace, 2005). However, the manner in which an intervention is implemented can also lead to negative outcomes. For example, one study that grouped high-risk youths before exposing them to an intervention found iatrogenic effects. Further analysis of moment-to-moment videotaped interactions revealed an undercurrent among youths of subtle positive behaviors, such as head nods and grins, during discussions of inappropriate behaviors (Dishion, McCord, & Poulin, 1999; Dishion, Poulin, & Burraston, 2001). These subtle actions were found to reinforce the continuation of negative behavior patterns. Thus, attention to the composition of intervention groups can be an important element of effectiveness.

The current state of knowledge has clearly shown that skills and competency development interventions are the most potent strategies in terms of prevention effectiveness throughout the childhood and adolescent years. In addition, intervention delivery processes are critical to achieving positive results. On one hand, programs with interactive activities that provide participants opportunities to learn and practice skills and then reinforce those skills over time have been found to be the most successful in facilitating the desired behavior change; on the other hand, information delivered only in a lecture format has shown little effect (Dusenbury et al., 2003; N. S. Tobler, 2000; N. S. Tobler et al., 2000). This is consistent with the literature on implementation science in education and other social service fields (cf. Fixsen et al., 2005; Joyce & Showers, 2002). Moreover, the amount of intervention or dose received by the intended audience is important. Receiving half of some interventions has demonstrated modest effects, but even greater effects were achieved when more of the program was experienced (Botvin, Griffin, & Nichols, 2006; Griffin, Botvin, & Nichols, 2006). Finally, it is important that prevention efforts be consistent across contexts. That is, efforts at the individual, family, school, and community levels should reinforce one another. Inconsistency across contexts creates confusion and may result in the discounting of all efforts (Ringwalt et al., 2003).

OTHER OPPORTUNITIES FOR DRUG ABUSE PREVENTION SCIENCE

In this chapter, we have reviewed fundamental definitions of drug abuse prevention and highlighted some of the knowledge underlying prevention interventions. We conclude with a discussion of two additional topics: opportunities for expanded prevention activities during the current era of health care reform and potential areas of emphasis for future directions of NIDA-supported prevention research.

Drug Abuse Prevention in an Era of Health Care Reform

The passage of the Patient Protection and Affordable Care Act (ACA; 2010) brought the prevention capabilities of the health care system to national prominence. Although relatively little has been discussed regarding the role of health care providers and the health care system in reducing the initiation and progression of drug use, the ACA has significant implications for drug abuse prevention. Most children and youths, as well as many adults, interact with a medical care provider periodically, if not regularly. Medical care providers have a unique opportunity to influence their patients' health-risk behaviors, including those influencing drug use. Through health care reform, primary medical providers will have increased opportunity to screen patients for risks that may lead to substance abuse behaviors.

A small but growing body of intervention research is being conducted in medical offices, clinics, and hospitals, including the use of tools to screen for potential drug-related problem behaviors. For example, one recent line of research has tested an intervention for women who have been raped and is intended to reduce the trauma caused by both the rape itself and the postrape forensic evidence collection procedures. It is believed that these experiences may lead to the initiation or exacerbation of substance abuse problems. Before undergoing the postrape forensic exam, women view a two-part video presentation that addresses the process of the forensic examination, aiming to reduce stress and future emotional problems. It also provides information and skills to reduce postrape substance use and abuse. Early findings have suggested reductions in alcohol and marijuana use among women who were active drug users before the rape compared with the nonviewers (Resnick, Acierno, Kilpatrick, & Holmes, 2005).

The ACA emphasizes and encourages prevention across the health care system to achieve two overarching goals: controlling the spiraling escalation in health care costs and improving the overall health of the U.S. population. Two broad mechanisms are used: (a) direct insurance funding of prevention practices found to be effective in primary care and (b) the Prevention and Public Health Fund. Direct funding may support the implementation of practices such as screening as prevention services become integral to routine medical care. Thus, there is potential for the implementation of and payment for services, including existing EBIs, through innovations in health care reform, especially in states that have received waivers to implement novel practices among Medicaid patients (e.g., family-based interventions).

The Prevention and Public Health Fund was created to promote wellness, prevent disease, and protect against public health emergencies. These efforts are coordinated at the federal level by the National Prevention Council, which consists of the lead executives from 17 federal departments, agencies, and offices; the council is advised by an appointed external group of scientists and medical professionals. In 2011, the council released the *National Prevention Council Action Plan: Implementing the National Prevention Strategy: America's Plan for Better Health and Wellness*. The strategy identified four strategic directions and seven strategy priorities that are most likely to reduce the nation's leading behavioral causes of illness and death. The council viewed implementation of the strategy as a way to "accelerate high impact areas to move

America from a system of sick care to one based on wellness and prevention" (National Prevention Council, 2011, p. 4). Figure 1.3 depicts the directions and priorities envisioned in the National Prevention Strategy.

The four strategic directions provide a foundation for the overall prevention efforts through engaging communities, health care practitioners, and individuals in actively refocusing health care on the prevention of the major causes of illness and injury, whereas the seven priorities provide recommendations based on the latest scientific evidence with the greatest potential to reduce the leading causes of preventable death and illness. Each of the strategic directions is germane to substance abuse prevention. For example, promoting healthy and safe communities is about meeting the basic needs of humans for safety, shelter, nutritious food, worthwhile and accessible work, and safe, healthful recreation, the core elements of theories of human development on which drug abuse prevention is based. Furthermore, the seven strategy priorities are intended to improve health and wellness by reducing the leading causes of mortality. The relevance of the two alcohol, tobacco, and other drug priorities to drug abuse prevention is obvious, and the links between the remaining priorities and drug use have been well established. Findings from drug abuse epidemiologic, etiologic, and prevention intervention research over the past 20 years have

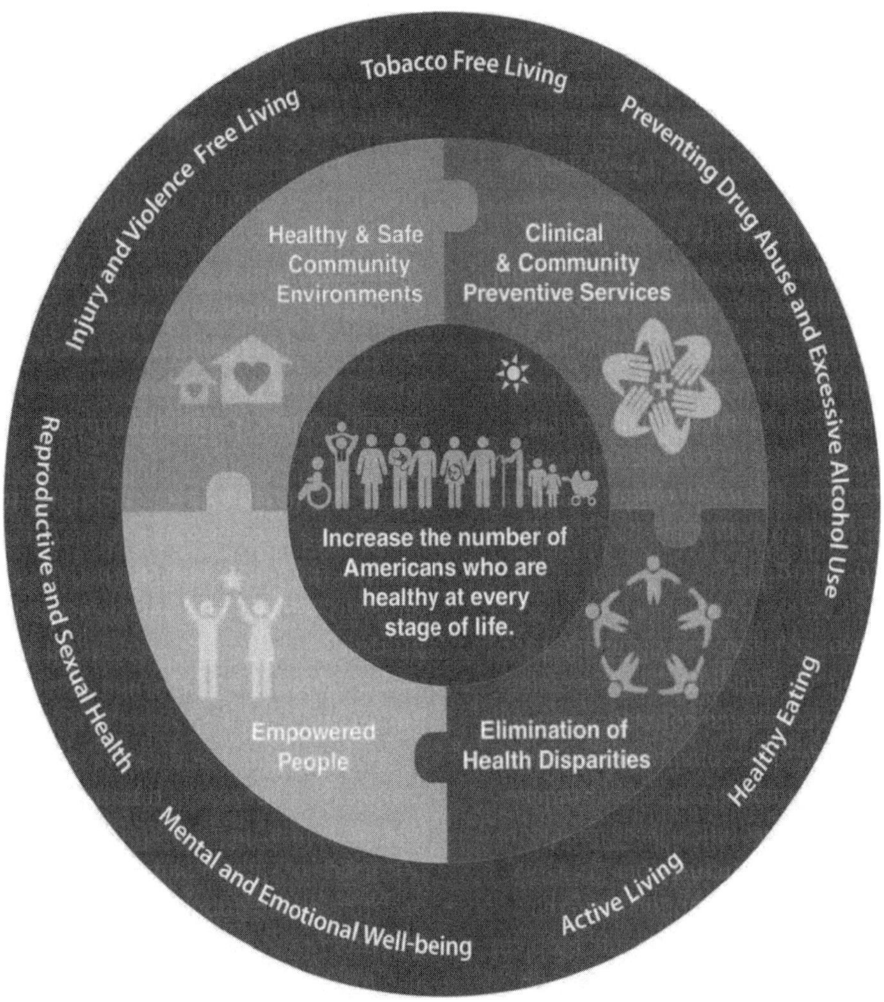

FIGURE 1.3. National prevention strategy. From *National Prevention Strategy: America's Plan for Better Health and Wellness*, 2011 by the National Prevention Council. In the public domain.

demonstrated the commonalities among multiple problem behaviors. Moreover, the 2009 IOM report stressed the salience of the full constellation of risk factors that predict multiple negative outcomes, including substance abuse, delinquency, violence, sexual risk behaviors, and other mental, emotional, and behavioral problems (NRC & IOM, 2009). Drug abuse prevention interventions often target multiple risk factors, and within a particular intervention the knowledge, skills, and competencies addressed could prevent multiple problem behaviors in addition to substance abuse.

Although the healthy eating and active living priorities may seem to have less well-established links to drug abuse prevention, recent advances in prevention research have demonstrated strong connections. For example, aspects of physical activity, such as controlled breathing and relaxation, are emerging as strategies for preventing or delaying initiation of drug use through improved self-regulation (e.g., Mendelson et al., 2010). In addition, research on the epidemiology and etiology of obesity and eating disorders has linked these nutrition problems with substance abuse and addiction (e.g., Riggs, Spruijt-Metz, Chou, & Pentz, 2012; Volkow, Wang, Tomasi, & Baler, 2013). Interestingly, one long-standing evidence-based drug prevention program, the Midwestern Prevention Project, has been adapted for use as an obesity prevention intervention (Sakuma, Riggs, & Pentz, 2012).

In sum, drug abuse prevention research and the EBIs tested through this work have much to offer toward fulfilling the goals and priorities for health care reform. The adoption of an evidence-based focus for the accomplishment of the strategic priorities heightens the importance of implementation and dissemination research to accelerate uptake of EBIs in the next few years.

Prevention Science at NIDA

As noted earlier, NIDA's prevention research mission is focused on increasing knowledge on preventing or delaying the initiation of drug use, the progression to abuse and dependence, and the transmission of drug-related HIV infection. A recent expert panel review of the NIDA prevention research portfolio noted the proactive role that the institute has taken in building the field of prevention science, "creating a diverse portfolio that encompasses basic research, statistical methodology, efficacy trials, effectiveness research, systems research, and services research" (NIDA, 2009, p. iii). NIDA's scientific program staff follows progress in the field and identifies the current state of knowledge as well as research questions and directions that warrant continued and increased attention. Findings from the NIDA portfolio have demonstrated that a great deal is known about how to prevent or delay the initiation of drug use and its progression, and many prevention interventions have proven effective over both the short and long terms. By and large, however, these interventions have not been put into sustained practice in the venues for which they were intended. Therefore, one significant goal for NIDA prevention science is to increase the focus on implementation science to improve knowledge of how EBIs can be adopted more broadly, taken to scale, and sustained in practice. Implementation science in the context of prevention research is at the forefront of groundbreaking research through the development of risk-related data platforms, identification of best practices, systems testing, public–private partnerships, and measurement and methods. These advances are encouraged by the era of health care reform that highlights prevention as the future of a system of wellness. However, for this to become a reality, new approaches are needed to support the implementation and measurement of quality evidence-based interventions in health- and community-based settings. At the same time, basic science translational research on preventive interventions remains a critical and prominent focus. One important research goal is the identification and refinement of core components and mechanisms that account for the effectiveness of EBIs. Another frontier is both the frontward and the backward translation of findings associated with genetically controlled negative behaviors, including substance abuse.

NIDA prevention research continues to focus on innovative and emergent advances in methodology as well as new technologies. These can include innovative uses of existing and new data sources, such as genetic, imaging, and social media data;

innovative research designs, such as optimization strategies, adaptive designs, and microtrials; and emergent technologies, such as smartphone, web-based, or social media technologies. Finally, NIDA will continue to pay close attention to developing the human capital for prevention research and practice, including training prevention investigators and facilitating collaborations and linkages across scientific disciplines, between various organizations and entities, and among stakeholders such as scientists, community stakeholders, service providers, and policymakers.

CLOSING NOTE

As have many other fields of scientific inquiry, prevention science has evolved over time. New tools and technologies help us to understand both observed and theorized behavior patterns in relation to actual internal processes that our prior models only referred to as inside the black box. The increasing precision of these tools pinpoints biological mechanisms that, in combination with environmental characteristics, are associated with behaviors that can affect life course trajectories and help in refining theories of human behavior and improve innovative prevention interventions.

A second major evolution is the dissemination and implementation of evidence-based interventions and systems. For much of the past 30 years, prevention science has focused primarily on the development of interventions as well as on systems for the dissemination of interventions. In recent years, prevention experts have recognized the critical importance of focusing more clearly on variables that facilitate or inhibit the uptake and adoption of prevention interventions and systems. Recent and impending changes in health care open up the potential for broader adoption of prevention interventions with strong scientific support providing an unprecedented opportunity for public health benefit. For efforts in these areas to be fruitful in improving the health of Americans, it is critical that prevention science continue to ask—and answer—the complex practice and policy questions that underlie the successful dissemination and implementation of evidence-based practices.

References

Anthony, J. C. (2010). Epidemiology and etiology hand in hand. In L. M. Scheier (Ed.), *Handbook of drug use etiology: Theory, methods, and empirical findings* (pp. 113–124). Washington, DC: American Psychological Association.

Barrera, M., Biglan, A., Taylor, T. K., Gunn, B. K., Smolkowski, K., Black, C., . . . Fowler, R. C. (2002). Early elementary school intervention to reduce conduct problems: A randomized trial with Hispanic and non-Hispanic children. *Prevention Science, 3*, 83–94. doi:10.1023/A:1015443932331

Bierman, K., Bruschi, C., Domitrovich, C., Fang, G., & Miller-Johnson, S. (2004). Early disruptive behaviors associated with emerging antisocial behavior among girls. In M. Putallaz & K. L. Bierman (Eds.), *Aggression, antisocial behavior and violence among girls: A developmental perspective* (pp. 137–161). New York, NY: Guilford Press.

Bierman, K. L., Coie, J. D., Dodge, K. A., Foster, E. M., Greenberg, M. T., Lochman, J. E., . . . Pinderhughes, E. E. (2004). The effects of the Fast Track program on serious problem outcomes at the end of elementary school. *Journal of Clinical Child and Adolescent Psychology, 33*, 650–661. doi:10.1207/s15374424jccp3304_1

Bierman, K. L., Coie, J. D., Dodge, K. A., Greenberg, M. T., Lochman, J. E., McMahon, R. J., & Pinderhughes, E. (2010). The effects of a multiyear universal social–emotional learning program: The role of student and school characteristics. *Journal of Consulting and Clinical Psychology, 78*, 156–168. doi:10.1037/a0018607

Biglan, A., Ary, D., & Wagenaar, A. C. (2000). The value of interrupted time-series experiments for community intervention research. *Prevention Science, 1*, 31–49. doi:10.1023/A:1010024016308

Bornstein, M. H. (1989). Sensitive periods in development: Structural characteristics and causal interpretations. *Psychological Bulletin, 105*, 179–197. doi:10.1037/0033-2909.105.2.179

Botvin, G. J., Epstein, J. A., Baker, E., Diaz, T., & Ifill-Williams, M. (1997). School-based drug abuse prevention with inner-city minority youth. *Journal of Child & Adolescent Substance Abuse, 6*, 5–19. doi:10.1300/J029v06n01_02

Botvin, G. J., Griffin, K. W., & Nichols, T. D. (2006). Preventing youth violence and delinquency through a universal school-based prevention approach. *Prevention Science, 7*, 403–408. doi:10.1007/s11121-006-0057-y

Botvin, G. J., Griffin, K. W., Paul, E., & Macaulay, A. P. (2003). Preventing tobacco and alcohol use among elementary school students through Life Skills

Training. *Journal of Child & Adolescent Substance Abuse, 12*, 1–17. doi:10.1300/J029v12n04_01

Brody, G. H., Yu, T., Chen, Y., Kogan, S. M., & Smith, K. (2012). The Adults in the Making program: Long-term protective stabilizing effects on alcohol use and substance use problems for rural African American emerging adults. *Journal of Consulting and Clinical Psychology, 80*, 17–28. doi:10.1037/a0026592

Bronfenbrenner, U. (1979). *The ecology of human development: Experiments by nature and design*. Cambridge, MA: Harvard University Press.

Bronfenbrenner, U. (2005). Ecological systems theory. In U. Bronfenbrenner (Ed.), *Making human beings: Bioecological perspectives on human development* (pp. 106–173). Thousand Oaks, CA: Sage.

Brown, C. H., Ten Have, T. R., Jo, B., Dagne, G., Wyman, P. A., Muthén, B., & Gibbons, R. D. (2009). Adaptive designs for randomized trials in public health. *Annual Review of Public Health, 30*, 1–25. doi:10.1146/annurev.publhealth.031308.100223

Caplan, G. (1964). *Principles of preventive psychiatry*. New York, NY: Basic Books.

Caruthers, A. S., Van Ryzin, M. J., & Dishion, T. J. (2014). Preventing high-risk sexual behaviors in early adulthood with family interventions in adolescence: Outcomes and developmental processes. *Prevention Science, 15*, 59–69. doi:10.1007/s11121-013-0383-9

Catalano, R. F., Haggerty, K. P., Hawkins, J. D., & Elgin, J. (2011). Prevention of substance use and substance use disorders: The role of risk and protective factors. In Y. Kaminer & K. C. Winters (Eds.), *Clinical manual of adolescent substance abuse treatment* (pp. 25–63). Washington, DC: American Psychiatric Publishing.

Catalano, R. F., & Hawkins, J. D. (1996). The social development model: A theory of antisocial behavior. In J. D. Hawkins (Ed.), *Delinquency and crime: Current theories* (pp. 149–197). New York, NY: Cambridge University Press.

Chakraborty, B., Collins, L. M., Strecher, V. J., & Murphy, S. A. (2009). Developing multicomponent interventions using fractional factorial designs. *Statistics in Medicine, 28*, 2687–2708. doi:10.1002/sim.3643

Cicchetti, D., & Blender, J. A. (2006). A multiple-levels-of-analysis perspective on resilience. *Annals of the New York Academy of Sciences, 1094*, 248–258. doi:10.1196/annals.1376.029

Cicchetti, D., & Rogosch, F. A. (1996). Equifinality and multifinality in developmental psychopathology. *Development and Psychopathology, 8*, 597–600. doi:10.1017/S0954579400007318

Collins, L. M., Baker, T. B., Mermelstein, R. J., Piper, M. E., Jorenby, D. E., Smith, S. S., . . . Fiore, M. C. (2011). The multiphase optimization strategy for engineering effective tobacco use interventions. *Annals of Behavioral Medicine, 41*, 208–226. doi:10.1007/s12160-010-9253-x

Cowen, E. L., & Work, W. C. (1988). Resilient children, psychological wellness, and primary prevention. *American Journal of Community Psychology, 16*, 591–607. doi:10.1007/BF00922773

Dishion, T. J., & Kavanagh, K. (2000). A multilevel approach to family-centered prevention in schools. *Addictive Behaviors, 25*, 899–911. doi:10.1016/S0306-4603(00)00126-X

Dishion, T. J., McCord, J., & Poulin, F. (1999). When interventions harm: Peer groups and problem behavior. *American Psychologist, 54*, 755–764. doi:10.1037/0003-066X.54.9.755

Dishion, T. J., Poulin, F., & Burraston, B. (2001). Peer group dynamics associated with iatrogenic effects in group interventions with high-risk young adolescents. In C. Erdley & D. W. Nangle (Eds.), *Damon's new directions in child development: The role of friendship in psychological adjustment* (pp. 79–92). San Francisco, CA: Jossey-Bass. doi:10.1002/cd.6

Durlak, J. A., Taylor, R. D., Kawashima, K., Pachan, M. K., DuPre, E. P., Celio, C. I., . . . Weissberg, R. P. (2007). Effects of positive youth development programs on school, family, and community systems. *American Journal of Community Psychology, 39*, 269–286. doi:10.1007/s10464-007-9112-5

Dusenbury, L., Brannigan, R., Falco, M., & Hansen, W. B. (2003). A review of research on fidelity of implementation: Implications for drug abuse prevention in school settings. *Health Education Research, 18*, 237–256. doi:10.1093/her/18.2.237

Eckenrode, J., Campa, M., Luckey, D. W., Henderson, C. R., Cole, R., Kitzman, H., . . . Olds, D. (2010). Long-term effects of prenatal and infancy nurse home visitation on the life course of youths: 19-year follow-up of a randomized trial. *Archives of Pediatrics & Adolescent Medicine, 164*, 9–15. doi:10.1001/archpediatrics.2009.240

Farmer, A. D., & Bierman, K. L. (2002). Predictors and consequences of aggressive-withdrawn problem profiles in early grade school. *Journal of Clinical Child and Adolescent Psychology, 31*, 299–311. doi:10.1207/S15374424JCCP3103_02

Fixsen, D. L., Naoom, S. F., Blase, K. A., Friedman, R. M., & Wallace, F. (2005). *Implementation research: A synthesis of the literature* (FMHI Pub. No. 231). Tampa: University of South Florida, Louis de la Parte Florida Mental Health Institute, National Implementation Research Network.

Gordon, R. S. (1983). An operational classification of disease prevention. *Public Health Reports, 98*, 107–109.

Greenberg, P., & Kusche, C. (1998). Preventive interventions for school-age deaf children: The PATHS curriculum. *Journal of Deaf Studies and Deaf Education, 3*, 49–63. doi:10.1093/oxfordjournals.deafed.a014340

Griffin, K. W., Botvin, G. J., & Nichols, T. R. (2004). Long-term follow-up effects of a school-based drug abuse prevention program on adolescent risky driving. *Prevention Science, 5*, 207–212. doi:10.1023/B:PREV.0000037643.78420.74

Griffin, K. W., Botvin, G. J., & Nichols, T. R. (2006). Effects of a school-based drug abuse prevention program for adolescents on HIV risk behavior in young adulthood. *Prevention Science, 7*, 103–112. doi:10.1007/s11121-006-0025-6

Hansen, W. B., Giles, S. M., & Fearnow-Kenney, M. (2000). *Improving prevention effectiveness*. Greensboro, NC: Tanglewood Research.

Hawkins, J. D., Catalano, R. F., Kosterman, R., Abbott, R., & Hill, K. G. (1999). Preventing adolescent health-risk behaviors by strengthening protection during childhood. *Archives of Pediatrics & Adolescent Medicine, 153*, 226–234. doi:10.1001/archpedi.153.3.226

Hawkins, J. D., Catalano, R. F., & Miller, J. Y. (1992). Risk and protective factors for alcohol and other drug problems in adolescence and early adulthood: Implications for substance abuse prevention. *Psychological Bulletin, 112*, 64–105. doi:10.1037/0033-2909.112.1.64

Hawkins, J. D., Jenson, J. M., Catalano, R. F., & Lishner, D. M. (1988). Delinquency and drug abuse: Implications for social services. *Social Service Review, 62*, 258–284. doi:10.1086/644546

Hawkins, J. D., & Weis, J. G. (1985). The social development model: An integrated approach to delinquency prevention. *Journal of Primary Prevention, 6*, 73–97. doi:10.1007/BF01325432

Hunter, F. T., & Youniss, J. (1982). Changes in functions of three relations during adolescence. *Developmental Psychology, 18*, 806–811. doi:10.1037/0012-1649.18.6.806

Ialongo, N., Poduska, J., Werthamer, L., & Kellam, S. (2001). The distal impact of two first-grade preventive interventions on conduct problems and disorder in early adolescence. *Journal of Emotional and Behavioral Disorders, 9*, 146–160. doi:10.1177/106342660100900301

Ialongo, N. S., Werthamer, L., Kellam, S. G., Brown, C. H., Wang, S., & Lin, Y. (1999). Proximal impact of two first-grade preventive interventions on the early risk behaviors for later substance abuse, depression, and antisocial behavior. *American Journal of Community Psychology, 27*, 599–641. doi:10.1023/A:1022137920532

Joyce, B., & Showers, B. (2002). *Student achievement through staff development* (3rd ed.). Alexandria, VA: Association for Supervision and Curriculum Development.

Kellam, S. G. (1975). *Mental health and going to school: The Woodlawn program of assessment, early intervention, and evaluation*. Chicago, IL: University of Chicago Press.

Kellam, S. G., Mackenzie, A. C. L., Brown, C. H., Poduska, J. M., Wang, W., Petras, H., & Wilcox, H. D. (2011). The good behavior game and the future of prevention and treatment. *Addiction Science & Clinical Practice, 6*, 73–84.

Kellam, S. G., Wang, W., Mackenzie, A. C. L., Brown, C. H., Ompad, D. C., Or, F., . . . Windham, A. (2014). The impact of the good behavior game, a universal classroom-based preventive intervention in first and second grades, on high-risk sexual behaviors and drug abuse and dependence disorders into young adulthood. *Prevention Science, 15*(1, Suppl.), 6–18. doi:10.1007/s11121-012-0296-z

Khoury, M. J., Gwinn, M., Yoon, P. W., Dowling, N., Moore, C. A., & Bradley, L. (2007). The continuum of translation research in genomic medicine: How can we accelerate the appropriate integration of human genome discoveries into health care and disease prevention? *Genetics in Medicine, 9*, 665–674. doi:10.1097/GIM.0b013e31815699d0

Kitzman, H. J., Olds, D. L., Cole, R. E., Hanks, C. A., Anson, E. A., Arcoleo, K. J., . . . Holmberg, J. (2010). Enduring effects of prenatal and infancy home visiting by nurses on children: Follow-up of a randomized trial among children at age 12 years. *Archives of Pediatrics & Adolescent Medicine, 164*, 412–418. doi:10.1001/archpediatrics.2010.76

Lilienfeld, A. M., & Lilienfeld, D. E. (1980). *Foundations of epidemiology*. New York, NY: Oxford University Press.

Masten, A. S. (2011). Resilience in children threatened by extreme adversity: Frameworks for research, practice, and translational synergy. *Development and Psychopathology, 23*, 493–506. doi:10.1017/S0954579411000198

Masten, A. S. (2012). Resilience in children: Vintage Rutter and beyond. In P. Slater & A. Quinn (Eds.), *Developmental psychology: Revisiting the classic studies* (pp. 204–221). London, England: Sage.

Mendelson, T., Greenberg, M. T., Dariotis, J. K., Gould, L. F., Rhoades, B. L., & Leaf, P. J. (2010). Feasibility and preliminary outcomes of a school-based mindfulness intervention for urban youth. *Journal of Abnormal Child Psychology, 38*, 985–994. doi:10.1007/s10802-010-9418-x

Miller-Johnson, S., Coie, J. D., Maumary-Gremaud, A., & Bierman, K. (2002). Peer rejection and aggression and early starter models of conduct disorder. *Journal of Abnormal Child Psychology, 30*, 217–230. doi:10.1023/A:1015198612049

Moffitt, T. E. (2003). Life-course persistent and adolescence-limited antisocial behavior: A 10-year research review and a research agenda. In B. B. Layey, T. E.

Moffitt, & A. Caspi (Eds.), *Causes of conduct disorder and juvenile delinquency* (pp. 49–75). New York, NY: Guilford Press.

National Institute on Drug Abuse. (2009). *Report from the NIDA Prevention Research Review Work Group: Review of the prevention research portfolio.* Rockville, MD: Author. Retrieved from http://www.drugabuse.gov/sites/default/files/prr_rpt.pdf

National Institute on Drug Abuse. (2011). *PA-11-311: Drug abuse prevention intervention research (R01).* Retrieved from http://grants.nih.gov/grants/guide/pa-files/PA-11-311.html

National Prevention Council. (2011). *National prevention strategy: America's plan for better health and wellness.* Washington, DC: Author. Retrieved from http://www.surgeongeneral.gov/initiatives/prevention/strategy/report.pdf

National Research Council and Institute of Medicine. (2009). *Preventing mental, emotional, and behavioral disorders among young people.* Washington, DC: National Academies Press.

Olds, D. L., Kitzman, H. J., Cole, R. E., Hanks, C. A., Arcoleo, K. J., Anson, E. A., . . . Stevenson, A. J. (2010). Enduring effects of prenatal and infancy home visiting by nurses on maternal life course and government spending: Follow-up of a randomized trial among children at age 12 years. *Archives of Pediatrics & Adolescent Medicine, 164*, 419–424. doi:10.1001/archpediatrics.2010.49

Palmgreen, P., Donohew, L., Lorch, E. P., Hoyle, R. H., & Stephenson, M. T. (2001). Television campaigns and adolescent marijuana use: Tests of sensation seeking targeting. *American Journal of Public Health, 91*, 292–296. doi:10.2105/AJPH.91.2.292

Palmgreen, P., Donohew, L., Lorch, E. P., Hoyle, R. H., & Stephenson, M. T. (2002). Television campaigns and sensation seeking targeting of adolescent marijuana use: A controlled time series approach. In R. C. Hornik (Ed.), *Public health communication: Evidence for behavior change* (pp. 35–56). Mahwah, NJ: Erlbaum.

Patient Protection and Affordable Care Act, Pub. L. 111–148, 42 U.S.C. §§ 18001-18121 (2010).

Pentz, M. A. (2000). Institutionalizing community-based prevention through policy change. *Journal of Community Psychology, 28*, 257–270. doi:10.1002/(SICI)1520-6629(200005)28:3<257::AID-JCOP3>3.0.CO;2-L

Pentz, M. A. (2010). Anti-drug-abuse policies as prevention strategies. In Z. Sloboda & W. J. Bukoski (Eds.), *Handbook of drug abuse prevention: Theory, science, and practice* (pp. 217–237). New York, NY: Kluwer Academic.

Ramey, C. T., & Campbell, F. A. (1991). Poverty, early childhood education, and academic competence: The Abecedarian experiment. In A. Huston (Ed.), *Children in poverty* (pp. 190–221). New York, NY: Cambridge University Press.

Resnick, H., Acierno, R., Kilpatrick, D. G., & Holmes, M. (2005). Description of an early intervention to prevent substance abuse and psychopathology in recent rape victims. *Behavior Modification, 29*, 156–188. doi:10.1177/0145445504270883

Riemer, M., Kelley, S. D., Casey, S., & Taylor Haynes, K. (2012). Developing effective research-practice partnerships for creating a culture of evidence-based decision making. *Administration and Policy in Mental Health and Mental Health Services Research, 39*, 248–257. doi:10.1007/s10488-011-0368-6

Riggs, N. R., Spruijt-Metz, D., Chou, C.-P., & Pentz, M. A. (2012). Relationships between executive cognitive function and lifetime substance use and obesity-related behaviors in fourth grade youth. *Child Neuropsychology, 18*, 1–11. doi:10.1080/09297049.2011.555759

Ringwalt, C. L., Ennett, S., Johnson, R., Rohrbach, L. A., Simons-Rudolph, A., Vincus, A., & Thorne, J. (2003). Factors associated with fidelity to substance use prevention curriculum guides in the nation's middle schools. *Health Education & Behavior, 30*, 375–391. doi:10.1177/1090198103030003010

Robertson, E. B., Sims, B. E., & Reider, E. E. (2012). Partnerships in drug abuse prevention services research: Perspectives from the National Institute on Drug Abuse. *Administration and Policy in Mental Health and Mental Health Services Research, 39*, 327–330. doi:10.1007/s10488-011-0400-x

Rutter, M. (1985). Resilience in the face of adversity. Protective factors and resistance to psychiatric disorder. *British Journal of Psychiatry, 147*, 598–611. doi:10.1192/bjp.147.6.598

Sakuma, K. L., Riggs, N. R., & Pentz, M. A. (2012). Translating evidence based violence and drug use prevention to obesity prevention: Development and construction of the Pathways program. *Health Education Research, 27*, 343–358. doi:10.1093/her/cyr095

Scheier, L. M. (Ed.). (2010). *Handbook of drug use etiology: Theory, methods and empirical findings.* Washington, DC: American Psychological Association.

Spoth, R., Redmond, C., Shin, C., Greenberg, M., Feinger, M., & Schainker, L. (2013). PROSPER community–university partnership delivery system effects on substance misuse through 6 ½ years past baseline from a cluster randomized controlled intervention trial. *Preventive Medicine, 56*, 190–196. doi:10.1016/j.ypmed.2012.12.013

Spoth, R., Trudeau, L., Shin, C., Ralston, E., Redmond, C., Greenberg, M., & Feinberg, M. (2013).

Longitudinal effects of universal preventive intervention on prescription drug misuse: Three randomized controlled trials with late adolescents and young adults. *American Journal of Public Health, 103*, 665–672. doi:10.2105/AJPH.2012.301209

Spoth, R., Trudeau, L., Shin, C., & Redmond, C. (2008). Long-term effects of universal preventive interventions on prescription drug misuse. *Addiction, 103*, 1160–1168. doi:10.1111/j.1360-0443.2008.02160.x

Spoth, R. L., Guyll, M., & Day, S. X. (2002). Universal family-focused interventions in alcohol-use disorder prevention: Cost-effectiveness and cost-benefit analyses of two interventions. *Journal of Studies on Alcohol, 63*, 219–228.

Spoth, R. L., Redmond, C., & Shin, C. (2000). Reducing adolescents' aggressive and hostile behaviors: Randomized trial effects of a brief family intervention 4 years past baseline. *Archives of Pediatrics & Adolescent Medicine, 154*, 1248–1257. doi:10.1001/archpedi.154.12.1248

Spoth, R. L., Redmond, C., & Shin, C. (2001). Randomized trial of brief family interventions for general populations: Adolescent substance use outcomes 4 years following baseline. *Journal of Consulting and Clinical Psychology, 69*, 627–642. doi:10.1037/0022-006X.69.4.627

Swisher, J. D., & Clayton, R. (2000). Sustainability of prevention. *Addictive Behaviors, 25*, 965–973. doi:10.1016/S0306-4603(00)00124-6

Tobler, A. L., & Komro, K. A. (2010). Trajectories or parental monitoring and communication and effects on drug use among urban young adolescents. *Journal of Adolescent Health, 46*, 560–568. doi:10.1016/j.jadohealth.2009.12.008

Tobler, N. S. (2000). Lessons learned. *Journal of Primary Prevention, 20*, 261–274. doi:10.1023/A:1021362620740

Tobler, N. S., Roona, M. R., Ochshorn, P., Marshall, D. G., Streke, A. V., & Stackpole, K. M. (2000). School-based adolescent drug prevention programs: 1998 meta-analysis. *Journal of Primary Prevention, 20*, 275–336. doi:10.1023/A:1021314704811

Volkow, N. D., Wang, G.-J., Tomasi, D., & Baler, R. D. (2013). Obesity and addiction: Neurobiological overlaps. *Obesity Reviews, 14*, 2–18. doi:10.1111/j.1467-789X.2012.01031.x

Wilcox, H. C., Kellam, S. G., Brown, C. H., Poduska, J. M., Ialongo, N. S., Wang, W., & Anthony, J. C. (2008). The impact of two universal randomized first- and second-grade classroom interventions on young adult suicide ideation and attempts. *Drug and Alcohol Dependence, 95*(Suppl. 1), S60–S73. doi:10.1016/j.drugalcdep.2008.01.005

CHAPTER 2

A HISTORY OF DRUG ABUSE PREVENTION SCIENCE

William Bukoski

In this chapter, I recount the story of prevention science from its early institutional foundations, outlining its social philosophies and discussing the competing political (and social) agendas that were central to the establishment of the National Institute on Drug Abuse (NIDA). The chapter begins with a discussion of the early growing pains in prevention, including both program development and evaluation. I then narrate how early discoveries from several program evaluation studies eventually forged the scientific foundations of prevention. This discussion highlights the contributions of drug policy experts and scientists who had a formative influence on the fledgling origins of prevention science. At its most fundamental level, the chapter represents a compendium or institutional history spanning several decades both before and during the time I worked in various capacities, including as chief of the Prevention Research Branch and associate director for prevention research at NIDA. During my 3-decade tenure at NIDA, I was fortunate to be able to work closely with some of the most promising scholars of our time and watch the institute, the field of prevention science, and the science of drug prevention grow in remarkable albeit somewhat unheralded ways.

BIRTH OF DRUG PREVENTION, PREVENTION EVALUATION, AND PREVENTION SCIENCE

The foundation of drug abuse prevention research shares its early conceptual history with the mental hygiene movement of the 1920s and 1930s, which began to focus on primary prevention through a richer understanding of the positive social, psychological, and physical development of children (Albee & Joffee, 1977). At that time, concern shifted from just preventing emotional or social disturbances or negative behaviors to promoting practices that improve self-concept, stress reduction, communication skills, family-rearing practices, and general well-being (Spaulding & Balch, 1983). Mental health's focus on the prevention of psychopathology was energized in the mid-1970s by the annual Vermont Conferences on the Primary Prevention of Psychopathology led by George Albee (Albee & Joffee, 1977; Heffernan & Albee, 1985). Even with the push for mental health to take center stage in public health debates, critics reinforced the need for evidence of program efficacy through production of methodologically rigorous and scientifically sound evaluation studies. There was at that time a growing skepticism over the evaluation strengths of primary prevention, and this concern

http://dx.doi.org/10.1037/14550-003
Handbook of Adolescent Drug Use Prevention: Research, Intervention Strategies, and Practice, L. M. Scheier (Editor)

persisted in the field of mental health through the 1980s (Snow & Swift, 1985).

GUIDING PRINCIPLES AND INITIAL FORMATIVE DEFINITIONS

The categorization of public health initiatives into primary, secondary, and tertiary prevention was an important legacy to modern prevention science (Commission on Chronic Illness, 1957; Gordon, 1983). The purpose of primary prevention is to eliminate or minimize the appearance of new cases of a disorder (incidence); secondary prevention identifies and successfully treats those afflicted with the disorders and thereby reduces existing cases (prevalence); tertiary prevention rehabilitates recuperating individuals and returns them to a productive life in society (Simeonsson, 1991). This conceptual framework was highly influential in the emergence of prevention as a credible medical science and formed the foundation of subsequent mental health and substance abuse policies, legislation, funding priorities, health practices, evaluations, and research (Last & Wallace, 1992).

Nearly 40 years after the first publication of the public health prevention model, and following the lead of mental health, a new conceptualization of prevention emerged to shape the continued evolution of prevention science. This new model was prompted by a substantial body of research that identified key predictive risk and protective factors contributing to subsequent mental health and substance abuse disorders. This new concept of prevention was articulated and promoted by the Institute of Medicine in its landmark publication *Reducing Risks for Mental Disorders* (Mrazek & Haggerty, 1994). The Institute of Medicine prevention model advanced universal interventions appropriate for the general population consisting of individuals who are not identifiable by risk level; selective interventions that are appropriate for individuals or groups at measurable and above-average risk of developing a disorder, and indicated interventions that are appropriate for individuals or groups with measurably higher levels of risk for a disorder (Mrazek & Haggerty, 1994). This new conceptualization of prevention was soon adopted in the fields of drug and alcohol abuse prevention to guide prevention policy, principles, program development, evaluation, and research studies (Sloboda & David, 1991).

AN EMERGING SCIENCE OF PREVENTION ANCHORED IN EPIDEMIOLOGY

A careful historical analysis shows that technically sound and rigorous scientific epidemiological methods in preventive medicine were adopted in prevention science to include observation of health events and outcomes; counting cases; estimating associations of possible population risks with observed events; formation of hypotheses; testing of hypotheses through case control, cohort, or experimental studies; and formulation of inferences from gathered evaluative data (Tyler & Last, 1992). Both Schuster and Kilbey (1992) and, more recently, Sloboda (2005) have described the lasting contributions of public health epidemiological methods to prevention of drug abuse.

The period from 1960 to 1970 highlighted the concerted use of drug surveys, community surveillance methods, and data-oriented community workgroups to characterize the national drug problem. This work provided much-needed information on the populations at risk and the nature, extent, and costs of ever-increasing drug consumption and its effects on public health, criminality, and national economic development. To illustrate, Ball and Chambers (1970) conducted a landmark study of opiate addiction in the United States. They drew important data on heroin use from three sources: the Federal Bureau of Narcotics file of active addicts based on reports from police departments, the health registry of the New York City health department, and admission reports from the National Institute of Mental Health's drug treatment hospitals located in Fort Worth, Texas, and Lexington, Kentucky. Ball and Chambers reported a current prevalence of 108,424 heroin and opiate addicts in the United States in 1967, which included 30,885 first-time reported addicts. They also found that for most heroin users, marijuana use preceded first injections of heroin and that most addicts' first use of marijuana occurred primarily during adolescence. The circumstances of marijuana use involved socializing peer groups and occurred in recreational areas or on the street.

DISCONTENT AND SOCIAL UPHEAVAL: STIMULUS FOR FEDERAL ACTION IN DRUG PREVENTION

The 1960s and 1970s were a time of great social upheaval, characterized by massive antiwar protests and the antiestablishment, counterculture hippie movement. Drug surveillance and street ethnography also heralded this unique epoch of U.S. history that witnessed dramatic increases in recreational drug use. Drug epidemics included dramatic upsurges in use of heroin, LSD, cocaine, amphetamines, methaqualone, and PCP and the resurgence of marijuana (Inciardi, 1990). Drug use became popularized by "reefer madness," stories of wild orgiastic parties, and the escapades of the beatnik generation (e.g., Kerouac, 1955). This was also a period in which New Journalism glorified drug use (Wolfe, 1969). More important, drug use was no longer restricted to the inner-city, the entertainment industry, or underground cultures but had also reached Middle America, with increased use reported by adolescents and young adults from all regions and walks of life (Inciardi, 1990). Drug-seeking behavior appeared to be expanding and was unchecked by law enforcement, the threat of incarceration, and sweeping antidrug activities conducted by the Federal Bureau of Narcotics (Musto, 1999).

National attention was now focused on the frightening increase in drug abuse with gripping newspaper headlines and vociferous antidrug editorials. These efforts fomented politically charged debate over the seeming failure of federal government efforts to mount successful interdiction and curtail the flow of dangerous illegal drugs into the country (Musto & Korsmeyer, 2002). Two prominent features of drug abuse generated public sentiment.

First was a rapid increase in street crime that affected both urban centers and rural communities. Until this time, many of the United States' bucolic rural settings had been spared the ravages of drug abuse. Media stories sensationalized linkages between crime (theft, robbery, assaults) and the heroin epidemic, suggesting that heroin addicts supported their addictions by resorting to crime (Brown, 1990). Drug use was demonized in a massive antidrug frenzy that preceded the much-heralded War on Drugs that was yet to come in the mid-1980s.

Second was increasing evidence that the heroin problem had migrated from the impoverished inner city to Middle America and was threatening a new class of users: affluent young adults attending college (Brown, 1990). Adding fuel to the fire was increased media attention in the *New York Times* and *Time* magazine to the many Vietnam veterans who returned stateside addicted to heroin. Fear spread that the heroin addiction of our nation's heroes would substantially increase drug-related street crimes (Brown, 1990). Lee Robins's (1973; Robins, Davis, & Goodwin, 1974) landmark study of Vietnam veteran heroin addicts showed this depiction was erroneous and reinforced that most heroin-addicted Vietnam veterans recovered and abstained from use. Needless to say, the picture painted of heroin and other illicit drug use continued to reinforce the linkages between crime and drug abuse.

Out of concern over these trends, President Nixon created the White House Special Action Office for Drug Abuse Prevention (SAODAP). The goal of this federal agency was to promote prevention of drug abuse through research, education, training, treatment, and rehabilitation (DuPont, 2010; Musto, 1999). Nixon named Jerome Jaffe as the nation's first drug czar. Jaffe was a highly regarded medical researcher with expertise in treating heroin addiction with methadone. Nixon charged SAODAP to effectively coordinate all federal efforts to reduce drug addiction by expanding effective drug treatment nationwide and supporting methadone clinics. To formalize this prevention mission nationwide and to enhance federal prevention funding, federal legislation (the Drug Abuse Office and Treatment Act of 1972; Pub. L. No. 92–255) was crafted and signed into law by President Nixon in March 1972 (DuPont, 2010).

The Drug Abuse Office and Treatment Act authorized the creation of NIDA in September 1972 with statutory authority in 1973, combining drug abuse program components from SAODAP, the Division of Narcotic Abuse and Drug Addiction, and the Addiction Research Center. The latter two drug abuse research and treatment agencies had formerly been housed in the National Institute of Mental Health. NIDA operated under the mandate of the newly formed Alcohol, Drug Abuse, and Mental Health Administration along with the National

Institute on Alcohol Abuse and Alcoholism previously established by Congress in 1970 and the National Institute of Mental Health (DuPont, 2010).

CRAFTING NIDA'S MISSION: A FEDERAL PREVENTION AGENCY

Robert L. DuPont, a prominent drug abuse treatment researcher and Harvard-trained psychiatrist, was appointed as the first director of NIDA (DuPont, 2009). On completion of his psychiatry residency, DuPont joined the District of Columbia Department of Corrections, where he managed its correction halfway houses and parole program. DuPont conducted a seminal study by drug testing all jail inmates and used this information to document the heroin epidemic sweeping the country. His analysis linked heroin addiction to the burgeoning crime rate in the nation's capital, and the study findings were subsequently published in the *New England Journal of Medicine* (DuPont, 1971). Within months of the release of DuPont's report in 1969, the District of Columbia government created a citywide series of methadone drug clinics that would lead to the successful treatment of more than 2,000 heroin addicts and contribute to the 50% reduction in the District's serious crime rate.

As NIDA's new director, DuPont developed an innovative staffing plan, formulated an effective division and branch structure, and prepared the necessary federal budget that would enable NIDA to orchestrate cutting-edge drug abuse prevention science in basic and applied research, training, and prevention programming (DuPont, 2009). During fall 1973 and the early months of 1974, DuPont recruited key senior staff to shape NIDA organizationally, including Karst Besteman as deputy director. Besteman was a well-respected expert in drug treatment methods and familiar with government operations. DuPont also hired the best drug abuse prevention staff from the U.S. Department of Education, SAODAP, the Division of Narcotic Abuse and Drug Addiction, and the Office of Economic Opportunity (Robert DuPont, personal communication, March 20, 2012).

To provide effective leadership in prevention, DuPont selected John Olsen to serve as the first chief of the Drug Prevention Branch at NIDA. Olsen, who previously served at SAODAP, was a retired Air Force officer with extensive experience in drug prevention programming and community training activities. Olsen then hired Bernard McColgan as his deputy branch chief. McColgan was a respected drug abuse prevention bureaucrat from the U.S. Department of Education's drug prevention program, then under the leadership of Helen Knowles. DuPont then hired me (in January 1977) to assist Olsen and create a scientifically sound evaluation program in drug abuse prevention, thereby initiating a theory-driven program of prevention evaluation research (Robert DuPont, personal communication, March 20, 2012).

NIDA LAUNCHES THE PREVENTION BRANCH

Under its new leadership, NIDA provided nationwide technical assistance in primary prevention, funding for innovative primary prevention models in the form of E07 federal education grants, and assistance in planning future demonstration models using the Delphi process (Bukoski, 1990). The Delphi process convened meetings for national, state, and local primary prevention service providers. These meetings provided a platform to discuss, debate, and reach consensus on a new lexicon of prevention terms and establish a series of recommendations for future primary prevention activities that would eventually be funded by NIDA's Prevention Branch. The Delphi process results were summarized in a publication titled *Toward a National Strategy for Primary Drug Abuse Prevention* (NIDA, 1975), which codified the current knowledge base of primary prevention strategies targeting school-age youths. Several promising programs were recommended to include values clarification and affective education to enhance self-esteem, promote prosocial values, and enhance academic motivation and youth alternatives to drug use (Bukoski, 1990). At that time, primary prevention shunned the use of the terms *drug use* and *drug abuse* (all drug use was illicit and abusive) and did not measure changes in drug use risk or drug use behaviors resulting from exposure to primary prevention (Schaps, Cohen, & Resnick, 1975). Interestingly, the three primary prevention strategies (values clarification, affective education, and alternatives) shared common program features with efforts undertaken by the mental hygiene movement fostered decades earlier to improve the competency and social development of youths (Bukoski, 1990).

Shortly thereafter, NIDA's Prevention Branch funded several technical assistance contracts. The intention was to advance training to the local community and disseminate primary prevention programs that promoted values clarification, affective education, and drug alternatives expertise. The first contract was Project Pyramid, which developed a series of publications that described primary prevention techniques and provided concise examples of their effective implementation in communities across the nation. Project Pyramid also provided local communities with experts in primary prevention techniques to train and motivate local staff implementers. NIDA's Prevention Branch also supported a contract to implement the Center for Multicultural Awareness, which provided multicultural primary prevention strategies and expert consultation to varied racial and ethnic groups across the country.

Within a short period of time, program staff at NIDA quickly recognized the importance of providing scientific advice to state and local prevention service providers. This assistance would encompass teaching local providers how to structure sound evaluation plans, implement data collection procedures, and engage in rigorous data analysis methods. These combined efforts would promote the first round of efficacy evaluations and eventually result in the accumulated body of knowledge today regarding the effectiveness of drug abuse prevention programs. The first National Prevention Evaluation Resource Network technical assistance contract was funded by a consortium of three drug abuse single-state agencies (New Jersey, Pennsylvania, and Wisconsin). The network created well-crafted manuals and publications that captured the best research measures and methods to evaluate primary prevention (J. F. French, Fisher, & Costa, 1983; J. G. French & Kaufman, 1981).

NIDA's Prevention Branch also provided a stream of funding through prevention education (E07) and research demonstration (R18) grants. John Swisher, professor of educational and psychological counseling at Pennsylvania State University, served as the first chairman of the prevention grant application review committee. These grant programs stimulated the development of new and innovative primary prevention educational and alternative programs in schools and communities and promoted research evaluation studies (Robert DuPont, personal communication, March 20, 2012).

MISSION OF THE PREVENTION RESEARCH BRANCH

The Omnibus Budget Reconciliation Act of 1981 (Pub. L. 97–35) created new federal block funding that shifted the planning and administration of drug treatment and prevention services to state governments. The same congressional legislation created NIDA's Division of Clinical Research in 1982 and for the first time carved out a Prevention Research Branch directed by Carl Leukefeld. Bernard McColgan was appointed Prevention Branch chief within a new Division of Prevention and Communications (Bukoski, 1990).

The Prevention Research Branch raised the visibility and credibility of drug abuse prevention research with a professional staff of prevention scientists and a dedicated prevention research budget. The branch's mission included creating a scientific knowledge base for drug abuse prevention through a series of competitive, peer-reviewed research grants that would result in systematic and controlled testing of theory-based prevention interventions. Over the course of these early years, the program budgets for prevention research to carry out these important formative scientific prevention studies were relatively meager. The Prevention Research Branch's program budgets were, for example, for Fiscal Year 1982, $2.87 million; Fiscal Year 1983, $3.94 million; Fiscal Year 1984, $4.57 million; Fiscal Year 1985, $5.95 million; Fiscal Year 1986, $6.19 million; and Fiscal Year 1987, $10.13 million (Bukoski, 1990). By comparison, the 2013 fiscal year budget for NIDA exceeded $1 billion with $246 million earmarked for the Epidemiology and Prevention Research Branch.

Over the course of the next 3 decades, NIDA's leadership in prevention research was spearheaded by a number of federal research administrators who served as chief of the Prevention Research Branch, including Carl Leukefeld, Robert Battjes, Catherine Bell, William Bukoski, and Elizabeth Robertson. Special recognition is also provided for Zili Sloboda, who served as director of the Division of Epidemiology and Prevention Research. In 1992, NIDA, along with National Institute on Alcohol

Abuse and Alcoholism and the National Institute of Mental Health, was transferred from the Alcohol, Drug Abuse, and Mental Health Administration to the National Institutes of Health (1999). This organizational shift meant that drug abuse prevention research was now formally included as part of the nation's premiere scientific medical enterprise. With the National Institutes of Health seal of recognition, approval, and budgeting security, it was only a matter of time until drug prevention research gained national and international recognition as a noteworthy field of science.

THE DIFFICULT ROAD FOR EARLY PREVENTION STUDIES AND THE EVOLUTION OF PREVENTION SCIENCE

A series of drug prevention evaluation studies conducted in the 1960s and 1970s were unable to provide unequivocal support for drug prevention program effectiveness (Leukefeld, 1991). In fact, few prevention programs actually mentioned drug prevention as one of their objectives in fear that the topic might stimulate youth curiosity about drug use. Instead, early prevention programs emphasized improving youth development, strengthening self-esteem, clarifying positive values, enhancing decision making, and providing youths with alternatives to substance use, such as using carpentry skills in community restoration projects. A review by Schaps, DeBartolo, Moskowitz, Palley, and Churgin (1981) of 127 drug prevention evaluation studies documented problems with research designs and lack of randomization associated with most early prevention trials. Nathan (1983) also recounted the failures of prevention to remedy the devastation of alcoholism and drug addiction, especially for high-risk subgroups such as women, fetuses and newborn infants, youths, minorities, and older adults. Furthermore, policy change as a communitywide intervention was also not at that time prominently discussed in the drug research literature. However, in the 1980s prevention science took a radical shift, broadening its base to include epidemiology and developing stronger ties to biologic, social, and environmental studies. Blending insight from these different disciplines provided new approaches to examining the role of many putative risk and protective factors that underlie the onset and progression of adolescent substance abuse (Sloboda, Cottler, Hawkins, & Pentz, 2009).

LANDMARK RESEARCH IN PREVENTION SCIENCE: THE NAPA PROJECT

Before the move to the National Institutes of Health, NIDA had already funded a groundbreaking research study evaluating school-based drug abuse prevention programs. The Napa Project represented a collaboration designed to test the efficacy of seven different prevention modalities in middle and junior high schools located in Napa, California (Moskowitz, Schaps, Malvin, & Schaeffer, 1984; Schaps & Moskowitz, 1984; Schaps, Moskowitz, Condon, & Malvin, 1982). Six of the seven programs focused on school instructional methods and social factors hypothesized to promote school bonding and affective skills. By design, none of these programs included instructional materials emphasizing drug use. A seventh program targeting junior high school youths taught individual decision-making skills, effects of media advertising, and drug refusal techniques to counter peers' offers to use drugs and provided information on the negative consequences of drug use.

The Napa Project provided a novel approach to prevention for several reasons. First, the research involved different levels of random assignment using schools (classroom management and Magic Circle programs), students (cross-age tutoring and school store programs), and classrooms (drug education) for the different program components. This effort resulted in hierarchically nested data (e.g., school as the unit of assignment and student as the unit of observation). Methodologically, and to avoid inflated Type I error rates (Murray, 1998), this required appropriate statistical controls for clustering (behavioral similarity that arises from socially intact groups). Second, the researchers also used process (fidelity) evaluations to assess the quality of teacher training and program implementation in the classroom. This effort helps provide insight into program delivery factors that can affect adoption (and adaptation). Third, the evaluation also used a wide range of outcomes assessing both teacher-level (e.g., faculty cohesiveness, teacher satisfaction, teaching climate) and student-level (e.g., self-esteem, social norms, drug use) measures to gauge program success.

Program evaluation findings indicated that affective education (consisting of six interventions), primarily emphasizing positive youth development, did not produce favorable program outcomes for drug use. Indeed, only the drug education program resulted in specious, albeit favorable, program effects, and for girls only. The researchers concluded that the body of evidence from this project brought into question the validity and utility of generic prevention programs targeting youth drug use (Malvin, Moskowitz, Schaps, & Schaeffer, 1985; Moskowitz, Malvin, Schaeffer, & Schaps, 1984; Schaps, Moskowitz, Malvin, & Schaeffer, 1986).

VITAL ROLE OF TESTING RELEVANT DRUG ABUSE PREVENTION THEORIES

The Napa Project provided rich insight into the need for theory-based prevention programs. It also raised issues related to implementation, process evaluation, and the need for capacity building to sustain prevention efforts. Since that time, NIDA has funded numerous randomized controlled trial prevention studies. Many of these programs are covered in considerable detail in this handbook (see Chapters 9–12, 15, 19, and 21), including descriptions of their history from the point of conception to implementation, evaluation, and even refinement. Fueling program development at this time were several landmark articles that provided needed structure to the field in terms of coalescing action theory with information detailing adolescent drug etiology (Flay & Petraitis, 1991; Hawkins, Catalano, & Miller, 1992).

Flay and Petraitis (1991) detailed how well-articulated prevention (action) theory supports intervention and program development. First, a rationally sound theory signals what intervening variables program curricula should directly address. These are the hypothesized developmental processes or targets of program instruction leading to behavior change. Second, theory establishes realistic magnitudes of effect in the intervening mechanisms that should be expected with program exposure. Third, theory explicates the complexity of drug abuse behaviors and encourages researchers to use comprehensive programs with doses sufficient to counteract developmental forces (i.e., peer pressure and resistance skills training) and provide veridical information to counteract social norms (i.e., drug consequences information). Added to this, prevention theory guides evaluation researchers to use advanced measures (behavioral and otherwise) and rigorous research designs. Prevention theory development and testing directly reflect salient risk and protective factors and processes identified in etiologic and epidemiological research.

EMERGENCE OF A SCIENCE OF DRUG PREVENTION INTERVENTIONS

Guided by prevention theory, specific drug abuse risk, protective, and resiliency factors have been identified (Bachman, Johnston, & O'Malley, 1998; Glantz & Johnson, 1999; Hawkins et al., 1992), leading to the design and testing of specific theory-based prevention interventions through randomized controlled research studies (Coie et al., 1993; Sloboda & Bukoski, 2003). These prevention programs include the use of drug information, persuasive communications, affective education, alternatives, social influences, life skills training, and comprehensive community-based interventions.

Drug Information Programs

Drug education programs that provide scientific knowledge about how drugs affect brain and behavior have been an essential part of drug abuse prevention throughout its history (Bukoski, 1985; Schuster & Kilbey, 1992). In the 1970s and 1980s, researchers provided drug information as an effective deterrent to youth drug use. The theoretical basis for drug information education draws from social persuasion theory (Hovland, Janis, & Kelley, 1953; McGuire, 1964) and research in mass media communication (Wartella & Middlestadt, 1991). One of the most compelling persuasive communication theories of the 1970s was the theory of reasoned action (Ajzen & Fishbein, 1973, 1977; M. Fishbein & Ajzen, 1975). According to this theory, intentions (i.e., future anticipation) are potent predictors of whether a person will engage in a particular behavior. Other factors include a person's beliefs about the social acceptability of drug use (and the perceived consequences or benefits of drug use) and the prevailing attitudes toward drug use (the perceived importance and pleasantness of drugs). One of the major points made by TRA is that attitudes and beliefs do not directly influence behavior; rather, their influence is mediated entirely through intentions. On the basis of the theory of reasoned action, persuasive communications should be aimed at moderating normative beliefs (prevalence) and expectancies (anticipated outcomes) regarding drug use. The combined influence of these will lead to changes in a person's intention to engage in a behavior.

Affective Education Prevention Programs

A second major approach to drug abuse prevention in the 1970s and 1980s involved affective education, which targeted underlying personal characteristics such as self-esteem, interpersonal communication skills, values clarification, decision making, problem solving, and attitudes toward schooling (Ahlgren & Norem-Hebeisen, 1979; Norem-Hebeisen, 1975; Schaps et al., 1975). The theoretical basis for affective education derives from numerous research studies examining a wide range of personality, family, social interactional, and environmental correlates of drug abuse (Brook, Lukoff, & Whiteman, 1977; Gorsuch & Butler, 1976; Jessor & Jessor, 1977; Kandel, 1978).

Alternatives to Drug Use

A third salient approach to drug abuse prevention implemented alternative life, work, outdoor, and community program experiences to counter vulnerability to drug use. Researchers hypothesized that youths who were provided alternative experiences to drug use would develop increased levels of confidence, self-reliance, and optimistic feelings about themselves (Bry, 1982; Cohen, 1973; Cook, Lawrence, Morse, & Roehl, 1984; Malvin et al., 1985; Swisher & Hu, 1983).

Social Influences Prevention Programs

A fourth prevention strategy involved the social influences model including psychological inoculation, correcting perceived social norms, and peer–media resistance skills training (Botvin & Griffin, 2004). According to a social inoculation approach, adolescent smoking behavior is the result of peer and adult social influences and media advertising that promotes cigarette use as socially acceptable and normative (Evans et al., 1978). Drawing from the theoretical work of McGuire (1964), Evans et al. (1978) trained or inoculated nonsmoking adolescents to recognize and resist prosmoking messages in the media and practice refusing peer or adult offers to smoke cigarettes. Evans et al. used normative education to confront youth perceptions that smoking was normative and corrected their misperceptions about how many of their friends and adults really smoked. The social influence approach also teaches students resistance skills to refuse drug offers. Students practice and role-play skills in the classroom and are provided corrective feedback from teachers and other students within the safe environment of the classroom. The "just say no" strategy owes a great deal to the influence of Evans et al. and also to the social learning–social influence model of Bandura (1977). A key tenet of social learning theory stresses the importance of observational learning (vicarious or direct), which occurs when new behaviors are primarily learned from another person who models the behavior in question (Bandura, 1986).

Early formative adolescent smoking prevention intervention research studies (Evans et al., 1981; Klepp, Halper, & Perry, 1986; Luepker, Johnson, Murray, & Pechacek, 1983; McAlister, Perry, Killen, Slinkard, & Maccoby, 1980) successfully included peers in the classroom who had been trained by researchers to teach and role-play scripted responses with their classmates to resist offers to use tobacco.

Competence Enhancement Prevention Programs

A fifth type of prevention intervention involves competence enhancement and life skills training (Botvin & Griffin, 2004). This multicomponent prevention approach expands on social influence models by combining competence enhancement with social assertiveness and resistance skills training. Implemented in the classroom by trained teachers, the model taught general life skills to enhance decision making, problem solving, goal setting, self-directed actions, stress and anxiety management, assertiveness, general interpersonal skills to improve conversing and interacting with other youths, and drug resistance (refusal) skills. This approach blends Bandura's (1977) social learning and self-efficacy model with problem behavior theory (Jessor & Jessor, 1977). Unlike the social influences model, which teaches skills to resist pressures to use drugs, competence enhancement provides general skills for prosocial development that are effective for potentially vulnerable youths with low self-esteem who may experiment with drugs as they interact within their social environment.

EFFICACY AND EFFECTIVENESS OF PROTOTYPIC DRUG PREVENTION PROGRAMS

Meta-analyses have become a favorite tool of drug prevention researchers because they collectively summarize empirical findings across several studies and use this to determine comparative effect sizes (Glass, McGaw, & Smith, 1981; Hedges & Olkin, 1985). Several meta-analyses now help summarize and tabulate effects across numerous well-conducted prevention studies. Tobler (1986), for instance, summarized findings from 143 drug abuse prevention program modalities (tested in 98 independent studies). She assigned each prevention study to one of five program models: (a) drug knowledge only; (b) affective education only; (c) peer focused, including resistance training and social and life skills; (d) knowledge plus affective; and (e) alternatives including community activities and training in job or personal competence. When controlling for differences in experimental design, the statistical assessment of effect size by modality on drug use showed that peer programs had a significantly larger effect size (.40) than any of the other program modality types. For example, the effect size for knowledge only was .03; for affective education, .07; for knowledge plus affective education, .15; and for alternatives, .22.

In a follow-up meta-analysis of drug prevention programs, Tobler et al. (2000) reported on the efficacy of 207 school-based drug prevention programs that were evaluated from 1978 through 1998 and a subset of 93 high-quality prevention research designs. Tobler et al. classified the 207 prevention programs into eight program models defined by prevention approach tested and method of instruction (noninteractive or interactive). Instruction in noninteractive classes was usually conducted by a teacher (or a police officer, as with the Drug Abuse Resistance Education Program) with content provided by lectures and student questions and answers. Teaching methods in interactive instruction used a variety of techniques, including peer-led role-plays teaching social resistance skill acquisition through learning, practice, and rehearsal; role play with peers in realistic but within-class settings; corrective feedback; training for skill generalization to real-world settings; and peer group discussions, presentations, or projects.

Results of the meta-analyses of drug use outcomes for all 207 programs showed an overall weighted effect size of .05 for noninteractive programs and .15 for interactive programs. For the subset of 93 high-quality research studies, the overall drug use weighted effect size was .03 for the noninteractive prevention programs and .16 for the interactive prevention programs. Tobler et al. (2000) indicated that, overall, some of the most innovative and promising school-based drug prevention programs produced relatively small effect sizes. The Drug Abuse Resistance Education Program showed little, if any, favorable effect preventing youth drug use. Didactic classroom lectures or noninteractive teaching of drug prevention content were substantially less effective than interactive teaching methods that used trained peers within the classroom (Tobler, 1992; Tobler et al., 2000).

Bruvold's (1993) meta-analysis of 94 school-based cigarette smoking prevention programs indicated that only two types of prevention programs were effective (with small effect sizes). The first program was categorized as social reinforcement and included teaching recognition of peer pressure to smoke, resistance skills training, and appreciation of the immediate physical and social consequences of drug use. The second effective prevention approach was labeled *alternatives* or *social norms* and attempted to increase self-esteem, reduce alienation, and quell boredom. Although this was not a strict meta-analysis, Hansen (1992) reviewed published research on drug prevention from 1980 to 1990 and reported that most prevention education strategies fell short of desired program effects on drug outcomes and only social influence programs and competence enhancement were effective.

EMERGENCE OF A SCIENCE OF PREVENTION IMPLEMENTATION

Research on the dose and fidelity of prevention program implementation has evolved into a vital component of prevention science. Ennett et al. (2003) reported that evidence-based drug prevention programs were not widely used by public school systems across the country. They assessed the data on prevention implementation from the School-Based Substance Use Prevention Study for the 1998–1999 school year to determine the frequency of use of many nationally known prevention programs: Life Skills Training, Project ALERT, Project Northland, STAR/ISTAR, Project Toward No Tobacco Use, Seattle Social Development Project, Adolescent Training and Learning to Avoid Steroids, Adolescent Alcohol Prevention Trial, and Michigan Model. The authors indicated that 62.25% of schoolteachers and administrators stated they provided some coverage of social skills or competence-enhanced instructional components in their lesson plans. Yet the vast majority of teachers (79.5%) reported that they used ineffective noninteractive or didactic teaching methods in their classrooms. In fact, only 14.23% of schoolteachers and administrators responded that they used both effective prevention content and effective interactive teaching methods in their classes.

FAILURE OF THEORY OR INSUFFICIENT PROGRAM IMPLEMENTATION DOSE OR FIDELITY

It is conceivable that the small effect sizes reported in the literature result from failure in theory or programmatic constraints that hinder implementation. Theory failure can arise if the action theory does not correctly specify risk or protective factors in a developmentally consistent manner. A table of specification should spell out the developmental and instructional linkage between the intervention strategies (e.g., specific skills being taught) and the target risk mechanisms. For instance, various instructional training methods including skits and behavioral rehearsal can teach youths how to initiate conversations, ask for change at a convenience store, and politely refuse drug offers. These are the basic tenets of social learning theory that guide many current prevention programs. Implementation failure can arise with inconsistent training methods, poor program adherence (not following the training materials), or varying dose. These relevant fidelity concerns (Dusenbury, Brannigan, Falco, & Hansen, 2003) are discussed in considerable detail in other chapters of this handbook (see Chapters 17, 23, 25, 28, and 29).

COMPREHENSIVE COMMUNITY-BASED DRUG PREVENTION PROGRAMS

Throughout the 1980s, both program staff at NIDA and researchers alike acknowledged the complexities of drug abuse. Discussion ensued regarding the numerous risk and protective factors implicated in drug use and the need for more comprehensive, multicomponent interventions. In response, NIDA published in 1984 a research funding announcement titled "Community Research in Alcohol and Drug Abuse." The announcement called for rigorous controlled research to study the individual and combined effects of theory-based multiple-component and comprehensive drug prevention strategies implemented at the community level, including media campaigns, drug policy, drug education in the schools, family interventions, and community organization strategies to directly involve and empower local prevention practitioners. Program staff at NIDA recognized that these innovative studies would be breaking new ground and might encounter challenges with implementation and finding appropriate methods to test efficacy and effectiveness.

Midwestern Prevention Project

The Midwestern Prevention Project (Pentz et al., 1989), a comprehensive, community-based drug abuse prevention research study, was one of several projects funded through the community research request for application. This quasi-experimental study was conducted in 15 metropolitan communities (Standard Metropolitan Statistical Area) and involved 50 schools located in Kansas City (Kansas and Missouri). The project began in 1984 and was expanded in 1987 to the Standard Metropolitan Statistical Area representing Indianapolis, Indiana, to replicate the prevention model with a randomized experimental design. The program included a 10-session school-based social influences and competence enhancement drug prevention curriculum for sixth and seventh graders, community-wide mass media, coordinated parent–child homework and discussion sessions with other parents, formation of community-level prevention coalitions, and implementation of preventive health policy supportive of the study's objectives. Statistical analysis of baseline to 1-year follow-up differences in drug prevalence between students in the treatment and control groups were assessed using covariance and change score models and used the proportion and logit of each proportion as the metric of effectiveness. Statistical comparison showed that for all drug use types and levels, the proportion of students reporting drug use was significantly higher in control than in treatment schools ($p < .05$; Pentz et al., 1989).

Communities That Care

The Community Youth Development Study based on the Communities That Care (CTC) prevention strategy is also a comprehensive and community-based drug abuse prevention program (Hawkins et al., 2008) and stands as another important contribution to prevention science. Briefly, the Community Youth Development Study was evaluated using a longitudinal study of 12 pairs of matched communities randomly assigned to treatment or control conditions (Hawkins et al., 2008). CTC finds traction in the social development model (Catalano & Hawkins, 1996; Hawkins & Weis, 1985) and draws from three basic theoretical perspectives: control theory (Hirschi, 1969), differential association (Matsueda, 1988), and social learning theory applied to delinquency (Akers, Krohn, Lanza-Kaduce, & Radosevich, 1979). The collective strength of these theories suggests that prosocial bonding will occur for youths who (a) have an opportunity to interact in positive social groups they may find in school and among peers, their family, and local community organizations; (b) have developed social skills to participate in group activities; and (c) receive positive reinforcement for demonstrated prosocial behaviors. CTC is a prevention system that organizes and trains coalitions consisting of community leaders and stakeholders to identify unique community risk and protective factors to problem behaviors through administration of CTC's Youth Survey (Arthur et al., 2007). Each community coalition is trained by CTC to assess important bellwether indicators of community risk and protection and select from CTS's *Guide to Prevention Strategies* (Hawkins & Catalano, 2004) appropriate evidence-based prevention programs to reduce the specific risk factors unique to that community (Hawkins et al., 2008).

CTC findings from Pennsylvania communities that focused on a multilevel assessment of 15 risk factors and six drug use and delinquency outcomes for sixth-, eighth-, 10th-, and 12th-grade CTC cohorts ($N = 98{,}436$ students) indicated reduced rates of risk factors and problem behavior outcomes for CTC communities in comparison with non-CTC communities (Feinberg, Greenberg, Osgood, Sartorius, & Bontempo, 2007). The effects of CTC were assessed prospectively for nondrug initiates (alcohol, cigarettes, smokeless tobacco, marijuana, and inhalants) and for students who had evidenced delinquent behavior by the fifth grade (Hawkins et al., 2009). Overall, significant statistical effects favoring CTC communities were found when measuring the incidence rates of alcohol, cigarettes, and smokeless tobacco.

Monahan, Hawkins, and Abbott (2013) recently published a meta-analysis of the effects of CTC on eighth-grade delinquent behavior. Results of the analysis within each matched pair of communities indicated that CTC communities had lower delinquency in the eighth grade than matched control communities, with an overall weighted effect size of −.31.

LEGACY OF DISTINGUISHED SENIOR DRUG ABUSE PREVENTION SCIENTISTS

The publication of the watershed prevention science article by Coie et al. (1993) proclaimed the fact that prevention had reached a new plateau of accomplishment and recognition and should henceforth be considered a science of prevention. Notwithstanding, the transformation of this new science required much hard work and diligence by a cadre of researchers and federal research administrators. Over the past several decades, drug prevention research has evolved and matured into a sophisticated science. Much credit and professional praise is merited by the large number of senior drug abuse prevention scientists who crafted the design of their own unique theory-based preventive interventions and went through the arduous and rigorous process of applying for and securing federal funding for their research studies. The work of many of these scientists is showcased in this handbook. Table 2.1

TABLE 2.1

Distinguished Prevention Scientists

Scientists	Contribution	Reference
Bardo, Michael	Sensation seeking as a risk factor to drug abuse	Bardo & Mueller (1991)
Botvin, Gilbert	Life Skills Training program	Botvin, Baker, Filazzola, & Botvin (1990)
Brook, Judith	Child precursor risk factors to drug abuse	Brook, Whiteman, Cohen, & Tanaka (1992)
Clayton, Richard	Director of the first NIDA-funded prevention research center; legendary work on the epidemiology of drug abuse	Clayton (1986)
Collins, Linda	Innovative work in statistical analysis and director of NIDA's first prevention methodology center	Collins & Horn (1991); Collins & Seitz (1994)
Dishion, Thomas	Clinical and prevention research on parent and peer factors in drug abuse	Dishion & Kavanagh (2003)
Donohew, Louis	Theoretical study of persuasive communications related to sensation seeking and drug abuse prevention	Donohew, Lorch, & Palmgreen (1991)
DuPont, Robert	Distinguished history of drug testing research in industry and in public and private education	DuPont & Saylor (2003)
Flay, Brian	Development of the theory of triadic influence of smoking and mass media and intervention research	Flay (1986, 1999)
Goldberg, Linn	Groundbreaking study of adolescent steroid prevention	Goldberg et al. (1996)
Hansen, William	Intervention research on social influences to adolescent drug abuse and for development of the All-Stars prevention program	Hansen & Graham (1991); Hansen (1996)
Johnson, C. Anderson	Inspiration for and development and testing of the Self Management and Resistance Training drug abuse prevention strategy and scientific advocacy for comprehensive community-based drug prevention	Hansen, Johnson, Flay, Graham, & Sobel (1988); Johnson et al. (1990)
Johnston, Lloyd, and colleagues	Monumental contributions to prevention and epidemiology resulting from the Monitoring the Future studies	Johnston, O'Malley, Bachman, Schulenberg, & Miech (2014)
Kellam, Sheppard	Landmark studies of the early antecedents of drug abuse	Kellam, Ensminger, & Simon (1980); Kellam, Rebok, Ialongo, & Mayer (1994)
Kumpfer, Karol	Development and testing of the Strengthening Families Program; international studies of dissemination	Kumpfer, Molgaard, & Spoth (1996)
Oetting, Gene	Development of peer cluster theory	Oetting & Beauvais (1987)
Ringwalt, Chris	Highly informative surveys that measure the adoption of evidence-based drug prevention in schools across the country	Ringwalt et al. (2011)
Scheier, Lawrence	Extensive study of drug abuse etiology	Scheier (2010)
Schinke, Steven	Drug intervention research	Schinke, Botvin, & Orlandi (1991)
Sloboda, Zili	Brilliant and inspired NIDA leadership to drug abuse research directly leading to the creation of prevention science; scientific writings, critical research studies, and untiring dedicated service to the Society for Prevention Research	Sloboda (2005); Sloboda & David (1991); Sloboda, Stephens, et al. (2009)
Spoth, Richard	Seminal studies of family and systemwide programs for drug abuse prevention	Spoth, Redmon, Shing, & Azevedo (2004)
Tarter, Ralph	Innovative investigation of the genetics of drug abuse	Tarter (2002); Vanyukov et al. (2012)
Wills, Thomas	Risk factors for adolescent drug abuse	Wills, Windle, & Cleary (1998)

Note. NIDA = National Institute on Drug Abuse.

shows the distinguished prevention scientists who deserve special recognition from the scientific community and from the thousands of communities and hundreds of thousands of students, families, media broadcasters, and community stakeholders who have benefited from their (and their colleagues') tireless efforts.

FUTURE OF DRUG ABUSE PREVENTION SCIENCE

On the basis of its rich legacy of innovative theory, rigorous controlled trials of prevention interventions, practical translation studies, and a dynamic and rapidly growing Society for Prevention Research, prevention science has a bright and promising future. As an organization, the Society for Prevention Research serves an important professional function, providing stimulus for future growth, sophistication, and maturation of the field into an authentic science. The society now has its own peer-reviewed journal, *Prevention Science;* counts among its members a growing cadre of research scientists; has an affiliated association of early career scientists and mentors; and holds annual scientific meetings and training workshops on emerging technical issues. As a field, prevention science will continue to provide unlimited and challenging opportunities not only to enhance drug abuse prevention, but also to promote tremendous gains in neuroscience, genetics, developmental epidemiology, nutrition and obesity, HIV/AIDS, violence, and kindergarten through 12th-grade education through transdisciplinary research (Bukoski, 2003).

This new approach to prevention science recognizes that complex human behavior such as drug abuse reflects a dynamic interaction and developmental unfolding of genetics and neurochemistry within the influences of social and environmental factors (D. H. Fishbein & Ridenour, 2013). D. H. Fishbein and Ridenour (2013) suggested that involvement and collaboration within and across scientific domains is crucial to create better understanding of the etiology, epidemiology, and prevention of drug behaviors and perhaps leading in the future to formulation of personalized prevention strategies.

In summary, the future advancement of prevention science is strengthened through continued mentored training of new investigators, innovative scientific inquiries by a dedicated cadre of senior prevention scientists, and continued scientific leadership and funding support from a collection of National Institutes of Health institutes and offices.

References

Ahlgren, A., & Norem-Hebeisen, A. A. (1979). Self-esteem patterns distinctive of groups of drug abusing and other dysfunctional adolescents. *Substance Use & Misuse, 14*, 759–777. doi:10.3109/10826087909041906

Ajzen, I., & Fishbein, M. (1973). Attitudinal and normative variables as predictors of specific behaviors. *Journal of Personality and Social Psychology, 27*, 41–57. doi:10.1037/h0034440

Ajzen, I., & Fishbein, M. (1977). Attitude-behavior relations: A theoretical analysis and review of empirical research. *Psychological Bulletin, 84*, 888–918. doi:10.1037/0033-2909.84.5.888

Akers, R. L., Krohn, M., Lanza-Kaduce, L., & Radosevich, M. (1979). Social learning and deviant behavior: A specific test of a general theory. *American Sociological Review, 44*, 636–655. doi:10.2307/2094592

Albee, G. W., & Joffee, J. M. (Eds.). (1977). *Primary prevention of psychopathology: Vol. 1. The issues.* Hanover, NH: University Press of New England.

Arthur, M. W., Briney, J. S., Hawkins, J. D., Abbott, R. D., Brooke-Weiss, B., & Catalano, R. F. (2007). Measuring community risk and protection using the Communities That Care Youth Survey. *Evaluation and Program Planning, 30*, 197–211. doi:10.1016/j.evalprogplan.2007.01.009

Bachman, J. G., Johnston, L. D., & O'Malley, P. M. (1998). Explaining recent increases in students' marijuana use: Impacts of perceived risks and disapproval, 1976 through 1996. *American Journal of Public Health, 88*, 887–892. doi:10.2105/AJPH.88.6.887

Ball, J. C., & Chambers, C. D. (Eds.). (1970). *The epidemiology of opiate addiction in the United States.* Springfield, IL: Charles C Thomas.

Bandura, A. (1977). Self-efficacy: Toward a unifying theory of behavioral change. *Psychological Review, 84*, 191–215. doi:10.1037/0033-295X.84.2.191

Bandura, A. (1986). *Social foundations of thought and action: A social cognitive theory.* Englewood Cliffs, NJ: Prentice-Hall.

Bardo, M. T., & Mueller, C. W. (1991). Sensation seeking and drug abuse prevention from a biological perspective. In L. Donohew, H. E. Sypher, & W. J. Bukoski (Eds.), *Persuasive communication and drug and drug abuse prevention* (pp. 195–208). Hillsdale, NJ: Erlbaum.

Botvin, G. J., Baker, E., Filazzola, A. D., & Botvin, E. M. (1990). A cognitive behavioral approach to substance abuse prevention: One-year follow-up. *Addictive Behaviors, 15*, 47–63. doi:10.1016/0306-4603(90)90006-J

Botvin, G. J., & Griffin, K. W. (2004). Life Skills Training: Empirical findings and future directions. *The Journal of Primary Prevention, 25*, 211–232. doi:10.1023/B:JOPP.0000042391.58573.5b

Brook, J. S., Lukoff, I. F., & Whiteman, M. (1977). Peer, family, and personality domains as related to adolescents' drug behavior. *Psychological Reports, 41*, 1095–1102. doi:10.2466/pr0.1977.41.3f.1095

Brook, J. S., Whiteman, M., Cohen, P., & Tanaka, J. S. (1992). Childhood precursors of adolescent drug use: A longitudinal analysis. *Genetic, Social, and General Psychology Monographs, 118*, 195–213.

Brown, B. S. (1990). The growth of drug abuse treatment systems. In J. A. Inciardi (Ed.), *Handbook of drug control in the United States* (pp. 29–50). New York, NY: Greenwood Press.

Bruvold, W. H. (1993). A meta-analysis of adolescent smoking prevention programs. *American Journal of Public Health, 83*, 872–880. doi:10.2105/AJPH.83.6.872

Bry, B. H. (1982). Reducing the incidence of adolescent problems through preventive intervention: One- and five-year follow-up. *American Journal of Community Psychology, 10*, 265–276. doi:10.1007/BF00896494

Bukoski, W. J. (1985). School-based substance abuse prevention: A review of program research. *International Journal of the Addictions, 20*, 1693–1706.

Bukoski, W. J. (1990). The federal approach to primary drug abuse prevention and education. In J. A. Inciardi (Ed.), *Handbook of drug control in the United States* (pp. 93–114). New York, NY: Greenwood Press.

Bukoski, W. J. (2003). The emerging science of drug abuse prevention. In Z. Sloboda & W. J. Bukoski (Eds.), *Handbook of drug abuse prevention: Theory, science, and practice* (pp. 3–24). New York, NY: Kluwer Academic.

Catalano, R. F., & Hawkins, J. D. (1996). The social development model: A theory of antisocial behavior. In J. D. Hawkins (Ed.), *Delinquency and crime: Current theories* (pp. 149–197). New York, NY: Cambridge University Press.

Clayton, R. R. (1986). Multiple drug use: Epidemiology, correlates, and consequences. *Recent Developments in Alcoholism, 4*, 7–38. doi:10.1007/978-1-4899-1695-2_1

Cohen, A. Y. (1973). *Alternatives to drug abuse: Steps toward prevention.* Washington, DC: U.S. Government Printing Office. Retrieved from ERIC database. (ED099750)

Coie, J. D., Watt, N. F., West, S. G., Hawkins, J. D., Asarnow, J. R., Markman, H. J., . . . Long, B. (1993). The science of prevention: A conceptual framework and some directions for a national research program. *American Psychologist, 48*, 1013–1022. doi:10.1037/0003-066X.48.10.1013

Collins, L. M., & Horn, J. L. (1991). *Best methods for the analysis of change: Recent advances, unanswered questions, future directions.* Washington, DC: American Psychological Association.

Collins, L. M., & Seitz, L. A. (Eds.). (1994). *Advances in data analysis for prevention intervention research* (NIDA Research Monograph 142, Publication No. NIH 94-3599). Rockville, MD: National Institute on Drug Abuse.

Commission on Chronic Illness. (1957). *Chronic illness in the United States* (Vol. 1). Cambridge, MA: Harvard University Press.

Cook, R., Lawrence, H., Morse, C., & Roehl, J. (1984). An evaluation of the alternatives approach to drug abuse prevention. *Substance Use & Misuse, 19*, 767–787. doi:10.3109/10826088409057222

Dishion, T. J., & Kavanagh, K. (2003). *Intervening in adolescent problem behavior: A family centered approach.* New York, NY: Guilford Press.

Donohew, L., Lorch, E., & Palmgreen, P. (1991). Sensation seeking and targeting of televised anti-drug PSAs. In L. Donohew, H. E. Sypher, & W. J. Bukoski (Eds.), *Persuasive communication and drug abuse prevention* (pp. 209–228). Hillsdale, NJ: Erlbaum.

Drug Abuse Office and Treatment Act of 1972, Pub. L. No. 92–255, 21 U.S.C. 1101 *et seq.*

DuPont, R. L. (1971). Profile of a heroin-addiction epidemic. *New England Journal of Medicine, 285*, 320–324. doi:10.1056/NEJM197108052850605

DuPont, R. L. (2009). Reflections on the early history of the National Institute on Drug Abuse (NIDA): Implications for today. *Journal of Drug Issues, 39*, 5–14. doi:10.1177/002204260903900101

DuPont, R. L. (2010). Present at the creation—NIDA's first five years. *Drug and Alcohol Dependence, 107*, 82–87. doi:10.1016/j.drugalcdep.2009.05.007

DuPont, R. L., & Saylor, K. E. (2003). Drug tests in prevention research. In Z. Sloboda & W. J. Bukoski (Eds.), *Handbook of drug abuse prevention: Theory, science, and practice* (pp. 199–216). Hillsdale, NJ: Erlbaum.

Dusenbury, L., Brannigan, R., Falco, M., & Hansen, W. B. (2003). A review of research on fidelity of implementation: Implications for drug abuse prevention in school settings. *Health Education Research, 18*, 237–256. doi:10.1093/her/18.2.237

Ennett, S. T., Ringwalt, C. L., Thorne, J., Rohrbach, L. A., Vincus, A., Simons-Rudolph, A., & Jones, S.

(2003). A comparison of current practices in school-based substance use prevention programs with meta-analysis findings. *Prevention Science, 4*, 1–14. doi:10.1023/A:1021777109369

Evans, R. I., Rozelle, R. M., Maxwell, S. E., Raines, B. E., Dill, C. A., Guthrie, T. J., . . . Hill, P. C. (1981). Social modeling films to deter smoking in adolescents: Results of a three-year field investigation. *Journal of Applied Psychology, 66*, 399–414. doi:10.1037/0021-9010.66.4.399

Evans, R. I., Rozelle, R. M., Mittlemark, M. B., Hansen, W. B., Bane, A. L., & Havis, J. (1978). Deterring the onset of smoking in children: Knowledge of immediate physiological effects and coping with peer pressure, media pressure, and parent modeling. *Journal of Applied Social Psychology, 8*, 126–135. doi:10.1111/j.1559-1816.1978.tb00771.x

Feinberg, M. E., Greenberg, M. T., Osgood, D. W., Sartorius, J., & Bontempo, D. (2007). Effects of the Communities That Care model in Pennsylvania on youth risk and problem behaviors. *Prevention Science, 8*, 261–270. doi:10.1007/s11121-007-0073-6

Fishbein, D. H., & Ridenour, T. A. (2013). Advancing transdisciplinary translation for prevention of high-risk behaviors: Introduction to the special issue. *Prevention Science, 14*, 201–205. doi:10.1007/s11121-013-0394-6

Fishbein, M., & Ajzen, I. (1975). *Belief, attitude, intention and behavior: An introduction to theory and research.* Reading, MA: Addison-Wesley.

Flay, B. R. (1986). Mass media linkages with school-based programs for drug abuse prevention. *Journal of School Health, 56*, 402–406. doi:10.1111/j.1746-1561.1986.tb05782.x

Flay, B. R. (1999). Understanding environmental, situational and intrapersonal risk and protective factors for youth tobacco use: The theory of triadic influence. *Nicotine & Tobacco Research, 1*(Suppl.1), S111–S114. doi:10.1080/14622299050011911

Flay, B. R., & Petraitis, J. (1991). Methodological issues in drug use prevention research: Theoretical foundations. In C. G. Leukefeld & W. J. Bukoski (Eds.), *Drug abuse prevention intervention research: Methodological issues* (NIDA Research Monograph 107, Publication No. ADM 91-1761, pp. 81–109). Rockville, MD: National Institute on Drug Abuse.

French, J. F., Fisher, C. C., & Costa, S. J. (Eds.). (1983). *Working with evaluators: A guide for drug abuse prevention program managers* (Publication No. ADM 83-1233). Rockville, MD: National Institute on Drug Abuse.

French, J. G., & Kaufman, N. J. (Eds.). (1981). *Handbook for prevention evaluation* (Publication No. ADM 84-1145). Rockville, MD: National Institute on Drug Abuse.

Glantz, M. D., & Johnson, J. L. (Eds.). (1999). *Resilience and development.* New York, NY: Kluwer Academic.

Glass, G., McGaw, B., & Smith, M. (1981). *Meta-analysis in social research.* Beverly Hills, CA: Sage.

Goldberg, L., Elliot, D. L., Clarke, G. N., MacKinnon, D. P., Moe, E. L., Zoref, L., . . . Lapin, A. (1996). Effects of a multidimensional anabolic steroid prevention intervention: The Adolescents Training and Learning to Avoid Steroids (ATLAS) program. *JAMA, 276*, 1555–1562. doi:10.1001/jama.1996.03540190027025

Gordon, R. S. (1983). An operational classification of disease prevention. *Public Health Reports, 98*, 107–109.

Gorsuch, R. L., & Butler, M. C. (1976). Initial drug abuse: A review of predisposing social psychological factors. *Psychological Bulletin, 83*, 120–137. doi:10.1037/0033-2909.83.1.120

Hansen, W. B. (1992). School-based substance abuse prevention: A review of the state of the art in curriculum, 1980-1990. *Health Education Research, 7*, 403–430. doi:10.1093/her/7.3.403

Hansen, W. B. (1996). Pilot test results comparing the All Star Program with seventh grade D.A.R.E.: Program integrity and mediating variable analysis. *Substance Use & Misuse, 31*, 1359–1377. doi:10.3109/10826089609063981

Hansen, W. B., & Graham, J. W. (1991). Preventing alcohol, marijuana, and cigarette use among adolescents: Peer pressure resistance training versus establishing conservative norms. *Preventive Medicine, 20*, 414–430. doi:10.1016/0091-7435(91)90039-7

Hansen, W. B., Johnson, C. A., Flay, B. R., Graham, J. W., & Sobel, J. (1988). Affective and social influences approaches to the prevention of multiple substance abuse among seventh grade students: Results from Project SMART. *Preventive Medicine, 17*, 135–154. doi:10.1016/0091-7435(88)90059-X

Hawkins, J. D., & Catalano, R. F. (2004). *Communities that care: Prevention strategies guide.* South Deerfield, MA: Channing Bete.

Hawkins, J. D., Catalano, R. F., Arthur, M. W., Egan, E., Brown, E. C., Abbott, R. D., & Murry, D. M. (2008). Testing Communities That Care: The rationale, design and behavioral baseline equivalence of the Community Youth Development Study. *Prevention Science, 9*, 178–190. doi:10.1007/s11121-008-0092-y

Hawkins, J. D., Catalano, R. F., & Miller, J. Y. (1992). Risk and protective factors for alcohol and other drug problems in adolescence and early adulthood: Implications for substance abuse prevention. *Psychological Bulletin, 112*, 64–105. doi:10.1037/0033-2909.112.1.64

Hawkins, J. D., Oesterle, S., Brown, E., Arthur, M., Abbott, R. D., Fagan, A. A., & Catalano, R. F. (2009). Results of a Type 2 translational research trial to prevent adolescent drug use and delinquency: A test of Communities That Care. *Archives of Pediatrics & Adolescent Medicine, 163*, 789–798. doi:10.1001/archpediatrics.2009.141

Hawkins, J. D., & Weis, J. G. (1985). The social development model: An integrated approach to delinquency prevention. *The Journal of Primary Prevention, 6*, 73–97. doi:10.1007/BF01325432

Hedges, L., & Olkin, I. (1985). *Statistical methods for meta-analysis.* New York, NY: Academic Press.

Heffernan, J. A., & Albee, G. W. (1985). Prevention, perspectives: From Vermont to Washington. *American Psychologist, 40*, 202–204. doi:10.1037/0003-066X.40.2.202

Hirschi, T. (1969). *Causes of delinquency.* Berkeley: University of California Press.

Hovland, C., Janis, L., & Kelley, H. (1953). *Communication and persuasion.* New Haven, CT: Yale University Press.

Inciardi, J. A. (Ed.). (1990). *Handbook of drug control in the United States.* New York, NY: Greenwood Press.

Jessor, R., & Jessor, S. L. (1977). *Problem behavior and psychosocial development—A longitudinal study of youth.* New York, NY: Academic Press.

Johnson, C. A., Pentz, M. A., Weber, M. D., Dwyer, J. H., Baer, N., MacKinnon, D. P., . . . Flay, B. R. (1990). Relative effectiveness of comprehensive community programming for drug abuse prevention with high-risk and low-risk adolescents. *Journal of Consulting and Clinical Psychology, 58*, 447–456. doi:10.1037/0022-006X.58.4.447

Johnston, L. D., O'Malley, P. M., Bachman, J. G., Schulenberg, J. E., & Miech, R. A. (2014). *Monitoring the Future national survey results on drug use, 1975–2013: Vol. I. Secondary school students.* Ann Arbor: University of Michigan.

Kandel, D. B. (1978). *Longitudinal research on drug use: Empirical findings and methodological issues.* New York, NY: Hemisphere.

Kellam, S. G., Ensminger, M. E., & Simon, M. B. (1980). Mental health in first grade and teenage drug, alcohol, and cigarette use. *Drug and Alcohol Dependence, 5*, 273–304. doi:10.1016/0376-8716(80)90003-4

Kellam, S. G., Rebok, G. W., Ialongo, N., & Mayer, L. (1994). The course and malleability of aggressive behavior from early first grade into middle school: Results of a developmental epidemiologically-based preventive trial. *Journal of Child Psychology and Psychiatry, 35*, 259–281. doi:10.1111/j.1469-7610.1994.tb01161.x

Kerouac, J. (1955). *On the road.* New York, NY: Penguin Books.

Klepp, K.-I., Halper, A., & Perry, C. L. (1986). The efficacy of peer leaders in drug abuse prevention. *Journal of School Health, 56*, 407–411. doi:10.1111/j.1746-1561.1986.tb05783.x

Kumpfer, K. L., Molgaard, V., & Spoth, R. (1996). The Strengthening Families Program for the prevention of delinquency and drug use. In R. D. Peters & R. J. McMahon (Eds.), *Preventing childhood disorders, substance abuse, and delinquency* (pp. 241–267). Thousand Oaks, CA: Sage.

Last, J. M., & Wallace, R. B. (Eds.). (1992). *Public health and preventive medicine* (13th ed.). Norwalk, CT: Appleton & Lange.

Leukefeld, C. G. (1991). The role of the National Institute on Drug Abuse in drug abuse prevention research. In L. Donohew, H. E. Sypher, & W. J. Bukoski (Eds.), *Persuasive communication and drug abuse prevention* (pp. 21–34). Hillsdale, NJ: Erlbaum.

Luepker, R. V., Johnson, C. A., Murray, D. M., & Pechacek, T. F. (1983). Prevention of cigarette smoking: Three-year follow-up of an education program for youth. *Journal of Behavioral Medicine, 6*, 53–62. doi:10.1007/BF00845276

Malvin, J. H., Moskowitz, J. M., Schaps, E., & Schaeffer, G. A. (1985). Evaluation of two school-based alternative programs. *Journal of Alcohol and Drug Education, 30*, 98–108.

Matsueda, R. L. (1988). The current state of differential association theory. *Crime & Delinquency, 34*, 277–306. doi:10.1177/0011128788034003005

McAlister, A., Perry, C., Killen, J., Slinkard, L. A., & Maccoby, N. (1980). Pilot study of smoking, alcohol and drug abuse prevention. *American Journal of Public Health, 70*, 719–721. doi:10.2105/AJPH.70.7.719

McGuire, W. J. (1964). Inducing resistance to persuasion: Some contemporary approaches. In L. Berkowitz (Ed.), *Advances in experimental social psychology* (pp. 192–227). New York, NY: Academic Press.

Monahan, K. C., Hawkins, J. D., & Abbott, R. D. (2013). The application of meta-analysis within a matched-pair randomized control trial: An illustration testing the effects of Communities That Care on delinquent behavior. *Prevention Science, 14*, 1–12. doi:10.1007/s11121-012-0298-x

Moskowitz, J. M., Malvin, J. H., Schaeffer, G. A., & Schaps, E. (1984). An experimental evaluation of a drug education course. *Journal of Drug Education, 14*, 9–22. doi:10.2190/R977-NCC7-9ET5-3PLX

Moskowitz, J. M., Schaps, E., Malvin, J. H., & Schaeffer, G. A. (1984). The effects of drug education at follow-up. *Journal of Alcohol and Drug Education, 30*, 45–49.

Mrazek, P. J., & Haggerty, R. J. (Eds.). (1994). *Reducing risks for mental disorders.* Washington, DC: National Academy Press.

Murray, D. M. (1998). *Design and analysis of group-randomized trials*. New York, NY: Oxford University Press.

Musto, D. F. (1999). *The American disease*. New York, NY: Oxford University Press.

Musto, D. F., & Korsmeyer, P. (2002). *The quest for drug control: Politics and federal policy in a period of increasing substance abuse, 1963-1981*. New Haven, CT: Yale University Press. doi:10.12987/yale/9780300090369.001.0001

Nathan, P. E. (1983). Failures in prevention: Why we can't prevent the devastating effect of alcoholism and drug abuse. *American Psychologist, 38*, 459–467. doi:10.1037/0003-066X.38.4.459

National Institute on Drug Abuse. (1975). *Toward a national strategy for primary drug abuse prevention: Final report: Delphi II*. Rockville, MD: National Institute on Drug Abuse.

National Institutes of Health. (1999). *NIH almanac 1999* (Publication No. NIH 99-5). Bethesda, MD: Author.

Norem-Hebeisen, A. A. (1975). Self-esteem as a predictor of adolescent drug abuse. In D. Lettieri (Ed.), *Predicting adolescent drug abuse: A review of issues, methods, and correlates* (NIDA Research Issues 11, Publication No. ADM 76-299, pp. 193–206). Rockville, MD: National Institute on Drug Abuse.

Omnibus Budget Reconciliation Act of 1981, Pub. L. 97–35, 95 Stat. 357.

Oetting, E. R., & Beauvais, F. (1987). Peer cluster theory, socialization characteristics, and adolescent drug use: A path analysis. *Journal of Counseling Psychology, 34*, 205–213. doi:10.1037/0022-0167.34.2.205

Pentz, M. A., Dwyer, J. H., MacKinnon, D. P., Flay, B. F., Hansen, W. B., Yu, E., . . . Johnson, C. A. (1989). A multicommunity trial for primary prevention of adolescent drug abuse: Effects on drug use prevalence. *JAMA, 261*, 3259–3266. doi:10.1001/jama.1989.03420220073030

Ringwalt, C., Vincus, A. A., Hanley, S., Ennett, S. T., Bowling, J. M., & Haws, S. (2011). The prevalence of evidence-based drug use prevention curricula in U.S. middle schools in 2008. *Prevention Science, 12*, 63–69. doi:10.1007/s11121-010-0184-3

Robins, L. N. (1973). *A follow-up of Vietnam drug users* (White House Special Action Office Monograph, Series A, No. 1). Washington, DC: U.S. Government Printing Office.

Robins, L. N., Davis, D. H., & Goodwin, D. W. (1974). Drug use in U.S. Army enlisted men in Vietnam: A follow-up on their return home. *American Journal of Epidemiology, 99*, 235–249.

Schaps, E., Cohen, A., & Resnick, H. (1975). *Balancing head and heart: Sensible ideas for the prevention of drug and alcohol abuse*. Lafayette, CA: Pacific Institute for Research and Evaluation.

Schaps, E., DeBartolo, R. D., Moskowitz, J., Palley, C. S., & Churgin, S. (1981). A review of 127 drug abuse prevention program evaluations. *Journal of Drug Issues, 11*, 17–43.

Schaps, E., & Moskowitz, J. M. (1984). *The Napa Project, 1978-1981* (ERIC Report No. ED 293014). Washington, DC: U.S. Department of Education.

Schaps, E., Moskowitz, J. M., Condon, J. W., & Malvin, J. H. (1982). Process and outcome evaluation of a drug education course. *Journal of Drug Education, 12*, 353–364. doi:10.2190/VKMG-GHKG-NEP7-FKVD

Schaps, E., Moskowitz, J. M., Malvin, J. H., & Schaeffer, G. A. (1986). Evaluation of seven school-based prevention programs: A final report on the Napa Project. *Substance Use & Misuse, 21*, 1081–1112. doi:10.3109/10826088609077256

Scheier, L. M. (Ed.). (2010). *Handbook of drug use etiology: Theory, methods, and empirical findings*. Washington, DC: American Psychological Association.

Schinke, S. P., Botvin, G. J., & Orlandi, M. A. (1991). *Substance abuse in children and adolescents: Evaluation and intervention*. Thousand Oaks, CA: Sage.

Schuster, C. R., & Kilbey, M. M. (1992). Sensation seeking and targeting of televised anti-drug PSAs. In J. M. Last & R. B. Wallace (Eds.), *Public health and preventive medicine* (13th ed., pp. 769–786). Norwalk, CT: Appleton & Lange.

Simeonsson, R. J. (1991). Primary, secondary, and tertiary prevention in early intervention. *Journal of Early Intervention, 15*, 124–134. doi:10.1177/105381519101500202

Sloboda, Z. (Ed.). (2005). *Epidemiology of drug abuse*. New York, NY: Springer + Business Media.

Sloboda, Z., & Bukoski, W. J. (Eds.). (2003). *Handbook of drug abuse prevention: Theory, science, and practice*. New York, NY: Kluwer Academic.

Sloboda, Z., Cottler, L. B., Hawkins, J. D., & Pentz, M. A. (2009). Reflections on 40 years of drug abuse prevention research. *Journal of Drug Issues, 39*, 179–195. doi:10.1177/002204260903900114

Sloboda, Z., & David, S. L. (1991). *Preventing drug use among children and adolescents: A research-based guide* (Publication No. NIH 97-4212). Rockville, MD: National Institute on Drug Abuse.

Sloboda, Z., Stephens, R. C., Stephens, P. C., Grey, S. F., Teasdale, B., Hawthorne, R. D., . . . Marquette, J. F. (2009). The Adolescent Substance Abuse Prevention Study: A randomized field trial of a universal substance abuse prevention program. *Drug and Alcohol Dependence, 102*, 1–10. doi:10.1016/j.drugalcdep.2009.01.015

Snow, D. L., & Swift, C. F. (1985). Consultation and education in community health: A historical analysis. *Journal of Primary Prevention, 6*, 3–30. doi:10.1007/BF01325338

Spaulding, J., & Balch, P. (1983). A brief history of primary prevention in the twentieth century: 1908-1980. *American Journal of Community Psychology, 11*, 59–80. doi:10.1007/BF00898419

Spoth, R., Redmon, C., Shing, C., & Azevedo, K. (2004). Brief family intervention effects on adolescent substance initiation: School-level growth curve analyses 6 years following baseline. *Journal of Consulting and Clinical Psychology, 72*, 535–542. doi:10.1037/0022-006X.72.3.535

Swisher, J. D., & Hu, T. (1983). Alternatives to drug abuse: Some are and some are not. In T. J. Glynn, C. G. Leukefeld, & J. P. Ludford (Eds.), *Preventing adolescent drug abuse: Intervention strategies* (NIDA Research Monograph 47, Publication No. ADM 83-1280, pp. 141–153). Rockville, MD: National Institute on Drug Abuse.

Tarter, R. E. (2002). Etiology of adolescent substance abuse: A developmental perspective. *American Journal on Addictions, 11*, 171–191. doi:10.1080/10550490290087965

Tobler, N. S. (1986). Meta-analysis of 143 adolescent drug prevention programs: Quantitative outcome results of program participants compared to control or comparison group. *Journal of Drug Issues, 16*, 537–567.

Tobler, N. S. (1992). Drug prevention programs can work: Research findings. *Journal of Addictive Diseases, 11*, 1–28. doi:10.1300/J069v11n03_01

Tobler, N. S., Roona, M. R., Ochshorn, P., Marshall, D. G., Streke, A. V., & Stackpole, K. M. (2000). School-based adolescent drug prevention programs: 1998 meta-analysis. *The Journal of Primary Prevention, 20*, 275–336. doi:10.1023/A:1021314704811

Tyler, C. W., & Last, J. M. (1992). Epidemiology. In J. M. Last & R. B. Wallace (Eds.), *Public health and preventive medicine* (13th ed., pp. 11–41). Norwalk, CT: Appleton & Lange.

Vanyukov, M. M., Tarter, R. E., Kirillova, G. P., Kirisci, L., Reynolds, M. D., Kreek, M. J., . . . Ridenour, T. A. (2012). Common liability to addiction and "gateway hypothesis": Theoretical, empirical and evolutionary perspective. *Drug and Alcohol Dependence, 123*(Supp. 1), S3–S17. doi:10.1016/j.drugalcdep.2011.12.018

Wartella, E., & Middlestadt, S. (1991). Mass communication and persuasion: The evolution of direct effects, limited effects, information process, and affect and arousal models. In L. Donohew, H. E. Sypher, & W. J. Bukoski (Eds.), *Persuasive communication and drug abuse prevention* (pp. 53–70). Hillsdale, NJ: Erlbaum.

Wills, T. A., Windle, M., & Cleary, S. D. (1998). Temperament and novelty seeking in adolescent substance use: Convergence of dimensions of temperaments with constructs from Cloninger's theory. *Journal of Personality and Social Psychology, 74*, 387–406. doi:10.1037/0022-3514.74.2.387

Wolfe, T. (1969). *The electric Kool-Aid acid test.* New York, NY: Farrar, Straus, & Giroux.

Part II

EPIDEMIOLOGY AND ETIOLOGY: RISK AND PROTECTIVE FACTORS

CHAPTER 3

TRENDS IN DRUG USE AMONG YOUTH IN THE UNITED STATES

Megan E. Patrick and Patrick M. O'Malley

This chapter presents data on recent averages of substance use among U.S. adolescents and historical substance use trends since the mid-1970s. The data are derived from the Monitoring the Future (MTF) study, one of the most consistent sources of information on drug among youth in the United States. MTF includes annual in-school assessments of national samples of eighth-, 10th-, and 12th-grade students (Johnston, O'Malley, Bachman, & Schulenberg, 2012a). The project yields high-quality data on the prevalence of, and grade-level differences in, substance use and on the historical changes in drug use over time.

We first provide an overview of the MTF design, survey, and sampling procedures. Then, we use MTF to describe the historical trends (from 1976 to 2011) in prevalence of marijuana, other illegal drugs, inhalants, nonmedical use of prescription drugs, the most commonly used substances of alcohol and tobacco, and other substances that have raised concern or reached national notoriety in recent years (e.g., synthetic marijuana, hookah). We present 2011 data on current use of marijuana, other illicit drugs, alcohol, and cigarettes by grade, gender, and race/ethnicity. We selected results presented in this chapter from a broader range of data to provide an overall summary of trends in drug use among American youth. Details about the use of individual drugs are available from annually released study monographs describing rates of drug use among adolescents in eighth, 10th, and 12th grades (Johnston et al., 2012a). Similar data, based on follow-up surveys from a subsample of 12th graders, are available for college students, young adults, and adults to age 50 (Johnston, O'Malley, Bachman, & Schulenberg, 2012b). We conclude with a discussion of how findings from MTF have contributed and continue to advance the field of prevention science.

DESIGN AND PROCEDURES OF MONITORING THE FUTURE

Annual surveys from MTF provide point estimates of drug use from any given year, reveal historical changes over time, and show variation in drug use across subgroups. Twelfth graders have been surveyed in school during the spring of each year since 1976 (with an initial pilot survey in 1975). About 16,000 of them in roughly 130 public and private high schools were selected to provide a representative cross-section throughout the coterminous United States.

Although not the focus of this chapter, a longitudinal panel has been followed into adulthood. Each year since 1976, a subsample of 12th-grade students has been invited to complete questionnaires every 2 years through age 30 and every 5 years thereafter

Preparation of this chapter was supported by grants from the National Institute on Drug Abuse (R01 DA 001411 and R01 DA 016575). The content of this chapter is solely the responsibility of the authors and does not necessarily represent the official views of the National Institute on Drug Abuse.

http://dx.doi.org/10.1037/14550-004
Handbook of Adolescent Drug Use Prevention: Research, Intervention Strategies, and Practice, L. M. Scheier (Editor)

(Johnston et al., 2012b). The longitudinal design provides valuable data on the long-term consequences of high school substance use, patterns in substance use behaviors over time, college attendees and nonattendees in the United States, and predictors of health and behavior in adulthood. In 1991, MTF was expanded to younger ages to include nationally representative samples of eighth- and 10th-grade students. Each year, about 17,000 eighth-grade students in approximately 150 schools (mostly middle schools) and about 16,000 10th-grade students in approximately 130 schools are surveyed. The multistage random sampling and data collection procedures are described fully elsewhere (Bachman, Johnston, O'Malley, & Schulenberg, 2011; Johnston et al., 2012a).

THE BIG PICTURE

In the broadest terms, what have we learned about drug use among U.S. adolescents over the nearly 40 years of the MTF study? Figure 3.1 shows the percentage of eighth, 10th, and 12th graders who have used any *illicit drug*—marijuana, LSD, other hallucinogens, crack, other cocaine, heroin, narcotics other than heroin, amphetamines, sedatives (barbiturates), or tranquilizers not under a doctor's orders—during their lifetime. According to the data, 12th graders generally use substances at higher rates than 10th-grade students, who use at higher rates than eighth graders. Although mostly age-graded, the differences are almost surely understated because high school dropouts are not included in the 12th-grade data, but most eventual dropouts are included in the lower grades, particularly the eighth grade. (Although dropouts are excluded from the surveyed population of 12th graders, their inclusion would likely have a modest effect on prevalence rates due to the relatively small proportion who drop out [see Johnston et al., 2012a, Appendix A, for an extended discussion], and any effect would be even smaller for estimation of trends.) Furthermore, as of 2011, substantial portions of U.S. adolescents have reported

FIGURE 3.1. Trends in lifetime prevalence of using any illegal drug (including marijuana), by grade. For 12th graders, it includes any use of marijuana, LSD, other hallucinogens, crack, other cocaine, or heroin; or any use of other narcotics other than heroin, amphetamines, sedatives (barbiturates), methaqualone (excluded since 1990), or tranquilizers not under a doctor's orders. For eighth and 10th graders, the use of narcotics other than heroin and sedatives (barbiturates) has been excluded because these younger respondents appear to over-report use (perhaps because they include the use of nonprescription drugs in their answers).

using any illicit drug: 20% of eighth graders, 38% of 10th graders, and 50% of 12th graders.

Five different historical periods seem to reflect consolidated trends in drug use since 1976, thus resulting in four inflection points: (1) an increase in the late 1970s with a peak in 1981; (2) a decline in the 1980s that reached a low point around 1992; (3) an increase between 1992 and 1997; (4) a period of gradual decline from 1997 to 2007; and (5) a period of stability or perhaps a slight increase through 2011. Among 10th and 12th graders, the level of lifetime drug use in the most recent year (2011) was higher than the lowest year (1992) by eight or nine percentage points, whereas, for eighth graders, the level of use in 2011 was only about one percentage point higher than the low year (1991). On the other hand, the 2011 level among 12th graders was lower than the peak year of 1981 by 16 percentage points. The trend periods have been roughly similar for the three grades, with some differences: The eighth graders started to increase in 1992, whereas the 10th and 12th graders were still declining in reported levels of drug use.

These overall trends in the use of any illicit drug have been driven largely by the most commonly used drug, marijuana, and mask many differences among specific illicit drugs. For example, cocaine, ecstasy, and LSD all have different profiles.

Trends in Use of Specific Drugs

Marijuana use. MTF surveys contain items probing the use of marijuana with the instruction that "marijuana is sometimes called weed, pot, dope" and hashish is "sometimes called hash, hash oil." Figure 3.2 shows the prevalence of marijuana use in the past year for eighth, 10th, and 12th graders in the United States by historical year since 1976. The peak level of annual marijuana use among 12th graders was 51% in 1979. Prevalence fell thereafter to a low of 22% in 1992, a remarkable drop of more than one half. The sharp increase in marijuana use across the mid-1990s mirrors trends in other substance use during that period. For annual marijuana use, rates nearly doubled among eighth, 10th, and 12th graders. Following a slow decline in rates from 1997 to 2006, marijuana use has shown increases again in recent years: More than 36% of 12th graders reported use in the past year. The use of marijuana on a daily or almost daily basis (i.e., 20 or more occasions within a 30-day period) has reached the highest level in the past 30 years: at 6.6% of 12th graders in 2011, although still below the peak of 10.7% reached in 1978.

Use of illegal drugs other than marijuana. MTF surveys include questions that explore patterns of use for a range of drugs. For purposes of describing

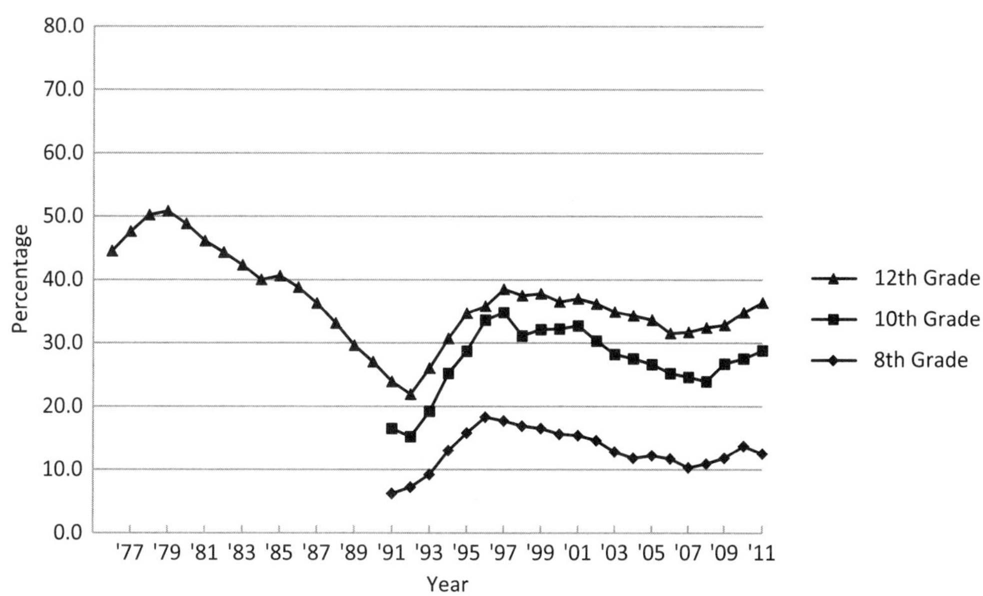

FIGURE 3.2. Trends in annual prevalence of marijuana use, by grade.

overall prevalence of illegal drug use, an index was created for use of any illegal drug other than marijuana. Trends in annual use, by grade level, of illicit drugs other than marijuana are shown in Figure 3.3. For 12th graders, these drugs included LSD, other hallucinogens, crack, other cocaine, heroin, other narcotics, amphetamines, sedatives (barbiturates), or tranquilizers, all without a doctor's orders. About 80% of 12th graders who reported using illegal drugs other than marijuana also reported marijuana use. Use of illegal drugs other than marijuana in the past year peaked in 1981 at 34% of 12th graders, before declining until about 1991. Rates of substance use for most types of drugs increased across the 1990s from 15% in 1992 to 22% in 2001 among 12th graders. Since 2001, rates of illegal drug use other than marijuana, reported as past-year use, have fallen but, over the past few years, have leveled around 18% for 12th graders. Since the mid-1990s, rates of illegal drug use among eighth graders has fallen by about half.

Specific illegal drugs. In addition to the most commonly reported types of substance use (i.e., alcohol, cigarettes, marijuana, and any illegal drugs other than marijuana), MTF gathers a wealth of information on more specific substances and trends. Details regarding these prevalence rates, subgroup differences, and historical changes are available elsewhere (Johnston et al., 2012a), so only the broadest overview is provided in this chapter.

Concern about individual illegal drugs often arises from media coverage or the public's perception that use of a drug is increasing. MTF provides empirical documentation of actual rates of use and drugs of widest use. Trends in individual drugs may ebb and flow, and uptake of a new drug may replace use of another substance. LSD use peaked in 1996 at 8.8% of 12th graders reporting past-year use, with low rates since: 2.7% of 12th graders in 2011. After more than doubling in the 3 previous years, ecstasy (3,4-methylenedioxy-methamphetamine, or MDMA) peaked in 2001 at 9.2% of 12th graders. A

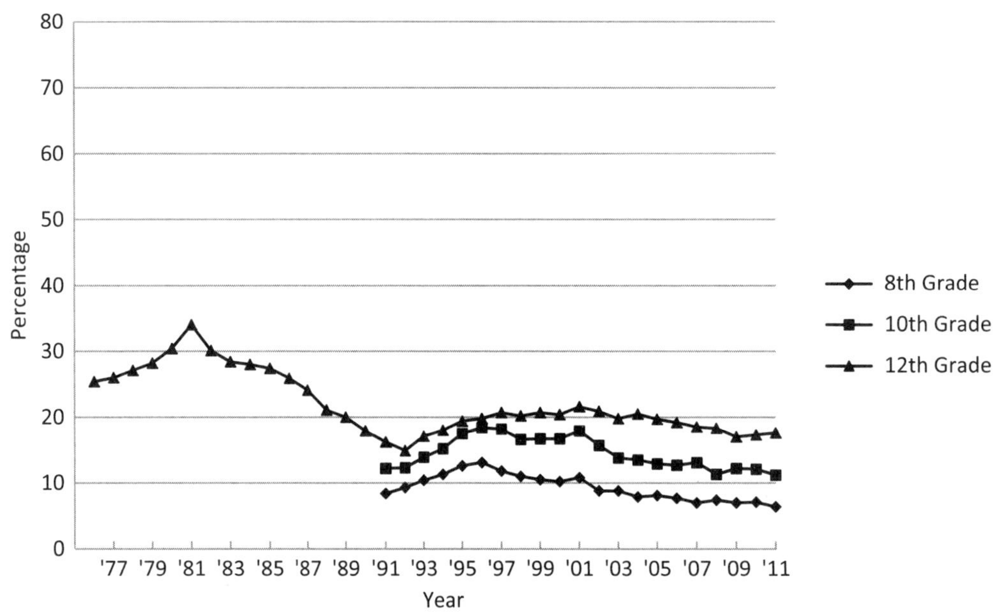

FIGURE 3.3. Trends in annual prevalence of use of any illicit drug other than marijuana, by grade. For 12th graders, it includes any use of marijuana, LSD, other hallucinogens, crack, other cocaine, or heroin; or any use of other narcotics other than heroin, amphetamines, sedatives (barbiturates), methaqualone (excluded since 1990), or tranquilizers not under a doctor's orders. For eighth and 10th graders, the use of narcotics other than heroin and sedatives (barbiturates) has been excluded because these younger respondents appear to over-report use (perhaps because they include the use of nonprescription drugs in their answers). Beginning in 2001, revised sets of questions on other hallucinogen and tranquilizer use were introduced. From 2001 on, data points are based on revised questions.

concern is that ecstasy use may be rebounding, given the slight increases in 2011: 5.3% of 12th graders. Methamphetamine questions were added to the MTF survey in 1999; since then, declines in use across all grades have been noted (e.g., 1.4% of 12th graders in 2011). Crystal meth (also called ice) questions were added in 1990 and captured increases across the decade, but use never reached high levels (e.g., 3.0% of 12th graders in 2002) and has declined since to 1.2% of 12th graders in 2011. Crack cocaine use increased rapidly in the 1980s to a peak of 4.1% of 12th graders in 1986; use has since fallen to 1.0% of 12th graders in 2011. Heroin use has decreased across the MTF study, except for some increase along with other illegal drugs during the 1990s, with consistently low rates: 0.8% of 12th graders in 2011. Club drugs, including Rohypnol (added in 1996), ketamine (added in 2000), and gamma hydroxybutyrate, or GHB (added in 2000), have had very low rates with declines in recent years: 1.3%, 1.7%, and 1.4% of 12th graders in 2011, respectively.

Inhalants. The use of *inhalants*—fumes or gases released by common household substances, such as glues, aerosols, butane, and solvents—to get high continues to be a national concern (National Institute on Drug Abuse [NIDA], 2012a). MTF asks participants how often they have "sniffed glue, or breathed the contents of aerosol spray cans, or inhaled any other gases or sprays in order to get high." Inhalants are unique in that use tends to be more common among eighth graders than among 10th and 12th graders. In 2011, 7.0% of eighth graders reported past-year inhalant use compared with 3.2% of 12th graders.

Nonmedical use of prescription drugs. Nonmedical use of prescription drugs among U.S. youth is also a current concern (NIDA, 2012b). MTF asks about the use of amphetamines, sedatives (barbiturates), narcotics other than heroin, or tranquilizers without a doctor's orders. In 2011, 22% of 12th graders reported nonmedical use of prescription drugs in their lifetime, and 15% reported use in the past year. Questions have been added regarding the amphetamines Ritalin (added in 2001, with declines since to 2.6% of 12th graders reporting past-year use in 2011) and Adderall (added in 2009, with little change in the past few years: 6.5% of 12th graders reporting past-year use in 2011). Questions about the narcotics Vicodin and OxyContin were added in 2002. Vicodin use in the past year peaked to 10.5% of 12th graders in 2003 and has seen decreases since. OxyContin use has remained near its highest levels: 4.9% of 12th graders in 2011 compared with the peak of 5.5% in 2005. In 2001, the tranquilizers question was revised to include Xanax, although rates dropped in 2011 to 5.6% of 12th graders.

Alcohol use. The MTF survey asks about "alcoholic beverages, including beer, wine, liquor, and any other beverage that contains alcohol." Overall, frequency of alcohol use among adolescents has declined in recent years to historically low levels. Trends from 1976 to 2011 in the use of any alcohol within a 30-day period are shown in Figure 3.4. Trends in drunkenness within a 30-day period from 1991, when questions were added, through 2011 are shown in Figure 3.5. In the late 1970s, about 70% of 12th graders reported consuming alcohol within a 30-day period. Levels remained similarly high until the late 1980s, when a precipitous drop occurred in past 30-day drinking, followed by a small increase from 1993 through the late 1990s, and then further decline to the present. In 2011, 40% of 12th graders reported drinking in the past 30 days and 25% reported being drunk in the past 30 days. As shown in Figures 3.4 and 3.5, similar trends have occurred for alcohol use and drunkenness among eighth and 10th graders. *Binge drinking*, or consuming five or more drinks in a row in the past 2 weeks, was reported by about 40% of 12th graders in the late 1970s and early 1980s and by about 22% of 12th graders in 2011.

Tobacco use. Trends in cigarette smoking within a 30-day period are shown in Figure 3.6. Following a drop in cigarette use among 12th graders in the late 1970s, smoking rates remained stable at about 30%. Cigarette use then escalated across the 1990s to a high of 37% in 1997 of 12th graders who reported smoking within a 30-day period. Following the peak in the late 1990s, cigarette use in all three grade levels decreased appreciably to 19% of 12th graders in 2011, although the rate of decrease is decelerating. In 2011, daily cigarette use declined to 10.3% of 12th graders.

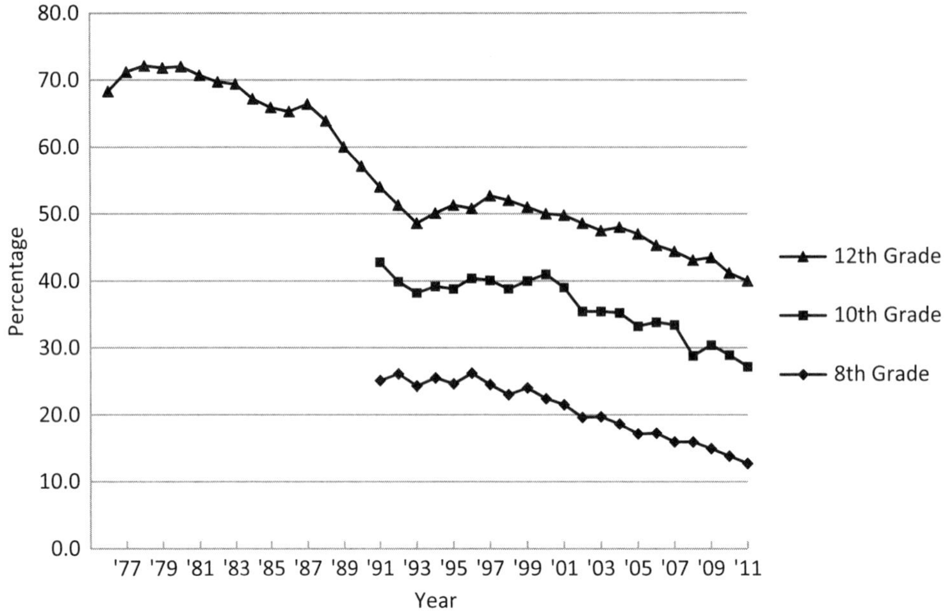

FIGURE 3.4. Trends in 30-day prevalence of use of alcohol, by grade. In 1993, a revised set of questions on alcohol use was introduced. From 1993 on, data points are based on the revised question.

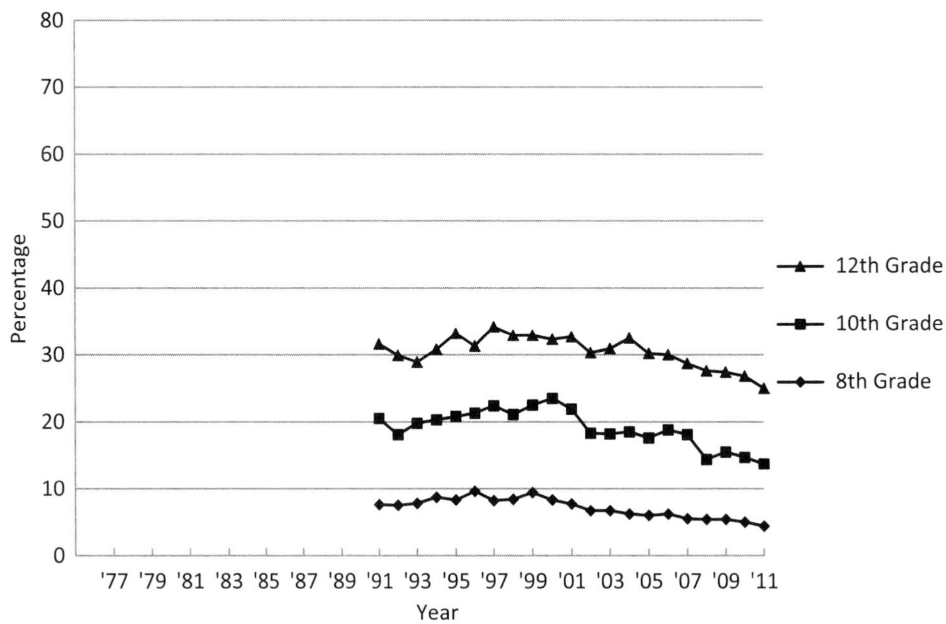

FIGURE 3.5. Trends in 30-day prevalence of being drunk, by grade.

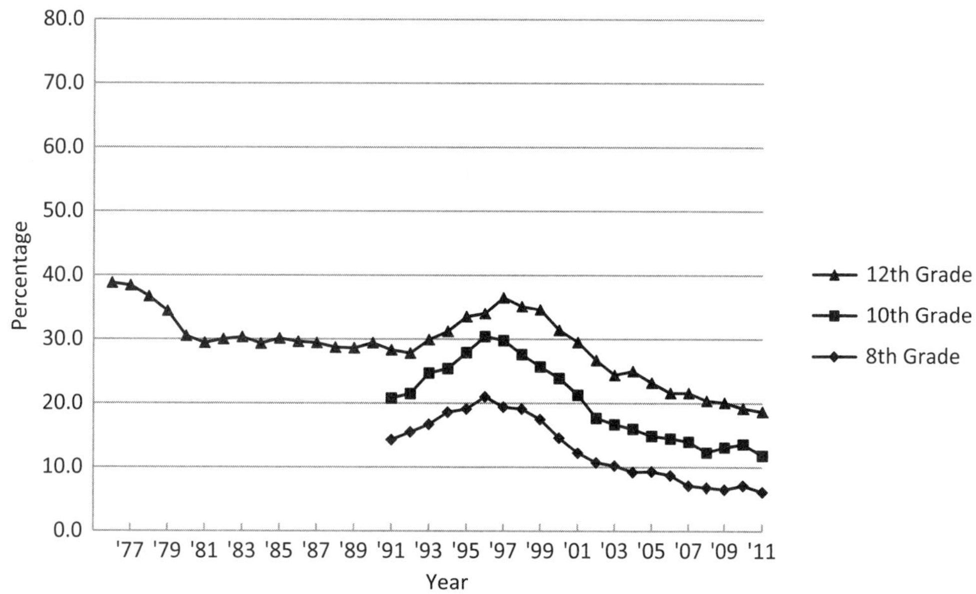

FIGURE 3.6. **Trends in 30-day prevalence of use of cigarettes, by grade.**

Questions about additional tobacco products have been added to MTF over the past few years. In 2011, about 19% of 12th graders reported hookah smoking in the past year and about 20% reported smoking small cigars in the past year. Use of snus (7.9%) and dissolvable tobacco (1.5%) in the past year was lower than other forms of tobacco use.

Substances with recent trends. Additional substances, sometimes not yet regulated by the Food and Drug Administration, are being added to the MTF study as they emerge. Synthetic marijuana is one such substance; it was measured for the first time in 2011. After natural marijuana, synthetic marijuana is the next most used illicit drug: 11.4% of 12th graders reported using it in the past year. Questions about the use of salvia were added in 2009; about 6% of 12th graders reported using it in the past year. Use of stay-awake pills rose in the 1980s—in 1988, 26% of 12th graders reported past-year use—but has shown declines over time to 4% of 12th graders reporting past-year use in 2011.

Epidemiology of Substance Use Among Adolescents in the United States—2011

Table 3.1 provides prevalence estimates (in percentages) of marijuana use in the past year, marijuana use within a 30-day period, daily marijuana use, use of other illicit drugs in the past year, and use of other illicit drugs within a 30-day period. Table 3.2 provides the prevalence of alcohol use in the past year, alcohol use within a 30-day period, drunkenness within a 30-day period, binge drinking in the past 2 weeks, cigarette use within a 30-day period, and daily cigarette use. Prevalence estimates are given by grade (eighth, 10th, and 12th) and by gender and race/ethnicity (White, African American, and Hispanic).

Grade-level differences. For all measures of alcohol use, cigarettes, marijuana use, and the composite measure of the use of any illicit drugs other than marijuana, eighth graders have the lowest prevalence and 12th graders have the highest prevalence; that is, age-graded increases in substance use exist across adolescence. For example, Figure 3.7 shows, throughout the life of the MTF study, the prevalence of marijuana use, by grade, based on retrospective reports of grade at first use. Rates of marijuana use among 6th graders are low with a clear pattern of steady increase in use from 6th grade to 12th grade each year, despite historical changes in the levels of use by 12th grade. Inhalant use (not included in the table) is the only example of eighth graders' having higher prevalence than 12th graders.

TABLE 3.1

Prevalence of Marijuana Use and Use of Any Illicit Drug Other Than Marijuana[a] for Eighth, 10th, and 12th Graders, by Gender and Race/Ethnicity, in 2013

	Marijuana			Other illicit drugs	
	Past year	Past 30 days	Daily	Past year	Past 30 days
8th graders					
Total	12.7	7.0	1.1	5.8	3.3
Gender					
Boys	12.6	6.7	1.3	4.8	2.6
Girls	12.5	7.2	0.9	6.6	3.7
Race/ethnicity[b]					
White	9.1	4.7	0.8	4.9	2.3
African American	13.6	8.2	1.0	4.0	2.8
Hispanic	16.8	10.0	1.7	7.4	3.7
10th graders					
Total	29.8	18.0	4.0	10.9	5.1
Gender					
Boys	32.7	20.6	6.2	12.2	5.8
Girls	27.0	15.3	2.0	9.5	4.3
Race/ethnicity[b]					
White	27.3	16.5	3.5	11.2	5.1
African American	30.5	19.1	4.7	6.5	3.8
Hispanic	33.4	20.0	3.7	12.4	5.6
12th graders					
Total	36.4	22.7	6.5	17.3	8.4
Gender					
Boys	39.8	26.4	8.9	18.9	9.2
Girls	32.4	18.7	3.8	15.1	7.0
Race/ethnicity[b]					
White	35.6	21.8	6.5	18.7	9.0
African American	35.0	24.0	6.2	9.5	5.1
Hispanic	39.2	24.3	6.1	14.7	6.9

Note. The prevalence of marijuana use (in percentages) is shown for the past year, within a 30-day period, and daily; use of any illicit drug other than marijuana is shown for the past year and past 30-day period. For eighth graders, the approximate weighted *N* is 14,600. For 10th graders, the approximate weighted *N* is 12,900. For 12th graders, the approximate weighted *N* is 12,600.

[a]For 12th graders, includes any use of LSD, other hallucinogens, crack, other cocaine, or heroin; or any use of narcotics other than heroin, amphetamines, sedatives (barbiturates), or tranquilizers not under a doctor's orders. For eighth and 10th graders, the use of narcotics other than heroin and sedatives (barbiturates) has been excluded because these younger respondents appear to over-report use. [b]To derive percentages for each racial subgroup, data for the specified year and the previous year have been combined to increase subgroup sample sizes and thus provide more stable estimates.

TABLE 3.2

Prevalence of Alcohol Use, Drunkenness, Five or More Drinks in a Row, and Cigarettes Use for Eighth, 10th, and 12th Graders, by Gender and Race/Ethnicity, in 2013

	Alcohol		Been drunk	5+ drinks	Cigarettes	
	Past year	Past 30 days	Past 30 days	Past 2 weeks	Past 30 days	Daily
8th graders						
Total	22.1	10.2	3.5	5.1	4.5	1.8
Gender						
Boys	20.7	9.3	3.0	4.5	4.0	1.7
Girls	23.5	11.2	4.0	5.7	4.7	1.8
Race/ethnicity[a]						
White	21.2	9.5	3.3	4.2	4.7	2.0
African American	20.2	9.7	3.0	4.5	3.5	1.5
Hispanic	28.8	14.3	4.5	7.8	4.0	1.4
10th graders						
Total	47.1	25.7	12.8	13.7	9.1	4.4
Gender						
Boys	46.2	26.0	13.2	14.7	10.5	5.4
Girls	48.1	25.3	12.4	12.5	7.5	3.4
Race/ethnicity[a]						
White	49.7	28.2	15.4	15.7	11.4	5.7
African American	39.1	19.0	7.2	8.6	5.3	2.6
Hispanic	51.3	28.8	13.1	16.9	8.3	2.6
12th graders						
Total	62.0	39.2	26.0	22.1	16.3	8.5
Gender						
Boys	62.6	41.8	29.1	26.1	18.4	9.7
Girls	61.3	36.3	22.7	18.1	13.2	6.5
Race/ethnicity[a]						
White	65.6	43.6	30.6	25.6	19.4	10.9
African American	50.6	28.4	13.4	12.5	9.6	5.3
Hispanic	62.9	39.0	22.7	22.4	12.4	4.7

Note. The prevalence of alcohol use (in percentages) is shown for the past year and within a 30-day period; reported drunkenness is shown for a 30-day period; binge drinking (five or more drinks) is shown for the past 2 weeks; use of cigarettes is shown for a 30-day period and daily. For eighth graders, the approximate weighted *N* is 14,600. For 10th graders, the approximate weighted *N* is 12,900. For 12th graders, the approximate weighted *N* is 12,600.
[a]To derive percentages for each racial subgroup, data for the specified year and the previous year have been combined to increase subgroup sample sizes and thus provide more stable estimates.

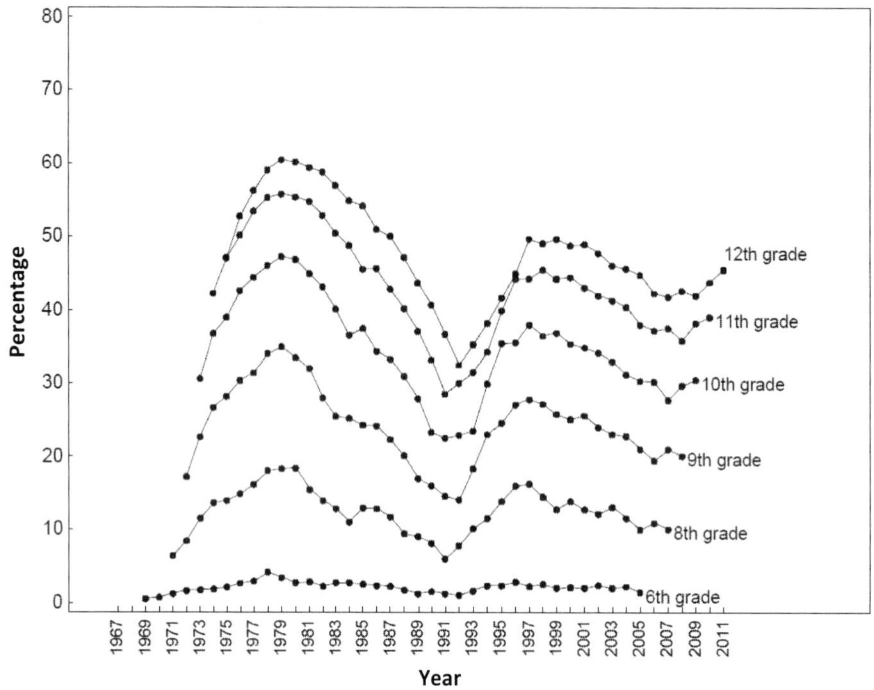

FIGURE 3.7. Trends in lifetime prevalence in marijuana use, based on retrospective reports from 12th graders.

Gender differences. Males tend to use drugs more frequently and at higher levels than females. Gender differences are more pronounced at heavier levels of use and among 12th graders than among younger adolescents. For example, 26.2% of eighth-grade boys and 27.1% of eighth-grade girls reported using alcohol in the past year. In contrast, 25.5% of 12th-grade boys and only 17.6% of 12th-grade girls reported binge drinking in the past 2 weeks. Gender differences in substance use seem to have narrowed: For example, differences between males and females in alcohol use have decreased over the past decade. The gender difference in past 30-day use of alcohol was 9.6% in 2001, with 54.7% of boys and 45.1% of girls reporting use, and 4.6% in 2011, with 42.1% of boys and 37.5% of girls reporting use.

Race/ethnicity differences. White Americans have the highest prevalence of using most drugs, although Hispanics tend to have the highest rates at younger ages. For example, in eighth grade, 16.9% of Hispanics, 13.6% of African Americans, and 11.4% of Whites reported using marijuana in the past year. By the 12th grade, however, the order changed: 36.6% of Whites, 34.4% of Hispanics, and 32.4% of African Americans reported past-year marijuana use. African Americans tend to have lower rates of drug and alcohol use than Whites or Hispanics.

IMPLICATIONS FOR PREVENTION

The MTF study has played an important role in providing information on drug use among adolescents in the United States. Prevalence rates, subgroup differences, and changing trends indicate the most important priorities for public health initiatives and help track progress in intervention success over time. Tobacco is typically illegal for people under 18, and alcohol is illegal for those under 21, although the legal status for adults provides many opportunities to control use of these products. In the case of tobacco, MTF data have been used to demonstrate the value of numerous preventive actions in reducing tobacco use, such as higher taxes (Chaloupka & Pacula, 1999), media campaigns (Emery et al., 2005; Terry-McElrath et al., 2007, 2013; Wakefield et al., 2006), state-level laws restricting smoking areas (Tworek et al., 2010), and restrictions on marketing practices (Slater, Chaloupka, Wakefield, Johnston, & O'Malley, 2007). In the case of alcohol, MTF data have been used to show that certain laws and policies can reduce youthful drinking, including a higher minimum drinking age (Carpenter, Kloska, O'Malley, & Johnston, 2007; O'Malley & Wagenaar, 1991), higher taxes on alcohol (Carpenter et al., 2007), and lower legal blood alcohol limits for young drivers (Carpenter et al., 2007; Wagenaar, O'Malley, & LaFond, 2001).

Perhaps the best example of how MTF has contributed to prevention science is an understanding of the importance of certain beliefs and attitudes in explaining trends in drug use. Studies that have examined psychosocial predictors of substance use, including self-reported reasons for using and not using specific drugs (Johnston & O'Malley, 1986; Terry-McElrath, O'Malley, & Johnston, 2009), have shown, for example, that adolescents with multiple reasons for using drugs are most likely to use in problematic ways (e.g., before 4 p.m.; Coffman, Patrick, Palen, Rhoades, & Ventura, 2007). Our own examination of age-related trends in reasons for using alcohol and marijuana from ages 18 to 30 have revealed that the majority of reasons for use, including social and coping reasons, has shown decreased prevalence as adolescents move toward young adulthood, with a smaller number of reasons (e.g., to relax) increasing in prevalence with age (Patrick & Schulenberg, 2011; Patrick, Schulenberg, O'Malley, Johnston, & Bachman, 2011). In addition, reasons for alcohol and marijuana use reported in high school have been associated with substance use and related problems reported 17 years later at age 35 (Patrick, Schulenberg, O'Malley, Maggs, et al., 2011). These studies, which examined the pivotal role of self-reported reasons for using substances, provide insight into the motivational context of substance use over time, therefore providing foundational information for prevention and intervention efforts.

Trends in use of marijuana provided the basis for an early understanding of the role attitudes play in predicting and forecasting use. Marijuana use by high school seniors had been increasing in the late 1970s, but that trend reversed fairly dramatically and decreased in the early 1980s. One explanation for the reversal was suggested by trends in other variables: a rise in perceived risk of harm and disapproval associated with marijuana use, particularly regular use. (Measures of these variables were available because the researchers who started the MTF study—Lloyd Johnston and Jerald Bachman—developed a conceptual framework that considered such variables to be likely explanatory factors in substance use.)

Johnston, Bachman, and O'Malley (1981) first advanced the possible connection between perceived risk and disapproval to actual use of marijuana. They hypothesized that a decline in daily marijuana use in 1980 was because of a continuing increase in health concerns (perceived risk of harm) related to regular use of marijuana and a decrease in perceived peer acceptance (i.e., a rise in perceived peer disapproval of use, or a changing injunctive norm). In a series of publications during the years that followed, the MTF investigators provided analytic evidence to support that hypothesis (Bachman, Johnston, & O'Malley, 1998; Bachman, Johnston, O'Malley, & Humphrey, 1988; Johnston, 1985). Bachman et al. (1988) compared two alternative explanations for the changes in marijuana use between 1976 and 1986: One was that young people became more conservative and less prone to engaging in risk behaviors in general, and the second posited changes in views that were specific to marijuana. The first explanation, offered by Jessor (1985), suggested that the decline in marijuana use could have been because of an increase in adolescents' general conventional behavior, which would be indicated by factors such as academic performance, truancy, religiosity, time spent in non–adult-supervised recreation, delinquent behaviors, and conservative as opposed to radical political beliefs. Extensive analyses led to the conclusion that changes in general factors could not explain the decline in use but changes in perceived risk and disapproval of marijuana could. A later analysis concluded that an increase in marijuana use during the 1990s among eighth, 10th, and 12th graders could be explained by trends in perceived risk and disapproval (Bachman et al., 1998); and again, changes in general factors, including individual lifestyle factors that correlated substantially with marijuana use, could not account for changes in use.

Those and related findings have clear implications for prevention (Bukoski, 1991; Johnston, 1985, 1991; Sloboda, 2005). It is imperative to communicate to adolescents the real potential harm resulting from drug use. In addition, perceptions of peer acceptance of substance use are important; the information must be accurate to be accepted. Another variable considered to be a possible explanatory factor for drug use trends is availability; however, a measure of perceived availability (i.e., how easy it would be to get some marijuana) does not vary with actual use to the extent that perceived risk and disapproval do. This concept is illustrated in Figure 3.8, which shows trends among 12th graders in perceived risk, availability, and actual use of marijuana. Perceived risk and marijuana use are almost a perfect complement: As one increases, the other decreases. Perceived risk is something of a leading indicator that often presages the change in use by a year. Availability, on the other hand, does not covary so closely with marijuana use.

An important point about the salient role of perceived risk and disapproval is that they are specific to individual drugs. Thus, changes in attitudes related to marijuana predict changes in marijuana use and not necessarily changes in other substances. Bachman, Johnston, and O'Malley (1990) presented analyses showing that changes in cocaine use could be attributed to changes in disapproval and especially to perceived risk associated with cocaine. The changes in perceived risk were likely attributable to a great deal of negative publicity about cocaine and in particular to the highly publicized death of Len Bias, a young athlete who had just been drafted into professional basketball to play for the Boston Celtics. His death was widely cited as having been due to an overdose of cocaine by an inexperienced user (Schmidt & Kenworthy, 1986). Figure 3.9 shows the association of the perceived risk of cocaine use, availability of cocaine use, and reported cocaine use.

The demonstration that measures of perceived harm at the individual level relate strongly to actual consumption is compelling, but evidence from MTF exists that measures at the aggregate level can be instrumental in determining drug use behavior. Social norms and attitudes regarding marijuana

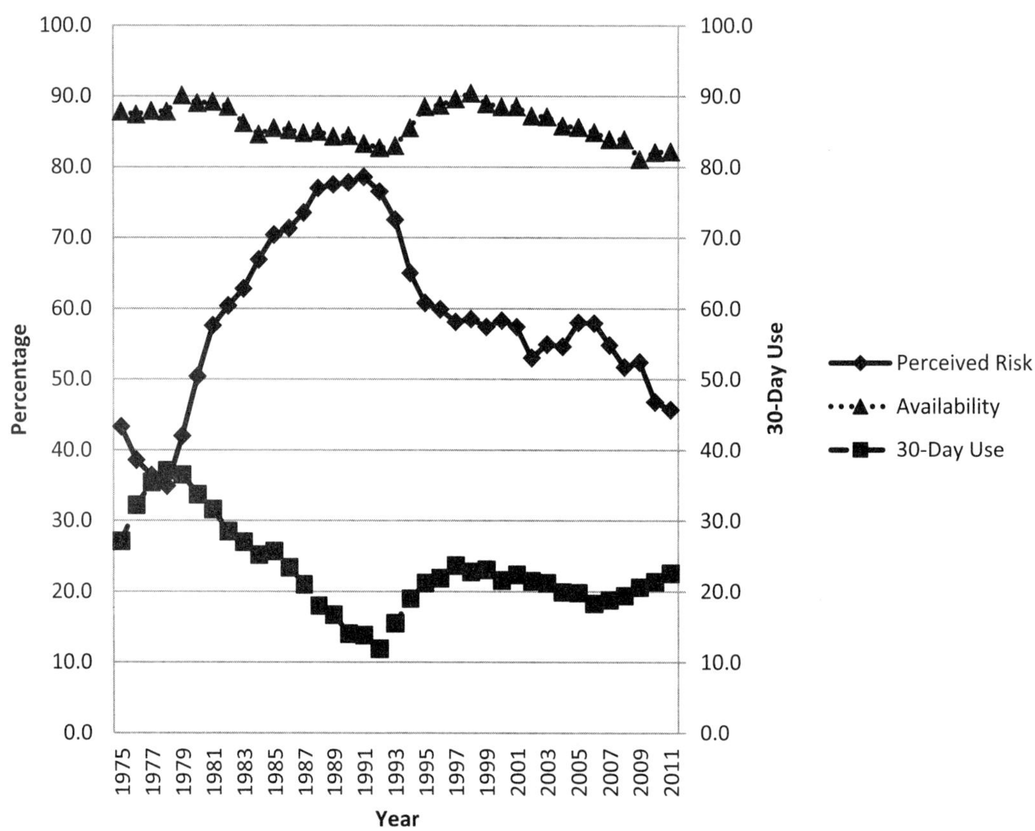

FIGURE 3.8. Trends in use, perceived risk, and availability of marijuana among 12th graders. The trend in use refers to 30-day use of marijuana. The trend in perceived risk refers to regular marijuana use.

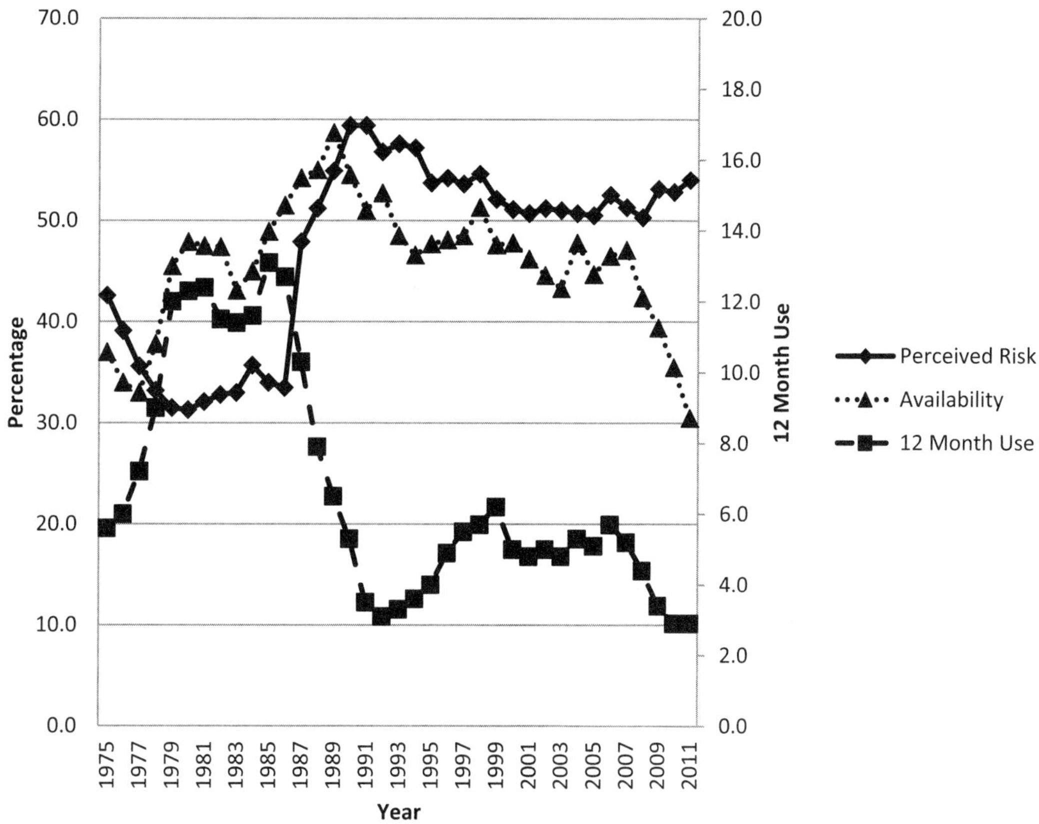

FIGURE 3.9. Trends in use, perceived risk, and availability of cocaine among 12th graders. The trend in use refers to annual use of cocaine among 12th graders. The trend in perceived risk refers to one to two times the use of cocaine. The percentages for perceived risk and availability are plotted against the *y*-axis on the left (0%–70%), whereas the use of cocaine is plotted against the *y*-axis on the right (0%–20%), thus allowing for a comparison of the trend lines while clearly conveying, at the lower percentages, the trend in use.

use vary by birth cohort, with some cohorts being, for example, more disapproving of marijuana than others. This cohort-level norm can have a significant effect on use, even after controlling for all individual level effects (Keyes et al., 2011).

Given that attitudes and beliefs at the individual and aggregate levels are important determinants of drug use behaviors, it is natural to consider what factors influence attitudes and beliefs. In the case of cocaine, it seems clear that a large amount of media attention, including highly publicized drug-related fatalities, were instrumental in raising the perceived risk of cocaine use. The presence of a number of cohort effects in the MTF data has suggested another, very different, possible mechanism for change: Newer (younger) cohorts may have different exposure to the dangers of certain drugs. In the case of LSD, for example, older cohorts, such as youth growing up in the late 1960s and early1970s, had the opportunity to see and hear about the risks associated with LSD use when such use was more common. Adolescents in the 1990s, though, had much less direct or indirect experience; in essence, *generational forgetting*—a lack of exposure to the risks related to a drug because of less exposure to or experience with the drug—of potential harms can occur (Johnston, O'Malley, & Bachman, 1993). Generational forgetting can lead to increased use of the drug by the current generation.

CONCLUSION

Overall, trends in substance use have shown favorable improvements over time, with fewer adolescents reporting substance use in recent years. However, marijuana use appears to have been on the rise in recent years, and illicit drug use (other than marijuana) is at similar levels in 2011 as it was 20 years earlier. Alcohol use and cigarette use are currently at historic lows among U.S. adolescents. Recent increases in the use of marijuana and ecstasy indicate that a new upsurge in drug use among youth in the United States may be on the horizon. Levels of perceived risk of harm associated with those drugs are falling (Johnston et al., 2012a); these declines are a leading indicator of generational forgetting and a warning to prevention scientists about a possible resurgence.

A review of the MTF findings shows that more work is needed. Although alcohol use is less than in the past, one quarter of high school seniors reported being drunk in the past month and nearly as many (23%) reported using marijuana during the past month. One out of every 10 high school seniors said they use cigarettes daily and 9% reported using illegal drugs other than marijuana in the past month. This type of substance use among adolescents continues to be a concern. In addition, the landscape of substance use is constantly changing. The available and popular drugs vary over time; prime examples are the synthetic drugs and the nonmedical use of prescription drugs that have been of recent concern. The trend toward legalizing marijuana for medical and recreational use poses new challenges for prevention of marijuana use among U.S. adolescents. Monitoring the substance use of adolescents continues to be important to identifying areas of concern and providing data for targeting prevention and intervention efforts.

References

Bachman, J. G., Johnston, L. D., & O'Malley, P. M. (1990). Explaining the recent decline in cocaine use among young adults: Further evidence that perceived risks and disapproval lead to reduced drug use. *Journal of Health and Social Behavior, 31*, 173–184. doi:10.2307/2137171

Bachman, J. G., Johnston, L. D., & O'Malley, P. M. (1998). Explaining the recent increases in students' marijuana use: The impacts of perceived risks and disapproval from 1976 through 1996. *American Journal of Public Health, 88*, 887–892. doi:10.2105/AJPH.88.6.887

Bachman, J. G., Johnston, L. D., O'Malley, P. M., & Humphrey, R. H. (1988). Explaining the recent decline in marijuana use: Differentiating the effects of perceived risks, disapproval, and general lifestyle factors. *Journal of Health and Social Behavior, 29*, 92–112. doi:10.2307/2137183

Bachman, J. G., Johnston, L. D., O'Malley, P. M., & Schulenberg, J. E. (2011). *The Monitoring the Future project after thirty-seven years: Design and procedures* (Monitoring the Future Occasional Paper No. 76). Ann Arbor, MI: Institute for Social Research.

Bukoski, W. J. (1991). A definition of drug abuse prevention research. In L. Donohew, H. E. Sypher, & W. J. Bukoski (Eds.), *Persuasive communication and drug abuse prevention* (pp. 3–19). Hillsdale, NJ: Erlbaum.

Carpenter, C. S., Kloska, D. D., O'Malley, P. M., & Johnston, L. D. (2007). Alcohol control policies and youth alcohol consumption: Evidence from 28 years of Monitoring the Future. *B.E. Journal of Economic Analysis & Policy, 7*(1). doi:10.2202/1935-1682.1637

Chaloupka, F. J., & Pacula, R. L. (1999). Sex and race differences in young people's responsiveness to price and tobacco control policies. *Tobacco Control, 8*, 373–377. doi:10.1136/tc.8.4.373

Coffman, D. L., Patrick, M. E., Palen, L., Rhoades, B. L., & Ventura, A. (2007). Why do high school seniors drink? Implications for a targeted approach. *Prevention Science, 8*, 241–248. doi:10.1007/s11121-007-0078-1

Emery, S., Wakefield, M. A., Terry-McElrath, Y., Saffer, H., Szczypka, G., O'Malley, P. M., . . . Flay, B. (2005). Televised state-sponsored anti-tobacco advertising and youth smoking beliefs and behavior in the United States, 1999–2000. *Archives of Pediatrics & Adolescent Medicine, 159*, 639–645. doi:10.1001/archpedi.159.7.639

Jessor, R. (1985). Bridging etiology and prevention in drug abuse research. In C. L. Jones & R. J. Battjes (Eds.), *Etiology of drug abuse: Implications for prevention.* National Institute on Drug Abuse Research Monograph No. 56. PsycCRITIQUES, *31*(9), 257–268. doi:10.1037/025079

Johnston, L. D. (1985). The etiology and prevention of substance use: What can we learn from recent historical changes? In C. L. Jones & R. J. Battjes (Eds.), *Etiology of drug abuse: Implications for prevention.* National Institute on Drug Abuse Research Monograph No. 56. PsycCRITIQUES, *31*(9), 155–177. doi:10.1037/025079

Johnston, L. D. (1991). Toward a theory of drug epidemics. In R. L. Donohew, H. Sypher, & W. Bukoski (Eds.), *Persuasive communication and drug abuse prevention* (pp. 93–132). Hillsdale, NJ: Erlbaum.

Johnston, L. D., Bachman, J. G., & O'Malley, P. M. (1981). *Highlights from student drug use in America, 1975–1980.* Washington, DC: National Institute on Drug Abuse.

Johnston, L. D., & O'Malley, P. M. (1986). Why do the nation's students use drugs and alcohol? Self-reported reasons from nine national surveys. *Journal of Drug Issues*, *16*, 29–66.

Johnston, L. D., O'Malley, P. M., & Bachman, J. G. (1993). *National survey results on drug use from the Monitoring the Future study, 1975–1992. Volume I: Secondary school students* (DHHS Publication No. 93-3597). Rockville, MD: National Institute on Drug Abuse.

Johnston, L. D., O'Malley, P. M., Bachman, J. G., & Schulenberg, J. E. (2012a). *Monitoring the Future national survey results on drug use, 1975–2011: Vol. I. Secondary school students.* Ann Arbor, MI: Institute for Social Research.

Johnston, L. D., O'Malley, P. M., Bachman, J. G., & Schulenberg, J. E. (2012b). *Monitoring the Future national survey results on drug use, 1975–2011: Vol. II. College students and adults ages 19–50.* Ann Arbor, MI: Institute for Social Research.

Keyes, K. M., Schulenberg, J. E., O'Malley, P. M., Johnston, L. D., Bachman, J. G., Li, G., & Hasin, D. (2011). The social norms of birth cohorts and adolescent marijuana use in the United States, 1976–2007. *Addiction*, *106*, 1790–1800. doi:10.1111/j.1360-0443.2011.03485.x

National Institute on Drug Abuse. (2012a). *Inhalants* (Research Report Series, NIH Publication No. 12-3818). Rockville, MD: National Institute on Drug Abuse. Retrieved from http://www.drugabuse.gov/sites/default/files/inhalantsrrs.pdf

National Institute on Drug Abuse. (2012b). *Prescription drug abuse: Young people at risk.* Retrieved from http://www.drugabuse.gov/related-topics/trends-statistics/infographics/prescription-drug-abuse-young-people-risk

O'Malley, P. M., & Wagenaar, A. C. (1991). Effects of minimum drinking age laws on alcohol use, related behaviors, and traffic crash involvement among American youth: 1976–1987. *Journal of Studies on Alcohol*, *52*, 478–491.

Patrick, M. E., & Schulenberg, J. E. (2011). How trajectories of reasons for alcohol use relate to trajectories of binge drinking: National panel data spanning late adolescence to early adulthood. *Developmental Psychology*, *47*, 311–317. doi:10.1037/a0021939

Patrick, M. E., Schulenberg, J. E., O'Malley, P. M., Johnston, L., & Bachman, J. (2011). Adolescents' reported reasons for alcohol and marijuana use as predictors of substance use and problems in adulthood. *Journal of Studies on Alcohol and Drugs*, *72*, 106–116.

Patrick, M. E., Schulenberg, J. E., O'Malley, P. M., Maggs, J. L., Kloska, D. D., Johnston, L. D., & Bachman, J. G. (2011). Age-related changes in reasons for using alcohol and marijuana from ages 18 to 30 in a national sample. *Psychology of Addictive Behaviors*, *25*, 330–339. doi:10.1037/a0022445

Schmidt, S., & Kenworthy, T. (1986, June 25). Cocaine caused Bias' death, autopsy reveals. *Los Angeles Times.* Retrieved from http://articles.latimes.com/1986-06-25/sports/sp-20106_1_len-bias

Slater, S. J., Chaloupka, F. J., Wakefield, M., Johnston, L. D., & O'Malley, P. M. (2007). The impact of retail cigarette marketing practices on youth smoking uptake. *Archives of Pediatrics & Adolescent Medicine*, *161*, 440–445. doi:10.1001/archpedi.161.5.440

Sloboda, Z. (2005). Implications of epidemiologic information for effective drug abuse prevention strategies. In Z. Sloboda (Ed.), *Epidemiology of drug abuse* (pp. 211–223). New York, NY: Springer. doi:10.1007/0-387-24416-6_14

Terry-McElrath, Y. M., Emery, S., Wakefield, M. A., O'Malley, P. M., Szczypka, G., & Johnston, L. D. (2013). Effects of tobacco-related media campaigns on smoking among 20–30 year old adults: Longitudinal data from the USA. *Tobacco Control: An International Journal*, *22*, 38–45. doi:10.1136/tobaccocontrol-2011-050208

Terry-McElrath, Y. M., O'Malley, P. M., & Johnston, L. D. (2009). Reasons for drug use among American youth by consumption level, gender, and race/ethnicity: 1976–2005. *Journal of Drug Issues, Summer*, 677–714.

Terry-McElrath, Y. M., Wakefield, M. A., Emery, S., Saffer, H., Szczypka, G., O'Malley, P. M., . . . Flay, B. R. (2007). State anti-tobacco advertising and smoking outcomes by gender and race/ethnicity. *Ethnicity & Health*, *12*, 339–362. doi:10.1080/13557850701300723

Tworek, C., Yamaguchi, R., Kloska, D. D., Emery, S., Barker, D., Giovino, G., . . . Chaloupka, F. J. (2010). State-level tobacco control policies and youth smoking cessation measures. *Health Policy*, *97*, 136–144. doi:10.1016/j.healthpol.2010.04.009

Wagenaar, A. C., O'Malley, P. M., & LaFond, C. (2001). Lowered legal blood alcohol limits for young drivers: Effects on drinking, driving, and driving-after-drinking behaviors in 30 states. *American Journal of Public Health*, *91*, 801–804. doi:10.2105/AJPH.91.5.801

Wakefield, M., Terry-McElrath, Y., Emery, S., Saffer, H., Chaloupka, F., Szczypka, G., . . . Johnston, L. (2006). Impact of televised tobacco industry smoking prevention advertising on youth smoking-related beliefs, intentions and behavior. *American Journal of Public Health*, *96*, 2154–2160. doi:10.2105/AJPH.2005.083352

CHAPTER 4

THEORETICAL MODELS OF DRUG USE ETIOLOGY: FOUNDATIONS OF PREVENTION

Lawrence M. Scheier

The chapter begins with a few words on the role of theory in scientific endeavor, clarifies the concept of theory testing, and references the tenets of logical positivism. It discusses two prominent psychosocial theories that have been the cornerstone of modern school-based drug prevention: social influence/social learning and self-efficacy formulations of human behavior, and problem behavior theory (PBT). The chapter addresses the major axioms and postulates of each theory as they bear on the discussion of experimental manipulation checks required for program evaluation. The final section emphasizes the need for harmony between basic studies of etiology and efforts to develop applied prevention models.

THEORY AS CONFIRMATION OF REALITY

There are many ways to cast definitions of *theory.* Some, like Bandura (1978), have regarded theory as "a device for organizing diverse bodies of evidence and for guiding the search for more integrative generalizations" (p. 252). This approach comports with the need for theory to be broad and encompassing rather than built around specific instances of events that may reflect sampling error or inconsistencies. From an epidemiological perspective, Kellam, Koretz, and Moscicki (1999) suggested that the "role of theory is to provide the empirically validated story of how mental health problems develop" (p. 471). According to developmental psychologists, theory is "the instrument of explanation or understanding, a source of meaning for facts or observation that endows them with a wider significance" (Jessor & Jessor, 1977, p. 10).

Philosophers of science have posited that theory provides a framework for testing propositions emanating from observations of the real world (Popper, 1963). From a utilitarian point of view, theories must be useful; if they are unable to explain important phenomena, they have no place in the real order of things. Theories are a tacit rejection of the "ultimate knowledge" that exists within nature (*veracitas naturae*). In their broadest sense, theories are human conventions and arise in their multiplicity because our knowledge lacks authority (i.e., no one known truth exists). Theories are born of prejudices, ignorance, and error, and, according to Popper (1963), are bold conjectures that are a product of "ignorant cocksureness" (p. 17). Popper, who founded critical rationalism, has suggested that "theories are our own inventions, our own ideas; they are not forced upon us, but are our self-made instruments of thought" (p. 157). In critical rationalism, theories are a form of validation that represents the path to truth, but not truth in and of itself. Truth is veiled by our own ignorance, education, and tradition, and is, in essence, beyond our reach.

Historians of science have indicated that theory stems from a long tradition of testing and validation considered to be part and parcel of normal science

http://dx.doi.org/10.1037/14550-005
Handbook of Adolescent Drug Use Prevention: Research, Intervention Strategies, and Practice, L. M. Scheier (Editor)

(Kuhn, 1970). Theory also assumes that people believe they know what the world is like because they readily observe it daily. However, when people attempt explanations of the world, they may contrive faulty testimonial because they lack precision in understanding and because the world is complex. One of the crucial elements of a valid theory is the ability to make testable and specific predictions based on explicit axioms and postulates. Given a testable theoretical framework, and if the theory is valid and withstands empirical refutation, an investigator should be able to draw specific conclusions about the outcomes. In a rationalist's perspective, theories must be refutable; otherwise, they are not scientifically verifiable. The combination of testability, falsifiability, or refutability is what composed Popper's (1963) *criterion of demarcation:* creating the distinction between theory and the conceivable, the possible, and what people observe.

According to Popper's (1963) falsification hypothesis, good scientific theories forbid things from happening as much as they predict what will or should happen. That is the mark of a good theory: its ability to make precise predictions that bear relevance to the real world. Through the falsification process, a good theory will eliminate poor explanations that do not fit the world. Perhaps Popper's greatest epistemological contribution was the distinction between origin and validity. Popper brought to mind the epistemological question, Will we ever know? Because people cannot truly know the origin of something (like the world), they must focus instead on their energies on the way in which they accept assertions about the world, that is, the means through which people determine whether a theory has any authority. When this discussion is placed on a grand scale, a researcher can posit cosmological theories that account for creation of the universe (e.g., Davies, 1992). On a relatively smaller scale, a prevention researcher can provide an overarching theoretical framework for health behaviors (Flay & Petraitis, 1994) or seamlessly weave together several theoretical propositions into an organized framework to account for drug use (e.g., Petraitis, Flay, & Miller, 1995).

In placing such tremendous emphasis on the process of critical examination (i.e., Kant's autonomy of thought), Popper (1963) reinstated a reliance on theory testing and the methods of induction as the sine qua non of modern science. Indeed, Popper has suggested that, at the very least, a theory must attend to elements of causal propositions that are malleable, measurable or observable, distinct, subject to statistical validation, and replicable in similar environmental contexts and also under different conditions. A good discussion of these points and the role of theory in everyday thinking can be found in Godfrey-Smith (2003).

Broad Theoretical Foundations of Adolescent Drug Use

Prevention science relies heavily on theory because the assessment methods do not allow for observation of the precise mechanisms through which interventions bring about behavior change. The basic plan of action (i.e., a causal chain of events) that leads to behavior change cannot be observed in the traditional sense of the word. Indeed, following intervention exposure, the researcher infers changes in youth's attitudes, beliefs, or knowledge, for instance, from self-reports, or, in some cases, observation of skills demonstrated using role-playing. If anything, these changes are located "inside the head," thus creating the specter of events transpiring within a *black box*, that is, the precise mechanisms are unknown but inferred based on theoretical exposition.

The first part of this causal chain of events has been termed *action*, *program*, or *intervention theory* (Chen, 1990; West & Aiken, 1997). In the case of preventing drug use, intervention or action theory specifies how various features of the instructional strategies (e.g., materials, activities, handouts, videos, role-playing, didactic instruction) will change the target risk mechanisms that give rise to drug use (e.g., low self-esteem, perceived social acceptability of drug use, social assertiveness, drug refusal skills). Assuming the program developer has a theory, such as social learning theory, in hand, this first theoretical component requires developing a table of specification that outlines in detail the mechanisms linking instructional modalities (i.e., teaching skills) with intended behavior change. This approach is common practice in achievement test development, provides a basis to determine content validity, and is used to acquire information about discriminability of items with regard to the target domains (e.g., Chase, 1999).

To provide a substantive example, a developer might posit that teaching youth social skills will improve their ability to ward off negative social influences, such as drug use offers. That is, ensuring that youth can resist negative peer influences provides a good foundation for drug prevention. The curriculum usually involves some role-playing and behavioral rehearsal in which students rely on skits, and real-life examples of situations in which they should refuse drug offers. Practicing skills in classroom situations, watching videos of youth engaging these skills, and discussing the underlying nature of peer influences (i.e., peer conformity processes) are strategies for improving drug refusal skills. The program developer bases the curriculum on a strong body of empirical evidence linking peer social influence with drug use (e.g., Andrews & Hops, 2010; Graham, Marks, & Hansen, 1991). Lesson plans are structured around teaching youth how to artfully decline drug offers, deflect conversation about drugs, and defend their rights (e.g., assertiveness) in socially acceptable ways that will reduce their vulnerability to drug offers.

The researcher reinforces the construction of a table of specifications by selecting psychometrically sound metrics to assess behavior. Here, the researcher may have in mind a reliable scale of assertiveness that assesses youth's defense of rights. A learning module strengthening defense of rights would teach youth age-appropriate ways to tell people they cannot cut in line while waiting for a movie, to return defective merchandise to a store, to ask for correct change, or to ask a friend to return something borrowed (e.g., Gambrill & Richey, 1975). To illustrate, L. M. Scheier, Botvin, and Griffin (2001) showed that the effects of the Life Skills Training program on drug use were mediated through social skills (i.e., assertiveness). They modeled a latent construct of social competence reflected by drug refusal skills, a measure of assertiveness confidence, and assertiveness skills (i.e., defense of rights). The latent construct taps social competence by blending an efficacy component, that is, a belief in skill execution, with frequency measures of actual behavior that comports with social learning theory. Duration of favorable program effects were shown over 1 and 2 years postintervention (seventh to ninth grades) with associated decreases in self-reported alcohol and polydrug use (controlling for baseline measures of skills and drug use).

Constructing an intervention around the different components of the causal chain is necessary but insufficient for successful program development. A program developer must also concentrate on factors influencing program delivery and adoption. Implementation theory describes the organizational processes undergirding program delivery, including adherence to training (i.e., fidelity), adoption, diffusion, and sustainability. A significant portion of this handbook elaborates on how these different intervention implementation components work to improve program outcomes.

Etiology

Intervention theory is only one part of the causal chain that links program instructional modalities with changes in behavior. Another crucial component is psychosocial (etiological) theory, which provides knowledge of developmental mechanisms that link skills with drug use. This information indicates the core features of vulnerability—what makes one youth more susceptible to negative peer influence than another. Psychosocial theory draws heavily from epidemiology and etiology in building a synthesized picture of risk and protective factors (e.g., Hawkins, Catalano, & Miller, 1992). Epidemiology and etiology are like brick and mortar: Each binds or strengthens the other. Epidemiology is vitally important because, through it, the researcher can detail the features or characteristics of risk associated with a disease state or health condition in various subgroups (Lilienfeld & Lilienfeld, 1980). The primary focus of epidemiology is generally concerned with studying the *incidence*, or new cases, and *prevalence*, or cases within defined boundaries of population or time, of risk or disease. Through etiology, though, one extends this focus by examining the natural developmental course of risk and its influence on drug use, or any health condition such as HIV or spousal aggression. A naturalistic observation study of youth development at a critical juncture in the life span that gathers information on drug use is akin to the counterfactual condition in an experiment, which helps paint a picture of what happens to youth when no treatment is administered over time (L. M. Scheier, 2010).

Etiology has intrinsic value to prevention because it informs program developers about lifespan development. This effort offers insight into child development, family relations, peer influences, identity, psychosocial maturational processes, and the various means through which youth gather information about themselves and the world. Armed with this knowledge and coupled with epidemiological information on risk at the population level, program developers can develop specific strategies to intercede and curtail behavior by limiting risk and boosting protection (e.g., Clayton, 1992; Sloboda, Glantz, & Tarter, 2012). This view is consistent with a concept that has dominated developmental psychology: *sensitive periods* (Bornstein, 1989), which suggests that key inflection points exist at which well-timed interventions can correct wayward behaviors and promote youth adaptation.

Although etiology mostly concerns an examination of causal pathways to drug use, program developers can also benefit from examining the consequences of drug use. Through good theories of drug use, they not only can identify effects of drug use on performance during the early stages of adolescence (e.g., L. M. Scheier & Botvin, 1995) but also can go beyond this developmental period and specify possible later outcomes that can adversely influence adult role socialization (e.g., Brook et al., 2013; Newcomb, Scheier, & Bentler, 1993; L. M. Scheier & Botvin, 1995). This information can be bundled into intervention strategies under information about the consequences of drug use and conveyed to youth as evidence of potential disruption to their lives (for more on using this type of strategy to dispel myths, see Chapters 9 and 10 of this handbook).

The next section of this chapter illustrates two psychosocial theories that have guided development of drug prevention interventions: social learning theory and PBT. Although this review is not meant to be exhaustive, it should be useful to the discussion of how drug prevention works and should also elaborate whether the body of knowledge gathered so far from etiology can critically inform prevention. An important distinction is that this review identifies theories that are primarily cognitive in nature at the exclusion of those that rely on contextual or environmental influences. Other chapters in this handbook emphasize more ecological models of drug use or incorporate cognitive theories as one step in the intervention process and then include broader transactional models of drug use.

SOCIAL LEARNING THEORY

Social learning theory is perhaps the most empirically scrutinized motivational framework from which to understand the causes of human behavior (Bandura, 1969, 1986). It departs from several of its contemporary rival theories (e.g., Bolles, 1975; Rotter, 1966) through its assertion that motivation for behavior (i.e., activation and persistence) occurs. Rather than explain behavior in terms of the generalized expectance of control or as resulting from learned reinforcement contingencies (i.e., behavior reflects the anticipation of benefits or aversion of problems), social learning theory posits that self-regulation occurs through the expectance of self-efficacy, a cognitive symbolic representation that takes shape as a belief in performance capability.[1] Indeed, Bandura was less inclined to believe that people are controlled as weather vanes by the whim of perceptions of control or reward structures. Instead, he painstakingly outlined a model of human self-efficacy that involves reliance on cognitive schemas or mental representations of how people will perform in similar situations based on our past

[1]An *efficacy expectance* and an *outcome expectance*, motivational enterprises within a self-efficacy formulation, convey different meanings. An efficacy expectance, which precedes an outcome expectance, is based solely on the cognitive formulation of whether a person has the right skills to execute a task. An outcome expectance refers to one's estimation of whether he or she will achieve a desired goal (i.e., a judgment of the likelihood that consequences will occur) and does not require deliberation over whether the right assets or capability is present to achieve it. Outcome expectancies can interest or disinterest a person in a task; however, the motivation to engage the task is based on the efficacy, and not the incentivized, expectance. According to Bandura, basing behavior on the anticipation of rewards and reinforcement is too deterministic or fatalistic. The cognitive architecture of a self-efficacy formulation suggests that self-regulatory influences provide a better explanation to account for human action.

history (i.e., performance) and the rewards or outcomes associated with that history (Bandura, 1997).

People learn from watching others—from modeling their behaviors and retaining this information in memory symbolically (Bandura & Walters, 1963). The key feature of this symbolic representation is that performance information provides individuals with a reliable indication of whether they can engage a particular task and have the confidence to obtain a particular outcome. This process can be as simple as teaching a young boy (or girl) to swing a baseball bat by first showing him the mechanics and then letting him hold and swing the bat. The youngster will take a few rudimentary swings and more than likely miss, but with practice and determination, he will soon learn the smooth rotation of the torso, turning of the wrists, visual focus on the ball, and physical power required to hit a ball. If a parent pitches a few easy balls, the youngster will benefit from the joy of making contact and swinging for the fences. These efficacy formulations, or expectances regarding the ability to execute a specific activity, are what guides behavior—they provide internal standards—and not the judgment of outcomes or likely consequences from enacting the behavior. In addition to formulating a unified cognitively mediated model of behavior, Bandura (1997) was clear to suggest that the self-reflective thinker and the doer are not separate people; rather, they are the same coherent being who reviews their performance capability as a prelude to action.

Source of Efficacy

In its simplest form, social learning theory suggests that people actively formulate their expectations of personal efficacy from four sources: modeling and vicarious learning, enactive mastery involving practice, verbal or exhortative instruction (i.e., social persuasion), and physiological states (i.e., emotional arousal that helps individuals judge their levels of stress and anxiety in the face of performance). Enactive mastery and personal accomplishments based on performance are perhaps the best source of efficacy information because the individual gains firsthand, authentic knowledge of his or her own capabilities. In keeping with a social learning formulation, self-efficacy is especially potent as a motivator of behavior when the individual perceives that performance occurred because of skill and not due to an external source or aid. Self-efficacy also arises as a powerful motivational force when the individual believes the task was challenging and that his or her diligence and effort paid off (a modicum of failure may be useful to teach persistence).

Within the broad rubric of modeling, individuals can vicariously learn by monitoring others' performance or experiences, or they can actively model the desired level of performance. By itself, vicarious or observational learning is somewhat weaker and less effective than personal mastery but can still inform the individual of the requirements for obtaining mastery. As a source of learning, modeling relies heavily on identification and social comparison processes (e.g., Festinger, 1954). A core principle of modeling suggests that individuals profit greatly from seeing others they value perform a particular task with positive consequences and who have similar personal characteristics. Wills (1992) discussed this process in terms of upward social comparison as opposed to reflecting on downward social comparison. The evaluative process will likely increase the expectation that the observer can improve and obtain the same outcomes if he or she values the comparison, persists, and applies the same skills (e.g., Bandura, 1973; Bandura, Ross, & Ross, 1963).

Implications of Social Learning Theory

Many examples relevant to drug prevention drawing from the experimental literature reinforce a modeling and self-efficacy formulation. For instance, many youth learn about the effects of drugs by vicariously observing their peers or close friends. Social learning theory suggests that, once these behaviors occur, the observing youth engages a form of anticipatory self-evaluation, reflecting on whether he or she can engage this behavior and obtain similar outcomes (i.e., gain social approval from friends for smoking cigarettes or drinking alcohol). The constructive evaluation and social comparison presage an individual's decision to act and take shape as self-directed cognitive prompts to smoke cigarettes or drink alcohol. After some time, the imitative behavior possesses intrinsic reward value, and the observed model no longer needs to be present.

Vicarious social reinforcement also comes into in play: Many youth will observe peer models perform behavior (i.e., drink alcohol at a Friday night party) and then witness the social reinforcements some time later (i.e., when the same alcohol-abusing youth return to school on Monday and a group of chummy pals discuss their weekend frolicking and social experiences).

Past performance also strengthens an individual's willingness to engage a particular task. The eventual formation of an individual's conviction or belief that he or she can execute a task conveys tremendous motivational significance. In an efficacy formulation, a youth can decide, by evaluating his or her past performance, whether he or she possesses or lacks the necessary skills to refuse a drug offer. People actively contribute to their actions through self-reflection (i.e., organized constructions), which is what distinguishes a self-efficacy formulation from control theories (Rotter, 1966). In a self-efficacy formulation, a person becomes engrossed in a task, evaluates the challenges, and thinks about what course of action is required to solve a task, social or otherwise. A drug prevention program built on self-efficacy teaches youth skills to avoid setbacks and failure. The program invests in the skills that help youth navigate tasks (social or otherwise) and puts into motion belief in success (i.e., judgments of capability). Performance and proficiency of action are the active ingredients of a self-efficacy formulation, not intention or the determination of control. Youth who believe they can mobilize the necessary skills to solve a problem will be more likely to engage the task at hand than youth who deliberate over whether they can control the outcome or render a decision to engage on the basis of whether something was likely happening to them.

In addition to engaging a cognitive evaluation, feelings of inadequacy can cause anxiety or distress, and the desire to remove this distress may encourage acquiescence to peer pressure. Through extensive focus group work, program developers often learn that many youth would just rather not be bothered by friends who offer them drugs. By taking a hit on a marijuana joint or a swig of alcohol, they defuse any potential intolerable situations, thus limiting inferences that they are weak or a group outsider. In a self-efficacy formulation, changing youths' propensity to use refusal skills will only come through improving their performance (i.e., learning appropriate ways to refuse drug offers) and increasing their conviction that they can implement this skill. This is critical feature of many current prevention programs that rely on behavioral rehearsal and practice (i.e., homework) to ensure that youth have opportunities to hone their refusal and social assertiveness skills. It is also likely that youth may learn to use drugs as a form of palliative coping (e.g., to assuage anxiety or to relieve stress). Research backs this assertion and especially links emotional stress and drinking and other forms of drug use (e.g., Swaim, Chen, Deffenbacher, & Newcomb, 2001; Swaim, Oetting, Edwards, & Beauvais, 1989). This body of knowledge suggests that informing youth that drugs do not allay anxiety but, rather, exacerbate it provides one means of education. In the case of several programs described in this handbook (see Chapter 9), considerable program content emphasizes that continued use of drugs leads to tolerance, and ineffective coping can result in addiction.

Social learning theory provides a clear means to understand why interventions that emphasize "just say no" do not work—they are not targeting important factors associated with drug use. In particular, in keeping with a self-efficacy formulation, any type of campaign or prevention modality that wants youth to improve their refusal skills has to also consider the importance of improving their social competencies (i.e., enactive mastery). The opportunity to practice their social skills will, in turn, influence the belief, or self-efficacy expectation, that they can implement these skills in a socially adept manner. In a social learning formulation, it is the belief in perceived competence that regulates behavior, not the mere verbal statement of inoculation.

Bandura (1997) was quite clear in his pronouncement of self-efficacy theory; he suggested that people are not creatures who move from means to outcomes in the absence of internal cognitive deliberation. Rather, the more veridical framework suggests that effort is intended to produce valued outcomes through performance attainments (i.e., good grades); the performance attainments provide the intended outcomes (i.e., praise from parents).

The reason people differ in our efficacy formulations (and ability to refuse drug offers) is that we differ in the amount of effort we apply and the knowledge we bring to the situation. People also differ with regard to the command over subskills required to execute the task at hand, the resources we have at hand (i.e., training), and the emotional capability we have to diminish interference from anxiety or factors that displace effort (i.e., cognitive interference). The following section makes clear how drug prevention programs should approach teaching self-efficacy to increase the likelihood youth will refuse drug offers.

Social Learning Theory and Prevention

Social learning theory has had a tremendous influence on current prevention programs, particularly those involving social skills resistance training and competence-based programs that teach generic life skills (e.g., Botvin, 2000; Ellickson & Bell, 1990; Pentz, 1985). The basic thrust of many of these programs involves teaching youth a range of social skills, some specific to drugs (i.e., refusal skills) and others that entail more general assertiveness, social confrontation, and ways to avoid or reduce social anxiety. Assertiveness skills include teaching youth to initiate conversations, approach adults and ask for information, and assert themselves in a socially appropriate manner. As I alluded to previously, specific instructional components might include teaching youth to politely ask friends to return borrowed items, how to return defective merchandise to the store, and to speak up when people cut in line or fail to return a borrowed item. Many programs also buttress these skills with general communication skills and teach a bevy of life skills, such as decision making, goal adaptation, self-reinforcement, and problem solving, that reinforce the application of specific social skills.

As part of their training, youth also learn how to refuse drug offers and to detect and learn to respond correctly to popular media advertising that promote sales of liquor, beer, wine, and tobacco products. Program modules that directly attend to media influences are based on identification theory, which suggests that some models, symbolic or otherwise, can induce imitative behaviors on the mere grounds of their perceived social power, as is often the case with fashion models, actors, and high-profile media personnel (see Gerrard, Gibbons, Stock, Vande Lune, & Cleveland, 2005, and also Gerrard, Gibbons, Houlihan, Stock, & Pomery, 2008, for an example of etiology models involving risk prototypes). In some cases, especially with multimodal competence enhancement programs, youth also learn anxiety reduction techniques, including progressive relaxation, meditation, and other forms of behavioral control strategies (i.e., using self-statements to reward themselves and achieve a measure of calm), that help them allay fears that may accompany poor coping skills. By learning deep breathing exercises and alternative relaxation strategies, youth can avoid the anticipated stress that can follow social confrontation with peers. The various prevention modalities for social skills and personal competence training can be taught through didactic teaching methods, behavioral role-rehearsal, homework assignments, and small group learning that involves modeling and practice.

Important Lessons

Important lessons can be gained from applying the strict tenets of social learning theory. For instance, according to Bandura (1997), it is best to conceptualize performance as a successive accretion of skills (i.e., dividing performance into proximal subgoals). In this manner, an individual can break performances into their components and practice each one until achieving a point of mastery. Complexity often results in failure and can induce anxiety, which is why Bandura suggested giving options to youth rather than creating the belief in multiple selves—that is, avoid having youth divide their mind-set on the basis of whether, at one moment, they believe they can execute a task and, at another moment, fear failure because they do not possess the requisite skills. That approach might strap youth into nonaction because they will waffle over engagement. Youth are much better off learning they are the core determinant of their behavior (i.e., efficacy results from their own doing), but, in certain situations, they can turn to options if they lack the belief (i.e., efficacy formulation) that they can refuse a drug offer. In that case, if performance dictates that some anxiety may arise from refusing peers' overtures to smoke cigarettes, youth will be better positioned if they learn alternative ways to deflect drug offers—perhaps by teaching self-determination or some other program feature that weakens the importance of the offer.

The emphasis on multiple tiers of intervention to improve efficacy formulations will also lessen the impact of negative affect that may arise from perceived failure. Recognize that an efficacy formulation hinges on incorporating motivation at every step; youth who are motivated to develop efficacy (e.g., social skills) will apply these skills, when needed, if they perceive their own efficacy and anticipate reward (i.e., beneficial outcomes). That is why it is so crucial to inform adolescents of other alternatives, or lifestyle choices, besides drug use; provide normative education in combination with skills training to motivate youth toward a more conservative antidrug mind-set); and shore up their internal resources (i.e., goal adaptation and decision making) at the same time they learn new skills to refuse offers.

Beneath the Hood

At some point, recognizing one's efficacy and evaluating mastery performance may become part of habitual learned behavior but will not detract from an efficacy formulation, which relies on self-evaluation or explicit rational thinking processes. Rather, the distinction between a System I and II type of cognitive framework (Kahneman, 2011) suggests that new ways must be learned to bring these processes from beneath the radar of consciousness to more rational surface levels as part of training programs that influence self-evaluative thinking. This approach can be done fairly effortlessly through programs that highlight repeated performance aligned with positive and enduring, that is, desired, reward structures. Consider that repeated performance is a basis of mastery and that people do not break down the individual skills required to perform most complex tasks. For instance, people rely on rote knowledge when driving a car and rarely decompose the performance into subskills (e.g., putting on a seatbelt, adjusting the mirror, inserting a key into the ignition, starting the engine, putting the car in gear, stepping on the gas); instead, we examine our general belief in driving on the basis of an overall sense of mastery performance ("I can drive safely"). Many of these performance-oriented behaviors operate silently and are not routinely subject to conscious reflection.

Youth operate the same way. Watching young kids play soccer at age 8 is very different from the same experience with 12- or 14-year-old players. Over time, the young athletes learn dribbling skills and how to pass using different parts of their foot. They also learn how to trap the ball using different parts of their body and eventually how to pass accurately over long distances. They do this without thinking or breaking down the performance into muscle microprocesses, but, rather, they gain proficiency based on practice (i.e., rehearsal). In the beginning, when training youngsters, a person may show them basic muscle movement, how to turn the foot to receive a ball, and touch dribbling maneuvers. This is one of the principles of the Dutch Ajax training: to break down the muscle movements and teach soccer in bits and pieces, one touch at a time (e.g., Smink, 2004). Speed and agility change dramatically with increasing age, and so too does efficacy, which responds to new performance evaluations. In light of this formulation, it is essential to teach youth task persistence, even in the face of dissuasive factors or competing influences, and link effort with positive reward structures as a means of increasing efficacy beliefs. Efficacy sustains effort, and effort promotes efficacy (reciprocal determinism at its best).

It is also essential to teach youth to master what skills are readily accessible and highlight the competencies they have rather than push them to develop competencies possibly beyond their immediate reach (i.e., trainers do not teach 6-year-olds to head soccer balls). This is perhaps the single most important reason to teach developmentally appropriate skills (i.e., social assertiveness) and then time interventions so they are specific to current skill levels rather than match them to faddish social trends or cultural nuances that have no lasting power. Furthermore, it is important to teach youth skills that have tremendous temporal relevance to the behavior(s) in question. Teaching at a specific level encourages youth to use these skills in similar social transactions, although this does not mean that youth will not generalize their efficacy beliefs. Both efficacy and optimism contribute to psychological well-being. When thinking about teaching efficacy through skill performance, consider encouraging optimism and a brighter outlook—even in the face of despair (i.e., resilience training). An optimistic sense of efficacy (e.g., Karademas, 2006; M. F. Scheier & Carver, 1985) will ward off depression (i.e., a perceived lack of control) because it will assure individuals that they can and do have the necessary resources to exercise control over outcomes (through performance mastery).

Efficacy will also contribute to learning, and an important component of training youth to be more efficacious is to find ways to improve the learning environment. Although beyond the scope of this chapter, considerable evidence suggests that efficacy prompts learning by teaching youth that they can apply the correct strategies rather than rely on practice alone (Schunk & Rice, 1987, 1992). What is important to glean from these studies is the students' careful attention to their use of mental strategies, or step-by-step processes to solve problems, rather than verbal exhortations by teachers that students "can learn." Teaching youth to apply strategies gives them a sense of internal reliance and self-determination (Ryan & Deci, 2000).

PROBLEM BEHAVIOR THEORY

PBT provides a dramatically different example of developmental theory in the context of drug prevention. For one thing, it is not steeped in learning theory; rather, it reflects historical forces shaping ideas about deviance and prominent contemporaneous social psychological theories of personality. PBT was shaped by the social and political activism of the 1960s, with a particular emphasis on drug use, sexual activity, drinking, activism, and protest (i.e., highlighting the social norms of the time, including antiestablishment and social and political criticism). One way to think about PBT is as a social psychological framework designed to support theoretical inquiry into deviance. Its framework reflects several influences, including Lewin's (1951) field theoretical approach to human behavior, Merton's (1957) structural analysis and formulations of social anomie, and Rotter's (1954) social learning theory (Rotter, Chance, & Phares, 1972). Together, these frameworks provide a basis from which to understand individual differences in personality as it influences problem behaviors or behaviors that deviate from social norms. PBT also emphasizes factors influencing conforming behaviors, including academic performance, law abidance, and church involvement.

PBT began as a study of primarily White, middle-class youth and their families drawn from the Rocky Mountain region of Colorado (Jessor, Graves, Hanson, & Jessor, 1968). Two age cohorts were followed initially for 4 years: one from junior high school and a smaller college sample. The junior high school sample was followed annually from 1969 over four successive annual waves and thereafter, on less frequent occasions, through young adulthood (Jessor, Donovan, & Costa, 1991). The sample is noted for its high retention rates across time (exceeding 82% over multiple follow-ups), the quality of data provided by participants, and the students' willingness to respond to a lengthy self-report questionnaire with personal questions about candor and honesty.

The overriding theoretical framework of PBT suggests that three systems of social psychological processes interact to produce behavior: personality, environment, and behavior. A key postulate in the PBT model is that the dynamic interplay between systems creates a proneness to problem behavior in which different instigations and motivations are balanced against various protections and controls. When the balance is out of kilter (i.e., the variables dynamically interact), youth engage in deviant activities, become attracted to political activism (i.e., social protest), engage in precocious sex (i.e., losing one's virginity at an early age), get drunk, smoke marijuana, and engage in aggressive (i.e., getting into fights) or delinquent (i.e., stealing, lying, and petty theft) activities.

Personality System

The personality system contains cognitive processes that primarily reflect values, beliefs, expectations, and orientations toward self and others. The balance within this system revolves around motivations or instigations to use drugs and protections, or controls, that minimize opportunities for drug use. Foremost among motivational instigations are values meaningful to youth, such as academic achievement, independence, and affection. Youth striving for autonomy, showing little deference to their parents, and showing little interest in conventional institutions such as school are more prone to engage in problem behaviors. Beliefs about self and society tap self-esteem, alienation, and social criticism, which encompass how youth give social meaning and relate to the world. The personality system contains three component structures: motivational-instigation, personal belief, and personal control, all of which compose the nature of the person and, in PBT, are considered more proximal to the behaviors considered transgressions.

The motivational-instigation structure is based on orientation of action, the goals toward which an individual strives, and the directionality of these goals (e.g., low value on achievement could be reflected through measures of school bonding). A measure of discrepancy in goals is important and involves pairing, for instance, academic motivation with independence. By creating these discrepancies, investigators could develop a picture of whether youth value their autonomy and like or dislike school. Youth who dislike school and are rarely monitored by their parents might be prone to problem behaviors.

The personal belief structure involves restraints on participating in unconventional behavior that are tethered to a person's beliefs about his or her role in society (i.e., the deviant identity; see Kaplan & Cheng-Hsien, 2000) and how that person sees his or her actions in terms of conventional beliefs. Taken together, the four variables in this component structure—social criticism, alienation, self-esteem, and internal-external locus of control—capture an individual's stake in or willingness to participate in society and the person's desire to engage in positive activities, accept the values of the larger society (i.e., commitment), find meaning in daily roles/activities, and maintain high self- and social regard.

The personal control structure represents the constraints against nonnormative behavior and, compared with the personal belief structure, is more directly linked with problem behaviors. For instance, attitudinal tolerance of deviance, religiosity, and the discrepancy between the perceived positive and negative functions of engaging in deviant behaviors (i.e., drug use) are the principal elements of this control structure. Tolerance of deviance deals with the perceived wrongness of behavior, such as lying or stealing, drinking, or using drugs. *Religiosity* refers to the moral sanctions—taught through institutions such as the church or family—that an individual weighs before engaging in problem behaviors. The positive-versus-negative function is a complex weighing of the costs and effects of engaging in problem behaviors. For instance, two young minor youth might want to have sexual relations, but one believes it is morally wrong and could lead to unwanted pregnancy, thus preventing the pair from consummating this intimate act.

Perceived Social Environment

A second major system in PBT that interacts with personality in producing behavior reflects the perceived social environment. Reliance on the concept of *perceived* means the environment in terms of its meaning for the actor (i.e., his or her own interpretation of how the environment works). This is a more phenomenological interpretation that fits with the concepts of life space or press that are part of Lewin's (1951) field theory. The environment comprises different elements; however, those of concern in PBT are the social agents that can encourage or discourage problem behaviors, perceived supports, and opportunities that encourage problem behaviors. The salience of opportunity in producing delinquency is also a part of the Gottfredson and Hirschi (1990) general theory of crime. The difference between the environmental elements is the *texture* they provide to a youth's life—how a youth actively constructs his or her self, which entails, in part, whether a youth's parents support a deviant identity or attempt to thwart deviant activities by instituting controls to regulate behavior. A more recent conceptualization of deviant identity builds off the notion of labeling and how meaning is derived from unconventional behaviors (e.g., Brownfield & Thompson, 2005).

Elements of the social environment include distal structures, such as parental supports (i.e., help being available), and also controls that take shape as regulations or sanctions that parents or peers might disapprove of deviance and drug use, compatibility (i.e., consensus) between parents and peers in their expectations for youth, and perceived influence of parents versus peers. When a youth's parents and peers agree on expected sanctions for behavior, she or he has more certainty about how to act. If a youth feels pushed or pulled by parents or peers, respectively, and has great uncertainty about behavior, anxiety and disenfranchisement (i.e., anomie) result. The relative weight of peers versus parents is easy to grasp in the context of sanctions toward problem behavior. Parental influence precedes peers; when peers exact greater control over a youth's behavior, however, that indicates that the youth has distanced herself or himself from parental influence. Spending more time with peers and less time with parents only encourages problem behaviors, which arise in this age group because of poor supervision and lack of regulatory controls.

Proximal influences take shape as opportunity: social approval, social pressures, and affective ties with friends, and role models. Opportunity is about the chances youth have to learn about problem behaviors such as drug use vicariously and by direct experience. Hanging out with older youth who have access to alcohol or being around friends who smoke cigarettes represents opportunity and is positioned in PBT as proximal to the behavior in question. A youth will not smoke cigarettes merely because he or she associates with other friends who smoke, although research has shown that such proximity through socialization does dramatically increase the odds (e.g., Aloise-Young, Graham, & Hansen, 1994). The operative term in PBT is *approvals* and entails the social milieu youth engage, the strength of the approval for drug use, cajoling and encouragement, and the emotional bonds (i.e., affection) youth have with their friends. Conformity processes also play a large role in deviance (Cialdini & Trost, 1998; Kosten, Scheier, & Grenard, 2013). As with the other systems in PBT, the perceived environment works in a dynamic manner: pitting the social controls against problem behaviors against the youth's perception of role models and supports for problem behaviors. If a youth is raised in a home with strict social controls against problem behaviors and finds support for these actions in his or her immediate peer network, he or she will abide by conventional norms. Conversely, the discordance between controls in the home and peer role models can induce discrepancy that orients the youth toward deviance. All it takes, for instance, is for a youth to spend unsupervised time away from home in the company of delinquent peers who model unconventional behaviors. The social acceptability of the behaviors combined with opportunity (e.g., staying out late on school nights) is enough sometimes to encourage youth toward delinquency.

Behavior System

The behavior system primarily emphasizes behaviors that are undesirable by societal standards and contrary to adult authority and social expectations, including social transgressions such as sexual intercourse, marijuana use, drinking (including problem or excessive drinking), activist protest, and general deviance (i.e., stealing, lying, aggression). According to PBT, these transgressions are regarded collectively and individually as "behavior that departs from regulatory norms" (Jessor & Jessor, 1978, p. 46). Also included in the behavior system are conventional behaviors related to socially approved activities that reflect the individual's close ties to normatively expected and more traditional functions, such as school and church attendance. Considerable evidence collected over the years has supported the psychometric validity of a common problem behavior syndrome based on the moderate statistical overlap among these behaviors (Donovan & Jessor, 1985; Donovan, Jessor, & Costa, 1988; McGee & Newcomb, 1992; Newcomb & Bentler, 1988).

Across several studies using different combinations of follow-up years, Jessor and colleagues have reported clear personality differences in problem-prone youth compared to their more conventional counterparts. For instance, youth who reported they used marijuana or drank alcohol did not favor their academic progress (i.e., had poor grades and low achievement motivation), placed greater emphasis on their independence, felt self-criticism, maintained weak religious ties, valued the upside of certain problem behaviors (i.e., perceived positive benefits to using drugs), and were more tolerant of deviance. Although these data reflected trends occurring in the late 1960s and 1970s, more recent evidence has shown their relevance to current drug consumption trends (e.g., Jessor, Chase, & Donovan, 1980; Jessor, Turbin, & Costa, 1998; Jessor, Van Den Bos, Vanderryn, Costa, & Turbin, 1995). In addition, studies have now been extended to affirm these findings with minority youth (e.g., Farrell, Danish, & Howard, 1992; Farrell, Kung, White, & Valois, 2000; L. M. Scheier & Botvin, 1996). Cross-national comparisons have also reinforced the importance of the three social psychological systems in accounting for youth problem behaviors in places such as China (e.g., Jessor, Turbin, Costa, Dong, Zhang, & Wang, 2003) and Kenya (e.g., Kabiru, Beguy, Ndugwa, Zulu, & Jessor, 2012; Ndugwa et al., 2011).

Many of the measures embodied by PBT reflect the tumultuous period youth experience as they seek autonomy and independence. Regulation of behavior comes in many shapes and forms, one of which is the close bond between a youth and conventional institutions. When tolerance for deviance is high, bonds to conventional institutions weaken, and peer models encourage drug use, youth get caught up transgressing against societal rules. When the transgressions are normative and restricted to lying, minor petty concerns (e.g., taking money from a parent's purse), and disobedience (e.g., refusing curfews), they are not troublesome. However, these transgressions can become more aggravated and persistent to the degree that they are noticeable by authorities and warrant prosecution, if not remand. When parents offer few incentives to remain committed to family and school, friends take on added meaning and tug on the youths' conventional allegiances and weaken bonds that might otherwise be protective. Drug-abusing youth are intolerant, seek risks, feel alienated, and push the limit with regard to controls in the home and in other conventional settings.

Implications of PBT for Prevention

Different facets of PBT can be incorporated into a drug prevention program. In terms of instigations and constraints, bonding to school is one way of instructing youth about conventional behavior. When youth feel strong ties to conventional institutions and do not feel alienated from important institutions, they are more likely to adhere to the rules and regulations that dictate social order. This is a main theoretical component of the Seattle Social Development Project (e.g., Fleming, Catalano, Oxford, & Harachi, 2002; Hawkins et al., 1992), a program that has shown favorable long-term outcomes for intervention youth (e.g., Hawkins, Guo, Hill, Battin-Pearson, & Abbott, 2001; Hawkins et al., 2007).

In addition, many programs that teach youth that drugs have serious addictive properties do not avail youth of the problems they may encounter as they negotiate adolescence. It is clear that youth develop expectancies for drugs ("If I smoke pot, I will get high and feel good; my problems will go away") primarily from social engagement with friends, from the media, and from personal experience. That said, many programs (covered in this handbook) contain instructional modules to counter the effects of media (i.e., portraying drug and alcohol use as glamorous) or modules that offer instruction detailing the negative consequences of drug use. Other programs teach youth they can be independent and self-affirming. For instance, Reconnecting Youth (Eggert & Nicholas, 2010) incorporates many of the essential components of PBT (e.g., social alienation) in a peer-led program to reduce school dropout, drug use, suicidal behavior, and other externalizing behaviors in high-risk youth. The program teaches youth to be independent but also conventional, to reduce their distress by engaging in prosocial activities, implement positive emotion-focused coping strategies, and develop peer friendship networks that revolve around positive youth adaptation.

As another example of how PBT can be used in prevention, the Office of National Drug Control Policy's National Youth Anti-Drug Media Campaign incorporated themes targeting parents with public service announcements via radio and television to encourage them to spend more time with their children, monitor their children, and engage in family activities. The goal of these activities was to promote family bonding, encourage parent–child communication about life and drugs, and create opportunities for children to bond with their parents. The "antidrug" in this case, a moniker for the campaign from 1999 to 2004, was parental involvement. Evidence from the campaign program evaluation indicated that parents reported more favorable attitudes toward and beliefs in the role of monitoring as a deterrent to youth drug use following exposure to the campaign messages (e.g., Hornik et al., 2003). The campaign continues today with the new moniker "Above the Influence" but with federal government funding cutbacks and no formal evaluation component.

THEORETICAL WRAP-UP

In this chapter, two theories were used to illustrate the supportive and intricate relations between etiology and prevention. However, any number of additional theories that have gained traction in the field could have been used, and many are discussed in the chapters throughout this handbook (see also L. M. Scheier, 2012, for a review of primary prevention). Over the past decade or so, theories of drug prevention have become considerably more ecological and blended developmental models that stem from etiology to include broader contextual influences. Theories have also become more transactional and have included references to family dynamics and processes that involve supportive socialization agents that influence child and youth behavior (L. M. Scheier & Hansen, 2014). These theories represent important additions to the field and are not covered in this handbook because of space limitations.

The interface of theory and drug prevention involves a two-step process: a marriage between specification of an intervention theory and psychosocial theory. Intervention theory strikes a chord with instructional practices, whereas psychosocial theory accentuates developmental processes that link targets of intervention theory (i.e., putative risk factors) with behavior. Social learning theory and its reliance on self-efficacy formulations is one of the best representations of this two-step interface, because instructional methods that improve self-efficacy also change behavior. The process of providing youth with instructional methods that focus on skills development and teach them functional strategies to reduce negative peer influence (i.e., refusal skills or social assertiveness) dampens their enthusiasm for engaging in unconventional behavior, including drug use. The instructional strategies, which teach youth to be more diligent, persistent, and successful, also net youth who believe they maintain greater internal control over their performance (i.e., the seeds of self-regulation). These types of self-reliant youth, buoyed by their own performance and who are reaping the fruits of their labor, will be less inclined to associate with deviant peers and less likely to engage in rules-transgressing behaviors (e.g., aggression, minor infractions at school, vandalism, petty theft). These same youth will desire and strive for more optimal outcomes in life (i.e., goal setting), make better decisions, and be more self-reinforcing and less prone to depression. They also will be willing to work toward these goals by relying on their own internal standards for performance.

Efficacy breeds a sense of benevolence and comfort to engage the world, which, in turn, provides a basis for perceived competence that White (1959) argued was the core ingredient to achievement. The combination of efficacy, mastery, and achievement represents a solid deterrent to deviance and drug use.

References

Aloise-Young, P. A., Graham, J. W., & Hansen, W. B. (1994). Peer influence on smoking initiation during early adolescence: A comparison of group members and group outsiders. *Journal of Applied Psychology, 79*, 281–287. doi:10.1037/0021-9010.79.2.281

Andrews, J. A., & Hops, H. (2010). The influence of peers on substance use. In L. M. Scheier (Ed.), *Handbook of drug use etiology: Theory, methods, and empirical findings* (pp. 403–420). Washington, DC: American Psychological Association.

Bandura, A. (1969). Social learning theory of identificatory processes. In D. A. Goslin (Ed.), *Handbook of socialization theory and research* (pp. 213–262). Chicago, IL: Rand McNally.

Bandura, A. (1973). *Aggression: A social learning analysis.* Englewood Cliffs, NJ: Prentice-Hall.

Bandura, A. (1978). Reflections on self-efficacy. *Advances in Behaviour Research and Therapy, 1*, 237–269. doi:10.1016/0146-6402(78)90012-7

Bandura, A. (1986). *Social foundations of thought and action: A social cognitive theory.* Englewood Cliffs, NJ: Prentice-Hall.

Bandura, A. (1997). *Self-efficacy: The exercise of control.* New York, NY: Freeman.

Bandura, A., Ross, D., & Ross, S. A. (1963). Imitation of film-mediated aggressive models. *Journal of Abnormal and Social Psychology, 66,* 3–11. doi:10.1037/h0048687

Bandura, A., & Walters, R. H. (1963). *Social learning and personality development.* New York, NY: Holt, Rinehart & Winston.

Bolles, R. C. (1975). *Learning theory.* New York, NY: Holt, Rinehart & Winston.

Bornstein, M. H. (1989). Sensitive periods in development: Structural characteristics and causal interpretations. *Psychological Bulletin, 105,* 179–197. doi:10.1037/0033-2909.105.2.179

Botvin, G. J. (2000). Preventing drug abuse in schools: Social and competence enhancement approaches targeting individual-level etiological factors. *Addictive Behaviors, 25,* 887–897. doi:10.1016/S0306-4603(00)00119-2

Brook, J. S., Lee, J. Y., Rubenstone, E., Finch, S. J., Seltzer, N., & Brook, D. W. (2013). Longitudinal determinants of substance use disorders. *Journal of Urban Health, 90,* 1130–1150. doi:10.1007/s11524-013-9827-6

Brownfield, D., & Thompson, K. (2005). Self-concept and delinquency: The effects of reflected appraisals by parent and peers. *Western Criminology Review, 6,* 22–29.

Chase, C. I. (1999). *Contemporary assessment for educators.* New York, NY: Longman.

Chen, H. T. (1990). *Theory-driven evaluations.* Newbury Park, CA: Sage.

Cialdini, R. B., & Trost, M. R. (1998). Social influence: Social norms, conformity, and compliance. In D. T. Gilbert, S. T. Fiske, & G. Lindzey (Eds.), *The handbook of social psychology* (Vol. 2, pp. 151–192). Boston, MA: McGraw-Hill.

Clayton, R. (1992). Transitions in drug use: Risk and protective factors. In M. Glantz & R. Pickens (Eds.), *Vulnerability to drug abuse* (pp. 15–51). Washington, DC: American Psychological Association. doi:10.1037/10107-001

Davies, P. C. W. (1992). *The mind of God: The scientific basis for a rational world.* New York, NY: Simon and Schuster.

Donovan, J. E., & Jessor, R. (1985). Structure of problem behavior in adolescence and young adulthood. *Journal of Consulting and Clinical Psychology, 53,* 890–904. doi:10.1037/0022-006X.53.6.890

Donovan, J. E., Jessor, R., & Costa, M. (1988). Syndrome of problem behavior in adolescence: A replication. *Journal of Consulting and Clinical Psychology, 56,* 762–765. doi:10.1037/0022-006X.56.5.762

Eggert, L. L., & Nicholas, L. (2010). *Reconnecting youth: A peer group approach to building life Skills.* Bloomington, IN: Solution Tree.

Ellickson, P. L., & Bell, R. M. (1990). Drug prevention in junior high: A multi-site longitudinal test. *Science, 247,* 1299–1305. doi:10.1126/science.2180065

Farrell, A. D., Danish, S. J., & Howard, C. W. (1992). Risk factors for drug use in urban adolescents: Identification and cross-validation. *American Journal of Community Psychology, 20,* 263–286. doi:10.1007/BF00937910

Farrell, A. D., Kung, E. M., White, K. S., & Valois, R. F. (2000). The structure of self-reported aggression, drug use, and delinquent behaviors during early adolescence. *Journal of Clinical Child Psychology, 29,* 282–292. doi:10.1207/S15374424jccp2902_13

Festinger, L. (1954). A theory of social comparison processes. *Human Relations, 7,* 117–140. doi:10.1177/001872675400700202

Flay, B. R., & Petraitis, J. (1994). The theory of triadic influence: A new theory of health behavior with implications for preventive interventions. In G. S. Albrecht (Ed.), *Advances in medical sociology, Vol. IV: A reconsideration of models of health behavior change* (pp. 19–44). Greenwich, CT: JAI Press.

Fleming, C. R., Catalano, R. F., Oxford, M. L., & Harachi, T. W. (2002). A test of generalizability of the social development model across gender and income groups with longitudinal data from the elementary school developmental period. *Journal of Quantitative Criminology, 18,* 423–439. doi:10.1023/A:1021173711746

Gambrill, E. D., & Richey, C. A. (1975). An assertion inventory for use in assessment and research. *Behavior Therapy, 6,* 550–561. doi:10.1016/S0005-7894(75)80013-X

Gerrard, M., Gibbons, F. X., Houlihan, A. E., Stock, M. L., & Pomery, E. A. (2008). A dual-process approach to health risk decision making: The prototype willingness model. *Developmental Review, 28,* 29–61. doi:10.1016/j.dr.2007.10.001

Gerrard, M., Gibbons, F. X., Stock, M. L., Vande Lune, L. S., & Cleveland, M. J. (2005). Images of smokers and willingness to smoke among African American pre-adolescents: An application of the prototype/willingness model of adolescent health risk behavior to smoking initiation. *Journal of Pediatric Psychology, 30,* 305–318. doi:10.1093/jpepsy/jsi026

Godfrey-Smith, P. (2003). *Theory and reality.* Chicago, IL: University of Chicago Press. doi:10.7208/chicago/9780226300610.001.0001

Gottfredson, M. R., & Hirschi, T. (1990). *A general theory of crime*. Stanford, CA: Stanford University Press.

Graham, J. W., Marks, G., & Hansen, W. B. (1991). Social influence processes affecting adolescent substance use. *Journal of Applied Psychology*, *76*, 291–298. doi:10.1037/0021-9010.76.2.291

Hawkins, J. D., Catalano, R. F., & Miller, J. Y. (1992). Risk and protective factors for alcohol and other drug problems in adolescence and early adulthood: Implications for substance abuse prevention. *Psychological Bulletin*, *112*, 64–105. doi:10.1037/0033-2909.112.1.64

Hawkins, J. D., Catalano, R. F., Morrison, D. M., O'Donnell, J., Abbott, R. D., & Day, L. E. (1992). The Seattle Social Development Project: Effects of the first four years on protective factors and problem behaviors. In J. McCord & R. E. Tremblay (Eds.), *Preventing antisocial behavior: Interventions from birth through adolescence* (pp. 139–161). New York, NY: Guilford Press.

Hawkins, J. D., Guo, J., Hill, K. G., Battin-Pearson, S., & Abbott, R. D. (2001). Long-term effects of the Seattle Social Development Intervention on school bonding trajectories. *Applied Developmental Science*, *5*, 225–236. doi:10.1207/S1532480XADS0504_04

Hawkins, J. D., Smith, B. H., Hill, K. G., Kosterman, R., Catalano, R. F., & Abbott, R. D. (2007). Promoting social development and preventing health and behavior problems during the elementary grades: Results from the Seattle Social Development Project. *Victims & Offenders*, *2*, 161–181. doi:10.1080/15564880701263049

Hornik, R., Maklan, D., Cadell, D., Barmada, C., Jacobsohn, L., Henderson, V., . . . Steele, D. (2003). *Evaluation of the National Youth Anti-Drug Media Campaign: 2003 Report of Findings*. Bethesda, MD: National Institute on Drug Abuse. Retrieved from http://archives.drugabuse.gov/initiatives/westat/pdf/1203report.pdf

Jessor, R., Chase, J. A., & Donovan, J. E. (1980). Psychosocial correlates of marijuana use and problem drinking in a national sample of adolescents. *American Journal of Public Health*, *70*, 604–613. doi:10.2105/AJPH.70.6.604

Jessor, R., Donovan, J. E., & Costa, F. M. (1991). *Beyond adolescence: Problem behavior and young adult development*. Cambridge, England: Cambridge University Press.

Jessor, R., Graves, T. D., Hanson, R. C., & Jessor, S. L. (1968). *Society, personality and deviant behavior: A study of a tri-ethnic community*. New York, NY: Holt, Rinehart & Winston.

Jessor, R., & Jessor, S. L. (1977). *Problem behavior and psychosocial development: A longitudinal study of youth*. New York, NY: Academic Press.

Jessor, R., & Jessor, S. L. (1978). Theory–testing in longitudinal research on marijuana use. In D. B. Kandel (Ed.), *Longitudinal research on drug use: Empirical findings and methodological issues* (pp. 41–71). Washington, DC: Hemisphere.

Jessor, R., Turbin, M. S., & Costa, F. M. (1998). Protective factors in adolescent health behavior. *Journal of Personality and Social Psychology*, *75*, 788–800. doi:10.1037/0022-3514.75.3.788

Jessor, R., Turbin, M. S., Costa, F. M., Dong, Q., Zhang, H., & Wang, C. (2003). Adolescent problem behavior in China and the United States: A cross-national study of psychosocial protective factors. *Journal of Research on Adolescence*, *13*, 329–360. doi:10.1111/1532-7795.1303004

Jessor, R., Van Den Bos, J., Vanderryn, J., Costa, F. M., & Turbin, M. S. (1995). Protective factors in adolescent problem behavior: Moderator effects and developmental change. *Developmental Psychology*, *31*, 923–933.

Kabiru, C. W., Beguy, D., Ndugwa, R. P., Zulu, E. M., & Jessor, R. (2012). "Making it": Understanding adolescent resilience in two informal settlements (slums) in Nairobi, Kenya. *Child & Youth Services*, *33*, 12–32. doi:10.1080/0145935X.2012.665321

Kahneman, D. (2011). *Thinking fast and slow.* New York, NY: Farrar, Strauss, & Giroux.

Kaplan, H. B., & Cheng-Hsien, L. (2000). Deviant identity as a moderator of the relation between negative self-feelings and deviant behavior. *Journal of Early Adolescence*, *20*, 150–177. doi:10.1177/0272431600020002003

Karademas, E. C. (2006). Self-efficacy, social support and well-being: The mediating role of optimism. *Personality and Individual Differences*, *40*, 1281–1290. doi:10.1016/j.paid.2005.10.019

Kellam, S. G., Koretz, D., & Moscicki, E. K. (1999). Core elements of developmental epidemiologically based prevention research. *American Journal of Community Psychology*, *27*, 463–482. doi:10.1023/A:1022129127298

Kosten, P. A., Scheier, L. M., & Grenard, J. L. (2013). Latent class analysis of peer conformity: Who is yielding to pressure and why? *Youth & Society*, *45*, 565–590. doi:10.1177/0044118X12454307

Kuhn, T. S. (1970). *The structure of scientific revolutions* (3rd ed.). Chicago, IL: University of Chicago Press.

Lewin, K. (1951). *Field theory in social science; selected theoretical papers* (D. Cartwright, Ed.). New York, NY: Harper & Row.

Lilienfeld, A. M., & Lilienfeld, D. E. (1980). *Foundations of epidemiology*. New York, NY: Oxford University Press.

McGee, L., & Newcomb, M. D. (1992). General deviance syndrome: Expanded hierarchical evaluations at four ages from early adolescence to adulthood. *Journal of Consulting and Clinical Psychology*, *60*, 766–776. doi:10.1037/0022-006X.60.5.766

Merton, R. K. (1957). *Social theory and social structure* (rev. ed.). New York, NY: Free Press.

Ndugwa, R. P., Kabiru, C. W., Cleland, J., Beguy, D., Egondi, T., Zulu, E. M., & Jessor, R. (2011). Adolescent problem behavior in Nairobi's informal settlements: Applying problem behavior theory in Sub-Saharan Africa. *Journal of Urban Health*, *88*, S298–317. doi:10.1007/s11524-010-9462-4

Newcomb, M. D., & Bentler, P. M. (1988). *Consequences of adolescent drug use: Impact on the lives of young adults*. Thousand Oaks, CA: Sage.

Newcomb, M. D., Scheier, L. M., & Bentler, P. M. (1993). Effects of adolescent drug use on adult psychopathology: A prospective study of a community sample. *Experimental and Clinical Psychopharmacology*, *1*, 215–241. doi:10.1037/1064-1297.1.1-4.215

Pentz, M. A. (1985). Social competence and self-efficacy as determinants of substance use in adolescence. In T. A. Wills & S. Shiffman (Eds.), *Coping and substance use* (pp. 117–142). San Diego, CA: Academic Press.

Petraitis, J., Flay, B. R., & Miller, T. Q. (1995). Reviewing theories of adolescent substance abuse: Organizing the pieces of the puzzle. *Psychological Bulletin*, *117*, 67–86. doi:10.1037/0033-2909.117.1.67

Popper, K. R. (1963). *Conjectures and refutations: The growth of scientific knowledge*. London, England: Routledge & Kegan Paul.

Rotter, J. B. (1954). *Social learning and clinical psychology*. Englewood Cliffs, NJ: Prentice-Hall. doi:10.1037/10788-000

Rotter, J. B. (1966). Generalized expectancies for internal versus external control of reinforcement. *Psychological Monographs*, *80*(1, Whole No. 609).

Rotter, J. B., Chance, J. E., & Phares, E. J. (1972). *Applications of a social learning theory of personality*. New York, NY: Holt, Rinehart & Winston.

Ryan, R. M., & Deci, E. L. (2000). Self-determination theory and the facilitation of intrinsic motivation, social development, and well-being. *American Psychologist*, *55*, 68–78. doi:10.1037/0003-066X.55.1.68

Scheier, L. M. (Ed.). (2010). *Handbook of drug use etiology: Theory, methods, and empirical findings*. Washington, DC: American Psychological Association.

Scheier, L. M. (2012). Primary prevention models: The essence of drug abuse prevention in schools. In H. J. Shaffer (Ed.), *APA addiction syndrome handbook, Vol. 2: Recovery, prevention, and other issues* (pp. 197–223). Washington, DC: American Psychological Association.

Scheier, L. M., & Botvin, G. J. (1995). Effects of early adolescent drug use on cognitive efficacy in early-late adolescence: A developmental structural model. *Journal of Substance Abuse*, *7*, 379–404. doi:10.1016/0899-3289(95)90011-X

Scheier, L. M., & Botvin, G. J. (1996). Purpose in life, cognitive, efficacy, and general deviance as determinants of drug abuse in urban black youth. *Journal of Child & Adolescent Substance Abuse*, *5*, 1–26. doi:10.1300/J029v05n01_01

Scheier, L. M., Botvin, G. J., & Griffin, K. W. (2001). Preventive intervention effects on developmental progression in drug use: Structural equation modeling analyses using longitudinal data. *Prevention Science*, *2*, 91–112. doi:10.1023/A:1011543730566

Scheier, L. M., & Hansen, W. B. (Eds.). (2014). *Parenting and teen drug use: The most recent findings from research, prevention, and treatment*. New York, NY: Oxford University Press.

Scheier, M. F., & Carver, C. S. (1985). Optimism, coping, and health: Assessment and implications of generalized outcome expectancies. *Health Psychology*, *4*, 219–247. doi:10.1037/0278-6133.4.3.219

Schunk, D. H., & Rice, J. M. (1987). Enhancing comprehension skill and self-efficacy with strategy value information. *Journal of Reading Behavior*, *19*, 285–302.

Schunk, D. H., & Rice, J. M. (1992). Influence of reading-comprehension strategy information on children's achievement outcomes. *Learning Disability Quarterly*, *15*, 51–64. doi:10.2307/1510565

Sloboda, Z., Glantz, M. D., & Tarter, R. E. (2012). Revising the concepts of risk and protective factors for understanding the etiology and development of substance use and substance use disorders: Implications for prevention. *Substance Use & Misuse*, *47*, 944–962. doi:10.3109/10826084.2012.663280

Smink, J. (2004). *Ajax training sessions*. Spring City, PA: Reedswain.

Swaim, R. C., Chen, J., Deffenbacher, J. L., & Newcomb, M. D. (2001). Negative affect and alcohol use among non-Hispanic White and Mexican American adolescents. *Journal of Child & Adolescent Substance Abuse*, *11*, 55–75. doi:10.1300/J029v11n01_03

Swaim, R. C., Oetting, E. R., Edwards, R. W., & Beauvais, F. (1989). Links from emotional distress to adolescent drug use: A path model. *Journal of Consulting and Clinical Psychology*, *57*, 227–231. doi:10.1037/0022-006X.57.2.227

West, S. G., & Aiken, L. S. (1997). Toward understanding individual effects in multicomponent prevention programs: Design and analysis strategies. In K. J. Bryant, M. Windle, & S. G. West (Eds.), *The science of prevention: Methodological advances from alcohol and substance abuse research* (pp. 167–209). Washington, DC: American Psychological Association. doi:10.1037/10222-006

White, R. W. (1959). Motivation reconsidered: The concept of competence. *Psychological Review*, *66*, 297–333. doi:10.1037/h0040934

Wills, T. A. (1992). Social comparison and self change. In J. Fisher, J. Chinsky, Y. Klar, & A. Nadler (Eds.), *Self-change: Social-psychological and clinical perspectives* (pp. 231–252). New York, NY: Springer-Verlag. doi:10.1007/978-1-4612-2922-3_12

Chapter 5

VULNERABILITY AND RISKS: IMPLICATIONS FOR UNDERSTANDING ETIOLOGY AND DRUG USE PREVENTION

Zili Sloboda

This chapter reviews the major currents that have fueled the development of prevention science and focuses on the formative and contributing roles of epidemiology and etiology. It also provides a developmental framework within which to better understand how the concept of risk has shaped current prevention efforts and discusses how the field has integrated the role of protective factors. Subsequent sections explore how epidemiology and etiology have helped to formulate the basis for developing rationally guided and sound intervention strategies. The chapter also examines how the present understanding of vulnerability has expanded to include contributions from neurobiological science and genetics. Concluding the chapter is a discussion of how interventions shape socialization at the family, institutional, and individual levels.

HISTORY OF ETIOLOGIC RESEARCH ON DRUG USE

Many of the early epidemiological studies designed to understand factors associated with the onset of drug use and addiction involved studies of drug-abusing populations. Samples were identified primarily through treatment or drawn from detained populations (i.e., criminal institutions or addiction facilities) using matched non–drug-using controls or case studies. Both approaches depended on skillful retrospective interviewing to reconstruct the respondents' lives and drug use habits. Through careful inspection of the drug users' narratives, drug abuse researchers learned about putative risk factors for drug involvement and instigators of first drug use.

Between 1950 and 1970, a rash of studies provided information on the lives of drug users. Sociologists were instrumental in this effort and used a combination of detailed clinical interviews, street ethnography, and in-depth qualitative studies to address important questions about drug use, addiction, crime, and natural recovery. In their now classic book *The Road to H*, Chein, Gerard, Lee, Rosenfeld, and Wilner (1964) produced the first detailed account of the antecedents of delinquency and heroin use by studying adolescent drug users living in New York City (Chein, 1966). One goal of their study was to learn more about factors that prompted heroin use and whether crime and drug use were related, as many had come to believe.

During the mid-1970s, a team of sociologists (O'Donnell, Voss, Clayton, Slatin, & Room, 1976) examined pathways to drug use by studying a randomly drawn sample of young men born between 1944 and 1955; the sample was obtained from selective service records. Guided by research suggesting that marijuana was causally related to heroin use,

I would like to thank Hanno Petras for his thoughtful contribution to the concept of prevention as a socialization process and for his efforts in helping me present these ideas to influence our current understanding of prevention science.

http://dx.doi.org/10.1037/14550-006
Handbook of Adolescent Drug Use Prevention: Research, Intervention Strategies, and Practice, L. M. Scheier (Editor)

O'Donnell et al. (1976). were inspired to study the lives of drug users. A popular theme at that time was the *gateway hypothesis* that drug involvement progresses in an invariant stage-like pattern: beginning with alcohol, cigarettes, and then marijuana, and eventually progressing to harder drug use, including pills, cocaine, and heroin (Kandel, 1975; Kandel & Faust, 1975; Kandel, Treiman, Faust, & Single, 1976; see also Kandel, 2002, for a more recent update on the gateway hypothesis).

Both Chein's (1966; Chein et al., 1964) work with youthful heroin users and the O'Donnell et al. (1976) study of young men contradicted commonly held myths about drug use and showed that crime was not an essential component of supporting drug addiction. Indeed, both studies went far in dispelling many existing negative perceptions about the characteristics of heroin and marijuana users. These and related etiology and epidemiology studies that examined drug subcultures (e.g., Goode, 1974; Johnson, 1973) offset the government's approach to drug use. The evidence countered claims made by Harry Anslinger, then director of the Federal Bureau of Narcotics in the Department of the Treasury (predecessor to the Office of National Drug Control Policy), who vocally suggested that marijuana was associated with malingering and violence, and was causally related to heroin use (Galliher, Keys, & Elsner, 1998).

The Drug Surveillance Era

In the late 1960s and early 1970s, two major population-based surveys were established: the National Household Survey on Drug Abuse and the Monitoring the Future (MTF) study. The National Household Survey on Drug Abuse became the first epidemiological source of information detailing the prevalence of substance use in a representative sample of the U.S. general population ages 12 and older. Originally housed in the Special Action Office on Drug Abuse Prevention in 1972, the Household Survey was moved to the just-created National Institute on Drug Abuse (NIDA, n.d.) in 1974. Currently, the funding and administration of the National Drug Use and Health Survey (the new title for the National Household Survey on Drug Abuse) fall under the aegis of the Substance Abuse and Mental Health Services Administration.

At about the same time, a collaborative group of researchers at the University of Michigan were awarded an NIDA grant to support MTF, which is part of the U.S. government's effort to monitor drug trends among secondary school students and use the surveillance to inform policy and formulate prevention goals (see Chapter 3, this volume, for details on MTF). Ongoing surveys of students attending a nationally representative sample of public and private schools have been conducted every spring since 1975. MTF, as well as the National Household Survey, continues to provide annual drug surveillance information detailing prevalence rates for a variety of licit and illicit drugs; who uses them (by age group, region of the country, ethnicity, and gender); and modes of administration. In addition, both surveys include information on age of first use by drug category, friends' use of drugs, perceptions of harm associated with drug use, and perceptions of social approval or tolerance for the use of drugs. Findings from these and related studies provide prevention researchers and intervention developers information about what drugs to target, messages about the normative nature of drug use and the potential harm associated with drug use, and the most developmentally appropriate age level to receive the intervention (Johnston, 1997; Pentz, 2010; Sloboda, 2005).

Although descriptive epidemiological studies are informative, they do not specifically address the etiologic mechanisms associated with the onset of drug use or the progression to drug use disorders, including abuse and dependence. Descriptive epidemiology indicates that the initiation of substance use generally occurs during adolescence, which suggests that the precursors for many substance-using behaviors occur in early and mid-childhood. To address the need for prospective data, longitudinal studies of high-risk youth and young adults were funded in the mid-1970s by NIDA. That initial body of work tracked cohorts of early adolescents through the high drug initiation years (ages 13–16) and, in several cases, for lengthy periods beyond (e.g., Brook, Gordon, & Whiteman, 1985; Jessor & Jessor, 1977; Kaplan, Martin, & Robbins, 1984). In some cases, a few of those studies collected additional data on children and grandchildren of the original cohorts (e.g., Brook, Zhang, Balka, & Brook, 2012) and examined intergenerational transmission, biological markers of drug disorders, and additional family and peer socialization processes that may encourage behavior to pass from one generation to another.

Based on the findings from the accumulated research, several related theoretical frameworks regarding the antecedents of drug use have been developed and tested. In general, the components of these theories include the interaction of several interpersonal (e.g., family and peer processes) and intrapersonal domains (e.g., personality attributes). One of these frameworks, problem behavior theory (Jessor & Jessor, 1977), is covered extensively in Chapter 4 of this handbook. Kandel's seminal research extended studies that examined the psychosocial precursors to drug use by describing the stages of progression of substance use among young users (Kandel, 1975; Kandel & Faust, 1975). Termed the *gateway*, *developmental stage*, or *stepping-stone*, this hypothesis suggests that involvement in the use of various classes of drugs follows invariant paths, generally beginning with the use of licit substances (e.g., alcohol, tobacco) and then progressing to the use of illicit drugs (e.g., marijuana, pills, psychedelics, cocaine, heroin). The hypothesis does not imply that all youngsters who use tobacco and/or alcohol will move to the use of illicit drugs; rather, it suggests they are at high risk for such movement (Kandel, 2002).

Kandel and Jessor (2002) outlined three propositions regarding these relations: sequencing, association, and causation. *Sequencing* implies a fixed relation between the timing of use of two substances. Sequencing would occur, for instance, if alcohol use led to tobacco use in a fixed or invariant sequence. *Association* suggests that the initiation or use of one substance increases the likelihood of using a second. For instance, drinking alcohol places youth at risk for using another drug. *Causation* means that the use of a substance results in progression in the sequence. A large empirical literature supports the first two propositions, but the third one lacks concrete evidence (Kandel, 2003; Maldonado-Molina & Lanza, 2010). However, as a result of the consistent research findings across studies, most prevention programming targets all of the gateway drugs, including tobacco, alcohol, and marijuana.

Risk and Protection

In 1992, two landmark publications fostered new inroads into the discussion about risk and protective factors. One was a peer review journal publication by Hawkins, Catalano, and Miller (1992). The second was a volume edited by Glantz and Pickens (1992). Both scholarly pieces helped to systematically shape the present understanding of the different relations among risk, protective factors, and drug use. *Risk factors* were defined as measures of behavior or psychosocial functioning, including attitudes, beliefs, and personality, that were found to be associated with increased propensity to use drugs. *Protective factors* involved measures that appeared to prevent the use of drugs or reduce the untoward negative effects of risk (i.e., compensatory or ameliorative effects).

Hawkins et al. (1992) divided risk factors into two broad categories: those related to society and that reflected a range of cultural influences (essentially reflecting contextual, or environmental, factors), and those related to individual-level and interpersonal motivational factors. *Contextual factors* included laws and norms favorable to substance use behaviors: those related to availability, extreme economic deprivation, and neighborhood disorganization. *Individual and interpersonal factors* included physiological measures, family history of substance use and attitudes toward substance use, poor/inconsistent family management, family conflict, and, low family bonding. *Other individual and interpersonal factors* included early/persistent problem behaviors, academic failure, low commitment to school, and peer rejection during elementary grades, association with substance-using peers, alienation and rebelliousness, and early onset of drug (substance) use.

Hawkins et al. (1992) also reviewed the body of knowledge regarding the role of protective factors that both mitigate risk and lower vulnerability to drug use. In their words, these factors "mediate or moderate the effects of exposure to risk" (p. 86) and were constructed to incorporate dominant thinking about resilience at that time (e.g., Garmezy, 1985; Rutter et al., 1997; Werner, 1989). Their seminal article was published at a time when much less was known about the instrumental role of protective factors and little research could guide the field in that direction. Today, however, this area of inquiry has nearly caught up to the literature on risk factors (e.g., Griffin, Scheier, Botvin, & Diaz, 2000; Sloboda, Glantz, & Tarter, 2012).

Although the work of Hawkins and colleagues addressed the constellation of factors that precipitate drug use and, to some extent, drug abuse, Glantz and Pickens (1992) were more concerned about factors related to progression from use to drug abuse or drug use disorders. Their edited volume, *Vulnerability to Drug Abuse*, represented the first effort to use data from the aforementioned longitudinal studies to examine factors related to drug progression. Contributing to their organized volume collectively, the researchers reported that intrapersonal or biological, psychological, and psychiatric mechanisms played key roles in explaining the movement across the drug use continuum, from initial experimental use to abuse and even disordered drug use.

As important as the concepts of risk and protective factors have been to the progression of prevention programming, few attempts have been made to determine whether the constellation of risk and protective factors listed by Hawkins et al. (1992) can be grouped into meaningful clusters (Sloboda et al., 2012). It is also unclear whether knowledge of these factors sufficiently elucidates the actual relations of risk or protection to drug use disorders or drug use patterns per se (Catalano, Kosterman, Hawkins, Newcomb, & Abbott, 1996; Lacourse et al., 2002). Furthermore, many of the longitudinal studies supporting the risk and protective factors framework relied on adolescent samples and did not study putative etiological mechanisms using earlier age groups, a course that would have permitted prospective tracking of the developmental course of risk and protection.

What is known about many of the risk factors reported in the literature is that they most likely indicate other underlying psychosocial mechanisms. Clarity has been achieved for some, but not all, of these risk mechanisms. This effort has reinforced an earlier claim that suggested the need to distinguish between risk indicators and risk mechanisms (O'Connor & Rutter, 1996). Risk indicators are *markers*, that is, proxies for persistent conditions that can lead to problem behaviors, such as drug use. Divorce, for example, can be troubling for young children; however, knowing that a child is from a divorced home does not reveal how divorce contributes to drug use (a better picture can be obtained with knowledge about parental monitoring, communication, parenting skills, presence of both parents actively rearing the child, and so forth). The actual mechanism that contributes to drug use most likely represents a skein of experiences that reflect the intersection of faulty parenting and a child's emotional coping skills as he or she navigates childhood into adolescence.

Another level needs to be considered when earmarking risk factors, particularly those representing intrapersonal processes that capture biopsychological characteristics, such as low IQ, hyperactivity, and concentration problems that have likely developmental and neurobiological origins (Glantz & Pickens, 1992; Hawkins et al., 1992). These risk factors contribute to vulnerability, but not all youth with difficult temperaments or concentration problems end up using drugs. Other factors, including the social capital of the family, will weigh heavily on whether a youth struggling with attention-deficit/hyperactivity disorder or having some form of neurobiological deficit (e.g., attention problems) will end up using drugs. In addition, behavioral, and attitudinal elements (e.g., antisocial behavior, beliefs, and attitudes regarding drug use) are also represented as individual/peer risk factors, which are independent factors within the individual/peer domain with obvious potential for bidirectional influences. Additional risk factor domains (e.g., family, school, community) capture behaviors that impede positive socialization experiences. Such socialization failure may reflect challenged socialization agents or intrapersonal mechanisms that hinder socialization, including family conflict, academic failure, failure to attach and commit to prosocial organizations, and low neighborhood attachment. These occurrences act as stressors on individual and family performance.

Vulnerability and Its Role in Coping Behaviors

The concepts of risk and protection suggest that youth may be vulnerable, that is, susceptible, predisposed, or at heightened risk. Glantz (2010) defined *vulnerability* as "increased potential danger of an adverse condition or outcome resulting from some form of dysfunction or insufficiency" (p. 61). Evidence of the involvement of individual characteristics in the susceptibility to negative behaviors, such as drug use, is clear. Being vulnerable, however, is not sufficient for individuals to become involved in those negative behaviors. Indeed, as the resilience literature has underscored, successful adaptation is having the characteristics and skills to appropriately handle exposure to risks and risky situations (Garmezy, 1985; Masten, Best, & Garmezy, 1990; Rutter, 1985; Werner, 1989). It is the interaction of vulnerability and the environment and the lack of the adaptation characteristics and skills that increase the risk of drug use (National Research Council and Institute of Medicine, 2009).

New Directions

This new developmental and longitudinal perspective has encouraged researchers to move away from solely emphasizing a risk factor approach to explore three important and interrelated agendas. The first focuses on identifying impediments associated with cognitive, emotional, and social developmental processes that make individuals vulnerable to negative coping behaviors (Fishbein & Ridenour, 2013). The second, and perhaps less well-developed agenda, examines micro- and macrolevel environmental experiences that place vulnerable individuals at risk to engage in negative behaviors (Fishbein, 2013). Furthermore, the contribution of resiliency research has been the focus on the link between vulnerability and engaging in negative coping behaviors. Resiliency research has articulated the characteristics and skills that help individuals adapt to challenging experiences. This rethinking and reformulation of the processes associated with engagement in high-risk behaviors suggests a psychological chain reaction. For instance, developmental vulnerability and risk are necessary but insufficient to provide impetus for drug use. Adaptive skills and prosocial attitudes may serve to alter the path to engagement in negative behaviors for vulnerable individuals.

The following section builds on this chain of events concept (see Figure 5.1). It discusses how inadequate cognitive, emotional, and social development (i.e., being vulnerable) can impede the formation of prosocial attitudes and the ability of youth to acquire adaptive coping and decision-making skills (socialization), particularly when youth interact with stress-producing micro- and macrolevel environments, such as neglectful parents or resource-deficient neighborhoods and communities. Therefore, when faced with adverse or challenging experiences and situations, vulnerable youth who do not experience prosocial bonds with family and friends and lack important self-management and decision-making skills are more likely to engage in behaviors that yield negative social or health outcomes. The acquisition of these requisite decision-making and self-management skills and the desire to become contributing members of society are important components to this chain of events. This framework is an appropriate guide for prevention interventions.

Other essential components included in this framework are addressed in the next sections. An overview of socialization is presented within a developmental framework across early childhood to adolescence, rather than into adulthood, and includes the key socialization agents across these developmental stages. In addition, an overview of the barriers to effective socialization is provided that discusses developmental deficiencies and environmental influences.

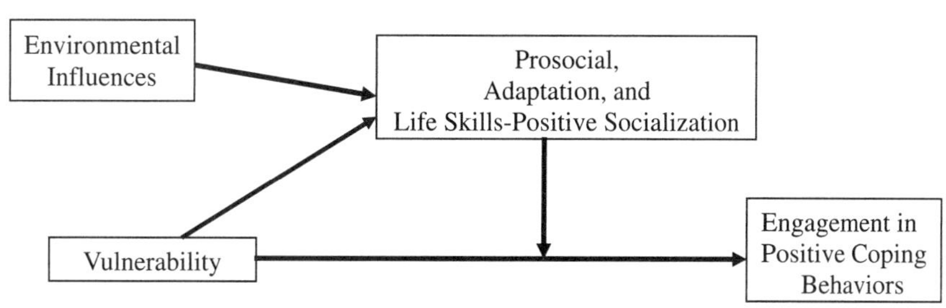

FIGURE 5.1. **Interrelationships among vulnerability, socialization, and engagement in coping behaviors.**

HUMAN DEVELOPMENT AND SOCIALIZATION

Acceptable social behaviors are learned from primary socialization agents, including parents, and through secondary socialization agents, such as schools and oftentimes faith or community organizations. Clausen (1968) defined *socialization* as "the means by which social and cultural continuity are attained" (p. 5); it includes the internalization of societal goals, norms, and values associated with what are acceptable behaviors, and age- and gender-related roles and responsibilities as a member of a society. These goals, norms, and values are the key factors influencing information processing, decision making, and behavioral selection.

Socialization is informed by societal benchmarks that are developmentally and culturally appropriate and apply to language, cognition, identity of self, and self-control. Not all of these benchmarks have equal weighting; some are more important than others. The valence of each factor may vary by culture and the complexity of the society in which an individual is born (Calzada, Brotman, Huang, Bat-Chava, & Kingston, 2009; Coll, Akerman, & Cicchetti, 2000; Rogoff, 2003). In general, documented societal benchmarks are based primarily on Western cultures and the needs of individuals within Eurocentric cultures to learn what is expected of them over their life span. Only recently have adaptations been made to accommodate cultural variations for non-Western and developing societies (e.g., Gladstone et al., 2010). Every society relies on a range of socializing agents that provide guidance, including parents, teachers, peer groups, religious groups, economic and political organizations, and mass media. Each agent serves a different role and applies different influences across the life span.

Early and Middle Childhood

Children's earliest social interactions occur in the family before the child begins his or her formal education. The parents, caregivers, and extended family are key socialization agents during this developmental phase. Children who experience interaction with parents or caregivers who fail to nurture, or who are exposed to ineffective parenting skills in a chaotic family setting (i.e., substance abusing or mentally deficient caregiver), grow up without forming the warm human attachments needed to bond to family and society. Even with positive parents or caregivers, young children who experience physical or emotional problems that may include a difficult temperament present challenges to unprepared parents. Failure to provide the support and guidance needed for children can impede developmental competencies and make a child vulnerable and at-risk for negative outcomes.

During middle childhood, increasingly greater amounts of time are spent most often in school and in the presence of same age peers—and away from the family. The parents and family retain a strong influence during this developmental phase, but other socialization agents, such as teachers, other adults, and peers, begin to assume significance. Therefore, competencies developed during infancy and early childhood will greatly influence the extent to which a school-age child will bond with and adapt to the challenges of school, develop prosocial attitudes, and engage in law-abiding and conventional activities. Mental disorders that have their onset during this period, including anxiety disorders, impulse control, and conduct disorders, may also impede the development of healthy attachment to school, reduce cooperative play with peers, and inhibit adaptive learning and self-regulation. Children of dysfunctional families who fail to acquire needed social skills often affiliate at this time with deviant peers, thus putting themselves at risk for negative life choices, including drug use, alcohol misuse, and involvement in delinquent activities. Parents and other adults play a significant role in children's development during this period by setting rules for acceptable behaviors; closely monitoring free time and friendship patterns; helping their child acquire skills to make informed decisions; and, serving as positive role models.

Adolescence

Adolescence is the developmental period when youth are exposed to new ideas and behaviors through increased associations with people and organizations beyond those experienced in childhood. Research findings have indicated that during this period of development, the plasticity and malleability of the adolescent brain result in a major expansion of neural connections and openness to new information and experiences. The desire to assume adult roles and obtain greater emotional and financial independence occur at the same time youth experience these significant brain changes that are spurred by hormonal and neuroendocrine flooding. Although they provide opportunities, the development of new pathways and brain circuitry in the underlying neural structure can also create conditions that may impair a youth's ability to make good decisions and engage in self-control processes. Poor self-control and lack of behavioral inhibition encourage youth toward risky behaviors when they are exposed to opportunistic situations, including precocious and unprotected sex, smoking and drinking, drinking while driving, and illicit drug use (Steinberg, 2007).

Adolescence is also a period of development associated with cognitive changes due to formal operational reasoning. Youth can now formulate a picture of themselves in the future and deliberate options for how they will live as adults. It is also a period of dramatic emotional changes, much of which can be attributed primarily to puberty and neurohormonally activated brain reorganization. The most remarkable and visible changes of adolescence take shape in terms of physical development (i.e., secondary sex characteristics, such as breasts, pubic hair, testes). At the same time, adolescents further expand their social network (peers) and undergo processes of identity reformulation (identity vs. role confusion). Older youth also gain emotional and physical independence when they obtain their driver's license, spend more time without adult supervision, and, as part of their freedoms, obtain part-time jobs. The search for autonomy and emergence of an independent self exposes youth to new ideas, beliefs, and attitudes. They also confront new ideologies and world perspectives introduced through encounters with adults other than their parents, including teachers, family friends, coaches, employers, and coworkers. In addition, during adolescence, peers, dating, and engaging in activities away from home, such as field trips, sports events, or summer camp, also strongly influence the development of new ideas, skills, and competencies.

NEUROBIOLOGICAL, GENETIC, AND PERSONALITY INFLUENCES ON DEVELOPMENT—AND ON INDIVIDUAL VULNERABILITY

The interrelationship between cultural definitions of societal benchmarks and normal biological development has been a great challenge to the fields of developmental psychology, neuroscience, and developmental anthropology (Jahoda, 2002). Understanding the human biological, cognitive, physiological, and emotional changes that take place between birth and late adolescence informs what society expects of its members. If not addressed early, any developmental delay or impairment can lead to problem behaviors in adulthood, when they are more trenchant and difficult to treat (Moffitt, 1993; Patterson, Forgatch, Voerger, & Stoolmiller 1998). Developmental delays can impede socialization efforts by parents, teachers, and others who can wield tremendous influence on prosocial development. Furthermore, the lack of acquiring appropriate socialization skills has been shown in multigenerational studies to be responsible for intergenerational transmission of negative or maladaptive behaviors (Brook et al., 2012; Smith & Farrington, 2004; Tarter et al., 2012).

Sources of developmental delay may occur at any time, for any reason. For instance, exposure to teratogens during gestation, such as common infectious agents (e.g., viruses, bacteria), chemicals (e.g., lead), certain medicinal drugs (e.g., thalidomide), and "abusable" drugs, enhance the risk for physical and neurological problems. Such problems impede normal physical, cognitive, emotional, or behavioral functioning (e.g., Cornelius & Day, 2009; Mendola, Selevan, Gutter, & Rice, 2002; Zhu, Kartiko, & Finnell, 2009). Teratogens are not the only barriers to normal development; any factor that impairs the development of an individual's brain or catalyzes deficits in physical, emotional, and social functioning during any developmental period can compromise later adjustment, including long-term maladaptive outcomes in adulthood (Gregory et al., 2007; Kellam, Ling, Merisca, Brown, & Ialongo, 1998).

Deficits arising from impaired neurological or neural development may be difficult to identify (Carter,

Briggs-Gowan, & Davis, 2004; Hielkema, de Winter, de Meer, & Reijneveld, 2011). These impairments can be overt, such as the lack of appropriate social skills, or more difficult to detect, such as deficits in decision-making skills. Tools and instruments are not readily available to make consistent early assessments to gauge neurological impairment in important life skills (Mardia, Bookstein, & Kent, 2013; Petras, Buckley, Leoutsakos, Stuart, & Ialongo, 2013).

Recent advances in the areas of neurobiological science, behavioral genetics, and personality development have furthered the understanding of the significant effects the aforementioned deficits have on cognitive, emotional, and social functioning. Neurobiological research involving the prefrontal and frontal cortex, and the hypothalamic pituitary adrenal and hypothalamic pituitary gonadal axes (McBurnett, Lahey, Rathouz, & Loeber, 2000; Yehuda, Halligan, & Grossman, 2001), and genetic studies (e.g., Kendler, Myers, & Prescott, 2007; Merikangas & Avenevoli, 2000; Tsuang et al., 1999) have suggested the strong influence of biological factors on development and cognitive functioning. Cognitive skills needed to engage in healthy and prosocial behaviors include decision-making and self-monitoring skills, abstract thinking, and the ability to form goal strategies, as well as resultant behavioral and affective regulation. A developmental problem can either be enhanced or reduced through natural interventions, such as skilled parenting and instructional strategies, or through interventions that directly address the impairment (Tremblay, 2002; Xiao et al., 2011).

Findings from neurobiological research have suggested that negative neurological processes hinder not only the successful achievement of developmental benchmarks but also successful socialization. Such developmental deficits make affected individuals more vulnerable to socialization failure either through failed societal bonding to family, schools, or community or poor decision making when attaching to social groups and when confronted with risk-prone situations. Such deficits increase the likelihood of engaging in negative behaviors, such as substance use (e.g., Bailey, Hill, Oesterle, & Hawkins, 2009; Paczkowski & Baker, 2007).

Evidence also exists of a relationship between cognitive functioning and temperament (e.g., Giancola, Mezzich, & Tarter, 1998; Healey, Brodzinsky, Bernstein, Rabinovitz, & Halpern, 2009). Wills (Wills & Ainette, 2010; Wills & Dishion, 2004) proposed that temperament or personality dimensions are related to different facets of self-control. In particular, the work of Wills and colleagues indicates that self-control or self-regulation consists of two dimensions: one that reflects behavioral capacities and one that emphasizes emotional functions. According to this dual regulatory framework, good self-regulation is demonstrated by planning ahead, being able to associate consequences with behavior, considering alternative behaviors to achieve the same outcome, being able to reduce excessive arousal, and being able to constructively deal with negative emotions, such as anger and sadness. Poor self-regulation involves being impatient, having difficulty delaying gratification, recovering from personal confrontation and inhibiting negative thoughts, being easily frustrated and distracted, being impulsive, and having unpredictable affect.

Other researchers have also described focus and attention as critical aspects of the cognitive effort required for self-regulation and have discussed using active cognitive strategies to minimize negative stimuli and to monitor one's level of emotional arousal (Rothbart, Sheese, Rueda, & Posner, 2011; Southam-Gerow & Kendall, 2002). More work refining these concepts and, in particular, developing adequate psychometric measures is ongoing. Such efforts will surely provide further insights into the mechanisms of self-regulation and lead to improved interventions that increase self-control and decision making for vulnerable individuals (Cole, Martin, & Dennis, 2004; see also Chapter 16, this handbook). Importantly, novel approaches that rely on neurobiological studies will eventually link self-regulation and temperament with cognitive processing in a single overarching framework.

Growing evidence has suggested that poorly formed or impaired neurobiological processes as a result of drug use itself may increase an adolescent's chances of progressing from drug initiation to drug abuse and dependence (e.g., Schepis, Adinoff, & Rao, 2008). However, at this time, the evidence is fairly inconsistent and seems to depend on the substance being studied and its neuropsychological effects (e.g., Meier et al., 2012). Most of these experimental studies have been conducted with animals for ethical reasons, whereas natural studies of adolescent drug users are more difficult to conduct (Winters & Arria, 2011). The available findings from both animal studies and the few natural studies of long-term drug users, though, have indicated that drug-specific neurobiological changes in the brain's gray and white matter can mitigate executive functioning and decision making (Solowij et al., 2011; Tapert, Schweinsburg, & Brown, 2008; Thoma et al., 2011). Although in the very early stages, recognition of the need to integrate findings from these multiple disciplines has formed a foundation for a transdisciplinary research agenda. The achievement of such an effort will delineate the etiologic processes and mechanisms associated with behaviors of concern to society, including drug using behaviors.

Micro- and Macrolevel Environmental Influences

The preceding sections discussed socialization, development, and the genetic and neurobiological factors that can affect individual development and the ability to achieve developmental benchmarks. The degree to which these benchmarks are achieved defines individual vulnerability. As individuals develop over time, they experience influences at the microlevel environment, or primary socialization agents—families, schools, churches, workplace—as well as the macrolevel environment, or secondary socialization agents—neighborhoods, region, nations. These experiences can be positive or negative. It is the interface between individual vulnerability and the micro- and macrolevel environments that determines risk or likelihood to become involved in negative behaviors, such as drug use. Risk is lowered when vulnerable children grow up in a positive family environment. However, when these same children experience a harsh, negligent family environment, they will most likely experience negative life trajectories. Children coming from these environments will have different experiences within school and later in life in their relationships with peers and within the workplace.

The macrolevel environment or structural influences, including poverty, disruption in the social environment, governmental policies, and poor quality physical environment, will influence children not only directly but also indirectly by affecting the competencies of key socialization agents. For instance, not only does poverty affect children and adolescents' safety, health, and opportunities, but the lack of social capital can hinder the ability of parents and teachers, for instance, to be effective socialization agents. Impoverished neighborhoods generally have high rates of unemployment, minimal access to community services, high rates of homelessness, single-parent families, poor quality educational facilities, and relatively higher rates of child abuse, social transiency, and crime (Blair, 2010; Manly, Lynch, Oshri, Herzog, & Wortel, 2013). Parents themselves may also feel the stresses of poverty. Economic hardship may disrupt parenting by limiting the time spent with children and the ability to provide appropriate nurturing for healthy development or to maintain a safe environment, and it may reduce opportunities to serve as positive role models (Jackson, Brooks-Gunn, Huang, & Glassman, 2000).

A child's neighborhood social environment also plays an important role in shaping norms and provides examples of positive role models that expose youth to acceptable behaviors (Furr-Holden, Milam, Young, MacPherson, & Lejuez, 2011). Any disruption of the physical environment, including lack of social cohesion and perceived racial or ethnic discrimination, can increase feelings of social marginalization and contribute to anomie (Sanders-Phillips, Settles-Reaves, Walker, & Brownlow, 2009).

Reconceptualization of Prevention

Prevention is concerned primarily with behaviors that can have a detrimental impact on the health and welfare of individuals, groups, and populations. Within this framework, the prevention of drug using behaviors, particularly for children and adolescents, is relevant no matter what policy discussions are ongoing. The perspective that drug use and other forms of negative behaviors, such as juvenile delinquency and academic failure, result from interrupted socialization suggests that prevention interventions play an important role in the socialization process. According to this framework, prevention interventions train individuals to make culturally sound, developmentally consistent, and context-appropriate behavioral choices.

Prevention interventions, therefore, can then be viewed in two ways. First, interventions train socialization agents (e.g., parents, teachers) by providing parenting and teaching techniques that reinforce prosocial attitudes and behavior and are shaped to children's needs and their vulnerabilities. Second, interventions take on features or characteristics of socialization agents. In this role, interventions teach targeted groups to use evidence-based practices in observing and interpreting children's cues within specific contexts, such as the performance of classroom exercises, anger control, or responses to requests to complete specific tasks. In addition, preventive interventions encourage parents and teachers to try on new behaviors and weigh the potential outcomes for the performance of these behaviors (Petras & Sloboda, 2014). Therefore, an essential component of effective preventive interventions is the internalization and reinforcement of good behavioral decisions through socialization processes that transfer culturally acceptable attitudes, norms, beliefs, and behaviors to societal members. In addition, effective interventions teach socially approved responses to environmental and social cues.

The foregoing discussion underscores the important contributions that findings from multiple disciplines make toward understanding the complex etiologic mechanisms associated with engagement in negative coping behaviors, such as drug use. These contributions go beyond simple risk and protective factors. These mechanisms may be related to serious neurological, environmental, and social detriments, or the natural development of the adolescent brain to manage conflicting emotions and progression toward self-regulation (e.g., Steinberg, 2010). Prevention interventions are not designed to alter these mechanisms per se but to provide information and skills to help susceptible children and adolescents avoid unhealthy behaviors. It is for this reason that the types of available prevention programming vary considerably.

The new conceptualization of prevention as a socialization intervention has two implications. First, it suggests that prevention interventions serve to enable key socialization agents, such as parents and teachers, to enhance their powerful regulatory and educational role through the provision of skills and knowledge. This new conceptualization also posits that prevention interventions serve as socialization agents themselves by reinforcing prosocial norms, attitudes, and behaviors. Accurate implementation of interventions suggests that, with prevention interventions, one must consider the developmental phase of the targeted group. To be maximally effective and combine the various resources available to the growing child, the short- and long-term outcomes and the content, structure, and delivery strategies of the intervention must be age- and developmentally appropriate.

Many evidence-based prevention programs target children who are potentially at high risk for engagement in negative behaviors because of poor socialization. For instance, the Nurse–Family Partnership (Olds, 1988; Olds et al., 2007) was one of the first intervention programs to offer services to new mothers with substance abuse problems. The intervention focuses on parenting skills training to help mothers attend to their baby's nutritional and developmental needs and provide a safe home environment. In addition, the program teaches these young mothers about birth control and family planning, and offers support to help them obtain the necessary education and skills to find adequate employment and become independent.

The Good Behavior Game (Kellam et al., 1998, 2008) trains teachers to socialize elementary students into conventional behaviors. The intervention uses specific strategies and rewards to teach children to sit still, wait their turn, and pay attention to classroom activities. Other evidence-based programs, such as Life Skills Training, serve as socialization agents by enhancing individual competencies and providing adolescents problem-specific knowledge and skills designed to strengthen prosocial attitudes and reinforce skills to resist pressures to initiate substance use (Botvin, Griffin, & Nichols, 2006).

Evidence also shows that highly vulnerable youth benefit greatly when interventions provide skills and support for behavioral regulation and good decision making. For instance, Dick et al. (2009) and Dodge and Pettit (2003) found that strong positive parenting and a supportive school climate can facilitate positive social development for youth with more self-regulatory problems. Brody, Beach, Philibert, Chen, and Murry (2009); Hawkins, Kosterman, Catalano, Hill, and Abbott, (2005); and others (Leve, Fisher, & Chamberlain, 2009; Petras et al., 2008) found that similar intervention strategies had favorable program effects on children with biological/behavioral precursors to negative behaviors (e.g., *5-HTTLPR* genotype, childhood aggression, poor self-regulation).

CONCLUSION

The field of drug use prevention has traditionally used the framework based on the risk and protective factors framework (i.e., universal, selective, and indicated) to distinguish the focus of prevention strategies (Mrazek & Haggerty, 1994). In recent years, discussion about the appropriateness of this classification system has extended beyond drug use prevention to include the wider public health debate over the definition of risk (e.g., Füssel, 2007; Schwartz, Bellinger, & Glass, 2011; Taylor-Gooby & Zinn, 2006). As this chapter indicates, alternative approaches have suggested that distinctions underlying prevention goals should incorporate the more encompassing and relevant concept of vulnerability (Frohlich & Potvin, 2008). Recognition that not all who may be vulnerable engage in negative behaviors implies that, at some level, protective mechanisms are in place and exerting an influence on behavior. The review presented in this chapter suggests that adherence to prosocial norms, attitudes, and behavioral expectations plays a significant role in preventing engagement in negative behaviors. Learning how to avoid transgressing behaviors and acting in a conventional manner are outcomes of socialization processes that begin within the family and extend into the community through schools, peer groups, and other social agencies. The chapter pointed out the different ways in which neurobiological, environmental, and behavioral mechanisms can disrupt the work of positive socialization agents.

Much research conducted in the past 2 decades since Hawkins et al. (1992) and Glantz and Pickens (1992) has shown how intrapersonal and environmental factors and processes interact to influence children's and adolescents' behavioral pathways. The findings from the research summarized in this chapter have suggested that, in stressful or challenging situations, cognitive, emotional, and developmental deficiencies increase vulnerability to engagement in negative coping behaviors. Risk can be attenuated through the acquisition of prosocial or life skills and through positive, developmentally appropriate socialization processes. Such a reconceptualization of the original risk and protection framework that has guided drug use prevention indicates an array of intervention points by targeting key socialization agents, such as parents and teachers, and also targeting individuals or their environments. The framework also suggests a comprehensive range of prevention programming.

Other chapters in this handbook go to great lengths to showcase the different sides of the arguments supporting behavioral interventions that emphasize individual-level risk and those supporting larger scale environmental interventions that target alteration of contextual factors (e.g., server interventions, media campaigns) with alternative methods. Environmental interventions are designed as social control measures to address the availability of and accessibility to drugs by increasing the costs of cigarettes through taxation, beer keg registration, and the implementation of no-smoking policies or drug-free zones near schools. Given the vulnerability–socialization–behavior conceptualization, it needs to be understood that although environmental interventions are commonly viewed as external to the individual, the individual is at the heart of the discussion. Indeed, a person is making decisions about whether to engage in a specific maladaptive behavior. For these reasons, to be effective in addressing behaviors such as drug use, multiple prevention programming and policies are needed within the community setting. Prevention and early interventions need to help parents through challenging times and with children who may require special attention. Prevention programming also should extend into schools, the community, and the workplace to help children, adolescents, and young adults function and perform their age-appropriate roles of being successful students, citizens, and employees.

To be more effective, the field of prevention science needs to extend research to examine the relations between vulnerability and factors that play an important role in drug use initiation. The reconceptualization of prevention presented in this chapter supports current efforts of the Society for Prevention Research to develop a new transdisciplinary translational research agenda. This agenda can further elucidate the underlying mechanisms that lead to drug use and also to progression to abuse and dependence. It is hoped that such research findings will improve responsiveness to the work done by prevention science and improve the desired outcomes (Fishbein & Ridenour, 2013).

References

Bailey, J. A., Hill, K. G., Oesterle, S., & Hawkins, J. D. (2009). Parenting practices and problem behavior across three generations: Monitoring, harsh discipline, and drug use in the intergenerational transmission of externalizing behavior. *Developmental Psychology*, *45*, 1214–1226. doi:10.1037/a0016129

Blair, C. (2010). Stress and the development of self-regulation in context. *Child Development Perspectives*, *4*, 181–188. doi:10.1111/j.1750-8606.2010.00145.x

Botvin, G. J., Griffin, K. W., & Nichols, T. R. (2006). Preventing youth violence and delinquency through a universal school-based prevention approach. *Prevention Science*, *7*, 403–408. doi:10.1007/s11121-006-0057-y

Brody, G. H., Beach, S. R., Philibert, R. A., Chen, Y.-F., & Murry, V. M. (2009). Prevention effects moderate the association of *5-HTTLPR* and youth risk behavior initiation: Gene × environment hypotheses tested via randomized prevention design. *Child Development*, *80*, 645–661. doi:10.1111/j.1467-8624.2009.01288.x

Brook, J. S., Gordon, A. S., & Whiteman, M. (1985). Stability of personality during adolescence and its relationship to stage of drug use. *Genetic, Social, and General Psychology Monographs*, *111*, 317–330.

Brook, J. S., Zhang, C., Balka, E. B., & Brook, D. W. (2012). Pathways to children's externalizing behavior: A three-generation study. *Journal of Genetic Psychology*, *173*, 175–197. doi:10.1080/00221325.2011.594821

Calzada, E. J., Brotman, L. M., Huang, K. Y., Bat-Chava, Y., & Kingston, S. (2009). Parent cultural adaptation and child functioning in culturally diverse, urban families of preschoolers. *Journal of Applied Developmental Psychology*, *30*, 515–524. doi:10.1016/j.appdev.2008.12.033

Carter, A. S., Briggs-Gowan, M. J., & Davis, N. O. (2004). Assessment of young children's social-emotional development and psychopathology: Recent advances and recommendations for practice. *Journal of Child Psychology and Psychiatry*, *45*, 109–134. doi:10.1046/j.0021-9630.2003.00316.x

Catalano, R. F., Kosterman, R., Hawkins, J. D., Newcomb, M. D., & Abbott, R. D. (1996). Modeling the etiology of adolescent substance use: A test of the social development model. *Journal of Drug Issues*, *26*, 429–455.

Chein, I. (1966). The chronic addict—and why he turned to drugs. *Rehabilitation Record*, *7*, 16–18.

Chein, I., Gerard, D. L., Lee, R. S., Rosenfeld, E., & Wilner, D. M. (1964). *The road to H: Narcotics, delinquency and social policy.* New York, NY: Basic Books.

Clausen, J. A. (1968). *Socialization and society.* Boston, MA: Little, Brown.

Cole, P. M., Martin, S. E., & Dennis, T. A. (2004). Emotion regulation as a scientific construct: Methodological challenges and directions for child development research. *Child Development*, *75*, 317–333. doi:10.1111/j.1467-8624.2004.00673.x

Coll, C. G., Akerman, A., & Cicchetti, D. (2000). Cultural influences in developmental process and outcomes: Implications for the study of development and psychopathology. *Development and Psychopathology*, *12*, 333–356. doi:10.1017/S0954579400003059

Cornelius, M. D., & Day, N. L. (2009). Developmental consequences of prenatal tobacco exposure. *Current Opinion in Neurology*, *22*, 121–125. doi:10.1097/WCO.0b013e328326f6dc

Dick, D. M., Latendresse, S., Lansford, J., Budde, J., Goate, A., Dodge, K., . . . Bates, J. E. (2009). Role of GABRA2 in trajectories of externalizing behavior across development and evidence of moderation by parental monitoring. *Archives of General Psychiatry*, *66*, 649–657. doi:10.1001/archgenpsychiatry.2009.48

Dodge, K. A., & Pettit, G. S. (2003). A biopsychosocial model of the development of chronic conduct problems in adolescence. *Developmental Psychology*, *39*, 349–371. doi:10.1037/0012-1649.39.2.349

Fishbein, D. H. (2013). *An introduction to the etiology of drug use and substance abuse.* Unpublished manuscript, United Nations Office on Drugs and Crime, Vienna, Austria.

Fishbein, D. H., & Ridenour, T. A. (2013). Advancing transdisciplinary translation for prevention of high-risk behaviors: Introduction to the Special Issue. *Prevention Science*, *14*, 201–205. doi:10.1007/s11121-013-0394-6

Frohlich, K. L., & Potvin, L. (2008). Transcending the known in public health practice. The inequality paradox: The population approach and vulnerable populations. *American Journal of Public Health*, *98*, 216–221. doi:10.2105/AJPH.2007.114777

Furr-Holden, C. D. M., Milam, A. J., Young, K. C., MacPherson, L., & Lejuez, C. W. (2011). Exposure to hazardous neighborhood environments in late childhood and anxiety. *Journal of Community Psychology*, *39*, 876–883. doi:10.1002/jcop.20461

Füssel, H.-M. (2007). Vulnerability: A generally applicable conceptual framework for climate change research. *Global Environmental Change*, *17*, 155–167. doi:10.1016/j.gloenvcha.2006.05.002

Galliher, J. F., Keys, D. P., & Elsner, M. (1998). Lindesmith v. Anslinger: An early government victory in the failed war on drugs. *Journal of Criminal Law & Criminology*, *88*, 661–682. doi:10.2307/1144292

Garmezy, N. (1985). Broadening research on developmental risk. In W. Frankenburg, R. Emde, & J. Sullivan (Eds.), *Early identification of children at risk: An international perspective* (pp. 45–58). New York, NY: Plenum Press. doi:10.1007/978-1-4899-0536-9_3

Giancola, P. R., Mezzich, A. C., & Tarter, R. E. (1998). Executive cognitive functioning, temperament, and antisocial behavior in conduct disordered adolescent females. *Journal of Abnormal Psychology*, *107*, 629–641. doi:10.1037/0021-843X.107.4.629

Gladstone, M., Lancaster, G., Umar, E., Nyirenda, M., Kayira, E., van den Broek, N., & Smyth, R. L. (2010). Perspectives of normal child development in rural Malawi—A qualitative analysis to create a more culturally appropriate developmental assessment tool. *Child: Care, Health and Development*, *36*, 346–353. doi:10.1111/j.1365-2214.2009.01008.x

Glantz, M. D. (2010). Touchstone issues for theories of substance abuse-dependence etiology. In L. M. Scheier (Ed.), *Handbook of drug use etiology: Theory, methods, and empirical findings* (pp. 51–69). Washington, DC: American Psychological Association.

Glantz, M. D., & Pickens, R. W. (1992). Vulnerability to drug abuse: Introduction and overview. In M. D. Glantz & R. W. Pickens (Eds.), *Vulnerability to drug abuse* (pp. 1–14). Washington, DC: American Psychological Association. doi:10.1037/10107-000

Goode, E. (1974). Marijuana use and the progression to dangerous drugs. In L. L. Miller (Ed.) *Marijuana effects on human behavior* (pp. 303–338). New York, NY: Academic Press.

Gregory, A. M., Caspi, A., Moffitt, T. E., Koenen, K., Eley, T. C., & Poulton, R. (2007). Juvenile mental health histories of adults with anxiety disorders. *The American Journal of Psychiatry*, *164*, 301–308. doi:10.1176/appi.ajp.164.2.301

Griffin, K. W., Scheier, L. M., Botvin, G. J., & Diaz, T. (2000). Ethnic and gender differences in psychosocial risk, protection, and adolescent alcohol use. *Prevention Science*, *1*, 199–212. doi:10.1023/A:1026599112279

Hawkins, J. D., Catalano, R. F., & Miller, J. Y. (1992). Risk and protective factors for alcohol and other drug problems in adolescence and early adulthood: Implications for substance abuse prevention. *Psychological Bulletin*, *112*, 64–105. doi:10.1037/0033-2909.112.1.64

Hawkins, J. D., Kosterman, R., Catalano, R. F., Hill, K. G., & Abbott, R. D. (2005). Promoting positive adult functioning through social development intervention in childhood: Long-term effects from the Seattle Social Development Project. *Archives of Pediatrics & Adolescent Medicine*, *159*, 25–31. doi:10.1001/archpedi.159.1.25

Healey, D. M., Brodzinsky, L. K., Bernstein, M., Rabinovitz, B., & Halperin, J. M. (2009). Moderating effects of neurocognitive abilities on the relationship between temperament and global functioning. *Child Neuropsychology*, *16*, 20–31. doi:10.1080/09297040902984490

Hielkema, M., de Winter, A. F., de Meer, G., & Reijneveld, S. A. (2011). Effectiveness of a family-centered method for the early identification of social-emotional and behavioral problems in children: A quasi experimental study. *BMC Public Health*, *11*, 636. doi:10.1186/1471-2458-11-636

Jackson, A. P., Brooks-Gunn, J., Huang, C. C., & Glassman, M. (2000). Single mothers in low-wage jobs: Financial strain, parenting, and preschoolers' outcomes. *Child Development*, *71*, 1409–1423. doi:10.1111/1467-8624.00236

Jahoda, G. (2002). Culture, biology and development across history. In H. Keller, Y. H. Poortinga, & A. Schulmerich (Eds.), *Between culture and biology: Perspectives on ontogenetic development* (pp. 13–29). Cambridge, England: Cambridge University Press. doi:10.1017/CBO9780511489853.002

Jessor, R., & Jessor, S. L. (1977). *Problem behavior and psychological development: A longitudinal study of youth.* San Diego, CA: Academic Press.

Johnson, B. D. (1973). *Marihuana users and drug subcultures.* New York, NY: Wiley.

Johnston, L. D. (1997). Contributions of drug epidemiology to the field of drug abuse prevention. *Substance Use & Misuse*, *32*, 1637–1642. doi:10.3109/10826089709035557

Kandel, D. (1975). Stages in adolescent involvement in drug use. *Science*, *190*, 912–914. doi:10.1126/science.1188374

Kandel, D. B. (2002). Examining the gateway hypothesis: Stages and pathways of drug involvement. In D. B. Kandel (Ed.), *Stages and pathways of drug involvement: Examining the gateway hypothesis* (pp. 3–16). New York, NY: Cambridge University Press. doi:10.1017/CBO9780511499777.003

Kandel, D. B. (2003). Does marijuana use cause the use of other drugs? *JAMA*, *289*, 482–483. doi:10.1001/jama.289.4.482

Kandel, D., & Faust, R. (1975). Sequence and stages in patterns of adolescent drug use. *Archives of General Psychiatry*, *32*, 923–932. doi:10.1001/archpsyc.1975.01760250115013

Kandel, D. B., & Jessor, R. (2002). The gateway hypothesis revisited. In D. B. Kandel (Ed.),

Stages and pathways of drug involvement: Examining the gateway hypothesis (pp. 365–372). New York, NY: Cambridge University Press. doi:10.1017/CBO9780511499777.018

Kandel, D. B., Treiman, D., Faust, R., & Single, R. (1976). Adolescent involvement in legal and illegal drug use: A multiple classification analysis. *Social Forces*, *55*, 438–458. doi:10.1093/sf/55.2.438

Kaplan, H. B., Martin, S., & Robbins, C. (1984). Pathways to adolescent drug use: Self-derogation, peer influence, weakening of social controls and early substance use. *Journal of Health and Social Behavior*, *25*, 270–289. doi:10.2307/2136425

Kellam, S. G., Brown, C. H., Poduska, J. M., Ialongo, N. S., Wang, W., Toyinbo, P., . . . Wilcox, H. C. (2008). Effects of a universal classroom behavior management program in first and second grades on young adult behavioral, psychiatric, and social outcomes. *Drug and Alcohol Dependence*, *95*(Suppl. 1), S5–S28. doi:10.1016/j.drugalcdep.2008.01.004

Kellam, S. G., Ling, X., Merisca, R., Brown, C. H., & Ialongo, N. (1998). The effect of level of aggression in the first grade classroom on the course and malleability of aggressive behavior into middle school. *Development and Psychopathology*, *10*, 165–185. doi:10.1017/S0954579498001564

Kendler, K. S., Myers, J., & Prescott, C. A. (2007). Specificity for genetic and environmental risk factors for symptoms of cannabis, cocaine, alcohol, caffeine, and nicotine dependence. *Archives of General Psychiatry*, *64*, 1313–1320. doi:10.1001/archpsyc.64.11.1313

Lacourse, E., Cote, S., Nagin, D., Vitaro, F., Brendgen, M., & Tremblay, R. (2002). A longitudinal–experimental approach to testing theories of antisocial behavior development. *Development and Psychopathology*, *14*, 909–924. doi:10.1017/S0954579402004121

Leve, L. D., Fisher, P. A., & Chamberlain, P. (2009). Multidimensional treatment foster care as a preventive intervention to promote resiliency among youth in the child welfare system. *Journal of Personality*, *77*, 1869–1902. doi:10.1111/j.1467-6494.2009.00603.x

Maldonado-Molina, M. M., & Lanza, S. (2010). A framework to examine gateway relations in drug use: An application of latent transition analysis. *Journal of Drug Issues*, *40*, 901–924. doi:10.1177/002204261004000407

Manly, J. T., Lynch, M., Oshri, A., Herzog, M., & Wortel, S. N. (2013). The impact of neglect on initial adaptation to school. Advance online publication. *Child Maltreatment*, *18*(3), 155–170. Retrieved from http://www.ncbi.nlm.nih.gov/pmc/articles/PMC3775317/

Mardia, K., Bookstein, F., & Kent, J. (2013). Alcohol, babies, and the death penalty: Saving lives by analyzing the shape of the brain. *Significance*, *10*, 12–16. doi:10.1111/j.1740-9713.2013.00659.x

Masten, A., Best, K., & Garmezy, N. (1990). Resilience and development: Contributions from the study of children who overcame adversity. *Development and Psychopathology*, *2*, 425–444. doi:10.1017/S0954579400005812

McBurnett, K., Lahey, B., Rathouz, P., & Loeber, R. (2000). Low salivary cortisol and persistent aggression in boys referred for disruptive behavior. *Archives of General Psychiatry*, *57*, 38–43. doi:10.1001/archpsyc.57.1.38

Meier, M. H., Ambler, A., Harrington, H., Houts, R., Keefe, R. S., McDonald, K., . . . Moffitt, T. E. (2012). Persistent cannabis users show neuropsychological decline from childhood to midlife. *PNAS: Proceedings of the National Academy of Sciences of the United States of America*, *109*, E2657–E2664. doi:10.1073/pnas.1206820109

Mendola, P., Selevan, S. G., Gutter, S., & Rice, D. (2002). Environmental factors associated with a spectrum of neurodevelopmental deficits. *Mental Retardation and Developmental Disabilities Research Reviews*, *8*, 188–197. doi:10.1002/mrdd.10033

Merikangas, K. R., & Avenevoli, S. (2000). Implications of genetic epidemiology for the prevention of substance use disorders. *Addictive Behaviors*, *25*, 807–820. doi:10.1016/S0306-4603(00)00129-5

Moffitt, T. E. (1993). Adolescence-limited and life-course-persistent antisocial behavior: A developmental taxonomy. *Psychological Review*, *100*, 674–701. doi:10.1037/0033-295X.100.4.674

Mrazek, P. J., & Haggerty, R. (Eds.). (1994). *Reducing risks for mental disorders: Frontiers for prevention intervention research*. Washington, DC: National Academy Press.

National Institute on Drug Abuse. (n.d.). *The NIH almanac*. Retrieved from http://www.nih.gov/about/almanac/organization/NIDA.htm

National Research Council and Institute of Medicine. (2009). *Preventing mental, emotional, and behavioral disorders among young people: Progress and possibilities*. Washington, DC: National Academies Press.

O'Connor, T. G., & Rutter, M. (1996). Risk mechanisms in development: Some conceptual and methodological considerations. *Developmental Psychology*, *32*, 787–795. doi:10.1037/0012-1649.32.4.787

O'Donnell, J. A., Voss, H. L., Clayton, R. R., Slatin, G. T., & Room, R. G. (1976). Young men and drugs—A nationwide survey. *NIDA Research Monograph*, *5*, 1–144.

Olds, D. (1988). The prenatal/early infancy project. In R. Price, E. Cowen, R. Lorion, & J. Ramos-McKay (Eds.), *Fourteen ounces of prevention: A casebook for practitioners* (pp. 9–23). Washington, DC: American Psychological Association. doi:10.1037/10064-001

Olds, D. L., Kitzman, H., Hanks, C., Cole, R., Anson, E., Sidora-Arcoleo, K., & Bondy, J. (2007). Effects of nurse home visiting on maternal and child functioning: Age-9 follow-up of a randomized trial. *Pediatrics*, *120*, e832–e845. doi:10.1542/peds.2006-2111

Paczkowski, E., & Baker, B. L. (2007). Parenting children with and without developmental delay: The role of self-mastery. *Journal of Intellectual Disability Research*, *51*, 435–446. doi:10.1111/j.1365-2788.2006.00894.x

Patterson, G. R., Forgatch, M. S., Voerger, K. L., & Stoolmiller, M. (1998). Variables that initiate and maintain an early-onset trajectory of offending. *Development and Psychopathology*, *10*, 531–547. doi:10.1017/S0954579498001734

Pentz, M. A. (2010). Translating research into practice and practice into research for drug use prevention. In L. M. Scheier (Ed.), *Handbook of drug use etiology: Theory, methods, and empirical findings* (pp. 581–596). Washington, DC: American Psychological Association.

Petras, H., Buckley, J., Leoutsakos, J.-M., Stuart, E., & Ialongo, N. (2013).The use of multiple versus single assessment time points to improve screening accuracy in identifying children at risk for later serious antisocial behavior. *Prevention Science, 14*, 423–436.

Petras, H., Kellam, S. G., Brown, C. H., Muthén, B. O., Ialongo, N. S., & Poduska, J. M. (2008). Developmental epidemiological courses leading to antisocial personality disorder and violent and criminal behavior: Effects by young adulthood of a universal preventive intervention in first- and second-grade classrooms. *Drug and Alcohol Dependence*, *95*(Suppl. 1), S45–S59. doi:10.1016/j.drugalcdep.2007.10.015

Petras, H., & Sloboda, Z. (2014). An integrated prevention science model: A conceptual foundation for prevention research. In Z. Sloboda & H. Petras (Eds.), *Advances in prevention science: Defining prevention* (pp. 251–273). New York, NY: Springer. doi:10.1007/978-1-4899-7424-2_11

Rogoff, B. (2003). *The cultural nature of human development*. New York, NY: Oxford University Press.

Rothbart, M. K., Sheese, B. E., Rueda, M. R., & Posner, M. I. (2011). Developing mechanisms of self-regulation in early life. *Emotion Review*, *3*, 207–213. doi:10.1177/1754073910387943

Rutter, M. (1985). Resilience in the face of adversity: Protective factors and resistance to psychiatric disorder. *British Journal of Psychiatry, 147*, 598–611.

Rutter, M., Dunn, J., Plomin, R., Simonoff, E., Pickles, A., Maughan, B., . . . Eaves, L. (1997). Integrating nature and nurture: Implications of person-environment correlations and interactions for developmental psychopathology. *Development and Psychopathology*, *9*, 335–364. doi:10.1017/S0954579497002083

Sanders-Phillips, K., Settles-Reaves, B., Walker, D., & Brownlow, J. (2009). Social inequality and racial discrimination: Risk factors for health disparities in children of color. *Pediatrics*, *124*, S176–S186. doi:10.1542/peds.2009-1100E

Schepis, T. S., Adinoff, B., & Rao, U. (2008). Neurobiological processes in adolescent addictive disorders. *American Journal on Addictions*, *17*, 6–23. doi:10.1080/10550490701756146

Schwartz, J., Bellinger, D., & Glass, T. (2011). Expanding the scope of risk assessments: Methods for studying differential vulnerability and susceptibility. *American Journal of Public Health*, *101*, S102–S109. doi:10.2105/AJPH.2011.300367

Sloboda, Z. (2005). Implications of epidemiologic information for effective drug abuse prevention strategies. In Z. Sloboda (Ed.), *Epidemiology of drug abuse* (pp. 211–223). New York, NY: Springer. doi:10.1007/0-387-24416-6_14

Sloboda, Z., Glantz, M. D., & Tarter, R. E. (2012). Revisiting the concept of risk and protective factors for understanding the etiology and development of drug abuse: Implications for prevention. *Substance Use & Misuse*, *47*, 944–962. doi:10.3109/10826084.2012.663280

Smith, C. A., & Farrington, D. P. (2004). Continuities in antisocial behavior and parenting across three generations. *Journal of Child Psychology and Psychiatry, 45*, 230–247. doi:10.1111/j.1469-7610.2004.00216.x

Solowij, N., Jones, K. A., Rozman, M. E., Davis, S. M., Ciarrochi, J., Heaven, P. C., . . . Yucel, M. (2011). Verbal learning and memory in adolescent cannabis users, alcohol users and non-users. *Psychopharmacology*, *216*, 131–144. doi:10.1007/s00213-011-2203-x

Southam-Gerow, M. A., & Kendall, P. C. (2002). Emotion regulation and understanding: Implications for child psychopathology and therapy. *Clinical Psychology Review*, *22*, 189–222. doi:10.1016/S0272-7358(01)00087-3

Steinberg, L. (2007). Risk taking in adolescence: New perspectives from brain and behavioral science. *Current Directions in Psychological Science*, *16*, 55–59. doi:10.1111/j.1467-8721.2007.00475.x

Steinberg, L. (2010). A dual systems model of adolescent risk-taking. *Developmental Psychobiology*, *52*, 216–224.

Tapert, S. F., Schweinsburg, A. D., & Brown, S. A. (2008). The influence of marijuana use on neurocognitive functioning in adolescents. *Current Drug Abuse Reviews*, *1*, 99–111. doi:10.2174/1874473710801010099

Tarter, R. E., Kirisci, L., Mezzich, A., Ridenour, T., Fishbein, D., Horner, M., . . . Vanyukov, M. (2012). Does the "gateway" sequence increase prediction of cannabis use disorder development beyond deviant socialization? Implications for prevention practice and policy. *Drug and Alcohol Dependence*, *123*(Suppl. 1), S72–S78. doi:10.1016/j.drugalcdep.2012.01.015

Taylor-Gooby, P., & Zinn, J. O. (2006). Current directions in risk research: New developments in psychology and sociology. *Risk Analysis*, *26*, 397–411. doi:10.1111/j.1539-6924.2006.00746.x

Thoma, R. J., Monnig, M. A., Lysne, P. A., Ruhl, D. A., Pommy, J. A., Bogenschutz, M., . . . Yeo, R. A. (2011). Adolescent substance abuse: The effects of alcohol and marijuana on neuropsychological performance. *Alcoholism: Clinical and Experimental Research*, *35*, 39–46. doi:10.1111/j.1530-0277.2010.01320.x

Tremblay, R. E. (2002). Prevention of injury by early socialization of aggressive behavior. *Injury Prevention*, *8*, iv17–iv21.

Tsuang, M. T., Lyons, M. J., Harley, R. M., Xian, H., Eisen, S., Goldberg, J., . . . Faraone, S. V. (1999). Genetic and environmental influences on transitions in drug use. *Behavior Genetics*, *29*, 473–479. doi:10.1023/A:1021635223370

Werner, E. E. (1989). High-risk children in young adulthood: A longitudinal study from birth to 32 years. *American Journal of Orthopsychiatry*, *59*, 72–81. doi:10.1111/j.1939-0025.1989.tb01636.x

Wills, T. A., & Ainette, M. G. (2010). Temperament, self-control, and adolescent substance use: A two-factor model of etiological processes. In L. M. Scheier (Ed.), *Handbook of drug use etiology: Theory, methods, and empirical findings* (pp. 127–146). Washington, DC: American Psychological Association.

Wills, T. A., & Dishion, T. J. (2004). Temperament and adolescent substance use: A transactional analysis of emerging self-control. *Journal of Clinical Child and Adolescent Psychology*, *33*, 69–81. doi:10.1207/S15374424JCCP3301_7

Winters, K. C., & Arria, A. (2011). Adolescent brain development and drugs. *Prevention Researcher*, *18*, 21–24.

Xiao, L., Bechara, A., Palmer, P. H., Trinidad, D. R., Wei, Y., Jia, Y., & Johnson, C. A. (2011). Parent–child engagement in decision making and the development of adolescent affective decision capacity and binge drinking. *Personality and Individual Differences*, *51*, 285–292. doi:10.1016/j.paid.2010.04.023

Yehuda, R., Halligan, S., & Grossman, R. (2001). Childhood trauma and risk for PTSD: Relationship to intergenerational effects of trauma, parental PTSD, and cortisol excretion. *Development and Psychopathology*, *13*, 733–753. doi:10.1017/S0954579401003170

Zhu, H., Kartiko, S., & Finnell, R. H. (2009). Importance of gene–environment interactions in the etiology of selected birth defects. *Clinical Genetics*, *75*, 409–423. doi:10.1111/j.1399-0004.2009.01174.x

Part III

PREVENTION OF CONDUCT DISORDERS

CHAPTER 6

PREVENTING CONDUCT DISORDERS AND RELATED PROBLEMS

Caroline L. Boxmeyer, John E. Lochman, Nicole P. Powell, and Cameron E. Powe

This chapter provides an overview of the etiology, prevalence, and risk factors for childhood conduct problems and describes the developmental relations between those problems and later substance use. It also reviews common elements of preventive interventions for childhood conduct problems and provides exemplars of such interventions for conduct problems in early, middle, and late childhood and early adolescence and discusses the extant research base for these interventions.

CHILDHOOD CONDUCT PROBLEMS AND SUBSTANCE USE

Once established in childhood, conduct problems become increasingly stable and predict later negative outcomes, including substance use (Fite, Colder, Lochman, & Wells, 2007; Lochman & Wayland, 1994). Therefore, to prevent substance use, it is important to address the empirical risk factors for conduct problems. Children at risk for substance use include those with a diagnosis of conduct disorder (CD), a repetitive and persistent pattern of behavior that violates others' rights or major age-appropriate societal norms or rules, and those with a diagnosis of oppositional defiant disorder (ODD), which reflects a recurrent pattern of negativistic, defiant, disobedient, and hostile behavior toward authority figures (American Psychiatric Association, 2013). Children with subclinical conduct problems (e.g., moderate levels of aggressive, impulsive behavior and negative emotionality) are also at risk for substance use, as are children with multiple environmental risk factors (Lochman & Wells, 2002a).

Prevalence estimates for CD range from 1% to 16%, based on the diagnostic system and gender (Loeber, Burke, Lahey, Winters & Zera, 2000). In the recent National Health and Nutrition Examination Survey, the 12-month prevalence of CD in youth ages 8 to 15 was 2.1% (Merikangas et al., 2010). Lifetime prevalence estimates for ODD range from 10% to 11% (Costello, Mustillo, Erkanli, Keeler, & Angold, 2003; Nock, Kazdin, Hiripi, & Kessler, 2007). Evidencing the link between conduct problems and substance use, nearly half (47.2%) of all individuals who met criteria for ODD in the National Comorbidity Survey Replication also met criteria for a lifetime substance use disorder (Nock et al., 2007). Individuals with conduct problems were 5 to 7 times more likely to develop a substance use disorder (Nock et al., 2007), a finding that underscores the importance of providing preventive

Preparation of this chapter was supported by grants from the National Institute on Drug Abuse (R01 DA023156 and R34 DA034295). The content of this chapter is solely the responsibility of the authors and does not necessarily represent the official views of the National Institute on Drug Abuse.

Correspondence concerning this chapter should be directed to Dr. Caroline Boxmeyer, Center for the Prevention of Youth Behavior Problems, The University of Alabama, Tuscaloosa, AL 35487-0348.

http://dx.doi.org/10.1037/14550-007
Handbook of Adolescent Drug Use Prevention: Research, Intervention Strategies, and Practice, L. M. Scheier (Editor)

intervention to children with conduct problems as a substance use prevention strategy. Conduct problems are linked to substance use through a mediational chain that includes peer rejection and peer delinquency (Fite et al., 2007) and has impulsivity and negative emotionality as key temperamental factors (Moeller & Dougherty, 2002; Pardini, Lochman, & Wells, 2004).

Etiology and Risk Factors for Childhood Conduct Problems

A contextual social–cognitive model has been used to summarize the empirically identified risk factors for conduct problems in children (Matthys & Lochman, 2010). Across development, a child can experience several of these risk factors, which can increase the likelihood that the child will display severe and persistent conduct problems and later substance use. These risk factors fall within five domains: (a) neurobiological, (b) family, (c) school and contextual, (d) peer, and (e) later-emerging child-level social cognitive and emotional regulation processes.

Neurobiological factors. Several prenatal factors can affect a child's developing brain and result in later conduct problems, including intrauterine drug and tobacco exposure, and severe maternal nutritional deficiencies (Brennan, Grekin, Mortensen, & Mednick, 2002; Delaney-Black et al., 2000; Kelly, Davis, & Henschke, 2000; Räsänen et al., 1999). Child-level neurobiological factors, such as androgen and serotonin levels, can affect the development of conduct problems and may influence the child's temperament; indeed, research has shown a positive correlation between higher androgen levels and aggression (Connor, 2002). Decreased levels of serotonin are related to less behavioral inhibition (Linnoila et al., 1983; Soubrié, 1986). Children's temperament can affect their subsequent aggressive behavior, but only when parents provide harsh discipline or low monitoring (Matthys, Vanderschuren, Schutter, & Lochman, 2012). For example, the following child temperaments are associated with conduct problems: those temperaments characterized by a lack of control (i.e., short attention span, negativism, restlessness, emotional lability; Caspi, Henry, McGee, & Moffitt, 1995); high emotional reactivity levels (Scaramella & Conger, 2003); and difficult temperaments in general (Coon, Carey, Corley, & Fulker, 1992); as well as fearful and highly active children (Colder, Lochman, & Wells, 1997).

Conduct problems and substance abuse have similar genetic and neural pathways (e.g., Comings et al., 2000). Genetic effects on children's development of conduct problems are primarily manifested in interaction with environmental risk factors, such as child maltreatment, marital problems, and parental substance abuse (Cadoret, Yates, Troughton, Woodworth, & Stewart, 1995; Caspi et al., 2002).

Family contextual factors. A wide range of family contextual factors lead to elevated risk of conduct problems during childhood, including poverty (Barry, Dunlap, Cotton, Lochman, & Wells, 2005); parent criminality, parental substance use, and maternal depression (Barry et al., 2005); marital conflict (Wolfe, Crooks, Lee, McIntyre-Smith, & Jaffe, 2003); single and teenage parenthood (Cuffe, McKeown, Addy, & Garrison, 2005); stressful life events (Barry et al., 2005); and controlling, ambivalent attachment between parent and child (Moss et al., 2006). These familial risk factors can affect parenting practices, which, in turn, can exert an effect on child behavior. For example, higher levels of maternal depression predict caregivers' use of inconsistent discipline, and inconsistent discipline predicts aggressive behavior in children (Barry, Dunlap, Lochman, & Wells, 2009).

Parenting practices associated with conduct problems in childhood (e.g., J. B. Reid, Patterson, & Snyder, 2002) include insensitive and nonresponsive parenting at age 1 year, that is, the reliability and pacing of parental reactions do not enable the parent to adequately meet the child's needs; increasingly coercive cycles of harsh parenting and noncompliance exhibited by the child, beginning in the preschool or toddler years, particularly for children who display challenging and difficult temperament styles; inconsistent, severe discipline; confusing or vague commands and directions; distinct lack of parental warmth and involvement; and absence of parental monitoring and supervision, especially as children mature into adolescence. The associations between child conduct problems and parenting factors are bidirectional: The behavior and temperament displayed by the child can also affect the behavior the parent adopts (Fite, Colder, Lochman, & Wells, 2006).

School and contextual factors. Distinct features of the school context can diminish or exacerbate a child's conduct problems. Schools and teachers can exercise positive influences on a student's behavior, even in the presence of substantial risk factors (McEvoy & Welker, 2000). In contrast, several school-level and classroom features have been connected to children's higher levels of disruptive and aggressive behavior. Schools with greater levels of overall student poverty (Thomas, Bierman, & Conduct Problems Prevention Research Group, 2006) and schools with lower levels of financial resources (Battistich, Solomon, Kim, Watson, & Schaps, 1995) have higher incidents of aggressive behavior exhibited by students and poorer child behavioral functioning, in general. Children who have previously been exposed to antisocial and violent activity have a greater risk of developing conduct problems (McCabe, Lucchini, Hough, Yeh, & Hazen, 2005).

Thomas, Bierman, Thompson, Powers, and the Conduct Problems Prevention Research Group (2008) examined the hypothesis that higher rates of student poverty add to underresourced and nonoptimal classroom contexts in which teachers' poor management skills and poor student–teacher relationships obstruct the effective social control of aggressive student behavior. The findings revealed that, although child characteristics (i.e., disruptive behavior at home, attention deficit problems) explained most of the variance in school aggression, school factors also explained significant variance, particularly for low-quality classroom contexts. Thomas et al. (2008) also found that classroom contexts characterized by teachers with disapproving attitudes and students who exhibit disengaged behavior destabilize the learning environment and, subsequently, can cause disruptive behavior in children. Similar to coercive interactions in families of children with conduct problems (Dishion & Patterson, 2006), teachers may use coercive, unsuccessful, and negative behavior control strategies (i.e., reprimands, threats, displays of anger, low use of behavioral contingencies and positive reinforcement). These often harsh tactics can escalate children's oppositional behavior and further contribute to behavior problems in school (Webster-Stratton, Reid, & Hammond, 2001).

In contrast, teachers who use positive, effective behavior management strategies often have students who exhibit fewer behavior problems. This result is especially evident when comparing to students of teachers who use more disciplinary strategies (Yates & Yates, 1990). Furthermore, when the teacher–student relationship is considered to be positive, warm, and supportive, children show less aggression at school (Rimm-Kaufman et al., 2002). Schools that serve high-poverty communities may also contain a higher number of students with disruptive and aggressive behavior overall, which poses an increased challenge, because having that higher percentage of students in the classroom increases the incidents of aggressive behavior displayed by other students (Barth, Dunlap, Dane, Lochman, & Wells, 2004). Evidence suggests that this effect can extend into future school years (Kellam, Ling, Merisca, Brown, & Ialongo, 1998).

Peer factors. Children with conduct problems are more at risk for having exaggerated or inaccurate perceptions of their levels of acceptance by their peers and for being rejected by their peers (Pardini, Barry, Barth, Lochman, & Wells, 2006). Children who are defined as only aggressive and children who are defined as only rejected show less severe antisocial behavior than children defined as both aggressive and socially rejected (Miller-Johnson, Coie, Maumary-Gremaud, Bierman, & Conduct Problems Prevention Research Group, 2002). The degree of social rejection that students experience can be influenced by the match between the race of students and their peers in a classroom (Jackson, Barth, Powell, & Lochman, 2006), and gender and race appear to moderate the relation between adolescent's negative outcomes and peer rejection. To further illustrate this point, one study (Lochman & Wayland, 1994) found that peer rejection ratings of African American children who were part of a mixed-race classroom did not predict later disruptive behavior in adolescence. However, peer rejection ratings of Caucasian children were associated with disruptive behavior in the future.

As children with conduct problems transition to adolescence, they are more likely to associate with deviant peers (Warr, 2002). If they lack the appropriate social skills necessary to affiliate with, and are continually rejected and/or ostracized by, prosocial peer groups, these adolescents are more likely to turn to a deviant peer group (Miller-Johnson et al., 2002). The inclination to associate with deviant peers substantially increases the risk for more severe conduct problems and risk behaviors in adolescence, such as substance use and delinquency (e.g., Fite et al., 2007).

Child-level social–cognitive and emotional regulation processes. As they develop, children begin to form steady patterns of social information processing and emotional regulation based on their biological disposition and temperament, and on their specific contextual experiences with their community, peers, and family. The contextual social–cognitive model (Lochman & Wells, 2002a) highlights the interactive and reciprocal relations among children's cognitive appraisal of problem situations, efforts to generate solutions to perceived problems, patterns of physiological arousal, and behavioral response in problem situations. Children with conduct problems often experience cognitive distortions at the appraisal phases of social information processing partly because of executive function deficits (Ellis, Weiss, & Lochman, 2009). These children also have difficulty correctly interpreting and processing others' intentions and social cues. In the appraisal phase, children with conduct problems recall fewer relevant nonhostile cues (Lochman & Dodge, 1994) and misperceive the levels of aggressive behavior that they or their peers exhibit in dyadic interactions (Lochman & Dodge, 1998). Children who are reactively aggressive often have a hostile attributional bias: They disproportionally infer that others are acting toward them in a hostile and provocative manner (Dodge, Lochman, Harnish, Bates, & Pettit, 1997; Lochman & Dodge, 1994).

Children with conduct problems also experience difficulty at the problem solution phase. They are more likely to endorse social goals related to revenge and dominance (Lochman, Wayland, & White, 1993), which then guide the nonverbal and maladaptive action-oriented solutions they use to solve perceived problems (Dunn, Lochman, & Colder, 1997; Lochman & Dodge, 1994). Aggressive children often have lower verbal skills, which can contribute to their difficulty accessing and making use of competent verbal assertion and compromise solutions. Children with conduct problems often assess aggressive solutions in a more positive light, believing that aggressive behavior will lead to more positive results for them (Lochman & Dodge, 1994). Those who display proactive aggressive behavior and callous–unemotional traits show especially deficient beliefs at this stage of information processing (Dodge et al., 1997; Pardini, Lochman, & Frick, 2003).

Their physiological arousal in response to social problem situations varies based on their biological sensitivity to context and interpretation of the activating event (Williams, Lochman, Phillips, & Barry, 2003). In turn, arousal level influences problem solving and works either to increase the fight or flight response or to block the child's ability to generate effective solutions. Because of the interactive nature of these highly ingrained thought and behavior patterns in children, they can be difficult to change and often require lengthy, multimodal interventions.

Common Mechanisms Targeted by Preventive Interventions

Preventive interventions for children at-risk for conduct problems are often multicomponent in nature; that is, they seek to influence as many key contextual domains as possible. By addressing the common elements of interventions at the parent/family, child, and contextual levels, as described in this section, the expected outcome is a reduction in risk for substance abuse.

Improving the parent–child relationship. An initial aim of parenting interventions is to strengthen the positive bond between parent and child. Parents are encouraged to reserve special time each day to connect with their child in a meaningful way and to minimize conflict during this time. Parents of younger children are taught to engage in child-directed play and follow the child's lead during unstructured play together. Parents of older children are encouraged to spend regular one-on-one time with their child, use this time to engage in an activity their child enjoys, be available to listen to their child's concerns, express warmth and affection for their child, and avoid criticizing their child or raising conflict-laden topics during this time. Once the parent and child have developed a stronger level of trust and affection, parents are taught additional behavioral parenting strategies.

Parental stress management. Parenting can be stressful, and parents of children with conduct problems often experience more psychosocial stressors. Thus, another important intervention focus is providing parents with support and training to manage those stressors. Emphasis is on describing how stress can undermine positive parenting behaviors and negatively affect the parent–child relationship. Parents are taught to recognize how their own stress can lead to overreactions to their child's behavior, and they are encouraged to find ways to take part in enjoyable, stress-reducing activities and schedule this time regularly. They are often introduced to relaxation techniques, including guided imagery, deep breathing, and progressive muscle relaxation. Parents are also taught how their own thoughts ("My child is driving me crazy" vs. "He is irritable today because he did not sleep well last night") and feelings affect their parenting behaviors. Those who have marked difficulty modulating their own emotions are also advised to seek adjunctive individual therapy. Some interventions provide practical support for parents and/or seek to increase their support from the community. Other interventions focus on increasing parents' support and stress management before focusing on strengthening the parent–child relationship.

Parental contingency management. Another overarching aim of parent interventions is to modify the contingencies in place that shape the child's behavior. Parents of children with conduct problems are often less clear and consistent in setting expectations for their child's behavior and in addressing problems as they arise. When combined with a child's challenging temperament, an escalating pattern of harsh, coercive interchanges often may result between the parent and child. Thus, a focus of parent/family interventions is to help parents learn to set and enforce clear contingencies for their child's behavior. Parents are taught to use labeled praise to reinforce specific positive behaviors (e.g., "I really appreciate your doing what I asked with a positive attitude") and to use planned ignoring to diffuse minor irritating behaviors that might otherwise lead to conflict. Parents practice setting clear behavior rules and expectations, giving clear instructions, and assessing child compliance. Parents also rehearse providing positive consequences for desired behaviors and using effective nonphysical punishment strategies that address noncompliance and other problem behavior.

An important goal is for parents to consistently convey their positive regard for their child as they also respond differentially to positive and negative child behaviors. This same contingency management process is mimicked in child- and classroom-focused interventions. Mental health clinicians and classroom teachers are trained to convey warmth and positive regard for the child, even in the face of challenging behaviors, and to use specific praise, collaborative problem solving, and valued incentives to increase positive child behavior, and to use strategic ignoring and consequences to decrease problem behavior.

Parental support for children's academic learning. Given the important role of school in children's lives, another common intervention focus is to help parents support their child's learning and behavior at school. Parents are taught to develop regular, proactive communication methods with their child's teacher. For example, parents learn to use a school-to-home notebook, closely monitor homework completion, and collaborate effectively with the teacher to address the child's behavioral functioning at school. Rather than wait for problems to arise, parents practice proactive strategies for communicating with their child's teacher. Child interventions often teach children organization and study skills to increase their academic success and decrease conflict with parents and teachers around academic issues.

Parental supervision to decrease delinquency. A specific risk factor for children's substance use initiation is their involvement with deviant peers. Thus, an important focus of parent/family interventions is to encourage parents to closely supervise their child's activities, be aware of the types of peers with whom their child is spending time, and continue these practices well into adolescence. Parents are encouraged to keep their child involved in supervised, structured activities and to develop systems for monitoring their child's activities during unstructured times. Avoiding deviant peer affiliation is important in preventing substance use.

Children's personal goal-setting. Building children's motivation for personal behavior change is a central aspect of intervention. One method for motivating children with conduct problems to improve their behavior is to help them learn to set personal goals and examine how their current behavior is preventing them from accomplishing their goals. When used regularly, this goal-setting process can make the intervention personally relevant, increase children's motivation to improve their behavior outside of intervention sessions, and facilitate their regular receipt of feedback about target behaviors and reinforcement for behavior gains. Parents and teachers can also use goal-setting to modify their interaction patterns with children who exhibit challenging behavior.

Children's emotional awareness and emotion regulation. Another key intervention target is to help children become better at detecting a range of emotions and recognizing the early signs of emotional arousal. Children are taught to recognize the physiological, behavioral, and cognitive manifestations of anger arousal and how they can use their own thoughts and behavior to reduce arousal. They practice reducing anger arousal using a range of coping strategies, including self-instruction, distraction, deep breathing, and relaxation. Children are then exposed to increasingly high levels of anger arousal during a series of graded in vivo exposure tasks and practice using one or more coping strategies to reduce their anger arousal.

Child and family social problem solving. Another common intervention focus is to teach children how to solve social problems more effectively. This process entails a series of steps: identifying the problem specifically and accurately, generating a range of potential solutions, thinking ahead about the likely consequences of each solution, and enacting the solution with the most positive expected outcome. Primary intervention aims are to help children use more deliberate (reasoned) rather than automatic processing and to practice using solutions most likely to yield positive social outcomes (e.g., verbal assertion, bargaining, compromise). As one step in this process, children are taught to consider problems from another individual's perspective and reduce common social–cognitive deficits, such as hostile attribution biases. In some cases, interventions teach parents the same problem-solving approach and encourage them to use it at home as an effective means to solve family problems.

School and contextual interventions. Children with conduct problems often experience difficulty both in their home and school environments. Accordingly, many interventions seek to improve the communication between home and school and ensure that consistent approaches are being used to shape the child's behavior across these settings. Interventions that focus directly on the teacher and school environment can be conducted informally, through a school-to-home communication plan, or formally through a Section 504 or Individualized Education Plan for children with more severe conduct problems. The intervention often identifies several measurable and attainable behavioral goals for the child and helps the teacher use a contingency management system that helps the child meet these goals. Classroom-wide curricula are also available to help teachers develop a positive classroom environment, use effective behavioral management strategies, and foster positive social–emotional learning in all classroom students.

PREVENTIVE INTERVENTIONS IN EARLY AND MIDDLE CHILDHOOD

Several well-established risk factors for conduct problems and substance use are present early in life, which suggests that prevention programs might be most efficiently delivered to the youngest children.

By targeting at-risk children in their first years, early intervention has the potential to improve functioning and reduce distress in young children's families, promote positive behavior in children, and prevent the occurrence of additional risk factors that, without intervention, might occur in high risk families (e.g., harsh or abusive parenting). In the following section, we review the evidence for several programs that seek to prevent negative outcomes by addressing early occurring risk factors in young children. By reducing aggression in young children and promoting effective parenting strategies, these programs decrease at-risk children's likelihood of later developing serious conduct problems and initiating substance use.

Universal Prevention Programs

Nurse home visitation programs. Two randomized controlled trials of a nurse home visitation program have been conducted in New York and Tennessee (Olds, Henderson, Kitzman, et al., 1998) to evaluate the effectiveness of a CD prevention program in reducing children's risk for later negative outcomes. Both studies targeted high-risk mothers, primarily low-income and unmarried, who were expecting their first child. Visits were conducted biweekly in the mothers' homes and extended from the first or second trimester of pregnancy through the child's second birthday. Visits included structured activities that focused on three primary risk areas: reducing maternal use of tobacco and other substances, promoting mothers' sensitivity and responsiveness to their children, and improving mothers' own personal development (e.g., completing education; obtaining employment; spacing future pregnancies).

In the 15 years following program completion, rates of child maltreatment were significantly lower for participating than comparison families (Olds et al., 1997). Furthermore, adolescents of participating mothers reported significantly fewer arrests, convictions, and parole violations, and reported lower rates of tobacco use and alcohol consumption than the comparison group (Olds, Henderson, Cole, et al., 1998). These results suggest that very early prevention, beginning during the prenatal period and extending through the toddler years, can significantly affect development and reduce the risk of later antisocial behavior and substance use.

Promoting Alternative THinking Strategies. Promoting Alternative THinking Strategies (PATHS) is a universal prevention program that provides developmentally appropriate curricula across age and grade levels, including the preschool period (Kusche & Greenberg, 1994). PATHS recognizes that children who demonstrate behavioral problems also tend to have deficits in their social–emotional skills and seeks to improve children's functioning and decrease their risk status by teaching core social and emotional competencies. The preschool/kindergarten program consists of 45 manualized lessons designed to be led by teachers during the school day. Extension activities and parent materials are provided to promote generalization of skills. The program is based on the ABCD (affective–behavioral–cognitive–dynamic) model of development (Greenberg & Kusche, 1993), which posits that children develop social and emotional competencies as they are increasingly able to integrate affect, behavior, and cognitive understanding. In addition to a focus on the children's own skill development, PATHS emphasizes the role of the environmental context.

A randomized trial indicated that preschool children who participated in PATHS had better emotion knowledge skills and were rated as more socially competent and less socially withdrawn compared with a non-PATHS comparison group (Domitrovich, Cortes, & Greenberg, 2007). In a second clinical trial, PATHS was implemented with 4-year-old children in Head Start classrooms. Children who received the PATHS curriculum demonstrated lower levels of aggressive behavior and greater levels of self-control and emotion regulation compared to children in the control group (Bierman et al., 2008). PATHS children also showed improvements in their social–emotional skills, social behavior, and problem-solving skills.

Evaluations of PATHS, implemented through the early elementary grades, have also yielded encouraging results. Children in the first through third grades who participated in PATHS in the United Kingdom demonstrated improvements at postintervention in emotional symptoms, conduct problems, hyperactivity, peer problems, and consideration of others, whereas children assigned to the control condition did not show improvements in these areas (Curtis & Norgate, 2007). In a study involving second and third graders in both self-contained and regular classes, participation in PATHS was linked to improvements in emotion understanding, ability to discuss emotional experiences, and self-efficacy for emotion management (Greenberg, Kusche, Cook, & Quamma, 1995). Use of PATHS with special education students across 3 years (first through third grades) has been shown to reduce aggressive and disruptive behaviors 2 years after the intervention (Kam, Greenberg, & Kusche, 2004).

In a large-scale, multisite, longitudinal study, children who participated in PATHS as first through third graders in the context of the Fast Track prevention program demonstrated reduced aggression, improved prosocial behavior, and increased academic engagement (i.e., increased teacher-rated self-control and on-task behavior) compared to controls (Bierman et al., 2010). Expanding on earlier results from the same trial, these findings demonstrated that participation in PATHS in first through third grade led to favorable prevention effects on conduct problems in the home and school settings (Conduct Problems Prevention Research Group, 1999).

Targeted Prevention and Treatment Programs

Incredible Years. The Incredible Years training series (Webster-Stratton & Reid, 2010) encompasses a range of programs designed to prevent and treat aggressive and disruptive behaviors in children from birth to age 12. The programs include universal, targeted prevention and treatment protocols; separate curricula are available for implementation with children, parents, and teachers. Originally designed for implementation with 4- to 8-year-old children, a substantial body of literature has provided solid evidence for the program's effectiveness in preventing and treating conduct problems in the preschool and early elementary school years.

Incredible Years for children from preschool through second grade includes child (Dinosaur School), parent, and teacher programs. The child component seeks to decrease aggressive and disruptive behaviors, and promote resilience through teaching concepts, including social skills, strategies for school success, emotional understanding, problem solving, and anger management. In support of primary prevention, the program is implemented in a classroom setting; for treatment of disruptive behavior symptoms, the program is implemented with small groups. In the parenting component, parents learn skills, including positive attention and praise, establishment of predictable rules and routines, and effective limit setting, to interrupt the cycle of negative parent–child interactions. The teacher component is designed to promote effective classroom management practices, including using praise and encouragement, providing incentives to address behavior problems, and establishing positive teacher–student relationships.

Multiple randomized controlled trials have supported the effectiveness of Incredible Years for the treatment and prevention of conduct problems. Results of numerous trials, conducted by the program developer, of the parent program for the treatment of conduct problems have demonstrated significant reductions in child disruptive behaviors and improvements in parenting skills compared to controls (for a review, see Webster-Stratton & Reid, 2010). Independent investigations (e.g., Larsson et al., 2009; Lavigne et al., 2008) have replicated these positive results on child behavior and parenting. Improvements in child behavior after the parenting intervention were maintained at a 3-year follow-up (Webster-Stratton, 1990). Combined child and parent intervention produced the most improvements in child behavior at posttreatment and at a 1-year follow-up (Webster-Stratton & Hammond, 1997). In addition, the child component, alone or in combination with the parenting program, has been shown to produce greater effects on children's social skills (Webster-Stratton & Hammond, 1997). Including the teacher training component has been shown to produce reductions in teachers' use of harsh, critical, and inconsistent methods, and bolster the effectiveness of the parenting program (Webster-Stratton, Reid, & Hammond, 2004).

Effectiveness of the parenting program for preventing conduct problems in at-risk children has also been demonstrated in three randomized trials with Head Start students (M. J. Reid, Webster-

Stratton, & Baydar, 2004; Webster-Stratton, 1998; Webster-Stratton, Reid, & Hammond, 2001). These studies support the program's effectiveness in improving parenting behaviors, preventing child conduct problems, and improving child prosocial behaviors. Independent replications have also demonstrated favorable preventive effects (e.g., Gross et al., 2003; Hutchings et al., 2007).

Parent–child interaction therapy. Parent–child interaction therapy (PCIT; Zisser & Eyberg, 2010) is an evidence-based treatment designed to address oppositional and disruptive behaviors in young children. The program seeks to improve child compliance through the promotion of warm, responsive parenting and effective limit-setting. Treatment sessions include the parent and child together, and are heavily focused on coaching parents to use specific child-rearing skills. Two main skill areas are taught: child-directed interaction skills (e.g., providing labeled praise and reflective statements, refraining from directive commands and critical statements) and parent-directed interaction skills (e.g., delivering effective instructions, following through with predictable consequences).

Two randomized controlled trials of PCIT with 3- to 6-year-old children have demonstrated the program's effectiveness in reducing child disruptive behaviors and increasing positive parent–child interactions (Bagner & Eyberg, 2007; Schuhmann, Foote, Eyberg, Boggs, & Algina, 1998). Follow-up studies have indicated that treatment gains persist up to 6 years following completion of treatment (Hood & Eyberg, 2003).

PREVENTIVE INTERVENTIONS ADMINISTERED IN LATER CHILDHOOD AND EARLY ADOLESCENCE

This section provides an overview of intervention programs that have been delivered with school and community populations, and staged as universal prevention programs. It also gives an overview of programs delivered to samples with, or at risk for, conduct problems (Matthys & Lochman, 2010), and describes later negative outcomes, including substance abuse.

Universal Prevention Programs

Seattle Social Development Project. The Seattle Social Development Project (SSDP) is a universal prevention program designed to reduce aggression by creating a positive school environment. Used predominantly for public elementary schools serving high-crime areas in Seattle, Washington, the program includes training for teachers to increase the use of nonpunitive classroom behavioral management, such as positive reinforcement. More recent versions of the intervention have included parent training and child problem-solving and social skills training (Hawkins, Catalano, Kosterman, Abbott, & Hill, 1999). Longitudinal efficacy evaluation studies of treated versus control children have found significant prevention effects with corresponding reductions in alcohol use (Hawkins et al., 1999) and delinquency, lower frequency of sexual intercourse and number of sexual partners, and decreased reports of pregnancy for females and males fathering children (Hawkins et al., 1999). In addition, students receiving the prevention reported more positive feelings and commitment to school compared to control groups, improved academic achievement, and less student-reported school misbehavior (Hawkins et al., 1999). Findings have primarily relied on youth self-report.

Positive behavioral support. A fairly new, but rapidly growing, approach to universal promotion of students' positive social and academic functioning is the school-wide application of Positive Behavioral Support (PBS, also known as Positive Behavioral Interventions and Supports; Sugai & Horner, 2002). The PBS approach has an established record of reducing challenging behaviors in children with developmental and intellectual disabilities, and research is beginning to emerge supporting the effectiveness of PBS as a school-wide preventive intervention to reduce the incidence of problem behaviors and increase student learning. For example, the teaching recess application promotes workshops for the entire school, including staff and students, that outline positive behavioral expectations for recess. Following such an intervention, recess-related office referrals were found to decrease by 80% (Todd, Haugen, Anderson, & Spriggs, 2002).

Olweus Bullying Prevention Program. The Olweus Bullying Prevention Program was a nationwide universal preventive intervention conducted in Norway. The program's objectives include reducing the acceptance of bullying among children and school staff, and improving school supervision and deterrence of bullying by instilling awareness with instructional booklets, providing suggestions for preventing bullying, initiating classroom meetings, and using videos (Olweus, 1993). Results from a clinical trial involving 42 Norwegian elementary and middle schools showed at least a 50% decrease in bullying and decreased reports of delinquency including vandalism, fighting, intoxication, theft, and truancy. Impressively, the results indicated even greater positive effects at a 2-year follow-up compared with a 1-year follow-up.

Targeted Prevention and Treatment Programs

Problem-Solving Skills Training Plus Parent Management Training. The full Problem-Solving Skills Training plus Parent Management Training (PSST + PMT) program has a component addressing parent training and one addressing prosocial problem-solving skills among children with disruptive behavior disorders. The program is targeted to school-age, antisocial children between ages 7 and 13 years, and children attend 25 weekly sessions lasting approximately 50 minutes each (Kazdin, Siegel, & Bass, 1992). PSST emphasizes the daily interpersonal situations that children face and focuses on individual interpersonal deficits. Techniques, such as role-playing, reinforcement, modeling, and feedback, are used to teach and reward effective problem-solving skills. Children are also given tasks called "super-solvers," which allow them to practice techniques from the sessions with other people outside of the group. Parent participation is a large component of the training, and parents attend their own training and also view the child sessions, serve as a coleader, and supervise the child's use of the new skills at home (Kazdin et al., 1992).

Outcome studies have suggested that PSST significantly reduces antisocial behavior during 1-year follow-up periods. Although PSST has been found to do better than PMT at increasing children's social competence at school and reducing self-reports of aggression and delinquency, a combination of both treatments is optimal for most outcomes (Kazdin et al., 1992). The combination of PSST with an increased parent-focused intervention was found to produce stronger outcome effects (in terms of both statistical and clinical significance) than PSST or parent-focused interventions alone (Kazdin et al., 1992). The accumulation of evidence suggests that PSST + PMT is an effective and long-lasting treatment for antisocial behavior in children.

Coping Power Program. The Coping Power Program was derived from the child-focused Anger Coping Program, which produced lower rates of alcohol, marijuana, and other drug use at a follow-up period 3 years postintervention, in comparison to a control condition (Lochman, 1992). The Coping Power Program is a comprehensive, multicomponent intervention based on the contextual social–cognitive model of risk for conduct problems (Lochman & Wells, 2002a). The program draws on the cognitive and behavioral techniques of well-established parent training programs and also incorporates techniques that target malleable child-level, social–cognitive risk factors for conduct problems. It includes 34 child sessions and 16 parent sessions designed to be delivered over a 16- to 18-month period.

Mental health professionals can implement the program in clinical settings, or school mental health personnel can carry out the program in schools. Although originally designed to be implemented with fourth- to sixth-grade children, the program has been successfully adapted for younger and older children. An abbreviated version that can be implemented in one academic year (24 child, 10 parent sessions) has produced significant reductions in children's aggressive behavior at a multiyear follow-up (Lochman et al., 2014). A version of the program for individual delivery (rather than group delivery) is being evaluated—with promising pilot results.

In an initial efficacy study of the Coping Power Program, Lochman and Wells (2002a, 2004) randomly assigned 183 aggressive boys (60% African

American, 40% White non-Hispanic) to one of three conditions: Coping Power Program child component, Coping Power Program child and parent components, and an untreated cell. The two intervention conditions took place during fourth to fifth or fifth to sixth grades, and the intervention lasted for 1.5 school years. At 1-year follow-up, in comparison to the control condition, the two Coping Power Program conditions produced reductions in children's self-reported delinquent behavior and in parent-reported alcohol and marijuana use by the child, and improved teacher-rated child functioning at school (Lochman & Wells, 2004).

Coping Power Program effects on parent-rated youth substance use and delinquent behavior were most apparent among participants who had received the combined child and parent Coping Power Program. In contrast, boys' teacher-rated behavioral improvements during the follow-up year appeared to be primarily influenced by the child component. The intervention effects on delinquency, parent-reported substance use, and teacher-rated improvement at 1-year follow-up were mediated by intervention-produced improvements in children's internal locus of control, their perceptions of their parents' consistency, their ability to make accurate attributions about social stimuli, person perception, and children's expectations that aggression would not work for them (Lochman & Wells, 2002a). These mediated effects were observed for both program modalities: the child component only and the child plus parent component.

Several types of effectiveness and dissemination studies have been conducted with the Coping Power Program. These studies have yielded significant positive intervention effects on aggressive behavior and problem-solving skills among aggressive deaf children in a residential setting (Lochman et al., 2001) and on the overt aggression of children with CDs in Dutch outpatient clinics compared to children receiving care-as-usual (van de Wiel et al., 2007). Four years postintervention, the Dutch version of the Coping Power Program (Utrecht Coping Power Program [UCPP]) had preventive effects by reducing adolescent marijuana and cigarette use (but not alcohol use). The rates of substance use among youth in UCPP were within the range of typically developing Dutch adolescents (Zonnevylle-Bender, Matthys, van de Wiel, & Lochman, 2007). Moreover, UCPP produced reductions in children's conduct problems at the end of intervention for 49% less cost than a care-as-usual condition (van de Wiel, Matthys, Cohen-Kettenis, & van Engeland, 2003).

Lochman and Wells (2002b) examined the effects of the Coping Power Program (combined child and parent components) as an indicated preventive intervention for high-risk children. A total of 245 male and female aggressive fourth-grade students were randomly assigned to one of four conditions: the Coping Power Program alone, the Coping Power Program plus universal classroom intervention, classroom intervention alone, and control. At postintervention, the three treatment intervention conditions produced lower rates of substance use than the control condition. Children who received both interventions displayed improvements in their social competence with peers, and their teachers rated these children as having the greatest increases in problem-solving and anger-coping skills. The program also produced reductions in parent-rated and teacher-rated proactive aggressive behavior, and increases in teacher-rated behavioral improvement.

A 1-year follow-up of this effectiveness trial sample replicated the findings of the prior efficacy study. Children in the Coping Power Program had lower rates of self-reported substance use and delinquency, and lower levels of teacher-rated aggressive social behavior at school compared to the control children (Lochman & Wells, 2003). Long-term effects on children's aggressive behavior at school were found 3 years after intervention (Lochman, Wells, Qu, & Chen, in press). Another dissemination study found that children participating in Coping Power Program groups run by school guidance counselors who received an intensive form of training had significant reductions in aggressive behavior at the end of intervention (Lochman et al., 2009) and less deterioration in academic outcomes 2 years later (Lochman et al., 2012).

Multisystemic therapy. Multisystemic therapy (MST) is an intensive family- and community-based treatment program that has been implemented with chronic and violent juvenile offenders, substance-abusing juvenile offenders, adolescent sexual offenders, youth in psychiatric crisis (i.e., homicidal, suicidal, psychotic), and maltreating families (Henggeler & Lee, 2003). MST is an individualized intervention that focuses on the interaction between adolescents and the multiple environmental systems that influence their antisocial behavior, including peers, family, school, and community. Strategies for changing the adolescent's behavior are developed in close collaboration with family members by identifying the major contextual forces that help maintain the deviant behavior. Program services, delivered in the family's natural environment, can include a variety of treatment approaches, such as parent training, family therapy, school consultation, marital therapy, and individual therapy. Although the techniques used in these treatment strategies can vary, many are either behavioral or cognitive–behavioral in nature (e.g., contingency management, behavioral contracting). Clinicians are guided by a set of nine MST principles, which include focusing on system strengths, delivering developmentally appropriate treatment, and improving effective family functioning. Throughout the intervention, MST experts consult weekly with clinicians to closely monitor their adherence to these treatment principles.

Evaluations of MST effectiveness with chronic and violent juvenile offenders have produced promising results. Several investigations have shown that families who receive MST have reported lower levels of adolescent behavior problems and improvements in family functioning at posttreatment compared to alternative treatment conditions. In the first of several randomized clinical trials, MST was compared with treatment-as-usual with a sample of 84 serious juvenile offenders. Juveniles in the MST condition had significantly fewer arrests ($M = .87$ vs. 1.52) and weeks of incarceration ($M = 5.8$ vs. 16.2) at a 59-week follow-up, and showed reduced recidivism at a 2-year follow-up. Results from a subsequent evaluation of MST found lower recidivism rates in juvenile offenders assigned to MST compared with youth who completed individual counseling at 4-year follow-up (Borduin et al., 1995). Among offenders who did recidivate, those assigned to MST had a lower number of total arrests and were charged with fewer serious offenses compared with youth assigned to individual counseling.

SUMMARY AND IMPLICATIONS FOR THE FUTURE

Childhood conduct problems are a strong and stable risk marker for later negative outcomes, including substance use (Lochman & Wayland, 1994). As indicated in this chapter's overview of the etiological risk factors for childhood conduct problems, a number of empirically supported programs ranging from universal prevention, targeted prevention, and treatment programs are able to modify the risk factors for childhood conduct problems in positive and lasting ways. These programs share many core elements. Going forward, it will be important to make these programs and their core elements widely available. They provide important strategies for fostering children's positive development, and preventing substance use and related problems.

Many of the previously described risk factors for conduct problems are also risk factors for substance abuse. For example, key predictors of substance abuse include children's lack of social competence and difficulty getting along with others, poor self-regulation and impulse control, weak social bond with school and academic difficulties, and less supportive and consistent caregiving environments (Lochman & Wells, 2002b). Conduct problems and substance abuse also have similar genetic and neural pathways (e.g., Comings et al., 2000). In light of these commonalities, Conner and Lochman (2010) have emphasized that a developmental pathways approach is central to improving the understanding of CD and substance abuse.

Three decades ago, Loeber (1990) theorized that as shared risk factors accumulate and aggressive behavior patterns become increasingly entrenched, later sequelae on the trajectory toward CD and substance abuse occur (e.g., as increased peer rejection, affiliation with deviant peer groups, poor parental supervision, involvement in delinquent acts, school failure). If substance abuse is downstream on a shared developmental pathway with child conduct problems, the prevention and treatment programs for children's conduct problems detailed in this chapter are then important tools for altering the developmental trajectories of at-risk children and preventing substance abuse.

References

American Psychiatric Association. (2013). *Diagnostic and statistical manual of mental disorders* (5th ed.). Arlington, VA: Author.

Bagner, D. M., & Eyberg, S. M. (2007). Parent–child interaction therapy for disruptive behavior in children with mental retardation: A randomized controlled trial. *Journal of Clinical Child and Adolescent Psychology*, *36*, 418–429. doi:10.1080/15374410701448448

Barry, T. D., Dunlap, S., Lochman, J. E., & Wells, K. C. (2009). Inconsistent discipline as a mediator between maternal distress and aggression in boys. *Child & Family Behavior Therapy*, *31*, 1–19. doi:10.1080/07317100802701186

Barry, T. D., Dunlap, S. T., Cotton, S. J., Lochman, J. E., & Wells, K. C. (2005). The influence of maternal stress and distress on disruptive behavior problems in children. *Journal of the American Academy of Child & Adolescent Psychiatry*, *44*, 265–273. doi:10.1097/00004583-200503000-00011

Barth, J. M., Dunlap, S. T., Dane, H., Lochman, J. E., & Wells, K. C. (2004). Classroom environment influences on aggression, peer relations, and academic focus. *Journal of School Psychology*, *42*, 115–133. doi:10.1016/j.jsp.2003.11.004

Battistich, V., Solomon, D., Kim, D., Watson, M., & Schaps, E. (1995). Schools as communities, poverty levels of student populations, and student attitudes, motives, and performance: A multilevel analysis. *American Educational Research Journal*, *32*, 627–658. doi:10.3102/00028312032003627

Bierman, K. L., Coie, J. D., Dodge, K. A., Greenberg, M. T., Lochman, J. E., McMahon, R. J., & Pinderhuges, E. (2010). The effects of a multiyear universal social–emotional learning program: The role of student and school characteristics. *Journal of Consulting and Clinical Psychology*, *78*, 156–168. doi:10.1037/a0018607

Bierman, K. L., Domitrovich, C. E., Nix, R. L., Gest, S. D., Welsh, J. A., Greenberg, M. T., . . . Gill, S. (2008). Promoting academic and social–emotional school readiness: The Head Start REDI Program. *Child Development*, *79*, 1802–1817. doi:10.1111/j.1467-8624.2008.01227.x

Borduin, C. M., Mann, B. J., Cone, L. T., Henggeler, S. W., Fucci, B. R., Blaske, D. M., & Williams, R. A. (1995). Multisystemic treatment of serious juvenile offenders: Long-term prevention of criminality and violence. *Journal of Consulting and Clinical Psychology*, *63*, 569–578. doi:10.1037/0022-006X.63.4.569

Brennan, P. A., Grekin, E. R., Mortensen, E., & Mednick, S. A. (2002). Relationship of maternal smoking during pregnancy with criminal arrest and hospitalization for substance abuse in male and female adult offspring. *The American Journal of Psychiatry*, *159*, 48–54. doi:10.1176/appi.ajp.159.1.48

Cadoret, R. J., Yates, W. R., Troughton, E., Woodworth, G., & Stewart, M. A. S. (1995). Genetic–environmental interaction in the genesis of aggressivity and conduct disorders. *Archives of General Psychiatry*, *52*, 916–924. doi:10.1001/archpsyc.1995.03950230030006

Caspi, A., Henry, B., McGee, R. O., & Moffitt, T. E. (1995). Temperamental origins of child and adolescent behavior problems: From age three to fifteen. *Child Development*, *66*, 55–68. doi:10.2307/1131190

Caspi, A., McClay, J., Moffitt, T. E., Mill, J., Martin, J., Craig, I. W., . . . Poulton, R. (2002). Role of genotype in the cycle of violence in maltreated children. *Science*, *297*, 851–854. doi:10.1126/science.1072290

Colder, C. R., Lochman, J. E., & Wells, K. C. (1997). The moderating effects of children's fear and activity level on relations between parenting practices and childhood symptomatology. *Journal of Abnormal Child Psychology*, *25*, 251–263. doi:10.1023/A:1025704217619

Comings, D. E., Gade-Andavolu, R., Gonzalez, N., Wu, S., Muhleman, D., Blake, H., . . . MacMurray, J. P. (2000). Comparison of the role of dopamine, serotonin, and noradrenaline genes in ADHD, ODD and conduct disorder: Multivariate regression analysis of 20 genes. *Clinical Genetics*, *57*, 178–196. doi:10.1034/j.1399-0004.2000.570304.x

Conduct Problems Prevention Research Group. (1999). Initial impacts of the Fast Track prevention trial for conduct problems: I. The high-risk sample. *Journal of Consulting and Clinical Psychology*, *67*, 631–647. doi:10.1037/0022-006X.67.5.631

Conner, B. T., & Lochman, J. E. (2010). Comorbid conduct disorder and substance use disorders. *Clinical Psychology: Science and Practice*, *17*, 337–349. doi:10.1111/j.1468-2850.2010.01225.x

Connor, D. F. (2002). *Aggression and antisocial behavior in children and adolescents: Research and treatment*. New York, NY: Guilford Press.

Coon, H., Carey, G., Corley, R., & Fulker, D. W. (1992). Identifying children in the Colorado Adoption Project at risk for conduct disorder. *Journal of the American Academy of Child & Adolescent Psychiatry*, *31*, 503–511. doi:10.1097/00004583-199205000-00018

Costello, E. J., Mustillo, S., Erkanli, A., Keeler, G., & Angold, A. (2003). Prevalence and development of psychiatric disorders in childhood and adolescence. *Archives of General Psychiatry*, *60*, 837–844. doi:10.1001/archpsyc.60.8.837

Cuffe, S. P., McKeown, R. E., Addy, C. L., & Garrison, C. Z. (2005). Family and psychosocial risk factors in a longitudinal epidemiological study of adolescents. *Journal of the American Academy of Child & Adolescent Psychiatry*, *44*, 121–129. doi:10.1097/00004583-200502000-00004

Curtis, C., & Norgate, R. (2007). An evaluation of the Promoting Alternate Thinking Strategies curriculum at key stage 1. *Educational Psychology in Practice*, *23*, 33–44. doi:10.1080/02667360601154717

Delaney-Black, V., Covington, C., Templin, T., Ager, J., Nordstrom-Klee, B., Martier, S., & Sokol, R. J. (2000). Teacher-assessed behaviour of children prenatally exposed to cocaine. *Pediatrics*, *106*, 782–791. doi:10.1542/peds.106.4.782

Dishion, T. J., & Patterson, G. R. (2006). The development and ecology of antisocial behavior in children and adolescents. In D. Cicchetti & D. J. Cohen (Eds.), *Developmental psychopathology, Vol. 3: Risk, disorder, and adaptation* (2nd ed., pp. 503–541). Hoboken, NJ: Wiley.

Dodge, K. A., Lochman, J. E., Harnish, J. D., Bates, J. E., & Pettit, G. S. (1997). Reactive and proactive aggression in school children and psychiatrically impaired chronically assaultive youth. *Journal of Abnormal Psychology*, *106*, 37–51. doi:10.1037/0021-843X.106.1.37

Domitrovich, C. E., Cortes, R. C., & Greenberg, M. T. (2007). Improving young children's social and emotional competence: A randomized trial of the preschool "PATHS" curriculum. *Journal of Primary Prevention*, *28*, 67–91. doi:10.1007/s10935-007-0081-0

Dunn, S. E., Lochman, J. E., & Colder, C. R. (1997). Social problem-solving skills in boys with conduct and oppositional defiant disorders. *Aggressive Behavior*, *23*, 457–469. doi:10.1002/(SICI)1098-2337(1997)23:6<457::AID-AB5>3.0.CO;2-D

Ellis, M. L., Weiss, B., & Lochman, J. E. (2009). Executive functions in children: Associations with aggressive behavior and social appraisal processing. *Journal of Abnormal Child Psychology*, *37*, 945–956. doi:10.1007/s10802-009-9321-5

Fite, P. J., Colder, C. R., Lochman, J. E., & Wells, K. C. (2006). The mutual influence of parenting and boys' externalizing behavior problems. *Journal of Applied Developmental Psychology*, *27*, 151–164. doi:10.1016/j.appdev.2005.12.011

Fite, P. J., Colder, C. R., Lochman, J. E., & Wells, K. C. (2007). Pathways from proactive and reactive aggression to substance use. *Psychology of Addictive Behaviors*, *21*, 355–364. doi:10.1037/0893-164X.21.3.355

Greenberg, M. T., & Kusche, C. A. (1993). *Promoting social and emotional development in deaf children: The PATHS Project.* Seattle: University of Washington Press.

Greenberg, M. T., Kusche, C. A., Cook, E. T., & Quamma, J. P. (1995). Promoting emotional competence in school-aged children: The effects of the PATHS curriculum. *Development and Psychopathology*, *7*, 117–136. doi:10.1017/S0954579400006374

Gross, D., Fogg, L., Webster-Stratton, C., Garvey, C., Julian, W., & Grady, J. (2003). Parent training with families of toddlers in day care in low-income urban communities. *Journal of Consulting and Clinical Psychology*, *71*, 261–278. doi:10.1037/0022-006X.71.2.261

Hawkins, J. D., Catalano, R. F., Kosterman, R., Abbott, R. D., & Hill, K. G. (1999). Preventing adolescent health-risk behaviors by strengthening protection during childhood. *Archives of Pediatrics & Adolescent Medicine*, *153*, 226–234. doi:10.1001/archpedi.153.3.226

Henggeler, S. W., & Lee, T. (2003). Multisystemic treatment of serious clinical problems. In A. E. Kazdin & J. R. Weisz (Eds.), *Evidence-based psychotherapies for children and adolescents* (pp. 301–322). New York, NY: Guilford Press.

Hood, K. K., & Eyberg, S. M. (2003). Outcomes of parent–child interaction therapy: Mothers' reports on maintenance three to six years after treatment. *Journal of Clinical Child and Adolescent Psychology*, *32*, 419–429. doi:10.1207/S15374424JCCP3203_10

Hutchings, J., Gardner, F., Bywater, T., Daley, D., Gardner, F., Whitaker, C., . . . Edwards, R. T. (2007). Parenting intervention in Sure Start services for children at risk of developing conduct disorder: Pragmatic randomized controlled trial. *British Medical Journal*, *334*, 678–682. doi:10.1136/bmj.39126.620799.55

Jackson, M. F., Barth, J. M., Powell, N., & Lochman, J. E. (2006). Classroom contextual effects of race on children's peer nominations. *Child Development*, *77*, 1325–1337. doi:10.1111/j.1467-8624.2006.00937.x

Kam, C., Greenberg, M. T., & Kusche, C. A. (2004). Sustained effects of the PATHS curriculum on the social and psychological adjustment of children in special education. *Journal of Emotional and Behavioral Disorders*, *12*, 66–78. doi:10.1177/10634266040120020101

Kazdin, A. E., Siegel, T. C., & Bass, D. (1992). Cognitive problem-solving skills training and parent management training in the treatment of antisocial behavior in children. *Journal of Consulting and Clinical Psychology*, *60*, 733–747. doi:10.1037/0022-006X.60.5.733

Kellam, S. G., Ling, X., Merisca, R., Brown, C., & Ialongo, N. (1998). The effect of the level of aggression in the first grade classroom on the course and malleability of aggressive behavior into middle school. *Development and Psychopathology*, *10*, 165–185. doi:10.1017/S0954579498001564

Kelly, J. J., Davis, P. O., & Henschke, P. N. (2000). The drug epidemic: Effects on newborn infants and health resource consumption at a tertiary perinatal centre. *Journal of Paediatrics and Child Health, 36*, 262–264. doi:10.1046/j.1440-1754.2000.00492.x

Kusche, C. A., & Greenberg, M. T. (1994). *The PATHS curriculum*. South Deerfield, MA: Channing-Bete.

Larsson, B., Fossum, B., Clifford, G., Drugli, M., Handegard, B., & Morch, W. (2009). Treatment of oppositional defiant and conduct problems in young Norwegian children: Results of a randomized controlled trial. *European Child & Adolescent Psychiatry, 18*, 42–52. doi:10.1007/s00787-008-0702-z

Lavigne, J. V., LeBailly, S. A., Gouze, K. R., Cicchetti, C., Pochyly, J., Arend, R., . . . Binns, H. J. (2008). Treating oppositional defiant disorder in primary care: A comparison of three models. *Journal of Pediatric Psychology, 33*, 449–461. doi:10.1093/jpepsy/jsm074

Linnoila, M., Virkkunen, M., Scheinen, M., Nuutila, A., Rimon, R., & Goodwin, F. K. (1983). Low cerebrospinal fluid 5-hydroxyindoleacetic acid concentration differentiates impulsive from nonimpulsive violent behavior. *Life Sciences, 33*, 2609–2614. doi:10.1016/0024-3205(83)90344-2

Lochman, J. E. (1992). Cognitive–behavioral intervention with aggressive boys: Three-year follow-up and preventive effects. *Journal of Consulting and Clinical Psychology, 60*, 426–432. doi:10.1037/0022-006X.60.3.426

Lochman, J. E., Baden, R. E., Boxmeyer, C. L., Powell, N. P., Qu, L., Salekin, K. L., & Windle, M. (2014). Does a booster intervention augment the preventive effects of an abbreviated version of the Coping Power Program for aggressive children? *Journal of Abnormal Child Psychology, 42*, 367–381. doi:10.1007/s10802-013-9727-y

Lochman, J. E., Boxmeyer, C., Powell, N., Qu, L., Wells, K., & Windle, M. (2009). Dissemination of the Coping Power Program: Importance of intensity of counselor training. *Journal of Consulting and Clinical Psychology, 77*, 397–409. doi:10.1037/a0014514

Lochman, J. E., Boxmeyer, C. L., Powell, N. P., Qu, L., Wells, K., & Windle, M. (2012). Coping Power dissemination study: Intervention and special education effects on academic outcomes. *Behavioral Disorders, 37*, 192–205.

Lochman, J. E., & Dodge, K. A. (1994). Social–cognitive processes of severely violent, moderately aggressive, and nonaggressive boys. *Journal of Consulting and Clinical Psychology, 62*, 366–374. doi:10.1037/0022-006X.62.2.366

Lochman, J. E., & Dodge, K. A. (1998). Distorted perceptions in dyadic interactions of aggressive and nonaggressive boys: Effects of prior expectations, context, and boys' age. *Development and Psychopathology, 10*, 495–512. doi:10.1017/S0954579498001710

Lochman, J. E., FitzGerald, D. P., Gage, S. M., Kannaly, M. K., Whidby, J. M., Barry, T. D., . . . McElroy, H. (2001). Effects of social–cognitive intervention for aggressive deaf children: The Coping Power Program. *Journal of the American Deafness and Rehabilitation Association, 35*, 39–61.

Lochman, J. E., & Wayland, K. K. (1994). Aggression, social acceptance and race as predictors of negative adolescent outcomes. *Journal of the American Academy of Child & Adolescent Psychiatry, 33*, 1026–1035. doi:10.1097/00004583-199409000-00014

Lochman, J. E., Wayland, K. K., & White, K. J. (1993). Social goals: Relationship to adolescent adjustment and to social problem solving. *Journal of Abnormal Child Psychology, 21*, 135–151. doi:10.1007/BF00911312

Lochman, J. E., & Wells, K. C. (2002a). Contextual social–cognitive mediators and child outcome: A test of the theoretical model in the Coping Power Program. *Development and Psychopathology, 14*, 945–967. doi:10.1017/S0954579402004157

Lochman, J. E., & Wells, K. C. (2002b). The Coping Power Program at the middle school transition: Universal and indicated prevention effects. *Psychology of Addictive Behaviors, 16*, S40–S54. doi:10.1037/0893-164X.16.4S.S40

Lochman, J. E., & Wells, K. C. (2003). Effectiveness study of Coping Power and classroom intervention with aggressive children: Outcomes at a one-year follow-up. *Behavior Therapy, 34*, 493–515. doi:10.1016/S0005-7894(03)80032-1

Lochman, J. E., & Wells, K. C. (2004). The Coping Power program for preadolescent aggressive boys and their parents: Outcome effects at the one-year follow-up. *Journal of Consulting and Clinical Psychology, 72*, 571–578. doi:10.1037/0022-006X.72.4.571

Lochman, J. E., Wells, K. C., Qu, L., & Chen, L. (in press). Three year follow-up of Coping Power intervention effects: Evidence of neighborhood moderation? *Prevention Science.*

Loeber, R. (1990). Development and risk factors of juvenile antisocial behavior and delinquency. *Clinical Psychology Review, 10*, 1–41. doi:10.1016/0272-7358(90)90105-J

Loeber, R., Burke, J. D., Lahey, B. B., Winters, A., & Zera, M. (2000). Oppositional defiant and conduct disorder: A review of the past 10 years, Part I. *Journal of the American Academy of Child & Adolescent Psychiatry, 39*, 1468–1484. doi:10.1097/00004583-200012000-00007

Matthys, W., & Lochman, J. E. (2010). *Oppositional defiant disorder and conduct disorder in childhood.* Oxford, England: Wiley-Blackwell.

Matthys, W., Vanderschuren, L. J. M. J., Schutter, D. J. L. G., & Lochman, J. E. (2012). Impaired neurocognitive functions affect social learning processes in oppositional defiant disorder and conduct disorder: Implications for interventions. *Clinical Child and Family Psychology Review, 15*, 234–246.

McCabe, K. M., Lucchini, S. E., Hough, R. L., Yeh, M., & Hazen, A. (2005). The relation between violence exposure and conduct problems among adolescents: A prospective study. *American Journal of Orthopsychiatry, 75*, 575–584. doi:10.1037/0002-9432.75.4.575

McEvoy, A., & Welker, R. (2000). Antisocial behavior, academic failure, and school climate: A critical review. *Journal of Emotional and Behavioral Disorders, 8*, 130–140. doi:10.1177/106342660000800301

Merikangas, K. R., He, J., Brody, D., Fisher, P. W., Bourdon, K., & Koretz, D. S. (2010). Prevalence and treatment of mental disorders among US children in the 2001–2004 NHANES. *Pediatrics, 125*, 75–81. doi:10.1542/peds.2008-2598

Miller-Johnson, S., Coie, J. D., Maumary-Gremaud, A., & Bierman, K., & Conduct Problems Prevention Research Group. (2002). Peer rejection and aggression and early starter models of conduct disorder. *Journal of Abnormal Child Psychology, 30*, 217–230. doi:10.1023/A:1015198612049

Moeller, F. G., & Dougherty, D. M. (2002). Impulsivity and substance abuse: What is the connection? *Addictive Disorders & Their Treatment, 1*, 3–10. doi:10.1097/00132576-200205000-00002

Moss, E., Smolla, N., Cyr, C., Dubois-Comtois, K., Mazzarello, T., & Berthiaume, C. (2006). Attachment and behavior problems in middle childhood as reported by adult and child informants. *Development and Psychopathology, 18*, 425–444. doi:10.1017/S0954579406060238

Nock, M. K., Kazdin, A. E., Hiripi, E., & Kessler, R. C. (2007). Lifetime prevalence, correlates, and persistence of oppositional defiant disorder: Results from the National Comorbidity Survey Replication. *Journal of Child Psychology and Psychiatry, 48*, 703–713. doi:10.1111/j.1469-7610.2007.01733.x

Olds, D. L., Eckenrode, J., Henderson, C. R., Kitzman, H., Powers, J., Cole, R., . . . Luckey, D. (1997). Long-term effects of nurse home visitation on maternal life course and child abuse and neglect: 15-year follow-up of a randomized trial. *JAMA, 278*, 637–643. doi:10.1001/jama.1997.03550080047038

Olds, D., Henderson, C. R., Cole, R., Eckenrode, J., Kitzman, H., Luckey, D., . . . Powers, J. (1998). Long-term effects of nurse home visitation on children's criminal and antisocial behavior: 15-year follow-up of a randomized trial. *JAMA, 280*, 1238–1244. doi:10.1001/jama.280.14.1238

Olds, D., Henderson, C. R., Kitzman, H., Eckenrode, J., Cole, R., & Tatelbaum, R. (1998). The promise of home visitation: Results of two randomized trials. *Journal of Community Psychology, 26*, 5–21. doi:10.1002/(SICI)1520-6629(199801)26:1<5::AID-JCOP2>3.0.CO;2-Y

Olweus, D. (1993). Bully/victim problems among schoolchildren: Long-term consequences and an effective intervention program. In S. Hodgins (Ed.), *Mental disorder and crime* (pp. 317–349). Thousand Oaks, CA: Sage.

Pardini, D., Lochman, J., & Wells, K. (2004). Negative emotions and alcohol use initiation in high-risk boys: The moderating effect of good inhibitory control. *Journal of Abnormal Child Psychology, 32*, 505–518. doi:10.1023/B:JACP.0000037780.22849.23

Pardini, D. A., Barry, T. D., Barth, J. M., Lochman, J. E., & Wells, K. C. (2006). Self-perceived social acceptance and peer social standing in children with aggressive-disruptive behaviors. *Social Development, 15*, 46–64. doi:10.1111/j.1467-9507.2006.00329.x

Pardini, D. A., Lochman, J. E., & Frick, P. J. (2003). Callous/unemotional traits and social cognitive processes in adjudicated youth. *Journal of the American Academy of Child & Adolescent Psychiatry, 42*, 364–371. doi:10.1097/00004583-200303000-00018

Räsänen, P., Hakko, H., Isohanni, M., Hodgins, S., Järvelin, M., & Tiihonen, J. (1999). Maternal smoking during pregnancy and risk of criminal behavior among adult male offspring in the northern Finland 1966 birth cohort. *The American Journal of Psychiatry, 156*, 857–862.

Reid, J. B., Patterson, G. R., & Snyder, J. (Eds.). (2002). *Antisocial behavior in children and adolescents: A developmental analysis and model of intervention*. Washington, DC: American Psychological Association. doi:10.1037/10468-000

Reid, M. J., Webster-Stratton, C., & Baydar, N. (2004). Halting the development of externalizing behaviors in Head Start children: The effects of parent training. *Journal of Clinical Child and Adolescent Psychology, 33*, 279–291. doi:10.1207/s15374424jccp3302_10

Rimm-Kaufman, S. E., Early, D. M., Cox, M. J., Saluja, G., Pianta, R. C., Bradley, R. H., & Payne, C. (2002). Early behavioral attributes and teachers' sensitivity as predictors of competent behavior in the kindergarten classroom. *Journal of Applied Developmental Psychology, 23*, 451–470. doi:10.1016/S0193-3973(02)00128-4

Scaramella, L. V., & Conger, R. D. (2003). Intergenerational continuity of hostile parenting and its consequences: The moderating influence of children's negative emotional reactivity. *Social Development, 12*, 420–439. doi:10.1111/1467-9507.t01-1-00241

Schuhmann, E. M., Foote, R., Eyberg, S. M., Boggs, S., & Algina, J. (1998). Parent–child interaction therapy: Interim report of a randomized trial with short-term maintenance. *Journal of Clinical Child Psychology, 27,* 34–45. doi:10.1207/s15374424jccp2701_4

Soubrié, P. (1986). Serotonergic nerves and behaviour. *Journal de Pharmacologie, 17,* 107–112.

Sugai, G., & Horner, R. H. (2002). Introduction to the special series on positive behavior support in schools. *Journal of Emotional and Behavioral Disorders, 10,* 130–135. doi:10.1177/10634266020100030101

Thomas, D. E., Bierman, K. L., & Conduct Problems Prevention Research Group. (2006). The impact of classroom aggression on the development of aggressive behavior in children. *Development and Psychopathology, 18,* 471–487. doi:10.1017/S0954579406060251

Thomas, D. E., Bierman, K. L., Thompson, C., Powers, C. J., & Conduct Problems Prevention Research Group. (2008). Double jeopardy: Child and school characteristics that predict aggressive-disruptive behavior in the first grade. *School Psychology Review, 37,* 516–532.

Todd, A., Haugen, L., Anderson, K., & Spriggs, M. (2002). Teaching recess: Low-cost efforts producing effective results. *Journal of Positive Behavior Interventions, 4,* 46–52. doi:10.1177/109830070200400108

van de Wiel, N. M. H., Matthys, W., Cohen-Kettenis, P. T., Maassen, G. H., Lochman, J. E., & van Engeland, H. (2007). The effectiveness of an experimental treatment when compared with care as usual depends on the type of care as usual. *Behavior Modification, 31,* 298–312. doi:10.1177/0145445506292855

van de Wiel, N. M. H., Matthys, W., Cohen-Kettenis, P., & van Engeland, H. (2003). Application of the Utrecht Coping Power program and care as usual to children with disruptive behavior disorders in outpatient clinics: A comparative study of cost and course of treatment. *Behavior Therapy, 34,* 421–436. doi:10.1016/S0005-7894(03)80028-X

Warr, M. (2002). *Companions in crime: The social aspects of criminal conduct.* Cambridge, England: Cambridge University Press. doi:10.1017/CBO9780511803956

Webster-Stratton, C. (1990). Long-term follow-up of families with young conduct problem children: From preschool to grade school. *Journal of Clinical Child Psychology, 19,* 144–149. doi:10.1207/s15374424jccp1902_6

Webster-Stratton, C. (1998). Preventing conduct problems in Head Start children: Strengthening parenting competencies. *Journal of Consulting and Clinical Psychology, 66,* 715–730. doi:10.1037/0022-006X.66.5.715

Webster-Stratton, C., & Hammond, M. (1997). Treating children with early-onset conduct problems: A comparison of child and parent training interventions. *Journal of Consulting and Clinical Psychology, 65,* 93–109. doi:10.1037/0022-006X.65.1.93

Webster-Stratton, C., & Reid, M. J. (2010). The Incredible Years parents, teachers, and children training series: A multifaceted approach for young children with conduct disorders. In J. R. Weisz & A. R. Kazdin (Eds.), *Evidence-based psychotherapies for children and adolescents* (2nd ed., pp. 194–210). New York, NY: Guilford Press.

Webster-Stratton, C., Reid, M. J., & Hammond, M. (2001). Preventing conduct problems, promoting social competence: A parent and teacher training partnership in Head Start. *Journal of Clinical Child Psychology, 30,* 283–302. doi:10.1207/S15374424JCCP3003_2

Webster-Stratton, C., Reid, M. J., & Hammond, M. (2004). Treating children with early-onset conduct problems: Intervention outcomes for parent, child, and teacher training. *Journal of Clinical Child and Adolescent Psychology, 33,* 105–124. doi:10.1207/S15374424JCCP3301_11

Williams, S. C., Lochman, J. E., Phillips, N. C., & Barry, T. (2003). Aggressive and nonaggressive boys' physiological and cognitive processes in response to peer provocations. *Journal of Clinical Child and Adolescent Psychology, 32,* 568–576. doi:10.1207/S15374424JCCP3204_9

Wolfe, D. A., Crooks, C. V., Lee, V., McIntyre-Smith, A., & Jaffe, P. G. (2003). The effects of children's exposure to domestic violence: A meta-analysis and critique. *Clinical Child and Family Psychology Review, 6,* 171–187. doi:10.1023/A:1024910416164

Yates, G. C., & Yates, S. M. (1990). Teacher effectiveness research: Towards describing user-friendly classroom instruction. *Educational Psychology, 10,* 225–238. doi:10.1080/0144341900100304

Zisser, A., & Eyberg, S. M. (2010). Parent–child interaction therapy. In J. R. Weisz & A. R. Kazdin (Eds.), *Evidence-based psychotherapies for children and adolescents* (2nd ed., pp. 179–193). New York, NY: Guilford Press.

Zonnevylle-Bender, M. J. S., Matthys, W., van de Wiel, N. M. H., & Lochman, J. (2007). Preventive effects of treatment of DBD in middle childhood on substance use and delinquent behavior. *Journal of the American Academy of Child & Adolescent Psychiatry, 46,* 33–39. doi:10.1097/01.chi.0000246051.53297.57

CHAPTER 7

SELF-CONTROL AND SUBSTANCE USE PREVENTION: A TRANSLATIONAL ANALYSIS

Thomas A. Wills, Jeffrey S. Simons, and Frederick X. Gibbons

This chapter examines the implications of self-regulation research for the prevention of early onset drug use. It outlines a dual-process approach to conceptualizing and assessing two regulation constructs that we term *self-control* and *dysregulation.* We summarize research that has related self-control or dysregulation measures to adolescent substance use and focus on both main effects and moderation effects. We also review available research that has implemented a self-control intervention and examined effects on outcome variables, including, but not limited to, smoking and alcohol use. We outline a translational model that suggests how to include self-regulation concepts in primary or secondary prevention programs. The chapter concludes with a discussion of several questions that could be addressed in further research on self-regulation and substance use prevention.

Recent research has shown the value of self-control concepts as an organizing factor for conceptualizing vulnerability or protection for substance use. The literature on adolescents now includes a number of studies that have found that measures of good self-control or poor regulation are related to early onset and progression of cigarette smoking (e.g., Audrain-McGovern, Rodriguez, Tercyak, Nenner, & Moss, 2006; Novak & Clayton, 2001), alcohol use (Brody & Ge, 2001; Patock-Peckham & Morgan-Lopez, 2006), or combined use of licit and illicit drugs (Gibbons et al., 2012; Wills, Walker, Mendoza, & Ainette, 2006). Several studies have also revealed that regulation measures predict substance use problems (e.g., Dvorak, Simons, & Wray, 2011; Simons, Carey, & Wills, 2009; Wills, Pokhrel, Morehouse, & Fenster, 2011). Research has shown that differences in regulation variables precede onset of substance use, both in human studies (e.g., Tarter et al., 2003; Wills, Ainette, et al., 2007) and in animal models (e.g., Belin, Mar, Dalley, Robbins, & Everitt, 2008; Dalley et al., 2007), thus indicating that the onset of use is attributable to premorbid influences.

Several different studies have shown that self-control can be modified. For example, training can improve basic executive functions in preschool children (Diamond & Lee, 2011), self-control training can reduce exam stress among college students (Oaten & Cheng, 2006a, 2006b), and a self-control training program can increase the likelihood of smoking cessation among adults (Muraven, 2010b). In addition, self-control has been indicated as a mechanism that mediates the impact of preventive programs for children (Raver et al., 2011; Ursache, Blair, & Raver, 2012) and dual-process concepts (described subsequently) have been incorporated in prevention program evaluations (Gerrard et al., 2006). These findings suggest that training in

Preparation of this chapter was supported by grants from the National Institute on Drug Abuse (R01 DA021856 and R01 DA021898) and the National Institute on Alcohol Abuse and Alcoholism (R01 AA020519). The content of this chapter is solely the responsibility of the authors and does not necessarily represent the official views of the National Institute on Drug Abuse or the National Institute on Alcohol Abuse and Alcoholism.

http://dx.doi.org/10.1037/14550-008
Handbook of Adolescent Drug Use Prevention: Research, Intervention Strategies, and Practice, L. M. Scheier (Editor)

self-control is a potentially valuable tool for drug prevention programs. Because of the significant translational potential, the need exists to explore in detail the implications of self-control concepts for prevention research.

SELF-REGULATION THEORY AS A CONCEPTUAL BRIDGE

Self-regulation theory provides a conceptual bridge that links early temperament characteristics known to predict substance use over considerable time intervals to complex self-control characteristics in adolescence and adulthood (e.g., Moffitt et al., 2011; Wills, Sandy, & Yaeger, 2000). Self-control abilities continue to develop throughout adolescence (Steinberg, 2008; Wills & Dishion, 2004), and research has shown that measures of good self-control and poor regulation are related to several proximal risk and protective factors for substance use or abuse (e.g., Simons et al., 2009; Wills et al., 2013). Thus, adolescence is a developmentally appropriate time for implementing prevention programs that incorporate these concepts. Moreover, self-regulation theory ties developmental neuroscience and social–cognitive research (Gibbons, Gerrard, & Lane, 2003; Lieberman, 2007) with research on the etiology and prevention of addictive behaviors (Perry & Carroll, 2008; Wills & Ainette, 2010).

DUAL-PROCESS THEORY AND THE TWO DOMAINS OF REGULATION PROCESSES

Dual-process theory posits that two distinct systems for processing information exist (e.g., see Gerrard, Gibbons, Houlihan, Stock, & Pomery, 2008; Hofmann, Friese, & Strack, 2009). One system, which in cognitive research is generally termed *rational, analytic*, or *cold cognition*, is based on conscious processing of relevant information and systematic consideration of risks and benefits; this approach is deliberative, takes time, and requires cognitive effort. The other system, generally termed *associative, heuristic*, or *hot cognition*, is largely automatic and is based more on simple judgmental heuristics and reactions to images rather than conscious reflection, an approach that is quick and more spontaneous in nature. The dual-process approach, which has been extended to health behavior research, posits that some behaviors related to substance use occur more through deliberative decision making, whereas other behaviors occur because of reactions to situations and reward orientations that a person may not be able to fully articulate (Gibbons, Houlihan, & Gerrard, 2009; Houben, Schoenmakers, & Wiers, 2010; Wiers et al., 2007).

Our research program is based on the proposition that complex self-control attributes, as they exist in adolescence, develop from a substrate of simple temperament characteristics in early childhood involving reactivity and regulation (e.g., Barkley, 1997; Rothbart, Ahadi, & Evans, 2000; Tarter et al., 1999). The *regulation domain* is grounded in four basic cognitive executive functions that are believed to underlie the development of more complex self-control abilities: focusing attention, updating representations in working memory, shifting between mental representations (cognitive flexibility), and inhibiting a prepotent response. The *reactivity domain* is based on emotional and reward-oriented systems involved in responses to stimuli and reactions to situations. With cognitive and social maturation, these temperament dimensions broaden in scope and complexity (Willem, Bijttebier, & Claes, 2010; Wills et al., 2000) to comprise two domains of correlated attributes: self-control and dysregulation (Dvorak et al., 2011; Pearson, Kite, & Henson, 2013; Wills et al., 2013).[1]

Properties of the Two Domains of Regulation

Measures of the two regulation domains have been developed through confirmatory analyses (e.g., Wills et al., 2001, 2006; Wills, Resko, Ainette, & Mendoza, 2004) that have tested the role of multiple indicators for hypothesized underlying constructs. Figure 7.1 shows that a latent construct for *self-control* is measured by indicators that tap information gathering, decision making, and problem solving (Kendall & Williams, 1982; Scheier & Botvin, 1995; Wills,

[1]In neuroscience theory focusing on problem behavior, these have been termed the *reflective* and *impulsive systems* (Bickel et al., 2007) or the *cognitive-control* and *socioemotional systems* (Steinberg, 2008).

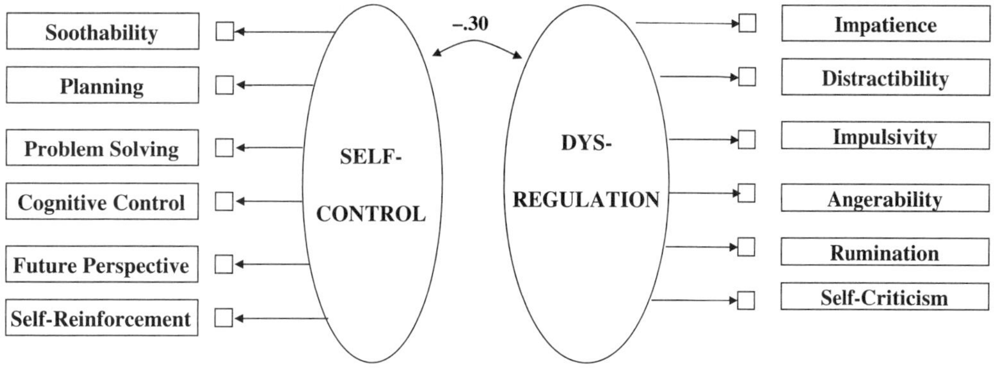

FIGURE 7.1. Schematic measurement model for constructs of self-control and dysregulation. Ovals represent latent constructs; squares, observed variables. Line with single-headed arrow indicates loading of observed variable on underlying construct; curved double-headed arrow indicates covariance of latent constructs.

McNamara, Vaccaro, & Hirky, 1996); delay of gratification (Shoda, Mischel, & Peake, 1990); linking behaviors and consequences over time, or future time perspective (Barkley, 1997; Zimbardo & Boyd, 1999); and reinforcing oneself for appropriate progress toward a goal, or self-reinforcement (Heiby, 1983). A latent construct for *dysregulation* is measured by indicators that tap attention problems and distractibility; a tendency to act without thinking, or impulsiveness; reactivity to situational cues, or present orientation; and an attraction to immediate rewards with discounting of alternative rewards in the future, or delay discounting (Eysenck & Eysenck, 1978; Kendall & Williams, 1982; Madden & Bickel, 2010; Zimbardo & Boyd, 1999).[2]

The two domains of regulation measured by these indicators are inversely related but moderately correlated, and make independent contributions to outcomes. This conclusion is supported by findings that, across studies, have indicated that the average correlation of self-control and dysregulation constructs is around $r = -.30$, and by multivariate analyses that have shown that the two constructs make independent contributions to other variables that constitute pathways in risk or protection for substance use (e.g., Pearson et al., 2013; Wills et al., 2011, 2013). The finding of a moderate inverse correlation indicates that the domains are bidimensional, not unidimensional, so a high score on self-control does not necessarily mean a low score on dysregulation. Initial studies had focused on behavioral regulation, but research has also included measures of emotional self-control based on sadness control and anger control (Southam-Gerow, 2013; Zeman, Shipman, & Penza-Clyve, 2001) and measures of emotional dysregulation based on indicators of angerability and affective lability (Simons & Carey, 2006; Wills et al., 2006). Behavioral and emotional regulation tend to be correlated (Wills et al., 2011), which suggests they are rooted in a common core of temperament attributes (Rothbart et al., 2000; Wills et al., 2000).

Research on Effects of Self-Control

In this section, we summarize research on regulation and substance use with a focus on studies of particular relevance to the theme of this chapter. Examples of the studies reviewed are included in Table 7.1. The review is selective because we could not cover all the studies that have related some kind of self-regulation measure to an index of substance use (see Lejuez et al., 2010; Perry & Carroll, 2008).

[2] Other types of regulation measures have been used. In addition to neuropsychological measures of attention or inhibition, these other types include generalized measures, such as the Barratt Impulsiveness Inventory and the Humphrey Scale, and specific performance measures such as Bechara's gambling task or Lejuez's balloon analogue task (see Lejuez et al., 2010; Perry & Carroll, 2008). Although these measures have shown correlations with substance use, the trait measures are unipolar and the performance measures typically do not correlate well with each other (see Reynolds, Ortengren, Richards, & de Wit, 2006). Thus, it is difficult to know which are most relevant for a dual-process model; our discussion is focused on research in which measures of self-control and dysregulation were included in the same study.

TABLE 7.1

Studies on Main Effects for Self-Control and Dysregulation Constructs

Citation	Sample (*N*), age	Measure(s)	Findings
Wills & Stoolmiller (2002)	1,526, 11–15 years	Latent constructs	Higher SC → less initiation Dysreg → more initiation, escalation
Wills, Murry, et al. (2007)	670, 11.2 years	Latent constructs	Higher SC → more academic competence, favorable perceptions of abstainers Dysreg → more deviance-prone attitudes
Griffin, Scheier, Acevedo, Grenard, & Botvin (2012)	692, 15–23 years	Kendall-Wilcox	Higher SC → high probability of being in low-risk (drinking/sex) group
Audrain-McGovern et al. (2009)	947, 15–20 years	Delay discounting	Higher discounting prospectively related to uptake of smoking
Simons, Maisto, & Wray (2010)	621, 20.2 years	Planfulness, impulsivity	Planning inversely related to sexual risk behavior, impulsiveness positively related to risk behavior
Shin, Hong, & Wills (2012)	6,337, 12–21 years	Distractibility	Child maltreatment → More distractibility Distractibility → More binge drinking
Simons, Gaher, Oliver, Bush, & Palmer (2005)	731, 20.2 years	Impulsivity, affective lability	Impulsivity → More alcohol problems Lability → coping motives → alcohol use
Piehler, Véronneau, & Dishion (2012)	997, 16–23 years	Attention/inhibition	Effortful control prospectively predicted fewer marijuana problems
Pearson, Kite, & Henson (2013)	278, college students	Latent constructs	Higher self-control → More use of drinking-protective strategies Dysreg → More alcohol use (direct)
Wills, Pokhrel, Morehouse, & Fenster (2011)	1,307, 16.0 years	Latent constructs	Behavioral SC → More academic competence Behavioral dysreg → More negative life events, deviant affiliations, substance problems Emotional dysreg → More negative events, substance problems (direct)
Isasi & Wills (2011)	1,771, 13.9 years	Latent constructs	Higher SC → More self-efficacy, fruit/vegetable intake, vigorous physical activity Dysreg → More junk food, sedentary behavior

Note. → = is related to; dysreg = dysregulation; SC = self-control.

Main Effects of Self-Control

Independent contributions to substance use. Self-control is inversely related to substance use, an observation that has been made for tobacco, alcohol, and marijuana. Multivariate analyses have shown that measures of dysregulation are independently, positively related to the onset and escalation of substance, and other types of risk behavior (e.g., Simons, Maisto, & Wray, 2010). Substantial changes in self-control may occur during adolescence for part of the population, and these changes are related to adolescents' substance use. For example, Wills and Stoolmiller (2002) found that an increase in good self-control was inversely related to change in adolescent substance use, whereas an increase in dysregulation was related to progression of use (cf. Hustad, Carey, Carey, & Maisto, 2009; King, Fleming, Monahan, & Catalano, 2011). Griffin, Scheier, Acevedo, Grenard, and Botvin (2012) used latent class analysis to examine relations of self-control to high-risk drinking and sexual behavior in a cohort of females. The authors found that a higher level of self-control in ninth grade differentiated a group with lower behavioral risk in young adulthood from a high-risk (drinking/sexual activity) group.

Mediated effects. Relations of self-control with substance use tend to be indirect ones that are mediated through other factors. The most common indirect pathway for good self-control is through higher levels of academic competence, which then is protective against involvement in substance use (cf. McClelland et al., 2007). Wills, Murry, et al. (2007) observed this pathway in a sample of younger African American adolescents and observed a pathway through more positive perceptions of abstainers from substance use. Dysregulation tends to be related to more negative life events and affiliation with deviant peers, which are risk factors for substance use (e.g., Wills et al., 2011). Behavioral and emotional dysregulation may also be related to positive perceptions of substance users and/or negative perceptions of abstainers (Wills et al., 2013). Isasi and Wills (2011) examined self-control and several health-related outcomes in an inner-city sample of adolescents. The authors found that self-control was related to a healthier pattern of dietary intake and higher levels of vigorous physical activity, whereas dysregulation was related to more junk food intake and higher levels of sedentary activity; effects for self-control were mediated through self-efficacy, whereas dysregulation had direct effects to outcomes (cf. Miller, Barners, & Beaver, 2011; Riggs, Spruijt-Metz, Sakuma, Chou, & Pentz, 2010).

Parenting and self-control. Several studies have suggested that family variables are an important influence on an individual's level of self-control (Wills & Bantum, 2012). For example, Wills, Resko, et al. (2004) found that the protective effect of parental support on adolescent substance use was mediated through a path from parental support to adolescents' self-control. Self-control, in turn, was related to higher academic competence, which represented the main protective pathway in that sample (e.g., Brody et al., 2005). In contrast, the development of dysregulation has been related to early adversity and child maltreatment. For example, Shin, Hong, and Wills (2012) found that an effect of early child abuse/neglect on binge drinking in adolescence was mediated through a path to an index of distractibility and inattentiveness, which then was related to heavy drinking.

Prediction of substance use problems. Regulation constructs have consistently been linked to substance use problems. For example, Piehler, Vérronneau, and Dishion (2012) found that a construct for self-control assessed in adolescence predicted less problem marijuana use at age 23. Simons, Gaher, Oliver, Bush, and Palmer (2005) found that emotional dysregulation was related to greater endorsement of coping motives for alcohol use, and motives then had a direct effect to more alcohol problems in a sample of college-age youth. In contrast, dysregulation had a direct effect to more alcohol problems that were not mediated through motives or level of use, findings that are similar to those by Pearson et al. (2013). Wills et al. (2011) found that behavioral self-control had an indirect protective effect for adolescent substance problems through higher academic competence and a lower level of substance use. Independently, behavioral dysregulation had indirect risk effects on problems through relations to more negative life events and more affiliation with deviant peers.

Social influences on self-regulation. A program of research with African American families has shown that racial discrimination is related to higher levels of substance use among parents and among children (Gibbons, Gerrard, Cleveland, Wills, & Brody, 2004). A recent study (Gibbons et al., 2012) focused on how discrimination acts as a constant stressor that erodes self-control ability. Results from a longitudinal field study showed that experiences with discrimination over the period 10–18 years were related to reductions in self-control, which resulted in increased levels of substance use. A laboratory study showed that imagined experiences of discrimination increased the accessibility of substance-related cognitions, especially for people low in self-control. A longitudinal study by Evans, Fuller-Rowell, and Doan (2012) found that the effect of social stress on weight gain was mediated by reduced delay of gratification. That research showed how experiences with the larger social system have implications for self-control.

Moderation Effects for Self-Control

Although main effects for self-control have been studied extensively, less attention has been paid to moderation effects. Table 7.2 showcases a few recent studies that have focused on this issue and shown buffering effects for self-control and vulnerability effects for dysregulation.

TABLE 7.2

Studies of Moderation Effects for Self-Control and Dysregulation Measures

Citation	Sample (*N*), age	Measure(s)	Findings
Wills, Sargent, Stoolmiller, Gibbons, & Gerrard (2008)	1,766, 11–15 years	Latent constructs	Higher SC: Less effect of negative life events, deviant peer affiliations on substance use
Gardner, Dishion, & O'Connell (2008)	803, 17–19 years	Attention, inhibition	Higher SC: Less effect of deviant peers on antisocial behavior index
Simons & Carey (2006)	823, 19.9 years	Impulsivity, affective lability	Higher dysreg: More effect of alcohol consumption on alcohol problems
Simons, Carey, & Wills (2009)	2,270, 19.6 years	Latent construct	Higher dysreg: More effect of alcohol consumption on alcohol abuse symptoms
Simons, Gaher, Oliver, Bush, & Palmer (2005)	56, 21.5 years	Impulsiveness (Eysenck)	Higher impulsiveness: More effect of daily negative affect, daily alcohol consumption on alcohol-related problems
Simons, Dvorak, et al. (2010)	102, 20.3 years	Impulsiveness (urgency)	Higher impulsiveness: More effect of daytime anxiety on nighttime intoxication
Fox, Bergquist, Gu, & Sinha (2010)	130, 33.4 years	Impulsiveness (Barratt)	Higher impulsiveness: More effect of life stress on problem drinking
Pearson, D'Lima, & Kelley (2011)	195, 18–19 years	Composite score	Higher SC: Less effect of parental alcoholism on offspring alcohol problems
Brody, Kogan, Chen, & Murry (2008)	667, 11.2 years	Composite (Humphrey)	Lower SC: More change in intervention-targeted youth protective behaviors

Note. dysreg = dysregulation; SC = self-control.

Buffering effects for self-control. Wills et al. (2008) studied a cohort of elementary school youth through high school. A higher level of self-control reduced the impact of negative life events and deviant peer affiliations on change in adolescents' substance use. A longitudinal study by Gardner, Dishion, and Connell (2008) found that the impact of affiliating with deviant peers on a composite index of antisocial behavior was reduced among individuals who scored higher on a composite indexing attention, persistence, and behavioral inhibition. A study of college students (Pearson, D'Lima, & Kelley, 2011) found that an overall statistical relation between parental alcohol status and students' alcohol problems was reduced considerably among students who reported a higher level of self-control.

Vulnerability effects for dysregulation. Several studies have demonstrated that dysregulation increases the impact of risk factors. For example, with a sample of college youth, Simons and Carey (2006) found that impulsivity moderated the association between level of alcohol use and number of alcohol-related problems, thus increasing the strength of the association. A subsequent study using latent-variable methods showed that a higher level of dysregulation increased the relation of alcohol consumption to abuse (but not dependence) symptoms; also, dysregulation increased the path from affective lability to abuse symptoms (Simons et al., 2009). Fox, Bergquist, Gu, and Sinha (2010), with a sample of adult regular drinkers, found that the impact of life stress on hazardous drinking patterns, as assessed by the Alcohol Use Disorders Identification Test, was greater among people who scored higher on the Barratt Impulsiveness Scale. Using an implicit measure of alcohol motivation, Farris, Ostafin, and Palfai (2010) found that distractibility increased the relation between alcohol motivation and hazardous drinking scores.

Moderation effects for daily drinking. Simons et al. (2005) conducted an experience sampling study with college students who were moderate drinkers. The students completed daily assessments of mood states and drinking behavior for 14 days. Impulsiveness was related to higher levels of alcohol problems in general. Moreover, the relations of daily negative affect and daily level of alcohol consumption with alcohol problems were stronger for people with higher levels of impulsivity. In a second study that used a 28-day study period (Simons, Dvorak, Batien, & Wray, 2010), a particular index of impulsiveness (negative urgency) increased the effect of anxiety during the day on drinking behavior and intoxication at night.

Differential intervention effects. Self-control was examined in the context of a family-based intervention study for prevention of early substance use and sexual risk behavior among African American adolescents (Brody, Kogan, Chen, & Murry, 2008). The intervention had a significant effect on a composite of youth protective behaviors among participants who initially scored lower on self-control as measured by the Humphrey scale. The intervention had little effect on people who were initially high on self-control, thus suggesting that they were well-functioning to begin with.

STUDIES OF SELF-CONTROL TRAINING

Investigators have recently begun to test intervention approaches to self-regulation, usually with the intent of enhancing aspects of self-control. Because this is a diverse group of studies, we summarize in the following section the ones most relevant to the chapter.

Mediation of School-Based Intervention Effects

Raver et al. (2011) examined how self-control was involved in mediating the impact of a school-based intervention program conducted with 4-year-olds in Head Start programs. The intervention was designed to enhance self-control through the provision of clear rules and routines and the provision of rewards for self-regulated behavior. Results from a randomized trial based on a standardized battery of regulation tasks (e.g., attention, impulse control, executive functions) showed that an intervention effect on academic performance was mediated through improvements in attention skills and improvements in executive functions.

Ursache et al. (2012) discussed mediation findings that were demonstrated in two other programs: the Promoting Alternative THinking Strategies curriculum (Riggs, Greenberg, Kusche, & Pentz, 2006) and the Tools curriculum (Diamond, Barnett, Thomas, & Munro, 2007). The Tools curriculum was based on the Vygotskian approach, in which children learn regulation by cooperatively planning out scenarios and acting them out according to the rules they had chosen to govern the story and the characters. Both programs have shown favorable program effects on academic performance, and, in a few cases on classroom environment, through improvements in children's self-regulation.

Cognitive Training Programs

Diamond and Lee (2011) discussed several approaches to enhancing self-control among young children in school-based contexts through cognitive and sometimes physical training. Computerized training to improve working memory with programs such as Cogmed has shown significant effects. Classroom-based interventions that approach self-control training through social pretend-play exercises, in which children learn rule-guided behavior through role-playing, have shown the most generalized effects, because the training becomes integrated into the classroom throughout the school year. Training in the traditional martial arts that emphasizes discipline and self-control (e.g., tae kwon do) has been shown to improve several indices of executive functions among 8- to 10-year-olds, as have programs using mindfulness meditation (Greenberg & Harris, 2012; Tang, Lu, Fan, Yang, & Posner, 2012; Tang, Yang, Leve, & Harold, 2012).

The neurological basis of laboratory training for improving cognitive executive functions among children, adolescents, and adults was discussed by Bryck and Fisher (2012). The typical approach was to use computer-based training with speeded choices targeted on a specific executive function. These studies showed that significant improvement in executive functions can be obtained with such programs and that some enhancement was observed for all four of the aforementioned functions, including working memory and attentional focusing. However, critiques have pointed to some limitations associated with these studies (e.g., Owen et al., 2010; Shipstead, Redick, & Engle, 2012). For instance, only a few studies have examined long-term retention of the training effects. In addition, the extent to which laboratory training on a specific task (e.g., working memory) will generalize to other tasks or settings is still not well understood. Nevertheless, intervention to strengthen self-control ability through executive functions enhancement is viewed as a promising approach because it has a plausible theoretical basis from knowledge about brain development (Berkman, Graham, & Fisher, 2012). Further research is currently proceeding in several directions to examine the robustness of laboratory training effects and their retention over time.

Self-Control Training for Health Behaviors

Oaten and Cheng (2006a, 2006b, 2007) focused on self-control training for college students during stressful exam periods. One study that examined academic skills had training in goal-setting and self-monitoring of study time, and external deadlines to improve discipline in preparation for exams. Visual aids provided feedback about any discrepancies between goals and behavior, and state assessments of self-control were obtained through a computerized visual tracking task performed under interference. Results from Oaten and Cheng (2006a) showed improvement in study time and in collateral behaviors, such as less smoking, perceived stress, and unhealthy eating. A second study that focused on physical exercise (Oaten & Cheng, 2006b) showed increases in the frequency and intensity of physical activity. A study focused on financial monitoring (Oaten & Cheng, 2007) also showed improvement in targeted behaviors (e.g., more savings). In these studies, the laboratory assessment of self-control showed improvement in the experimental group but deterioration in the control group. Riggs, Kobayakawa-Sakuma, and Pentz (2007) tested a curriculum for elementary school students in which intervention components focused on eating situations. The curriculum used both visual aids, such as a red/yellow light system (e.g., Tominey & McClelland, 2011) and group exercises dealing with food choices. Results showed that the experimental group increased their scores on a multidimensional inventory assessing attitudes toward self-regulation of eating behavior, so the findings have implications for obesity prevention.

Muraven (2010a) developed a self-control training paradigm to assist smoking cessation. Participants were instructed to practice self-control each day over a 2-week period by either avoiding sweet foods or squeezing a handgrip for as long as possible on several trials. The rationale was that either task requires the individual to override or inhibit a prepotent response, so regularly practicing small acts that involve inhibiting thoughts, moods, or urges should generalize to other larger tasks that require self-control. In the smoking cessation study (Muraven, 2010b), adult clients enrolled in a smoking cessation program first completed self-control training or a control training paradigm over a 14-day period. They then made a cessation effort on a target date and were followed for a 4-week period. The self-control training period and the cessation period were monitored through interactive voice response telephone reporting. Results from survival analyses showed that clients who received the self-control training showed a significantly longer abstinence time. In absolute terms, the self-control training doubled the odds of being abstinent at the end of the study period.

Self-Control Training and Aggressive Behavior

Finkel, DeWall, Slotter, Oaten, and Foshee (2009) conducted an experimental study designed to strengthen self-control and examine its implications in the interpersonal partner violence context. Similar to methods used by Muraven (2010a), training conducted over a 2-week period involved either a physical regulation task (using the nondominant hand to perform daily activities) or a verbal regulation task (following grammatical rules to achieve better expression in sentences). Participants in the experimental and control conditions then completed a questionnaire on their projected responses toward a partner in various provocation situations. Results showed that participants who received either of the self-control interventions had less inclination to use aggression under conditions of provocation. In a subsequent study, Denson, Capper, Oaten, Friese, and Schofield (2011) enrolled participants in a similar training program and then placed them in a situation in which they received provocation from another student (an experimental confederate). Results showed that dispositional aggression was related to retaliation against the confederate among people in the control condition, but in the experimental condition, dispositional aggression was unrelated to aggressive behavior (i.e., a buffering effect of training).

A SELF-CONTROL TRAINING MODEL FOR PREVENTION

A substantial base of evidence has indicated that self-control is related to substance use, and studies are beginning to evaluate training programs for enhancing self-control. The existing research indicates that self-control training can result in at least short-term improvements in self-regulation among children and adults. Although study designs are limited in some ways, these programs have demonstrated favorable program effects on a number of health-related outcomes, including smoking, exercise, and diet, thus creating an opportunity for researchers to use concepts from successful training programs to examine potential influences on substance use trajectories.

In this section, we outline how previous research examining self-control regulatory processes can be translated into workable prevention programs. We refer to *programs* because there may be no single approach that is best for all ages and stages of substance use. We first present a heuristic model of substance use prevention and then discuss crucial issues for how such programs can be developed and evaluated, with an emphasis on the implications of the dual-process framework for program design.

Our theoretical approach to a translational prevention program is outlined in Figure 7.2 and uses the multiple pathways for self-control constructs that have been demonstrated in prior research. The goal of the program design is to modify aspects of regulation constructs that are related to proximal risk or protective factors for substance use. So, one aspect that is focused on planfulness (Training Approach A) can target aspects of behavioral self-control that are strongly related to academic competence, a protective factor for substance use, and can target aspects of behavioral dysregulation that are related to negative life events and deviant peer affiliations, that is, risk factors for use. Another aspect that is focused on impulsiveness (Training Approach B) can be keyed to temptation situations

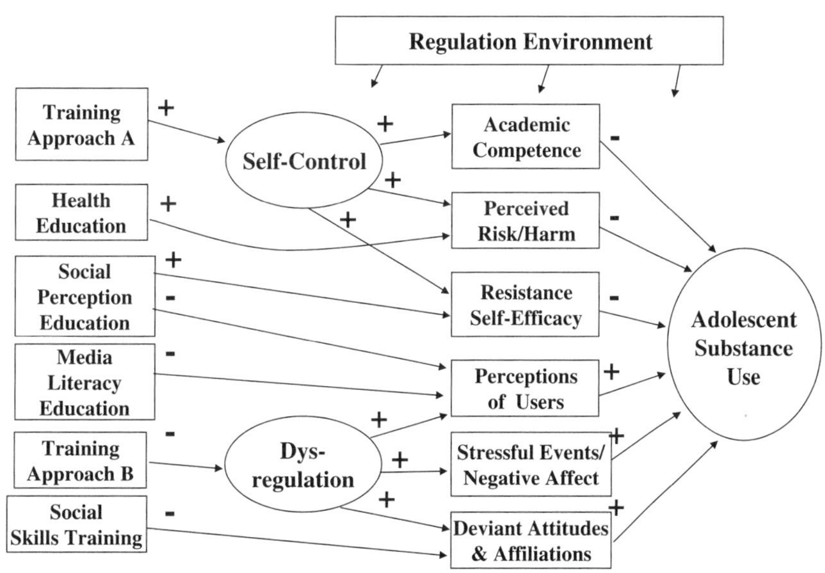

FIGURE 7.2. Heuristic model of the translational prevention approach. Rectangles at the left side of the figure represent program components; ovals represent regulation constructs influenced by program; rectangles near the right side of the figure represent mediators of program effects on substance use. Arrows from regulation constructs to mediators represent pathways for effects of self-control or dysregulation. Training Approach A = focus on planfulness, Training Approach B = focus on impulsiveness.

to strengthen efficacy for dealing with explicit or implicit pressures to smoke and drink, and aspects of dysregulation that increase the likelihood of particular negative events (e.g., talking back to teachers; Sussman, McCuller, & Dent, 2003).

The self-control components would be sequenced to gain maximal leverage from other components (Hansen & Altman, 2000) and the intervention would ideally be embedded in a school environment that encourages and rewards appropriate self-control (Diamond & Lee, 2011), using obvious visual cues (Tominey & McClelland, 2011) or more subtle environmental modifications that encourage people to direct their behavior in healthier directions (see Bennhold, 2013; Thaler & Sunstein, 2008). The present approach is based on a training model with individuals but could be extended to include parent-training components (Brody et al., 2006; Gerrard et al., 2006); this is a potentially important extension because families are a major source of influence on the development of self-control.

The program design model includes other components shown to be useful in evidence-based prevention programs (see Skara & Sussman, 2003) and that may not overlap with the effects of regulation constructs. It is essential to include an educational component that emphasizes imparting correct knowledge about the health effects of substances and their potential risks. The program design model also includes a component to correct common myths about substances that encourage initiation or deter cessation (Sussman & Ames, 2008). Components for modifying cognitive perceptions about the prevalence of substance use (commonly overestimated by adolescents) and perceptions of teens who smoke and drink (typically ambivalent among younger adolescents) also are essential for preventing early onset of use (see Gerrard et al., 2006). Because the media is a source of positive images of substance users, components for increasing resistance to the often subtle influences on smoking and drinking from movies and advertising are desirable (e.g., Wills, Sargent, Stoolmiller, Gibbons, & Gerrard, 2008). Components for enhancing social skills that are generally useful for teen social situations have been included in programs such as Life Skills Training and Toward No Drug Abuse (Skara & Sussman, 2003). Prior research has shown that regulation constructs are related to some of these variables but are not the sole influence on them (see, e.g., Wills, Murry, et al., 2007; Wills et al., 2013), so multiple modes of intervention are likely to increase and possibly synergize each other's effects.

This prevention approach assumes that modifying self-regulation will take time and effort, and will involve (depending on the age) a combination of computerized training and testing, cognitive–behavioral instruction and modeling, and small-group exercises to deal with social aspects of self-control. As discussed subsequently, implicit training procedures may be useful to deal with information processing biases and automatic approach motivations (Stacy & Wiers, 2010). The theoretical goal is to alter the way in which teens think about problems, in which they make decisions in emotionally neutral (cold) and emotionally-loaded (hot) situations, and in which they interact with peers who may be trying to tempt or provoke them. The intervention approaches can draw on the prevention literature on decision making and problem solving (e.g., Sussman et al., 2004) and on clinical literature on anger management and emotion regulation (e.g., Siegel, 2010; Southam-Gerow, 2013). The goal of an integrated prevention program is to have effects on participants' cognitive beliefs, perceptions of their own efficacy, and ability to use self-control skills across a variety of situations. Studies using this kind of prevention model should be designed to include tests for the generalizability of training effects and their durability over time.

The intervention targets are directly suggested by the measures of regulation constructs as used in previous research. Although that research has tended to view self-control simply as inhibition of impulses, findings from the confirmatory analyses have shown that regulation-related constructs are measured by a range of indicators. For example, indicators used to assess behavioral self-control assess planning, problem solving, time perspective, and delay of gratification. Each measure has a theoretical background and a set of items that provide targets for cognitions and behaviors to be modified. For poor regulation, items that assess impulsiveness, distractibility, and present orientation also provide intervention targets, and both types of items can serve as a basis for the evaluation of intervention effects. Whether behavioral regulation or emotional regulation should be emphasized is still a question, but current data have suggested the two approaches complement each other. Therefore, enhancement of emotional regulation skills should produce some improvement in self-regulation of behavior in addition to behavioral regulation training (see Wills et al., 2011, 2013).

ISSUES FOR PREVENTION PROGRAM DEVELOPMENT

Several issues about the development and implementation of prevention programs based on self-control concepts remain to be clarified in further research. In this section, we discuss issues that are most germane to the theoretical approach we have outlined.

Age Differences in Targets and Methods

Adolescence is characterized by rapid maturational changes relevant to self-regulation and rapid social–environmental changes relevant to substance use risk (Steinberg, 2008; Wills & Dishion, 2004). An important concern is to know more about what aspects of self-control training programs should target and precisely how these efforts can influence trajectories of key variables at different periods of development (see Bryck & Fisher, 2012; Tang, Yang, et al., 2012). Another valuable concern is how early interventions dealing with basic executive functions (Diamond & Lee, 2011) can dovetail with outcomes obtained from prevention programs delivered at later ages. Possibly, relatively small beneficial effects of an early training program can be amplified over time because of transactions between the individual and environment; that is, a small effect on initial status could translate to large effects over the developmental course. However, a question could be raised about whether effects of early training programs might be overwhelmed by the ongoing reorganization of adolescents' cognitive abilities and social environment. Both concerns are pressing and show how additional research is vitally needed to identify optimal periods for incorporating self-control training into substance use prevention.

Another question is the extent to which effects of self-control training programs vary as a function of motivational factors; that is, does self-control training matter more or less if the individual is motivated to use or abstain from drugs? One perspective, congruent with the mediation effects discussed earlier, is that good self-control promotes prosocial behavior and deters onset of use through higher academic involvement and lesser tendency to affiliate with disenfranchised peers. Alternatively, to the extent that self-control training improves inhibitory control and reduces coping motivations for drug use among current users, one may expect the effects to vary as a function of risk and motivation. This expectation would be consistent with some of the moderation effects discussed earlier that show effects primarily for people who score low on self-control. Research is needed that is directed to the primary prevention context, in which the great majority of the population has not engaged in risk behavior, and to secondary prevention contexts, in which the role of motivational factors among individuals using tobacco or alcohol with some regularity can be examined.

Another question for future research is the relative efficacy of programs that train basic executive functions (e.g., attention control) versus more complex characteristics (e.g., problem solving) that are particularly relevant for substance use in adolescence. One approach to this question would be to test training in executive functions itself as a method for preventing early onset of smoking or alcohol use. However, there may be a good rationale for studying whether adding training in executive functions enhances the outcome of an existing multimodal prevention program, such as Life Skills Training. The functions targeted in current cognitive training programs, such as improving working memory to link behaviors and consequences over time, have been suggested as the foundations of effective self-control. Thus, conducting computerized training as an add-on to an existing program for teaching complex psychosocial skills could result in greater retention and/or use of those skills. This kind of question could be tested within the context of ongoing prevention research. More generally, the issue is whether long-term programs can conduct interventions that target self-control at a current stage of development and change their approach as participants mature from childhood through adolescence. This issue raises the question of whether effects of training at one developmental period would generalize to effects at a later period.

Increasing Self-Control or Decreasing Impulsiveness: It's Not a Choice

Existing intervention studies have focused primarily on increasing self-control, for example, through training in executive functions (Bryck & Fisher, 2012; Diamond & Lee, 2011). Although done for a reason, from the dual-process model, it does not follow that a high level of self-control is equivalent to a low level of impulsiveness. Rather, this approach suggests that interventions should be designed to address both systems (see Figure 7.2). We have outlined several approaches to enhancing self-control, such as training in planning, self-monitoring, and systematic decision making (e.g., Oaten & Cheng, 2006a; Sussman et al., 2004). A different line of thinking suggests approaches designed to reduce dysregulation. Possibilities within the boundaries of current research include a minimal behavioral intervention, such as computerized training on a stop-signal task (Muraven, 2010a) or self-talk training to dampen emotional arousal and induce more delay in responding in potential conflict situations (Finkel et al., 2009). The emotion regulation literature may be useful in learning to identify and avoid triggers for impulsive responding or to design training based on the concept that, for some people, overreacting is a habit that is learned and, like other habits, can be unlearned (Siegel, 2010).

The dual-process prevention model raises a further question about whether self-control training would be most appropriate as a universal prevention strategy or as a secondary prevention approach targeted to higher risk youth. The only current precedent is the study by Brody et al. (2008), which found that a family-based intervention primarily had beneficial effects among youth who initially were low on self-control. However, that study leaves unclear whether a self-control training approach can net favorable findings across a range of self-control practices and with a heterogeneous sample of youth. Descriptive data are clear that self-control measures are normally distributed in the adolescent population, and the public health approach to prevention has had notable successes through the achievement of relatively small shifts in levels of risk factors throughout the general population. Answers to these questions can be obtained by using designs that test the relative impact of training programs on lower- and higher-risk youth.

Explicit Interventions for Implicit Cognitions?

Substance use prevention programs have almost invariably used intervention procedures that focused on explicit cognitions: reading instructional materials, listening to didactic lectures about skills, or following role-play instructions. Although these effects have an established record of success, some theorists have argued that substance use may be driven to a certain extent by automatic processes: motivations and approach tendencies of which people may not be entirely aware (see Stacy & Wiers, 2010; Wiers et al., 2007). This is an issue for all prevention programs, but particularly for a dual-process approach, which posits that substance use may be influenced not only by the reasoned (conscious) system but also by the reactive (less conscious) system. In theory, a prevention program based on a dual-process approach should also be trying to address implicit cognitions (De Houwer, 2006).

Although less attention has been paid to training procedures using implicit cognition concepts, one research group has developed a procedure to decrease alcohol motivation based on an evaluative conditioning approach (Houben et al., 2010; Wiers et al., 2011). It is assumed that an action that pulls something toward the self activates automatic approach cognitions, whereas an action that pushes something away from the self activates avoidance cognitions. On this assumption, a study was conducted with alcoholic patients. Some participants were given a joystick with instructions to push it away from themselves when pictures of alcohol were presented and to pull it toward themselves when pictures of soft drinks were presented. After the patients received treatment, a posttest was administered using both implicit and explicit measures. Results indicated that patients in an alcohol avoidance training group had more negative attitudes about alcohol and better clinical outcomes at a 1-year follow-up. An alternative procedure was to pair alcohol cues with one arm of a go/no-go task. This approach strengthened response inhibition and reduced drinking behavior at a 1-week follow-up (Houben, Nederkoorn, Wiers, & Jansen, 2011); it provides an experimental paradigm for procedures to deal with a stronger reward orientation that has been suggested as a factor in risk for substance use among impulsive people (Dawe & Loxton, 2004).

An alternative approach involves targeting attention biases for positive versus negative emotional stimuli. It has long been suggested that affective disorders such as anxiety and depression are grounded in an implicit bias for negative information, and recent training studies for cognitive bias modification (CBM) have aimed to change attentional biases toward positive stimuli (Hallion & Ruscio, 2011). For example, attention bias is altered in a computer-delivered task by placing a visual probe, to which the participant must respond, behind either a positive or a negative stimulus. If the probe differentially appears in the location of the positive stimulus, a habit of directing attention toward positive stimuli is encouraged. Several studies have shown that CBM paradigms improve affect and reduce risk for depression (Hertel & Mathews, 2011). Interestingly, experimental studies have indicated that CBM training is more effective when emotional stimuli are presented as faces rather than as words (Browning, Holmes, Charles, Cowen, & Harmer, 2012); this finding suggests that the training is working through the heuristic (image-based) pathway, rather than the analytic processing pathway. In addition, the results suggest that CBM procedures could be used to reduce levels of negative affect and increase levels of positive affect, which would serve indirectly to decrease risk for substance use (Colder, Chassin, Lee, Villalta, & Kassel, 2010). An attractive pragmatic aspect is that CBM training procedures can be delivered on smartphones or tablets; therefore, if necessary, a participant could receive intervention 7 days a week.

Transition From Use to Abuse

Although a proportion of the young adult population is vulnerable to substance abuse, the empirical correlation between level of substance use and number of substance-related problems (e.g., fighting, reckless driving) is generally moderate, meaning that some people are susceptible to abuse symptoms at lower levels of use (Simons et al., 2009). Self-control attributes have been suggested as an important factor in the relation between use and abuse, either through main effects or moderation effects (Dvorak et al., 2011; Simons et al., 2009; Wills, Sandy, & Yaeger, 2002). Self-control training may be considered as a secondary prevention approach for those at risk for substance use problems because of frequent consumption or a family history of substance abuse.

Determining what aspects of regulation processes are most relevant for preventing the transition from substance use to substance abuse is a topic of ongoing research, and few studies of self-control have been conducted at the daily level, where most of the variance in drinking occurs (Simons, Dvorak, et al., 2010; Simons, Wills, & Neal, 2014). People who score higher on good self-control may be better able to anticipate, and possibly avoid, problem situations (Wills et al., 2011), and evidence suggests that they use more protective strategies in drinking situations (Pearson et al., 2013). This finding suggests that training in reasoned approaches that are focused on identifying temptation situations and preparing alternative responses for such situations could be useful for deterring substance use problems. However, this approach could be more effective for people with relatively good self-control, who are less likely to get into such situations because they are more discerning in their choice of companions and/or have more alternative activities available that do not involve high rates of drinking or other substance use (Wills et al., 2011). Training approaches for more impulsive people would address that they are more reactive to situations, experience higher levels of negative emotions, and may be distracted from their original goals by intoxication and by influence from peer modeling of binge drinking behaviors. For such people, explicit training to enhance self-monitoring and resistance to social influences could be combined with implicit training to reduce the effect of automatic motivations for drinking (e.g., Sharbanee et al., 2013).

Will Self-Control Training Reduce Spontaneity and Intuitive Insight?

A possible concern about self-control training is that overreliance on the analytic system will lose the advantages of the associative system. In this scenario, self-control training could produce rigid, overcontrolled people who are not using their ability to react intuitively and spontaneously to situations, and no longer take the kinds of risks that will result in novel inventions and creative social systems. Indeed, one of the most striking aspects of psychological research is studies of the behavior of experts who can achieve complex intellectual or physical performances quickly and seemingly without effort (Gladwell, 2005). Existential psychologists have also emphasized how creativity and happiness arise from the spontaneous flow of activity (Csikszentmihalyi, 1996). Certainly, many positive benefits result from the ability to work intuitively and spontaneously. A valid concern also exists regarding risk taking, because adolescence is a time of experimentation and increasing independence. To the extent that improved self-control predicts social competence, this may increase age-appropriate experimentation (including with substances) and might not be an entirely unexpected outcome (Wills, Forbes, & Gibbons, 2014). No educator would want to design a system that discourages students from taking risks, and noted scientists have described how breakthroughs came from the recognition that they had the freedom to throw away the textbook and strike out in a new direction (see, e.g., Watson, 1968).

Although a complete discussion of this issue is beyond the scope of this chapter, we point out that the kind of impulsive behavior discussed as a risk factor is spontaneous but disorganized. The measures of good self-control described here show that planning and thought for the future are consistently related to psychological well-being, whereas poor regulation is related to higher levels of depression and anxiety (Simons et al., 2014). Indeed, the essence of fruitless risk taking is that it is based entirely on a reaction to the current situation, with little thought given to the consequences (see Steinberg, 2008). Hence, we would emphasize that the intuitive performances of expert artists and scientists are based on long years of disciplined training and practice. For example, Herrigel (1999) described how his training in archery eventually produced an "artless art" that flowed spontaneously, but not without years of coaching and discipline from a mentor. Similar experiences occur every day for musicians, dancers, and writers who go through years of practice, practice, and more practice to achieve what seems to the audience like an effortless performance. The key to such training is the support and motivation to persist at disciplined training to acquire complex skills that flow almost automatically. Another example is from research on mindfulness training, which shows how such training improves both behavioral and emotional regulation (Chiesa, Serretti, & Jakobsen, 2013; Greenberg & Harris, 2012; Keng, Smoski, & Robins, 2011). Therefore, improving self-control through discipline and organization does not imply that all spontaneity and intuition will be diminished; the evidence suggests the contrary. So, we do not see that training in self-control has a high risk of producing inhibited, overcontrolled people, but evaluation studies should include measures to examine for this possibility.

References

Audrain-McGovern, J., Rodriguez, D., Epstein, L. H., Cuevas, J., Roders, K., & Mileyto, E. P. (2009). Does delay discounting play an etiological role in smoking? *Drug and Alcohol Dependence, 103*, 99–106. doi:10.1016/j.drugalcdep.2008.12.019

Audrain-McGovern, J., Rodriguez, D., Tercyak, K. P., Nenner, G., & Moss, H. B. (2006). The impact of self-control indices on peer smoking and adolescent smoking progression. *Journal of Pediatric Psychology, 31*, 139–151.

Barkley, R. A. (1997). Behavioral inhibition, sustained attention, and executive functions: Constructing a unifying theory of ADHD. *Psychological Bulletin, 121*, 65–94. doi:10.1037/0033-2909.121.1.65

Belin, D., Mar, A. C., Dalley, J. W., Robbins, T. W., & Everitt, B. J. (2008). High impulsivity predicts the switch to compulsive cocaine-taking. *Science, 320*, 1352–1355. doi:10.1126/science.1158136

Bennhold, K. (2013, December 7). Britain's ministry of nudges. *New York Times*, pp. B1, B4.

Berkman, E. T., Graham, A. M., & Fisher, P. A. (2012). Training self-control: A domain-general neuroscience approach. *Child Development Perspectives, 6*, 374–384.

Bickel, W. K., Miller, M. L., Yi, R., Kowal, B. P., Lindquist, D. M., & Pitcock, J. A. (2007). Behavioral theories of drug addiction: Competing neural systems and temporal discounting processes. *Drug and Alcohol Dependence, 90*(Suppl. 1), S85–S91. doi:10.1016/j.drugalcdep.2006.09.016

Brody, G. H., & Ge, X. (2001). Linking parenting and self-regulation to functioning and alcohol use in early adolescence. *Journal of Family Psychology, 15*, 82–94. doi:10.1037/0893-3200.15.1.82

Brody, G. H., Kogan, S. M., Chen, Y.-F., & Murry, V. (2008). Effects of the Strong African American families program on conduct problems. *Journal of Adolescent Health, 43*, 474–481. doi:10.1016/j.jadohealth.2008.04.016

Brody, G. H., Murry, V., McNair, L., Chen, Y.-F., Gibbons, F. X., Gerrard, M., & Wills, T. A. (2005). Linking changes in parenting to parent-child relationship quality and youth self-control. *Journal of Research on Adolescence, 15*, 47–69. doi:10.1111/j.1532-7795.2005.00086.x

Brody, G. H., Murry, V. M., Kogan, S. M., Gerrard, M., Gibbons, F. X., Molgaard, V., . . . Wills, T. A. (2006). The Strong African American Families Program: A cluster-randomized prevention trail of long-term effects and a mediational model. *Journal of Consulting and Clinical Psychology, 74*, 356–366. doi:10.1037/0022-006X.74.2.356

Browning, M., Holmes, E. A., Charles, M., Cowen, P. J., & Harmer, C. J. (2012). Using attentional bias modification as a vaccine against depression. *Biological Psychiatry, 72*, 572–579. doi:10.1016/j.biopsych.2012.04.014

Bryck, R. L., & Fisher, P. A. (2012). Training the brain: Implications of neural plasticity for the intersection of neuroscience and prevention research. *American Psychologist, 67*, 87–100. doi:10.1037/a0024657

Chiesa, A., Serretti, A., & Jakobsen, J. C. (2013). Mindfulness: Top-down or bottom-up emotion regulation strategy? *Clinical Psychology Review, 33*, 82–96. doi:10.1016/j.cpr.2012.10.006

Colder, C. R., Chassin, L., Lee, M. R., Villalta, I. K., & Kassel, J. D. (2010). Affect and adolescent substance use. In J. D. Kassel (Ed.), *Substance abuse and emotion* (pp. 109–135). Washington, DC: American Psychological Association. doi:10.1037/12067-005

Csikszentmihalyi, M. (1996). *Creativity: Flow and the psychology of discovery and invention.* New York, NY: Harper Perennial.

Dalley, J. W., Fryer, T. D., Brichard, L., Robinson, E. S. J., Theobald, D. E. H., Laane, K., . . . Robbins, T. W. (2007). Nucleus accumbens D2/3 receptors predict trait impulsivity and cocaine reinforcement. *Science, 315*, 1267–1270. doi:10.1126/science.1137073

Dawe, S., & Loxton, N. J. (2004). The role of impulsivity in the development of substance use and eating disorders. *Neuroscience and Biobehavioral Reviews, 28*, 343–351. doi:10.1016/j.neubiorev.2004.03.007

De Houwer, J. (2006). What are implicit measures and why are we using them. In R. Wiers & A. Stacy (Eds.), *Handbook of implicit cognition and addiction* (pp. 11–28). Thousand Oaks, CA: Sage. doi:10.4135/9781412976237.n2

Denson, T. F., Capper, M. M., Oaten, M., Friese, M., & Schofield, T. P. (2011). Self-control training decreases response to provocation in aggressive individuals. *Journal of Research in Personality, 45*, 252–256. doi:10.1016/j.jrp.2011.02.001

Diamond, A., Barnett, W. S., Thomas, J., & Munro, S. (2007). Preschool program improves cognitive self-control. *Science, 318*, 1387–1388. doi:10.1126/science.1151148

Diamond, A., & Lee, K. (2011). Interventions shown to aid executive function development in children 4 to 12 years of age. *Science, 333*, 959–964. doi:10.1126/science.1204529

Dvorak, R. D., Simons, J. S., & Wray, T. B. (2011). Alcohol use and problem severity: Associations with dual systems of self-control. *Journal of Studies on Alcohol and Drugs, 72*, 678–684.

Evans, G. W., Fuller-Rowell, T. E., & Doan, S. N. (2012). Childhood cumulative risk and obesity: The mediating role of self-regulation. *Pediatrics, 129*, e68–e73. doi:10.1542/peds.2010-3647

Eysenck, S. B. G., & Eysenck, H. J. (1978). Impulsiveness and venturesomeness: A dimensional system for personality description. *Psychological Reports, 43*, 1247–1255. doi:10.2466/pr0.1978.43.3f.1247

Farris, S. R., Ostafin, B. D., & Palfai, T. P. (2010). Distractibility moderates the relation between automatic alcohol motivation and drinking. *Psychology of Addictive Behaviors, 24*, 151–156. doi:10.1037/a0018294

Finkel, E. J., DeWall, C., Slotter, E., Oaten, M., & Foshee, V. (2009). Self-regulation training and partner violence perpetration. *Journal of Personality and Social Psychology, 97*, 483–499. doi:10.1037/a0015433

Fox, H. C., Bergquist, K. L., Gu, P., & Sinha, R. (2010). Interactive effects of cumulative stress and impulsivity on alcohol consumption. *Alcoholism: Clinical and Experimental Research, 34*, 1376–1385.

Gardner, T. W., Dishion, T., & Connell, A. (2008). Adolescent self-regulation as resilience within the deviant peer context. *Journal of Abnormal Child Psychology, 36*, 273–284. doi:10.1007/s10802-007-9176-6

Gerrard, M., Gibbons, F. X., Brody, G. H., Murry, V. M., Cleveland, M. J., & Wills, T. A. (2006). A theory-based dual-focus alcohol intervention for preadolescents. *Psychology of Addictive Behaviors, 20*, 185–195. doi:10.1037/0893-164X.20.2.185

Gerrard, M., Gibbons, F. X., Houlihan, A. E., Stock, M. L., & Pomery, E. A. (2008). A dual-process approach to health risk decision making. *Developmental Review, 28*, 29–61. doi:10.1016/j.dr.2007.10.001

Gibbons, F. X., Gerrard, M., Cleveland, M. J., Wills, T. A., & Brody, G. H. (2004). Perceived discrimination and substance use in African-American parents and their children: A panel study. *Journal of Personality and Social Psychology, 86*, 517–529. doi:10.1037/0022-3514.86.4.517

Gibbons, F. X., Gerrard, M., & Lane, D. J. (2003). A social reaction model of adolescent health risk. In J. M. Suls & K. A. Wallston (Eds.), *Social psychological foundations of health and illness* (pp. 107–136). Oxford, England: Blackwell. doi:10.1002/9780470753552.ch5

Gibbons, F. X., Houlihan, A. E., & Gerrard, M. (2009). A dual-focus perspective on prevention of health risk behaviors. *British Journal of Health Psychology, 14*, 231–248. doi:10.1348/135910708X376640

Gibbons, F. X., O'Hara, R. E., Stock, M. L., Gerrard, M., Weng, C.-Y., & Wills, T. A. (2012). Self-control mediates the relation between racial discrimination and substance use in African American adolescents. *Journal of Personality and Social Psychology, 102*, 1089–1104. doi:10.1037/a0027404

Gladwell, M. (2005). *Blink: The power of thinking without thinking*. New York, NY: Little, Brown.

Greenberg, M. T., & Harris, A. R. (2012). Nurturing mindfulness in children and youth: Current state of research. *Child Development Perspectives, 6*, 161–166. doi:10.1111/j.1750-8606.2011.00215.x

Griffin, K. W., Scheier, L. M., Acevedo, B., Grenard, J. L., & Botvin, G. J. (2012). Long-term effects of self-control on alcohol use and sexual behavior among urban minority young women. *International Journal of Environmental Research and Public Health, 9*, 1–23. doi:10.3390/ijerph9010001

Hallion, L. S., & Ruscio, A. M. (2011). A meta-analysis of the effect of cognitive bias modification on anxiety and depression. *Psychological Bulletin, 137*, 940–958. doi:10.1037/a0024355

Hansen, W. B., & Altman, D. G. (2000). Sequencing issues in health behavior program development. In S. Sussman (Ed.), *Handbook of program development for health behavior research and practice* (pp. 361–386). Thousand Oaks, CA: Sage.

Heiby, E. M. (1983). Assessment of frequency of self-reinforcement. *Journal of Personality and Social Psychology, 44*, 1304–1307. doi:10.1037/0022-3514.44.6.1304

Herrigel, E. (1999). *Zen in the art of archery*. New York, NY: Vintage Books.

Hertel, P. T., & Mathews, A. (2011). Cognitive bias modification: Past perspectives, current findings and future applications. *Perspectives on Psychological Science, 6*, 521–536. doi:10.1177/1745691611421205

Hofmann, W., Friese, M., & Strack, F. (2009). Impulse and self-control from a dual-systems perspective. *Perspectives on Psychological Science, 4*, 162–176. doi:10.1111/j.1745-6924.2009.01116.x

Houben, K., Nederkoorn, C., Wiers, R. W., & Jansen, A. (2011). Resisting temptation: Decreasing alcohol-related affect and drinking behavior by training response inhibition. *Drug and Alcohol Dependence, 116*, 132–136. doi:10.1016/j.drugalcdep.2010.12.011

Houben, K., Schoenmakers, T. M., & Wiers, R. W. (2010). I didn't feel like drinking but I don't know why: The effects of evaluative conditioning on alcohol-related attitudes, craving and behavior. *Addictive Behaviors, 35*, 1161–1163. doi:10.1016/j.addbeh.2010.08.012

Hustad, J. T. P., Carey, K. B., Carey, M. P., & Maisto, S. A. (2009). Self-regulation, alcohol consumption, and consequences in college student heavy drinkers: A simultaneous latent growth model. *Journal of Studies on Alcohol and Drugs, 70*, 373–382.

Isasi, C. R., & Wills, T. A. (2011). Behavioral self-regulation and weight-related behaviors in inner-city adolescents: A model of direct and indirect effects. *Childhood Obesity, 7*, 306–315.

Kendall, P. C., & Williams, C. L. (1982). Assessing the cognitive and behavioral components of children's self-management. In P. Karoly & F. H. Kanfer (Eds.), *Self-management and behavior change* (pp. 240–284). New York, NY: Pergamon Press.

Keng, S.-L., Smoski, M. J., & Robins, C. J. (2011). Effects of mindfulness on psychological health: A review of empirical studies. *Clinical Psychology Review, 31*, 1041–1056. doi:10.1016/j.cpr.2011.04.006

King, K. M., Fleming, C. B., Monahan, K. C., & Catalano, R. F. (2011). Changes in self-control and attention problems during middle school predict alcohol, tobacco, and marijuana use during high school. *Psychology of Addictive Behaviors, 25*, 69–79. doi:10.1037/a0021958

Lejuez, C. W., Magidson, J. F., Mitchell, S. H., Sinha, R., Stevens, M. C., & de Wit, H. (2010). Behavioral and biological indicators of impulsivity in the development of alcohol use, problems, and disorders. *Alcoholism: Clinical and Experimental Research, 34*, 1334–1345.

Lieberman, M. D. (2007). The X- and C-systems: The neural basis of automatic and controlled social cognition. In E. Harmon-Jones & P. Winkelman (Eds.), *Integrating biological and psychological explanations of social behavior* (pp. 290–315). New York, NY: Guilford Press.

Madden, G. J., & Bickel, W. K. (2010). *Impulsivity: The behavioral and neurological science of discounting*. Washington, DC: American Psychological Association.

McClelland, M. M., Cameron, C. E., Connor, C. M., Farris, C. L., Jewkes, A. M., & Morrison, F. J. (2007). Links between behavioral self-regulation and preschoolers' literacy, vocabulary, and math skills. *Developmental Psychology*, *43*, 947–959. doi:10.1037/0012-1649.43.4.947

Miller, H. V., Barnes, J. C., & Beaver, K. M. (2011). Self-control and health outcomes in a national representative sample. *American Journal of Health Behavior*, *35*, 15–27. doi:10.5993/AJHB.35.1.2

Moffitt, T. E., Arsenault, L., Belsky, D., Dickson, N., Hancox, R. J., Harrington, H., . . . Caspi, A. (2011). A gradient of childhood self-control predicts health, wealth, and public safety. *PNAS Proceedings of the National Academy of Sciences of the United States of America*, *108*, 2693–2698. doi:10.1073/pnas.1010076108

Muraven, M. (2010a). Building self-control strength: Practicing self-control leads to improved self-control performance. *Journal of Experimental Social Psychology*, *46*, 465–468. doi:10.1016/j.jesp.2009.12.011

Muraven, M. (2010b). Practicing self-control lowers the risk of smoking lapse. *Psychology of Addictive Behaviors*, *24*, 446–452. doi:10.1037/a0018545

Novak, S. P., & Clayton, R. R. (2001). Influence of school environment and self-regulation on transitions between stages of cigarette smoking. *Health Psychology*, *20*, 196–207. doi:10.1037/0278-6133.20.3.196

Oaten, M., & Cheng, P. (2006a). Improved self-control: The benefits of a regular program of academic study. *Basic and Applied Social Psychology*, *28*, 1–16. doi:10.1207/s15324834basp2801_1

Oaten, M., & Cheng, K. (2006b). Longitudinal gains in self-regulation from regular physical exercise. *British Journal of Health Psychology*, *11*, 717–733. doi:10.1348/135910706X96481

Oaten, M., & Cheng, P. (2007). Improvements in self-control from financial monitoring. *Journal of Economic Psychology*, *28*, 487–501. doi:10.1016/j.joep.2006.11.003

Owen, A. M., Hampshire, A., Grahn, J. A., Stenton, R., Dajaniz, S., Burns, A. S., . . . Ballard, C. G. (2010). Putting brain training to the test. *Nature*, *465*, 775–778. doi:10.1038/nature09042

Patock-Peckham, J. A., & Morgan-Lopez, A. (2006). Links between parenting styles, impulse control, and drinking outcomes. *Psychology of Addictive Behaviors*, *20*, 117–125. doi:10.1037/0893-164X.20.2.117

Pearson, M. R., D'Lima, G. M., & Kelley, M. L. (2011). Self-regulation as a buffer of the relation between parental misuse and alcohol outcomes. *Addictive Behaviors*, *36*, 1309–1312. doi:10.1016/j.addbeh.2011.07.009

Pearson, M. R., Kite, B. A., & Henson, J. M. (2013). Predictive effects of good self-control and poor regulation on alcohol-related outcomes: Do protective behavioral strategies mediate? *Psychology of Addictive Behaviors*, *27*, 81–89. doi:10.1037/a0028818

Perry, J. L., & Carroll, M. E. (2008). The role of impulsive behavior in drug abuse. *Psychopharmacology*, *200*, 1–26. doi:10.1007/s00213-008-1173-0

Piehler, T. F., Véronneau, M.-H., & Dishion, T. J. (2012). Effortful control and substance use progression in adolescence. *Journal of Abnormal Child Psychology*, *40*, 1045–1058. doi:10.1007/s10802-012-9626-7

Raver, C., Jones, S., Li-Grining, C., Zhai, F., Bub, K., & Pressler, E. (2011). CSRP's impact on academic skills: Self-regulation as a mediating mechanism. *Child Development*, *82*, 361–378.

Reynolds, B., Ortengren, A., Richards, J. B., & de Wit, H. (2006). Dimensions of impulsive behavior. *Personality and Individual Differences*, *40*, 305–315. doi:10.1016/j.paid.2005.03.024

Riggs, N. R., Greenberg, M. T., Kusche, C. A., & Pentz, M. A. (2006). Outcomes of a social-emotional prevention program in elementary school students. *Prevention Science*, *7*, 91–102. doi:10.1007/s11121-005-0022-1

Riggs, N. R., Kobayakawa-Sakuma, K. L., & Pentz, M. A. (2007). Preventing risk for obesity by promoting self-regulation skills. *Evaluation Review*, *31*, 287–310. doi:10.1177/0193841X06297243

Riggs, N. R., Spruijt-Metz, D., Sakuma, K.-L., Chou, C.-P., & Pentz, M. (2010). Executive function and food intake in children. *Journal of Nutrition Education and Behavior*, *42*, 398–403. doi:10.1016/j.jneb.2009.11.003

Rothbart, M. K., Ahadi, S. E., & Evans, D. E. (2000). Temperament and personality: Origins and outcomes. *Journal of Personality and Social Psychology*, *78*, 122–135. doi:10.1037/0022-3514.78.1.122

Sharbanee, J. M., Stritzke, W. G. K., Wiers, R. W., Young, P., Rinck, M., & MacLeod, C. (2013). The interaction of approach action tendencies and working memory predicts the inability to regulate drinking behavior. *Psychology of Addictive Behaviors*. doi:10.1037/a0029982

Scheier, L. M., & Botvin, G. J. (1995). Effects of early adolescent drug use on cognitive efficacy in adolescence: A developmental structural model. *Journal of Substance Abuse*, *7*, 379–404. doi:10.1016/0899-3289(95)90011-X

Shin, S. H., Hong, H. G., & Wills, T. A. (2012). Examination of pathways from childhood maltreatment to adolescent binge drinking. *American Journal on Addictions*, *21*, 202–209. doi:10.1111/j.1521-0391.2012.00227.x

Shipstead, Z., Redick, T. S., & Engle, R. W. (2012). Is working memory training effective? *Psychological Bulletin, 138*, 628–654. doi:10.1037/a0027473

Shoda, Y., Mischel, W., & Peake, P. K. (1990). Predicting adolescent self-regulatory competencies from preschool delay of gratification. *Developmental Psychology, 26*, 978–986. doi:10.1037/0012-1649.26.6.978

Siegel, J. (2010). *Stop overreacting: Effective strategies for calming your emotions.* Oakland, CA: New Harbinger.

Simons, J. S., & Carey, K. B. (2006). An affective and cognitive model of marijuana and alcohol problems. *Addictive Behaviors, 31*, 1578–1592. doi:10.1016/j.addbeh.2005.12.004

Simons, J. S., Carey, K. B., & Wills, T. A. (2009). Alcohol abuse and dependence symptoms: A model of common and specific etiology. *Psychology of Addictive Behaviors, 23*, 415–427. doi:10.1037/a0016003

Simons, J. S., Dvorak, R. D., Batien, B. D., & Wray, T. B. (2010). Event-level associations between affect, alcohol intoxication, and acute dependence symptoms: Effects of urgency, self-control, and drinking experience. *Addictive Behaviors, 35*, 1045–1053. doi:10.1016/j.addbeh.2010.07.001

Simons, J. S., Gaher, R. M., Oliver, M. N. I., Bush, J. A., & Palmer, M. A. (2005). An experience sampling study of associations between affect and alcohol use and problems among college students. *Journal of Studies on Alcohol, 66*, 459–469.

Simons, J. S., Maisto, S. A., & Wray, T. B. (2010). Sexual risk taking among young adult alcohol and marijuana users. *Addictive Behaviors, 35*, 533–536. doi:10.1016/j.addbeh.2009.12.026

Simons, J. S., Wills, T. A., & Neal, D. J. (2014). The many faces of affect: A multilevel model of drinking frequency/quantity and alcohol dependence symptoms among young adults. *Journal of Abnormal Psychology, 123*, 676–694. doi:10.1037/a0036926

Skara, S., & Sussman, S. (2003). A review of 25 long-term adolescent tobacco and other drug use prevention program evaluations. *Preventive Medicine: An International Journal Devoted to Practice and Theory, 37*, 451–474. doi:10.1016/S0091-7435(03)00166-X

Southam-Gerow, M. A. (2013). *Emotion regulation in children and adolescents: A practitioner's guide.* New York, NY: Guilford Press.

Stacy, A. W., & Wiers, R. W. (2010). Implicit cognition and addiction: A tool for explaining paradoxical behavior. *Annual Review of Clinical Psychology, 6*, 551–575. doi:10.1146/annurev.clinpsy.121208.131444

Steinberg, L. (2008). A social neuroscience perspective on adolescent risk taking. *Developmental Review, 28*, 78–106. doi:10.1016/j.dr.2007.08.002

Sussman, S., & Ames, S. (2008). *Drug abuse: Concepts, prevention, and cessation.* New York, NY: Cambridge University Press.

Sussman, S., Earleywine, M., Wills, T., Cody, C., Biglan, A., Dent, C., & Newcomb, M. D. (2004). The motivation, skills, and decision-making model of drug abuse prevention. *Substance Use & Misuse, 39*, 1971–2016. doi:10.1081/JA-200034769

Sussman, S., McCuller, W. J., & Dent, C. W. (2003). The association of social self-control with drug use among high-risk youth. *Addictive Behaviors, 28*, 1159–1166. doi:10.1016/S0306-4603(02)00222-8

Tang, Y.-Y., Lu, Q., Fan, M., Yang, Y., & Posner, M. I. (2012). Mechanisms of white matter changes induced by meditation. *PNAS Proceedings of the National Academy of Sciences of the United States of America, 109*, 10570–10574. doi:10.1073/pnas.1207817109

Tang, Y.-Y., Yang, L., Leve, L., & Harold, G. T. (2012). Improving executive function and its neurobiological mechanisms through a mindfulness-based intervention: Advances within the field of developmental neuroscience. *Child Development Perspectives, 6*, 361–366.

Tarter, R., Vanyukov, M., Giancola, P., Dawes, M., Blackson, T., Mezzich, A., & Clark, D. B. (1999). Etiology of early age onset substance use disorder. *Development and Psychopathology, 11*, 657–683. doi:10.1017/S0954579499002266

Tarter, R. E., Kirisci, L., Mezzich, A., Cornelius, J. R., Pajer, K., Vanyukov, M., . . . Clark, D. (2003). Neurobehavioral disinhibition in childhood predicts early age onset of substance use disorder. *The American Journal of Psychiatry, 160*, 1078–1085. doi:10.1176/appi.ajp.160.6.1078

Thaler, R. H., & Sunstein, C. R. (2008). *Nudge: Improving decisions about health, wealth, and happiness.* New York, NY: Penguin Books.

Tominey, S. L., & McClelland, M. M. (2011). A randomized trial using circle time games to improve self-regulation in preschool. *Early Education and Development, 22*, 489–519. doi:10.1080/10409289.2011.574258

Ursache, A., Blair, C., & Raver, C. C. (2012). The promotion of self-regulation as a means for enhancing school readiness. *Child Development Perspectives, 6*, 122–128. doi:10.1111/j.1750-8606.2011.00209.x

Watson, J. D. (1968). *The double helix.* New York, NY: Atheneum Press.

Wiers, R. W., Bartholow, B., van den Wildenberg, E., Thush, C., Engels, R., Sher, K., . . . Stacy, A. (2007). Automatic and controlled processes and the development of addictive behaviors in adolescents. *Pharmacology, Biochemistry and Behavior, 86*, 263–283. doi:10.1016/j.pbb.2006.09.021

Wiers, R. W., Ebert, C., Rinck, M., Becker, E. S., & Lindenmeyer, J. (2011). Retraining automatic action tendencies changes alcoholic patients' approach bias for alcohol and improves treatment outcome. *Psychological Science, 22*, 490–497.

Willem, L., Bijttebier, P., & Claes, L. (2010). Reactive and self-regulatory temperament dimensions in relation to alcohol use in adolescence. *Addictive Behaviors, 35*, 1029–1035. doi:10.1016/j.addbeh.2010.06.023

Wills, T. A., & Ainette, M. G. (2010). Temperament, self-control, and adolescent substance use: A two-factor model of etiological processes. In L. M. Scheier (Ed.), *Handbook of drug use etiology: Theory, methods, and empirical findings* (pp. 127–-146). Washington, DC: American Psychological Association.

Wills, T. A., Ainette, M. G., Mendoza, D., Gibbons, F. X., & Brody, G. H. (2007). Self-control and substance use precursors. *Psychology of Addictive Behaviors, 21*, 205–215. doi:10.1037/0893-164X.21.2.205

Wills, T. A., & Bantum, E. O. (2012). Self-regulation and resilience among adolescents and adult cancer survivors. *Journal of Social and Clinical Psychology, 31*, 568–592. doi:10.1521/jscp.2012.31.6.568

Wills, T. A., Bantum, E. O., Pokhrel, P., Maddock, J. E., Ainette, M. G., Morehouse, E., & Fenster, B. (2013). A dual-process model of early substance use: Tests in two diverse populations of adolescents. *Health Psychology.* doi:10.1037/a0027634

Wills, T. A., Cleary, S. D., Filer, M., Shinar, O., Mariani, J., & Spera, K. (2001). Temperament and self-control related to early-onset substance use. *Prevention Science, 2*, 145–163. doi:10.1023/A:1011558807062

Wills, T. A., & Dishion, T. (2004). Temperament and adolescent substance use: An analysis of emerging self-control. *Journal of Clinical Child and Adolescent Psychology, 33*, 69–81. doi:10.1207/S15374424JCCP3301_7

Wills, T. A., Forbes, M., & Gibbons, F. X. (2014). Parent and peer support and substance use. In L. M. Scheier & W. B. Hansen (Eds.), *Parenting and teen drug use: The most recent findings from research, prevention, and treatment* (pp. 148–165). New York, NY: Oxford University Press.

Wills, T. A., McNamara, G., Vaccaro, D., & Hirky, A. E. (1996). Escalated substance use: A longitudinal grouping analysis. *Journal of Abnormal Psychology, 105*, 166–180. doi:10.1037/0021-843X.105.2.166

Wills, T. A., Murry, V. M., Brody, G. H., Gibbons, F. X., Gerrard, M., & Walker, C. (2007). Ethnic pride and self-control related to protective/risk factors. *Health Psychology, 26*, 50–59. doi:10.1037/0278-6133.26.1.50

Wills, T. A., Pokhrel, P., Morehouse, E., & Fenster, B. (2011). Behavioral and emotional regulation and adolescent substance use problems. *Psychology of Addictive Behaviors, 25*, 279–292. doi:10.1037/a0022870

Wills, T. A., Resko, J., Ainette, M., & Mendoza, D. (2004). The role of parent and peer support in adolescent substance use: A test of mediated effects. *Psychology of Addictive Behaviors, 18*, 122–134.

Wills, T. A., Sandy, J. M., & Yaeger, A. (2000). Temperament and adolescent substance use: An epigenetic approach to risk and protection. *Journal of Personality, 68*, 1127–1151. doi:10.1111/1467-6494.00129

Wills, T. A., Sandy, J. M., & Yaeger, A. (2002). Moderators of the relation between substance use level and problems. *Journal of Abnormal Psychology, 111*, 3–21. doi:10.1037/0021-843X.111.1.3

Wills, T. A., Sargent, J. D., Stoolmiller, M., Gibbons, F. X., & Gerrard, M. (2008). Movie smoking exposure and smoking onset. *Psychology of Addictive Behaviors, 22*, 269–277. doi:10.1037/0893-164X.22.2.269

Wills, T. A., & Stoolmiller, M. (2002). The role of self-control in escalation of substance use: A time-varying analysis. *Journal of Consulting and Clinical Psychology, 70*, 986–997. doi:10.1037/0022-006X.70.4.986

Wills, T. A., Walker, C., Mendoza, D., & Ainette, M. G. (2006). Behavioral and emotional self-control: Relations to substance use in samples of middle- and high-school students. *Psychology of Addictive Behaviors, 20*, 265–278.

Zeman, J., Shipman, K., & Penza-Clyve, S. (2001). Development and validation of the Children's Sadness Management scale. *Journal of Nonverbal Behavior, 25*, 187–205. doi:10.1023/A:1010623226626

Zimbardo, P. G., & Boyd, J. N. (1999). Time perspective: A valid, reliable individual-differences metric. *Journal of Personality and Social Psychology, 77*, 1271–1288. doi:10.1037/0022-3514.77.6.1271

CHAPTER 8

PREVENTIVE INTERVENTION TO REDUCE YOUTH CONDUCT PROBLEMS AND SUBSTANCE USE: LINKING THE INTERESTS OF FAMILIES AND TEACHERS (LIFT)

J. Mark Eddy, Susan E. Barkan, and Lindsay Lanham

This chapter illustrates a popular genre of universal prevention programs for youth problem behaviors: multimodal interventions that address challenges that children and the adults who interact with them face during childhood and adolescence. We specifically highlight Linking the Interests of Families and Teachers (LIFT; Reid, Eddy, Fetrow, & Stoolmiller, 1999). LIFT is an evidence-informed universal prevention program that comprises behavioral interventions for the home and school contexts; it was designed specifically to decrease the likelihood that a child will develop conduct problems, conduct disorder, and commonly co-occurring problems, such as early substance use. Universal programs target a general population of children and are intended to be beneficial in some way to all members of that population, including those at high risk for exhibiting a psychiatric disorder (Mrazek & Haggerty, 1994). We present the rationale behind LIFT, describe program components, and discuss the effects of the program on conduct problems and substance use.

BACKGROUND

Most children display disobedience, defiance, aggression, and temper tantrums at various points during childhood. They are considered typical child behaviors, at least at certain ages and within certain contexts, such as the family. Some children, however, behave in these ways so frequently and in so many different settings that they persistently break the basic rules of social relationships and violate others' rights. During their primary school years, such children may be labeled "aggressive," "emotionally disturbed," or "socially maladjusted." When aggressive and maladjusted children reach adolescence and come into contact with the police and the courts, they are often labeled "delinquent." Psychiatrists and psychologists consider such children to have conduct problems, and in extreme cases, they may be diagnosed with *conduct disorder*, a general term often used to refer to several diagnoses listed in the various iterations of the *Diagnostic and Statistical Manual of Mental Disorders, Fifth Edition* (*DSM–5;* American Psychiatric

Preparation for this chapter was supported by grants from the National Institute of Child Health and Human Development (R01 HDD05554880) and the Administration for Children and Families (90CA1781). The content of this chapter is solely the responsibility of the authors and does not necessarily represent the official views of the National Institute of Child Health and Human Development or the Administration for Children and Families.

Support for the development and testing of LIFT was provided by grants from the National Institute of Mental Health (R01 MH 54248 and P30 MH 46690) and by the Department of Scientific and Industrial Research (RO1 MH 59127).

http://dx.doi.org/10.1037/14550-009
Handbook of Adolescent Drug Use Prevention: Research, Intervention Strategies, and Practice, L. M. Scheier (Editor)

Association, 2013), including conduct disorder, oppositional defiant disorder, and disruptive behavior disorder not elsewhere classified.

Conduct disorder encompasses an ongoing pattern of antisocial behaviors during childhood and/or adolescence, such as fighting, bullying, stealing, vandalizing, and lying for personal gain (Lahey & Waldman, 2012). Concern about child conduct is one of the most common reasons for child mental health consultation (Breslau, Miller, Chung, & Schweitzer, 2011; Kazdin, 1995; Morcillo et al., 2012), and across the decades has been present in half of all referrals (Robins, 1991; Wolff, 1961). The prevalence of conduct disorder varies by gender, age, and study; boys are estimated to have a higher prevalence than girls during childhood (generally, 2.0%–13.0% for boys vs. 1.0%–5.0% for girls; Lahey et al., 2000; Lahey & Waldman, 2012; Loeber, Burke, Lahey, Winters, & Zera, 2000; Loeber, Farrington, Stouthamer-Loeber, & Van Kammen, 1998; Maughan, Rowe, Messer, Goodman, & Meltzer, 2004). By adolescence, Merikangas et al. (2010) estimated the lifetime prevalence of conduct disorder at 6.8% (i.e., girls, 5.8%; boys, 7.9%), whereas Costello, Mustillo, Erkanli, Keeler, and Angold (2003) estimated a cumulative prevalence of 9.0% (i.e., 3.8% for girls; 14.1% for boys).

A hallmark feature of conduct disorder is that it often co-occurs with other childhood mental disorders (Costello et al., 2003; Feehan, McGee, Raja, & Williams, 1994; Lahey & Waldman, 2012; Loeber et al., 2000; Maughan et al., 2004, Merikangas et al., 2010; Offord et al., 1992). The most frequently discussed co-occurring disorder is attention-deficit/hyperactivity disorder (ADHD; persistent and persuasive difficulties with inattention, impulsivity, and/or hyperactivity; Loeber et al., 2000). Some clinicians and researchers view ADHD as either a precursor to the early initiation of conduct disorder (e.g., Loeber et al., 2000; Loeber & Keenan, 1994) or as part of the same externalizing behavior problem syndrome (e.g., Hinshaw, 1987). Children with conduct disorder and ADHD tend to exhibit conduct problems at a younger age, display higher rates of aggression, and continue conduct problems for longer periods (Hinshaw, Lahey, & Hart, 1993). Other disorders that commonly co-occur with conduct disorder include mood disorders and anxiety disorders (Costello et al., 2003; Fergusson, Lynskey, & Horwood, 1996; Lahey & Waldman, 2012; Loeber et al., 2000; Loeber & Keenan, 1994; Maughan et al., 2004; Merikangas et al., 2010; Zoccolillo, 1992).

Conduct problems can begin during early childhood and may extend into adulthood. Approximately half to two thirds of children diagnosed with conduct disorder in childhood continue to have a conduct disorder during adolescence; similarly, regardless of diagnosis, 40% to 75% of adolescents exhibiting high levels of conduct problems continue to do so during young adulthood (INSERM Collective Enterprise Centre, 2005). The persistence of conduct disorder puts children at risk for numerous concurrent and future difficulties during adolescence and adulthood. Notably, in terms of this volume, childhood conduct problems elevate risk during adulthood for substance abuse (Breslau, Saito, Tancredi, Nock, & Gilman, 2012; Lahey & Waldman, 2012; Loeber et al., 2000; Robins & McEvoy, 1990), a variety of other mental disorders (Burke, Loeber, & Birmaher, 2002; Loeber et al., 2000; Robins & Price, 1991; Zoccolillo, 1992), and physical health problems (Bardone, Moffitt, Caspi, Dickson, & Silva, 1998; Colman et al., 2009; Odgers et al., 2007). Conduct problems are also related to difficulties in other important areas of adult life, such as educational failure (Colman et al., 2009; Odgers et al., 2007), intimate relationships (Colman et al., 2009; Kessler, Walters, & Forthofer, 1998), work performance problems (Colman et al., 2009; Zoccolillo, Pickles, Quinton, & Rutter, 1992), underemployment, and social marginalization (Colman et al., 2009; Emerson, Einfeld, & Stancliffe, 2011). Probably most striking is that children with conduct disorder are at risk for adult adjustment problems not just in one of these areas but in multiple areas simultaneously (Maughan, Pickles, & Quinton, 1995; Quinton, Pickles, Maughan, & Rutter, 1993; Zoccolillo et al., 1992). For example, a significant number of incarcerated adults not only have extensive histories of youth delinquency and adult criminality but also persistent substance abuse histories (e.g., Kjellstrand, Cearley, Eddy, Foney, & Martinez, 2012).

Given this picture, it is not surprising that the social and economic costs related to conduct disorder make it one of the most expensive child mental health issues (Kazdin, 1995). Children with conduct disorder receive ongoing services from a multitude of sectors throughout their lives that go beyond mental health, and include, but are not limited to, juvenile justice, education, substance abuse treatment, criminal justice, and public health. Knapp, Scott, and Davies (1999) estimated the average yearly cost of a child diagnosed with conduct disorder to be about $26,000. During the same period, Cohen (1998) estimated that one child with serious conduct problems may cost society as much as $1.7 million to $2.3 million over a lifetime. Of particular note is that the majority of the subgroup of adult male chronic offenders who commit a large proportion of official and serious crimes each year displayed serious conduct problems as children, accruing costs along the way (Blumstein, Cohen, Roth, & Visher, 1986; Farrington & Wikström, 1994; Wolfgang, Figlio, & Sellin, 1972). On top of estimable costs are the immeasurable costs of the emotional and physical injuries inflicted by individuals with conduct disorder on others, including family and friends, through the course of their antisocial "careers."

Because of its significant and long-term implications for a child and his or her family, community, culture, and society, preventing the genesis of conduct disorder has been of ongoing interest to practitioners, researchers, granting agencies and foundations, administrators, and policymakers. As noted in Chapter 6 of this handbook, a variety of prevention programs targeting conduct disorder have been developed and tested, and some have been found to have favorable outcomes. In a recent meta-analysis of findings from rigorous comparison group studies of outcomes related to 45 prevention programs targeting conduct disorder, more favorable effects were found for programs that used behavioral intervention techniques (effect size of Cohen's $d = 0.54$) and/or comprised multiple modes of intervention (Cohen's $d = 0.21$; Grove, Evans, Pastor, & Mack, 2008). LIFT is a behavioral, multimodal intervention that was included in the Grove et al. (2008) analysis.

DEVELOPMENTAL THEORY BEHIND LIFT

A variety of risk factors for conduct problems and conduct disorder have been identified within child, family, peer, and community domains (for a review, see Chapter 6, this volume). The relationship of each of these factors to concurrent or subsequent conduct problems and disorder varies across the stages of development. Although factors that protect against conduct disorder are also extremely important in theoretical conceptions, to date, less attention has been given to studies of protective factors. In a meta-analysis of 34 longitudinal studies on the predictors of violent and serious conduct problems during late adolescence and young adulthood, Lipsey and Derzon (1998) found that, when children were 6 to 11 years old, the risk factors most predictive of later problems were centered in the child and family, namely, child conduct problems, child substance use, child sex (boys), family socioeconomic status (low), and parental conduct problems. In contrast, when children were ages 12 to 14, the most predictive risk factors were centered in the child and extrafamilial settings, namely, child conduct problems, child problems at school, child association with other children with conduct problems (so called deviant peers), and low popularity with peers.

At the community level, conduct disorders may be more common in urban versus rural areas for younger children, but rates appear similar across areas by adolescence (e.g., Offord, Boyle, & Racine, 1991; Osborn, Butler, & Morris, 1984; Rutter, 1981; Rutter, Cox, Tupling, Berger, & Yule, 1975). Conduct disorder tends to be more prevalent in impoverished, socially disorganized, high adult-crime neighborhoods (e.g., Farrington, 1986; Hawkins et al., 1998; Herrenkohl et al., 2000; Lahey, Miller, Gordon, & Riley, 1999; Loeber et al., 2000; Sampson, Raudenbush, & Earls, 1997). Stressful life events (e.g., Mathijssen, Koot, & Verhulst, 1999) and exposure to certain environmental toxins (e.g., Needleman, Riess, Tobin, Biesecker, & Greenhouse, 1996)—both of which tend to be more common in impoverished neighborhoods—are also related to conduct problems. However, whether these factors cause conduct disorder is unclear. Although poverty in itself is not a risk factor, extreme poverty is associated with multiple risk factors and may influence whether the family has access to the resources needed to deal with basic needs and stressors and the physical and mental health issues that may arise. All of these factors can have an effect on parenting behavior (Emerson et al., 2011).

What is useful in terms of designing a prevention program is having a framework for how risk and protective factors initiate and shape the development of conduct disorder. In this regard, a variety of researchers have shared a relatively similar conception of a developmental model for conduct problems (e.g., Coie & Jacobs, 1993; Dodge, 2000; Hawkins & Weis, 1985; Kellam & Rebok, 1992; Patterson, 1982). Common to the models is that the social interactions between the child and others—most notably, parental figures, siblings, peers, and teachers—are hypothesized to be a potent force in exacerbating child conduct problems once they have begun. What is less clear is what initiates conduct problems. Generally, initiation is thought to result from an interaction between the response tendencies of the child—which themselves are due to interactions among biological, environmental, and social factors—and the response tendencies of the other key people in the child's life.

The developmental model underlying the LIFT program is coercion theory (Patterson, Reid, & Dishion, 1992; Reid & Eddy, 1997). Within this model, the life of a child who begins to display conduct problems early in life is hypothesized to follow a predictable course, if protective mechanisms are not present. Early child difficulties result when the challenges presented by a child and the prevailing environment are inadequately negotiated by parents and other caregiving adults (hereafter referred to simply as "parents"). For example, if a child with a difficult temperament is born to depressed and irritable parents who live in extremely stressful circumstances, chances are increased that, over time, parent–child interactions will inadvertently teach the child and the parents to become increasingly coercive (i.e., displaying negative behavior toward a person until that person backs down) to have their needs and desires met. Child coercive behavior patterns are at the core of conduct problems, and when persistent and serious, are likely to elicit a conduct disorder diagnosis when a mental health professional comes into contact with the child.

Unfortunately, a tendency to behave in defiant, negative, and aggressive ways at home sets up a child to behave similarly in other settings. Patterson (1982) referred to this process as "basic training." Most notably, on school entry, child aggressive and coercive behaviors typically lead peers to dislike, and eventually socially reject, the child. As coercive behaviors continue at home and in other community settings, the child also may be rejected by parents and other adults because many adults find the child's behavior distracting, out of line, offensive, and disruptive. One result is that the dominant modes of social interaction for a child with conventional adults and peers are conflict and avoidance. These actions, in turn, decrease the number of opportunities the child has to be involved in prosocial situations in which he or she can learn the nuances of getting along well with others.

Social interactions influence the cognitive development of a child (Vygotsky, 1978). In this regard, the loss of close contact with prosocial adults can have far reaching significance. Adults can provide children with frameworks by *scaffolding* their cognitive development: that is, the parent interprets the child's developmental capabilities and then slowly increments the child's skill set, encouraging the child to progressively acquire and refine new cognitive and problem-solving skills (Rogoff, 1990). Parents can also provide children with social and cultural capital (Dubas & Snider, 1993), and help them to view their futures from different perspectives by seeing the various possible selves they may become (e.g., Markus & Nurius, 1986). The absence of these rewarding self-actualizing experiences greatly reduces a child's options.

Failure to thwart the developmental trajectory can have significant and lasting consequences. Despite how intelligent the child is, he or she may fail academically because of the child's behavioral style and the responses it invokes from others. Teaching a child who is often fussy, argumentative, and disobedient is difficult and unpleasant, and a common result is that basic skills in reading, writing, and mathematics are often not nurtured adequately. Children who are not reading well by the end of the third grade are more likely than proficient readers to suffer a variety of significant negative consequences during adolescence and emerging adulthood (National Reading Panel, 2000). With decreasing access to normative situations, the central social influence in the child's life often becomes his or her deviant peers, children who have similar problems and have experienced similar life course trajectories (Reid, Patterson, & Snyder, 2002).

Surrounded by deviant peers, unsupervised by parents and other caregivers, and rejected by prosocial classmates and adults, the "difficult" child is now in a situation conducive to learning new types of conduct problems. Within such a context, a child eventually begins to exhibit other behaviors that are extremely problematic at relatively young ages, such as substance use. If these behaviors continue, interaction with the juvenile justice system is likely, providing a medium for continued and concentrated exposure to deviant peers. Furthermore, youth with conduct problems often exhibit other mental health problems. This close alliance arises because the social interactional processes related to conduct problems, particularly within the family context, also appear to be intimately involved in the development of depression and anxiety in children (Kaslow, Deering, & Racusin, 1994) and other family members. Failures and problems in one area of a child's life contribute to failures in other areas, and soon what began as a problem with oppositional and defiant behavior during early childhood may lead to academic failure, depression, school dropout, substance abuse, early sexual behavior, teen parenthood, and a host of other covert and overt conduct problems.

Coercion theory describes an early starter pathway to conduct disorder (e.g., Reid et al., 2002). However, the majority of children who have conduct problems do not start to have these problems early in life. Conduct disorder may begin later due to a combination of child and parent factors most notably related to the introduction of some intense stressor or set of stressors that significantly disrupts the lives of child and parent(s) and shifts each toward less adaptive life pathways. Of greatest concern are circumstances that significantly decrease parental involvement with the child, particularly when no other caregiver is available to fill the void in terms of supervision, monitoring, discipline, and positive reinforcement. Situations such as divorce, parental substance abuse, prolonged separation, and mental disability are often precursors that instigate decreased parental involvement.

Decreased parental involvement can lead to poor outcomes in child conduct, especially if the child seeks to fill the social vacuum through friendships with deviant peers. Exposure to deviant peer networks without parental supervision increases the opportunities both for intense exposure to negative behavioral standards and for high levels of reinforcement of the display of antisocial behaviors. Once a child enters a pathway to conduct disorder, the course is relatively similar, a phenomenon referred to by researchers as *interactional continuity* (e.g., Reid et al., 2002), because a relatively limited number of ways to be antisocial exist and, thus, the general model sketches out a common pathway even for these late-starter youth. The predicted difference, over the long run, is that, in contrast to early starters, children who enter the pathway later already had the opportunity to develop a base of prosocial skills and knowledge, and may, later in life, be able to reengage these skills and knowledge, and ease their reentry into the conventional world.

THE LIFT PROGRAM

LIFT targets risk and protective factors relevant to current and future conduct problems and disorder in elementary school-age children. The program primarily focuses on developing the social and problem-solving skills of children and parents relevant to the home, school, and peer group settings. LIFT was designed to be relatively simple to deliver, to be easy to integrate into a typical public elementary school schedule, and to minimize cost to provider and participant. Of key importance is that all families and children in a targeted grade are invited to participate in the program. Children considered at risk or high risk for problems are not siphoned off into special programs, thus decreasing the risks related to labeling and numerous other detrimental effects of social marginalization.

LIFT is one of a variety of programs that has been listed as a best practice or an evidence-based practice by several panels of scientists and practitioners (e.g., the U.S. Department of Education's Safe and Drug Free Schools panel; the Office of Juvenile Justice and Delinquency Prevention Blueprints for Violence Prevention panel) that reviewed the prevention and intervention literatures on youth problem behaviors in the late 1990s and early 2000s. Each panel had a somewhat different focus (e.g., some focused on one specific child problem behavior, others focused on a variety of such behaviors), and each panel used a slightly different definition for what constituted the best, so conclusions regarding programs varied.

To find the programs about which there was agreement, Metzler, Taylor, Eddy, Lichtenstein, and Hoeven (2002) cross-referenced 11 best practice lists that met three criteria: (a) the list was created through a national-level panel (usually funded by a federal agency or a large private foundation); (b) the list used specified and rigorous scientific standards of program efficacy or effectiveness; and (c) the list was designed to focus on one or more of a set of related child outcomes, including child conduct problems, academic achievement, and substance use/abuse. If a program appeared on at least three of the 11 lists, it was considered a solid indication of scientific support for the potential promise of the program for prevention or intervention. Forty-one programs appeared on at least three of the lists, including LIFT. The majority (i.e., 24) of those programs targeted children in the early and/or middle childhood periods, the age group that is targeted by LIFT. About half of them (i.e., 13) were multimodal, with the two most likely program components being parent management training and child social skills training. Most of the multimodal programs were designed as universal interventions and included at least some components delivered within the school context.

LIFT is a universal school-based intervention that includes three components that are delivered simultaneously: parent management training offered to all parents in a family, child social skills training offered to all children in the child's regular classroom, and a version of the Good Behavior Game, which is delivered on the playground to all children during the regular class recess time (Eddy, Reid, & Fetrow, 2000; Eddy, Reid, Fetrow, Lathrop, & Dickey, 2005; Reid et al., 1999). Over the 10-week program period, these components are tied together through a proactive communication plan designed to increase the flow of information between parents and teachers. Each component used in LIFT is an adaptation of interventions that had been tested in prior studies and that have been shown to lead to reduced conduct problems in children. Not surprisingly, LIFT shares key similarities with all of the preventive interventions highlighted in Chapter 6 of this handbook that target elementary school children and with programs highlighted in prevention chapters in other recent volumes on the conduct disorders (e.g., Murrihy, Kidman, & Ollendick, 2012).

Parent Management Training Component

Parent management training programs (e.g., Patterson, Reid, Jones, & Conger, 1975) focus on the development and strengthening of parenting skills to reinforce effective monitoring and supervision, positive involvement and encouragement, consistent and nonviolent discipline, and constructive family problem solving. Such programs were originally created for families of children with serious conduct problems and often lasted for as long as was required until clinically significant progress had been made. Across numerous high-quality studies, these programs have been found to be efficacious treatments, at least in the short run, for child conduct problems (Brestan & Eyberg, 1998; Litschge, Vaughn, & McCrea, 2010). For example, in a meta-analysis of 26 methodologically rigorous studies that compared outcomes for children whose parents/caregivers had received parent management training versus a comparison group, the average effect size for child conduct problems immediately following intervention was Cohen's $d = 0.80$ (Serketich & Dumas, 1996).

LIFT uses an adapted group-based version of parent management training. Program content focuses on skills in encouragement, discipline, supervision and monitoring, and family problem solving. Each of the six, 2-hour sessions follows the same format: brief review of parent experiences in home practice of parenting skills from the previous week;

brief lecture on new parenting skills, group discussion, and role-play practice; and presentation of the home practice assignment for the following week. At various points throughout the 6-week program, video clips are used to illustrate key parenting skills. Sessions take place in school classrooms and are offered several times per week in case parents miss their planned group meeting time. To reduce economic burdens for parents, child care and snacks are provided. If all parents in a family miss all sessions offered in a given week, they are offered a home visit makeup session. If a home visit is not possible, materials (e.g., handouts, video clips) are sent in the mail. Regardless of how a session was delivered, all parents are given a check-in call several days after their weekly session and provided consultation and support around their assigned home practice. If requested by a family at any time during the program, additional phone call or in-person sessions are held to discuss specific problems facing a family and to provide appropriate clinical referrals.

Child Social Skills Training Component

Child social skills training programs (e.g., Shure & Spivack, 1988) focus on the development and strengthening of cognitive and behavioral skills that may help children excel in social situations. Skills taught are related to empathy, interpersonal problem solving, and anger management. Numerous versions of these programs have been created for clinical and preventive applications. In terms of clinical treatment, in a meta-analysis of 84 studies that compared a child social skills training condition to a comparison group condition, the average effect size for conduct problems immediately postintervention was Cohen's $d = 0.38$, and at follow-up was Cohen's $d = 0.28$ (Lösel & Beelmann, 2003). In terms of preventive applications, in a meta-analysis of 213 school-based studies, the average effect size on conduct problems was Cohen's $d = 0.22$ (Durlak, Weissberg, Dymnicki, Taylor, & Schellinger, 2011; Grove et al., 2008).

In LIFT, program content focuses on listening; identifying and managing emotions; following directions, rules and other forms of cooperation; dealing with groups of peers; and solving problems. Twice each week for 10 weeks, 1-hour sessions are conducted within the child's classroom during the regular school day. The session at the beginning of each week focuses on teaching new skills. Each session follows the same format: brief lecture and role-plays on a specific set of social and problem-solving skills, structured small and large group skills practice, free play on the playground, and skills review and presentation of daily rewards. The session at the end of the week includes a class problem-solving session and free play on the playground.

Good Behavior Game Component

The Good Behavior Game provides positive behavior support to children as they practice and refine prosocial behaviors with peers and adults (Barrish, Saunders, & Wolfe, 1969). The game was originally developed for use in the classroom and has been applied with modest success as a preventive intervention during elementary school. For example, in a randomized trial, the game was found to result in reductions in teacher ratings of child aggression for boys and girls and in peer ratings of aggression for boys by the end of the school year (Dolan et al., 1993). In long-term follow-up, favorable program effects were found on teacher ratings of child aggression for boys, but only for those who were originally highest in aggressive behavior (e.g., Kellam, Rebok, Mayer, Ialongo, & Kalodner, 1994). Other studies of the game have also found positive impacts (for a review, see Embry, 2002).

In LIFT, the Good Behavior Game occurs during the free play, or class recess, portion of each session of the child social skills training program. Within a class of students, children are divided into small groups. During the game, individuals, groups, and the entire class can earn various rewards for displaying positive behaviors and not displaying negative behaviors. Individual and class rewards are given for the display of positive behaviors. Playground monitors, who give individual rewards, are taught to actively move about the playground during the recess period, closely monitor child behavior, and catch children exhibiting positive behaviors. When a monitor observes a child acting in an overtly positive manner toward peers, the monitor names the behavior, praises the child, and publicly acknowledges the behavior by giving the child a colorful nylon armband. At the end of recess, all armbands earned by class members are put into a class jar. When the jar is full, the entire class earns a highly desired reward, such as an extra recess period.

In contrast, rewards for small groups depend on the ability of group members to inhibit their negative interactions with peers. Throughout recess, each time a child is observed behaving in a negative manner, his or her behavior is noted. At the end of recess, the total number of negative points earned by a group is subtracted from a preset number of "good faith" positive points that each group was given at the beginning of recess. If a small group manages to retain a predetermined percentage of their positive points, each member earns a sticker. When the group earns a certain number of total points after several recesses, each member has the opportunity to select a small prize. In short, during the game, simple rewards formally acknowledge and reinforce both individual and group performance of positive social skills.

Parent–Teacher Communication

Communication between parents and teachers is widely considered to be vital to the success of a child during the primary and secondary grades (Barge & Loges, 2003). LIFT uses a variety of means of communication to maximize parent involvement. During each of the 10 weeks of child social skills training, parents receive weekly newsletters that describe LIFT activities at school and suggest complementary family activities. To supplement the newsletter, phone and answering machines are installed in each classroom (the program was designed before widespread use of cell phones and the Internet). Teachers are encouraged to leave daily messages about class activities and homework assignments on the "LIFT Line." Parents are encouraged to call for these messages and to leave messages for the teacher. Teachers can then respond as they choose. During their weekly phone contact throughout the parent management training component, parents are encouraged to call the LIFT Line and seek additional contact with teachers, as desired.

Training and Supervision

LIFT was designed to be taught by laypeople, teachers, or other helping professionals. During the randomized trial described in the following section, the instructors for the various program components were not serving as teachers in the study schools. LIFT instructors had a wide variety of educational experiences, from high school diplomas to doctorates in clinical psychology. Not only was initial training provided to instructors, recess monitors, and classroom teachers about the content and process of LIFT, but each of these individuals was also provided with ongoing supervision and support through a combination of weekly team and individual meetings.

PROGRAM OUTCOMES

Randomized Controlled Trial

Outcomes due to the LIFT program were examined in a community-based randomized controlled trial (see Reid et al., 1999). The trial focused on randomly chosen public elementary schools located in neighborhoods with households that were identified to be at or above the local median in terms of youth delinquency (defined as contact with police due to child misbehavior). Six schools were randomly assigned to a LIFT program group, six schools to a no LIFT control group, and six schools to serve as alternatives, if needed, should one or more schools refuse to participate (only three schools refused because of prior commitments to other programs or research studies). After school selection and agreement to participate, six schools (i.e., three LIFT schools, three control schools) were randomly assigned to have all fifth-grade classrooms participate in the trial, and six schools to have all first-grade classrooms participate. Because of different developmental challenges facing students, the LIFT program had slightly different content for first graders and their parents/caregivers versus fifth graders and their parents/caregivers (see Eddy et al., 2000).

Across the 12 schools, parents in 88% of eligible families agreed to participate in the study. The final sample included 671 children (50% girls) and at least one of their parents. Families tended to be from the lower-to-middle socioeconomic classes.

Similar to the local geographic area, 85% of children and parents were White. Demographic characteristics were similar between the intervention and control groups. Participants were assessed via interview, questionnaire, and direct observation before and after the 10-week intervention, and then on a yearly basis throughout childhood and adolescence. Participants were compensated for their time in participating in the assessments, but not for attending the program.

Initial Outcomes

More than 90% of the home and school content was delivered to more than 90% of children and parents (Reid et al., 1999). This unusually high level of participation was achieved because of the decision to provide home visits and mailings to parents when they were unable to attend group parenting sessions; only 28% of parents received all parent management training component materials through their attendance at the group sessions. Consumer satisfaction in terms of parent and teacher reports was quite high: 94% of parents stated they would recommend LIFT to other parents and 75% of teachers stated they would recommend LIFT to other teachers.

In terms of immediate program effects on children and parents, LIFT significantly decreased observed child physical aggression during free play with classmates and observed parent negative verbal behavior during family problem-solving interactions. LIFT also significantly increased teacher ratings of child socially skilled behaviors toward classmates 1 year after the program (Reid et al., 1999). Favorable impacts were observed for both first- and fifth-grade children and families, and for boys and girls, and effect sizes ranged from Cohen's $d = 0.12$ to $d = 0.57$. The positive effects during free play were particularly pronounced for the children who exhibited the highest levels of physical aggression on the playground before the start of the LIFT program (Stoolmiller, Eddy, & Reid, 2000).

Follow-Up Outcomes

Because of the significant differences in developmental challenges facing the first- and fifth-grade participants, follow-up analyses for the two age groups were conducted separately. In the first-grade sample, relative to controls, participants in the LIFT group displayed significantly less growth in ADHD behaviors during the first 3 years following the intervention (Reid & Eddy, 2002). In the fifth-grade sample, significant effects were found during the first 3 years on indicators of delinquency and early substance use. In terms of their relative risk ratios, compared with LIFT participants, control participants were 1.5 times more likely to be detained for the first time by police and 1.5 times more likely to report patterned alcohol use (Eddy, Reid, Stoolmiller, & Fetrow, 2003). However, no differences were found in reports of tobacco or marijuana use initiation.

As first graders reached middle and high school, favorable effects of LIFT were found on indicators of conduct problems. At ages 15 to 16, the DISC-IV, a clinical diagnostic interview based on the *Diagnostic and Statistical Manual of Mental Disorders, Fourth Edition* (*DSM–IV*; American Psychiatric Association, 1994) was administered to participants (Shaffer, Fisher, Lucas, Dulcan, & Schwab-Stone, 2000). A significant difference ($p < .05$) between the groups was found in terms of conduct disorder, in which 2.6% of LIFT program participants met criteria versus 5.5% of control participants. The evaluation team also used survival analysis to examine time to first detainment by police by the age of 14 years. A nonsignificant trend was found ($p <. 10$), with a total of 6.0% of intervention participants detained versus 11.0% of control participants. As fifth graders reached the end of high school, effects were examined on growth in conduct problems and depression, and on latent classes of growth curves for each (Kerr, Reinke, & Eddy, 2013; Reinke, Eddy, Dishion, & Reid, 2012). Across adolescence, LIFT was not found to favorably influence growth in either type of problem or latent class membership. Effects were also examined on substance use across the full period of adolescence. LIFT was associated with a 10% reduction in risk in terms of initiating alcohol use or tobacco use (DeGarmo, Eddy, Reid, & Fetrow, 2009). The program also significantly reduced the rate of growth in use of illicit drugs and tobacco, and lowered average levels of use of tobacco, alcohol, and illicit drugs during adolescence among LIFT compared with control youth.

Favorable program effects in LIFT were greater for both the first- and fifth-grade samples among children who displayed the highest levels of conduct problems before LIFT began. For example, for an initial examination, a configural frequency analysis was conducted to examine patterns of dichotomized scores of parent, teacher, and peer ratings of conduct problems made before the intervention (see Bergman & Magnusson, 1987; Cairns & Cairns, 1994). For each rater, continuous ratings were recoded 1 (if the score for a given child was in the top 20% of all scores in the sample) and 0 (if the score was in the bottom 80%). Only two patterns occurred more than would be expected by chance: 000 (parents, teachers, and peers all scored the child low on conduct problems) and 111 (parents, teachers, and peers all scored the child high on conduct problems).

Once patterns were identified, the relations between predisposing risk status and police detainment resulting from child misbehavior during adolescence were examined. For the fifth-grade sample, boys and girls exposed to the LIFT program who were rated high on conduct problems were less likely to be detained by police by age 14 years compared with control boys and girls (i.e., boys: 100% control vs. 75% LIFT; girls: 50% control vs. 0% LIFT). However, police detainment rates were similar across groups for those youth for whom everyone agreed were low on conduct problems (i.e., boys: 9% control vs. 6% LIFT; girls: 4% control vs. 4% LIFT). Results for the first-grade sample were similar for boys and girls: 50% of high conduct problem control participants detained versus only 20% of similar LIFT participants, and with 11% of low conduct problems control participants detained versus 3% of similar LIFT participants.

CONCLUSION

The LIFT program is a multimodal preventive intervention package encompassing parent management training, child social skills training, and the Good Behavior Game. Before the creation of LIFT, versions of each of these components had been tested in multiple randomized trials with favorable effects on relevant youth outcomes. LIFT is well liked by participants and appears to fit well within the regular daily schedule of public elementary schools, at least within the targeted community. Within the context of a randomized trial, the program had an effect on a variety of important precursors to more serious conduct problems, such as physical aggression on the playground and on related problems over the long run, such as contact with police during early adolescence and substance use across adolescence. However, to date, longer term effects on growth in conduct problems have not been found.

The findings illustrate the potential promise, and limitations, of brief universal prevention programs, such as LIFT. Particularly promising is that initial positive effects are possible from universal programs, even for the highest-risk children. This finding alone is encouraging for a 10-week program conducted during one grade in primary school. In terms of limits, not surprisingly, one systematic and short term attempt like LIFT to prevent such a complicated outcome as conduct disorder is not enough to fully inoculate a population. Additional approaches are needed, and they are needed over the long run as key players (e.g., peers, siblings, parents/caregivers, teachers) enter and leave the child's social world.

Nevertheless, although the effects of a program like LIFT on conduct problems and substance use are modest, if promising programs such as LIFT were disseminated widely, some children would likely be diverted from embarking on paths that lead to delinquency as well as crime and substance abuse. Preventing even a small number of criminal acts and/or substance abuse cases during adulthood could result in substantial savings, given the high emotional and financial toll related to these interrelated issues (Greenwood, Model, & Rydell, 1996).

Despite the potential gains from the delivery of evidence-based programs such as LIFT, disseminating evidence-based programs continues to be a challenging endeavor. For example, between 2005 and 2008, the prevalence of U.S. schools that used evidence-based drug use prevention curricula (some of which share similarities with LIFT) rose from 23% to 26%, but the prevalence of untested curricula rose from 18% to 28% (Ringwalt et al., 2009, 2011), even though the federal No Child Left Behind Act of 2001 (Pub. L. No. 107–110) mandates the implementation of evidence-based drug prevention curricula in the nation's schools. Thus, even with federal (and state) statutes directing the consideration of research evidence when choosing programs, a variety of barriers remain to bringing evidence-based programs into practice.

One major problem, and one that currently appears to be getting worse given the continued financial instability in the United States and around the world, is limited financial resources to support the purchase and delivery of evidence-based programs in schools. Creative solutions are needed to facilitate the movement of evidence-based practices—in contrast to programs—into the ongoing, day-to-day work of teachers and other school staff. The components used in LIFT, for example, were first developed more than 40 years ago and have been examined in randomized trials numerous times with positive outcomes. The pressing question is, how long is reasonable to wait to move an evidence-based practice into standard practice?

One alternative would be to bring knowledge and skill instruction about evidence-based practices into the regular curricula of colleges and universities. Rather than evidence-based programs being something that a professional receives training and certification in after graduation (i.e., through continuing education), training in evidence-based practices, including effective techniques for ongoing supervision, support, and use, could become part of standard practice in teacher, administrator, counselor, and school psychologist training. An additional, and synergistic, change would be to bring the cost of necessary materials (e.g., curricula, handouts) and training down to an affordable price for all schools. Finding ways for schools to more effectively support and supervise personnel in the delivery of evidence-based practices, and to fund such activities on an ongoing basis, is also crucial. In short, a variety of factors is limiting the spread of evidence-based practices, and something needs to change.

Whatever happens in the future in terms of evidence-based programs and practices, it would behoove the field to remember the words of Carroll (2012):

> The point of training providers in evidence-based practices is not to have them simply go through the motions of using motivational language or teaching coping skills but to use these techniques, and others, to produce the most successful outcomes in the largest number of cases possible. (p. 1031)

If evidence-based practices do not achieve this goal, they are not useful. The evidence for the effectiveness of programs in the field is slim, mostly because few studies have examined evidence-based programs under truly real-world conditions. Evidence-based programs are a place to start, but much work lies ahead in terms of whether they are a place to end. The only way to find out is to build a truly reliable and valid evidence base through multiple research groups and within multiple communities, and by conducting multiple rigorous research studies on the outcomes of promising programs. In terms of conduct problems, conduct disorder, and co-occurring problems, such as early substance use, it is time for the field to value replication over novelty and implementation studies over efficacy studies.

References

American Psychiatric Association. (1994). *Diagnostic and statistical manual of mental disorders* (4th ed.). Washington, DC: Author.

American Psychiatric Association. (2013). *Diagnostic and statistical manual of mental disorders* (5th ed.). Arlington, VA: Author.

Bardone, A. M., Moffitt, T. E., Caspi, A., Dickson, N., & Silva, P. A. (1998). Adult physical health outcomes of adolescent girls with conduct disorder, depression, and anxiety. *Journal of the American Academy of Child & Adolescent Psychiatry*, *37*, 594–601. doi:10.1097/00004583-199806000-00009

Barge, J. K., & Loges, W. E. (2003). Parent, student, and teacher perceptions of parental involvement. *Journal of Applied Communication Research*, *31*, 140–163. doi:10.1080/0090988032000064597

Barrish, H. H., Saunders, M., & Wolfe, M. D. (1969). Good behavior Game: Effects of individual contingencies for group consequences and disruptive behavior in a classroom. *Journal of Applied Behavior Analysis*, 2, 119–124. doi:10.1901/jaba.1969.2-119

Bergman, L. R., & Magnusson, D. (1987). A person approach to the study of the development and adjustment problems: An empirical example and some research strategy considerations. In D. Magnusson & O. Ohman (Eds.), *Psychopathology: An interactional perspective* (pp. 383–401). New York, NY: Academic Press.

Blumstein, A., Cohen, J., Roth, J. A., & Visher, C. A. (Eds.). (1986). *Criminal careers and "career criminals."* Washington, DC: National Academy Press.

Breslau, J., Miller, E., Chung, W. J., & Schweitzer, J. B. (2011). Childhood and adolescent onset psychiatric disorders, substance use and failure to graduate high school on time. *Journal of Psychiatric Research*, *45*, 295–301. doi:10.1016/j.jpsychires.2010.06.014

Breslau, J., Saito, N., Tancredi, D. J., Nock, M., & Gilman, S. E. (2012). Classes of conduct disorder symptoms and their life course correlates in a US national sample. *Psychological Medicine*, *42*, 1081–1089. doi:10.1017/S003329171100198X

Brestan, E. V., & Eyberg, S. M. (1998). Effective psychosocial treatments of conduct-disordered children and adolescents: 29 years, 82 studies, and 5,272 kids. *Journal of Clinical Child Psychology*, *27*, 180–189. doi:10.1207/s15374424jccp2702_5

Burke, J. D., Loeber, R., & Birmaher, B. (2002). Oppositional defiant disorder and conduct disorder: A review of the past 10 years, part II. *Journal of the American Academy of Child & Adolescent Psychiatry*, *41*, 1275–1293. doi:10.1097/00004583-200211000-00009

Cairns, R. B., & Cairns, B. D. (1994). *Lifelines and risks.* New York, NY: Cambridge University Press.

Carroll, K. M. (2012). Dissemination of evidence-based practices: How far we've come, and how much further we've got to go. *Addiction*, *107*, 1031–1033. doi:10.1111/j.1360-0443.2011.03755.x

Cohen, M. A. (1998). The monetary value of saving a high risk youth. *Journal of Quantitative Criminology*, *14*, 5–33. doi:10.1023/A:1023092324459

Coie, J. D., & Jacobs, M. R. (1993). The role of social context in the prevention of conduct disorder. *Development and Psychopathology*, *5*, 263–275. doi:10.1017/S0954579400004387

Colman, I., Murray, J., Abbott, R. A., Maughan, B., Kuh, D., Croudace, T. J., & Jones, P. B. (2009). Outcomes of conduct problems in adolescence: 40 year follow-up of national cohort. *British Medical Journal*, *338*, 208–211. doi:10.1136/bmj.a2981

Costello, E. J., Mustillo, S., Erkanli, A., Keeler, G., & Angold, A. (2003). Prevalence and development of psychiatric disorders in childhood and adolescence. *Archives of General Psychiatry*, *60*, 837–844. doi:10.1001/archpsyc.60.8.837

DeGarmo, D. S., Eddy, J. M., Reid, J. B., & Fetrow, R. A. (2009). Evaluating mediators of the impact of the Linking the Interests of Families and Teachers (LIFT) multimodal preventive intervention on substance use initiation and growth across adolescence. *Prevention Science*, *10*, 208–220. doi:10.1007/s11121-009-0126-0

Dodge, K. A. (2000). Conduct disorder. In A. J. Sameroff, M. Lewis, & S. M. Miller (Eds.), *Handbook of developmental psychopathology* (2nd ed., pp. 447–463). New York, NY: Kluwer Academic/Plenum. doi:10.1007/978-1-4615-4163-9_24

Dolan, L. J., Kellam, S. G., Brown, C. H., Werthamer-Larsson, L., Rebok, G. W., . . . Wheeler, L. (1993). The short-term impact of two classroom-based preventive interventions on aggressive and shy behaviors and poor achievement. *Journal of Applied Developmental Psychology*, *14*, 317–345. doi:10.1016/0193-3973(93)90013-L

Dubas, J. S., & Snider, B. A. (1993). The role of community-based youth groups in enhancing learning and achievement through non-formal education. In R. M. Lerner (Ed.), *Early adolescence: Perspectives on research, policy, and intervention* (pp. 150–174). Hillsdale, NJ: Erlbaum.

Durlak, J. A., Weissberg, R. P., Dymnicki, A. B., Taylor, R. D., & Schellinger, K. B. (2011). The impact of enhancing students' social and emotional learning: A meta-analysis of school-based universal interventions. *Child Development*, *82*, 405–432. doi:10.1111/j.1467-8624.2010.01564.x

Eddy, J. M., Reid, J. B., & Fetrow, R. A. (2000). An elementary school-based prevention program targeting modifiable antecedents of youth delinquency and violence: Linking the Interests of Families and Teachers (LIFT). *Journal of Emotional and Behavioral Disorders*, *8*, 165–176. doi:10.1177/106342660000800304

Eddy, J. M., Reid, J. B., Fetrow, R. A., Lathrop, M., & Dickey, C. (2005). The Linking the Interests of Families and Teachers (LIFT) prevention program for youth antisocial behavior: Description, outcomes, and feasibility in the community. In M. H. Epstein, K. Kutash, & A. J. Duchnowski (Eds.), *Outcomes for children and youth with emotional and behavioral disabilities and their families: Program and evaluation best practices* (2nd ed., pp. 479–499). Austin, TX: Pro-Ed.

Eddy, J. M., Reid, J. B., Stoolmiller, M., & Fetrow, R. A. (2003). Outcomes during middle school for an elementary school-based preventive intervention for conduct problems: Follow-up results from a randomized trial. *Behavior Therapy*, *34*, 535–552. doi:10.1016/S0005-7894(03)80034-5

Embry, D. D. (2002). The Good Behavior Game: A best practice candidate as a universal behavioral vaccine.

Clinical Child and Family Psychology Review, *5*, 273–297. doi:10.1023/A:1020977107086

Emerson, E., Einfeld, S., & Stancliffe, R. J. (2011). Predictors of the persistence of conduct difficulties in children with cognitive delay. *Journal of Child Psychology and Psychiatry*, *52*, 1184–1194. doi:10.1111/j.1469-7610.2011.02413.x

Farrington, D. P. (1986). Stepping stones to adult criminal careers. In D. Olweus, J. Block, & M. R. Yarrow (Eds.), *Development of antisocial and pro-social behaviour* (pp. 359–384). New York, NY: Academic Press.

Farrington, D. P., & Wikström, P. O. H. (1994). Criminal careers in London and Stockholm: A cross-national comparative study. In E. G. M. Weitekamp & H. J. Kerner (Eds.), *Cross-national longitudinal research on human development and criminal behavior* (pp. 65–89). The Netherlands: Kluwer Academic. doi:10.1007/978-94-011-0864-5_2

Feehan, M., McGee, R., Raja, S. N., & Williams, S. M. (1994). DSM-III-R disorders in New Zealand 18-year-olds. *Australian and New Zealand Journal of Psychiatry*, *28*, 87–99. doi:10.3109/00048679409075849

Fergusson, D. M., Lynskey, M. T., & Horwood, L. J. (1996). Origins of comorbidity between conduct and affective disorders. *Journal of the American Academy of Child & Adolescent Psychiatry*, *35*, 451–460. doi:10.1097/00004583-199604000-00011

Greenwood, P. W., Model, K. E., & Rydell, C. P. (1996). *Diverting children from a life of crime: Measuring costs and benefits*. Berkeley: University of California.

Grove, A. B., Evans, S. W., Pastor, D. A., & Mack, S. D. (2008). A meta-analytic examination of follow-up studies of programs designed to prevent the primary symptoms of oppositional defiant and conduct disorders. *Aggression and Violent Behavior*, *13*, 169–184. doi:10.1016/j.avb.2008.03.001

Hawkins, J. D., Herrenkohl, T., Farrington, D. P., Brewer, D., Catalano, R. F., & Harachi, T. W. (1998). A review of predictors of youth violence. In R. Loeber & D. P. Farrington (Eds.), *Serious and violent juvenile offenders: Risk factors and successful intervention* (pp. 107–146). Thousand Oaks, CA: Sage.

Hawkins, J. D., & Weis, J. G. (1985). The social development model: An integrated approach to delinquency prevention. *Journal of Primary Prevention*, *6*, 73–97. doi:10.1007/BF01325432

Herrenkohl, T. I., Maguin, E., Hill, H. G., Hawkins, J. D., Abbott, R. D., & Catalano, R. F. (2000). Developmental risk factors for youth violence. *Journal of Adolescent Health*, *26*, 176–186. doi:10.1016/S1054-139X(99)00065-8

Hinshaw, S. P. (1987). On the distinction between attentional deficits/hyperactivity and conduct problems/aggression in child psychopathology. *Psychological Bulletin*, *101*, 443–463. doi:10.1037/0033-2909.101.3.443

Hinshaw, S., Lahey, B. B., & Hart, E. (1993). Issues of taxonomy and comorbidity in the development of conduct disorder. *Development and Psychopathology*, *5*, 31–49. doi:10.1017/S0954579400004247

INSERM Collective Expertise Centre. (2005). *Conduct disorder in children and adolescents* (INSERM Collective Expert Reports [Internet]). Retrieved from http://www.ncbi.nlm.nih.gov/books/NBK7133/

Kaslow, N. J., Deering, C. G., & Racusin, G. R. (1994). Depressed children and their families. *Clinical Psychology Review*, *14*, 39–59. doi:10.1016/0272-7358(94)90047-7

Kazdin, A. E. (1995). *Conduct disorders in childhood and adolescence* (2nd ed.). Thousand Oaks, CA: Sage. doi:10.4135/9781483345406

Kellam, S. G., & Rebok, G. W. (1992). Building developmental and etiological theory through epidemiologically based preventive intervention trials. In J. McCord & R. E. Tremblay (Eds.), *Preventing antisocial behavior: Interventions from birth though adolescence* (pp. 162–195). New York, NY: Guilford Press.

Kellam, S. G., Rebok, G. W., Mayer, L. S., Ialongo, N., & Kalodner, C. R. (1994). Depressive symptoms over first grade and their response to a developmental epidemiologically based preventive trial aimed at improving achievement. *Development and Psychopathology*, *6*, 463–481. doi:10.1017/S0954579400006052

Kerr, D. C. R., Reinke, W. M., & Eddy, J. M. (2013). Trajectories of depressive symptoms and externalizing behaviors across adolescence: Associations with histories of suicide attempt and ideation in early adulthood. *Suicide and Life-Threatening Behavior*, *43*, 50–66. doi:10.1111/j.1943-278X.2012.00127.x

Kessler, R. C., Walters, E. E., & Forthofer, M. S. (1998). The social consequences of psychiatric disorders, III: Probability of marital stability. *The American Journal of Psychiatry*, *155*, 1092–1096.

Kjellstrand, J., Cearley, J., Eddy, J. M., Foney, D., & Martinez, C. R. (2012). Characteristics of incarcerated fathers and mothers: Implications for preventive interventions targeting children and families. *Children and Youth Services Review*, *34*, 2409–2415. doi:10.1016/j.childyouth.2012.08.008

Knapp, M. R. J., Scott, S., & Davies, J. (1999). The cost of antisocial behavior in younger children: A pilot study of economic and family impact. *Clinical Child Psychology and Psychiatry*, *4*, 457–473. doi:10.1177/1359104599004004003

Lahey, B. B., Miller, T. L., Gordon, R. A., & Riley, A. W. (1999). Developmental epidemiology of the disruptive behavior disorders. In H. C. Quay &

A. E. Hogan (Eds.), *Handbook of disruptive behavior disorders* (pp. 23–48). New York, NY: Kluwer Academic. doi:10.1007/978-1-4615-4881-2_2

Lahey, B. B., Schwab-Stone, M., Goodman, S. H., Waldman, I. D., Canino, G., Rathouz, P. J., . . . Jensen, P. S. (2000). Age and gender differences in oppositional behavior and conduct problems: A cross-sectional household study of middle childhood and adolescence. *Journal of Abnormal Psychology, 109*, 488–503. doi:10.1037/0021-843X.109.3.488

Lahey, B. B., & Waldman, I. D. (2012). Annual research review: Phenotypic and causal structure of conduct disorder in the broader context of prevalent forms of psychopathology. *Journal of Child Psychology and Psychiatry, 53*, 536–557. doi:10.1111/j.1469-7610.2011.02509.x

Lipsey, M. W., & Derzon, J. H. (1998). Predictors of violent or serious delinquency in adolescence and early adulthood: A synthesis of longitudinal research. In R. Loeber & D. P. Farrington (Eds.), *Serious and violent juvenile offenders: Risk factors and successful interventions* (pp. 86–105). Thousand Oaks, CA: Sage.

Litschge, C. M., Vaughn, M. G., & McCrea, C. (2010). The empirical status of treatments for children and youth with conduct problems: An overview of meta-analytic studies. *Research on Social Work Practice, 20*, 21–35. doi:10.1177/1049731508331247

Loeber, R., Burke, J. D., Lahey, B. B., Winters, A., & Zera, M. (2000). Oppositional defiant and conduct disorder: A review of the past 10 years, part I. *Journal of the American Academy of Child & Adolescent Psychiatry, 39*, 1468–1484. doi:10.1097/00004583-200012000-00007

Loeber, R., Farrington, D. P., Stouthamer-Loeber, M., & Van Kammen, W. B. (Eds.). (1998). *Antisocial behavior and mental health problems: Explanatory factors in childhood and adolescence.* Mahwah, NJ: Erlbaum.

Loeber, R., & Keenan, K. (1994). Interaction between conduct disorder and its comorbid conditions: Effects of age and gender. *Clinical Psychology Review, 14*, 497–523. doi:10.1016/0272-7358(94)90015-9

Lösel, F., & Beelmann, A. (2003). Effects of child skills training in preventing antisocial behavior: A systematic review of randomized evaluations. *Annals of the American Academy of Political and Social Science, 587*, 84–109. doi:10.1177/0002716202250793

Markus, H., & Nurius, P. (1986). Possible selves. *American Psychologist, 41*, 954–969. doi:10.1037/0003-066X.41.9.954

Mathijssen, J. J. P., Koot, H. M., & Verhulst, F. C. (1999). Predicting change in problem behavior from child and family characteristics and stress in referred children and adolescents. *Development and Psychopathology, 11*, 305–320. doi:10.1017/S0954579499002072

Maughan, B., Pickles, A., & Quinton, D. (1995). Parental hostility, childhood behavior, and adult social functioning. In J. McCord (Ed.), *Coercion and punishment in long-term perspectives* (pp. 34–58). New York, NY: Cambridge University Press.

Maughan, B., Rowe, R., Messer, J., Goodman, R., & Meltzer, H. (2004). Conduct disorder and oppositional defiant disorder in a national sample: Developmental epidemiology. *Journal of Child Psychology and Psychiatry, 45*, 609–621. doi:10.1111/j.1469-7610.2004.00250.x

Merikangas, K. R., He, J. P., Burstein, M., Swanson, S. A., Avenevoli, S., Cui, L., . . . Swendsen, J. (2010). Lifetime prevalence of mental disorders in U.S. adolescents: Results from the National Comorbidity Survey Replication—Adolescent Supplement. *Journal of the American Academy of Child & Adolescent Psychiatry, 49*, 980–989. doi:10.1016/j.jaac.2010.05.017

Metzler, C., Taylor, T., Eddy, J. M., Lichtenstein, D., & Hoeven, M. (2002, May). Finding common ground among "best practices" lists: The evidence base and program elements of top family-focused and school-based programs. In C. Metzler (Chair), *Finding common ground among "best practice" lists.* Symposium conducted at the Tenth Annual Meeting of the Society for Prevention Research, Seattle, WA.

Morcillo, C., Duarte, C. S., Sala, R., Wang, S., Lejuez, C. W., Kerridge, B. T., & Blanco, C. (2012). Conduct disorder and adult psychiatric diagnoses: Associations and gender differences in the U.S. adult population. *Journal of Psychiatric Research, 46*, 323–330. doi:10.1016/j.jpsychires.2011.10.012

Mrazek, P. G., & Haggerty, R. J. (Eds.). (1994). *Reducing risks for mental disorders: Frontiers for preventive intervention research.* Washington, DC: National Academy Press.

Murrihy, R. C., Kidman, A. D., & Ollendick, T. H. (Eds.). (2012). *Clinical handbook of assessing and treating conduct problems in youth.* New York, NY: Springer.

National Reading Panel. (2000). *Teaching children to read: An evidence-based assessment of the scientific literature on reading and its implications for reading instruction.* Washington, DC: National Institute on Child Health and Human Development.

Needleman, H. L., Riess, J. A., Tobin, M. J., Biesecker, G. E., & Greenhouse, J. B. (1996). Bone lead levels and delinquent behavior. *JAMA, 275*, 363–369. doi:10.1001/jama.1996.03530290033034

No Child Left Behind Act of 2001, Pub. L. No. 107-110, 20 U.S.C. §§ 6301-8962 (2002).

Odgers, C. L., Caspi, A., Broadbent, J. M., Dickson, N., Hancox, R. J., Harrington, H., . . . Moffitt, T. E. (2007). Prediction of differential adult health burden by conduct problem subtypes in males. *Archives of General Psychiatry*, *64*, 476–484. doi:10.1001/archpsyc.64.4.476

Offord, D. R., Boyle, M. H., & Racine, Y. A. (1991). The epidemiology of antisocial behavior in childhood and adolescence. In D. J. Pepler & K. H. Rubin (Eds.), *The development and treatment of childhood aggression* (pp. 31–54). Hillsdale, NJ: Erlbaum.

Offord, D. R., Boyle, M. H., Racine, Y. A., Fleming, J. E., Cadman, D. T., Blum, H. M., . . . Woodward, C. A. (1992). Outcome, prognosis, and risk in a longitudinal follow-up study. *Journal of the American Academy of Child & Adolescent Psychiatry*, *31*, 916–923. doi:10.1097/00004583-199209000-00021

Osborn, A. F., Butler, N. R., & Morris, A. C. (1984). *The social life of Britain's five-year-olds: A report of the child health and education study.* London, England: Routledge & Kegan Paul.

Patterson, G. R. (1982). *Coercive family process.* Eugene, OR: Castalia.

Patterson, G. R., Reid, J. B., & Dishion, T. (1992). *Antisocial boys. A social interaction approach* (Vol. 4). Eugene, OR: Castalia.

Patterson, G. R., Reid, J. B., Jones, R. R., & Conger, R. E. (1975). *A social learning approach to family intervention: Families with aggressive children* (Vol. 1). Eugene, OR: Castalia.

Quinton, D., Pickles, A., Maughan, B., & Rutter, M. (1993). Partners, peers and pathways: Assortative pairing and continuities in conduct disorder. *Development and Psychopathology*, *5*, 763–783. doi:10.1017/S0954579400006271

Reid, J. B., & Eddy, J. M. (1997). The prevention of antisocial behavior: Some considerations in the search for effective interventions. In D. M. Stoff, J. Breiling, & J. D. Maser (Eds.), *Handbook of antisocial behavior* (pp. 343–356). New York, NY: Wiley.

Reid, J. B., & Eddy, J. M. (2002). Preventive efforts during the elementary school years: The Linking the Interests of Families and Teachers project. In J. B. Reid, G. R. Patterson, & J. Snyder (Eds.), *Antisocial behavior in children and adolescents: A developmental analysis and model for intervention* (pp. 219–233). Washington, DC: American Psychological Association. doi:10.1037/10468-011

Reid, J. B., Eddy, J. M., Fetrow, R. A., & Stoolmiller, M. (1999). Description and immediate impacts of a preventive intervention for conduct problems. *American Journal of Community Psychology*, *27*, 483–518. doi:10.1023/A:1022181111368

Reid, J. B., Patterson, G. R., & Snyder, J. (Eds.). (2002). *Antisocial behavior in children and adolescents: A developmental analysis and model for intervention.* Washington, DC: American Psychological Association. doi:10.1037/10468-000

Reinke, W. M., Eddy, J. M., Dishion, T. J., & Reid, J. B. (2012). Joint trajectories of symptoms of disruptive behavior problems and depressive symptoms during early adolescence and adjustment problems during emerging adulthood. *Journal of Abnormal Child Psychology*, *40*, 1123–1136. doi:10.1007/s10802-012-9630-y

Ringwalt, C., Vincus, A. A., Hanley, S., Ennett, S. T., Bowling, J. M., & Haws, S. (2011). The prevalence of evidence-based drug use prevention curricula in U.S. middle schools in 2008. *Prevention Science*, *12*, 63–69. doi:10.1007/s11121-010-0184-3

Ringwalt, C., Vincus, A. A., Hanley, S., Ennett, S. T., Bowling, J. M., & Rohrbach, L. (2009). The prevalence of evidence-based drug use prevention curricula in U.S. middle schools in 2005. *Prevention Science*, *10*, 33–40. doi:10.1007/s11121-008-0112-y

Robins, L. N. (1991). Conduct disorder. *Child Psychology & Psychiatry & Allied Disciplines*, *32*, 193–212.

Robins, L. N., & McEvoy, L. (1990). Conduct problems as predictors of substance abuse. In L. N. Robins & M. Rutter (Eds.), *Straight and devious pathways from childhood to adulthood* (pp. 182–204). New York, NY: Cambridge University Press.

Robins, L. N., & Price, R. K. (1991). Adult disorders predicted by childhood conduct problems: Results from the NIMH Epidemiologic Catchment Area project. *Psychiatry: Interpersonal and Biological Processes*, *54*, 116–132.

Rogoff, B. (1990). *Apprenticeship in thinking: Cognitive development in social context.* New York, NY: Oxford University Press.

Rutter, M. (1981). Epidemiological/longitudinal strategies and causal research in child psychiatry. *Journal of the American Academy of Child Psychiatry*, *20*, 513–544. doi:10.1016/S0002-7138(09)61643-5

Rutter, M., Cox, A., Tupling, C., Berger, M., & Yule, W. (1975). Attainment and adjustment in two geographical areas: I. The prevalence of psychiatric disorder. *British Journal of Psychiatry*, *126*, 493–509. doi:10.1192/bjp.126.6.493

Sampson, R. J., Raudenbush, S. W., & Earls, F. (1997). Neighborhoods and violent crime: A multilevel study of collective efficacy. *Science*, *277*, 918–924. doi:10.1126/science.277.5328.918

Shaffer, D., Fisher, P., Lucas, C., Dulcan, M. K., & Schwab-Stone, M. (2000). NIMH Diagnostic Interview Schedule for Children, Version IV (NIMH DISC-IV): Description, differences from previous versions and reliability of some common diagnoses. *Journal of the American Academy of Child & Adolescent Psychiatry*, *39*, 28–38. doi:10.1097/00004583-200001000-00014

Shure, M. B., & Spivack, G. (1988). Interpersonal cognitive problem solving. In R. H. Price, E. L. Cowen, R. P. Lorion, & J. Ramos-McKay (Eds.), *Fourteen ounces of prevention: A casebook for practitioners* (pp. 69–82). Washington, DC: American Psychological Association. doi:10.1037/10064-006

Serketich, W. J., & Dumas, J. E. (1996). The effectiveness of behavioral parent training to modify antisocial behavior in children: A meta-analysis. *Behavior Therapy*, *27*, 171–186. doi:10.1016/S0005-7894(96)80013-X

Stoolmiller, M., Eddy, J. M., & Reid, J. B. (2000). Detecting and describing preventive intervention effects in a universal school-based randomized trial targeting delinquent and violent behavior. *Journal of Consulting and Clinical Psychology*, *68*, 296–306. doi:10.1037/0022-006X.68.2.296

Vygotsky, S. (1978). *Mind in society.* Cambridge, MA: Harvard University Press.

Wolff, S. (1961). Symptomatology and outcome of preschool children with behavior disorders attending a child guidance clinic. *Child Psychology & Psychiatry, and Allied Disciplines*, *2*, 269–276. doi:10.1111/j.1469-7610.1961.tb02031.x

Wolfgang, M. E., Figlio, R. M., & Sellin, T. (1972). *Delinquency in a birth cohort.* Chicago, IL: University of Chicago Press.

Zoccolillo, M. (1992). Co-occurrence of conduct disorder and its adult outcomes with depressive and anxiety disorders: A review. *Journal of the American Academy of Child & Adolescent Psychiatry*, *31*, 547–556. doi:10.1097/00004583-199205000-00024

Zoccolillo, M., Pickles, A., Quinton, D., & Rutter, M. (1992). The outcome of childhood conduct disorder: Implications for defining antisocial personality disorder and conduct disorder. *Psychological Medicine*, *22*, 971–986. doi:10.1017/S003329170003854X

Part IV

SCHOOL-BASED DRUG USE PREVENTION PROGRAMS

CHAPTER 9

EVALUATING THE EFFICACY OF PROJECT TND: EVIDENCE FROM SEVEN RESEARCH TRIALS

Steve Y. Sussman

There is a tremendous need for ongoing dialogue as to whether drug abuse prevention programs work in the manner hypothesized. This crucial discussion gives traction to the field with regard to factors that may enhance or impede program efficacy. Toward this end, the present chapter provides the primary developer's perspective on how Project Towards No Drug Abuse (TND) may be working to reduce drug use among youth. First, the history of the project is described. This is followed by discussion of the intervention theory, a motivation enhancement, life-skills decision making (MSD) model of behavior change. Program contents are then described within the context of the intervention protocol. Seven cluster-randomized controlled trials (C-RCTs) using Project TND are then summarized in chronological order. Next, the chapter includes a broad discussion outlining how program material provides a social-interactional context through which behavior "change talk" is elicited, leading to behavior change. The chapter closes with a discussion of notable similarities and differences between Project TND and motivational interviewing (MI) and provides suggestions for future process research that can enhance youth drug abuse prevention.

Project TND is a 12-session school-based prevention program developed to deter youth from smoking cigarettes; drinking alcohol; and using illicit substances, including marijuana and other drugs (e.g., cocaine, methamphetamine, painkillers). The program was developed specifically for older teens, particularly those at relatively high risk for drug abuse (e.g., alternative high school youth). Since its inception in 1992, Project TND has undergone seven different C-RCTs that have experimentally manipulated different aspects of the program. A consistent body of evidence has shown favorable program effects on 30-day substance use at the 1-year or longer follow-up (Dent, Sussman, McCuller, & Stacy, 2001; Rohrbach, Sun, & Sussman, 2010; Sun, Skara, Sun, Dent, & Sussman, 2006; Sun, Sussman, Dent, & Rohrbach, 2008; Sussman, Dent, Simon, Stacy, & Craig, 1998; Sussman, Dent, & Stacy, 2002; Sussman, Sun, McCuller, & Dent, 2003; Sussman, Sun, Rohrbach, & Spruijt-Metz, 2012; Valente et al., 2007). Favorable program effects on hard drug use (a composite of cocaine, hallucinogens, stimulants, inhalants, ecstasy, painkillers, tranquilizers, and other drugs [i.e., PCP, steroids, GHB, and K]) have been found in all seven trials at 1-year follow-up. In addition, favorable program effects on hard drug use have been demonstrated in the two RCTs that involved 2-year follow-up and likewise in one 5-year follow-up study (Sun et al., 2006; Sussman, Sun, et al., 2003). A composite of hard drug use is often necessary analytically because of the relatively low base rates for

Preparation for this chapter was supported by a grant from the National Institute on Drug Abuse (R01 DA020138). The content of this chapter is solely the responsibility of the author and does not necessarily represent the official views of the National Institute on Drug Abuse.

http://dx.doi.org/10.1037/14550-010
Handbook of Adolescent Drug Use Prevention: Research, Intervention Strategies, and Practice, L. M. Scheier (Editor)

many hard drug types. Bundling these drug types is one means of offsetting the highly skewed responses associated with hard-drug types, providing sufficient variance to examine—and not strain—the robustness of the statistical analyses. Conceptually speaking, aggregating across several drug categories captures a propensity toward extreme—and often risky—involvement with multiple drugs.

The program's ability to achieve preventive effects with other substances has been less consistent across trials, with favorable effects on alcohol use observed in four of seven trials (Sussman et al., 1998, 2002, 2012; Sussman, Sun, et al., 2003; Valente et al., 2007), favorable effects on marijuana use obtained in three trials (Rohrbach et al., 2010; Sussman et al., 2002; Sussman, Sun, et al., 2003; Valente et al., 2007), and favorable program effects on cigarette smoking demonstrated in two trials (Sussman et al., 2002, 2012; Sussman, Sun, et al., 2003), at 1- or 2-year follow-up. Many practitioners use Project TND in their school systems without considering the collective body of evidence from all seven trials, which span a 20-year period. Given the specious, albeit favorable, nature of the program evaluation findings, it seemed prudent to revisit the conceptual framework underlying the experimental manipulations, critically explore the program's "active ingredients," and reexamine what might be responsible for the varied pattern of findings. As a result of a trial-by-trial analysis, we may be poised to make stronger inferences regarding why the program works—when it does work.

HISTORY OF PROJECT TND

Project TND was originally developed to apply to older at-risk teens. The term *at-risk* was intended to broadly include youth unable to remain in the regular/comprehensive school system. Functional roadblocks that impeded attending normal high schools for many youth included achieving insufficient school credits (related to absenteeism, or poor academic performance), exhibiting conduct problems (e.g., repeated suspensions), or violating zero tolerance drug use policies. In many of our nation's school systems, youth meeting these criteria are transferred to an alternative high school (AHS). From an educational standpoint, the concept of the AHS was intended to address the academic and emotional needs of these high-risk youth, through more individualized instruction in addition to group instruction, short school days (e.g., 4–6 hours per day), and relatively high teacher-to-student ratios.

Despite the good intentions of educators, a higher prevalence of negative health-related behaviors has been previously documented among youth from AHSs compared to regular high schools (RHSs). Examining 30-day drug use, researchers have found that students in AHSs are much more likely than students in RHSs to have smoked cigarettes (70.1% vs. 36.3%), drank alcohol (64.9% vs. 50.8%), engaged in episodic heavy drinking (51.5% vs. 33.4%), used marijuana (53.9% vs. 26.2%), and used cocaine (15.9% vs. 3.3%). Unfortunately, very few drug abuse prevention or cessation programs have been conducted with this population of youth (for a review, see Sussman, Arriaza, & Grigsby, in press). Project TND was originally developed to combat drug misuse within the AHS population, although three out of seven Project TND trials examined the generalizability of the program to an RHS context, as is discussed below.

The state education system in California uses the term *continuation* to reference AHSs. There is concrete evidence showing that youth attending continuation high schools (CHSs) follow the pattern of youth in AHSs and that compared to the general population of high school youth are at relatively high risk for drug abuse and risky sexual behavior (Black, Sun, Rohrbach, & Sussman, 2011; Sussman, Dent, Simon, et al., 1995). The fact that these youth experiment with a variety of drugs at a much higher prevalence than the RHS system suggested that prevention efforts were needed that went beyond addressing the gateway drugs (i.e., tobacco, alcohol, and sometimes marijuana) addressed by primary prevention programs.

Additional concerns include whether the type of social resistance or comprehensive social influences programming would benefit older at-risk teens in these specialized educational environments. In fact, both preliminary program development efforts (Sussman, Dent, Simon, et al., 1995) as well as more recent findings (Sussman, Earleywine, et al., 2004) indicated that older teens asked to practice drug refusal offers during classroom activities might react negatively. Older teens are more focused on examining their identity and developing a worldview rather than on examining social pressures. Also, social influences activities are generally more suitable for contexts in which a majority of youth don't use drugs. In these contexts, social resistance skills serve to inoculate youth prior to engaging the behavior in question. Within at-risk contexts like CHSs, a greater number of youth are likely to have already misused drugs. These contextual and program development concerns suggested that a different prevention approach, relevant to older, at-risk teens, was needed. This led to the MSD approach (Sussman, Earleywine, et al., 2004).

THEORETICAL RATIONALE AND CONCEPTUAL FRAMEWORK

Project TND was initiated with a series of four program development studies from 1992 to 1993. This work used a total of 1,326 continuation (alternative) high school students from 21 schools, and 706 regular (comprehensive) high school students from six schools, located in Southern California (see Sussman, 1996; Sussman, Rohrbach, & Mihalic, 2004). This opportunity fueled development of a drug prevention model that blended previous theory with instructional methods believed to have greater relevance for at-risk teens. The Project TND curriculum drew from behavioral-therapy-related, cognitive psychology, social psychology, sociology, and recovery or chemical dependency treatment-related approaches (for details, see Sussman, 2010; Sussman, Earleywine, et al., 2004; Sussman, Rohrbach, & Mihalic, 2004). The model incorporated (a) prosocial motivation enhancement, (b) life and social skills, and (c) decision-making components as intermediate cognitive behavioral processes that decrease vulnerability to a wide range of deviant outcomes (Sussman, Earleywine, et al., 2004). Modification of these intermediate processes was considered optimal to reduce risk and protect continuation students from drug misuse and engagement in other high-risk behaviors that can interfere with learning and can also be personally destructive.

Motivation Enhancement

Motivation enhancement focuses on techniques to clarify desire for change and reduce ambivalence toward change. This may include, but is not restricted to, a specific strategy such as MI (Miller & Rollnick, 2002), which is described later in this chapter. The motivation enhancement approach dedicates a significant amount of programming to dissuade youth from starting drug use (i.e., change a youth's intentions, for those curious about starting drug use), decrease their intentions to escalate drug use, or increase their willingness to quit drug use. Motivation enhancement approaches assist individuals in clarifying their direction of change and increase their willingness to change. One central feature of motivation enhancement in Project TND is to make youth aware of their equivocation regarding using drugs. Once this equivocation is made explicit, the participant can examine how using or not using drugs may be associated with other likely life outcomes. The goal here is for youth to realize that upon close examination (using a step-by-step analysis) their rationale for using drugs is flawed, leading to the conclusion that not misusing drugs is the best course of action (Sussman, Earleywine, et al., 2004). Project TND uses several motivation enhancement activities including drug use myth correction, counteracting stereotyping, valuing health and achievement of health goals, and clarification of attitudinal perspectives. Each of these motivation enhancement program strategies is briefly explained below (Sussman, 1996).

Drug use myths. This program strategy describes questionable or dysfunctional expectancies and beliefs that serve to justify drug use. For example, users may mistakenly believe that the ability to regulate subjective drug use effects affords them control over their drug use. In reality, true cessation of bodily warning signals (e.g., coughing, dizziness, nausea) experienced the first few times youth try a drug such as cigarettes or alcohol may indicate physical deterioration as addiction begins. So, as drug users acclimate to the effects of a drug (i.e., no longer feel sick), they may actually be experiencing tolerance to the drug—one of several physical dependence symptoms. Furthermore, a drug user may require increasingly larger amounts to gain the felt experience of being high. Challenging a person's drug use myths should help prevent them from continuing to use drugs to the point of dependence. The process of cognitive restructuring is used to target the correction of faulty or self-defeating cognitive structures ("myths"). In particular, elaborating on the logical steps involved in the construction of a drug use myth may help prevent youth from engaging in detrimental behaviors. Program materials address the "kernel of truth" embedded in a myth (subjective experiences that indicate tolerance) and why it is still a myth (signs of physical dependence).

To illustrate this program goal, a common myth suggests that having trouble finding one's car after getting drunk is a humorous event. Many adults recall situations where a friend or close associate had one too many drinks and could not remember where they parked their car. When the module is taught, students are challenged regarding certain myth elements. For example, posing the following questions: (a) "Did you want to find your car?" (b) "Were you too drunk to find it for a long time?" and (c) "And that's funny?" Confronted by these myth elements, the apparent humor of the situation may dissipate. Furthermore, students can be taught to delineate the kernel of truth in the myth (not finding one's car is an odd event) and separate this from the false aspects of the myth (not finding one's car indicates failure of functioning, which is sad, not funny; Sussman, 2010; Sussman, Earleywine, et al., 2004).

Stereotyping. Lower risk and more conventional peers tend to perceive AHS students as more deviant than they actually are. Of course, younger children and even adults may view high school youth in general as more deviant than they really are. High school students often test their newfound freedoms by rebelling against conventional standards. Many youth test limits by pushing curfews, engaging in alternative personal mores, and experimenting with radical changes to their appearance such as adopting unique clothing styles (e.g., the Goth look). Delinquency increases during this developmental period (Hasking, Scheier, & Abdallah, 2011), and many youth report greater levels of parental conflict particularly as they test the extent of parental control in moral, personal, and prudential domains (Smetana & Asquith, 1994). Indeed, this premise was suggested in early interview work that preceded the development of Project TND modules (cf. Sussman, 1996).

Understandably, high school students may resent this stereotype, which casts a negative pall on their activities. Addressing this stereotype may help prevent drug abuse. If high school students are persuaded to this negative stereotyping through conformity processes, the situation could lead to a self-fulfilling prophecy, as if they were buying into the stereotype. For instance, a delinquent youth may think, "You think I'm bad—I'll show you how bad I can be." A stereotype-oriented lesson may accomplish an important goal. If high-risk youth do not view themselves as deviant as they assume others have judged them, possibly, reactions against this stereotype—such as rebelling against it—may energize an effort to avoid drug use as well as portray oneself in a more favorable and conventional limelight. Further, correcting the misperception that regular drug use is normative among teenagers, especially among their peers, can go a long way toward modifying erroneous perceptions and encourage youth to not buy into the stereotype.

Valuing life and health goals. Many AHS youth report that they plan to graduate from high school, pursue additional education, or find a job. In fact, there is evidence showing that most high school youth do not view "hanging out," absent life goals, as a desirable option (Sussman, Rohrbach, & Mihalic, 2004). Many youth also recognize that drug use can interfere with achieving their life's goals by interfering with their personal health. The TND program builds on this premise by suggesting that enhancing consideration of the value of health in deliberate cognition can increase motivation for learning adaptive coping strategies that can positively direct youth toward maximizing life goals (which precludes drug misuse).

Attitudinal perspectives. Consistent with attitudinal perspective theory (Upshaw & Ostrom, 1984), most youth view themselves as holding moderate views (i.e., occupying the political middle, balanced on most attitudes). These same youth tend to identify regular drug use as a form of deviant, immoderate ("radical") behavior (Olds, Thombs, & Tomasek, 2005; Sussman, Earleywine, et al., 2004). Showcasing for these youth the disparity between their general self-attitude ratings as "moderates" versus engaging in more extreme specific behaviors (e.g., drug use) can push the pendulum and motivate them to engage in more temperate behavior.

Intervention Skills

Even if at-risk youth desire not to misuse drugs, there may be social-contextual variables that serve as barriers to being able to engage in lower risk behaviors. The central goal of skills training is to help youth create bridges to a wider (prosocial) network of peers. Direct instruction, modeling, practice, and group reinforcement enhance learning of social and life skills (Hansen, Watson-Perczel, & Christopher, 1989; Sussman, Rohrbach, & Mihalic, 2004). At least three basic kinds of skills require instruction: self-control, communication, and resource acquisition. The ability to control one's behavior in sensitive situations, communicate effectively to achieve certain goals, and acquire needed resources from one's social and physical environment are paramount to a comfortable transition into adulthood, and deviations from a productive transition may lead to drug misuse (Arnett, 2004).

Social self-control skills. Good self-control protects against substance use and buffers against the impact of risk factors (e.g., Cooper, Agocha, & Sheldon, 2000; Wills, Walker, Mendoza, & Ainette, 2006). As several other chapters in this handbook suggest, poor self-control contributes to behavioral, affective, and cognitive deficits. Self-control strategies cross physiological and personality boundaries because self-control also relates to coping motives for substance use—a strong malleable predictor of substance use problems (Cooper et al., 2000; Wills et al., 2006). In certain situations, youth lack restraint or fail to plan accordingly. In these situations, coping skills instruction may help increase individual self-control. In social self-control programming, youth learn to assess their self-control in social situations (e.g., learn to modulate their tendency to make provocative statements, blurt out or say things they "did not mean" in stressful situations, suppress their tendency for attention-grabbing opportunities; Sussman, McCuller, & Dent, 2003). Youth learn the importance of thinking ahead and anticipating problem social situations so that they are prepared beforehand to deal with problems that may arise. They also learn the importance of social context and to respect cultural mores (e.g., not seeming joyful or not laughing at a funeral). Finally, they learn assertiveness and anger management to help them better control their reactions in social settings (Sussman, Rohrbach, & Mihalic, 2004).

Listening and communication skills. Youth genuinely benefit from listening to information with an open mind and asking open-ended questions to keep a conversation going. They can improve their communication skills by learning how to ask various types of open-ended questions, establish eye contact appropriately (i.e., when listening and when speaking, the latter to observe reactions to what they are saying), nodding their head to indicate active listening, and orienting their body toward the other speaker. Overall, increasing communication skills will have protective effects for high-risk teens (Cooper et al., 2000).

Resource acquisition. Adults often assume that teens can access community services (e.g., vocational, educational, recreational, transportation, mental health and drug counseling; see Sussman, Skara, & Pumpuang, 2008) with little effort. In fact, few teens recognize the availability of health services or other community assistance. Learning how to obtain simple information, including phone numbers and locations, can assist teens immensely (Sussman et al., 2008). Coaching teens on techniques for receiving assistance can prove productive. Public assistance for drug problems and other life problems can help tremendously. Negotiating the bureaucratic difficulties inherent in many of these systems can require considerable skill, but learning how to make attempts to acquire assistance is a major step forward towards getting one's needs met.

Decision Making

Learning how to make good decisions is an important part of transitioning through older adolescence and into emerging adulthood (Arnett, 2004). Indeed, youth must learn to make self-fulfilling choices and engage in a future orientation that goes beyond the here and now (e.g., Barnett et al., 2013). As a result, drug misuse prevention programs have employed decision-making strategies that help youth develop goal adaptation skills and think about the consequences of their actions (Beyth-Marom, Fischhoff, Quadrel, & Furby, 1991; Byrnes, 2002). In keeping with these themes, Project TND's decision-making session involves four steps: (1) brainstorming (making a list of ideas without judging them); (2) weighing the pros and cons (learning how to evaluate the benefits and costs of each idea); (3) selecting the best option; and (4) following through (trying a particular option and then reevaluating the decision). Training in decision making by design operates on variables that are intermediate in the causal process and thereby strengthen individual profiles of self-control abilities so that youth are more resilient in the face of proximal risk factors for drug use, such as life stressors (Slovic, Lichtenstein, & Fischhoff, 1988).

BRIEF DESCRIPTION OF THE PROJECT TND INTERVENTION

The MSD model guided program development efforts and construction of the Project TND curriculum. The current version of the Project TND curriculum contains 12 separate 40-minute interactive sessions. Session 1 (Active Listening) teaches youth how to communicate effectively and listen to material with an open mind (motivation and skills material). Session 2 (Stereotyping) targets making high-risk youth aware that they may increase their vulnerability to substance abuse by engaging in a self-fulfilling prophecy and that they can counteract negative stereotyping by not abusing drugs. Youth are also provided current prevalence information regarding their own age cohort with the intent of demonstrating to them their tendency to overestimate drug use among peers, perhaps reflecting the beginnings of a self-fulfilling prophecy (motivation material).

Session 3 (Myths and Denials) confronts myths, using the myth deconstruction strategy described earlier, that facilitate drug use (e.g., people get used to a drug). In addition, this session confronts denial regarding drug use (i.e., tendency to blame others, deny injury, deny effects on others, reinterpret negative effects as not so bad or even funny), to minimize the perceptions of positive functions of drug use (motivation and decision-making material). Session 4 (Chemical Dependency) uses the acronym TRAP (Trial use, Recreational use, Abuse, "Pinned" down [addicted]) in order to provide information about the course of negative consequences associated with chemical dependency. In addition, Session 4 discusses the family and social contexts of drug abuse (family roles, enabling) and the availability of assistance to individuals who may be affected by a drug abuser (motivation material and self-assistance toolkit—some skills material).

Session 5 (Talk Show) has the goal of providing students with an empathetic and cognitive understanding of the negative consequences of drug abuse, through the use of a "talk show" activity. The talk show session is constructed like a Dr. Phil or Oprah television segment. Guests on the show (student volunteers from the class) enact various roles (e.g., current alcoholic/drug addict, alcoholic/drug addict's girlfriend/boyfriend, parent of teenager who was a victim of a drunk driving accident, recovering drug addict/alcoholic, DUI jail inmate, and best friend of someone who died from an accidental overdose). This session also permits active review of prior information (e.g., applies the TRAP sequence to marijuana use specifically) and teaches perspective taking (how to experience empathy) regarding drug abuse effects (motivation and decision-making material). Session 6 (Stress, Health, & Goals) emphasizes the importance of health as a long-term value for a happy life and ties youths' ability to attain near-future life goals to health. Youth are taught that living a healthy life in pursuit of personal goals requires balance, and to also recognize that drug abuse can injure their current health. The decisions they must make about healthy living pivot around the need to temper drug use or give up their near-future goals. In addition, program content provides coping alternatives to drug abuse to help people proactively or reactively deal with stress, using a mnemonic: Consider lifestyle alternative, Other's support, Problem solving, and Esteem building, or COPE (motivation and skills material). Helpful resource information is provided, as well (e.g., websites for general drug information, drug abuse recovery groups, emotional support).

Session 7 (Tobacco Basketball and Use Cessation) provides information on the consequences of cigarette smoking using the framework of a "tobacco basketball" question game. Two teams play competitive basketball with questions worth 1 to 3 points, and the team scoring the most points wins. Afterward, youth read a brief quit manual (e.g., how to withdraw from nicotine, motivation and skills material). Project TND also references other quit material from the National Cancer Institute. Session 8 (Self Control) has the goal of teaching youth to be aware of different social contexts and match the social behavior to the context. This session also teaches youth to not act in ways that alienate others (e.g., social self-control, prosocial assertiveness) and improve their chances of creating durable social bonds and achieve personal goals (skills material).

Session 9 (Marijuana Panel) teaches students about the consequences of marijuana use through a group panel activity involving a talk show format with students playing different roles, such as an ex-user, a boy/girlfriend of a marijuana user, a parent of a marijuana user, and a scientist (motivation material). Session 10 (Positive & Negative Thought & Behavior Loops) shows how positive thinking, making choices, and resulting behavior—or negative thinking—choices, and behavior are tied together as process "loops" (motivation and decision-making material). In addition, reasons why people get exposed to violent situations and methods for avoiding violence (e.g., make use of trusted adult mediators, learn to keep calm, practice assertiveness) are presented (skills and decision making material).

Session 11 (Perspectives) considers that most people generally portray themselves as "moderates" (in between, less extreme, balanced; as opposed to "radicals," who want major changes, or "conservatives," who desire limited change). Accordingly, most people also use appropriate self-statements to reflect this position. When students examine their specific attitudes and behaviors toward drug use in the context of their general self-statements, they can form a more conservative, anti–drug-abuse perspective (motivation and decision-making material). Session 12 (Decision Making and Commitment) involves motivating youth to think through the pros and cons of drug use and to make a healthy commitment to their own lives. This commitment is regarding whether or not they desire to avoid drug abuse or engage in other anti–drug-use behaviors (e.g., think about the dangers or consequences of drug use, discuss dangers of drug use with others). Since students may choose any number of commitments, it is likely that they can select one antidrug commitment they feel comfortable endorsing (decision-making material).

EFFICACY EVALUATIONS OF PROJECT TND

To date, seven independent research trials have evaluated the efficacy of Project TND. Each of these trials examined an experimental manipulation in a C-RCT design. Together, these trials suggest a mixture of favorable and less-than-optimal findings supporting the efficacy of Project TND. Certainly, there are many confounders that can limit interpretability or comparison across trials (e.g., time, regional location, type of school, number of sessions increased from nine to 12 beginning with the third trial). However, all of the trials compared programmatic variations to a standard care control condition, and a general pattern of effects does emerge. This section of the chapter briefly describes each of the seven trials, presented in chronological order. Underlying reasons why programming is working emerge across trials, as is discussed.

Trial 1: Efficacy of School-as-Community Component in CHSs

The first trial evaluating Project TND involved a nine-session program and was conducted from 1992 to 1997. In this trial, a three-group C-RCT design was used, with a total of 21 CHSs, comparing TND with or without use of a limited outreach to the community component ("school-as-community"), against a standard care control condition (Sussman et al., 1998, 2002; $N = 1{,}074$ students). The school-as-community component was derived from notions that suggest that preventive effects can be obtained through encouraging participants to engage in more healthful interconnections with others throughout a school and beyond its borders (Sussman et al., 1998).

The standard care condition involved whatever program the school usually provided as drug abuse prevention material (i.e., primarily health class textbook material, Red Ribbon Week). The school-as-community component involved weekly Associated Student Body (ASB) meetings (for 4 to 8 months; an average of 10 student ASB members per school), six school-wide drug-free events (e.g., field trips to nearby community worksites, fundraisers, drug-free sporting events, drug-free dances, environmental events worksite, recreational activities), a newsletter that was provided to the seven schools assigned to that condition, and school-wide assemblies (Sussman et al., 1997).

The program evaluation failed to find a significant incremental effect for the school-as-community condition. In addition, there was also no main intervention effect for cigarette, alcohol, and marijuana use when comparing the program conditions (combined) with the standard care control condition. However, there was a significant and favorable program effect for hard drug use (a composite of stimulant and depressant pill use, cocaine, psychedelics, and club drugs). Indeed, students exposed to the intervention reported nearly half the monthly hard drug use frequency at follow-up compared with those in the control group. Furthermore, the same evaluation indicated a significant interaction between pretest alcohol use level and condition. No favorable program effect was obtained among pretest nonusers of alcohol and at the lower levels of consumption, with the regression intercept values all roughly equal (average value = 11.64, standard error of the alcohol intercepts = 2.33). These findings notwithstanding, at higher pretest levels of alcohol use, intervention students exhibited significantly lower alcohol use at 1-year follow-up compared with the control condition students at comparable pretest drinking levels (Sussman et al., 1998). Results generalized to victimization and weapons-carrying among males at the 1-year follow-up (Simon et al., 2002). In addition, there was a durable program effect on hard drug use maintained at the 5-year follow-up (Sun et al., 2006).

In summary, the initial program evaluation of Project TND offered several important pieces of evidence suggesting that conducting drug abuse prevention with continuation students was feasible and efficacious. For one thing, prior to engaging in this project, it was not at all clear that at-risk youth could be engaged in a drug-abuse-related study, or for that matter any research due to either lack of cooperation or high truancy. Contrary to our initial concern, these at-risk youth were willing to complete questionnaires and also were motivated to participate in a structured prevention study. In addition, the evaluation showed that it was possible to elicit changes in drug use behavior (at least for hard drug use and alcohol use among baseline drinkers) via exposure to a theory-based drug prevention program.

We also learned that attempts to elicit incremental effects via changes in the school environment outside of the classroom were not successful even though manipulation checks indicated the school-as-community component successfully expanded drug prevention efforts outside the classroom (Sussman et al., 1997). Findings such as these led to speculation that something favorable happens in the classroom that potentially elicits behavior change. However, it was unknown what specific behavior change processes mediated classroom program effects. Tentatively, it was assumed that the MSD model guided the effects obtained, as it served as the theoretical template for program development and curriculum construction (Sussman, Rohrbach, & Mihalic, 2004).

Trial 2: Generalization Trial of Classroom Program to RHSs

Having achieved a favorable 1-year program effect in the CHS context, we inquired whether the program would be able to achieve program effects among regular (comprehensive) high school youth who were older but not at particular risk for drug misuse (other than their age). Thus, the next step in program development involved a second validity trial conducted at three RHSs (1995–1997). The RHS delivery involved a two-condition experimental design: TND-curriculum and standard care conditions, with a pre- and posttest, and 1-year follow-up evaluation (Dent et al., 2001; Sussman et al., 2002). The experimental design involved assigning students to experimental conditions at the classroom level (i.e., 13 classrooms were assigned to each of the two experimental conditions; $N = 679$). Mixed-model analysis of variance was used to control for clustering effects and control the Type I error rate. The results of this trial matched those obtained for the CHS study just reviewed. Favorable program effects were found on higher levels of alcohol use (up to a 60%

relative reduction at the highest levels of baseline use) and at all levels of hard drug use (a 60%–75% relative reduction). In summary, for a 1-year follow-up period, the effects in RHSs replicated the findings found at CHSs (Dent et al., 2001; Sussman et al., 2002). Possibly, whatever was working in Project TND was applicable to older teens in general.

Trial 3: Efficacy of a Self-Instruction Component in CHSs

Project TND-2 represented a third group-randomized trial (1997–2001). Based on pilot testing work, three new sessions were added (a 25% increase in curriculum length) to try to elicit effects on cigarette smoking and marijuana use. One and one-half sessions focused on preventing marijuana use. A second new session focused on cigarette smoking cessation, with provision of key concepts from the Project Towards No Tobacco Use (TNT) cessation trial component (Sussman, Dent, Stacy, Burton, & Flay, 1995), and also included use of a self-help booklet. Additional new material expanded on self-control and decision-making material (to emphasize violence prevention). In addition to lengthening the program, two modes of delivery were contrasted in the study: an efficacy condition (health educator–led classroom program) and a treatment effectiveness condition (i.e., health educator–assisted self-instruction program, the program modality generally used at CHSs at that time). These two experimental conditions were compared with a standard care (control) condition, in a three-condition randomized design ($N = 18$ schools; $N = 715$ subjects), with a 2-year follow-up. This project was able to assess the importance of classroom interaction in eliciting effects on self-reported drug use behavior.

We were surprised to find that, while similar session knowledge increases were obtained as the health educator–led condition, the self-instruction condition fared no better than the control condition (Sussman et al., 2002; Sussman, Sun, et al., 2003) at 1-year follow-up. However, the health educator–led condition showed favorable program effects, compared with the other two conditions, for cigarette, alcohol (among baseline drinkers), marijuana, and the hard drug use composite (Sussman et al., 2002). Program effects were maintained at 2-year follow-up (27 months) on hard drug use and cigarette smoking, and for marijuana use among baseline male nonusers (Sussman, Sun, et al., 2003).

To summarize, the first three drug abuse prevention trials showed that efforts outside of the classroom within the school environment and outside to the local community failed to elicit changes in behavior and, at the other extreme, material delivered in the classroom within a self-instruction package also failed to elicit behavior changes. Material delivered in the classroom that involved interaction between teenagers and also between youth and health educators showed favorable program effects. Features of interactional programming that may have produced favorable effects include the material being relatively fun and involving, with students generating their own answers and therefore more likely to "own" their behavior, the material becoming more "real and lifelike" as conversation permits adjustments to specific features of youth populations, and such interactive programming permitting practice and emulation of prosocial behavior (Sussman, Rohrbach, Patel, & Holiday, 2003).

Sussman, Rohrbach, et al. (2003) then examined the curriculum-based, teacher-student interactional process to address what factors might be successfully mediating program effects. These authors suggested that explicit, structured action on the part of the teacher that directs students to make statements and ask questions of one another may be a driving force in effective drug education program delivery. The statements or questions that may have been producing interactions resulting in program effects included curriculum instructions that requested the teacher to (a) ask partially open-ended questions (which require one-sentence responses from students; e.g., questions related to providing definitions of terms), (b) ask open-ended questions (which require more than one-sentence responses from students; e.g., "What would you do about the drug problem in this country?"), (c) make use of "other-question messages" (direct student to ask questions of other students; e.g., "Do you have any questions for him/her?"), and (d) make use of "other-statement messages" (direct students to make statements to other students; e.g., "Please tell him/her what your experiences were like").

There were also student-to-student or student-to-teacher interactions that were not explicitly written into the program that might have benefited program success. For example, students might (a) disclose remedial personal experiences to the class, (b) check with other students to provide the right answers to questions posed by the teacher on a class game, and (c) express cohesion with each other supporting their moderate antidrug stances. These types of statements may elicit rational normative stances toward drug use (Sussman, Rohrbachet et al., 2003).

Trial 4: Program Material Mediation and Efficacy of Classroom Teachers in CHSs and RHSs

In all of the trials thus far, health educators delivered the program materials. This left unresolved whether program materials could be effectively delivered by classroom teachers. In addition, only one of the three trials was delivered in a regular classroom context. We desired to see whether program effects might be replicated in CHS and RHS classrooms in the same trial and with the 12-session program. Finally, of even greater importance, we were not sure what facets of the program content actually produced drug use effects. For example, it was not clear whether or not correction of cognitive misperception-type material and decision making was the main reason for change or whether youth also needed to learn behavioral skills. To address this point, we conducted a fourth trial that examined variation in program outcomes by teacher type (trained health educators vs. school teachers), school type (RHS vs. CHS), and program content type (cognitive misperception only vs. combined Project TND curriculum).

This project involved a three-condition design (*N* = 18 schools; *N* = 2,064 students), which manipulated program content type (standard care control, TND combined [i.e., cognitive misperception and behavioral skills material], and TND cognitive misperception-only) with 1-year follow-up (Sun et al., 2008). Teacher type and school type (there were three CHS and three RHS per condition) were crossed and nested within each of the program conditions. One goal of this trial involved determining whether school teachers could deliver the TND curriculum with as much fidelity as health educators. Multiple trained observers' coding of at least two sessions, student process ratings of teaching effectiveness, and knowledge change scores were used to compare program delivery. With 10 hours of training, we found that classroom teachers delivered TND as well as trained health educators (Rohrbach et al., 2007).

Second, we wanted to know whether the 12-session program effects generalized to the RHS context (thus far, we had only demonstrated such effects with the nine-session program). This was the case, as effects failed to interact with school type. Also, using componential analysis techniques, we tested whether the complete program (cognitive misperception and behavioral skill instruction) provides a greater effect compared with the provision of cognitive misperception information only. Across all program schools, the two different curricula failed to significantly reduce dichotomous (yes/no) measures of cigarette, alcohol, marijuana, and hard drug use at 1-year follow-up. Both curricula exerted an effect only on the continuous measure of hard drug use, indicating a 42% ($p = .02$) reduction in the number of times hard drugs were used in the last 30 days in the program groups relative to the control, but the two program groups failed to differ from each other (Sun et al., 2008).

These findings suggest that explicit behavioral skills instruction was not a key ingredient involved in the efficacy of TND. Rather, experimental manipulation of drug use misperceptions (see Sussman, 2010) in the classroom that take place in a highly interactive but structured context may be responsible for eliciting behavior change. In other words, activities that attempted to alter youths' thinking about drug use and their motivations not to misuse drugs (e.g., counteracting stereotyping, correcting drug use myths, creating discrepancy regarding placing an importance on health as a value vs. using drugs regularly, and providing attitudinal perspectives material ["moderate" people don't misuse drugs]) elicited an impact on behavior regardless of whether youth received modules to improve behavior skills (e.g., effective communication, stress coping, social self-control). We speculated that teacher-facilitated structured interactions in the classroom (e.g., prompting youth to answer open-ended questions about drug use, and to speak with each other about drug use during the stereotyping, drug use myths, health as a value, and talk show sessions) may catalyze deeper social interactions that are supporting conventional behaviors and responsible for the effects obtained.

Trial 5: Efficacy of Peer Leader and Enhanced Interaction Components in CHSs

Valente et al. (2007) tested whether the addition of social network peer leader selection and increased classroom group interaction (termed *TND Network*) provided an incremental effect compared with the use of standard TND or a standard care control condition at a 1-year follow-up. Indeed, use of peer-nominated peer leaders to lead peer-group interactions within the class facilitated greater processing and influence of TND program material. The 1-year follow-up data were collected at 14 CHSs (classroom level of assignment; $N = 75$ classrooms, $N = 541$ students) in a three-condition experimental design. Exposure to the standard TND program was not associated with changes in any substance use or the composite score relative to control students. Receiving TND Network, in the context of a peer environment that supports nonuse, was associated with decreased marijuana ($\beta = -0.64$, 95% CI [−1.09, −0.19]; $p < .05$) and cocaine use ($\beta = -0.37$, 95% CI [−0.63, −0.10]; $p < .05$) relative to the control condition. TND Network was also associated with decreased composite drug use (considering all drug categories) relative to the control condition ($\beta = -0.37$, 95% CI [−0.54, −0.20]; $p < .01$). The findings of this trial were relatively difficult to interpret because it appeared that the standard TND program failed to elicit significant intervention effects. However, the TND networked condition suggested that maximizing the classroom interaction among peers was vital to obtaining behavioral effects a year or more later. This result was supportive of our speculations regarding the social interactional nature of Project TND's active ingredients, evident in the first four trials.

Trial 6: National Dissemination Trial in Primarily RHSs With Classroom Teachers

While all of the previous trials obtained favorable program effects on hard drug use, and several obtained effects on other drugs, all of the previous trials were conducted in California. In a sixth, dissemination trial, we used a three-condition experimental design. We recruited a total of 65 high schools from 14 school districts in the United States were recruited as a convenience sample (58 were RHSs, seven were AHSs). We recruited schools from four regions of the country (Northeast, South, Central, and West) in equal proportions to those represented in our database of organizations that had adopted Project TND since we made the program commercially available.

This sixth trial assessed the amount of training needed to best implement the program with fidelity and achieve target behavioral effects. The experimental conditions contrasted the efficacy of a multicomponent, comprehensive training package with a standard training package that involved a 1-day in-person workshop and general teaching tips. A third experimental condition provided a means to determine whether the standard training package might be superior to a 1-year wait-list control condition (Rohrbach, Sun, & Sussman, 2010). The multicomponent condition involved (a) telephone and in-person coaching, (b) provision of an Internet page (which provided answers to specific questions on implementation), (c) in-person training, (d) monitoring and coaching, and (e) general teaching tips. Physical education and health teachers from these schools delivered the program to students ($N = 2{,}538$). Program effectiveness was assessed using dichotomous measures of 30-day substance use at both baseline and 1-year follow-up.

Comparing the comprehensive, multicomponent intervention against the control condition, the program showed a marginally significant effect in lowering marijuana use from baseline to 1-year follow-up. Significant program effects on hard drug use were observed for baseline nonusers only. There were no differences in the effects of the two intervention conditions (i.e., comprehensive or standard training). Analyses of the differential program effects by baseline substance use status indicated that program effects on marijuana and hard drug use were achieved for baseline nonusers ($p < .10$ and $p < .05$, respectively), but not for baseline users. Post hoc comparisons of the effects of the two intervention conditions indicated a stronger effect on alcohol use among baseline nonusers for comprehensive program implementation training relative to the standard training condition, but a relatively weaker effect of the comprehensive training condition on hard drug use among baseline users. Overall, this trial indicated that TND could elicit favorable program effects when delivered by regular classroom teachers at primarily RHSs across the United States, although effects were somewhat weaker than in research trials with highly structured program delivery. Also, basic training without ongoing coaching, a key feature that differentiated the comprehensive, multicomponent training from the standard training, appeared sufficient (Rohrbach et al., 2010).

Trial 7: Efficacy of a Motivational Interviewing Booster Component in CHSs

Previous research has suggested that school-based drug abuse prevention programs have a greater chance of long-term success if youth are exposed to additional contacts with program providers of some type after delivery of the core program (Sussman et al., 2012). MI is a reasonable choice as the booster component approach for Project TND because the development of motivation to change is the core objective of MI (Miller & Rollnick, 2002). Motivation to change is created by developing discrepancy between current behavior and future goals, similar to goals of Project TND. In the seventh trial, a total of 24 schools were randomized to one of three conditions: Standard Care Control (SCC), TND classroom program only (TND only), and TND plus MI booster (TND+MI). A total of 1,186 participants completed baseline and 1-year follow-up surveys. Following the classroom program, youth in the TND+MI condition received up to three sessions of one-on-one MI in person and by telephone. Effects were examined for 30-day prevalence rates for cigarette, alcohol, marijuana, and hard drug use, as well as measures of risky sexual behavior (number of sex partners, condom use, having sex while using drugs or alcohol). Collapsed across the two program conditions, results showed significant reductions in prevalence of alcohol, hard drug use, and cigarette smoking relative to controls. These effects were also observed for a composite substance use index.

Although the TND+MI booster condition was implemented with high fidelity (Barnett, Spruijt-Metz, Unger, Sun, Rohrbach, & Sussman, 2012) the program did not provide significant incremental effects on drug use at 1-year follow-up. The failure to find a significant difference between the two program conditions was not due to a difference in perceived quality of the classroom program, which was controlled in the analysis. However, booster programming with MI following a classroom-based drug prevention program for youth had not been tested to date. Given the results of this trial, it is possible that booster programming is not an essential feature of drug use prevention interventions with older at-risk teens. These teens simply may not have the time or the inclination to participate extensively in such programming. Alternatively, perhaps the use of MI as an effective booster would have been more relevant if youth voluntarily approached a treatment agent to address their drug use.

Summary

The findings of these seven trials suggest that the active ingredients that make Project TND effective in reducing drug use occur in the classroom context involving interactions between the facilitator and youth, and also involving youth-to-youth as they engage in program activities. These engaging social interactions provide impetus for youth to envision changes in lifestyle. As a prominent example, across all trials, the favorite program session was the talk show. Scripted and nonscripted interaction as depicted in the talk show session provides students with an empathetic understanding of the negative consequences of drug abuse. After one talk show session some years ago, a youth commented, “Both of my parents are alcoholics; maybe I shouldn’t drink.” During another talk show session, one youth commented that they only used “meth” on weekends, so that wasn’t drug misuse. Another youth said to that same student, “No, that is drug abuse.” In other words, it is likely that spontaneous and heartfelt corrective statements made by youth about their own behavior, or a classmate’s behavior, elicited by the classroom process demands, leads to favorable program effects. Self-report questionnaires administered at pre- and posttests would not likely tap such changes in classroom process, reinforcing the need for more qualitative work to discern these program features. Unfortunately, direct observation, recording, and analysis of this process had not yet been completed in Project TND.

Similar types of spontaneous corrective processes like the talk show example appear to be operative in other sessions, as observed anecdotally by staff. In Session 2, youth have stated their desire to act against a self-fulfilling prophesy and their resistance to being stereotyped. In Session 3, youth have noted in discussion that temporary happiness and emotional protection from drug use was a myth. Also in Session 3, youth stated agreement with the existence of the concept of reinterpretation. For example, they mentioned that some youth would attempt to reinterpret getting sick in a car as not being sad, but being funny. In Session 4, some youth became emotional when participating in the discussion of family roles. For example, someone spontaneously reported, "I don't want to end up like him." In Session 5, some youth discussed knowing someone who is chemically dependent and recalled the personal stress caused by that person's drug use. In Session 11, some youth reported not wanting to appear as a radical by using drugs regularly. Also, in Session 12, several youth made various statements showing their willingness to avoid drug misuse. A few youth spontaneously mentioned their need to change their drug use behavior.

MOTIVATIONAL INTERVIEWING AND THE MECHANISM OF TND EFFECTS

At this point, it is worth speculating how Project TND might really be working and to deliberate these mechanisms in the context of the original MSD model. I suggest that Project TND activities rely on the social-interactional context and stimulate motivation enhancement and decisions to avoid drug misuse. It is also worth noting that the active ingredients of Project TND comport with the goals of MI, which blends principles of cognitive therapy with Carl Rogers's client-centered approach (Miller & Rollnick, 2002). Accordingly, MI facilitates collaboration between the counselor (facilitator) and the client (participant) based on respect for the client's perspective. One major assumption of this approach is that the resources and motivation for behavior change reside within the client. The major tasks of the counselor are to (a) express empathy, (b) help the client to verbalize discrepancy between his or her current undesirable behavior and their stated personal goals, (c) "roll with resistance" (i.e., avoid arguing or case-building, inviting the client to explore their own perspectives and develop their own answers and solutions), and (d) support client self-efficacy to change behavior (Miller & Rollnick, 2002; Moyers et al., 2007). In MI, desire (e.g., "I want to quit doing drugs"), efficacy (e.g., "I can do it"), and reasons (e.g., "I'm killing myself") for change language predict commitment strength language (e.g., "I won't be using"), which appears to be the strongest predictor of behavior change (Amrhein et al., 2003).

Often, MI has been used at critical and/or teachable moments (e.g., when individuals are mandated to treatment) and when treatment occurs within very short time spans. Brief motivational intervention models are developmentally appropriate for youth and emerging adults because MI can provide opportunities to increase youths' sense of control over their lives, is particularly effective for younger populations that are typically at a low level of readiness to change their behavior, and can be tailored to individual needs and circumstances (Baer & Peterson, 2002). One report aggregating several studies of young people suggested limited advantage to MI over receiving no treatment or other program modalities (in 30% of 17 trials reviewed by Grenard et al., 2006). However, a more recent review by Barnett, Sussman, et al. (2012) indicated higher success among young people (MI was effective in 66% of 39 trials examined using drug abuse prevention and treatment).

Similarities and Differences Between Project TND and Group MI

Project TND involves a group classroom situation, whereas most MI research and practice have involved one-on-one treatment contexts (Hettema, Steele, & Miller, 2005). Recently, some work has examined situations where MI is offered in a group setting. Group MI is conducted rather similarly to individual-based MI, although there are several notable differences. In particular, in group MI the interpersonal dynamics of a group are critical concerns including consideration of group structure (size, formalized leadership), roles (expressive and instrumental leaders), and individual experiences that filter into the group process. Group MI requires resolution of equivocation and production of commitment language among group members, at a group as well as an individual level (Cimini et al., 2009; D'Amico, Osilla, & Hunter, 2010; Engle, Macgowan, Wagner, & Amrhein, 2010; Pensuksan, Taneepanichskul, & Williams, 2010).

There have only been a few group MI studies with adolescents (most have been with college-age youth). Engle and colleagues (2010) collected audio recordings and transcripts from 19 eight- to 10-session school-based treatment groups composed of 108 substance-abusing youth aged 10 to 19 years. Group commitment language (e.g., "I'm going to cut way down now") and positive peer response (e.g., "That's cool") predicted marijuana use outcomes and mediated facilitator empathy. Other research has found that more positive and less negative peer responses, and group leader empathy, are associated with reduced marijuana use or more positive commitment language. D'Amico, Osilla, and Hunter (2010) reported that first-time adolescent offenders were highly receptive to a six-session group MI intervention. This "free talk" intervention involves providing personalized feedback about teens' alcohol and other drug use and various skills-training activities, goal planning, and role-play making healthy choices—all conducted within a group MI structure.

Conceivably, Project TND may work by eliciting similar drug-use-related "change talk" (i.e., statements revealing consideration of, motivation for, or commitment to change) effects in a group situation. Group MI involves a counseling structure, establishing trust in the group, providing individual and normative feedback within the group context, a discussion of reasons for using and not using alcohol or other drugs, a decisional-balance exercise, and the setting of personal goals that occur in one to six sessions (LaBrie, Cail, Pedersen, & Migliuri, 2010; Santa Ana, Wulfert, & Nietert, 2007). Also, youth may identify discrepancies between their own personal goals and perceived consequences of alcohol or drug use (Cimini et al., 2009). Project TND also involves establishing trust in the group, provides individual and normative feedback regarding one's tendency to self-stereotype, and teaches social self-control. Discrepancy confrontation is evident in several of the motivation enhancement activities in TND such as the sessions that examine stereotyping and perspectives. Discussion of reasons for avoiding drugs is interlaced throughout sessions and is vital to the talk show activity. Decision making and making a personal commitment is also a central component to Project TND.

However, Project TND is different in some important ways from group MI. In particular, Project TND involves 12 relatively structured sessions, provides more directed, structured instruction and more educational information (e.g., on coping strategies), and truly reflects a blend of health education with principles of counseling. There are also directed manipulations to enhance motivation of the group and elicit discussion. These features are different from the client-driven, relatively unstructured use of MI (see Barnett, Sussman et al., 2012). In addition, MI generally is used when subjects have suffered some type of negative consequence and are seeking assistance in a clinical context. TND is used solely for prevention purposes and is offered in educational contexts.

Still, the potential overlap between the underlying change mechanisms in MI, or group MI, and the group process in Project TND, is of interest, and could potentially be monitored in the classroom setting. There are at least five peripheral features of Project TND that might be central to inducing change. First, in the TND classroom, youth are encouraged to speak, and even vent their feelings, all in a trustful environment (e.g., Norcross, 2010; Santa Ana et al., 2007). Relevant to Rogers's client-centered notions, feeling safe in an environment is one necessary condition for change (Miller & Rollnick, 2002). Second, health educators offering TND may guide youth and encourage them to receive understanding, social support, and empathy from other students. This gradual encouragement offered in a safe environment is, in client-centered therapy, essential to promote behavior change.

Third, some students may be doing relatively well in school and not misusing drugs. In the context of the curriculum material provided, these students provide effective role models for other students. In other words, non-drug using youth may serve as "pathfinders" and exert positive peer influence, helping to motivate or fuel self-efficacy enhancement for others to change (LaChance, Feldstein-Ewing, Bryan, & Hutchison, 2009). Fourth, youth may provide corrective feedback to each other within the context of the program (change talk/healing talk/corrective feedback). In this respect, youth are receiving what MI researchers have referred to as a type of normative feedback to counteract misperceptions about drug use. Finally, the emotional input of the material, which is incredibly poignant to many youth, can encourage change (e.g., family roles identification, identification with characters in the talk show session). Also, it is possible that the teacher is able to help participants link their comments (about which they personally identify) to the program material (e.g., see Giles et al., 2008; Sussman, Rohrbach et al., 2003).

CONCLUSION: FUTURE RESEARCH IN PROJECT TND—EXAMINING GROUP PROCESS LANGUAGE

It is possible that Project TND material and guided interaction in the project (e.g., through the use of partially open-ended questions, open-ended questions, other-directed questions, and other-directed statements) stimulate verbal behavior that precedes behavior change in drug misuse. As Amrhein and colleagues (2003) described, such behavior signaling impending change may include (a) reasons to change; (b) readiness; (c) need; and (d) ability, desire, and commitment. Each or some of the sessions might contain material that elicits these types of change talk. The change talk might refer directly to drug use, or it might refer to a behavior that is associated with drug use (e.g., regarding social self-control self-ratings, a student may say, "I guess I am provocative and maybe I should try to be less so"). It is possible that specific material, such as engaging in a self-rating of social self-control, may elicit such change-related talk, effecting positive change. A vicarious domino effect may also occur where change talk elicited by one participant in a classroom situation may be heard by other participants, who adopt these strategies as part of their own behavioral repertoire.

A process analysis of Project TND may be very useful and involve several developmental steps. First, audiotaped recordings or direct observation and coding of a naturally occurring classroom process may assist in ascertaining critical moments in TND material that elicits change. In addition, aspects of teacher–participant interaction, which may show examples of empathy (the teacher making an effort to understand the youths' perspectives), spirit (support of youths' autonomy in decision making), or which facilitates change talk (elicited by the teacher or other youth), may be noted across points in the material. Second, if such critical moments occur more than once, they may be explored through focus group discussions on why certain material elicits certain interactions of change talk-related responses. Such work may be accomplished within the context of a two-group experimental design with a 1-year follow-up (TND vs. SSC) to provide a replication of program effects and identify change talk in the classroom that is associated with behavior change. Eventually, there may be an attempt to eliminate some material, removing pieces that do not appear to elicit change talk, and to determine whether program efficacy is compromised. If not, this would suggest that active ingredients of Project TND can be distilled and included in a briefer program format. There is still much to learn in future TND research.

References

Amrhein, P. C., Miller, W. R., Yahne, C. E., Palmer, M., & Fulcher, L. (2003). Client commitment language during motivational interviewing predicts drug use outcomes. *Journal of Consulting and Clinical Psychology, 71*, 862–878. doi:10.1037/0022-006X.71.5.862

Arnett, J. J. (2004). *Emerging adulthood: The winding road from the late teens through the twenties*. New York, NY: Oxford University Press.

Baer, J. S., & Peterson, P. L. (2002). Motivational interviewing with adolescents and young adults. In W. R. Miller & G. A. Rollnick (Eds.), *Motivational interviewing: Preparing people for change* (2nd ed.; pp. 320–332). New York, NY: Guilford Press.

Barnett, E., Spruijt-Metz, D., Unger, J., Sun, P., Rohrbach, L. A., & Sussman, S. (2012). Boosting a teen substance use prevention program with Motivational Interviewing. *Substance Use & Misuse*, *47*, 418–428. doi:10.3109/10826084.2011.641057

Barnett, E., Spruijt-Metz, D., Unger, J. B., Rohrbach, L. A., Sun, P., & Sussman, S. (2013). Bidirectional associations between future time perspective and substance use among continuation high-school students. *Substance Use & Misuse*, *48*, 574–580. doi:10.3109/10826084.2013.787092

Barnett, E., Sussman, S., Smith, C., Rohrbach, L. A., & Spruijt-Metz, D. (2012). Motivational interviewing for adolescent substance use: A review of the literature. *Addictive Behaviors*, *37*, 1325–1334. doi:10.1016/j.addbeh.2012.07.001

Beyth-Marom, R., Fischhoff, B., Quadrel, M. J., & Furby, L. B. (1991). Teaching decision making to adolescents: A critical review. In J. Baron & R. V. Brown (Eds.), *Teaching decision making to adolescents* (pp. 19–59). Hillsdale, NJ: Erlbaum.

Black, D. S., Sun, P., Rohrbach, L. A., & Sussman, S. (2011). Decision-making style and gender moderation of the self-efficacy—condom use link among adolescents and young adults. *Archives of Pediatrics & Adolescent Medicine*, *165*, 320–325. doi:10.1001/archpediatrics.2011.17

Byrnes, J. P. (2002). The development of decision-making. *Journal of Adolescent Health*, *31*(Suppl), 208–215. doi:10.1016/S1054-139X(02)00503-7

Cimini, M. D., Martens, M. P., Larimer, M. E., Kilmer, J. R., Neighbors, C., & Monserrat, J. M. (2009). Assessing the effectiveness of peer-facilitated interventions addressing high-risk drinking among judicially mandated college students. *Journal of Studies on Alcohol and Drugs*, (Supplement No. 16), 57–66.

Cooper, M. L., Agocha, V. B., & Sheldon, M. S. (2000). A motivational perspective on risky behaviors: The role of personality and affect regulatory processes. *Journal of Personality*, *68*, 1059–1088. doi:10.1111/1467-6494.00126

D'Amico, E. J., Osilla, K. C., & Hunter, S. B. (2010). Developing a group motivational interviewing intervention for adolescents at-risk for developing an alcohol or drug use disorder. *Alcoholism Treatment Quarterly*, *28*, 417–436. doi:10.1080/07347324.2010.511076

Dent, C. W., Sussman, S., McCuller, W. J., & Stacy, A. W. (2001). Project Towards No Drug Abuse: Generalizability to a general high school sample. *Preventive Medicine*, *32*, 514–520. doi:10.1006/pmed.2001.0834

Engle, B., Macgowan, M. J., Wagner, E. F., & Amrhein, P. C. (2010). Markers of marijuana use outcomes within adolescent substance abuse group treatment. *Research on Social Work Practice*, *20*, 271–282. doi:10.1177/1049731509347855

Giles, S., Jackson-Newsom, J., Pankratz, M. M., Hansen, W. B., Ringwalt, C. L., & Dusenbury, L. (2008). Measuring quality of delivery in a substance use prevention program. *The Journal of Primary Prevention*, *29*, 489–501. doi:10.1007/s10935-008-0155-7

Grenard, J. L., Ames, S. L., Pentz, M. A., & Sussman, S. (2006). Motivational interviewing with adolescents and young adults for drug-related problems. *International Journal of Adolescent Medicine and Health*, *18*, 53–67. doi:10.1515/IJAMH.2006.18.1.53

Hansen, D. J., Watson-Perczel, M., & Christopher, J. S. (1989). Clinical issues in social-skills training with adolescents. *Clinical Psychology Review*, *9*, 365–391. doi:10.1016/0272-7358(89)90062-7

Hasking, P. A., Scheier, L. M., & Abdallah, A. (2011). The three latent classes of adolescent delinquency and the risk factors for membership in each class. *Aggressive Behavior*, *37*, 19–35. doi:10.1002/ab.20365

Hettema, J., Steele, J., & Miller, W. R. (2005). Motivational interviewing. *Annual Review of Clinical Psychology*, *1*, 91–111. doi:10.1146/annurev.clinpsy.1.102803.143833

LaBrie, J. W., Cail, J., Pedersen, E. R., & Migliuri, S. (2010). Reducing alcohol risk in adjudicated male college students: Further validation of a group motivational interviewing enhancement intervention. *Journal of Child & Adolescent Substance Abuse*, *20*, 82–98. doi:10.1080/1067828X.2011.534369

LaChance, H., Feldstein-Ewing, S. W., Bryan, A. D., & Hutchison, K. E. (2009). What makes group MET work? A randomized controlled trial of college student drinkers in mandated alcohol diversion. *Psychology of Addictive Behaviors*, *23*, 598–612. doi:10.1037/a0016633

Miller, W. R., & Rollnick, S. (2002). *Motivational interviewing*. New York, NY: Guilford Press.

Moyers, T. B., Martin, T., Christopher, P. J., Houck, J. M., Tonigan, J. S., & Amrhein, P. C. (2007). Client language as a mediator of motivational interviewing efficacy: Where is the evidence? *Alcoholism: Clinical and Experimental Research*, *31*, 40s–47s. doi:10.1111/j.1530-0277.2007.00492.x

Norcross, J. C. (2010). Therapy relationship in treating addictions: Evidence-based practices. Part of symposium "Evidence-based practice in addictions-valuing RCTs and therapeutic relationships" presented at the *2010 Annual Convention of the American Psychological Association*, San Diego, California.

Olds, R. S., Thombs, D. L., & Tomasek, J. R. (2005). Relations between normative beliefs and initiation intentions toward cigarette, alcohol and marijuana. *Journal of Adolescent Health*, *37*, 75e7–75e13.

Pensuksan, W. C., Taneepanichskul, S., & Williams, M. A. (2010). A peer-drinking group motivational intervention among Thai male undergraduate students. *International Journal of Drug Policy*, *21*, 432–436. doi:10.1016/j.drugpo.2010.02.005

Rohrbach, L. A., Dent, C. W., Skara, S., Sun, P., & Sussman, S. (2007). Fidelity of implementation in Project Towards No Drug Abuse (TND): A comparison of classroom teachers and program specialists. *Prevention Science*, *8*, 125–132. doi:10.1007/s11121-006-0056-z

Rohrbach, L. A., Sun, P., & Sussman, S. (2010). One-year follow-up evaluation of the Project Towards No Drug Abuse (TND) dissemination trial. *Preventive Medicine*, *51*, 313–319. doi:10.1016/j.ypmed.2010.07.016

Santa Ana, E. J., Wulfert, E., & Nietert, P. J. (2007). Efficacy of group motivational interviewing (GMI) for psychiatric inpatients with chemical dependence. *Journal of Consulting and Clinical Psychology*, *75*, 816–822. doi:10.1037/0022-006X.75.5.816

Simon, T. R., Sussman, S., Dahlberg, L. L., & Dent, C. W. (2002). Influence of a substance abuse prevention curriculum on violence-related behavior. *American Journal of Health Behavior*, *26*, 103–110. doi:10.5993/AJHB.26.2.3

Slovic, P., Lichtenstein, S., & Fischhoff, B. (1988). Decision making. In R. C. Atkinson, R. J. Hernstein, G. Lindzey, & D. Luce (Eds.), *Stevens' handbook of experimental psychology* (2nd ed., pp. 673–738). New York, NY: Wiley.

Smetana, J. G., & Asquith, P. (1994). Adolescents' and parents' conceptions of parental authority and adolescent autonomy. *Child Development*, *65*, 1147–1162. doi:10.2307/1131311

Sun, P., Sussman, S., Dent, C. W., & Rohrbach, L. A. (2008). One-year follow-up evaluation of Project Towards No Drug Abuse (TND4). *Preventive Medicine*, *47*, 438–442. doi:10.1016/j.ypmed.2008.07.003

Sun, W., Skara, S., Sun, P., Dent, C. W., & Sussman, S. (2006). Project Towards No Drug Abuse: Long-term substance use outcomes evaluation. *Preventive Medicine*, *42*, 188–192. doi:10.1016/j.ypmed.2005.11.011

Sussman, S. (1996). Development of a school-based drug abuse prevention curriculum for high-risk youths. *Journal of Psychoactive Drugs*, *28*, 169–182. doi:10.1080/02791072.1996.10524389

Sussman, S. (2010). Cognitive misperceptions and drug misuse. In L. M. Scheier (Ed.), *Handbook of drug use etiology: Theory, methods, and empirical findings* (pp. 617–629). Washington, DC: American Psychological Association.

Sussman, S., Arriaza, B., & Grigsby, T. (in press). Alcohol, tobacco and drug misuse (ATOD) prevention and cessation programming for alternative high school youth: A review. *Journal of School Health.*

Sussman, S., Dent, C. W., Simon, T. R., Stacy, A., & Craig, S. (1998). One year outcomes of Project Towards No Drug Abuse. *Preventive Medicine, 27*, 632–642 (Erratum: 27 (5. Pt. 1), 766).

Sussman, S., Dent, C. W., Simon, T. R., Stacy, A. W., Galaif, E. R., Moss, M. A., . . . Johnson, C. A. (1995). Immediate impact of social influence-oriented substance abuse prevention curricula in traditional and continuation high schools. *Drugs & Society*, *8*, 65–81. doi:10.1300/J023v08n03_06

Sussman, S., Dent, C. W., Stacy, A. W., Burton, D., & Flay, B. R. (1995). *Developing school-based tobacco use prevention and cessation programs.* Thousand Oaks, CA: Sage.

Sussman, S., Dent, C. W., & Stacy, S. (2002). Project Towards No Drug Abuse: A review of the findings and future directions. *American Journal of Health Behavior*, *26*, 354–365. doi:10.5993/AJHB.26.5.4

Sussman, S., Earleywine, M., Wills, T., Cody, C., Biglan, T., Dent, C. W., & Newcomb, M. D. (2004). The motivation, skills, and decision-making model of "drug abuse" prevention. *Substance Use & Misuse*, *39*, 1971–2016. doi:10.1081/JA-200034769

Sussman, S., Galaif, E. R., Newman, T., Hennesy, M., Pentz, M. A., Dent, C. W., . . . Simon, T. R. (1997). Implementation and process evaluation of a student "school-as-community" group: A component of a school-based drug abuse prevention program. *Evaluation Review*, *21*, 94–123. doi:10.1177/0193841X9702100106

Sussman, S., McCuller, W. J., & Dent, C. W. (2003). The associations of social self-control, personality disorders, and demographics with drug use among high risk youth. *Addictive Behaviors*, *28*, 1159–1166. doi:10.1016/S0306-4603(02)00222-8

Sussman, S., Rorhbach, L., & Mihalic, S. (2004). *Blueprints for violence prevention. Book twelve: Project Towards No Drug Abuse.* Boulder, CO: Institute of Behavioral Science, Regents of the University of Colorado.

Sussman, S., Rohrbach, L., Patel, R., & Holiday, K. (2003). A look at an interactive classroom-based drug abuse prevention program: Interactive contents and suggestions for research. *Journal of Drug Education*, 33, 355–368.

Sussman, S., Skara, S., & Pumpuang, P. (2008). Project Towards No Drug Abuse (TND): A needs assessment of a social service referral telephone program for high risk youth. *Substance Use & Misuse*, *43*, 2066–2073. doi:10.1080/10826080802290208

Sussman, S., Sun, P., McCuller, W. J., & Dent, C. W. (2003). Project Towards No Drug Abuse: Two-year outcomes of a trial that compares health educator delivery to self-instruction. *Preventive Medicine*, *37*, 155–162. doi:10.1016/S0091-7435(03)00108-7

Sussman, S., Sun, P., Rohrbach, L., & Spruijt-Metz, D. (2012). One-year outcomes of a drug abuse prevention program for older teens and emerging adults: Evaluating a motivational interviewing booster component. *Health Psychology*, *31*, 476–485. doi:10.1037/a0025756

Upshaw, H. S., & Ostrom, T. M. (1984). Psychological perspective in attitude research. In J. R. Eiser (Ed.), *Attitudinal judgment* (pp. 23–41). New York, NY: Springer-Verlag. doi:10.1007/978-1-4613-8251-5_2

Valente, T. W., Ritt-Olson, A., Stacy, A., Unger, J. B., Okamoto, J., & Sussman, S. (2007). Peer acceleration: Effects of a social network tailored substance abuse prevention program among high-risk adolescents. *Addiction*, *102*, 1804–1815. doi:10.1111/j.1360-0443.2007.01992.x

Wills, T. A., Walker, C., Mendoza, D., & Ainette, M. G. (2006). Behavioral and emotional self-control: Relations to substance use in samples of middle and high school students. *Psychology of Addictive Behaviors*, *20*, 265–278. doi:10.1037/0893-164X.20.3.265

Chapter 10

LIFE SKILLS TRAINING: A COMPETENCE ENHANCEMENT APPROACH TO TOBACCO, ALCOHOL, AND DRUG ABUSE PREVENTION

Gilbert J. Botvin and Kenneth W. Griffin

This chapter examines Life Skills Training (LST), a school-based preventive intervention designed to prevent adolescent substance use and abuse. LST targets key etiologic factors as described in a conceptual framework derived from social learning theory and problem behavior theory. The LST program consists of three major components: (a) a personal competence component that teaches self-management skills, (b) a social competence component that teaches an array of social skills, and (c) a drug resistance component that teaches health-related content, resistance skills, and pro-health attitudes and norms. LST has been extensively tested in a series of randomized trials and found effective in preventing the use/misuse of tobacco, alcohol, marijuana, and other psychoactive drugs. Over 30 years of research shows that LST works with a wide range of students, cuts the use of psychoactive substances in half, and reduces other health-risk behaviors. Findings indicate that the program is effective when implemented under different delivery conditions, by different program providers, with different age groups, and with different populations. Follow-up studies have provide evidence of the long-term effectiveness of LST. Independent economic analysis indicates that LST produces cost savings of $38 for every dollar invested. Finally, LST offers the potential for reducing other health-risk behaviors and fostering academic success.

Given the public health imperative to reduce the mortality and morbidity associated with substance use and abuse, and the growing body of high-quality prevention research, the National Institutes of Health and other leading government agencies have convened expert panels to identify effective prevention programs and policies in an effort to guide practitioners, policymakers, and other decision makers. The LST program has been identified by multiple expert panels as meeting the standard of evidence required to be considered effective. In addition to being one of the most rigorously and extensively tested substance abuse prevention approaches, LST is also one of the most widely disseminated evidence-based programs available. To date, it has been implemented throughout the United States and in 35 countries worldwide.

This chapter describes the LST approach, discusses its theoretical foundations, and reviews its content, materials, provider training, and intervention methods. The chapter summarizes the results from a large body of empirical research demonstrating the effectiveness of the LST in preventing the

Correspondence concerning this chapter should be directed to Gilbert J. Botvin, Department of Healthcare Policy and Research, Weill Medical College of Cornell University, 402 East 67th Street, Concourse 1, New York, NY 10065 or at gjbotvin@med.cornell.edu. See http://www.lifeskillstraining.com for more information about Life Skills Training.

http://dx.doi.org/10.1037/14550-011
Handbook of Adolescent Drug Use Prevention: Research, Intervention Strategies, and Practice, L. M. Scheier (Editor)

use/misuse of tobacco, alcohol, and other drugs. It also describes the research methods used and summarizes findings on mediation that illustrate potential mechanisms of the intervention effects. Finally, it describes the application of LST to different populations, settings, and health-risk behaviors, and discusses potential educational benefits and findings from several cost–benefit studies.

THEORETICAL FOUNDATIONS

Early research testing the effectiveness of tobacco, alcohol, and illicit drug abuse prevention approaches produced disappointing results (Tobler & Stratton, 1997). One reason for the failure of those approaches was that they were not well-grounded in theory and etiologic research, a necessary precondition for developing effective preventive interventions. Etiology research indicates that there is no single necessary and/or sufficient cause that invariably leads to adolescent substance use. Instead, the use of one or more substances is the result of a combination of cognitive, social, personality, pharmacological, biological, and developmental factors, along with an array of environmental or contextual influences (Botvin, 2000; Cicchetti & Luthar, 1999; Hawkins, Catalano, & Miller, 1992; Scheier, 2010).

Although tobacco, alcohol, drug abuse, violence, and other health-risk behaviors are multiply determined, the most effective contemporary approaches to prevention are well-grounded in psychosocial theory. LST relies primarily on social learning theory (Bandura, 1977) and problem behavior theory (Jessor & Jessor, 1977). Social learning theory posits that learning occurs within a social context and results from a process of observation, imitation, and modeling. Problem behavior theory is an extension and application of social learning theory to adolescent problem behaviors. Social factors, particularly from peers and high-status role models (e.g., entertainment celebrities), can be a source of influence encouraging a range of problem behaviors, including health-risk behaviors. Intrapersonal factors affect motivation to engage in these behaviors and interact with interpersonal (social) factors to increase (or decrease) risk. Intrapersonal factors are also important because some can moderate the impact of negative social factors by affecting susceptibility to those influences (Botvin, 2000; Flay, 1987).

Social learning theory and problem behavior theory have both been applied to health-risk behaviors such as tobacco, alcohol, and illicit drug use. From the perspective of these theories, substance use is a socially learned and functional behavior that is acquired through a process of observation, modeling, and reinforcement, and results from the interaction of social factors and intrapersonal factors, including cognitions (i.e., knowledge, attitudes, and expectancies), skills, and personality factors. Social influences to engage in substance use may come from family members (e.g., parents, older siblings), peers, and/or the mass media. For example, adolescents are at increased risk of initiating substance use if their family members or friends smoke, drink, or use drugs and/or convey positive attitudes and expectancies regarding these behaviors. Furthermore, risk for substance use can be increased through exposure to celebrities and other high-status role models in the media who smoke, drink, or use drugs or promote positive attitudes and expectancies regarding substance use.

The risk of substance use initiation is influenced by a constellation of additional intrapersonal factors. Adolescents are more likely to engage in substance use if they are unaware of its potential deleterious effects on health, physical performance, or appearance; if they have positive attitudes toward or believe there are important beneficial outcomes (i.e., expectancies) associated with substance use; or if they have inaccurate (i.e., elevated) normative beliefs regarding the prevalence and social acceptability of substance use. Adolescents are more likely to engage in substance use if they lack the resistance skills necessary to identify, avoid, and/or resist high-risk social situations involving peer or media pressures to smoke, drink, or use drugs. The risk of substance use initiation is higher among adolescents who have poor self-management skills (e.g., lacking in adequate skills for making decisions and solving problems, coping with anxiety and stress) and poor social skills (e.g., lacking in general assertiveness skills and/or adequate skills for communicating effectively, meeting people, developing social relationships). Finally, adolescents are more vulnerable to prodrug social influences from peers or the media if they possess certain personality characteristics (e.g., low self-esteem, poor self-efficacy, high anxiety, impulsivity, rebelliousness).

CONCEPTUAL MODEL GUIDING LST

Figure 10.1 presents a conceptual model of drug use initiation that incorporates key elements of social learning theory and problem behavior theory. The model provides a useful framework for organizing key etiologic domains, identifying potential points of intervention (e.g., school, family, individual), as well as targets of intervention within a given domain of interest (e.g., specific intrapersonal, etiologic factors). In the model, several contextual and psychosocial domains are conceptualized as superordinate constructs that comprise a causal framework of drug initiation. The left side of the figure includes contextual factors. On the top left of the figure, the sociocultural domain consists of key demographic factors (e.g., age, gender, social class), and cultural factors (e.g., ethnic identity, acculturation). The family domain consists of factors such as family-management practices, family communication, discipline, parental monitoring, family substance use, and family attitudes toward substance use. The social-environment domain includes community factors (e.g., community resources, neighborhood organizations); school factors (e.g., school bonding, school size, school climate); media influences that foster positive attitudes, expectancies, and norms that promote substance use (e.g., movies, TV shows, advertising, music, the Internet); peer influences (i.e., peer drug use and prodrug attitudes); and drug availability.

Together, these social-environmental factors shape and interact with intrapersonal factors, which are organized into three major domains: two relate to generic skills and competencies and one relates specifically to drug abuse and other health-risk behaviors. Starting from the top middle of the figure, these domains include personal competence skills (e.g., self-management skills such as decision making), social competence skills (e.g., communication skills, assertive skills), and the drug resistance domain which includes cognitive and attitudinal factors (e.g., knowledge, norms, expectancies related to drug use) and a set of skills specific to resisting peer and media influences to smoke, drink, or use illicit drugs. The next domain includes personality and other psychological factors (e.g., self-efficacy, self-esteem, impulsivity) that mediate the influence of social-environmental factors and intrapersonal factors on tobacco, alcohol, drug abuse, and other

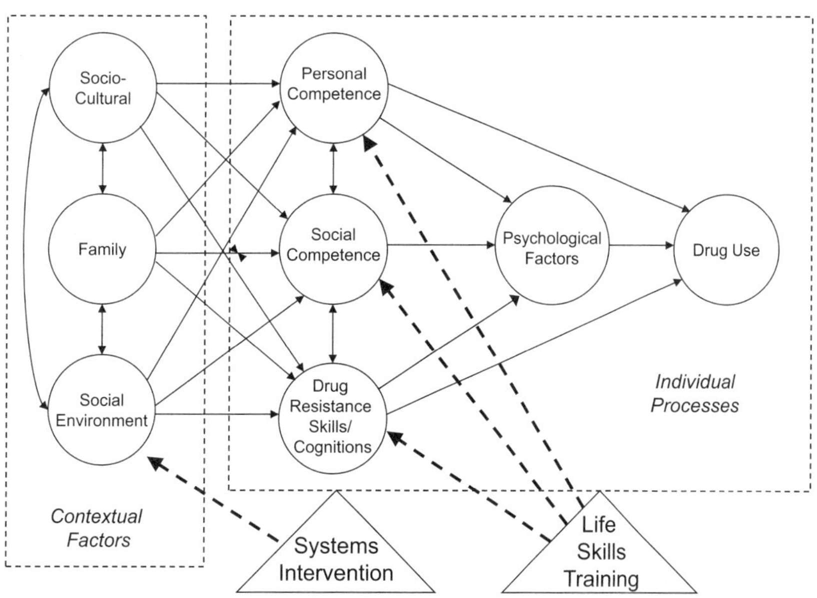

FIGURE 10.1. Model of individual and contextual factors in adolescent drug use and targets of intervention.

health-risk behaviors. This conceptual model helped guide the development of the LST program and illustrates how components of LST target specific intrapersonal etiologic factors.

PROGRAM DESCRIPTION

The LST program is a school-based intervention designed to prevent tobacco, alcohol, and drug abuse. LST is primarily conceptualized as a universal prevention program intended to be implemented with all students on a grade level. However, LST can also be used as a selective prevention program for high-risk youth. LST was originally developed to prevent cigarette smoking. Over the years, the program was expanded to include a focus on alcohol, marijuana, and other illicit drugs, as well as aggression and violence. Studies indicate that favorable program effects from LST generalize to other health-risk behaviors, such as risky driving and sexual behaviors that increase risk for HIV/AIDS. In its original form, LST consisted of 10 class sessions. As the content increased, so did the number of sessions. Moreover, booster years were added in order to maintain and/or enhance the initial prevention effects. Currently the LST middle/junior high school program consists of 15 class periods in the first year, 10 class periods in the second year, and five class periods in the third year. The LST program is designed to be taught in a logical sequence at a rate of one or more sessions per week.

PROGRAM COMPONENTS

The LST program consists of three major components: (a) a personal competence component that teaches self-management skills; (b) a social competence component that teaches an array of social skills; and (c) a drug resistance component that teaches health-related content, resistance skills, and prohealth attitudes and norms. Each component consists of several units designed to be taught in one or more class periods. Many of the skills taught in the LST program are derived from cognitive behavior therapy (CBT). However, instead of using these CBT skills in a therapeutic setting to remediate existing problems, they are taught in an educational setting to prevent the development of potential problems. The LST program components are designed to work in synergy to help young people successfully navigate developmental tasks, to increase resilience, and to facilitate healthy psychosocial development.

Personal Competence

The personal competence component is designed to teach an array of individual self-management skills. One unit contains material designed to foster the development of problem-solving and decision-making skills. For example, the program teaches students how to identify problem situations or important decisions they need to make, identify goals, generate alternative solutions, consider potential consequences, make a final decision, and take the appropriate action. In another unit, students are taught to identify media influences that can influence their behavior, such as those coming from movies, TV, and the Internet. Students are taught skills for identifying, analyzing, interpreting, and resisting these various sources of influence from the media.

The unit on advertising is designed to increase awareness of the purpose and function of advertising as a means of influencing consumer behavior (e.g., influencing consumers to buy a particular product or service), identify specific advertising techniques, increase the ability to analyze and interpret ads, and formulate counterarguments to common advertising appeals. Another unit is designed to provide students with skills for coping with stress and anxiety (e.g., relaxation training, deep breathing), as well as emotional self-regulation skills designed to manage feelings of anger/frustration (e.g., inhibiting impulsive reactions, reframing, using positive self-statements).

A final unit in the personal competence component is designed to provide students with the basic principles of personal behavior change and a general approach to self-improvement (e.g., self-assessment, goal setting, self-monitoring, self-reinforcement). Students identify something they would like to improve that is measurable and achievable before the end of the program (i.e., usually the end of the semester), set a realistic goal, break that goal down into a series of subgoals, work toward achieving their goal, and use self-monitoring to assess progress and self-reinforcement to reward success. Examples of typical items selected for self-improvement include losing weight, improving grades, becoming more physically fit, improving musical or athletic skills, and improving family relationships.

Social Competence

The social competence component teaches an important set of social skills in an effort to promote overall social competence. One unit focuses on teaching general communication skills so that students learn to communicate clearly and avoid misunderstandings. Some of the material taught involves recognizing the importance of nonverbal communication, maintaining consistency between verbal and nonverbal channels of communication, learning to be specific when giving instructions or making arrangements, and using paraphrasing as a way to ensure that students understand a message being communicated by someone else. Another unit within the social skills component focuses on overcoming shyness, initiating social interactions through common greetings, initiating brief social interactions, and teaching skills for meeting new people, making new friends, and developing healthy relationships. In another unit, students are taught complimenting skills (both giving and receiving compliments) and general conversational skills (i.e., techniques for starting, sustaining, and concluding a conversation). In a final unit, students are taught general assertiveness skills (e.g., skills for making requests, refusing unreasonable requests, and standing up for one's rights).

Drug Resistance

The drug resistance component teaches health information and skills designed to increase students' ability to resist social pressures to smoke cigarettes, drink alcohol, and use illicit drugs. Included in this component is material concerning (a) the adverse consequences of tobacco, alcohol, and illicit drug use; (b) the current prevalence of drug use among both youth and adults in order to correct or modify normative expectations about drug use; (c) the changing social acceptability of cigarette smoking and illicit drugs; and (d) the immediate physiological effects of cigarette smoking. In addition to material in specific units relating to tobacco, alcohol, and drugs, material related to health topics is also integrated into other units of the program. For example, the unit focusing on media influences includes material concerning media pressures to smoke, drink, or use illicit drugs. Similarly, in the unit focusing on advertising, students are taught to identify and form counterarguments to common advertising messages. Finally, students are taught the use of assertiveness skills to resist direct peer pressure to smoke cigarettes, drink alcohol, or use illicit drugs (these skills are framed as "defense of rights").

BOOSTER INTERVENTION

Results from school-based studies indicate that prevention effects often decay over time (Resnicow & Botvin, 1993). However, booster interventions can maintain and even enhance initial prevention effects (Botvin, Renick, & Baker, 1983). Therefore, the LST middle/junior high school program currently consists of a primary year of intervention (i.e., Grade 6 in middle school, Grade 7 in junior high school) and a booster intervention in the subsequent 2 years that is designed to reinforce material covered during the primary year of intervention. Correspondingly, the 15 sessions in the first year of LST are followed by 10 booster sessions in Year 2 and five booster sessions in Year 3. The booster sessions provide developmentally appropriate content that focuses on the continued development and reinforcement of personal self-management skills, general social skills, and drug refusal skills, with an emphasis on skills to help students cope effectively with the many pressures and problems they are likely to confront during the middle/junior high school years.

MATERIALS, DELIVERY METHODS, AND PROVIDER TRAINING

Curriculum Materials

The LST program is designed to be self-contained, easy to use, and engaging for students. In order to standardize the intervention and enhance fidelity, the program materials include a teacher's manual and student guide for each year of the intervention. The teacher's manuals contain carefully designed and easy-to-follow lesson plans that provide developmentally appropriate content and activities for each class session. The student guides contain content and activities relating to class sessions and behavioral homework assignments. The material in the student guides is designed for use both in and out of class to reinforce material covered in the program and to help consolidate the skills taught and practiced in the classroom. Capitalizing on feedback from both teachers and students, these materials have been refined and improved over the years to foster implementation fidelity and promote student engagement. These refinements involved improving the presentation of LST content and activities in the various program materials, rather than substantive changes to the underlying prevention strategy. The prevention program was also expanded over the years from its original focus on tobacco to one that includes content and activities related to alcohol, illicit drugs, and violence.

Delivery Methods

Several different intervention methods are used to implement the LST program, with an emphasis on interactive techniques. These include the use of traditional didactic teaching methods, facilitation and group discussion, classroom demonstrations, and cognitive–behavioral skills training. While lecturing and conventional didactic teaching methods are appropriate for some of the material in the LST program, much of the material can be taught most effectively using interactive methods such as facilitating group discussions and skills training, with skills training being the primary intervention method. Since a major emphasis of the LST program is on the teaching of general personal self-management skills, social skills, and skills for resisting social influences to use drugs, the central role of teachers and other program providers is that of a skills trainer or coach. The LST cognitive–behavioral skills-training approach consists of instruction, demonstration, behavioral rehearsal (i.e., practice), feedback, social reinforcement (e.g., praise), and extended practice in the form of behavioral homework assignments.

Provider Training

Provider training typically consists of a 1- or 2-day training workshop and is delivered by a national pool of certified trainers. The purpose of the training is to familiarize intervention providers with the prevention program content, materials, teaching methods, and underlying intervention theory. It also provides an opportunity for trainees to learn and practice the skills needed to successfully implement the prevention program. Research shows that different training formats (e.g., face-to-face workshops vs. packaged videotaped training) can produce comparable results (Botvin, Baker, Dusenbury, Botvin, & Diaz, 1995). Online training is becoming an increasingly popular alternative to conventional face-to-face workshops, especially for remote sites.

EVIDENCE OF EFFECTIVENESS

The LST approach to tobacco, alcohol, and illicit drug abuse prevention has been rigorously and extensively tested in a series of studies over more than three decades. These studies have been conducted in a logical sequence in order to develop and test the effectiveness of this prevention approach with different substance use behaviors, different types of program providers, different age groups, and different populations.

HISTORY AND OVERVIEW

LST was originally developed as a cigarette smoking prevention program and was tested with White middle-class students residing in suburban New York (Botvin & Eng, 1980). In this initial formulation, the program was designed to modify perceived tobacco use norms, decrease social influences to smoke cigarettes, and increase personal and social competence in an effort to address a number of important social and psychological factors related to the onset of cigarette smoking. Subsequent research tested this approach with other forms of substance use and other health-risk behaviors. LST has been tested when implemented using different delivery formats (e.g., weekly or multiple times per week), different program providers (e.g., teachers, health professionals, peer leaders), with different age groups (i.e., elementary, middle/junior high, and high school students), and with different populations (i.e., suburban, urban, and rural populations; White, Black, and Hispanic youth). Research with the LST program has also tested its long-term durability; the effectiveness of booster sessions for maintaining and enhancing program effects; its impact on hypothesized mediating variables; and issues related to dissemination, adoption, implementation—particularly the importance of implementation fidelity, and sustainability.

Studies testing LST include both efficacy and effectiveness trials, and have ranged from small-scale pilot studies involving only a few schools and several hundred students to large-scale randomized controlled trials (RCTs) involving as many as 56 schools and nearly 6,000 students. These studies have varied in length from short- and intermediate-term studies lasting from a few months to a few years to long-term studies lasting up to 12 years in our most recent follow-up. The compilation of studies shows not only that LST has an immediate impact on students who receive the program in middle/junior high school but also that these effects are durable and can last well into young adulthood.

Thus far, evidence for the effectiveness of LST has been documented by 32 outcome studies (involving 18 separate cohorts of students) published in peer-reviewed scientific journals. While the majority of these studies were conducted by investigators at Cornell University's Weill Medical College, studies conducted and published by other research groups provide independent evidence of LST's effectiveness. Table 10.1 summarizes the research designs, sample descriptions, and primary outcomes of these various studies.

TABLE 10.1

Studies Testing the Effects of Life Skills Training on Substance Use and Related Outcomes

Authors, year published, journal	Dataset/ cohort[a]	Randomized trial	No. of schools	No. of LST sessions	Years of follow-up[b]	No. of students	Sampled description	Intervention effects
Efficacy trials								
Botvin et al., 1980, *Preventive Medicine*	1	●	2	10	0	281	W,S	S
Botvin et al., 1980, *The Journal of School Health*	1	●	2	10	.25	281	W,S	S
Botvin et al., 1982, *Preventive Medicine*	2	●	2	12	1	426	W,S	S
Botvin et al., 1983, *Journal of Behavioral Medicine*	3	●	7	15	1	902	W,S	S
Botvin, Baker, Renick, et al., 1984, *Addictive Behaviors*	4	●	10	20	0	1311	W,S	S,A,C
Botvin, Baker, Botvin, et al., 1984, *Journal of Studies on Alcohol*	5	●	2	20	1	239	W,U	A

(continued)

TABLE 10.1 (*cont.*)

Authors, year published, journal	Dataset/ cohort[a]	Randomized trial	No. of schools	No. of LST sessions	Years of follow-up[b]	No. of students	Sampled description	Intervention effects
Botvin, Dusenbury, et al., 1989, *Journal of Behavioral Medicine*	6	●	8	15	0	471	M,U	S
Botvin, Batson, et al., 1989, *Public Health Reports*	7	●	9	12	0	608	M,U	S
Botvin, Baker, Dusenbury, et al., 1990, *Addictive Behaviors*	4	●	10	30	1	998	W,S	S,A,C
Botvin et al., 1992, *Health Psychology*	8	●	47	15	0	3153	M,U	S
Botvin et al., 1994, *Psychology of Addictive Behaviors*	9	●	6	15	0	639	M,U	
Botvin, Schinke, et al., 1995, *Psychology of Addictive Behaviors*	9	●	6	23	2	456	M,U	A
Botvin et al., 1997, *Journal of Child & Adolescent Substance Abuse*	10	●	7	30	0	721	M,U	S,A,C,I
Botvin et al., 2003, *Journal of Child & Adolescent Substance Abuse*	11	●	20	24	0	1090	W,S	S,A
Zollinger et al., 2003, *The Journal of School Health*	12		16	15	2	1598	M,U	S
Effectiveness trials								
Botvin, Baker, Dusenbury, et al., 1990, *Journal of Consulting and Clinical Psychology*	13	●	56	30	2	3684	W,S	S,A,C
Botvin et al., 1999, *JAMWA*	14	●	29	25	1	2209	M,U	S
Botvin et al., 2000, *Addictive Behaviors*	13	●	56	30	6	447	W,S	I
Botvin et al., 2001, *Prevention Science*	14	●	29	25	1	3621	M,U	S,A,I

TABLE 10.1 (*cont.*)

Authors, year published, journal	Dataset/ cohort[a]	Randomized trial	No. of schools	No. of LST sessions	Years of follow-up[b]	No. of students	Sampled description	Intervention effects
Botvin et al., 2001, *Psychology of Addictive Behaviors*	14	●	29	25	2	3041	M,U	A
Scheier et al., 2001, *Prevention Science*	13	●	56	30	5	2288	W,S	S,A,C,I
Spoth et al., 2002, *Psychology of Addictive Behaviors*[c]	15	●	24	30	1	1115	W,R	C,I
Griffin et al., 2003, *Preventive Medicine*	14	●	29	25	1	758	M,U	S,A
Trudeau et al., 2003, *Prevention Science*	15	●	24	30	1.5	847	W,R	S,A,C
Fraguela et al., 2003, *Psychology in Spain*	16	●	5	16	4	1029	W,U	S,A,C,I
Griffin et al., 2004, *Prevention Science*	13	●	56	30	6	2042	W,S	R
Spoth et al., 2005, *Psychology of Addictive Behaviors*[b]	17	●	36	15	2	1109	W,R	A,C,I
Spoth et al., 2006, *Archives of Pediatrics & Adolescent Medicine*[b]	17	●	36	20	5.5	398	W,R	I
Griffin et al., 2006, *Prevention Science*	13	●	56	30	6	2042	W,S	H
Botvin et al., 2006, *Prevention Science*	18	●	41	18	0	4858	W,U	V,D
Spoth et al., 2008, Drug Alcohol Depend[b]	17	●	36	20	5.5	398	W,R	I

Note. M = Predominantly Minority; W = Predominantly White; U = Urban; S = Suburban; R = Rural; S = Smoking; A = Alcohol; C = Cannabis; I = Illicit Drugs Other Than Cannabis; V = Violence; D = Delinquency; R = Risky Driving; H = HIV Risk Behavior

[a]Publications with same number represent studies on same cohort of students. [b]Years of follow-up after posttest assessment. [c]Results presented are for LST only vs. control condition.

RESEARCH METHODS

All of the LST studies conducted at Cornell University were RCTs, with schools being randomly assigned to experimental or control conditions. This methodology affords strict controls for potential biases, such as contamination across conditions and other threats to internal validity. In the large-scale randomized trials, schools were blocked on relevant covariates (e.g., cigarette smoking rates, reading levels, percent receiving school lunch, racial/ethnic composition) prior to random assignment in order to increase pretest equivalence and improve analytic precision (Murray, 1998). Students in the experimental condition received the LST program, while students in the control condition received no experimental manipulation (in some early studies) or "treatment as usual" (in more recent studies in which students received the drug education programs normally provided by their schools).

Students were typically pretested and posttested by self-report questionnaires designed to collect data on demographic characteristics, substance use, and hypothesized mediating variables associated with substance use risk. Survey questionnaires were tested for reliability and validity, and shown to have good psychometric properties. Data collection and program implementation were standardized using detailed research protocols to protect against potential threats to internal validity. Particular attention was placed on procedures to enhance the validity of self-report data. For example, biochemical indicators of behavior (i.e., expired air or saliva) were collected simultaneously using bogus pipeline procedures to enhance the validity of self-reports (Evans, Hansen, & Mittlemark, 1977). In addition, data collectors with racial and ethnic backgrounds similar to the study participants were recruited and trained using standardized protocols to ensure high-quality data collection. Carefully developed procedures were used to track study participants in order to maintain the highest possible sample retention rates and to reduce attrition. Moreover, attrition analyses were conducted in all large-scale randomized trials to rule out the possibility of sample bias due to differential attrition (by experimental condition and prior risk status). Data from these studies were analyzed using well-accepted statistical methods for preventive intervention evaluations. Most studies used multivariate techniques that adjust for relevant covariates to improve model precision. To account for school-level clustering in large-scale effectiveness trials, data were analyzed either at the school level or involved statistical techniques controlling for clustering effects. As a whole, this body of research provides clear and consistent evidence that the LST approach can decrease tobacco, alcohol, drug use, and other health-risk behaviors.

EFFICACY TRIALS

Studies testing LST found that the program can reduce the proportion of tobacco, alcohol, and marijuana users by about 50% and, in some cases, by as much as 80%. The early studies testing LST demonstrated its efficacy as a cigarette smoking prevention program (Botvin & Eng, 1982; Botvin, Eng, & Williams, 1980). Subsequent studies found prevention effects for the use of alcoholic beverages (Botvin, Baker, Botvin, Filazzola, & Millman, 1984; Botvin, Baker, Renick, Filazzola, & Botvin, 1984) and/or marijuana (Botvin, Baker, Renick, et al., 1984). In addition, research showed that booster sessions could maintain and, in some cases, even enhance initial prevention effects (Botvin et al., 1983). With respect to program providers, the LST approach was shown to be effective when implemented by outside health professionals (Botvin, Eng, & Williams, 1980), peer leaders (Botvin & Eng, 1982), or classroom teachers (Botvin et al., 1983).

A series of RCTs tested LST with predominantly African American and Hispanic students from urban junior high schools. Similar to earlier LST research initiatives, the initial intent was to determine the program's efficacy for preventing cigarette smoking. Two studies found that LST prevented cigarette smoking among Hispanic junior high school students (Botvin, Dusenbury, Baker, James-Ortiz, Botvin, & Kerner, 1992; Botvin, Dusenbury, Baker, James-Ortiz, & Kerner, 1989). Another study demonstrated the efficacy of LST with a sample of African American youth (Botvin, Batson, et al., 1989). In addition, a study testing both culturally focused and generic versions of LST in a population of inner-city, multiethnic minority youth found that while both conditions were effective, the culturally focused version produced stronger prevention effects with respect to the frequency and amount of alcohol use (Botvin, Schinke, Epstein, & Diaz, 1994; Botvin, Schinke, Epstein, Diaz, & Botvin, 1995). Further research testing the efficacy of LST with inner-city minority youth found that it reduced use of tobacco, alcohol, marijuana, and multiple drugs (Botvin, Epstein, Baker, Diaz, & Ifill-Williams, 1997). Taken together, these studies show that LST works well with multiple populations including White, African American, and Hispanic youth, and that tailoring it to specific populations can increase the program's efficacy.

EFFECTIVENESS TRIALS

The LST program also has been tested in several large-scale, group-randomized effectiveness trials, with the school as the unit of assignment to experimental conditions. These studies were designed to be methodologically rigorous and to provide important data concerning the short- and long-term effectiveness of LST on tobacco, alcohol, and drug use; its impact on more serious levels of drug involvement; and whether the program works in the hypothesized manner by modifying targeted risk factors associated with change in behavior.

The largest randomized trial involved 56 schools in New York State randomly assigned to one of three conditions: (a) LST and live (in-person) teacher training workshops, (b) LST and videotaped teacher training, and (c) treatment-as-usual control condition. For schools assigned to the two experimental treatment conditions, students receive the LST program in the seventh grade with booster sessions in the eighth and ninth grades. Students were pretested and post-tested in the seventh grade with annual follow-up assessments. Initial results at the end of junior high school showed that students who received LST had significantly less cigarette smoking, alcohol abuse (i.e., drunkenness), and marijuana use (Botvin, Baker, et al., 1990). Five-year follow-up data collected at the end of high school showed similar results (Botvin, Baker, et al., 1995).

Several hypotheses were tested in this study: (a) live (in-person) teacher-training workshops would produce stronger prevention effects than packaged (videotaped) teacher training; (b) prevention effects would last until the end of high school; (c) targeting early-stage drug use would reduce one or more forms of more serious (i.e., later-stage) drug use, such as heavy (e.g., pack-a-day) cigarette smoking, heavy (e.g., binge) drinking, drunkenness, and multiple (i.e., polydrug) use; and (d) higher implementation fidelity would yield stronger prevention effects. The first three hypotheses were tested using data from the full follow-up sample. Furthermore, since no differences were found for the two teacher training conditions, they were combined for all subsequent analyses. The fourth hypothesis was tested using a high fidelity subsample, which was operationally defined as students who received 60% or more of the prevention program based on classroom observations of teacher implementation fidelity.

Analyses of data from the full follow-up sample of 3,597 students found that LST students had significantly lower rates of cigarette smoking, alcohol abuse (i.e., drunkenness), and polydrug use (i.e., tobacco, alcohol, and marijuana) than controls. The strongest prevention effects were found when implementation fidelity was taken into account. Analyses of data from the high-fidelity sample indicated that LST students had significantly lower rates of substance use than controls on nearly every measure of tobacco, alcohol, marijuana, and polydrug use. Virtually all of the statistical comparisons between the LST students and the controls were significant, and the effects were larger for students in the high-fidelity sample. Additional follow-up data were collected 6 months later (after high school) from a random sample of students. Students were mailed a follow-up survey to assess illicit drug use. Results found that, relative to controls, students who participated in the LST program during middle/junior high school had lower rates of illicit drug use overall and lower rates of hallucinogen, heroin, and narcotic use (Botvin, Griffin, Diaz, Scheier, Williams, & Epstein, 2000).

A second large-scale, randomized trial was conducted with inner-city, minority youth attending 29 New York City middle/junior high schools. In order to ensure that LST was culturally appropriate for the target audience, the program materials were adapted in several ways. The Teacher's Manual and Student Guide were modified to include (a) relevant graphics and illustrations of minority youth; (b) language and reading levels of materials appropriate for the target population; (c) role-play scenarios adapted to best reflect the lives of minority youth; and (d) materials that were focus-group-tested with teachers, parents, and students from the participating communities. Posttest and 1-year follow-up results indicated that students who received the LST program reported less cigarette smoking, alcohol use, inhalant use, and polydrug use relative to controls (Botvin, Griffin, Diaz, & Ifill-Williams, 2001a). Additional analyses showed that LST reduced binge drinking (i.e., five or more drinks per drinking occasion) by 50% or more at the 1-year and 2-year follow-up assessments (Botvin, Griffin, Diaz, & Ifill-Williams, 2001b). Furthermore, analysis of data from a subsample of high-risk youth (i.e., students with poor academic performance and drug-using friends) who received the LST program were less likely than controls to engage in cigarette smoking, drinking, inhalant use, or polydrug use (Griffin, Botvin, Nichols, & Doyle, 2003).

LONG-TERM EFFECTIVENESS: 12-YEAR FOLLOW-UP

Twelve-year follow-up data were collected from the longitudinal sample of 3,597 students described above (Botvin, Baker, et al., 1995). Tracking procedures used to locate students from the original study included directory assistance searches, telephone matching services, Department of Motor Vehicles databases, mailings with address correction requests, and searches of spider-linked credit databases. After obtaining confirmed addresses on more than half of the original sample, follow-up surveys were mailed and completed surveys obtained on over 2,200 students. Several analyses were conducted to determine the comparability of the final follow-up sample by condition. First, the follow-up sample was tested to determine its comparability by condition in terms of demographic characteristics, pretest substance use, and academic performance (i.e., grades). Second, the follow-up sample was examined in terms of marital or cohabitation status, college graduation rates, and income status. Third, analyses were conducted to test for differential attrition by experimental condition. No significant differences were found for any of these analyses. Moreover, the final young adult follow-up sample was approximately half male and half female, with an average age of 24. Significant intervention effects were found for several measures of substance use, including overall illicit drug use, marijuana use, nonmedical pill use, and tranquilizer use (Botvin & Griffin, 2012). The results of this follow-up study demonstrate the long-term effectiveness of LST in a sample of young adults who received LST during middle/junior high school.

INDEPENDENT EVIDENCE

Although much of the research testing LST has been conducted by our research team at Cornell, several independent studies by other research groups have provided additional evidence for the effectiveness of LST. In a series of RCTs, Spoth and his colleagues tested LST in a large-scale effectiveness trial involving Iowa youth. The first of these studies tested the effectiveness of a school-based prevention program (LST) alone and in combination with a family-focused prevention program. While there were significant prevention effects for both conditions, there were stronger effects for the condition with both LST and the family-focused intervention (Spoth, Redmond, Trudeau, & Shin, 2002). Interestingly, there were also significant prevention effects for marijuana use 1 year after the end of the intervention for the group receiving only the LST program when compared with the control group.

In a follow-up study measuring students substance use 6 months later, students who received the LST program reported slower growth in substance use initiation (measured by rates of smoking, drinking, and marijuana use) relative to controls (Trudeau, Spoth, Lillehoj, Redmond, & Wickrama, 2003). In a third study conducted by Spoth and colleagues, the long-term impact of LST was assessed both alone and in combination with a family-focused prevention program. The researchers found decreased rates of methamphetamine use for both conditions (relative to controls) at the 4.5- and 5.5-year follow-ups (Spoth, Clair, Shin, & Redmond, 2006).

In another independent study conducted with 1,598 students in Grades 6 to 8, Zollinger, Saywell, Muegge, Wooldridge, Cummings, and Caine (2003) found lower rates of cigarette smoking and greater intentions to remain smoke-free for students who received LST relative to controls who did not. Finally, researchers in Spain conducted a 4-year longitudinal study involving 1,029 students from five secondary schools. Prevention effects were found first for cigarette smoking and alcohol use, followed later by prevention effects for the use of cannabis, tranquilizers, and amphetamines (Fraguela, Martin, & Trinanes, 2003).

In sum, there is a substantial literature involving methodologically rigorous, well-executed studies testing the effectiveness of LST—some conducted by researchers at Cornell and others conducted by independent investigators. Together, these studies provide consistent evidence of LST's effectiveness with White, African American, and Hispanic/Latino youth as well as with suburban, urban, and rural youth. Of the published studies testing LST listed in Table 10.1, there are 20 studies showing that the program decreases tobacco use, 15 studies showing that it decreases alcohol use, 10 studies showing that it decreases marijuana use, and 10 studies showing that it produces significant reductions in illicit drug use other than marijuana.

MEDIATING AND MODERATING MECHANISMS

A series of studies examined the links between substance use outcomes and key hypothesized mediators and moderators outlined in the LST conceptual model. Below is a brief review of findings that support specific pathways of the LST conceptual model, first from an etiologic perspective and then from an intervention perspective.

Personal Competence Skills

A number of etiology studies focused on the protective role that personal self-management skills—including decision making, problem solving, behavioral self-control, and self-reinforcement—may play in terms of adolescent substance use. In two studies using latent growth modeling, the protective effects of self-management skills were examined longitudinally over the course of middle school and high school. Findings indicated that early self-management skills slowed growth in substance use (i.e., alcohol, cigarettes, and marijuana) over time, and that increases in self-management skills were inversely related to growth in substance use over time (Griffin, Scheier, & Botvin, 2009; Lowe, Acevedo, Griffin, & Botvin, 2013).

Several studies examined the mediating mechanisms through which personal self-management skills are protective. These skills had a direct protective effect on later substance use, and this protective effect was fully mediated by greater psychological well-being but not psychological distress (Griffin, Botvin, Scheier, Epstein, & Diaz, 2002; Griffin, Scheier, Botvin, & Diaz, 2001). These findings support the LST conceptual model by suggesting that personal competence during early adolescence reflects an underlying psychosocial resiliency in which youth with better self-management skills experience greater levels of well-being that reduces substance use involvement. Other studies have identified moderating effects where self-management skills (including decision-making and self-reinforcement skills) buffered the impact of negative social influences such as prodrug attitudes and behaviors among peers and parents (Botvin, Malgady, Griffin, Scheier, & Epstein, 1998). These findings provide further support for the intervention model.

Social Competence and Drug Resistance Skills

Other studies illustrate the mediating mechanisms through which social competence skills can protect young people from substance use. For example, one study found that students who were more socially confident, assertive, and had better communication skills reported less cigarette smoking and drinking; this direct effect was fully mediated by higher expectancies of social benefits arising from drug use (Griffin, Epstein, Botvin, & Spoth, 2001). These findings support the conceptual intervention model by showing that youth lacking competence skills may engage in substance use in an attempt to achieve increased social status or other perceived social benefits.

While drug refusal skills can have direct protective effects on substance use, an individual's ability to utilize refusal skills may stem from a variety of factors. General competencies in areas such as decision-making skills and perceived self-efficacy enhance adolescents ability to draw upon specific drug refusal skills (Epstein, Griffin, & Botvin, 2000a, 2000b, 2000c) and media resistance skills (Epstein & Botvin, 2008). Moreover, a study using latent growth modeling to analyze 4-year longitudinal data provided support for a dual process model indicating that growth in poor refusal skills and personal self-control skills was paralleled by increasing rates of alcohol involvement (Scheier, Botvin, Griffin, & Diaz, 1999).

Finally, studies have identified moderating effects where drug refusal skills buffer the impact of negative social influences associated with drug use. Among youth with friends that drink alcohol, those who engaged in less frequent use of refusal skills were at greater risk for future drinking than youth who engaged in more frequent use of refusal skills (Epstein & Botvin, 2002; Epstein, Zhou, Bang, & Botvin, 2007). Taken together, these findings support the LST intervention model by showing that drug refusal skills and related competencies can offset perceived and actual prodrug influences in the social environment.

Intervention Effects on Hypothesized Mediators

In addition to etiology studies testing the conceptual model, intervention studies have examined the impact of LST on hypothesized mediators. In studies focusing on cigarette smoking prevention, intervention effects were observed on hypothesized mediators including antismoking knowledge (Botvin & Eng, 1982; Botvin, Batson, et al., 1989; Botvin, Dusenbury, et al., 1989; Botvin et al., 1983, 1992; Zollinger et al., 2003), perceived peer and/or adult smoking norms (Botvin, Baker, et al., 1990; Botvin, Dusenbury, et al., 1989; Botvin et al., 1992), cigarette smoking refusal skills and smoking intentions (Zollinger et al., 2003), decision making (Botvin, Batson, et al., 1989), assertiveness and self-esteem (Botvin et al., 1983), and social anxiety (Botvin & Eng, 1980, 1982; Botvin et al., 1983).

In the studies focusing more broadly on substance use, intervention effects were observed on hypothesized mediators, including antidrug knowledge (Botvin, Baker, Dusenbury, et al., 1990; Botvin, Baker, Renick, et al., 1984; Botvin, Schinke, et al., 1995; Botvin et al., 2001b, 2003), antidrug attitudes (Botvin, Baker, Botvin, et al., 1984; Botvin, Baker, Filazzola, et al., 1990; Botvin et al., 2001b, 2003), perceived peer and/or adult drug use norms (Botvin, Baker, Dusenbury, et al., 1990; Botvin et al., 2001b, 2003), drug refusal skills (Trudeau et al., 2003), locus of control (Botvin, Baker, Dusenbury, et al., 1990; Botvin, Baker, Renick, et al., 1984), risk taking (Botvin, Schinke, et al., 1995), and self-esteem (Botvin, Baker, Renick, et al., 1984; Botvin et al., 2003).

Direct Tests of Mediating Mechanisms

Several studies provided a direct test of mediation using the statistical criteria outlined by Baron and Kenny (1986). Studies examining the mediating mechanisms of the LST program can be grouped into those focused on the impact of LST on cigarette smoking and those focused on the impact of LST on substance use more broadly. The former studies found that the intervention prevents smoking through its effect on smoking knowledge, perceived peer and/or adult smoking norms (Botvin et al., 1992, 1999), and refusal skills, smoking intentions, and risk taking (Botvin et al., 1999). Studies testing mediation of LST on substance use showed that the intervention prevents substance use through its effects on antidrug attitudes (Botvin et al., 1994; Botvin, Schinke, et al., 1995), peer normative expectations (Botvin et al., 1997, 2001a), drug refusal skills (Botvin et al., 1997), behavioral intentions (Botvin et al., 1994, 2001a), social competence (Scheier et al., 2001), and risk taking (Botvin et al., 1994, 1997, 2001a).

Implications for Theory

In summary, data from etiology and intervention studies provide support for the LST prevention model. The conceptual model posits that specific personal and social competence skills lead to reduced drug use via a process that enhances psychosocial resilience. Adolescents with better competence skills are more effective in social interactions or achieve greater success in academic pursuits as well as other developmental tasks. These mastery experiences promote self-efficacy and expectations of future success, contributing to a sense of self-esteem and well-being. This process of resilience reduces vulnerability to negative social environmental influences such as prodrug social messages, media portrayals, adult role models, and peer influences. Likewise, it also may reduce internal motivational forces that promote drug use such as the desire to appear mature, rebellious, and independent. Because this resilience process involves a general set of social and self-management competencies, it offers the potential for preventing a variety of problem or health-risk behaviors that share a similar constellation of risk and protective factors. To the extent that these competence skills promote success in developmental tasks, they also would be expected to have the potential to promote positive youth development more broadly.

APPLICATION OF LST TO OTHER AGE GROUPS

Age-appropriate interventions using the LST approach were developed, tested, and proven to be effective with several different age groups. Although most research testing LST was conducted with middle/junior high school students, LST has also been tested with elementary school students and high school students. These interventions were designed to be used either alone or in combination with one another.

Elementary School

Since many of the same etiologic factors appear to play a role in promoting the onset of tobacco and alcohol use among younger populations (O'Loughlin, Paradis, Renaud, & Gomez, 1998), a reasonable hypothesis is that prevention approaches found effective with middle/junior high school students might also be effective with younger populations. Therefore, the LST program was adapted for upper elementary school students in Grades 3 through 5. The goal of the program was to reduce tobacco and alcohol use. Similar to the LST middle-school program, the prevention program for elementary school students was designed to teach students the knowledge and skills necessary to resist social influences to use one or more substances, as well as to teach material designed to promote personal and social competence using interactive teaching methods. The LST elementary-school program consists of 24 classes (approximately 30 to 45 minutes each) designed to be taught over the course of 3 years at a rate of eight classes per year. The program materials and activities were intended for students in the last 3 years of elementary school (either Grades 3–5 or Grades 4–6). Results of a randomized trial involving 20 elementary schools and 1,097 students demonstrated the effectiveness of the LST program for preventing tobacco and alcohol use among elementary school students and also demonstrated the utility of intervening during the preadolescent years (Botvin, Griffin, Paul, & Macaulay, 2003).

High School

Two studies show that LST is also effective with high school students. These two studies involved students attending suburban schools in the ninth and 10th grades as well as some students in the eighth grade. In the initial study, participating students were pretested and posttested by self-report questionnaires probing their cigarette smoking, health knowledge, and several psychosocial variables (Botvin, Eng, & Williams, 1980). The intervention reduced cigarette smoking by 60% among ninth and 10th graders. A follow-up study collected data 3 months after the initial posttest to determine the stability of these findings. Overall, follow-up results indicated that the students who received the intervention continued to have significant and substantial reductions in smoking rates (Botvin & Eng, 1980). The LST materials for high school students have been updated and refined to make them more appealing to this age group.

WORKPLACE

The Life Skills Training Wellness Program (LST-WP) is an extension and adaptation of the LST approach suitable for the workplace. LST-WP is based on the same theory, prevention approach, and methods of the school-based program. It is designed to provide comprehensive skills training for adolescent and young adult employees in many of the same key areas as the school-based program. LST-WP is an eight-session program that focuses on teaching self-management skills (e.g., goal setting in the workplace, problem solving in the workplace, stress and anger management), social skills (e.g., effective communication, conflict resolution), and work-life skills (e.g., time and money management, drug resistance skills, building a safe and drug-free workplace). LST-WP was tested in a 20-site randomized trial with a diverse sample of 16- to 24-year-old employees at a large supermarket chain (Williams, Samuolis, Griffin, & Botvin, 2011). Six-month and 18-month follow-up results indicated that employees who participated in the LST-WP program were 1.6 times more likely than controls to score high on job satisfaction and quality of work, and lower on health care utilization and symptoms of stress and depression.

BEYOND DRUG ABUSE PREVENTION

Multiple Health-Risk Behaviors

With the accumulation of evidence from different areas of research, it has become increasingly clear that many health-risk behaviors cluster together. Not only are these risk behaviors highly associated with one another, but many also share overlapping etiologic factors and a similar developmental course. As a consequence, the same individuals are often at risk for multiple health problems (Biglan, Brennan, Foster, & Holder, 2004). This suggests the exciting possibility that rather than developing separate preventive interventions for each of these various health-risk behaviors, a single prevention approach targeting these shared etiologic factors may have the potential for preventing or reducing risk for multiple health problems. For example, rather than developing and implementing separate programs, all competing for time and resources, a single intervention may prevent or reduce risk for a wide range of health-risk behaviors. In addition to the existing etiologic evidence and theoretical formulations, research with the LST indicates that it can have favorable prevention effects on multiple health-risk behaviors. The evidence discussed in this chapter documents the effectiveness of LST for preventing the use/abuse of tobacco, alcohol, marijuana, and other illicit drugs. In addition, studies testing LST have also found that it can significantly reduce risky driving (Griffin, Botvin, & Nichols, 2004), violence and delinquency (Botvin, Griffin, & Nichols, 2006), and HIV/AIDS risk behaviors (Griffin, Botvin, & Nichols, 2006).

Academic Benefits

Academic performance is often adversely affected by drug use, violence, and other problem behaviors. Tobacco, alcohol, and illicit drug use are associated with lower academic performance, higher absenteeism, and higher dropout rates. Prevention programs that effectively deter or reduce drug use may also help students avoid the deleterious effects of drug use on academic performance and other educational outcomes. Similarly, competence-based prevention programs, such as LST, that are designed to teach a range of life skills may facilitate overall educational success. Information garnered from the fields of health, psychology, and education suggests that LST may have the potential for producing a positive impact on several key educational outcomes.

First, LST has the potential for improving school attendance, engagement, and commitment. LST can contribute to a sense of mastery that enhances school bonding by not only preventing problem behaviors but also by providing students with the requisite skills to be resilient and successful in the face of new challenges. Second, LST also offers the potential for improving school safety (e.g., by decreasing aggression and violence) and fostering the development of a supportive learning environment. Students who feel safe and secure are likely to be better able to learn and thrive at school. Third, LST can increase students' ability to handle academic pressures through the acquisition of problem-solving and decision-making skills, goal-setting and self-reinforcement skills, and skills for coping with stress and anxiety. Fourth, by teaching general social skills, LST can improve students' ability to interact with one another, work collaboratively with teachers and other students, and both request and provide social support to and from peers. Fifth, LST teaches self-regulation, persistence, and management of emotions, which are necessary for effective classroom learning. Finally, LST provides students with the skills necessary to resist pressure from peers and the media to smoke, drink, or use drugs or engage in other health-risk behaviors. In addition, students are taught critical-thinking, decision-making and problem-solving skills, which can lead to making more appropriate health-related decisions. Together, these skills not only help students avoid the pitfalls of drug use and related problem behaviors, but also can provide students with the social and emotional skills needed to support academic success.

Economic Benefits

Tobacco, alcohol, and illicit drug abuse cost the United States over $500 billion per year (Miller & Hendrie, 2008). As such, it is one of the most expensive health problems facing our nation. Nationwide implementation of effective prevention programs offers not only the potential for significantly reducing tobacco, alcohol, and drug abuse, along with the associated mortality and morbidity, but also the potential for considerable cost savings. Just as the effectiveness of different prevention approaches varies, so too do the potential economic benefits. Thus, in addition to conducting research to identify effective prevention approaches, it is also important that educators, health professionals, and policymakers become cognizant of the costs and potential economic benefits of different prevention approaches in order to make informed decisions about the allocation of increasingly scarce resources.

In addition to effectiveness, a useful metric for decision makers when comparing different programs or policy options is *cost–benefit*. Cost–benefit provides a means of assessing the cost savings that may accrue from financial expenditures on an effective tobacco, alcohol, or drug abuse prevention program (i.e., the return on investment). Cost–benefit is expressed as the ratio of expenditures to deliver a program (i.e., costs) and the social/economic savings monetized over time (i.e., benefits). Several recent cost–benefit analyses have been conducted to determine the potential cost savings of effective prevention programs. These studies show that effective prevention programs are a good investment and that LST, in particular, can produce significant cost savings (Aos, Lieb, Mayfield, Miller, & Pennucci, 2004; Jones, Bumbarger, Greenberg, Greenwood, & Kyler, 2008). Moreover, a recent cost–benefit analysis found a $38 benefit for every dollar spent on LST (Lee, Aos, Drake, Pennucci, Miller, & Anderson, 2012). Based on these cost–benefit analyses, it is evident that prevention is well worth the investment, and that LST can produce considerable cost savings. In view of the rapidly escalating costs of health care, it would be prudent for policymakers to place a much greater emphasis on promoting the use of prevention programs and policies that have been tested and proven effective.

SUMMARY AND CONCLUSIONS

Life Skills Training (LST) addresses a number of key etiologic factors using a theoretical framework derived from social learning theory and problem behavior theory. LST has been extensively tested in a series of randomized trials and found effective in preventing cigarette smoking, alcohol, and drug use as well as violence and other health-risk behaviors, such as risky driving. Research demonstrates that it is effective when delivered using different implementation formats, by different program providers, with different age groups, and with different populations. Follow-up studies conducted at the end of high school, after high school, and/or among young adults in their mid-20s support the long-term effectiveness of LST. Moreover, independent cost–benefit studies show that LST produces a cost savings of as much as $38 for every dollar invested. Finally, LST offers the potential for reducing other health-risk behaviors and improving educational outcomes.

The growing availability of effective prevention programs has resulted in new tools for transforming prevention practice, improving public health, and reducing health care costs. Yet, funding for prevention has declined precipitously in recent years, putting the fruits of three decades of prevention research at risk. Given the rapidly escalating costs of health care, it is crucial that policymakers significantly increase funding for prevention and vigorously promote the use of programs and policies that have been tested and proven effective.

References

Aos, S., Lieb, R., Mayfield, J., Miller, M., & Pennucci, A. (2004). *Benefits and costs of prevention and early intervention programs for youth.* Olympia, WA: Washington State Institute for Public Policy.

Bandura, A. (1977). *Social learning theory.* Englewood Cliffs, NJ: Prentice Hall.

Baron, R. M., & Kenny, D. A. (1986). The moderator-mediator variable distinction in social psychological research: Conceptual, strategic and statistical considerations. *Journal of Personality and Social Psychology, 51*, 1173–1182. doi:10.1037/0022-3514.51.6.1173

Biglan, A., Brennan, P. A., Foster, S. L., & Holder, H. D. (2004). *Helping adolescents at risk: Prevention of multiple problem behaviors.* New York, NY: Guilford.

Botvin, G. J. (2000). Preventing drug abuse in schools: Social and competence enhancement approaches targeting individual-level etiological factors. *Addictive Behaviors, 25*, 887–897. doi:10.1016/S0306-4603(00)00119-2

Botvin, G. J., Baker, E., Botvin, E. M., Filazzola, A. D., & Millman, R. B. (1984). Prevention of alcohol misuse through the development of personal and social competence: A pilot study. *Journal of Studies on Alcohol, 45*, 550–552.

Botvin, G. J., Baker, E., Dusenbury, L., Botvin, E. M., & Diaz, T. (1995). Long-term follow-up results of a randomized drug abuse prevention trial in a White middle-class population. *JAMA, 273*, 1106–1112. doi:10.1001/jama.1995.03520380042033

Botvin, G. J., Baker, E., Dusenbury, L., Tortu, S., & Botvin, E. M. (1990). Preventing adolescent drug abuse through a multimodal cognitive-behavioral approach: Results of a three-year study. *Journal of Consulting and Clinical Psychology, 58*, 437–446. doi:10.1037/0022-006X.58.4.437

Botvin, G. J., Baker, E., Filazzola, A., & Botvin, E. M. (1990). A cognitive-behavioral approach to substance abuse prevention: A one-year follow-up. *Addictive Behaviors, 15*, 47–63. doi:10.1016/0306-4603(90)90006-J

Botvin, G. J., Baker, E., Renick, N., Filazzola, A. D., & Botvin, E. M. (1984). A cognitive-behavioral approach to substance abuse prevention. *Addictive Behaviors, 9*, 137–147. doi:10.1016/0306-4603(84)90051-0

Botvin, G. J., Batson, H., Witts-Vitale, S., Bess, V., Baker, E., & Dusenbury, L. (1989). A psychosocial approach to smoking prevention for urban black youth. *Public Health Reports, 104*, 573–582.

Botvin, G. J., Dusenbury, L., Baker, E., James-Ortiz, S., Botvin, E. M., & Kerner, J. (1992). Smoking prevention among urban minority youth: Assessing effects on outcome and mediating variables. *Health Psychology, 11*, 290–299. doi:10.1037/0278-6133.11.5.290

Botvin, G. J., Dusenbury, L., Baker, E., James-Ortiz, S., & Kerner, J. (1989). A skills training approach to smoking prevention among Hispanic youth. *Journal of Behavioral Medicine, 12*, 279–296. doi:10.1007/BF00844872

Botvin, G. J., & Eng, A. (1980). A comprehensive school-based smoking prevention program. *The Journal of School Health, 50*, 209–213. doi:10.1111/j.1746-1561.1980.tb07378.x

Botvin, G. J., & Eng, A. (1982). The efficacy of a multicomponent approach to the prevention of cigarette smoking. *Preventive Medicine, 11*, 199–211. doi:10.1016/0091-7435(82)90018-4

Botvin, G. J., Eng, A., & Williams, C. L. (1980). Preventing the onset of cigarette smoking through life skills training. *Preventive Medicine, 9*, 135–143. doi:10.1016/0091-7435(80)90064-X

Botvin, G. J., Epstein, J. A., Baker, E., Diaz, T., & Ifill-Williams, M. (1997). School-based drug abuse prevention with inner-city minority youth. *Journal of Child & Adolescent Substance Abuse, 6*, 5–19. doi:10.1300/J029v06n01_02

Botvin, G. J., & Griffin, K. W. (2012, April). *Long-term outcomes from Blueprints model programs: Life Skills Training.* Paper presented at 2012 Blueprints for Violence Prevention conference, San Antonio, Texas.

Botvin, G. J., Griffin, K. W., Diaz, T., & Ifill-Williams, M. (2001a). Drug abuse prevention among minority adolescents: One-year follow-up of a school-based preventive intervention. *Prevention Science, 2*, 1–13. doi:10.1023/A:1010025311161

Botvin, G. J., Griffin, K. W., Diaz, T., & Ifill-Williams, M. (2001b). Preventing binge drinking during early adolescence: One- and two-year follow-up of a school-based preventive intervention. *Psychology of Addictive Behaviors, 15*, 360–365. doi:10.1037/0893-164X.15.4.360

Botvin, G. J., Griffin, K. W., Diaz, T., Miller, N., & Ifill-Williams, M. (1999). Smoking initiation and escalation in early adolescent girls: One-year follow-up of a school-based prevention intervention for minority youth. *Journal of the American Medical Women's Association, 54*, 139–143.

Botvin, G. J., Griffin, K. W., Diaz, T., Scheier, L. M., Williams, C., & Epstein, J. A. (2000). Preventing illicit drug use in adolescents: Long-term follow-up data from a randomized control trial of a school population. *Addictive Behaviors, 25*, 769–774. doi:10.1016/S0306-4603(99)00050-7

Botvin, G. J., Griffin, K. W., & Nichols, T. R. (2006). Preventing youth violence and delinquency through a universal school-based prevention approach. *Prevention Science, 7*, 403–408. doi:10.1007/s11121-006-0057-y

Botvin, G. J., Griffin, K. W., Paul, E., & Macaulay, A. P. (2003). Preventing tobacco and alcohol use among elementary school students through Life Skills Training. *Journal of Child & Adolescent Substance Abuse*, *12*, 1–17. doi:10.1300/J029v12n04_01

Botvin, G. J., Malgady, R. G., Griffin, K. W., Scheier, L. M., & Epstein, J. A. (1998). Alcohol and marijuana use among rural youth: Interaction of social and intrapersonal influences. *Addictive Behaviors*, *23*, 379–387. doi:10.1016/S0306-4603(98)00006-9

Botvin, G. J., Renick, N. L., & Baker, E. (1983). The effects of scheduling format and booster sessions on a broad-spectrum psychosocial smoking prevention program. *Journal of Behavioral Medicine*, *6*, 359–379. doi:10.1007/BF00846324

Botvin, G. J., Schinke, S. P., Epstein, J. A., & Diaz, T. (1994). The effectiveness of culturally-focused & generic skills training approaches to alcohol and drug abuse prevention among minority youth. *Psychology of Addictive Behaviors*, *8*, 116–127. doi:10.1037/0893-164X.8.2.116

Botvin, G. J., Schinke, S. P., Epstein, J. A., Diaz, T., & Botvin, E. M. (1995). Effectiveness of culturally-focused and generic skills training approaches to alcohol and drug abuse prevention among minority adolescents: Two-Year follow-up results. *Psychology of Addictive Behaviors*, *9*, 183–194. doi:10.1037/0893-164X.9.3.183

Cicchetti, D., & Luthar, S. S. (1999). Developmental approaches to substance use and abuse. *Development and Psychopathology*, *11*, 655–656. doi:10.1017/S0954579499002254

Epstein, J. A., & Botvin, G. J. (2002). The moderating role of risk-taking and refusal assertiveness on social influences in alcohol use among inner-city adolescents. *Journal of Studies on Alcohol*, *63*, 456–459.

Epstein, J. A., & Botvin, G. J. (2008). Media resistance skills and drug skill refusal techniques: What is their relationship with alcohol use among inner-city adolescents? *Addictive Behaviors*, *33*, 528–537. doi:10.1016/j.addbeh.2007.11.001

Epstein, J. A., Griffin, K. W., & Botvin, G. J. (2000a). A model of smoking among inner-city adolescents: The role of personal competence and perceived benefits of smoking. *Preventive Medicine: An International Journal Devoted to Practice and Theory*, *31*, 107–114. doi:10.1006/pmed.2000.0674

Epstein, J. A., Griffin, K. W., & Botvin, G. J. (2000b). Competence skills help deter smoking among inner-city adolescents. *Tobacco Control*, *9*, 33–39. doi:10.1136/tc.9.1.33

Epstein, J. A., Griffin, K. W., & Botvin, G. J. (2000c). Role of general and specific competence skills in protecting inner-city adolescents from alcohol use. *Journal of Studies on Alcohol*, *61*, 379–386.

Epstein, J. A., Zhou, X. K., Bang, H., & Botvin, G. J. (2007). Do competence skills moderate the impact of social influences to drink and perceived social benefits of drinking on alcohol use among inner-city adolescents? *Prevention Science*, *8*, 65–73. doi:10.1007/s11121-006-0054-1

Evans, R. I., Hansen, W. B., and Mittlemark, M. B. (1977). Increasing the validity of self-reports of behavior in a smoking in children investigation. *Journal of Applied Psychology*, *62*, 521–523.

Flay, B. R. (1987). Social psychological approaches to smoking prevention: Review and recommendations. In W. B. Ward & P. D. Mullen (Eds.), *Advances in Health Education and Promotion*, 2, 121–180. Greenwich, CT: JAI Press.

Fraguela, J. A., Martin, A. L., & Trinanes, E. A. (2003). Drug-abuse prevention in the school: Four-year follow-up of a programme. *Psychology in Spain*, *7*, 29–38.

Griffin, K. W., Botvin, G. J., & Nichols, T. R. (2004). Long-term follow-up effects of a school-based drug abuse prevention program on adolescent risky driving. *Prevention Science*, *5*, 207–212. doi:10.1023/B:PREV.0000037643.78420.74

Griffin, K. W., Botvin, G. J., & Nichols, T. R. (2006). Effects of a school-based drug abuse prevention program for adolescents on HIV risk behaviors in young adulthood. *Prevention Science*, *7*, 103–112. doi:10.1007/s11121-006-0025-6

Griffin, K. W., Botvin, G. J., Nichols, T. R., & Doyle, M. M. (2003). Effectiveness of a universal drug abuse prevention approach for youth at high risk for substance use initiation. *Preventive Medicine: An International Journal Devoted to Practice and Theory*, *36*, 1–7. doi:10.1006/pmed.2002.1133

Griffin, K. W., Botvin, G. J., Scheier, L. M., Epstein, J. A., & Diaz, T. (2002). Personal competence skills, distress, and well-being as determinants of substance use in a predominantly minority urban adolescent sample. *Prevention Science*, *3*, 23–33. doi:10.1023/A:1014667209130

Griffin, K. W., Epstein, J. A., Botvin, G. J., & Spoth, R. L. (2001). Social competence and substance use among rural youth: Mediating role of social benefit expectancies of use. *Journal of Youth and Adolescence*, *30*, 485–498. doi:10.1023/A:1010449300990

Griffin, K. W., Scheier, L. M., & Botvin, G. J. (2009). Developmental trajectories of self-management skills and adolescent substance use. *Salud y Drogas*, *9*, 15–37.

Griffin, K. W., Scheier, L. M., Botvin, G. J., & Diaz, T. (2001). The protective role of personal competence skills in adolescent substance use: Psychological well-being as a mediating factor.

Psychology of Addictive Behaviors, 15, 194–203. doi:10.1037/0893-164X.15.3.194

Hawkins, J. D., Catalano, R. F., & Miller, J. Y. (1992). Risk and protective factors for alcohol and other drug problems in adolescence and early adulthood: Implications for substance abuse prevention. *Psychological Bulletin, 112,* 64–105. doi:10.1037/0033-2909.112.1.64

Jessor, R., & Jessor, S. L. (1977). *Problem behavior and psychosocial development: a longitudinal study of youth.* New York, NY: Academic Press.

Jones, D., Bumbarger, B., Greenberg, M., Greenwood, P., & Kyler, S. (2008). *The economic return on PCCD's research-based programs: A cost–benefit assessment of delinquency prevention in Pennsylvania.* University Park: Pennsylvania State University.

Lee, S., Aos, S., Drake, E., Pennucci, A., Miller, M., & Anderson, L. (2012). *Return on investment: Evidence-based options to improve statewide outcomes, October 2012* (Document No. 12-04-1201). Olympia, WA: Washington State Institute for Public Policy.

Lowe, S. R., Acevedo, B. P., Griffin, K. W., & Botvin, G. J. (2013). Longitudinal relationships between self-management skills and substance use in an urban sample of predominantly minority adolescents. *Journal of Drug Issues, 43,* 103–118. doi:10.1177/0022042612462221

Miller, T., & Hendrie, D. (2008). *Substance abuse prevention dollars and cents: A cost–benefit analysis* (DHHS Pub. No. [SMA] 07-4298). Rockville, MD: Center for Substance Abuse Prevention, Substance Abuse and Mental Health Services Administration.

Murray, D. M. (1998). *Design and analysis of group-randomized trials.* New York, NY: Oxford University Press.

O'Loughlin, J., Paradis, G., Renaud, L., & Gomez, L. S. (1998). One-year predictors of smoking initiation and of continued smoking among elementary schoolchildren in multiethnic, low-income, inner-city neighborhoods. *Tobacco Control, 7,* 268–275. doi:10.1136/tc.7.3.268

Resnicow, K., & Botvin, G. J. (1993). School-based substance use prevention programs: Why do effects decay? *Preventive Medicine: An International Journal Devoted to Practice and Theory,* 22, 484–490. doi:10.1006/pmed.1993.1039

Scheier, L. M. (2010). *Handbook of drug use etiology: Theory, methods, and empirical findings.* Washington, DC: American Psychological Association.

Scheier, L. M., Botvin, G. J., & Griffin, K. W. (2001). Preventive intervention effects on developmental progression in drug use: Structural equation modeling analyses using longitudinal data. *Prevention Science, 2,* 91–112. doi:10.1023/A:1011543730566

Scheier, L. M., Botvin, G. J., Griffin, K. W., & Diaz, T. (1999). Latent growth models of drug refusal skills and adolescent alcohol use. *Journal of Alcohol and Drug Education, 44,* 21–48.

Spoth, R. L., Clair, S., Shin, C., & Redmond, C. (2006). Long-term effects of universal preventative interventions on methamphetamine use among adolescents. *Archives of Pediatrics & Adolescent Medicine, 160,* 876–882. doi:10.1001/archpedi.160.9.876

Spoth, R. L., Randall, G., Trudeau, L., Shin, C., & Redmond, C. (2008). Substance use outcomes 5 1/2 years past baseline for partnership-based, family school preventive interventions. *Drug and Alcohol Dependence, 96,* 57–68.

Spoth, R., Randall, G. K., Shin, C., & Redmond, C. (2005). Randomized study of combined universal family and school preventive interventions: Patterns of long-term effects on initiation, regular use, and weekly drunkenness. *Psychology of Addictive Behaviors, 19,* 372–381.

Spoth, R. L., Redmond, C., Trudeau, L., & Shin, C. (2002). Longitudinal substance initiation outcomes for a universal preventive intervention combining family and school programs. *Psychology of Addictive Behaviors, 16,* 129–134. doi:10.1037/0893-164X.16.2.129

Tobler, N., & Stratton, H. (1997). Effectiveness of school based drug prevention programs: A meta-analysis of the research. *The Journal of Primary Prevention, 18,* 71–128. doi:10.1023/A:1024630205999

Trudeau, L., Spoth, R. L., Lillehoj, C., Redmond, C., & Wickrama, K. (2003). Effects of a preventive intervention on adolescent substance use initiation, expectancies, and refusal intentions. *Prevention Science, 4,* 109–122. doi:10.1023/A:1022926332514

Williams, C., Samuolis, J., Griffin, K. W., & Botvin, G. J. (2011). Life Skills Training Wellness Program: An application for young adults in supermarkets. In J. W. Bray, D. M. Galvin, & L. A. Cluff (Eds.), *Young adults in the workplace: A multisite initiative of substance use prevention programs* (RTI Press Publication No. BK-0005-1103; pp. 117–132). Research Triangle Park, NC.

Zollinger, T. W., Saywell, R. M., Muegge, C. M., Wooldridge, J. S., Cummings, S. F., & Caine, V. A. (2003). Impact of the Life Skills Training curriculum on middle school students' tobacco use in Marion County, Indiana, 1997–2000. *The Journal of School Health, 73,* 338–346. doi:10.1111/j.1746-1561.2003.tb04190.x

CHAPTER 11

ALL STARS: A CONCEPTUAL HISTORY

William B. Hansen

This chapter explores the development, evaluation, and refinement of the All Stars program, a school-based drug prevention program. The chapter begins with a description of the research that preceded the development of All Stars, including both research on earlier programs and etiologic research that defined the rationale for selecting the mediators targeted by the intervention. The chapter concludes with research findings about All Stars, including a description of strategies employed for improving program effectiveness.

ORIGINS AND THEORETICAL UNDERPINNINGS

The All Stars middle-school–based alcohol and drug prevention program began as a distinct intervention in 1993. The program now includes additional foci preventing violence, bullying, and premature sexual activity. Since its inception, the program has been updated over 20 times and has been expanded to include multiple booster programs. Our goal is to keep the program relevant culturally, technologically, and developmentally and improve the effectiveness of the intervention. This effort includes adopting promising new content and methods as well as discarding content and methods that hinder program effectiveness. All Stars incorporates empirical research that continues to evolve both because of innovations in prevention science and the changing nature of the world in which adolescents live.

All Stars' origins stretch back to the earliest federally funded drug prevention research studies. In 1975, Dr. Richard I. Evans at the University of Houston received funding to test psychosocial approaches to preventing tobacco use. Evans et al. (1978) considered five psychosocial prevention modalities as part of a randomized controlled trial (RCT), including the following:

1. students learning about consequences of smoking cigarettes, such as increased carbon monoxide in the breath (Higbee, 1969);
2. students learning skills to resist peer pressure based on McGuire's (1964) inoculation approach to inducing resistance to persuasion and Bandura and Walter's theory of social learning;
3. students learning skills to counter susceptibility to media portrayals of smoking, based on Festinger and Maccoby's (1964) research on resisting persuasive communications;
4. students learning how to challenge negative parental role models based on Bandura and Walters (1963) theory of vicarious reinforcement; and
5. the intervention correcting exaggerated perceptions of cigarette prevalence among peers and important

I would like to thank the National Institute on Alcohol Abuse and Alcoholism and the National Institute on Drug Abuse for the funding they provided to complete research on the All Stars drug prevention program. I also appreciate my many colleagues, including everyone with whom I have been a coauthor on peer review articles and published books. Mostly, I appreciate my wife, Kathy, who has supported me throughout my research career.

http://dx.doi.org/10.1037/14550-012
Handbook of Adolescent Drug Use Prevention: Research, Intervention Strategies, and Practice, L. M. Scheier (Editor)

adults based on Maccoby, Maccoby, Romney, and Adams's (1961) notion and Asch's (1956) seminal research on conformity processes that suggested that students develop a false consensus about what is perceived to be normative for young adolescents.

Schools were recruited and randomized to either treatment or control conditions. Interventions consisted of videotaped programs and posters that encapsulated messages plus feedback about the extent of cigarette smoking in their class (i.e., normative education). This information was provided to students by trained research assistants. The results of this 10-week intervention suggested that a psychosocial intervention might have promise for deterring the onset of cigarette smoking, with students in the treatment group reporting reduced rates of cigarette smoking onset (10.0%) compared with students in the control group (18.3%).

The late 1980s witnessed a proliferation of drug prevention trials (see also Chapter 2, this handbook). Several studies in particular had bearing on the development of All Stars, including Project SMART (Hansen, Johnson, Flay, Graham, & Sobel, 1988) and the Tobacco and Alcohol Prevention Program (TAPP; Hansen, Fielding, & Malotte, 1988).

Project SMART (Hansen, Johnson, et al., 1988) was a 5-year NIDA-funded RCT that involved two multicomponent approaches to drug prevention. The *affective* education approach addressed self-management skills teaching youth how to improve self-esteem, manage stress, make decisions, set goals, and clarify values. The *social influences* program taught youth how to deal with social influences (i.e., peer, parent and media pressures to use alcohol, tobacco and other drugs), providing them information about the prevalence of drug use to correct erroneous perceptions of social norms (i.e., addressing whether drug use is acceptable and popular among teenagers). Results suggested that the affective approach had negative (i.e., boomerang) effects, with treated youth reporting more frequent alcohol, tobacco, and marijuana use compared with control students. The social influence approach, on the other hand, reduced the onset of substance use among experimentally treated compared with control students.

TAPP (Hansen, Malotte, & Fielding, 1988) also applied a multicomponent approach to prevention. This intervention included peer and media pressure resistance skills training, provided information about short-term consequences of alcohol and tobacco use, and introduced a process for making decisions and committing to avoid alcohol and tobacco use. Compared with no-treatment controls, TAPP deterred the onset of tobacco use. At final posttest, assessed 30 months after the pretest, 26% of experimentally treated students reported cigarette smoking compared with 34% of students in the control condition.

THE ADOLESCENT ALCOHOL PREVENTION TRIAL

The Adolescent Alcohol Prevention Trial (AAPT), a randomized longitudinal drug prevention project, went further by isolating the "mediating" mechanisms that account for preventive effects (Hansen, Graham, Wolkenstein, et al., 1988). Mediating mechanisms, which were considered here to be the causal agents of change, link the intervention modules (i.e., skills training) with behavioral outcomes (drug use). The design of AAPT compared the effectiveness of peer-pressure resistance skills training with an intervention to promote positive peer group norms and instill youth with antidrug attitudes.

Intervention components were first pilot tested with 1,428 fifth- and seventh-grade students to examine the differential effects of each program component on targeted mediating variables. In the pilot test, students who received the normative education component believed that drinking alcohol was less likely to result in positive social outcomes. The same youth were less likely to believe that adults drank alcohol every day and that their peers had tried smoking marijuana and cigarettes. There were no differences, however, between treated students exposed to the resistance skills-training curriculum and control youth (information about the consequences of drug use) in perceived self-efficacy to refuse offers to use substances.

Following the pilot test, we conducted a longitudinal study involving 12 junior high schools randomly assigned to one of four conditions: Information Only (ICU), Information + Resistance Skills Training (RT+ICU), Information + Normative Education (NE+ICU), or Information + Resistance Skills Training + Normative Education (NE+RT+ICU).

Trained health educators delivered each program. Students were pretested prior to the program in seventh grade and then posttested annually through the 11th grade. Students provided self-reported alcohol use, drunkenness, and problems associated with drinking alcohol, tobacco and marijuana use.

At the 1-year posttest (eighth grade), there were significant main effects of normative education for all frequency of use measures (alcohol, cigarette, and marijuana use) but no significant main effects attributable to the resistance training intervention (Hansen & Graham, 1991). There were interaction effects that revealed the combined program (NE+RT+ICU) was superior to all other program types for preventing 30-day alcohol use and 30-day marijuana use.

Taylor, Graham, Cumsille, and Hansen (2000) demonstrated the longitudinal effectiveness of the normative education approach using growth-modeling techniques with students followed from Grades 7 to 11. These analyses revealed whether students assigned to a particular program component (RT vs. NORM or ICU) differed not only in their respective levels of drug use from year to year (which would reflect program effects) but also whether they differ in their rates of growth (i.e., acceleration) utilizing the full five annual assessments from Grades 7 to 11. Controlling for gender and ethnicity, normative education had a beneficial effect on the levels of all types of drug use. When compared with the ICU control condition, the combined program also had a positive effect on the slope of the three alcohol use measures.

Importantly, when we modeled pretest drug use as part of the growth curve, the normative education program decreased growth for all five measures of drug use. Normative education also had a favorable program effect when growth in drug use was modeled with a quadratic effect. The pattern of findings indicates that normative education works more strongly in the initial years of the program by tempering youths' estimates of the social acceptability and perceived prevalence of drug use.

STUDIES OF POTENTIAL MEDIATORS

Analyses of AAPT data elucidate mediating mechanisms by estimating the effects of both resistance skills training and normative education on targeted risk factors (Donaldson, Graham, & Hansen, 1994). Results of the process analysis (Lipsey & Pollard, 1989) revealed that the resistance skills training program improved drug refusal skills when compared with control students who did not receive this training; however, the same analyses showed that resistance skills were not related significantly to subsequent drug use. Unexpectedly, normative education had a significant crossover effect and was positively associated with the development of refusal skills. The only statistically significant paths from mediators to program outcomes were those between estimated prevalence and students' beliefs that drug use was not socially acceptable and self-reported drug use. These analyses corroborated our growing belief that normative education, which involves the correction of erroneous perceptions regarding the prevalence and social acceptability of drug use, represents an essential element of effective drug prevention.

Subsequent analyses examined the efficacy of resistance skills training under two conditions: (a) when students had a predisposition to not use substances based on their answers to questions about perceived prevalence and social acceptability of drugs and (b) when students had no such predisposition (Donaldson, Graham, Piccinin, & Hansen, 1995). Results suggested that peer-pressure resistance training was only effective when adolescents had a positive predisposition and was actually counterproductive when this was not the case.

MIDWESTERN PREVENTION PROJECT

Pentz et al. (1989) combined the program materials from Project SMART and AAPT into a school-based curriculum implemented as part of the Midwestern Prevention Project (MPP). This multicomponent school- and community-based drug prevention trial included student pre- and posttest surveys that assessed alcohol, cigarette, and marijuana use and a variety of mediators targeted by the curriculum. The target risk factors included beliefs about the (a) negative and (b) positive consequences of using substances, (c) self-efficacy to refuse offers to use substances, (d) communication skills, (e) perceived prevalence of drug use among peers, (f) the anticipated reaction of friends to hypothetical substance use and (g) future drug use intentions. Program evaluation (manipulation checks) and mediation (process) analyses followed conventions outlined by Sobel (1982, 1986) and further described by Judd and Kenny (1981).

Findings indicated that the intervention did not affect all mediators equally. MacKinnon et al. (1991) showed that the intervention achieved reduced rates of onset of alcohol and cigarettes primarily by changing friends' anticipated reactions to substance use and making substance use less socially desirable among treated students. Process analyses showed that prevention effects for cigarette smoking and marijuana use were achieved through changes in youths' intentions to avoid drugs and by suppressing their beliefs about the positive consequences of using substances.

CODIFICATION OF RULES GOVERNING PROGRAM EFFECTS

As a consequence of this accumulation of knowledge, Hansen and McNeal (1996) introduced two "laws" that describe how prevention programs achieve their effects. The *law of indirect effect* states that behaviors are not changed directly, but rather, all changes in behavior are produced by changing psychosocial or environmental mediators. The *law of maximum expected potential effect* states that the magnitude of change in behavioral outcomes that can be produced by an intervention reflects the combined function of two factors: the ability of the program to change targeted mediators and the strength of relation that exists between the mediator and the behaviors of interest. The latter law is a direct outgrowth of mediating variable analysis methods (i.e., MacKinnon et al., 1991) and can be expressed mathematically:

$$ES_{pb} = ES_{pm} \times \beta_{mb}$$

The effect size an intervention is expected to have on behavior (ES_{pb}) is the product of the relation observed between the magnitude of program effect on the mediator or set of mediators (ES_{pm}) and the natural relation that exists between mediators and the behavior (β_{mb}).

Introduction of this mediation framework sparked increased emphasis on finding risk and protective factors that were amenable to change through an intervention and that had strong predictive relations with behavioral outcomes. Numerous longitudinal research studies have examined a wide range of putative risk factors as predictors of adolescent drug use (e.g., Ary & Biglan, 1988; Bry, McKeon, & Pandina, 1982; Conrad, Flay, & Hill, 1992; Chassin et al., 1984; Newcomb & Bentler, 1988; Weber et al., 1989). Despite the significant inroads made by these studies, no single compendium of measures existed that incorporated the body of knowledge from prior intervention studies and provided a means to compare plausible mediators across different samples, using different research designs, and examining different program modalities.

Hansen (1992) compiled a review of school-based drug prevention studies to address this gap. A framework was created using touchstone issues that had served as the conceptual focus of numerous interventions. The list included (a) alternatives to drug use, (b) beliefs about the social and psychological consequences of drug use, (c) commitment and intentionality, (d) decision-making and problem-solving skills training, (e) goal-setting skills training, (f) normative education, (g) peer- and media-pressure resistance skills training, (h) self-esteem building, (i) skills for giving and getting assistance with problems, (j) social skills and communication training, (k) stress management training, and (l) values clarification (later denoted to be lifestyle incongruity). Mediating variables that correspond to these concepts are listed in Table 11.1.

The next logical step involved determining precisely which mediators satisfied the second leg of the equation (β_{mb}) and would be responsive to preventive intervention. A study of middle- and high-school students in Forsyth County, North Carolina, included annual assessments of potential mediators and drug use behaviors. Table 11.1 shows the results of analyses that examined the effects of Year 1 mediators on Year 2 behavioral outcomes, controlling for Year 1 drug use (Hansen, Uebersax, & Rose, 1995). Targeting normative beliefs through norm setting continued to be an important potential mediator. Targeting the development of commitments and intentions to avoid drug use also emerged as an important mediator, which is not surprising given

TABLE 11.1

Cross-Lagged Correlations and Standardized Regression (Path) Coefficients Between Postulated Mediating Variables in Year 1 and Substance Use in Year 2 ($N = 2{,}639$)

		Alcohol path		Tobacco path		Other drugs path	
Topic	Postulated mediator	$r_{(m1,s2)}$	Coefficient	$r_{(m1,s2)}$	Coefficient	$r_{(m1,s2)}$	Coefficient β
f	Normative Beliefs	–0.445	–0.196	–0.390	–0.134	–0.197	–0.145
c	Commitment	–0.398	–0.185	–0.369	–0.129	–0.187	–0.155
l	Lifestyle Incongruence	–0.400	–0.170	–0.376	–0.123	–0.198	–0.151
b	Beliefs about Consequences	–0.318	–0.085	–0.293	–0.071	–0.176	–0.121
g	Resistance Skills Training	–0.270	–0.093	–0.208	–0.033	–0.134	–0.093
h	Self-Esteem	–0.151	–0.071	–0.169	–0.059	–0.079	–0.059
e	Goal-Setting Skills	–0.146	–0.064	–0.141	–0.043	–0.064	–0.043
d	Decision-Making Skills	–0.115	–0.036	–0.113	–0.027	–0.076	–0.055
a	Alternatives	–0.104	–0.019	–0.120	–0.024	–0.066	–0.040
k	Stress Management Skills	–0.079	–0.021	–0.089	–0.033	–0.032	–0.012
i	Assistance Skills	0.080	0.021	0.033	0.011	0.018	0.008
j	Social and Communication Skills	0.073	0.045	0.024	0.013	0.030	0.031
Average		–0.189	–0.073	–0.184	–0.054	–0.097	–0.070

the findings reported by MacKinnon et al. (1991). On the other hand, it was surprising to see that lifestyle incongruence, which represented the mediator targeted by values clarification programs, was also an efficient mediator. In part, this surprise came from the fact that our own prior work with Project SMART (Hansen, Johnson, Flay, et al., 1988) and other researchers' programs (e.g., Goodstadt, Sheppard, & Chan, 1982; Moskowitz, Malvin, Schaeffer, & Schaps, 1983) that had featured values clarification approaches had not shown promise in evaluation studies. Beliefs about consequences, which focused on the social and psychological consequences of drug use (not severe health consequences), was also highly related to drug use onset. Analysis showed that these four variables loaded on a single well-defined factor. This factor reflecting "motivational components" at Year 1 was negatively associated with alcohol and other drug use ($\beta = -.30$) 1 year later. The other factors, personal and social skills, did not account for these outcomes and had standardized regression weights near zero (Hansen et al., 1995).

Path analyses were repeated with separate models being estimated for alcohol, tobacco, and marijuana use. Fearnow-Kenney, Hansen, and McNeal (2002) reported separate analyses demonstrating that the same "motivational components" accounted for Year 2 alcohol use (mediated effect $\beta = -0.68$), cigarette smoking (mediated effect $\beta = -0.13$), and marijuana use at Time 2 (mediated effect $\beta = -0.39$). In contrast, personal and social skills either failed to predict Year 2 use or, in some cases, had small but significant positive relations with the designated outcomes, suggesting that they may actually be contraindicated for prevention.

McNeal and Hansen (1999) extended this work by examining risk of becoming a drug user among students, who—at the Year 1 test—had not used a substance. Analyses were conducted on students who were nonusers of alcohol ($n = 1{,}348$), tobacco ($n = 1{,}630$), marijuana ($n = 1{,}975$), and inhalants ($n = 1{,}910$) in the past 30 days. Among alcohol nonusers 29.2% of the panel sample initiated alcohol use 1 year later. Similarly, 18.5% began using tobacco, 10.3% began using marijuana, and 5.3% began using inhalants. The goal of analysis was to calculate effect size differences for each of the 12 variables and identify which ones accounted for the risk of drug use onset between eighth and ninth grades.

When averaged across all substances, the largest effect sizes (ES) in order of decreasing magnitude were obtained for commitment to avoid drug use

(ES = 0.33), having normative beliefs that drug use is not prevalent and socially acceptable (ES = 0.28), viewing one's lifestyle as being incongruent with drug use (ES = 0.28), and having beliefs about consequences that make drug use unattractive (ES = 0.28). Other variables had smaller ES values. Thus, the variables that showed the greatest promise as potential mediators were, once again, normative beliefs, commitment, lifestyle incongruence, and beliefs about the consequences of using drugs.

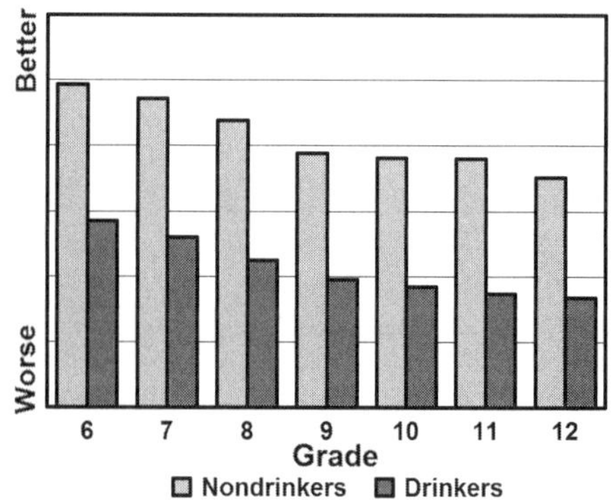

FIGURE 11.2. Normative beliefs among drinkers and nondrinkers at different grades.

ALL STARS CURRICULUM DESIGN

All Stars curriculum design capitalized on the knowledge gained from these mediating variable and process evaluation studies. For All Stars, the mediators associated with the highest level of observed β_{mb} were selected: normative beliefs, commitment to avoid drug use, lifestyle incongruence, and beliefs about salient consequences. Attention was then focused on how to influence targeted mediating variables so that ES_{pm} might be maximized.

These data allowed us to discern several other characteristic patterns relevant to drug use onset. For example, when sampled over time, each of the targeted mediators had similar developmental trajectories. Figure 11.1 shows there is "temporal erosion" for each of the putative risk factors over time. The most profound changes occur in students' normative beliefs. When they are in the sixth grade, students believe few of their peers engage in drug use and that drug use is socially unacceptable. Over time, without intervention, the perception that drug use is rare and unacceptable wanes considerably. Similar decays occur to students' beliefs about consequences, their stated commitment to avoid drug use, and the degree to which they view drug use interfering with the lifestyle they seek.

These age-related changes provide graphic evidence of the natural processes at work that a drug prevention program needs to alter. The decay observed in Figure 11.1 primarily reflects changes in target risk factors that co-occur with behavioral changes. However, among those who are nonusers at any age or grade, their self-reported status vis-à-vis key mediating variables remains consistently positive. For example, Figures 11.2 and 11.3 depict observed differences between nondrinkers and drinkers on two mediators emphasized by All Stars. There is a slight temporal erosion among both nondrinkers

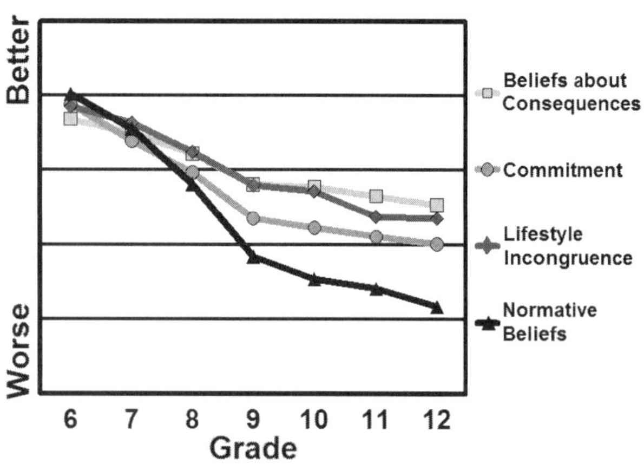

FIGURE 11.1. Changes in targeted mediators as a function of age.

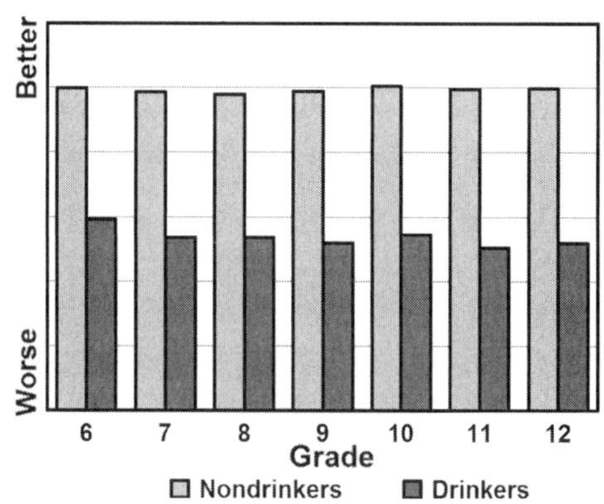

FIGURE 11.3. Lifestyle incongruence among drinkers and nondrinkers at different grades.

and drinkers normative beliefs; however, Figure 11.3 shows there is practically no erosion of expressed lifestyle incongruence among nondrinkers across time. Commitment to avoid drug use follows the patterns of normative beliefs with slight erosion between the sixth and ninth grades among all students, but with clear distinctions between drug users and nonusers. Beliefs about the social and psychological consequences of drug use follow the pattern observed for lifestyle incongruence; nonusers at any grade are consistently positive while users are consistently less so.

All Stars seeks to maintain or improve students' antidrug normative beliefs, reinforce their commitments to avoid drug use, alter the perceived incongruence between their desired lifestyle and one that would result from using drugs, and promote beliefs that drug use will have negative social and personal consequences.

Normative Education

As indicated earlier, there has been substantial empirical work examining normative development and also prevention efforts showing that normative beliefs play a crucial role in drug etiology (Evans et al., 1978; Hansen & Graham, 1991). In the Houston project, the experimental intervention consisted of doing an in-class analysis of students' survey responses and presenting results to students several weeks later. These interventions took less than 10 minutes of classroom time. There were multiple feedback sessions per classroom, one that followed each survey administration. Whereas the film-based intervention had netted a significant reduction in final posttest prevalence compared with the control group (10.0% vs. 18.3%), the prevalence for the feedback-only group was 8.6%.

All Stars begins by collecting students' anonymous reports about recent alcohol, cigarette, and marijuana use. This survey also includes narrative assessments of opinions about alcohol, tobacco, and marijuana related topics. The teacher uses findings from classroom surveys in an activity titled "The Opinion Poll Game" that reveals class norms. Students play the game on two occasions. All Stars also directs students to establish general normative rules of behavior that address drug use and other high-risk behaviors.

All Stars' customers routinely collect student pre- and posttest surveys and fidelity data as part of their delivery of the program using a system we developed known as *Evaluation Lizard* (Hansen et al., 2006). Evaluation Lizard allows teachers to have rapid access to summary classroom prevalence data. Teachers receive supplemental instructions about how to provide feedback to their classrooms about alcohol, tobacco, marijuana, and inhalant use. Because surveys are available for many middle school drug prevention programs, this opens the possibility that teachers delivering programs other than All Stars may also provide this feedback.

Lifestyle Incongruence

Previous attempts for addressing lifestyle incongruence, typically conceptualized as values clarification, had not been successful in preventing alcohol and drug use (Goodstadt et al., 1982; Hansen, Johnson, Flay, et al., 1988). Therefore, the traditional values clarification approach was entirely abandoned and a new approach was developed. To avoid the stigma associated with values clarification (Kinnier, 1995), we used the term *idealism* to describe the approach. The program component drew heavily upon Milton Rokeach's (1973, 1979) values theory and Leon Festinger's (1957) cognitive dissonance theory.

Rokeach (1979) proposed 18 idealized end states or *terminal values* that provide motivation for human behavior. Rokeach's methodology requires participants to rank order their values, with the expectation that those ranked highest would motivate behavior. To incorporate this perspective into All Stars, we modified the linguistic and conceptual content of his values. For instance, Rokeach's values *mature love* and *a world of beauty* were unlikely to be relevant concepts for young people. We also created a set of "negative" values that youth would want to avoid, such as *addiction, poverty, disease, conflict,* and *prejudice.* Instead of rank ordering all values as Rokeach proposed, students were asked to select two sets of values, one set consisting of the four that were most desired and one set consisting of the four that were least desired.

Rokeach was prescriptive about how to identify values. We used guidance from Festinger's theory of cognitive dissonance to augment the dissonance between what students valued and participation in risky behaviors. Thus, consonant behaviors that supported ideal futures were highlighted and encouraged and dissonance was created between negative behaviors and idealized futures. A series of activities encourage students to think about their ideal personal futures in light of the habits and reputations they wish to develop.

Commitment

Ajzen and Fishbein's (1977) theory of reasoned action suggests that attitudes play a central role in motivating behavior through behavioral intentions. This theory assesses intentions as the "likelihood" of future behavior. This is distinctly different from motivational intentions, which reflects an individual's desire or motivation to act, irrespective of the probability that they will act. In etiologic studies of drug use onset (e.g., compare Chassin et al., 1981, with MacKinnon et al., 1991), there is ambiguity about whether behavioral or motivational intentions are assessed. From a program development perspective, motivational intentions need to be the focus of intervention. The primary goal is to promote the adoption of a commitment that reflects a person's willingness to pursue a path related to an idealized future in which they engage in health-promoting behaviors and avoid risk-engendering behaviors.

There is a body of research that supports the underlying relevance of building commitment that was considered important to incorporating this strategy in All Stars. Early research by Hovland, Janis, and Kelley (1953) supported the notion that making a public statement promoted attitudes that aligned with the message that was delivered. Commitments are strengthened when the message being delivered is already one that is supported (Cook & Berrenberg, 1981). Thus, there was a body of research that supported strategies for making public commitments that served as a basis for program design.

Prior research conducted as part of Project SMART (Hansen, Johnson, et al., 1988) and likewise as part of the MPP (Johnson et al., 1990) had incorporated video-recorded statements made by students that detailed their personal commitments. This method basically provides students with an outline to develop a script defining their commitments which are then read in front of a camera. In prior interventions, there was no opportunity provided for students to think more deeply about their motivations. All Stars remedied this by including discussions about the importance of making commitments and the negative consequences that occur when individuals fail to make commitments in life or when they make but cannot keep these commitments.

Beliefs About Social and Psychological Consequences

Prior drug prevention programs have included dedicated activities that provide direct instruction about drug use consequences. Programs that have incorporated this approach include TAPP (Hansen, Malotte, & Fielding, 1988), Project SMART (Hansen, Johnson, et al., 1988), the information component of AAPT (Hansen & Graham, 1991), the MPP (Pentz et al., 1989), as well as numerous other well-known drug prevention programs (e.g., Life Skills Training [Botvin, Baker, Dusenbury, Tortu, & Botvin, 1990]; Project TNT [Dent, Sussman, Stacy, Craig, Burton, & Flay, 1995]). All Stars takes a slightly different instructional tactic. The program does not include teaching sessions that detail the short-term social and psychological consequences of drug use. Instead, instruction that targets consequences is integrated into each of the other component pieces of the intervention. Thus, when students consider social norms, lifestyle incongruence, and making commitments, they also consider the social and psychological implications related to each of these topics. This integration allowed All Stars to avoid being "preachy" while at the same time providing a forum for ensuring that students think about how drug use and non-use would influence their own personal lives.

Additional Program Components

All Stars was designed to take advantage of two other aspects that prior prevention research supported: parental attentiveness (i.e., monitoring, supervision, and communication) and bonding to prosocial institutions. Hansen (1992) excluded these components from his review of mediating variables because no school-based drug prevention program had included them as target mediators. Evidence for each is considered here.

BLENDING FACTORS RELATED TO PARENTING WITH ALL STARS

The idea of involving parents in prevention results from empirical studies that reinforce the positive role parents play in protecting youth from harm. For example, Richardson et al. (1989) found that eighth-grade students without parental supervision and who took care of themselves after school were at twice the risk of alcohol, tobacco, and marijuana use when compared to teens that were supervised. Parental monitoring had also been established as a strong predictor of delinquent behavior (e.g., Dishion & Loeber, 1985). Further, children from authoritative families, characterized by warmth, reasonableness, open communication, and having high expectations about behavior are also protected from engaging in drug use (for a review, see Scheier & Hansen, 2014).

To address this important literature, All Stars includes program materials that targets parents and parenting from three perspectives. First, on nearly every worksheet, there is a corresponding parent–child section that is to be completed at home. These home activities receive dedicated discussion time during the classroom-based program. The rationale is that students can be better prepared with classroom discussion to engage these assignments and also for staff to detect potential problems at home when these assignments are left unfinished. The inclusion of home assignments is intended to promote parent-child discussion of relevant topics covered by the program in the home environment and provides parents with prompts for establishing communication, support, and expectations for behavior.

Second, All Stars includes a parent session that may be conducted as a separate after-school group meeting for parents. Key elements common to many parenting programs are included: understanding adolescent growth and development, showing love during the teenage years, promoting positive attachments, setting clear standards for behavior, monitoring friendships and providing supervision, providing discipline, and setting an example through positive role modeling. There are suggestions for dealing with the challenges common to hosting parenting meetings, notably the challenges all parent drug-prevention programs face with recruitment (Spoth & Redmond, 1993).

Third, a set of ancillary materials have been developed, which include a written parenting guide, *When It Comes From You*, and an audio CD, *7 Strategies for Parenting*. The written materials briefly summarize the same material covered in the parenting session. The audio CD presents stories from parents that cover these same topics.

There is less compelling evidence in the research literature about the importance of bonding. From data collected as part of the evaluation of All Stars from clients who have used Evaluation Lizard, the magnitude of correlation between bonding and alcohol use (at the same time point) is $r = -.19$ (Hansen, 2014). In elementary schools, improvements in school bonding are achieved through proactive classroom management, interactive teaching, and cooperative learning techniques in their classrooms (Hawkins, Guo, Hill, Battin-Pearson, & Abbott, 2001). A similar approach for middle schools would be laudable but could not be completed through a program like All Stars. Nonetheless, to the extent possible, promoting school bonding is a worthwhile goal.

Given what we have learned so far, the approach adopted in All Stars contains two instructional facets. First, activities are designed to be engaging and structured so that, if they are implemented correctly, teachers will solicit and listen to students as they make comments and answer questions. The meta-analysis by Tobler and colleagues (Tobler, 1986; Tobler & Stratton, 1997) showed that programs promoting engagement are more successful than didactic programs. We expected that an added benefit of promoting interactivity would be increased bonding to school. Second, the original version of All Stars called for one-on-one meetings between the student and teacher. These meetings had the goal of building a positive personal relationship and reinforcing key content of the program. As the program has morphed into one that can be delivered either by specialists or in situ teachers, the one-on-one meetings have been relegated to the class of supplemental activities.

ALL STARS CORE AND BOOSTER PILOT STUDIES AND RANDOMIZED FIELD TRIAL

Core Pilot Study

The Core program for All Stars consists of 13 activities plus a session devoted to celebration and review. The latter session also includes handing out commitment certificates as rewards for completing the program. With the development of the Core curriculum, the first step to be accomplished was a pilot test to examine the impact of the intervention on targeted mediators. One school was recruited to participate in this study (Hansen, 1996). Half of the students in this school had received the middle school Drug Abuse Resistance Education (D.A.R.E.) program during the fall semester in their health class. This version of D.A.R.E. was under revision and, as a consequence, the local D.A.R.E. officer had not yet been provided with either the revised curriculum guide or student materials. All Stars was delivered in the spring semester health class by a certified and experienced teacher.

Student surveys assessed four of the six targeted mediators (i.e., normative beliefs, lifestyle incongruence, commitment, and bonding to school). Students in both the All Stars and D.A.R.E. conditions were surveyed at the beginning of the spring semester and posttested at the end of the semester, a period of 4 months. At pretest, students in both conditions were equivalent on all measures. At posttest, students receiving All Stars improved on each of the mediators whereas students who had received the fall semester D.A.R.E. intervention show declines on each of these measures. At posttest, students also rated their All Stars experience more positively than did those rating their D.A.R.E. experience.

The Kentucky Field Trial of All Stars Core

Following the completion of the pilot study, the next phase involved conducting a longitudinal RCT. The program evaluation was conducted by an independent evaluation team, headed by Dr. Nancy Harrington of the University of Kentucky. Eight middle schools served as test sites that received the intervention. Five schools received All Stars delivered by trained specialists. In three schools, All Stars was taught by in situ classroom teachers. Six schools served as no-treatment controls.

One-year posttest findings (Harrington, Giles, Hoyle, Feeney, & Yungbluth, 2001) showed positive results for targeted mediators, with in situ teachers outperforming specialists (see Figure 11.4). Analysis of control students showed temporal erosion for the targeted mediating variables. Students who received All Stars from a visiting specialist had less severe downturns. For lifestyle incongruence, commitment to avoid drugs, and bonding to school, students who received All Stars from an in situ teacher improved their scores. The only mediator to show decay for these students was their normative beliefs, which had a modest downturn from pretest to posttest.

The All Stars intervention showed favorable program effects on targeted drug use behaviors (Harrington et al., 2001) primarily for the condition in which regular classroom teachers taught the program (see Figure 11.5). For this field trial, the content of the intervention was expanded to include preventing violence and premature sexual activity. There was a significant change in the slope of involvement in precoital sexual behaviors measured using the Adolescent Sexual Activity Index (Hansen, Paskett, & Carter, 1999) among both the teacher and specialist conditions when compared with the control condition.

A subsequent analysis (McNeal, Hansen, Harrington, & Giles, 2004) demonstrated that

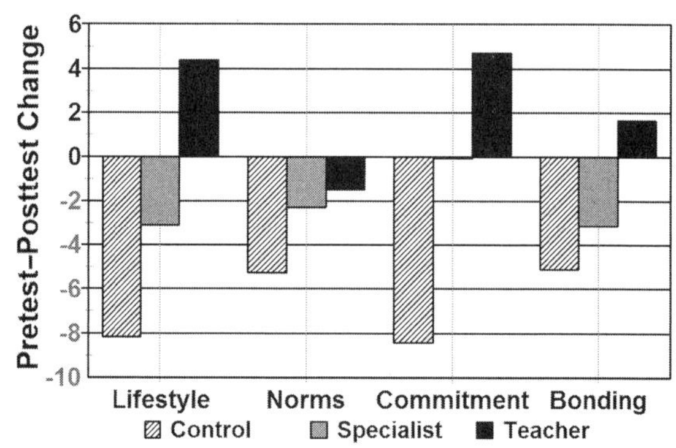

FIGURE 11.4. Results of the All Stars Kentucky field trial on changing four targeted mediators. From "Evaluation of the All Stars Character Education and Problem Behavior Prevention Program: Pretest–Posttest Effects on Mediator and Outcome Variables for Middle School Students," by N. G. Harrington, S. M. Giles, R. H. Hoyle, G. J. Feeney, and S. C. Yungbluth, 2001, *Health Education & Behavior*, *28*, p. 540. Copyright 2001 by Sage. Adapted with permission.

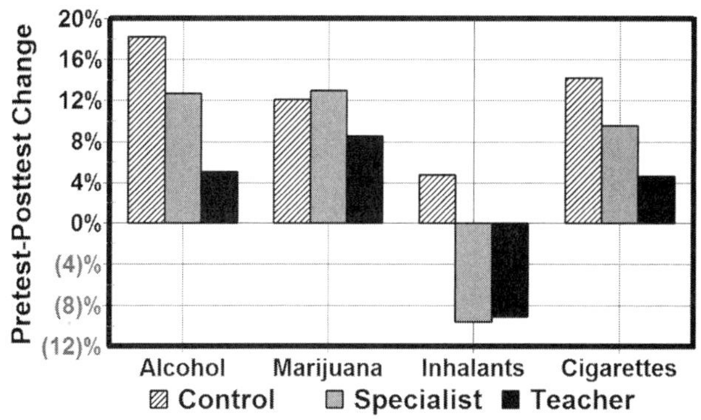

FIGURE 11.5. Results of the All Stars Kentucky field trial on changing targeted behavioral outcomes. From "How All Stars Works: An Examination of Program Effects on Mediating Variables," by R. B. McNeal, W. B. Hansen, N. G. Harrington, and S. M. Giles, 2004, *Health Education & Behavior*, *31*, p. 173. Copyright 2004 by Sage. Reprinted with permission.

three target risk factors—normative beliefs, lifestyle incongruence, and commitment—all mediated program effects on drug use and sexual behaviors. Lifestyle incongruence accounted for the largest magnitude of effect for improved rates of alcohol, cigarette, and inhalant use, and for reducing sexual activity. Relatively speaking, commitment had the largest mediated effect on marijuana use. Normative beliefs consistently mediated drug outcomes, but not to the same magnitude as other target risk mechanisms. Bonding to school did not significantly mediate any of the behavioral outcomes. From these analyses, it is clear that it was only when targeted mediators were significantly changed was there a resulting benefit in terms of reduced drug use and sexual activity. These findings also go to great lengths to explain why teachers were more successful than specialists; they had a meaningful effect in changing mediators, which then translated into meaningful effects on deterring the onset of drug use, and in the case of inhalants, actually promoting a reduction in the prevalence of use.

The Booster Field Trial

The primary challenge that resulted from the Kentucky field trial was that effects were short-lived. By eighth grade, there were no longer significant differences between either of the treatment conditions and the control group. To remedy this situation, we developed a booster program to reinforce the intervention. The booster program is structured as a 1-year follow-up intervention and contains the same program content offered in the Year 1 materials delivered in a nine-session program. The booster program is not only abbreviated, it also has activities that are structured so as to not entirely repeat Core activities.

To test the potential of a booster program to augment outcomes, a study was conducted using a single-cohort longitudinal design with pretest, posttest, 1- and 2-year follow-up measurements. This study was conducted in community settings with agencies that provide after-school and weekend programming for youth. Seven community agencies from six states in the eastern United States took part in this study. Each agency recruited a minimum of three groups of adolescents ranging in age from 11 to 15 to receive either All Stars in Year 1 only, the program with follow-up booster sessions in Year 2, or serve as a no-treatment control group. As with the Kentucky field trial, Dr. Nancy Harrington independently conducted the program evaluation.

Pretest data were collected from 308 adolescents. Posttest data were collected within 1 month of program completion. Approximately one year from posttest, follow-up data were collected. The final wave of follow-up data was collected approximately one year after the initial follow-up. In the analysis of the final survey for drug use, a significant interaction emerged with drug use among control participants having increased from pretest to posttest and continued to increase at both follow-up assessments. In contrast, there was no change in drug use among All Stars participants in either the All Stars Only or All Stars plus Booster condition.

TECHNOLOGICAL ENHANCEMENTS

One challenge observed by in situ teachers and agency prevention specialists alike in their delivery of All Stars Core was the time-consuming nature of some of the activities. For example, in order to deliver the lesson that focused on giving feedback to students about their opinions, teachers are required to analyze students' responses to 38 opinion survey items and identify similar responses that can logically be grouped together before they can use the information in their teaching. In response to such needs, we designed a number of enhancements to All Stars that would make teacher and student participation easier through the use of online technologies (Bishop, Bryant, Giles, Hansen, & Dusenbury, 2006; Hansen, Bishop, & Bryant, 2009). Our specific goal was to increase fidelity by making elements of a program easier to implement by reducing complexity and the demands on teachers' time. Reducing preparation time and automating the more tedious tasks of the program would increase teachers' support for the program and increase the likelihood that all aspects of the program would be completed. This was in turn expected to increase the potential to be delivered as intended.

Twelve schools and one community group were assigned to the All Stars Technology condition. Eleven schools and one community group were assigned to deliver the program using traditional methods. All teachers had prior experience teaching All Stars Core. Teachers in both conditions were surveyed at pretest and posttest regarding the degree to which they completed activities of the program for which online components were available. The survey also measured the perceived ease of program delivery.

For the most part, program-related attitudes remained fairly stable or slightly improved for teachers in the technology condition, whereas attitudes among teachers who continued to teach the standard program showed a slight decrease. Teachers in both conditions reported completing 90% of the program activities. However, two thirds of technology teachers reported being able to complete more of the activities than they had when they used the standard version of the program.

There remain interesting challenges for using online technologies in classroom environments. All teachers who order student materials are now provided with access to the online components of the program. It is not clear how many teachers choose—or are able—to take advantage of these enhancements. In some cases, school systems have set up firewalls and other methods that severely limit student and teacher access to online materials. Thus, while there were significant improvements associated with the online version of All Stars, not every teacher who desires access to these components will be able to do so.

ALL STARS PLUS PROGRAM DEVELOPMENT

Given the strong attachment to the motivational mediators selected for All Stars Core and Booster programs, the development of All Stars Plus, which focuses on teaching decision-making, goal-setting, and peer-pressure resistance skills, may seem somewhat incongruous. After all, as noted in Table 11.1, these three mediators ranked only in the second tier of those that might be meaningful targets of intervention. The answer to this concern lies in two explanations. First, as Donaldson et al. (1995) pointed out, resistance skills training may actually be beneficial for individuals who already have appropriate antidrug attitudes. Social and personal skills may benefit youth who have already developed an antidrug attitude. For example, McNeal and Hansen (1999) found that there were ESs comparable to those of mediators targeted by All Stars Core for predicting maintaining nonuse versus initiation for several drugs. The ES difference between those who maintained nondrinking alcohol and resistance skills training was ES = −0.23. Resistance skills were also moderately important for those who initially drank alcohol and quit (ES = −0.27) as were goal-setting skills (ES = −0.22; Hansen & McNeal, 2001).

The second explanation focuses on how second-tier mediators could be theoretically "harnessed" with first-tier mediators. There is a conceptual link between understanding that pressure to use alcohol, tobacco, and other drugs is minimized both by creating an antidrug social norm and by increasing students' personal confidence that they can avoid drug use (Donaldson et al., 1995). There is also a conceptual link between making commitments and the process of making decisions. Making commitments can be bolstered by going through a process of weighing alternatives and finding a course of action that fits with prior commitments and deeply held values (Janis & Mann, 1977). Building this mind-set in youth requires teaching decision making and goal setting. In the Kentucky field trial, McNeal et al. (2004) reported that impulsive decision-making mediated program effects on marijuana and inhalant use. Finally, there is a theoretical link between holding specific values and striving to achieve goals that are consonant with those values (Eccles & Wigfield, 1995, 2002).

All Stars Plus Field Trial

All Stars Plus is intended to be a third-year booster program. Eight schools participated in a field trial of the Plus program during the spring semester in 2003 (Hansen & Dusenbury, 2004). Assignment to conditions was not randomized but rather was based on convenience. There were either within-school controls (in the cases where classes were organized by semester the fall-semester classes served as controls) or, in some cases, entire schools were solicited to serve as controls. Among the latter were schools that had initially been invited to participate, but because of administrative issues, were not able to deliver the program. Classrooms in treatment conditions were assigned to receive either All Stars Core or a combined intervention consisting of All Stars Core and Plus.

Student surveys included measures targeted by Core as well as decision-making skills, impulsivity, goal setting skills, persistence, and diligence in pursuing goals, and skills for refusing offers to use drugs. Students responded to questions assessing lifetime, past 30-day participation, and amount consumed for five drug use behaviors (i.e., drinking alcohol, getting drunk, using marijuana, using inhalants, and smoking cigarettes).

The addition of Plus to the Core intervention improved student outcomes (see Figure 11.6). All Stars Core and Core with the addition of Plus each reduced alcohol consumption and drunkenness, primarily by reducing the frequency of participation in these behaviors. Core with Plus reduced marijuana use and inhalant use and resulted in no pretest to posttest increase in participation in smoking cigarettes. Thus, the addition of lessons that targeted goal setting, decision making, and refusing peer pressure to use substances augmented the effectiveness of All Stars Core.

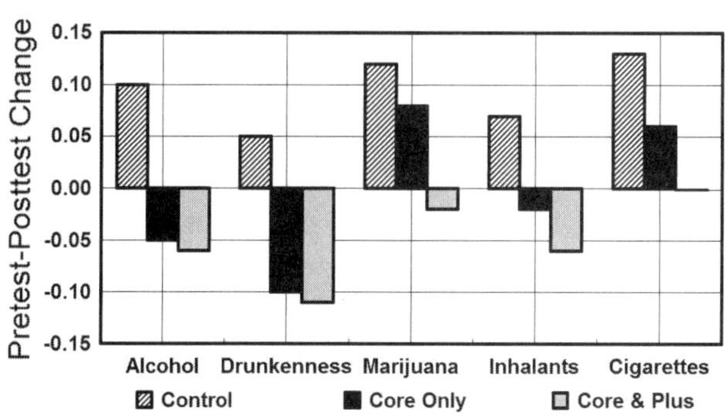

FIGURE 11.6. Results of the Core v. Core and Plus field trial on changing targeted behavioral outcomes. Data from Hansen and Dusenbury (2004).

Both Core and the combined Core and Plus programs improved goal-setting skills when compared with controls. Neither program differentially improved students' decision-making skills, impulsivity, or students' ability to resist peer pressure. Compared with controls, neither program had an impact on normative beliefs; however, there was a strong positive impact on lifestyle incongruence that was equivalent for both interventions. Similarly, both Core and Core with Plus had favorable program effects on school bonding when compared with controls. Core (but not Core with Plus) improved commitments to avoid drug use; students who received Core with Plus were no different than controls. We concluded that the primary strength of All Stars Plus was to strengthen mediators targeted by All Stars Core. All Stars Plus is now offered as a booster.

DISSEMINATION STUDIES

Chicago Coaching Study

The dissemination of evidence-based programs into a real-world setting is of tremendous concern (see the chapters in Part IX, this handbook), with considerable concern about quality of implementation in nonresearch settings (Swisher, 2000). Because drug-prevention programs involve psychosocial concepts, and because there is a general tendency to reinvent innovations (Rogers, 1995), there is a concern that programs will be poorly implemented when disseminated. To test an approach to mitigate these issues, we recruited 48 teachers in 44 schools in Chicago to participate in a 3-year cycle of All Stars Core intervention.

In each cycle of teaching, students completed pretest and posttest surveys that included standardized-mediating variable and drug-use behavior assessments. In addition, posttest surveys included questions that asked about student engagement in and enjoyment of All Stars, attitudes toward their teacher, and perceptions of their teachers' skills (Ringwalt, Pankratz, Gottfredson, et al., 2009).

Teachers used camcorders to record their implementation of all program sessions. Coders viewed recordings and documented whether teachers attempted each step within each activity (Ringwalt, Pankratz, Hansen, et al., 2009). Coders also noted changes and omissions in the program.

One key finding in this study related to the variability of teachers' performance over time. In general, teachers tended to regress to the grand mean over time. With few exceptions, teachers whose performance was judged to be superior in Cycle 1, based on assessments of adherence, had generally poorer performance over time. Those who were judged to be poorer initially gradually improved (Ringwalt, Pankratz, Hansen, et al., 2009).

Approximately half of the teachers were assigned to receive personal coaching that could guide their performance (Dusenbury et al., 2010; Ringwalt, Pankratz, Gottfredson, et al., 2009). Coaches viewed teachers' video recordings and identified positive qualities and issues for which there might be improvement. They attempted to meet with teachers three times during the course of teaching each cycle in order to provide them with feedback and suggestions.

Students who were taught by a teacher who had been coached had a lower rate of escalation of cigarette use than was the case for students who received All Stars from a teacher who had not been coached. This same finding was not observed for alcohol and marijuana use. A disappointing finding was that coaching did not specifically improve targeted mediating variables.

While the results of coaching as a main effect were limited, there were other outcomes that reveal possible future strategies that may make coaching more effective. Topics selected for coaching were based on joint decisions between the coach and the teacher. We identified 23 different topics that coaches and teachers considered. Amount of time spent coaching on seven of the topics (i.e., time management, using humor, skipping content or activities, getting parents involved, building self-confidence to teach, movement in the classroom, and engaging high-risk youth) related to changes in student mediators and behavior. Coaching about not skipping content and appropriately using humor was positively associated with changes in parental attentiveness. Coaching teachers to not skip content was also associated with positive outcomes for lifestyle incongruence and parental attentiveness. Coaching intended to help teachers build self-confidence in teaching ability was associated with improvements in students' bonding to school. Coaching to help teachers get parents involved and coaching to help teachers manage high-risk students was associated with reduced drug use (Dusenbury et al., 2010).

Coaching may have benefits, but it also carries considerable costs. The value of a study examining coaching was first and foremost that we acquired new information regarding how All Stars was delivered under dissemination conditions. This research provided an opportunity to learn about the role that observations can play in helping understand program implementation in the real world. Without dedicated funds to maintain this high-intensity form of training, coaching is not expected to be a readily adopted feature of standard practice.

Adaptation and Implementation Study

We conducted a two-phase study to examine the role of implementation quality and adaptation on the effectiveness of All Stars. Measuring fidelity has an extensive history (Durlak & DuPre, 2008); however, a universal method that has the potential of being applied to multiple school-based prevention programs had not been developed and validated (Hansen, 2014). Using feedback from prevention-program developers, prevention researchers, administrators from prevention-service organizations, and governmental-prevention policymakers, lists of potential topics were first solicited and then validated (Hansen, 2011). From these lists, standardized forms were created that could be adapted to assess adherence, percentage completed, achievement of objectives, dosage, participant engagement, quality of teaching, teacher understanding, potential impact-targeted mediators and behaviors, classroom or group management and adaptations to methods and messages.

During the first phase, we used video recordings from nine teachers who taught All Stars for 3 consecutive years. Teachers were selected whose classroom results spanned the spectrum of mediating variable outcomes observed. Two or more coders made ratings for 324 video recordings. Interrater agreement and the correlation between paired coders' score were acceptable (i.e., *r*s above .70) for all measures with the exception of student engagement (Bishop, Pankratz, Hansen, Albritton, Albritton, & Strack, 2013).

These granular data were used to examine the role of fidelity and adaptation on program outcomes. We completed a comparison of classrooms in which there had been a high versus low amount of adaptation and an average of positive versus negative adaptation. Classrooms in which All Stars Core had been taught with relatively little program adaptation (maintaining high fidelity) and in which the adaptations that were introduced were positive had significantly more students remain as nondrug users (Hansen et al., 2013). In contrast, when teachers made a greater than average number of adaptations (altering program content), program efficacy was reduced. Even when few adaptations were made, but those adaptations tended to be negative in terms of their potential impact on targeted mediators, efficacy was also reduced.

There were other benefits to documenting how teachers implemented All Stars. Weaknesses were identified and corrected in the subsequent iteration of the curriculum guide. Somewhat overly complicated activities were revamped and simplified. Points to emphasize during class instruction were also added. Further, from the catalog of positive adaptations teachers introduced, we identified added features such as insightful questions and clarifying steps that were readily included in the revised curriculum. Having access to these data has proved extremely valuable in terms of helping achieve the goal of continued quality improvement.

During the second phase, we applied the assessment methods to examine the degree to which teachers who had purchased All Stars implemented the program. In this phase of the study, teachers initially taught All Stars using an earlier version of the curriculum and then taught the program using the revised version of the program. Based on teachers' self-reports (unpublished), there were only modest gains in fidelity. Using the older version of the program, teachers reported teaching an average of 91.9% of prescribed activities, which rose to 93.5% with the revised curriculum. Teachers' greatest improvements came in their reports of student engagement (77.2% of optimum before and 80.0% of optimum after) and their estimates of how effective the program would be (72.8% of optimum before and 76.2% of optimum after). These and related findings suggest there is yet room for improvement either through improving the program or helping teachers improve their delivery of the program.

While fidelity showed only modest improvement, there were significantly fewer self-reported adaptations by teachers using the revised curriculum when compared with earlier versions used. Average numbers of self-reported adaptations dropped from 25.0 to 10.6 (Cohen's $d = 1.25$) using the revised curriculum. There were fewer method adaptations and fewer message adaptations. It was gratifying that teachers needed to make fewer adaptations to the program.

Support for Local Evaluations

With the development of a national registry for effective prevention programs (i.e., NREPP), the field of prevention has embarked on an era of national, if not global, dissemination. For at least some programs, being "on the NREPP list" of model programs is deemed sufficient; no further research or documentation is required. We have taken a somewhat different perspective. The research that supports All Stars helps us understand that prevention is a challenging and ongoing enterprise even when conducted under the auspices of a relatively well-controlled RCT. Well-designed, theoretically consonant, and methodologically rigorous programs sometimes fail. Even more important, the conditions that lead to success or failure are not yet fully understood. Our research on implementation and adaptation points out some of the issues that surround understanding how and when an intervention succeeds and fails (Hansen et al., 2013). Nonetheless, there are significant gaps in our knowledge about how programs such as All Stars fare in the real world under conditions of normal practice.

We provide schools and prevention agencies that adopt All Stars with the ability to conduct meaningful local program evaluation. Classical RCTs have served as the gold standard for assessing efficacy and effectiveness of preventive interventions (Flay et al., 2005). In contrast, many local evaluations of drug prevention programs are small-scale implementations without the ability to randomize to condition or the ability to enlist a control or comparison group. For such evaluations, standards have not yet been widely adopted.

We propose three solutions to this challenge. The first is to routinely collect student pretest and posttest data (Hansen et al., 2006). The second is to routinely collect fidelity data from teachers (Bishop et al., 2006). Both solutions are relatively straightforward. The third proposed solution is to develop methods for allowing local evaluations to estimate effectiveness compared with prior local evaluations, an approach we refer to as *synthetic comparators* (Hansen, Derzon, & Reese, 2012). The synthetic comparator strategy involves identifying the similarity between a given local evaluation and prior archived evaluations in order to construct a comparison group against which current outcomes can be measured (see also Chapter 28, this handbook).

Four requirements support this method. First, we need data from previous local evaluations. Second, similar outcome measures need to have been employed. Third, we need standardized methods to establish pretest equivalence. Fourth, we need analytic tools for making comparisons. With the development of Evaluation Lizard, we are ready to fulfill these requirements (Hansen et al., 2012). Since 2005, All Stars' clients have routinely collected student pretest and posttest surveys. To date, over 1,400 local evaluation projects have collected pretest and posttest surveys assessing student behaviors and mediators. These projects represent not only local evaluations of All Stars, but other programs as well. Most of these local evaluations do not have resources for long-term tracking and follow-up. Therefore, the data typically available for analysis only include pretest and immediate posttest survey data.

For this chapter, we sampled recent All Stars local evaluation projects to assess typical patterns of pretest to posttest change in alcohol and cigarette use. Figures 11.7 and 11.8 reveal the typical pattern of change associated with the implementation of All Stars Core. The modal result was "no onset" with 33% and 53% of projects having no onset of alcohol or cigarettes, respectively, among their pretest nonusing students. Further, 53% of projects had fewer than 5% of students start drinking alcohol and 79% had fewer than 5% start smoking cigarettes.

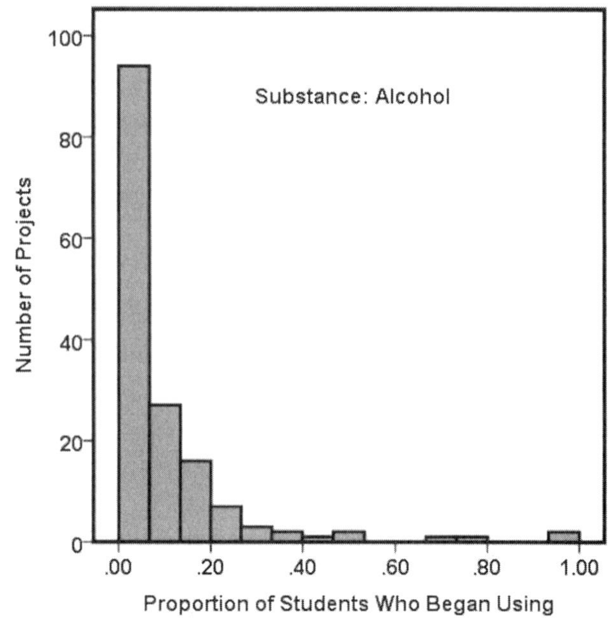

FIGURE 11.7. Onset of alcohol use from pretest to posttest among students who did not drink alcohol at pretest who received All Stars Core, aggregated at the project level ($N = 156$ projects).

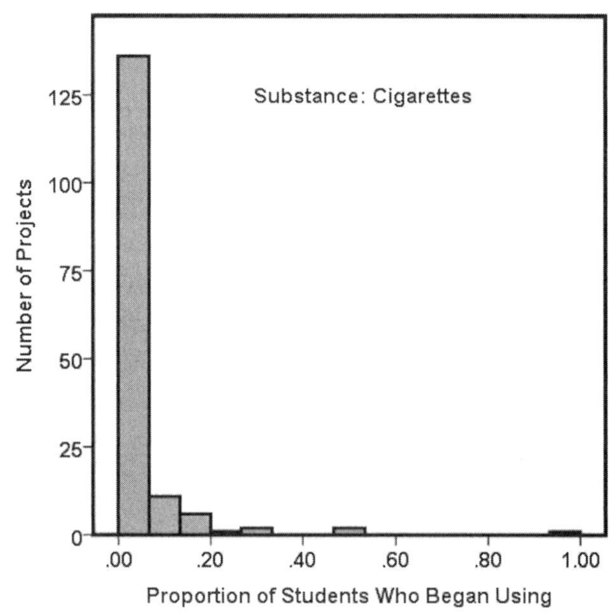

FIGURE 11.8. Onset of cigarette use from pretest to posttest among students who did not smoke cigarettes at pretest who received All Stars Core, aggregated at the project level ($N = 159$ projects).

CONCLUSION

All Stars has a long history of development that began with the earliest prevention studies conducted in the 1970s. The foundation of All Stars is a focus on target risk mechanisms that have a strong predictive relation with alcohol, tobacco, and other drug use. The primary targeted mediators—lifestyle incongruence, normative beliefs, commitment to avoid drug use—have been consistently shown to predict drug use. When these mediators are changed as a result of program exposure, success in preventing drug use follows. There is evidence that the program can have an impact on these primary mediators as well as the secondary mediators also included as a focus of intervention—positive parental attentiveness and bonding to prosocial institutions.

The challenge with all evidence-based prevention programs is to promote effectiveness under real-world conditions. All Stars is unique in the degree to which real-world outcomes have been used to improve the program. Curriculum design has clearly benefitted from our observations via video recordings of teachers as they deliver the program. An equally important source of real-world information is now beginning to emerge as part of our continued efforts that focus on local evaluation.

References

Ajzen, I., & Fishbein, M. (1977). Attitude-behavior relations: A theoretical analysis and review of the research. *Psychological Bulletin, 84*, 888–918. doi:10.1037/0033-2909.84.5.888

Ary, D. V., & Biglan, A. (1988). Longitudinal changes in adolescent cigarette smoking behavior: Onset and cessation. *Journal of Behavioral Medicine, 11*, 361–382. doi:10.1007/BF00844936

Asch, S. E. (1956). Studies of independence and conformity: A minority of one against a unanimous majority. *Psychological Monographs: General and Applied, 70*, 1–70. doi:10.1037/h0093718

Bandura, A., & Walters, R. H. (1963). *Social learning and personality development.* New York, NY: Holt, Rinehart and Winston.

Bishop, D., Bryant, K. S., Giles, S. M., Hansen, W. B., & Dusenbury, L. (2006). Simplifying the delivery of a prevention program with web-based enhancements. *The Journal of Primary Prevention, 27*, 433–444. doi:10.1007/s10935-006-0042-z

Bishop, D. C., Pankratz, M. M., Hansen, W. B., Albritton, J., Albritton, L., & Strack, J. (2013). Measuring fidelity and adaptation: Reliability of a standardized instrument. *Evaluation & the Health Professions, 37*, 231–257. doi:10.1177/0163278713476882

Botvin, G. J., Baker, E., Dusenbury, L., Tortu, S., & Botvin, E. M. (1990). Preventing adolescent drug abuse through a multimodal cognitive-behavioral approach: Results of a three-year study. *Journal of Consulting and Clinical Psychology, 58*, 437–446. doi:10.1037/0022-006X.58.4.437

Bry, B. H., McKeon, P., & Pandina, R. J. (1982). Extent of drug use as a function of number of risk factors. *Journal of Abnormal Psychology, 91*, 273–279. doi:10.1037/0021-843X.91.4.273

Chassin, L., Presson, C. C., Bensenberg, M., Corty, E., Olshavsky, R. W., & Sherman, S. J. (1981). Predicting adolescents' intentions to smoke cigarettes: An application of the Ajzen and Fishbein and Jessor and Jessor Models. *Journal of Health and Social Behavior, 22*, 445–455. doi:10.2307/2136684

Chassin, L., Presson, C. C., Sherman, S. J., Corty, E., & Olshavsky, R. W. (1984). Predicting the onset of cigarette smoking in adolescents: A longitudinal study. *Journal of Applied Social Psychology, 14*, 224–243. doi:10.1111/j.1559-1816.1984.tb02233.x

Conrad, K. M., Flay, B. R., & Hill, D. (1992). Why children start smoking cigarettes: Predictors of onset. *British Journal of Addiction, 87*, 1711–1724. doi:10.1111/j.1360-0443.1992.tb02684.x

Cook, S. W., & Berrenberg, J. L. (1981). Approaches to encouraging conservation behavior: A review and conceptual framework. *Journal of Social Issues, 37*, 73–107. doi:10.1111/j.1540-4560.1981.tb02627.x

Dent, C. W., Sussman, S., Stacy, A. W., Craig, S., Burton, D., & Flay, B. R. (1995). Two-year behavior outcomes of Project Toward No Tobacco Use. *Journal of Consulting and Clinical Psychology, 63*, 676–677. doi:10.1037/0022-006X.63.4.676

Dishion, T. J., & Loeber, R. (1985). Adolescent marijuana and alcohol use: The role of parents and peers revisited. *The American Journal of Drug and Alcohol Abuse, 11*, 11–25. doi:10.3109/00952998509016846

Donaldson, S. I., Graham, J. W., & Hansen, W. B. (1994). Testing the generalizability of intervening mechanism theories: Understanding the effects of adolescent drug use prevention interventions. *Journal of Behavioral Medicine, 17*, 195–216. doi:10.1007/BF01858105

Donaldson, S. I., Graham, J. W., Piccinin, A. M., & Hansen, W. B. (1995). Resistance skills training and onset of alcohol use: Evidence for beneficial and potentially harmful effects in public schools and in private Catholic schools. *Health Psychology, 14*, 291–300. doi:10.1037/0278-6133.14.4.291

Durlak, J. A., & DuPre, E. (2008). Implementation matters: A review of research on the influence of implementation on program outcomes and the factors affecting implementation. *American Journal of Community Psychology*, *41*, 327–350. doi:10.1007/s10464-008-9165-0

Dusenbury, L., Hansen, W. B., Jackson-Newsom, J., Pittman, D., Wilson, C., Simley, K., . . . Giles, S. (2010). Coaching to enhance quality of implementation in prevention. *Health Education*, *110*, 43–60. doi:10.1108/09654281011008744

Eccles, J., & Wigfield, A. (1995). In the mind of the actor: The structure of adolescents' achievement task values and expectancy-related beliefs. *Personality and Social Psychology Bulletin*, *21*, 215–225. doi:10.1177/0146167295213003

Eccles, J. S., & Wigfield, A. (2002). Motivational beliefs, values, and goals. *Annual Review of Psychology*, *53*, 109–132. doi:10.1146/annurev.psych.53.100901.135153

Evans, R. I., Rozelle, R. M., Mittelmark, M. B., Hansen, W. B., Bane, A. L., & Havis, J. (1978). Deterring the onset of smoking in children: Knowledge of immediate physiological effects and coping with peer pressure, media pressure, and parent modeling. *Journal of Applied Social Psychology*, *8*, 126–135. doi:10.1111/j.1559-1816.1978.tb00771.x

Fearnow-Kenney, M., Hansen, W. B., & McNeal, R. B. (2002). Comparison of psychosocial influences on substance use in adolescents: Implications for prevention programming. *Journal of Child & Adolescent Substance Abuse*, *11*, 1–24. doi:10.1300/j029v11n04_01

Festinger, L. (1957). *A theory of cognitive dissonance.* Evanston, IL: Harper, Row & Peterson.

Festinger, L., & Maccoby, N. (1964). On resistance to persuasive communications. *The Journal of Abnormal and Social Psychology*, *68*, 359–366. doi:10.1037/h0049073

Flay, B. R., Biglan, A., Boruch, R. F., Castro, F. G., Gottfredson, D., Kellam, S., . . . Ji, P. (2005). Standards of evidence: Criteria for efficacy, effectiveness and dissemination. *Prevention Science*, *6*, 151–175. doi:10.1007/s11121-005-5553-y

Goodstadt, M. S., Sheppard, M. A., & Chan, G. C. (1982). An evaluation of two school-based alcohol education programs. *Journal of Studies on Alcohol*, *43*, 352–369.

Hansen, W. B. (1992). School-based substance abuse prevention: A review of the state of the art curriculum 1980-1990. *Health Education Research*, *7*, 403–430. doi:10.1093/her/7.3.403

Hansen, W. B. (1996). Pilot test results comparing the All Stars program with seventh grade D.A.R.E.: Program integrity and mediating variable analysis. *Substance Use & Misuse*, *31*, 1359–1377. doi:10.3109/10826089609063981

Hansen, W. B. (2011). *Assessing fidelity: What program developers, policy makers, practitioners and researchers think is important.* Unpublished manuscript, Tanglewood Research, Greensboro, NC.

Hansen, W. B. (2014). [Correlation between bonding and alcohol use]. Unpublished raw data.

Hansen, W. B. (2014). Measuring fidelity. *Defining prevention science.* New York, NY: Springer. doi:10.1007/978-1-4899-7424-2_15

Hansen, W. B., Bishop, D., & Bryant, K. S. (2009). Using online components to facilitate program implementation: Impact of technological enhancements to All Stars on ease and quality of program delivery. *Prevention Science*, *10*, 66–75. doi:10.1007/s11121-008-0118-5

Hansen, W. B., Derzon, J. H., & Reese, E. L. (2012). A synthetic comparator approach to local evaluation of school-based substance abuse prevention programming. *Evaluation & the Health Professions*, *37*, 258–282. doi:10.1177/0163278712464772

Hansen, W. B., & Dusenbury, L. (2004). All Stars Plus: A competence and motivation enhancement approach to prevention. *Health Education*, *104*, 371–381. doi:10.1108/09654280410564141

Hansen, W. B., Fielding, J. E., & Malotte, C. K. (1988). Evaluation of a tobacco and alcohol abuse prevention curriculum for adolescents. *Health Education Quarterly*, *15*, 93–114. doi:10.1177/109019818801500109

Hansen, W. B., & Graham, J. W. (1991). Preventing alcohol, marijuana, and cigarette use among adolescents: Peer pressure resistance training vs. establishing conservative norms. *Preventive Medicine*, *20*, 414–430. doi:10.1016/0091-7435(91)90039-7

Hansen, W. B., Graham, J. W., Wolkenstein, B. H., Lundy, B. Z., Pearson, J., Flay, B. R., & Johnson, C. A. (1988). Differential impact of three alcohol prevention curricula on hypothesized mediating variables. *Journal of Drug Education*, *18*, 143–153. doi:10.2190/FLQ5-9KNJ-92TH-WCDF

Hansen, W. B., Johnson, C. A., Flay, B. R., Graham, J. W., & Sobel, J. L. (1988). Affective and social influences approaches to the prevention of multiple substance abuse among seventh grade students: Results from Project SMART. *Preventive Medicine*, *17*, 135–154.

Hansen, W. B., & McNeal, R. B. (1996). The law of maximum expected potential effect: Constraints placed on program effectiveness by mediator relationships. *Health Education Research*, *11*, 501–507. doi:10.1093/her/11.4.501

Hansen, W. B., & McNeal, R. B. (2001). Self-initiated cessation from substance use: A longitudinal study of the relationship between postulated mediators and quitting. *Journal of Drug Issues*, *31*, 957–975. doi:10.1177/002204260103100408

Hansen, W. B., Malotte, C. K., & Fielding, J. E. (1988). Evaluation of a tobacco and alcohol abuse prevention curriculum for adolescents. *Health Education & Behavior*, 15, 93–114. doi:10.1177/109019818801500109

Hansen, W. B., Pankratz, M. M., Dusenbury, L., Giles, S. M., Bishop, D. C., Albritton, J., . . . Strack, J. (2013). Styles of adaptation: The impact of frequency and valence of adaptation on preventing substance use. *Health Education*, *113*, 345–363. doi:10.1108/09654281311329268

Hansen, W. B., Paskett, E. D., & Carter, L. J. (1999). The adolescent sexual activity index (ASAI): A standardized strategy for measuring interpersonal heterosexual behaviors among youth. *Health Education Research*, *14*, 485–490. doi:10.1093/her/14.4.485

Hansen, W. B., Reese, E., Wyrick, C. H., Jackson-Newsom, J., Bryant, K. S., & Dyreng, D. I. (2006). An online strategy for evaluating educational and social intervention programs. *IPSI BgD Transactions on Internet Research*, *2*, 27–32.

Hansen, W. B., Uebersax, J. S., & Rose, L. A. (1995). *Comparison of postulated mediators of school-based substance use prevention in adolescents: A longitudinal examination.* Unpublished Manuscript.

Harrington, N. G., Giles, S. M., Hoyle, R. H., Feeney, G. J., & Yungbluth, S. C. (2001). Evaluation of the All Stars character education and problem behavior prevention program: Pretest-posttest effects on mediator and outcome variables for middle school students. *Health Education & Behavior*, *28*, 533–546. doi:10.1177/109019810102800502

Hawkins, J. D., Guo, J., Hill, K. G., Battin-Pearson, S., & Abbott, R. D. (2001). Long-term effects of the Seattle Social Development intervention on school bonding trajectories. *Applied Developmental Science*, *5*, 225–236. doi:10.1207/S1532480XADS0504_04

Higbee, K. L. (1969). Fifteen years of fear arousal: Research on threat appeals: 1953-1968. *Psychological Bulletin*, *72*, 426–444. doi:10.1037/h0028430

Hovland, C. I., Janis, I. L., & Kelley, H. H. (1953). *Communication and persuasion.* New Haven, CT: Yale University Press.

Janis, I. L., & Mann, L. (1977). *Decision making: A psychological analysis of conflict, choice, and commitment.* New York, NY: Free Press.

Johnson, C. A., Pentz, M. A., Weber, M. D., Dwyer, J. H., Baer, N., MacKinnon, D. P., . . . Flay, B. R. (1990). Relative effectiveness of comprehensive community programming for drug abuse prevention with high-risk and low-risk adolescents. *Journal of Consulting and Clinical Psychology*, *58*, 447–456. doi:10.1037/0022-006X.58.4.447

Judd, C. M., & Kenny, D. A. (1981). Process analysis: Estimating mediation in treatment evaluations. *Evaluation Review*, *5*, 602–619. doi:10.1177/0193841X8100500502

Kinnier, R. T. (1995). A reconceptualization of values clarification: Values conflict resolution. *Journal of Counseling & Development*, *74*, 18–24. doi:10.1002/j.1556-6676.1995.tb01817.x

Lipsey, M. W., & Pollard, J. A. (1989). Driving toward theory in program evaluation: More models to choose from. *Evaluation and Program Planning*, *12*, 317–328. doi:10.1016/0149-7189(89)90048-7

Maccoby, E. E., Maccoby, N., Romney, A. K., & Adams, J. S. (1961). Social reinforcement in attitude change. *The Journal of Abnormal and Social Psychology*, *63*, 109–115. doi:10.1037/h0043154

MacKinnon, D. P., Johnson, C. A., Pentz, M. A., Dwyer, J. H., Hansen, W. B., Flay, B. R., & Wang, E. Y. (1991). Mediating mechanisms in a school-based drug prevention program: First year effects of the Midwestern Prevention Project. *Health Psychology*, *10*, 164–172. doi:10.1037/0278-6133.10.3.164

McGuire, W. J. (1964). Inducing resistance to persuasion. *Advances in Experimental and Social Psychology*, *1*, 191–229.

McNeal, R. B., & Hansen, W. B. (1999). Developmental patterns associated with the onset of drug use: Changes in postulated mediators during adolescence. *Journal of Drug Issues*, *29*, 381–400.

McNeal, R. B., Hansen, W. B., Harrington, N. G., & Giles, S. M. (2004). How All Stars works: An examination of program effects on mediating variables. *Health Education & Behavior*, *31*, 165–178. doi:10.1177/1090198103259852

Moskowitz, J. M., Malvin, J., Schaeffer, G. A., & Schaps, E. (1983). An evaluation of a junior high school student primary prevention program. *Addictive Behaviors*, *8*, 393–401. doi:10.1016/0306-4603(83)90040-0

Newcomb, M. D., & Bentler, P. M. (1988). *Consequences of adolescent drug use: Impact on the lives of young adults.* Newbury Park, CA: Sage.

Pentz, M. A., MacKinnon, D. P., Dwyer, J. H., Wang, E. Y. I., Hansen, W. B., Flay, B. R., & Johnson, C. A. (1989). Longitudinal effects of the Midwestern Prevention Project (MPP) on regular and experimental smoking in adolescents. *Preventive Medicine*, *18*, 304–321. doi:10.1016/0091-7435(89)90077-7

Richardson, J. L., Dwyer, K., McGuigan, K., Hansen, W. B., Dent, C., Johnson, C. A., . . . Flay, B. R. (1989). Substance use among eighth-grade students who take care of themselves after school. *Pediatrics*, *84*, 556–566.

Ringwalt, C., Pankratz, M., Gottfredson, N., Jackson-Newsom, J., Dusenbury, L., Giles, S., . . . Hansen, B. (2009). The effects of students' curriculum engagement, attitudes towards their teachers, and perception of their teachers' skills on school-based prevention curriculum outcomes. *Journal of Drug Education, 39*, 223–237. doi:10.2190/DE.39.3.a

Ringwalt, C. L., Pankratz, M. M., Hansen, W. B., Dusenbury, L., Jackson-Newsom, J., Giles, S. M., & Brodish, P. H. (2009). The potential of coaching as a strategy to improve the effectiveness of school-based substance use prevention curricula. *Health Education & Behavior, 36*, 696–710. doi:10.1177/1090198107303311

Rogers, E. M. (1995). *Diffusion of innovations* (4th ed.). New York, NY: The Free Press.

Rokeach, M. J. (1973). *The nature of human values.* New York, NY: The Free Press.

Rokeach, M. J. (1979). *Understanding human values.* New York, NY: Free Press.

Scheier, L. M., & Hansen, W. B. (2014). Parenting styles and adolescent drug use. In L. M. Scheier & W. B. Hansen (Eds.), *Parenting and teen drug use: The most recent findings from research, prevention, and treatment* (pp. 62–91). New York, NY: Oxford University Press.

Sobel, M. E. (1982). Asymptotic confidence intervals for indirect effects in structural equation models. In S. Leinhardt (Ed.), *Sociological methodology* (pp. 290–312). Washington, DC: American Sociological Association. doi:10.2307/270723

Sobel, M. E. (1986). Some new results on indirect effects and their standard errors in covariance structure models. In N. Tuma (Ed.), *Sociological methodology* (pp. 159–186). Washington, DC: American Sociological Association. doi:10.2307/270922

Spoth, R., & Redmond, C. (1993). Study of participating barriers in family-focused prevention: Research issues and preliminary results. *International Quarterly of Community Health Education, 13*, 365–388. doi:10.2190/69LM-59KD-K9CE-8Y8B

Swisher, J. D. (2000). Sustainability of prevention. *Addictive Behaviors, 25*, 965–973. doi:10.1016/S0306-4603(00)00124-6

Taylor, B. J., Graham, J. W., Cumsille, P., & Hansen, W. B. (2000). Modeling prevention program effects on growth in substance use: Analysis of five years of data from the Adolescent Alcohol Prevention Trial. *Prevention Science, 1*, 183–197. doi:10.1023/A:1026547128209

Tobler, N. S. (1986). Meta-analysis of 143 adolescent drug prevention programs: Quantitative outcome results of program participants compared to a control or comparison group. *Journal of Drug Issues, 16*, 537–567.

Tobler, N. S., & Stratton, H. (1997). Effectiveness of school-based drug prevention programs: A meta-analysis of the research. *The Journal of Primary Prevention, 17*, 1–6.

Weber, M. D., Graham, J. W., Hansen, W. B., Flay, B. R., & Johnson, C. A. (1989). Evidence for two paths of alcohol use onset in adolescents. *Addictive Behaviors, 14*, 399–408. doi:10.1016/0306-4603(89)90027-0

Chapter 12

PEER GROUP CONNECTION: A PEER-LED PROGRAM TARGETING THE TRANSITION INTO HIGH SCHOOL

Robert J. Pandina, Valerie L. Johnson, and Sherry L. Barr

Schools are a logical and important setting for conducting programs aimed at preventing a myriad of problems among youth, including tobacco use (Campbell et al., 2008), bullying (Farrington & Ttofi, 2009), HIV (Griffin, Botvin, & Nichols, 2006), suicide (Cooper, Clements, & Holt, 2011; Wyman et al., 2010), and substance use (Faggiano et al., 2008). Alcohol and recreational drug use typically begins during adolescence, thus, schools provide access to the appropriate age groups to target prevention activities (U.S. Office of the Surgeon General, 2006). Schools also offer the most systematic and efficient way to reach large numbers of young people each year, especially when programs are integrated into the school day and become a component of the standard curriculum. When integrated into the fabric of the school's offerings, programming is also more likely to be sustained over time.

In a national survey of 1,392 school districts, Ringwalt et al. (2008) found that 43% indicated that they did not use any prevention curricula, and of those schools that were using prevention curricula, only 10% were using evidence-based programs. Although a range of school-based interventions have been developed to prevent or delay the onset of alcohol and other drug use, the majority of these school-based programs have been developed for and delivered in middle schools, leaving a gap in programming for elementary and high schools. These findings, along with estimates released annually by *Monitoring the Future's* school-based surveys of adolescent substance use (Johnston, O'Malley, Bachman, & Schulenberg, 2012), reveal that initiation of substance use increases rapidly across the middle and high school grades, indicating a compelling need for more high school–focused programs. In 2011, one third of the surveyed eighth-grade students reported that they had used alcohol. By 10th grade, this percentage increased to 56%, and by senior year of high school 70% indicated use (Johnston et al., 2012). Although there has been an overall decrease over the past decade in lifetime prevalence of alcohol and any illicit drug use among high school students, the results of the most recent *Monitoring the Future* survey indicate that there are still substantial portions of youth engaging in harmful use behaviors.

INTERVENING DURING A CRITICAL DEVELOPMENTAL TRANSITION PERIOD

The transition from middle school to high school represents an important developmental period linked to a broad range of risk factors typically

Preparation of this chapter was supported by grants from the National Institute on Drug Abuse (P20 DA017552) and the State of New Jersey (10-767-ADA-0). Correspondence concerning this chapter should be directed to Dr. Robert J. Pandina, Center of Alcohol Studies, Rutgers University, Piscataway, NJ 08854.

http://dx.doi.org/10.1037/14550-013
Handbook of Adolescent Drug Use Prevention: Research, Intervention Strategies, and Practice, L. M. Scheier (Editor)

associated with onset and escalation of alcohol and drug use. By intervening during this period, key risk factors can be reduced and protective factors can be enhanced, with the net effect being a sustained reduction in antecedents and mediators of harmful behaviors. The transition to a new educational setting requires major adaptations that can be quite stressful for students. Research has demonstrated that the stress often accompanying the transition from middle school to high school is associated with lowered achievement and school attendance (Akos & Galassi, 2004) and contributes to a significant decline in school connectedness, one of the most important predictors of student success (Blum, 2005) and a protective factor that decreases risks for negative outcomes. Hence, those students who begin the process of transition to high school with higher levels of attachment to a prosocial school environment may be protected from negative outcomes (Dedmond, 2006). As students make the transition into high school, they face increased academic demands for which an alarming number are unprepared academically (Cohen & Smerdon, 2009).

Simultaneously, youth must make important academic and social decisions that determine their likelihood of graduating from high school, going to college, or successfully entering the workforce. During the transition from middle to high school, students often lose contact with important support systems, including their middle school teachers and peers; they experience fewer opportunities to interact with teachers; experience a more competitive, impersonal, grade-oriented environment; develop a more negative view of themselves; and feel an increased need for peer friendships (Brown, 2004). The transition from middle to high school often marks the initiation of a number of problem behaviors, including substance use, aggressive and violent behavior, and high-risk sexual behavior. For many youth, the transition proves too difficult, and they leave school altogether, increasing the likelihood of a troubled adulthood. More students fail ninth grade than any other grade (Kennelly & Monrad, 2007), and promotion rates between ninth and 10th grades are much lower than rates between any other grades (Wheelock & Miao, 2005).

Overall, there is demonstrated weakness in social support that is provided to students during the transition into high school. By the time students reach high school, more than half are "chronically disengaged" from school (Blum, 2005). Research consistently demonstrates that students are most vulnerable for dropping out of school during and immediately after their first year of high school (Cohen & Smerdon, 2009). By focusing on the transition from middle to high school, this period of heightened vulnerability has the potential for being transformed into a window of opportunity to prevent the consequences of poor decisions and overwhelming stress.

The school environment also provides an important socialization environment during adolescence (Pellerin, 2005). Students have an increasing need for autonomy and participation in decisions regarding their experiences and, paradoxically, have a need for strong social supports and close, trusting relationships with peers and adults (Klem & Connell, 2004). Hence, negotiating the peer environment is a major facet of adaptation to this new context. Particularly salient are the roles that the peer group and the need to adjust to a new peer environment play in influencing the development of drug use behaviors. One of the most consistent results in the substance abuse literature is the importance and complexity of peer influences and peer social interactions on the development of drug use behaviors particularly during key transitional periods.

Sustained programming into and throughout high school is arguably a necessary component of maintaining earlier benefits of elementary and middle school programming, as was demonstrated by the high school component of Project Northland (Perry et al., 2002). Focused efforts to prevent problematic patterns of alcohol use, such as heavy drinking and binge drinking, are also warranted during high school. School-based interventions are often designed to reduce risk factors for early alcohol use primarily at the individual level (e.g., by enhancing student's knowledge and skills), although others, the most successful ones (many are discussed in this handbook), also address social and environmental risk factors (e.g., alcohol-related norms). Some school-based programs focus on the general population of adolescents (i.e., are universal programs), whereas others target adolescents who are particularly at risk (i.e., are selective or indicated programs).

The research literature that examines the efficacy of school-based substance use prevention programs is fairly large, encompassing several decades of empirical study. Past evidence suggests that comprehensive school-based prevention approaches that appear to be effective are so because of the synergistic combination of social influence and competence enhancement elements (Epstein, Griffin, & Botvin, 2002), including norm setting (Kumar, O'Malley, Johnston, Schulenberg, & Bachman, 2002), refusal skills, self-management skills, and general social skills. Tobler (1986) and Tobler and Stratton (1997) conducted the first of a series of meta-analyses of school-based prevention programs and found that interactive programs reported better outcomes than noninteractive programs. Their meta-analysis work demonstrated support for a youth involvement approach, which seeks to promote protective mediators such as self-empowerment, leadership, planning, decision making, opportunities for success, and team-building skills. Ennett et al. (2003) found that teachers comfortable using interactive teaching methods were likely to deliver effective content.

Wilson, Gottfredson, and Najaka (2001) conducted a meta-analysis of 165 school-based prevention practices and found that instructional techniques that do not use cognitive behavioral or behavioral instructional strategies such as mentoring, tutoring, work-study programs, and recreational programs are not effective in reducing high-risk behaviors. Social competency instruction using cognitive behavioral and behavioral instructional methods or environmentally focused programs were all particularly effective. Beyond the general agreement that something works, there is much uncertainty about the specific magnitude of the effects, as well as the specific components of the program and specific segments of the population with which prevention works. Cuijpers' (2002) meta-analysis of a dozen peer- and adult-led, school-based, drug prevention programs concluded that effectiveness of these programs is determined by several factors, including content, number of regular and booster sessions, and the person who leads the implementation. Programs that involve youth directly in the implementation may not only enhance skills transmission but may also change the social climate of the school, as suggested by DeJong and Langford's (2002) research, which showed that peer-led programs helped to change students' social norms (see Chapter 9, this handbook).

Faggiano et al. (2008) conducted a systematic review of 29 studies that met rigorous standards for design quality and investigated the effectiveness of drug use prevention programs. Most of the programs that met the stringent inclusion criteria were developed for middle school students. Results of the review demonstrated that programs that develop individual social skills are most effective in having a positive impact on mediating variables (e.g., drug knowledge, decision making, self-esteem, peer pressure resistance) and drug use. Peer-led programs were found to be more effective than teacher-led programs with regard to marijuana use.

Stigler, Neusel, and Perry (2011) reviewed effective school-based approaches to alcohol prevention. Their review indicated that to be most effective, interventions should be theory driven, address social norms around substance use, build personal and social skills that help students resist pressure to use, involve interactive teaching approaches (e.g., small group activities and role plays), use peer leaders to facilitate delivery of the program, integrate other segments of the community (e.g., parents) into the program, be delivered over multiple sessions and years, provide adequate training and support to program facilitators, and be culturally and developmentally appropriate for the students they serve.

USING PEER LEADERS IN SUBSTANCE USE PREVENTION

Research findings from the past few decades have identified key program components that are more effective than others in achieving desired student outcomes. One component that has consistently emerged as promising is the use of properly selected and trained peer leaders for program delivery (Stigler et al., 2011). The concept of peer leadership in substance abuse prevention has been a staple part of the drug prevention literature for more than 40 years (e.g., Capone, McLaughlin, & Smith, 1973; Lawler, 1971; Smart, Bennett, & Fejer, 1976). In the early 1970s, attempts were made to develop, implement, and evaluate peer group drug abuse prevention programs. By and large, research demonstrated that these programs had favorable effects on levels of information known about drug use, facilitated peer friendships, developed individual responsibility, and instilled student confidence. Unfortunately, these programs showed no favorable effects on drug using behaviors. Programs showing some promise of success exhibited a common ingredient—student involvement in decision making. The shortcomings of these first attempts at peer-led prevention programming have been outlined in the above cited literature and are briefly summarized here.

First, there were high levels of teacher facilitator attrition. Usually, there was only one advisor for the program, making stable institutionalization of the program quite difficult. Although the teacher served as a resource person, typically this person was neither trained nor compensated. Second, although the programs were student implemented, students were not selected carefully on the basis of their demonstrated promise for responsible action with minimal teacher direction. Third, the programs were not integrated into a core curriculum; therefore, time limitations hindered the extent to which leadership skills were fostered. Fourth, there was limited flexibility and adaptability as to the content of the program. The emphasis was on drug abuse to the exclusion of other areas of concern, including other problem behaviors and important protective and mediating factors. Fifth, students who were most at risk for substance abuse did not benefit from the programs because of their high absenteeism and their low motivation to participate in any activities associated with the school. Finally, there was no involvement of any stakeholders or advisory group to provide assistance in an advisory capacity, either from schools, parents, or community groups. Kam, Greenberg, and Walls (2003) found that one of the most important factors contributing to the success of program implementation is adequate support from the school principal. Support from stakeholders is regarded as essential for the long-term survival of prevention programs. Part of the barrier of successful continuation of an effective prevention program is that schools traditionally have had no or limited infrastructure for such programming.

Several programs that use peers as facilitators in addressing substance use have been deemed model programs and have shown that the use of peers for delivering positive messages about avoiding substance use can be promising. Life Skills (National Health Promotion Associates, 2014; see also Chapter 10, this handbook) was developed to work with elementary, middle, and junior high students. The program targets both protective and risk factors in the teaching of personal and social skills to build resilience. Sessions are interactive and use facilitated discussions, structured small-group activities, and role playing (Botvin, Baker, Renick, Fiazzola, & Botvin, 1984).

The Project Towards No Drug Abuse program (see Chapter 9, this volume) attempts to enhance both prosocial norms and those norms opposed to the use of substances. Valente et al. (2007) found that a peer-led group exhibited lower rates of substance use than the teacher-led group when assessed 1 year later. Although researchers found that peer-led interactive substance prevention programs can enhance peer influences, they noted that among students who are close to other peers who support drug use, such an interactive program may have deleterious effects. (For additional discussions on the issues surrounding peer clustering of high-risk youth, see Dishion, McCord, & Poulin, 1999; Weiss, Little, & Bouffard, 2005.)

Project ALERT is a school-based drug use prevention program for middle or junior high school students. It was designed to instruct youth in the skills they need to resist social influences by building norms against use. Two major evaluations of this program involved over 85 schools and revealed some positive results regarding substance use attitudes (Ghosh-Dastidar, Longshore, Ellickson, & McCaffrey, 2004). Finally, Project Northland is a multilevel intervention model that involved students, peers, parents, and the community and focused on alcohol use. The peer-led curriculum emphasized resistance skills and normative expectations. Overall, the results suggested that some of Project Northland's effectiveness in influencing a student's decision to use or to abstain was because of its favorable deterrent effect on negative peer influences (Komro et al., 2001).

Similarities among these programs and with peer group connection (PGC) include a focus on developing many of the same skills and competencies among students. Curriculum dose and content of each program differ, but one of the features that distinguishes PGC from the other programs is its focus on older age peers as the main mode of delivery to incoming high school students during their period of transition. PGC intensively trains peer leaders to deliver the program to ninth-grade students. Peer leaders are trained through participation in a leadership retreat and a daily credit-bearing course. PGC also develops a team of school stakeholders to support the implementation, sustainability, and expansion of the program. In addition, PGC includes family night events that directly involve family members in the program and a daylong (4–5 hours) activity day for ninth-grade students that focuses on team building. The program incorporates a service learning component and booster sessions in the sophomore year to reinforce learning from the freshman year.

PEER GROUP CONNECTION OVERVIEW

Goals

Given the noted gap in high school drug prevention programming, the evidence showing the effectiveness of a peer leadership approach and the importance of intervening during the transition from middle to high school, a well-designed, peer-led, skills-focused program that is implemented during the ninth-grade year has potential to make a positive impact on student decision making, behaviors, and high school completion. Such a program must also consider the following: (a) the teachers–advisors–mentors in the program are well trained and duly compensated; (b) the students selected to lead the program are chosen using stringent criteria and are well trained; (c) the program is incorporated into the school's curriculum; (d) the content is broad and flexible, focusing on a variety of risk and protective factors and issues facing adolescents; (e) the program is developmentally appropriate (both in terms of age of the individual and the developmental stage of drug involvement); and (f) the program is integrated into the school's mission, and a supporting infrastructure is in place (Zavela, 2002). The PGC high school transition program provides one example of a program that incorporates each of these mission critical features.

PGC uses selected and trained older students that are drawn from the same school in which the program is implemented to create a nurturing environment for younger students in transition. The program was developed by the Princeton Center for Leadership Training (now Supportive Schools), a nonprofit organization that works in partnership with schools to implement the program. The program's mechanism for change is to train selected school faculty to prepare 11th- and 12th-grade students to mentor and educate small groups of freshmen. As part of this program, student peer leaders participate in comprehensive training to prepare them to conduct weekly outreach sessions designed to develop skills, promote a respectful school culture, nourish meaningful connections, and strengthen relationships among students across grades.

Theoretical Framework

The PGC program model is grounded in the theories of social and emotional learning (SEL), which "teaches the skills we all need to handle ourselves, our relationships, and our work, effectively and ethically" (Background on Social and Emotional Learning, 2007, p. 1). A mounting body of evidence clearly indicates that compared with students who do not participate in such programs, students who receive SEL programming academically outperform their peers, get better grades, and graduate at higher rates (Background on Social and Emotional Learning, 2007). SEL has been found to improve academic attitudes (motivation and commitment), behaviors (attendance, study habits, cooperative learning), and performance (grades, test scores and subject mastery; Zins, Weissberg, Wang, & Walberg, 2004). Peer group interactions and school culture and climate have consistently been named among the most influential factors on student learning (Garringer & MacRae, 2008).

In addition, the PGC program is grounded in social learning theory, incorporating observational learning, imitation, and modeling, all well-researched motivational constructs. Diverse groups of students from different levels of risk for problem behaviors, including substance use, are identified to collectively participate in the program. Youth at both high and moderate risk for problem behaviors and academic failure benefit from exposure to more motivated and academically successful students in a supportive, structured setting and benefit from observational learning and imitation of these peer role models (Gregoric & Owens, 2008). Lower risk students, who demonstrate fewer overt signs of distress but may be vulnerable in less obvious ways to academic or behavioral problems, also receive peer support to overcome obstacles that could eventually lead to more serious problems.

PGC also integrates the best practice recommendations for SEL, high school transition, and peer mentoring programs. Research indicates that SEL programs with the best outcomes are multiyear in duration, use interactive rather than purely knowledge-based instructional methods, and are integrated into the life of the school rather than being implemented as marginal add-ons (Zins et al., 2004). Effective high school transition programs support and guide students throughout the transition, not as a one-time event; facilitate caring relationships; create a culture of support and a sense of community; and provide students with mentoring, life skills, and opportunities to get to know and develop positive relationships with older students and other incoming students (Feller, 2003; Mizelle & Irvin, 2000; Smith, 2006). Finally, effective peer mentoring programs carefully assess and select peer–cross-age leaders, allow for adult support and supervision for peer mentors in the structure of the program, make training materials developmentally appropriate and engaging, and set high expectations for peer leaders (U.S. Department of Education Mentoring Resource Center, 2005).

Curriculum

The curriculum is designed to address mediating factors, which have been shown through research to influence risk reduction behaviors and produce positive student outcomes. Targeted mediators include those needed to (a) enhance a sense of school attachment; (b) create a kinship to other prosocial peers; (c) provide skills necessary to make healthy decisions; (d) resist negative influences; (e) set realistic goals; (f) manage anger and stress; and (g) develop a belief system consistent with an achievement orientation. The curriculum includes two primary resources: (a) the *Training Curriculum for Peer Leaders* contains the materials used by faculty advisors in the daily peer leadership class and two peer leader retreats, to prepare peer leaders for their role in delivering the program to ninth-grade students; and (b) the *Freshman Outreach Curriculum* contains the materials used by the peer leaders when they are conducting the weekly peer leader outreach sessions with freshmen, the activity day for freshmen, and the family nights. The Freshman Outreach Curriculum includes 34 modules. In Table 12.1, we present the overview of the topics and sequences.

RANDOMIZED TRIAL OF THE PEER GROUP CONNECTION PROGRAM

Funding for implementing and evaluating the PGC program in two urban high schools was obtained in 2004 as part of a National Institute on Drug Abuse–funded Prevention Research Center grant.[1] This research project was part of a larger effort funded by the National Institutes of Health with two key aims in mind. The first aim was the development, refinement, and enhancement of prevention intervention processes and strategies targeting key transitional phases. The second aim was the development of an interactive model environment that promotes interactions between basic and applied researchers and prevention practitioners and facilitates translation and integration of knowledge between etiologic research and prevention programming.

Two inner city public high schools serving largely minority populations participated in the study. School A consisted of 157 ninth-grade students from a low-income (70% free or reduced-price lunch) mid-Atlantic urban high school. Students who were scheduled to receive physical education during first period were assigned to a no-program control group

[1] Transdisciplinary Prevention Research Center Grant P20 DA017552.

TABLE 12.1

Program Modules Delivered to Address Protective–Risk Factors

Week/session	Factors addressed
1	SA, SC
2	SA, PA, SC
3	SA, PA, SC
4	SA, AO, DM, PS
5	SA, PA, SC
6	SA, PA, SC
7	SA, PA, SC
8	SA, SC, CS, EX
9	SS
10	SA, PS
11	SC, CS, DM
12	SC, CS, EX, DM
13	AO, SC, CS, EX, DM
14	SA, PA, SC
15	AO, SM, SC, CS, DM, GS
16	SC, CS, DM
17	AO, SC, CS, EX, SS, DM
18	AO, CS, EX, PS
19	PG
20	SC, CS, DM
21	SA
22	SA, SC, PS
23	SC, CS, DM
24	SC, CS, DM
25	SA, AO, PA, SC, CS, DM
26	SA, EX
27	SA, PA, SC, CS, EX, AH, DM, PG
28	SA, PA, SC, CS, EX, AH, DM, PG
29	SA, PS
30	SA, PS
31	SA, PA, SC, PG
32	SA
33	SA, SC, PS
34	SA, SC

Note. SA = school attachment (sense of belonging–school bonding); SC = social competence (competence in interpersonal relationships); PA = peer acceptance (understanding and tolerance of differences); AO = achievement orientation–motivation (academic self-concept, value of education, plans to stay in school); DM = decision making; PS = involvement in prosocial–extracurricular activities; CS = coping skills; EX = expectancies (to the consequences of negative behaviors); SS = sensation seeking and impulsivity; GS = goal-setting strategies; AH = anger–hostility management; SM = stress management; PG = peer group (behaviors of friends and attitude toward friends' behaviors).

($n = 60$), and freshmen students who were scheduled to receive physical education during seventh period ($n = 97$) were assigned to the program treatment group. There were slightly more female (54%) than male (46%) students in the study, and the majority of the participants were Latino–Hispanic (47%) and African American (40%). At the beginning of their freshman year, 157 students completed the baseline assessment, and 129 completed the posttest at the end of the school year.

School B consisted of 269 ninth-grade students (136 male and 133 female) from a low-income (ranked by the Brookings Institute as one of the top 100 most economically depressed localities in the United States), mid-Atlantic, urban high school. The total high school enrollment of ninth-through-12th-grade students was approximately 1,440. The majority of the participants in this high school were Hispanic–Latino (92%). The school committed three teachers to serve as program instructors, also known as faculty advisors, and designated 14 senior students to be trained as peer leaders. This allowed for a total of seven program groupings (two peer leaders conducting each group), with 12 to 14 first-year students included per group. Incoming ninth-grade students were randomly assigned to the program group ($n = 94$). The remaining 175 students were designated as part of the control group. There were approximately equal proportions of females and males in the program and control groups. A total of 269 students completed assessments at the beginning of their freshman year and before programming, 253 students completed the survey at the end of their freshman year, 200 completed the third at follow-up, and 168 students completed the assessment at the end of junior year.

PROGRAM IMPLEMENTATION

Development of Stakeholder Team

Before program implementation, a group of school stakeholders were assembled in each school to prepare and plan. Stakeholders included the principal, the vice principal responsible for student scheduling, other administrators, and faculty representatives.

Selection of Faculty Advisors

The stakeholder team from both School A and School B selected three teachers from the faculty of the school to become faculty advisors. The stakeholder team sought to identify three teachers who each exhibited certain characteristics of commitment and ability. The selected faculty members from each school participated in an intensive 11-day training regimen before program start-up. Training focused on the process for recruiting and selecting students to become peer leaders and planning and preparing for program implementation.

Selection of Peer Leaders

The faculty advisors team taught a daily year-long leadership course in which 16 students from School A and 14 students from School B who were in their senior year of high school were trained to become peer leaders for freshmen. Peer leaders were chosen based on various leadership qualities and the degree to which they were on track to graduate. Students who were selected to become peer leaders earned course credit toward their graduation requirements for their participation in the program. During the daily leadership course, peer leaders learned to deliver the outreach sessions and earned a grade based on mastery of leadership skills, role-modeling behaviors, class participation, and self-assessments.

Delivering Program Activities During Freshman Year

Each week throughout the school year, three class sessions of the daily leadership course for peer leaders were used as interactive practice sessions, the fourth class period was used by the peer leaders to conduct the outreach sessions with freshmen, and the final class was used to debrief the outreach session that had been conducted with the freshmen on the previous day. In the 40-minute freshman outreach sessions that took place once per week during the ninth grade, each of the two-person teams of peer leaders facilitated activities for a group of 12 to 14 freshmen. Of the 34 manual-based sessions, 24 outreach sessions were delivered over the course of the year. Truncated programming was primarily because of school holidays and alternative programs, including assemblies and state-mandated proficiency testing.

Program Activities During Sophomore Year

During the following school year in School B only, three 2.5-hour booster sessions were conducted with the sophomore students who participated in the program as freshmen. Booster sessions were designed to reinforce program skills.

Monitoring Dosage and Implementation Fidelity

To provide support to faculty advisors and to help ensure implementation fidelity, faculty advisors received on-site technical assistance and consultation from the program developers. Developers observed advisors while they team-taught the daily leadership course and provided specific feedback to the advisors about strengths and areas in need of improvement. Program developers monitored the peer leaders conducting outreach sessions and coached the faculty advisors on how to provide effective feedback on the peer leaders' performance as leaders and facilitators. Rating scales, which assessed teaching effectiveness, were completed during all technical assistance visits.

Observers completed rating scales to capture the degree to which the faculty advisors and peer leaders were implementing the program with fidelity and high-quality instruction. Analyses of fidelity data indicated that ratings of the overall effectiveness of the faculty advisors were *excellent* or *good* in 87% (13 of 15) of the observations. Observer ratings of the overall effectiveness of the peer leaders in conducting the outreach sessions indicated that 89% of the observed sessions were rated as satisfactory or above (i.e., comported with the instructional materials supporting high-program fidelity).

Data Collection

All study participants completed a baseline self-report survey during the orientation day in small group administrations at the beginning of ninth grade. Students were instructed that the purpose of the survey was to learn about their opinions and experiences to improve curriculum. The survey administration was completed with written answers and overseen by study staff with human subject certifications and institutional research board approval. To maximize the accuracy of student reports and to assure confidentiality, we assigned students unique identifiers, and personal identification was not requested. The survey took between 40 and 80 min to complete. Surveys were translated into Spanish and were available if necessary along with the assistance of bilingual survey administrators. In addition, school records provided additional information on attendance, grades, and disciplinary referrals.

Survey Measures

The survey instrument was composed of a battery of questions assessing students' behaviors and attitudes. The items collected were those believed to be important for determining risk for a variety of school problems, including substance use and abuse. Questionnaire items included nonmalleable demographic variables including gender and race but also putative risk (and protective) factors hypothesized as mediators of substance use, including discipline and absentee history, personality measures such as sensation seeking, academic achievement, motivation, decision making, goal setting, and attitudes toward school and peer groups (see Table 12.2 for a sampling of key measures).

SUMMARY OF RESULTS

In our study of School A (Johnson, Holt, Bry, & Powell, 2008), we found several statistically significant positive program effects. Given the relatively small sample size of a pilot program and findings that show risk status can serve as a moderating factor of program effectiveness, we examined participant outcomes as a function of an index of baseline grades and days absent from school. Using the criteria of a grade point average below 70 or absences (range = 0–16) in excess of eight for the first marking period as a baseline measure of school performance risk, the freshmen receiving no program were categorized as either low-risk controls ($n = 39$) or high-risk controls ($n = 21$), whereas those who were receiving the program were likewise categorized as either low-risk participants ($n = 54$) or high-risk participants ($n = 43$).

There was also evidence that the program significantly increased students' ability to resist peer pressure among students who were at high academic risk at the beginning of the school year. A positive trend was also observed toward the program having a dampening effect on tolerance for friends' substance use among those same high-risk students, compared with high-risk control students. In addition, the program exhibited a preventive effect on school-related misconduct and discipline referrals among the high-risk PGC students. Finally, analysis of School A revealed that program students increased their level of school bonding and the same students gained self-assertiveness, which in turn resulted in less intention to use alcohol compared to the control group.

Results of analyses on data obtained from School B showed that the proportion of program participants who had not used alcohol by the 1-year follow-up was significantly higher than control group students, who in comparison were more likely to continue their alcohol use (Johnson, Pandina, & Bry, 2008). In examining the proportions of students surveyed at freshman and junior years, we found that among both the program group and the control group students approximately one in 10 students reported that they started using alcohol over the course of the past 3 years. However, one third of the program students, compared with one fifth of the control students, reported that they had stopped using alcohol over the 3-year period. In another analysis, we found that treated students were less likely to engage in fighting, have greater abilities to seek out help to solve a problem, and more likely to use cognitive coping skills than students in the control group.

At the 2-year follow-up in School B, experimentally treated students exhibited higher levels of competence than their control counterparts and were more likely to have refrained from alcohol use in the past year. Competence skills include those that are both social (resist peer influences, ability to make friends, ability to self express, ability to solicit help from adults) and personal (goal setting, decision making, use of thoughtful and positive coping methods). In addition, program students with improved competency did not exhibit the same severe increase in absenteeism or decrease in academic performance over time as their control counterparts (Johnson,

TABLE 12.2

Description of Measures

Behavioral measures	
Measure	**Metric**
Cigarette use	Not used–used
Intent to use cigarettes	Not likely–somewhat likely–very likely
Alcohol use	Not used–used
Intent to use alcohol	Not likely–somewhat likely–very likely
Marijuana use	Not used–used
Intent to use marijuana	Not likely–somewhat likely–very likely
Cut class	Never—1–2 times—>2 times
Cut school	Never—1–2 times—>2 times
Late for class	Never—1–2 times—>2 times
Sent out of class	Never—1–2 times—>2 times
School warnings	Never—1–2 times—>2 times
Fighting	Never—1–2 times—>2 times
In-school suspension	Never—1–2 times—>2 times
Out-of-school suspension	Never—1–2 times—>2 times

Psychosocial measures			
Measure	**No. of items**	α	**Principal source**
Academic self-efficacy[a]	7	.83	Bandura, 1990
Expressive self-efficacy[a]	3	.67	Bandura, 1990
Help seeking[a]	4	.69	Bandura, 1990
Refusal skills[a]	6	.89	Bandura, 1990
Social competence[a]	6	.63	McNeal & Hansen, 1999
Goal setting[b]	5	.74	McNeal & Hansen, 1999
Decision making[b]	3	.76	McNeal & Hansen, 1999
Negative coping styles[b]	5	.55	Pandina, Labouvie, & White, 1984
Problem solving[b]	8	.84	Pandina, Labouvie, & White, 1984
Quality of relationship with caregiver[b]	3	.78	Paulson, Hill, & Holmbeck, 1991
Academic motivation[a]	4	.52	Vallerand et al., 1993
School bonding[a]	13	.82	Goodenow, 1993
School-related positive attitudes and behaviors[b]	5	.82	Libbey, 2004
School-related negative attitudes and behaviors[b]	7	.75	Libbey, 2004
Classmate acceptance[a]	6	.79	Bowen & Richman, 1997
Time spent in prosocial activities[a]	8	.74	Borden, Donnerymeyer, & Scheer, 2001
Peer deviance[b]	3	.82	Pandina, Labouvie, & White, 1984
Tolerance of peer deviance[b]	8	.94	Pandina, Labouvie, & White, 1984
Sensation seeking[b]	9	.80	Schafer, Blanchard, & Fals-Stewart, 1994

[a]Scores ranging from 1 to 4. [b]Scores ranging from 1 to 5.

Mun, & Pandina, 2008). It appeared that the booster sessions provided to program students during sophomore year were also helpful in increasing the level of help-seeking behavior and use of cognitive coping methods (problem solving) to deal with age-appropriate transitions.

Finally, analyses showed that the PGC program can effectively improve graduation rates among Latino males, especially those identified at-risk for school dropout before entering ninth grade (Johnson, Simon, & Mun, 2014). To determine whether the program had a favorable effect for students who vary in their baseline risk for school dropout, we calculated a score using a logistic regression analysis with graduation status as the binary outcome (graduated–not graduated) and 35 participant characteristics at baseline as predictors. The results of this analysis provided a single summary score (range = .05–.98) that estimates the probability of graduation for each participant. This level of higher graduation probability represented approximately 70% of the sample and was believed to reflect the area's typical graduation rate. The remaining 30% were deemed at greatest risk for dropout based on the scalar equivalent of their baseline measures. Although fewer than half of the Latino males who enter ninth grade will graduate from high school nationwide (Green & Winters, 2006), male students participating in PGC had a graduation rate of 81%. Males who exhibited a low probability for graduating but then became part of the PGC program had a better chance of graduating (60%) compared with their control group counterparts (30%). Among those students who entered ninth grade with a high probability of graduating, students in the PGC treatment group had a better chance of graduating. Approximately nine out of 10 of the students assigned to the treatment group who started ninth grade exhibiting a low-baseline risk score completed high school within 4 years, compared with only 75% of the low-baseline risk control group students. These findings suggest that there are distinct benefits to providing high school transition support to all incoming ninth-grade students, not just those who are seemingly most at risk for dropping out of school.

LESSONS LEARNED

Throughout the implementation and research process, important findings have emerged related to lessons learned. In this section, we summarize the most salient observations obtained from the investigation, both in terms of the ingredients required for successful execution of the intervention and intended changes in outcomes and mediators on the part of freshmen participants.

Program Implementation Issues

Program start-up. Several preimplementation tasks must be completed to ensure successful program completion, including selecting appropriate faculty advisors, scheduling the weekly freshman outreach sessions, recruiting, selecting and scheduling peer leaders for the daily leadership course, identifying appropriate physical space in the building for the multiple groups, and obtaining schoolwide faculty buy-in for the program. Convening a committed team of stakeholders to focus on ensuring these tasks are successfully completed is essential.

Selecting faculty advisors and peer leaders. Advisors who are enthusiastic and committed to the program's goals and are willing to attend all program training and to implement the program with fidelity to the intervention model are necessary to support the integration of a prevention program into a school. Peer leaders need to be enthusiastic and credible ambassadors for the program and exhibit positive role-modeling characteristics. Careful attention to widely publicizing the opportunity to become a peer leader to the pool of eligible students is likely to lead to a group of peer leaders who are representative of the larger student body.

Using data to inform modifications. Data collected from key program constituents are essential to inform revisions and adaptations. Data collected through pre- and postprogram surveys, student feedback forms, school records, fidelity observations, advisor interviews, and student focus groups were used to examine each module in the outreach curriculum.

Finding Program Effects

Sample size and individual randomization. Our investigation is one of many evaluations of school-based programs that have shown that prevention curricula produced favorable effects on mediators of substance use but displayed limited effects in changes in consumption measures themselves (Gandhi, Murphy-Graham, Petrosino, Schwartz Chrismer, & Weiss, 2007). This is especially true of longitudinal studies that encompass several years of follow-up postprogram delivery. The reasons for lack of large effect sizes can be numerous and varied. In our study, we did not randomize intact units such as schools or school districts to experimental treatment condition; instead, we randomized individual subjects within a given school. We wished to avoid the problem of students naturally sharing common characteristics within classrooms while being assigned to a treatment or control condition. Although we believe the contagion effect of peer leadership qualities and norms can be an advantage to the school culture at large, such contamination within individuals within the school may have resulted in posttest differences in treated versus control subjects being masked or diluted.

Data collection. The PGC program was evaluated by independent investigators, and funding was obtained for 3 years of follow-up at School B. Data regarding graduation status were obtained for study subjects in School B, but additional post–high school follow-up has not been done. Researchers have opined about the lack of long-term follow-up of subjects who have participated in school-based drug prevention programs (Gandhi et al., 2007). However, finding (i.e., tracking) and surveying subjects post high school is a labor intensive and expensive undertaking. It is also possible that the self-report of use of alcohol and marijuana may have been underreported by many of our minority students. This issue of the underreporting of illegal behaviors (and the race specific nature of these findings) has been debated in the literature as far back as the 1990s (Bauman & Ennett, 1994; Shillington & Clapp, 2000; Wallace & Bachman, 1993). This suggests the possible utility of using information from peer social network analysis to validate substance use rates and changes over time, a daunting but potentially valuable task.

Data analysis. In our examination of substance use outcome measures, we chose not to use a large number of variables so as to not run the risk of capitalizing on chance by conducting scores of analyses. The most robust findings in this investigation were for several alcohol use outcome measures as well as for important mediators, especially when we controlled for baseline at-risk status among the study participants. The identification of students exhibiting probability of failure in important skill sets appeared to us to be critical in tailoring additional programming. It was these students who gained the most by participation in the program.

CONCLUDING COMMENTS

The importance of peer influences on substance use during adolescence has been studied widely over the past several decades (Crosnoe, Muller, & Frank, 2004). More recent research findings have demonstrated that social learning variables have an effect on both frequency of alcohol use and abuse for adolescents (Preston & Goodfellow, 2006) and that the unique groups of best friendships, peer cliques, and social crowds differentially predict adolescent substance use (Hussong, 2002). McIntosh, MacDonald, and McKeganey (2006) argued that normative definitions regarding drug use change from that of a risk-taking behavior to one of drug use as a recreational activity.

We recognize the importance of considering the differential impact of peers on use behaviors at various development stages. For example, distinctions should be made about the influence of peers at the time of initiation when use behavior is relatively novel and serves in part as an *entrance* requirement to a group, versus the *maintenance* stage, when behavior becomes more related to an individual's identity or their psychological composition. If an intervention is aimed at eliminating or limiting use in an individual or a peer cluster, where use behavior is well established, programs aimed at use initiation would be expected to have limited potential (see Chapter 9, this volume). These issues of transitions have obvious implications for evaluators who are attempting to determine accurately the impact of planned interventions.

We are in agreement with, and our program experience supports, the views of Stigler et al. (2011), who posited eight critical elements for effective school-based programs. We believe that the PGC program has adhered to each one of them. The program is theory driven, addresses social norms, builds skills, uses interactive teaching approaches, integrates community and family elements into the program (stakeholders meet regularly to plan, troubleshoot, and ensure the sustainability of the initiative), spans multiple sessions and years throughout school (it is integrated into the school day, and each pair of peer leaders meets with the same group of freshmen weekly throughout the entire ninth-grade year; sophomore year booster sessions reinforce the learning from freshman activities), adequately supports and trains teachers (faculty members participate in an 11-day train-the-trainer course over a 1.5-year period), contains culturally and developmentally appropriate materials (PGC is a structured, manual-based curriculum), and especially important for PGC is that it uses peer leaders. Research indicates that peers play a critical role in the lives of adolescents, serving as support for one another, formal and informal models of behaviors, and trusted sources of information (Maxwell, 2002; Whitaker & Miller, 2000). Peer-mentoring programs positively affect students' connectedness to school and parents and improve social skills, self-esteem, and academic achievement, and both mentors and mentees benefit from participation in the programs (U.S. Department of Education Mentoring Resource Center, 2005). The contagion of positive peer leadership can change the culture of a school.

All in all, our investigations have added to the mounting body of evidence suggesting that preventive programming for urban high school students may be most effective when it is targeted, tailored, and integrated across risk levels. Of particular note is that the variables observed to have the most robust effects reflected the best practices of the PGC program.

We believe that if important mediators of substance use display a positive change after program participation, but survey results can find no significant change in self-reported use behaviors, it is not advisable to "throw out the baby with the bathwater." As several chapters in this handbook make patently clear, changes in important mediators, including school bonding, competence and resistance skills, increased attendance and decreased disciplinary problems among high school students, have been linked to changes in the trajectories of long-term alcohol and other drug use, as well as to changes in academic achievement and other vital outcomes. In our study, the PGC program was instrumental in improving the probability of graduating high school, which in itself is a factor in substance use reduction.

Limited large effect sizes of many of the current prevention programs have been discussed at length (Gandhi et al., 2007; Gorman, 1995) and raise the question as to whether any school-based drug prevention program alone will substantially reduce the number of youth who experiment with substances. Over a decade ago, Gottfredson (1997) advocated for embedding prevention programs within more comprehensive programs. Schools must embrace the need for wraparound services, which are expensive, and resources are scarce. A broader scale community-wide effort is needed to assemble the resources of numerous stakeholders and agencies to tackle our nation's substance abuse problems.

In spite of decades of theory-driven and evidence-based programs submitted to rigorous experimental examination, the research and prevention communities have uncovered no magic bullets or secret weapons to eradicate or dramatically reduce the many potentially damaging outcomes that are evidenced among the youth of this country. It would be a mistake to believe, however, that a number of otherwise vulnerable youth have not positively benefited from the existing programs. It is likely that they have benefited but that technology is not yet sophisticated enough to detect the favorable program effects. A final point is the need to understand our current generation of young people as they attempt to navigate the complexity of our culture and the need to incorporate the reality of their everyday experiences into our future programs not only for navigating substance abuse but also for navigating life in 21st-century America.

References

Akos, P., & Galassi, J. P. (2004). Middle and high school transitions as viewed by students, parents, and teachers. *Professional School Counseling, 7*, 213–221.

Background on Social and Emotional Learning. (SEL). (2007). *CASEL briefs*. Retrieved from http://casel.org/wp-content/uploads/SELCASELbackground.pdf

Bandura, A. (1990). *Multidimensional scales of perceived academic efficacy.* Stanford, CA: Stanford University.

Bauman, K. E., & Ennett, S. E. (1994). Tobacco use by Black and White adolescents: The validity of self-reports. *American Journal of Public Health, 84*, 394–398. doi:10.2105/AJPH.84.3.394

Blum, R. (2005). School connectedness: Improving students' lives. *Military Child Initiative*, 1–18.

Borden, L. M., Donnerymeyer, J. F., & Scheer, S. D. (2001). The influence of extra-curricular activities and peer influence on substance use. *Adolescent & Family Health, 2*, 12–19.

Botvin, G. J., Baker, E., Renick, N. L., Fiazzola, A. D., & Botvin, E. M. (1984). A cognitive-behavioral approach to substance use prevention. *Addictive Behaviors, 9*, 137–147. doi:10.1016/0306-4603(84)90051-0

Bowen, G. L., & Richman, J. M. (1997). *The school success profile.* Chapel Hill: University of North Carolina.

Brown, B. (2004). Adolescents' relationships with peers. In R. M. Lerner & L. Steinberg (Eds.), *Handbook of adolescent psychology* (pp. 363–394). Hoboken, NJ: Wiley.

Campbell, R., Starkey, F., Holliday, J., Audrey, S., Bloor, M., Parry-Langdon, N., & Moore, L. (2008). An informal school-based peer-led intervention for smoking prevention in adolescence (ASSIST): A cluster randomized trial. *The Lancet, 371*, 1595–1602. doi:10.1016/S0140-6736(08)60692-3

Capone, T., McLaughlin, J. H., & Smith, F. (1973). Peer group leadership program in drug abuse prevention, 1970-1971 academic year. *Journal of Drug Education, 3*, 201–245. doi:10.2190/9DFA-RM0L-CPX1-2NX3

Cohen, J., & Smerdon, B. (2009). Tightening the dropout tourniquet: Easing the transition from middle to high school. *Preventing School Failure, 53*, 177–184. doi:10.3200/PSFL.53.3.177-184

Cooper, G. D., Clements, P. T., & Holt, K. (2011). A review and application of suicide prevention programs in high school settings. *Issues in Mental Health Nursing, 32*, 696–702. doi:10.3109/01612840.2011.597911

Crosnoe, R., Muller, C., & Frank, K. (2004). Peer context and the consequences of adolescent drinking. *Social Problems, 51*, 288–304. doi:10.1525/sp.2004.51.2.288

Cuijpers, P. (2002). Peer-led and adult-led school drug prevention: A meta-analytic comparison. *Journal of Drug Education, 32*, 107–119. doi:10.2190/LPN9-KBDC-HPVB-JPTM

Dedmond, R. (2006). Freshman transition programs: Long-term and comprehensive. *Principal's Research Review, 1*, 1–8.

DeJong, W., & Langford, L. M. (2002). A typology for campus-based alcohol prevention: Moving toward environmental management strategies. *Journal of Studies on Alcohol. Supplement, 14*, 140–147.

Dishion, T. J., McCord, J., & Poulin, F. (1999). When interventions harm: Peer groups and problem behavior. *American Psychologist, 54*, 755–764. doi:10.1037/0003-066X.54.9.755

Ennett, S. T., Ringwalt, C. L., Thorne, J., Rohrbach, L. A., Vincus, A., Simons-Rudolph, A., & Jones, S. (2003). A comparison of current practice in school-based substance use prevention programs with meta-analysis findings. *Prevention Science, 4*, 1–14. doi:10.1023/A:1021777109369

Epstein, J. A., Griffin, K. W., & Botvin, G. (2002). Positive impact of competence skills and psychological wellness in protecting inner city adolescents from alcohol use. *Prevention Science, 3*, 95–104. doi:10.1023/A:1015479216401

Faggiano, F., Vigna-Taglianti, F. D., Versino, E., Zambon, A., Borraccino, A., & Lemma, P. (2008). School-based prevention for illicit drugs use: A systematic review. *Preventive Medicine, 46*, 385–396. doi:10.1016/j.ypmed.2007.11.012

Farrington, D. P., & Ttofi, M. M. (2009). School-based programs to reduce bullying and victimization. *Campbell Systematic Reviews*, 6.

Feller, R. W. (2003). Aligning school counseling, the changing workplace, and career development assumptions. *Professional School Counseling, 6*, 262–271.

Gandhi, A. G., Murphy-Graham, E., Petrosino, A., Schwartz Chrismer, S., & Weiss, C. (2007). The devil is in the details: Examining the evidence for "proven" school-based drug abuse prevention programs. *Evaluation Review, 31*, 43–74. doi:10.1177/0193841X06287188

Garringer, M., & MacRae, P. (2008). Building effective peer mentoring programs in schools: An introductory guide. *The Mentoring Resource Center.* Retrieved from http://educationnorthwest.org/webfm_send/169

Ghosh-Dastidar, B., Longshore, D. L., Ellickson, P. L., & McCaffrey, D. F. (2004). Modifying pro-drug risk factors in adolescents: Results from Project ALERT. *Health Education & Behavior, 31*, 318–334. doi:10.1177/1090198104263333

Goodenow, C. (1993). Classroom belonging among early adolescent students: Relationships to motivation and achievement. *The Journal of Early Adolescence, 13*, 21–43. doi:10.1177/0272431693013001002

Gorman, D. M. (1995). On the difference between statistical and practical significance in school based drug abuse prevention. *Drugs: Education, Prevention, and Policy, 2*, 275–283.

Gottfredson, D. C. (1997). School-based crime prevention. In L. W. Sherman et al. (Eds.), *Preventing crime: What works, what doesn't, what's promising: A report to the United States Congress* (pp. 5-1–5-14). Washington, DC: U.S. Department of Justice Office of Justice Programs.

Green, J. P., & Winters, M. A. (2006). Leaving boys behind: Public high school graduation rates. *Civic Report, 48*, 1–10.

Gregoric, C., & Owens, L. (2008). The effectiveness of peer support leadership training in a south Australian school. *International Journal of Adolescence and Youth, 14*, 93–112. doi:10.1080/02673843.2008.9747997

Griffin, K. W., Botvin, G. J., & Nichols, T. R. (2006). Effects of a school-based drug abuse prevention program for adolescents on HIV risk behavior in young adulthood. *Prevention Science, 7*, 103–112. doi:10.1007/s11121-006-0025-6

Hussong, A. (2002). Differentiating peer contexts and risk for adolescent substance use. *Journal of Youth and Adolescence, 31*, 207–220. doi:10.1023/A:1015085203097

Johnson, V., Pandina, R. J., & Bry, B. (2008). Changes in social norms, harm perception and reasons for alcohol use among high school students participating in a peer-led prevention program. *Alcoholism: Clinical and Experimental Research, 32*, 241A (923).

Johnson, V. L., Holt, L. J., Bry, B. H., & Powell, S. R. (2008). Effects of an integrated prevention program on urban youth transitioning into high school. *Journal of Applied School Psychology, 24*, 225–246. doi:10.1080/15377900802089999

Johnson, V. L., Mun, E. Y., & Pandina, R. J. (2008, March). *A longitudinal evaluation of a peer-led transition program in a predominately Latino high school.* Paper presented at the Society for Research on Adolescence annual meeting, Chicago, IL.

Johnson, V. L., Simon, P., & Mun, E. Y. (2014). A peer-led high school transition program increases graduation rates among Latino males. *Journal of Educational Research, 107*, 186–196. doi:10.1080/00220671.2013.788991

Johnston, L. D., O'Malley, P. M., Bachman, J. G., & Schulenberg, J. E. (2012). *Monitoring the Future National Survey Results on Drug Use, 1975-2011: Vol. I, Secondary school students.* Ann Arbor, MI: Inter-university Consortium for Political and Social Research.

Kam, C.-M., Greenberg, M. T., & Walls, C. T. (2003). Examining the role of implementation quality in school based prevention using the PATHS curriculum. *Prevention Science, 4*, 55–63. doi:10.1023/A:1021786811186

Kennelly, L., & Monrad, M. (2007). *Easing the transition to high school: Research and best practices designed to support high school learning.* Retrieved from http://www.betterhighschools.org/docs/NHSC_TransitionsReport.pdf

Klem, A. M., & Connell, J. P. (2004). Relationships matter: Linking teacher support to student engagement and achievement. *Journal of School Health, 74*, 262–273. doi:10.1111/j.1746-1561.2004.tb08283.x

Komro, K. A., Perry, C. L., Williams, C. L., Stigler, M. H., Farbakhsh, K., & Veblen-Mortenson, S. (2001). How did Project Northland reduce alcohol use among adolescents? Analysis of mediating variables. *Health Education Research, 16*, 59–70. doi:10.1093/her/16.1.59

Kumar, R., O'Malley, P. M., Johnston, L. D., Schulenberg, J. E., & Bachman, J. G. (2002). Effects of school level norms on student substance use. *Prevention Science, 3*, 105–124. doi:10.1023/A:1015431300471

Lawler, J. M. (1971). Peer group approach to drug education. *Journal of Drug Education, 1*, 63–76. doi:10.2190/PD4T-92YQ-XYNL-JLKA

Libbey, H. P. (2004). Measuring student relationship to school: Attachment, bonding, connectedness and engagement. *Journal of School Health, 74*, 274–283. doi:10.1111/j.1746-1561.2004.tb08284.x

Maxwell, K. A. (2002). Friends: The role of peer influence across adolescent risk behaviors. *Journal of Youth and Adolescence, 31*, 267–277. doi:10.1023/A:1015493316865

McIntosh, J., MacDonald, F., & McKeganey, N. (2006). Why do children experiment with illegal drugs? The declining role of peer pressure with increasing age. *Addiction Research & Theory, 14*, 275–287. doi:10.1080/16066350500330465

McNeal, R. B., & Hansen, W. B. (1999). Developmental patterns associated with the onset of drug use: Changes in postulated mediators during adolescence. *Journal of Drug Issues, 29*, 381–400.

Mizelle, N. B., & Irvin, J. L. (2000). Transition from middle school into high school. *Middle School Journal, 31*, 57–61.

National Health Promotion Associates. (2014). *LifeSkills training*. White Plains, NY: Author. Retrieved from http://www.lifeskillstraining.com

Pandina, R. J., Labouvie, E. W., & White, H. R. (1984). Potential contributions of the life span developmental approach to the study of adolescent alcohol and drug use: The Rutgers Health and Human Development Project, a working model. *Journal of Drug Issues, 14*, 253–268.

Paulson, S. E., Hill, J. P., & Holmbeck, G. N. (1991). Distinguishing between perceived closeness and warmth in families of seventh-grade boys and girls. *The Journal of Early Adolescence, 11*, 276–293. doi:10.1177/0272431691112007

Pellerin, L. A. (2005). Student disengagement and the socialization styles of high schools. *Social Forces, 84*, 1159–1179. doi:10.1353/sof.2006.0027

Perry, C. L., Williams, C. L., Komro, K. A., Veblen-Mortenson, S., Stigler, M. H., Munson, K. A., . . . Forster, J. L. (2002). Project Northland: Long-term outcomes of community action to reduce adolescent alcohol use. *Health Education Research, 17*, 117–132. doi:10.1093/her/17.1.117

Preston, P., & Goodfellow, M. (2006). Cohort comparisons: Social learning explanations for alcohol use among adolescents and older adults. *Addictive Behaviors, 31*, 2268–2283. doi:10.1016/j.addbeh.2006.03.005

Ringwalt, C., Hanley, S., Vincus, A. A., Ennett, S. T., Rohrbach, L. A., & Bowling, J. M. (2008). The prevalence of effective substance use prevention curricula in the nation's high schools. *The Journal of Primary Prevention, 29*, 479–488. doi:10.1007/s10935-008-0158-4

Schafer, J., Blanchard, L., & Fals-Stewart, W. (1994). Drug use and risky sexual behavior. *Psychology of Addictive Behaviors, 8*, 3–7. doi:10.1037/0893-164X.8.1.3

Shillington, A. M., & Clapp, J. D. (2000). Self-report stability of adolescent substance use: Are there differences for gender, ethnicity and age? *Drug and Alcohol Dependence, 60*, 19–27. doi:10.1016/S0376-8716(99)00137-4

Smart, R. G., Bennett, C., & Fejer, D. (1976). A controlled study of the peer group approach to drug education. *Journal of Drug Education, 6*, 305–311. doi:10.2190/WA9A-APT7-X3BY-JCEY

Smith, J. S. (2006). *Research summary: Transition from middle school to high school*. Retrieved from http://www.nmsa.org/research/ResearchSummaries/TransitionfromMStoHS/tabid/1087

Stigler, M. H., Neusel, E., & Perry, C. L. (2011). School-based programs to prevent and reduce alcohol use among youth. *Alcohol Research & Health, 34*, 157–162.

Tobler, N. S. (1986). Meta-analysis of 143 adolescent drug prevention programs: Quantitative outcome results of program participants compared to a control or comparison group. *Journal of Drug Issues, 16*, 537–567.

Tobler, N. S., & Stratton, H. H. (1997). Effectiveness of school-based drug prevention programs: A meta-analysis of the research. *The Journal of Primary Prevention, 18*, 71–128. doi:10.1023/A:1024630205999

U.S. Department of Education Mentoring Resource Center, Office of Safe and Drug-Free Schools. (2005). *Mentoring Fact Sheet* (No. 7). Folsom, CA: Author.

U.S. Office of the Surgeon General. (2006). *Surgeon General's call to action to prevent underage drinking*. Washington, DC: Author.

Valente, T. W., Ritt-Olson, A., Stacy, A., Unger, J. B., Okamoto, J., & Sussman, S. (2007). Peer acceleration: Effects of a social network tailored substance abuse prevention program among high-risk adolescents. *Addiction, 102*, 1804–1815. doi:10.1111/j.1360-0443.2007.01992.x

Vallerand, R. J., Pelletier, L. G., Blais, M. R., Brière, N. M., Sénécal, C., & Vallières, E. F. (1993). On the assessment of intrinsic, extrinsic, and amotivation in education: Evidence on the concurrent and construct validity of the Academic Motivation Scale. *Educational and Psychological Measurement, 53*, 159–172. doi:10.1177/0013164493053001018

Wallace, J. M., & Bachman, J. G. (1993). Validity of self reports in student based studies on minority populations: Issues and concerns. Drug abuse among minority youth: Methodological issues and recent research advances. *NIDA Monograph Series, 130*, 167–194.

Weiss, H. B., Little, P. M. D., & Bouffard, S. M. (2005). More than just being there: Balancing the participation equation. *New Directions for Youth Development, 2005*, 15–31. doi:10.1002/yd.105

Wheelock, A., & Miao, J. (2005). The ninth-grade bottleneck: An enrollment bulge in a transition year that demands careful attention and action. *School Administrator, 62*, 36–40.

Whitaker, D. J., & Miller, K. S. (2000). Parent-adolescent discussions about sex and condoms: Impact on peer influences of sexual risk behaviors. *Journal of Adolescent Research, 15*, 251–273. doi:10.1177/0743558400152004

Wilson, D. B., Gottfredson, D. C., & Najaka, S. S. (2001). School-based prevention problem behaviors: A meta-analysis. *Journal of*

Quantitative Criminology, 17, 247–272. doi:10.1023/A:1011050217296

Wyman, P. A., Brown, C. H., LoMurray, M., Schmeelk-Cone, K., Petrova, M., Yu, Q., & Wang, W. (2010). An outcome evaluation of the sources of strength suicide prevention program delivered by adolescent peer leaders in high schools. *American Journal of Public Health, 100*, 1653–1661. doi:10.2105/AJPH.2009.190025

Zavela, K. J. (2002). Developing effective school-based drug abuse prevention programs. *American Journal of Health Behavior, 26*, 252–265. doi:10.5993/AJHB.26.4.2

Zins, J. E., Weissberg, R. P., Wang, M. C., & Walberg, H. J. (Eds.). (2004). *Building academic success on social and emotional learning: What does the research say?* New York, NY: Teachers College Press.

Part V

FAMILY-BASED DRUG USE PREVENTION PROGRAMS

CHAPTER 13

A POPULATION APPROACH TO PARENTING AND FAMILY INTERVENTION

Ronald J. Prinz

The population approach to parenting and family intervention described in this chapter is useful for a number of goals, including the reduction of risk for youth substance abuse. Parental influence is pervasive in many areas of child development and well-being, including risk for adolescent substance abuse. Parenting practices during early childhood, child behavior problems emanating from parenting difficulties, and parenting gone awry in the form of child maltreatment all heighten risk for subsequent substance abuse. On the other hand, evidence-based parenting interventions that reduce problems during early childhood can mitigate that risk.

This chapter offers a rationale and key principles for the adoption of a public health strategy in the area of parenting intervention. An example of such an approach, the Triple P—Positive Parenting Program system, is described with respect to structure, conceptualization, and utility. This multilevel, multiple format strategy provides an evidence-driven exemplar for reaching large segments of the population. The large and growing evidence base for Triple P is summarized. Two population studies of Triple P are delineated, and cost–benefit considerations are briefly addressed. A public health approach to parenting has the potential to reduce family-based risk factors associated with subsequent substance abuse. By addressing multiple goals within the same intervention, the cost-efficiency of a population approach to parenting and family support such as Triple P makes such an effort viable.

INITIAL PREMISE

Parenting and family interventions are an important part of prevention efforts targeting youth substance abuse (Hawkins, Catalano, & Miller, 1992; Lochman & van den Steenhoven, 2002). Unlike other areas of substance abuse prevention (e.g., peer and school interventions), however, the points of intervention for parenting and family functioning can come many years before adolescence and substance-use onset.

PARENTING, CHILD DEVELOPMENT, SUBSTANCE ABUSE, AND PREVENTION

Parental influence is pervasive in many areas of child development (Biglan, Brennan, Foster, & Holder, 2004; Collins, Maccoby, Steinberg, Hetherington, & Bornstein, 2000; Farah et al., 2008; Jones & Prinz, 2005; Komro, Flay, & Biglan, 2011; Patterson, Reid, & Dishion, 1992). Parents affect key risk and protective factors that influence children's language and communication, emotion regulation, social skills and

The author of this chapter has served as a consultant to Triple P International and to the Centers for Disease Control and Prevention. The content of this chapter is solely the responsibility of the author and does not necessarily represent the official views of Triple P International or the Centers for Disease Control and Prevention.

http://dx.doi.org/10.1037/14550-014
Handbook of Adolescent Drug Use Prevention: Research, Intervention Strategies, and Practice, L. M. Scheier (Editor)

associated peer relationships, physical health and well-being, the development of sustained attention, problem-solving processes, school achievement, and modes of coping with adversity and life transitions.

Parenting and its impact on child development affect risk for youth substance abuse in multiple ways. Effective engagement and involvement by parents when children are young predict parental monitoring practices in early adolescence that mitigates risk for substance abuse (Racz & McMahon, 2011). Child behavior problems, which tend to be either the result of or exacerbated by parenting difficulties, contribute to risk for youth substance abuse (Hawkins et al., 1992).

Parenting exerts influence on development and adverse outcomes in other ways. For example, child maltreatment, which by definition is associated with parenting practices gone awry, is a powerful contributor to and predictor of factors linked to youth substance abuse. Until recently, child maltreatment research and youth substance abuse research have operated in separate orbits. There is now much greater recognition in the research and policy arenas that child maltreatment in all its forms contributes substantially to youth substance abuse. It is important also to note that risk from child maltreatment is not restricted to official child protective services (CPS) cases—particularly in light of evidence that child maltreatment actually occurs at a much higher rate than official records reflect (Theodore et al., 2005).

Child maltreatment is associated with subsequent affect-regulation difficulties and poor self-concept (Ialongo et al., 2006), depressive symptomatology in adolescence that contributes to youth substance abuse (Blumberg, 1981; Harkness & Lumley, 2008; Kazdin, Moser, Colbus, & Bell, 1985; Stone, 1993), mental health disorders in adolescence and adulthood (Afifi, Boman, Fleisher, & Sareen, 2009), and substance abuse in particular (Anda et al., 2006; Corso, Edwards, Fang, & Mercy, 2008; Dube et al., 2006). More generally, research has indicated that 95% of maltreated children experience demonstrable problems in middle childhood and early adolescence (Bolger & Patterson, 2003). It is becoming abundantly clear that, to be most effective, parenting interventions in early childhood must address both child maltreatment and parenting more broadly.

Evidence-based parenting interventions can help reduce or prevent mental, emotional, and behavioral problems in early childhood and promote children's readiness for school entry. And parenting and family interventions help reduce the risk for later adverse outcomes such as substance abuse, delinquency, academic difficulties and school dropout, and teen parenthood. At a population level, parenting and family support interventions have the potential to reduce the prevalence of child maltreatment. More generally, evidence-based parenting interventions reduce family-related risk factors and strengthen family-based protective factors (Barrett & Ollendick, 2004; Biglan et al., 2004; Donovan & Spence, 2000; Essau, 2003; Lochman & van den Steenhoven, 2002; Petrie, Bunn, & Byrne, 2007; Prinz, 2007; Prinz & Dumas, 2004; Prinz & Jones, 2003; Sutton, 2007).

TOWARD A PUBLIC HEALTH APPROACH

The widespread nature of child social, emotional, and behavioral problems as well as substance abuse and other adverse conditions in adolescence underscores the need for strategies that can cost-effectively reach large segments of the population. The ubiquitous role that parenting plays in the early risk for many of these problems provides a strong rationale for the adoption of a public health approach to parenting and family-based preventive intervention.

A public health strategy builds on several key facets and principles. An overarching goal is to reach large segments of the population. This is consistent with a central aim for any public health intervention: to reduce prevalence. Any plan for meeting these goals requires at least (a) enactment of the principle of minimal sufficiency, (b) a plan that optimizes program access and reach, and (c) an approach that engages several sectors of the community.

To begin with, an effective public health strategy draws on the principle of *minimal sufficiency*. Contrary to a clinical strategy that might apply substantial programming to each individual, family, or case, the principle of minimal sufficiency involves a more parsimonious approach. The notion is to apply just enough intervention to solve the problem at hand—without applying excessive and presumably unnecessary programming. This principle also builds on the premise that individuals in the population vary in how much intervention is needed to produce favorable preventive effects.

A public health strategy needs a plan that optimizes program access and satisfies population reach. In practice, this means that programming needs to be located in many settings involving professionals from a variety of disciplines across multiple service sectors. Rather than constrain a program to a single service sector, it makes more sense to engage multiple sectors including health care and public health, mental health, education, social services, juvenile justice, and nongovernmental organizations.

The Centers for Disease Control and Prevention (CDC; 1999) identified the top 10 greatest public health achievements in the United States during the 20th century. Included in the CDC's list are the recognition of tobacco as a major health hazard, improved motor vehicle safety, control of infectious diseases, vaccination, and family planning. The top 10 public health achievements share several strategies in common: viable ways to affect the entire population, combination of lower and higher intensity interventions, media components, and multipronged facets. Although many of these achievements involved behavioral changes by the public, noticeably absent from the CDC's list was a focus on strengthening parenting (including the reduction of problematic parenting practices). This is not because of a lack of interest on the CDC's part; on the contrary, the CDC is heavily engaged in the prevention of injury and violence, with a major emphasis on parenting and family strategies.

There are several reasons to take a public health approach to parenting and family intervention. From a philosophical perspective, such an approach builds toward a strong societal commitment to children. Parents vary in their preferences for delivery modalities and ways to access parenting support. A public health approach might be better able to meet parental preferences. Making parenting and family support normative and broadly accessible has the potential for reducing or at least sidestepping the issue of stigma that prevents some parents from seeking support. Finally, a public health approach to parenting and family intervention has the potential to create efficiencies by addressing several goals and outcome domains with the same core intervention. Community-wide, evidence-driven parenting intervention can contribute to the prevention of (a) child maltreatment; (b) early behavioral and emotional problems; (c) difficulties at school entry; and (d) subsequent adverse outcomes such as substance abuse, academic problems, school dropout, teen parenthood, and delinquency.

In their seminal report *Preventing Mental, Emotional and Behavioral Disorders Among Young People: Progress and Possibilities*, the Institute of Medicine and National Research Council (2009) endorsed a population health perspective and the importance of giving families easy access to evidence-based preventive interventions while minimizing stigma. Increasingly, there is evidence that a population approach to parenting and family support that aims to make such support commonplace and accessible in the community is gaining momentum.

AN EXAMPLE OF A PUBLIC HEALTH APPROACH TO PARENTING AND FAMILY SUPPORT

Developed by Matthew Sanders and colleagues at the University of Queensland, Triple P is an example of a broad strategy for parenting and family intervention through a multilevel system involving varying levels of intensity and a wide variety of delivery formats and modalities. Triple P is not a single program but a coordinated system of parenting interventions.

On occasion, Triple P has been inaccurately labeled as strictly a universal preventive intervention. Although it does include universal facets, Triple P might more aptly be described as building on a blended model of prevention. The tiered, multilevel nature of the program in conjunction with its variations produces blend of various components of universal, selected, and indicated interventions. It is fair to say that Triple P is intended to be a whole-of-population approach, with some components intended for universal application and other components intended for more targeted use.

In the Triple P lexicon, *level* refers to the degree of intervention intensity. There are five levels of intensity going from the lowest intensity level,

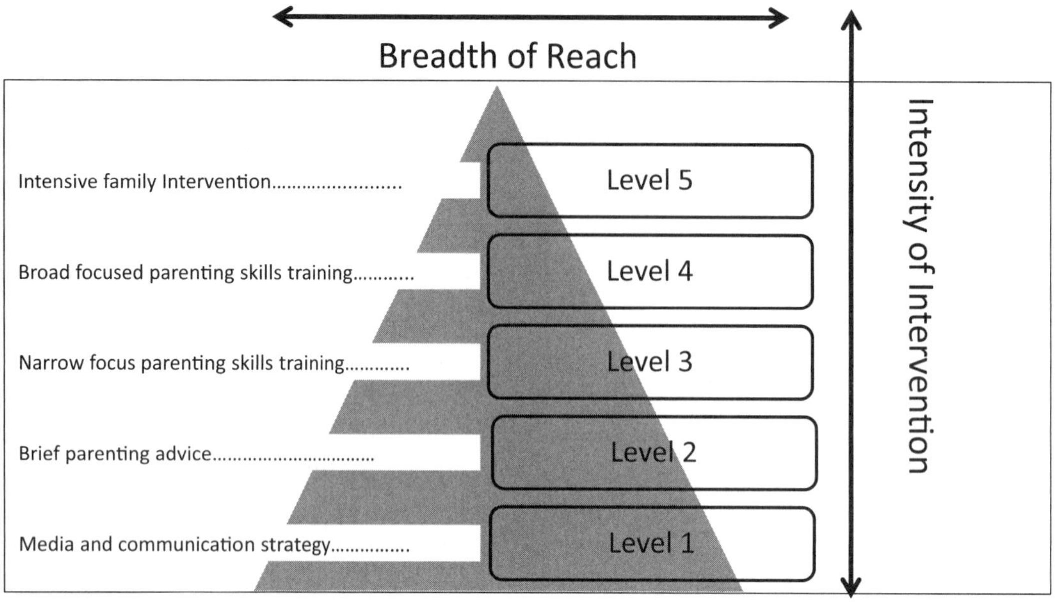

FIGURE 13.1. Schematic of the Triple P system of tiered levels of intervention.

with a broad reach, to the highest intensity level, with the narrowest reach (see Figure 13.1), as described in more detail below. *Format* refers to the delivery modality, such as individual consultation, group intervention, or self-directed program. *Variant* refers to a version of Triple P that is tailored to a specific need or segment of the population (e.g., parents with a child having a developmental disability or parents being treated through the CPS system).

Level 1 Triple P, sometimes referred to as Universal Triple P, pertains to coordinated media and communication strategies. These strategies serve several purposes: (a) normalizing and destigmatizing the process of seeking and participating in parenting support interventions, (b) empowering parents to solve child-related problems, (c) connecting parents with community resources and programs, and (d) validating positive parenting concepts with parents and professionals alike (Sanders & Prinz, 2008). Level 1 can also involve Triple P's Stay Positive communications strategy, which includes a website, brochures and flyers, posters, parent newspapers (with parenting tips), media and communication kits, production of radio spots, a television spot, and support resources for the media coordinators.

Level 2 Triple P is a brief parenting consultation, delivered either to individual parents in one to two brief contacts or to a large group of parents (parenting seminar). This level has utility for many parents seeking assistance for relatively minor, subclinical, and discrete child problem behaviors without engaging in more intensive levels of intervention.

Level 3 Triple P, a more extended version of Level 2, involves up to four contacts typically delivered to individual parents in the form of brief consultation. An alternate format for Level 3 involves a series of 2-hour, stand-alone group discussion sessions dealing with common topics such as disobedience, hassle-free shopping, mealtime, and so forth. Level 3 Triple P is mainly for the management of discrete child problems that are not complicated by other major behavioral challenges or significant family dysfunction. One variant of Level 3 Triple P is Teen Primary Care Triple P for parents with adolescents. Level 2 and Level 3 interventions are designed to be efficacious, but it is also recognized that some families require more intensive programming.

Level 4 Triple P is intended to benefit children with various social, emotional, and behavioral problems (whether or not the problems have yet to meet diagnostic criteria for a disorder) and parents who are struggling with parenting-related challenges. One format of Level 4 is delivered to individual families in 10 sessions, in a clinic or community center, or in the parent's home. The group format of Level 4 involves eight sessions with no more than four to eight families. A third format version is self-directed Triple P that parents accomplish on their own with a workbook. Variants of Level 4 Triple P include Baby Triple P for first-time parents undertaking the transition to parenthood and Stepping Stones Triple P for parents of a child with a developmental disability.

Level 5 Triple P, also called Enhanced Triple P, is an optional augmentation to Level 4 for families with additional risk factors that might need to be addressed through the intervention. Level 5 in its basic form includes optional intervention modules on partner support and communication, parental mood management and stress coping skills, and additional practice sessions for parent–child issues. Variants of Level 5 include Pathways Triple P for parents at risk of child abuse, Lifestyle Triple P for parents of overweight or obese children, and Family Transitions Triple P for parents going through separation or divorce.

All levels and variants of Triple P subscribe to a foundational set of principles (Sanders, 2012). These principles, which are universal and somewhat elastic, include the following:

1. *safe and engaging environment*—children need a safe, supervised, and protective environment in which to be raised;
2. *positive learning environment*—parents are children's first teachers and as such can build a family environment that is conducive to learning;
3. *assertive discipline*—effective parenting requires child-behavior management strategies that are preferred alternatives to coercive discipline practices such as threatening, shouting, or corporal punishment;
4. *realistic expectations*—the expectations, beliefs and assumptions about child behavior can be adjusted so that parents choose goals that are developmentally appropriate for their children and practical for themselves; and
5. *parental self-care*—teaches parents to take good care of themselves as part of their poise and emphasis on providing effective parenting.

Attributes Triple P Shares With Other Evidence-Based Parenting Interventions

In practice, Triple P shares several attributes with other evidence-supported parenting interventions.

- *Action focused.* Parents actually engage in activities during the intervention, rather than simply talking with the staff member. Activities take the form of asking questions and raising issues, practicing during a session, and trying parenting strategies at home.
- *Problem-solving oriented.* Parenting interventions generally focus on specific challenges and problems. A problem-solving orientation nonetheless involves building on child, parent, and family strengths. Solving the challenges parents face in child rearing entails solving the issues they raise. Effective parenting interventions apply problem-solving strategies that have a reasonable probability of ameliorating the problems at hand rather than just talking about the child's problems without generating action plans.
- *Specific, concrete, and practical parenting strategies.* Although it is important for parents to induce general principles that they can apply in future situations, parenting and family interventions still try to focus on practical parenting strategies that parents can readily implement. Parents need and want suggestions for action. Parenting and family interventions typically offer a menu of specific parenting strategies so that parents can find the best fit for their personal style and still address the issue at hand. Instead of vague generalities (e.g., "Show your child a lot of love") the interventions focus, for example, on specific ways to build closer and more affectionate parent–child relationships. For more complex situations, interventionists walk parents through specific but straightforward steps to implement a strategy.
- *Collaborative goal setting.* Parenting interventions seem to work better if parents play a major role in setting the specific goals for themselves and their children in consultation with the interventionist. The staff member asks facilitative questions and helps the parent articulate useful and specific goals. Parents' role in this process is essential. Parents are not passive participants but consumers who have a major stake in what happens with their children. The interventions typically involve identifying and sharpening parents' goals for their children. Parents often

begin sessions with distress and concern as they discuss their children's adjustment. It is the interventionist's job to join with the parent and help them figure out what the needs are in terms of the specific challenges relevant to their children's development and functioning.

- *Consultative rather than prescriptive.* Although not all parenting interventions subscribe to this concept equally, there is a general trend toward making the intervention consultative rather than telling parents what they must do. A consultative approach provides menu options, answers parents' questions, and emphasizes the staff member's role as a facilitating consultant to the parent.
- *Adopting a positive frame.* Parents do not need to feel blamed or inept for an intervention to be successful. Successful parenting and family interventions adopt a positive frame about the child, the parent, the program tasks, and the intervention itself.

Consistent with these attributes and derived from the aforementioned core principles, Triple P draws from 40 core parenting skills that cluster into eight categories: encouraging desirable behavior, teaching new child skills and behaviors, managing misbehavior, parent–child relationship enhancement skills, anticipating and planning, self-regulation skills, mood and coping skills, and partner support skills. Most of the parenting strategies in the Triple P system include variations that are tailored to different developmental levels (i.e., infants, toddlers, preschoolers, elementary school age, and early adolescence).

Evidence Base for Triple P

The evidence base for Triple P has been accruing for well over 30 years. The forerunners of Triple P parenting strategies were developed and tested in a series of controlled single-subject and multiple-baseline design studies. These focused studies examined a number of issues, such as the viability of home-delivered programming to teach parents ways to alter young children's disruptive behavior patterns; the generalization of acquired parenting skills across settings (e.g., home vs. shopping trip) as well as across time of day, behaviors, and siblings; the refinement of specific parenting strategies; and the utility of procedures for unique problems, such as child recurring abdominal pain.

Since that early period, the evidence base for facets of Triple P has grown substantially. To date, there have been over 200 published studies, including over 100 randomized controlled trials associated with Triple P. Various components of the Triple P system have been subjected to a series of controlled evaluations that have shown positive effects on observed and parent-reported child behavior problems, parenting practices, and parents' adjustment (de Graaf, Speetjens, Smit, de Wolff, & Tavecchio, 2008a, 2008b; Nowak & Heinrichs, 2008; Sanders, 2012; Thomas & Zimmer-Gembeck, 2007). Independent appraisals of the evidence for Triple P have led to its recognition by the National Institute of Clinical Excellence (2006), the World Health Organization's (2009) recommended programs for global violence reduction, the United Nations task force on family-based treatment for prevention of substance abuse (United Nations Office on Drugs and Crime, 2009), Blueprints for Healthy Youth Development (2013), and the California Evidence-Based Clearinghouse for Child Welfare (2013).

The strength of the scientific evidence supporting Triple P has been established through systematic replication of findings across sites, investigators, countries, and cultures. The evidence is based on many years of sound empirical research, including randomized trials looking at efficacy and effectiveness as well as many service–field evaluations. An integrated series of controlled outcome studies has provided considerable evidence demonstrating the benefits of the levels of intervention and modes of delivery in a variety of populations. In these studies, outcomes were positive for children whose parents were exposed to Triple P versus comparison conditions receiving no treatment, being on a waitlist, or receiving usual care conditions. This program of research has shown successful outcomes with a number of populations and problem areas: preschool-age children and conduct problems (Sanders, Markie-Dadds, Tully, & Bor, 2000), children with attention problems (Bor, Sanders, & Markie-Dadds, 2002), children of depressed parents (Sanders & McFarland, 2000), children from marital discordant homes (Dadds, Schwartz, & Sanders, 1987), children in stepfamilies (Nicholson & Sanders, 1999), children with developmental disabilities (Sanders & Plant, 1989), and children in rural and remote areas where access to community or mental health services is limited (Connell, Sanders, & Markie-Dadds, 1997). Triple P interventions also have demonstrated favorable program effects on other behavioral and developmental problems, such as persistent feeding difficulties (Turner, Sanders, & Wall, 1994), sleep disorders (Sanders, Bor, & Dadds, 1984), recurrent pain (Sanders, Shepherd, Cleghorn, & Woolford, 1994), and habit disorders (Christensen & Sanders, 1987).

A large number of outcome studies have collectively demonstrated that Triple P is effective in strengthening the quality of parenting practices; reducing coercive parenting; and reducing early social, emotional, and behavioral problems in children. Furthermore, there have been several independent replications of Triple P implementation and findings in diverse cultural contexts (Bodenmann, Cina, Ledermann, & Sanders, 2008; Cann, Rogers, & Matthews, 2003; Crisante & Ng, 2003; Gallart & Matthey, 2005; Heinrichs et al., 2009; Leung, Sanders, Leung, Mak, & Lau, 2003; Matsumoto, Sofronoff, & Sanders, 2007; Tehrani-Doost, Shahrivar, Gharaie, & Alaghband-Rad, 2009; Turner, Richards, & Sanders, 2007). The robustness of the main findings for improved child outcomes across diverse cultural groups and contexts is particularly important.

In addition to support for each component of Triple P, which provides a sound foundation for population-level implementation of the whole system, more recent research has moved toward the broader implementation of Triple P as a population strategy. For example, implementation of the Triple P system has been shown to reduce the prevalence of conduct problems in preschool age children from high-risk neighborhoods (Zubrick et al., 2005). Several effectiveness and dissemination studies have been conducted with Triple P demonstrating portability and broad utility in multiple settings (Sanders, Murphy-Brennan, & McAuliffe, 2003; Sanders, Tully, Turner, Maher, & McAuliffe, 2003; Turner & Sanders, 2006; Zubrick et al., 2005).

POPULATION-LEVEL PREVENTION TRIALS

Every Family Study

In a population-based initiative, Sanders et al. (2008) in the Every Family prevention study examined the impact of Triple P on the prevention of children's social, emotional, and behavioral problems on school entry in children 4 to 7 years old, conducted in 20 catchment areas. Using a quasi-experimental design, all levels of Triple P were implemented including a local media strategy, the brief consultation levels, and large-group (seminar) and small-group programming. More intensive programming was also available for parents when needed. Across all levels, 375 practitioners were trained to deliver Triple P, including child health nurses, physicians, school nurses, mental health services staff, and family intervention specialists. After 2 years of intervention in 10 of the 20 catchment areas, parents in the 10 intervention areas showed significantly lower rates of coercive parenting, parental depressed affect, and child emotional and psychosocial difficulties compared with the 10 control areas. Overall, this study demonstrated the potential for population-level impact on child behavior problems at school entry without selecting out a small segment of the age cohort for special intervention.

U.S. Triple P System Population Trial

A place randomization trial, called the U.S. Triple P System Population Trial, tested the impact of Triple P on child-maltreatment prevention with funding from the CDC (Prinz, Sanders, Shapiro, Whitaker, & Lutzker, 2009). The basic thrust of this population trial included disseminating the Triple P system to entire communities by training the existing workforce in several service sectors and then systematically evaluating whether and to what extent the prevalence of child-maltreatment related indicators could be reduced.

A key premise of the population trial—that a parenting intervention disseminated to an entire community would help to prevent child maltreatment—flies in the face of convention within the child abuse field, which tends to focus only on high-risk families. An important part of the problem is that official child maltreatment cases in the CPS system tend to grossly underestimate problematic parenting practices in the population. Theodore et al. (2005) found in a random household telephone survey that self-reports of physical abuse by surveyed parents were 40 times greater than actual official records of abuse. Given that problematic parenting is much more common than the CPS system reflects, and undermines child development regardless, efforts at prevention need to take a broader approach.

The population trial involved random assignment of 18 mid-sized South Carolina counties (controlling for population size, child abuse rate, and poverty rate) either to dissemination of the Triple P system (treatment) or to services as usual (control). The Triple P condition involved training more than 600 service providers in the different sectors (i.e., health care and public health, education including preschools, mental health, family services, and nongovernmental organizations), as well as implementation of the Level 1 Triple P media and communication strategies. To make parenting support widely accessible while diminishing stigma, Triple P was disseminated without couching the program's goals in terms of child-abuse reduction.

The focus of the intervention was on maltreatment of children younger than 8 years old. At any given time, there were approximately 85,000 families with at least one child birth to 8 years of age in the nine counties exposed to Triple P. About 15% of those households in the experimental catchment area participated in the direct delivery of Triple P.

Three population indicators were analyzed: (a) child out-of-home placements, reported by the state Foster Care System; (b) hospital treated child maltreatment injuries, reported by hospitals; and (c) substantiated cases of child maltreatment, reported by CPS. All three indicators showed stable preintervention baselines during the 5-year period before the trial, and the two groups of counties (i.e., Triple P and control) did not differ significantly on any of the indicators. Controlling for baseline after 2.5 years of intervention exposure, counties in the Triple P intervention condition showed significantly lower prevalence rates of child out-of-home placements and hospital-treated maltreatment injuries. The Triple P counties also showed a significantly slowing in the growth of prevalence rates for substantiated child maltreatment cases, in comparison with the control counties and also relative to the other 28 South Carolina counties that were not part of the population trial.

The Washington State Institute for Public Policy (WSIPP) conducted a cost–benefit analysis of Triple P in the context of the child welfare system. On the basis of the population trial, which implemented all five levels of the Triple P system, WSIPP estimated that the benefit-to-cost ratio was $6.06 return on each dollar (Lee, Aos, & Drake, 2012). Overall, the population trial results were promising and demonstrated the viability of a public health approach to parenting and family support as a cogent strategy for reducing the prevalence of child maltreatment indicators at a population level.

CONCLUSION

There is little doubt that parenting plays a major role in child development; in the etiology of child social, emotional, and behavioral problems; and in the generation or mitigation of other risk factors. Prevention during the early years of childhood must include the strengthening of parenting and child rearing. A public health approach to parenting has the potential to reduce family-based risk factors associated with subsequent substance abuse. By attempting to bring under a single roof multiple goals with the same intervention, the cost-efficiency of a population approach to parenting and family support makes such an effort viable.

References

Afifi, T. O., Boman, J., Fleisher, W., & Sareen, J. (2009). The relationship between child abuse, parental divorce, and lifetime mental disorders and suicidality in a nationally representative adult sample. *Child Abuse & Neglect, 33*, 139–147. doi:10.1016/j.chiabu.2008.12.009

Anda, R. F., Felitti, V. J., Bremner, J. D., Walker, J. D., Whitfield, C., Perry, B. D., . . . Giles, W. H. (2006). The enduring effects of abuse and related adverse experiences in childhood: A convergence of evidence from neurobiology and epidemiology. *European Archives of Psychiatry and Clinical Neuroscience, 256*, 174–186. doi:10.1007/s00406-005-0624-4

Barrett, P. M., & Ollendick, T. H. (Eds.). (2004). *Handbook of interventions that work with children and adolescents: Prevention and treatment*. London, England: Wiley. doi:10.1002/9780470753385

Biglan, A., Brennan, P. A., Foster, S. L., & Holder, H. D. (2004). *Helping adolescents at risk: Prevention of multiple problem behaviors*. New York, NY: Guilford Press.

Blueprints for Healthy Youth Development. (2013). Retrieved from http://www.colorado.edu/cspv/blueprints/

Blumberg, M. L. (1981). Depression in abused and neglected children. *American Journal of Psychotherapy, 35*, 342–355.

Bodenmann, G., Cina, A., Ledermann, T., & Sanders, M. R. (2008). The efficacy of the Triple P–Positive Parenting Program in improving parenting and child behavior: A comparison with two other treatment conditions. *Behaviour Research and Therapy, 46*, 411–427. doi:10.1016/j.brat.2008.01.001

Bolger, K. E., & Patterson, C. J. (2003). Sequelae of child maltreatment: Vulnerability and resilience. In S. S. Luthar (Ed.), *Resilience and vulnerability: Adaptation in the context of childhood adversities* (pp. 156–181). New York, NY: Cambridge University Press. doi:10.1017/CBO9780511615788.009

Bor, W., Sanders, M. R., & Markie-Dadds, C. (2002). The effects of the Triple P-Positive Parenting Program on preschool children with co-occurring disruptive behavior and attentional/hyperactive difficulties. *Journal of Abnormal Child Psychology, 30*, 571–587. doi:10.1023/A:1020807613155

California Evidence-Based Clearinghouse for Child Welfare. (2013). *Welcome to the CEBC: California Evidence-Based Clearinghouse for Child Welfare*. Retrieved from http://www.cebc4cw.org/

Cann, W., Rogers, H., & Matthews, J. (2003). Family intervention services program evaluation: A brief report on initial outcomes for families. *Australian e-Journal for the Advancement of Mental Health, 2*, 208–215.

Centers for Disease Control and Prevention. (1999, April 2). Ten great public health achievements—United States, 1900–1999. *Morbidity and Mortality Weekly Report, 48*, 241–243.

Christensen, A. P., & Sanders, M. R. (1987). Habit reversal and differential reinforcement of other behaviour in the treatment of thumbsucking: An analysis of generalization and side-effects. *Journal of Child Psychology and Psychiatry, 28*, 281–295. doi:10.1111/j.1469-7610.1987.tb00211.x

Collins, W. A., Maccoby, E. E., Steinberg, L., Hetherington, E. M., & Bornstein, M. H. (2000). Contemporary research on parenting: The case for nature and nurture. *American Psychologist, 55*, 218–232. doi:10.1037/0003-066X.55.2.218

Connell, S., Sanders, M. R., & Markie-Dadds, C. (1997). Self-directed behavioral family intervention for parents of oppositional children in rural and remote areas. *Behavior Modification, 21*, 379–408. doi:10.1177/01454455970214001

Corso, P. S., Edwards, V. J., Fang, X., & Mercy, J. A. (2008). Health-related quality of life among adults who experienced maltreatment during childhood. *American Journal of Public Health, 98*, 1094–1100. doi:10.2105/AJPH.2007.119826

Crisante, L., & Ng, S. (2003). Implementation and process issues in using Group Triple P with Chinese parents: Preliminary findings. *Australian e-Journal for the Advancement of Mental Health, 2*, 101–113.

Dadds, M. R., Schwartz, S., & Sanders, M. R. (1987). Marital discord and treatment outcome in behavioral treatment of childhood conduct disorders. *Journal of Consulting and Clinical Psychology, 55*, 396–403. doi:10.1037/0022-006X.55.3.396

de Graaf, I., Speetjens, P., Smit, F., de Wolff, M., & Tavecchio, L. (2008a). Effectiveness of the Triple P Positive Parenting Program on behavioral problems in children: A meta-analysis. *Behavior Modification, 32*, 714–735. doi:10.1177/0145445508317134

de Graaf, I., Speetjens, P., Smit, F., de Wolff, M., & Tavecchio, L. (2008b). Effectiveness of the Triple P Positive Parenting Program on parenting: A meta-analysis. *Family Relations, 57*, 553–566. doi:10.1111/j.1741-3729.2008.00522.x

Donovan, C. L., & Spence, S. H. (2000). Prevention of childhood anxiety disorders. *Clinical Psychology Review, 20*, 509–531. doi:10.1016/S0272-7358(99)00040-9

Dube, S. R., Miller, J. W., Brown, D. W., Giles, W. H., Felitti, V. J., Dong, M., & Anda, R. F. (2006). Adverse childhood experiences and the association with ever using alcohol and initiating alcohol use during adolescence. *Journal of Adolescent Health, 38*, 444.e1–444.e10. doi:10.1016/j.jadohealth.2005.06.006

Essau, C. A. (Ed.). (2003). *Conduct and oppositional defiant disorders: Epidemiology, risk factors, and treatment*. Mahwah, NJ: Erlbaum.

Farah, M. J., Betancourt, L., Shera, D. M., Savage, J. H., Giannetta, J. M., Brodsky, N. L., . . . Hurt, H. (2008). Environmental stimulation, parental nurturance and cognitive development in humans. *Developmental Science, 11*, 793–801. doi:10.1111/j.1467-7687.2008.00688.x

Gallart, S. C., & Matthey, S. (2005). The effectiveness of Group Triple P and the impact of four telephone calls. *Behaviour Change, 22*, 71–80. doi:10.1375/bech.2005.22.2.71

Harkness, K. L., & Lumley, M. N. (2008). Child abuse and neglect and the development of depression in children and adolescents. In J. R. Z. Abela & B. L. Hankin (Eds.), *Handbook of depression in children and adolescents* (pp. 466–488). New York, NY: Guilford Press.

Hawkins, J. D., Catalano, R. F., & Miller, J. Y. (1992). Risk and protective factors for alcohol and other drug problems in adolescence and early adulthood: Implications for substance abuse prevention. *Psychological Bulletin, 112*, 64–105. doi:10.1037/0033-2909.112.1.64

Heinrichs, N., Hahlweg, K., Naumann, S., Kuschel, A., Bertram, H., & Stander, D. (2009). Universal prevention of child behavior problems through parent training. *Zeitschrift für Klinische Psychologie und Psychotherapie, 38*, 79–88. doi:10.1026/1616-3443.38.2.79

Ialongo, N. S., Rogosch, F. A., Cicchetti, D., Toth, S. L., Buckley, J., Petras, H., & Neiderhiser, J. (2006). A developmental psychopathology approach to the prevention of mental health disorders. In D. Cicchetti & D. J. Cohen (Eds.), *Developmental psychopathology: Vol. 1. Theory and method* (2nd ed., pp. 968–1018). Hoboken, NJ: Wiley.

Institute of Medicine and National Research Council. (2009). *Preventing mental, emotional, and behavioral disorders among young people: Progress and possibilities.* Washington, DC: National Academies Press.

Jones, T. L., & Prinz, R. J. (2005). Potential roles of parental self-efficacy in parent and child adjustment: A review. *Clinical Psychology Review, 25*, 341–363. doi:10.1016/j.cpr.2004.12.004

Kazdin, A. E., Moser, J., Colbus, D., & Bell, R. (1985). Depressive symptoms among physically abused and psychiatrically disturbed children. *Journal of Abnormal Psychology, 94*, 298–307. doi:10.1037/0021-843X.94.3.298

Komro, K. A., Flay, B. R., & Biglan, A., (2011). Creating nurturing environments: A science-based framework for promoting child health and development within high-poverty neighborhoods. *Clinical Child and Family Psychology Review, 14*, 111–134. doi:10.1007/s10567-011-0095-2

Lee, S., Aos, S., & Drake, E. (2012). *Return on investment: Evidence-based options to improve statewide outcomes* (Document No. 12-04-1201). Olympia: Washington State Institute for Public Policy.

Leung, C., Sanders, M. R., Leung, S., Mak, R., & Lau, J. (2003). An outcome evaluation of the implementation of the Triple P-Positive Parenting Program in Hong Kong. *Family Process, 42*, 531–544. doi:10.1111/j.1545-5300.2003.00531.x

Lochman, J. E., & van den Steenhoven, A. (2002). Family-based approaches to substance abuse prevention. *Journal of Primary Prevention, 23*, 49–114. doi:10.1023/A:1016591216363

Matsumoto, Y., Sofronoff, K., & Sanders, M. R. (2007). The acceptability and effectiveness of the Triple P–Positive Parenting Program in a cross-cultural context: Results of an efficacy trial. *Behaviour Change, 24*, 205–218. doi:10.1375/bech.24.4.205

National Institute of Clinical Excellence. (2006). *Parent-training/education programmes in the management of children with conduct disorders.* London, England: Author.

Nicholson, J. M., & Sanders, M. R. (1999). Randomized controlled trial of behavioral family intervention for the treatment of child behavior problems in stepfamilies. *Journal of Divorce & Remarriage, 30*, 1–23. doi:10.1300/J087v30n03_01

Nowak, C., & Heinrichs, N. (2008). A comprehensive meta-analysis of Triple P–Positive Parenting Program using hierarchical linear modeling: Effectiveness and moderating variables. *Clinical Child and Family Psychology Review, 11*, 114–144. doi:10.1007/s10567-008-0033-0

Patterson, G. R., Reid, J. B., & Dishion, T. J. (1992). *Antisocial boys.* Eugene, OR: Castalia.

Petrie, J., Bunn, F., & Byrne, G. (2007). Parenting programmes for preventing tobacco, alcohol or drug misuse in children under 18: A systematic review. *Health Education Research, 22*, 177–191. doi:10.1093/her/cyl061

Prinz, R. J. (2007). Parenting and the prevention of childhood injuries. In L. S. Doll, S. E. Bonzo, J. A. Mercy, & D. A. Sleet (Eds.), *Handbook of injury and violence prevention* (pp. 333–346). New York, NY: Springer Science+Business Media.

Prinz, R. J., & Dumas, J. E. (2004). Prevention of oppositional defiant disorder and conduct disorder in children and adolescents. In P. M. Barrett & T. H. Ollendick (Eds.), *Handbook of interventions that work with children and adolescents* (pp. 475–488). Chichester, England: Wiley. doi:10.1002/9780470753385.ch19

Prinz, R. J., & Jones, T. L. (2003). Family-based interventions. In C. A. Essau (Ed.), *Conduct and oppositional defiant disorders: Epidemiology, risk factors, and treatment* (pp. 279–298). Mahwah, NJ: Erlbaum.

Prinz, R. J., Sanders, M. R., Shapiro, C. J., Whitaker, D. J., & Lutzker, J. R. (2009). Population-based prevention of child maltreatment: The U.S. Triple P system population trial. *Prevention Science, 10*, 1–12. doi:10.1007/s11121-009-0123-3

Racz, S. J., & McMahon, R. J. (2011). The relationship between parental knowledge and monitoring and child and adolescent conduct problems: A 10-year update. *Clinical Child and Family Psychology Review, 14*, 377–398. doi:10.1007/s10567-011-0099-y

Sanders, M. R. (2012). Development, evaluation, and multinational dissemination of the Triple P–Positive Parenting Program. *Annual Review of Clinical*

Psychology, 8, 345–379. doi:10.1146/annurevclinpsy-032511-143104

Sanders, M. R., Bor, W., & Dadds, M. R. (1984). Modifying bedtime disruptions in children using stimulus control and contingency management procedures. *Behavioural Psychotherapy, 12*, 130–141. doi:10.1017/S0141347300009800

Sanders, M. R., Markie-Dadds, C., Tully, L. A., & Bor, W. (2000). The Triple P–Positive Parenting Program: A comparison of enhanced, standard, and self-directed behavioral family intervention for parents of children with early onset conduct problems. *Journal of Consulting and Clinical Psychology, 68*, 624–640. doi:10.1037/0022-006X.68.4.624

Sanders, M. R., & McFarland, M. (2000). Treatment of depressed mothers with disruptive children: A controlled evaluation of cognitive behavioral family intervention. *Behavior Therapy, 31*, 89–112. doi:10.1016/S0005-7894(00)80006-4

Sanders, M. R., Murphy-Brennan, M., & McAuliffe, C. (2003). The development, evaluation and dissemination of a training programme for general practitioners in evidence-based parent consultation skills. *International Journal of Mental Health Promotion, 5*, 13–20. doi:10.1080/14623730.2003.9721914

Sanders, M. R., & Plant, K. (1989). Generalization effects of behavioral parent training to high and low risk parenting environments. *Behavior Modification, 13*, 283–305. doi:10.1177/01454455890133001

Sanders, M. R., & Prinz, R. J. (2008). Using the mass media as a population level strategy to strengthen parenting skills. *Journal of Clinical Child and Adolescent Psychology, 37*, 609–621. doi:10.1080/15374410802148103

Sanders, M. R., Ralph, A., Sofronoff, K., Gardiner, P., Thompson, R., Dwyer, S., & Bidwell, K. (2008). Every family: A population approach to reducing behavioral and emotional problems in children making the transition to school. *The Journal of Primary Prevention, 29*, 197–222. doi:10.1007/s10935-008-0139-7

Sanders, M. R., Shepherd, R. W., Cleghorn, G., & Woolford, H. (1994). The treatment of recurrent abdominal pain in children: A controlled comparison of cognitive-behavioral family intervention and standard pediatric care. *Journal of Consulting and Clinical Psychology, 62*, 306–314. doi:10.1037/0022-006X.62.2.306

Sanders, M. R., Tully, L. A., Turner, K. M. T., Maher, C., & McAuliffe, C. (2003). Training GPs in parent consultation skills: An evaluation of training for the Triple P-Positive Parenting Program. *Australian Family Physician, 32*, 763–768.

Stone, N. (1993). Parental abuse as a precursor to childhood onset depression and suicidality. *Child Psychiatry and Human Development, 24*, 13–24. doi:10.1007/BF02353714

Sutton, J. M. (2007). Prevention of depression in youth: A qualitative review and future suggestions. *Clinical Psychology Review, 27*, 552–571. doi:10.1016/j.cpr.2007.01.014

Tehrani-Doost, M., Shahrivar, Z., Gharaie, J., & Alaghband-Rad, J. (2009). Efficacy of positive parenting on improving children's behavior problems and parenting styles. *Iranian Journal of Psychiatry and Clinical Psychology, 14*, 371–379.

Theodore, A. D., Chang, J. J., Runyan, D. K., Hunter, W. M., Bangdiwala, S. I., & Agans, R. (2005). Epidemiologic features of the physical and sexual maltreatment of children in the Carolinas. *Pediatrics, 115*, e331–e337. doi:10.1542/peds.2004-1033

Thomas, R., & Zimmer-Gembeck, M. J. (2007). Behavioral outcomes of parent-child interaction therapy and Triple P–Positive Parenting Program: A review and meta-analysis. *Journal of Abnormal Child Psychology, 35*, 475–495. doi:10.1007/s10802-007-9104-9

Turner, K. M. T., Richards, M., & Sanders, M. R. (2007). A randomised clinical trial of a group parent education program for Australian indigenous families. *Journal of Paediatrics and Child Health, 43*, 429–437. doi:10.1111/j.1440-1754.2007.01053.x

Turner, K. M. T., & Sanders, M. R. (2006). Dissemination of an evidence-based, population-level parenting and family support strategy: Our experience with the Triple P–Positive Parenting Program. *Aggression and Violent Behavior, 11*, 176–193. doi:10.1016/j.avb.2005.07.005

Turner, K. M. T., Sanders, M. R., & Wall, C. R. (1994). Behavioural parent training versus dietary education in the treatment of children with persistent feeding difficulties. *Behaviour Change, 11*, 242–258.

United Nations Office on Drugs and Crime. (2009). *Guide to implementing family skills training programs for drug abuse prevention*. New York, NY: Author.

World Health Organization. (2009). *Preventing violence through the development of safe, stable and nurturing relationships between children and their parents and caregivers*. Geneva, Switzerland: Author.

Zubrick, S. R., Ward, K. A., Silburn, S. R., Lawrence, D., Williams, A. A., Blair, E., . . . Sanders, M. R. (2005). Prevention of child behavior problems through universal implementation of a group behavioral family intervention. *Prevention Science, 6*, 287–304. doi:10.1007/s11121-005-0013-2

CHAPTER 14

BRIEF STRATEGIC FAMILY THERAPY: THIRTY-FIVE YEARS OF INTERPLAY AMONG THEORY, RESEARCH, AND PRACTICE IN ADOLESCENT BEHAVIOR PROBLEMS AND DRUG ABUSE

Viviana E. Horigian and José Szapocznik

In this chapter, we present brief strategic family therapy (BSFT), a family therapy model developed and tested with over 35 years of research to address adolescent drug abuse and behavior problems. As an integrative model based on structural and systems theory, and understanding that family is the most influential system within which adolescent change can be brought about, this problem-focused, directive, and practical approach has the goal of changing the family patterns of interaction that are responsible for adolescent problem behavior. BSFT treatment parameters, systems diagnostic approach, and therapeutic techniques are explained. Research on efficacy and effectiveness of the intervention and current implementation strategy are described.

Adolescent substance abuse represents a major national public health problem that results in harmful behaviors, impaired health, and social and economic burden. Recent trends indicate that our nation's teenagers continue to use illicit drugs at an increasing rate (Johnston, O'Malley, Bachman, & Schulenberg, 2013). According to national statistics, nearly 52% of U.S. adolescents are current alcohol users. Of these adolescents, about 61% had their first drink in early adolescence, and 40% of high school students have used marijuana in their lifetime (Eaton et al., 2012; Substance Abuse and Mental Health Services Administration, 2012a). Although most adolescents who use substances do so in moderation and on a time-limited basis, a subset of these youth will continue to use into their adult years and will develop substance use careers. In general, adolescents who are most at risk for these substance-abuse trajectories into adult life are those who initiate substance use at young ages (usually before age 14 or 15), whose involvement is especially severe, and who have experienced traumatic events or come from families with maladaptive interactional patterns. Early detection of substance use is challenging because many youth are not identified as "substance-use involved" until their consumption progresses to abuse or dependence. Therefore, the spectrum of adolescent substance use problems, from experimentation to dependence, calls for a continuum of care approach that includes prevention, screening, and brief identification efforts to successfully refer youth to appropriate levels of care and treatment programs.

Adolescence is also a developmental stage when risk and protective factors for emerging adult substance abuse can be targeted. Studies in the early

Preparation of this chapter was supported by a grant from the National Institute on Drug Abuse (U10-DA13720). The content of this chapter is solely the responsibility of the author and does not necessarily represent the official views of the National Institute on Drug Abuse.

http://dx.doi.org/10.1037/14550-015
Handbook of Adolescent Drug Use Prevention: Research, Intervention Strategies, and Practice, L. M. Scheier (Editor)

1990s focused on risk and protective factors associated with adolescent substance use. Since then, there has been a growing body of research on the young adult developmental period, examining adolescent predictors of substance use. In a recent review of risk and protective factors of substance use and problem use in emerging adults, Stone, Becker, Huber, and Catalano (2012) summarized that (a) high levels of family bonding and support during adolescence predict decreased young adult alcohol involvement and drug use, (b) poor family functioning predicts problem drinking by age 22, and (c) parental monitoring is associated with decreased risk of alcohol use and dependence by age 21.

The BSFT model described in this chapter builds on the body of evidence gathered on adolescent development and drug use. BSFT addresses family interactions associated with adolescent substance use and related behavior problems such as delinquency, affiliation with antisocial peers, and unsafe sexual activity. In BSFT, adolescent symptoms are considered to be rooted in maladaptive family interactions such as inappropriate family alliances, overly rigid or overly permeable family boundaries, and parents' tendency to believe that a single individual (usually the adolescent) is responsible for the family's troubles. These maladaptive patterns of family interactions may result in the symptoms or merely prevent the family from effectively correcting the symptoms. As a consequence, transforming family interactions and improving family functioning lead to improvements in the youth's presenting problem.

Several reasons for the inclusion of BSFT are described in this handbook. First, adolescents targeted by the BSFT model may fall in the drug use spectrum described above (i.e., might engage in occasional use, abuse, or dependence). Second, the BSFT model's main mechanism of action is through the improvement of family functioning, including effective parental leadership and management, positive parenting, and parent involvement; all of which are risk factors linked to emerging adulthood substance use. Third, there is an accumulation of empirical evidence supporting the efficacy of this approach and reinforcing the pivotal role of family relations in adolescent drug use.

THEORETICAL FOUNDATIONS OF BSFT

Adolescent drug use is multidetermined with biological, social, environmental, psychological, and genetic contributing factors. However, the family is perhaps the strongest and most enduring influence on adolescent behavior and development (Gorman-Smith, Tolan, Henry, & Florsheim, 2000; Steinberg, 2001; Szapocznik & Coatsworth, 1999). A cohesive family, positive parenting and involvement, effective parental leadership, and other adaptive family characteristics can offset the effects of deviant friends, neighborhood crime, and underperforming schools on adolescent drug use (Hawkins, Catalano, & Miller, 1992; Hemovich, Lac, & Crano, 2011; Kodjo & Klein, 2002). Research shows that the family context influences adolescents' attitudes, beliefs, and sense of self (Benson & Johnson, 2009). A compilation of evidence strongly suggests that the family is the most promising target for interventions aimed at preventing (Kumpfer & Alvarado, 2003; Kumpfer, Smith, & Summerhays, 2008) and/or treating adolescent drug use and abuse (Rowe, 2012; Tanner-Smith, Wilson, & Lipsey, 2013; Waldron & Turner, 2008).

BSFT is a family treatment model developed and tested for over 35 years of research conducted at the University of Miami's Center for Family Studies. The Center for Family Studies was established in 1972 as the Spanish Family Guidance Clinic with the goal of developing a richer understanding of the drug abuse problem among Cuban youth residing in Miami. From the onset, factors contributing to youth drug use and related problem behaviors were perceived as resulting from dissonance experienced by immigrant Hispanic families that had been immersed in mainstream Westernized culture. The BSFT approach was consistent with systems theory that suggested that behavior is better understood in the social context in which it occurs (Szapocznik & Kurtines, 1993). Early formative research conducted at the Center for Family Studies (Szapocznik, Scopetta, & King, 1978a, 1978b; Szapocznik, Scopetta, Kurtines, & Aranalde, 1978) indicated that Cuban families residing in Miami tended to value family connectedness over individual autonomy and that they tended to focus on the present rather than on the past. These findings provided the challenge of developing a treatment model that would align with these cultural values.

The BSFT program was therefore formulated as an integrative model that combined structural and strategic family therapy techniques to address systemic–relational (primarily family) interactions that are associated with adolescent problem behaviors. The structural components of the BSFT treatment draw on the work of Salvador Minuchin (1974; Minuchin & Fishman, 1981), and the strategic aspects are based on work by Jay Haley (1976) and Chloe Madanes (1981). With the use of structural and strategic techniques, the goal of the BSFT model is to change the patterns of family interactions that encourage problematic adolescent behavior. By working with families, BSFT not only decreases youth problems but also creates better functioning families (Santisteban et al., 2003). Because changes are brought about in family patterns of interactions, these changes in family functioning are more likely to endure after treatment completion because multiple family members have changed the way they interact with and respond to each other. In keeping with the integration of structural and strategic principles, BSFT is a present problem-focused, directive, and practical approach, focusing on identifying and enacting the changes in patterns of family interactions necessary to ameliorate the adolescent's presenting problems. Because of its problem focus, other family issues such as problems between the parent figures are not addressed in BSFT unless they are directly related to the adolescent's drug use and related problems such as delinquency and sexual risk behaviors.

BSFT CONCEPTUAL PRINCIPLES

The BSFT intervention is based in three core principles: system, structure–patterns of interactions, and strategy. The first principle rests on the foundation that the family is a system. This core principle reinforces that family members are mutually influential and responsive to one other (interdependent), and their actions are interrelated. In other words, what one family member says or does affects everyone else in the family. In essence, problem behavior or drug use does not belong to the youth in question, but rather it is a manifestation of the family system. Owning the behaviors and interactions that form the family system is a necessary first step.

The second BSFT principle provides that repetitive family patterns of interaction affect individual family member's development and behavior. *Patterns of interaction* are defined as the sequential behaviors among family members that become habitual and repeat over time and are idiosyncratic to a family system. A maladaptive family structure is characterized by repetitive family interactions that persist even when these interactions fail to meet the goals of the family or its individual members. As part of this principle, the BSFT model holds that improvements in family members' experience and behaviors require strengthening adaptive family interactions and transforming–restructuring maladaptive family interactions. The identification and recognition of these patterns is a crucial task for the BSFT therapist. To do so, the therapist brings the family together and asks them to carry out an interactional task, such as discussing with each other what brings them to therapy.

As this process unfolds, the family inevitably will engage in the typical patterns of their family interaction, including those that are adaptive and maladaptive, giving the therapist the opportunity to identify and diagnose both adaptive and maladaptive patterns. To illustrate, as parents engage in discussion about what brought them to therapy they may argue vehemently about their disagreements with regard to rules and consequences for their adolescent child's behavior. As this dialogue occurs, their child acts disruptively to attract attention. This acting out routine distracts the parents from their conflict and redirects their attention to the adolescent. In extreme cases, adolescents may suffer a drug overdose or get arrested as a way of distracting their parents when they are engaged in a severe conflict. The therapist identifies both the role of the adolescent in preventing the parents from discussing and mutually resolving their disagreements and the inability of the parents to resolve differences of opinion with regard to the rules and consequences for their teen.

The third basic principle of BSFT reflects its strategic nature because the therapeutic intervention is planned, problem focused, and practical to achieve certain goals. For example, according to plan, adaptive patterns of interactions will be strengthened (e.g., nurturing behavior), whereas maladaptive patterns of interactions (e.g., inability of parents to speak in a single voice regarding parenting) will be corrected specifically because they impact the adolescent's behavior (problem focused). For BSFT to be effective, yet brief, only family interactions directly linked to the adolescent's problem behaviors become the target for intervention. Recognition of how these patterns unfold, their clinical caricature, and their basic nature are part of an extensive training program in BSFT. In effect, there is no surrogate for clinical acumen and the combined emphasis on decades of research that has identified recurring patterns of maladaptive behavior (Szapocznik & Kurtines, 1989; Szapocznik, Rio, Hervis, Mitrani, Kurtines, & Faraci, 1991) and therapists behaviors to address them (Robbins, Alexander, & Turner, 2000; Robbins, Feaster, Horigian, Puccinelli, et al., 2011).

TABLE 14.1

Goals of Brief Strategic Family Therapy

Structural level	Specific goals
Family	Increase parental figures involvement with one another and balance the involvement of the parent figures with the child
	Improve effective parenting, including successful management of children's behavior
	Improve family cohesiveness, collaboration, and affect, and reduce family negativity
	Improve family communication, conflict resolution and problem-solving skills
	Correct assignment and effective performance of the roles and responsibilities of the family
Individual child–adolescent	Reduce behavior problems
	Reduce substance use
	Reduce associations with antisocial peers
	Improve self-control
	Promote prosocial behaviors
	Promote good school attendance, conduct, and achievement

BSFT GOALS

In addition to adhering to these basic principles, BSFT is predicated on several key research findings. First, changing family interaction patterns is an effective way of changing individual behavior. Second, changing an individual and then having them return to the dysfunctional family environment increases the risk of behavior problems reemerging. Third, changes in one powerful individual can result in changes in the rest of the family. For both individual and family change to be successful and maintained over time, BSFT proposes a treatment model that addresses the behavior of the individual in the context of family interactions. Goals targeted in therapy include eliminating or reducing the use of drugs and associated problem behaviors and changing family members' behaviors that are linked to each other and related to adolescent drug abuse. Table 14.1 lists the specific change goals targeted in BSFT.

THE BSFT INTERVENTION

BSFT is a manual driven intervention developed specifically for children and adolescents ages 8 to 17 (Szapocznik, Hervis, & Schwartz, 2003). The intervention is appropriate for behavior problems such as drug use, conduct problems at home and at school, oppositional behavior, delinquency, sexually risky behavior, aggressive–violent behavior, and association with antisocial peers. BSFT is a relatively short-term program usually implemented in 12 to 16 (range 8–24) sessions typically delivered once a week for 1 to 1.5 hours over a 4-month period. The actual number of sessions and length of service are based on the therapist's ability to achieve the necessary improvements in specific behavioral criteria and the corresponding severity of family problems. Sessions may occur more frequently around crises times because these are opportune moments for change. Treatment involves the entire family, which typically includes everyone who lives in the adolescent's household as well as other individuals with whom the adolescent has regular contact and who function in family roles.

BSFT is a flexible approach that can be used with a broad range of family situations (e.g., two-parent families, single-parent families, step families, multigenerational families), different service settings (e.g., mental health clinics, drug abuse treatment programs, other social service settings), and treatment modalities (e.g., as a primary outpatient intervention, in combination with residential or day treatment, as an after-care–continuing-care service to residential treatment). A critical aspect of service delivery is that location of service is flexible and should not become an obstacle in the delivery of BSFT. This aspect is critical because of the many impediments to treatment; getting disorganized families to the treatment setting is a challenge. Home-based treatment is one approach to overcome these barriers to treatment.

BSFT follows a prescribed process format that is flexible and adapted to the content of each family's central concerns. BSFT therapeutic strategies are organized into four theoretically and empirically supported intervention techniques that are called *domains: joining, tracking and diagnostic enactments, reframing*, and *restructuring* (Robbins, Feaster, Horigian, Puccinelli, et al., 2011; Szapocznik & Kurtines, 1989). Although some intervention techniques are more likely to occur earlier or later, in general all intervention domains are used throughout therapy, and there is a sequence in which different interventions may be more prevalent (see Figure 14.1). Earlier sessions are characterized by joining efforts designed to establish a therapeutic alliance with each family member and with the family as a whole. This process requires that the therapist accept and respect each individual family member and the way in which the family unit is organized as a whole.

The early phases of therapy are also more likely to include tracking and diagnostic enactment to systematically identify adaptive and maladaptive family interactional patterns, which are then used to formulate a treatment plan. A central feature of tracking and diagnostic enactment is that the therapist encourages family members to behave in their usual manner, as if the therapist was not present. Family members are encouraged to talk with one other about the issues that brought them to therapy rather than commenting to the therapist. When family members do address the therapist, the therapist asks the family members to redirect the statement or question to the person referenced in the statement. By observing the family's patterns of interaction—the ways in which family members behave with each other repeatedly—the therapist identifies those interactions that are either adaptive or maladaptive (the latter contribute to adolescent problem behaviors). Therapists can then formulate an initial treatment plan to transform family interactional patterns in specific ways that will reduce or eliminate the adolescent's drug use and related problem behaviors. As the family transforms (broadens its repertoire of behaviors–interactions) throughout treatment, the treatment plan is revised to keep abreast of the family's changes.

Reframing strategies are essential to the treatment model and are used to reduce family conflict by transforming negative affect in ways that create a motivational context for change. For example, anger can be recast as hurt or concern. Consider a case where a mother gets very angry and upset because

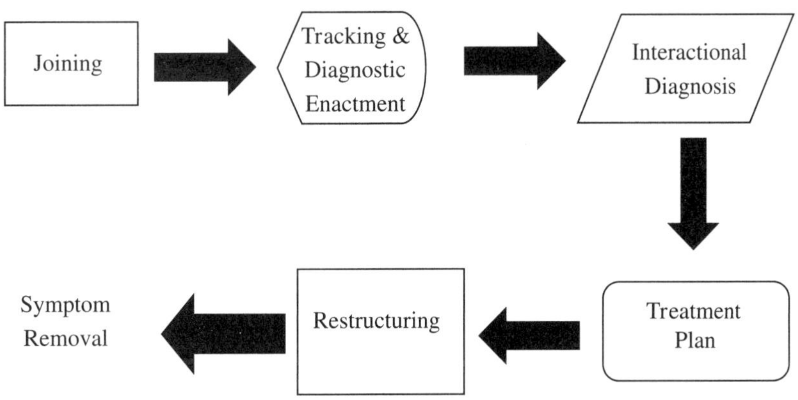

FIGURE 14.1. Brief strategic family therapy circular theory of change.

her daughter informs her that she is now pregnant. The therapist can reframe the mother's anger by saying,

> I can see how concerned you are for your daughter. You had so many dreams for her, and you are worried that they are not possible now. You must have a great deal of love for your daughter that her actions would make you so angry.

This intervention creates the opportunity for family members to perceive one other in new ways and thereby behave with one other in new ways. Once more tender emotions are expressed the therapist can use them as a foundation to build positive family interactions. By promoting constructive interactions, reframing creates a motivational context of change; it serves as a natural springboard for restructuring interventions that transform family relations from problematic to naturally supportive.

Over the course of treatment, therapists maintain an effective working relationship with family members through joining, facilitate within-family interactions through tracking, continuously assess evolving patterns of interactions through diagnostic enactment, and transform negative family interactions (while creating a motivational context for change) through reframing. However, during the later stages of treatment, the focus shifts to implementing restructuring strategies to transform family relations from problematic to effective and mutually supportive. These strategies include (a) directing, redirecting, or blocking communication; (b) shifting family alliances; (c) promoting conflict resolution skills; (d) developing effective behavior management skills; and (e) fostering parenting and parental leadership skills. All of these intervention approaches involve assigning in-session tasks, followed by out-of-session homework tasks once the in-session tasks are proceeding well.

To illustrate the course of therapy, parent figures might be asked to engage in a conversation about managing the adolescent's behavior. The adolescent may attempt to interfere with the dyadic interaction between the parent figures in which case the therapist will block the adolescent from interfering with the conversation. Subsequently, the therapist coaches the parent figures to block the adolescent from interfering in their discussions. Once parent figures are successful in achieving this within-session task, the homework task may consist of parents repeating this task at home whenever the adolescent attempts to interfere when the parents are having a conversation, particularly conversations revolving around issues germane to their youth. As another example, an adolescent and a disengaged father figure might be asked to engage in collaborative tasks, together first in the session and then out of session, as a way of building a durable and meaningful father–child bond.

DIAGNOSIS

Considerable work has gone into defining the structural diagnostic classifications on which the treatment plan is built (Szapocznik et al., 1991). To derive a diagnosis of the family, interactions are assessed along six dimensions: organization, resonance, developmental stage, life context, identified patient-hood, and conflict resolution.

Organization refers to repetitive patterns of interactions that give the family a specific form, and three categories of organization are examined: leadership, subsystem organization, and communication flow. Leadership is assessed by evaluating the distribution of authority and responsibility within the family, including who takes charge of the family's directorship and whether it is in the appropriate hands. Subsystem organization is evaluated by the patterns of alliances between and among family members, and communication flow is assessed by directness and specificity of communication.

Resonance refers to the sensitivity and connection of family members to one and another. When evaluating resonance, therapists evaluate permeability of boundaries and differentiation between individuals in the family. At one extreme, boundaries can be too rigid and impermeable, resulting in the lack of connectedness or disengagement among family members. At the opposite extreme, boundaries can be too open or permeable resulting in overconnectedness or enmeshed family interactions. Perhaps more than any of the other dimensions, resonance must be considered within the family's cultural context.

Many immigrant families, for example, come from regions of the world in which people are more collectivistic and interdependent and where familial closeness is especially valued. In contrast, in more individualistic cultural contexts, high levels of family closeness could be interpreted as overinvolvement and may be experienced as suffocating and maladaptive. Overinvolvement or underinvolvement is detrimental when it causes problems for the family or for a specific family member.

Developmental stage refers to the appropriateness of family members' interactions with respect to roles and tasks assigned to various family members, taking into consideration their age and role within the family. A maladaptive pattern may include a youth who is overburdened with parental tasks. Given this position and assigned such important duties, a youth will eventually acquire power within the family. Imbued with such power in a family, if the youth chooses to rebel against his or her parents, the parents who have endowed the youth with adult responsibilities will be unable to set limits on the youth. In a home without limits and porous boundaries, with little parental monitoring and no means of asserting parental authority, a child could easily begin to stretch rules, ask for special dispensation, and deny parents a means to assert parental control. The combined effect of these actions and the lack of careful supervision places the youth at risk for drug abuse and related problems. Times of developmental transitions, in general, and adolescence, to be specific, represent moments of increased risk for families and children, creating new challenges that require adaptation.

Flexibility to change patterns of interactions to adapt to new developmental moments is critical at times of transitions to avoid eliciting symptomatic behaviors, such as drug use and delinquency in the adolescent. *Life context* refers to the situation in which the family and its members find themselves. For example, parents might be working long hours, or adolescents may attend a school in a neighborhood with high rates of drug use and crime. Parents who are consumed with work or by necessity work more than one job are often less available to supervise and monitor their child's peer associations and activities. This requires greater effort on the part of both parent and child to carve out sufficient time to constructively build a positive bond. Similarly, a youth living in a high drug use or crime neighborhood will need more support from the parent. In addition to support, there is a tremendous need for effective parent–youth communication and parental monitoring to help ward off negative social influences. The child needs adult role models that can help steward her or him toward prosocial opportunities, avoid rules transgressing behaviors, and reduce motivations for deviant peer associations.

Identified patient-hood refers to the extent to which the family is convinced that their primary problem is all the fault of the person exhibiting the symptom (identified patient [IP]) and organizes itself around this person, therefore the IP is largely at the center of the interaction. In fact from the BSFT perspective, problems arise from interdependent patterns of interactions and as such are not typically believed to rest with a single family member.

Conflict resolution refers to the family's style for managing disagreements. A family can approach and attempt to manage conflicts in five different ways: denial, avoidance, diffusion, conflict emergence without resolution, and conflict emergence with resolution. An adaptive family uses the full range of styles.

Diagnosis of family interactions is based on what families do in therapy sessions—not necessarily what they report they do at home, and as noted content plays a minimal role in the diagnostic process. The therapist must create a therapeutic context where in family members are free to interact in their typical style. These enactments permit the therapist to directly observe how the family behaves, are critical for accurately identifying the characteristics patterns of social interactions, arrive to a clinical formulation, and establish a treatment plan.

CHALLENGE OF ENGAGING FAMILIES IN TREATMENT

Lack of agreement between the family members as to how they should handle their child's negative behavior often makes it difficult for the same family members to agree that therapy provides a viable remedy. Moreover, if family members believe that the adolescent is the problem, they may think that only the adolescent needs to be in therapy. Definitely, the same interactional problems that maintain the adolescent's symptoms are also associated with resistance to coming to treatment (Szapocznik & Kurtines, 1989). The BSFT model involves highly specialized engagement techniques that have been extensively validated (Coatsworth, Santisteban, McBride, & Szapocznik, 2001; Santisteban et al., 2003; Szapocznik et al., 1988). The same intervention domains used in BSFT treatment—joining, tracking and diagnostic enactment, and reframing—are also used to engage families into therapy. The therapist begins to explore family interactions during an initial call by tasking the caller to bring all the members of the family into the first session.

The organization of the family will become apparent by the caller's response. It is not uncommon for callers making contact with the therapist to present impediments and spin off a list of reasons for why they cannot bring other family members. This usually involves a powerful youth or an alienated parent (often a father) that may not want to attend family therapy. In other cases, the caller is ambivalent to bring one or more family members into treatment—which typically represents the family patterns of interactions that are problematic to the family. For example, when a mother believes that her husband is unreasonably harsh with their child and wants to present her husband's behavior as part of the problem, but she does not dare do so in front of him. With the caller's approval, the therapist will insert herself–himself into the family process by reaching directly to the family member who either does not want to come to treatment or who the caller is not eager to bring to treatment as a way of getting around the initial obstacles that prevent all family members from attending.

The use of the specialized engagement strategies, which are an integral component of BSFT, have resulted in much higher rates of family treatment engagement and treatment completion compared with standard engagement strategies. Research (presented below) on how BSFT therapists achieve treatment engagement has evidenced that negativity among family members is a strong predictor of dropout and that the most effective way to reduce negativity is through reframing. Also, maintaining an adequate balance between therapist–father alliance and therapist–adolescent alliance reduces the likelihood of adolescent dropout in treatment.

CULTURE AND BSFT

The BSFT model was originally developed to address acculturation discrepancies between Cuban adolescents and their parents residing in Miami (Szapocznik et al., 1978a, 1978b). At the time BSFT was developed, the program developers found that nearly all of the drug abusing and delinquent adolescents referred for treatment evidenced cultural and normative developmental conflicts with their parents. The majority of subsequent BSFT efficacy research (Coatsworth et al., 2001; Santisteban et al., 1996, 2003; Szapocznik et al., 1988, 1989) continued to focus almost exclusively on Hispanic families. A single condition study (BSFT only) later evidenced the extent to which the model could be used with African American youth, revealing that BSFT significantly reduced adolescent behavior problems and improved family functioning (Santisteban et al., 1997).

Later stages in BSFT research suggested that the model is equally applicable to a diverse set of groups, including White, African American, and Hispanic youth and their families (Robbins, Feaster, Horigian, Rohrbaugh, et al., 2011). The BSFT model is currently being implemented with a variety of populations in the United States and applied in several European countries. This wide sphere of application in different cultural groups rests of the foundation that BSFT principles and intervention techniques are relatively culture independent. Concepts such as systems, structure, and problem focus can be used across cultures. What varies across cultures is the diagnostic interpretation of the domains assessed in BSFT and the content that characterizes families across cultures. For example, evaluating the organization of the family will take into consideration whether a family is immersed in a highly patriarchal culture; from a highly interdependent culture; or from a culture that rewards independence, strength of character, and willfulness.

Consequently, joining techniques might require a sensitive approach to the therapeutic alliance between therapist and parent (father) and therapist and adolescent. The alliance has to consider these triangulated relationships and their appropriateness within a patriarchal system. Developmental appropriateness may also differ across cultures, therefore what might be expected for adolescents in terms of responsibilities and independence in one culture (e.g., migrant worker children working in the field at an early age) might not be expected in another. BSFT calls for therapists to possess sufficient knowledge of the families' cultural background to enable them to ascertain to what extent they may be able to move the family away from cultural customs to change family interactions that may be causing symptoms in a family member.

The BSFT model is well suited for families immersed in cultural change and where intergenerational or cultural conflicts occur between parents and adolescents. In many immigrant families, children and adolescents adapt quickly to the new cultural context, but parents often do not. One strategy that has been useful in BSFT is to initially include a psychoeducational component that teaches parents and children the differences between the parent's culture of origin and the American culture that is contributing to the dissonance. This is extremely poignant if the family is emigrating to the United States from an extremely hierarchical culture. Understanding the differences between cultures might create the motivational context for parents to openly discuss with their children the habits and challenges of the new culture.

THERAPY PROCESS AND OUTCOME RESEARCH ON THE BSFT MODEL

BSFT has been evaluated in a number of randomized clinical trials. The first generation of evaluations tested the efficacy of the model and of specialized engagement techniques. The success of these initial studies led the U.S. Department of Health and Human Services to label the BSFT approach as one of its "model programs" and to list it as part of the National Registry of Evidence-Based Programs and Practices (Substance Abuse and Mental Health Services Administration, 2012b). The next generation of evaluations included the identification of therapist's behaviors that were associated with the best adolescent outcomes and effectiveness testing. More recent observations include outcome evaluations of BSFT as implemented currently across the United States and Europe.

EFFICACY TRIALS

The efficacy of the BSFT model in reducing behavior problems and drug abuse has been tested in two randomized, controlled clinical trials (RCTs). In the first trial, Szapocznik et al. (1989) randomized Cuban boys with behavior and emotional problems to the BSFT model (ages 6–11), individual psychodynamic child therapy, or a recreational placebo control condition. The two treatment conditions, implemented by highly experienced therapists, were found to be equally efficacious, and both were more efficacious than the recreational control group in reducing children's behavioral and emotional problems and in maintaining these reductions at 1-year follow-up. Comparisons between the two treatment conditions at 1-year follow-up showed that the BSFT condition was associated with a significant improvement in independently rated family functioning, whereas individual psychodynamic child therapy was associated with a significant deterioration in family functioning.

In a second RCT, Santisteban et al. (2003) randomly assigned Hispanic (half Cuban and half from other Hispanic countries) behavior-problem and drug abusing youth to receive either the BSFT model or adolescent group counseling. The BSFT condition was significantly more efficacious than group counseling in reducing conduct problems, associations with antisocial peers, marijuana use, and improving observer ratings of family functioning. Baseline family functioning was found to moderate treatment effects. For families entering the study with comparatively high levels of family functioning, family functioning remained high in the BSFT condition, whereas family functioning deteriorated in the families of adolescents assigned to group therapy. For families entering the study with comparatively low levels of family functioning, the BSFT condition significantly improved family functioning, whereas family functioning did not improve in families assigned to adolescent group therapy. Furthermore, adolescent group counseling was associated with clinically significant increases in reported levels of marijuana use.

BSFT Engagement

The efficacy of BSFT engagement was tested in three separate studies with Hispanic behavior problem adolescents and their families. In the first study (Szapocznik et al., 1988), Hispanic (mostly Cuban) families with drug abusing adolescents were randomly assigned to BSFT with engagement as usual (the control condition) or to BSFT + BSFT engagement module (the experimental condition). The BSFT engagement module consisted of the application of the specialized engagement techniques described above. The engagement as usual condition was modeled after community-based adolescent outpatient programs' approaches to engagement in the Miami area. The results of the study revealed that 93% of the families in the BSFT engagement condition, compared with only 42% of the families in the engagement as usual condition, were engaged into treatment (defined as attending an admission session). Moreover, 75% of families in the BSFT engagement condition completed treatment (defined as the family and the therapist reaching a mutual decision that treatment could be terminated), compared with only 25% of families in the treatment as usual (TAU) condition.

In a second study (Santisteban et al., 1996), families were randomly assigned to a BSFT engagement or engagement control (no specialized engagement) condition. In the BSFT engagement condition, 81% of families were successfully engaged, compared with 60% of the families in the engagement control condition (defined as attending the admission session plus one family therapy session). One of several key findings from this study was that the effectiveness of BSFT engagement procedures was moderated by Hispanic nationality. Among the non-Cuban Hispanic groups (composed primarily of Nicaraguan, Colombian, and Puerto Rican families) assigned to the BSFT engagement condition, the rate of engagement was high (97%) compared with the much lower rate (64%) found in the Cuban group assigned to this same BSFT Engagement condition ($ps < .002$). Most of the Cuban families had U.S.-born adolescents, whereas the majority of adolescents from other national backgrounds were foreign born. Evidence suggests that U.S.-born Hispanic adolescents tend to be more Americanized compared with adolescents born outside the United States (Schwartz, Pantin, Sullivan, Prado, & Szapocznik, 2006). There is also evidence that acculturation to American values and behaviors among Hispanic families is associated with decreased orientation toward family (Sabogal, Marin, Otero-Sabogal, Marin, & Perez-Stable, 1987). As a result, it is possible that the lower engagement rate found for Cuban individuals was because of higher rates of Americanization in the Cuban families. It is possible that more Americanized families perceive less need for family involvement in adolescent drug abuse treatment. This finding resulted in the incorporation of specific family reconnection strategies into the current version of BSFT engagement. These new modules focused on reorientation toward the importance of family.

In a third study, Coatsworth et al. (2001) tested the ability of BSFT + BSFT engagement to engage and retain adolescents and their families in comparison to a community control condition. An important feature of this study was that the control condition was implemented by a community treatment agency, and as such this was a hybrid efficacy–effectiveness study with the experimental condition controlled in the university setting and the control condition provided in the community as would usually be provided by the agency involved in the study. The Hispanic adolescents and families in this study were primarily Cuban or Nicaraguan. Findings indicated that BSFT engagement successfully engaged 81% of families into treatment—significantly higher than the 61% rate in the community control condition. Likewise, among families who were successfully engaged, 71% of BSFT cases, compared with 42% in the community control condition, were retained to treatment completion.

BSFT Effectiveness

An effectiveness trial (Robbins, Feaster, Horigian, Rohrbaugh, et al., 2011) of BSFT was conducted as part of the National Institute on Drug Abuse's Clinical Trials Network (CTN). With the intent to test the intervention under real world conditions, the study compared BSFT and TAU (whatever treatment the agency typically provided for drug using adolescents) by randomizing 480 families of adolescents (213 Hispanics, 148 White, and 110 Black; 377 male, 103 female) referred to drug abuse treatment at eight community treatment agencies located around the United States. Seventy-two percent of these adolescents were referred for treatment by the juvenile justice system, and most of the remaining cases were referred from residential treatment. Sixty-nine percent of the youth had diagnoses of drug abuse or dependence. Services in both conditions were delivered by therapists in community agencies. These therapists were randomized within agency to deliver either the BSFT or TAU. The study design deviated from the approach used in implementation of family-based treatments such as multisystemic therapy, functional family therapy, and our own implementation work with the BSFT approach.

Typically in the implementation of family-based approaches and in our own BSFT implementation, the family-based empirically supported treatment is provided in small clinical units of typically four therapists each dedicated to the BSFT approach. Instead, because of the historical approach in which CTN studies have been conducted and to comply with design requirements, we randomly assigned therapists to the BSFT approach or TAU within intact clinic units. This resulted in clinics housing both BSFT and non-BSFT therapists. Moreover, in contrast to usual implementation work in family-based models, BSFT therapists were allowed and sometimes required by their agencies to have BSFT and non-BSFT cases. These deviations from the usual BSFT and other family-based treatment approaches created considerable challenges to fidelity.

Consistent with prior findings on BSFT efficacy, this intent-to-treat study design showed that BSFT was significantly more effective than TAU in engaging and retaining families in treatment. Families in TAU were 2.33 times (11.4% BSFT, 26.8% TAU) more likely to fail to engage (defined as not completing at least two sessions) compared with families in the BSFT condition. Families in TAU were 1.41 times (40.0% BSFT, 56.6% TAU) more likely to fail to retain (defined in this study as completing fewer than eight sessions) compared with families in BSFT. These differences were significant and consistent across ethnic groups. It is important to note that therapy took much longer to administer than expected. The usual expectation is that BSFT therapy should last approximately 4 months, which is consistent with how BSFT is implemented in practice. However, the median length of treatment for those participants who were retained in treatment across both conditions was approximately 8 months. With respect to adolescent drug use outcomes, the effectiveness study showed no significant differences between conditions on the number of drug using days per 28-day periods 1-year postrandomization. However, nonparametric analyses showed that the median number of self-reported drug use days per month at the 12-month follow-up was significantly higher in the TAU condition (3.5 days) than in the BSFT condition (2 days). It is important to note that the median number of drug use days was low and restricted, with an interquartile range between 1 and 3 days of self-reported use per month. Such a restricted range made it difficult to detect statistically significant or clinically meaningful effects. As detailed above, an overwhelming majority of adolescents in the study were referred from juvenile justice or from residential treatment, both of which involved surveillance (and limited opportunities to engage in) drug use. These referral sources may have been responsible for the relatively low baseline rates of drug use, and in the case of the juvenile justice referrals, continued surveillance may have been responsible for the low levels of drug use over time.

The same study also showed that findings differed based on the reporting source. The BSFT condition produced significantly greater improvements in parent-reported family functioning (defined as positive parenting, parental monitoring, effectiveness of parental discipline, parental willingness to discipline adolescents when necessary, family cohesion, and absence of family conflict) compared with the TAU condition. Adolescents in both conditions reported significant improvements in family functioning with no statistically significant differences by treatment condition.

Post hoc analyses of the BSFT effectiveness study evidenced that BSFT was more effective than TAU in reducing alcohol use in parents and that this effect was mediated by parental reports of family functioning. In addition, BSFT as compared with TAU had its strongest effect in reducing adolescent drug use among youth whose parents used drugs at baseline (Horigian et al., 2014).

THERAPIST BEHAVIORS, THERAPY PROCESS, AND OUTCOMES

Process research has demonstrated that negativity in family interactions in the first session leads to failure to retain families in treatment past the first session (Fernandez & Eyberg, 2009). Moreover, families are more likely to engage into treatment if negativity is reduced (Robbins et al., 2000), and reframing is the technique that is least likely to damage therapists' rapport (alliance, bond) with family members (Robbins et al., 2006). Process research has also evidenced that early engagement requires therapists to maintain a balanced bond with the parent (often the father figure) and the problem youth. If, in the first session, the strength of the bond the therapist develops with the parent and the youth is not balanced, this unbalance leads to early dropout from treatment (Robbins et al., 2000). These findings have been incorporated into BSFT treatment as conducted today.

EFFECTS OF THERAPIST ADHERENCE AND BEHAVIORS ON TREATMENT OUTCOMES

Using data from the BSFT effectiveness trial, Robbins, Feaster, Horigian, Puccinelli, et al. (2011) examined the extent to which BSFT therapists adhered to the BSFT model. To do this, adherence items were assessed along four theoretically and clinically relevant/prescribed therapist behaviors: joining, tracking and eliciting enactments, reframing, and restructuring. The scales for the four domains of adherence used in the study were confirmed through factor analyses. These items were assessed by trained independent raters who watched randomly selected videos of therapy sessions.

Results of these analyses revealed that higher levels of restructuring and reframing (reducing negativity and creating a motivational context for change) significantly increased the likelihood of families being engaged into treatment. Furthermore, higher levels of each of the four BSFT technique domains, therapist joining, tracking and enactment, reframing, and restructuring predicted significantly higher rates of retention, defined as a family attending at least eight sessions. A 1 *SD* increase in reframing predicted a 19% increase in the likelihood of retention; a 1 *SD* increase in joining predicted a 22% increase in the likelihood of retention; a 1 *SD* increase in restructuring predicted a 59% increase in the likelihood of retention; and a 1 *SD* increase in tracking and eliciting enactment predicted a 62% increase in the likelihood of retention. This study revealed that overall joining levels predicted improvements in observer-reported family functioning.

The effect of prescribed therapist behaviors on adolescent drug use outcomes was somewhat complex. Across time, as would be expected, joining decreased and restructuring increased. Smaller declines in joining and larger increases in restructuring predicted significantly less adolescent drug use at the 12-month follow-up. That is, therapists who were high in joining in early sessions and remained so throughout treatment were associated with better adolescent drug use outcomes. Therapists whose attempts to restructure maladaptive family interactions increased most during the course of treatment were also associated with better adolescent drug use outcomes. Thus, therapists who failed to maintain high levels of joining or implement sufficient numbers of restructuring interventions were less able to affect the youths' drug use.

These results demonstrated that the specific therapist behaviors prescribed by the BSFT approach are needed to engage families into treatment, retain them, improve family functioning, and reduce adolescent drug use. When therapists did not engage sufficiently in these behaviors, adolescent outcomes tended to suffer. Robbins, Feaster, Horigian, Puccinelli, et al.'s (2011) experience during the trial led them to conclude that adherence levels were affected by a number of within-agency systemic factors, including overburdened therapists, therapists not dedicated to BSFT, and therapists not embedded within BSFT-dedicated units. These conclusions have been confirmed in subsequent experience with implementation of BSFT in real-world settings.

BSFT AS IMPLEMENTED IN CLINICAL PRACTICE

The results of the BSFT effectiveness study have highlighted some challenges that allowed shaping the manner in which BSFT is implemented in clinical practice (Szapocznik, Schwartz, Muir, & Brown, 2012a). Some of these challenges are consistent with those described in the multilevel, complex, and interactive processes involved in the adoption and implementation of other evidence-based practices (Fixsen, Naoom, Blase, Friedman, & Wallace, 2005; Glisson & Schoenwald, 2005). There are multiple processes and levels of influence, including agency and program administrators, funders, model consultants functioning at an organizational level, model trainers–supervisors, therapists and target population. Palinkas and Aarons (2009) identified six critical determinants of successful evidence-based practice implementation: (a) availability of adequate financial and staff resources; (b) positive relations with community partners; (c) agency leadership support for EBPs, including willingness to engage in new and innovative endeavors; (d) creating high motivation–low resistance in staff including selecting and selectively removing staff based on their support for change and innovation as a way to achieve improvements in client outcomes; (e) tangible benefits for staff including development of new clinical skills; and (f) perceived benefits outweigh perceived costs—specifically that improvements in service delivery and client outcomes are worth the trouble of changing the agency's culture and operating procedures. In our current implementation work, all of these factors are taken into consideration when an organization expresses interest in obtaining training in the BSFT intervention to ensure successful adoption, fidelity, and sustainability of the model (Saldana, Chamberlain, Wang, & Brown, 2012). Most important to note, agencies become the target of a systemic intervention for BSFT implementation.

To conceptualize the need for an additional intervention focusing on BSFT implementation, we find it is useful to refer back to the systemic foundation of the BSFT model. There is an inevitable relationship between changes in the behavior of the system and changes desired in a target unit. In the BSFT model, the system is the family and the target unit is the adolescent (Szapocznik, Schwartz, Muir, & Brown, 2012b). However, in implementing an evidence-based intervention, the system is the agency that must change to support the adoption and sustainability of the BSFT model, and the target unit is the team of therapists trained to implement the BSFT approach with fidelity. Moreover, consistent with the overall model, systems are interrelated as well. Therefore, a change in one of the levels can facilitate or impede a change in target unit at a different level. Therefore, what happens at the agency level can impact adolescent outcomes as systems at these grossly different levels are also interrelated. To promote adoption and sustainability, the agency must also target funders, judges, and legislators whose support is needed to facilitate the use of the BSFT in the community (Szapocznik, Muir, Schwartz, Johnathan, & Hendricks, 2013).

BSFT implementation begins with a site readiness assessment. *Site readiness* refers to the process of engaging organizational leaders, agency staff, and community stakeholders in preparing them to adopt the BSFT program. The goal of the site readiness process is for agency staff at all levels, from therapists to agency leaders, to obtain a full understanding of the requirements (including changes in therapist behavior and organizational structure) that are needed to implement the BSFT program. Site readiness activities begin with joining strategies to ensure that the BSFT model manager, housed at the Center for Family Studies' BSFT Institute, is viewed as a member of the agency team, working to produce better adolescent outcomes that would support continued funding for the program. Once this is achieved, it is possible to discuss therapist eligibility, select the BSFT team, and explain and establish training and supervision requirements and obtain the agencies commitment to these requirements. Because the vast majority of agencies implementing the BSFT program are adopting an evidence-based program for the first time, changes in their standard practices are required to successfully implement the BSFT model. Some examples of the changes that are necessary for successful implementation of BSFT are at the funding level, shifting from a pay per contact to pay per case, and the agency level, allowing and supporting time for supervision as well as for therapists to review their own videotapes on a consistent basis to ensure fidelity and, in turn, treatment outcomes, which will result in sustained funding opportunities.

The next phase in the implementation of BSFT is the constitution of the unit of four to five therapists, selected on their academic training (master's level), openness to adopt a systemic training, and experience in working with adolescents. This is followed by the training phase, which includes three 3-day workshops conducted at the agency site and 2 hours of weekly group supervision of videotaped sessions for approximately one year. Workshops cover the research evidence supporting the BSFT model, the philosophy of the model, and theoretical principles such as understanding the family as a system; that patterns of interaction in a family are repetitive and predictable; and that lasting change can be created by carefully planning interventions targeting those patterns of interaction that are directly linked to the adolescent's problem behavior. Ultimately, BSFT trainers must demonstrate to therapists that the BSFT approach will better help them to reach their own clinical goals. Each workshop includes interactive lectures, taped demonstrations of family therapy sessions, live case consultations, and interactive class exercises. Weekly supervision helps therapists integrate the didactic information into their behaviors during therapy.

Another critical step toward an agency's BSFT sustainability is the selection of a BSFT on-site supervisor. A competent BSFT therapist will emerge within the group and will be nominated as a supervisor whose role will involve leading weekly group supervision sessions. The BSFT on-site supervisor is selected during the first year and trained during the second year of BSFT implementation. The BSFT on-site supervisor is selected jointly by the BSFT model manager and the agency leadership. The primary responsibility of the BSFT on-site supervisor is to ensure fidelity to the model, which is crucial given the research linking BSFT adherence to good clinical outcomes. The BSFT on-site supervisor is guided and supported through weekly supervision meetings with the BSFT model manager. During these weekly meetings, the BSFT model manager provides guidance and coaching on how to supervise and maintain fidelity to the BSFT model, offers techniques to implement when therapists drift away from the model, presents guidelines for successful case closures, and supports the BSFT on-site supervisor in monthly meetings with agency leaders.

The next step also critical to the sustainability of BSFT involves officially licensing the agency's BSFT unit. Agencies are granted a license to practice the BSFT model once staff has been achieved a predesignated level of competency and once the agency possesses the necessary resources to implement the model. In the second year of licensure and beyond, to maintain the licensure, agencies are required to participate in an annual 2-day booster workshop and an annual 2-day advanced training visit. Booster workshops address areas where the therapists may have drifted away from the treatment model. Live consultation occurs wherever therapy is being delivered (usually at the clinic office or in clients' homes).

A final aspect of sustainability is supporting agency leadership with funders and other stakeholders by presenting the BSFT model and the accompanying research evidence. As we stated above, joining with funders and stakeholders is essential because their support is needed to facilitate therapist training and good clinical outcomes for adolescents and their families.

CONCLUSIONS AND FUTURE DIRECTIONS

Nearly four decades have passed since the initial development of the BSFT model. The model has been rigorously tested following the stages of research described for psychotherapy interventions (Rounsaville, Carroll, & Onken, 2001). Originally developed to address conflicted parent and adolescent relationships in immigrant families, the model has evolved and been tested in response to specific clinical needs: Specialized engagement techniques were added to bring reluctant families into treatment, reframing became increasingly prominent as a way to reduce negativity, there was an increase motivational context for change, and there was an increase in engagement and retention. In addition, an implementation program supported by the creation of the BSFT Institute was established. The experience of BSFT implementation with the insights provided by the effectiveness trial has made clear that an organizational-level systemic approach is critical in ensuring successful adoption, fidelity, and sustainability of BSFT. This approach is used in BSFT implementation today. The next stage for BSFT research is to investigate the efficacy and effectiveness of BSFT implementation interventions.

References

Benson, J. E., & Johnson, M. K. (2009). Adolescent family context and adult identity formation. *Journal of Family Issues, 30*, 1265–1286. doi:10.1177/0192513X09332967

Coatsworth, J. D., Santisteban, D. A., McBride, C. K., & Szapocznik, J. (2001). Brief strategic family therapy versus community control: Engagement, retention, and an exploration of the moderating role of adolescent symptom severity. *Family Process, 40*, 313–332. doi:10.1111/j.1545-5300.2001.4030100313.x

Eaton, D. K., Kann, L., Kinchen, S., Shanklin, S., Flint, K. H., Hawkins, M. A., . . . Wechsler, H. (2012). Youth risk behavior surveillance—United States, 2011. *Morbidity and Mortality Weekly Report, 61*(4), 1–162.

Fernandez, M. A., & Eyberg, S. M. (2009). Predicting treatment and follow-up attrition in parent-child interaction therapy. *Journal of Abnormal Child Psychology, 37*, 431–441. doi:10.1007/s10802-008-9281-1

Fixsen, D. L., Naoom, S. F., Blase, K. A., Friedman, R. M., & Wallace, F. (2005). *Implementation research: A synthesis of the literature. The national implementation research network* (FMHI Publication No. 231). Tampa: University of South Florida, Louis de la Parte Florida Mental Health Institute.

Glisson, C., & Schoenwald, S. K. (2005). The ARC organizational and community intervention strategy for implementing evidence-based children's mental health treatments. *Mental Health Services Research, 7*, 243–259. doi:10.1007/s11020-005-7456-1

Gorman-Smith, D., Tolan, P. H., Henry, D. B., & Florsheim, P. (2000). Patterns of family functioning and adolescent outcomes among urban African American and Mexican American families. *Journal of Family Psychology, 14*, 436–457. doi:10.1037/0893-3200.14.3.436

Haley, J. (1976). *Problem-solving therapy.* San Francisco, CA: Jossey-Bass.

Hawkins, J. D., Catalano, R. F., & Miller, J. Y. (1992). Risk and protective factors for alcohol and other drug problems in adolescence and early adulthood: Implications for substance abuse prevention. *Psychological Bulletin, 112*, 64–105. doi:10.1037/0033-2909.112.1.64

Hemovich, V., Lac, A., & Crano, W. D. (2011). Understanding early-onset drug and alcohol outcomes among youth: The role of family structure, social factors, and interpersonal perceptions of use. *Psychology, Health & Medicine, 16*, 249–267. doi:10.1080/13548506.2010.532560

Horigian, V. E., Feaster, D. J., Brincks, A., Robbins, M. S., Perez, M. A., & Szapocznik, J. (2014). *The effects of brief strategic family therapy (BSFT) on parent substance use and its impact on adolescent substance use.* Manuscript submitted for publication.

Johnston, L. D., O'Malley, P. M., Bachman, J. G., & Schulenberg, J. E. (2013). *Monitoring the future national results on adolescent drug use: Overview of key findings, 2012.* Ann Arbor: The University of Michigan.

Kodjo, C. M., & Klein, J. D. (2002). Prevention and risk of adolescent substance abuse: The role of adolescents, families, and communities. *Pediatric Clinics of North America, 49*, 257–268. doi:10.1016/S0031-3955(01)00003-7

Kumpfer, K. L., & Alvarado, R. (2003). Family-strengthening approaches for the prevention of youth problem behaviors. *American Psychologist, 58*, 457–465. doi:10.1037/0003-066X.58.6-7.457

Kumpfer, K. L., Smith, P., & Summerhays, J. F. (2008). A wakeup call to the prevention field: Are prevention programs for substance use effective for girls? *Substance Use & Misuse, 43*, 978–1001. doi:10.1080/10826080801914261

Madanes, C. (1981). *Strategic family therapy.* San Francisco, CA: Jossey-Bass.

Minuchin, S. (1974). *Families and family therapy.* Cambridge, MA: Harvard University Press.

Minuchin, S., & Fishman, H. C. (1981). *Family therapy techniques.* Cambridge, MA: Harvard University Press.

Palinkas, L. A., & Aarons, G. A. (2009). A view from the top: Executive and management challenges in a statewide implementation of an evidence-based practice to reduce child neglect. *International Journal of Child Health and Human Development, 2*, 47–55.

Robbins, M. S., Alexander, J. F., & Turner, C. W. (2000). Disrupting defensive family interactions in family therapy with delinquent adolescents. *Journal of Family Psychology, 14*, 688–701. doi:10.1037/0893-3200.14.4.688

Robbins, M. S., Feaster, D. J., Horigian, V. E., Puccinelli, M. J., Henderson, C., & Szapocznik, J. (2011). Therapist adherence in brief strategic family therapy for adolescent drug abusers. *Journal of Consulting and Clinical Psychology, 79*, 43–53. doi:10.1037/a0022146

Robbins, M. S., Feaster, D. J., Horigian, V. E., Rohrbaugh, M., Shoham, V., Bachrach, K., . . . Szapocznik, J. (2011). Brief strategic family therapy versus treatment as usual: Results of a multisite randomized trial for substance using adolescents. *Journal of Consulting and Clinical Psychology, 79*, 713–727. doi:10.1037/a0025477

Robbins, M. S., Liddle, H. A., Turner, C. W., Dakof, G. A., Alexander, J. F., & Kogan, S. M. (2006). Adolescent and parent therapeutic alliances as predictors of dropout in multidimensional family therapy. *Journal of Family Psychology, 20*, 108–116. doi:10.1037/0893-3200.20.1.108

Rounsaville, B. J., Carroll, K. M., & Onken, L. S. (2001). A stage model of behavioral therapies research: Getting started and moving on from Stage I. *Clinical Psychology: Science and Practice, 8*, 133–142. doi:10.1093/clipsy.8.2.133

Rowe, C. L. (2012). Family therapy for drug abuse: Review and updates 2003–2010. *Journal of Marital and Family Therapy, 38*, 59–81. doi:10.1111/j.1752-0606.2011.00280.x

Sabogal, F., Marin, G., Otero-Sabogal, R., Marin, B. V., & Perez-Stable, E. J. (1987). Hispanic familism and acculturation: What changes and what doesn't? *Hispanic Journal of Behavioral Sciences, 9*, 397–412. doi:10.1177/07399863870094003

Saldana, L., Chamberlain, P., Wang, W., & Brown, C. H. (2012). Predicting program start-up using the stages of implementation measure. *Administration and Policy in Mental Health and Mental Health Services Research, 39*, 419–425. doi:10.1007/s10488-011-0363-y

Santisteban, D. A., Coatsworth, J. D., Perez-Vidal, A., Kurtines, W. M., Schwartz, S. J., LaPerriere, A., & Szapocznik, J. (2003). Efficacy of brief strategic family therapy in modifying Hispanic adolescent behavior problems and substance use. *Journal of Family Psychology, 17*, 121–133. doi:10.1037/0893-3200.17.1.121

Santisteban, D. A., Coatsworth, J. D., Perez-Vidal, A., Mitrani, V., Jean-Gilles, M., & Szapocznik, J. (1997). Brief structural strategic family therapy with African American and Hispanic high risk youth: A report of outcome. *Journal of Community Psychology, 25*, 453–471. doi:10.1002/(SICI)1520-6629(199709)25:5<453::AID-JCOP6>3.0.CO;2-T

Santisteban, D. A., Szapocznik, J., Perez-Vidal, A., Kurtines, W. M., Murray, E. J., & LaPerriere, A. (1996). Efficacy of intervention for engaging youth and families into treatment and some variables that may contribute to differential effectiveness. *Journal of Family Psychology, 10*, 35–44. doi:10.1037/0893-3200.10.1.35

Schwartz, S. J., Pantin, H., Sullivan, S., Prado, G., & Szapocznik, J. (2006). Nativity and years in the receiving culture as markers of acculturation in ethnic enclaves. *Journal of Cross-Cultural Psychology, 37*, 345–353. doi:10.1177/0022022106286928

Steinberg, L. (2001). We know some things: Parent–adolescent relationships in retrospect and prospect. *Journal of Research on Adolescence, 11*, 1–19. doi:10.1111/1532-7795.00001

Stone, A. L., Becker, L. G., Huber, A. M., & Catalano, R. F. (2012). Review of risk and protective factors of substance use and problem use in emerging adulthood. *Addictive Behaviors, 37*, 747–775. doi:10.1016/j.addbeh.2012.02.014

Substance Abuse and Mental Health Services Administration. (2012a). *Results from the 2011 national survey on drug use and health: Summary of national findings* (NSDUH Series H-44, HHS Publication No. SMA 12-4713). Rockville, MD: Substance Abuse and Mental Health Services Administration.

Substance Abuse and Mental Health Services Administration. (2012b). *SAMSHA's national registry of evidence-based programs and practices–brief strategic family therapy (April 2008)*. Retrieved from http://nrepp.samhsa.gov/ViewIntervention.aspx?id=151

Szapocznik, J., & Coatsworth, J. D. (1999). An eco-developmental framework for organizing the influences on drug abuse: A developmental model of risk and protection. In M. D. Glantz & C. R. Hartel (Eds.), *Drug abuse: Origins and interventions* (pp. 331–366). Washington, DC: American Psychological Association. doi:10.1037/10341-014

Szapocznik, J., Hervis, O. E., & Schwartz, S. (2003). *Brief strategic family therapy for adolescent drug abuse* (NIH Publication No. 03-4751). Rockville, MD: National Institute on Drug Abuse.

Szapocznik, J., & Kurtines, W. M. (1989). *Breakthroughs in family therapy with drug abusing and problem youth.* New York, NY: Springer.

Szapocznik, J., & Kurtines, W. M. (1993). Family psychology and cultural diversity: Opportunities for theory, research, and application. *American Psychologist, 48*, 400–407. doi:10.1037/0003-066X.48.4.400

Szapocznik, J., Muir, J., Schwartz, S., Johnathan, D., & Hendricks, C. B. (2013). Brief Strategic Family Therapy: Implementing evidence-based models in community settings. *Psychotherapy Research.* Advance online publication.

Szapocznik, J., Perez-Vidal, A., Brickman, A. L., Foote, F. H., Santisteban, D., Hervis, O., & Kurtines, W. M. (1988). Engaging adolescent drug abusers and their families in treatment: A strategic structural systems approach. *Journal of Consulting and Clinical Psychology, 56*, 552–557. doi:10.1037/0022-006X.56.4.552

Szapocznik, J., Rio, A., Hervis, O. E., Mitrani, V. B., Kurtines, W. M., & Faraci, A. M. (1991). Assessing change in family functioning as a result of treatment: The structural family systems rating scale (SFSR). *Journal of Marital and Family Therapy, 17*, 295–310. doi:10.1111/j.1752-0606.1991.tb00897.x

Szapocznik, J., Santisteban, D., Rio, A., Perez-Vidal, A., Santisteban, D., & Kurtines, W. M. (1989). Family effectiveness training: An intervention to prevent drug abuse and problem behaviors in Hispanic adolescents. *Hispanic Journal of Behavioral Sciences, 11*, 4–27. doi:10.1177/07399863890111002

Szapocznik, J., Schwartz, S. J., Muir, J. A., & Brown, C. H. (2012a). Brief strategic family therapy: An intervention to reduce adolescent risk behavior. *Couple and Family Psychology, 1*, 134–145.

Szapocznik, J., Schwartz, S. J., Muir, J. A., & Brown, C. H. (2012b). *Implementation of an evidence-based intervention: Brief strategic family therapy.* Unpublished manuscript.

Szapocznik, J., Scopetta, M. A., & King, O. E. (1978a). The effect and degree of treatment comprehensiveness with a Latino drug abusing population. In D. E. Smith et al. (Eds.), *A multicultural view of drug abuse* (pp. 563–573). Cambridge, MA: G. K. Hall.

Szapocznik, J., Scopetta, M. A., & King, O. E. (1978b). Theory and practice in matching treatment to the special characteristics and problems of Cuban immigrants. *Journal of Community Psychology, 6*, 112–122. doi:10.1002/1520-6629(197804)6:2<112::AID-JCOP2290060203>3.0.CO;2-R

Szapocznik, J., Scopetta, M. A., Kurtines, W. M., & Aranalde, M. A. (1978). Theory and measurement of acculturation. *Interamerican Journal of Psychology, 12*, 113–130.

Tanner-Smith, E. E., Wilson, S. J., & Lipsey, M. W. (2013). The comparative effectiveness of outpatient treatment for adolescent substance abuse: A meta-analysis. *Journal of Substance Abuse Treatment, 44*, 145–158. doi:10.1016/j.jsat.2012.05.006

Waldron, H. B., & Turner, C. W. (2008). Evidence-based psychosocial treatments for adolescent substance abuse. *Journal of Clinical Child and Adolescent Psychology, 37*, 238–261. doi:10.1080/15374410701820133

CHAPTER 15

RESEARCH ON THE STRENGTHENING FAMILIES PROGRAM FOR PARENTS AND YOUTH AGES 10–14: LONG-TERM EFFECTS, MECHANISMS, TRANSLATION TO PUBLIC HEALTH, PROSPER PARTNERSHIP SCALE UP

Richard Spoth, Cleve Redmond, W. Alex Mason, Lisa Schainker, and Lauren Borduin

About 10 years ago, a special issue of the journal *Prevention Science* reviewed the "great progress" that had occurred in the subfield of family-focused preventive intervention research. The summary of almost two decades of effort highlighted how, in particular, the scientific community was well poised to seize an opportunity for larger scale implementation and greater public health impact (Spoth, Kavanagh, & Dishion, 2002). Over a decade later, the field has further progressed, and the opportunity for public health impact is even greater, although many challenges remain. In part, one of the articles (Spoth & Redmond, 2002) featured in the special issue reviewed the research to date on the Iowa Strengthening Families Program (subsequently revised and renamed the Strengthening Families Program: For Parents and Youth 10–14 [SFP 10-14]). In this chapter, we recapitulate and update this program of research. Most important, the chapter reflects the progress in the broader field of prevention science. It also illustrates critical opportunities that, when properly seized, could better achieve the public health impact through family-focused prevention. These opportunities are suggested by knowledge gaps addressed through the SFP 10-14 program of research.

GAPS ADDRESSED BY THE PROGRAM OF RESEARCH

Three decades ago, one of the most salient gaps in the empirical literature on family-focused interventions was the lack of research on universal interventions' effectiveness and on the viability of their sustained, quality implementation. A key reason for the development and subsequent research on the SFP 10-14 was to address these issues.

Preparation of this chapter was supported by grants from the National Institute on Drug Abuse (DA013709, DA10815, DA007029, and DA028879), the National Institute on Alcohol Abuse and Alcoholism (AA14702), the National Institute of Mental Health (MH49217), the Centers for Disease Control (DP002279), and the Annie E. Casey Foundation. The content of this chapter is solely the responsibility of the authors and does not necessarily represent the official views of the sponsors.

We gratefully acknowledge the Partnerships in Prevention Science Institute staff, contributing colleagues from collaborating universities, the adolescent and young adult participants in the studies, and collaborating schools.

http://dx.doi.org/10.1037/14550-016
Handbook of Adolescent Drug Use Prevention: Research, Intervention Strategies, and Practice, L. M. Scheier (Editor)

In light of the limited research on universal preventive interventions, Offord, Kraemer, Kazdin, Jensen, and Harrington (1998); Biglan (1995); and others (see Institute of Medicine and National Research Council, 2009) have assessed the primary tradeoffs to be considered in achieving public health impact with *universal* interventions, as compared with *selected* interventions (for individuals or a population subgroup in which risk is higher than average) or *indicated* interventions (for high-risk individuals identified or having minimal signs or symptoms foreshadowing disorders). Considering these tradeoffs, widespread implementation of a universal intervention is indicated when it is justified by the likelihood of public health impact based on four conditions: (a) the extent to which highly prevalent public health problems are targeted; (b) the effectiveness of the intervention; (c) the viability of its cost; and (d) the likely extent of widespread implementation in the targeted population (see Offord et al., 1998).

In the case of the SFP 10-14 program of research, the prospects for meeting conditions like those described above motivated the formative phases of family-focused program development and related research. An especially important condition for impact is the likely extent of translation to widespread implementation, frequently described in terms of intervention scale-up that is guided by translation research. In this context, *scale-up* is defined as strategic efforts to extend the reach and benefits of evidence-based interventions (EBIs) in their targeted populations at an increasing rate through intervention adoption and quality sustained implementation with increasingly larger numbers of intervention beneficiaries. The SFP 10-14 program of research has addressed a range of factors related to widespread implementation or scale-up. This effort is part of an emerging translation-oriented research paradigm. One way of articulating this paradigm and characterizing the primary gaps addressed by the SFP 10-14 program of research is that it entails increased attention to the "4 Es" of long-range intervention impact during intervention design, development, and testing phases (Spoth, 2008). These 4 Es are *effectiveness*, particularly long term; *extensiveness* of coverage of the population segments that could benefit from family-focused prevention, targeting all developmental stages warranting intervention; *efficiency*, including generalization of effects and economic benefits; and *engagement*, of prospective adopters and participants.

In connection with knowledge gaps concerning program scale-up, the SFP 10-14 program of research specifically has addressed (a) factors influencing family engagement in preventive intervention research (Prinz & Miller, 1996; Spoth & Redmond, 2002), (b) universal intervention implementation barriers (Bierman et al., 1997), and (c) the effectiveness of community-based collaborative research on sustained implementation of these programs (Molgaard, 1997).

A final important gap addressed by the SFP 10-14 program of research is the limited attention to preventive interventions with rural populations (see Robertson, Sloboda, Boyd, Beatty, & Kozel, 1997). As summarized by Spoth (2007), the community–university partnership-based program of research, of which the early SFP 10-14 studies were a part, was designed to address these rural population-related gaps.

To summarize how the SFP 10-14 program of research has addressed these gaps, we organize the remainder of the chapter under three main topics: (a) SFP 10-14 development and outcomes, (b) the public health framework and empirical findings that led to the development of the partnership delivery system called PROSPER (PROmoting School-community-university Partnerships to Enhance Resilience), and (c) future directions in addressing selected challenges in this subfield of research.

PROGRAM OF RESEARCH: DEVELOPMENT, OUTCOMES, MECHANISMS OF EFFECTS OVERVIEW OF THE PROGRAM

SFP 10-14 is a seven-session universal intervention that uses a skill-building approach to prevent substance use and other problem behaviors in young adolescents. Unlike many home-based or parent-focused interventions targeting adolescent substance use that are presented only to parents, the SFP 10-14 includes parent- and youth-relevant topics and activities that are addressed in independent groups, as well as activities that are done together as a family. In addition to the core set of seven sessions, four booster sessions can be delivered 3 months to a year after the last session to reinforce the key messages of the intervention. The program activities were designed to work best with between eight and 13 families per group.

Parent segments center on how to deal effectively with adolescents in everyday situations, providing nurturance while setting appropriate limits, as well as clearly articulating their beliefs and expectations related to alcohol and drug use. Parent program content is presented through DVD instruction with intermittent discussion facilitated by the group leader. Youth segments focus on goals and dreams for the future, appreciating parents, dealing with stress and emotions, and building skills to deal with peer pressure. These topics are covered using a combination of active games and projects that encompass session objectives followed by discussions that highlight the related take-home message. Family segments include games and projects that allow parents and youth to practice communicating and problem solving.[1]

Development of the SFP 10-14

The version of the SFP 10-14 curriculum that is currently available for commercial use has undergone a few minor revisions since its predecessor, the Iowa Strengthening Families Program (ISFP), and it was adapted from the original Strengthening Families Program (SFP; Kumpfer, DeMarsh, & Child, 1989). The original SFP was designed for 6- to 12-year-olds and their parents who were being treated for substance abuse disorders. The ISFP retained the 2-hour structure of the original SFP but was reduced from 14 sessions to seven sessions, which was more appropriate for universal populations, logistically more feasible, and less expensive to deliver. Developers used three main conceptual frameworks to guide their revision of the intervention: the biopsychosocial vulnerability model, the resiliency model of Kumpfer (1994), and the family process model (Conger et al., 1991). Each of these models supports family risk-reduction and youth-resiliency approaches to preventing substance use and other problem behaviors (Molgaard, Spoth, & Redmond, 2000).

Focus groups were used to solicit input on content appropriateness, and implementation feasibility was tested by delivering the ISFP to groups of Iowa families. The ISFP was then evaluated in a randomized controlled trial (RCT) called Project Family and proved to be efficacious by producing a wide range of positive outcomes, as detailed subsequently. As a next step, program developers worked toward rendering the intervention more appropriate for ethnically diverse families. This process involved the addition of African American and Latino families to the DVDs and other program-related materials. Additional changes, such as resequencing topics; increasing the number of interactive, game-like activities for youth; and the addition of separate parent and youth components in the seventh session were made based on feedback garnered during earlier implementations. This revised ISFP curriculum became the Strengthening Families Program: For Parents and Youth 10–14 and was tested in the Capable Families and Youth (CaFaY) Project as part of a multicomponent intervention that also included a school-based program. In addition, the SFP 10-14 was one of three family-focused interventions on a menu of programs in the PROSPER Project, summarized below.

Effectiveness Trials Demonstrating Longitudinal Outcomes

There have been three primary RCTs examining ISFP/SFP 10-14-related outcomes. The first of these trials, Project Family, focused solely on family-focused interventions and evaluated the ISFP as a stand-alone intervention. In the second trial, CaFaY, the SFP 10-14 was evaluated as part of a multicomponent intervention in which the intervention was combined with a school-based program. In the third trial, PROSPER, the SFP 10-14 was evaluated within a broader test of community–university partnership-based implementation of family- and school-based interventions selected by community teams.[2] Table 15.1 summarizes articles reporting on outcomes from these three longitudinal

[1] Further summary detail on the SFP 10-14 can be found at http://www.ncjrs.gov/pdffiles1/ojjdp/182208.pdf

[2] All participating community teams chose the SFP 10-14 from a program menu also including the Guiding Good Choices and Adolescent Transitions programs. Community teams were based in school districts with K–12 enrollments ranging from approximately 1,300 to 5,200 students.

TABLE 15.1

Summary of Selected Reports of Outcomes Across Multiple Waves of Data Collection Up to 14 Years Past Baseline in Longitudinal Prevention Trials Conducted Over 23 Years

Authors	Data collection points; analyzed sample	Method–procedures–outcomes	Key findings
		Project Family	
Spoth, Redmond, & Shin, 1998	6th grade (posttest, 0.5 years past baseline); *n* = 357 families	Latent variable SEM analysis of direct and indirect ISFP effects on parenting outcomes assessed using observational and self-report measures	Significant direct ISFP effects were found on intervention-targeted parenting behaviors; significant indirect ISFP effects through intervention-targeted parenting behaviors were found on parent–child affective quality and on general child management.
Redmond, Spoth, Shin, & Lepper, 1999	7th-grade follow-up (1.5 years past baseline); *n* = 280 families	Replication of Spoth et al., 1998, analysis: Latent variable SEM analysis of direct and indirect ISFP effects on parenting outcomes assessed using observational and self-report measures	Significant direct ISFP effects were found on intervention-targeted parenting behaviors; significant indirect ISFP effects through intervention-targeted parenting behaviors were found on parent–child affective quality and on general child management—demonstrating that effects observed at posttest were sustained for an additional year.
Spoth, Redmond, & Lepper, 1999	7th- and 8th-grade follow-ups (2.5 years past baseline); *n* = 316 7th graders/*n* = 294 8th graders	Mixed-model ANCOVA test of ISFP effects on adolescent alcohol initiation (assessed through index of youth-reported alcohol behaviors); dose-effect studied	Significantly lower levels of alcohol initiation behaviors were reported by ISFP group adolescents than by controls at the 7th- and 8th-grade follow-up assessments; effects associated with intervention dosage (attendance rate) were significant at the 7th-grade assessment but not in 8th grade.
Spoth, Reyes, Redmond, & Shin, 1999	6th-, 7th-, 8th-grade follow-ups (2.5 years past baseline); *n* = 329 adolescents	Stage-sequential model and intervention-control differences in progression of multiple substance use tested using latent transition and log-linear analyses	Adolescents who attended the ISFP were less likely to progress in initiation of substance use between the 7th- and 8th-grade follow-up assessments than were control group adolescents.
Spoth, Redmond, & Shin, 2000	10th grade follow-up (4 years past baseline); *n* = 303 families	Mixed-model ANCOVA test of ISFP effects on adolescent aggressive and hostile behaviors, assessed through parent and youth reports and observational ratings	Adolescents in the ISFP condition showed significantly lower levels of observer-rated aggression, hostility, and self-reported aggressive and destructive conduct than did adolescents in the control condition; results for family-member reported aggression and hostility also favored the ISFP condition, but not significantly so—relative reduction rates (RRRs) of aggressive and destructive conduct ranged from 32% to 77%.

TABLE 15.1 (*cont.*)

Authors	Data collection points; analyzed sample	Method–procedures–outcomes	Key findings
Spoth, Redmond, & Shin, 2001	10th-grade follow-up (4 years past baseline); $n = 302$ adolescents	Mixed-model ANCOVA and *z* tests of ISFP effects on multiple substance use; preliminary growth curve analyses	Significantly lower levels of past month alcohol and tobacco use were found for ISFP (vs. control) group adolescents. Significantly lower proportions of ISFP adolescents had initiated alcohol use, used alcohol without parental permission, been drunk, smoked cigarettes, and used marijuana since baseline—RRRs ranged from 26% to 56%.
Spoth, Redmond, Shin, & Azevedo, 2004	7th- to 12th-grade follow-ups (6.5 years past baseline); $n = 304$ adolescents	Nonlinear growth curve analyses of ISFP effects on multiple lifetime substance use assessed using parent and youth reports	Overall, results indicated significantly slower growth in lifetime use of alcohol, cigarettes, and marijuana among ISFP-condition adolescents relative to controls. Significant differences were observed in times to inflection points for alcohol composite use index, lifetime drunkenness, and lifetime cigarette use.
Trudeau, Spoth, Randall, & Azevedo, 2007	6th- to 12th-grade follow-ups (6.5 years past baseline); $n = 383$ adolescents	An SEM analysis of ISFP effects on growth patterns of adolescent internalizing symptoms and monthly polysubstance use and the association between internalizing symptom and polysubstance growth factors through self-reported measures	ISFP group adolescents had a significantly slower rate of increase in internalizing symptoms (anxiety and depression) and polysubstance use (alcohol, tobacco, marijuana, inhalants, and other illicit drugs) than control condition adolescents did. ISFP slowed the rate of increase in polysubstance use significantly more for girls than for boys, whereas overall levels of substance use were lower in the ISFP group for both genders (vs. controls).
Spoth, Randall, & Shin, 2008	8th- and 12th-grade follow-ups (6.5 years past baseline); $n = 293$ 8th graders/ $n = 308$ 12th graders	A group-coded approach and chi-square difference tests of nested models were used to assess ISFP effects on school engagement (8th grade) and academic success (12th grade)	Significant effects of the ISFP were found on proximal intervention outcomes, intermediate school engagement, and the academic success of 12th graders. Specifically, ISFP increased parenting competencies, reduced students' substance-related risk in 6th grade, and was indirectly and positively associated with changes in 12th grade academic performance through positive effects on school engagement measured in 8th grade.

(continued)

TABLE 15.1 (*cont.*)

Authors	Data collection points; analyzed sample	Method–procedures–outcomes	Key findings
Spoth, Guyll, & Shin, 2009	7th- to 12th-grade follow-ups (6.5 years past baseline); *n* = 446 adolescents	Odds ratio analyses and growth curve modeling were used to examine protective shield/ adolescents' exposure to use and long-term illicit substance use	ISFP was significantly associated with reduced 12th-grade substance use. ISFP reduced the rate of increase in exposure across adolescence, which was significantly indirectly associated with the likelihood of 12th-grade illicit substance use. The RRR for exposure was 49%.
Spoth, Trudeau, Guyll, Shin, & Redmond, 2009	6th to 12th grade and 21 years of age follow-ups (10 years past baseline); *n* = 331 adolescents/YAs	Hierarchical latent growth curve models used to test growth factor effects on subsequent YA substance use outcomes through self-reports	Indirect long-term intervention effects on YA outcomes through adolescent substance initiation growth factors were significant. ISFP RRRs ranged from 19% (*drunkenness*) to 31% (*illicit drug use*).
Spoth, Clair, & Trudeau, 2014	Seven waves from 6th grade through age 21 follow-ups (10 years past baseline); *n* = 666 adolescents/YAs	Latent growth curve models and chi-square tests were used to assess ISFP effects on adolescent initiation growth factors and initiation growth factor effects on YA health-risking sexual behaviors and STD outcomes measured with self-reports	ISFP showed significant indirect effects on number of sexual partners, lifetime sexually transmitted diseases, and substance use during sex but not number of condoms used, through adolescent substance initiation growth factors. Singles in the ISFP group were significantly less likely to combine substances with sex than singles in the control group.
Spoth, Trudeau, Guyll, & Shin, 2012	6th to 12th grade, and 21 years of age follow-ups (10 years past baseline); *n* = 331 adolescents/YAs	Growth curve modeling was used to assess indirect ISFP intervention effects on YAs through effects on growth of protective shield/adolescent substance exposure	Long-term ISFP effects associated with reductions of illicit substance use were mediated by protective shield effects. The RRR was 28.2%.
Trudeau, Spoth, Randall, Mason, & Shin, 2012	Six follow-ups occurred from 6th grade through age 21 (10 years past baseline); *n* = 374 6th grade families/ *n* = 331 21-year-olds	Latent growth curve modeling was used to examine YA internalizing ISFP effects YA on growth factors of adolescent internalizing symptoms measured with self-reports	ISFP effects were observed on growth factors for adolescent internalizing symptoms (Grades 6–12); the ISFP's effect on internalizing symptoms in YA was mediated through growth factors of adolescents' internalizing symptoms. Moderation of ISFP effects by risk status was found, with higher risk adolescents (early substance initiators) benefitting more from the intervention (RRR = 28%).

TABLE 15.1 (*cont.*)

Authors	Data collection points; analyzed sample	Method–procedures–outcomes	Key findings
		Capable Families and Youth Project (CaFaY)	
Spoth, Redmond, Trudeau, & Shin, 2002	8th-grade follow-up (1.5 years past baseline); *n* = 1,372 adolescents	Mixed-model ANCOVA tests for SFP 10-14 + LST effects on an adolescent-reported substance initiation index and new user rates of alcohol, tobacco, and marijuana	Adolescents in the SFP 10-14 + LST intervention group reported lower substance initiation index scores and new user rates of marijuana than controls; intervention adolescents reported lower new user rates of alcohol use than adolescents in the control group.
Spoth, Randall, Shin, & Redmond, 2005	8th- and 9th-grade follow-ups (2.5 years past baseline); *n* = 1361 8th graders/ *n* = 1198 9th graders	Multilevel analysis of covariance conducted growth curve and point-in-time analyses of SFP 10-14 + LST effects on lifetime initiation of substances, regular alcohol use, and weekly drunkenness	Growth of substance initiation for the SFP 10-14 + LST group was significantly slower than for the control group. SFP 10-14 + LST group adolescents had significantly lower point-in-time weekly drunkenness than adolescents in the control group. No significant intervention effects were found for regular alcohol use measures.
Spoth, Randall, Trudeau, Shin, & Redmond, 2008	8th- through 12th-grade follow-ups (5.5 years past baseline); *n* = 1237 adolescents	Repeated-measures analyses with linear slope contrasts were used to test for linear slope differences between SFP 10-14 + LST and control conditions using adolescent reports of substance initiation and more serious substance use	Significantly lower mean levels and a slower rate of increase in alcohol, cigarette, and marijuana initiation was found for the SFP 10-14 + LST condition versus the control condition at the 12th-grade follow-up.
Spoth, Trudeau, Redmond, & Shin (in press)	Follow-ups from 7th grade through age 22 (9.5 years past baseline); *n* = 984 adolescents/YAs	Two-step hierarchical latent growth curve models were used to examine SFP 10-14 + LST intervention effects on YA substance misuse outcomes	Analyses indicated significant indirect intervention effects on the average levels of drunkenness, alcohol-related problems, cigarette use, and illicit substance use, through effects on adolescent substance initiation growth factors, along with intervention by risk interaction effects favoring the higher risk subsample.

(continued)

TABLE 15.1 (*cont.*)

Authors	Data collection points; analyzed sample	Method–procedures–outcomes	Key findings
		PROSPER Project	
Spoth, Redmond, Shin, Greenberg, Clair, & Feinberg, 2007	8th-grade follow-up (2.5 years past baseline); $n = 12{,}022$ adolescents	Multilevel-model ANCOVA tests of the PROSPER Model SFP 10-14 + school intervention effects on past-month, past-year, and lifetime use of multiple substances	Substance initiation and past-year marijuana and inhalant use rates were significantly lower for adolescents in the SFP 10-14 + school intervention compared with those in the control condition. Intervention-control comparisons showed positive trends for alcohol, cigarettes, marijuana, methamphetamines, ecstasy, and inhalants. For some outcomes, intervention effects were stronger for higher versus lower risk students.
Redmond, Spoth, Shin, Schainker, Greenberg, & Feinberg, 2009	6th through 9th grade follow-ups (3.5 years past baseline); $n = 11{,}931$ 6th graders/ $n = 10{,}706$ 7th graders/ $n = 10{,}170$ 8th graders/ $n = 9{,}438$ 9th graders	Multilevel ANCOVA tests for differences in youth, parent, and family competencies, and risk and protective factors for PROSPER Model SFP 10-14 + school intervention group versus control group	Significant differences were found for almost all measured outcomes through the 8th-grade follow-up, including parenting outcomes, parent–child affective quality, and youth attitude and skill outcomes. The 9th grade follow-up showed positive significant intervention effects on general child management, parent–child activities, most youth attitude and skill outcomes, and substance refusal intentions.
Spoth, Redmond, Clair, Shin, Greenberg, & Feinberg, 2011	6th- through 10th-grade follow-ups (4.5 years past baseline); $n = 11{,}960$ adolescents	Multilevel ANCOVA to test for effects of the PROSPER Model SFP 10-14 + school intervention on lifetime, past-month, and past-year use of multiple substances	Significantly lower substance use was found in the intervention group for 12 of the 15 point-in-time substance-use-related outcomes, with RRRs of up to 51.8%. Slower substance use growth in the intervention group was found for 14 of the 15 measures versus the control group.
Spoth, Redmond, Shin, Greenberg, Feinberg, & Schainker, 2013	11th- and 12th-grade follow-ups were conducted (6.5 years past baseline); $n = 11{,}960$ adolescents	Multilevel ANCOVA procedures were used to assess the effects of the PROSPER Model's SFP 10-14 + school intervention on multiple current and lifetime substance misuse	The SFP 10-14 + school intervention produced significantly lower current and lifetime rates of misuse and slower growth in misuse initiation for most outcomes; RRRs were up to 31.4%. Greater benefits for higher risk adolescents were found for growth and point-in-time misuse.

TABLE 15.1 (*cont.*)

Authors	Data collection points; analyzed sample	Method–procedures–outcomes	Key findings
Spoth, Trudeau, Redmond, Shin, Greenberg, Feinberg, & Hyun, 2014	6th- through 12th-grade follow-ups performed (6.5 years past baseline); $n = 1{,}064$ families	Zero-inflation Poisson model tests for effects of the PROSPER model SFP 10-14 + school intervention on frequency of conduct problem behaviors	Significant differences in conduct behavior problems between the PROSPER intervention group and the control group were found at all follow-ups. The combined SFP 10-14 + school intervention reduced conduct problems with an RRR up to 15.2%. Higher frequency problem behaviors also were reduced: RRRs were between 6.9% and 18.1%.
		Multiproject articles	
Spoth, Clair, Shin, & Redmond, 2006	Study 1: 12th-grade follow-up (6.5 years past baseline); $n = 457$ 12th graders Study 2: 11th- and 12th-grade follow-ups (5.5 years past baseline); $n = 588$ 11th graders/ $n = 597$ 12th graders	Fisher's exact test was used to assess differences in supplemental methamphetamine measure between the intervention and control conditions in each study (Study 1: ISFP, controls/Study 2: SFP 10-14 + LST, controls)	Study 1: In 12th grade, the ISFP condition past-year rate of methamphetamine use was 0.0% compared with 3.2% for the control condition. Study 2: SFP 10-14 + LST condition adolescents had significantly lower rates of lifetime and past-year use at the 4.5-year follow up than control condition adolescents. Intervention condition adolescents maintained significantly lower lifetime use rates at the 5.5-year follow-up.
Spoth, Trudeau, Shin, & Redmond, 2008	Study 1: 12th-grade and 21-year-old follow-ups (10 years past baseline); $n = 457$ 12th graders/ $n = 483$ 21-year-olds Study 2: 11th- and 12th-grade follow-ups (5.5 years past baseline); $n = 1{,}443$ 11th graders/ $n = 1{,}212$ 12th graders	Fisher's exact test was used to assess intervention-control differences (Study 1: ISFP vs. controls/Study 2: SFP 10-14 + LST vs. controls) in lifetime and past-year prescription drug misuse assessed through self-reports	Study 1: ISFP 12th graders' past year narcotic misuse was significantly less than that of controls, as were ISFP 21-year-olds' lifetime narcotic and barbiturate misuse rates. Study 2: SFP 10-14 + LST showed significant effects on lifetime prescription drug misuse at the 11th grade follow-up, while effects at the 12th grade follow-up were only marginally significant.

(continued)

TABLE 15.1 (*cont.*)

Authors	Data collection points; analyzed sample	Method–procedures–outcomes	Key findings
Spoth, Trudeau, Shin, Ralston, Redmond, Greenberg, & Feinberg, 2013	Study 1: Follow-ups performed from 6th grade through age 25 (14 years past baseline); *n* = 304 adolescents/YAs Study 2: Follow-ups performed from 7th grade through ages 21 to 25 (13 years past baseline); *n* = 1,440 adolescents/YAs Study 3: Follow-ups performed from 6th through 12th grade (6.5 years past baseline); *n* = 8,000 adolescents	Fisher's exact test (Study 1) and multilevel analyses (Studies 2 and 3) were used to assess intervention effects on POM and PDMO. Multilevel ANCOVA procedures for dichotomous outcomes were used to assess risk moderation of intervention effects (Study 1: ISFP vs. controls/Study 2: SFP 10-14 + LST vs. controls/Study 3: SFP 10-14 + school intervention vs. controls)	Study 1: The ISFP showed significant effects on POM and PDMO with RRRs of 65%. There were comparable effects for both higher and lower risk subgroups. Study 2: The SFP 10-14 + LST showed marginally to highly significant effects on POM and PDMO outcomes across all ages measured. Higher risk participants showed significantly stronger effects from the intervention than lower risk participants. Study 3: The SFP 10-14 + school intervention showed significant effects on POM and PDMO. Comparable effects were found for lower and higher risk groups.

Note. SEM = structural equation modeling; ISFP = Iowa Strengthening Families Program; ANCOVA = analysis of covariance; SFP 10-14 = Strengthening Families Program: For Parents and Youth 10–14; LST = Life Skills Training; PROSPER = PROmoting School-community-university Partnerships to Enhance Resilience; RRR = relative reduction rate; POM = prescription opioid misuse; PDMO = prescription drug misuse overall; YA = young adult.

studies conducted over the past 23 years, across multiple outcomes and waves of data collection, up to 14 years past baseline.[3]

Summary of Outcomes

An illustrative finding from Project Family concerns reductions in substance initiation, the primary target of the intervention. Reductions in initiation remained significant in studies conducted 4 and 6 years after intervention delivery, when participants were in the 10th and 12th grades (Spoth, Redmond, & Shin, 2001; Spoth, Redmond, Shin, & Azevedo, 2004). Findings revealed proportions of new substance users (initiators) were significantly lower in the ISFP condition than in the control group for lifetime alcohol, tobacco, marijuana use, drunkenness, and drinking without parental permission (Spoth, Redmond, et al., 2004); results for these lifetime substance use outcomes indicated slower growth in initiation among ISFP condition youth relative to controls through 6 years past baseline, as illustrated in Figure 15.1 for the lifetime drunkenness outcome (Spoth, Redmond, et al., 2004).

The practical significance of these and related findings is indicated by the relative reduction rates (RRRs) for lifetime drunkenness and other types of substance initiation. For example, the ISFP's RRRs for lifetime drunkenness, marijuana use, and drinking without parental permission were 40%, 56%, and 55%, respectively, at the 10th grade follow-up (Spoth et al., 2001). In the case of drunkenness, for instance, if the RRR were to hold when scaling up the program, for every 100 general population 10th graders in nonintervention school districts reporting drunkenness, there would be only approximately 60 students in intervention school districts reporting this behavior.

[3] To conserve space, the more detailed summary, along with a more comprehensive list of citations, is available at http://www.ppsi.iastate.edu/APAChapter/SFP10-14_Trials-Outcomes.pdf

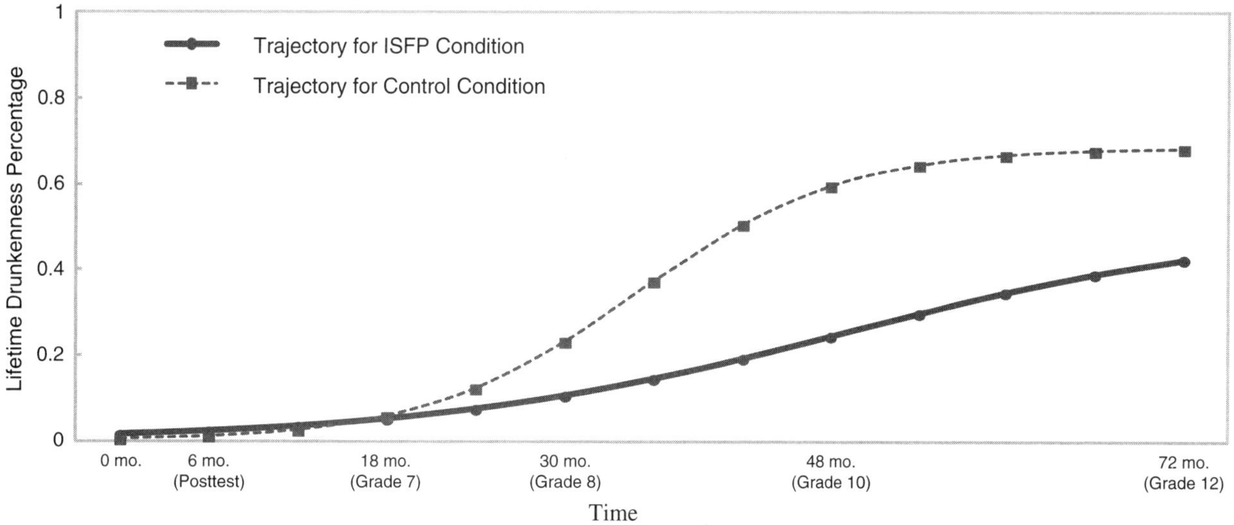

FIGURE 15.1. Lifetime drunkenness through 6 years past baseline: Logistic curve results. ISFP = Iowa Strengthening Families Program.

An important feature of all three trials examining longitudinal outcomes of the SFP 10-14 was that many aspects of these projects were coordinated through local partnerships with representatives from the Cooperative Extension System (CES). The CES has been characterized as the largest informal education system in the world. The benefits of CES-assisted partnerships and system supports for preventive intervention research were summarized by Molgaard (1997; Spoth & Molgaard, 1999). In the case of the SFP 10-14 program of research, benefits of this collaborative approach were enhanced through linkages with the public school systems (Spoth, Redmond, et al., 2004). Conducting the SFP 10-14 program of research through the use of these partnerships has contributed greatly to its quality and ecological validity, as described later.

Long-Term Effects With Emerging Adults

Theory suggests and research is increasingly confirming that early developmentally well-timed preventive interventions can function as catalysts that initiate a sequence of events leading to positive outcomes in the long term. The notion of long-term prevention effects is consistent with the developmental cascades perspective (Dodge et al., 2009). This developmentally framed model suggests behaviors that flourish in one developmental period are linked to the same and related behaviors in subsequent developmental periods. The SFP 10-14 has demonstrated hypothesized effects for delayed substance initiation and reduced substance misuse among adolescents. Drawing on developmental theory and research, as part of the Project Family trial, Spoth, Trudeau, Guyll, Shin, and Redmond (2009) examined whether ISFP effects on substance use and misuse in adolescence continued into early adulthood, 10 years after implementation of the intervention. This and similar types of investigations are challenging for at least two reasons.

First, very-long-term effects are not expected to be large in magnitude, and small effect sizes, although still potentially practically significant, can raise concerns related to statistical power in intervention tests (Shrout & Bolger, 2002). Second, the developmental cascades perspective and similar theories propose that interventions set in motion a complex sequence of events that unfold over time, leading to long-term outcomes. This theory suggests that long-term prevention effects will be primarily indirect, operating through more proximal intervention outcomes. In this vein, Spoth, Trudeau, et al. (2009) reported latent growth model findings (see Figure 15.2) that showed ISFP reduced substance misuse in early adulthood (frequency of drunkenness, alcohol problems, cigarette smoking, illicit drug use, and polysubstance use), through delayed substance initiation during adolescence.

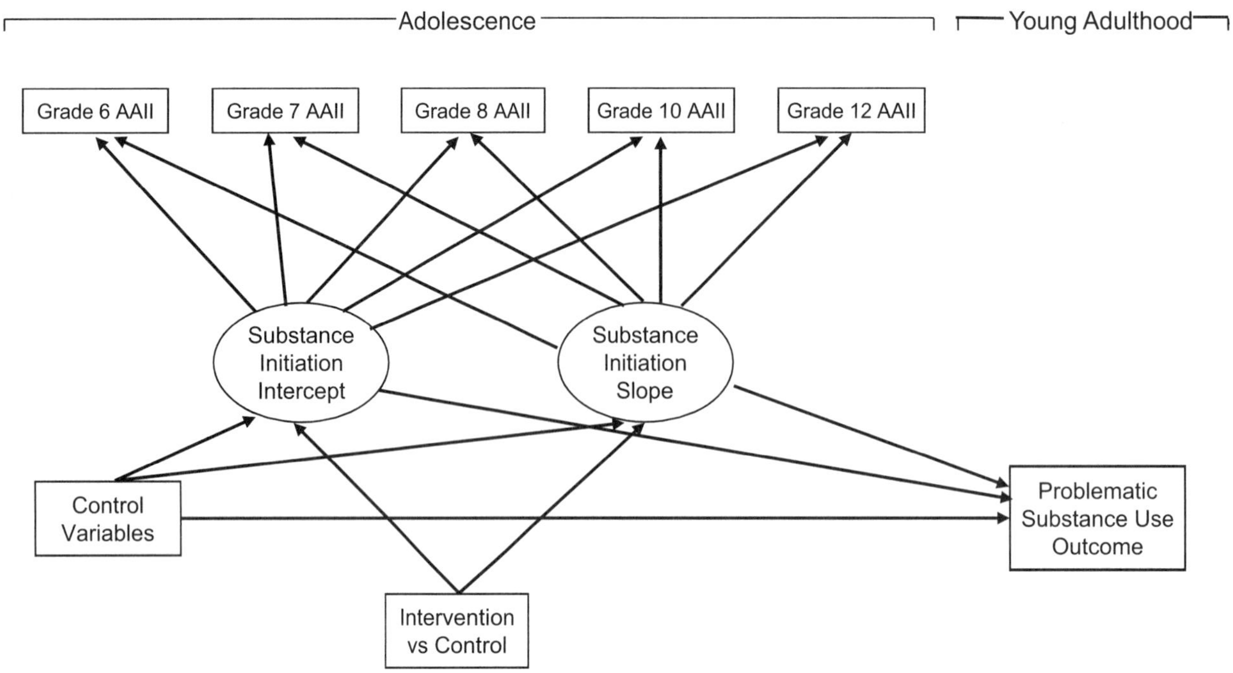

FIGURE 15.2. Model of universal intervention effects on substance misuse in young adulthood via growth in substance initiation during adolescence. Model control variables include pretest AAII, gender, parent marital status, parent education, and family income. AAII = Adolescent Alcohol, Tobacco, and Other Drug Initiation Index. From "Universal Intervention Effects on Substance Use Among Young Adults Mediated by Delayed Adolescent Substance Initiation," by R. Spoth, L. Trudeau, M. Guyll, C. Shin, and C. Redmond, 2009, *Journal of Consulting and Clinical Psychology, 77*, p. 625. Copyright 2009 by the American Psychological Association.

Similar analyses in the CaFaY trial also showed indirect effects of the ISFP on reduced illicit drug use at age 21, ten years postintervention. This effect was achieved through a reduced rate of increase in adolescent substance use exposure, which we termed a *protective shield* (see Spoth, Trudeau, Guyll, & Shin, 2012). Further support for this mechanism was provided through a replication and extension of the developmental model tested in the Project Family trial, summarized above, using follow-up data through age 24 (Spoth, Trudeau, Redmond, & Shin, in press).

Long-term ISFP/SFP 10-14 effects are not limited to substance use outcomes but also include indirect effects on lifetime sexually transmitted diseases, number of sexual partners, and substance use during sex in early adulthood through reduced substance use exposure in adolescence (Spoth, Clair, & Trudeau, 2014). Taken together, results from these studies provide evidence of long-term benefits from brief, universal family-focused preventive intervention and support a developmental model positing that proximal effects during adolescence can extend over adolescence and into early adulthood.

Crossover Effects

There is growing evidence that substance misuse preventive interventions can have effects that generalize to nontargeted substances and other outcomes. Such *crossover effects* have been demonstrated for the SFP 10-14. Nontargeted substance misuse outcomes for the ISFP/SFP 10-14 include both prescription drug misuse and methamphetamine (meth) use. Long-term follow-up studies have shown that ISFP condition participants compared with control participants reported less narcotic use in the 12th grade as well as less narcotic and barbiturate use at age 21 (Spoth, Trudeau, Shin, & Redmond, 2008). In analyses of the effects of the multicomponent SFP 10-14 + Life Skills Training (LST), intervention group members reported significantly less lifetime prescription drug misuse than their control counterparts in late adolescence (see Spoth, Trudeau, et al., 2013), as shown in Figure 15.3. This combined intervention

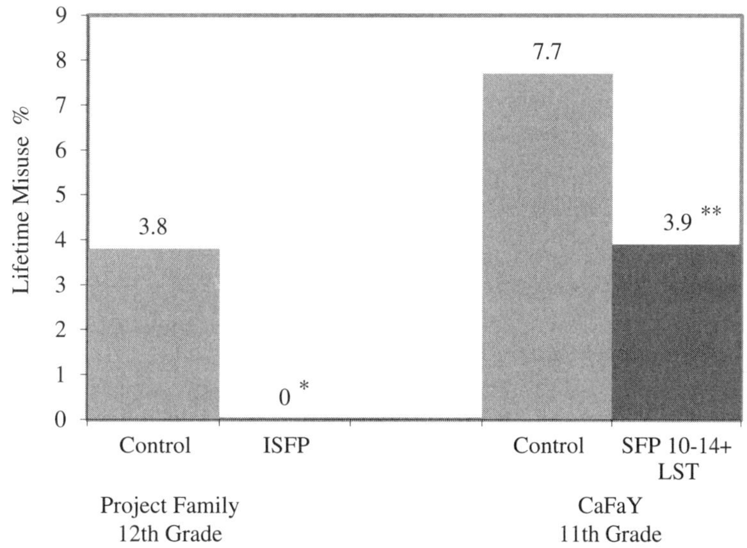

FIGURE 15.3. **Lifetime prescription drug misuse: Project Family and CaFaY Trials. ISFP = Iowa Strengthening Families Program; SFP 10-14 + LST = Strengthening Families Program: For Parents and Youth 10–14 + Life Skills Training. From "Long-Term Effects of Universal Preventive Interventions on Prescription Drug Misuse," by R. Spoth, L. Trudeau, C. Shin, and C. Redmond, 2008, *Addiction, 103,* p. 1166. Copyright 2008 by the Society for the Study of Addiction. Reprinted with permission.**
$^{*}p < .05$. $^{**}p < .01$, one-sided, for test of intervention-control difference.

approach also has demonstrated significant effects on lifetime and past-year meth use among youth (Spoth, Clair, Shin, & Redmond, 2006).

ISFP/SFP 10-14 crossover effects are not limited to nontargeted substance misuse outcomes but also have been shown to generalize to health-risking sexual behaviors in young adults (Spoth, Clair, et al., 2014) and to internalizing symptoms (depression and anxiety). For example, Trudeau, Spoth, Randall, and Azevedo (2007) found that ISFP group participants demonstrated a significantly slower rate of increase in adolescent polydrug use and internalizing symptoms than did those in the control group. Further analyses demonstrated that the ISFP had significant indirect effects on young adult internalizing symptoms through reduced growth in such symptoms across adolescence. The reasons for crossover effects of family-focused preventive interventions on internalizing symptoms are not yet fully understood. However, it is likely that such effects are partially because of intervention content addressing risk and protective factors that are common across these distinct but related outcomes. Shared risk and protective factors for substance misuse and internalizing symptoms addressed by the SFP 10-14 include family conflict, parental warmth–acceptance, parental behavioral control, and deficits in adolescent coping skills. The program also has had promising effects on adolescent academic outcomes, as indicated in a study of model mediators (e.g., school engagement, parenting competency) of long-term intervention effects on outcomes. Spoth, Randall, and Shin (2008) found significant indirect effects of the ISFP on increased school engagement in eighth grade and academic success in 12th grade through proximal intervention-targeted outcomes, including increased parenting competencies and decreased student substance-related risk.

Crossover effects further illustrate the value of the SFP 10-14 and other universal family-focused preventive interventions (e.g., Preparing for the Drug Free Years [PDFY]; Mason, Hitchings, & Spoth, 2007) by demonstrating that EBIs targeting multiple salient risk and protective processes for youth and families can have salutary effects on a range of public health and other relevant outcomes, both targeted and nontargeted. Communities are challenged by multiple public health concerns: Implementing family-focused EBIs, such as the SFP 10-14 with demonstrated crossover effects is one strategy for maximizing existing resources to prevent and reduce multiple health-compromising outcomes.

MECHANISMS OF EFFECTS

How preventive EBIs affect targeted outcomes is a critical consideration for prevention science. Mediation analysis (MacKinnon, 2008) is a valuable methodological tool for examining intervention-induced sequences of events and has been used to understand the mechanisms of SFP 10-14 effects. This work has been guided by an outcome model summarized in several reports. For example, Spoth, Redmond, and Shin (1998) analyzed longitudinal self-report and observational data collected at pre- and posttest from 523 families to test indirect ISFP effects on parent–child affective quality and general child management through intervention-targeted behaviors (e.g., communication of substance use rules or consequences, anger management). Results from latent-variable structural equation modeling supported the hypothesized mediation model by demonstrating that the ISFP increased intervention targeted behaviors, which were associated in turn with increased parent–child affective quality as well as improved general child management. These analyses were extended, and findings were replicated out to a 1-year follow-up (Redmond, Spoth, Shin, & Lepper, 1999).

Spoth and Redmond (2002) further extended the latent variable parenting model by incorporating an intervention-targeted adolescent behavior, alcohol refusal skills, and an adolescent substance use outcome, propensity to use alcohol, based on four waves of prevention trial data. Specifically, they tested a mediation model examining indirect effects of the ISFP on adolescent alcohol propensity through targeted parent and adolescent behaviors and effective general child management, finding support for these factors as hypothesized intervention-related mechanisms of change. The analyses were distinguished by their latent-variable representation of key constructs, which accounted for the influences of parent-report and observational method factors.

Mediation analysis also has been an important tool for understanding the long-term effects of the SFP 10-14. Long-term effects of brief universal family-focused preventive interventions are not expected to be large in magnitude and are hypothesized on the basis of developmental theory to be predominantly indirect. As summarized previously, Spoth, Trudeau, et al. (2009) found indirect effects of ISFP on problem substance use in young adulthood mediated through reduced growth in substance initiation during adolescence. Similar analyses have replicated this basic pattern of findings (Spoth, Clair, et al., 2014). These studies demonstrate a strategy based on meditational models for parsimoniously addressing the complex interplay of developmental processes, including multiple proximal intervention targets that unfold in a sequence of events over time. This unfolding leads to long-term outcomes through the primary mechanism of delayed substance initiation and reduced adolescent substance use exposure. Results have provided clear support for the hypothesis that protective effects from interventions delivered during the adolescent years extend into early adulthood, providing benefits in the form of reduced problematic substance use, offending behaviors, and health-risking sexual behaviors.

MODERATION OF EFFECTS

There often are variations in an intervention's reach and impact across subgroups within a population, suggesting the presence of moderating variables, including participant or environmental characteristics (MacKinnon, Weber, & Pentz, 1988). Moderation analyses of the effects of universal preventive interventions generally have shown either the presence of very few moderators of intervention impact (Spoth et al., 1998) or a compensatory effect in which higher risk participants receive greater benefit than their lower risk counterparts (Conduct Problems Prevention Research Group, 1999). Moderation tests are critically important for the advancement of our understanding of universal family-focused prevention in that they can identify subgroups that could benefit most from the intervention or for whom intended intervention effects might be attenuated, suggesting program modifications to enhance population impact.

Guyll, Spoth, Chao, Wickrama, and Russell (2004) examined parental social–emotional maladjustment (i.e., parent internalizing and externalizing problems) as a potential moderator of ISFP effects on trajectories of adolescent substance use over a 4-year period. Investigators considered the possibility that parental risk might be associated with poorer intervention outcomes by potentially decreasing engagement in and compliance with program activities. However, results from growth curve analyses showed that the effects of the ISFP on reduced alcohol use were not moderated by parental risk. In a further extension, Spoth et al. (2006) conducted logistic growth curve analyses to test for family-related risk moderation of ISFP effects on substance initiation over a 6-year period extending from early to late adolescence. Results demonstrated effects of the ISFP on reduced alcohol and illicit substance initiation but provided no evidence of significant moderation by family risk status.

Despite research demonstrating gender differences in social development and in social developmental predictors (including family factors) of substance misuse and related problems, the degree to which gender may influence family program effects remains relatively unexplored (Kumpfer, Pinyuchon, de Melo, & Whiteside, 2008). Evidence to date indicates that family involvement and bonding, monitoring, and praise (Yeh, Chiang, & Huang, 2006); peer influences and norms (Andrews, 2005); and conventionality, depression, self-esteem, and stress (Windle, 1990) are stronger predictors of substance use and misuse for girls. Shyness, aggression, delinquency, and parent substance use are stronger predictors of these outcomes for boys (Ensminger, Juon, & Fothergill, 2002; Mason et al., 2007). These findings suggest that interventions designed to reduce family risks and increase protective factors may have stronger effects on targeted outcomes for girls than boys. Consistent with this possibility, growth curve analyses conducted by Trudeau et al. (2007) showed that the ISFP slowed the rate of increase in adolescent polydrug use significantly more for adolescent girls than for boys. Such gender differences may suggest that program modifications are needed to enhance the impact of universal family-focused interventions on outcomes for boys compared with girls or that gender-specific intervention models may be valuable (Schinke, Cole, & Fang, 2009).

Frameworks and Findings on Translation to Public Health Impact

The literature on family-focused preventive intervention research over the past 2 decades has evolved contemporaneously with theoretical development and research directed toward broader implementation of effective preventive interventions. The latter effort clarifies an important aspect of the context for both family-focused preventive intervention research efforts in general and the SFP 10-14 program of research in particular. Indeed, the burgeoning growth of implementation science highlights the potential public health impact and suggests the future course for a wide range of family-based programs. Relevant advancements in prevention science over the previous couple of decades were crystallized in the 1994 Institute of Medicine report on "frontiers for preventive intervention research" (Mrazek & Haggerty, 1994) and in a more recent, updated report (Institute of Medicine and National Research Council, 2009). The advancements summarized were placed squarely in a public health framework, with considerable attention to the family-focused intervention research like that presented herein.

More specifically, the seminal Preventive Intervention Research Cycle summarized in the 1994 report is oriented toward the translation of intervention research into broader public health or population-level impact; the 2009 report details that purpose and the research that informs it. Grounded in the 2009 report, the Society for Prevention Research Task Force on Type 2 Translation Research has summarized how to progress with broader integration of science into practice, to better achieve population-level impact. It does so through the presentation of a conceptual framework (called the Translation Science to Population Impact or TSci Impact framework; Spoth, Rohrbach, et al., 2013). This framework addresses Type 2 translation research. Although this type of research has been defined and classified in various ways in the health research literature, we define it as investigation of the complex processes and mechanisms through which tested and proven interventions are integrated into practice and policy on a large scale and in a sustainable way, across targeted populations and settings.

The individual components of the Type 2 Translation Research framework form the structure for the subsequent sections of this chapter. To elaborate, the framework outlines the intervention development and effectiveness research that is followed by (a) four translation-to-practice functions (preadoption, adoption, implementation, sustainability), optimally shaped through research-based informational feedback loops across all phases of translation; (b) the multiple (national, state, community) contexts for this work; and (c) necessary infrastructural supports (both practice based and research based). The framework is grounded in the diffusion of innovation theory (Rogers, 1995) with its core concept being that EBIs diffuse across multiple, interrelated stages. Specifically, the translation science to population impact framework articulates a translation process that entails the four translation-to-practice functions as phases of research. The success of each phase is influenced by a wide range of factors that warrant systematic study. Studies within the SFP 10-14 program of research have addressed each of these phases. Moreover, these studies have been responsive to two strong recommendations in the article presenting the framework. One recommendation is that translation-oriented research be embedded in effectiveness trials. Such has been the case with the SFP 10-14 program of research, as indicated in the previous section on program outcomes. In addition, the article highly recommends research conducted through practitioner–scientist partnerships, highlighting their many benefits. In the case of the SFP 10-14 program of research, the partnership model evolved across the three RCTs described previously.

The first generation structure for collaborative partnership-based research began with the Project Family trial (Spoth & Redmond, 2002). During this study, community-based extension agents provided assistance in hiring and coordinating local school staff as well as coordinating with the university-based researchers to implement and evaluate the ISFP. This experience was instructive in optimizing strategies for involving extension agents who could assist in coordinating intensive program implementation and evaluation research across communities. This optimizing led to a second-generation partnership structure for the next project directed toward the study of the SFP 10-14 combined with a school-based intervention (the CaFaY project). This partnership included an extension agent along with a loosely knit group of local community residents that helped organize and implement the interventions, assisted by regional extension-based coordinators.

Taking lessons learned from the first- and second-generation partnerships in hand, the partnership developed for the PROSPER project incorporated organized community teams oriented toward *sustainability*. This partnership of schools, universities, and communities, called the PROSPER Partnership Model, facilitated the use of existing public education infrastructures for the purpose of training, technical assistance, and other resources to enhance the capacity for sustained implementation of EBIs (Spoth, Greenberg, Bierman, & Redmond, 2004). A somewhat unique feature of the PROSPER approach is the use of relatively small community teams designed to be strategic and maintain focused intervention delivery goals. A second model component designed to maximize program sustainability is a continuously operating team of extension-based program implementation technical assistants.

The following section summarizes research on each of the key components of the translational research framework. Notably, seizing the opportunities for public health impact will require addressing a number of challenges in family-focused preventive intervention research, also highlighted by our research on the SFP 10-14. These challenges are summarized in the closing section of the chapter, along with a discussion of future opportunities.

TRANSLATION TO PUBLIC HEALTH IMPACT: ADOPTION, IMPLEMENTATION, AND SUSTAINABILITY

Even the most effective preventive intervention will have very limited public health impact if it is not delivered well, is poorly attended, or is implemented without quality. To achieve maximum public health impact, a universal prevention program such as the SFP 10-14 (a) must be appealing to potential participants, as well as program providers; (b) must have sufficient numbers of participants successfully recruited; and (c) be consistently delivered with sufficiently high quality to produce favorable effects. In addition, if population-level impact is to be maximized, high-quality delivery must be sustained over time. And, of course, the program must be appropriate to the targeted population, both in terms of content and participant acceptance.

Program Adoption: Economic Benefits

Ultimately, the decision to adopt and implement a program most frequently falls to program funders and service providers. Although evidence of program effectiveness is a critical consideration, it is not the only factor of relevance. Economic investment versus expected benefit is often a factor that is considered. To help address such consideration with regard to the ISFP/SFP 10-14, a number of cost analyses have been conducted.

The economic benefits of the ISFP were examined for a study that reported the estimated benefits and costs of the ISFP associated with the prevention of alcohol disorders (Spoth, Guyll, & Day, 2002). Estimates of cases prevented, costs per case prevented, benefit–cost, and net benefit were calculated based on (a) observed ISFP effects delaying the initiation of alcohol use among adolescents, (b) estimated reductions in likelihood of lifetime alcohol disorders associated with each year of delayed alcohol initiation, (c) estimates of the monetary costs associated with alcohol disorders, and (d) estimates of intervention costs. Findings indicated an economic savings of $119,633.00 per case prevented and a resulting benefit–cost ratio of $9.60 per $1.00 invested in ISFP programming, an average benefit of $5,923.00 per participating family. Sensitivity analyses suggested that these estimates were robust over a range of assumptions, including cost and program efficacy.

A second study (Guyll, Spoth, & Cornish, 2012) focused on the prevention of meth use and its subsequent benefits to employers. This study considered the ISFP and the multicomponent SFP 10-14 + LST intervention. Estimates of intervention cost, cost-effectiveness, benefit–cost ratio, and net benefit were calculated, following analyses of 12th-grade meth use rates and meth-related employer costs. On the basis of intervention effects demonstrated in the Project Family trial, cost analyses showed that the ISFP lowered meth use by 3.9%, cost $25,385 to prevent each case, and had a benefit–cost ratio of 3.84, yielding an estimated net benefit of $2,813 per youth. Drawing on results from the CaFaY project, the multicomponent SFP 10-14 + LST lowered meth use rates by 1.8%, cost $62,697 to prevent each case, and had a benefit–cost ratio of 1.56, yielding an estimated net benefit of $620 per youth. Findings were robust across a range of plausible values for key parameters. Results supported the economic use of the ISFP and multicomponent SFP 10-14 for the prevention of substance misuse and related problems.

A recent analysis examined the economic viability of the PROSPER model for the dissemination of preventive EBIs, including the SFP 10-14 (Crowley, Jones, Greenberg, Feinberg, & Spoth, 2012) guided by a cost–procedure–process–outcome analysis model (Yates, 2009). Analyses included estimates of the financial and economic costs of the PROSPER delivery system, with results suggesting that the implementation costs of delivering the SFP 10-14 are lower when using the PROSPER approach than the costs of standard (non-PROSPER supported) program delivery, by 59% to 67%. These results highlight progress in delivery-system development that can be used to increase the broader public health impact of the SFP 10-14 and similar EBIs.

Program Participation: Participation Factors and Recruitment

The public health impact of a program also is contingent on participation by a sufficient proportion of the targeted population. A number of studies have been conducted of direct relevance to family recruitment and participation in the ISFP/SFP 10-14. These studies have included (a) an examination of family participation factors using consumer preference research methods, as well as prospective and retrospective surveys of families targeted for later recruitment into prevention trials and programs, and (b) the study of community-based SFP 10-14 recruitment strategies.

Family participation factors. Consumer preference research was undertaken to evaluate how prospective participants' preferences for various program characteristics influence participation decisions. A range of program-specific attributes, such as program location, content, packaging or promotion, and time requirements, were examined through conjoint analysis. Derived from mathematical psychology and psychometrics, conjoint analysis allows measurement of the relative importance of program attributes (e.g., program duration), as well as the relative importance of preferences for specific program features or attribute levels (e.g., program durations of 5 weeks vs. 10 weeks). Results based on an examination of 39 individual family-focused prevention program features describing 11 program attributes (e.g., program meeting time, facilitator background) showed the program attributes most important to parents were meeting time, facilitator background, program duration, research base, and meeting location. Findings highlighted the importance that parents placed on the practical aspects (e.g., meeting time and duration) of family prevention programs and are consistent with findings from a study of families refusing to participate in a parent skills-training program in which time and scheduling conflicts were more often cited as reasons for nonparticipation than were parent perceptions of program efficacy (Spoth & Redmond, 1992–1993).

A range of factors influencing family participation in the SFP 10-14 and similar family-focused programs also have been examined through prospective participation factor surveys. Findings concerning family socioeconomic influences on participation and participation-related beliefs and attitudes have been mixed. Family income has generally not been found to be strongly associated with participation; on the other hand, parent education has shown small but consistently positive associations with participation-relevant beliefs and attitudes, such as parenting skill support seeking, the perceived benefits of family-focused programs, and actual program participation (Redmond et al., 2002, 2004; Spoth, Redmond, Kahn, & Shin, 1997). In contrast to mixed or weak socioeconomic status effects, findings concerning the importance of family time and scheduling constraints have been consistent and substantial, likely placing practical limits on the recruitment rates that can be achieved for the SFP 10-14 and similar family-focused interventions (Spoth et al., 1996).

Community-based program recruitment. Issues of effective and sustainable community-based SFP 10-14 recruitment were addressed directly in the PROSPER trial. When compared with community-based recruitment rates reported in the literature for other multisession universal interventions, rates in the PROSPER trial were high, averaging 17% during the first 2 years of implementation (see Spoth, Clair, Greenberg, Redmond, & Shin, 2007, for more detail on relevant recruitment studies). Factors associated with higher recruitment rates included the quality of program promotional materials, effective collaboration with technical assistance providers, and the frequency of technical assistance requests, after controlling for community and school district contextual influences (Spoth, Clair, et al., 2007). Findings support the viability of successful family-focused program recruitment by community teams that are provided with technical assistance.

Findings across multiple effectiveness trials and from the PROSPER trial in particular suggest that the strategic application of substantial resources devoted to recruitment is critical to the successful diffusion of preventive EBIs for families (Spoth & Redmond, 2000). Tactics to enhance recruitment include personal contacts, the use of well-trained recruitment personnel, convenient intervention locations, and endorsements by influential community members, as well as the use of participation incentives, such as free meals and transportation (Spoth, Clair, et al., 2007). Nonetheless, time and scheduling demands often are the primary barriers to recruitment, highlighting the importance of implementation strategies that maximize schedule flexibility and minimize time demands.

Implementation Quality

Previous research has shown that many family-focused preventive interventions have failed to maintain high-quality implementation over numerous years. This is problematic because low-quality implementation has been found to result in less positive outcomes (Durlak & DuPre, 2008). Because it is central to program efficacy, implementation quality has been monitored across SFP 10-14 trials. As reported in previously published studies, the SFP 10-14 can be delivered by community implementers with a high degree of adherence to the content specified in intervention manuals. In the Project Family trial, trained observers monitored program content delivery by recording adherence ratings; in addition to 100% coverage of broad program content areas (core elements), adherence has averaged 80% or higher for detailed content coverage (Spoth, Guyll, Trudeau, & Goldberg-Lillehoj, 2002; Spoth et al., 1998). These earlier reports of high adherence levels emphasize the benefits of the school/community–researcher collaboration for high-quality implementation. Partnership-based implementation of the research projects likely contributed to these results, including local collaborator assistance with recruitment and training of local implementers, the cultural sensitivity and user friendliness of the written materials, and local implementer training that emphasized the importance of adherence.

More recently, SFP 10-14 implementation adherence has been examined within the PROSPER trial. This is a more real-world implementation setting in which researchers are further removed from program delivery, providing technical assistance only indirectly to program facilitators who are supervised by community team leaders. On the basis of reports from trained observers, results showed uniformly high rates of SFP 10-14 implementation adherence, which averaged over 90%, as well as high ratings on other indicators of implementation quality (group participation, facilitation quality) that were sustained across the first two programming years. It is interesting to note that community team member attitudes regarding prevention showed a positive correlation of .43 with facilitation quality ratings (Spoth, Guyll, Lillehoj, Redmond, & Greenberg, 2007). More recent findings from the PROSPER trial have shown sustained SFP 10-14 implementation adherence ratings of nearly 90% across 14 community sites through 6 years of program delivery (Spoth, Guyll, Redmond, Greenberg, & Feinberg, 2011). Figure 15.4 shows that adherence levels were generally high and relatively stable, averaging above 90%. Facilitation quality also was at the upper end of the scale.

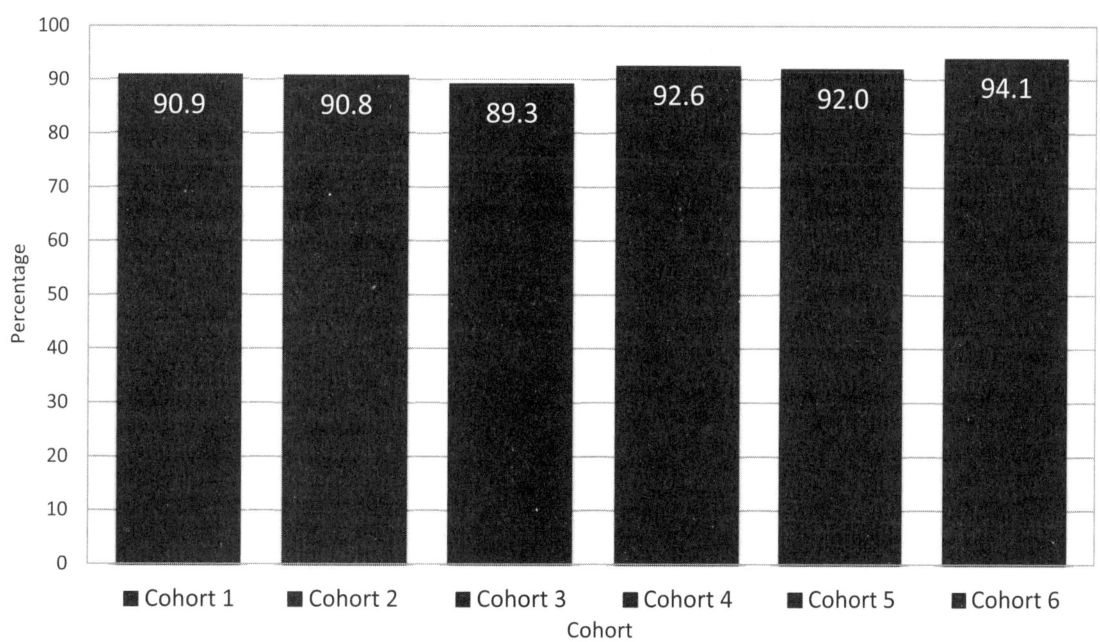

FIGURE 15.4. Long-term adherence for SFP 10-14 observer ratings for Cohorts 1–6. From "Six-Year Sustainability of Evidence-Based Intervention Implementation Quality by Community-University Partnerships: The PROSPER Study," by R. Spoth, M. Guyll, C. Redmond, M. Greenberg, and M. Feinberg, 2011, *American Journal of Community Psychology, 48*, p. 419. Copyright 2011 by Springer. Reprinted with permission.

Culturally competent implementation. Research has demonstrated that interventions designed for a White, middle-class American population may not be well-received by cultural subgroups that do not relate to program materials or messages inconsistent with the values and beliefs of their community (Kumpfer, Alvarado, Smith, & Bellamy, 2002). The majority of evidence-based parent-training interventions have been guided by European American cultural norms and values and may not capture the full breadth of ethnic minority parenting practices (Calzada, 2010). A number of researchers have suggested that EBIs should undergo an adaptation process to increase their cultural relevancy before dissemination (Domenech Rodriguez, Baumann, & Schwartz, 2011). This process should include guidance from empirical research with the target population, quantitative or qualitative, to ensure that relevant cultural issues are included and addressed in the intervention. Thus, it is important that adaptations to existing family-focused EBIs be made and tested to ensure they are culturally relevant and appropriate for all subcultural groups within a general population. A number of adaptations have been made to the SFP 10-14 curriculum to render the program relevant and appropriate for a wide range of subpopulations within the United States and all over the world. Notably, SFP 10-14 adaptations have been developed for African American (Strong African-American Families) and Latino families (Familias Fuertes Program) in the United States and South America.[4]

Sustainability of Delivery

Sustainability is one of the key challenges to achieving community-level impact through EBIs (Spoth & Greenberg, 2011). Most PROSPER community teams have been successfully implementing programming for 11 years. And, although PROSPER programming involves both the SFP 10-14 and a school-based drug-prevention program, the vast majority of community teams' efforts and financial resources are devoted to delivery of the family-focused SFP 10-14. As such, the sustained functioning of community teams and sustained delivery of SFP 10-14 are closely linked. To sustain team operations and ongoing delivery of SFP 10-14, teams have used a range of strategies for generating financial and in-kind resources, managing program-delivery quality, strengthening partnerships with the local school district and other community organizations, creating communication and marketing plans, monitoring team functioning, conducting regular meetings, and providing recognition and rewards to sustain interest and support in PROSPER programming. A focus on these strategies, supported by the PROSPER partnership-based technical assistance structure, has successfully contributed to the success of SFP 10-14 and school-based programming demonstrated in PROSPER communities.

CURRENT AND PLANNED EFFORTS TO ADDRESS KEY RESEARCH CHALLENGES

An earlier review (Spoth, Greenberg, & Turrisi, 2009) highlighted a range of challenges in preventive intervention science that are broadly applicable to the subfield of family-focused preventive intervention. These challenges concerned (a) limited longitudinal study, (b) lack of specificity in logic models, (c) a need for greater specificity in self-reported outcome measures and related measurement issues, (d) limited replication study, (e) limited study of active ingredients or core components and outcome mediators, (f) limited economic analyses, and (g) limited study of factors that moderate effects. Many of these challenges have been salient and addressed in the SFP 10-14 program of research; they can be divided into two categories. The first category involves challenges that are currently being addressed in ongoing studies and have already been discussed. These challenges include, for example, limited study of mediators, factors that moderate program effects, and economic cost analyses. A second category of challenges are central to the rationale for specific research efforts planned for the future, as discussed below.

Selected Challenges for Planned Projects

Challenge of limited longitudinal study across developmental stages. Most studies of family-focused preventive interventions, particularly

[4] For more detail see http://www.ppsi.iastate.edu/APAChapter/SFP10-14_Adaptations.pdf

selected and universal types, have limited longitudinal follow-up assessments (Foxcroft, Ireland, Lister-Sharp, Lowe, & Breen, 2003). In this context, it is especially important to examine the broader effects (beyond those on substance misuse) on young-adult functioning during the transitional period from late adolescence through young adulthood.

Research has documented adverse consequences of prior substance misuse on life-course roles and transitions, such as postsecondary education, work, marriage, and having children, which in turn influence adult substance misuse patterns (Schulenberg, O'Malley, Bachman, & Johnston, 2005). Consequently, life-course pathways defined by those roles and transitions have important implications for continued substance misuse and for ongoing health and well-being in other areas of functioning throughout adulthood. Given findings showing that SFP 10-14 implementation with young adolescents can reduce substance misuse among adolescents, with effects carrying forward into emerging adulthood, it will be worthwhile to examine the potential for preventive intervention with young adolescents to influence life-course pathways and improve subsequent young adult health and functioning. To examine this question, research is planned that will follow-up the Project Family panel sample as they move into their early 30s, a time at which many adult roles such as those related to family formation and career development have been established. The collection of that follow-up data will allow the examination of how adolescent and emerging adult substance misuse affects the successful transition into adult roles, and also important, how preventive intervention effects on adolescent and emerging adult substance misuse may alter the sequence, timing, and successful adoption of those roles.

Needed culturally competent adaptations. Castro, Barrera, and Martinez (2004) suggested that interventions can be made culturally relevant to a subcultural group by making content understandable (e.g., using the group's language), interesting and important to the group, and applicable to the group's everyday life. A challenge to creating cultural adaptations to EBIs is the heterogeneity that exists within each cultural group, including level of acculturation (Castro, Barrera, & Holleran Steiker, 2010). Once program materials have been modified for culturally relevant and appropriate use with a wide range of ethnic groups, an important next step is to determine whether the culturally adapted curriculum produces the same effects in the new target population as were found in the original research trial. Along these lines, Castro and colleagues are planning to collaborate with other researchers to conduct a RCT of the Familias Fuertes Program. Although this adaptation of the SFP 10-14 for South American families (and also for Latino families living in the United States) has been evaluated with smaller pilot studies in Latino populations in the United States (Reidy, Orpinas, & Davis, 2012) and South America (Correa, Zubarew, Valenzuela, & Salas, 2012), it has not yet undergone a rigorous trial testing its efficacy.

Limited attention to scale-up infrastructures and factors. In earlier sections, this challenge has been framed in terms of the limited research on factors influencing the key translation functions at the pre-adoption, adoption, implementation, and sustainability phases. Although substantial scale-up progress has been made in the cases of some family-focused preventive interventions (see Dishion, 2012), new frameworks and models are needed to guide future research in this area (Sandler et al., 2005). Addressing how to reach additional populations in a culturally sensitive and competent way is one key aspect of future research on the SFP 10-14, as just illustrated. In addition to a scale-up approach that is culturally sensitive and competent, translation-oriented research requires broader ecological sensitivity to the multiple contexts in which the SFP 10-14 is being implemented (Spoth, Rohrbach, et al., 2013).

Our future research will focus on how to optimize all translation functions through PROSPER partnership-based delivery of the SFP 10-14 and companion school-based programs. Specifically, a collaborative effort with the lead SFP 10-14 dissemination program staff at our university is being planned that will entail a multisite randomized controlled effectiveness study in selected states. In addition to longitudinal evaluation of the primary outcomes specified in the outcome section of this chapter, multiple translation research studies will be embedded in the effectiveness trial. These studies will address high-priority research questions in each of the areas of adoption, implementation, and sustainability research including economic analysis (see corresponding recommendations in Spoth, Rohrbach, et al., 2013). For example, a planned adoption-related study to be conducted early in the trial will use a consumer research technique (conjoint analysis) to inform improved strategies for increasing consumer demand for the SFP 10-14, following a model applied in earlier research (see Cunningham et al., 2009; Spoth & Redmond, 1992–1993). In addition, social network analyses of social influence factors in extension-based administrators' decision making about adopting and implementing the SFP 10-14 will be conducted, extending an earlier pilot study. Finally, a planned study will examine the use of social media and text messaging to cue home-based application of techniques about which youth and parents receive instruction in the SFP 10-14. Technological adaptations relevant to program delivery also will be tested; most notably, the effectiveness of web-based program facilitator training to support high-quality program delivery as a more convenient and cost-effective alternative to the current in-person group trainings.

CONCLUSION

As emphasized in our introduction, there is a compelling case for advancing the subfield of family-focused preventive intervention research. The case is strikingly evident in the data on unacceptably high rates of health-compromising problem behaviors among our youth, along with the numerous threats to their positive development and the many challenges caregivers confront in optimally nurturing their development. The case is further underscored by all of the negative social, health, and economic consequences of the high rates of youth problem behaviors. Public health–oriented intervention research is well suited to the amelioration of these negative consequences. There are, however, gaps in the relevant research base that have been identified over the past 30 years; many remain to be filled, and there are challenges to surmount in filling these gaps.

In this chapter, we have highlighted our attempts to address the research gaps and related challenges through a series of SFP 10-14 studies over the past 23 years. This program of research has yielded many instructive patterns of findings concerning the SFP 10-14's development, outcomes, mechanisms of effects, cultural adaptations, and factors in its translation to widespread practice. Among others, some key findings from studies of the SFP 10-14 (as a stand-alone intervention or when combined with school-based interventions), include (a) achievement of long-term point-in-time effects on substance misuse, up to 14 years past baseline, into young adulthood; (b) positive changes of problem behavior trajectories across multiple developmental stages; (c) accomplishment of a wide range of crossover effects that were not directly targeted (e.g., school attachment, academic performance, reducing internalizing problems, health-risking sexual behaviors); (d) demonstration of cost-effectiveness and other economic benefits; (e) effective engagement of families who can benefit; and (f) quality, sustained implementation, in the context of community–university partnerships. These key sets of findings are informing plans for future research, including those focusing on long-term life-course effects, effectiveness of cultural adaptations, and multisite scale-up research.

Most important to note, it is worth underscoring how the progress in the subfield overall and our SFP 10-14 program of research in particular highlight future potential for public health impact. This potential is especially clear in recent work showing the viability of partnership-based scale-up efforts designed to reach increasing numbers of youth and families who could benefit from the SFP 10-14. By carefully building on the work of other researchers in this promising area of preventive intervention, by addressing the evident research challenges and applying what has been learned from SFP 10-14 research to date, we hope the next generation of SFP 10-14 research will provide further dividends on the resources invested. In this way, the progress of research could contribute to the larger effort to improve the health and well-being of the youth and families potentially served for the present generation and those to come.

References

Andrews, J. A. (2005). Substance abuse in girls. In D. J. Bell, S. L. Foster, & E. J. Mash (Eds.), *Handbook of behavioral and emotional problems in girls* (pp. 181–209). New York, NY: Springer. doi:10.1007/0-306-48674-1_6

Bierman, K. L., Cole, J. D., Dodge, K. A., Greenberg, M. T., Lochman, J. E., & McMahon, R. J. (1997). Implementing a comprehensive program for the prevention of conduct problems in rural communities: The Fast Track experience. *American Journal of Community Psychology, 25*, 493–514. doi:10.1023/A:1024659622528

Biglan, A. (1995). Choosing a paradigm to guide prevention research and practice. *Drugs and Society, 8*, 149–160. doi:10.1300/J023v08n03_13

Calzada, E. J. (2010). Bringing culture into parent training with Latinos. *Cognitive and Behavioral Practice, 17*, 167–175. doi:10.1016/j.cbpra.2010.01.003

Castro, F. G., Barrera, M., & Holleran Steiker, L. K. (2010). Issues and challenges in the design of culturally-adapted evidence-based interventions. *Annual Review of Clinical Psychology, 6*, 213–239. doi:10.1146/annurev-clinpsy-033109-132032

Castro, F. G., Barrera, M., Jr., & Martinez, C. R., Jr. (2004). The cultural adaptation of prevention interventions: Resolving tensions between fidelity and fit. *Prevention Science, 5*, 41–45. doi:10.1023/B:PREV.0000013980.12412.cd

Conduct Problems Prevention Research Group. (1999). Initial impact of the Fast Track prevention trial for conduct problems: I. The high-risk sample. *Journal of Consulting and Clinical Psychology, 67*, 631–647. doi:10.1037/0022-006X.67.5.631

Conger, R. D., Lorenz, F., Elder, G., Melby, J., Simmons, R., & Conger, K. (1991). A process model of family economic pressure and early adolescent alcohol use. *The Journal of Early Adolescence, 11*, 430–449. doi:10.1177/0272431691114003

Correa, M. L., Zubarew, T., Valenzuela, M. T., & Salas, F. (2012). Evaluation of the program "Strong Families: Love and Limits" in families with teenagers aged 10 to 14 years. *Revista Medica de Chile, 140*, 726–731.

Crowley, D. M., Jones, D. E., Greenberg, M. T., Feinberg, M. E., & Spoth, R. L. (2012). Resource consumption of a dissemination model for prevention programs: The PROSPER delivery system. *Journal of Adolescent Health, 50*, 256–263. doi:10.1016/j.jadohealth. 2011.07.001

Cunningham, C. E., Valliancourt, T., Rimas, T., Deal, K., Cunningham, L., Short, K., & Chen, Y. (2009). Modeling the bullying prevention program preferences of educators: A discrete choice conjoint experiment. *Journal of Abnormal Child Psychology, 37*, 929–943. doi:10.1007/s10802-009-9324-2

Dishion, T. J. (2012). Juvenile forensic psychology and psychiatry: The movement toward data-based innovations. In E. Grigorenko (Ed.), *Handbook of juvenile forensic psychology and psychiatry* (pp. 579–584). New York, NY: Springer. doi:10.1007/978-1-4614-0905-2_37

Dodge, K. A., Malone, P. S., Lansford, J. E., Miller, S., Pettit, G. S., & Bates, J. E. (2009). A dynamic cascade model of the development of substance-use onset. *Monographs of the Society for Research in Child Development, 74*(Serial No. 294).

Domenech Rodriguez, M. M., Baumann, A. A., & Schwartz, A. L. (2011). Cultural adaptation of an evidence based intervention: From theory to practice in a Latino/a community context. *American Journal of Community Psychology, 47*, 170–186. doi:10.1007/s10464-010-9371-4

Durlak, J. A., & DuPre, E. (2008). Implementation matters: A review of research on the influence of implementation on program outcomes and the factors affecting implementation. *American Journal of Community Psychology, 41*, 327–350. doi:10.1007/s10464-008-9165-0

Ensminger, M. E., Juon, H. S., & Fothergill, K. (2002). Childhood and adolescent antecedents of substance use in early adulthood. *Addiction, 97*, 833–844. doi:10.1046/j.1360-0443.2002.00138.x

Foxcroft, D. R., Ireland, D., Lister-Sharp, D. J., Lowe, G., & Breen, R. (2003). Longer-term primary prevention for alcohol misuse in young people: A systematic review. *Addiction, 98*, 397–411. doi:10.1046/j.1360-0443.2003.00355.x

Guyll, M., Spoth, R., Chao, W., Wickrama, K., & Russell, D. (2004). Family-focused preventive interventions: Evaluating parental risk moderation of substance use trajectories. *Journal of Family Psychology, 18*, 293–301. doi:10.1037/0893-3200.18.2.293

Guyll, M., Spoth, R., & Cornish, M. (2012). Substance misuse prevention and economic analysis: Challenges and opportunities regarding international utility. *Substance Use & Misuse, 47*, 877–888. doi:10.3109/10826084.2012.663276

Institute of Medicine and National Research Council. (2009). *Preventing mental, emotional, and behavioral disorders among young people: Progress and possibilities.* Washington, DC: The National Academies Press.

Kumpfer, K. (1994). *Strengthening America's Families: Promising parenting and family strategies for delinquency prevention: User's guide.* Silver Spring, MD: Office of Juvenile Delinquency Prevention, U.S. Department of Justice.

Kumpfer, K. L., Alvarado, R., Smith, P., & Bellamy, N. (2002). Cultural sensitivity in universal family-based prevention interventions. *Prevention Science, 3*, 241–246. doi:10.1023/A:1019902902119

Kumpfer, K. L., DeMarsh, J. P., & Child, W. (1989). *Strengthening Families Program: Children's skills training curriculum manual, parenting training manual, children's skill training manual, and family skills training manual*

(*Prevention Services to Children of Substance-Abusing Parents*). Salt Lake City: University of Utah, Social Research Institute, Graduate School of Social Work.

Kumpfer, K. L., Pinyuchon, M., de Melo, A. T., & Whiteside, H. O. (2008). Cultural adaptation process for international dissemination of the Strengthening Families Program. *Evaluation & The Health Professions, 31*, 226–239. doi:10.1177/0163278708315926

MacKinnon, D. P. (2008). *Introduction to statistical mediation analysis*. Mahwah, NJ: Erlbaum.

MacKinnon, D. P., Weber, M. D., & Pentz, M. A. (1988). How do school-based drug prevention programs work and for whom? *Drugs and Society, 3*, 125–143.

Mason, W. A., Hitchings, J. E., & Spoth, R. L. (2007). Emergence of delinquency and depressed mood throughout adolescence as predictors of late adolescent problem substance use. *Psychology of Addictive Behaviors, 21*, 13–24. doi:10.1037/0893-164X.21.1.13

Molgaard, V. K. (1997). The Extension Service as key mechanism for research and services delivery for prevention of mental health disorders in rural areas. *American Journal of Community Psychology, 25*, 515–544. doi:10.1023/A:1024611706598

Molgaard, V. K., Spoth, R., & Redmond, C. (2000). *Competency training: The Strengthening Families Program for Parents and Youth 10-14. OJJDP Juvenile Justice Bulletin* (NCJ 182208). Washington, DC: U.S. Department of Justice, Office of Juvenile Justice and Delinquency Prevention.

Mrazek, P. J., & Haggerty, R. J. (Eds.). (1994). *Reducing risks for mental disorders: Frontiers for preventive intervention research*. Washington, DC: National Academy Press.

Offord, D. R., Kraemer, H. C., Kazdin, A. E., Jensen, P. S., & Harrington, R. (1998). Lowering the burden of suffering from child psychiatric disorder: Trade-offs among clinical, targeted, and universal interventions. *Journal of the American Academy of Child & Adolescent Psychiatry, 37*, 686–694. doi:10.1097/00004583-199807000-00007

Prinz, R. J., & Miller, G. E. (1996). Parental engagement in interventions for children at risk for conduct disorder. In R. D. Peters & R. J. McMahon (Eds.), *Preventing childhood disorders, substance abuse, and delinquency* (pp. 161–183). Newbury Park, CA: Sage. doi:10.4135/9781483327679.n8

Redmond, C., Spoth, R., Shin, C., & Hill, G. (2004). Engaging rural parents in family-focused programs to prevent youth substance abuse. *Journal of Primary Prevention, 24*, 223–242. doi:10.1023/B:JOPP.0000018047.58778.d1

Redmond, C., Spoth, R., Shin, C., & Lepper, H. (1999). Modeling long-term parent outcomes of two universal family-focused preventive interventions: One-year follow-up results. *Journal of Consulting and Clinical Psychology, 67*, 975–984. doi:10.1037/0022-006X.67.6.975

Redmond, C., Spoth, R., & Trudeau, L. (2002). Family- and community-level predictors of parent support seeking. *Journal of Community Psychology, 30*, 153–171. doi:10.1002/jcop.10002

Redmond, C., Spoth, R. L., Shin, C., Schainker, L., Greenberg, M., & Feinberg, M. (2009). Long-term protective factor outcomes of evidence-based interventions implemented by community teams through a community-university partnership. *Journal of Primary Prevention, 30*, 513–530.

Reidy, M. C., Orpinas, P., & Davis, M. (2012). Successful recruitment and retention of Latino study participants. *Health Promotion Practice, 13*, 779–787. doi:10.1177/1524839911405842

Robertson, E. B., Sloboda, Z., Boyd, G., Beatty, L., & Kozel, N. (Eds.). (1997). *Rural substance abuse: State of knowledge and issues*. Rockville, MD: National Institute on Drug Abuse.

Rogers, E. M. (1995). *Diffusion of innovations* (4th ed.). New York, NY: Free Press.

Sandler, I., Ostrom, A., Bitner, M. J., Ayers, T. S., Wolchik, S., & Daniels, V. S. (2005). Developing effective prevention services for the real world: A prevention service development model. *American Journal of Community Psychology, 35*, 127–142. doi:10.1007/s10464-005-3389-z

Schinke, S. P., Cole, K. C. A., & Fang, L. (2009). Gender-specific intervention to reduce underage drinking among early adolescent girls: A test of a computer-mediated, mother-daughter program. *Journal of Studies on Alcohol and Drugs, 70*, 70–77.

Schulenberg, J., O'Malley, P. M., Bachman, J. G., & Johnston, L. D. (2005). Early adult transitions and their relation to well-being and substance use. In R. Settersten, Jr., F. Furstenberg, Jr., & R. Rumbaut (Eds.), *On the frontier of adulthood: Theory, research, and public policy* (pp. 417–453). Chicago, IL: University of Chicago Press. doi:10.7208/chicago/9780226748924.003.0013

Shrout, P. E., & Bolger, N. (2002). Mediation in experimental and nonexperimental studies: New procedures and recommendations. *Psychological Methods, 7*, 422–445. doi:10.1037/1082-989X.7.4.422

Spoth, R. (2007). Opportunities to meet challenges in rural prevention research: Findings from an evolving community-university partnership model. *The Journal of Rural Health, 23*, 42–54. doi:10.1111/j.1748-0361.2007.00123.x

Spoth, R. (2008). Translating family-focused prevention science into effective practice. Toward a translational impact paradigm. *Current Directions in Psychological Science, 17*, 415–421. doi:10.1111/j.1467-8721.2008.00617.x

Spoth, R., Clair, S., Greenberg, M., Redmond, C., & Shin, C. (2007). Toward dissemination of evidence-based family interventions: Maintenance of community-based partnership recruitment results and associated factors. *Journal of Family Psychology*, *21*, 137–146. doi:10.1037/0893-3200.21.2.137

Spoth, R., Clair, S., & Trudeau, L. (2014). Universal family-focused intervention with young adolescents: Effects on health-risking sexual behaviors and STDs among young adults. *Prevention Science, 15*(Suppl. 1), s47–s58. doi:10.1007/s11121-012-0321-2

Spoth, R., & Greenberg, M. (2011). Impact challenges in community science-with-practice: Lessons from PROSPER on transformative practitioner–scientist partnerships and prevention infrastructure development. *American Journal of Community Psychology, 48*, 106–119. doi:10.1007/s10464-010-9417-7

Spoth, R., Greenberg, M., Bierman, K., & Redmond, C. (2004). PROSPER Community–university partnership model for public education systems: Capacity-building for evidence-based, competence-building prevention. *Prevention Science, 5*, 31–39. doi:10.1023/B:PREV.0000013979.52796.8b

Spoth, R., Greenberg, M., & Turrisi, R. (2009). Overview of preventive interventions addressing underage drinking: State of the evidence and steps toward public health impact. *Alcohol Research & Health, 32*, 53–66.

Spoth, R., Guyll, M., & Day, S. X. (2002). Universal family-focused interventions in alcohol-use disorder prevention: Cost-effectiveness and cost-benefit analyses of two interventions. *Journal of Studies on Alcohol, 63*, 219–228.

Spoth, R., Guyll, M., Lillehoj, C. J., Redmond, C., & Greenberg, M. (2007). PROSPER study of evidence-based intervention implementation quality by community–university partnerships. *Journal of Community Psychology, 35*, 981–999. doi:10.1002/jcop.20207

Spoth, R., Guyll, M., Redmond, C., Greenberg, M., & Feinberg, M. (2011). Six-year sustainability of evidence-based intervention implementation quality by community-university partnerships: The PROSPER study. *American Journal of Community Psychology, 48*, 412–425. doi:10.1007/s10464-011-9430-5

Spoth, R., Guyll, M., & Shin, C. (2009). Universal intervention as a protective shield against exposure to substance use: Long-term outcomes and public health significance. *American Journal of Public Health, 99*, 2026–2033.

Spoth, R., Guyll, M., Trudeau, L., & Goldberg-Lillehoj, C. (2002). Two studies of proximal outcomes and implementation quality of universal preventive interventions in a community–university collaboration context. *Journal of Community Psychology, 30*, 499–518. doi:10.1002/jcop.10021

Spoth, R., & Molgaard, V. (1999). Project Family: A partnership integrating research with the practice of promoting family and youth competencies. In T. R. Chibucos & R. Lerner (Eds.), *Serving children and families through community–university partnerships: Success stories* (pp. 127–137). Boston, MA: Kluwer Academic. doi:10.1007/978-1-4615-5053-2_18

Spoth, R., Randall, G. K., & Shin, C. (2008). Increasing school success through partnership-based family competency training: Experimental study of long-term outcomes. *School Psychology Quarterly, 23*, 70–89. doi:10.1037/1045-3830.23.1.70

Spoth, R., Randall, G. K., Shin, C., & Redmond, C. (2005). Randomized study of combined universal family and school preventive interventions: Patterns of long-term effects on initiation, regular use, and weekly drunkenness. *Psychology of Addictive Behaviors, 19*, 372–381.

Spoth, R., Randall, G. K., Trudeau, L., Shin, C., & Redmond, C. (2008). Substance use outcomes 5.5 years past baseline for partnership-based, family-school preventive interventions. *Drug and Alcohol Dependence, 96*, 57–68.

Spoth, R., & Redmond, C. (1992–1993). Study of participation barriers in family-focused prevention: Research issues and preliminary results. *International Quarterly of Community Health Education, 13*, 365–388. doi:10.2190/69LM-59KD-K9CE-8Y8B

Spoth, R., & Redmond, C. (2000). Research on family engagement in preventive interventions: Toward improved use of scientific findings in primary prevention practice. *Journal of Primary Prevention, 21*, 267–284. doi:10.1023/A:1007039421026

Spoth, R., Redmond, C., Clair, S., Shin, C., Greenberg, M. & Feinberg, M. (2011). Preventing substance misuse through community-university partnerships: Randomized controlled trial outcomes 4.5 years past baseline. *American Journal of Preventive Medicine, 40*, 440–447. doi:10.1016/j.amepre.2010.12.012.

Spoth, R., Redmond, C., Hockaday, C., & Shin, C. (1996). Barriers to participation in family skills preventive interventions and their evaluations: A replication and extension. *Family Relations, 45*, 247–254. doi:10.2307/585496

Spoth, R., Redmond, C., & Lepper, H. (1999). Alcohol initiation outcomes of universal family-focused preventive interventions: One- and two-year follow ups of a controlled study. *Journal of Studies on Alcohol, 13*, 103–111.

Spoth, R., Redmond, C., & Shin, C. (1998). Direct and indirect latent-variable parenting outcomes of two universal family-focused preventive interventions: Extending a public health-oriented research base. *Journal of Consulting and Clinical Psychology, 66*, 385–399. doi:10.1037/0022-006X.66.2.385

Spoth, R., Redmond, C., & Shin, C. (2000). Modeling factors influencing enrollment in family-focused preventive intervention research. *Prevention Science, 1*, 213–225.

Spoth, R., Redmond, C., Shin, C., & Azevedo, K. (2004). Brief family intervention effects on adolescent substance initiation: School-level curvilinear growth curve analyses six years following baseline. *Journal of Consulting and Clinical Psychology, 72*, 535–542. doi:10.1037/0022-006X.72.3.535

Spoth, R., Redmond, C., Shin, C., Greenberg, M., Feinberg, M., & Schainker, L. (2013). PROSPER community-university partnership delivery system effects on substance misuse through 6 1/2 years past baseline from a cluster randomized controlled intervention trial. *Preventive Medicine, 56*, 190–196. doi:10.1016/j.ypmed.2012.12.013.

Spoth, R., Redmond, C., Shin, C., Greenberg, M., Clair, S., & Feinberg, M. (2007). Substance use outcomes at 18 months past baseline: The PROSPER community-university partnership trial. *American Journal of Preventive Medicine, 32*(5), 395–402.

Spoth, R., Reyes, M. L., Redmond, C., & Shin, C. (1999). Assessing a public health approach to delay onset and progression of adolescent substance use: Latent transition and loglinear analyses of longitudinal family preventive intervention outcomes. *Journal of Consulting and Clinical Psychology, 67*, 619–630.

Spoth, R., Rohrbach, L. A., Greenberg, M., Leaf, P., Brown, C. H., Fagan, A., . . . Hawkins, J. D. (2013). Addressing core challenges for the next generation of type 2 translation research and systems: The Translation Science to Population Impact (TSci Impact) framework. *Prevention Science, 14*, 319–351. doi:10.1007/s11121-012-0362-6

Spoth, R., Trudeau, L., Guyll, M., Shin, C., & Redmond, C. (2009). Universal intervention effects on substance use among young adults mediated by delayed adolescent substance initiation. *Journal of Consulting and Clinical Psychology, 77*, 620–632. doi:10.1037/a0016029

Spoth, R., Trudeau, L., Redmond, C., & Shin, C. (in press). Replication RCT of early universal prevention effects on young adult substance misuse. *Journal of Consulting and Clinical Psychology.*

Spoth, R., Trudeau, L., Redmond, C., Shin, C., Greenberg, M., Feinberg, M., & Hyun, G. (2014). *PROSPER partnership delivery system: Effects on conduct problem behavior outcomes through 6.5 years past baseline.* Manuscript submitted for publication.

Spoth, R., Trudeau, L., Shin, C., Ralston, E., Redmond, C., Greenberg, M., & Feinberg, M. (2013). Longitudinal effects of universal preventive intervention on prescription drug misuse: Three RCTs with late adolescents and young adults. *American Journal of Public Health, 103*, 665–672. doi:10.2105/AJPH.2012.301209

Spoth, R., Trudeau, L., Shin, C., & Redmond, C. (2008). Long-term effects of universal preventive interventions on prescription drug misuse. *Addiction, 103*, 1160–1168. doi:10.1111/j.1360-0443.2008.02160.x

Spoth, R. L., Clair, S., Shin, C., & Redmond, C. (2006). Long-term effects of universal preventive interventions on methamphetamine use among adolescents. *Archives of Pediatrics & Adolescent Medicine, 160*, 876–882. doi:10.1001/archpedi.160.9.876

Spoth, R. L., Kavanagh, K., & Dishion, T. (2002). Family-centered preventive intervention science: Toward benefits to larger populations of children, youth, and families. *Prevention Science, 3*, 145–152. doi:10.1023/A:1019924615322

Spoth, R. L., & Redmond, C. (2002). Project Family prevention trials based in community–university partnerships: Toward scaled up preventive interventions. *Prevention Science, 3*, 203–221. doi:10.1023/A:1019946617140

Spoth, R. L., Redmond, C., Kahn, J. H., & Shin, C. (1997). A prospective validation study of inclination, belief, and context predictors of family-focused prevention involvement. *Family Process, 36*, 403–429. doi:10.1111/j.1545-5300.1997.00403.x

Spoth, R. L., Redmond, C., & Shin, C. (2001). Randomized trial of brief family interventions for general populations: Adolescent substance use outcomes four years following baseline. *Journal of Consulting and Clinical Psychology, 69*, 627–642. doi:10.1037/0022-006X.69.4.627

Spoth, R. L., Redmond, C., Trudeau, L., & Shin, C. (2002). Longitudinal substance initiation outcomes for a universal preventive intervention combining family and school programs. *Psychology of Addictive Behaviors, 16*, 129–134.

Spoth, R. L., Trudeau, L., Guyll, M., & Shin, C. (2012). Benefits of universal intervention effects on a youth protective shield 10 years after baseline. *Journal of Adolescent Health, 50*, 414–417. doi:10.1016/j.jadohealth.2011.06.010

Trudeau, L., Spoth, R., Randall, G. K., & Azevedo, K. (2007). Longitudinal effects of a universal family-focused intervention on growth patterns of adolescent internalizing symptoms and polysubstance use: Gender comparisons. *Journal of Youth and Adolescence, 36*, 725–740. doi:10.1007/s10964-007-9179-1

Trudeau, L., Spoth, R., Randall, K., Mason, W. A., & Shin, C. (2012). Internalizing symptoms: Effects of a preventive intervention on developmental pathways from early adolescence to young adulthood. *Journal of Youth & Adolescence, 41*, 788–801.

Windle, M. (1990). A longitudinal study of antisocial behaviors in early adolescence as predictors of late adolescent substance use: Gender and ethnic group differences. *Journal of Abnormal Psychology, 99*, 86–91. doi:10.1037/0021-843X.99.1.86

Yates, B. T. (2009). Cost-inclusive evaluation: A banquet of approaches for including costs, benefits, and cost-effectiveness and cost-benefit analyses in your next evaluation. *Evaluation and Program Planning, 32*, 52–54. doi:10.1016/j.evalprogplan.2008.08.007

Yeh, M. Y., Chiang, I. C., & Huang, S. Y. (2006). Gender differences in predictors of drinking behavior in adolescents. *Addictive Behaviors, 31*, 1929–1938. doi:10.1016/j.addbeh.2005.12.019

Chapter 16

FAMILY-CENTERED PREVENTION OF ADOLESCENT DRUG ABUSE: TRANSLATIONAL RESEARCH IN A PUBLIC HEALTH FRAMEWORK

Thomas J. Dishion, Marie-Hélène Véronneau, Elizabeth A. Stormshak, and Kathryn Kavanagh

During the past 20 years research, on the contribution of the family to the etiology of adolescent drug use has evolved tremendously in terms of sophistication of measurement, research design, and experimental rigor. Several recent randomized prevention trials that have targeted parenting practices have suggested benefits with regard to reducing problem behavior and drug use in adolescence and young adulthood. In this chapter, we provide an overview of the literature canvassing the contribution of the family in general and parenting in particular to adolescent drug use. We then review recent developments in translating these findings into interventions that prevent and treat adolescent drug and alcohol use.

Before the 1970s, longitudinal studies on the contribution of the family to adolescent problem behavior focused primarily on delinquency. These studies, conducted largely by criminologists, strongly implicated disorganized, harsh, or lenient parenting as among the strongest predictors of delinquent behavior in adolescence. Another powerful predictor, as might be suspected, is antisocial behavior in childhood, consisting of unconventional rules-transgressing behaviors rated by teachers or parents (Loeber & Dishion, 1983). McCord (1981) published an important longitudinal study of preadolescent boys residing in the Boston area and documented that problem drinking and criminal behavior in adulthood are associated with early aggression, harsh and punitive parenting, conflict in the family, and poor supervision after school. Adults with problem drinking who had no history of arrests had childrearing histories similar to those of adults with moderate or little alcohol use. A notable feature of the McCord study was the use of home visitors' observations when measuring parenting practices. A methodological weakness of early studies on adolescent drug use was reporting bias because only youths described their problem behavior and their perceptions of parent and peer influences.

The McCord (1981) study is also a good example of scientific progress in the etiological studies of problematic substance use. In fact, it was not until the 1970s that an empirically supported connection was made between the etiology of adolescent problem behavior and multiple forms of substance use, such as marijuana use (e.g., Smith & Fogg, 1979). Carefully conducted longitudinal research with epidemiologically defined samples of youth confirmed that problem behavior (e.g., aggression) and

Preparation of this chapter was supported by grants from the National Institute on Drug Abuse (DA07031, DA16110, and DA018374). The content of this chapter is solely the responsibility of the authors and does not necessarily represent the official views of the National Institute on Drug Abuse.

http://dx.doi.org/10.1037/14550-017
Handbook of Adolescent Drug Use Prevention: Research, Intervention Strategies, and Practice, L. M. Scheier (Editor)

emotional adjustment (e.g., shyness) preceded both tobacco and marijuana use in adolescence (Kellam, Brown, Rubin, & Ensminger, 1983). Findings from longitudinal research also suggested that aggression and parenting practices both preceded adult alcohol abuse (McCord, 1988). Findings such as these were a beacon to an emerging field of drug prevention research that targeted aggression in schools and family management practices.

The shared developmental pathway of problem behavior and substance use suggests shared genetic and environmental etiologies (Cadoret, 1992; Cloninger & Gottesman, 1987; McCord, 1988). Genetic and environmental models of influence posit that parental drug use is a principal antecedent to adolescent substance use and abuse. One of the barriers to identifying a significant relationship between parental behaviors and adolescence outcome was the weak measurement of parental drug use, which often relied on single-item measures. Studies that measured parental substance use more intensively have revealed more robust connections between parent and adolescent use (Chassin, Presson, Sherman, Corty, & Olshansky, 1984). However, as longitudinal studies progressed to include a wider array of risk factors, including peer influences (Kandel, 1973), it was generally found that a shift occurred in early adolescence toward peer influences exceeding those of parents in predicting adolescent substance use (Chassin, Presson, Sherman, Montello, & McGrew, 1986; Patterson, 1993). Moreover, when parental influence was separated into parental substance use and parental monitoring practices, evidence strongly favored the weight of parental monitoring over parental substance use as a more direct influence on adolescent drug use (Baumrind, 1985; Dishion & Loeber, 1985). Longitudinal models became more sophisticated over time and revealed that parental substance-use effects on adolescent drug use were mediated by factors such as parental monitoring (Chassin, Pillow, Curran, Molina, & Barrera, 1993a, 1993b).

DEVELOPMENTAL CASCADES

The converging perspective of shared environmental etiology of problem behavior and the role of parenting and peer environments naturally led to a broader ecological view of adolescent drug use etiology (Bronfenbrenner, 1989). Dishion, Capaldi, and Yoerger (1999) studied the impact of 200 boys' behavior patterns and ecology on the initiation of tobacco, alcohol, and marijuana use. As expected, the onset of alcohol and marijuana use was predicted by the boys' antisocial behavior, parents' poor discipline practices, and parental substance use. The onset of tobacco use was predicted not only by antisocial behavior but also by family low socioeconomic status and the boys' low social preference according to peer nominations. In this longitudinal study, parental monitoring and involvement with drug using peers did not emerge as strong predictors of adolescent substance use until ages 13 to 14 (Dishion, Capaldi, Spracklen, & Li, 1995).

A developmental perspective on the emergence of adolescent drug use suggests that a series of behavioral stages begins in early childhood that can result in increasingly serious forms of adolescent problem behavior and substance use (see Figure 16.1). In early childhood, behaviors such as defiance and poor self-regulation are prognostic of antisocial behavior in elementary school (Shaw, Gilliom, Ingoldsby, & Nagin, 2003). As described earlier, antisocial behavior in childhood is a strong predictor of more serious forms of problem behavior in adolescence, including substance use. In this cascade of outcomes each stage of development leads to a series of adaptations, each of which forms the foundation for behavior that follows (Patterson, Reid, & Dishion, 1992). In this model, the downward direction of youth adjustment involves engagement in behaviors that are increasingly self-destructive and antisocial.

Figure 16.1 illustrates two important features of the developmental cascade perspective. First, each stage of development is accompanied by amplifying mechanisms (e.g., Patterson & Bank, 1989). In childhood, poor performance (i.e., lack of school readiness) and peer rejection in school of children with relatively high levels of antisocial behavior at school entry are particularly problematic. Poor academic skills and peer rejection are the two best predictors of early deviant peer involvement (Dishion, Patterson, Stoolmiller, & Skinner, 1991). As such, the dynamics of peer rejection and peer clustering begin much earlier than in early adolescence. Snyder et al. (2005)

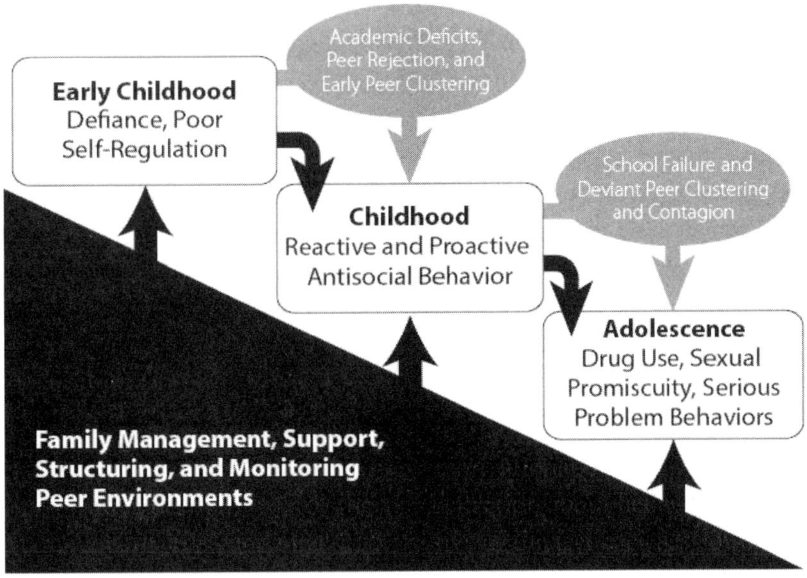

FIGURE 16.1. A developmental cascade model: Parenting contributions and amplifying mechanisms.

found that children in kindergarten were beginning the process of deviancy training by supporting one another when they enacted deviant behavior in the school setting, including mimicking adult behaviors such as cigarette smoking. Cairns, Cairns, Neckerman, Gest, and Gariepy (1988) also found that early aggression was associated with clustering in elementary school and these groups often formed the core social network of the school. School contexts that have a high prevalence of problem behavior are also those that confer high social status to children who are antisocial (Stormshak et al., 1999).

The early shift from aggressive behavior to other forms of problem behavior has been given various labels, including *covert* antisocial behavior and *overt* antisocial behavior (Loeber & Schmaling, 1985; Patterson et al., 1992). The terms *proactive* antisocial behavior and *reactive* antisocial behavior may be more accurate because in this definitional framework the first term suggests a modicum of planning and masking, whereas the latter term suggests that behavior that is emotionally driven and impulsive. The two types of antisocial behaviors are obviously correlated, but the key is that proactive antisocial behavior is highly embedded within a deviant peer environment, and it is often furtive and avoidant of detection (Poulin & Boivin, 2000).

The movement from antisocial behavior in childhood to more serious forms of problem behavior is amplified by the increasing tendency for youths to self-organize into groups that directly support, model, reinforce, and provide resources to engage in drug use and other forms of antisocial behavior. In one longitudinal study, daily telephone interviews were conducted with adolescents and their parent during which time they were asked to recall their experiences in the family and the peer group in the previous 24 hours. "Number of unsupervised hours with peers" was the best predictor of growth in substance use in early adolescence and was stronger than youth and parent report of exchanges of affection, talking about the day's activities, and having meals together (Dishion, Bullock, & Kiesner, 2008).

The central role of parenting from early childhood through adolescence is the second important feature of the developmental cascade in preventing or reducing progression of the high-risk trajectory (see Figure 16.1). In early childhood, direct socialization of children requires more intense daily teaching and positive behavior support (Shaw et al., 2003), whereas in adolescence, monitoring and structuring of peer environments comes increasingly into play (Dishion, Nelson, & Bullock, 2004). Several studies have suggested the importance of family management and parental monitoring, particularly with respect to adolescent drug use, and its pivotal role holds across cultural groups (Barrera, Castro, & Biglan, 1999; Catalano et al., 1992).

Most of the links in the developmental cascade model from early childhood through adolescence have been investigated in unique research studies. Dodge et al. (2009) tested much of the model depicted in Figure 16.1 by using a sample of 585 youths first assessed in early childhood and followed through adolescence. As expected, early childhood behavior difficulties led to later behavior problems at school age, which in turn predicted peer relationship difficulties. Peer relationship difficulties and deviant peer involvement were prognostic of adolescent drug use. Early parenting in this study was assessed primarily by conducting interviews. Laird, Criss, Pettit, Dodge, and Bates (2008) examined the same sample and found that youths whose parents maintained their monitoring practices were less influenced by deviant peer involvement in adolescence. Thus, the consequential role of parenting through adolescence was confirmed longitudinally after a person-centered approach was used to analyze the youths' developmental trajectories. Later, Dick et al. (2009) analyzed the European American subset of this sample and found evidence that parental monitoring moderates the impact of genetic susceptibility (*GABRA2* polymorphism) on the emergence and course of a high-risk trajectory for problem behavior and substance use. This finding fits the general perspective that genetic risk for problem behavior is most likely a tendency for some children to be more susceptible than others to risky environments (Belsky, Bakermans-Kranenburg, & van Ijzendoorn, 2007).

Although interest in the developmental progression to adolescence and young adulthood has been well studied, there are two major limitations to the existent science. First, the vast majority of research about adolescent substance use is based on youth self-reports at long temporal intervals, often every year. In only a handful of studies, researchers have examined adolescent substance use in shorter time intervals, which could potentially identify different predictors. For example, the Dishion and Medici Skaggs (2000) study of monthly "bursts" of adolescent substance use involved a combination of monthly parent and youth report. The maximum score of each reporting agent was used, and then monthly covariates were identified using generalized estimation equations. It was found that variation in time in unsupervised time with peers predicted monthly bursts in substance use. In general, the development of ecological momentary assessments will lend itself to a renewed appreciation of the covariates of substance use (e.g., Stone & Shiffman, 1994). The second major limitation is that models that incorporate molecular–genetic effects are limited with respect to the amount of variation accounted for by genetic factors. Although these pioneering studies suggest interesting and potentially important gene × environment interactions, there is less evidence that such findings will inform future intervention research. One of the key scientific benchmarks in family-based research about substance use is to also identify the endophenotype or temperament factor that accurately describes the mediation of genetic effects on adolescent drug use (Rutter, 2006; Wills & Dishion, 2004). It is likely that the application of diverse methodological strategies for studying substance use will define new directions for the study of family contributions to adolescent substance use.

TRANSLATIONAL RESEARCH

There is an inherent weakness to developmental science that does not experimentally manipulate putative causal variables (Cook & Campbell, 1979); that is, prevention experiments and developmental research are mutually informative. When developmental hypotheses are translated into prevention experiments, we can test the extent to which manipulation of a developmental dynamic confers reduced risk on participating children (Dishion & Patterson, 1999; McCord & Tremblay, 1992). To date, several longitudinal intervention experiments have provided empirical support for interventions that target parenting and result in reductions in adolescent substance use (e.g., Kosterman, Hawkins, Guo, Catalano, & Abbott, 2000; Liddle, 2010; Spoth, Redmond, & Shin, 2001; Spoth, Reyes, Redmond, & Shin, 1999; Waldron & Brody, 2010).

In the late 1980s, Dishion, Reid, and Patterson (1988) embarked on a first effort to apply the developmental model shown in Figure 16.1 to prevent the emergence of substance use among high-risk adolescents. This National Institute on Drug Abuse (NIDA)–funded study tested two model-driven intervention paradigms to formulate the core components of what became the Adolescent Transitions Program (ATP).

The program of research randomly assigned high-risk youths to a combination of two interventions: one that would emphasize family management skills and another that would emphasize the support of adolescent self-regulation. In making the shift from treatment to prevention, our research group improved the efficiency of the intervention program by delivering both intervention components in groups. We randomly assigned 120 youths to (a) family management only, (b) self-regulation only, (c) both family management and self-regulation, or (d) materials only. Families in the materials-only condition received only intervention materials that consisted of six newsletters and five brief videotapes that covered the informational content of the sessions and addressed the parent and teen skills targeted in the intervention. Later, we added a group of 39 youths as quasi-experimental controls who were contacted only for assessment purposes. High-risk youths and their families were selected on the basis of parent report about a number of risk factors, including youth problem behavior, academic adjustment, and family relationships. We followed the youths from ages 12 to 15 to evaluate whether we were successful in preventing the emergence of drug use and other problem behavior.

We met with success and also encountered some unexpected findings executing this initial field experiment. In terms of success, the family management component clearly led to reductions in problem behavior at home and at school, reduced early onset of substance use, and improved family interaction (Dishion & Andrews, 1995; Dishion, Andrews, Kavanagh, & Soberman, 1996). Moreover, for the first time, we documented that changes in observed parent–adolescent conflict mediated reductions in antisocial behavior at school (Dishion, Patterson, & Kavanagh, 1992).

Unfortunately, there were iatrogenic and counterintuitive effects in this intervention as well. In the analysis of change from baseline to termination (3-month time period), random assignment to the self-regulation group led to reductions in parent–child negative interactions, as revealed by pre- and postintervention measures (Dishion & Andrews, 1995). However, much to our dismay, we also found quite early in our follow-up assessments that youths randomly assigned to the self-regulation groups increased cigarette smoking behavior (Dishion & Andrews, 1995). Unfortunately, this trend only worsened over time, and cigarette smoking and school reports of delinquent behavior increased for up to 3 years following the intervention. Alarmed by these initial findings, our research team began to deliberate the reasons for the findings and then converged on an explanation. We hypothesized that aggregating high-risk peers in the intervention was responsible for the increase in negative outcomes. Collaboration with Joan McCord and the reanalysis of the Cambridge Somerville youth study provided even more compelling evidence that aggregating youths who engage in problem behavior may, indeed, be iatrogenic; that is, it may result in unanticipated negative effects (Dishion, McCord, & Poulin, 1999; Poulin, Dishion, & Burraston, 2001). Videotaping our intervention groups turned out to be critical for linking the implementation of the model to the negative outcomes and confirmed that deviancy training interactions with peers in the group led to increases in problem behavior (Dishion, Poulin, & Burraston, 2001). Although the finding of iatrogenic effects for aggregation of high-risk youths was troubling, reporting these findings led to a series of studies that were both confirmatory (Feldman, Stiffman, Evans, & Orme, 1982; Palinkas, Atkins, Miller, & Fereira, 1996) and validating. Clearly, deviant peer influences must be taken very seriously when designing universal, selected, and indicated interventions (Dishion & Dodge, 2005; Dodge, Dishion, & Lansford, 2006).

Under these circumstances we eliminated the self-regulation intervention component delivered in peer groups and strengthened the parenting intervention of the ATP. Our next step was to take the intervention from a community treatment center and implement the program in schools. To do this, it was necessary to make several revisions to our implementation model. First, we created a context for the parent intervention in the public school environment that was feasible yet empirically validated. Second, it was necessary to make our parent intervention more efficient so that parent groups were not the only format in which we delivered family management materials. Third, we designed a strategy in which a combination of teacher and parent reports would be used to proactively identify youths in the context of schools who would be offered a selected family intervention. Fourth, we created an adaptive and tailored approach to family intervention in which assessments are used to identify the level and type of intervention that would be optimal for each family (Dishion, Kavanagh, & Kiesner, 1998).

We concluded that (a) it is critical to design interventions that are integrated into service systems that reach the general population of children and families (e.g., public schools; Women, Infants, and Children; Head Start); (b) prevention and treatment work best when they are integrated, in that an integrated approach that links universal, selected, and indicated components would increase reach and effectiveness; (c) interventions must be adapted and tailored to optimize the potential to address the child's specific needs; and (d) family-centered interventions are most likely to have enduring effects when they are provided repeatedly during a developmental transition (Dishion, Kavanagh, Schneiger, Nelson, & Kaufman, 2002). This ecological approach to family-centered intervention and treatment became the Family Check-Up (FCU) model (Dishion & Stormshak, 2007; Stormshak & Dishion, 2002).

THE FAMILY CHECK-UP MODEL IN PUBLIC MIDDLE SCHOOLS

The three levels of the FCU model are summarized in Figure 16.2. The first level of the program, a universal intervention, established a family resource center in each of the three participating public middle schools. The entire intervention group had access to parent-centered services of the family resource center, but this center was not promoted to the families assigned to the control group, who therefore did not request its services. These services included brief consultations with parents, such as telephone consultations, FCUs with parents, and access to videotapes and books relevant to parents' concerns. Parent consultants were selected to match the most prevalent ethnic groups in the sample (European American, African American, and Hispanic). The parent consultant also engaged students in six in-class lessons called the SHAPe Curriculum (see Dishion & Kavanagh, 2003).

This intervention was modeled on the Life Skills Training program described by Botvin, Baker, Dusenbury, Tortu, and Botvin (1990), but it was reduced in scope (six lessons in SHAPe vs. 16 in Life Skills Training). Each component of the SHAPe was accompanied by a home practice exercise that emphasized parent–student interactions to support

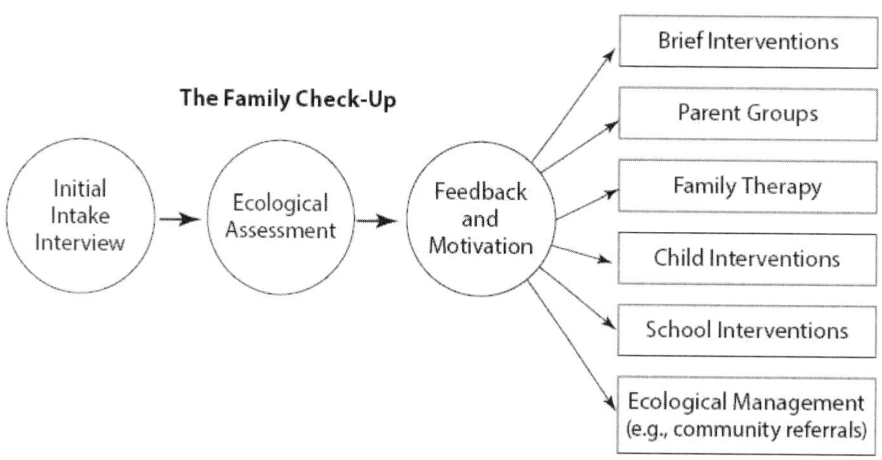

FIGURE 16.2. The Family Check-Up: A brief intervention with linked services.

family management. The six sessions focused on the following topics: (a) school success, (b) health decisions, (c) building positive peer groups, (d) the cycle of respect, (e) coping with stress and anger, and (f) solving problems peacefully. Brief parent–student activities designed to motivate and engage discussions supportive of family management were included in this intervention.

The selected intervention consisted of the FCU. This brief, three-session intervention is based on motivational interviewing and was modeled on the Drinker's Check-Up (Miller & Rollnick, 2002). All families in the intervention could request an FCU, but families of high-risk youths, as determined by teacher ratings, were specifically approached and offered the FCU in Grades 7 and 8. Youths deemed to be at high risk had been rated as such by teachers using the TRISK measure. Participants were selected as at risk on the basis of their relative ranking within their self-identified ethnic group and by gender. Risk behaviors included troublesome behavior at school, perceived tobacco use, and deviant peer associations. High-risk youths represented 27.4% of the participants assigned to the intervention group, and families of high-risk adolescents represented 40.9% of those who engaged in the intervention.

The three FCU sessions included (a) an initial interview (20–30 minutes), (b) an assessment session (60 minutes), and (c) a feedback session involving the consultant and the parents (usually 60 minutes or longer, if needed). The three sessions were scheduled as close in time as possible, usually within 1 to 2 weeks. However, when families' availability was limited, it could take up to 3 months to complete all three sessions. In the initial interview, a parent consultant explored parent concerns and stage of change and encouraged the parents to engage in a family assessment in the home. In the assessment session, family members were videotaped while they engaged in discussions about eight topics that were meant to help evaluate parent–child interactions. Topics included planning a family fun activity, discussing a family problem identified by the parent, and discussing how parents could help their adolescent improve in an area of personal growth identified by the youth. During the feedback session with the parent, the therapist summarized the results of the assessment while using motivational interviewing strategies to support reflection about behavior change. An essential objective of the feedback session was to explore potential intervention services to support family management practices.

The major focus of the FCU was a collaborative decision reached by the parent and parent consultant about the indicated services most appropriate for their family. Services included a tailored approach to parent management training based on the everyday parenting curriculum (EPC; Dishion, Stormshak, & Kavanagh, 2011). The EPC is grounded in the ATP parenting intervention (Dishion & Andrews, 1995) and the Parent Management Training–Oregon group parent training (Forgatch & Patterson, 2010). Although parents were the primary target in families that required indicated services, a minority of youths (about 10 of them) were involved in a curriculum called the Teen Focus (Dishion & Andrews, 1995), which had been developed in a randomized trial to help adolescents develop self-regulatory skills, especially teens struggling with depression, anxiety, or problem behavior. A combination of strategies was periodically used to train parent consultants, including didactic instruction, role play, and videotaped supervision while the intervention was available to the families.

During the past 15 years, we completed two randomized trials, Project Alliance 1 and Project Alliance 2, both of which involved sixth-grade students in multiethnic public middle schools. In both trials, the sixth-grade populations of metropolitan middle schools were randomly assigned at the individual level to the FRC versus public middle school as usual. A parent consultant was assigned to each school to engage parents of youths who were identified as at risk by teachers. Services were provided primarily in the seventh and eighth grades of middle school. The research design is summarized in Figure 16.3. We also conducted an effectiveness trial, the Next Generation Project, which was based on the same intervention model.

In Project Alliance 1, we actively engaged 25% of the families assigned to the treatment group in the FCU during the 2 years of service, across the three schools. We had contact with an additional 25% of

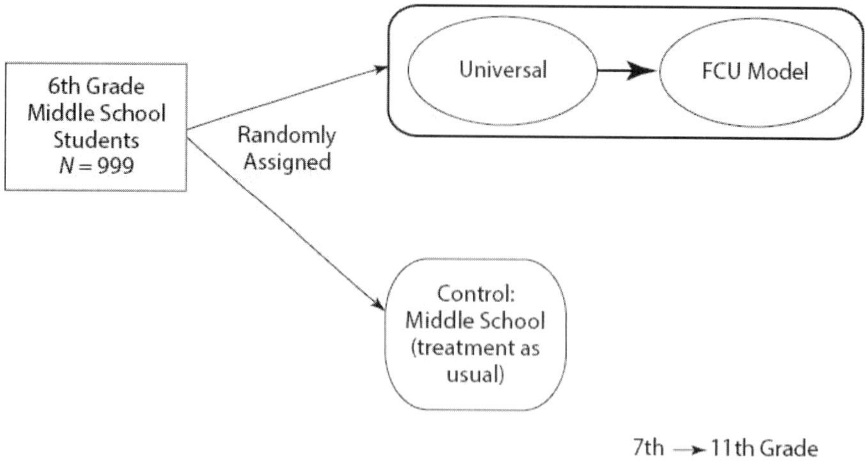

FIGURE 16.3. Multilevel prevention design for Adolescent Transitions Program study: Project Alliance 1.

the families but did not conduct the FCU with them. By and large, we found that the families at highest risk were the most likely to participate in the FCU. Connell, Dishion, and Deater-Deckard (2006) found that single-parent families, those with students involved in a deviant peer group, and those rated by teachers as at high risk were the most likely to engage in the FCU.

During the course of the 2 years, families at highest risk had an average of 6 hours of parent consultant contact. As one would expect, amount of contact time correlated with the student's risk level. Families with students at moderate risk engaged in approximately 3.5 hours of contact, and families at low risk averaged less than 1 hour of contact. Contact included telephone calls and personal contact and was recorded by the parent consultants by the minute (Dishion, Kavanagh, et al., 2002).

The covariation between engagement levels and risk suggested to us that a response to intervention framework was appropriate for family interventions in school. The lowest risk families received minimal, universal support. Moderate-risk families used more services, and high-risk families tended to engage in more intensive services, including the FCU. Another aspect of the adaptive and tailored approach is that the parent consultant was flexible in terms of the time of day, place (home vs. school), and type (individual vs. group) of the intervention. In addition, community referrals were used to address other aspects of the family ecology, such as parent depression, substance use, and/or psychiatric mediation. This flexibility and menu approach to intervention ensure that we are responsive to the ecology of families.

Intervention effects on parent engagement were also examined in the Next Generation project, which was conducted in another set of four public middle schools. In this study, we also carefully counted the minutes of contact with parents of students. Parent consultants often used creative means to engage parents. In one middle school, the parent consultant established a coffee cart for parents and would meet parents as they dropped off their middle school child and picked up coffee. In this study, we found that simply the number of parent contacts in sixth, seventh, and eighth grades was associated with reductions in the growth of teacher-rated risk (Stormshak, Dishion, Light, & Yasui, 2005).

Several reports from these trials have been published regarding intervention effects on substance use. The first revealed that randomization to the FRC in sixth grade was associated with reductions in substance use (Dishion, Kavanagh, et al., 2002) and in deviant peer involvement (Dishion, Bullock, & Granic, 2002) over a 4-year period. We found that for the youth at highest risk, reductions in drug use were mediated by changes in parental monitoring practices rated by independent observers (Dishion, Nelson, & Kavanagh, 2003). A key issue in this research is the proportion of the population who were engaged in intervention at the community level. One of the strengths of intervention trials was that 90% of the identified population were included in the study, with 80% retention over a 10-year period. Thus, a 25% engagement rate with the highest risk participants suggests that the FCU intervention strategy is a viable component of a public health approach to reduce the prevalence of substance abuse.

In the past 10 years, our research group augmented the analysis of family intervention effects by using complier average causal effect (CACE; Jo, 2002) modeling to systematically study how engagement in the FCU augments prevention outcomes for youth. This special application of mixture modeling estimates engagement and nonengagement in the randomized control group, based on defining a group of participants from the control group that resemble the nonengagers in the intervention group. In mixture modeling, estimates of engagers and nonengagers in the control group provide a latent variable of engagement for all participants. In this framework, engagement status is modeled as a moderator of growth and change in problem behavior.

Using CACE modeling, we found that engagement in the FCU predicted long-term reductions in several indices of adolescent problem behavior. Moreover, the most dramatic effects of EcoFIT was with sixth-grade students who were most severely problematic and whose families were most in need of services (Connell, Dishion, Yasui, & Kavanagh, 2007). When we used an intention-to-treat (ITT) design in which participants' outcomes were analyzed and reported on the basis of initial placement in the control or intervention group regardless of whether or not they actually engaged in the offered treatment, the outcomes to age 17 were modest. However, when we considered families who were actively engaged in the intervention and compared outcomes with those of control participants who would also have likely engaged in the FCU, the positive effects of the family intervention were in the moderate to large range.

The different sets of findings we attained from an ITT design and a CACE model point out the challenge for many randomized prevention trials: Many participants do not actually engage in the intervention, especially when it is offered on a voluntary basis. As mentioned earlier, when we tested the efficacy of the EcoFIT intervention in public middle schools, 25% of all families in the randomized intervention group engaged in the FCU. In the context of CACE modeling, preliminary analyses revealed that single-parent families whose sixth-grade student reported deviant peer involvement and family conflict at baseline were the most likely to eventually engage in the intervention condition.

Two outcome studies in which CACE models were used to evaluate adolescent outcomes associated with family participation in the FCU are summarized in Table 16.1. Outcomes for the four groups described earlier are presented in the table, but participants from both the control group and the intervention group who were identified as nonengagers were aggregated into one group because the findings for these groups were nearly identical. In our analysis of problem behavior, we found a marked reduction in the percentage of youths arrested among participants from the engager group

TABLE 16.1

Summary of Outcomes Applying EcoFIT to Public Middle Schools

11th-grade outcomes	Observed engagers (intervention group only)	Latent engagers (control group only)	Nonengagers (intervention and control groups together)
Participants arrested at least once in their lifetime (%)	15	100	5
Frequency of marijuana use during the past month (age 18)	1 time	5 times	0.3 time
Days absent from school	13	32	12

who actually received the FCU (15% arrested), compared with those who would have engaged (on the basis of their high-risk profile) but who were assigned to the control group (100% arrested). Thus, sixth-grade students at high risk whose parents were in need of support were 6 times as likely to be arrested within the next 5 years if they were not offered the FCU. Similarly, these youth used marijuana 5 times more frequently during a 1-month period than did the intervention group. These findings were extended to marijuana and to tobacco dependence by age 18 as well. Analyses revealed the EcoFIT intervention reliably reduced substance use, antisocial behavior, and the probability of arrest (Connell et al., 2007).

Table 16.1 also reveals that random assignment to the intervention resulted in a 50% reduction in days absent from school from sixth through 11th grade. Engagers in the control group missed an average of 32 days during the school year, and engagers in the intervention group missed only 13 (Stormshak, Connell, & Dishion, 2009).

A new set of CACE analyses was performed to verify if the beneficial effects of the intervention on at-risk participants' substance use were maintained into early adulthood, that is, more than 10 years after the beginning of the study (Véronneau, Dishion, & Connell, 2014). Results confirmed that engagers assigned to the control group used more alcohol throughout adolescence until age 21 (see Figure 16.4), and they presented more symptoms of alcohol abuse and dependence at age 23–24 than did at-risk students from the treatment group who engaged in the intervention. The same pattern of results emerged for tobacco use. Even though engagers who were assigned to the control group started to reduce their use of tobacco in late adolescence–early adulthood, their tobacco use was still estimated to be almost 2 times as much as that of engagers in the treatment group who benefited from the FCU (see Figure 16.5), and they presented more symptoms of tobacco dependence at age 23–24.

Regarding marijuana use, engager participants assigned to the control group were marginally more likely to report symptoms of marijuana abuse or dependence at age 23–24 than were engagers who benefited from the treatment. Even more

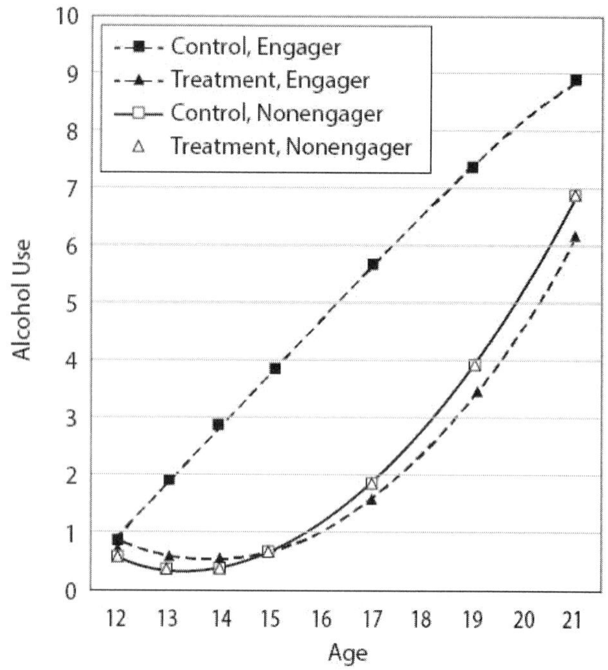

FIGURE 16.4. Complier average causal effect model results for change in alcohol use from adolescence through early adulthood.

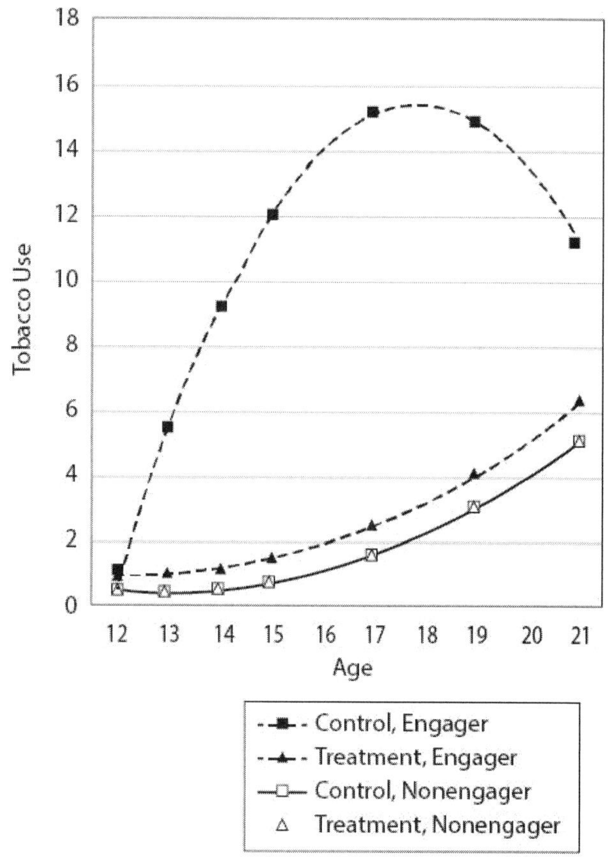

FIGURE 16.5. Complier average causal effect model results for change in tobacco use from adolescence through early adulthood.

compelling, engagers assigned to the control group increased their marijuana use throughout adolescence at a much faster pace than did their counterparts who received the intervention, such that by age 21 the estimated use of this substance for engagers in the control group was three times greater than it was for their counterparts whose families had engaged in the FCU (see Figure 16.6).

Another trend is particularly important to consider in these three CACE analyses. Although it is often said that families who are at low or no risk are most likely to engage in family-based services offered in the school, we did not find this to be the case. Our proactive approach to offering the FCU suggested that, in fact, the families who declined participation were those who were at lowest risk. In other words, those parents accurately assessed their young adolescents' risk status and did not feel the need to receive information or support regarding behavior management strategies. This finding is optimistic because it suggests that if the appropriate outreach and engagement strategies are in place for caregivers of the highest risk students, we are likely to reduce their long-term risk by motivating parental monitoring and positive behavior support.

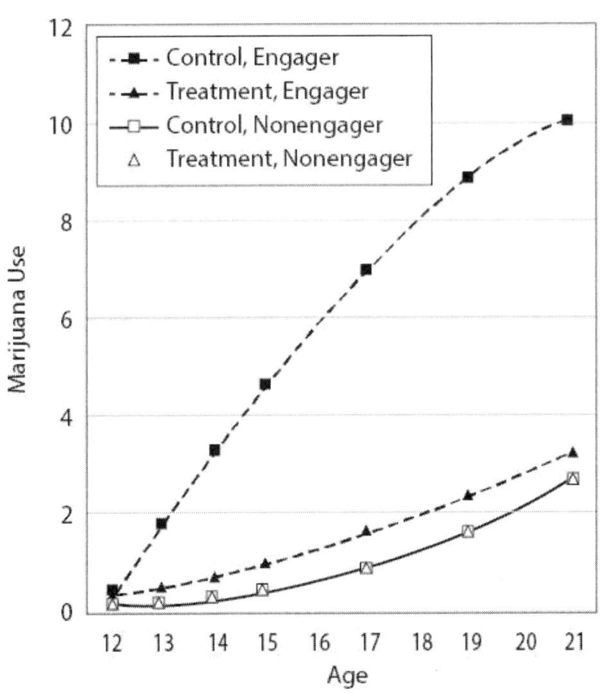

FIGURE 16.6. Complier average causal effect model results for change in marijuana use from adolescence through early adulthood.

Because the highest risk parents engaged in the FCU services, collaboration between parents and schools seems possible and advisable. It is noteworthy that in this study, we initially recruited 90% of the entire school population to participate. Overall, this study suggests the public health utility of the EcoFIT model offered in a public school environment.

In a second randomized trial, Project Alliance 2, we randomly assigned 593 youths at the beginning of sixth grade to either the EcoFIT model or middle school as usual. We examined the efficacy of the EcoFIT regarding a number of outcomes related to successful youth development. Using CACE modeling, we found that participation in the EcoFIT intervention substantially reduced the increase of substance use and problem behavior during the middle school years (Stormshak et al., 2011). ITT analyses revealed that the intervention improved self-regulation skills, which in turn predicted decreased depression and increased school engagement (Fosco, Frank, Stormshak, & Dishion, 2013; Stormshak, Fosco, & Dishion, 2010). One of our goals was to engage a high percentage of families in the treatment model, and in meeting that goal, we also successfully recruited a robust number of families of ethnic minority status (64%). The percentage of families receiving the FCU or other intervention support was similar across ethnic groups, and the intervention was equally successful with all ethnic minority groups and across genders (Stormshak et al., 2010). Furthermore, the rate of engagement in the FCU was nearly double that of Project Alliance 1, with 42% of families in the intervention group receiving the entire FCU intervention, compared with 25% in the earlier project (Connell et al., 2007). We speculate that the increased level of engagement in Project Alliance 2 compared with that of Project Alliance 1 was the result of parent consultants' efforts to actively engage families and to match the ethnicity of the parent consultant to that of each family. We also worked closely with schools to attend behavior support meetings and coordinate our services with those provided in the middle school setting.

We carefully examined the role of parenting in the development of problem behavior and maintenance of problem behavior over time in this sample. Several studies have revealed that parental monitoring and positive family relationships reduce the risk of depression (Margolis, Fosco, & Stormshak, 2011) and lead to positive changes in self-regulation and reductions in problem behavior (Fosco et al., 2013), whereas poor parental monitoring and negative family relationships predict declines in self-regulation and are associated with poor outcomes, such as substance use and affiliation with deviant peers (Fosco, Stormshak, Dishion, & Winter, 2012). Results from this series of studies underscore the importance of the parent–child relationship during the adolescent years, both as a risk factor and as a protective factor.

SUMMARY

Family environments in general and parenting in particular are key contributors to the developmental trajectory leading to adolescence-onset drug use and future drug dependence. In the past 30 years, developmental studies and intervention trial research have evolved in an iterative fashion and have evoked a compelling scientific argument suggesting that parenting practices can be targeted in prevention trials, and reductions in adolescent substance use follows. Our research group's work on developing family interventions began with testing structured parent groups and youth groups and progressed into designing an intervention that targets parenting and that can be embedded in public schools. The original ATP model evolved into a general approach to family intervention that is applicable to children and families across the developmental spectrum. We recently found that random assignment to the FCU, for example, improved parenting and reduced problem behavior in early childhood (Dishion, Shaw, et al., 2008; Gardner, Shaw, Dishion, Burton, & Supplee, 2007; Shaw, Dishion, Supplee, Gardner, & Arnds, 2006). By virtue of a data-driven, iterative approach, the intervention model has contributed to advances in prevention science at many levels, including the following:

1. *Effectiveness:* We improved the effectiveness of the intervention by eliminating the peer aggregation component of the original model and by designing the FCU. Statistical analysis strategies that incorporate intervention engagement have revealed significant intervention effects 4 years and 10 years postintervention.
2. *Efficiency:* The current version of the intervention program requires only about 6 hours of intervention time for the highest risk families, and during this brief exposure period it maintains and even enhances intervention effects.
3. *Expense:* Because families at high risk tend to select themselves into the intervention and because of the modest number of sessions for all families regardless of risk status, we believe the intervention is more cost effective than parent groups or other conventional parenting programs. One key issue to consider when comparing the cost-effectiveness of intervention models is the cost of engaging the highest risk parents who are most in need of the intervention services. By design, many prevention studies focusing on parenting do not engage the highest risk parents.
4. *Ethics:* In light of the ethnic diversity in the United States, it is unethical to provide family interventions that were developed with a monocultural bias. We have developed measurement and intervention protocols that are unbiased and that are experienced as respectful by a wide range of culturally heterogeneous families.

Progress in translational research will be made if it adheres to the following three principles. The first is *iteration:* To make developmental research progressively more useful for the design of empirically effective intervention services, it is necessary to repeatedly engage in the process described in Figure 16.7. As such, one must persevere in a program of research and work in a research group that has a shared focus and investigative or institutional history. The second principle is that family-based prevention research should be *problem focused:* It is important to attempt to solve a human problem that is amenable to the integration of developmental and intervention research. For example, Patterson set out to develop an effective intervention for aggressive children, because at that time all interventions were found to be ineffective (Patterson, Dishion, & Chamberlain, 1993). As the field progresses, some basic issues will evolve, such as measurement, conceptualization, and definition. However, keeping

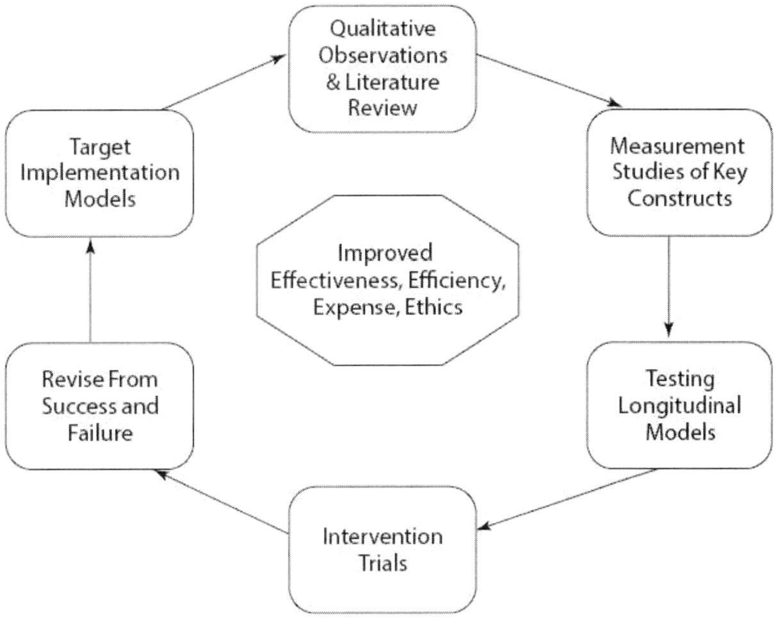

FIGURE 16.7. A model-building strategy for translational research for children and families.

an eye on the long-term goal helps one's research progress. The last principle is *integrity:* It is critical that we look for weaknesses and inaccuracies in our models and not simply confirm the successes. It is relatively rare for scientific research to publish failures to translate developmental models into successful interventions. This is unfortunate because it is almost certain that other investigators will repeat the mistakes, and progress will be undermined. In this sense, success in applied research requires some comfort with failure.

References

Barrera, M., Castro, F. G., & Biglan, A. (1999). Ethnicity, substance use and development: Exemplars for exploring group differences and similarities. *Development and Psychopathology, 11*, 805–822. doi:10.1017/S0954579499002333

Baumrind, D. (1985). Familial antecedents of adolescent drug use: A developmental perspective. In C. L. Jones & R. J. Battjes (Eds.), *Etiology of drug abuse: Implications for prevention* (Research Monograph No. 56, pp. 14–44). Washington, DC: Government Printing Office.

Belsky, J., Bakermans-Kranenburg, M. J., & van Ijzendoorn, M. H. (2007). For better and for worse: Differential susceptibility to environmental influences. *Current Directions in Psychological Science, 16*, 300–304. doi:10.1111/j.1467-8721.2007.00525.x

Botvin, G. J., Baker, E., Dusenbury, L., Tortu, S., & Botvin, E. M. (1990). Preventing adolescent drug abuse through a multimodal cognitive–behavioral approach: Results of a 3-year study. *Journal of Consulting and Clinical Psychology, 58*, 437–446. doi:10.1037/0022-006X.58.4.437

Bronfenbrenner, U. (1989). Ecological systems theory. In R. Vasta (Ed.), *Annals of child development: Vol. 6. Six theories of child development: Revised formulations and current issues* (pp. 187–249). London, England: Jai Press.

Cadoret, R. J. (1992). Genetic and environmental factors in initiation of drug use and the transition to abuse. In M. D. Glantz & R. W. Pickens (Eds.), *Vulnerability to drug abuse* (pp. 99–113). Washington, DC: American Psychological Association. doi:10.1037/10107-004

Cairns, R. B., Cairns, B. D., Neckerman, H. J., Gest, S. D., & Gariepy, J. (1988). Social networks and aggressive behavior: Peer support or peer rejection. *Developmental Psychology, 24*, 815–823. doi:10.1037/0012-1649.24.6.815

Catalano, R. F., Morrison, D. M., Wells, E. A., Gilmore, M. R., Irritani, B., & Hawkins, J. D. (1992). Ethnic differences and family factors related to early drug initiation. *Journal of Studies on Alcohol, 53*, 208–217.

Chassin, L., Pillow, D. R., Curran, P. J., Molina, B. S., & Barrera, M. (1993a). Relation of parental alcoholism to early adolescent substance use: A test of three mediating mechanisms. *Journal of Abnormal Psychology, 102*, 3–19. doi:10.1037/0021-843X.102.1.3

Chassin, L., Pillow, D. R., Curran, P. J., Molina, B. S., & Barrera, M. (1993b). Relation of parental alcoholism to early adolescent substance use: A test of three mediating mechanisms: Correction. *Journal of Abnormal Psychology, 102*, 558. doi:10.1037/0021-843X.102.4.533

Chassin, L., Presson, C., Sherman, S., Corty, E., & Olshansky, R. (1984). Predicting the onset of cigarette smoking in adolescents: A longitudinal study. *Journal of Applied Social Psychology, 14*, 224–243. doi:10.1111/j.1559-1816.1984.tb02233.x

Chassin, L., Presson, C. C., Sherman, S. J., Montello, D., & McGrew, J. (1986). Changes in peer and parent influence during adolescence: Longitudinal versus cross-sectional perspectives on smoking initiation. *Developmental Psychology, 22*, 327–334. doi:10.1037/0012-1649.22.3.327

Cloninger, C. R., & Gottesman, I. I. (1987). Genetic and environmental factors in antisocial behavior disorders. In S. A. Mednick, T. E. Moffitt, & S. A. Stack (Eds.), *The causes of crime: New biological approaches* (pp. 92–109). Cambridge, England: Cambridge University Press. doi:10.1017/CBO9780511753282.008

Connell, A. M., Dishion, T. J., & Deater-Deckard, K. (2006). Variable- and person-centered approaches to the analysis of early adolescent substance use: Linking peer, family, and intervention effects with developmental trajectories. [Special Issue]. *Merrill-Palmer Quarterly, 52*, 421–448. doi:10.1353/mpq.2006.0025

Connell, A. M., Dishion, T. J., Yasui, M., & Kavanagh, K. (2007). An adaptive approach to family intervention: Linking engagement in family-centered intervention to reductions in adolescent problem behavior. *Journal of Consulting and Clinical Psychology, 75*, 568–579. doi:10.1037/0022-006X.75.4.568

Cook, T. D., & Campbell, D. T. (1979). *Quasi-experimentation design and analysis issues for field settings*. Boston, MA: Houghton Mifflin.

Dick, D. M., Latendresse, S. J., Lansford, J. E., Budde, J. P., Goate, A., Dodge, K. A., . . . Bates, J. E. (2009). Role of GABRA2 in trajectories of externalizing behavior across development and evidence of moderation by parental monitoring. *Archives of General Psychiatry, 66*, 649–657. doi:10.1001/archgenpsychiatry.2009.48

Dishion, T. J., & Andrews, D. (1995). Preventing escalations in problem behaviors with high-risk young adolescents: Immediate and 1-year outcomes. *Journal of Consulting and Clinical Psychology, 63*, 538–548. doi:10.1037/0022-006X.63.4.538

Dishion, T. J., Andrews, D. W., Kavanagh, K., & Soberman, L. H. (1996). Preventive interventions for high-risk youth: The Adolescent Transitions Program. In B. McMahon & R. D. Peters (Eds.), *Conduct disorders, substance abuse and delinquency: Prevention and early intervention approaches* (pp. 184–214). Newbury Park, CA: Sage. doi:10.4135/9781483327679.n9

Dishion, T. J., Bullock, B. M., & Granic, I. (2002). Pragmatism in modeling peer influence: Dynamics, outcomes, and change processes. *Development and Psychopathology, 14*, 969–981. doi:10.1017/S0954579402004169

Dishion, T. J., Bullock, B. M., & Kiesner, J. (2008). Vicissitudes of parenting adolescents: Daily variations in parental monitoring and the early emergence of drug use. In M. Kerr, H. Stattin, & R. C. M. E. Engels (Eds.), *What can parents do? New insights into the role of parents in adolescent problem behavior* (pp. 113–133). Chichester, England: Wiley. doi:10.1002/9780470774113.ch5

Dishion, T. J., Capaldi, D., Spracklen, K. M., & Li, F. (1995). Peer ecology of male adolescent drug use. *Development and Psychopathology, 7*, 803–824. doi:10.1017/S0954579400006854

Dishion, T. J., Capaldi, D. M., & Yoerger, K. (1999). Middle childhood antecedents to progression in male adolescent substance use: An ecological analysis of risk and protection. *Journal of Adolescent Research, 14*, 175–205. doi:10.1177/0743558499142003

Dishion, T. J., & Dodge, K. A. (2005). Peer contagion in interventions for children and adolescents: Moving toward an understanding of the ecology and dynamics of change. *Journal of Abnormal Child Psychology, 33*, 395–400. doi:10.1007/s10802-005-3579-z

Dishion, T. J., & Kavanagh, K. (2003). *Intervening with adolescent problem behavior: A family-centered approach*. New York, NY: Guilford Press.

Dishion, T. J., Kavanagh, K., & Kiesner, J. (1998). Prevention of early adolescent substance use among high-risk youth: A multiple gating approach to parent intervention. Drug abuse prevention through family interventions. In R. S. Ashery, E. B. Robertson, & K. L. Kumpfer (Eds.), *Drug abuse prevention through family interventions* (pp. 208–228). Rockville, MD: National Institute on Drug Abuse.

Dishion, T. J., Kavanagh, K., Schneiger, A., Nelson, S. E., & Kaufman, N. (2002). Preventing early adolescent substance use: A family-centered strategy for the public middle-school ecology. *Prevention Science, 3*, 191–201.

Dishion, T. J., & Loeber, R. (1985). Adolescent marijuana and alcohol use: The role of parents and peers revisited. *The American Journal of Drug and Alcohol Abuse, 11*, 11–25. doi:10.3109/00952998509016846

Dishion, T. J., McCord, J., & Poulin, F. (1999). When interventions harm: Peer groups and problem behavior. *American Psychologist, 54*, 755–764. doi:10.1037/0003-066X.54.9.755

Dishion, T. J., & Medici Skaggs, N. (2000). An ecological analysis of monthly "bursts" in early adolescent substance use. *Applied Developmental Science, 4*, 89–97. doi:10.1207/S1532480XADS0402_4

Dishion, T. J., Nelson, S. E., & Bullock, B. M. (2004). Premature adolescent autonomy: Parent disengagement and deviant peer process in the amplification of problem behavior. *Journal of Adolescence, 27*, 515–530. doi:10.1016/j.adolescence.2004.06.005

Dishion, T. J., Nelson, S. E., & Kavanagh, K. (2003). The family check-up with high-risk adolescents: Preventing early-onset substance use by parent monitoring. *Behavior Therapy, 34*, 553–571. doi:10.1016/S0005-7894(03)80035-7

Dishion, T. J., & Patterson, G. R. (1999). Model-building in developmental psychopathology: A pragmatic approach to understanding and intervention. *Journal of Clinical Child Psychology, 28*, 502–512. doi:10.1207/S15374424JCCP2804_10

Dishion, T. J., Patterson, G. R., & Kavanagh, K. (1992). An experimental test of the coercion model: Linking theory, measurement, and intervention. In J. McCord & R. Trembley (Eds.), *The interaction of theory and practice: Experimental studies of interventions* (pp. 253–282). New York, NY: Guilford Press.

Dishion, T. J., Patterson, G. R., Stoolmiller, M., & Skinner, M. (1991). Family, school, and behavioral antecedents to early adolescent involvement with antisocial peers. *Developmental Psychology, 27*, 172–180. doi:10.1037/0012-1649.27.1.172

Dishion, T. J., Poulin, F., & Burraston, B. (2001). Peer group dynamics associated with iatrogenic effects in group interventions with high-risk young adolescents. In D. W. Nangle & C. A. Erdley (Eds.), *The role of friendship in psychological adjustment* (pp. 79–92). San Francisco, CA: Jossey-Bass. doi:10.1002/cd.6

Dishion, T. J., Reid, J. B., & Patterson, G. R. (1988). Empirical guidelines for the development of a treatment for early adolescent substance use. In R. E. Coombs (Ed.), *The family context of adolescent drug use* (pp. 189–224). New York, NY: Haworth.

Dishion, T. J., Shaw, D., Connell, A., Gardner, F., Weaver, C., & Wilson, M. (2008). The family check-up with high-risk indigent families: Preventing problem behavior by increasing parents' positive behavior support in early childhood. *Child Development, 79*, 1395–1414. doi:10.1111/j.1467-8624.2008.01195.x

Dishion, T. J., & Stormshak, E. A. (2007). *Intervening in children's lives: An ecological, family-centered approach to mental health care*. Washington, DC: American Psychological Association.

Dishion, T. J., Stormshak, E. A., & Kavanagh, K. A. (2011). *Everyday parenting: A professional's guide to building family management skills*. Champaign, IL: Research Press.

Dodge, K. A., Dishion, T. J., & Lansford, J. E. (Eds.). (2006). *Deviant peer influences in programs for youth: Problems and solutions*. New York, NY: Guilford Press.

Dodge, K. A., Malone, P. S., Lansford, J. E., Miller, S., Pettit, G. S., & Bates, J. E. (2009). A dynamic cascade model of the development of substance-use onset: Early peer relations problem factors. *Monographs of the Society for Research in Child Development, 74*, 51–54.

Feldman, R. A., Stiffman, A. R., Evans, D. A., & Orme, J. G. (1982). Prevention research, social work, and mental illness. *Social Work Research & Abstracts, 18*, 4–13. doi:10.1093/swra/18.3.4

Forgatch, M. S., & Patterson, G. R. (2010). Parent management training–Oregon model: An intervention for antisocial behavior in children and adolescents. In J. R. Weisz & A. E. Kazdin (Eds.), *Evidence-based psychotherapies for children and adolescents* (pp. 159–178). New York, NY: Guilford Press.

Fosco, G. M., Frank, J. L., Stormshak, E. A., & Dishion, T. J. (2013). Opening the "Black Box": Family Check-Up intervention effects on self-regulation that prevents growth in problem behavior and substance use. *Journal of School Psychology, 51*, 455–468. doi:10.1016/j.jsp.2013.02.001

Fosco, G. M., Stormshak, E. A., Dishion, T. J., & Winter, C. (2012). Family relationships and parental monitoring during middle school as predictors of early adolescent problem behavior. *Journal of Clinical Child and Adolescent Psychology, 41*, 202–213. doi:10.1080/15374416.2012.651989

Gardner, F., Shaw, D., Dishion, T. J., Burton, J., & Supplee, L. (2007). Randomized prevention trial for early conduct problems: Effects on proactive parenting and links to toddler disruptive behavior. *Journal of Family Psychology, 21*, 398–406. doi:10.1037/0893-3200.21.3.398

Jo, B. (2002). Model misspecification sensitivity analysis in estimating causal effects of interventions with noncompliance. *Statistics in Medicine, 21*, 3161–3181. doi:10.1002/sim.1267

Kandel, D. (1973). Adolescent marihuana use: Role of parents and peers. *Science, 181*, 1067–1070. doi:10.1126/science.181.4104.1067

Kellam, S. G., Brown, C. H., Rubin, B. R., & Ensminger, M. E. (1983). Paths leading to teenage psychiatric symptoms and substance use: Developmental epidemiological studies in Woodlawn. In S. R. Guze, F. J. Earns, & J. E. Barrett (Eds.), *Childhood psychopathology and development* (pp. 17–51). New York, NY: Raven Press.

Kosterman, R., Hawkins, J. D., Guo, J., Catalano, R. F., & Abbott, R. D. (2000). The dynamics of alcohol and marijuana initiation: Patterns and predictors of first use in adolescence. *American Journal of Public Health, 90*, 360–366. doi:10.2105/AJPH.90.3.360

Laird, R. D., Criss, M. M., Pettit, G. S., Dodge, K. A., & Bates, J. E. (2008). Parents' monitoring knowledge attenuates the link between antisocial friends and adolescent delinquent behavior. *Journal of Abnormal Child Psychology, 36*, 299–310. doi:10.1007/s10802-007-9178-4

Liddle, H. A. (2010). Treating adolescent substance abuse using multidimensional family therapy. In J. R. Weisz & A. E. Kazdin (Eds.), *Evidence-based psychotherapies for children and adolescents* (2nd ed., 416–432). New York, NY: Guilford Press.

Loeber, R., & Dishion, T. J. (1983). Early predictors of male delinquency: A review. *Psychological Bulletin, 94*, 68–99. doi:10.1037/0033-2909.94.1.68

Loeber, R., & Schmaling, K. B. (1985). Empirical evidence for overt and covert patterns of antisocial conduct problems: A meta-analysis. *Journal of Abnormal Child Psychology, 13*, 337–353. doi:10.1007/BF00910652

Margolis, K. L., Fosco, G. M., & Stormshak, E. A. (2011). *The Circle of Care: Extending beyond the nuclear family to examine the role of collaborative caretaking in adolescent development.* Manuscript in revision.

McCord, J. (1981). Consideration of some effects of a counseling program. In S. E. Martin, L. B. Sechrest, & R. Redner (Eds.), *New directions in the rehabilitation of criminal offenders* (pp. 394–405). Washington, DC: National Academy of Sciences.

McCord, J. (1988). Identifying developmental paradigms leading to alcoholism. *Journal of Studies on Alcohol, 49*, 357–362.

McCord, J., & Tremblay, R. E. (Eds.). (1992). *Preventing antisocial behavior: Interventions from birth through adolescence.* New York, NY: Guilford Press.

Miller, W. R., & Rollnick, S. (2002). *Motivational interviewing: Preparing people for change* (2nd ed.). New York, NY: Guilford Press.

Palinkas, L. A., Atkins, C. J., Miller, C., & Fereira, D. (1996). Social skills training for drug prevention in high-risk female adolescents. *Preventive Medicine, 25*, 692–701. doi:10.1006/pmed.1996.0108

Patterson, G. R. (1993). Orderly change in a stable world: The antisocial trait as a chimera. *Journal of Consulting and Clinical Psychology, 61*, 911–919. doi:10.1037/0022-006X.61.6.911

Patterson, G. R., & Bank, L. (1989). Some amplifying mechanisms for pathologic processes in families. In M. R. Gunnar & E. Thalen (Eds.), *Systems and development: The Minnesota symposia on child psychology* (Vol. 22, pp. 167–209). Hillsdale, NJ: Erlbaum.

Patterson, G. R., Dishion, T. J., & Chamberlain, P. (1993). Outcomes and methodological issues relating to treatment of antisocial children. In T. R. Giles (Ed.), *Effective psychotherapy: A handbook of comparative research* (pp. 43–88). New York, NY: Plenum. doi:10.1007/978-1-4615-2914-9_3

Patterson, G. R., Reid, J. B., & Dishion, T. J. (1992). *Antisocial boys.* Eugene, OR: Castalia.

Poulin, F., & Boivin, M. (2000). The role of proactive and reactive aggression: The formation and development of friendships in boys. *Developmental Psychology, 36*, 233–240. doi:10.1037/0012-1649.36.2.233

Poulin, F., Dishion, T. J., & Burraston, B. (2001). 3-year iatrogenic effects associated with aggregating high-risk adolescents in cognitive–behavioral preventive interventions. *Applied Developmental Science, 5*, 214–224. doi:10.1207/S1532480XADS0504_03

Rutter, M. (2006). *Genes and behavior: Nature–nurture interplay explained.* Malden, MA: Blackwell.

Shaw, D. S., Dishion, T. J., Supplee, L., Gardner, F., & Arnds, K. (2006). Randomized trial of a family-centered approach to the prevention of early conduct problems: Two-year effects of the family check-up in early childhood. *Journal of Consulting and Clinical Psychology, 74*, 1–9. doi:10.1037/0022-006X.74.1.1

Shaw, D. S., Gilliom, M., Ingoldsby, E. M., & Nagin, D. (2003). Trajectories leading to school-age conduct problems. *Developmental Psychology, 39*, 189–200. doi:10.1037/0012-1649.39.2.189

Smith, G. M., & Fogg, C. P. (1979). Psychological antecedents of teenage drug use. In R. G. Simmons (Ed.), *Research in community and mental health* (Vol. 1, pp. 87–102). Greenwich, CT: JAI Press.

Snyder, J., Schrepferman, L., Oeser, J., Patterson, G., Stoolmiller, M., Johnson, K., & Snyder, A. (2005). Deviancy training and association with deviant peers in young children: Occurrence and contribution to early-onset conduct problems. *Development and Psychopathology, 17*, 397–413. doi:10.1017/S0954579405050194

Spoth, R., Reyes, M. L., Redmond, C., & Shin, C. (1999). Assessing a public health approach to delay onset and progression of adolescent substance use: Latent transition and log-linear analyses of longitudinal family preventive intervention outcomes. *Journal of Consulting and Clinical Psychology, 67*, 619–630. doi:10.1037/0022-006X.67.5.619

Spoth, R. L., Redmond, C., & Shin, C. (2001). Randomized trial of brief family interventions for general populations: Adolescent substance use outcomes 4 years following baseline. *Journal of Consulting and Clinical Psychology, 69*, 627–642. doi:10.1037/0022-006X.69.4.627

Stone, A. A., & Shiffman, S. (1994). Ecological momentary assessment (EMA) in behavioral medicine. *Annals of Behavioral Medicine, 16*, 199–202.

Stormshak, E. A., Bierman, K. L., Bruschi, C. J., Dodge, K. A., Coie, J. D., & the Conduct Problems

Prevention Research Group. (1999). The relation between behavior problems and peer preference in different classroom contexts. *Child Development, 70*, 169–182. doi:10.1111/1467-8624.00013

Stormshak, E. A., Connell, A. M., & Dishion, T. J. (2009). An adaptive approach to family-centered intervention in schools: Linking intervention engagement to academic outcomes in middle and high school. *Prevention Science, 10*, 221–235. doi:10.1007/s11121-009-0131-3

Stormshak, E. A., Connell, A. M., Véronneau, M.-H., Myers, M. W., Dishion, T. J., Kavanagh, K., & Caruthers, A. S. (2011). An ecological approach to promoting early adolescent mental health and social adaptation: Family-centered intervention in public middle schools. *Child Development, 82*, 209–225. doi:10.1111/j.1467-8624.2010.01551.x

Stormshak, E. A., & Dishion, T. J. (2002). An ecological approach to child and family clinical and counseling psychology. *Clinical Child and Family Psychology Review, 5*, 197–215. doi:10.1023/A:1019647131949

Stormshak, E. A., Dishion, T. J., Light, J., & Yasui, M. (2005). Implementing family-centered interventions within the public middle school: Linking service delivery change to change in problem behavior. *Journal of Abnormal Child Psychology, 33*, 723–733. doi:10.1007/s10802-005-7650-6

Stormshak, E. A., Fosco, G. M., & Dishion, T. J. (2010). Implementing interventions with families in schools to increase youth school engagement: The Family Check-Up model. *School Mental Health, 2*, 82–92. doi:10.1007/s12310-009-9025-6

Véronneau, M.-H., Dishion, T. J., & Connell, A. M. (2014). *The prevention of problematic substance use in early adulthood: A randomized trial of the Family Check-Up in public middle schools.* Manuscript in preparation.

Waldron, H. B., & Brody, J. L. (2010). Functional family therapy for adolescent substance use disorders. In J. R. Weisz & A. E. Kazdin (Eds.), *Evidence-based psychotherapies for children and adolescents* (pp. 401–415). New York, NY: Guilford Press.

Wills, T. A., & Dishion, T. J. (2004). Temperament and adolescent substance use: A transactional analysis of emerging self-control. *Journal of Clinical Child and Adolescent Psychology, 33*, 69–81. doi:10.1207/S15374424JCCP3301_7

Part VI

PREVENTION FROM AN ENVIRONMENTAL AND POLICY PERSPECTIVE

CHAPTER 17

LESSONS FROM COMPREHENSIVE ENVIRONMENTAL COMMUNITY PREVENTION TRIALS

Robert F. Saltz, Joel W. Grube, and Andrew J. Treno

This chapter is dedicated to the memory of our colleague and coauthor, Dr. Andrew Treno, who passed away unexpectedly in April 2014. Andrew was a senior research scientist at the Prevention Research Center of the Pacific Institute for Research and Evaluation, where he had worked since 1992. Andrew was perhaps best known in the field of alcohol studies for his research and writings on environmental and community-based approaches to preventing alcohol-related problems. His work helped establish the evidence base for community efforts to ameliorate problems related to alcohol use and abuse. We will miss Andrew's thoughtfulness and insights and his cheerful collegiality.

INTRODUCTION

This chapter examines comprehensive environmental community interventions for preventing alcohol use and associated problems. A community systems conceptual framework is described that provides a model for understanding how these interventions can be effective. Examples of successful comprehensive community interventions are reviewed. The preponderance of evidence indicates that multicomponent, community-level interventions can reduce alcohol consumption and problems. A number of central questions, however, remain unanswered. In particular, it is unclear what specific components of these interventions are effective and through what mechanisms they work. Importantly, little research has addressed the mechanisms through which community change can be accomplished. Finally, although this chapter focuses on community interventions targeting alcohol use and problems, many of these approaches may be relevant to preventing tobacco and other drug use. The available research on community approaches to tobacco and other drug prevention is limited and results are mixed (e.g., Carson et al., 2011; Gates, McCambridge, Smith, & Foxcroft, 2006). Nonetheless, comprehensive community approaches to preventing tobacco and other drug use may be increasingly important given the changing political and social environment, especially as it relates to marijuana use.

Alcohol is the most commonly used and abused drug by youth and young adults in the United States. Although rates of alcohol use by young people have fallen dramatically since the 1980s, consumption remains high. On the basis of the 2013 Monitoring the Future (MTF) surveys, 39% of high school seniors, 63% of college students, and 69% of young adults (ages 19–28) report drinking in the past 30 days (Johnston, O'Malley, Bachman, Schulenberg,

Preparation of this chapter was supported by grants from the National Institute on Abuse and Alcoholism (P60-AA006282) and the National Institute on Drug Abuse (R01 DA015966). The content of this chapter is solely the responsibility of the authors and does not necessarily represent the official views of the National Institute on Abuse and Alcoholism or the National Institute on Drug Abuse.

http://dx.doi.org/10.1037/14550-018
Handbook of Adolescent Drug Use Prevention: Research, Intervention Strategies, and Practice, L. M. Scheier (Editor)

& Miech, 2014a, 2014b). Moreover, alcohol use far surpasses use of tobacco, marijuana, and other illicit drugs. The 2013 MTF data, for example, showed that between 1.5 and 4.5 times as many high school seniors, college students, and young adults reported recent use of alcohol compared with tobacco, marijuana, or other illicit drugs.

The consumption patterns of young drinkers may be particularly problematic. Overall, 22% of high school seniors, 35% of college students, and 35% of young adults report heavy episodic drinking (five or more drinks in a row) during the previous 2 weeks; 26%, 40%, and 38% of them, respectively, report being drunk at least once in the past month (Johnston et al., 2014a, 2014b). Thus, among those individuals who drank in the past month, 67% of seniors, 65% of college students, and 55% of young adults reported being drunk on at least one occasion. It has been estimated that more than 90% of drinking occasions among young adolescent drinkers are heavy drinking episodes (U.S. Department of Health and Human Services, 2007). These drinking patterns are substantially different from those of adults age 30 and older, who tend to drink more frequently but have fewer heavy drinking occasions (National Research Council & Institute of Medicine, 2004).

The pattern of heavy episodic drinking by adolescents and young adults is associated with an array of problems (Brown & Tapert, 2004; Hingson & Kenkel, 2004; Hingson & White, 2014). Each year, as many as 5,000 youth younger than 21 years old in the United States die as a result of drinking-related motor vehicle crashes, homicides, suicide, and other injuries such as falls, burns, and drowning (National Institute on Alcohol Abuse and Alcoholism, 2014). In 2012, 4,211 drivers younger than the age of 21 years were involved in alcohol-related fatal motor vehicle crashes (National Highway Traffic Safety Administration, 2013). In addition, early onset of drinking is associated with an increased likelihood of negative consequences later in life, including dependence and abuse, drinking and driving, unwanted or unplanned sex, unintended pregnancy, sexually transmitted infections, violence, and unintentional injury (e.g., Hingson & Kenkel, 2004; Hingson & White, 2014). Overall, excessive alcohol consumption in the United States is responsible for as many as 80,000 deaths annually and is estimated to cost $223.5 billion each year (Sacks et al., 2013). The estimated costs of underage drinking alone may reach as much as $61.9 billion annually (Miller, Levy, Spicer, & Taylor, 2006).

Interventions to prevent drinking and drinking problems among adolescents and college students traditionally have relied on education programs that focus on individual risk factors, such as increasing knowledge of the consequences of drinking, changing attitudes toward drinking, improving social and refusal skills, and correcting misperceptions of drinking norms. Although some education programs have showed success in delaying onset or reducing alcohol use among youth, critical reviews have concluded that little evidence has demonstrated that most alcohol education programs by themselves lead to long-term reductions in alcohol use and problems among young people (Elder et al., 2005; Foxcroft, Ireland, Lister-Sharp, Lowe, & Breen, 2003; Foxcroft & Tsertsvadze, 2011b). Evidence is inconclusive that education programs targeting multiple settings (e.g., schools and family) are more effective that those targeting single settings (Foxcroft & Tsertsvadze, 2011a).

ENVIRONMENTAL APPROACHES TO PREVENT YOUTH DRINKING AND DRINKING PROBLEMS

In contrast to education programs, environmental approaches to prevention are population based rather than targeting individual risk factors. For the most part, environmental approaches focus on implementing or enforcing policies to limit the availability of alcohol or to deter young drinkers and those individuals who supply them with alcohol. Broadly defined, alcohol policy includes (a) formal legal and regulatory mechanisms, rules, and procedures for reducing the consumption of alcohol or risky drinking behaviors; and (b) enforcement of these measures (Grube, 2010; Grube & Nygaard, 2005). Alcohol policies can be implemented at many levels, including national (e.g., excise taxes), state (e.g., limitations on retail or wholesale distribution), local (e.g., zoning ordinances), or institutional (e.g., school policies, responsible service practices in stores, bars, and restaurants). The primary purposes of such policies are to increase the "full price" of alcohol to youth, including the resources necessary for underage youth to obtain alcohol, the potential costs to youth for possessing or consuming it, and the potential costs to adults for selling or supplying alcohol to youth (Grube, 2010; Grube & Nygaard, 2005). Many policies have both availability and deterrence properties. For example, minimum drinking age laws make it more difficult for young people to purchase alcohol from retailers and also include penalties for possession or consumption of alcohol by underage youth. Similarly, compliance checks may impose fines or license revocation on local retailers who sell alcohol to underage youth and, consequently, increase the difficulties (i.e. opportunity cost) experienced by youth who attempt to purchase alcohol. Regulatory policies, practices, and enforcement also may reinforce norms against underage drinking or supplying alcohol to underage drinkers (Perry et al., 2000; Toomey, Lenk, & Wagenaar, 2007).

Policy approaches, and prevention more generally, have begun to focus on harm reduction (Marlatt & Witkiewitz, 2002, 2010; Riley & O'Hare, 2000; Stockwell, Gruenewald, Toumbourou, & Loxely, 2005). Harm reduction policies attempt to prevent or reduce alcohol problems by promoting moderate drinking and discouraging heavy drinking and drinking in risky situations. Such approaches do not necessarily target overall consumption. Thus, for example, responsible beverage service (RBS) programs attempt to prevent heavy drinking and impairment, rather than drinking *per se*.

Commercial and Social Availability of Alcohol

Despite a uniform drinking age of 21 years in all 50 states and the District of Columbia, young people can still readily obtain alcohol. Data from the 2012 MTF, for example, show that 91% of high school seniors report that alcohol is "fairly easy" or very easy to obtain (Johnston et al., 2014a). Purchase surveys routinely show that 30% or more of alcohol outlets will sell to underage buyers (e.g., Freisthler, Gruenewald, Treno, & Lee, 2003; Paschall, Grube, Black, Flewelling, Ringwalt, & Biglan, 2007; Wagenaar, Toomey, & Erickson, 2005). In part, these high sales rates result from low and inconsistent levels of enforcement (Wagenaar & Wolfson, 1994, 1995). Social sources of alcohol, however, appear to be more important than commercial sources, especially for underage drinkers (Paschall, Grube, Black, & Ringwalt, 2007). The most common social alcohol sources are friends and parties. Successful community interventions, then, need to address social as well as commercial availability of alcohol through multiple strategies.

Community Systems Approaches

A community systems approach to prevention recognizes that drug and alcohol use, and associated problems, are the result of a complex interplay among multiple factors that influence both supply and demand. Figure 17.1 depicts a simplified model of how individual, social, and commercial interests interact in determining supply of alcohol to and demand for alcohol by adolescents within a community context. Community-level preventive interventions can be implemented targeting each of these levels. Thus, for example, compliance checks and social host ordinances may influence commercial and social availability of alcohol, and the enforcement of minor-in-possession laws may directly deter minors from drinking. In general, systems such as this comprise a host of relationships based on economic theory, deterrence, peer influence, social learning theory, and other conceptual approaches that underlie the hypothetical sources of organizational and individual behavior change depicted in the comprehensive model. Although the model in Figure 17.1 is oriented specifically toward underage alcohol use and problems, this general framework may be relevant to the prevention of tobacco and other drug use as well (Birckmayer, Fisher, Holder, & Yacoubian, 2008; Birckmayer, Holder, Yacoubian, & Friend, 2004). Community systems approaches, in fact, may be increasingly relevant to important adolescents' drug use given current trends toward liberalization of laws regarding recreational marijuana.

Standards of Evidence

Although randomized controlled trials generally are considered to be the gold standard for evaluating

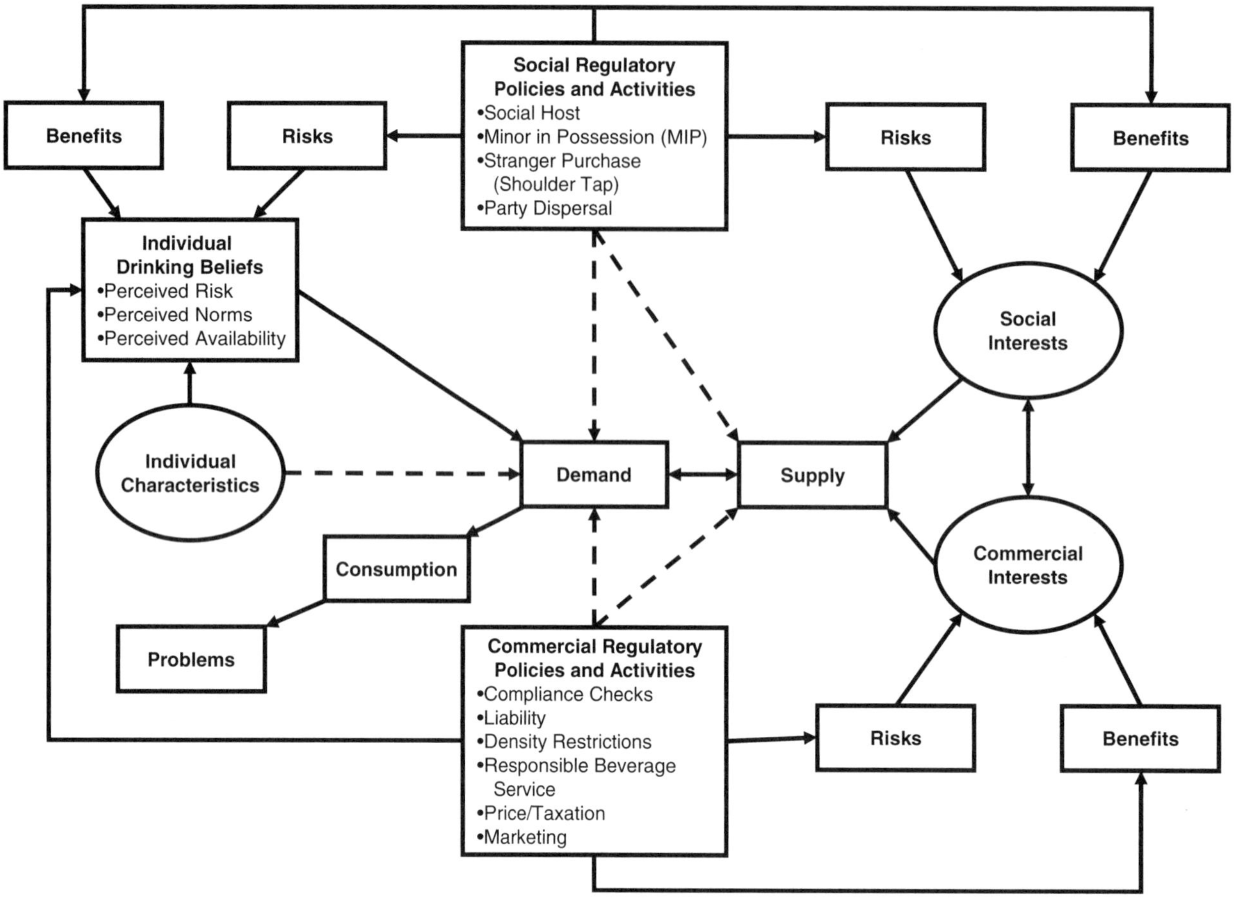

FIGURE 17.1. Community systems model of underage drinking.

preventive interventions, they often may be too expensive or impractical in community settings (Biglan, Ary, & Wagenaar, 2000; Flay et al., 2005). This is particularly the case in evaluations of interventions in which random assignment of communities to experimental and control conditions simply is not feasible. In some instances, random assignment actually would work to the detriment of external validity by ignoring the processes through which community-level interventions are developed and implemented. As a result of these considerations, community-level interventions and alcohol policies often are evaluated using quasi-experimental designs, such as interrupted or multiple baseline time-series. These designs can provide strong evidence for policy effectiveness if controls are adequate for confounding factors that may co-occur with the policy of interest. The ability to draw conclusions from such studies is enhanced to the extent that results are replicated across time or geographic units.

Naturalistic Studies

A considerable body of research has investigated the potential effects of alcohol policies through the evaluation of natural experiments or by analyzing naturally existing policy differences across clearly demarcated jurisdictions. Overall, these studies provide strong evidence that alcohol policies can reduce alcohol consumption and problems among adolescents and young adults. A recent international study, for example, found that adolescents living in countries with stronger alcohol policies were less likely to drink heavily or have their first drink by age 13, even after controlling for adult consumption levels and other factors (Paschall, Grube, & Kypri, 2009). Similarly, in a study of 50 California communities, adolescent alcohol use and heavy drinking were negatively related to the enforcement of underage drinking laws and positively related to alcohol outlet density and community levels of adult alcohol use (Paschall, Grube, Thomas, Cannon, & Treffers, 2012). Other research has examined the relations between community measures of youth access to alcohol, enforcement of possession laws, and the frequency of youth alcohol use and related problems (Dent, Grube, & Biglan, 2005). The perceived rate of illegal merchant sales in the communities was directly related to 30-day frequency of alcohol use, heavy drinking, using alcohol at school, and drinking and driving. Evidence also indicated that communities with higher perceived minor-in-possession law enforcement had lower rates of alcohol use and heavy drinking. Another study used purchase surveys to investigate possible effects of commercial alcohol availability on high school students' use of commercial and social alcohol sources, perceived ease of obtaining alcohol, and drinking (Paschall, Grube, Black, & Ringwalt, 2007). The school district-level alcohol sales rate was not related directly to students' drinking. The associations between students' use of commercial alcohol sources and their drinking behaviors, however, were stronger in districts with higher alcohol sales rates, whereas relations between use of social alcohol sources and drinking behaviors were diminished in those districts.

An example of a natural experiment is provided by recent studies of alcohol policy changes in the Canadian province of British Columbia. Before 2000, the number of private liquor licenses was allowed to increase slowly, followed by a moratorium in new licenses from 2000 to 2002. After the moratorium was lifted, there was a 33% increase in private outlets between 2002 and 2008 (Stockwell et al., 2009). Not surprisingly, as the number of private stores increased, the average price for alcoholic beverages decreased. Specifically, a doubling of the number of private liquor stores in a geographic jurisdiction was associated with a 3.7% decrease in prices relative to government-run stores (Treno et al., 2013). In addition, it was estimated that a 10% increase in the number of private outlets was related to increases in population-level alcohol consumption between 0.3% (private stores) and 2.3% (restaurants). Importantly, a 10% increase in private store density was associated with 2.5%, 2.4%, and 2.0% increases in acute, chronic, and total alcohol-attributable mortality rates (Zhao et al., 2013). Similarly, it was associated with about a 9% increase in both acute and chronic alcohol-related hospital admissions 2 years later (Stockwell et al., 2013).

As a final example of a naturalistic community-level experiment, a study in the Brazilian city of Diadema, where alcohol sales had been largely unregulated, suggests that a new law prohibiting alcohol sales after 11:00 P.M. was related to a decrease of almost nine murders per month (Duailibi et al., 2007). Assaults against women also decreased, but this effect was not significant when underlying trends were controlled.

Interventions With Retailers

Other studies indicate that interventions that provide feedback to clerks and managers regarding their performance relating to sales to buyers can significantly reduce sales of tobacco and alcohol to minors. These programs reward clerks who refuse sales to young-appearing customers who cannot provide an identification (I.D.) card and provide a reminder regarding the law to clerks who do sell. In contrast to enforcement efforts (e.g., compliance checks), no formal sanctions are involved. Most notably, a randomized community trial using this approach suggests that increasing retailer compliance with age identification for underage tobacco sales not only reduced tobacco sales to minors and youth smoking but also had a similar effect on underage drinking (Biglan, Ary, Smolkowski, Duncan, & Black, 2000). In general, these programs show significant effects decreasing sales of tobacco and alcohol to minors (e.g., Krevor, Ponicki, Grube, & DeJong, 2011; Moore et al., 2012), although the available evidence for effects on adolescents' drinking and smoking is not definitive.

Community Intervention Studies

Although natural experiments and studies of naturally occurring policy differences are suggestive, purposeful interventions in randomized community trials provide better evidence of the importance of policy approaches to preventing alcohol problems. In the following sections, we briefly review a handful of interventions, although these are not meant to be exhaustive. In addition, although some of the projects discussed are now somewhat dated, they are included to show how such prevention strategies have evolved and what core components have carried over through to the most recent examples.

Saving Lives. The Saving Lives project (Hingson et al., 1996), conducted in six communities in Massachusetts, was designed to reduce alcohol-impaired driving and related problems such as automobile speeding. Programs were designed locally and involved a host of activities, including media campaigns, business information programs, speeding and drunk driving awareness days, speed watch telephone hotlines, police training, high school peer-led education, Students Against Drunk Driving chapters, and college prevention programs. The program evaluation involved a quasi-experimental design with five communities serving as controls. Although the control communities were slightly more affluent than the experimental sites, they had similar demographic characteristics, rates of traffic citations, and fatal crashes. The study found that Saving Lives cities experienced a 25% decline in fatal crashes when compared with the rest of Massachusetts (i.e., a downturn from 178 crashes to 120), a 42% reduction in fatal motor vehicle crashes within the experimental communities, a 47% reduction in the number of fatally injured drivers who tested positive for alcohol, and an 8% decline in crash injuries among 15- to 25-year-olds. In addition, there was a decline in self-reported driving after drinking (specifically among youth). The greatest fatal and injury crash reductions occurred in the 15- to 25-year-old age-group.

Communities Mobilizing for Change on Alcohol. The Communities Mobilizing for Change on Alcohol (CMCA) project was designed to reduce access to alcohol among youth under the legal drinking age of 21 years. The project was composed of five core components intended to influence (a) community policies, (b) community practices, (c) youth alcohol access, (d) youth alcohol consumption, and subsequently (e) youth alcohol problems. Although the project clearly was communitywide in terms of the institutions involved, it focused on youth younger than 21 years of age. The CMCA project recruited 15 communities in Minnesota and western Wisconsin; matched them on size, state, proximity to a college or university, and baseline data from an alcohol purchase survey; and then randomly assigned members of each pair to intervention or control groups (Wagenaar, Murray, & Toomey, 2000). The CMCA project hired a part-time local organizer from within each community who was responsible for organizing activities that activated the community members, who, in turn, would select interventions designed to influence underage access to alcohol. The interventions that could be selected included a broad array of programs that affect youth access: decoy operations with alcohol outlets, citizen monitoring of outlets selling to youth, keg registration, sponsorship of alcohol-free events for youth, policy action to shorten hours of sale for alcohol, implementation of RBS training programs, and development of educational programs for youth and adults. The experimental sites were free to shape these interventions to fit their own ends. Evaluation data were collected at baseline and at about 30 months after the interventions began. Results showed that merchants increased the frequency of checks for age identification, reduced sales to minors, and reported more care in controlling alcohol sales to youth. A telephone survey of 18- to 20-year-olds showed reductions in attempts to purchase alcohol, reduced levels of alcohol use, and reduced propensity to provide alcohol to other teens. In addition, the study found a statistically significant decline in drinking and driving arrests among 18- to 20-year-olds and disorderly conduct violations among 15- to 17-year-olds in the CMCA cities compared with the controls (Wagenaar et al., 2000).

Community Trials. The Community Trials (CT) project was a five-component, community-level intervention conducted in three experimental communities matched to three control communities (Holder et al., 2000) located in California and South Carolina. Intervention components were designed to reduce alcohol-related harm among all people in the three experimental communities. The outcomes assessed in the project represented five primary sources of acute injury and harm related to alcohol use: injuries and fatalities related to drinking and driving, violence, drowning, burns, and falls. The design of each intervention component was based on prior scientific evidence and was intended to affect different aspects of community systems underlying use, abuse, and problems in community settings. The five intervention components included (a) a *media and mobilization* component to develop community organization and support for the goals and strategies of the project, (b) a *responsible beverage service* component to reduce service to intoxicated patrons at bars and restaurants, (c) a *sales to youth* component designed to reduce underage access, (d) a *drinking and driving* component to increase enforcement activities related to driving while intoxicated offenses, and (e) an *access* component designed to reduce the availability of alcohol for underage youth. The final evaluation of the project covered key problem areas through data collected in a large population survey and also from archival sources and hospital emergency room department records. Comparison of the effects of the interventions on relative risks of injury outcomes between matched communities showed significant reductions in nighttime injury crashes (10%) and crashes in which the driver was found by police to "have been drinking" (6%). Assault injuries observed in hospital emergency room departments declined by 43% and all hospitalized assault injuries declined by 2%. Analyses of the survey data showed a 49% decline in episodes of driving after "having had too much to drink" and a 51% decline in self-reports of driving when "over the legal limit." Importantly, although the drinking population increased slightly in the experimental sites over the course of the study, there was a significant reduction in problematic alcohol use; the average number of drinks per occasion declined by 6%, and the variance in drinking patterns (an indirect measure of heavy drinking) declined by 21% (Holder et al., 2000).

Sacramento Neighborhood Alcohol Prevention. The primary goal of the Sacramento Neighborhood Alcohol Prevention Project (SNAPP) was to implement and evaluate neighborhood-level interventions intended to reduce youth and young-adult access to alcohol, risky drinking, and associated problems, particularly in low-income ethnically diverse neighborhoods. SNAPP represented an extension of the CT project in that it posed three basic questions. First, could an environmental approach be tailored to the unique needs of economically and ethnically diverse populations? Second, could environmental strategies address the problem of intentional injuries (i.e., assaultive violence) in the context of more economically and ethnically diverse settings? Third, could these more specifically tailored interventions be implemented at the neighborhood level? To address these questions, SNAPP established the goals of reducing alcohol access, drinking, and related problems in two low-income, predominantly ethnic minority neighborhoods, focusing on individuals between the ages of 15 and 29 years.

SNAPP implemented five interventions: a mobilization component, a community awareness component, a responsible beverage service (RBS) component, an underage-access law enforcement component, and an intoxicated-patron law enforcement component. These different program modalities were fielded in one area of the city early in the project and fielded in another similar area about 2 years later. To mobilize the neighborhoods in support of the overall project goals and interventions, project lead agencies worked with collaborative advisory committees, composed of members drawn from each of the two geographic areas and that worked to ensure intervention implementation and fidelity to the project design. The community awareness component intended to increase awareness of the problems associated with youth and young-adult drinking and catalyze support for community mobilization efforts. Activities included neighborhood presentations of research findings and showcasing local statistics related to underage and problematic drinking to parents and other community groups, distribution of informational flyers and brochures, and youth participation as volunteers in data collection activities related to neighborhood alcohol availability.

The RBS component was designed to help retailers develop policies and train staff to reduce alcohol sales to minors and intoxicated persons. This component increased compliance with existing alcohol policies by obtaining sponsorship and support from local and state hospitality organizations, providing manager and server training for all on- and off-premise licensed alcohol outlets in the selected neighborhoods using a standard curriculum, developing a process to increase enforcement of existing laws regarding service to intoxicated customers, and obtaining endorsement of RBS from neighborhood bodies and organizations. The underage-access law enforcement component focused on increasing actual and perceived enforcement of laws prohibiting alcohol sales to minors and was accomplished by working with neighborhood police to increase the number of off-premise sting operations. These efforts were designed to parallel those of the off-premise intervention. Letters from the local police were sent to all premises in and around the study sites informing them that stepped-up enforcement of laws regarding sales to intoxicated patrons and minors would become a regular police activity.

A program efficacy evaluation showed that the neighborhood interventions led to an estimated reduction of 3.9% in police calls related to assaults and a 33.4% reduction in emergency medical system (e.g., ambulance) responses related to motor vehicle crashes in the first relative to the second intervention site. Subsequently, the program evaluation found an estimated reduction of 36.5% in police calls related to assaults and an estimated reduction of 37.4% in emergency medical system responses related to assaults in the second intervention site over preintervention levels (Treno, Gruenewald, Lee, & Remer, 2007).

Operation Safe Crossing. The goal of the Operation Safe Crossing project was to implement and evaluate a large drunk-driving enforcement program at the U.S.–Mexico border to reduce the number of youths crossing the border to drink in the city of Tijuana (across the border from the large metropolitan area of San Diego, California). The intervention activities for this project included both enforcement of drinking and driving laws through the use of sobriety checkpoints near the border and enforcing laws barring youth from reentering the U.S. without parents or other adult guardians through special patrols conducted about every 60 days (Voas, Tippetts, Johnson, Lange, & Baker, 2002). Data from a border breath-test assessment were used to dramatize the problem and gain public support for action. The data also were used to help design the enforcement effort and measure progress in reducing the cross-border drinking problem. Analysis of data from this pre–post study involved observations on more than 2 million pedestrians returning from Tijuana. Operation Safe Crossing reduced the number of late-night crossers by 31.6% relative to rates before the intervention. In addition, the proportion of pedestrians with blood alcohol concentrations at .08 declined by 29% and there was a decline in the number of 16- to 20-year-olds who had been drinking and were involved in automobile crashes relative to other drivers of the same age-group who had not been drinking and crashed.

Safer California Universities. The aim of Safer California Universities was to determine whether environmental prevention strategies targeting specific off-campus settings would reduce the incidence of student intoxication on college campuses. Fourteen large public universities were recruited to participate in the project, campuses were matched on student demographic and community characteristics and one member of each campus pair was assigned randomly to the intervention condition. The intervention campuses implemented five environmental interventions: (a) nuisance party enforcement operations to reduce problems related to off-campus parties, (b) minor decoy operations at on- and off-premise outlets to reduce underage sales and sales to intoxicated persons, (c) police roadside checkpoints testing for intoxicated drivers, (d) development of social host ordinances to discourage provision of alcohol to underage drinkers in social gatherings, and (e) the use of campus and local media to increase the visibility of all these environmental strategies. Significant reductions in the incidence and likelihood of intoxication at off-campus parties and bars or restaurants were observed among intervention campuses compared with controls. A lower likelihood of intoxication also was observed among intervention campuses for the last time students drank at an off-campus party, a bar or restaurant, or another (undesignated) setting. No increase in intoxication appeared in any setting; a sign that heavy drinking and intoxication were not displaced to other drinking contexts. Finally, stronger intervention effects were observed at those intervention campuses with the highest intensity of implementation (Saltz, Paschall, McGaffigan, & Nygaard, 2010).

Reducing Youth Access to Alcohol. The Oregon Reducing Youth Access to Alcohol project incorporated a mix of law enforcement and other community-based activities. The intervention was initiated as a collaborative effort involving researchers, local community actors, and the Addictions and Mental Health Division (AMHD) of Oregon's Department of Health and Human Services. The five specific program programs included (a) community mobilization, (b) the Reward and Reminder Program, (c) media advocacy, (d) enforcement, and (e) coordination and community outreach.

The study design involved 36 Oregon communities defined by public school districts that participated in the annual in-school Oregon Healthy Teens surveys of 8th- and 11th-grade students. Communities were assigned randomly to intervention and control conditions. Because of limited resources, the interventions were implemented consecutively in two cohorts of communities. During the initial stage of project interventions, project staff and community prevention coordinators secured community support and endorsement for the project. Specific mobilization activities included presentations highlighting local underage drinking data, education to increase awareness of the risks associated with underage alcohol consumption, and highlights of proposed project activities. In each intervention community, as a part of the Reward and Reminder Program, off-premise outlets in each community were visited by buyers youthful in appearance that reinforced proper alcohol I.D. checking practices and provided constructive feedback to clerks, managers, and owners when proper I.D. checking procedures were not followed. In the weeks preceding these visits, merchant education visits were conducted to each alcohol outlet. The media advocacy component included a series of newspaper articles and community and school newsletters focusing on such topics as county-specific underage drinking statistics, underage drinking during prom and graduation, the dangers of underage drinking at home, social host liability, and project law enforcement activities. Enforcement activities included compliance checks, which were completed once per year for 2 years in each of the off-premise alcohol outlets in the project communities, along with shoulder tap operations, third-party purchase surveillance, and enforcement of minor in possession laws, driving under the influence (DUI) enforcement, and controlled party dispersal. Throughout the program, staff and coalition members worked with key stakeholders in each community to ensure program implementation.

Evaluation data consisted of student surveys administered annually to 11th-grade students as well as underage purchase surveys. For evaluation purposes, four primary outcome measures were identified. These included measures of any prior 30-day alcohol use, prior 30-day binge drinking, and perceived availability to alcohol for the student survey, and "successful" purchases from the purchase survey. Statistically significant effects were found only for the underage sales outcome measure. Additional analyses, however, showed that enforcement activities, which varied considerably between sites, had a moderating effect on both 30-day drinking and underage binge drinking (Flewelling et al., 2013). Specifically, significant reductions in the designated outcomes were observed in communities with the highest levels of implementation. No changes were observed in communities with only modest levels of implementation.

Study to Prevent Alcohol-Related Consequences. The Study to Prevent Alcohol-Related Consequences (SPARC) was a comprehensive intervention using a community organizing approach to implement environmental strategies in and around college campuses (Wolfson et al., 2012). The ultimate goal was to reduce high-risk drinking and alcohol-related consequences among college students. Eight public and two private universities in North Carolina were randomized to the intervention or comparison condition. A repeated cross-sectional design was used to assess the program's efficacy. Each intervention school was assigned a campus or community organizer. The organizer worked to form a campus-community coalition, which developed and implemented a unique strategic plan implemented over a 3-year period.

Although each campus developed its own prevention plan, they were required to choose three of four program modalities or "strategy domains" that could (a) reduce alcohol availability, (b) address price and marketing of alcoholic beverages, (c) improve social norms, and (d) minimize harm related to alcohol. Within each of the selected program modalities, the interventions were expected to be comprehensive, including policy, enforcement, and public awareness. Examples of specific components include social norms marketing (to correct students' misperception of peer drinking), restricting alcohol at campus events, and enforcing compliance to laws prohibiting sales to underage persons. The researchers found decreases in the intervention group compared with the control group in severe consequences resulting from students' own drinking as well as in alcohol-related injuries caused to others. At the population level, these reductions translate to approximately 228 fewer severe consequences per month on each campus, and 107 fewer injuries caused to others in a month, a meaningful impact. In further analyses, higher levels of implementation of the intervention were associated with reductions in interpersonal consequences because of others' drinking and alcohol-related injuries caused to others.

Enforcing Underage Drinking Laws. The Enforcing Underage Drinking Laws (EUDL) program was established in 1998 by the U.S. Office of Juvenile Justice and Delinquency Prevention (OJJDP) to support and enhance efforts by states, territories, and communities to prevent the sale of alcoholic beverages to and the purchase and consumption of alcoholic beverages by minors. Although the interventions that are implemented across EUDL sites are varied, the program broadly promotes environmental strategies, including (a) controlling the type, location, and number of commercial alcohol outlets; (b) implementing responsible sales and service practices; (c) enforcing underage sales laws (i.e., compliance checks); (d) limiting minors' access to noncommercial sources of alcohol (e.g., enforcement of social host ordinances, party dispersal programs); (e) impaired driving enforcement; and (f) controlling alcohol pricing and promotion.

In addition, major foci of the EUDL program include the development of local coalitions and media advocacy. One of the few formal evaluations of EUDL investigated the efficacy of this program in five communities surrounding U.S. Air Force bases. This study found that the program was associated with significantly greater decreases in the percentage of junior officers with a positive Alcohol Use Disorders Identification Test score for two of the five intervention communities compared with matched comparison communities or with the Air Force overall (Spera et al., 2010). No significant program effects were found for the other three EUDL communities. Decreases in the rates of sales to minors, minor in possession arrests, and arrests for DUI were found in some of the five intervention communities but not in others (Spera, Barlas, Szoc, Prabhakaran, & Cambridge, 2012). To some extent, changes in these outcomes appeared to be related to intensity of implementation, with greater effects observed in communities with more EUDL activities. Although suggestive, the results of these studies are not definitive because of the small number of communities, the mixed patterns of findings, and the use of piecemeal analytic approaches that limit the ability to draw firm conclusions about overall program efficacy.

Stockholm Prevents Alcohol and Drug Problems. The Stockholm Prevents Alcohol and Drug Problems (STAD) program was developed in 1996 as a project of the Stockholm, Sweden, City Council and the Karolinska Institute. A major focus of STAD is preventing risky alcohol use in licensed restaurants, bars, and nightclubs. The program includes a combination of strategies, including community mobilization, implementation of RBS training and practices to prevent overservice, and enforcement. The program has shown substantial effects on alcohol sales to pseudo-intoxicated patrons, increasing service refusal rates from 5% before the program to 70% five years later (Wallin, Gripenberg, & Andréasson, 2005). Importantly, there was a 29% decrease in violent crimes reported to the police in the intervention area compared with the control area (Wallin, Norström, & Andréasson, 2003). The program significantly increased the likelihood that club doormen would refuse entrance to apparently drug-impaired patrons (Gripenberg, Wallin, & Andréasson, 2007). In addition, it reduced the prevalence of self-reported drug use among staff at the clubs (Gripenberg Abdon, Wallin, & Andréasson, 2011a). These outcomes were maintained for up to 5 years after the intervention was initiated (Gripenberg Abdon, Wallin, & Andréasson, 2011b). Taking implementation costs into account, it has been estimated that the program would lead to a savings of as much as €31 million (approximately $42 million) over 10 years because of reductions in judicial system costs, lost productivity, health care costs, and costs associated with other damage (Månsdotter, Rydberg, Wallin, Lindholm, & Andréasson, 2007). The program has gained good public acceptance and has been more broadly disseminated throughout Stockholm County (Wallin, 2007).

Environmental Strategies: A Fair Shake?

It is easy to understand any community's reluctance to adopt environmental prevention strategies, given the number of obstacles that often have to be surmounted. Some of these have to do with community perceptions relevant to prevention, including various individuals that may be critical to implementation (e.g., law enforcement agencies). Many individuals believe, for instance, that prevention efforts should target only the "heavy" drinkers and that a modest level of alcohol consumption is part and parcel of a society tolerant of social drinking. Although chronic heavy-drinking individuals do have elevated risks associated with their consumption practices, they usually constitute a minority of drinkers, all of whom are at some risk. As a result, in what some have called the "prevention paradox" (Kreitman, 1986; Skog, 2006), drinkers who typically consume low or moderate levels of alcohol, but occasionally drink heavily, produce the majority of negative alcohol-related consequences at the population level.

Another fairly prevalent attitude held by many stakeholders is that environmental strategies will not work. These sentiments usually are associated with phrases, such as "drinkers are always going to find a way," or something to the effect that alcohol problems will merely shift to some other time or location. These beliefs are likely related to the idea that negative consequences are concentrated among the heaviest, if not dependent, drinkers. The prevention field has sufficient empirical evidence to demonstrate that such pessimism is not warranted. One commonly may find an ambivalence about how bad the problems really are and perhaps a concern that "too much" prevention will destroy the perceived positive consequences associated with drinking. Finally, many environmental strategies appear to require more coordination and resources than other forms of prevention that appear, in contrast, to have clear guidelines (if not manuals) that make implementation simpler.

Still, the case for environmental strategies as part of a comprehensive approach to prevention does stand on solid ground. First, many of the individual-level approaches are best suited for people who are, in fact, risky or problematic drinkers, leaving a need to address the harms that accrue to the majority of drinkers for whom such interventions or programs are not appropriate. Second, many of the individual-level interventions are quite labor intensive and difficult to implement with fidelity. Third, evidence is limited that the impact of individual-level strategies may be compromised by "hostile" environments. DeJong et al. (2009), for instance, were able to show that an otherwise efficacious college drinking prevention program involving a social marketing approach was moderated by the density of alcohol outlets around the intervention campus.

Finally, the case could be made in a more positive light by arguing that we should expect to find a synergistic effect of combining individual-level and environmental prevention strategies in a thoughtful way so that each will support the other. It is easy to imagine, for instance, that various drinking contexts (e.g., restaurants) could be much better designed to support those in recovery of alcohol addiction as well as those who would choose to drink little, if at all.

COMPREHENSIVE COMMUNITY PREVENTION: FUTURE DIRECTIONS

At this point, and from the evidence accrued, we can offer a few summary statements. First, consistent themes are associated with the few programs reviewed in this chapter. One in particular is relevant to the efficacy of environmental approaches, suggesting that almost all of the interventions reviewed involve regulating availability, punishing or deterring "bad" drinkers, or punishing purveyors of alcohol. This is a rather small and crude repertoire but also is understandable within the context of these studies needing to show effects within a limited time frame (typically 2 or 3 years). Future studies may be able to evaluate the effects of a purposeful reduction of alcohol outlet density, for example, an intervention that may take more time to implement and also may have a more enduring if not larger effect.

Second, greater theoretical sophistication is needed both to consolidate these studies and to guide their future. This would help distinguish between general principles for prevention (e.g., reducing availability of alcohol) and the specific instances of those principles (e.g., using decoy operations to reduce sales to minors). This type of theoretical richness is key to helping practitioners make decisions about how much adaptation of specific practices can be made without jeopardizing the fundamental strategy (i.e., where the boundaries for maintaining "fidelity" may be found).

Third, the examples given in this chapter show a trend of increasingly rigorous research design, moving from simpler case-study designs to group-randomized trials. Still, the field needs to make further progress on building models of mediation and moderation of community-level effects as well as to refine measures of target risk mechanisms and designated outcomes. Outcome measures, however, are often among the strengths of these approaches, for example, in using archival evidence detailing the prevalence of injuries and deaths in the community in addition to self-reported measures of alcohol consumption or associated harms.

Fourth, there is a critical need for translational research in community-level interventions. To date, there has been an improvised quality to how the comprehensive interventions are designed, planned, and implemented. No doubt, individual researchers and teams have gained a great deal of valuable experience in conducting these trials, but rarely is that experience documented, much less systematically examined in formal research designs. There is a vast, uncharted territory for research into such questions as how to achieve enhanced enforcement of laws against serving minors or intoxicated persons, for example. Frankly, much of the innovation in alcohol control measures comes from communities and regulatory or policy control advocates themselves, leaving researchers to catch up to the latest developments in targeted hosts of private parties or new ordinances for controlling nuisance retail alcohol outlets.

The major achievement of the research to date has been to establish the efficacy of environmental community prevention in general. Although much remains to be done to enhance the impact and efficiency of these strategies, it was not too many years ago that many individuals (including stakeholders) discounted the entire approach as either unlikely to achieve its goals (e.g., as drinkers will easily find a way around the obstacles) or even illegitimate by virtue of the assumption that alcohol-related harm was limited entirely to those who were dependent on alcohol. With these assumptions and others effectively refuted, community prevention research should now turn its attention to the many conceptual issues that need to be addressed and the many significant questions that remain to be answered.

An important future direction for community-level intervention research is a shift in focus from establishing program efficacy (i.e., determining whether such programs can work) to examining the mechanisms that underlie effective programs (i.e., examining *how* such programs work). Recent efforts to explicate these relationships have considered the social and psychological mechanisms that affect the social use of alcohol outlets, shape regulation of those outlets, and affect rates of alcohol consumption and problems in communities (e.g., Gruenewald & Remer, 2006; Gruenewald, Remer, & LaScala, 2014). Recently, research has begun to explore *how* community-level programs and policies to reduce alcohol availability to minors affect drinking and drinking problems among adolescents (e.g., Flewelling et al., 2013; Lipperman-Kreda, Grube, & Paschall, 2010; Paschall, Grube, & Kypri, 2009) and college students (Saltz, Paschall, McGaffigan, & Nygaard, 2010). Understanding these mechanisms will help in the development and implementation of more effective environmental strategies (Treno, Gruenewald, Grube, Saltz, & Paschall, 2014). Similarly, community-level approaches almost always involve multiple intervention components. As a result, although these approaches have been shown to be effective in reducing alcohol consumption and problems, it often is unclear which particular components were more or less effective. Although a few studies have made progress toward identifying which components of such programs are related most closely to changes in outcomes (e.g., Stigler, Perry, Komro, Cudeck, & Williams, 2006), much remains to be done. Future research in this area needs to focus on ascertaining which specific interventions are most effective in which circumstances. This is a difficult task given the expense and effort involved in mounting community-level intervention projects. Finally, a majority of community-level prevention approaches have focused on alcohol consumption and problems. The evidence for the effectiveness of these approaches for tobacco and other drug use is inconclusive (e.g., Carson et al., 2011; Gates, McCambridge, Smith, & Foxcroft, 2006). Nonetheless, comprehensive community approaches to preventing tobacco and other drug use may be increasingly important given the changing political and social environment, especially as it relates to marijuana use. Future research should explore how to tailor these interventions for these substances.

This discussion would not be complete without acknowledging the gap in our knowledge regarding the mechanisms by which community-level change can be accomplished. In nearly all the research involving community prevention, researchers have been guided by conventional wisdom, personal experience, and theoretical perspectives or combinations of these in their efforts to implement preventive interventions so they can be evaluated. As we build registries of effective community interventions, we need to turn out attention to research focused specifically and rigorously on implementation. There is no reason why rigorous experimental and quasi-experimental designs cannot be used to determine the efficacy of differing approaches to achieving community change. For now, this territory is wide open to exploration.

References

Biglan, A., Ary, D., & Wagenaar, A. C. (2000). The value of time-series experiments for community intervention research. *Prevention Science*, *1*, 31–49. doi:10.1023/A:1010024016308

Biglan, A., Ary, D. V., Smolkowski, K., Duncan, T., & Black, C. (2000). A randomized controlled trial of a community intervention to prevent adolescent tobacco use. *Tobacco Control*, *9*, 24–32. doi:10.1136/tc.9.1.24

Birckmayer, J., Fisher, D. A., Holder, H. D., & Yacoubian, G. S., Jr. (2008). Prevention of methamphetamine abuse: Can existing evidence inform community prevention? *Journal of Drug Education*, *38*, 147–165. doi:10.2190/DE.38.2.d

Birckmayer, J. D., Holder, H. D., Yacoubian, G. S., Jr., & Friend, K. B. (2004). A general causal model to guide alcohol, tobacco, and illicit drug prevention: Assessing the research evidence. *Journal of Drug Education*, *34*, 121–153. doi:10.2190/PYL2-FF8N-6B6C-A57R

Brown, S. A., & Tapert, S. F. (2004). Health consequences of adolescent alcohol involvement. In R. J. Bonnie & M. E. O'Connell (Eds.), *Reducing underage drinking: A collective responsibility* (pp. 383–401). Washington, DC: National Academies Press.

Carson, K. V., Brinn, M. P., Labiszewski, N. A., Esterman, A. J., Chang, A. B., & Smith, B. J. (2011). Can community interventions deter young people from starting to smoke? *Cochrane Database of Systematic Reviews*, *7*, CD001291.

DeJong, W., Schneider, S. K., Towvim, L. G., Murphy, M., Doerr, E., Simonsen, N., . . . Scribner, R. (2009). A multisite randomized trial of social norms marketing campaigns to reduce college student drinking: A replication failure. *Substance Abuse*, *30*, 127–140. doi:10.1080/08897070902802059

Dent, C. W., Grube, J. W., & Biglan, A. (2005). Community level alcohol availability and enforcement of possession laws as predictors of youth drinking. *Preventive Medicine: An International Journal Devoted to Practice and Theory*, *40*, 355–362. doi:10.1016/j.ypmed.2004.06.014

Duailibi, S., Ponicki, W., Grube, J. W., Pinsky, I., Laranjeira, R., & Raw, M. (2007). The effect of restricting opening hours on alcohol-related violence. *American Journal of Public Health*, *97*, 2276–2280. doi:10.2105/AJPH.2006.092684

Elder, R. W., Nichols, J. L., Shults, R. A., Sleet, D. A., Barrios, L. C., & Compton, R. (2005). Effectiveness of school-based programs for reducing drinking and driving and riding with drinking drivers: A systematic review. *American Journal of Preventive Medicine*, *28*(Suppl.), 288–304. doi:10.1016/j.amepre.2005.02.015

Flay, B. R., Biglan, A., Boruch, R. F., Castro, F. G., Gottfredson, D., Kellam, S., . . . Ji, P. (2005). Standards of evidence: Criteria for efficacy, effectiveness and dissemination. *Prevention Science, 6*, 151–175. doi:10.1007/s11121-005-5553-y

Flewelling, R. L., Grube, J. W., Paschall, M. J., Biglan, A., Kraft, A., Black, C., . . . Ruscoe, J. (2013). Reducing youth access to alcohol: Findings from a community-based randomized trial. *American Journal of Community Psychology, 51*, 264–277. doi:10.1007/s10464-012-9529-3

Foxcroft, D. R., Ireland, D., Lister-Sharp, D. J., Lowe, G., & Breen, R. (2003). Longer-term primary prevention for alcohol misuse in young people: A systematic review. *Addiction, 98*, 397–411. doi:10.1046/j.1360-0443.2003.00355.x

Foxcroft, D. R., & Tsertsvadze, A. (2011a). Universal multi-component prevention programs for alcohol misuse in young people. *Cochrane Database of Systematic Reviews, 9*, CD009307.

Foxcroft, D. R., & Tsertsvadze, A. (2011b). Universal school-based prevention programs for alcohol misuse in young people. *Cochrane Database of Systematic Reviews, 5*, CD009113.

Freisthler, B., Gruenewald, P. J., Treno, A. J., & Lee, J. (2003). Evaluating alcohol access and the alcohol environment in neighborhood areas. *Alcoholism: Clinical and Experimental Research, 27*, 477–484. doi:10.1097/01.ALC.0000057043.04199.B7

Gates, S., McCambridge, J., Smith, L. A., & Foxcroft, D. (2006). Interventions for prevention of drug use by young people delivered in non-school settings. *Cochrane Database of Systematic Reviews, 1*, CD005030.

Gripenberg, J., Wallin, E., & Andréasson, S. (2007). Effects of a community-based drug use prevention program targeting licensed premises. *Substance Use and Misuse, 42*, 1883–1898. doi:10.1080/10826080701532916

Gripenberg Abdon, J. G., Wallin, E., & Andréasson, S. (2011a). The "Clubs Against Drugs" program in Stockholm, Sweden: Two cross-sectional surveys examining drug use among staff at licensed premises. *Substance Abuse Treatment, Prevention, and Policy, 6*. Retrieved from http://www.substanceabusepolicy.com/content/6/1/2

Gripenberg Abdon, J. G., Wallin, E., & Andréasson, S. (2011b). Long-term effects of a community-based intervention: 5-year follow-up of "Clubs Against Drugs." *Addiction, 106*, 1997–2004. doi:10.1111/j.1360-0443.2011.03573.x

Grube, J. W. (2010). Environmental approaches to preventing adolescent drinking. In L. M. Scheier (Ed.), *Handbook of drug use etiology: Theory, methods, and empirical findings* (pp. 493–509). Washington, DC: American Psychological Association.

Grube, J. W., & Nygaard, P. (2005). Alcohol policy and youth drinking: Overview of effective interventions for young people. In T. Stockwell, P. J. Gruenewald, J. Toumbourou, & W. Loxley (Eds.), *Preventing harmful substance use: The evidence base for policy and practice* (pp. 113–127). New York, NY: Wiley. doi:10.1002/9780470713624.ch10

Gruenewald, P. J., & Remer, L. (2006). Changes in outlet densities affect violence rates. *Alcoholism: Clinical and Experimental Research, 30*, 1184–1193. doi:10.1111/j.1530-0277.2006.00141.x

Gruenewald, P. J., Remer, L. G., & LaScala, E. A. (2014). Testing a social ecological model of alcohol use: The California 50-city study. *Addiction, 109*, 736–745. doi:10.1111/add.12438

Hingson, R., & Kenkel, D. (2004). Social, health, and economic consequences of underage drinking. In R. J. Bonnie & M. E. O'Connell (Eds.), *Reducing underage drinking: A collective responsibility* (pp. 351–382). Washington, DC: National Academies Press.

Hingson, R., McGovern, T., Howland, J., Heeren, T., Winter, M., & Zakocs, R. (1996). Reducing alcohol-impaired driving in Massachusetts: The Saving Lives Program. *American Journal of Public Health, 86*, 791–797. doi:10.2105/AJPH.86.6.791

Hingson, R., & White, A. (2014). New research findings since the 2007 Surgeon General's call to action to prevent and reduce underage drinking: A review. *Journal of Studies on Alcohol and Drugs, 75*, 158–169.

Holder, H. D., Gruenewald, P. J., Ponicki, W. R., Grube, J. W., Saltz, R. F., Voas, R. B., . . . Treno, A. J. (2000). Effect of community-based interventions on high-risk drinking and alcohol-related injuries. *JAMA, 284*, 2341–2347. doi:10.1001/jama.284.18.2341

Johnston, L. D., O'Malley, P. M., Bachman, J. G., Schulenberg, J. E., & Miech, R. A. (2014a). *Monitoring the Future national survey results on drug use, 1975–2013: Vol. I. Secondary school students.* Ann Arbor: University of Michigan.

Johnston, L. D., O'Malley, P. M., Bachman, J. G., Schulenberg, J. E. & Miech, R. A. (2014b). *Monitoring the Future national survey results on drug use, 1975–2013: Vol. II. College students and adults ages 19–55.* Ann Arbor: Institute for Social Research, University of Michigan.

Kreitman, N. (1986). Alcohol consumption and the preventive paradox. *British Journal of Addiction, 81*, 353–363. doi:10.1111/j.1360-0443.1986.tb00342.x

Krevor, B. S., Ponicki, B., Grube, J. W., & DeJong, W. (2011). The impact of mystery shopper reports on age verification for tobacco purchases. *Journal of Health Communication, 16*, 820–830. doi:10.1080/10810730.2011.561912

Lipperman-Kreda, S., Grube, J. W., & Paschall, M. J. (2010). Community norms, enforcement of minimum legal drinking age laws, personal beliefs and underage drinking: An explanatory model. *Journal of Community Health: The Publication for Health Promotion and Disease Prevention*, *35*, 249–257. doi:10.1007/s10900-010-9229-6

Månsdotter, A. M., Rydberg, M. K., Wallin, E., Lindholm, L. A., & Andréasson, S. (2007). A cost-effectiveness analysis of alcohol prevention targeting licensed premises. *European Journal of Public Health*, *17*, 618–623. doi:10.1093/eurpub/ckm017

Marlatt, G. A., & Witkiewitz, K. (2002). Harm reduction approaches to alcohol use: Health promotion, prevention, and treatment. *Addictive Behaviors*, *27*, 867–886. doi:10.1016/S0306-4603(02)00294-0

Marlatt, G. A., & Witkiewitz, K. (2010). Update on harm-reduction policy and intervention research. *Annual Review of Clinical Psychology*, *6*, 591–606. doi:10.1146/annurev.clinpsy.121208.131438

Miller, T. R., Levy, D. T., Spicer, R. S., & Taylor, D. M. (2006). Societal costs of underage drinking. *Journal of Studies on Alcohol*, *67*, 519–528.

Moore, R. S., Roberts, J., McGaffigan, R., Calac, D., Grube, J. W., Gilder, D. A., & Ehlers, C. L. (2012). Implementing a reward and reminder underage drinking prevention program in convenience stores near Southern California American Indian reservations. *American Journal of Drug and Alcohol Abuse*, *38*, 456–460. doi:10.3109/00952990.2012.696758

National Highway Traffic Safety Administration. (2013). *Traffic safety facts. Alcohol 2012 data. Alcohol-impaired driving*. Washington, DC: Department of Transportation. Retrieved from http://www-nrd.nhtsa.dot.gov/Pubs/811870.pdf

National Institute on Alcohol Abuse and Alcoholism. (2014, June). *Statistics on underage drinking*. Retrieved from http://www.niaaa.nih.gov/alcohol-health/special-populations-co-occurring-disorders/underage-drinking

National Research Council & Institute of Medicine. (2004). *Reducing underage drinking: A collective responsibility*. Washington, DC: National Academies Press.

Paschall, M. J., Grube, J. W., Black, C., Flewelling, R. L., Ringwalt, C. L., & Biglan, A. (2007). Alcohol outlet characteristics and alcohol sales to youth: Results of alcohol purchase surveys in 45 Oregon communities. *Prevention Science*, *8*, 153–159. doi:10.1007/s11121-006-0063-0

Paschall, M. J., Grube, J. W., Black, C. A., & Ringwalt, C. L. (2007). Is commercial alcohol availability related to adolescent alcohol sources and alcohol use? Findings from a multi-level study. *Journal of Adolescent Health*, *41*, 168–174. doi:10.1016/j.jadohealth.2007.03.009

Paschall, M. J., Grube, J. W., & Kypri, K. (2009). Alcohol control policies and alcohol consumption by youth: A multi-national study. *Addiction*, *104*, 1849–1855. doi:10.1111/j.1360-0443.2009.02698.x

Paschall, M. J., Grube, J. W., Thomas, S., Cannon, C., & Treffers, R. (2012). Relationships between local enforcement, alcohol availability, drinking norms and adolescent alcohol use in 50 California cities. *Journal of Studies on Alcohol and Drugs*, *73*, 657–665.

Perry, C. L., Williams, C. L., Komro, K. A., Veblen-Mortenson, S., Forster, J. L., Bernstein-Lachter, R., . . . McGovern, P. (2000). Project Northland high school interventions: Community action to reduce adolescent alcohol use. *Health Education and Behavior*, *27*, 29–49. doi:10.1177/109019810002700105

Riley, D., & O'Hare, P. (2000). Harm reduction: History, definition, and practice. In J. A. Inciardi & L. D. Harrison (Eds.), *Harm reduction: National and international perspectives* (pp. 1–26). Thousand Oaks, CA: Sage. doi:10.4135/9781452220680.n1

Sacks, J. J., Roeber, J., Bouchery, E. E., Gonzales, K., Chaloupka, F. J., & Brewer, R. D. (2013). State costs of excessive alcohol consumption, 2006. *American Journal of Preventive Medicine*, *45*, 474–485. doi:10.1016/j.amepre.2013.06.004

Saltz, R. F., Paschall, M. J., McGaffigan, R. P., & Nygaard, P. M. O. (2010). Alcohol risk management in college settings: The Safer California Universities randomized trial. *American Journal of Preventive Medicine*, *39*, 491–499. doi:10.1016/j.amepre.2010.08.020

Skog, O.-J. (2006). Alcohol and the so-called prevention paradox: How does it look today? *Addiction*, *101*, 155–158. doi:10.1111/j.1360-0443.2006.01319.x

Spera, C., Barlas, F., Szoc, R. Z., Prabhakaran, J., & Cambridge, M. H. (2012). Examining the influence of the Enforcing Underage Drinking Laws (EUDL) program on alcohol-related outcomes in five communities surrounding Air Force bases. *Addictive Behaviors*, *37*, 513–516. doi:10.1016/j.addbeh.2011.11.016

Spera, C., Franklin, K., Uekawa, K., Kunz, J. F., Szoc, R. Z., Thomas, R. K., & Cambridge, M. H. (2010). Reducing drinking among junior enlisted Air Force members in five communities: Early findings of the EUDL program's influence on self-reported drinking behaviors. *Journal of Studies on Alcohol and Drugs*, *71*, 373–383.

Stigler, M. H., Perry, C. L., Komro, K. A., Cudeck, R., & Williams, C. L. (2006). Teasing apart a multiple component approach to adolescent alcohol prevention: What worked in Project Northland? *Prevention Science*, *7*, 269–280. doi:10.1007/s11121-006-0040-7

Stockwell, T., Gruenewald, P. J., Toumbourou, J. W., & Loxely, W. (2005). Preventing risky drug use and related harms: The need for a synthesis of knowledge. In T. Stockwell, P. J. Gruenewald, J. Toumbourou, & W. Loxley (Eds.), *Preventing harmful substance use: The evidence base for policy and practice* (pp. 3–16). New York, NY: Wiley. doi:10.1002/9780470713624.ch1

Stockwell, T., Zhao, J., Macdonald, S., Pakula, B., Gruenewald, P., & Holder, H. (2009). Changes in per capita alcohol sales during the partial privatization of British Columbia's retail alcohol monopoly 2003–2008: A multi-level local area analysis. *Addiction, 104*, 1827–1836. doi:10.1111/j.1360-0443.2009.02658.x

Stockwell, T., Zhao, J., Martin, G., Macdonald, S., Vallance, K., Treno, A., . . . Buxton, J. (2013). Minimum alcohol prices and outlet densities in British Columbia, Canada: Estimated impacts on alcohol-attributable hospital admissions. *American Journal of Public Health, 103*, 2014–2020. doi:10.2105/AJPH.2013.301289

Toomey, T. L., Lenk, K. M., & Wagenaar, A. C. (2007). Environmental policies to reduce college drinking: An update of research findings. *Journal of Studies on Alcohol and Drugs, 68*, 208–219.

Treno, A. J., Gruenewald, P. J., Grube, J. W., Saitz, R., & Paschall, M. J. (2014). Environmental approaches to prevention: A community-based perspective. In R. K. Ries, D. A. Fiellin, S. C. Miller, & R. Saitz (Eds.), *Principles of addiction medicine* (5th ed., pp. 353–362). Chevy Chase, MD: American Society of Addiction Medicine.

Treno, A. J., Gruenewald, P. J., Lee, J. P., & Remer, L. G. (2007). The Sacramento Neighborhood Alcohol Prevention Project: Outcomes from a community prevention trial. *Journal of Studies on Alcohol and Drugs, 68*, 197–207.

Treno, A. J., Ponicki, W. R., Stockwell, T., Macdonald, S., Gruenewald, P. J., Zhao, J., . . . Greer, A. (2013). Alcohol outlet densities and alcohol price: The British Columbia experiment in the partial privatization of alcohol sales off-premise. *Alcoholism: Clinical and Experimental Research, 37*, 854–859. doi:10.1111/acer.12065

U.S. Department of Health and Human Services. (2007). *The surgeon general's call to action to prevent and reduce underage drinking*. Rockville, MD. Office of the Surgeon General. Retrieved from http://www.ncbi.nlm.nih.gov/books/NBK44360/

Voas, R. B., Tippetts, A. S., Johnson, M. B., Lange, J. E., & Baker, J. (2002). Operation Safe Crossing: Using science within a community intervention. *Addiction, 97*, 1205–1214. doi:10.1046/j.1360-0443.2002.00183.x

Wagenaar, A. C., Murray, D. M., & Toomey, T. L. (2000). Communities mobilizing for change on alcohol (CMCA): Effects of a randomized trial on arrests and traffic crashes. *Addiction, 95*, 209–217. doi:10.1046/j.1360-0443.2000.9522097.x

Wagenaar, A. C., Toomey, T. L., & Erickson, D. J. (2005). Preventing youth access to alcohol: Outcomes from a multi-community time-series trial. *Addiction, 100*, 335–345. doi:10.1111/j.1360-0443.2005.00973.x

Wagenaar, A. C., & Wolfson, M. (1994). Enforcement of the legal minimum drinking age in the United States. *Journal of Public Health Policy, 15*, 37–53. doi:10.2307/3342606

Wagenaar, A. C., & Wolfson, M. (1995). Deterring sales and provision of alcohol to minors: A study of enforcement in 295 counties in four states. *Public Health Reports, 110*, 419–427.

Wallin, E. (2007). Dissemination of prevention: Community action targeting alcohol use-related problems at licensed premises. *Substance Use and Misuse, 42*, 2085–2097. doi:10.1080/10826080701533245

Wallin, E., Gripenberg, J., & Andréasson, S. (2005). Overserving at licensed premises in Stockholm: Effects of a community action program. *Journal of Studies on Alcohol, 66*, 806–814.

Wallin, E., Norström, T., & Andréasson, S. (2003). Alcohol prevention targeting licensed premises: A study of effects on violence. *Journal of Studies on Alcohol, 64*, 270–277.

Wolfson, M., Champion, H., McCoy, T. P., Rhodes, S. D., Ip, E. H., Blocker, J. N., . . . Durant, R. H. (2012). Impact of a randomized campus/community trial to prevent high-risk drinking among college students. *Alcoholism: Clinical and Experimental Research, 36*, 1767–1778. doi:10.1111/j.1530-0277.2012.01786.x

Zhao, J., Stockwell, T., Martin, G., Macdonald, S., Vallance, K., Treno, A., . . . Buxton, J. (2013). The relationship between minimum alcohol prices, outlet densities and alcohol-attributable deaths in British Columbia, 2002-09. *Addiction, 108*, 1059–1069.

CHAPTER 18

ALCOHOL POLICY: INTERVENTIONS TO PREVENT YOUTH ALCOHOL USE

Sarah D. Lynne-Landsman and Alexander C. Wagenaar

This chapter reviews the evidence base behind the effectiveness of policies and laws in reducing underage access to alcohol with implications for future studies of alcohol prevention. First, it describes the scope of the problem of youth alcohol use and discusses the various sources of alcohol to youth. Standards of evidence are explicated, followed by a review of the evidence supporting policy interventions related to both social and commercial access to alcohol. The importance of considering the influence of the macrolevel context (laws and policies) as interventions and as potential moderators or mediators of school or family-based interventions to prevent underage alcohol use and related harms is discussed.

Alcohol use among youth under the age of 21 years is prevalent, with 66% of high school students reporting ever having drunk alcohol and 35% reporting drinking alcohol in the past month (Kann et al., 2014). Alcohol remains the most commonly used substance among youth despite recent declines in use and binge drinking (Johnston, O'Malley, Bachman, & Schulenberg, 2012). Numerous studies have linked alcohol use and adolescent risk behaviors, academic problems, social and emotional problems, unplanned and risky sex, aggression and victimization, legal problems, car crashes, and other alcohol-related unintentional injuries, deaths, and medical problems (Brown et al., 2008; Hingson, Heeren, Winter, & Wechsler, 2005). In addition, adolescent alcohol use is associated with damage to the brain, neurocognitive deficits, and increased risk of alcohol dependence in adulthood (Brown et al., 2008). The serious health, social, and personal consequences of teen drinking emphasize the importance of prevention efforts aimed at delaying and preventing alcohol use among youth.

Although it is illegal for individuals under the age of 21 years to purchase alcohol in the United States, youth are obtaining alcohol from both social and commercial sources (see Figure 18.1). In early adolescence, social sources of alcohol are the most common (Wagenaar et al., 1993). Social sources include parents, older siblings, older peers, older coworkers, and strangers. Parents and other individuals over age 21 may have alcohol easily accessible in homes, where youth obtain it with or without permission. And, of course, alcohol is often available at parties (e.g., graduation, birthday, holiday parties).Young people sometimes approach strangers outside of commercial retailers that sell alcohol (e.g., liquor stores, grocery chains, and corner markets or sundry stores) and convince them to make the purchase. In later adolescence, youth obtain

Preparation of this chapter was supported by the Institute for Child Health Policy at the University of Florida. The content of this chapter is solely the responsibility of the authors and does not necessarily represent the official views of the University of Florida.

http://dx.doi.org/10.1037/14550-019
Handbook of Adolescent Drug Use Prevention: Research, Intervention Strategies, and Practice, L. M. Scheier (Editor)

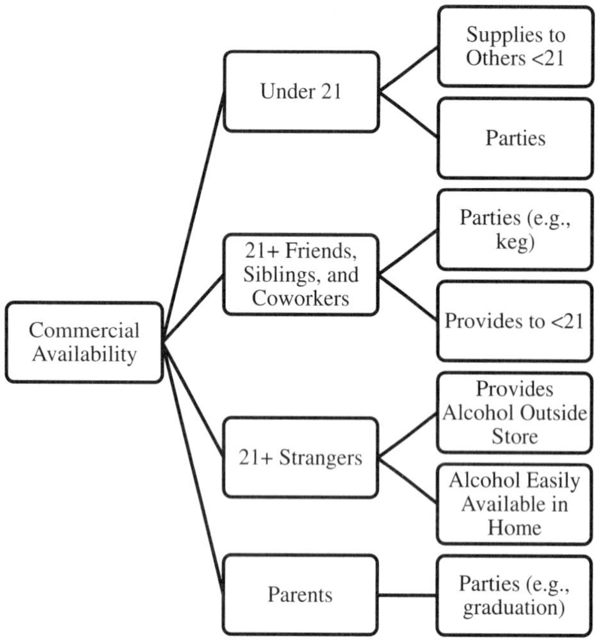

FIGURE 18.1. Sources of alcohol for youth.

alcohol directly from commercial sources, despite such sales being illegal (Wagenaar et al., 1993). Underage youth may attempt to purchase alcohol directly from retailers either without identification or using false identification, and they often pass alcohol along to their underage peers as well, providing a "trickle-down" flow of alcohol to younger teens.

Comprehensive efforts to reduce teen drinking include demand reduction and supply reduction components. This chapter focuses on the use of local and state laws to reduce the supply of alcohol to underage youth. Effective use of legal interventions has led to major reductions in health problems across a variety of health-risk behaviors, including safety belt use, tobacco exposure, and alcohol use. Communities can influence access to alcohol and subsequent alcohol use among adolescents through numerous well-formed policy strategies. Enacting and enforcing these policies, however, requires active mobilization of the community, continuous effort, and quality implementation. Therefore, it is important to identify those policy strategies with the strongest evidence of effectiveness in reducing, delaying, and preventing underage alcohol use.

STANDARDS OF EVIDENCE

The Society for Prevention Research developed criteria to aid in distinguishing those strategies for which sufficient scientific evidence of effectiveness already exists from those for which more research is needed (Flay et al., 2005). Establishing evidence of causal relations between policies and health outcomes was a primary consideration, but several other criteria were also important (e.g., size of effects, importance of outcomes, duration of effects). Applying the criteria developed by Flay et al. (2005), this chapter reviews policies to reduce underage drinking that fall into three broad categories: (a) meets criteria for policy effectiveness, (b) demonstrates consistent evidence from observational studies, and (c) has insufficient evidence but is plausible.

Criteria for assessing policy effectiveness are based on the developmental appropriateness and psychometric properties of designated outcomes, research design, and replication. To meet these criteria, a strong research design that strengthens causal inference must be used in an evaluation. This includes high-quality experimental or quasi-experimental research designs with a comparison group or the use of an interrupted time-series design. In addition, there should be at least one other independent replication with consistent positive results across the two (or more) studies. Policies that have not had this level of rigorous evaluation still may meet criteria for consistent evidence from observational studies. High-quality observational studies can provide evidence of consistent associations between enactment of policy and reductions in youth drinking; however, these studies fall short of providing strong evidence of causal relations. Nevertheless, many of the policies studied are considered promising and worth consideration by communities and policymakers despite the continuing need for further research with stronger research designs. The final category heralds strategies that do not meet the criteria for the aforementioned categories and thus lack sufficient evidence to date of the policy's effectiveness in reducing youth drinking. These strategies are plausible, based on established theory or analogous research in other areas, but need additional rigorous research to establish effectiveness.

STRATEGIES THAT ADDRESS SOCIAL SOURCES OF ALCOHOL FOR YOUTH

Given the prominence of social sources of alcohol for underage youth, especially during early adolescence (Dent, Grube, & Biglan, 2005; Wagenaar et al., 1993), the following strategies should be considered a critical part of a more comprehensive effort to reduce youth access to alcohol.

Meet Criteria for Policy Effectiveness

Hot-spot policing. Crime and infractions are not evenly dispersed across communities but tend to cluster in smaller geographic regions or "hot-spots" (Braga, 2001). *Hot-spot policing* refers to a more efficient use of law enforcement resources by focusing attention on high-infraction hot-spots as opposed to evenly dispersing police resources across a defined region. In prior research, hot-spots have been identified by evaluating the number of citizen calls to police for service at specific geographic locations. Those with the highest number of calls over a specified period of time are designated *hot-spots* (Braga, 2001). Hot-spots originally were assessed for effects on overall crime. The concept of hot-spots, however, can be applied to underage drinking because specific locations can be identified readily in communities as areas with high rates of underage drinking (e.g., parks, certain parking lots, sports fields) or particular commercial establishments or areas of multiple establishments with higher than average frequency of (illegal) sales to underage youth. Focusing law enforcement efforts on these hot-spots should reduce youth access to alcohol.

A review of five randomized trials and four quasi-experimental studies found that hot-spot policing was effective in reducing crime and that crime was not simply displaced from one location to another (Braga, 2001). In fact, there is some evidence of a geographic diffusion of benefits—that is, improvement in surrounding areas beyond the hot-spots as a result of this strategy (Weisburd & Eck, 2004). Given the strong research designs and consistent findings across studies reported in the Braga (2001) review, hot-spot policing meets criteria for policy effectiveness regarding crime reduction. Three of the studies included in the review, two randomized trials and one quasi-experimental trial, based hot-spot identification on drug activity (Hope, 1994; Sherman & Rogan, 1995; Weisburd & Green, 1995). None of these studies, however, specifically focused on alcohol or involved youth. Despite this limitation, hot-spot policing has many strengths, such as clearly demonstrated consistent evidence of effectiveness across diverse crimes, including those related to substance use; it further appears to be an efficient use of limited enforcement resources.

Consistent Evidence From Observational Studies

Social host liability. *Social host policies* establish that a host who serves alcohol can be held financially liable for damages caused by their guests. These efforts grew out of statutory and case law that holds alcohol retailers and dispensers accountable for damages caused by intoxicated patrons. The function of social host liability in reducing underage drinking is to provide a penalty to adults (e.g., parents, older peers) who provide alcohol to a minor, deterring such actions. A related policy is open house assembly local ordinances or state laws that hold adults accountable for underage drinking that occurs on their property, for example, during a party (defined as a gathering of three or more individuals), even though they might not have directly provided the alcohol to the teens.

As with almost any arena of state or local law, there is considerable variability in the components of social host liability policies and the degree of negligence that a host must meet to be held liable. In some circumstances, hosts can be held liable only if it can be demonstrated that they were aware of the underage drinking; at the other end of the spectrum, a host can be held liable if the drinking occurs on their property regardless of their knowledge (e.g., strict liability). Some social host policies fall in between these two extremes, holding the host liable if a reasonable adult should have known that underage individuals were consuming alcohol on their property (e.g., negligence). In a nationally representative sample of adults in the United States, respondents agreed that a host who provides alcohol to a minor should share some of the culpability with the minor for any damages incurred after drinking (Wagenaar, Denk, Hannan, Chen, & Harwood, 2001), and social host laws are a key component formalizing this shared responsibility.

In theory, social host liability policies should deter adults from providing alcohol to underage youth given that they may be held accountable for serious damages that the youth may cause while intoxicated (e.g., alcohol-related fatalities or motor vehicle crashes). Some parents assert that it may be safer for their adolescent and his or her friends to drink alcohol in a supervised environment as a justification for providing alcohol to underage youth in their homes. Research, however, does not support the argument that parents' providing alcohol in the home is healthy. Studies show that access to or parental provision of alcohol in the home is associated with greater adolescent alcohol use (Komro, Maldonado-Molina, Tobler, Bonds, & Muller, 2007; Tobler, Komro, & Maldonado-Molina, 2009) and parental prohibition of alcohol use in the home reduces youth alcohol consumption (Yu, 2003). An observational study of associations between social host policies and adult drinking behaviors found lower rates of heavy drinking and lower rates of drinking and driving; however, the study did not specifically evaluate outcomes related to underage youth (Stout, Sloan, Liang, & Davies, 2000). Whetten-Goldstein, Sloan, Stout, and Liang (2000) used a quasi-experimental time-series analysis and found that social host policies were not associated with fewer total or alcohol-related traffic fatalities involving minors. In part, this effect may be attributable to poor enforcement of social host policies, highlighting a need for strong community publicity efforts regarding social host policies and more rigorous police enforcement. A more recent evaluation compared states that had passed social host policies by 2005 with those that had not passed these policies on trends in both alcohol-related and non-alcohol-related traffic fatalities (Dills, 2010). The author found that these policies were associated with a 9% reduction in the drunk-driving fatality rate among minors, but note that this study did not employ a control group comparison. There may be fundamental differences between the types of states that pass a social host policy and those that do not, which could be related to the outcome of interest, in this case alcohol-related traffic fatalities among minors (Dills, 2010).

Despite a fair amount of consistent evidence that social host policies reduce underage alcohol-related traffic problems, only one study meets the criteria for policy effectiveness (Whetten-Goldstein et al., 2000), and as such, this does not yet meet the Standards of Excellence (Flay et al., 2005) replication criteria necessary for policy effectiveness. Yet, given the consistent effects across observational studies, with proper community education and enforcement, social host liability policies hold considerable promise for reducing underage alcohol consumption.

Insufficient Evidence but Plausible

Keg registration. Focus groups with youth under age 21 have identified kegs as an important source of alcohol given the low cost per drink (Wagenaar et al., 1993). This research, along with media coverage of fatal crashes involving underage youth who attended keg parties, led to the development of keg registration policies. These laws generally require commercial alcohol retailers that sell beer kegs to record key information about the purchasers (e.g., name, address, driver's license number), mark each keg with a unique identifying tag linked to the purchaser, and retain the record of this purchase for a specified period of time. In practice, keg registration policies vary widely in provisions and implementation across states and localities (Wagenaar, Harwood, Silianoff, & Toomey, 2005). Initial research evaluated the effect of the presence of a keg registration law on underage traffic fatalities and found an iatrogenic effect such that the presence of the policy was associated with more fatal crashes (Fell, Fisher, Voas, Blackman, & Tippetts, 2009). This evaluation, however, did not take into account differences by locality in the provisions and implementation of the keg registration policies. A more recent study of keg registration policies found that more stringent and comprehensive policies were associated with lower rates of adolescent binge drinking, drinking and driving, and riding with a drunk driver (Ringwalt & Paschall, 2011). A replication of this association is necessary to meet the criteria for consistency across observational studies; however, these findings are promising and highlight the importance of developing comprehensive policies with appropriate enforcement to maximize policy effectiveness.

Alcohol restrictions on public property. Restricting or prohibiting the consumption of alcohol at public events or on public property, such as at festivals, sporting events, parks, beaches, parking lots, and recreation centers, may reduce alcohol access to underage youth. In a study of alcohol access to underage youth at public festivals, Toomey et al. (2005) found that individuals who appeared under age 21 years successfully purchased alcohol without identification at 50% of the attempts. Similarly, individuals who appeared underage were successful at purchasing alcohol without identification during sporting events in both the stands (30% of attempts) and at concession booths (13% of attempts; Toomey, Erickson, Lenk, & Kilian, 2008). This demonstrates that public events and locations are plausible targets for reducing underage access to alcohol.

Evidence is limited that policies aimed at reducing alcohol consumption at public events such as festivals (e.g., limiting the number of drinks per sale) are associated with reduced sales to underage individuals (Toomey et al., 2005); however, policies were not implemented consistently across events (e.g., restricting area of alcohol consumption, having alcohol-free areas, stopping sales of alcohol early). Replication of this finding is necessary before meeting the criterion of consistent evidence of effectiveness across observational studies. Banning or prohibiting alcohol consumption at public events could be an important influence on reducing underage drinking; by eliminating alcohol in such venues, communities communicate a strong social norm of insulating teens from alcohol.

In some cases, complete bans on alcohol use in public places and events are not feasible. In these cases, conditional-use permits can be issued that allow for restricted alcohol consumption or sale at specific events (e.g., weddings, company picnics, other private parties) on public property. These permits allow communities to set standards for when, where, and how alcohol may be sold or consumed on public property, limiting the risks to youth and adults (National Research Council and Institute of Medicine, 2004). Exhibit 18.1 lists websites with information on the various environmental strategies that are discussed in this chapter.

Special event licenses and restrictions. Patterns of alcohol use among youth suggest that binge drinking on special occasions (e.g., birthdays, sport events, spring break, prom, graduation, holidays) is of concern. Prevention efforts that aim to reduce alcohol use overall would benefit from targeting prevention efforts at specific events known to be associated with heavy drinking or celebration. Most of the research on this topic has focused exclusively

Exhibit 18.1
Websites With Information on Alcohol-Related Environmental Prevention Strategies

Domain	Website URL
Social host laws	http://www.aep.umn.edu/index.php/aep-tools/underage-access/ http://www.socialhostliability.org/news/ http://alcoholpolicy.niaaa.nih.gov/Prohibitions_Against_Hosting_Underage_Drinking_Parties.html
Restricting alcohol use on public property	http://www.aep.umn.edu/index.php/aep-tools/underage-access/
Home delivery and enactment of alcohol restrictions and enforcement policies	http://www.aep.umn.edu/index.php/aep-tools/underage-access/
Enforcement checks	http://www.aep.umn.edu/index.php/aep-tools/underage-access/
Responsible beverage service training	http://www.aep.umn.edu/index.php/aep-tools/underage-access/
Enforcing underage drinking laws	http://www.aep.umn.edu/index.php/aep-tools/underage-access/
Minimum age of seller	http://www.aep.umn.edu/index.php/aep-tools/underage-access/

on college-age student populations, many, but not all, of whom are under the legal drinking age (Neighbors et al., 2007). The translation of these efforts for prevention of all underage alcohol use (both college and noncollege contexts) on special occasions is plausible and in need of direct evaluation. Neighbors et al. (2007) reviewed the event-specific prevention efforts empirically evaluated to date and offered guidance to community coalitions interested in developing their own strategies to reduce event-specific binge drinking. Of note is an emphasis on interventions that address multiple levels (e.g., individuals, groups, institutions, communities, society). Focusing on environmental strategies in particular, Neighbors et al. suggested offering and promoting alcohol-free alternative events; creating a social environment that promotes healthy norms; limiting alcohol availability; restricting marketing and promotion of alcohol at special events; and developing and enforcing local, state, and federal policies. For example, high school or college graduation weekend may be a particularly high-risk weekend for binge drinking. Suggested environmental strategies to reduce binge drinking include sponsoring a large alcohol-free graduation party, coordinating internship programs that begin before graduation, and sponsoring a career fair for new graduates (Neighbors et al., 2007).

In addition to personal events, community events also may be circumstances under which the risk for underage alcohol consumption increases. As discussed previously, a study at community festivals found that buyers appearing underage were able to purchase alcohol without identification at 50% of their attempts (Toomey et al., 2005). This highlights the need to develop initiatives around community events to minimize underage alcohol access and use as discussed in the prior section on alcohol restrictions on public property.

Noisy assembly. *Noisy assembly policies* are a method by which police can address a social disturbance that may be associated with parties that include underage consumption of alcohol. These policies generally contain components related to both distance (e.g., beyond a public residence) and time of day (e.g., 24 hours a day, 8:00 p.m.–6:00 a.m., etc.). To influence underage drinking, a violation of noisy assembly would need to provide police officers with legal cause to enter a private residence and gather evidence related to underage drinking within the premises. Although noisy assembly policies have the potential to reduce underage drinking and the accompanying social disturbance, very little research has evaluated the effectiveness of these legal ordinances. Gebhardt, Kaphingst, and DeJong (2000), evaluating the influence of a community-based coalition approach on reducing underage college student drinking behaviors, found that the approach was associated with a decrease in noise ordinance violations over time. This effect, however, could have been due to increased reluctance to report noise violations. It is also plausible that the underage students changed their noisy behavior but not their drinking behavior. The noisy assembly strategy is a plausible method for addressing underage drinking, but more empirical research is needed.

Home alcohol delivery restrictions. Delivery of alcohol to private residences has been identified as a source of alcohol for underage youth. A survey of underage youth from 15 Midwestern communities in the United States found that 10% of 12th graders and 7% of 18- to 20-year-olds had obtained alcohol via home delivery within the past year (Fletcher, Toomey, Wagenaar, Short, & Willenbring, 2000). Home delivery is a fairly private transaction and requires special enforcement efforts to ensure that there are no sales to minors or deliveries to underage drinking parties. As such, policy initiatives aimed at prohibiting or restricting home deliveries of alcohol have the potential to reduce alcohol access and associated harms to underage youth. No research to date, however, has empirically evaluated the effects of restricting home deliveries of alcohol on underage alcohol use.

Exterior parking lot lighting. *Shoulder-tapping* is a method whereby underage youth approach adults outside of alcohol retail outlets and ask them to purchase alcohol for them. One study found that 8% of approached adults purchased alcohol for youth who appeared underage after being approached outside of a retail establishment. When men in their 20s were specifically targeted by teens for such purchases, underage-appearing youth received the alcohol 19% of the time (Toomey, Fabian, Erickson, & Lenk, 2007). One method to reduce the ability of youth to approach strangers outside of alcohol retail establishments is to enforce lighting regulations in the parking lots and areas surrounding these facilities. Improved lighting will enhance the ability of both alcohol retail employees' and police patrol units to observe the shoulder-tap transactions taking place and potentially prevent the sale; however, empirical research is needed to evaluate this hypothesis.

STRATEGIES THAT ADDRESS COMMERCIAL SOURCES OF ALCOHOL FOR YOUTH

In later adolescence and with increasing physical maturation many youth are able to obtain alcohol directly from commercial retail sellers in addition to the social sources of alcohol available beginning in early and mid-adolescence (Wagenaar et al., 1993). Mosher (1995) reviewed evidence that policies targeting merchants more directly influence underage drinking than policies targeting underage purchasers. The following policies, in combination with the previously discussed policies aimed at decreasing social access to alcohol by underage youth, typically are combined in a comprehensive community plans to limit youth access to alcohol and prevent teen drinking. The Enforcing Underage Drinking Laws Randomized Community Trial (EUDL-CT) evaluated the combined effect of enforcing a variety of strategies aimed at reducing underage alcohol use, including compliance checks, enforcement of driving while intoxicated (DWI) laws, social availability of alcohol to youth, and policy enactment (Wolfson et al., 2011). Overall, communities with greater levels of EUDL-CT implementation had better outcomes; however, these were limited to social norms and expectations rather than behavior, with one exception. Intervention communities showed a greater decrease in alcohol-related motor vehicle crashes involving underage drivers compared with control communities (Wolfson et al., 2011). One limitation of the EUDL-CT implementation regarding social strategies is that enforcement activities, such as party patrols or alcohol outlet parking lot surveillance, disproportionately penalized the underage youth rather than the adult sources of alcohol. Information regarding specific commercial strategies of the EUDL-CT is discussed in the following sections.

Meet Criteria for Policy Effectiveness

Increasing alcohol excise and sales taxes. There is a very large body of scientific literature on the effects of alcohol taxes over the past half century. The evidence is overwhelming that increases in the retail price of alcohol resulting from an increase in alcohol tax rates significantly reduce drinking as well as a wide range of deleterious consequences of drinking, from chronic diseases such as cirrhosis and alcohol-related cancers, to acute alcohol problems such as traffic crashes, violence, and sexually transmitted infections. This large literature is summarized effectively in two meta-analyses (Wagenaar, Salois, & Komro, 2009; Wagenaar, Tobler, & Komro, 2010). In short, tax increases are passed through to consumers via an increase in retail price, and a 10% increase in price results in 5% to 7% less drinking, followed by similar reductions in the whole range of alcohol-related health and social outcomes. Results show tax effects on both the general adult population as well as the youth population. Alcohol taxes are effectively implemented at the state and national levels, and in some states, localities also are authorized to implement alcohol taxes. The preventive effectiveness of alcohol-specific taxes is supported by the largest body of scientific evidence of any preventive intervention studied to date.

Licensing restrictions and zoning ordinances. *Alcohol outlet density* refers to the number of on-premise (e.g., bars and restaurants) and off-premise (e.g., liquor stores, convenience stores) alcohol retail outlets within a specific geographic region. Numerous evaluations have found that areas with higher alcohol outlet density also tend to have more alcohol-related problems and crime (Campbell et al., 2009; Reboussin, Song, & Wolfson, 2011; Resko et al., 2010; Toomey et al., 2012). Campbell et al. (2009) reviewed the literature and found 10 time-series studies that evaluated the effects of changes in alcohol outlet density on alcohol-related harms. The authors reported that greater outlet density was associated with greater alcohol consumption and related harms (e.g., traffic crashes, crime) among both adult and youth populations. A more recent study of associations between alcohol outlet density and underage drinking behaviors found that increased density was associated with more alcohol purchase attempts as well as more success in purchasing alcohol, frequency of alcohol consumption, drinking and driving, and nonviolent consequences among youth ages 14–20 years old (Reboussin et al., 2011). Given consistent findings replicated across studies over time using strong study designs, regulating alcohol outlet density through the use of licensing and zoning ordinances is an effective strategy for reducing underage alcohol use and related harms.

Enforcement compliance checks. Enforcement compliance checks occur when police officers organize a "decoy" operation in which underage youth who are working with the police attempt to purchase alcohol at a specific retail outlet. If the merchant sells alcohol to the underage youth, the establishment is subject to citation and penalties. Underage youth generally are instructed not to try and make themselves look older and to provide valid identification if requested. Under these circumstances, it is not considered entrapment to conduct enforcement compliance checks (Mosher, 1995).

Research on tobacco has found strong evidence that enforcement compliance checks are effective in reducing sales of tobacco to underage youth (Mosher, 1995). Studies on alcohol are consistent with results from the tobacco research, lending further credibility to this strategy. One study compared the rate of underage alcohol sales across successive waves of enforcement checks and found that underage youth were able to purchase alcohol 59% of the time prior to the start of enforcement checks (Preusser, Williams, & Weinstein, 1994). This rate dropped to 32% after the first wave of enforcement and dropped to 26% after the second and third waves of enforcement. In a study employing a quasi-experimental time-series design, enforcement checks were found to reduce the propensity for alcohol retail establishments to sell alcohol to underage buyers by 17% (Wagenaar, Toomey, & Erickson, 2005). Unfortunately, this effect decayed over the course of 3 months, highlighting the need for consistent and frequent enforcement checks to maintain the effect. In addition, Wagenaar, Toomey, and Erickson (2005) did not find evidence of diffusion of the effect to the rest of the outlets within the same community that did not receive compliance checks. Compliance checks were the most consistently implemented enforcement strategy in the EUDL-CT project, as the program specified that 90% of off-premise alcohol outlets be checked at least two times a year (Wolfson et al., 2011).

Keep in mind, however, the results of the Wagenaar et al. (2005) study, which showed that compliance checks should be conducted in every outlet every 3 months to maintain reductions in sales of alcohol to underage youth. This may be one reason why the EUDL-CT influenced youth perceptions of alcohol-related social norms and expectations but did not have larger effects on underage alcohol use. Another quasi-experiment using a repeated-intervention design found evidence that compliance checks resulted in reduced access to alcohol by underage youth at alcohol establishments that received a citation as well as a reduction in access to youth at alcohol establishments exposed to media coverage about the citations for sales to underage youth (Scribner & Cohen, 2001). This finding shows that the effects of compliance checks might be enhanced by including media coverage of the enforcement compliance checks within communities, which could facilitate a broader diffused effect across establishments. Multiple studies with strong research designs have found enforcement checks to reduce alcohol use and access, indicating that this is an effective strategy for reducing access to alcohol by underage youth.

Consistent Evidence From Observational Studies

Responsible beverage service training. *Responsible beverage service (RBS) training* generally refers to programs aimed at educating individuals at the forefront of alcoholic beverage retail (e.g., servers, managers, owners) with the goal of preventing sales to underage and intoxicated patrons. There is large variability in programs across states (e.g., voluntary vs. mandatory, length of program, required attendees, enforcement, penalties, benefits), which contributes to differences in the effectiveness of these programs in reducing sales of alcohol to underage youth (Toomey et al., 1998). Mosher, Toomey, Good, Harwood, and Wagenaar (2002) outlined criteria for the development of effective RBS training programs that can serve as a source of guidance to public health professionals and others who are drafting RBS legislation to make such training compulsory. Mosher et al. (2002) reviewed the status of state laws mandating such training.

Research on the effectiveness of RBS training has yielded mixed results, which can be attributed, in part, to variability in program components and implementation (Wagenaar & Tobler, 2007). For instance, numerous reports have found that RBS programs are associated with decreased sales to individuals without identification who appear to be underage (Paschall et al., 2007; Toomey, Erickson, Lenk, Kilian, Perry, & Wagenaar, 2008; Toomey et al., 2001), an increase in checking identification (Buka & Birdthistle, 1999), and a decrease in the number of car crashes (Holder & Wagenaar, 1994). Other studies, however, have found that an RBS training program had little influence on underage alcohol sales beyond the effect of increased law enforcement compliance checks on underage alcohol sales (Grube, 1997; Wagenaar, Toomey, et al., 2005). Communities and states interested in implementing RBS training programs should consider them to be part of a more comprehensive effort that includes enforcement checks to reduce underage access to alcohol, as RBS training alone appears to have little effect.

Insufficient Evidence but Plausible

Administrative penalties. Enforcement of underage alcohol violations disproportionately targets underage youth rather than the commercial establishments that and adults who provide the alcohol (Wagenaar & Wolfson, 1994). Enforcement focused on commercial and social sources of alcohol, however, appears to be more important for reducing underage alcohol consumption than targeting just the youth themselves (Mosher, 1995). The intervention communities in the EUDL-CT more frequently cited employees rather than businesses for compliance check violations (Wolfson et al., 2011). Holding merchants accountable for sales of alcohol to underage youth, rather than employees, will have a greater long-term influence on commercial access to alcohol by youth because changing the management-determined conditions in the outlet will affect all servers—not just the individual one cited. Given the high rate of staff turnover, citing the alcohol sales license owners and managers is better than citing an individual clerk or server. Enforcing administrative penalties associated with selling alcohol to an underage buyer is one strategy to hold merchants accountable. To be effective, these penalties need to be severe enough to have a deterrent effect on commercial businesses.

Currently, the types of administrative penalties incurred for an underage sale violation vary widely across states, as does the probability that alcohol retailers will be monitored for violations. Administrative penalties include fines, mandatory RBS training, suspensions, and revocation of one's alcohol license for repeat violations. In some cases, the fines and suspensions levied against the commercial businesses are so low as to not be effective. Given that commercial establishments may earn thousands of dollars in a given month because of underage alcohol sales, these penalties are only minor deterrents. In conjunction with enforcement compliance checks and media publicity to draw attention to the enforcement of underage sale violations, the application of administrative penalties to businesses for violations is a plausible method for combating commercial access to alcohol by youth.

Employment of minors. Underage youth have more success purchasing alcohol from younger sellers (Wagenaar et al., 1993). This may be due to pressure that more youthful sellers feel to sell alcohol to their underage peers. Restricting the employment of minors in establishments that sell alcohol may be one method of combating illegal alcohol sales to underage youth. There is little research on this topic, but it appears to be a plausible strategy worth consideration by communities and future research.

Warning signs in alcohol establishments. Posting warning signs in establishments that sell alcohol is one strategy that has been suggested to reduce sales of alcohol to underage youth or to adults who are purchasing alcohol for underage youth. The content of these warning signs can vary and can include establishment policies on checking customer identification as well as the legal penalties for and consequences of providing or selling alcohol to underage youth. Evidence regarding effectiveness of warning signs in alcohol retail establishments is mixed. Early studies found that warning signs were associated with increased probability of alcohol sales to minors (Forster, Murray, Wolfson, & Wagenaar, 1995; Wolfson et al., 1996), whereas more recent research has found that the presence of warning signs is associated with reduced sales to minors (Britt, Toomey, Dunsmuir, & Wagenaar, 2006; Paschall et al., 2007). It is possible that enforcement of underage sale policies has increased over time, explaining changes in the observed effectiveness of the warning signs. In addition, the signs may provide a reminder to both sales staff and customers, serving to deter sales without identification to younger customers. While promising, the strategy has produced mixed evidence to date and may be effective only in combination with other strategies, such as enforcement compliance checks at alcohol retail establishments regarding sales to underage youth.

CONCLUSION

Alcohol is not only the most commonly used substance for youth under age 21 years but also is associated with numerous of preventable health, social, and personal consequences (Brown et al., 2008; Johnston et al., 2012). Given the multiple sources of alcohol for youth, preventing alcohol use by minors under the age of 21 years requires multifaceted prevention strategies. Many laws and policies can be used to minimize both social and commercial access to alcohol by underage youth. Policy contexts and interventions shape the social environment and norms, and these interventions should be implemented and evaluated as part of a comprehensive effort, including school and family interventions, to reduce the negative outcomes associated with alcohol and other substance use. It is recommended that future studies of school and family interventions to prevent alcohol and substance use also measure some of the macrolevel policy contexts to determine the extent to which policy and structural factors moderate or mediate intervention effects.

Communities should consider the strategies discussed in this chapter when developing a comprehensive plan to reduce underage access to alcohol, teen drinking, and the harms that result. The EUDL program, sponsored by the Office of Juvenile Justice and Delinquency Prevention, part of the U.S. Department of Justice, has provided states and communities with grants aimed at enacting and enforcing laws and policies around preventing underage access to alcohol from 1998 to 2007. The evaluation of this program, conducted by Wake Forest University School of Medicine, aimed to determine the effect of a local, coalition-based approach in implementing the best strategies to reduce underage alcohol use. The EUDL communities were required to implement compliance checks, enforcement of DWI laws, reduction of social availability of alcohol to youth, and policy enactment (Wolfson et al., 2011). Out of 34 intervention sites, only 53% met all four requirements. This may be one explanation for the limited effects of the EUDL project on behavioral outcomes, other than the significant reduction in alcohol-related motor vehicle crashes involving underage youth. Sites with higher levels of implementation had better outcomes, however, highlighting the importance of consistently and thoroughly implementing and enforcing the underage alcohol prevention policies in place. The Pacific Institute for Research and Evaluation currently provides a variety of tools, resources, and services for community leaders who want to enhance their underage drinking prevention and enforcement efforts (see http://www.udetc.org).

References

Braga, A. A. (2001). The effects of hot spots policing on crime. *Annals of the American Academy of Political and Social Science*, *578*, 104–125. doi:10.1177/0002716201578001007

Britt, H., Toomey, T. L., Dunsmuir, W., & Wagenaar, A. C. (2006). Propensity for and correlates of alcohol sales to underage youth. *Journal of Alcohol and Drug Education*, *50*, 25–42.

Brown, S. A., McGue, M., Maggs, J., Schulenberg, J., Hingson, R., Swartzwelder, S., . . . Murphy, S. (2008).

A developmental perspective on alcohol and youths 16 to 20 years of age. *Pediatrics, 121*, S290–S310. doi:10.1542/peds.2007-2243D

Buka, S. L., & Birdthistle, I. J. (1999). Long-term effects of a community-wide alcohol server training intervention. *Journal of Studies on Alcohol, 60*, 27–36.

Campbell, C. A., Hahn, R. A., Elder, R., Brewer, R., Chattopadhyay, S., Fielding, J., . . . Middleton, J. C. (2009). The effectiveness of limiting alcohol outlet density as a means of reducing excessive alcohol consumption and alcohol-related harms. *American Journal of Preventive Medicine, 37*, 556–569. doi:10.1016/j.amepre.2009.09.028

Dent, C. W., Grube, J. W., & Biglan, A. (2005). Community level alcohol availability and enforcement of possession laws as predictors of youth drinking. *Preventive Medicine, 40*, 355–362. doi:10.1016/j.ypmed.2004.06.014

Dills, A. K. (2010). Social host liability for minors and underage drunk-driving accidents. *Journal of Health Economics, 29*, 241–249. doi:10.1016/j.jhealeco.2009.12.001

Fell, J. C., Fisher, D. A., Voas, R. B., Blackman, K., & Tippetts, A. S. (2009). The impact of underage drinking laws on alcohol-related fatal crashes of young drivers. *Alcoholism: Clinical and Experimental Research, 33*, 1208–1219. doi:10.1111/j.1530-0277.2009.00945.x

Flay, B. R., Biglan, A., Boruch, R. F., Castro, F. G., Gottfredson, D., Kellam, S., . . . Ji, P. (2005). Standards of evidence: Criteria for efficacy, effectiveness and dissemination. *Prevention Science, 6*, 151–175. doi:10.1007/s11121-005-5553-y

Fletcher, L. A., Toomey, T. L., Wagenaar, A. C., Short, B., & Willenbring, M. L. (2000). Alcohol home delivery services: A source of alcohol for underage drinkers. *Journal of Studies on Alcohol, 61*, 81–84.

Forster, J. L., Murray, D. M., Wolfson, M., & Wagenaar, A. C. (1995). Commercial availability of alcohol to young people: Results of alcohol purchase attempts. *Preventive Medicine, 24*, 342–347. doi:10.1006/pmed.1995.1056

Gebhardt, T. L., Kaphingst, K., & DeJong, W. (2000). A campus-community coalition to control alcohol-related problems off campus: An environmental management case study. *Journal of American College Health, 48*, 211–215. doi:10.1080/07448480009599306

Grube, J. W. (1997). Preventing sales of alcohol to minors: Results from a community trial. *Addiction, 92*, S251–S260. doi:10.1111/j.1360-0443.1997.tb02995.x

Hingson, R., Heeren, T., Winter, M., & Wechsler, H. (2005). Magnitude of alcohol-related mortality and morbidity among U.S. college students ages 18-24: Changes from 1998 to 2001. *Annual Review of Public Health, 26*, 259–279. doi:10.1146/annurev.publhealth.26.021304.144652

Holder, H. D., & Wagenaar, A. C. (1994). Mandated server training and reduced alcohol-involved traffic crashes: A time series analysis of the Oregon experience. *Accident Analysis and Prevention, 26*, 89–97. doi:10.1016/0001-4575(94)90071-X

Hope, T. J. (1994). Problem-oriented policing and drug-market locations: Three case studies. In R. V. Clarke (Ed.), *Crime prevention studies* (Vol. 2, pp. 5–31). Monsey, NY: Criminal Justice Press.

Johnston, L. D., O'Malley, P. M., Bachman, J. G., & Schulenberg, J. E. (2012). *Monitoring the future: Overview of key findings 2011.* Ann Arbor, Michigan: University of Michigan.

Kann, L., Kinchen, S., Shanklin, S. L., Flint, K. H., Hawkins, J., Harris, W. A., . . . Zaza, S. (2014). Youth risk behavior surveillance—United States, 2013. *Morbidity and Mortality Weekly Report, 63*(SS-4): 1–168.

Komro, K. A., Maldonado-Molina, M. M., Tobler, A. L., Bonds, J. R., & Muller, K. E. (2007). Effects of home access and availability of alcohol on young adolescents' alcohol use. *Addiction, 102*, 1597–1608. doi:10.1111/j.1360-0443.2007.01941.x

Mosher, J. F. (1995). The merchants, not the customers: Resisting the alcohol and tobacco industries' strategy to blame young people for illegal alcohol and tobacco sales. *Journal of Public Health Policy, 16*, 412–432. doi:10.2307/3342619

Mosher, J. F., Toomey, T. L., Good, C., Harwood, E., & Wagenaar, A. C. (2002). State laws mandating or promoting training programs for alcohol servers and establishment managers: An assessment of statutory and administrative procedures. *Journal of Public Health Policy, 23*, 90–113. doi:10.2307/3343120

National Research Council and Institute of Medicine. (2004). *Reducing underage drinking: A collective responsibility.* Committee on Developing a Strategy to Reduce and Prevent Underage Drinking, R. J. Bonnie & M. E. O'Connell (Eds.). Board on Children, Youth, and Families, Division of Behavioral and Social Sciences and Education. Washington, DC: National Academies Press.

Neighbors, C., Walters, S. T., Lee, C. M., Vader, A. M., Vehige, T., Szigethy, T., & DeJong, W. (2007). Event-specific prevention: Addressing college student drinking during known windows of risk. *Addictive Behaviors, 32*, 2667–2680. doi:10.1016/j.addbeh.2007.05.010

Paschall, M. J., Grube, J. W., Black, C., Flewelling, R. L., Ringwalt, C. L., & Biglan, A. (2007). Alcohol outlet characteristics and alcohol sales to youth: Results of alcohol purchase surveys in 45 Oregon communities. *Prevention Science*, *8*, 153–159. doi:10.1007/s11121-006-0063-0

Preusser, D. F., Williams, A. F., & Weinstein, H. B. (1994).Policing underage alcohol sales. *Journal of Safety Research*, *25*, 127–133. doi:10.1016/0022-4375(94)90069-8

Reboussin, B. A., Song, E. Y., & Wolfson, M. (2011). The impact of alcohol outlet density on the geographic clustering of underage drinking behaviors within census tracts. *Alcoholism: Clinical and Experimental Research*, *35*, 1541–1549.

Resko, S. M., Walton, M. A., Bingham, C. R., Shope, J. T., Zimmerman, M., Chermack, S. T., & Cunningham, R. M. (2010). Alcohol availability and violence among inner-city adolescents: A multi-level analysis of the role of alcohol outlet density. *American Journal of Community Psychology*, *46*, 253–262. doi:10.1007/s10464-010-9353-6

Ringwalt, C. L., & Paschall, M. J. (2011). The utility of keg registration laws: A cross-sectional study. *Journal of Adolescent Health*, *48*, 106–108.

Scribner, R., & Cohen, D. (2001). The effect of enforcement on merchant compliance with the minimum legal drinking age law. *Journal of Drug Issues*, *31*, 857–866.

Sherman, L. W., & Rogan, D. (1995). Deterrent effects of police raids on crack houses: A randomized controlled experiment. *Justice Quarterly*, *12*, 755–781. doi:10.1080/07418829500096281

Stout, E. M., Sloan, F. A., Liang, L., & Davies, H. H. (2000). Reducing harmful alcohol-related behaviors: Effective regulatory methods. *Journal of Studies on Alcohol*, *61*, 402–412.

Tobler, A. L., Komro, K. A., & Maldonado-Molina, M. M. (2009). Relationship between neighborhood context, family management practices and alcohol use among urban, multi-ethnic, young adolescents. *Prevention Science*, *10*, 313–324. doi:10.1007/s11121-009-0133-1

Toomey, T. L., Erickson, D. J., Carlin, B. P., Lenk, K. M., Quick, H. S., Jones, A. M., & Harwood, E. M. (2012). The association between density of alcohol establishments and violent crime within urban neighborhoods. *Alcoholism: Clinical and Experimental Research*, *36*, 1468–1473. doi:10.1111/j.1530-0277.2012.01753.x

Toomey, T. L., Erickson, D. J., Lenk, K. M., & Kilian, G. R. (2008). Likelihood of illegal alcohol sales at professional sport stadiums. *Alcoholism: Clinical and Experimental Research*, *32*, 1859–1864.

Toomey, T. L., Erickson, D. J., Lenk, K. M., Kilian, G. R., Perry, C. L., & Wagenaar, A. C. (2008). A randomized trial to evaluate a management training program to prevent illegal alcohol sales. *Addiction*, *103*, 405–413. doi:10.1111/j.1360-0443.2007.02077.x

Toomey, T. L., Erickson, D. J., Patrek, W., Fletcher, L. A., & Wagenaar, A. C. (2005). Illegal alcohol sales and use of alcohol control policies at community festivals. *Public Health Reports*, *120*, 165–173.

Toomey, T. L., Fabian, L. E., Erickson, D. J., & Lenk, K. M. (2007). Propensity for obtaining alcohol through shoulder tapping. *Alcoholism: Clinical and Experimental Research*, *31*, 1218–1223. doi:10.1111/j.1530-0277.2007.00420.x

Toomey, T. L., Kilian, G. R., Gehan, J. P., Perry, C. L., Jones-Webb, R., & Wagenaar, A. C. (1998). Qualitative assessment of training programs for alcohol servers and establishment managers. *Public Health Reports*, *113*, 162–169.

Toomey, T. L., Wagenaar, A. C., Gehan, J. P., Kilian, G., Murray, D. M., & Perry, C. L. (2001). Project ARM: Alcohol risk management to prevent sales to underage and intoxicated patrons. *Health Education and Behavior*, *28*, 186–199. doi:10.1177/109019810102800205

Wagenaar, A. C., Denk, C. E., Hannan, P. J., Chen, H., & Harwood, E. M. (2001). Liability of commercial and social hosts for alcohol-related injuries. *Public Opinion Quarterly*, *65*, 344–368. doi:10.1086/322848

Wagenaar, A. C., Finnegan, J. R., Wolfson, M., Anstine, P. S., Williams, C. L., & Perry, C. L. (1993). Where and how adolescents obtain alcoholic beverages. *Public Health Reports*, *108*, 459–464.

Wagenaar, A. C., Harwood, E. M., Silianoff, C., & Toomey, T. L. (2005). Measuring public policy: The case of beer keg registration laws. *Evaluation and Program Planning*, *28*, 359–367. doi:10.1016/j.evalprogplan.2005.07.001

Wagenaar, A. C., Salois, M. J., & Komro, K. A. (2009). Effects of beverage alcohol price and tax levels on drinking: A meta-analysis of 1003 estimates from 112 studies. *Addiction*, *104*, 179–190. doi:10.1111/j.1360-0443.2008.02438.x

Wagenaar, A. C., & Tobler, A. L. (2007). Alcohol sales and service to underage youth and intoxicated patrons: Effects of responsible beverage service training and enforcement interventions. In *Transportation Research Circular: Traffic Safety and Alcohol Regulation* (Report No. E-C123). Washington, DC: Government Printing Office.

Wagenaar, A. C., Tobler, A. L., & Komro, K. A. (2010). Effects of alcohol tax and price policies on morbidity and mortality: A systematic review. *American Journal of Public Health*, *100*, 2270–2278. doi:10.2105/AJPH.2009.186007

Wagenaar, A. C., Toomey, T. L., & Erickson, D. J. (2005). Preventing youth access to alcohol: Outcomes from a multi-community time-series trial. *Addiction*, *100*, 335–345. doi:10.1111/j.1360-0443.2005.00973.x

Wagenaar, A. C., & Wolfson, M. (1994). Enforcement of the legal minimum drinking age in the United States. *Journal of Public Health Policy*, *15*, 37–53. doi:10.2307/3342606

Weisburd, D., & Eck, J. E. (2004). What can police do to reduce crime, disorder, and fear? *Annals of the American Academy of Political and Social Science*, *593*, 42–65. doi:10.1177/0002716203262548

Weisburd, D. L., & Green, L. (1995). Policing drug hot spots: The Jersey City drug market analysis experiment. *Justice Quarterly*, *12*, 711–735. doi:10.1080/07418829500096261

Whetten-Goldstein, K., Sloan, F. A., Stout, E., & Liang, L. (2000). Civil liability, criminal law, and other policies and alcohol-related motor vehicle fatalities in the United States: 1984–1995. *Accident Analysis and Prevention*, *32*, 723–733. doi:10.1016/S0001-4575(99)00122-0

Wolfson, M., Song, E., Martin, B. A., Wagoner, K., Pleasants, D., & Nieberg, R., . . . Hulme, S. (2011). *National evaluation of the enforcing underage drinking laws randomized community trial: Final report.* Wake Forest University, School of Medicine.

Wolfson, M., Toomey, T. L., Murray, D. M., Forster, J. L., Short, B. J., & Wagenaar, A. C. (1996). Alcohol outlet policies and practices concerning sales to underage people. *Addiction*, *91*, 589–602. doi:10.1111/j.1360-0443.1996.tb02316.x

Yu, J. (2003). The association between parental alcohol-related behaviors and children's drinking. *Drug and Alcohol Dependence*, *69*, 253–262. doi:10.1016/S0376-8716(02)00324-1

Chapter 19

ENACTING PREVENTIVE INTERVENTIONS AT THE COMMUNITY LEVEL: THE COMMUNITIES THAT CARE PREVENTION SYSTEM

Abigail A. Fagan and J. David Hawkins

This chapter provides an overview of the effectiveness of and challenges associated with implementing community-level interventions to reduce alcohol and other drug use among children, adolescents, and young adults. We focus on coalition-based strategies that rely on community members to plan, implement, and oversee prevention activities in a manner that ensures services are well coordinated, locally supported, and broadly implemented in the community. The Communities That Care (CTC) prevention system is described in detail to illustrate the potential benefits of community-based efforts. We discuss the training and technical assistance provided to CTC community members to support their efforts to collect data on local needs, address prioritized needs using prevention services with evidence of effectiveness, and monitor the quality of these implementation efforts. We also describe the results of a randomized controlled evaluation of CTC, undertaken in 24 communities in seven states, to reduce the initiation and prevalence of substance use and delinquency among youth, fostering community collaboration and support for prevention, and increasing the use and sustainability of evidence-based interventions. The chapter concludes with recommendations for additional research to identify and describe the specific mechanisms that foster communitywide changes in substance use and the cost-effectiveness of this type of prevention approach.

Benefits as well as challenges are associated with communitywide efforts to prevent youth alcohol and drug use (Backer & Guerra, 2011; Hallfors, Cho, Livert, & Kadushin, 2002; Wandersman, 2003). In contrast to more narrow prevention efforts seeking to change individual factors related to substance use for a discrete number of individuals, communitywide strategies try to alter contextual as well as individual factors and to achieve population-level impacts (Woolf, 2008). Such efforts are likely to require mobilization of community members to plan, implement, and oversee prevention efforts, but doing so can be difficult. This chapter reviews community-based mobilization strategies that have relied on participation from community residents to reduce alcohol and other drug use among children,

Preparation for this chapter was supported by a grant from the National Institute on Drug Abuse (R01 DA015183-03) with cofunding from the National Cancer Institute, the National Institute of Child Health and Human Development, the National Institute of Mental Health, the Center for Substance Abuse Prevention, and the National Institute on Alcohol Abuse and Alcoholism. The content of this chapter is solely the responsibility of the authors and does not necessarily represent the official views of the sponsors.

The authors gratefully acknowledge the ongoing participation in the study and data collection efforts of the residents of the 24 communities described in this chapter.

http://dx.doi.org/10.1037/14550-020
Handbook of Adolescent Drug Use Prevention: Research, Intervention Strategies, and Practice, L. M. Scheier (Editor)

adolescents, and young adults. We discuss in detail the CTC prevention system (Hawkins & Catalano, 1992; Hawkins, Catalano, & Arthur, 2002), which has been demonstrated as effective in lowering the initiation and prevalence of youth alcohol and tobacco use when implemented in small- to medium-size communities (e.g., 1,600–40,000 residents) participating in a randomized trial in seven states (Hawkins et al., 2009, 2012) and in a quasi-experimental study across counties in Pennsylvania (Feinberg, Greenberg, Osgood, Sartorius, & Bontempo, 2007; Feinberg, Jones, Greenberg, Osgood, & Bontempo, 2010). CTC provides tools and a guided process for communities to assess their drug prevention needs; select, implement, and monitor the implementation quality of evidence-based preventive interventions that will target these needs; and ensure broad participation in change efforts in order to create an environment that fosters healthy youth development.

WHY IMPLEMENT COMMUNITY-BASED PREVENTION STRATEGIES?

To date, numerous interventions have been developed, tested, and shown to be effective in reducing alcohol and other drug use among youth (O'Connell, Boat, & Warner, 2009; Spoth, Greenberg, & Turrisi, 2008). Although widespread dissemination of these interventions across communities has not yet been achieved (Spoth et al., 2013), some progress has been made in the adoption of discrete, evidence-based drug prevention programs by schools and other community agencies (Ringwalt et al., 2011; Sloboda et al., 2008). Given the ability of agencies to purchase and implement programs at their own discretion, why advocate for community-based approaches to prevention, which typically require that multiple agencies and individual stakeholders agree on prevention needs and take action to address these needs in a coordinated, collaborative manner? These types of initiatives can be difficult to enact, given that they rely on cooperation and collective decision making from multiple parties, who come from diverse professional and personal backgrounds and who often have conflicting or competing goals and ideas about what is needed to prevent youth substance use (Merzel & D'Afflitti, 2003; Stith et al., 2006; Wandersman & Florin, 2003). Furthermore, community-level strategies, especially compared with discrete preventive interventions, are likely to require significant effort, resolve, and financial resources, as producing communitywide outcomes likely involves the provision of multiple interventions to a significant proportion of the targeted population over many years (Arthur & Blitz, 2000; Woolf, 2008).

These challenges should not be underestimated, but they may be offset by several benefits. The biggest advantage of communitywide efforts is the potential to achieve widespread and long-term reductions in substance use and other problem behaviors across entire community populations. The typical approach to prevention in communities is for an individual professional to provide services to a particular client using a particular intervention (often an untested model), or for an agency to provide a discrete program or practice to a particular population (e.g., middle school students or parents of newborn babies) in a single context. These actors tend to work in isolation from one another and may be unaware of other services provided in their community. In contrast, community-based efforts usually rely on coalitions of stakeholders from diverse organizations and backgrounds to collectively plan, implement, and monitor prevention activities. This collaborative approach allows for the pooling of information and resources across agencies and can enhance community support for prevention initiatives, minimize duplication of services, and potentially offer more cost-effective services that are better implemented and more likely to be sustained (Hawkins et al., 2002; Specter, 2008; Wandersman & Florin, 2003).

Community-based efforts usually result in the delivery of multiple discrete interventions and policies that target for change multiple factors related to substance use (Flewelling et al., 2005; Wandersman & Florin, 2003). This approach increases the scope of programming in terms of the number of individuals reached and in the number of risk and protective factors addressed, which should translate into greater benefits for the entire community. Empirical research has shown that the effect sizes of individual drug prevention programs are relatively small (Foxcroft, Ireland, Lister-Sharp, Lowe, & Breen,

2003) and that many factors can promote drug use (Hawkins, Catalano, & Miller, 1992). Thus, synergistic efforts that also provide greater opportunities to target more of these factors have a greater potential to create change.

Another benefit of community-based efforts is their potential to change not only immediate or proximal factors that can influence substance use (e.g., individual motivations to use illegal substances or positive family relationships that may inhibit substance use) but also the long-term, structural, and environmental influences associated with such behaviors (Stevenson & Mitchell, 2003; Wagenaar & Perry, 1994). Community-based strategies, for example, may seek changes in local ordinances and policies to reduce access to alcohol and drugs or try to alter community norms to reduce support for underage drinking. To the degree that such efforts change the environment in which the majority or entirety of the population resides, they will necessarily increase exposure to prevention efforts, which should, in turn, increase the likelihood of community-wide changes. Communitywide efforts also can help bolster the effectiveness of discrete interventions by creating a more supportive context and infrastructure for their delivery and ensuring that the larger environment reinforces their prevention messages (Flay, 2000; Stevenson & Mitchell, 2003; Wagenaar & Perry, 1994).

Finally, community-based efforts have the advantage of ensuring that preventive interventions are a good fit with local needs, resources, and norms (Arthur & Blitz, 2000; Stith et al., 2006). What is most needed in one community to reduce youth drug use may not be what is needed in another community (Hawkins, Van Horn, & Arthur, 2004). For example, not all communities will necessarily benefit from implementing a particular school- or family-focused program, even if it has been tested and shown to be effective. Many community-based models, including CTC, emphasize the need to identify the conditions that foster substance use locally and then address these specific needs via implementation of interventions that have been shown to significantly affect such conditions (Arthur & Blitz, 2000; Saul et al., 2008; Stith et al., 2006). By implementing interventions that are tailored to the specific needs of the local community, ensuring they are well coordinated and target multiple risks faced in multiple contexts, and creating more supportive environments, community-based efforts have the potential to achieve population-level reductions in youth substance use.

EXAMPLES OF EFFECTIVE COMMUNITY-BASED SUBSTANCE USE PREVENTION STRATEGIES

As the preceding discussion suggests, community-based strategies can take many forms. Given their scope and complexity, these prevention models are challenging and costly to evaluate (Stith et al., 2006). As a result, knowledge regarding "what works" in community-based prevention is somewhat limited. We previously conducted a comprehensive review of community-based strategies intended to reduce alcohol and drug use among youth less than 21 years old, which were evaluated using well-conducted quasi-experimental or true experimental designs (Fagan & Hawkins, 2012). A total of 14 interventions met the specified search criteria; nine had one or more significant effects indicating reductions in alcohol and other drug use, and five were not demonstrated as effective in reducing youth substance use. We summarize next the characteristics associated with effective and ineffective strategies.

Although they relied on diverse change strategies, all nine effective models involved the use of community-based coalitions to plan and implement activities. Most of the ineffective models did so as well, however, which suggests that simply gathering local stakeholders and asking them to do their best to solve local drug problems is not enough to prevent adolescent substance use, even if coalitions are provided with significant resources. Evaluations of the Fighting Back (Hallfors et al., 2002) and Community Partnership coalition initiatives (Yin, Kaftarian, Yu, & Jansen, 1997), for example, demonstrated no significant changes in youth drug use. Although these projects were successful in creating broad-based coalitions of community members concerned about substance use, coalitions were described as having received insufficient guidance in how to enact preventive interventions, having varied widely in the nature and amount of services provided, and having relied largely on locally created preventive interventions that likely had not been evaluated previously for effectiveness in reducing drug use.

In contrast, coalition models that provide a more structured process to guide prevention efforts, including the provision of proactive training and technical assistance, and that emphasize high-quality implementation of effective preventive interventions appear to lower rates of youth substance use. Evaluations of CTC (Hawkins et al., 2009, 2012) and Promoting School-Community-University Partnerships to Enhance Resilience (PROSPER; Spoth, Guyll, Redmond, Greenberg, & Feinberg, 2011; Spoth et al., 2007), which support these characteristics, have been shown in randomized controlled evaluations to reduce the initiation and prevalence of alcohol and drug use among adolescents, as based on self-reported surveys with the majority of youth living in study communities. Reductions in teenage substance use also have been demonstrated in evaluations of coalition models funded by State Incentive Grants from the Center for Substance Abuse Prevention in Kentucky (Collins, Johnson, & Becker, 2007) and Vermont (Flewelling et al., 2005), both of which involved implementation of tested and effective prevention programs.

Our review of the evidence indicated that coalitions that focused explicitly and solely on changing community norms or policies related to alcohol use were not successful in preventing alcohol use among youths under the age of 18 years. The Communities Mobilizing for Change on Alcohol and A Matter of Degree interventions, for example, train communities to implement environmental-change approaches, including educating alcohol sales establishments about the penalties for selling to minors, tracking keg sales, restricting alcohol sales in venues accessible to youth, increasing enforcement of community laws and policies related to youth alcohol use, prohibiting alcohol advertising and promotions at public events that include youth, and increasing media coverage about the consequences of underage drinking (see Chapter 18, this volume). Although evaluations of these two interventions (Wagenaar et al., 2000; Weitzman, Nelson, Lee, & Wechsler, 2004) indicated some benefits to communities, they did not show significant ($p < .05$) differences in the proportion of youth under age 18 years who reported alcohol use. Given the limited number of large-scale, well-conducted evaluations of these types of strategies, additional research is warranted.

When used in isolation, environmentally focused efforts combined with universal, school-based drug prevention curricula have not demonstrated the ability to reduce alcohol use among teens, but they do appear to be successful. Our review demonstrated positive effects on youth substance use for community-based efforts that combined activities designed to change community norms and policies with curricula delivered to students in elementary school (the Native American Project; see Schinke, Tepavac, & Cole, 2000), middle school (the Midwestern Prevention Project; see Pentz et al., 1989; the Drug Abuse Resistance Education [D.A.R.E.] Plus; see Perry et al., 2003), and middle through high school (Project Sixteen; see Biglan, Ary, Smolkowski, Duncan, & Black, 2000; Project Northland; see Perry et al., 1996, 2000). School-based programs may be particularly important to success because they can reach a large proportion of the youth population in the community. In addition, such curricula tend to target proximal influences, such as peer relationships and individual attitudes regarding substance use, which are among the strongest risk factors for drinking and drug use (Hawkins et al., 1992; Tobler & Stratton, 1997).

The PROSPER project also emphasizes the importance of embedding school curricula in larger community efforts, and it too has been found to be effective at preventing substance use among adolescents (Spoth, Redmond, et al., 2011; Spoth et al., 2007). Importantly, these effects were evidenced in a well-conducted randomized trial involving 28 communities, and outcomes were assessed using reports from a longitudinal panel of youth representing 90% of all sixth-grade students in study communities at baseline. In the PROSPER model, local university Cooperative Extension Service agents and school district personnel, with assistance from academic researchers, jointly oversee local coalitions of youth, parents, and community members (see Chapter 15, this volume). Coalitions select and monitor the implementation of universal school-based prevention programs as well as programs that seek to improve parenting practices and parent–child interactions. PROSPER does not advocate for the implementation of particular school- and family-focused programs; rather, community coalitions select programs from a relatively short menu of evidence-based interventions that target youth substance use (Spoth, Greenberg, Bierman, & Redmond, 2004). By fostering collaboration among community members, using preexisting infrastructures (e.g., state cooperative extension offices and local school districts), and linking practitioners and academic scientists, the PROSPER model seeks to improve local capacity to effectively deliver interventions, promote their widespread delivery, and increase the likelihood that practices will be sustained (Spoth & Greenberg, 2011).

THE CTC PREVENTION SYSTEM

The CTC prevention system has been demonstrated as effective in reducing adolescent substance use, according to a quasi-experimental study in Pennsylvania (Feinberg et al., 2007, 2010) and a randomized controlled trial conducted in seven states (Hawkins, Catalano, et al., 2008; Hawkins et al., 2009, 2012). The CTC system seeks to translate scientific information regarding the putative risk and protective factors that contribute to problem behaviors and the results of scientific evaluations of interventions that address those factors into clear, manageable action steps that can be enacted locally (Hawkins et al., 2002). The process involves five phases: (a) assessing community readiness to undertake collaborative prevention activities, (b) forming a diverse and representative coalition to coordinate prevention efforts, (c) using local epidemiologic data to identify elevated risk factors and depressed protective factors in the community, (d) choosing evidence-based prevention policies and programs that target these factors, and (e) implementing the new interventions with fidelity and evaluating their impact on youth problem behaviors.

Like many other community-based prevention models, CTC seeks to create change by transforming community context and practice. Unlike some of the other models (including PROSPER), a key component of CTC is the collection of local data to identify the specific prevention needs of the community. In addition, CTC provides a broader menu of effective interventions from which communities can choose and emphasizes that strategies must be linked closely to the needs assessment (e.g., targeting areas of highest need) to have maximum impact (Hawkins et al., 2002; Hawkins & Catalano, 1992). Finally, CTC trains coalition members to monitor and evaluate the effectiveness of their prevention activities and to make changes as necessary in service delivery to ensure that outcomes are achieved. Given the inherent challenges of this work, and in effectively engaging community members, CTC relies on user-friendly materials to decode scientific facts; a series of training workshops that include didactic instruction, opportunities for discussion and decision making, and ample planning time; ongoing and proactive technical assistance; and a structured process that proceeds sequentially from planning, to implementation, to maintenance of prevention activities. The next sections describe these aspects of the CTC system in more detail. Before doing so, however, we discuss the empirical and theoretical basis of CTC.

Risk and Protective Factors and the Science of Substance Use Prevention

CTC builds on insights from the fields of medicine and public health that the best way to prevent a public health problem, such as substance use, is to identify the factors that contribute to its development and then seek to reduce or minimize their occurrence and influence through preventive interventions (Catalano et al., 2012; Coie et al., 1993). Empirical research has identified many factors contributing to the initiation, escalation, and deceleration of alcohol and drug use. *Risk factors* are conditions, experiences, and attributes that, when present, increase the likelihood of substance use (Hawkins et al., 1992). These factors exist across all areas of life and include individual characteristics (e.g., poor impulse control or believing that using drugs is not harmful), peer influences (e.g., having friends who use drugs or who believe that substance use is acceptable), family experiences (e.g., substance use by parents or siblings, inadequate monitoring of children by parents), school factors (e.g., academic failure, having a low commitment to school or education), and neighborhood experiences (e.g., availability of drugs, community norms that support substance use; Catalano, Haggerty, Hawkins, & Elgin, 2011; Donovan, 2004; Durlak, 1998; Hawkins et al., 1992; Newcomb, Maddahian, & Bentler, 1986). Although exposure to a particular risk factor does not guarantee that substance use will occur, the likelihood of use increases additively as the number of risk factors increases (Bry, McKeon, & Pandina, 1982; Coie et al., 1993; Pollard, Hawkins, & Arthur, 1999).

Protective factors are conceptually distinct from, and not simply the absence or opposite of, risk factors (Catalano & Hawkins, 1996; Hawkins et al., 1992). They typically are defined as experiences that reduce the negative impact of exposure to risk factors (Rutter, 1985), although they also may have direct effects in predicting abstinence or low involvement in substance use (also referred to as *promotive factors;* e.g., Sameroff, 2006). Protective factors have received much less empirical research than risk factors. Examples include having a resilient temperament, healthy beliefs and clear standards regarding substance use, a strong commitment to school and education, attachments to prosocial individuals and institutions, and reinforcements for prosocial behavior (Hawkins et al., 1992; Rutter, 1985).

Research has indicated that the emergence and influence of risk and protective factors vary developmentally, such that particular factors are more or less influential at different ages or developmental stages. For example, during infancy and early childhood, family factors (e.g., maternal use of alcohol and drugs), emotional warmth and nurturing, and parenting practices (e.g., monitoring, supervision, reinforcement) may be most important. During middle childhood and adolescence, school and peer experiences become more influential. Community factors tend to gain precedence during middle to late adolescence (Catalano & Hawkins, 1996; Hawkins et al., 1992). The developmental nature of risk and protection suggests that when measuring the prevalence of these factors in a community, it is important to collect data from youth of different ages. Likewise, preventive interventions must be developmentally appropriate, targeting the factors most salient for a particular age group, and these services must then be delivered to the right audience to have maximum impact (Fagan & Hawkins, 2013).

Both the influence and levels of risk and protective factors can vary across population groups (e.g., gender, race or ethnicity) and communities (Hawkins et al., 2004; Kellam, Ling, Merisca, Brown, & Ialongo, 1998). That is, these factors may not have the same meaning or influence across individuals or groups, and risk and protective factors may not be experienced at the same rates for all individuals or communities. In the CTC system, coalitions conduct local needs assessments to measure exposure to risk and protective factors across youth in the community and collaboratively decide which factors to address and which populations should be targeted for services on the basis of these assessments.

Empirical research also has shown that substance use, delinquency, and mental health problems share common antecedents (Coie et al., 1993; Hawkins et al., 2002). That is, a risk factor can lead to a variety of negative outcomes; for example, poor family management can impair school performance, lead to mental health deficits, and increase the likelihood of substance use, delinquency, and violence (Steinberg, 2001). Importantly, from the standpoint of prevention, reducing or altering the impact of one risk factor potentially can reduce multiple, related outcomes. For example, an intervention that improves academic performance may reduce not only a child's likelihood of engaging in substance use but also delinquency, dropping out of school, and mental health problems such as depression. By extension, offering multiple interventions in a coordinated fashion should greatly enhance communitywide reductions in diverse problem behaviors.

Theoretical Foundations of the CTC Prevention System

Theoretical perspectives of adolescent development, particularly the social development model (SDM), also have guided the development of CTC. The SDM is an integrated theory that recognizes that multiple risk and protective factors contribute to the etiology of prosocial and antisocial behaviors over the life span (Catalano & Hawkins, 1996; Hawkins & Weis, 1985). According to the SDM, it is important to provide youth with opportunities to actively participate in prosocial groups (in the family, school, peer, and community settings), teach them the skills they need to participate successfully in these groups, and favorably recognize their efforts in doing so. Youth develop strong bonds to individuals and groups who make these provisions. When bonding occurs, youth are more likely to subscribe to the healthy beliefs and clear standards for behavior communicated by those to whom they are bonded, are more likely to display positive and prosocial behaviors, and are less likely to engage in antisocial activities. Not coincidently, the types of activities thought to promote bonding are those typically found in the preventive interventions advocated in CTC. By increasing the use of such programs, communities enhance their chances of fostering healthy youth development.

The processes outlined in the SDM also suggest that participation in local CTC coalitions will promote bonding among adult members of the community. All interested community stakeholders should have the opportunity to participate in the CTC coalition. The specific number and types of members is not proscribed but will vary locally. CTC coalitions, however, are to be broad based and representative of the community in terms of demographic characteristics and in representing key sectors of the community, including elected officials, parents, law enforcement, school personnel, public health officials, faith organizations, social services agencies, business community, young people, and other stakeholders (Quinby et al., 2008). The local boundaries or definitions of the "community" also are decided on locally (Hawkins et al., 2002). CTC has been implemented in small towns, large cities, and specific neighborhoods or smaller regions of large cities.

In the early stages of CTC, coalitions develop a common vision for positive youth development and agree on the mechanisms that will be used to achieve this vision. Subsequent CTC training workshops provide coalition members with the skills necessary to plan and successfully implement effective preventive interventions. These actions should help ensure that community goals are achieved, and these positive results then can be widely communicated and celebrated. By increasing opportunities for stakeholders to work together, building skills, and ensuring that they receive positive recognition, CTC seeks to promote closer social bonds and greater collaboration among coalition members and the community as a whole (Hawkins et al., 2002). The active involvement of local residents in community planning and intervention has the added benefit of enhancing the likelihood that preventive actions are broadly supported, well implemented, and sustained over time, all of which should improve the health and well-being of community youth (Hawkins et al., 2002; Wandersman & Florin, 2003).

By fostering agreement on the collective norms to guide behavior and encouraging collaborative actions to prevent problem behaviors, CTC also can be seen as a mechanism for enhancing collective efficacy, which has been shown to reduce youth substance use and delinquency and to counteract the negative impact of environmental risk factors, such as poverty and disorder (Sampson, Raudenbush, & Earls, 1997). Communities with high levels of collective efficacy have residents who are closely connected and who agree on standards (i.e., norms) for appropriate and inappropriate behaviors. Residents also have a shared sense of responsibility for taking action to enforce these standards. Thus, in a neighborhood with high collective efficacy, residents will be more likely to communicate to youth that adults care about the healthy development of young people, disapprove of wrongdoing, and will take collective action to ensure that such behaviors do not occur (Sampson et al., 1997). Youth in such communities should refrain from delinquency because they feel supported by adults and do not want to disappoint them (i.e., they have strong attachment to the community) and because they believe their misdeeds will be discovered and punished (Fagan & Hawkins, 2013).

In the CTC system, collective efficacy is enhanced through the provision of materials, training, and technical assistance to community coalitions. The system fosters shared norms and cohesion by helping residents reach agreement regarding the actual levels of problem behaviors occurring in their communities and the degree to which local youth face risk and protective factors that contribute to problems. The CTC system also ensures effective community action by emphasizing the delivery of science-based, proven prevention models, which are selected to address specific community needs and monitored over time to ensure quality delivery, as described next.

Conducting Local Needs Assessments

Similar to other community-based prevention models (e.g., see Meyers, Durlak, & Wandersman, 2012), needs assessment is central to CTC. This emphasis on the systematic collection and analysis of data to guide prevention activities represents a shift from earlier community-based models, which tended to assume that community members knew instinctively what was best for their residents. The collection of data also helps ensure that decisions are driven by objective facts rather than by the potentially biased assumptions, political pressures, or the particular whims of those participating in the community coalition.

Given its reliance on volunteer members of diverse backgrounds and levels of experience, the CTC system seeks to simplify data collection and needs assessment processes. It requires the collection of epidemiologic data using an anonymous school-wide survey of students, specifically, the CTC Youth Survey or a similar survey that can provide comprehensive data on risk and protective factors. Extensive development work has shown that administration of the CTC Youth Survey will result in reliable and valid community-level indicators of risk, protection, and problem behaviors, including substance use, delinquency, and school problems (Arthur, Hawkins, Pollard, Catalano, & Baglioni, 2002; Glaser, Van Horn, Arthur, Hawkins, & Catalano, 2005). These efforts included a systematic review and selection of multiple survey items previously shown to have adequate psychometric properties in measuring risk and protective factors; cognitive pretesting with public school students to learn how they interpreted the meaning of the items included in the survey; and statistical analyses examining the reliability and validity of the risk and protective factors across gender, race or ethnicity, and age. This work has indicated that information from the survey is applicable to males and females, youth from diverse racial or ethnic groups (African American, Asian American, Latino, Native American, and European American), and students in Grades 6 through 12 (Arthur et al., 2002; Glaser et al., 2005).

Because the CTC Youth Survey was developed for use in middle and high schools, for communities to identify risk and protective factors faced by younger children, they must collect data from additional sources (e.g., archival data from health and social service agencies, community surveys of parents). Communities are encouraged to supplement the self-reported information with archival data that measure such community factors as residential turnover and poverty. The CTC Youth Survey does ask youth to report on some aspects of their communities, such as the presence of crime and disorder, the availability of drugs and weapons, and community norms about teenage substance use. Although these reports can be combined across youth to produce valid measures of community conditions (which have been shown to correlate with information from community key leaders and to predict substance use; see Van Horn, Hawkins, Arthur, & Catalano, 2007), youth may be less able to report on structural conditions, necessitating the collection of data from objective sources like the U.S. Census Bureau. Administrative data also can be collected on behavioral outcomes of concern (e.g., rates of teenage pregnancies or criminal arrests), assuming that such information can be linked to the community in which the coalition is based (e.g., state-level data will not be useful).

During the CTC Community Assessment Training, a subcommittee of the community coalition learns how to administer repeated, cross-sectional surveys and how to interpret these data. Communities are advised to administer the survey in all public middle and high schools in the community. Typically, teachers administer the survey during a single class period, using standardized protocols to ensure anonymity. Items built into the survey and multiple screening criteria are used to identify students who may be dishonest in completing the survey. Responses to each of the risk and protective factors on the survey are aggregated across all participating students, by grade, and are dichotomized to differentiate students reporting high and low levels of each factor (Arthur et al., 2007). In addition, the percentages of students who engage in various substances and delinquent behaviors are reported by grade. Data are aggregated across all participating schools to generate the community-wide profiles of risk and protection.

Communities are guided to focus on risk factors that are particularly elevated and protective factors that are particularly depressed, as well as trends over time (if data from multiple time points are available), and to prioritize those factors for prevention efforts. If profiles differ for students in different grades, different priorities may be identified for these age groups. At a subsequent CTC training workshop attended by the full coalition, the results are discussed and consensus is reached regarding the most important factors to be addressed. Although it can be challenging to collect data and reach communitywide consensus on the specific risk and protective factors to prioritize (e.g., see Fagan, Hawkins, & Catalano, 2008), these are critical components of the CTC system. The creation of a shared understanding of what needs to occur is an important change in the community itself. Consensus builds collective efficacy; helps communities move toward action; generates support for the use of preventive interventions; and should enhance the implementation, sustainability, and effectiveness of these interventions.

Linking Needs Assessments to Implementation, Monitoring, and Evaluation of Preventive Interventions

After agreeing on community priorities, coalition members assess programs, policies, and resources that are currently in place to address the prioritized risk and protective factors. Training and technical assistance are provided to guide the coalition in procedures for conducting interviews and written surveys of service providers. These data are reviewed to assess gaps in prevention services, particularly the degree to which interventions used in the community have been tested and shown to be effective, are being implemented with quality, and are reaching the populations for whom they are most appropriate. On the basis of this review, community coalitions decide whether or not current services should be improved (e.g., by increasing their implementation fidelity or scope), and they reach consensus regarding which new interventions should be implemented to fill identified gaps and address priorities. Achieving community consensus on new interventions to be adopted also can be arduous (for more description, see Fagan, Hawkins, et al., 2008), even when communities have clearly identified needs, information on potential strategies, and technical assistance to facilitate conversations.

The selection of new programs takes place during the CTC Community Plan Training workshop. During this meeting, coalition members are provided with lists and summaries of interventions that have been tested in well-conducted research trials and shown to alter risk and protective factors and reduce problem behaviors. In the past, about 100 programs were provided in the CTC *Prevention Strategies Guide* (http://www.communitiesthatcare.net). That list has become outdated, however, and communities now are guided to select programs listed on the Blueprints for Healthy Youth Development website (http://www.colorado.edu/cspv/blueprints/). Both sources contain information on a range of effective preventive interventions that can be implemented in school, family, and community settings and with youth across development, from programs serving mothers during their pregnancy and their babies' infancy to programs offered during childhood, early to midadolescence, late adolescence, and early adulthood. Effective interventions also have been identified for use with diverse groups, including universal populations as well as high-risk youth and families.

CTC does not mandate that coalitions choose particular interventions to implement or that they offer services to particular types of individuals. The primary emphasis is on ensuring that selected interventions are aligned to the community's particular needs—that is, the new programs should address risk factors that are prevalent and protective factors that are not prevalent in the community, as indicated by the archival data and the CTC Youth Survey. The CTC system recommends that communities provide services to youth of all ages, from early childhood through early adulthood, in which each new intervention is directed at a particular age group or developmental period, and the risk and protective factors targeted by the intervention match those identified in the needs assessment as elevated or depressed by that particular age group. Communities also are encouraged to implement interventions with both low- and high-risk populations—for example, by selecting (a) universal classroom curricula that could be delivered in schools to all children in a particular grade, (b) tutoring or mentoring services that selectively target children who have been identified as facing one or more risk factors (e.g., in the school or family environment), or (c) indicated interventions designed for youth who have begun to engage in problem behaviors but do not yet need treatment. Providing a range of services to youth varying in age and levels of risk and protection ensures that needs are addressed for all types of youth.

The CTC system recommends that communities consider enacting local policies and ordinances (e.g., by restricting alcohol sales in venues accessible to youth) designed to reduce substance use among a large proportion of residents. Unfortunately, to date, relatively few policies have been evaluated rigorously and shown to be effective in lowering drinking and drug use by those under age 18 years, as discussed at the beginning of this chapter (see also Chapter 18, this handbook). Furthermore, many policies that have been demonstrated as effective in reducing substance use, such as increasing taxes on alcohol and raising the minimum age at which it is legal to consume alcohol, cannot be implemented at a local community level.

In CTC, to facilitate the spread of prevention services, coalitions are advised to implement discrete, structured programs to as many members of the eligible population as possible. For example, if a coalition elects to adopt a new parent training intervention, they are guided to move beyond implementation "as usual" (e.g., offering the program to small groups of parents a few times a year) and to seek communitywide participation. To do so, they may encourage all agencies that have contact with parents to deliver or publicize the intervention, ask all program graduates or respected community members to recruit participants, and use multiple media outlets to promote the service and make participation a norm in the community. Likewise, a community that selects a school-based intervention is encouraged to implement the program in all grades for which the intervention is appropriate and in all schools in the community. At this level, implementation of a specific intervention is transformed into a communitywide change strategy with greater potential to achieve communitywide changes.

It is well established that the adoption of even the most effective intervention will not produce its intended outcomes unless it is implemented with fidelity—that is, in accordance with the key components, content, dosage, and manner of delivery specified by program developers (Durlak & DuPre, 2008; Fixsen, Naoom, Blase, Friedman, & Wallace, 2005). The CTC system emphasizes the importance of implementation fidelity and provides training and technical assistance to coalition members in methods for tracking implementation quality. As described elsewhere (Fagan, Hanson, Hawkins, & Arthur, 2008), protocols for assessing implementation include self-assessments by program implementers and observations conducted by coalition members, program administrators, and community members. CTC coalitions review data collected by these raters, provide feedback (positive and negative) to staff regarding their performance, and make implementation changes as necessary to overcome identified barriers to implementation.

As a final step in the feedback and quality improvement process, coalitions administer the CTC Youth Survey every 2 to 3 years to monitor levels of risk, protection, and problem behaviors. These results are added to the original community profile to assess changes over time, particularly whether or not the risk and protective factors targeted by prevention efforts have improved, the degree to which problem behaviors have decreased, and whether or not new areas of concern have emerged. If improvements are not evidenced, communities are advised to make changes to their prevention activities, either enhancing the quality or reach of current services (also using the results of the program monitoring system) or replacing these programs with new interventions. If positive results are evidenced, coalitions can publicize this information, generate greater community support for activities, and seek additional funding for prevention efforts, all of which should promote sustainability of these efforts and the likelihood of long-term effects.

The Effectiveness of the CTC Prevention System

Hypotheses regarding CTC's ability to help transform community practice and produce communitywide changes in youth substance use and related problem behaviors have been tested most rigorously in a randomized controlled evaluation involving 24 communities (Hawkins, Catalano, et al., 2008). In the Community Youth Development Study, small- to medium-size incorporated towns (with a mean population size of about 15,000 residents) with clear geographic boundaries were randomized to implement CTC ($n = 12$) or to a control condition ($n = 12$) in which prevention services operated as usual. For the first 5 years of the study (the efficacy phase), from spring 2003 through spring 2008, each of the 12 intervention communities was provided with training in the CTC model, proactive technical assistance via telephone calls and site visits two to three times per year, and funding for a full-time CTC coordinator. In Years 2 through 5, the CTC sites received up to $75,000 annually to implement tested and effective interventions targeting fifth- to ninth-grade students and their families. Restricting communities to programs for youth in early to midadolescence is not typical in CTC, but focusing efforts on this development period, which precedes the onset and peak of drug use, was considered the best way to observe potential preventive effects on the initiation of problem behaviors during the relatively short period of the study.

Consistent with the CTC system, coalitions selected interventions from a menu that included universal and selective programs (for a list of all 44 options, see Hawkins, Catalano, et al., 2008). Across all 12 CTC communities, 17 different school- and community-based interventions targeting youth, schools, and families were supported using study funding (with an average of about three programs implemented each year in each community, as described in Fagan, Hanson, Hawkins, & Arthur, 2009). In Years 6 through 10, data collection continued in intervention and control communities to assess the sustainability of effects on community practices, coalition functioning, and youth behaviors. No financial assistance and only limited technical assistance was provided to the 12 intervention communities during this phase (Hawkins et al., 2012).

Desired changes in community collaboration and prevention practices were evidenced during the efficacy phase of the trial. According to process evaluation data, intervention sites successfully implemented all components of the CTC system (Fagan et al., 2009). Broad-based coalitions were formed in all 12 intervention communities, and members reported high rates of coalition functioning and support for the CTC system (Quinby et al., 2008). Coalitions implemented preventive interventions that targeted the particular risk and protective factors that were reported as elevated or depressed by youth on the CTC Youth Survey, with different sets of interventions being implemented by different communities. Across intervention communities, these programs were implemented with high levels of fidelity (Fagan et al., 2009). On the basis of reports from a census of service providers in all intervention and control communities, communities utilizing the CTC system were found to implement a significantly greater number of effective interventions (Fagan, Arthur, Hanson, Briney, & Hawkins, 2011). In addition, surveys of key leaders in CTC communities compared with control communities reported greater levels of collaboration (E. C. Brown, Hawkins, Arthur, Briney, & Abbott, 2007) as well as adoption of a science-based framework for prevention that emphasizes needs assessment and evidence-based programming targeting risk and protective factors (E. C. Brown et al., 2007; E. C. Brown, Hawkins, Arthur, Briney, & Fagan, 2011).

Communitywide reductions in student substance use, delinquency, and violence also were evidenced, as based on data from a longitudinal cohort of students representing 76% of all eligible fifth- and sixth-grade students in all 24 communities. Students were surveyed annually beginning in Grade 5 with very high retention rates (over 90%) through Grade 10 (Hawkins et al., 2012). According to the longitudinal cohort data, students in CTC compared with control communities reported significant reductions in the initiation and prevalence of alcohol and other drug use (Hawkins, Brown, et al., 2008; Hawkins et al., 2009). For example, at Grade 8, significantly fewer students in the CTC communities who never had used drugs before Grade 5 had initiated alcohol use, tobacco use, or smokeless tobacco use. Among the full sample, favorable intervention effects also were found, with students in CTC communities reporting lower rates of recent alcohol use, binge drinking, and smokeless tobacco use compared with those in the control communities (Hawkins et al., 2009).

The results of the randomized evaluation indicated that when provided training and technical assistance, communities using the CTC prevention system realized long-term, communitywide reductions in adolescent substance use. We cannot easily pinpoint which specific components of the CTC system were essential for producing change because the randomized controlled trial was designed to determine the degree to which implementation of the system as a whole produced outcomes. That is, the evaluation tested the combination, but not the independent effects, of forming broad-based coalitions, conducting needs assessments, matching the delivery of effective interventions to locally identified risk and protective factors, and monitoring and evaluating prevention activities.

Nonetheless, recent analyses have identified an important community-level mechanism responsible for producing positive changes in youth outcomes (E. C. Brown et al., in press). Approximately 1.5 years after the CTC trial began, community leaders of all major sectors (e.g., mayors, police chiefs, superintendents, heads of social services agencies) in all 24 communities, as well as individuals nominated by leaders as being “most knowledgeable about” local prevention efforts, were asked to report the degree to which their community had adopted a science-based approach to prevention as indicated by use of epidemiologic data to identify and address elevated risk factors and the use of tested and effective preventive interventions. Key leaders’ reports of community adoption of a science-based approach to prevention mediated the effects of CTC on problem behaviors (i.e., substance use and delinquency), as reported by eighth-grade students in the longitudinal panel. This finding indicated that communitywide adoption of a science-based approach to prevention was a community-level change produced by CTC, which, in turn, produced improvements in youth outcomes.

Sustainability of effects on community processes and student outcomes in CTC versus control communities also has been demonstrated. On the basis of surveys of coalition leaders conducted between 1 and 2 years after the provision of training and technical assistance to CTC communities ended, 11 of the 12 coalitions were still operating, two thirds still employed a paid coordinator, and coalition activities still were well aligned with the CTC model (Gloppen, Arthur, Hawkins, & Shapiro, 2012). At this same time point, service providers reported using a significantly greater number of tested, effective programs in intervention versus control communities and were more likely to sustain the evidence-based programs reported 3 years earlier (Fagan, Hanson, Briney, & Hawkins, 2012). Furthermore, 18 months after the intervention phase ended, key leaders continued to report higher levels of adoption of a science-based approach to prevention in CTC compared with control communities (Rhew, Brown, Hawkins, & Briney, 2013).

Communitywide reductions in youth substance use also have been sustained. At Grade 10, analyses of data from the longitudinal panel indicated significantly lower mean levels of risk factors targeted by intervention communities and a slower rate of growth in these factors from Grades 5 through 10 for students in CTC versus control communities. In addition, there were significant reductions in the initiation of alcohol and cigarettes among baseline nonusers and lower levels of recent cigarette use for students in CTC communities compared with control communities. The intervention also had significant prevention effects on delinquency and violence, with students in CTC sites less likely to report involvement in these types of behaviors at Grade 10 (Hawkins et al., 2012).

RECOMMENDATIONS FOR COMMUNITY-BASED DRUG PREVENTION EFFORTS

As discussed earlier in the chapter, based on our systematic review of the evidence (Fagan & Hawkins, 2012), models that rely solely on community mobilization, without guidance, structure, and ample technical assistance for *how* to take action using evidence-based preventive interventions, do not significantly reduce youth alcohol and drug use. Similarly, focusing solely on changing community norms or policies related to youth substance use, such as enforcing underage drinking sales and consumption laws, restricting access to alcohol, or increasing media coverage about the consequences of underage drinking, does not appear to produce significant communitywide reductions in alcohol or drug use by youth under age 18 years (Fagan & Hawkins, 2012). The addition of tested and effective school-based substance use prevention curricula to these communitywide efforts improves outcomes, however. In addition, when prevention programs targeting individual, peer, school, family, and community factors are implemented in a collaborative and coordinated fashion, or in combination with strategies seeking to change community norms and practices, communitywide reductions in youth substance use are more likely.

Taken as a whole, this body of research suggests that the most promising way to change communities is to ask both community members and program developers to work "harder and smarter" in their prevention efforts. At the community level, this requires the active participation of diverse stakeholders in prevention activities and changes in "business as usual," such that efforts are better aligned with scientific evidence about what leads to substance use and which policies and programs are effective for preventing it. Coalitions should engage in careful planning for implementation to ensure that new interventions are a good fit for their community, and comprehensive, local needs assessments can help to identify risk factors that are elevated and protective factors that are depressed within a specific community. The implementation of interventions that have been well tested and shown to be effective also must be prioritized. These programs and policies should seek to reach as many individuals as possible and should be implemented in close adherence to their stated protocols to increase the likelihood of success. Finally, communities should monitor the delivery of their chosen strategies, improve the delivery of interventions when problems are identified, and assess communitywide changes and youth outcomes periodically to refine their prevention practices, celebrate successes, and promote long-term, sustainable changes in desired outcomes.

Empirically, more work must be done to expand scientific evidence of how to effectively reduce substance use and problem behaviors, at both the individual and community levels. Although the number of effective programs available for implementation has been increasing (Fagan & Eisenberg, 2012), the creation and evaluation of more interventions is needed to expand the number of options available to be implemented by communities. Furthermore, given some evidence that intervention effects can vary according to characteristics of participants (e.g., by age, gender, or race or ethnicity), evaluations should seek to identify differences in effectiveness across groups (C. H. Brown & Liao, 1999; Flay et al., 2005). This information then must be shared with practitioners to ensure that appropriate populations are targeted for services.

Additional evaluation of community-based strategies and systems like PROSPER and CTC also is warranted. The results described in this chapter are encouraging, but replication of such findings can increase our confidence in the effects and improve our understanding of exactly how and why these multifaceted systems actually benefit communities. Although we have assessed some of the community-level processes that may affect change in communities using CTC (E. C. Brown et al., in press), additional key questions to explore include the following: how to best train and support community members in their coalition efforts, whether or not different combinations of programs are associated with different outcomes, the degree of reach (i.e., participation) needed to produce communitywide outcomes, and what types of needs assessment tools and methodologies can help identify levels of risk and protection among hard-to-reach populations (e.g., families with very young children, youth who have dropped out of school). Policies intended to have broad effects on community residents must be evaluated, given the limited amount of evidence that such policies can reduce youth substance use.

Evaluation of the financial costs and benefits of community-based prevention efforts is needed. The Washington State Institute of Public Policy (Aos et al., 2011) has demonstrated that when well implemented, many prevention programs are cost beneficial in the long term, particularly given that their costs are offset by savings such as those related to reduced need for drug treatment services and less involvement in the juvenile and criminal justice systems. Sharing this information with communities is likely to positively influence their decisions to adopt effective preventive interventions (Beardslee, Chien, & Bell, 2011;

Catalano et al., 2012). Cost–benefit analyses based on longitudinal data from youth participating in the CTC randomized evaluation trial have indicated a monetary return of $5.30 for every dollar invested in the CTC system (Kuklinski, Briney, Hawkins, & Catalano, 2012). These results are promising not only because they provide further evidence of the effectiveness of the CTC system but also because they suggest that implementation of a coordinated set of effective prevention programs, adopted and monitored by community members working in concert, can produce communitywide changes in youth behaviors in a manner that is cost beneficial to society.

Few cost–benefit analyses of other community-based prevention systems have been conducted, which is understandable given the complexity of these efforts and the varying forms they take across communities. Information about the costs and benefits of community prevention systems is particularly important given that these strategies are likely to be more expensive to implement than discrete prevention policies or programs. At the same time, community-based systems may be more effective in improving youth outcomes compared with single programs or policies because they can target multiple risk factors and reach more individuals with services. If financial benefits are demonstrated, community prevention systems will become even more attractive to communities.

References

Aos, S., Lee, S., Drake, E. K., Pennucci, A., Klima, T., Miller, M. G., & Burley, M. (2011). *Return on investment: Evidence-based options to improve statewide outcomes* (Document No. 11-07-1201). Olympia, WA: Washington State Institute for Public Policy.

Arthur, M. W., & Blitz, C. (2000). Bridging the gap between science and practice in drug abuse prevention through needs assessment and strategic community planning. *Journal of Community Psychology, 28*, 241–255. doi:10.1002/(SICI)1520-6629(200005)28:3<241::AID-JCOP2>3.0.CO;2-X

Arthur, M. W., Briney, J. S., Hawkins, J. D., Abbott, R. D., Brooke-Weiss, B., & Catalano, R. F. (2007). Measuring community risk and protection using the Communities That Care Youth Survey. *Evaluation and Program Planning, 30*, 197–211. doi:10.1016/j.evalprogplan.2007.01.009

Arthur, M. W., Hawkins, J. D., Pollard, J. A., Catalano, R. F., & Baglioni, A. J. (2002). Measuring risk and protective factors for substance use, delinquency, and other adolescent problem behaviors: The Communities That Care Youth Survey. *Evaluation Review, 26*, 575–601.

Backer, T. E., & Guerra, N. G. (2011). Mobilizing communities to implement evidence-based practices in youth violence prevention: The state of the art. *American Journal of Community Psychology, 48*, 31–42. doi:10.1007/s10464-010-9409-7

Beardslee, W. R., Chien, P. L., & Bell, C. C. (2011). Prevention of mental disorders, substance abuse, and problem behaviors: A developmental perspective. *Psychiatric Services, 62*, 247–254. doi:10.1176/appi.ps.62.3.247

Biglan, A., Ary, D. V., Smolkowski, K., Duncan, T., & Black, C. (2000). A randomised controlled trial of a community intervention to prevent adolescent tobacco use. *Tobacco Control, 9*, 24–32. doi:10.1136/tc.9.1.24

Brown, C. H., & Liao, J. (1999). Principles for designing randomized preventive trials in mental health: An emerging developmental epidemiology paradigm. *American Journal of Community Psychology, 27*, 673–710. doi:10.1023/A:1022142021441

Brown, E. C., Hawkins, J. D., Arthur, M. W., Briney, J. S., & Abbott, R. D. (2007). Effects of Communities That Care on prevention services systems: Findings from the Community Youth Development Study at 1.5 years. *Prevention Science, 8*, 180–191. doi:10.1007/s11121-007-0068-3

Brown, E. C., Hawkins, J. D., Arthur, M. W., Briney, J. S., & Fagan, A. A. (2011). Prevention service system transformation using Communities That Care. *Journal of Community Psychology, 39*, 183–201. doi:10.1002/jcop.20426

Brown, E. C., Hawkins, J. D., Rhew, I. C., Shapiro, V. B., Abbott, R. D., Oesterle, S., . . . Catalano, R. F. (in press). Prevention system mediation of Communities That Care: Effects on youth outcomes. *Prevention Science*. doi:10.1007/s11121-013-0413-7

Bry, B. H., McKeon, P., & Pandina, R. J. (1982). Extent of drug use as a function of number of risk factors. *Journal of Abnormal Psychology, 91*, 273–279. doi:10.1037/0021-843X.91.4.273

Catalano, R. F., Fagan, A. A., Gavin, L. E., Greenberg, M. T., Irwin, J., Charles, E., . . . Shek, D. T. L. (2012). Worldwide application of prevention science in adolescent health. *The Lancet, 379*, 1653–1664. doi:10.1016/S0140-6736(12)60238-4

Catalano, R. F., Haggerty, K. P., Hawkins, J. D., & Elgin, J. (2011). Prevention of substance use and substance use disorders: The role of risk and protective factors. In Y. Kaminer & K. C. Winters (Eds.), *Clinical manual of adolescent substance abuse treatment* (pp. 25–63). Washington, DC: American Psychiatric Publishing.

Catalano, R. F., & Hawkins, J. D. (1996). The Social Development Model: A theory of antisocial behavior. In J. D. Hawkins (Ed.), *Delinquency and crime: Current theories* (pp. 149–197). New York, NY: Cambridge University Press.

Coie, J. D., Watt, N. F., West, S. G., Hawkins, J. D., Asarnow, J. R., Marman, H. J., . . . Long, B. (1993). The science of prevention: A conceptual framework and some directions for a national research program. *American Psychologist*, *48*, 1013–1022. doi:10.1037/0003-066X.48.10.1013

Collins, D., Johnson, K., & Becker, B. J. (2007). A meta-analysis of direct and mediating effects of community coalitions that implemented science-based substance abuse prevention interventions. *Substance Use and Misuse*, *42*, 985–1007. doi:10.1080/10826080701373238

Donovan, J. E. (2004). Adolescent alcohol initiation: A review of psychosocial risk factors. *Journal of Adolescent Health*, *35*, e7–e18. doi:10.1016/j.jadohealth.2004.02.003

Durlak, J. A. (1998). Common risk and protective factors in successful prevention programs. *American Journal of Orthopsychiatry*, *68*, 512–520. doi:10.1037/h0080360

Durlak, J. A., & DuPre, E. P. (2008). Implementation matters: A review of the research on the influence of implementation on program outcomes and the factors affecting implementation. *American Journal of Community Psychology*, *41*, 327–350. doi:10.1007/s10464-008-9165-0

Fagan, A. A., Arthur, M. W., Hanson, K., Briney, J. S., & Hawkins, J. D. (2011). Effects of Communities That Care on the adoption and implementation fidelity of evidence-based prevention programs in communities: Results from a randomized controlled trial. *Prevention Science*, *12*, 223–234. doi:10.1007/s11121-011-0226-5

Fagan, A. A., & Eisenberg, N. (2012). Latest developments in the prevention of crime and anti-social behaviour: An American perspective. *Journal of Children's Services*, *7*, 64–72. doi:10.1108/17466661211213689

Fagan, A. A., Hanson, K., Briney, J. S., & Hawkins, J. D. (2012). Sustaining the utilization and high quality implementation of tested and effective prevention programs using the Communities That Care prevention system. *American Journal of Community Psychology*, *49*, 365–377. doi:10.1007/s10464-011-9463-9

Fagan, A. A., Hanson, K., Hawkins, J. D., & Arthur, M. W. (2008). Bridging science to practice: Achieving prevention program fidelity in the Community Youth Development Study. *American Journal of Community Psychology*, *41*, 235–249. doi:10.1007/s10464-008-9176-x

Fagan, A. A., Hanson, K., Hawkins, J. D., & Arthur, M. W. (2009). Translational research in action: Implementation of the Communities That Care prevention system in 12 communities. *Journal of Community Psychology*, *37*, 809–829. doi:10.1002/jcop.20332

Fagan, A. A., & Hawkins, J. D. (2012). Community-based substance use prevention. In B. C. Welsh & D. F. Farrington (Eds.), *Oxford handbook on crime prevention* (pp. 247–268). New York, NY: Oxford University Press.

Fagan, A. A., & Hawkins, J. D. (2013). Preventing substance use, delinquency, violence, and other problem behaviors over the life-course using the Communities That Care System. In C. L. Gibson & M. D. Krohn (Eds.), *Handbook of life-course criminology* (pp. 277–296). New York, NY: Springer-Verlag. doi:10.1007/978-1-4614-5113-6_16

Fagan, A. A., Hawkins, J. D., & Catalano, R. F. (2008). Using community epidemiologic data to improve social settings: The Communities That Care prevention system. In M. Shinn & H. Yoshikawa (Eds.), *The power of social settings: Promoting youth development by changing schools and community programs* (pp. 292–312). New York, NY: Oxford University Press. doi:10.1093/acprof:oso/9780195327892.003.0016

Feinberg, M. E., Greenberg, M. T., Osgood, D. W., Sartorius, J., & Bontempo, D. (2007). Effects of the Communities That Care model in Pennsylvania on youth risk and problem behaviors. *Prevention Science*, *8*, 261–270. doi:10.1007/s11121-007-0073-6

Feinberg, M. E., Jones, D., Greenberg, M. T., Osgood, D. W., & Bontempo, D. (2010). Effects of the Communities That Care model in Pennsylvania on change in adolescent risk and problem behaviors. *Prevention Science*, *11*, 163–171. doi:10.1007/s11121-009-0161-x

Fixsen, D. L., Naoom, S. F., Blase, K. A., Friedman, R. M., & Wallace, F. (2005). *Implementation research: A synthesis of the literature* (FMHI Publication No. 231). Tampa: University of South Florida, Louis de la Parte Florida Mental Health Institute, The National Implementation Research Network.

Flay, B. R. (2000). Approaches to substance use prevention utilizing school curriculum plus social environment change. *Addictive Behaviors*, *25*, 861–885. doi:10.1016/S0306-4603(00)00130-1

Flay, B. R., Biglan, A., Boruch, R. F., Castro, F. G., Gottfredson, D. C., Kellam, S. G., . . . Ji, P. (2005). Standards of evidence: Criteria for efficacy, effectiveness, and dissemination. *Prevention Science*, *6*, 151–175. doi:10.1007/s11121-005-5553-y

Flewelling, R. L., Austin, D., Hale, K., LaPlante, M., Liebig, M., Piasecki, L., & Uerz, L. (2005). Implementing research-based substance abuse prevention in communities: Effects of a coalition-based prevention initiative in Vermont. *Journal of Community Psychology*, *33*, 333–353. doi:10.1002/jcop.20052

Foxcroft, D. R., Ireland, D., Lister-Sharp, D. J., Lowe, G., & Breen, R. (2003). Longer-term primary prevention for alcohol misuse in young people: A systematic review. *Addiction*, *98*, 397–411. doi:10.1046/j.1360-0443.2003.00355.x

Glaser, R. R., Van Horn, M. L., Arthur, M. W., Hawkins, J. D., & Catalano, R. F. (2005). Measurement properties of the Communities That Care Youth Survey across demographic groups. *Journal of Quantitative Criminology*, *21*, 73–102. doi:10.1007/s10940-004-1788-1

Gloppen, K. M., Arthur, M. W., Hawkins, J. D., & Shapiro, V. B. (2012). Sustainability of the Communities That Care prevention system by coalitions participating in the Community Youth Development Study. *Journal of Adolescent Health*, *51*, 259–264. doi:10.1016/j.jadohealth.2011.12.018

Hallfors, D., Cho, H., Livert, D., & Kadushin, C. (2002). Fighting back against substance use: Are community coalitions winning? *American Journal of Preventive Medicine*, *23*, 237–245. doi:10.1016/S0749-3797(02)00511-1

Hawkins, J. D., Brown, E. C., Oesterle, S., Arthur, M. W., Abbott, R. D., & Catalano, R. F. (2008). Early effects of Communities That Care on targeted risks and initiation of delinquent behavior and substance use. *Journal of Adolescent Health*, *43*, 15–22. doi:10.1016/j.jadohealth.2008.01.022

Hawkins, J. D., & Catalano, R. F. (1992). *Communities That Care: Action for drug abuse prevention.* San Francisco, CA: Jossey-Bass.

Hawkins, J. D., Catalano, R. F., & Arthur, M. W. (2002). Promoting science-based prevention in communities. *Addictive Behaviors*, *27*, 951–976. doi:10.1016/S0306-4603(02)00298-8

Hawkins, J. D., Catalano, R. F., Arthur, M. W., Egan, E., Brown, E. C., Abbott, R. D., & Murray, D. M. (2008). Testing Communities That Care: Rationale and design of the Community Youth Development Study. *Prevention Science*, *9*, 178–190. doi:10.1007/s11121-008-0092-y

Hawkins, J. D., Catalano, R. F., & Miller, J. Y. (1992). Risk and protective factors for alcohol and other drug problems in adolescence and early adulthood: Implications for substance abuse prevention. *Psychological Bulletin*, *112*, 64–105. doi:10.1037/0033-2909.112.1.64

Hawkins, J. D., Oesterle, S., Brown, E. C., Arthur, M. W., Abbott, R. D., Fagan, A. A., & Catalano, R. F. (2009). Results of a type 2 translational research trial to prevent adolescent drug use and delinquency: A test of Communities That Care. *Archives of Pediatrics and Adolescent Medicine*, *163*, 789–798. doi:10.1001/archpediatrics.2009.141

Hawkins, J. D., Oesterle, S., Brown, E. C., Monahan, K. C., Abbott, R. D., Arthur, M. W., & Catalano, R. F. (2012). Sustained decreases in risk exposure and youth problem behaviors after installation of the Communities That Care prevention system in a randomized trial. *Archives of Pediatrics and Adolescent Medicine*, *166*, 141–148. doi:10.1001/archpediatrics.2011.183

Hawkins, J. D., Van Horn, M. L., & Arthur, M. W. (2004). Community variation in risk and protective factors and substance use outcomes. *Prevention Science*, *5*, 213–220. doi:10.1023/B:PREV.0000045355.53137.45

Hawkins, J. D., & Weis, J. G. (1985). The social development model: An integrated approach to delinquency prevention. *Journal of Primary Prevention*, *6*, 73–97. doi:10.1007/BF01325432

Kellam, S. G., Ling, X., Merisca, R., Brown, C. H., & Ialongo, N. S. (1998). The effect of the level of aggression in the first grade classroom on the course and malleability of aggressive behavior into middle school. *Development and Psychopathology*, *10*, 165–185. doi:10.1017/S0954579498001564

Kuklinski, M. R., Briney, J. S., Hawkins, J. D., & Catalano, R. F. (2012). Cost-benefit analysis of Communities That Care Outcomes at eighth grade. *Prevention Science*, *13*, 150–161. doi:10.1007/s11121-011-0259-9

Merzel, C., & D'Afflitti, J. (2003). Reconsidering community-based health promotion: Promise, performance, and potential. *American Journal of Public Health*, *93*, 557–574. doi:10.2105/AJPH.93.4.557

Meyers, D. C., Durlak, J. A., & Wandersman, A. (2012). The quality implementation framework: A synthesis of critical steps in the implementation process. *American Journal of Community Psychology*, *50*, 462–480. doi:10.1007/s10464-012-9522-x

Newcomb, M. D., Maddahian, E., & Bentler, P. M. (1986). Risk factors for drug use among adolescents: Concurrent and longitudinal analyses. *American Journal of Public Health*, *76*, 525–531. doi:10.2105/AJPH.76.5.525

O'Connell, M. E., Boat, T., & Warner, K. E. (Eds.). (2009). *Preventing mental, emotional, and behavioral disorders among young people: Progress and possibilities.* Washington, DC: National Academies Press.

Pentz, M. A., Dwyer, J. H., MacKinnon, D. P., Flay, B. R., Hansen, W. B., Wang, E. Y. I., & Johnson, C. A. (1989). A multicommunity trial for primary prevention of adolescent drug abuse. *JAMA*, *261*, 3259–3266. doi:10.1001/jama.1989.03420220073030

Perry, C. L., Komro, K., Veblen-Mortenson, S., Bosma, L. M., Farbakhsh, K., Munson, K. A., . . . Lytle, L. A. (2003). A randomized controlled trial of the middle and junior high school D.A.R.E. and D.A.R.E. Plus programs. *Archives of Pediatrics and Adolescent Medicine*, *157*, 178–184. doi:10.1001/archpedi.157.2.178

Perry, C. L., Williams, C. L., Komro, K. A., Veblen-Mortenson, S., Forster, J. L., Bernstein-Lachter, R., . . . McGovern, P. (2000). Project Northland high school interventions: Community action to reduce adolescent alcohol use. *Health Education and Behavior*, *27*, 29–49. doi:10.1177/109019810002700105

Perry, C. L., Williams, C. L., Veblen-Mortenson, S., Toomey, T. L., Komro, K., Anstine, P. S., . . . Wolfson, M. (1996). Project Northland: Outcomes of a communitywide alcohol use prevention program during early adolescence. *American Journal of Public Health*, *86*, 956–965. doi:10.2105/AJPH.86.7.956

Pollard, J. A., Hawkins, J. D., & Arthur, M. W. (1999). Risk and protection: Are both necessary to understand diverse behavioral outcomes in adolescence? *Social Work Research*, *23*, 145–158. doi:10.1093/swr/23.3.145

Quinby, R., Fagan, A. A., Hanson, K., Brooke-Weiss, B., Arthur, M. W., & Hawkins, J. D. (2008). Installing the Communities That Care prevention system: Implementation progress and fidelity in a randomized controlled trial. *Journal of Community Psychology*, *36*, 313–332. doi:10.1002/jcop.20194

Rhew, I. C., Brown, E. C., Hawkins, J. D., & Briney, J. S. (2013). Sustained effects of the Communities That Care system on prevention service system transformation. *American Journal of Public Health*, *103*, 529–535.

Ringwalt, C., Vincus, A. A., Hanley, S., Ennett, S. T., Bowling, J. M., & Haws, S. (2011). The prevalence of evidence-based drug use prevention curricula in U.S. middle schools in 2008. *Prevention Science*, *12*, 63–69. doi:10.1007/s11121-010-0184-3

Rutter, M. (1985). Resilience in the face of adversity: Protective factors and resistance to psychiatric disorder. *British Journal of Psychiatry*, *147*, 598–611. doi:10.1192/bjp.147.6.598

Sameroff, A. (2006). Identifying risk and protective factors for health child development. In A. Clarke-Stewart & J. Dunn (Eds.), *Families count: Effects on child and adolescent development* (pp. 53–76). Cambridge, England: Cambridge University Press. doi:10.1017/CBO9780511616259.004

Sampson, R. J., Raudenbush, S. W., & Earls, F. (1997). Neighborhoods and violent crime: A multilevel study of collective efficacy. *Science*, *277*, 918–924. doi:10.1126/science.277.5328.918

Saul, J., Duffy, J., Noonan, R., Lubell, K., Wandersman, A., Flaspohler, P., . . . Dunville, R. (2008). Bridging science and practice in violence prevention: Addressing ten key challenges. *American Journal of Community Psychology*, *41*, 197–205. doi:10.1007/s10464-008-9171-2

Schinke, S. P., Tepavac, L., & Cole, K. C. (2000). Preventing substance use among Native American youth: Three-year results. *Addictive Behaviors*, *25*, 387–397. doi:10.1016/S0306-4603(99)00071-4

Sloboda, Z., Pyakuryal, A., Stephens, P. C., Teasdale, B., Forrest, D., Stephens, R. C., & Grey, S. F. (2008). Reports of substance abuse prevention programming available in schools. *Prevention Science*, *9*, 276–287. doi:10.1007/s11121-008-0102-0

Specter, A. (2008). Making youth violence prevention a national priority. *American Journal of Preventive Medicine*, *34*, S3–S4. doi:10.1016/j.amepre.2007.12.018

Spoth, R. L., & Greenberg, M. T. (2011). Impact challenges in community science-with-practice: Lessons from PROSPER on transformative practitioner-scientist partnerships and prevention infrastructure development. *American Journal of Community Psychology*, *48*, 106–119. doi:10.1007/s10464-010-9417-7

Spoth, R. L., Greenberg, M. T., Bierman, K. L., & Redmond, C. (2004). PROSPER Community-University partnership model for public education systems: Capacity-building for evidence-based, competence-building prevention. *Prevention Science*, *5*, 31–39. doi:10.1023/B:PREV.0000013979.52796.8b

Spoth, R. L., Greenberg, M. T., & Turrisi, R. (2008). Preventive interventions addressing underage drinking: State of the evidence and steps towards public health impact. *Pediatrics*, *121*, S311–S336. doi:10.1542/peds.2007-2243E

Spoth, R. L., Guyll, M., Redmond, C., Greenberg, M. T., & Feinberg, M. E. (2011). Six-year sustainability of evidence-based intervention implementation quality by community-university partnerships: The PROSPER study. *American Journal of Community Psychology*, *48*, 412–425. doi:10.1007/s10464-011-9430-5

Spoth, R. L., Redmond, C., Clair, S., Shin, C., Greenberg, M. T., & Feinberg, M. E. (2011). Preventing substance misuse through community–university partnerships randomized controlled trial outcomes 4½ years past baseline. *American Journal of Preventive Medicine*, *40*, 440–447. doi:10.1016/j.amepre.2010.12.012

Spoth, R. L., Redmond, C., Shin, C., Greenberg, M. T., Clair, S., & Feinberg, M. E. (2007). Substance use outcomes at eighteen months past baseline from the PROSPER community-university partnership trial. *American Journal of Preventive Medicine*, *32*, 395–402. doi:10.1016/j.amepre.2007.01.014

Spoth, R., Rohrbach, L. A., Greenberg, M. T., Leaf, P., Brown, C. H., Fagan, A., . . . Society for Prevention Research Type 2 Translational Task Force. (2013). Addressing core challenges for the next generation of type 2 translation research and systems: The translation science to population impact (TSci impact) framework. *Prevention Science*, *14*, 319–351. doi:10.1007/s11121-012-0362-6

Steinberg, L. (2001). We know some things: Parent–adolescent relationships in retrospect and prospect.

Journal of Research on Adolescence, *11*, 1–19. doi:10.1111/1532-7795.00001

Stevenson, J. F., & Mitchell, R. E. (2003). Community-level collaboration for substance abuse prevention. *Journal of Primary Prevention*, *23*, 371–404. doi:10.1023/A:1021397825740

Stith, S., Pruitt, I., Dees, J., Fronce, M., Green, N., Som, A., & Linkh, D. (2006). Implementing community-based prevention programming: A review of the literature. *Journal of Primary Prevention*, *27*, 599–617. doi:10.1007/s10935-006-0062-8

Tobler, N. S., & Stratton, H. H. (1997). Effectiveness of school-based drug prevention programs: A meta-analysis of the research. *Journal of Primary Prevention*, *18*, 71–128. doi:10.1023/A:1024630205999

Van Horn, M. L., Hawkins, D., Arthur, M. W., & Catalano, R. F. (2007). Assessing community effects on adolescent substance use and delinquency. *Journal of Community Psychology*, *35*, 925–946. doi:10.1002/jcop.20204

Wagenaar, A. C., Murray, D. M., Gehan, J. P., Wolfson, M., Forster, J. L., Toomey, T. L., . . . Jones-Webb, R. (2000). Communities Mobilizing For Change on Alcohol: Outcomes from a randomized community trial. *Journal of Studies on Alcohol*, *61*, 85–94.

Wagenaar, A. C., & Perry, C. L. (1994). Community strategies for the reduction of youth drinking: Theory and application. *Journal of Research on Adolescence*, *4*, 319–345. doi:10.1207/s15327795jra0402_8

Wandersman, A. (2003). Community science: Bridging the gap between science and practice with community-centered models. *American Journal of Community Psychology*, *31*, 227–242. doi:10.1023/A:1023954503247

Wandersman, A., & Florin, P. (2003). Community intervention and effective prevention. *American Psychologist*, *58*, 441–448. doi:10.1037/0003-066X.58.6-7.441

Weitzman, E. R., Nelson, T. F., Lee, H., & Wechsler, H. (2004). Reducing drinking and related harms in college: Evaluation of the “A Matter of Degree” program. *American Journal of Preventive Medicine*, *27*, 187–196.

Woolf, S. H. (2008). The power of prevention and what it requires. *JAMA*, *299*, 2437–2439. doi:10.1001/jama.299.20.2437

Yin, R. K., Kaftarian, S. J., Yu, P., & Jansen, M. A. (1997). Outcomes from CSAP’s Community Partnership Program: Findings from the National Cross-Site Evaluation. *Evaluation and Program Planning*, *20*, 345–355. doi:10.1016/S0149-7189(97)00014-1

Part VII

MEDIA CAMPAIGNS AND THEIR IMPACT

CHAPTER 20

SURVIVAL OF PUBLIC HEALTH SOCIAL MARKETING CAMPAIGNS: LESSONS LEARNED FROM TOBACCO

Jennifer K. Ibrahim

This chapter examines the creation and sustainability of public health social marketing campaigns in the face of political opposition and the influence of special interest groups. Using tobacco control media campaigns to illustrate key points, the chapter relies on brief case studies of several states and one national media campaign to discuss efforts to limit the effectiveness of social marketing efforts. The chapter also introduces several suggestions for health officials engaging social marketing campaigns and advocates specific methods for responding to them successfully.

Social marketing can be a powerful public health tool to prevent high-risk behaviors, including substance use, alcohol abuse, and tobacco consumption (Grier & Bryant, 2005). In the same way that peer pressure can be a powerful driver of experimentation and initiation of high-risk behaviors at the individual level, social marketing (also referred to here as media campaigns) can be a way to modify beliefs and social norms at the population level (Wakefield, Loken, & Hornik, 2010). Social marketing efforts can take several different forms, ranging from community-level programs to state-level media campaigns and nationwide warning labels. In the case of tobacco, since the 1964 Surgeon General's Report when the hazards of tobacco were first officially confirmed in the United States (U.S. Department of Health, Education, and Welfare, 1964), health officials have been seeking ways to inform and educate the public about the dangers of smoking (and later on, the dangers of exposure to secondhand smoke for nonsmokers) as well as to counter the tobacco industry's marketing efforts (Centers for Disease Control and Prevention, 2013). Following the Framework Convention on Tobacco Control (World Health Organization, 2003), nations around the globe began implementing graphic warning labels on packs of cigarettes; subsequent evaluations have shown that larger text and graphic warnings are more effective in eliciting cognitive and behavioral change than are text-only warnings (the only warnings used in the United States as of 2014; Borland et al., 2009; Hammond, Fong, McNeill, Borland, & Cummings, 2006). However, the development, implementation, and survival of even the most effective population-based public health efforts in the face of the tobacco industry are not easy to sustain and not always successful.

The purpose of this chapter is to consider the creation and sustainability of effective media campaigns in the face of political opposition and the influence of special interest groups. A full discussion of the effectiveness and the messaging styles of substance use media campaigns is given in Chapters 21 and 22. The present chapter focuses on tobacco-control media campaigns as an illustration and uses several brief, state-level case studies to discuss efforts to weaken or destroy tobacco-control media campaigns and the lessons learned from observing those efforts.

http://dx.doi.org/10.1037/14550-021
Handbook of Adolescent Drug Use Prevention: Research, Intervention Strategies, and Practice, L. M. Scheier (Editor)

The decision to focus on tobacco is fueled in part by the astonishing insights generated by the release of internal tobacco industry documents as part of the 1998 Master Settlement Agreement (National Association of Attorneys General, 1998). No similar revelations would be available in considering alcohol and other substance use media efforts. The chapter first provides a historical context for public health media campaigns. Next, the chapter examines several state case studies of tobacco media campaigns. The chapter then ends with a discussion of the broader lessons learned and the strategies that can be used by public health officials and advocates to defend and support public health social marketing campaigns.

ONCE UPON A TIME . . . A HISTORICAL CONTEXT OF MEDIA CAMPAIGNS

In 1949, the Federal Communications Commission (FCC) decided that all licensed radio and television stations were obligated to present both sides of a controversial issue. Named the "Fairness Doctrine," this law was created to ensure that all sides of an issue would be given access to the airwaves, even if one side could not afford to pay for access (Federal Communications Commission, 1948). In 1967, when the FCC declared cigarette advertising "controversial" (*Banzhaf v. Federal Communications Commission*, 1968), it provided antitobacco advertising airtime to provide accurate information on the dangers of tobacco use and to counter the marketing efforts of the multimillion-dollar tobacco industry. Although free public service announcements had previously been aired, they were rare and generally not given prime-time radio slots and thus reached a smaller segment of the population. Between 1967 and 1970, the Fairness Doctrine resulted in an estimated $75 million in free airtime for public health antismoking messages (Hamilton, 1972); there was an almost immediate drop in cigarette consumption, largely attributed to the media messages (Glantz, 1999; Hamilton, 1972).

As a result of the drop in tobacco consumption, the tobacco industry decided that it was worth dropping traditional broadcast cigarette advertising to reduce the equal time afforded antitobacco advertising (Snitzer, 1969) and focus their marketing efforts elsewhere. Between 1970 and 1971, cigarette advertising decreased by 20% to 30%, thereby also decreasing airtime for antismoking messages; surveillance data showed an increase in cigarette consumption at the same time (Hamilton, 1972). Then, beginning in January 1970, the FCC ordered the removal of all forms of cigarette advertising on television and radio (U.S. Food and Drug Administration, 1996). On its face, the removal of cigarette advertising was viewed as a public health victory because such legislative action would mean less public exposure to tobacco advertising on the television and radio airwaves. However, by removing its own advertisements, the tobacco industry eliminated antitobacco advertisements as well. With the loss of direct broadcast advertising, the tobacco industry shifted its advertising efforts elsewhere, such as sports sponsorship (Federal Trade Commission, 2011). Although no longer directly "advertising" on television, the tobacco industry logos and other tobacco-related images appeared on television during broadcast sporting events. The public health community did not have the resources to buy counter advertising on billboards, in magazines, and at other venues. Along with the industry's shift in marketing tactics, there occurred a rise in the prevalence rates of tobacco use once again (U.S. Food and Drug Administration, 1996).

With the elimination of tobacco-control advertisements at the national level in 1970, social marketing efforts shifted to the state level. Beginning in the mid-1980s, states began to establish tobacco-control programs, many of which included paid media campaigns of varying sizes. The states served as a quasi-laboratory to test antitobacco messaging and placement; they also served as a venue for the tobacco industry to test strategies to offset media campaigns (Ibrahim & Glantz, 2007). Minnesota was the first state to implement a statewide tobacco-control media campaign and also served as the first illustration of how political, economic, and legal challenges were made against the campaign in an attempt to weaken or destroy it.

Minnesota

In 1982, the Minnesota Commissioner of Health convened the Technical Advisory Committee on

Nonsmoking and Health to formulate recommendations for the promotion of nonsmoking and healthy individuals, including a communications plan (Minnesota Department of Public Health, 1984b). As the plan was being finalized, the Tobacco Institute, a lobbying arm for the tobacco industry headquartered in Washington, DC, characterized Minnesota's plan as "a revolutionary attack on our industry" (Brozek, 1985). The Tobacco Institute intended to destroy the Minnesota plan by claiming that it was "unnecessary, expensive, and impractical" and to de-legitimize it by questioning the validity of the underlying research (Minnesota Department of Public Health, 1984a). The Tobacco Institute turned to collaboration with third-party tobacco industry allies, such as Minnesota business and labor coalitions. The intent was to secure false estimates from advertising firms to claim that the Health Department's budget for the media campaign was too low and far more taxpayer dollars would be needed to support antitobacco media advocacy in the hopes of turning public support for the campaign into opposition (Minnesota Department of Public Health, 1984a).

The tobacco industry allies also claimed that state-level efforts duplicated national-level media efforts. Ironically, the national campaign referred to was actually run by the tobacco companies to discourage youth from smoking; it was called "Helping Youth Decide" (HYD; Landman, Ling, & Glantz, 2002; Mozingo, 1984; Minnesota Department of Public Health, 1984a). Targeted mailings were sent through the Tobacco Institute to "state legislators, educators, and allies" seeking endorsement of the HYD program (Minnesota Department of Public Health, 1984a). While being publicly touted as a program to prevent smoking by youth, it was regarded by the tobacco industry as a "legislative program" to assist with political efforts to counter tobacco control ("Helping Youth Decide," 1986). In the public's eye, a seemingly positive media campaign run by a special interest group may be viewed (on the surface) as socially responsible, but it is necessary to look below the surface to find underlying evidence or evaluations of effect; such "goodwill" campaigns can often be marketing for the product in disguise.

The tobacco industry also worked to shift the debate away from health to "areas in which we have the most credible arguments, e.g., economics, government intervention, etc." (Minnesota Department of Public Health, 1984a). To do so, the tobacco industry staged several editorial roundtable discussions involving representatives from Minnesota businesses, labor, education, and police groups. The meetings included discussion of the impact of engaging in such a plan, mobilization of voters to speak out against such government intrusion, and demonstration that a statewide media campaign was not necessary in light of numerous national programs already in place and not financed with Minnesota taxpayer dollars. Moreover, "local efforts are duplicative, a waste of taxpayers' money and unnecessary" (Minnesota Department of Public Health, 1984a). All of these strategies were planned or in action before the media campaign ever began, in the hopes of preventing the campaign from ever materializing. A key to the tobacco company efforts was to work behind the scenes so as not to ruin their public image; if health advocates are aware of such tactics, it is in their best interest to reveal such deceptive practices to the public.

In May 1985, the Minnesota State Legislature passed the Omnibus Act, which outlined funding and administrative responsibilities to implement the tobacco-control plan, with a cigarette tax increase partly allocated to public health programs including tobacco control (Minnesota Department of Health, 1989). The legislation also authorized the Commissioner of Health to run a long-term public communications campaign to promote nonsmoking (Minnesota Department of Health, 1987). From 1985 to 1990, the Department of Health ran a media campaign to promote nonsmoking among youth ages 8 to 18 years (Minnesota Department of Health, 1987, 1989). Media efforts at this time were focused on preventing smoking, but over time, messaging changed to focus on the tobacco industry's deceptive business practices (Lavack, 2001; Mahood, 2004).

Beginning in 1988, the tobacco industry successfully recruited new allies from several Minnesota business and labor organizations within specific legislative districts to build up grassroots political opposition to the antismoking media campaign

(Brozek & Nelson, 1988). The tobacco industry also worked diligently to secure political allies, intensifying campaign contributions and lobbying after the start of the first media campaign in 1986 (Tsoukalas, Ibrahim, & Glantz, 2003). The tobacco industry spent about $63,000 per year, on average, for lobbying from1980 through 1985, but it spent more than three times as much while the first media campaign was in full swing (1987–1992), averaging about $230,000 annually (Tsoukalas et al., 2003). In 1990, the legislature reduced the tobacco-control program's budget from $1.5 million to $1 million (Minnesota Department of Health, 1991). The governor used the state health department's successes in reducing the rate of smoking to recommend the cut in order to "meet the state budget shortfall and to pay for drug-prevention efforts" (Parker, 1990). In 1993, Governor Carlson, who received nearly $5,000 in tobacco contributions from 1989 through 1993 (Tsoukalas et al., 2003), eliminated the antismoking media campaign altogether, claiming a state fiscal crisis; in fact, the "crisis" was over the size of the reserve fund (McGrath, 1993).

The conclusion of the nation's first statewide tobacco-control media campaign was not without consequence. The Centers for Disease Control and Prevention (2013) concluded that while the Minnesota Plan, including the first antismoking media campaign, was in place (1985–1992), per capita tobacco in Minnesota consumption declined 26%, more than the national average (Gordon & Hamburger, 1999). After the program was ended (1993–1997), per capita consumption in Minnesota increased 3.1%, whereas the national rate decreased (Gordon & Hamburger, 1999).

California

As Minnesota's tobacco campaign was slowly being dismantled, California was just getting started on implementing social marketing efforts to prevent and reduce tobacco use. The California Tobacco Control Program was created in 1988 as a result of Proposition 99, a voter initiative that increased the state excise tax on cigarettes by $0.25 per pack and allocated 20% of the revenues to programs to reduce smoking (Begay & Glantz, 1991; Glantz & Balbach, 2000). A central component of the new statewide tobacco-control program, intended to reduce tobacco use through the promotion of an antitobacco social norm, was a media campaign administered by the California Tobacco Control Program (n.d.) of the state's Department of Public Health. The media campaign included television, radio, print, billboards, transit, and print, with messages on the tobacco industry practices, secondhand smoke, addiction, cessation, cigarette additives, smokeless tobacco, general health, pregnancy, and prevention among youth (California Tobacco Control Program, n.d.). Early on, the media campaign invested substantial resources in exposing how the tobacco industry manipulated the public to smoke and interfered with the policy-making process to create a protobacco industry policy environment (California Tobacco Control Program, n.d.; C. Stevens, personal communication, October 15, 2002).

One of the elements that helped to maintain media efforts in the early days was political willingness to delegate authority to administer the media campaign to the director of the Department of Health Services; Governor Deukmejian did not play a role in message development or advertising approval, so there were fewer opportunities for political interference by the tobacco industry. Health Director Kizer was also a strong supporter of the media campaign, obtaining the necessary contracts issued to implement the campaign in an expeditious fashion (Glantz, 1999). There was a short period of 59 days between the time the governor signed Proposition 99 implementing legislation and the time when the Department of Health Services released the request for bids from advertising agencies for the media campaign (California Department of Health Services, 2003).

In January 1989, the Los Angeles advertising firm of keye/donna/pearlstein was selected to develop the media campaign and the first antitobacco advertisements were run four months later (Glantz & Balbach, 2000). In addition to the rapid start of the media campaign, the content of the first advertisement was also important. Rather than using a health message, the advertising agency decided to directly address the practices of the tobacco companies. Paul Keye, the advertising agency principal, explained that the tobacco companies were not the original focus for content but, as they began to develop materials and saw the arguments from the wealthy tobacco companies, they were irritated and decided to focus on revealing those elements (Keye, 1993).

The first antitobacco advertisement that was aired was called "Industry Spokesman" and portrayed a smoke-filled boardroom of tobacco industry executives and the leader saying,

> Gentlemen, gentlemen. The tobacco industry has a very serious multi-billion dollar problem. We need more cigarette smokers. Pure and simple. Every day, 2,000 Americans stop smoking and another 1,110 also quit. Actually, technically they die. That means that this business needs 3,000 fresh new volunteers every day. So, forget about all that cancer, heart disease, stroke stuff. We're not in this for our health. (S. Glantz, personal communication, October 1, 2004)

This blunt approach had never been used before, and it infuriated the tobacco industry. Tobacco experts quickly reacted by considering legal action against the media campaign (Ibrahim & Glantz, 2006). The power of the ad was that it turned the tobacco industry executives' own words (as secured from internal tobacco industry documents) on themselves; the public was given a firsthand look at what the industry thought of their customers. On April 18, 1990, just 8 days after Industry Spokesman first aired, Kurt Malmgren, senior vice president of state activities for the Tobacco Institute, wrote to Samuel Chilcote Jr., president of the Tobacco Institute:

> As previously reported, [the Tobacco Institute's national legal counsel] Covington and Burling and California legal counsel have been reviewing possible grounds for a legal attack on the ad program. Among the possible bases for suit that have been reviewed are that the ad campaign is an improper expenditure of funds under Prop 99 and AB 75, that it is defamatory, that it is deceptive advertising, and presents First Amendment concerns.
>
> Aside from tactical questions as to the desirability of pursuing any legal action, the considered judgment of counsel here and on the ground in California is that there is no basis for a suit which would have a realistic chance of success.
>
> It is also our considered opinion that the industry should not attempt a "dollar-for-dollar" response in the media. Our goal is to keep the advertisements—not the tobacco industry—at the center of the controversy. If the industry attempts to meet the Department of Health Services head on in the media, the controversy is likely to shift from the advertisements to the industry. (Malmgren, 1990, p. 3)

The tobacco industry realized that a direct and public attack on the media campaign would be counterproductive and that there was not sufficient legal ground for such an attack. Reminiscent of efforts in Minnesota (Tsoukalas et al., 2003), the tobacco industry recruited allies and used the state's fiscal crisis to enable third parties to divert the media campaign's funds. In a memo from Terry Eagan from the Government Affairs Division of Philip Morris USA to Roger Mozingo in the State Government Relations Division of R.J. Reynolds, Eagan wrote,

> The tobacco industry has decided that the timing is excellent for an attempt to divert money from the antismoking media campaign into other programs that are doomed to suffer because of the current fiscal crisis. . . . Currently a host of groups interested in chasing the media money have surfaced. These groups include: the counties (from both urban and rural perspectives), the Black Health Network (walk-in clinics), the California Health Federation (clinics), the Department of Education (defending their existing tobacco revenue

> sources), the doctors, the hospitals, the dentists, and the ambulance operators. Literally dozens of other interest groups can be expected to surface when the money goes into play. (Philip Morris Companies Inc. Inter-Office Correspondence, 1990)

The tobacco industry was not successful in defunding the media campaign. In fact, the media campaign had received an almost $2 million increase in funding, from $14.3 million in 1990–1991 to $16.0 million in 1991–1992 (California Tobacco Control Program, 2002). However, newly elected Republican governor Pete Wilson, who was known to be a tobacco ally (Philip Morris Companies Inc. Inter-Office Correspondence, 1990), took action to reduce the number of ads that were being produced (California Tobacco Control Program, 2002) and in his 1992–1993 fiscal year (FY) budget, he suspended funds for the media campaign, claiming that the media campaign was of "secondary" significance (California Department of Finance, 1992) and lacked credible evidence for its efficacy. Four days after the budget was introduced, evidence from the California Tobacco Survey indicated that there was a 17% decrease in the percentage of adult smokers in California since Proposition 99 began, with the media campaign being a major program component (Pierce, 1992). From this example, it is easy to see that special-interest dollars and political allies can be a major driving force for decision making, even in the face of evidence to demonstrate effect.

After the Department of Health Services put the media contract out for rebidding in 1991, the Wilson administration declined to sign it (C. Stevens, personal communication, October 15, 2002). On February 21, 1992, the American Lung Association fought back by filing a lawsuit against Governor Wilson and the Director of the Department of Health Services, Molly Coye, stating that by preventing the advertising contract from being signed, they were violating Proposition 99, which stated that the state would run an antitobacco media campaign (Glantz & Balbach, 2000). On April 24, 1992, Judge James Ford of the Sacramento Superior Court ruled that Governor Wilson did not have the authority to take funds that had been appropriated for one purpose and use them for another. Following the court ruling, the Department of Health Services was permitted to sign the contract with the advertising agency on May 29, 1992 (C. Stevens, personal communication, October 15, 2002). The staunch and highly public opposition by health advocates to the bureaucratic tinkering with the tobacco-control social marketing was a major factor in the sustainability of the media campaign. Although this was a win for Californians, the courts having upheld the will of the people as demonstrated in the initial ballot initiative, it is important to keep in mind that not all states have this mechanism for advancing policy.

To further encumber the process, Governor Wilson implemented a formal review process over the media campaign by the Health and Welfare Agency (which includes the Department of Health Services) and the governor's office. In 1996, the Department of Health Services, under Governor Wilson, prohibited the use of the following four terms in the development of advertisements: "tobacco industry," "profit," "nicotine addiction," and "lies" (Glantz & Balbach, 2000). The reduction in the size and aggressiveness of the campaign was associated with a reduction in the rate of decline in cigarette consumption (and reduction in rate of decline of associated deaths from heart disease; Fichtenberg & Glantz, 2000). This reduction in effectiveness after 1994 was associated with 840 million packs of cigarettes (worth about $1.2 billion to the tobacco industry) being smoked between 1994 and 1998 that would not have been smoked otherwise. The same reduced effectiveness was associated with more than 15,000 deaths from heart disease that might not have occurred had the program remained as effective as it was between 1989 and 1994 (Fichtenberg & Glantz, 2000; Glantz & Balbach, 2000; Healton, 2001). The ability to quantify the effects and present them in clear terms is an important element in defending tobacco-control media campaigns; without this type of communication, it allows special interests to infer as they wish.

A consortium conducting an independent evaluation in 1998 found that the media campaign increased young people's belief that the tobacco industry was working to get kids addicted to cigarettes and recommended that the media campaign educate the public about the negative impact of tobacco marketing (Independent Evaluation Consortium, 1998b). A second evaluation revealed that almost all youth and adults were exposed to the media campaign in 1998 and that the exposure was significantly greater in 1998 than in 1996. Likewise, the evaluation also found that exposure to the messages of the media campaign was associated with more negative attitudes toward the tobacco industry and more support among youth for policies restricting tobacco marketing (Independent Evaluation Consortium, 1998a).

Governor Wilson's efforts to eliminate or reduce the effectiveness of the media campaign continued until his last days in office when, in the summer of 1998, he chose not to approve produced advertisements for placement and, instead, left them to newly elected Democratic governor Gray Davis, who took office in January 1999 (personal communication, October 15, 2002). Governor Davis reversed Wilson's ban on attacks on the tobacco industry after complaints from health advocates, but the number of advertisements focused on the tobacco industry's behavior remained relatively small and the cumbersome process for approving advertisements remained in place (Givel, Dearlove, & Glantz, 2001). Furthermore, the media campaign's budget was reduced from $23.3 million in 1998–99 to $19.6 million in 1999–2000, partly because of declining Proposition 99 revenues associated with lower cigarette consumption. While Governor Davis did not try to cut funds allocated to the media campaign, he refused to use funds from the $500 million allocated to California from the annual Master Settlement Agreement payments.

In March 2001, the American Heart Association and Americans for Nonsmokers' Rights launched a lobbying and newspaper campaign to strengthen California's Tobacco Control Program, specifically earmarking the media campaign to counter the effects of the tobacco industry's marketing and promotion. It was an important and effective strategy for public health officials and advocates to engage the public in these types of issues, particularly when it was the will of the people (as demonstrated through the voter initiative) to reduce tobacco use. In response, Governor Davis increased the funding for the media campaign to $45.3 million for FY 2000–2001 and FY 2001–2002 by releasing funds that had been tied up in litigation from the challenges brought by health groups against the diversions of funds from the Health Education Account during the Wilson administration (Givel & Glantz, 2001). However, subsequent budgets continued to reduce funds for the media campaign (California Department of Finance, 2001, 2002).

On April 1, 2003, R. J. Reynolds and Lorillard sued the State of California, claiming that the media campaign had violated their First Amendment rights, interfered with their right to a fair trial, and tarnished their reputation (*R. J. Reynolds Tobacco Company v. Diana M. Bonta*, 2003a). After a year-long legal battle, on September 28, 2004, the Ninth Circuit Court of Appeals rejected the tobacco companies' argument, saying, "A mere link between an excise tax and a government-sponsored advertising campaign, absent a claim that either the tax or the advertising is unconstitutional, does not violate the First Amendment" (*R. J. Reynolds Tobacco Company v. Diana M. Bonta*, 2003b). The other legal arguments brought by the tobacco companies were rejected as well. In this instance, it was crucial that health officials fully understood the legal authority granted through Proposition 99 and were willing to fight for it. Despite nominally being protected by the fact that the voters enacted Proposition 99, strong and repeated political and legal interventions by the health advocates in California were required to keep the program alive and aggressive.

Arizona

The experience in Arizona is an example of the tobacco industry's efforts to weaken efforts from the tobacco-control program's inception by limiting its scope. Voters in Arizona passed Proposition 200 on November 8, 1994, increasing the cigarette excise tax by $0.40 per pack, and dedicated 23% of the new revenues to a health education account for tobacco prevention and education programs (Bialous & Glantz, 1997). Republican governor Fife Symington and Senate President John Greene (R-Phoenix), both recipients of tobacco campaign contributions (Bialous & Glantz, 1997, 1999), opposed the creation of Arizona's Tobacco Education and Prevention Program (AzTEPP), stating that the tax proposed by Proposition 200 should be handled by the legislature, not the public via voter initiative (Bialous & Glantz, 1999). In April 1994, during a meeting with health advocates, Governor Symington and Senator Greene threatened the removal of nonprofit status and the blocking of any future legislation proposed by the health advocates who spearheaded Proposition 200, which included the American Heart Association, the American Lung Association, the American Cancer Society, and the Arizona for a Healthy Future Coalition (Bush, 1994a, 1994b; Cannella, 1994).

After failing to defeat the passage of Proposition 200, Governor Symington and Senator Greene worked to weaken AzTEPP through membership on the Tobacco Use Prevention Advisory Committee (TUPAC), the state commission that provided oversight for the tobacco control program. HB 2275, the implementing legislation for Proposition 200 (Arizona State Legislature, 1995), required that TUPAC be composed of the director of the Arizona Department of Health Services, two individuals appointed by the governor, four individuals appointed by the president of the Senate, and four individuals appointed by the speaker of the House. Governor Symington's appointees were from the Arizona Retailers Association and the Golden Eagle Distributors Association, both parties that have financial interests in tobacco (Bialous & Glantz, 1999). Senator Greene appointed Senators Guz Arzberger and Janice Brewer, both of whom were supporters of the tobacco industry (Bialous & Glantz, 1997).

An antitobacco media campaign was developed and implemented in December 1995. Under HB 2275 (Arizona State Legislature, 1995), the Arizona Department of Health Services was charged with the authority to oversee the media campaign. Rather than the broad approach used in California, the Arizona Department of Health Services severely limited the campaign, in both audience and message. The Department of Health Services determined that the media campaign should not address nicotine addiction and that the "target population of the media program during the first year of the contract shall be pre-adolescents and adolescents, pregnant women and their partners" (Administrative and Financial Services—Procurement Office, 1995; Bialous & Glantz, 1997, 1999). Given that only a small fraction of the population is pregnant at any given time (about 104 women per 1,000 women, U.S. data; Ventura et al., 2001) and a youth-focused advertising approach is unlikely to influence the majority of smokers who are adults (Hill, 1999), this was not considered the most effective approach to use in administering the media campaign. It was not until 1998 that the Health Department broadened the scope of the media campaign and began addressing adult cessation, in addition to pregnant women and children (Bialous & Glantz, 1997). Despite the narrow focus of the media campaign, Proposition 200 was associated with a decline in Arizona's tobacco use prevalence from 23.1% in 1996 to 18.3% in 1999 (Porter et al., 2001).

Florida

Following the lead of the attorney general in Mississippi in 1994, the Attorney General of Florida filed a lawsuit against the tobacco industry to cover the costs associated with treating Florida's Medicaid patients for tobacco-related illnesses. The intent was to fund smoking cessation programs, restrict tobacco marketing, and fund an antitobacco education program (*The State of Florida v. The American Tobacco Company*, 1995). Florida's case was settled on August 25, 1997, with the tobacco industry agreeing to pay $11.3 billion to the State of Florida over 25 years and provide $200 million for a 2-year-long Tobacco Pilot Program, "the elements of which shall be aimed specifically at the reduction of the use of Tobacco Products by persons under the age of 18 years" (*The State of Florida v. The American Tobacco Company*, 1997).

Having learned certain lessons in California, the tobacco industry worked to restrict the target audience of the campaign by incorporating language in the settlement stating,

> the $200 million amount payable by Settling Defendants in support of the Pilot Program shall be used only after approval by the Court and at the rate

> of approximately $100 million per 12-month period for general enforcement, media, educational and other programs directed to the underage users or potential underage users of Tobacco Products. (*The State of Florida v. The American Tobacco Company*, 1997)

The industry sought to prevent the media campaign from highlighting tobacco industry conduct by including a "vilification clause" that stated that funds "shall not be directed against the tobacco companies or any particular tobacco company or companies or any particular brand of Tobacco Products" (*The State of Florida v. The American Tobacco Company*, 1997).

Governor Lawton Chiles (D), an enthusiastic supporter of the lawsuit (Givel & Glantz, 2000), took on the task of creating a Tobacco Pilot Program within the governor's office in 1998 in hopes of deterring any efforts by the tobacco companies or protobacco forces to undermine such an effort. As in the California program, this high priority in the administration cleared the bureaucratic way to put an aggressive antitobacco marketing program in place quickly. The first step in the program's creation was the Governor's Summit on Tobacco Education of more than 600 youth participants, at which they decided on five components for the program, including youth programs and community partnerships, education and training, marketing and communications, enforcement, and research and evaluation (Givel & Glantz, 1999). Health officials who carefully considered the target audience for the media campaign were wise to bring youth into the development phase to ensure that the messages would resonate well with youth.

The objectives of the marketing component of the tobacco-control program emphasized maintaining tobacco-free youth, informing youth of the dangers of secondhand smoke and the addictive nature of tobacco, creating awareness of the Tobacco Pilot Program, linking popular athletes and teams with antitobacco messages, deglamorizing tobacco use, developing a communication network on the Internet, and helping youth to see that peer pressure to smoke can be successfully countered (Givel & Glantz, 1999). The advertising firm of Crispin, Porter and Bogusky from Miami, Florida, worked with youth to develop a campaign that would effectively speak to youth. The result was that youth clearly stated that they wanted the truth, facts, and not to be manipulated through social marketing by the tobacco industry (Hicks, 2001).

Although the Florida settlement vilification clause prevented the campaign from attacking any particular tobacco company (*The State of Florida v. The American Tobacco Company*, 1997), the campaign still adopted the powerful theme of "Truth" with the tagline "Their brand is lies. Our brand is Truth" (Givel & Glantz, 1999). *Whose* brand was left purposefully vague. Although the campaign could not directly attack the tobacco industry, it featured phone calls asking industry spokespersons embarrassing questions and directly attacked the industry's support network, including advertising agencies and scientists.

The vilification clause was lifted in September 1998 when the State of Texas settled its lawsuit against the tobacco industry in a way that did not include this restrictive language (*The State of Texas v. The American Tobacco Company*, 1998). Because the Florida settlement contained a "most favored nation" clause that said the more favorable terms in subsequent settlements would apply retroactively to Florida, "[T]he terms of this Settlement Agreement will be revised so that the State of Florida will obtain treatment at least as relatively favorable as any such nonfederal governmental entity" (*The State of Florida v. The American Tobacco Company*, 1997), the vilification clause was removed from the Florida settlement.

In April 1998, the so-called Truth campaign began with print and broadcast advertisements, expanding to billboard advertisements in summer 1998. In July 1998, the "Truth Train" filled with youth toured the state for 13 days to build awareness of the campaign and to recruit new members for Students Working Against Tobacco, as well as to call for Hollywood to stop glamorizing tobacco in the movies (Givel & Glantz, 2000). In fall 1998, Florida State University released the results of a survey assessing youth awareness of the Truth campaign which showed that since its inception, 57% of youth reported being aware of the campaign, 87% reported being aware of specific messages, and 47% believed that tobacco companies were using deceptive practices in their advertising (Florida Anti-Tobacco Media Evaluation, 1998). In the program's first 2 years, cigarette smoking prevalence dropped from 18.5% to 11.1% among middle school students and from 27.4% to 22.6% among high school students (Bauer, Johnson, Hopkins, & Brooks, 2000).

Despite strong signs of success, Florida House Appropriations chair James King (R-Jacksonville), one of the top recipients of tobacco industry campaign contributions in 1997–1998 (Givel & Glantz, 1999), called for reduced funding of the program (McKinnon, 1998). The claims of ineffectiveness were made despite the September evaluation (Florida Anti-Tobacco Media Evaluation, 1998), which reported broad exposure and awareness among youth and a growing belief that the tobacco industry used deceptive practices in advertising. Despite the program's success and popularity (Bauer et al., 2000; Niederdeppe, Farrelly, & Haviland, 2004; Sly, Heald, & Ray, 2001; Sly, Trapido, & Ray, 2002), Governor Jeb Bush did propose cutting the program when he included only $61.5 million in his budget to the legislature as opposed to the $70.5 million level at which it was funded the previous year ("Florida's key legislative issues," 1999). The Florida Senate Budget Subcommittee for Health and Human Services proposed to cut the program to $50 million (Kennedy & Perez, 1999), and the House Budget Subcommittee on Health and Human Services Appropriations proposed to eliminate the program altogether, claiming there was no evidence the program was working (Kennedy, 1999). Although the health advocates accepted Governor Bush's budget proposal (Givel & Glantz, 2000), the American Nonsmokers' Rights Foundation responded to these cuts by running a newspaper campaign urging the public to hold Governor Bush accountable for his budget cuts to the Truth campaign.

The tobacco industry found some success in the limitations placed on the Florida media campaign from its inception. Although the vilification clause was lifted as a restriction in Florida when Texas settled its lawsuit with the tobacco companies, the restriction on targeting youth under the age of 18 (*The State of Florida v. The American Tobacco Company*, 1997) remained in place under the terms of the Florida settlement. Health advocates and officials effectively responded to this limitation by creating the cutting-edge Truth campaign. However, despite the documented success of the campaign in reducing youth smoking (Friend & Levy, 2002; Institute for Social Research, 1999), the tobacco industry prevailed through campaign contributions, ultimately leading to the defunding of the media campaign in 1999 (Givel & Glantz, 2000). Health officials and advocates should absolutely use evaluation measures to demonstrate campaign effectiveness, but they should not expect those measures to stand on their own; rather, evaluation data should be used as a part of a more comprehensive strategy to defend a media campaign.

The American Legacy Foundation

On November 23, 1998, attorneys general for 46 states, the District of Columbia, and five territories that had sued the tobacco industry over smoking-related Medicaid costs announced the Master Settlement Agreement (MSA). This agreement settled the remaining state-level litigation against the tobacco industry (National Association of Attorneys General, 1998). The MSA provided the states with money in perpetuity based on their estimated Medicaid costs due to smoking and cigarette sales and adjusted these sums for inflation. The suit imposed limitations on tobacco industry advertising to youth; in addition, a national public health foundation was established with $250 million paid over the course of 10 years, and a national public education campaign was established with $1.45 billion over the next 5 years (National Association of Attorneys General, 1998).

The national public health foundation, named the American Legacy Foundation (hereinafter Legacy), was created to support programs to reduce youth tobacco use and to study educational programs to prevent tobacco-related disease (National Association of Attorneys General, 1998). The MSA required that its education account would be used only for

> public education and advertising regarding the addictiveness, health effects, and social costs related to the

> use of tobacco products and shall not be used for any personal attack on, or vilification of, any person, company, or governmental agency, whether individually or collectively. (National Association of Attorneys General, 1998).

This much broader "vilification clause" was intended to make it difficult for Legacy to use advertising portraying deleterious tobacco industry practices. However, Legacy acted aggressively and adopted the same approach used in the successful Florida Truth campaign (Givel & Glantz, 2000). Under the direction of Legacy, the national Truth campaign was effective in reducing smoking among teens (Farrelly, Davis, Haviland, Messeri, & Healton, 2005; Niederdeppe et al., 2004) and increasing antitobacco attitudes and beliefs (Farrelly et al., 2002). Between 1999 and 2002, youth smoking prevalence decreased from 25.3% to 18.0%, and 22% of this decline was attributed to the Truth campaign (Farrelly et al., 2005).

The vilification clause in the MSA provided a platform for the tobacco industry to later attack Legacy (Ibrahim & Glantz, 2006). On January 18, 2002, Lorillard gave notice (required under the terms of the MSA) to Legacy, stating that it was going to file suit against the foundation on the basis that the Truth antismoking advertising campaign violated the terms of the MSA through personal attacks and vilification of the company. Legacy filed a preemptive suit against Lorillard on February 13, 2002 (*American Legacy Foundation v. Lorillard Tobacco Company*, 2002). With knowledge of Lorillard's complaints, Legacy asked the court for a declaratory judgment. On January 31, 2003, the Delaware Chancery Court denied Legacy's motion for summary judgment, moving the case to trial. The court ultimately ruled in favor of Legacy, finding that criticizing the tobacco industry did not amount to "vilification," and provided a clear definition of the term *vilification*. Lorillard appealed to the Delaware Supreme Court, which upheld the lower court's decision (Ibrahim & Glantz, 2006). Here was a good example of health officials and attorneys doing their due diligence in advance to fully understand the law, to maximize the media messages without violating the law.

In addition to direct attacks on the Legacy media campaign, the tobacco companies also created duplicate antitobacco education programs targeting youth to displace evidence-based tobacco-control marketing efforts (Landman et al., 2002). As noted earlier, the tobacco industry introduced its own youth educational campaign ("Helping Youth Decide," 1986) in the mid-1980s in an attempt to delegitimize the utility and significance of the entire Minnesota Plan for Nonsmoking (Landman et al., 2002; Mozingo, 1984). In 1998, Philip Morris introduced "Think. Don't Smoke," which was shown to be associated with an increase in the intention to smoke (Farrelly et al., 2002); "Think. Don't Smoke" was discontinued in 2002 (Farrelly, Niederdeppe, & Yarsevich, 2003). Lorillard launched a youth smoking prevention program in 1999 with the slogan "Tobacco is whacko if you're a teen" (Farrelly et al., 2003). The tobacco companies saw such efforts as part of a larger plan to demonstrate social responsibility (Fooks et al., 2011; Friedman, 2009). As special interests try to distract public attention away from deceitful business practices, health interests must be prepared to investigate and reveal the true intent and face behind the program.

EXTENSIONS TO ALCOHOL AND OTHER SUBSTANCE USE SOCIAL MARKETING

The transition from tobacco social marketing to media campaign efforts related to alcohol and other substance use is fraught with difficulty for several reasons. First, the dangers to health and the legality of the drug products vary greatly. Alcohol, which individuals over age 21 can legally consume, has some reported health benefits and is socially acceptable when used in moderation (Karlamangla et al., 2008; Nova, Baccan, Veses, Zapatera, & Marcos, 2012; Thakker, 1998). The main focus of alcohol social marketing focuses on binge drinking, underage drinking, and drinking and driving (Perkins, Linkenbach, Lewis, & Neighbors, 2010; Smith & Foxcroft, 2009). Tobacco products, including cigarettes and smokeless tobacco, are by their very nature harmful to cardiovascular and respiratory health, regardless of the dose (U.S. Department of Health and Human Services, 2006). The social acceptability of these products has decreased over time as more information has become available about their harmful effects and the marketing practices of the tobacco industry (Mowery, Babb, Hobart, Tworek, & MacNeil, 2012). At the other end of the spectrum is "other drug use," which includes illegal substances for which there is less information on health effects, including legally controlled substances (e.g., prescription drug abuse) that can be abused. The lack of standardization for misuse of illicit drugs for youth makes it difficult to accurately assess health consequences. The variation in what is meant by "drugs" makes it difficult to conduct antidrug marketing because the target is constantly changing, resulting in very broad messaging. As seen with early tobacco efforts, broad marketing that simply focuses on a substance's being dangerous for one's health is not effective.

The second point has to do with the industry responsible for the target product. Powerful insights have been obtained into the tobacco industry's efforts from the release of internal tobacco industry documents through the MSA (National Association of Attorneys General, 1998). However, although we can see alcohol industry marketing firsthand, there is no way to know the research and motivations behind the advertising or the internal debates and discussions within the alcohol industry. There is growing research on the alcohol industry and their public relations efforts (Miller, de Groot, McKenzie, & Droste, 2011), which do seem to echo certain strategies used by the tobacco industry. For example, there are some duplicate social marketing programs sponsored by the alcohol industry that attempt to create a sense of social responsibility around alcohol-related issues (Babor & Robaina, 2013). Despite the differences between tobacco and alcohol marketing for "social responsibility," it is possible to draw from lessons learned in the case of tobacco and consider the implications for alcohol.

CONCLUSION

The intent of this chapter was to provide a macro-level overview of ways in which social marketing efforts that promote health can be attacked via special interest groups and political actors, as well as some strategies health officials and health advocates can use to defend those campaigns. The antitobacco media campaigns were used for illustration, but the lessons learned here can certainly be more broadly translated across media efforts against promoters of substances other than tobacco. In efforts to prevent population-level public health social marketing efforts, opponents can use three key approaches, which may be executed directly by the special interest group or through political or third-party allies (Ibrahim & Glantz, 2007, 2008).

1. The opposition can work to prevent the creation of media campaigns. In the examples provided, the tobacco industry worked to prevent voter initiatives to establish tobacco-control media campaigns or tried to infiltrate advisory committees so that the oversight and governance of the media campaigns was influenced by protobacco forces. The earlier the industry interests are threaded into the process, the more long-term that impact can be. Health officials and advocates must question the credentials and purpose of all individuals working early on to develop a media campaign; in addition to potentially having detrimental agendas, the developers should also have appropriate experience and insight into the health issue.
2. If the media campaign is created, special interest groups can work to lessen the impact through diversionary tactics, such as claims of a fiscal crisis or duplicative spending. This provides impetus for legislatures to shift funds in state budgets, particularly in light of poor empirical evidence linking media campaign expenditures with positive change in the addictive behavior. Public health officials should work with researchers to be able to share data, conduct systematic and rigorous evaluations, and effectively translate and disseminate evaluation findings so that the true effects are known and understood. Research should include cost-effectiveness analysis, and results should be shared so that elected officials can understand the impact for their constituents in an intuitive manner.
3. When media campaigns cannot be defunded, special interests can work to weaken the impact by watering down the messages being presented or limiting the audience so that the population

reached is minimal or even transitional, such as pregnant women. Preliminary needs assessments should help to guide the target audience for a media campaign and messaging should be determined through reviews of previous peer-reviewed findings or pilot testing for brand new messaging strategies.

The effective use of social marketing to protect and improve population health is contingent on many interrelated factors. Whereas previous chapters have addressed factors such as message content and mechanisms of delivery, this chapter has focused on political, legal, and special-interest-group challenges that threaten the sustainability of media campaigns. It is vital for the success of public health social marketing campaigns that health advocates and public health practitioners be aware of such tactics to prevent, weaken, or destroy evidence-based social marketing efforts. With continued fiscal uncertainty for states, public health programs are forced to do more with less, and media campaigns can be an effective means to modify high-risk behaviors such as substance use, including alcohol, tobacco, and other drugs, at the population level. Public health officials and advocates should be prepared to partner with researchers to conduct evaluations and demonstrate effectiveness in short- and long-term measurements (e.g., of behavior changes and disease states, respectively) and clearly communicate that to the public through earned media, op-eds, special reports, and other opportunities that may arise. Although evidence is a solid foundation for defending social marketing efforts, it alone is not enough. Health officials and advocates must be savvy and skeptical of unknown parties working to develop new media efforts or participate in advisory roles. In the end, speedy identification of the truth in media messages and the entities behind them, as well as sharing of that truth with the public, is the best way to defend public health social marketing efforts.

References

Administrative and Financial Services—Procurement Office. (1995). *Solicitation number H6-001: Media services.* Phoenix: Arizona Department of Health Services.

American Legacy Foundation v. Lorillard Tobacco Company, C.A. No. 19406-NC (Court of Chancery of the State of Delaware in and for New Castle County 2002).

Arizona State Legislature. (1995). Chapter 275—tobacco tax. Arizona Health Care Cost Containment System (H.B. 2275). *Arizona Revised Statutes.* Phoenix, AZ: Author.

Babor, T. F., & Robaina, K. (2013). Public health, academic medicine, and the alcohol industry's corporate social responsibility activities. *American Journal of Public Health, 103*(2), 206–214. doi:10.2105/AJPH.2012.300847

Banzhaf v. Federal Communications Commission, No. 405 F.2d 1082 (U.S. Court of Appeals District of Columbia Circuit 1968).

Bauer, U. E., Johnson, T., Hopkins, R., & Brooks, R. (2000). Changes in youth cigarette use and intentions following implementation of a tobacco control program. *Journal of the American Medical Association, 284*(6), 723–728. doi:10.1001/jama.284.6.723

Begay, M. E., & Glantz, S. A. (1991). *Political expenditures by the tobacco industry in California state politics.* San Francisco: Institute for Health Policy Studies, School of Medicine, University of California.

Bialous, S. A., & Glantz, S. A. (1997). *Tobacco control in Arizona, 1973–1997.* Retrieved from http://repositories.cdlib.org/ctcre/tcpmus/AZ1997

Bialous, S. A., & Glantz, S. A. (1999). Arizona's tobacco control initiative illustrates the need for continuing oversight by tobacco control advocates. *Tobacco Control, 8,* 141–151. doi:10.1136/tc.8.2.141

Borland, R., Wilson, N., Fong, G., Hammond, D., Cummings, K., Yong, H.-H., . . . McNeill, A. (2009). Impact of graphic and text warnings on cigarette packs: Findings from four countries over five years. *Tobacco Control, 18,* 358–364.

Brozek, M. (1985, April 11). *Memorandum to Roger Mozingo regarding Minnesota legislative status.* Tobacco Institute Collection, Legacy Tobacco Documents Library. Retrieved from http://legacy.library.ucsf.edu/action/document/page?tid-xzs42f00

Brozek, M., & Nelson, D. C. Tobacco Institute. (1988, January 6). *Memorandum to William A. Cannell regarding Minnesota plan/status report.* Tobacco Institute Collection, Legacy Tobacco Documents Library. Retrieved from http://legacy.library.ucsf.edu/cgi/getdoc?tid=jqs42f00&fmt=tif&ref=results

Bush, C. (1994a, January 7). Senate president speaks out against tobacco tax initiative. *Arizona Capitol Times,* p. 84.

Bush, C. (1994b, May 6). Tobacco tax promoters publicize allegations of industry conspiracy. *Arizona Capitol Times,* pp. 1, 2, 3.

California Department of Finance. (1992). *Governor's budget 1992–1993*. Sacramento, CA: Governor's Office, State of California. Retrieved from https://archive.org/stream/governorsbudget1992cali#page/n1/mode/2up

California Department of Finance. (2001). *Governor's budget, 2002–2003*. Sacramento, CA: Governor's Office, State of California. Retrieved from http://www.dof.ca.gov/budget/historical/2002-03

California Department of Finance. (2002). *Governor's budget, 2003–2004*. Sacramento, CA: Governor's Office, State of California. Retrieved from http://www.dof.ca.gov/budget/historical/2003-04

California Department of Health Services. (2003). *Proposition 99 Health Education Account, TCS Funding, CDE, and TRDRP Budget Appropriation Summary*. Sacramento, CA: Author.

California Tobacco Control Program. (2002). *Tobacco education media campaign scripts*. Sacramento, CA: California Department of Public Health.

California Tobacco Control Program. (n.d.). *Mission statement*. Sacramento, CA: California Department of Public Health. Retrieved from http://www.cdph.ca.gov/programs/Tobacco/Pages/default.aspx

Cannella, D. (1994, May 4). Cigarette-tax backers assail Symington. *Arizona Republic*, p. B1.

Centers for Disease Control and Prevention. (2013). *Smoking and tobacco use: Media campaign resource center.* Retrieved from http://www.cdc.gov/tobacco/media_campaigns

Farrelly, M. C., Davis, K. C., Haviland, M. L., Messeri, P., & Healton, C. G. (2005). Evidence of a dose-response relationship between "Truth" antismoking ads and youth smoking prevalence. *American Journal of Public Health, 95*, 425–431. doi:10.2105/AJPH.2004.049692

Farrelly, M. C., Healton, C. G., Davis, K. C., Messeri, P., Hershey, J. C., & Haviland, M. L. (2002). Getting to the truth: Evaluation national tobacco countermarketing campaigns. *American Journal of Public Health, 92*, 901–907. doi:10.2105/AJPH.92.6.901

Farrelly, M. C., Niederdeppe, J., & Yarsevich, J. (2003). Youth tobacco prevention mass media campaigns: Past, present and future directions. *Tobacco Control, 12*(Suppl. 1), i35–i47. doi:10.1136/tc.12.suppl_1.i35

Federal Communications Commission. (1948). *Docket No. 8516—In the matter of editorializing by broadcast licenses: Report by the commission*. Retrieved from http://transition.fcc.gov/ftp/Bureaus/Mass_Media/Databases/documents_collection/490608.pdf

Federal Trade Commission. (2011). *Federal Trade Commission cigarette report for 2007 and 2008.* Retrieved from http://www.ftc.gov/reports/federal-trade-commission-cigarette-report-2011

Fichtenberg, C. M., & Glantz, S. A. (2000). Association of the California Tobacco Control Program with declines in cigarette consumption and mortality from heart disease. *The New England Journal of Medicine, 343*, 1772–1777. doi:10.1056/NEJM200012143432406

Florida Anti-Tobacco Media Evaluation. (1998). *Report on September 1998 survey results*. Tallahassee: Florida State University.

Florida's key legislative issues for 1999. (1999, February 28). *Tallahassee Democrat*, p. A9.

Fooks, G. J., Gilmore, A. B., Smith, K. E., Collin, J., Holden, C., & Lee, K. (2011). Corporate social responsibility and access to policy elites. *PLoS Medicine*. Retrieved from http://www.plosmedicine.org/article/info%3Adoi%2F10.1371%2Fjournal.pmed.1001076

Friedman, L. C. (2009). Tobacco industry use of corporate social responsibility: Tactics as a sword and a shield on secondhand smoke issues. *The Journal of Law, Medicine & Ethics, 37*, 819–827. doi:10.1111/j.1748-720X.2009.00453.x

Friend, K., & Levy, D. (2002). Reductions in smoking prevalence and cigarette consumption associated with mass-media campaigns. *Health Education Research, 17*, 85–98. doi:10.1093/her/17.1.85

Givel, M. S., Dearlove, J., & Glantz, S. A. (2001). *Tobacco policy making in California 1999–2001: Stalled and adrift*. San Francisco: Institute for Health Policy Studies, University of California San Francisco.

Givel, M. S., & Glantz, S. A. (1999). *Tobacco industry political power and influence in Florida from 1979 to 1999*. San Francisco: Institute for Health Policy Studies, University of California San Francisco.

Givel, M. S., & Glantz, S. A. (2000). Failure to defend a successful state tobacco control program: Policy lessons from Florida. *American Journal of Public Health, 90*, 762–767. doi:10.2105/AJPH.90.5.762

Givel, M. S., & Glantz, S. A. (2001). Tobacco lobby political influence on U.S. state legislature in the 1990s. *Tobacco Control, 10*, 124–134. doi:10.1136/tc.10.2.124

Glantz, S. A. (1999). *Tobacco: Biology and politics*. Waco, TX: HealthEdCo.

Glantz, S. A., & Balbach, E. D. (2000). *Tobacco war: Inside the California battles*. Berkeley: University of California Press.

Gordon, G., & Hamburger, T. (1999, 23 May). Minnesota no longer leads the pack; health experts cite decline in antismoking efforts. *Minneapolis Star-Tribune*, p. 1B.

Grier, S., & Bryant, C. A. (2005). Social Marketing in Public Health. *Annual Review of Public Health, 26*, 319–339. doi:10.1146/annurev.publhealth.26.021304.144610

Hamilton, J. (1972). The demand for cigarettes: Advertising, the health scare and the cigarette advertising ban. *The Review of Economics and Statistics, 54*, 401–411. doi:10.2307/1924567

Hammond, D., Fong, G., McNeill, A., Borland, R., & Cummings, K. (2006). Effectiveness of cigarette warning labels in informing smokers about the risks of smoking: Findings from the International Tobacco Control (ITC) Four Country Survey. *Tobacco Control, 15*, iii19–iii25. doi:10.1136/tc.2005.012294

Healton, C. (2001). Who's afraid of the truth? *American Journal of Public Health, 91*, 554–558. doi:10.2105/AJPH.91.4.554

"Helping Youth Decide": A presentation for communications committee. (1986, October 30). Tobacco Institute Collection, Legacy Tobacco Documents Library. Retrieved from http://legacy.library.ucsf.edu/tid/wul13b00

Hicks, J. J. (2001). The strategy behind Florida's "Truth" campaign. *Tobacco Control, 10*, 3–5. doi:10.1136/tc.10.1.3

Hill, D. (1999). Why we should tackle adult smoking first. *Tobacco Control, 8*, 333–335. doi:10.1136/tc.8.3.333

Ibrahim, J. K., & Glantz, S. A. (2006). Tobacco industry litigation strategies to oppose tobacco control media campaigns. *Tobacco Control, 15*, 50–58. doi:10.1136/tc.2005.014142

Ibrahim, J. K., & Glantz, S. A. (2007). The rise and fall of tobacco control media campaigns, 1967–2006. *American Journal of Public Health, 97*, 1383–1396. doi:10.2105/AJPH.2006.097006

Ibrahim, J. K., & Glantz, S. A. (2008). Tobacco industry efforts to influence tobacco control media interventions. In National Cancer Institute (Ed.), *The role of the media in promoting and reducing tobacco use* (Chapter 13, pp. 549–576). NCI Tobacco Control Series, Monograph 19. Bethesda, MD: National Cancer Institute.

Independent Evaluation Consortium. (1998a). *Final report of the Independent Evaluation of the California Tobacco Control Prevention and Education Program: Wave I data, 1996–1997.* Rockville, MD: The Gallup Organization.

Independent Evaluation Consortium. (1998b). *Final report of the Independent Evaluation of the California Tobacco Control Prevention and Education Program: Wave 2 data, 1998; Wave 1 and 2 data comparisons, 1996–1998.* Rockville, MD: The Gallup Organization.

Institute for Social Research, University of Michigan. (1999). *Monitoring the Future: 1999 Data from in-school surveys of eighth, tenth, and twelfth graders.* Retrieved from http://monitoringthefuture.org/data/99data/pr99cig1.pdf

Karlamangla, A. S., Sarkisian, C. A., Kado, D. M., Dedes, H., Liao, D. H., Kim, S., . . . Moore, A. A. (2008). Light to moderate alcohol consumption and disability: Variable benefits by health status. *American Journal of Epidemiology, 169*, 96–104. doi:10.1093/aje/kwn294

Kennedy, J. (1999, March 18). "Truth" drive director is kicked out. *Orlando Sentinel.* Retrieved from http://articles.orlandosentinel.com/1999-03-18/news/9903180172_1_peter-mitchell-smoking-tobacco

Kennedy, J., & Perez, R. (1999, March 12). *State house may pull plug on "truth."* Retrieved from http://archive.tobacco.org/articles.php?mode-printable&article_ids%SB%5D-17389&submit-Button-Show+Selected+For+Printing

Keye, P. (1993). *What don't we know, and when haven't we known it?* Speech presented at Health Communications Day, Johns Hopkins University, Baltimore, MD.

Landman, A., Ling, P., & Glantz, S. A. (2002). Tobacco industry youth smoking prevention programs protect the tobacco industry and hurt tobacco control. *American Journal of Public Health, 92*, 917–930. doi:10.2105/AJPH.92.6.917

Lavack, A. M. (2001). *Tobacco industry denormalization campaigns: A review and evaluation.* Winnipeg, Canada: University of Winnipeg.

Mahood, G. (2004). *Tobacco industry denormalization: Telling the truth about the tobacco industry's role in the tobacco epidemic.* Toronto, ON: Non-Smokers' Rights Association.

Malmgren, K. (1990, April 18). *California's anti-tobacco advertising campaign.* American Tobacco Collection, Legacy Tobacco Documents Library. Retrieved from http://legacy.library.ucsf.edu/tid/aes90c00

McGrath, D. J. (1993, May 23). Behind the budget fight: Politics and prudence. *Minneapolis Star-Tribune*, p. 1B.

McKinnon, J. (1998, November 11). Lawmaker questions the effectiveness of antismoking ads, *Wall Street Journal*, p. F4.

Miller, P. G., de Groot, F., McKenzie, S., & Droste, N. (2011). Vested interests in addiction research and policy. Alcohol industry use of social aspect public relations organizations against preventative health measures. *Addiction, 106*, 1560–1567. doi:10.1111/j.1360-0443.2011.03499.x

Minnesota Department of Health. (1987). *The Minnesota nonsmoking initiative, June 1985–December 1986: A report to the 1987 legislature.* Minneapolis, MN: Author.

Minnesota Department of Health. (1989). *The Minnesota tobacco-use prevention initiative, 1987–1988: A report to the 1989 legislature.* Minneapolis, MN: Author.

Minnesota Department of Health. (1991). *Minnesota tobacco-use prevention initiative, 1989–1990: A report to the 1991 legislature*. Minneapolis, MN: Author.

Minnesota Department of Public Health. (1984a, September). *Public relations strategies to address the Minnesota plan for nonsmoking and health*. Legacy Tobacco Documents Library. Retrieved from http://legacy.library.ucsf.edu/cgi/getdoc?tid=nia92f00&fmt=tif&ref=results

Minnesota Department of Public Health. (1984b, September). *The Minnesota plan for nonsmoking and health: Report and recommendations of the technical advisory committee on nonsmoking and health*. Legacy Tobacco Documents Library. Retrieved from http://legacy.library.ucsf.edu/tid/nwb92f00

Mowery, P. D., Babb, S., Hobart, R., Tworek, C., & MacNeil, A. (2012). The impact of state pre-emption of local smoking restrictions on public health protections and changes in social norms. *Journal of Environmental Health and Public Health*. Retrieved from http://www.hindawi.com/journals/jeph/2012/632629/abs

Mozingo, R. (1984, August 13). *Confidential information on new TI program*. Tobacco Institute Collection, Legacy Tobacco Documents Library. Retrieved from http://legacy.library.ucsf.edu/cgi/getdoc?tid=poy82f00&fmt=tif&ref=results

National Association of Attorneys General. (1998). *Multistate settlement with the tobacco industry*. Retrieved from http://www.naag.org/backpages/naag/tobacco/msa/msa-pdf/MSA%20with%20Sig%20Pages%20and%20Exhibits.pdf/file_view

Niederdeppe, J., Farrelly, M. C., & Haviland, M. L. (2004). Confirming "truth": More evidence of a successful tobacco countermarketing campaign in Florida. *American Journal of Public Health, 94*, 255–257. doi:10.2105/AJPH.94.2.255

Nova, E., Baccan, G. C., Veses, A., Zapatera, B., & Marcos, A. (2012). Potential health benefits of moderate alcohol consumption: Current perspectives in research. *The Proceedings of the Nutrition Society, 71*, 307–315. doi:10.1017/S0029665112000171

Parker, W. (1990, 18 April). Antismoking budget cut one-third. *St. Paul Pioneer Press*, p. 6B.

Perkins, H. W., Linkenbach, J. W., Lewis, M. A., & Neighbors, C. (2010). Effectiveness of social norms media marketing in reducing drinking and driving: A statewide campaign. *Addictive Behaviors, 35*, 866–874. doi:10.1016/j.addbeh.2010.05.004

Philip Morris Companies Inc. Inter-Office Correspondence. (1990, April 24). Phillip Morris Collection, Legacy Tobacco Documents Library. Retrieved from http://legacy.library.ucsf.edu/tid/fqo95c00

Pierce, J. P. (1992, January). *Evaluating Proposition 99 in California*. Paper presented at the American Heart Association's Nineteenth Science Writers Forum, Galveston, TX.

Porter, R. S., Gowda, V. R., Kotchou, K., Nodora, K., Leischow, R., Arizona Department of Health Services Office on Smoking and Health, . . . Centers for Disease Control and Prevention. (2001). Tobacco use among adults—Arizona, 1996 and 1999. *Morbidity and Mortality Weekly Report, 50*, 402–406.

R. J. Reynolds Tobacco Company v. Diana M. Bonta. Application of amicus curiae for leave to file brief in support of Defendants' opposition to plaintiffs' motion for preliminary injunction, No. S-03-659 LKK GGH (U.S. District Court, Eastern District of California 2003).

R. J. Reynolds Tobacco Company v. Diana M. Bonta. Plaintiffs' response to amicus curiae brief of American Cancer Society, American Lung Association and American Heart Association (U.S. District Court, Eastern District of California 2003).

Sly, D. F., Heald, G. R., & Ray, S. (2001). The Florida "truth" anti-tobacco media evaluation: Design, first year results, and implications for planning future state media campaigns. *Tobacco Control, 10*, 9–15. doi:10.1136/tc.10.1.9

Sly, D. F., Trapido, E., & Ray, S. (2002). Evidence of the dose effects of an antitobacco counter-advertising campaign. *Preventive Medicine: An International Journal Devoted to Practice and Theory, 35*, 511–518. doi:10.1006/pmed.2002.1100

Smith, L. A., & Foxcroft, S. R. (2009). The effect of alcohol advertising, marketing and portrayal on drinking behaviour in young people: Systematic review of prospective cohort studies. *BMC Public Health*, 9(51). Retrieved from http://www.biomedcentral.com/1471-2458/9/51

Snitzer, M. (1969, October 14). *Corporate advertising for Philip Morris*. Phillip Morris Collection, Legacy Tobacco Documents Library. Retrieved from http://legacy.library.ucsf.edu/tid/kfl68e00

The State of Florida v. The American Tobacco Company, No. 95-1466AO (Circuit Court of the Fifteenth Judicial Circuit in and for the County of Palm Beach, State of Florida 1995).

The State of Florida v. The American Tobacco Company, No. 95-1466 AH (Circuit Court of the Fifteenth Judicial Circuit in and for Palm Beach County, Florida 1997).

The State of Texas v. The American Tobacco Company, No. 5-96CV-91 (U.S. District Court for the Eastern District of Texas, Texarkana Division 1998).

Thakker, K. D. (1998). An overview of health risks and benefits of alcohol consumption. *Alcoholism: Clinical and Experimental Research*, 22(Suppl. 7), 285s–298s. doi:10.1111/j.1530-0277.1998.tb04381.x

Tsoukalas, T., Ibrahim, J., & Glantz, S. (2003). *Shifting tides: Minnesota tobacco politics*. Retrieved from http://repositories.cdlib.org/ctcre/tcpmus/MN2003

U.S. Department of Health and Human Services. (2006). *The health consequences of involuntary exposure to tobacco smoke: A report of the Surgeon General*. Rockville, MD: U.S. Dept. of Health & Human Services, Centers for Disease Control & Prevention, National Center for Chronic Disease Prevention & Health Promotion, Office on Smoking & Health.

U.S. Department of Health, Education, and Welfare. (1964). *Smoking and health: Report to the Advisory Committee to the Surgeon General of the Public Health Service*. Washington, DC: U.S. Public Health Service.

U.S. Food and Drug Administration. (1996). *Children and tobacco, executive summary, final rule*. Retrieved from the Advertising Law Resource Center website: http://www.lawpublish.com/fdarule.html

Ventura, S. J., Mosher, W. D., Curtin, S. C., Abma, J. C., & Henshaw, S. (2001). Trends in pregnancy rates for the United States, 1976–1997: An update. *National Vital Statistics Reports*, *49*(4), 1–9.

Wakefield, M. A., Loken, B., & Hornik, R. C. (2010). Use of mass media campaigns to change health behaviour. *The Lancet*, *376*, 1261–1271. doi:10.1016/S0140-6736(10)60809-4

World Health Organization. (2003). *WHO Framework Convention on Tobacco Control*. Retrieved from http://www.who.int/fctc/text_download/en

CHAPTER 21

MESSAGE DESIGN APPROACHES TO HEALTH RISK BEHAVIOR PREVENTION

Nancy Grant Harrington, Donald W. Helme, and Seth M. Noar

Efforts to prevent adolescent drug use have involved many different kinds of interventions, including classroom-based programs, community-level initiatives, and public communication campaigns. At this point in time, researchers know a great deal about how to design and implement various types of interventions to promote their effectiveness. For example, programs that target youth in school classrooms should be interactive (Botvin & Griffin, 2007), community initiatives should involve participatory approaches (Bracht & Rice, 2013), and media campaigns should attain adequate reach and frequency (Atkin & Rice, 2013). No matter what the intervention, theory and formative research should play central roles in the development process. That development includes attention to the design of the messages that compose the intervention.

The purpose of this chapter is to provide a review and analysis of some of the major approaches to message design that have application to adolescent drug prevention efforts. Specifically, we address message sensation value, narrative messaging, message framing, and message tailoring. After describing each approach, we examine the theoretical mechanisms for message effects on important process and outcome variables. Then we consider how message design strategies have been applied to adolescent drug prevention interventions and review exemplar studies. At the end of the chapter, we consider important directions for future research and some of the challenges facing message design research. To begin, though, we provide an overview of some important message design considerations.

MESSAGE DESIGN CONSIDERATIONS

Persuasive messages incorporate dimensions of content, format, and structure. In terms of content, a message could address the health risks of smoking cigarettes or the self-esteem benefits of rejecting tobacco industry influence. In terms of format, a message could be conveyed as a loud and flashy 30-second public service announcement (PSA) on television or a 30-foot × 40-foot black-and-white billboard. In terms of structure, a message could tell the story of a boy who died of a cocaine overdose or present statistics on the number of deaths from cocaine each year. Beyond these major dimensions, other design considerations include the extent to which messages contain spoken or written language, static or dynamic visual images, and audio such as music or sound effects; whether or not the source of the message is identified; whether the message argument is explicit or implicit; and a host of other attribute (present or absent) or variable (present to some degree) dimensions. Cappella (2006) aptly noted that

http://dx.doi.org/10.1037/14550-022
Handbook of Adolescent Drug Use Prevention: Research, Intervention Strategies, and Practice, L. M. Scheier (Editor)

the variations on message design are seemingly limitless.

Although challenging, the possibilities for variations in message design should not be considered daunting. Indeed, researchers and practitioners can exercise considerable control over the messages they design for mass media–based interventions. The challenge comes in identifying precisely which elements of a message will influence the target variables. Several theoretical, conceptual, and empirical formulations help uncover the different features underlying message effects. For example, McGuire's (1981) seminal work on the hierarchy of message effects and the communication-persuasion matrix (McGuire, 2013) has shown that messages and audiences interact along a continuum ranging from initial exposure and attention to the message through integration of changed behavior into individuals' daily lives. The transtheoretical model and stages of health behavior change (Prochaska & DiClemente, 1983) have shown that individuals in the target audience may range from not even being aware that a health problem is relevant to them to having already integrated and sustained recommended changes in their lifestyles. Further, processes of change and work to integrate compatible behavior change theories into the stages-of-change framework suggest that different message strategies are more appropriate at different stages along the behavior change continuum (Slater, 1999). The more researchers know about their audience, and the clearer they are about their objectives, the more guidance the field will have in terms of message design.

As researchers look to theory to help guide the design of persuasive messages, they need to consider the important distinction between message design theories, information processing theories, and health-behavior change theories (Cappella, 2006). Message design theories provide a foundation on which to craft persuasive messages, addressing the kinds of content that should be included and how the content should be presented to attain optimal effects. Information processing theories emphasize cognitive and affective responses to messages and suggest what processes messages should influence to enhance effects, such as attracting and holding an audience's attention. Health-behavior change theories inform what topics messages should address, such as particular normative beliefs or attitudes or self-efficacy to refuse drug offers. Table 21.1 lists theories or frameworks relevant to persuasive messages, describes the major premises of each theory or framework, and cites publications that provide more detailed background.

Researchers also must recognize that messages do not operate in a vacuum. Especially in today's intensely saturated media environment, drug use prevention messages must cut through a great deal of clutter to have any hope of attracting adolescents' attention, much less of influencing their behavior. Hardly anyone, especially young people, consumes media for the advertisements or PSAs. Even if prevention messages attract and hold the attention of the target audience, they must compete with ads and entertainment media that promote the very behaviors in question. There is evidence to demonstrate the counterproductive effects that exposure to substance use through ads, television programs, and movies can have on adolescent behavior (Dalton et al., 2003; Stoolmiller, Gerrard, Sargent, Worth, & Gibbons, 2010).

Although messages by themselves can only do so much, what they can do is important. When messages reach large numbers of people through channels such as television, radio, and the Internet, small amounts of behavior change can have a large impact (Snyder et al., 2004). Further, although televised media campaigns can be successful on their own (e.g., Palmgreen, Donohew, Lorch, Hoyle, & Stephenson, 2001), they also can be coupled with classroom and community-based efforts to further enhance their effects (e.g., Hecht et al., 2003; Slater, Kelly, Lawrence, Stanley, & Comello, 2011). The take-home message here is that even though health promotion and risk reduction messages, in particular, adolescent drug prevention messages, face considerable odds, they can positively influence behavior. Prevention scientists, therefore, must learn how to craft theoretically sound persuasive messages and disseminate them appropriately and effectively so that the field as a whole has the best chance of promoting positive health behavior.

TABLE 21.1

Theories and Frameworks Relevant to the Design of Persuasive Messages

Theory or framework	Major premises	Publications
Message Design		
Emotional Appeals	Messages may elicit a range of emotional response from viewers; emotions influence persuasion through multiple pathways	Dillard & Nabi (2006)
Entertainment-Education	Extended storylines on television and radio programs can both educate and entertain; attention, parasocial interaction, identification, self- and collective efficacy, and communication in the social system promote individual and community change	Singhal & Rogers (1999)
Exemplification Theory	Messages containing qualitative evidence are more persuasive than those containing quantitative evidence; single instances in a narrative may be processed as evidence of a larger group's experiences	Zillmann & Brosius (2000)
Message Framing (Prospect Theory)	Messages can emphasize positive (gain-framed) or negative (loss-framed) consequences of behavior; gain-framed messages are more effective for low-risk prevention behaviors, whereas loss-framed messages are more effective for high-risk detection behaviors	Rothman & Salovey (1997)
Narratives (Transportation Theory)	Stories influence persuasion through transportation, which engenders parasocial relationships and identification with characters, reduced negative cognitive responses, and increased perceived realism	Hinyard & Kreuter (2007)
Tailoring	Messages that match individual demographic, psychological, or sociocultural traits influence persuasion through increased personal relevance	Rimer & Kreuter (2006)
Information Processing		
Activation Model of Information Exposure (Message Sensation Value)	Attention is a function of need for stimulation and the stimulation provided by a message; to attract and hold attention, a message must help audience members reach their optimal level of arousal	Donohew, Lorch, & Palmgreen (1998)
Elaboration Likelihood Model	There are two routes to persuasion: central (argument-driven) and peripheral (cue-driven); messages that increase the amount of thinking (through enhancing motivation and personal relevance) will increase central message processing	Petty & Cacioppo (1986)
Expectancy-Value Theory	Behavior is a function of expectations regarding outcomes and the value placed on the outcomes	Fishbein & Ajzen (1975)
Extended Parallel Process Model	Messages must produce high levels of threat and efficacy in audience members to persuade them to adopt a health behavior	Witte (1992)
Limited Capacity Model (LC4MP)	Audiences have a limited capacity to process information; processing demands from dynamic and multi-sensory messages can overwhelm limited cognitive resources	Lang (2000)
Media Priming Theory	Messages can alter the relative importance of variables that underlie persuasion by changing the strength of association between a predictor (e.g., attitude) and its related outcome (e.g., behavioral intention)	Domke, Shah, & Wackman (1998)
Unimodel	There is one route to persuasion in which individuals "more or less" evaluate any evidence presented in a stimulus message, be it argument-based or cue-based; when traditionally cue-related information is sufficiently detailed, results parallel those found for central processing	Kruglanski & Thompson (1999)
Health Behavior Change		
Health Belief Model	Behavior is predicted by perceived severity, perceived susceptibility, and perceived benefits of and barriers to engaging in the health behavior; cues to action are internal or external triggers to prompt behavior	Janz & Becker (1984)
Integrative Model of Behavior Prediction (Theory of Reasoned Action) (Theory of Planned Behavior)	Behavior is predicted by behavioral intention, skills, and environmental constraints; behavioral intention is influenced by attitudes, perceived norms, and self-efficacy, which are in turn influenced by their respective attitudinal, normative, and self-efficacy beliefs	Fishbein et al. (2002)
Social Cognitive Theory	Behavior is predicted by persons' beliefs that they are capable of engaging in the behavior (self-efficacy) and beliefs about expected outcomes of engaging in the behavior (outcome expectations)	Bandura (1986)
Transtheoretical Model	A person's readiness for behavior change varies along five stages from precontemplation to maintenance; different processes of change apply at different stages of the change process	Prochaska & DiClemente (1983)

Note. Data from Cappella (2006).

APPROACHES TO MESSAGE DESIGN

In the following sections, we review research from four of the most prominent theory-based strategies for the design of a health-behavior change message: message sensation value, narrative messaging, message framing, and message tailoring. Of these four approaches, message sensation value is most directly associated with adolescent drug use prevention efforts. Narratives and framing, although typically not central to prevention research design, are nevertheless ubiquitous in drug use prevention messaging. Message tailoring is one of the newest and most promising approaches to message design, and it has figured prominently in both adult smoking cessation interventions and smoking prevention interventions targeted at adolescent populations. Below, we review research and discuss theoretical foundations for each of these approaches.

Message Sensation Value

It is no great secret that young people tend to prefer excitement and novelty over the banal or common. Therefore, when designing messages to attract and hold the attention of youth, researchers need to consider ways to make their messages as appealing as possible—without sacrificing the quality and strength of their argument. One such strategy, based in decades of theory-based empirical research, is to manipulate the sensation value of a message. Message sensation value (MSV) is defined by the degree to which a message is able to elicit sensory, affective, and arousal responses in audience members (Palmgreen, Stephenson, Everett, Baseheart, & Francies, 2002). High sensation value (HSV) messages are novel, creative, unusual, and intense. Low sensation value (LSV) messages are familiar, predictable, calm, and clear.

In early research, MSV was operationally defined in terms of research participants' subjective responses to messages. The 17-item Perceived Message Sensation Value scale (PSMV; Palmgreen et al., 2002) assesses messages according to whether individuals *perceive* that a message elicits emotional arousal, has dramatic impact, and contains novelty, rather than coding the message to determine the presence or amount of these factors directly. Although obtaining viewers' subjective assessments of a message's sensation value is important, having a more objective indicator of precisely which features constitute HSV messages would be helpful for message designers. Thus, Morgan, Palmgreen, Stephenson, Hoyle, and Lorch (2003) worked to identify specific message content, format, and structural features that could define the sensation value of a video message.

Their MSV coding system considers visual, audio, and content features of messages. The visual dimension assesses the number of cuts and the use of special visual effects, slow motion, unusual colors, and intense images. The audio dimension assesses sound saturation and use of music and sound effects. The content dimension considers whether the PSA was acted out as a narrative or presented as a testimonial and whether it uses an unexpected format and has a surprise or twist ending. Morgan and colleagues (2003) found that MSV and PMSV were related moderately ($r = .46$). They also found moderate associations between MSV and PMSV's three subscales of emotional arousal, dramatic impact, and novelty (rs from .38 to .48). The objective MSV features most strongly related to PMSV were intense images, sound saturation, being acted out, and having an unexpected format and a surprise or twist ending.

Theoretical mechanisms for message sensation value effects. According to the activation model of information exposure (AMIE; Donohew, Lorch, & Palmgreen, 1998), attention to a stimulus is in part a function of an individual's level of need for stimulation and the level of stimulation provided by a stimulus source. If individuals do not achieve or maintain an optimal level of arousal upon exposure to a message—if the message is too powerful or too pallid—they very likely will turn away and seek another source of stimulation. If activation remains within some acceptable range, however, individuals will be more likely to continue paying attention to the information. In other words, creating persuasive messages with sufficient levels of arousal value increases the likelihood that receivers will attend to the message, both initially when attention is first captured and throughout the duration of the message (Donohew, Palmgreen, & Lorch, 1994).

MSV functions to attract and hold the attention of individuals on the basis of their sensation-seeking needs (Donohew et al., 1998). Sensation seeking is a measure of variability that quantifies an individual's need for stimulation. It is a trait defined by "the seeking of varied, novel, complex, and intense sensations and experiences, and the willingness to take physical, social, legal, and financial risks for the sake of such experience" (Zuckerman, 1994, p. 27). High sensation seekers (HSS) are receptive to stimuli that are intense, novel, and arousing. Low sensation seekers (LSS) tend to prefer the familiar and less arousing.

AMIE posits that HSV messages are more likely to attract and hold the attention of HSS, whereas LSV messages are more likely to be preferred by LSS. Laboratory research has shown support for these preferences, although in certain circumstances LSS also attend to HSV messages almost as much as HSS (e.g., Lorch et al., 1994). Given these findings, along with numerous findings that HSS are more likely to engage in risky health behaviors (see Zuckerman, 1994, for a review), it follows that HSV prevention messages should be targeted to HSS (Donohew, Palmgreen, Lorch, Zimmerman, & Harrington, 2002).

Message sensation value in adolescent drug use prevention. Use of HSV message design principles is now ubiquitous in drug prevention campaign research. Whereas early PSAs were typically slow-paced and pedantic, today's messages more often reflect the hard-hitting, novel, and graphic approach that is recommended to reach an at-risk HSS audience. Research has grown precipitously around the notion of HSS and HSV messages. Paek, Kim, and Hove (2010), for instance, found 934 antismoking video clips on YouTube and coded them for MSV. The authors discovered that HSV videos had a higher number of viewers (14,696) than LSV videos (4,804). Further, HSV videos had a higher viewer rating and a higher number of viewer comments than LSV videos. Although popularity may be one indicator of message impact, researchers are more concerned with message influence on attitude, behavioral intention, and behavior. To decipher the role of message influence, we turn to media campaign studies.

Some of the most compelling evidence for the effectiveness of using HSV messages to reduce adolescent substance abuse comes from a study by Palmgreen et al. (2001). The study tested the effectiveness of a targeted television-only PSA campaign in reducing marijuana use among HSS adolescents. It used a controlled interrupted time-series design and implemented the campaign in two comparable Midwestern cities, twice in one city and once in the other city (which served as the control for the first city during the first campaign implementation). Data, including self-report of marijuana use, were collected from random samples of 100 adolescents in each city every month for 32 months. Results showed that the campaigns reversed the upward developmental trends in 30-day marijuana use among HSS adolescents; no campaign effects were evident among LSS teens given the low levels of marijuana use observed in this audience.

Palmgreen, Lorch, Stephenson, Hoyle, and Donohew (2007) provided further evidence of the effectiveness of HSV prevention messages targeted at high-risk youth when they examined effects of the Marijuana Initiative implemented in 2002 as part of the Office of National Drug Control Policy's (ONDCP) National Youth Anti-Drug Media Campaign. The PSAs were designed to closely follow the principles of HSV message design, using novelty and hard-hitting drama to depict the negative consequences of marijuana use. Modeling the design of their 2001 study, Palmgreen and colleagues (2007) collected data from 100 randomly selected adolescents monthly over a 48-month period in each of two communities. This sampling frame overlapped the first 6 months of the Marijuana Initiative. Results showed that the HSV PSAs were effective in reversing the upward developmental trend in 30-day marijuana use and reducing positive marijuana attitudes and beliefs among HSS teens. Consistent with the 2001 study, there was no discernible impact on LSS given their low levels of marijuana use.

Narrative Messages

A long oral and written history shows that human beings are storytellers (Fisher, 1984). Indeed, telling stories is a universal way of sharing information, and in many respects is the backbone of cultural transmission. Whereas didactic communication conveys information through arguments and evidence, narrative communication conveys information through characters, conflict, and plot. More specifically, *narrative* is defined as "a cohesive and coherent story with an identifiable beginning, middle, and end that provides information about scene, characters, and conflict; raises unanswered questions or unresolved conflict; and provides resolution" (Hinyard & Kreuter, 2007, p. 777).

Carefully constructed narratives may be conveyed in as few as 30 seconds via PSAs (Palmgreen et al., 2001), incorporated through videos included in school curricula (Hecht & Miller-Day, 2009) or woven throughout multiple episodes of radio or television programs via entertainment-education initiatives (Singhal & Rogers, 1999). Narratives may be entirely fictional, entirely factual, or a combination of both. In this respect, what matters for the influence of the narrative appears to be its plausibility more than its actuality (Strange, 2002).

Theoretical mechanisms for narrative effects. Transportation theory (Green & Brock, 2000) explains the persuasive effects of narrative. *Transportation* is the process through which audience members are brought into the narrative world, "an integrative melding of attention, imagery, and feelings, focused on story events" (Green, 2006, p. S164). Transportation can result in changes in attitudes, beliefs, and behaviors through three mechanisms: (a) establishing parasocial relationships with characters, (b) reducing negative cognitive responses, and (c) increasing perceived realism.

When audience members feel as though they have a relationship with characters in the narrative, the characters may serve as role models whose behavior the audience members wish to emulate; social cognitive theory explains how such vicarious modeling influences behavior (Bandura, 1986). Narrative characters can also influence normative perceptions through the behavior in which they engage; normative perceptions, of course, are related to behavior change according to several major psychological theories (Noar & Zimmerman, 2005). Depending on the story situation, characters may also elicit an emotional response from the audience; increased emotion also can influence attitude and behavior change (Oatley, 2002). Audience members' identification with characters because of perceived similarities in demographic, psychosocial, or behavioral characteristics also facilitates transportation (Green, 2004).

Transportation into a story is an enjoyable experience, regardless of the valence of the story itself (Green, Brock, & Kaufman, 2004). When transported into a story, audiences—because they are in a pleasurable mental state—are less likely to experience negative cognitive reactions such as counterarguing (Dal Cin, Zanna, & Fong, 2004). In addition, because information is presented in story form and not as an obvious attempt at persuasion, the audience is less likely to experience psychological resistance (Dal Cin et al., 2004). Negative cognitive reactions also are less likely because cognitive resources (Lang, 2000) are being allocated to processing story events as they unfold and therefore are less available for other purposes.

Narratives enhance persuasion by providing audiences realistic examples of health-related situations. Realistic examples can enhance audience members' ability to imagine themselves in similar situations, which in turn can influence future behavior (Gregory, Cialdini, & Carpenter, 1982). Further, the visual imagery evoked by a narrative can be quite powerful and more likely to have longer lasting impact than information presented through nonnarrative means (Green, 2006).

Narrative messages in adolescent substance abuse prevention. The health-behavior change literature typically takes two approaches to investigating the effects of narrative. The first approach usually compares narrative messages to statistical messages (messages that present arguments based on statistical data, such as the prevalence of a health-related behavior and associated negative health effects) to determine message influence on outcome variables. The evidence in support of the narrative versus statistical message strategy is decidedly mixed, with some studies showing support for narratives and others showing support for statistics, often depending on which outcome variable is considered (e.g., cognitive vs. affective responses). The second approach is through entertainment-education (E-E), which uses entertainment formats such as television programs and comics to educate audiences about health and social issues (Singhal & Rogers, 1999). The E-E literature is characterized by a strong focus on social change, almost exclusively directed at family planning, gender equality, and HIV prevention. Although drug use prevention sometimes appears in a story, it is usually not the main focus. Research has shown E-E interventions can attract large audiences and have strong effects on behavior change—as long as the interventions are produced and implemented effectively (Singhal & Rogers, 1999).

Narrative messages are ubiquitous in adolescent drug prevention efforts, with PSAs featuring testimonials of (former) users or conveying vignettes of characters confronting conflicts related to drug use. The adolescent drug use prevention literature, however, has not really investigated narrative messaging using the comparative or E-E approaches. Indeed, a literature search revealed only one example of a study exploring the comparative effects of narrative on adolescent drug use, and that study compared narratives to a more comprehensive didactic approach instead of comparing them to statistical messages. Specifically, Epstein, Thomson, Collins, and Pancella (2009) compared narrative (interactive DVD) and didactic (interactive CD-ROM) versions of a curriculum to teach the science of drug addiction to African American adolescents. Results showed that both curricula had favorable gains for knowledge. The didactic version, however, resulted in greater mastery of the curriculum than the narrative version.

The clearest application of narrative in adolescent drug use prevention comes from Hecht et al. (2003), who developed the *keepin' it R.E.A.L.* program for middle school students. The curriculum teaches drug abuse resistance skills (Refuse, Explain, Avoid, and Leave) through adolescent narratives of experiences with offers of drugs and resistance of those offers. Five of the 10 lessons in the curriculum are taught through videos, four of which feature narratives of adolescents demonstrating each of the resistance strategies. The curriculum is offered in three versions: Mexican American, White/Black, and multicultural (Hecht & Raup Krieger, 2006). The cultural emphasis acknowledges that values, norms, motivations, resistance strategies, and perceptions of what constitutes communication competence differ across cultures, and in that sense, the curriculum reflects the importance of message targeting.

Evaluations of *keepin' it R.E.A.L.* have been positive, with favorable program effects on substance use, use of resistance strategies, and expectations and norms regarding drug use. Indeed, the program is considered a model program (Hecht & Raup Krieger, 2006) and is listed on the Substance Abuse and Mental Health Services (SAMHSA) National Registry of Evidence-Based Programs and Practices (see http://www.nrepp.samhsa.gov/), available and updated online. Nonetheless, there is little evidence to suggest that the cultural targeting enhances program efficacy. Instead, the effect is larger with the multicultural and Mexican American versions regardless of student ethnicity (Hecht et al., 2003; Hecht, Graham, & Elek, 2006). Hecht and his colleagues suggested that the effectiveness of the program resulted from its being culturally grounded instead of culturally adapted. That is, the formative and participatory research that went into program development involved adolescents' crafting program narratives based on their own real experiences with substance use offers and refusals, resulting in a program "from kids through kids to kids" (Hecht & Raup Krieger, 2006, p. 315). Such authenticity is a theoretically important component of effective narratives.

Message Framing

Message framing research involves the extent to which the consequences of a behavior are emphasized in a persuasive message. Gain-framed messages emphasize the positive consequences of adopting a healthy behavior or avoiding a risky behavior; loss-framed messages emphasize the negative consequences of not adopting a healthy behavior or engaging in a risky behavior. A consequence involves obtaining or not obtaining a desirable or undesirable outcome. In other words, message frames can be operationally defined in one of four ways: (a) attaining a desirable outcome (gain frame), (b) not attaining an undesirable outcome (gain frame), (c) attaining an undesirable outcome (loss frame), or (d) not attaining a desirable outcome (loss frame). The first and third frames have been most extensively investigated (Salovey, Schneider, & Apanovitch, 2002), although one study of sunscreen use compared all four frames and found both gain-framed messages to be equally more effective and both loss-framed messages to be equally less effective (Detweiler, Bedell, Salovey, Pronin, & Rothman, 1999).

Arguably, any prevention message that emphasizes the negative consequences of engaging in substance use or the positive consequences of avoiding substance use could be said to be framed. For example, if a PSA depicts a teenage boy losing his girlfriend because he will not quit smoking pot or depicts a teenage girl competing successfully in sports because she remains abstinent from alcohol, these messages could be said to be framed. Very few studies in the adolescent drug use prevention literature, however, actually report using message framing, per se, as a theoretical foundation for their research.

Still, the framing question is an important one in drug use prevention message design because it represents two distinct perspectives in the campaign literature. One perspective, representing the *loss frame camp*, emphasizes the risks of substance use to deter potential users. Advocates argue that emphasizing the physical, social, and relational risks of using drugs will lead target audiences to conclude that the risks of use outweigh the benefits. This perspective was especially apparent in the ONDCP National Media Campaign's implementation of the previously mentioned Marijuana Initiative. The PSAs in this phase of the media campaign strongly emphasized the negative consequences of marijuana use. Palmgreen et al. (2007) reported that these messages were effective in reversing upward development trends in marijuana use among HSS, as well as reducing positive marijuana attitudes and beliefs in this important target group.

Another perspective, representing the *gain frame camp*, promotes an approach that emphasizes the benefits of nonuse. Advocates argue that the adolescents most likely to use drugs are not risk averse but are actually risk seeking, so loss-framed messages that point out the risks of use may actually lead to iatrogenic effects (Hornik, Jacobsohn, Orwin, Piesse, & Kalton, 2008). Gain-framed messages that emphasize the benefits of remaining drug free, however, may be more effective with adolescents who are striving to gain autonomy. The gain-framing perspective was especially apparent in the "Above the Influence" component of the ONDCP campaign and the "Be Under Your Own Influence" campaign designed by Slater and colleagues (2011). Messages in these campaigns emphasized how avoiding marijuana use increases opportunity to achieve personal aspirations and gain autonomy. Results of evaluations showed that campaign exposure was related to reduced marijuana use and that the ONDCP campaign indirectly affected marijuana use through its effects on aspiration- and autonomy-related beliefs (Slater et al., 2011).

Theoretical mechanisms for framing effects. Prospect theory explains decisions made under conditions of uncertainty when outcomes are presented in terms of potential gains or losses (Kahneman & Tversky, 1979). Early research showed that people are more likely to make *risk-averse* decisions when outcomes are presented in terms of gains, whereas people are more likely to make *risk-seeking* decisions when outcomes are presented in terms of losses—even when the objective outcome is probabilistically identical. In a seminal article laying the foundation for this model, Tversky and Kahneman (1981) showed that when given a choice between a program that saved 200 people and a program that had a one-third probability of saving 600 people, 72% of respondents chose the first program. However, when given a choice between a program that resulted in 400 deaths and a program that offered a one-third probability that none of 600 people would die, 78% of respondents chose the second program. In other words, when the outcome was presented as a gain (200 people live), respondents preferred the sure bet, but when the outcome was presented as a loss (400 people die), respondents were willing to take a risk—even though they saved the same 200 people by making their choice.

Given the complexities of applying this theory to health-behavior decisions, the original focus of risk as outcome probability usually is translated to risk as outcome unpleasantness (Rothman & Salovey, 1997). Gain-framed messages, therefore, emphasize unpleasant outcomes that can be avoided or pleasant outcomes that can be obtained, and loss-framed messages emphasize the opposite. Consistent with this translation, the literature has tended to demonstrate that gain-framed messages are more effective in promoting disease prevention (risk averse) behaviors and loss-framed messages are more effective in promoting disease detection (risk seeking) behaviors (Rothman & Salovey, 1997). However, recent meta-analyses have been mixed. O'Keefe and Jensen (2007) considered disease prevention studies and found advantages for gain-framed messages but only with dental hygiene behaviors. O'Keefe and Jensen (2009) considered disease detection studies and found evidence supporting loss-framed messages but only with breast cancer screening. Gallagher and Updegraff (2012) found support for gain-framed messages on prevention behaviors but not attitudes or intentions. Finally, Covey (2014) suggested that individual differences are critical to understanding message effects in this area.

Message framing in adolescent substance abuse prevention. The framing literature on the whole suggests that because drug use prevention is, by definition, a prevention behavior and prevention entails little risk, antidrug messages should be gain framed and take shape as "Don't do drugs and you'll graduate from high school," "Avoid trouble with the law," "Succeed in sports," and "Don't anger your parents." As mentioned, however, some framing literature suggests that there is nothing inherent in the prevention/detection distinction that defines low or high risk but, rather, that it is the audience's perception of the situation that defines risk. For example, adolescents could perceive saying no to their peers as exceptionally risky (and carrying great personal costs if they are rejected). In that case, a loss frame should be applied. What do the adolescent drug use prevention studies that have investigated framing suggest?

In a study on the potential effect of normative influence and past behavior on response to gain- and loss-framed messages, Cho and Boster (2008) exposed 246 adolescents to a set of either gain- or loss-framed antidrug messages. Results showed main effects for perceived norms and loss framing on attitude toward and intentions to use alcohol, tobacco, and marijuana, but these main effects were consistently qualified by interactions. For adolescents with high levels of perceived peer drug use, loss-framed messages were more effective than gain-framed messages. For adolescents with low perceived peer drug use, both types of framing were effective. Prior drug use influenced the direct effect of loss framing. For adolescents who reported prior drug use, loss-framed messages were more effective in influencing their attitudes toward drug use than gain-framed messages. For adolescents who did not report prior drug use, both types of framing were effective. Overall, the results of this study lend support for the use of a loss-framing strategy for drug prevention, particularly among youth who had used drugs.

Goodall and Appiah (2008) investigated gain- and loss-framed messages in the context of graphic cigarette warning labels. In addition to considering smoking status on the impact of framing, the researchers considered the two variations on gain-framed messages: benefits (attain a desirable outcome) and avoidance (not attain an undesirable outcome). The messages emphasized smoking's effects on teeth and breathing. Of the 210 high school students who participated in the study, more reported positive attitudes toward the loss-framed messages than toward the gain-framed messages and perceived the former as more effective at reducing smoking and helping smokers to quit; there was no difference between the two versions of the gain-framed messages. Framing had no impact on attitude and behavioral intention overall. However, interaction effects for the messages depicting cigarette smoking's effect on teeth revealed that smokers reported lower intentions to smoke after seeing the loss-framed message than the gain-framed avoidance message. Furthermore, although smokers and nonsmokers alike believed that the loss-framed messages would be most effective in helping smokers to quit and increasing their likelihood of quitting, the actual effects were more pronounced among smokers.

The results of these drug use prevention framing studies with adolescents clearly contradict the broad hypothesis that gain-framed messages will be more effective with prevention behaviors. Instead, they reveal the importance of accounting for individual differences in risk perception, whether those differences stem from the influence of peers or personal behavior.

Message Tailoring

Tailored communication is defined as "any combination of strategies and information intended to reach one specific person, based on characteristics that are unique to that person, related to the outcome of interest, and derived from an individual assessment" (Kreuter, Strecher, & Glassman, 1999, p. 277). A tailored message is uniquely designed for each individual on the basis of select demographic (e.g., sex, age, ethnicity), psychosocial (e.g., stage of change, self-efficacy), or behavioral characteristics (e.g., past drug use). These characteristics should be (and often are) chosen according to a prevailing theory. Participants complete a questionnaire that assesses the characteristics, and then a tailoring algorithm chooses messages from a library that has been designed for the intervention. The resulting messages are specifically designed for the individuals on the basis of their questionnaire responses. For example, if a tailored intervention considered gender, sensation seeking, and attitudes about smoking for a tobacco prevention program, a message for an HSS female with positive attitudes about smoking would be very different from a message for an LSS male with negative attitudes about smoking.

Message tailoring is distinct from message *targeting*, which designs messages for particular groups of people (e.g., adolescent girls), and generic messaging, which designs messages to fit everyone (a "one size fits all" approach). The first studies in message tailoring compared print materials that were tailored on determinants from prominent health-behavior theories (e.g., social cognitive theory [Bandura, 1986], theory of reasoned action [Ajzen & Fishbein, 1980]; transtheoretical model [Prochaska & DiClemente, 1983]) to materials that were generic or targeted. These studies showed tailored materials to be superior to targeted and generic materials in promoting behavior change in areas such as smoking cessation and dietary practices (Skinner, Campbell, Rimer, Curry, & Prochaska, 1999). Since those early studies, the tailoring literature has expanded rapidly. Tailoring has been applied across different formats (e.g., letters, calendars) and channels (e.g., computer kiosk, Internet, mobile device), to more than 20 health behaviors (e.g., alcohol use, bullying, immunization) and to a variety of populations (e.g., adolescents, military personnel, medical patients; Noar, Harrington, & Aldrich, 2009). Overall, interventions that involve tailoring tend to show stronger effects for attitude, behavioral intention, and behavior change than generic or targeted interventions (Noar et al., 2009).

Theoretical mechanisms for tailoring effects. The elaboration likelihood model (ELM; Petty & Cacioppo, 1986; see also Kreuter & Wray, 2003) provides a theoretical explanation for message tailoring effects. The ELM suggests that individuals engage in two types of message processing: central route and peripheral route. Central route processing involves careful examination of arguments contained in a message, whereas peripheral route processing relies on heuristics or cues to inform decisions. Petty and Cacioppo (1986) argued that central route processing results in attitudes that are more persistent, resistant to counterarguing, and more strongly related to behavior.

An important process measure associated with increased central route processing is termed *personal relevance* (Petty & Cacioppo, 1986). Along the message design continuum, tailored messages are theoretically the most personally relevant. In practice, tailored messages are often viewed as highly relevant by target audiences (i.e., activating attention and effortful processing), and thus they are more likely to be centrally processed and to have an impact on attitude, behavioral intention, and behavior change (Kreuter & Wray, 2003).

Rimer and Kreuter (2006) presented four approaches to tailoring health-related messages that can increase personal relevance: (a) matching content to the information needs and interests of the individual; (b) placing information in a context that is meaningful to the individual; (c) using design, production, and channel elements to capture the individual's attention and enhance message processing; and (d) presenting the type and structure of information preferred by the individual (also see Noar et al., 2009). In the context of drug use prevention, message content could be tailored to address an adolescent's refusal skill self-efficacy. Messages could be placed in different types of reading materials preferred by adolescents (e.g., comic books produced through a print-enabled kiosk or through an online, interactive "choose your own adventure" program). A message's sensation value could be varied to meet the arousal needs of HSS or LSS. Messages also could be designed as gain framed or loss framed, depending on how an adolescent perceives risk associated with drug use or nonuse.

Message tailoring in adolescent drug use prevention. As a whole, most of the studies of tailored drug use prevention programs for adolescents focus on cigarette smoking prevention and cessation. Indeed, four out of the five studies we found focused on preventing cigarette smoking. We briefly review two representative studies here.

Norman, Maley, Li, and Skinner (2008) evaluated the effects of a web-based tailored smoking prevention and cessation intervention on 1,402 students in Grades 9 through 11 at 14 secondary schools located in Toronto, Canada. The intervention included a five-stage interactive web-based program that employed quizzes and self-assessments with tailored feedback to increase self-efficacy and resistance to smoking. The program also involved students' keeping journals for use in small-group-based motivational interviewing during one class period and receiving tailored e-mail messages for 6 months. The web-based messages were tailored according to students' smoking status (non-smoker, experimental/social smoker, and smoker) and their readiness to change (i.e., quit or reduce their smoking levels). Participants were randomly assigned to the tailored condition or web-based comparison condition, and they were assessed at baseline, postintervention, and 3- and 6-month follow-up periods on resistance to smoking, behavioral intention to not smoke, and cigarette use. Results showed that, among students receiving the tailored intervention, nonsmokers had a significantly decreased likelihood of starting smoking at all follow-up points and smokers had higher resistance to smoking and lower likelihood of intention to smoke at all follow-up points but had no change in actual cigarette use.

Patten et al. (2006) compared a clinic-based individual counseling intervention with an Internet-only tailored intervention, recruiting 139 adolescent smokers ages 11 through 18 years to participate. The tailored intervention featured 38 different interactive components (e.g., quizzes, personalized quit plan) and information services (e.g., e-mail question and answer). Following baseline assessments, outcomes were assessed at Weeks 8, 12, 24, and 36. Results showed that at Week 24 tailored intervention participants had significantly fewer smoking days than counseling participants, and the difference in the number of cigarettes smoked per day approached significance, with tailored intervention participants smoking fewer cigarettes per day than participants in the counseling condition.

On the basis of this limited literature, there does appear to be some promise for the effectiveness of tailored drug abuse interventions for adolescents. Clearly, however, much more work needs to be done to investigate the most efficacious ways to design and disseminate these interventions for youth.

CONCLUSIONS AND FUTURE DIRECTIONS

In this chapter, we have addressed four major approaches to message design: MSV, narrative messaging, message framing, and message tailoring. We reviewed the theoretical foundations of these approaches and presented a selective review of the adolescent drug use prevention literature featuring these approaches. We also revealed a number of challenges inherent in research that focuses on the design of persuasive messages. In this concluding section, we reflect upon some of these challenges and offer suggestions for efficaciously employing these techniques in future research.

We selected MSV, narrative, framing, and tailoring because they are major approaches to message design that have clear implications for adolescent drug use prevention efforts. However, these different message design strategies are, so to speak, the tip of the iceberg. The number of other elements that factor into message design is considerable. For example, we can ask about any of the following: figurative language, such as metaphor; emotion, ranging from fear to guilt to humor; grammar, such as the use of first, second, or third person; type and order of claim and argument; message sidedness; consequence type, duration, and target. All of these elements and more have been studied in the message design literature.

Although considering all such elements is not possible (Cappella, 2006), researchers need to keep two things in mind. First, even though we cannot possibly consider (and test) the vast variety of and limitless variations on message design elements, all messages do embody these elements, either as variables (more or less of something, e.g., MSV) or as attributes (presence or absence of something, such as visual images). Second, we need to develop more message design theories that direct our attention to those cognitive or emotional elements that matter and explain how they influence the outcomes of interest, such as attitude and behavior change.

In developing message design theories, we need a clear and coherent taxonomy to classify the various message elements. In this chapter, we have referred to content, format, and structure dimensions, but that is merely a convenient rubric, not a theoretically driven one. What are message content, format, and structure, and which message elements fall under each? Are there other message dimensions to consider? Basic, descriptive work is called for here—but it is critical work because when studies do not take relevant variables into consideration, results can be jeopardized. A study by Kang, Cappella, and Fishbein (2006), which considered the effect of MSV on high- and low-quality argument processing, provides one example. A post hoc analysis the researchers conducted of the antidrug PSAs used in their study revealed substantive differences in message elements beyond MSV and argument quality: HSV/high-argument-quality messages were less likely than HSV/low-argument-quality messages to mention positive outcomes and more likely to include arguments that started with "Don't." Such content differences may have introduced additional variance that affected message processing.

As researchers move forward to better understand the effect that messaging has on youth, they also need to be aware of the potential for new technology and its impact on message design research (Noar & Harrington, 2012). The Internet, social media, and mobile communication devices are quite well suited as channels for delivering drug use prevention messages. To what extent do the platforms and features of these channels, including the extent of their interactivity (Chung, 2012), accommodate the message elements that researchers wish to manipulate? The Internet has seemingly endless possibilities, offering visual, audio, and print capacity, interactivity, and adaptability. Further, the Internet is available via mobile platforms such as smartphones, so message reach is potentially enhanced. A number of research-based prevention programs have been developed for the Internet, including *RealTeen* (Schwinn, Schinke, & Di Noia, 2010), and peerx.com, an interactive prescription-drug-abuse prevention program offered through the National Institute on Drug Abuse website (see http://teens.drugabuse.gov/peerx). These programs, though, are ones that must be actively accessed by the audience, a limiting factor that may compromise their potential reach.

New technologies such as mobile communication devices, however, can disseminate prevention messages directly to the audience, overcoming the need for the audience to come to the program. Text messaging, for example, offers a relatively simple and effective means of reaching cell phone users (Head, Noar, Iannarino, & Harrington, 2013). Although users would need to sign up for a program initially, subsequent prevention messages could be disseminated on whatever schedule is deemed appropriate. The question then becomes whether the physical or technological limits of a text message place too many restrictions on message design. For example, is it possible to use text messaging to convey a tailored, HSV, gain-framed narrative? Or is the 160-character limit imposed by smartphones too much of a restriction? Do we get creative and break the narrative into 160-character episodes? Or do we conclude that text messaging and narrative are incompatible?

Social media also offer a number of exciting intervention possibilities. Not only can prevention messages be disseminated through platforms like Facebook but also social networking capacity offers innovative strategies for leveraging persuasive attempts. In a report of a randomized controlled trial assessing the impact of political mobilization messages disseminated through Facebook, Bond et al. (2012) discovered that people who received a social message that included images of their Facebook friends who had clicked an "I Voted" button were more likely to also click the "I Voted" button, click on a link to polling place information, and actually vote than people who received an informational message. There also was evidence that the social message influenced voting-related behavior of Facebook friends, as well as friends of friends. Investigating the power of social networking to enhance the reach and impact of adolescent drug prevention messages clearly warrants attention.

Research on social networking raises the issue of interpersonal communication in drug use prevention. Early campaign research tended to ignore the fact that people often talk about the media they consume and that such talk might have an impact on campaign effects. Research has begun to acknowledge this opportune fact and systematically explore how interpersonal communication about prevention campaign messages mediates and moderates campaign impact (Helme et al., 2011; Southwell & Yzer,

2007). For example, interpersonal communication may extend the reach of campaign messages when a person who has seen a PSA talks about it to a friend who has not seen it, or it may enhance a message's favorable effect if discussion reinforces campaign messages and therefore strengthens attitudes or normative perceptions against substance use. In an analysis of the Truth campaign effects, Hwang (2012) found that persons who lived in communities with higher campaign exposure talked more about the campaign and that conversation about the campaign positively influenced beliefs about cigarette smoking; there were also direct effects of campaign exposure on smoking beliefs. Of course, not all talk about campaigns may necessarily have positive effects. An experiment by David, Cappella, and Fishbein (2006) showed that participants who processed campaign ads in a biased manner were more likely to express prodrug opinions in subsequent online conversation, which in turn influenced attitudes and normative perceptions negatively. Investigating which message characteristics are more likely to promote unbiased processing and prompt positive interpersonal communication about campaign messages is an important direction for future research.

Finally, as we move forward with research on message design, we encourage researchers to follow sound reporting standards when they publish their studies (Harrington & Noar, 2012). Reports should clearly specify which message design, information processing, and health behavior change theories informed the study. In addition, reports should not only describe how messages were manipulated but also describe message channel, format, and dose. Including actual messages if channel/format and page space allow, or links to messages available online, would be extremely useful. Following reporting standards like these will more effectively convey research results, facilitate replication and synthesis, and help to promote a cumulative science of message design.

References

Ajzen, I., & Fishbein, M. (1980). *Understanding attitudes and predicting social behavior.* Englewood Cliffs, NJ: Prentice-Hall.

Atkin, C. K., & Rice, R. E. (2013). Theory and principles of public communication campaigns. In R. E. Rice & C. K. Atkin (Eds.), *Public communication campaigns* (4th ed., pp. 3–19). Los Angeles, CA: Sage.

Bandura, A. (1986). *Social foundations of thought and action: A social cognitive theory.* Englewood Cliffs, NJ: Prentice-Hall.

Bond, R. M., Fariss, C. J., Jones, J. J., Kramer, A. D. I., Marlow, C., Settle, J. E., & Fowler, J. H. (2012). A 61-million-person experiment in social influence and political mobilization. *Nature, 489,* 295–298. doi:10.1038/nature11421

Botvin, G. J., & Griffin, K. W. (2007). School-based programmes to prevent alcohol, tobacco, and other drug use. *International Review of Psychiatry, 19,* 607–615. doi:10.1080/09540260701797753

Bracht, N., & Rice, R. E. (2013). Community partnerships strategies in health campaigns. In R. E. Rice & C. K. Atkin (Eds.), *Public communication campaigns* (4th ed., pp. 289–304). Los Angeles, CA: Sage.

Cappella, J. N. (2006). Integrating message effects and behavior change theories: Organizing comments and unanswered questions. *Journal of Communication, 56,* S265–S279. doi:10.1111/j.1460-2466.2006.00293.x

Cho, H., & Boster, F. J. (2008). Effects of gain versus loss frame antidrug ads on adolescents. *Journal of Communication, 58,* 428–446. doi:10.1111/j.1460-2466.2008.00393.x

Chung, D. (2012). Interactivity: Conceptualizations, effects, and implications. In S. M. Noar & N. G. Harrington (Eds.), *eHealth applications: Promising strategies for behavior change* (pp. 37–55). New York, NY: Routledge.

Covey, J. (2014). The role of dispositional factors in moderating message framing effects. *Health Psychology, 33,* 52–65. doi:10.1037/a0029305

Dal Cin, S., Zanna, M. P., & Fong, G. T. (2004). Narrative persuasion and overcoming resistance. In E. S. Knowles & J. Linn (Eds.), *Resistance and persuasion* (pp. 175–191). Mahwah, NJ: Erlbaum.

Dalton, M. A., Sargent, J. D., Beach, M. L., Titus-Ernstoff, L., Gibson, J. J., Ahrens, M. B., . . . Heatherton, T. F. (2003). Effect of viewing smoking in movies on adolescent smoking initiation: A cohort study. *The Lancet, 362,* 281–285. doi:10.1016/S0140-6736(03)13970-0

David, C., Cappella, J. N., & Fishbein, M. (2006). The social diffusion of influence among adolescents: Group interaction in a chat room environment about anti-drug advertisements. *Communication Theory, 16,* 118–140. doi:10.1111/j.1468-2885.2006.00008.x

Detweiler, J. B., Bedell, B. T., Salovey, P., Pronin, E., & Rothman, A. J. (1999). Message framing and sunscreen use: Gain-framed messages motivate beachgoers. *Health Psychology, 18,* 189–196. doi:10.1037/0278-6133.18.2.189

Dillard, J. P., & Nabi, R. L. (2006). The persuasive influence of emotion in cancer prevention and detection messages. *Journal of Communication, 56*, S123–S139. doi:10.1111/j.1460-2466.2006.00286.x

Domke, D., Shah, D. V., & Wackman, D. B. (1998). Media priming effects: Accessibility, association, and activation. *International Journal of Public Opinion Research, 10*, 51–74. doi:10.1093/ijpor/10.1.51

Donohew, L., Lorch, E. P., & Palmgreen, P. (1998). Applications of a theoretic model of information exposure to health interventions. *Human Communication Research, 24*, 454–468. doi:10.1111/j.1468-2958.1998.tb00425.x

Donohew, L., Palmgreen, P., & Lorch, E. P. (1994). Attention, need for sensation, and health communication campaigns. *American Behavioral Scientist, 38*, 310–322. doi:10.1177/0002764294038002011

Donohew, L., Palmgreen, P., Lorch, E. P., Zimmerman, R., & Harrington, N. G. (2002). Attention, persuasive communication, and prevention. In W. D. Crano & M. Burgoon (Eds.), *Mass media and drug prevention: Classic and contemporary theories and research* (pp. 119–143). Mahwah, NJ: Erlbaum.

Epstein, J., Thomson, N. R., Collins, K. K., & Pancella, T. (2009). A longitudinal comparison of two versions of an interactive multimedia substance abuse education program. *Journal of Child & Adolescent Substance Abuse, 18*, 302–321. doi:10.1080/10678280902973286

Fishbein, M., & Ajzen, I. (1975). *Belief, attitude, intention, and behavior: An introduction to theory and research.* Reading, MA: Addison-Wesley.

Fishbein, M., Cappella, J. N., Hornik, R., Sayeed, S., Yzer, M. C., & Ahern, R. K. (2002). The role of theory in developing effective antidrug public service announcements. In W. D. Crano & M. Burgoon (Eds.), *Mass media and drug prevention: Classic and contemporary theories and research* (pp. 89–117). Mahwah, NJ: Erlbaum.

Fisher, W. (1984). Narration as a human communication paradigm: The case of public moral argument. *Communication Monographs, 51*, 1–22. doi:10.1080/03637758409390180

Gallagher, K. M., & Updegraff, J. (2012). Health message framing effects on attitudes, intentions, and behavior: A meta-analytic review. *Annals of Behavioral Medicine, 43*, 101–116. doi:10.1007/s12160-011-9308-7

Goodall, C., & Appiah, O. (2008). Adolescents' perceptions of Canadian cigarette package warning labels: Investigating the effects of message framing. *Health Communication, 23*, 117–127. doi:10.1080/10410230801967825

Green, M. C. (2004). Transportation into narrative worlds: The role of prior knowledge and perceived realism. *Discourse Processes, 38*, 247–266. doi:10.1207/s15326950dp3802_5

Green, M. C. (2006). Narratives and cancer communication. *Journal of Communication, 56*, S163–S183. doi:10.1111/j.1460-2466.2006.00288.x

Green, M. C., & Brock, T. C. (2000). The role of transportation in the persuasiveness of public narratives. *Journal of Personality and Social Psychology, 79*, 701–721. doi:10.1037/0022-3514.79.5.701

Green, M. C., Brock, T. C., & Kaufman, G. F. (2004). Understanding media enjoyment: The role of transportation into narrative worlds. *Communication Theory, 14*, 311–327. doi:10.1111/j.1468-2885.2004.tb00317.x

Gregory, W. L., Cialdini, R. B., & Carpenter, K. M. (1982). Self-relevant scenarios as mediators of likelihood estimates and compliance: Does imagining make it so? *Journal of Personality and Social Psychology, 43*, 89–99. doi:10.1037/0022-3514.43.1.89

Harrington, N. G., & Noar, S. M. (2012). Reporting standards for studies of tailored interventions. *Health Education Research, 27*, 331–342. doi:10.1093/her/cyr108

Head, K. J., Noar, S. M., Iannarino, N., & Harrington, N. G. (2013). Efficacy of text messaging-based interventions for health promotion: A meta-analysis. *Social Science & Medicine, 97*, 41–48. doi:10.1016/j.socscimed.2013.08.003

Hecht, M. L., Graham, J. W., & Elek, E. (2006). The drug resistance strategies intervention: Program effects on substance use. *Health Communication, 20*, 267–276. doi:10.1207/s15327027hc2003_6

Hecht, M. L., Marsiglia, F. F., Elek, E., Wagstaff, D. A., Kulis, S., Dustman, P., & Miller-Day, M. (2003). Culturally grounded substance use prevention: An evaluation of the *keepin' it R.E.A.L.* curriculum. *Prevention Science, 4*, 233–248. doi:10.1023/A:1026016131401

Hecht, M. L., & Miller-Day, M. (2009). The Drug Resistance Strategies Project: A communication approach to preventing adolescent drug use. In L. Frey & K. Cissna (Eds.), *Handbook of applied communication research* (pp. 535–557). Mahwah, NJ: Erlbaum.

Hecht, M. L., & Raup Krieger, J. L. (2006). The principle of cultural grounding in school-based substance abuse prevention: The drug resistance strategies project. *Journal of Language and Social Psychology, 25*, 301–319. doi:10.1177/0261927X06289476

Helme, D. W., Noar, S. M., Allard, S., Zimmerman, R. S., Palmgreen, P., & McClanahan, K. J. (2011). In-depth investigation of interpersonal discussions in response to a safer sex mass media campaign. *Health Communication, 26*, 366–378. doi:10.1080/10410236.2010.551582

Hinyard, L. J., & Kreuter, M. W. (2007). Using narrative communication as a tool for health behavior change: A conceptual, theoretical, and empirical overview. *Health Education & Behavior, 34*, 777–792. doi:10.1177/1090198106291963

Hornik, R., Jacobsohn, L., Orwin, R., Piesse, A., & Kalton, G. (2008). Effects of the national youth anti-drug media campaign on youths. *American Journal of Public Health*, *98*, 2229–2236. doi:10.2105/AJPH.2007.125849

Hwang, Y. (2012). Social diffusion of campaign effects: Campaign-generated interpersonal communication as a mediator of antitobacco campaign effects. *Communication Research*, *39*, 120–141. doi:10.1177/0093650210389029

Janz, N. K., & Becker, M. H. (1984). The health belief model: A decade later. *Health Education Quarterly*, *11*, 1–47. doi:10.1177/109019818401100101

Kahneman, D., & Tversky, A. (1979). Prospect theory: An analysis of decision under risk. *Econometrica*, *47*, 263–292. doi:10.2307/1914185

Kang, Y., Cappella, J., & Fishbein, M. (2006). The attentional mechanism of message sensation value: Interaction between message sensation value and argument quality on message effectiveness. *Communication Monographs*, *73*, 351–378. doi:10.1080/03637750601024164

Kreuter, M. W., Strecher, V. J., & Glassman, B. (1999). One size does not fit all: The case for tailoring print materials. *Annals of Behavioral Medicine*, *21*, 276–283. doi:10.1007/BF02895958

Kreuter, M. W., & Wray, R. J. (2003). Tailored and targeted health communication: Strategies for enhancing information relevance. *American Journal of Health Behavior*, *27*, S227–S232. doi:10.5993/AJHB.27.1.s3.6

Kruglanski, A. W., & Thompson, E. P. (1999). Persuasion by a single route: A view from the Unimodel. *Psychological Inquiry*, *10*, 83–109. doi:10.1207/S15327965PL100201

Lang, A. (2000). The limited capacity model of mediated message processing. *Journal of Communication*, *50*, 46–70. doi:10.1111/j.1460-2466.2000.tb02833.x

Lorch, E. P., Palmgreen, P., Donohew, L., Helm, D., Baer, S. A., & Dsilva, M. U. (1994). Program context, sensation seeking, and attention to televised anti-drug public service announcements. *Human Communication Research*, *20*, 390–412. doi:10.1111/j.1468-2958.1994.tb00328.x

McGuire, W. (1981). Theoretical foundations of campaigns. In R. E. Rice & W. Paisley (Eds.), *Public communication campaigns* (pp. 43–65). Newbury Park, CA: Sage.

McGuire, W. (2013). McGuire's classic input-output framework for constructing persuasive messages. In R. E. Rice & C. K. Atkin (Eds.), *Public communication campaigns* (4th ed., pp. 133–145). Los Angeles, CA: Sage.

Morgan, S. E., Palmgreen, P., Stephenson, M. T., Hoyle, R., & Lorch, E. P. (2003). Associations between message features and subjective evaluations of the sensation value of antidrug public service announcements. *Journal of Communication*, *53*, 512–526. doi:10.1111/j.1460-2466.2003.tb02605.x

Noar, S. M., & Harrington, N. G. (Eds.). (2012). *eHealth applications: Promising strategies for behavior change*. New York, NY: Routledge.

Noar, S. M., Harrington, N. G., & Aldrich, R. S. (2009). The role of message tailoring in the development of persuasive health communication messages. *Communication Yearbook*, *33*, 73–133.

Noar, S. M., & Zimmerman, R. S. (2005). Health behavior theory and cumulative knowledge regarding health behaviors: Are we moving in the right direction? *Health Education Research*, *20*, 275–290. doi:10.1093/her/cyg113

Norman, C. D., Maley, O., Li, X., & Skinner, H. A. (2008). Using the Internet to assist smoking prevention and cessation in schools: A randomized, controlled trial. *Health Psychology*, *27*, 799–810. doi:10.1037/a0013105

Oatley, K. (2002). Emotions and the story worlds of fiction. In M. C. Green, J. J. Strange, & T. C. Brock (Eds.), *Narrative impact: Social and cognitive foundations* (pp. 39–69). Mahwah, NJ: Erlbaum.

O'Keefe, D. J., & Jensen, J. D. (2007). The relative persuasiveness of gain-framed and loss-framed messages for encouraging disease prevention behaviors: A meta-analytic review. *Journal of Health Communication*, *12*, 623–644. doi:10.1080/10810730701615198

O'Keefe, D. J., & Jensen, J. D. (2009). The relative persuasiveness of gain-framed and loss-framed messages for encouraging disease detection behaviors: A meta-analytic review. *Journal of Communication*, *59*, 296–316. doi:10.1111/j.1460-2466.2009.01417.x

Paek, H.-J., Kim, K., & Hove, T. (2010). Content analysis of antismoking videos on YouTube: Message sensation value, message appeals, and their relationships with viewer responses. *Health Education Research*, *25*, 1085–1099. doi:10.1093/her/cyq063

Palmgreen, P., Donohew, L., Lorch, E. P., Hoyle, R. H., & Stephenson, M. T. (2001). Television campaigns and adolescent marijuana use: Tests of sensation seeking targeting. *American Journal of Public Health*, *91*, 292–296. doi:10.2105/AJPH.91.2.292

Palmgreen, P., Lorch, E. P., Stephenson, M. T., Hoyle, R. H., & Donohew, L. (2007). Effects of the Office of National Drug Control Policy's marijuana initiative campaign on high-sensation-seeking adolescents. *American Journal of Public Health*, *97*, 1644–1649. doi:10.2105/AJPH.2005.072843

Palmgreen, P., Stephenson, M. T., Everett, M. W., Baseheart, J. R., & Francies, R. (2002). Perceived message sensation value (PMSV) and the dimensions and validation of a PMSV scale. *Health Communication*, *14*, 403–428. doi:10.1207/S15327027HC1404_1

Patten, C. A., Croghan, I. T., Meis, T. M., Decker, P. A., Pingree, S., Colligan, R. C., . . . Gustafson, D. H. (2006). Randomized clinical trial of an Internet-based versus brief office intervention for adolescent smoking cessation. *Patient Education and Counseling, 64*, 249–258. doi:10.1016/j.pec.2006.03.001

Petty, R. E., & Cacioppo, J. T. (1986). *Communication and persuasion: Central and peripheral routes to attitude change.* New York, NY: Springer-Verlag. doi:10.1007/978-1-4612-4964-1

Prochaska, J. O., & DiClemente, C. C. (1983). Stages and processes of self-change of smoking: Toward an integrative model of change. *Journal of Consulting and Clinical Psychology, 51*, 390–395. doi:10.1037/0022-006X.51.3.390

Rimer, B. K., & Kreuter, M. W. (2006). Advanced tailored health communication: A persuasion and message effects perspective. *Journal of Communication, 56*, S184–S201. doi:10.1111/j.1460-2466.2006.00289.x

Rothman, A. J., & Salovey, P. (1997). Shaping perceptions to motivate healthy behavior: The role of message framing. *Psychological Bulletin, 121*, 3–19. doi:10.1037/0033-2909.121.1.3

Salovey, P., Schneider, T. R., & Apanovitch, A. M. (2002). Message framing in the prevention and early detection of illness. In J. P. Dillard & M. Pfau (Eds.), *The persuasion handbook: Developments in theory and practice* (pp. 391–406). Thousand Oaks, CA: Sage

Schwinn, T. M., Schinke, S. P., & Di Noia, J. (2010). Preventing drug abuse among adolescent girls: Outcome data from an internet-based intervention. *Prevention Science, 11*, 24–32. doi:10.1007/s11121-009-0146-9

Singhal, A., & Rogers, E. M. (1999). *Entertainment-education: A communication strategy for social change.* Mahwah, NJ: Erlbaum.

Skinner, C. S., Campbell, M. K., Rimer, B. K., Curry, S., & Prochaska, J. O. (1999). How effective is tailored print communication? *Annals of Behavioral Medicine, 21*, 290–298. doi:10.1007/BF02895960

Slater, M. D. (1999). Integrating application of media effects, persuasion, and behavior change theories to communication campaigns: A stage-of-change framework. *Health Communication, 11*, 335–354. doi:10.1207/S15327027HC1104_2

Slater, M. D., Kelly, K. J., Lawrence, F. R., Stanley, L. R., & Comello, M. L. G. (2011). Assessing media campaigns linking marijuana non-use with autonomy and aspirations: "Be Under Your Own Influence" and ONDCP's "Above the Influence." *Prevention Science, 12*, 12–22. doi:10.1007/s11121-010-0194-1

Snyder, L. B., Hamilton, M. A., Mitchell, E. W., Kiwanuka-Tondo, J., Fleming-Milici, F., & Proctor, D. (2004). A meta-analysis of the effect of mediated health communication campaigns on behavior change in the United States. *Journal of Health Communication, 9*, 71–96. doi:10.1080/10810730490271548

Southwell, B. G., & Yzer, M. C. (2007). The roles of interpersonal communication in mass media campaigns. *Communication Yearbook, 31*, 420–462.

Stoolmiller, M., Gerrard, M., Sargent, J. D., Worth, K. A., & Gibbons, F. X. (2010). R-rated movie viewing, growth in sensation seeking and alcohol initiation: Reciprocal and moderation effects. *Prevention Science, 11*, 1–13. doi:10.1007/s11121-009-0143-z

Strange, J. J. (2002). How fictional tales wag real world beliefs: Models and mechanisms of narrative influence. In M. C. Green, J. J. Strange, & T. C. Brock (Eds.), *Narrative impact: Social and cognitive foundations* (pp. 315–341). Mahwah, NJ: Erlbaum.

Tversky, A., & Kahneman, D. (1981). The framing of decisions and the psychology of choice. *Science, 211*, 453–458. doi:10.1126/science.7455683

Witte, K. (1992). Putting the fear back into fear appeals: The extended parallel process model. *Communication Monographs, 59*, 329–349. doi:10.1080/03637759209376276

Zillmann, D., & Brosius, H. B. (2000). *Exemplification in communication: The influence of case reports on the perception of issues.* Mahwah, NJ: Erlbaum.

Zuckerman, M. (1994). *Behavioral expressions and biosocial bases of sensation seeking.* Cambridge, England: Cambridge University Press.

CHAPTER 22

THE MEDIA CAMPAIGN AS A FOCAL PREVENTION STRATEGY: A GUIDE TO DESIGN, IMPLEMENTATION, AND EVALUATION

William D. Crano, Eusebio M. Alvaro, and Jason T. Siegel

In this chapter, we suggest ways in which media campaigns can be developed and designed so that the validity of their outcomes may be assessed with a greater degree of confidence. We first briefly discuss the National Youth Anti-Drug Media Campaign (NYAMC), one of the country's largest media-based campaigns using social marketing for health persuasion targeting youth drug prevention. This effort is intended to illustrate some of the decision points that must be navigated when mounting large-scale prevention campaigns of this type. We then turn to considerations of the nature of media effects, the outcomes that might be expected from health-persuasion social marketing campaigns, useful design options for developing and evaluating media campaigns, and a brief discussion of their strengths and weaknesses. The chapter is focused on design decisions that affect the quality of data obtained in evaluating campaign effects and on issues of message development that can make the difference between persuasive success or failure. The chapter also discusses quasi-experimental research designs that may prove useful when other rigorous design conditions are unavailable. The chapter is designed to cause readers to consider how, and the conditions under which, traditional mass media approaches should be exploited and when they should be avoided. We also provide an overview of theoretical issues in campaign development. Possessing this vital knowledge will help researchers elaborate the precise psychological mechanisms underlying campaign effects and their anticipated outcomes. By implication, theory also dictates which measures should be included in the campaign evaluation to accurately pinpoint the hypothesized causal processes that link social marketing efforts with behavior change.

The golden promise of the mass media has proved almost irresistible for drug prevention researchers and practitioners. Media campaigns offer the tantalizing possibility of reaching thousands, perhaps millions, of people at low cost, and even if their effect sizes are small, they may prove noteworthy when extrapolated to the larger population (Derzon & Lipsey, 2002). However, though mass-mediated tobacco prevention efforts have had positive effects (e.g., Farrelly, Nonnemaker, Davis, & Hussin, 2009; Richardson, Green, Xiao, Sokol, & Vallone, 2010; see also U.S. Department of Health and Human Services, 2012), the potential of the mass media for large-scale influence on drug-related behavior has been realized only rarely. Many earlier disappointments may be attributed to

The authors would like to acknowledge the assistance of Erin Kelly O'Brien, Candice Donaldson, Cara Tan, Elena Lyrintzis, and Brandon Nakawaki in the preparation of this chapter. The authors also thank the National Institute on Drug Abuse for their continued support of this research program.

http://dx.doi.org/10.1037/14550-023
Handbook of Adolescent Drug Use Prevention: Research, Intervention Strategies, and Practice, L. M. Scheier (Editor)

media campaigns that made use of research designs and evaluation models that could not produce unambiguous implications. As a result, the silver bullet of efficient and pervasive media-campaign influence on illicit drug use sometimes falls far short of its intended mark.

DESIGN OF MEDIA CAMPAIGNS

The goal of a methodologically rigorous research design is to create conditions that limit the ambiguity of inferences drawn from the analysis of study data. According to Campbell and Stanley (1963), *internal validity* is achieved when proper design renders implausible any alternative explanations of results attributed to the manipulation of independent variables. Discussion of threats to internal validity usually revolves around the nature and stringency of experimental designs, with the most rigorous sampling designs involving the random assignment of participants to treatment and control or comparison conditions (e.g., Crano, Brewer, & Lac, in press). When a host of important conditions are met (e.g., temporal precedence), a randomized design produces unbiased estimates of the causal effect (Rubin, 1974). The important point about randomization is that, with sufficient numbers, it ensures that naturally occurring and systematic variations in the sampling units are equivalent across study conditions.

In most research designs, individual participants usually are the units of analysis, although larger entities—including health catchment areas, clinics, schools, or even whole communities—may play this role as well (Donner & Klar, 2000). Noteworthy exceptions to the "necessity of randomization for causal inference" rule may be found in designs using regression-discontinuity, instrumental variable methods, interrupted time-series, or other forms of cluster-based designs (where data involving the unit of assignment and unit of analysis are hierarchically nested), but these are not common in studies of mass media communication effects (Cleland, 2012; Donohew, Palmgreen, Lorch, Zimmerman, & Harrington, 2002; Palmgreen, Donohew, Lorch, Hoyle, & Stephenson, 2002). When such multilevel designs are used, it is important that sufficient units of analysis be used to maintain statistical power.

The experimental orientation advocated by Crano, Brewer, and Lac (in press) is not characteristic of most media-based prevention studies, which rarely use more than one treatment and even more rarely assign respondents randomly to conditions formed by the factorial combination of multiple interventions. From the standpoint of causal inference of treatment effects, the common univariate design without random assignment is not ideal (Donaldson, Christie, & Mark, 2009). Attempts to derive unambiguous information from one-shot (treatment-measure) case study designs is not productive from an evaluation standpoint, but they are common in media-based prevention research (Bertrand, O'Reilly, Denison, Anhang, & Sweat, 2006; Kingsbury, Tessin, & Alexander, 2012; Noar, 2006, 2012). Nevertheless, the methodological requirements of simple laboratory experiments hold for large-scale media interventions as well, even when units of analysis are entire communities, not simply individuals, and they should be honored to ensure capture of reliable and valid data.

DECISION POINTS: THE NATIONAL YOUTH ANTI-DRUG MEDIA CAMPAIGN

Many campaigns have used nonexperimental approaches, which do not generally support unambiguous causal interpretation or precise identification of psychological processes responsible for designated outcomes. A creative design feature of the NYADMC involved the use of propensity score methods, an approach that has been invoked as a surrogate to achieve the main design features of randomization. Propensity score techniques mimic the desired goal of randomization by creating a coarse function (scalar weight) or propensity score obtained from regression analysis, based on a pool of candidate covariates, and then balancing participants on the basis of this scalar weight (Rosenbaum & Rubin, 1983). Membership in a particular subclass (homogeneous bins created by forming quintiles on the scalar weight) assumes a "nearest neighbor" effect, so that efficient matching on the multivariate distribution of the propensity score reduces potential sampling bias that might arise from preexisting confounding conditions.

The propensity score is typically based on the results of a logistic or probit regression analysis model that predicts treatment membership from a set of potentially confounding covariates. Under the stable unit-treatment value assumption (i.e., each individual receives only one treatment; see Rubin, 1980), the relation between treatment assignment and the endpoint is conditionally independent of the covariates. The resulting propensity score for each member of the sample then represents the estimated "conditional" probability of that individual's being exposed to the treatment (i.e., a valid unbiased estimate of the treatment effect). If the balancing works efficiently, then the arithmetic means of the estimated propensity score (a linear combination of covariates) will be equal between the treatment and control respondents.

Despite the overall importance of using covariate adjustments to equilibrate groups, there are some noteworthy drawbacks to the method. For instance, Rosenbaum and Rubin (1983), pioneers of propensity score methods in the social and life sciences, implicitly identified one of the method's limitations when they observed, "Both large and small sample theor[ies] show that adjustment for the scalar propensity score is sufficient to remove bias due to all *observed* covariates" (emphasis added; p. 41). A problem here is that "all observed covariates" used in an analysis may not include all the covariates that should be modeled, based on earlier empirical research and theory. It is conceivable that there remain uncontrolled factors that may bias either the treatment or control group participants without true randomization (in a normal regression framework these "hidden" unidentified covariates are reflected in the standard errors of the parameter estimates). This bias represents a threat to internal validity and can produce misleading findings and render subsequent inferences from the data invalid. Related to this problem, the use of large samples is recommended when deriving propensity scores because the balance on the covariates obtained through form subclasses will approximate the expected balance with increasing sample size.

A second potential problem with the propensity score approach is that the covariates used to derive the propensity score are no longer available for further analysis. In other words, the set of covariates used to create the coarse function are no longer viable candidates for exploring possible psychological mechanisms (mediation or moderation) that influence the behavior in question (i.e., drug use). Consider the case where a propensity score is formulated in part using a measure of perceived peer use of marijuana. Once this "candidate covariate" is used in creating the propensity score, it is no longer available to model as a putative risk factor in models predicting youth drug use or as a possible mediator of prevention campaign effects. Overall, propensity scoring is an important advance in minimizing the downside of using non- or quasi-experimental designs, but it is not a complete substitute for random assignment in creating equivalent groups and providing estimates of unbiased treatment effects.

There are important additional design features associated with the NYADMC that are worth noting and that may have influenced its evaluation. To begin with, the NYADMC was instituted in the early days of President Bill Clinton's first presidential term, and it continues today in altered form (U.S. Department of Health and Human Services, 2012). The campaign was designed to expose youth to a wide range of persuasive antidrug information through almost all known media channels. From 1999 through 2004, the effects of the campaign were assessed approximately annually in a nationally representative household panel sample of children (ages 9–11), youth (ages 12–18), and their parents (for details of the study's sampling model and design, see Hornik et al., 2000, 2001). The age ranges of the sample for children and youth provided a means to examine factors related to drug onset during the critical and vulnerable years of adolescence. The campaign targeted many of its antidrug advertisements to the 13-to-15-year-old age category, when social influences appear strong and drug use initiation begins (Alvaro et al., 2013; Crano, Siegel, Alvaro, Lac, & Hemovich, 2008). Using ACASI (audio computer-assisted self-interviewing) methods, matched parent–child or parent–youth dyads within each selected household responded to a survey, with different versions administered to children, youth, and parents. The survey tapped a wealth of putative risk factors associated with drug use.

It contained questions about general and specific levels of media campaign exposure, alcohol and tobacco use, attitudes toward and intentions to use drugs, and self-reported drug use. It also included a number of questions assessing family interactions, discussions about drug use, perceived parental control, parental monitoring and supervision, and items assessing parent–child communication.

Design

The NYADMC evaluation was designed to consider many factors, including the absence of randomization, the rapid turnaround required for assessing campaign effects (6 months between congressionally mandated reports), the health-persuasion logic model driving the campaign, and the need to collect accurate and valid data systematically from a panel sample of youth and their parents. Of considerable concern was the fact that the entire country was potentially exposed to the media intervention; there was no designated control or comparison group that was not exposed to the antidrug messages. To create such a blackout would have required closing public service media outlets or preventing airing of campaign advertisements in select regions of the country. Such activity runs counter to constitutional law regarding government censorship and free speech and would certainly have been legally challenged. In addition, to facilitate a rapid move from point of conception to actually airing campaign public service announcements (PSAs), there was limited vetting and pilot testing of the PSAs (U.S. Office of National Drug Control Policy, 1998). The rapid implementation and nationwide reach of the campaign may have been necessary, but the lack of experimental rigor undercut the capacity to make strong causal connections between campaign exposure and subsequent changes in drug use.

As a result, the evaluators were limited to a classic one-shot posttest-only design, an approach that Campbell and Stanley (1963) used as an example of what not to do when designing a study of high internal validity. With no control group and no pretest, the causal implications that could be drawn from the evaluation were limited. The campaign evaluation team could rely only on historical trend information from the period prior to the campaign as a benchmark of youth drug use. However, even this approach is subject to criticism, as historical trends and other uncontrolled events (e.g., the burgeoning use of drug prevention in schools) may affect internal validity in such cases. In addition, drug use trends may have been affected by other prevention efforts, changes in reporting methods (trend information obtained from school surveys do not always match household surveys; see, e.g., Fendrich & Johnson, 2001), and other extraneous factors. On the positive side, the campaign did attain one of its goals. The gross rating points (i.e., a measure of market saturation or exposure) linked to each of the ads aired throughout the campaign were high, and, importantly, the measure was associated significantly and positively with youths' self-reports of campaign ad exposures (Southwell, Barmada, Hornik, & Maklan, 2002).

Evaluation

The campaign's evaluator used two uniquely different composite measures of campaign exposure and recall to gauge the campaign's reach. The first method, assessing general exposure, asked youth (and separately their parents) questions about campaign brand recognition (saw or heard "My Anti-Drug" in recent months), including assessing their exposure to campaign themes (e.g., how often they saw recent antidrug ads on TV or heard them on radio). Questions about general exposure also queried respondents about their memory of having seen or heard about campaign themes in different media venues, including billboards, the Internet, newspapers and magazines, movie theater trailers, and television and radio, as well as recalling antitobacco ads on TV or the radio. Their answers then formed a composite indicating general exposure, which after weighting based on exposure level was then categorized into both three- and four-level ordinal scale scores.

The second method required parents and youth from each household to view brief clips of recently aired (in 60-day flights) campaign ads on a laptop monitor. Respondents were asked specific questions about recalling these PSAs (e.g., "In recent months, how many times have you seen or heard this ad?"). Additional items asked whether the ad "got their attention," "was convincing," "exaggerated the problem," and "said something important." A "ringer" ad that had not been aired during the prior 2-month flight also was included. Models predicting drug-relevant attitudes, intentions, and drug use controlled for many theoretically relevant factors using propensity score methods (Hornik, Jacobsohn, Orwin, Piesse, & Kalton, 2008). In the case of youth, the analyses examined whether those reporting either greater exposure to the campaign brand or recall of campaign ads were less likely to initiate or continue to use drugs than were youth who reported viewing fewer ads. The analyses provided no evidence of favorable campaign effects on adolescents' behaviors. The evaluation team reported that higher levels of campaign exposure were not favorably associated with lower reported levels of marijuana use over the 4-year evaluation period. Indeed, the evaluation even showed some evidence of iatrogenic effects, which indicated that during the 4-year period of the campaign, greater exposure was linked to weaker antidrug norms, higher perceptions of peer drug use, and at times, greater use of marijuana (but see Magura, 2012). In light of the evidence of pervasive campaign saturation, the absence of strong beneficial effects suggests that other elements of the campaign, specifically, the messages used to convey the drug-preventive effects, could have been improved (for an extended discussion of this possibility, see Crano, Siegel, & Alvaro, 2012).

Upon subsequent examination, a team of independent scientists conducting secondary analyses of the campaign, using slightly different evaluation approaches, indicated that the campaign had favorable effects on youths' reported drug use, their attitudes, and even parental behavior. Scheier and Grenard (2010) reported that growth in campaign exposure over the 4-year period was associated with corresponding declines in self-reported drug use (for certain drugs and specific forms of exposure). This particular study mined the longitudinal strengths of the data, which had not been done in the earlier evaluations. Furthermore, a study of youth participating in mall intercepts showed that theoretically plausible mechanisms of campaign effects were consistent with sample data, indicating that higher campaign recall was associated with a change in beliefs about the risks associated with drug use, including social norms, which in turn was associated with fewer intentions to use marijuana (Scheier, Grenard, & Holtz, 2011). This information, along with other studies validating the effectiveness of some features of the national media campaign for some respondents (Alvaro et al., 2013), could be used to inform the design, analysis, and persuasive message development of future drug prevention efforts.

AN ALTERNATE ROUTE

This brief overview suggests needed refinements to the one-shot mass media approach, previously described, that exposes an entire population to a single treatment. An alternative evaluation model might provide a less ambiguous picture of the effects of a nationwide social marketing drug prevention campaign. Such an approach would begin with a series of small-scale intervention experiments, with randomly assigned treatment and control groups conducted at the community level, across demographically and racially heterogeneous communities. Such a series could be viewed as a rollout, working up to a full-scale national media campaign. The NYADMC could not be designed in this way because of congressional mandate and the quick turnaround required in the evaluation phase. However, if the campaign design could be revisited with a steadier hand, we believe the alternative approach could produce insights and directions for future prevention efforts that would pay major dividends.

An important feature of the alternative plan is the use of a planned series of investigations that gradually refine the methodology and identify the types and formats of messages that operate most effectively. Mediators and moderators of effects could be identified in these studies (rather than only broad-brush main effects), and modifications based on these factors could be input into subsequent investigations and refinements that take place in the series. This sequential, cumulative process could uncover effective features of antidrug messages that would inform development and implementation of an effective large-scale media campaign, should such a campaign be deemed desirable. Although probably less costly, this approach is no less ambitious than the NYADMC in scope or aim. The advantages associated with accretion of knowledge over a longer time frame with smaller campaigns are obvious, and they include the use of randomized controlled trials, design amenable to standard and powerful evaluation methods, and resulting cause-effect inferences that are less ambiguous than those derived from quasi-experimental or nonexperimental designs.

The NYADMC evaluation did not correspond closely with the alternative outlined here; at the same time, given the less than ideal conditions under which it was conducted, it is fair to say that the evaluation was exemplary. Working with the tools they had at their disposal, the evaluators' use of sophisticated statistical techniques such as propensity scoring went a long way toward arriving at useful conclusions about campaign outcomes. Undoubtedly, the campaign evaluators and researchers from the behavioral science community at large would have liked the media campaign to use a fully randomized design, implement pretesting and posttesting, adopt psychometrically sound measures of hypothesized risk mechanisms, and design means a priori to incorporate refinements over time. The alternative methods described earlier detail one such approach, and should be considered in evaluation going forward.

QUASI-EXPERIMENTAL DESIGN CONSIDERATIONS

The advice regarding smaller scale, targeted interventions that enable more certain identification of causal operators may prove useful for prevention specialists working on a smaller scale, on projects that do not involve large nationwide samples and huge expenditures. In these cases, as in the national campaign, true experimental designs might not be possible. However, feasible evaluation designs may be implemented in developing and testing mass media prevention campaigns, and it is to these designs that we direct our attention for the remainder of this chapter. This material will be familiar to seasoned researchers, for whom this work may serve simply to keep important concerns top of mind, while perhaps introducing some new ideas. For others, especially those in positions to drive decisions about the design and implementation of campaigns, this chapter may serve as a source of guidance to maximize success.

The first order of business in developing any media-based prevention campaign is to understand the nature of the problem and to decide on the audience to which persuasive campaign messages are directed. These issues are equally important and equally indispensable. Then, designing persuasive communications that resonate with receivers is the next critical step. Discussing this feature is beyond the scope of this chapter, but we have covered some of the necessary bases in earlier writings (e.g., see Crano et al., 2012). Once these features have been planned, the next issue is the design of the study. A principal requirement of this phase is that the resulting data be reliable, valid, and amenable to evaluative analysis. Creating or locating measures of high reliability and validity should not prove overly demanding, but the fundamental design of the study, the focus of the remainder of this chapter, can be problematic.

There are many ways to evaluate the effects of social marketing media campaigns. Ideally, researchers can use experimental designs with random assignment and strict control over factors that compromise internal validity. However, as we have learned over the years, implementing experimental designs in applied field contexts—with some noteworthy exceptions (see Derzon, 2014)—is difficult. Failing to randomize introduces the possibility of incomparability between treatment and comparison groups, and thus causal inferences based on designs that do not use random assignment generally are not as secure as those drawn from true experimental designs, which inevitably involve randomization. However, even though the internal validity of most quasi-experimental designs may be less secure than that of experimental studies, minor additions to the standard designs can appreciably enhance the interpretability of results. With an appropriately circumspect mind-set, then, let us consider some useful designs for prevention research. The discussion of the designs that follow owes much to the work of Cook and Campbell (1979), and the updated version of this work (Shadish, Cook, & Campbell, 2002). Both works provide detailed information regarding quasi-experimental designs that should be required reading for researchers contemplating media interventions. With many of these designs, addition of relevant covariates that could be used in developing a propensity score, mediation, or moderation analysis is highly recommended (Harder, Stuart, & Anthony, 2010).

One-Group Pretest–Posttest Design

One of the simplest quasi-experimental designs involves administration of a pretest and posttest separated by the campaign (see Figure 22.1). Because there is no comparison or control group, and because there is only one treatment condition, respondents cannot be randomized to conditions. This design is a minor improvement over the one used in the NYAMC, as it includes a pretest. A difference between pretest and posttest scores provides a barometer of change over time possibly attributable to the campaign intervention. Unfortunately, this design is susceptible to almost all threats to internal validity, including history, maturation, selection, testing, the regression artifact, and so on. The design is not a total loss, however, as it is possible to compare the pretest-to-posttest behavioral changes with those found in comparable settings or communities, or to compare findings with archival data collected earlier from the treated setting. These comparisons do not allow causal inferences, but they provide information of some utility.

In drug prevention contexts, pretest-to-posttest differences in the absence of a control group are not particularly compelling. If the only information available suggests that youth drug use declined in a community receiving a media-based prevention intervention, one could reasonably attribute changes in usage to any of a number of possibilities: history (a celebrity died from an overdose, an unrelated educational outreach occurred), maturation (respondents were in their late 20s, after which drug use usually declines with or without a campaign), mortality (many drug users died during the campaign, so a loss of heavy users was responsible for the overall decline), secular trend (when the campaign aired, an ongoing decline in drug use simply continued), special treatment (community members were so honored to have the antidrug campaign aired in their community that they introduced measures to supplement campaign activity), and last but not least, actual benefits derived from the intervention, or what is termed *treatment effectiveness*. Without any additional design features, such as a nonequivalent control group or repeated drug usage measures, which followed theory-based expectations, an evaluator could state only that the campaign might have been responsible for the change.

FIGURE 22.1. One-group pretest and posttest design.

Nonequivalent Pretest–Posttest Control Group Design With Single or Double Pretests

Addition of a quasi-control condition adds considerably to the utility of a one-group design (see Figure 22.2). In the nonequivalent pretest–posttest design, we recognize that the groups may not be equivalent owing to the lack of randomization of respondents to conditions. However, groups can be roughly equated through propensity scores, for example, and if the variables used in the propensity analysis are well chosen, the comparison can be informative. Often, this design is used in comparisons of respondents tested in treated and nontreated communities (Palmgreen et al., 2002). The initial equivalence of pretest scores is a positive feature, though it is not a guarantor of initial equivalence on every factor that might affect response to the intervention (Campbell & Erlebacher, 1970).

Even when the intervention is delivered at the community level, differences between individual respondents within the treatment and control groups can be assessed and the effects of the nesting of respondents within communities determined

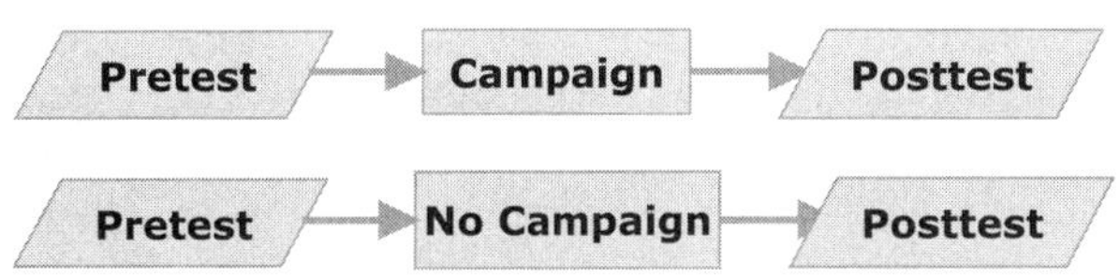

FIGURE 22.2. Nonequivalent pretest and posttest control group design.

via hierarchical linear analysis. These comparisons must be interpreted with caution, given the nonequivalence of the groups on which they are based. The "quasi-equating" of groups via propensity score methods is a useful possibility when using the nonequivalent pretest–posttest design, but it is most useful if both a pretest measure and a nonequivalent control group are available.

A problem that sometimes occurs when using this design is the result of the initial nonequivalence of the treated and comparison groups on the critical premeasure(s). Differences in rates of change on the critical measure can cause a spread of differences that appear to enhance or to suppress intervention effects. The classic achievement gap issue is an example of this bias in educational research (Cohen, Garcia, Apfel, & Master, 2006). Children from financially well-off homes begin the school year at a higher achievement level than their less economically fortunate peers, and the gap grows as time passes. One interpretation of the growing gap is that the educational system is failing the neediest students. An alternative possibility is that the growing gap reflects differences in maturation rates of high- and low-achieving children, and thus the gap would be expected to grow as time goes by. This does not mean that nothing should be done, but the two interpretations call for different solutions. Thus, caution is advised in interpreting the results of studies using the nonequivalent control group design; even so, the design can be useful in pointing to a likely relation while mitigating the plausibility of some rival alternative hypotheses.

A valuable addition to the nonequivalent pretest–posttest control group design involves the use of two or more pretests, an especially useful supplement when initial differences in maturation rates pose a strong rival alternative explanation of findings, as in the achievement gap literature. Multiple pretests help control for maturational trends and add an element of precision by reducing error (the use of repeated measures is likely to reduce model imprecision). This information can help render implausible explanations based on different maturation rates between conditions of the study.

Nonequivalent Groups Switching Replications Design

This design requires considerably more planning (and budget) than the nonequivalent pretest–posttest control group design, but it can provide the basis for useful inference of campaign effects. In the first phases of research, the design resembles the nonequivalent pretest–posttest scheme. The difference involves a switch of treated and nontreated groups after the first (or *n*th) posttest (see Figure 22.3). The design is appealing if predicted outcome patterns emerge. For example, finding an intervention effect from pretest to posttest in the initially treated group (top row, Figure 22.3) that replicates with exposure in the formerly untreated group (bottom row, Figure 22.3) strengthens the plausibility of inferring that the treatment is effective. Common threats to internal validity—history, maturation, secular trends, and so on—are rendered less plausible, given the appropriate data pattern, although they are not ruled out entirely (see Palmgreen et al., 2002).

Using more than one postintervention measure can enhance confidence of interpretation if the research is based on strong theory that specifies the likely outcomes of the interventions across time. Extended designs, which trace the decay patterns of treatment effects, require strong theory to realize the true value of this design. If data follow the gain or loss course prescribed by established theory, the plausibility of theory-based interpretations is enhanced, as is our understanding of the factors that might affect the behavior in question. The NYADMC

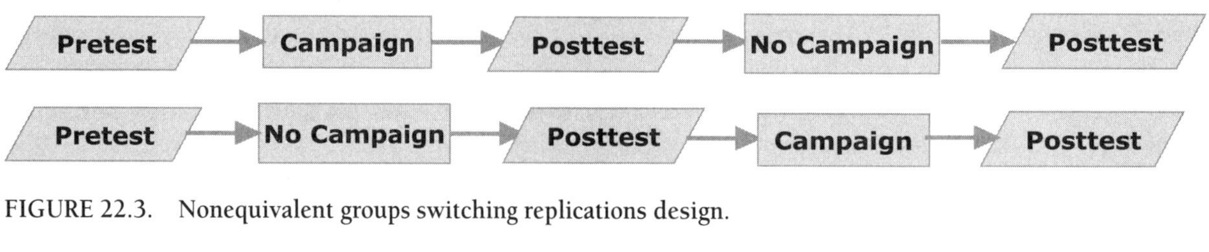

FIGURE 22.3. Nonequivalent groups switching replications design.

was not developed with these design considerations in mind. A switching replication was not possible because all respondents across the country were exposed, theoretically, to the same treatment. To switch interventions requires at least two groups that can be switched from intervention to control, and vice versa, over the course of the study.

Interrupted Time Series Design With and Without a Noncomparable Comparison Group

Interrupted time series designs can be useful in both primary and secondary research. The design can take one of two forms. The simple interrupted time series design resembles that of the nonequivalent pretest–posttest design. The extended version, the interrupted time series design with a noncomparable comparison group, resembles the nonequivalent pretest–posttest-control group design. In neither case are respondents randomly assigned to treatment conditions. To aid interpretation of interrupted time series designs, the interruption must be delivered at a discrete point in time.

California's "Three Strikes and You're Out" law provides a good example of a time-discrete interruption. The ballot measure that instituted the law was passed in 1994, following the public uproar over the murder of Polly Klaas, a 12-year-old girl who was taken from her home in the dead of night and murdered. The law went into effect in California on March 7, 1994. The statute imposed a sentence of 25 years to life for repeated perpetrators of serious "violent" crimes (e.g., rape, murder, armed robbery, child molestation); the second strike doubled the usual penalty, and the third strike practically mandated life imprisonment.

Data on serious crimes in California were available across many years, before and after passage of the law, and its effects were assessed by comparing crime rates before and after the interruption (Ramirez & Crano, 2003). Statistical treatment of interrupted time series data can be challenging, but most analytic issues can be addressed with sufficient observations (typically, 50 to 100 observations are recommended for the pretest and post-phases), especially if the variance of observations across time is not great (Lütkepohl, 1993; Wagner, Soumerai, Zhang, & Ross-Degnan, 2002). Simple interrupted time series designs (i.e., those without a nonequivalent no-treatment control group) compare time series data before and after the interruption or intervention. It is simplest to conceptualize the analysis process as involving a comparison of slope and intercept of the longitudinal data functions before and after the interruption (Berry & Lewis-Beck, 1986). Substantial differences between slope or intercept, or both, suggest the interruption had an effect. Changes in historical context present a rival alternative explanation of intervention effects, but if the change in intercept is abrupt, and the slopes on each side of the interruption differ markedly, the plausibility of this rival alternative is not strong.

In the context of drug prevention, suppose a researcher were interested in the effects of a pervasive antimarijuana advertising blitz (or the death of a well-loved celebrity from drug overdose). Considerable research on adolescent drug use suggests that marijuana use rates are relatively stable over time (Johnston, O'Malley, Bachman, & Schulenberg, 2012, 2013). Suppose then an intensive media intervention was initiated at a specific point in time. Monthly prevalence rates for marijuana could be collected across the study. The bottom function in Figure 22.4 represents the results of this hypothetical intervention study. For convenience, only 12 months of marijuana usage data on each side of the interruption are presented, but, as noted, having 50 or more data points on each side of the interruption is highly desirable.

In the interrupted time series design, the analysis is focused on the slopes and intercepts of the usage function (i.e., changes in mean or rate of drug use) before and after the interruption (i.e., the ad campaign). If there are substantial differences in the functions before and after the treatment, we might conclude that the campaign had an effect. As Figure 22.4 illustrates, the hypothetical intercept and the rate of marijuana use both dropped substantially after the campaign's start, suggesting that the campaign was effective. Alternative interpretations might suggest that some historical event occurred just as the intervention began, causing these changes. A famous musician might have been killed while driving under the influence of marijuana,

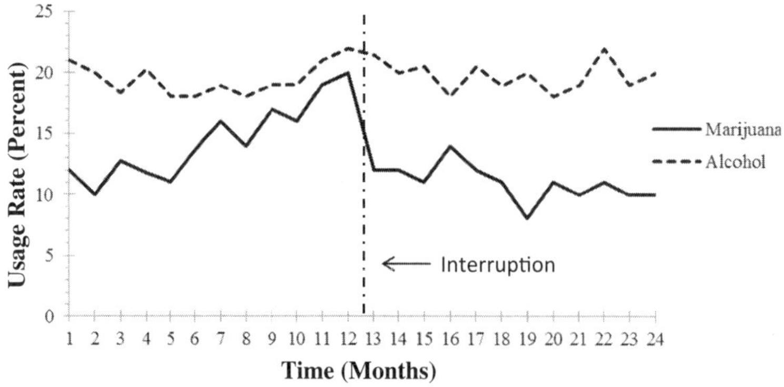

FIGURE 22.4. Hypothetical example of an interrupted time series with a noncomparable comparison group design relating marijuana and alcohol use rates over time.

or, owing to technological advances, new ways of detecting any illicit substance (e.g., alcohol, marijuana, methamphetamines) made it almost impossible to use any drug without being discovered, and so out of fear of being caught, youth moderated their use of illicit substances. One or both of these events, if the timing were exactly right, could have caused the observed differences. However, for this rival explanation to hold, both the alternative event and the interruption would have had to occur at the precise time of the intervention's initiation. The introduction of the interruption at a precise point in time, along with auxiliary research that delves into respondents' behavioral motivations, would facilitate assessing the plausibility of alternative interpretations.

The use of a nonequivalent no-treatment control group also simplifies interpretability in interrupted time series analyses. For example, suppose the developer of an antimarijuana media campaign had also implemented monthly measures of alcohol use for youth targeted by the antimarijuana campaign, even though the campaign did not address the dangers of adolescent alcohol use. If the results of the study were consistent with those of Figure 22.4, the rival alternative hypothesis that the contiguous introduction of a general drug-detection device explained the reduction in marijuana usage would be rendered implausible, insofar as the device was sensitive to both substances. If the device's introduction had affected marijuana use, it should have done so for alcohol as well.

Autocorrelation and cyclicality must be addressed in time series analyses. *Autocorrelation* refers to the typical finding that observations proximal in time and space are generally more strongly related than those separated by these factors. Consider, for instance, the ambient temperatures on contiguous days in June, which are more highly correlated than temperatures measured 6 months apart. Autocorrelation causes problems in time series analysis because almost all of the statistics used to study such data assume independence of observations, a requirement rarely met in practice.

A second analytic problem has to do with the cyclical nature of many phenomena. For example, petty crimes (e.g., shoplifting) seem to peak every December. Probably, this is attributable to some people's need to fund their holiday gift-giving. Such cyclical trends can wreak havoc on proper interpretation in time series analyses, depending on the point in the cycle at which they occur. If a cyclically related downward shift in petty crimes occurred at precisely the same time as the introduction of an intervention designed to deter them, inferences drawn from the simple interrupted time series analysis might be rendered ambiguous.

Again, we rely on Figure 22.4 to illustrate some further points. Suppose marijuana use declined from month 12 to 13 on an annual basis. In this case, the difference between the pretest and the postinterruption intercept might not indicate an intervention effect, though a change in the slope before and after the interruption would require cynics to generate some creative rival alternative hypotheses. These types of problems can be addressed through proper application of statistical models specifically designed to account for the distorting effects of autocorrelation and cyclicality (Box & Jenkins, 1976). Such analyses sometimes are made difficult by the form of the data, and some researchers object that they are overly conservative, rendering results nonsignificant when plotted findings clearly suggest otherwise (e.g., Berry & Lewis-Beck, 1986). Even so, in the appropriate circumstances, interrupted time series designs allow for analysis of effects whose explanations are compelling and that otherwise could not have been generated.

Use of Contextual Analysis and Unobtrusive Measures in Quasi-Experimentation

Uncontrolled variables may have considerable effects on the outcomes of quasi-experimental designs. Use of traditionally recommended approaches to address threats to internal validity (Shadish et al., 2002) such as design controls (e.g., random selection and assignment) or statistical controls (e.g., use of reliable and valid covariates) may be unavailable or constrained in quasi-experimental contexts. Using unobtrusive measures in a contextual analysis of intervention and comparison communities may shed light on validity threats and other design-related issues. Although all the implications of the integration of quasi-experimental designs with unobtrusive measures cannot be detailed in this chapter, a combination of methods lends itself to design considerations that may appreciably enhance the quality of interpretations derived from research outcomes. Considering history and reactivity, two general classes of threats to internal validity, will suggest how the integration might facilitate proper inference.

History. Threats to internal validity based on historical changes may weaken interpretations across a range of quasi-experimental designs. Archival data and community-wide indicators, however, may shed light on the extent to which activities related to the outcome of interest were present in nonrandomly assigned intervention and comparison groups or communities. Sources of data may include legislative actions, new social policies, hospitalizations, enforcement activity, media coverage of the campaign itself, or relevant issues that potentially influenced campaign participants. For example, relevant precampaign legislation (e.g., bans on smoking in public areas prior to a smoking cessation campaign) may provide a reasonable rival hypothesis to campaign effects if these activities are observed in an intervention but not a comparison site. On the other hand, postcampaign legislation may reasonably be considered a surrogate outcome measure indicating campaign success, given the absence of similar legislation in a comparison community (Lando, Bluhm, & Forster, 1991).

Reactivity. Although history is a major threat to internal validity in quasi-experiments, reactivity looms large as a threat to both internal and construct validity (Shadish et al., 2002). *Reactivity* refers to the problem of research arrangements that heighten respondents' self-conscious awareness of their being studied. Reactive research contexts may cause participants to misreport their true feelings or alter their normal behavioral reactions. Even in the early historical stages of questionnaire use, William James (1890) reflected on the possible unintended but negative consequences of their use: "The custom has spread, and it will be well for us in the next generation if such circulars be not ranked among the common pests of life" (p. 154).

The popular implicit-association test is popular precisely because it offers a method that possibly circumvents reactivity effects (Greenwald, McGhee, & Schwartz, 1998). It uses response latencies to infer the extent of cognitive conflict aroused when concepts (e.g., Black, White) are paired with valenced descriptors (e.g., pleasant, unpleasant).

The problem of reactivity also may be addressed through the use of unobtrusive measures. In many instances, given that they are almost by definition unnoticed by participants, unobtrusive measures evade respondents' awareness of being assessed, thus avoiding reactive responses and the threat of invalidity (Bouchard, 1976; Kazdin, 1979; Webb, Campbell, Schwartz, & Sechrest, 2000). In some instances, however, even unobtrusive measures may not be entirely nonreactive. Bouchard (1976) noted an intriguing scenario in which archival records assumed to be free from reactivity may actually be affected by a reactive response when they were first entered into the database. A record-keeper's desire to put on the best face or, conversely, underplay the negative implications of collected data may affect the manner in which data are entered into an archival source in the first place. However, this concern is relatively minor in light of the larger benefits of avoiding respondents' reactivity.

Community-level outcomes. Unobtrusive measures can often be assessed at levels other than the individual. As such, their use addresses calls for community or group-level effects, rather than individual reactions, to assess media campaign effects (Wallack, 1981). Moreover, this emphasis is in keeping with the use of quasi-experimental designs implemented at the group or community level, and it is particularly amenable to time-series designs. In drug prevention, measures of school disciplinary records, local drug-related crime statistics, hospitalizations, deaths, news coverage of drug issues, drug-related legislative actions, and content analyses of television programming or social media posts are all potentially useful data sources that may provide a valid means of assessing campaign effects beyond the individual level.

An added benefit of community-level outcomes is that they allow assessment of the behavioral outcomes associated with a campaign. Although some have argued for the adoption of physical indicators of drug use like salivary thiocyanate to provide a biochemical marker of marijuana use (e.g., Magura, 2012), these proposals have been met with well-argued objections (Hornik & Orwin, 2012). There is no doubt that physical indicators would provide a more certain indication of program success or failure, but there also is no doubt that such measures are costly and difficult to implement.

THEORIES OF MEDIA EFFECTS AND IMPLICATIONS FOR ASSESSING OUTCOMES

Our discussion to this point has shown that media campaigns can be designed in a variety of ways to take advantage of the contexts in which they are administered. How treatment effects are induced in mass media campaigns involves the application of one or another of the various theories of persuasion that have been developed over the years. Media interventions usually differ in important ways from face-to-face efforts, and tactics of persuasion may vary from context to context as well, though little research emphasis has been placed on understanding the dynamic individual-level processes responsible for media effects in prevention contexts (Crano, 2010). Moreover, information on how message effects affect persuasion directly and via interactions with target audience characteristics has been woefully underrepresented in the prevention literature (Crano et al., 2012). The design of the NYADMC invoked the theory of reasoned action, or theory of planned behavior (TPB; Ajzen, 2012). Essentially, TPB argues that behavior is most immediately affected by intentions, which in turn are affected by attitudes, subjective norms, and perceived behavioral control. Thus, changing youth's attitudes toward drugs, their perceptions of subjective norms, and their control over drug use were viewed as the surest ways to reduce intentions to use drugs in the near future. However, broad theoretical frameworks of this type, while exceptionally valuable, offer little guidance as to specific variations in the design of messages that will prove most persuasive for targeted audiences (e.g., Santa & Cochran, 2008).

Midrange theories and research on the specifics of the design of persuasive messages compatible with the requirements of higher level persuasion theories (e.g., TPB) for mass media are not well developed. However, considerations of persuasive ad design, while critically important, are well beyond the scope of this chapter. Even so, it is useful to pose the metaquestion of what reasonably may be expected from media campaigns, assuming well-developed persuasive messages, as this question should inform the campaign's evaluation. The evaluation design of a media campaign should be dictated by campaign goals, which in turn are determined by the theoretical framework used adopted, the messages used, and the general conduct of the work. This suggests that individually assessed self-reports of the indicators common in classic prevention research—knowledge, attitudes, and behavior—

may not be the best or only campaign outcomes that should be considered. Awareness of mass media theory is an important precursor to the development and use of approaches appropriate to the design and evaluation of prevention campaigns. Here it is worth considering two broad theories that illustrate how theory shapes or guides decisions regarding appropriate measures of drug prevention campaign effects.

Two (Multi)-Step Flow

More than a half-century ago, Lazarsfeld, Berelson, and Gaudet (1944) posited that media effects follow a two-step (or multistep) flow model whereby messages influence opinion leaders who subsequently influence others in their social network via direct communication. Support for the broad proposition that mass and interpersonal communication interact to attain persuasion goals has been found in a number of health contexts (Durkin & Wakefield, 2006; Gunther, Bolt, Borzekowski, Liebhart, & Dillard, 2006; Hafstad & Aaro, 1997). Moreover, while not commonly cited as a theoretical perspective, use of the two-step flow framework has been encouraged in the drug prevention literature for some time (e.g., Trager, 1976). As one illustration of the two-step flow model and the critical role of interpersonal discussion (a central feature of persuasion theory), Morton and Duck (2006) found that parents who perceived a campaign as having high message quality were more likely to discuss drug use with their children. Huansuriya, Siegel, and Crano (2014) used structural equation modeling and extended Morton and Duck's (2006) research by demonstrating that parental discussions were motivated by positive reactions to media prevention messages. These discussions, in turn, influenced marijuana-abstinent children's subsequent intentions to avoid using drugs. The findings suggest the impact of explicitly encouraging parent–child discussion of drug-relevant information, and empowering parents to do so is worthy of future research (Miller, Siegel, Hohman, & Crano, 2013; Ramirez et al., 2004). How interpersonal communication is best assessed will undoubtedly prove an important consideration in this research arena. One pressing concern is whether to depict communication processes in light of one's own self-reported communication behavior, as reflecting another person's behavior, or as a measure of concordance between dyadic parties.

Regardless of source, it is noteworthy that all of these options draw on self-reported information. Perhaps, following the lead of researchers like David, Cappella, and Fishbein (2006) and Walther, DeAndrea, Kim, and Anthony (2010), interpersonal communication may be assessed best by a third party observing and coding interactions either in the physical (school-based observational studies of student interactions) or the virtual world (drug discussions via social media). Furthermore, from a message-testing perspective, studies can be used to investigate conversational content in response to exposure to prevention messages (Walther et al., 2010). Current approaches to assessing interpersonal communication have only scratched the surface of these possibilities.

Agenda Setting

In the two-step flow model, media effects are conceptualized as minimal and indirect; that is, the effect size of media interventions is assumed to be small. Achieved effects of the intervention are thought to occur via an indirect process, insofar as they are mediated through an opinion leader. In contrast, the agenda-setting model holds that media effects can be large, while acknowledging that they may be indirect (McCombs & Shaw, 1972). The agenda-setting model conceptualizes mass media as setting the order of importance of social issues (e.g., issue X is extremely important, issue Y is of lesser consequence), while determining how these issues are contextualized (e.g., smoking as an individual choice rather than a health issue). In agenda-setting terms, mass media efforts are tools for telling audiences what to think about, not what to think. Hence, issue salience and framing, rather than overt attitude or behavioral change, are seen as the central immediate outcomes of the mass media.

Although traditionally applied to the study of news programming, the agenda-setting model has gained the attention of some prevention specialists. For example, in a national health evaluation program in the Netherlands, Brug, Tak, and Te Velde (2011) noted that mass media campaigns "could be most appropriate for agenda setting and public awareness" (p. 249). In the United States, communication researchers have begun to incorporate traditional agenda-setting methods in studies examining issues such as drug prevention (Jacobsohn, 2004; Lancaster, Hughes, Spicer, Matthew-Simmons, & Dillon, 2011; Shaw & McCombs, 1989).

The implications of the agenda-setting model for the evaluation of drug-use prevention campaign effects at the individual level suggest that perceived issue importance and self-interest may be crucial features of program evaluation. Measures can assess issue importance in both absolute (e.g., "List the top three health issues faced by today's youth") and relative terms (e.g., "Rank the following five health issues in terms of their importance for today's youth"). In the former case, one would expect either the appearance of a previously absent issue or an increase in ranking of the issue at hand; in relative terms, campaign success could be reflected in an improvement in the ranking of designated issues. Changes in individual perceptions of issue framing also could be assessed, as could feelings of self-interest, which have implications for consistency between beliefs and subsequent behavior (Crano, 1995; Johnson, Siegel, & Crano, 2014). Variations in perceptions of issue framing and self-interest could be assessed with open-ended items soliciting descriptions of target issues or with Likert-scaled attitudinal items assessing agreement with differing conceptualizations of the issue.

Importantly, an agenda-setting approach encourages conceptualizing campaign impact at the societal level. Here, one would be concerned with examining community- or society-wide data indicating that the campaign had elevated concern among the populace on the targeted issue. Indicators such as postcampaign increases in news coverage of the issue or in the framing of the issue (Wallack, 1981) in such coverage would be valuable. The now-classic Minnesota Heart Health Program, though not designed to affect health policy, nonetheless harnessed support for local smoking legislation and, ultimately, passage of a city ordinance banning cigarette vending machines (Lando et al., 1991). A focused campaign purposely designed from the outset with agenda-setting goals and measures could result in substantial societal changes, which ultimately could affect targeted behaviors.

CONCLUSION

Many mass media prevention campaigns share similar design flaws. They make use of poor pretest measures (or avoid pretests entirely), develop inadequate sampling plans, employ single modality interventions with no treatment combinations, and/or fail to consider the true underlying nature of how media effects are achieved. Campaign evaluations also use assessments that often do not ensure that respondents assigned to the intervention condition actually received it (Crano & Messé, 1985). Studies with just one of these design flaws usually fail; combining flaws raises the odds of disappointment.

The design of specific persuasive messages can begin after one has determined the general "shape and style" of the communications to be used in the campaign, the goal of the research (e.g., agenda setting, two-step flow of influence), and characteristics of the individuals who form the campaign's target audience. Some thought should be given to the accumulation of effects the campaign may create. Persuasive campaign messages, that is, should not be developed in isolation, independent of one another. A single persuasive message is rarely effective for long, but different messages all arguing the same position and reinforcing earlier communications create desirable cumulative effects. Message design is informed by experience, theory, and empirical research, and the more costly the campaign, the greater should be expenditures on up-front research and development. Creating strong and cumulative message effects fosters the persuasive goals of all media campaigns.

After determining the campaign's targets, researching variations in the targeted group's susceptibilities, and designing and testing the messages to be used, the task then involves the choice of proper research design, which is a major determinant of the scientific credibility and utility of findings. Design should be fitted to the particularities of the research context, the sample, and the messages to be used. It should not be the other way around, as when design is imposed on the context without consideration of contextual variations. When such oversights occur, creative minds are forced to do the best they can, implementing complex statistical analyses in place of basic design features to tease out campaign effects. Offsetting design problems with complex statistics rarely provides the basis for inferences as secure as those based on well-planned research. The return on well-designed studies will more than offset the costs incurred in their development.

In some contexts, it is even possible to use true experimental designs in developing media-based prevention campaigns, and in these cases the evaluation can be straightforward. However, such rigorous designs are rare in media research. More likely, given the large scope of many media-based interventions, quasi-experimental designs will prove more applicable, and, as noted, they should be developed so that specific features of the design reduce the severity and plausibility of the specific rival alternative hypotheses that may arise in situ. These alternatives will depend on the sample, the context, and the communications used, and the campaign designer must be mindful of these factors. When all of this has been accomplished, and fortune smiles, we may experience the joy of creating new and useful knowledge, an experience that will prove worth the price of the ticket.

References

Ajzen, I. (2012). The theory of planned behavior. In P. A. M. Van Lange, A. W. Kruglanski, & E. T. Higgins (Eds.), *Handbook of theories of social psychology* (Vol. 1, pp. 438–459). Thousand Oaks, CA: Sage. doi:10.4135/9781446249215.n22

Alvaro, E. M., Crano, W. D., Siegel, J. T., Hohman, Z., Johnson, I., & Nakawaki, B. (2013). Adolescents' attitudes toward anti-marijuana ads, usage intentions, and actual marijuana usage. *Psychology of Addictive Behaviors*. doi:10.1037/a0031960

Berry, W. D., & Lewis-Beck, M. S. (1986). *New tools for social scientists: Advances and applications in research methods*. Beverly Hills, CA: Sage.

Bertrand, J. T., O'Reilly, K., Denison, J., Anhang, R., & Sweat, M. (2006). Systematic review of the effectiveness of mass communication programs to change HIV/AIDS-related behaviors in developing countries. *Health Education Research, 21*, 567–597. doi:10.1093/her/cyl036

Bouchard, T. J. (1976). Unobtrusive measures: An inventory of uses. *Sociological Methods & Research, 4*, 267–300. doi:10.1177/004912417600400301

Box, G. E., & Jenkins, G. M. (1976). *Time-series analysis*. San Francisco, CA: Holden-Day.

Brug, J., Tak, N. I., & Te Velde, S. J. (2011). Evaluation of nationwide health promotion campaigns in The Netherlands: An exploration of practices, wishes and opportunities. *Health Promotion International, 26*, 244–254. doi:10.1093/heapro/daq058

Campbell, D. T., & Erlebacher, A. (1970). How regression artifacts in quasi-experimental evaluations can mistakenly make compensatory education look harmful. In J. Hellmuth (Ed.), *Compensatory education: A national debate* (Vol. 3, pp. 185–210).

Campbell, D. T., & Stanley, J. C. (1963). *Experimental and quasi-experimental designs for research*. Chicago, IL: Rand McNally.

Cleland, C. (2012). Charles Cleland on Steve Magura's "Failure of intervention or failure of evaluation: A meta-evaluation of the National Youth Anti-Drug Media Campaign evaluation." *Substance Use & Misuse, 47*, 1431–1433. doi:10.3109/10826084.2012.723490

Cohen, G. L., Garcia, J., Apfel, N., & Master, A. (2006). Reducing the racial achievement gap: A social-psychological intervention. *Science, 313*, 1307–1310. doi:10.1126/science.1128317

Cook, T. D., & Campbell, D. T. (1979). *Quasi-experimentation: Design and analysis issues in field settings*. Chicago, IL: Rand McNally.

Crano, W. D. (1995). Attitude strength and vested interest. In R. E. Petty & J. A. Krosnick (Eds.), *Attitude strength: Antecedents and consequences* (pp. 131–157). Hillsdale, NJ: Erlbaum.

Crano, W. D. (2010). Experiments as reforms: Persuasion in the nation's service. In J. P. Forgas, J. Cooper, & W. D. Crano (Eds.), *The psychology of attitudes and attitude change* (pp. 231–248). New York, NY: Psychology Press.

Crano, W. D., Brewer, M. B., & Lac, A. (in press). *Principles and methods of social research* (3rd ed.). New York, NY: Taylor & Francis.

Crano, W. D., & Messé, L. A. (1985). Assessing and redressing comprehension artifacts in social interaction research. *Evaluation Review, 9*, 144–172. doi:10.1177/0193841X8500900204

Crano, W. D., Siegel, J. T., & Alvaro, E. M. (2012). The siren's call: Mass media and drug prevention. In J. P. Dillard & L. Shen (Eds.), *The Sage handbook of persuasion: Developments in theory and practice* (2nd ed., pp. 296–313). Los Angeles, CA: Sage.

Crano, W. D., Siegel, J. T., Alvaro, E. M., Lac, A., & Hemovich, V. (2008). The at-risk adolescent marijuana nonuser: Expanding the standard distinction. *Prevention Science, 9*, 129–137. doi:10.1007/s11121-008-0090-0

David, C., Cappella, J., & Fishbein, M. (2006). The social diffusion of influence among adolescents: Group interaction in a chat room environment about antidrug advertisements. *Communication Theory, 16*, 118–140. doi:10.1111/j.1468-2885.2006.00008.x

Derzon, J. H. (2014). Differences-indifferences in approaches. In G. J. N. Bruinsma & D. L. Weisburd (Eds.), *Encyclopedia of criminology and criminal justice* (pp. 1054–1064). New York, NY: Springer Science+Business Media.

Derzon, J. H., & Lipsey, M. W. (2002). A meta-analysis of the effectiveness of mass-communication for changing substance-use knowledge, attitudes, and behavior. In W. D. Crano & M. Burgoon (Eds.), *Mass media and drug prevention: Classic and contemporary theories and research* (pp. 231–258). Mahwah, NJ: Erlbaum.

Donaldson, S. I., Christie, C. A., & Mark, M. M. (Eds.). (2009). *What counts as credible evidence in applied research and evaluation practice?* Newbury Park, CA: Sage. doi:10.4135/9781412995634

Donner, A., & Klar, N. (2000). *Design and analysis of cluster randomization trials in health research.* New York, NY: Wiley.

Donohew, L., Palmgreen, P., Lorch, E., Zimmerman, R., & Harrington, N. (2002). Attention, persuasive communication, and prevention. In W. D. Crano & M. Burgoon (Eds.), *Mass media and drug prevention: Classic and contemporary theories and research* (pp. 119–143). Mahwah, NJ: Erlbaum.

Durkin, S., & Wakefield, M. (2006). Maximizing the impact of emotive anti-tobacco advertising: Effects of interpersonal discussion and program placement. *Social Marketing Quarterly, 12*, 3–14. doi:10.1080/15245000600851334

Farrelly, M. C., Nonnemaker, J., Davis, K. C., & Hussin, A. (2009). The influence of the national truth campaign on smoking initiation. *American Journal of Preventive Medicine, 36*, 379–384. doi:10.1016/j.amepre.2009.01.019

Fendrich, M., & Johnson, T. P. (2001). Examining prevalence differences in three national surveys of youth: Impact of consent procedures, mode, and editing rules. *Journal of Drug Issues, 31*, 665–694.

Greenwald, A. G., McGhee, D. E., & Schwartz, J. (1998). Measuring individual differences in implicit cognition: The implicit association test. *Journal of Personality and Social Psychology, 74*, 1464–1480. doi:10.1037/0022-3514.74.6.1464

Gunther, A. C., Bolt, D., Borzekowski, D. L. G., Liebhart, J. L., & Dillard, J. P. (2006). Presumed influence on peer norms: How mass media indirectly affect adolescent smoking. *Journal of Communication, 56*, 52–68. doi:10.1111/j.1460-2466.2006.00002.x

Hafstad, A., & Aaro, L. E. (1997). Activating interpersonal influence through provocative appeals: Evaluation of a mass media–based antismoking campaign targeting adolescents. *Health Communication, 9*, 253–272. doi:10.1207/s15327027hc0903_4

Harder, V. S., Stuart, E. A., & Anthony, J. C. (2010). Propensity score techniques and the assessment of measured covariate balance to test causal associations in psychological research. *Psychological Methods, 15*, 234–249. doi:10.1037/a0019623

Hornik, R., Jacobsohn, L., Orwin, R., Piesse, A., & Kalton, G. (2008). Effects of the National Youth Anti-drug Media Campaign on youths. *American Journal of Public Health, 98*, 2229–2236. doi:10.2105/AJPH.2007.125849

Hornik, R., Maklin, D., Cadell, D., Judkins, D., Sayeed, S., Zador, P., . . . Steele, D. (2000). *Evaluation of the National Youth Anti-Drug Media Campaign: Campaign exposure and baseline measurement of correlates of illicit drug use from November 1999 through May 2000.* Bethesda, MD: National Institute on Drug Abuse.

Hornik, R., Maklin, D., Judkins, D., Cadell, D., Yanovitzky, I., Zador, P., . . . Zanutto, E. (2001). *Evaluation of the National Youth Anti-Drug Media Campaign: Second semi-annual report of findings.* Bethesda, MD: National Institute on Drug Abuse.

Hornik, R., & Orwin, R. (2012). On Stephen Magura's "Failure of intervention or failure of evaluation: A meta-evaluation of the National Youth Anti-Drug Media Campaign evaluation". *Substance Use & Misuse, 47*, 1436–1438. doi:10.3109/10826084.2012.719723

Huansuriya, T., Siegel, J. T., & Crano, W. D. (2014). Parent-child drug communication: Pathway from parents' ad exposure to youths' marijuana use intention. *Journal of Health Communication, 19*, 244–259. doi:10.1080/10810730.2013.811326

Jacobsohn, L. (2004, May). *Examining marijuana-related news coverage in the context of the National Youth Anti-Drug Media Campaign.* Presented at the annual meeting of the International Communication Association, New Orleans, LA.

James, W. (1890). *The principles of psychology.* New York, NY: Holt. doi:10.1037/11059-000

Johnson, I., Siegel, J. T., & Crano, W. D. (2014). Extending the reach of vested interest in predicting attitude-consistent behavior. *Social Influence, 9*, 20–36. doi:10.1080/15534510.2012.738243

Johnston, L. D., O'Malley, P. M., Bachman, J. G., & Schulenberg, J. E. (2012). *Monitoring the future: National survey results on drug use, 1975–2011: Vol. I. Secondary school students.* Ann Arbor: The University of Michigan.

Johnston, L. D., O'Malley, P. M., Bachman, J. G., & Schulenberg, J. E. (2013). *Monitoring the future: National results on adolescent drug use: Overview of key findings, 2012.* Ann Arbor: The University of Michigan.

Kazdin, A. E. (1979). Unobtrusive measures in behavioral assessment. *Journal of Applied Behavior Analysis, 12*, 713–724. doi:10.1901/jaba.1979.12-713

Kingsbury, N., Tessin, J., & Alexander, D. (2012). The evaluation worked and the campaign did not—A response from the Government Accountability Office. *Substance Use & Misuse, 47*, 1427–1428. doi:10.3109/10826084.2012.719726

Lancaster, K., Hughes, C. E., Spicer, B., Matthew-Simmons, F., & Dillon, P. (2011). Illicit drugs and the media: Models of media effects for use in drug policy research. *Drug and Alcohol Review, 30*, 397–402. doi:10.1111/j.1465-3362.2010.00239.x

Lando, H. A., Bluhm, J., & Forster, J. (1991). The ban on cigarette vending machines in Bloomington, Minnesota. *American Journal of Public Health, 81*, 1339–1340.

Lazarsfeld, P. F., Berelson, B., & Gaudet, H. (1944). *The people's choice.* Oxford, England: Duell, Sloan & Pearce.

Lütkepohl, H. (1993). *Introduction to multiple time series analysis.* New York, NY: Springer-Verlag. doi:10.1007/978-3-642-61695-2

Magura, S. (2012). Failure of intervention or failure of evaluation: A meta-evaluation of the National Youth Anti-Drug Media Campaign evaluation. *Substance Use & Misuse, 47*, 1414–1420. doi:10.3109/10826084.2012.705706

McCombs, M., & Shaw, D. L. (1972). The agenda-setting function of the mass media. *Public Opinion Quarterly, 36*, 176–185. doi:10.1086/267990

Miller, S. M., Siegel, J. T., Hohman, Z., & Crano, W. D. (2013). Factors mediating the association of the recency of parent's marijuana use and their adolescent children's subsequent initiation. *Psychology of Addictive Behaviors.* doi:10.1037/a0032201

Morton, T. A., & Duck, J. M. (2006). Enlisting the influence of others: Alternative strategies for persuasive media campaigns. *Journal of Applied Social Psychology, 36*, 269–296. doi:10.1111/j.0021-9029.2006.00008.x

Noar, S. M. (2006). A 10-year retrospective of research in health mass media campaigns: Where do we go from here? *Journal of Health Communication, 11*, 21–42. doi:10.1080/10810730500461059

Noar, S. M. (2012). An Audience–Channel–Message–Evaluation (ACME) framework for health communication campaigns. *Health Promotion Practice, 13*, 481–488. doi:10.1177/1524839910386901

Palmgreen, P., Donohew, L., Lorch, E. P., Hoyle, R. H., & Stephenson, M. T. (2002). Television campaigns and sensation seeking targeting of adolescent marijuana use: A controlled time series approach. In R. C. Hornik (Ed.), *Public health communication: Evidence for behavior change* (pp. 35–56). Mahwah, NJ: Erlbaum.

Ramirez, J. R., & Crano, W. D. (2003). Deterrence and incapacitation: An interrupted time-series analysis of California's three-strikes law. *Journal of Applied Social Psychology, 33*, 110–144. doi:10.1111/j.1559-1816.2003.tb02076.x

Ramirez, J. R., Crano, W. D., Quist, R., Burgoon, M., Alvaro, E. M., & Grandpre, J. (2004). Acculturation, familism, parental monitoring, and knowledge as predictors of marijuana and inhalant use in adolescents. *Psychology of Addictive Behaviors, 18*, 3–11. doi:10.1037/0893-164X.18.1.3

Richardson, A. K., Green, M., Xiao, H., Sokol, N., & Vallone, D. (2010). Evidence for Truth: The young adult response to a youth-focused anti-smoking media campaign. *American Journal of Preventive Medicine, 39*, 500–506. doi:10.1016/j.amepre.2010.08.007

Rosenbaum, P. B., & Rubin, D. R. (1983). The central role of the propensity score in observational studies for causal effects. *Biometrika, 70*, 41–55. doi:10.1093/biomet/70.1.41

Rubin, D. B. (1980). Discussion of paper by D. Basu. *Journal of the American Statistical Association, 75*, 591–593.

Rubin, D. B. (1974). Estimating causal effects of treatments in randomized and nonrandomized studies. *Journal of Educational Psychology, 66*, 688–701. doi:10.1037/h0037350

Santa, A. F., & Cochran, B. N. (2008). Does the impact of anti-drinking and driving Public Service Announcements differ based on message type and viewer characteristics? *Journal of Drug Education, 38*, 109–129. doi:10.2190/DE.38.2.b

Scheier, L. M., & Grenard, J. L. (2010). Influence of a nationwide social marketing campaign on adolescent drug use. *Journal of Health Communication, 15*, 240–271. doi:10.1080/10810731003686580

Scheier, L. M., Grenard, J. L., & Holtz, K. D. (2011). An empirical assessment of the Above the Influence advertising campaign. *Journal of Drug Education, 41*, 431–461. doi:10.2190/DE.41.4.f

Shadish, W. R., Cook, T. D., & Campbell, D. T. (2002). *Experimental and quasi-experimental designs for generalized causal inference.* Boston, MA: Houghton Mifflin Harcourt.

Shaw, D. L., & McCombs, M. E. (1989). Dealing with illicit drugs: The power—and limits—of mass media agenda setting. In P. J. Shoemaker (Ed.), *Communication campaigns about drugs: Government, media, and the public* (pp. 113–120). Hillsdale, NJ: Erlbaum.

Southwell, B. G., Barmada, C. H., Hornik, R. C., & Maklan, D. M. (2002). Can we measure encoded exposure? Validation evidence from a national campaign. *Journal of Health Communication*, *7*, 445–453. doi:10.1080/10810730290001800

Trager, R. (1976). Adolescent reactions to educational media messages regarding drug education. In R. E. Ostman (Ed.), *Communication research and drug education* (Vol. III, pp. 155–175). London, England: Sage.

U.S. Department of Health and Human Services, Centers for Disease Control and Prevention, National Center for Chronic Disease Prevention and Health Promotion, Office on Smoking and Health. (2012). *Preventing tobacco use among youth and young adults: A report of the Surgeon General.* Washington, DC: U.S. Government Printing Office. Retrieved from http://www.surgeongeneral.gov/library/reports/preventing-youth-tobacco-use/full-report.pdf

U.S. Office of National Drug Control Policy. (1998). *Testing the anti-drug message in 12 American cities National Youth Anti-Drug Media Campaign Phase I* (Report No. 1). Washington, DC: U.S. Government Printing Office.

Wagner, A. K., Soumerai, S. B., Zhang, F., & Ross-Degnan, D. (2002). Segmented regression analysis of interrupted time series studies in medication use research. *Journal of Clinical Pharmacy and Therapeutics*, *27*, 299–309. doi:10.1046/j.1365-2710.2002.00430.x

Wallack, L. M. (1981). Mass media campaigns: The odds against finding behavior change. *Health Education & Behavior*, *8*, 209–260. doi:10.1177/109019818100800302

Walther, J. B., DeAndrea, D., Kim, J., & Anthony, J. C. (2010). The influence of online comments on perceptions of anti marijuana public service announcements on YouTube. *Human Communication Research*, *36*, 469–492. doi:10.1111/j.1468-2958.2010.01384.x

Webb, E. J., Campbell, D. T., Schwartz, R. D., & Sechrest, L. (2000). *Unobtrusive measures: Nonreactive research in the social sciences.* Chicago, IL: Rand McNally.

Part VIII

EVALUATION OF DRUG USE PREVENTION: MODELING BEHAVIOR CHANGE AND PROGRAM EFFECTS

CHAPTER 23

LATENT VARIABLE MODELING AS A TOOL IN RESEARCH ON DRUG PREVENTION

Patrick S. Malone and Darren T. Woodlief

This chapter introduces and surveys some of the aspects of latent variable modeling (LVM) that make it particularly useful for research in drug prevention. A secondary goal is to lay the groundwork for the remaining chapters in this section, which summarily address latent class modeling, mediation, and growth modeling in the context of prevention science. The chapter begins with a brief presentation of LVM as a general case of regression analysis, highlighting the familiar and the potentially unfamiliar. It then discusses some strengths of LVM that may be particularly relevant in drug abuse prevention research, drawing on conceptual examples relevant to the field and citing empirical examples. Before the chapter closes, it also discusses certain limitations in LVM strategies (many of which apply to other common strategies in both social science statistics and biostatistics) and discusses some issues warranting caution, such as the links between LVM and causal inference as well as notes on statistical power and sample size needs of LVM.

STRENGTHS AND ADVANTAGES OF LVM FOR DRUG PREVENTION RESEARCH

Structural equation modeling (SEM) as a statistical tool has been available to applied researchers for decades (Jöreskog & Sörbom, 1976), and its predecessor, path analysis, long before that (Wright, 1920). Prevention science is one of the applied fields at the forefront of methodological sophistication. However, SEM—and LVM more generally—is far more versatile than most prevention scientists credit or apply. Prevention research often includes a number of complexities not addressed by the core statistics sequence in most traditional social science, public health, or medical graduate education programs. Most readers of this volume will be familiar with the fundamental principles of experimentation and the value of an appropriate sampling strategy, random assignment, and good instrumentation (although we will discuss these issues in the context of limiting factors). Even in the context of a randomized experiment, however, field prevention studies do not always conform to the prototype. As examples, prevention research may

- be randomized at the level of group, rather than individual;
- have multiple treatment conditions or multiple comparison conditions;
- incorporate longitudinal measurement of the outcome(s);
- have outcomes with nonstandard measurement (e.g., time to event; zero-inflated measurement; nominal outcomes, whether directly observed or latent);

The authors gratefully acknowledge support on a National Institute on Drug Abuse K award (K01-DA024116). Correspondence concerning this chapter should be directed to Patrick S. Malone at malone.ps@gmail.com.

http://dx.doi.org/10.1037/14550-024
Handbook of Adolescent Drug Use Prevention: Research, Intervention Strategies, and Practice, L. M. Scheier (Editor)

- interact with baseline characteristics—including levels of the planned outcome—that moderate the program impact;
- have open questions regarding proposed mechanism of the effects; or
- suffer from noncompliance or partial compliance with the random assignment (either a participant not following the protocol or contamination of the comparison group).

If the research is not randomized, these and other considerations proliferate. LVM is no panacea, but a good modeling strategy can mitigate many of these concerns.

LVM is an extension of the same general linear model as multiple regression and path analysis. LVM, however, is a much more powerful and versatile alternative. Instead of looking at the effect of one predictor variable on one criterion above and beyond any other predictors, as is the case in multiple regression, a researcher can simultaneously test a complex pattern of relations between multiple predictors (called exogenous variables) and criterion (endogenous) variables, distinguishing between indirect and direct relations. Path analysis does allow for such complex relations; however, it is limited by only allowing an investigator to model observed variables.

Conventional multiple regression models, as well as path analysis, require the assumption that all measures are error-free. One of the greatest advantages of LVM is the ability to avoid that untenable assumption by incorporating measurement error into the model. LVM allows the researcher to distinguish between the unreliability of measures of an underlying construct and nonrandom, unexplained variance. On the basis of tenets of classical test theory, the measurement portion of an LVM allows for the separation of the observed variables' common variances from their error variances (Jöreskog & Sörbom, 1979).

In addition, LVM is highly flexible in handling challenging data, such as nonnormally distributed or discretely scaled data. One of its biggest strengths, in comparison with conventional multiple regression, is the ability of LVM to handle missing data. Missing data often are manifest in the simplest data collection efforts, but they are almost inevitably in longitudinal studies when participants may drop out for any number of reasons. The lack of complete data, however, is poorly handled by most traditional methods of regression modeling based on ordinary least squares estimation. These methods, typically using listwise or pairwise deletion, can yield biased parameter estimates and inaccurate estimates of standard errors and confidence intervals, leading to faulty hypothesis tests (Graham, Hofer, & MacKinnon, 1996).

In contrast, the available options for dealing with missing data in the LVM framework (e.g. full-information maximum likelihood, multiple imputation) yield substantially less biased (or unbiased) parameter estimates and more accurate standard errors (Tomarken & Waller, 2005). This has been shown to be the case not just with observed values missing completely at random (MCAR) or missing at random (MAR), but also with data missing not at random (MNAR; Graham, 2009, Schafer, 1997).

LVM is of particular value to drug prevention researchers in a multiple group model setting. Traditionally, researchers have compared group means on observed variables using analysis of variance or multivariate analysis of variance. LVM is much more flexible, allowing for comparisons on latent constructs while also accounting for measurement error on the observed variables (Aiken, Stein, & Bentler, 1994). In addition, LVM not only can be used to test group means but also is able to test whether variances and covariances differ between groups by constraining to equality group parameter estimates. This ability to select and apply constraints in a principled ordered fashion, rather than by default, is a significant benefit of the LVM approach (Loehlin, 2004).

Growth Models

The noted advantages are general to LVM, regardless of application. One of the principal LVM tools used specifically in prevention research with longitudinal data is the latent growth model (LGM, also known as the latent trajectory model; Duncan, Duncan, & Strycker, 2006), its variants, and related models, such as the latent change score model (Hamagami & McArdle, 2001). Chapter 26 in this volume is dedicated to growth modeling, so we will not explore it in great depth here but rather will summarize and relate this methodology to drug prevention research.

The latent trait model. As a preface to our discussion of the LGM for prevention research, we present a simpler model: the latent trait model (Steyer, Ferring, & Schmitt, 1992). The latent trait model is a specific application of confirmatory factor analysis to longitudinal data. The *trait*, being construed as the enduring person-level quality across measurement, is simply a factor indicated by several repeated measures of a construct, such as drug refusal skills. By definition, a factor reflects the common shared variances of a set of specified indicators. In this respect, the aspect of drug refusal skills that is consistent over measurement occasions can be taken as the trait (i.e., social skill). Operationally, this is a factor with equal loadings (typically fixed to 1) for the repeated measures. This is analogous to a simple average of observed scores, but it has the advantages of a latent variable with respect to excluding the influence of time-specific variability. The latent trait variable has a mean (the mean of the repeated measures, aggregated across individuals) and a variance (the variability in the individual levels of the trait).

The linear growth model. The linear growth model is a straightforward extension of the latent trait model (Steyer et al., 1992) and commonly is used in drug prevention applications (e.g., Crawford, Pentz, Chou, Li, & Dwyer, 2003; Duncan et al., 2006). If the latent trait is the persistent, enduring quality being measured over repeated occasions, the linear growth model partitions the residual variability (after considering the level of the trait) by extracting a component that reflects steady change over time in the level of the manifest variable. A sample model is presented in Figure 23.1. The latent trait component commonly is referred to as the *intercept* (a common part of elementary geometry, in which a line is characterized by a slope indicating growth along the abscissa and a y-intercept on the ordinate; represented using the familiar $y = mx + b$). The fixed unit loadings to the intercept factor *define* the intercept factor as the trait at a given time of measurement—a point at which the *slope* factor's loading is equal to zero. In contrast, the fixed loadings for the slope factor typically are related to the time that elapses between measurements (equal time intervals are convenient but are not a requirement for modeling growth).

By way of example, this diagram might be suitable for modeling drug refusal skills developing in response to a multiple-week intervention, where the indicators are measures of refusal skills at baseline

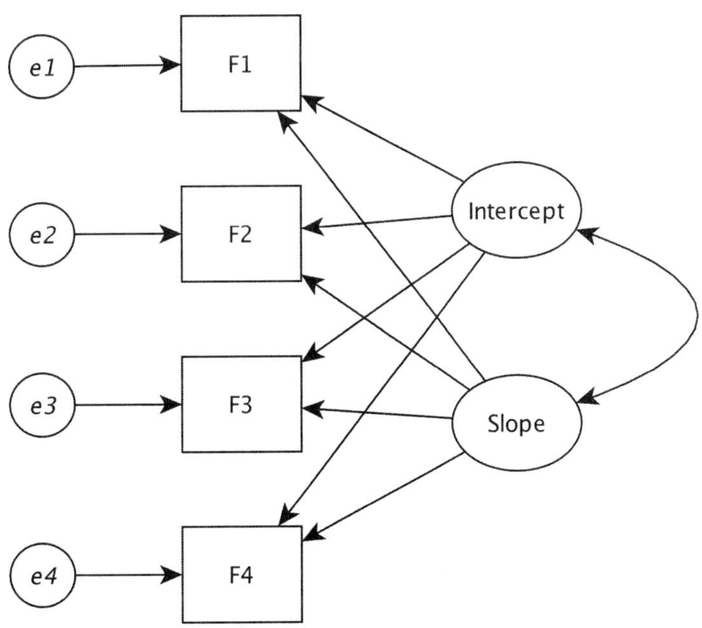

FIGURE 23.1. Basic framework of a linear growth model.

(Week 0), 1 week into the program, 2 weeks into the program, and so forth. The fixed loadings have the effect that the model-predicted skill score is equal to (1 *) the individual's intercept + (week number *) the individual's slope—the geometric definition of a line. Residual variances for the observed scores—or, in more complex *curve of factor* models, which posit latent variables as indicators—reflect the extent to which individual growth curves (trajectories) do not exactly fit the line implied by the combination of latent intercept and slope.

Truthfully, a more common measurement structure in drug use prevention is an intervention with long-term follow-up, assessed in intervals of months or sometimes years. A key advantage of LGM is the capacity to model the latent slope with unequally spaced or even individual-specific occasions of measurement. This advantage can and, we argue, should be taken into account in the data collection design. Using shorter measurement intervals in the period of and directly following the prevention program facilitates the detection of rapid postprogram changes in substance use and other phenomena of interest.

The relation of this model to a drug prevention controlled trial is made clear using the case of a multiple-group version of the LGM. In a randomized study, the means of the latent intercept factors are expected to be approximately identical in the intervention and comparison groups, given a sufficiently large sample size. This is, of course, a goal of randomization: to minimize any systematic differences between groups at baseline that might confound treatment outcomes. The effect of treatment is apparent in the difference between mean slopes between the groups. Regardless of the linear trend in drug refusal skills in a treatment-as-usual (TAU) comparison group, the expectation would be that the mean slope would be more positive—a greater increase in skills with time—in the intervention group compared with the comparison control group, if the intervention is in fact augmenting youths' resistance skills. This is testable in an LVM by positing a constraint that the latent slope factors have equal means across the two experimental groups. If applying this constraint results in a significant decrement in the model fit, that implies that the latent slope factors have different means.

Mediated Effects

Mediated, or indirect, effects also receive a more complete treatment in Chapter 25 in this volume; however, the SEM implementation warrants mention here as well. Given that an intervention shows an effect, program evaluation should be concerned with the precise mechanism of this effect. What proximal outcome is affected by the intervention, which in turn drives differences in the more distal outcome? This is the hypothesized mechanism (causal chain of events) that links the intervention modalities to intervening target risk mechanisms and eventual change in behavior. The first step applied by many prevention researchers utilizes SEM to test hypothesized causal agents of change. The core model of an indirect effect—an effect of an exogenous variable transmitted by an endogenous mediator—is shown in Figure 23.2.

This framework of program effects is easily modeled as an LVM, and in this case, both the mediator and outcome are construed as latent variables. In its simplest form (as depicted in Figure 23.2), the indirect effect is represented by the product of the *a* coefficient (the structural coefficient linking the predictor X to the mediator M) and the *b* coefficient (linking M to the outcome Y). The value of SEM is particularly notable, given reports by MacKinnon and Fairchild (2009) that measurement error in the mediator is particularly undesirable in the simpler path-analytic framework. The use of a confirmatory factor model for the mediator is a key workaround.

MacKinnon (2008; see also Chapter 25, this volume) provided an in-depth understanding of the testing and interpretation of the *ab* product. This product and its confidence interval have served as the standard means of testing mediated effects in many disciplines within prevention and social sciences, succeeding the simpler, classic formulation by Baron and Kenny (1986). Newer techniques rooted in perspectives on causal inference (e.g., Imai, Jo, & Stuart, 2011) are also taking hold, but many of those techniques still draw on an LVM implementation.

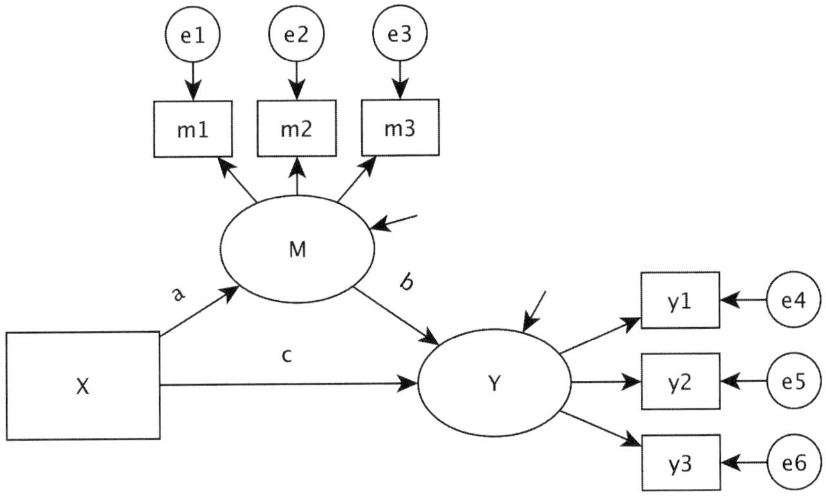

FIGURE 23.2. Graphic representation of latent variable mediation model.

Causal Inference

As an approach to causal inference, LVM is—as with any regression technique—a tool only as strong as the assumptions the researcher is willing to make. We will return to this issue in our discussion of cautions and limitations in the application of LVM, but we raise it here because of the historic associations between LVM (and particularly SEM, and even more particularly mediation analysis) and the concept of "causal modeling" (Cliff, 1983). The idea that a path and associated coefficient in an LVM represent a causal effect is intuitively appealing. However, it is no more necessarily true than would be if we regressed age on height. Although height regressed on age is plausible as an estimator of a causal effect, the reverse is just as straightforward to estimate, whether in linear regression or path analysis. With respect to mediation, most conceptions of indirect effects draw on causal reasoning and often use the language of causal inference: "the effect of *X* on *Y* that is due to the effect of *X* on *M*." However, several assumptions, not all of them intuitive, are required before one can appropriately conclude that the product of coefficients is an estimate of a causal pathway (for an excellent discussion of causation in drug prevention, see also Scheier, 2012).

Extensions

LVM is a tremendously flexible tool—or, rather, set of tools. The structural equation model is the most familiar to many social and prevention researchers; however, this section touches on a few extensions of particular relevance to drug prevention research.

Mixture modeling. One of the most important extensions to LVM, which has come into use in the past decade, is the finite mixture model (B. O. Muthén & Shedden, 1999). Mixture modeling is a general case of the latent class analysis (LCA) or latent profile analysis (LPA; Collins & Wugalter, 1992). LCA and LPA have long standing in quantitative methods. The finite mixture model allows the combination of LCA/LPA and SEM—that is, the combination of one or more *nominal* latent variables (classes or profiles) in modeling with one or more *continuous* latent variables (factors).

For a simple example of how a categorical latent factor approach can be applied in drug prevention research, consider the possibility that some members of a study sample are, for whatever reasons of background and circumstance, not at risk of initiating drug use. In a randomized experiment, this group would be expected to be composed of comparable proportions in both the experimental and comparison samples. In a conventional group-based analysis, as with an intent-to-treat approach, the presence of this subsample will dilute the size of any treatment effects, insofar as a segment of each sample will not differ after treatment. Using mixture modeling, the data analyst can partition the treatment and comparison groups into subgroups composed of either at-risk or nonvulnerable participants and focus the tests of intervention effects on those most at risk or most vulnerable. This could restore much of the statistical power lost to the "dilution," but not all, as the mixture model is probabilistic (i.e., subgroup membership is based on probabilities, not certainties of assignment).

Adding some complexity, a class of respondents—especially for youth participants—may be especially vulnerable to initiation of substance use because of multiple morbidities (e.g., attention deficit–hyperactivity disorder for tobacco use). Even in the absence of direct measures of these morbidities, mixture modeling may identify a higher risk class or classes that show reduced effects of the prevention intervention. Identifying this latent class again helps distinguish who among the participants is most affected by the program. Lanza and Rhoades (2013) recently discussed the use of mixture models in both prevention and treatment as a remedy to many of the more basic approaches that assume "homogeneity of effects."

Growth mixture modeling. An increasingly popular method for evaluating prevention effects, as well as descriptive modeling of change in a measure of a behavior or other construct, is the growth mixture model (GMM; B. O. Muthén & Muthén, 2000). As the label infers, this methodology combines properties of two models already discussed, the LGM and the finite mixture model. Recalling that growth modeling can be viewed as a data reduction technique by which a number of measures over time are abstracted into parameters describing a curve, GMM applies mixture modeling to those parameters. That is, in the simplest case, the classes (latent profiles) would be associated with means and variances of intercepts and slopes taken together—perhaps, for example, a low-stable class, a low-increasing class, and a high-stable class. An application to prevention is a straightforward extension of the hypothetical case described for mixture modeling generally: if a low-stable (i.e., never at risk of problematic levels of drug use) class exists in the population in the absence of intervention, it is reasonable to expect that this class will be found in similar proportion in both the treatment and comparison samples. The study participants in this class would not be expected to contribute to any treatment effect. By way of caution, however, the small-sample properties of this approach only recently are being explored, and there are indications that violations of distributional assumptions can have substantial impact at even moderately large sample sizes (Van Horn et al., 2009).

Multifacet longitudinal modeling. In the interests of illustrating the versatility of LVM tools, we touch on the multifacet longitudinal model (MFLM). Unpacking the term, a *facet* of an outcome is some longitudinal aspect, such as age of first alcohol use (a survival, or time-to-event indicator) or trajectory of growth in alcohol-related problems. Witkiewitz and Masyn (2008) combined multiple facets in studying a sample of postintervention alcohol users, modeling time to relapse and changes in use following relapse in a single model. Relatedly, B. O. Muthén and Masyn (2005) developed the discrete-time survival (also known as time-to-event) model in latent variable formulations. Furthermore, Malone, Lamis, Masyn, and Northrup (2010) demonstrated the use of a highly constrained associative latent transition analysis (Bray, Lanza, & Collins, 2010; Flaherty, 2008) model using mixture models to estimate discrete-time survival processes. Malone, Northrup, Masyn, Lamis, and Lamont (2012) combined these innovations to describe race and ethnicity as predictors of both age of first alcohol use and the subsequent persistence of use through adolescence, even when age of first use was observed only partially.

Prevention research with planned missing data. A different extension of this application is the use of LVM to accommodate research designs with planned missing data. For example, a prevention experiment might best be evaluated with bioassay methods, such as measuring salivary cotinine to detect tobacco use or thiocyanate levels to detect marijuana use in a prevention trial. Such measures, however, require either face-to-face meetings with the participants (to maintain chain of custody) or the participants' willingness to collect and mail samples themselves, and then subsequent laboratory analysis. This approach is more expensive and—because of its relative intrusiveness—more likely to lead to respondent refusal than, for example, telephone or online survey follow-ups.

The methods for accommodating unplanned missing data discussed previously, however, are equally—or even more—applicable to planned missing data. Graham et al. (1996) presented a selection of straightforward methods for improving cost-effectiveness by omitting some measurements for some recipients in a systematic way. In the current example, the online survey might be administered to the entire study sample and the more-expensive salivary assay to a smaller, randomly selected portion. By imputation or other data augmentation methods, prediction of or from cotinine levels can be estimated for the entire sample without bias or unnecessary loss of power. This statement can be made strongly because the mechanism of nonresponse is entirely known and, in this example, known to be completely at random (MCAR).

Conceptual Example

This section imagines a data set representing participants in a randomized controlled drug prevention trial. It applies different aspects of this hypothetical data set to illustrate some uses of LVM in drug use prevention and to highlight possible extensions.

Test of differences between two group means. The simplest, and often first-applied, test of program efficacy is a comparison between intervention and comparison groups on the level of a designated outcome (i.e., drug use). This design is the heart of the intent-to-treat analysis as applied to a randomized controlled trial (RCT)—prediction from the group of assignment. At least two straightforward methods to apply this design, each of which lays the building blocks for elaborations later in this section, and so we review both.

Path model with dichotomous predictor. The first model is an estimation of the "path model" depicted in Figure 23.3. This path model is trivially equivalent to a bivariate linear regression from a binary predictor—or, framed differently, yields the same information as a student's *t*-test. Of particular interest is the regression of *Y* on the treatment variable (a dichotomy signifying the respondent's treatment assignment). In most software, in the absence of explicit commands to the contrary, *Y* is treated as a continuous, normal variable, and the form of *X* (treatment) is unconstrained—in this case, most often coded 0/1, where 0 is the control group and 1 is the treatment condition (i.e., participants in the latter condition were exposed to the experimental intervention).

Most LVM programs provide detailed information in their output that allows researchers to check whether the model was configured and estimated correctly: in this case, an observed independent variable, *X*, predicting a continuous dependent variable, *Y*, in a single group of respondents. Most software would default to maximum likelihood estimation for this example. The output also will contain model fit information. In this example, there would be a perfect fit of the model to the data, χ^2 (0) = 0, $p = 1$. Only one statistical relation is modeled, the parameter indicating the relation between treatment and *Y*; and one freely estimated parameter can reproduce this perfectly. This is referred to as a *saturated* model, a point to which we will return.

A statistically significant regression parameter between treatment and *Y* suggests an effect of treatment assignment. The unstandardized regression coefficient (*b*) indicates the predicted difference in *Y* between respondents in the comparison control group, coded 0, and in the treatment group, coded 1. Because we have not established a meaningful unit of *Y*, the regression coefficient, β, standardized with

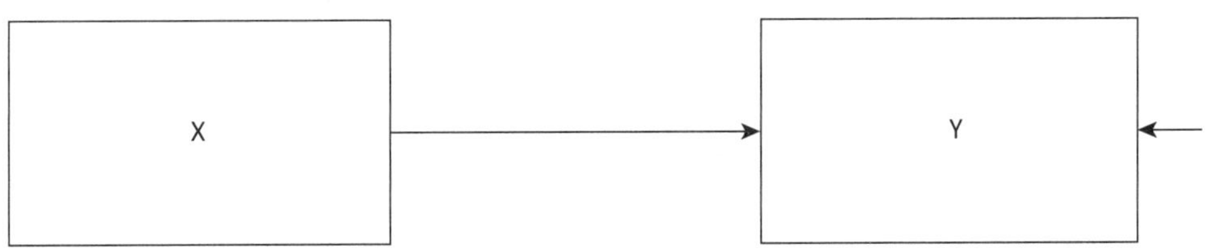

FIGURE 23.3. Simple path model.

respect to Y, is informative, indicating the predicted difference in Y scaled relative to standard deviations of Y.

Multiple group models with differences in means. The second model takes advantage of the multiple-group modeling facility found in almost all LVM software. Instead of regressing outcomes on the grouping variable (treatment), separate models are estimated for each group. The continuation of this example uses a trivial model within each group: simply the mean and variance of Y, with each parameter freely estimated. If the treatment condition defines group membership, the mean of Y would be allowed to differ between groups. The implementation of the next step would vary substantially by the software package, but it is conceptually simple: a test of the expected difference in model fit if the constraint of equal means across groups is applied. The resulting test, usually either a Wald test or a likelihood ratio test, is interpretable relative to the χ^2 distribution. The variance of y can be allowed to differ between groups. Doing so removes the assumption of homogeneity of variance that is implicit in the single-group model discussed earlier. We could as easily have maintained the constraint; this flexibility is an advantage of the multiple-group approach.

The overall model fit of a two-group model would be perfect because of the saturated model (unless the variances were constrained to be homogenous, in which case the test of model fit would be a one-degree-of-freedom test of that constraint, the only constraint implied in the modeling process). The Wald or likelihood ratio test is then compared with the χ^2 distribution with one degree of freedom (a single constraint being tested). Significance of this test indicates that the constraint harms model fit, and therefore it should be rejected.

Multiple group models with a latent continuous outcome. The next example goes beyond the realm of path analysis and ventures into SEM. That is, we will now assume we have multiple indicators (perhaps questionnaire items) of the designated outcome from our sample prevention program. There are several advantages to using multiple indicators. The latent variable (i.e., factor) captures variance common to the indicators. To illustrate, many drug prevention trials use the variance shared among alcohol, cigarettes, and marijuana use to reflect a latent construct of "polydrug use." In one example testing a school-based drug prevention program, Scheier, Botvin, and Griffin (2001) hypothesized a latent construct of "social competence" to reflect the shared variation between measures of refusal skill efficacy, assertiveness, and social skills. The same authors used measures of alcohol, tobacco, and marijuana use to reflect a latent construct of "polydrug use," capturing the common covariation underlying use of these drugs. The rest of the modeling approach, then, is focused on predicting that common variance, versus potentially misleading relations between the treatment condition and variance specific to a single measure or item. The analysis is otherwise essentially identical to the previous multiple-group example.

A key difference from previous iterations of this example is that the model is no longer saturated, and thus it is not expected to fit perfectly. Specifically, the assumption reflected in the measurement model (i.e., that the covariances between the observed variables are fully attributable to the relations to and among the sources) can be false, whether or not the structural model (the relations among the latent variables) is saturated. The use and interpretation of fit measures in LVM is an active topic of research and academic debate. Boomsma, Hoyle, and Panter (2012) provided a thorough overview of implications for reporting (see also McDonald & Ho, 2002).

Reporting the standardized solution in a latent variable model reflects convention in the factor analytic literature. Factor loadings, specifically, are traditionally standardized. As in most analytic strategies, however, unstandardized coefficients and their associated standard errors also should be reported (e.g., American Psychological Association, 2010). In the multiple-group model, the mean of the latent factor representing Y usually is constrained to zero in one group. In the absence of this constraint, or another with similar effects, the locations (i.e., means) of the factors in each group would not be identified. Most software packages have reasonable defaulting schemes to handle such issues with minimal intervention by the data analyst. The key result in this model, therefore, is the estimated mean of the outcome factor in the second (treatment) group. As in our previous examples, the hypothesis of equal outcome means is of interest. We also note that attending to the standardized solution has the side effect that the factor loadings—the strength of relations between the factor and the indicators—appear to differ between groups, even if they are constrained to equality in the analysis. This is to be expected as an effect of between-group differences in the factor variances.

The absence of measurement invariance—a situation in which a latent variable has different relations to its indicators between groups or measurement occasions—remains, however, a potential threat to validity in this analysis. For example, the correlations among different refusal-skill items, and therefore their factor loadings, may differ by gender, ethnicity, culture, or even time of measurement (Pentz & Chou, 1994). The reader confronted with this possibility is referred to Raykov, Marcoulides, and Li (2012) for a recent treatment.

Inclusion of covariates. The versatility of LVM makes the modeling of covariates (whether included as confounds, suppressors, or hypothesized third-variable causes) correspondingly flexible. In our example, we will focus on the most common case, that in which variance attributable to a covariate is partialled from both the predictors and all endogenous variables. This strategy is most closely parallel to the analysis of covariance, although models in which only some of the predictive relations from the covariates are modeled could be desirable in some circumstances. The modeling is straightforward: All variables of interest, including hitherto exogenous variables such as treatment status, are regressed on the covariates. In this example, we might include covariates intended to represent demographic features of the participants (e.g., gender), participation in prior substance-use-related programs, or an indicator of baseline substance use.

The two groups representing treatment assignment usually should be allowed to have different means for the exogenous predictors (covariates), thus enabling the association with the possible confound. The outcome measure *Y* also would be regressed on the three covariates. The regression relations with the covariates may or may not be constrained to equality across treatment conditions—allowing differences would allow treatment by covariate interactions.

An important caveat applies to LVM as much as to conventional multiple regression methods. MacKinnon, Krull, and Lockwood (2000) demonstrated that the functions of confounding, mediation, and suppression are statistically indistinguishable in regression models: Each serves to partition the variance in *Y* predicted by *X* into components accounted for by some third variable and those "residual" components attributable solely to *X*. The summary of this argument, as in our discussions of causal inference, is that the placement and role of variables in the model is at the discretion and judgment of the analyst, and not necessarily reflective of the population relations.

Tests of Differences in Alternative Outcomes

To this point, we have discussed tests of simple mean differences for drug prevention outcomes, whether modeled as a manifest score or a factor mean. The next section touches on alternative ways to model prevention outcomes and details one increasingly common model used in current prevention programs.

Structured continuous outcomes. Simple means (or proportions, discussed in the following section) are widespread outcome measures: in part due to ease of modeling but also due to the relative ease of data collection in most cases. If data collection resources permit, however, tests of prevention program outcomes can be much more detailed. We discussed earlier the latent trajectory as possible outcome. A difference in the rate of change over time, or even the shape and curvature of the trajectory of some specified outcome, can provide valuable information on the time-course of a prevention program's effect. Such a difference could result from a sleeper effect, a general change in response to TAU, or a decay of the program's effects over time, among other possibilities. Furthermore, even the relatively simple latent trait model can improve stability of the estimate of the outcome and thus can yield greater statistical power to detect modest prevention effects. The trade-offs in power between a greater number of participants and a greater number of occasions of measurement depend on the specifics of the study, but a detailed a priori power analysis can more than pay for itself in facilitating the optimal use of resources.

Simple and structured discrete outcomes. An obvious outcome of interest in drug use prevention research is the occurrence of drug use. Most modern LVM programs can accommodate a discretely measured outcome, using a logit or probit link function. This allows the full array of modeling possibilities discussed in this chapter, including modeling the outcome as a dichotomy (use vs. nonuse). Categorical data analysis, unfortunately, tends to be limited in power, especially with a skewed (very rare or very common) outcome, as often is encountered with measures of youth drug use.

An alternative to the simple use–nonuse dichotomy, and also frequently of interest in prevention research, is the timing of an event—for example, modeling the timing of first use of an illicit drug, or modeling factors that contribute to relapse after a program's end. Survival analysis (e.g., Singer & Willett, 2003, provided a detailed treatment) models the time to the outcome. Using a survival model as the structured model of a program outcome can show much more refined differences than a simple dichotomous indicator of substance use. This usage is not yet widespread in applied LVM, but it can be accommodated in software that permits use of dichotomous outcomes.

Combinations of outcome types. In many cases in substance use research, the optimal model of an outcome is neither strictly categorical nor continuous. For example, a researcher might be interested in the extent of use of a drug, but many participants may not use it at all—a type of floor effect. This *semicontinuous* outcome can be readily modeled using techniques detailed by Olsen and Schafer (2001). In this strategy, parallel models are constructed for the dichotomous portion of the outcome—use versus nonuse—and the continuous portion—quantity or frequency of use of the drug, given a nonzero amount. These techniques take advantage of modern tools for accommodating missing data, treating the quantity variable as missing for those youth who abstain. This is a particularly useful extension of LVM for drug use prevention in that a program might have a favorable prevention effect on abstinence but not show favorable effects on frequency of use among users, or vice versa.

A recent outgrowth of research that examines and extends the semicontinuous outcome approach falls under the general rubric of the MFLM. Applications in substance use appear in Witkiewitz and Masyn (2008) and in Malone et al. (2012). The use versus nonuse and extent of use in the previous example would be two facets of the progression of substance involvement. Other facets might include time to first use (a survival outcome), cessation of use, or extent of problematic use (e.g., heavy episodic drinking, beyond moderate drinking). The MFLM is a promising, although computationally intensive, approach to incorporating such multiple facets of possible outcomes of a prevention project in a single LVM.

Latent nominal outcomes. Latent nominal outcomes—latent class, latent profile, or a more general case—are increasing in popularity in LVM approaches to prevention. This approach could have been classed with the other *discrete outcomes*, but we wish to highlight this approach in its own section. The concept of a finite mixture model was discussed earlier; our purpose now is to illustrate its use as a dependent variable. Our prevention example continues with a mixture model, using the variable name *C* for the latent outcome. In addition to defining the variable *C* as a latent class (or profile), class membership is regressed on *TREAT* (capturing assignment to experimental conditions) as well as on important covariates.

Many potential obstacles to obtaining a good solution in mixture modeling are beyond the scope of this chapter; a recent treatment appears in Nylund, Asparouhov, and Muthén (2007). Given at least a three-class model solution, we now are working in the context of a multinomial logistic regression. The polytomous outcome requires two or more coefficients corresponding to the regression of *C* (latent categorical variable) on treatment: the logistic coefficient for the relative likelihood of membership in Class 1 versus Class 3 (assuming that Class 3 is the reference group) as a function of treatment, and the logistic coefficient indicating the comparison of Class 2 versus Class 3. Depending on the specific hypotheses of interest, a test of both coefficients with two degrees of freedom may be appropriate, corresponding to a null hypothesis of no difference in class proportions as a function of treatment.

Mediating and moderating variables in LVM. The role and testing of mediating variables are discussed in Chapter 25 in this volume, but, in brief, a variable modeled in a mediating role generally is assumed to play a causal or intervening role in the link between *X* (e.g., a prevention program) and an outcome (*Y*). The actual requirements for an inference of causal mediation can be strict, depending on the details of the study, but the incorporation in an LVM is straightforward: the mediator (*M*) is regressed on *X* and the outcome (*Y*) is regressed on the mediator. As an example, the hypothetical prevention program might teach cognitive behavior skills to improve social assertiveness, refusal skills, and social efficacy (i.e., communication skills). The improvement in skills, the target risk mechanisms, then is likely to boost youths' ability to refuse drug offers, thwarting negative peer social influences, and thus protect them from drug use.

Moderators play an entirely different role and are analogous to the epidemiologic concept of "effect modifiers." In the drug use prevention context, a moderator most often would be a variable (e.g., gender, ethnicity, current substance use) that varies the strength of the relation between the prevention program and the outcome (i.e., has a conditioning effect). As an example, our hypothetical prevention program might be particularly effective for participants who had no prior experience with illicit substance use. Modeling past use as a moderator of program effects would enable testing whether this predisposing risk condition matters in obtaining favorable program effects. The modeling of moderation in LVM takes many forms, depending especially on the measurement of the moderator (continuous vs. discrete, latent vs. manifest), and the optimal modeling strategy for moderators is an active topic of research. A recent discussion can be found in T. D. Little, Card, Bovaird, Preacher, and Crandall (2007).

Space precludes a full treatment of both moderators and mediators, along with their unique aspects in the context of both their statistical importance and their respective roles in the "developmental" processes underlying prevention effects. One commonality linking discussion of mediating and moderating variables is that both serve as "third variables" in an assessment of an $X \rightarrow Y$ relation; however, they do so in different ways. A given variable, however, can serve more than one role in a model, including the possibility of being both a mediator and a moderator (for a clear example of this in substance use research, see Pilgrim, Schulenberg, O'Malley, Bachman, & Johnston, 2006). The baseline-as-moderator example mentioned earlier is a common situation in prevention research. A mediator-as-moderator, to date, rarely is tested in applied research, but that may be as much due to the historical separation between the two concepts. A ready-to-hand example might be that a prevention program relies on a change in perceived peer norms regarding substance use. The baseline level of perceived norms, however, could easily alter the function of the intervention. Furthermore, even given that the prevention program affects perceived norms in the aggregate, the postintervention assessment of norms at the individual level might moderate the direct effect of the program on substance use. Preacher, Rucker, and Hayes (2007) presented several of these "dual-role" cases with notes on implementation.

Regression mixture models. Finally, the regression mixture model is an advanced technique that is gaining popularity as another means by which different elements of LVM can be brought together to best model the effects of a prevention program. Regression mixture modeling is not yet applied broadly in prevention research, in part because of the demands the methods place on sample size (Van Horn et al., 2009), but the appeal is clear. Such an approach models a latent nominal variable as the *moderator* of the program effect. That is, the researcher might hypothesize that different subgroups exist in the sampled population who are more or less responsive to the intervention, but who are not explicitly identified as members of those groups. Thus, the latent classification variable reflects difference in the regression coefficients in the body of the LVM.

EXTENSIONS OF LVM FOR DRUG USE PREVENTION RESEARCH

Many potential complicating program evaluation factors that are prevalent in drug use prevention research can require particular attention both at the statistical and conceptual level. This is true as much or more in LVM strategies as in other modeling approaches. This section addresses a few common cases, comments on the complicating nature, and provides direction to more specialized readings.

Clustered Designs

The nominal case of individual randomization to an intervention versus comparison (control) condition is actually, in our experience, relatively rarely implemented in prevention trials. Drug use prevention programs often have much larger samples than do treatment programs, making individual assignment unwieldy or infeasible. There are two easily distinguished cases of the clustered prevention experiment: clustered recruitment with individual assignment to treatment, and clustered treatment delivery. The distinction, however, can be deceptive, as the implications for analysis for the former are as strict in some ways as for the latter.

The clustered recruitment strategy is extremely common in prevention research. In simple terms, "clusters" of participants in the study have greater commonalities (that may or may not have to do with substance use) than with participants in other clusters because of some feature of the recruitment into the study. In a school-based program, the clusters might represent classrooms within the school, schools within the district, or even districts within a larger sampling frame. In a community-based program, recruitment might have been based on membership in specific churches, health care settings, or other community entities. In a national study, the design may have included stratified sampling of, for example, county or parish or Census tract, and random sampling within that unit. In any such case, commonalities among participants due to their respective higher-level sampling unit can distort results (usually in the direction of underestimated standard errors and therefore overstated significance of results) if not considered. Fortunately, this is relatively easily dealt with in most contemporary LVM software (Murray, 1998, has an excellent book that outlines the different statistical considerations and conceptual problems that arise from clustering in group randomized designs).

In the commercially available Mplus software (L. K. Muthén & Muthén, 2012), for example, two syntax commands are sufficient to identify the clustering variable and switch estimation methods to account for the complex or "nested" sample. This adjusts the standard errors and reduces the likelihood of making a Type I error (albeit often at the expense of lost power given shrinkage in degrees of freedom associated with the unit of assignment and cost of increased analysis time). More complex sampling designs, such as cross-classified designs in which a respondent may be a member of two clusters that do not perfectly overlap—perhaps a cohort in a weekend program that draws from several schools—can be more difficult to deal with, although technical advances in software are beginning to catch up with this case, as well. The reader confronted with this situation is referred to Asparouhov and Muthén (2012) and to Jeon and Rabe-Hesketh (2012).

The second case we mentioned is the cluster-*delivered* program. This is typically, although not necessarily, a subset of the cluster-based *recruitment* design just discussed. In this situation, commonly referred to as the *group-randomized trial*, the randomization to condition is at the level of the cluster, such as random assignment of entire classrooms to a program delivered to a class as a whole, but in which the respondent (the provider of data assessing results) is still an individual student. Failure to account for the clustered nature of this design will again likely result in underestimation of standard errors, but it also is highly likely to result in an overpowered statistical test resulting from an incorrect calculation of (numerator, in the case of *F* tests) degrees of freedom. Not all common LVM software programs include capacity for this situation, and the implications for degrees of freedom for the statistical test are a subject of much statistical research. This multilevel model is well described in Vermunt (2003); for current purposes, we will note that multilevel (vs. clustered) LVM is highly demanding in the higher-level sample size (i.e., number of "delivery units"), both in terms of statistical power and in terms of ease of reaching a stable solution.

A common fallacy in both cases is that a small observed effect of the cluster, perhaps measured as an intraclass correlation (ICC), means that the cluster does not need to be accounted in the analysis. Although this is strictly true, in the sense that a multilevel analysis of data where the ICC is 0 will return results identical to a nonclustered analysis, judging the ICC as small enough to disregard is often a mistake. Depending on the number of clusters (sampling or delivery units) in the design, even an ICC that appears to be small (e.g., 0.01, scaled as a correlation coefficient) can have a substantial effect on the standard error. In general, therefore, there is no advantage to ignoring clustering: If the clustering is important, then it should be modeled; if it is not, modeling it will have no consequence for the results. An exception might be called for in particularly large problems in which the clustering is affecting computer run-times or ease of convergence, but the guideline otherwise holds.

Survey Weights

A second element of the sampling design that can affect the use of LVM is a *weighted* sampling strategy, where even within the sampling, frame units (e.g., respondents) have systematically unequal chances of being included in the study. A common example might include oversampling ethnic minority youth from a specific population, or a case that involves oversampling individuals recording a particular diagnosis. In either case—ethnic origins or diagnosis—members of the specific group in question are disproportionately represented in the eventual sample. Most modern LVM software easily handles this situation, applying survey weights, although in some cases that combine additional features of the analysis, the inclusion of weights can significantly increase run-times.

Nonrandom Assignment

The final case we deal with related to sampling and recruitment is the nonrandom design. As many us have had drilled into our heads since undergraduate statistics training, the randomized experiment is the gold standard for inferring causal effects. Even in the case of the randomized experiment, there are necessary supporting assumptions for the transition to the inference that sometimes are overlooked in our training, but here we discuss the more obvious case. Even in a randomized prevention experiment, there is rarely (at least in the field) full compliance with the assignment to condition. Respondents randomized to the TAU condition often are less likely to respond to recruitment and to continue participation than those receiving the treatment being studied. Regardless, even in the treatment condition, 100% participation and compliance is the exception rather than the rule. In either of these cases, there may be systematic pretreatment differences in the resulting compliant samples, violating the assumptions associated with random assignment. Even aside from this case, RCTs are subject to other limitations—most obviously threats to generalizability but also others that are only beginning to be widely acknowledged. Derzon (2014) provided an accessible review of several limitations that may pose substantial concerns for prevention researchers as well as discussion of several recommendations for complementary approaches.

The methodological literature burgeons with theoretical and often-technical considerations of these problems and potential solutions. In recent years, the use of methods based on *propensity scores* has gained increasing popularity in drug prevention research (e.g., Scheier & Grenard, 2010). In its classic form, propensity-score matching is a potential solution to nonrandomized studies that is designed to result in comparable groups, as if the grouping had been fully the result of random assignment. The simplest—and most easily discussed in a brief treatment—approach is to take members of the originally assigned treatment group and predict actual uptake of treatment from baseline variables in a logistic regression. The regression coefficients then are used to generate post hoc probabilities of uptake among members of both treatment and comparison groups. That is, regardless of actual uptake, a given member of the treatment sample might be projected from baseline variables as having had, for example, a .835 probability of uptake. A member of the comparison group with a comparable probability is then matched to the treatment respondent and included in the group to be used in the statistical comparisons. This typically will result in the "loss" of some unmatched members of both groups, and thus some loss of generalizability. Should the model perform as expected, however, the process results in two groups that are comparable on an array of baseline characteristics, which is the scalar propensity score.

Recent methodological literature has seen many elaborations on these basic principles (e.g., Stuart, 2010) that have been demonstrated to improve performance (and generalizability) over this basic version, but the core methodology is the same—an adjustment to the samples being compared to compensate for nonrandomization of treatment (and thus the likely lack of pretest equivalence of members of the two or more groups).

Missing Data

LVM can be used when data are missing, but certain assumptions need to be considered. This is a complex topic handled well in several recent sources (Enders, 2010; Graham, 2009; Schafer, 1997). In the interests of facilitating understanding of the more technical sources, we mention here definitions based on the widely used, but sometimes nonintuitive, terminology of R. J. A. Little and Rubin (1987). In these conventions, data can be construed as MCAR, MAR, or MNAR (sometimes referred to as nonignorable, nonrandom missing data). These assumptions reflect the mechanism that results in observations (or data) being missing. The assumption of MCAR holds if and only when the likelihood of a data-point being missing is entirely unrelated to its true (unobserved) value. The less-restrictive MAR assumption is that the likelihood of a datum being missing is unrelated to its true value *after* conditioning on other variables in the model (i.e., the partial correlation between likelihood of being unobserved and its value). A simple example of MCAR might be data being missing if and only if a respondent has relocated geographically between observations in a longitudinal study and an indicator of relocation is incorporated in the model. MCAR data are also MAR, inasmuch as no conditioning is required in the MCAR case. Data sets in which the mechanism of missingness does *not* meet the definition of MAR are MNAR. When analyzing data from a design with planned missing data (e.g., a three-form design with partial overlap of questions on the different forms), the MCAR assumption still can be met provided the selection of who receives which form is nonsystematic.

Cautions and Limitations

Model fit. Much is known and has been written about the assessment of model fit in LVM; much less is agreed on. The gold standard of fit for most models is the χ^2 test of fit, in which a nonsignificant χ^2 statistic indicates that the null hypothesis of perfect fit cannot be rejected. The frequentist-trained user (i.e., most of those trained in social science traditions) will immediately note a discrepancy in this model from classic training: Our theory, as implemented in the model, predicts results consistent with the null hypothesis.

In LVM, the null hypothesis stipulates that the variances, covariances, and other statistics *implied* by the estimated parameters, given the model configuration, do not differ from the *observed* sample statistics. That is, given the estimated parameters linking any two variables via the relations specified by the model, an implied covariance can be calculated, which is hypothesized to match the observed covariance, and this is repeated across all sample statistics used in the model. There are, as many of us were trained, two principal sources of a nonsignificant test: (a) the null hypothesis is true in the population, or (b) the study lacked statistical power to reject the null, given the actual differences between the implied and observed statistics. There is no absolute means of distinguishing between the two cases in a given study.

The opposite side of this coin, however, is that many users (and many statisticians) are concerned about the χ^2 test being overpowered in a given study: The test can lead the researcher to reject the null even in the case of substantively trivial discrepancies. This problem is not unique to LVM, of course, and its relevance in other designs and analysis techniques underlies the emphasis on effect size in recent years. An LVM, however, easily can be complex enough to defy a simple characterization of effect size.

One result of this sensitivity of the χ^2 statistic to small discrepancies with large samples (where no one can quite say for all cases how small a discrepancy is "small" and how large a sample is "large") is a plethora of indices of *approximate* fit. The usual goals of the developers of these indices have been to characterize good (or ill) fit of a model to the data in a way that is not overly sensitive to sample size or model complexity. There are far too many measures of approximate fit to detail in this section, but we briefly describe two of the most common indices used, and refer to Hu and Bentler (1999) for details.

The comparative fit index (CFI) is extremely popular, in part because of its intuitive simplicity. For a given data set, the *saturated* model—that is, a model in which every bivariate relation in the data can be accommodated—results in a χ^2 statistic of 0 with zero degrees of freedom, indicating perfect fit to the data. For the same data set, the *null* model is a model in which no bivariate relations are accommodated—that is, a model of each variable assumed to be unrelated to all others—and results in the worst possible χ^2 statistic for the data set. The CFI is calculated as the point the estimated model occupies on the spectrum from worst to best possible fit, scaled from 0 (the null model) to 1 (the saturated model). In general, experience and research support a CFI of .95 or greater as indicative of good fit, with .90 commonly being viewed as a lower bound of acceptability (Hu & Bentler, 1999).

The estimated root mean square error of approximation (est. RMSEA) is also well regarded, since its development by Steiger and Lind (1980). The est. RMSEA is less easily detailed, but in essence, it uses properties of the χ^2 distribution to characterize the lack of fit of the model to the data scaled to the degrees of freedom in the model. We have not discussed LVM degrees of freedom, but for this purpose, a degree of freedom can be thought of as a constraint on the saturated model. Any such constraint will harm absolute fit, but at the same time it will increase parsimony as one less free parameter is being estimated. The est. RMSEA uses the degrees of freedom (the number of constraints) as an adjustment, and so it better reflects model parsimony as a desideratum than does the CFI. Estimated RMSEA has a further advantage over most indices of approximate fit in that its sampling distribution is known. Whereas CFI is a calculated point value, the calculation of the RMSEA generates a confidence interval. Common thresholds for est. RMSEA are a desired estimate below .06 (as an index of ill fit, 0 is perfect; Hu & Bentler, 1999). Estimates or upper confidences bounds greater than .10 typically are construed as ill fit.

We also note that resorting to measures of approximate fit is not the only approach to coping with a significance test that indicates poor fit. There is increasing interest in the methodological literature in localizing misfit (French & Finch, 2008, discuss this strategy in the context of testing measurement invariance). Axiomatically, lack of fit is determined by the impact of constraints in the LVM. These constraints most commonly involve either fixing certain parameter estimates to zero by omitting possible paths from the model or explicitly constraining two or more coefficient estimates to equality. As an alternative, albeit post hoc, response to lack of absolute fit, the researcher can examine the consequence for overall model fit obtained by relaxing individual constraints (e.g., by restoring omitted paths) to localize the problem indicated by the overall misfit. Confidence intervals derived in this process can help with the problem of estimating the practical significance of a given source of ill fit. The modification indices provided by most LVM software reflect an earlier implementation of this approach.

One more point should be made before leaving the subject of model fit. Even in the case of a nonsignificant χ^2 test with a well-powered study, the failure to reject the null does not guarantee that the model being estimated reflects the state of relations in the population. Empirical support for the model indicates consistency not only with the hypothesized structural model but also with any number of equivalent models that are based on the same variables, parameters, and data. This point is particularly concerning in models with few degrees of freedom for the test of fit, as few constraints on the structure are being tested. At the extreme, a model with no degrees of freedom (a saturated model) cannot fail to fit perfectly, regardless of how the variables are arranged. This underscores the importance of strong theoretical and empirical support for the researcher's structural model. By having this support and addressing any potentially viable alternative models, we lend further credence to our hypothesized model. In addition, any possible alternative models that fit as well or nearly as well as our model must be considered. This is an underacknowledged issue in many studies utilizing SEM (Bentler, 1978; Kline, 2010).

Statistical power in LVM. In the discussion of fit, we mentioned statistical power, but we did not go into detail. The first principle is that rules of thumb for power in LVM are largely unhelpful. In traditional discussion of statistical power, we learn that power depends on sample size, alpha, and the anticipated effect size. What often is left implicit is that it also depends on the model configuration, which is why power analysis texts separately tabulate many different kinds of analyses and model complexities (*df*). In the much less confined world of LVM, however, the variety of models defies tabulation. Rather than leaving the reader without hope, we will discuss the two primary ways power comes into play.

First, and touching on the discussion of model fit, there is the question of power to reject the estimated model. This now is largely a solved problem to the extent fit is assessed with estimated RMSEA. Preacher and Coffman (2006) published a utility that calculates power (or, alternatively, sample size) to reject hypotheses about the RMSEA. This utility can be used for absolute fit (i.e., power to reject a null hypothesis that the population RMSEA is 0) or for approximate fit (e.g., power to reject the hypothesis that the RSMEA is ≤ .05). The difference in RSMEA between that in the reference model (0, .05) and the model being tested is thus the effect size.

Power, however, comes into play in LVM in a second way. Even given an acceptable, good, or even perfect overall fit, what is the power to reject hypotheses regarding parameter estimates? For example, the key estimate being studied might be a structural regression coefficient corresponding to the program effect on a mediator or designated outcome. Even in a model with perfect fit, the structural relation of interest may not be observed to be significantly different from zero. The power to reject a hypothesis that the parameter is zero, however, could be very different from the power for a similar hypothesis for a second parameter elsewhere in the same model, depending on the measurement properties of the latent variables and many other fundamental aspects of covariance structure modeling. There is no simple answer to these issues. There is, though, one complicated one: simulation. The current gold standard for this sort of question of power relies on statistical simulation (i.e., "Monte Carlo study") of the model to be tested. Descriptions of the process are beyond the scope of this chapter but can be found in L. K. Muthén and Muthén (2002).

Causal Inference in LVM

We have discussed in different contexts the issue of causal inference from LVM. Our possibly undue stress is due to the common misconception that a well-fitting model necessarily reflects the "state of nature"—that is, the true directional relations operating in the population that give rise to observed covariances in the sample. Techniques do exist that can improve the confidence with which the user can draw causal inferences from LVM, although they are, by and large, not unique to the modeling strategy. Most treatments to date of the theory of causal inference—even those targeted to an audience of prevention scientists—are fairly technical in nature. A relatively accessible treatment reflecting the theoretical side is found in Sobel (1996).

One practical approach that is gaining traction in LVM and other applications is *propensity matching*. As we discussed in the section on Extensions, this procedure is designed to result in subsamples equivalent to each other on an array of observed background variables, allowing a mimicking of the strength of experimental random assignment even in observational studies. Stuart and colleagues (e.g., Harder, Stuart, & Anthony, 2010; Imai et al., 2011; Stuart, 2010) have presented a number of treatments using propensity matching that are easily combined with LVM.

Even true random assignment, however, as in a field experiment, is not a perfect guarantee of appropriate causal inference. Our discussion of indirect effects dealt with some aspects of this, but we highlight this point as especially relevant to data measured over time. For example, participants from a randomized clinical trial that are assigned to the treatment condition are (by standards of responsible conduct of research) free to continue participation in the intervention or not. The most common response to this in our reading of prevention science literature is to analyze data using the intent-to-treat approach, in which initial assignment is used as the predictor in all analyses, regardless of degree of participation. Sobel (1994) demonstrated how this strategy—usually argued for as the most conservative strategy—can yield misleading results in certain situations. The researcher conducting substance use prevention studies is urged to consider this problem, including potential solutions such as instrumental variable approaches to assessing causal effects when compliance is not perfect (e.g., Antonakis, Bendahan, Jacquart, & Lalive, 2010).

CONCLUSION

We have covered a great deal of material in this chapter—even if only surveying a vast literature—and a single chapter can provide only a cursory introduction to such a broad (and rapidly expanding) topic. We hope the reader has come away with a balanced perspective on the strengths, capacities, and limitations of LVM as a strategy in substance use prevention research. It is a tremendously flexible and versatile approach. Indeed, its flexibility can easily lead to misuse—in the sense of "use that may lead to poor inference"—in the absence of a careful awareness of those strengths, capacities, and limitations. Our limited space precluded a focus on some of the more practical, get-your-hands-dirty aspects of software and code. Narayanan (2012) completed a recent review of the strengths and weaknesses of major software packages with strong LVM capacities, and Byrne (1998, 2001, 2006, 2011) has produced a series of texts with didactic presentations for implementing LVM in several of those packages. The technical advances proceed at a pace that makes these references quickly dated, but the fundamentals in a given software option continue to apply. Finally, we refer to Hoyle's (2012) edited volume detailing many theoretical and practical aspects of LVM, most of which would be relevant to some strategies of drug use prevention research.

References

Aiken, L. S., Stein, J. A., & Bentler, P. M. (1994). Structural equation analysis of clinical subpopulation differences and comparative treatment outcomes: Characterizing the daily lives of drug addicts. *Journal of Consulting and Clinical Psychology*, *62*, 488–499. doi:10.1037/0022-006X.62.3.488

American Psychological Association (2010). *Publication manual of the American Psychological Association* (6th ed.). Washington, DC: Author.

Antonakis, J., Bendahan, S., Jacquart, P., & Lalive, R. (2010). On making causal claims: A review and recommendations. *Leadership Quarterly*, *21*, 1086–1120. doi:10.1016/j.leaqua.2010.10.010

Asparouhov, T., & Muthén, B. (2012, April). *General random effect latent variable modeling: Random subjects, items, contexts, and parameters.* Paper presented at the annual meeting of the National Council on Measurement in Education, Vancouver, British Columbia.

Baron, R. M., & Kenny, D. A. (1986). The moderator-mediator variable distinction in social psychological research: Conceptual, strategic, and statistical considerations. *Journal of Personality and Social Psychology*, *51*, 1173–1182. doi:10.1037/0022-3514.51.6.1173

Bentler, P. M. (1978). The interdependence of theory, methodology, and empirical data: Causal modeling as an approach to construct validation. In D. B. Kandel (Ed.), *Longitudinal drug research* (pp. 267–302). New York, NY: Wiley.

Boomsma, A., Hoyle, R. H., & Panter, A. T. (2012). The structural equation modeling research report. In R. H. Hoyle (Ed.), *Handbook of structural equation modeling* (pp. 341–358). New York, NY: Guilford Press.

Bray, B. C., Lanza, S. T., & Collins, L. M. (2010). Modeling relations among discrete developmental processes: A general approach to associative latent transition analysis. *Structural Equation Modeling*, *17*, 541–569. doi:10.1080/10705511.2010.510043

Byrne, B. M. (1998). *Structural equation modeling with LISREL, PRELIS, and SIMPLIS: Basic concepts, applications, and programming.* Mahwah, NJ: Erlbaum.

Byrne, B. M. (2001). *Structural equation modeling with AMOS: Basic concepts, applications, and programming.* Mahwah, NJ: Erlbaum.

Byrne, B. M. (2006). *Structural equation modeling with EQS*. Mahwah, NJ: Erlbaum.

Byrne, B. M. (2011). *Structural equation modeling with Mplus: Basic concepts, applications, and programming*. Mahwah, NJ: Erlbaum.

Cliff, N. (1983). Some cautions concerning the application of causal-modeling methods. *Multivariate Behavioral Research, 18*, 115–126. doi:10.1207/s15327906mbr1801_7

Collins, L. M., & Wugalter, S. E. (1992). Latent class models or stage-sequential dynamic latent-variables. *Multivariate Behavioral Research, 27*, 131–157. doi:10.1207/s15327906mbr2701_8

Crawford, A. M., Pentz, M. A., Chou, C. P., Li, C. Y., & Dwyer, J. H. (2003). Parallel developmental trajectories of sensation seeking and regular substance use in adolescents. *Psychology of Addictive Behaviors, 17*, 179–192. doi:10.1037/0893-164X.17.3.179

Derzon, J. H. (2014). Differences-in-differences in approaches. In G. J. N. Bruinsma & D. L. Weisburd (Eds.), *Encyclopedia of criminology and criminal justice* (pp. 1054–1064). New York, NY: Springer Science+Business Media.

Duncan, T. E., Duncan, S. C., & Strycker, L. A. (2006). *An introduction to latent variable growth curve modeling: Concepts, issues, and applications*. Mahwah, NJ: Erlbaum.

Enders, C. K. (2010). *Applied missing data analysis*. New York, NY: Guilford Press.

Flaherty, B. P. (2008). Testing the degree of cross-sectional and longitudinal dependence between two discrete dynamic processes. *Developmental Psychology, 44*, 468–480. doi:10.1037/0012-1649.44.2.468

French, B. F., & Finch, W. H. (2008). Multigroup confirmatory factor analysis: Locating the invariant referent sets. *Structural Equation Modeling, 15*, 96–113. doi:10.1080/10705510701758349

Graham, J. W. (2009). Missing data analysis: Making it work in the real world. *Annual Review of Psychology, 60*, 549–576. doi:10.1146/annurev.psych.58.110405.085530

Graham, J. W., Hofer, S. M., & MacKinnon, D. P. (1996). Maximizing the usefulness of data obtained with planned missing value patterns: An application of maximum likelihood procedures. *Multivariate Behavioral Research, 31*, 197–218. doi:10.1207/s15327906mbr3102_3

Hamagami, F., & McArdle, J. J. (2001). Advanced studies of individual differences linear dynamic models for longitudinal data analysis. In G. A. Marcoulides & R. E. Schumacker (Eds.), *New developments and techniques in structural equation modeling* (pp. 203–246). Mahwah, NJ: Erlbaum.

Harder, V. S., Stuart, E. A., & Anthony, J. C. (2010). Propensity score techniques and the assessment of measured covariate balance to test causal associations in psychological research. *Psychological Methods, 15*, 234–249. doi:10.1037/a0019623

Hoyle, R. H. (Ed.). (2012). *Handbook of structural equation modeling*. New York, NY: Guilford Press.

Hu, L. T., & Bentler, P. M. (1999). Cutoff criteria for fit indexes in covariance structure analysis: Conventional criteria versus new alternatives. *Structural Equation Modeling, 6*, 1–55. doi:10.1080/10705519909540118

Imai, K., Jo, B., & Stuart, E. A. (2011). Commentary: Using potential outcomes to understand causal mediation analysis. *Multivariate Behavioral Research, 46*, 861–873. doi:10.1080/00273171.2011.606743

Jeon, M., & Rabe-Hesketh, S. (2012). Profile-likelihood approach for estimating generalized linear mixed models with factor structures. *Journal of Educational and Behavioral Statistics, 37*, 518–542. doi:10.3102/1076998611417628

Jöreskog, K. G., & Sörbom, D. (1976). *LISREL III: Estimation of linear structural equation systems by maximum likelihood methods: A FORTRAN IV program*. Chicago, IL: National Educational Resources.

Jöreskog, K. G., & Sörbom, D. (1979). *Advances in factor analysis and structural equation models*. New York, NY: University Press of America.

Kline, R. B. (2010). *Principles and practice of structural equation modeling* (3rd ed.). New York, NY: Guilford Press.

Lanza, S. T., & Rhoades, B. L. (2013). Latent class analysis: An alternative perspective on subgroup analysis in prevention and treatment. *Prevention Science, 14*, 157–168. doi:10.1007/s11121-011-0201-1

Little, R. J. A., & Rubin, D. B. (1987). *Statistical analysis with missing data*. New York, NY: Wiley.

Little, T. D., Card, N. A., Bovaird, J. A., Preacher, K. J., & Crandall, C. S. (2007). Structural equation modeling of mediation and moderation with contextual factors. In T. D. Little, J. A. Bovaird, & N. A. Card (Eds.), *Modeling contextual effects in longitudinal studies* (pp. 207–230). Mahwah, NJ: Erlbaum.

Loehlin, J. C. (2004). *Latent variable models: an introduction to factor, path, and structural equation analysis* (4th ed.). Mahwah, NJ: Erlbaum.

MacKinnon, D. P. (2008). *Introduction to statistical mediation analysis*. New York, NY: Erlbaum.

MacKinnon, D. P., & Fairchild, A. J. (2009). Current directions in mediation analysis. *Current Directions in Psychological Science, 18*, 16–20. doi:10.1111/j.1467-8721.2009.01598.x

MacKinnon, D. P., Krull, J. L., & Lockwood, C. M. (2000). Equivalence of the mediation, confounding, and suppression effect. *Prevention Science*, *1*, 173–181. doi:10.1023/A:1026595011371

Malone, P. S., Lamis, D. A., Masyn, K. E., & Northrup, T. F. (2010). A dual-process discrete-time survival analysis model: Application to the gateway drug hypothesis. *Multivariate Behavioral Research*, *45*, 790–805. doi:10.1080/00273171.2010.519277

Malone, P. S., Northrup, T. F., Masyn, K. E., Lamis, D. A., & Lamont, A. E. (2012). Initiation and persistence of alcohol use in United States Black, Hispanic, and White male and female youth. *Addictive Behaviors*, *37*, 299–305. doi:10.1016/j.addbeh.2011.11.010

McDonald, R. P., & Ho, M.-H. R. (2002). Principles and practice in reporting structural equation analyses. *Psychological Methods*, *7*, 64–82. doi:10.1037/1082-989X.7.1.64

Murray, D. M. (1998). *Design and analysis of group-randomized trials*. New York, NY: Oxford University Press.

Muthén, B. O., & Masyn, K. (2005). Discrete-time survival mixture analysis. *Journal of Educational and Behavioral Statistics*, *30*, 27–58. doi:10.3102/10769986030001027

Muthén, B. O., & Muthén, L. K. (2000). Integrating person-centered and variable-centered analyses: Growth mixture modeling with latent trajectory classes. *Alcoholism: Clinical and Experimental Research*, *24*, 882–891. doi:10.1111/j.1530-0277.2000.tb02070.x

Muthén, B. O., & Shedden, K. (1999). Finite mixture modeling with mixture outcomes using the EM algorithm. *Biometrics*, *55*, 463–469. doi:10.1111/j.0006-341X.1999.00463.x

Muthén, L. K., & Muthén, B. O. (2002). How to use a Monte Carlo study to decide on sample size and determine power. *Structural Equation Modeling*, *9*, 599–620. doi:10.1207/S15328007SEM0904_8

Muthén, L. K., & Muthén, B. O. (2012). *Mplus user's guide* (7th ed.). Los Angeles, CA: Author.

Narayanan, A. (2012). A review of eight software packages for structural equation modeling. *American Statistician*, *66*, 129–138. doi:10.1080/00031305.2012.708641

Nylund, K. L., Asparouhov, T., & Muthén, B. O. (2007). Deciding on the number of classes in latent class analysis and growth mixture modeling: A Monte Carlo simulation study. *Structural Equation Modeling*, *14*, 535–569. doi:10.1080/10705510701575396

Olsen, M. K., & Schafer, J. L. (2001). A two-part random-effects model for semicontinuous longitudinal data. *Journal of the American Statistical Association*, *96*, 730–745. doi:10.1198/016214501753168389

Pentz, M. A., & Chou, C. (1994). Measurement invariance in longitudinal clinical research assuming change from development and intervention. *Journal of Consulting and Clinical Psychology*, *62*, 450–462. doi:10.1037/0022-006X.62.3.450

Pilgrim, C. C., Schulenberg, J. E., O'Malley, P. M., Bachman, J. G., & Johnston, L. D. (2006). Mediators and moderators of parental involvement on substance use: A national study of adolescents. *Prevention Science*, *7*, 75–89. doi:10.1007/s11121-005-0019-9

Preacher, K. J., & Coffman, D. L. (2006). *Computing power and minimum sample size for RMSEA*. [Software]. Retrieved from http://quantpsy.org/

Preacher, K. J., Rucker, D. D., & Hayes, A. F. (2007). Addressing moderated mediation hypotheses: Theory, methods, and prescriptions. *Multivariate Behavioral Research*, *42*, 185–227. doi:10.1080/00273170701341316

Raykov, T., Marcoulides, G. A., & Li, C.-H. (2012). Measurement invariance for latent constructs in multiple populations: A critical view and refocus. *Educational and Psychological Measurement*, *72*, 954–974. doi:10.1177/0013164412441607

Schafer, J. L. (1997). *Analysis of incomplete multivariate data*. London, England: Chapman & Hall. doi:10.1201/9781439821862

Scheier, L. M. (2012). Primary prevention models: The essence of drug abuse prevention in schools. In H. J. Schaffer, D. A. LaPlante, & S. E. Nelson (Eds.), *APA addiction syndrome handbook: Vol. 2. Recovery, prevention, and other issues* (pp. 197–223). Washington, DC: American Psychological Association.

Scheier, L. M., Botvin, G. J., & Griffin, K. W. (2001). Preventive intervention effects on developmental progression in drug use: Structural equation modeling analyses using longitudinal data. *Prevention Science*, *2*, 91–112. doi:10.1023/A:1011543730566

Scheier, L. M., & Grenard, J. L. (2010). Influence of a nationwide social marketing campaign on adolescent drug use. *Journal of Health Communication*, *15*, 240–271. doi:10.1080/10810731003686580

Singer, J. D., & Willett, J. B. (2003). *Applied longitudinal data analysis: Modeling change and event occurrence*. New York, NY: Oxford University Press. doi:10.1093/acprof:oso/9780195152968.001.0001

Sobel, M. E. (1994). Causal inference in latent variable models. In A. von Eye & C. C. Clifford (Eds.), *Latent variable analysis: Applications for developmental research* (pp. 3–35). Thousand Oaks, CA: Sage.

Sobel, M. E. (1996). An introduction to causal inference. *Sociological Methods and Research*, *24*, 353–379. doi:10.1177/0049124196024003004

Steiger, J. H., & Lind, J. C. (1980). *Statistically based tests for the number of common factors*. Paper presented at the annual meeting of the Psychometric Society, Iowa City, IA.

Steyer, R., Ferring, D., & Schmitt, M. J. (1992). States and traits in psychological assessment. *European Journal of Psychological Assessment*, *8*, 79–98.

Stuart, E. A. (2010). Matching methods for causal inference: A review and a look forward. *Statistical Science*, *25*, 1–21. doi:10.1214/09-STS313

Tomarken, A. J., & Waller, N. G. (2005). Structural equation modeling: Strengths, limitations, and misconceptions. *Annual Review of Clinical Psychology*, *1*, 31–65. doi:10.1146/annurev.clinpsy.1.102803.144239

Van Horn, M. L., Jaki, T., Masyn, K., Ramey, S. L., Smith, J. A., & Antaramian, S. (2009). Assessing differential effects: Applying regression mixture models to identify variations in the influence of family resources on academic achievement. *Developmental Psychology*, *45*, 1298–1313. doi:10.1037/a0016427

Vermunt, J. K. (2003). Multilevel latent class models. *Sociological Methodology*, *33*, 213–239. doi:10.1111/j.0081-1750.2003.t01-1-00131.x

Witkiewitz, K., & Masyn, K. E. (2008). Drinking trajectories following an initial lapse. *Psychology of Addictive Behaviors*, *22*, 157–167. doi:10.1037/0893-164X.22.2.157

Wright, S. (1920). Correlation and causation Part I. Method of path coefficients. *Journal of Agricultural Research*, *20*, 557–585.

CHAPTER 24

CIGARETTE SMOKING PATTERNS AS A CASE STUDY OF THEORY-ORIENTED LATENT CLASS ANALYSIS

Brian P. Flaherty

This chapter presents an exploratory latent class analysis (LCA) of cigarette smoking patterns in a U.S. national sample of adult White men and women. These analyses are a first step toward developing a psychometrically sound cigarette smoking pattern scale based on the latent class (LC) model. LCA, a statistical approach to identifying homogeneous subgroups (classes) in a population, has similarities to cluster analysis and factor analysis. Interest in and use of LCA has grown rapidly over the past several years, in part, due to the idea that prevention and intervention efforts may need to be tailored to different classes.

The chapter is organized in the following manner. First, LCA models are briefly reviewed, with an emphasis on measurement. Motivation for the analysis of cigarette smoking patterns is provided next, followed by a brief overview of the study methods and results. A discussion then ensues regarding model selection, class interpretation, and how researchers can confirm construct validity assessment by examining class membership covariate associations. The discussion further emphasizes measurement-focused and theoretically oriented use of LCA models. Additionally, model selection is highlighted and the potential weakness of solely relying on a single statistical decision criterion is discussed. The chapter concludes with a broad discussion of how LCA models can influence prevention science. This discussion revolves around the procedures and methodological insight garnered by giving serious thought to measurement techniques in drug prevention and how statistical models must be evaluated in a thoughtful and sophisticated manner.

Historically, measurement and psychometrics have focused largely on quantitative items and traits. Item response models (Embretson & Reise, 2000) brought categorical items into broader consideration, but generally speaking in psychology, the traits of interest primarily have been construed as continuous measures. Largely, categorical latent variable models, such as LCA (Goodman, 1974), latent profile analysis (Gibson, 1959), and normal distribution mixture models (Titterington, Smith, & Makov, 1985) have not been treated seriously as measurement models in prevention or health research. Furthermore, growth mixture (Muthén & Shedden, 1999) and factor mixture models (Lubke & Muthén, 2005) also typically have been employed as exploratory, data-partitioning analyses, rather than being rooted in substantive theory and measurement. In many LC applications, there is typically little or no discussion of measures or why certain items were selected for a particular study. The present chapter presents results from

Preparation for this chapter was supported by a grant from the National Institute on Drug Abuse (R37DA018673). The content of this chapter is solely the responsibility of the authors and does not necessarily represent the official views of the National Institute on Drug Abuse.

Correspondence concerning this chapter should be directed to Brian Flaherty at bxf4@u.washington.edu.

http://dx.doi.org/10.1037/14550-025
Handbook of Adolescent Drug Use Prevention: Research, Intervention Strategies, and Practice, L. M. Scheier (Editor)

exploratory analysis, but it focuses on measurement and latent construct meaning throughout. This chapter also initiates the development of an LC-based scale appropriate for identifying cigarette smoking patterns.

In addition to the need for developing the use of LC and mixture models explicitly as measurement models, there is a simultaneous need for scientific research and pedagogical writing that addresses the use of these models with real data. Empirical examples, including issues and challenges commonly encountered in the use of these models, inform the field as a whole. There has been an explosion of LC and other mixture model applications across social, behavioral, and health sciences, but the variety of models fit by current software has surpassed our knowledge of how well these models work across diverse research problems.

One key appeal of LC models is that they map onto many researchers' understanding that there are different types of people in the population and that these different types of people (i.e., classes) may require different interventions or treatments. This approach stands in direct contrast to the broad-brush primary prevention approaches that deliver a single program to all youth in some intact context (e.g., schools). These models allow one to identify subgroups or discrete classes of youth and test whether members of those classes respond differently to intervention. This refinement underscores the importance of thinking precisely about what we are measuring and how. Theoretically meaningful classes will not necessarily emerge from any collection of data analyzed, just as meaningful dimensions may not emerge from factor analyzing an arbitrary set of variables. If LC and mixture analyses are going to make substantial theoretical and subsequent health impacts, careful consideration of the items, measures, and data are required.

Cigarette smoking patterns and types of smokers have long been discussed in tobacco research, although there is no agreed-upon theory or specification of expected patterns or types in a well-defined parent population. Conceptually, types of smokers map well onto an LC framework. Accurate assessment of types of smokers requires the same measurement development that would go into developing a new continuous scale assessing self-efficacy, for example. The present chapter begins this process. Furthermore, the analytic problem that is the focus of this chapter represents a nearly optimal application in current research. The sample size used in the illustration is relatively large compared with many studies. All of the analyses are conducted in parallel in four demographic subgroups. Finally, the data come very close to possibly meeting the model assumptions. Therefore, model performance here is probably a best-case scenario for exploratory LCA in real and theoretically valuable data.

MEASUREMENT FOCUSED OVERVIEW OF LATENT CLASS MODELS

LC and mixture models are a class of multivariate statistical models that organize people or observations into homogeneous subgroups in a population (Collins & Lanza, 2010; McCutcheon, 1987). Subgroups are characterized and differentiated by response profiles to measured variables (i.e., item response distributions). For instance, data containing youth responses to questions about social skills or cigarette smoking may reveal underlying patterns that form the basis of discrete groups (low-, medium-, and high-skilled youth or youth with different levels of proficiency in different situations). Necessarily, this chapter includes only a brief overview of the LC model, with an emphasis on its use as a measurement models. In addition to the references provided herein, see Goodman (1974) for the first general statistical treatment of the LC model and Clogg (1995) for technical review of the model and related issues. Before turning to the LC model, however, it is important to briefly consider latent variable models and measurement error generally.

Latent Variable Models and Measurement Error

Many constructs of interest in psychology and other sciences are not directly observable or measurable, and therefore they must be inferred on the basis of fallible or incomplete data. One advantage of multiple indicator latent variable models over manifest variable analysis is the separation of random error from reliable variance (i.e., following the tenets of classical test theory). Another useful aspect to these models is the ability to consider richer and ideally purer latent constructs.

Why consider LCs or types? Psychology has a long history of measuring and modeling continuous latent traits, demonstrated by the wide use of factor analysis (Gorsuch, 1983) and item response models (Embretson & Reise, 2000). Latent trait models scale observations along a latent continuum. Measurement and psychometrics often have been a primary concern in the development, use, and evaluation of these models. In stark contrast, measurement considerations appear to rarely play a role in the development, use, and evaluation of LC and mixture models. Although fundamental similarities of factor analytic, item response, and LC models have been shown (Bartholomew, Knott, & Moustaki, 2011), substantive use of these models differs dramatically. In contrast to factor and item response theory models, LC models typically are used as data-partitioning procedures, not as latent variable measurement models. This need not always be the case. When substantive science focuses on subgroups, serious thought to measurement also should occur. Rather than laying out the notation and LC mathematical model, readers should refer to the cited sources. Consider instead Table 24.1, which contains fictional values that exemplify the LC model estimates and demonstrate some measurement considerations.

TABLE 24.1

Fictional Results of a Latent Class Analysis Highlighting Measurement Considerations

	Experimenters (20%)		Heavy smokers (80%)	
	p (No)	*p* (Yes)	*p* (No)	*p* (Yes)
Ever smoke 100 or more cigarettes?	.96	.04	.02	.98
Plan to smoke next year?	.55	.45	.20	.80
Like the color blue?	.52	.48	.51	.49

Note. Table contains conditional response probabilities. Latent class proportions are in parenthesis beneath class label.

The first row in Table 24.1 corresponds to the first item, "Have you ever smoked 100 or more cigarettes?" The four columns contain the response probabilities for the two hypothetical classes: experimenters and heavy smokers. The first two columns are the probabilities members of the experimenters class have of replying yes or no to each question. The last two columns are the parallel probabilities for the heavy smokers. Note that in this hypothetical example, the LC proportions are 20% and 80%, respectively.

The first item in Table 24.1 is an example of an item that effectively distinguishes both classes. Members of the experimenter class are 96% likely to indicate that they have never smoked 100 or more cigarettes. Four percent of this class is expected to reply to this question answering yes. One interpretation of this 4% is that this small percentage represents measurement error. That is, perhaps all people in this class have, in truth, smoked fewer than 100 cigarettes, but about 4% mistakenly indicated yes. Another interpretation is that there is some true within-class variability, and a small proportion of the individuals endorsing this item actually have smoked more than 100 cigarettes. In a case like this, the actual situation is probably a combination of the two: some random measurement error and some true within-class variability. The reasonableness of these two interpretations is likely to vary across substantive domains. The second item in Table 24.1 is an example of an item that is strongly associated with membership in one class (heavy smokers), but not the other. The third item does not measure members of either class well. Contrast this with good measurement in the standard factor model. If an item works well, it is assumed to work well for all members of the population. If it does not work well (i.e., is not strongly correlated with the factor), the item is discarded. In the LC situation, items can vary in their effectiveness at measuring members of each class (i.e., distinguishing one or more classes from others).

Table 24.1 also provides a basis to begin considering theoretically meaningful parameter restrictions that can further clarify and strengthen the underlying conceptual model. For example, consider another item and class supplementing those depicted already in the table. Suppose these hypothetical respondents also were asked about their intentions to quit. We might imagine the heavy smoker class splitting in two distinct groups: one class with high intentions to quit and another with little or no intention of quitting. In this case, it would be quite reasonable to specify a priori that members of these two heavy smoker classes (those with and those without intentions to quit) have equal response probabilities for the ever smoked 100 cigarettes item. That is, both classes might have equal error rates. The ever smoked 100 cigarettes item does not help distinguish those two heavy smoker classes from each other, but it does distinguish them from the experimental smoker class. Another example is the inclusion of a redundant indicator of smoking experience. Perhaps a priori constraints also would be possible within class, but across the redundant items. As a final point, the possible associations between quit intentions and class membership highlight that serious consideration of measurement in LC models forces one to think clearly about what constitutes an appropriate LC indicator, as opposed to what should be modeled as a predictor or outcome associated with class membership. Depending on the construct of interest, intentions to quit may or may not be an appropriate indicator.

Other important aspects about LC models include estimation, the number of model parameters, degrees of freedom, model fit, and model selection. (Again, detailed information on these and other issues should be sought elsewhere.) One important consideration that ties in with the underlying goals of this chapter is model selection. LC models are categorical data models; therefore, standard categorical data fit statistics, such as Pearson's χ^2 or the likelihood ratio statistic (e.g., see Upton, 1978) may be used. These models fit statistics test if statistical sampling variability is a plausible explanation for differences between our model estimates and observed data. Problems can arise, however, with the distribution of these statistics under the null model when data are sparse (Agresti & Yang, 1987). For this reason, other statistical assessment approaches, such as Akaike's information criterion (AIC; Akaike, 1987) or Bayes' information criterion (BIC; Schwarz, 1978), *p*-value adjustment (Lo, Mendell, & Rubin, 2001), bootstrapping (McLachlan, 1987), and posterior predictive check distributions (Rubin & Stern, 1994), have been proposed as methodologically rigorous ways to select best-fitting models. As with other latent variable models, multiple criteria commonly are examined together (Hu & Bentler, 1999; Tanaka, 1993). Additionally, the reasonableness and interpretability of the solution should contribute to model assessment and selection (Browne & Cudeck, 1993).

Besides beginning the development of an LC-based measurement scale for cigarette smoking patterns, another purpose of this chapter is to highlight decisions and issues likely to be encountered broadly in applied LCA. In exploratory work that addresses the beginning of typological theory development, model selection is likely to be a critical issue. The empirical example presented here is exploratory LCA but is based on previous substantive work.

Cigarette Smoking Patterns

Cigarette smoking continues to be the leading preventable cause of death in the United States. Every year, an estimated 443,000 people died in the United States from tobacco-related causes (Centers for Disease Control and Prevention, 2010). Globally, the World Health Organization has predicted that by 2025 three million people will die annually from tobacco-related causes in industrial countries and seven million will die annually in developing countries. The rate of increase of tobacco-related disease and death is much higher in developing countries (MacKay & Eriksen, 2002). Thus, even with tobacco control gains evidenced in the United States, tobacco use remains an immense health problem worldwide.

Historically, with the exception of studies of tobacco use etiology among youth, most tobacco research has focused on daily heavy smokers (Fagan & Rigotti, 2009). There is now interest in understanding variability in cigarette smoking patterns, for example, studies emphasizing light or intermittent smoking. Echoing Shiffman (1989), light or atypical smoking patterns (i.e., recreational or sporadic cigarette smoking at bars or social events) are interesting because people fitting this bill raise questions about our models of nicotine dependence. Furthermore, compared with daily heavy smokers, patterns of association between cigarette consumption and relevant predictors or outcomes may vary among atypical smokers. For example, public health programs and messages found to be effective with daily heavy smokers may not be as effective for other types of smokers. Research examining atypical smokers has tended to discuss different types of smokers, for example, light or intermittent smokers (Husten, McCarty, Giovino, Chrismon, & Zhu, 1998), chippers (Shiffman, 1989), low-consumption smokers (Zhu, Pulvers, Zhuang, & Báezconde-Garbanati, 2007), and low-rate smokers (Owen, Kent, Wakefield, & Roberts, 1995). This emphasis on different types or patterns of cigarette smoking motivates this chapter.

Because of the lack of theory or models, operational definitions of different types or groups of smokers vary across studies. Light smoking typically has been defined as smoking fewer than some cutoff amount of cigarettes per day on the days smoked, with cutoffs ranging from as low as four or five cigarettes per day (cpd) to 10 or higher (see Husten, 2009). Identifying prevalent cigarette smoking patterns and developing a standard measurement approach should benefit science by both clarifying our understanding of the phenomena and enhancing scientific progress (e.g., increase comparability and clearer communication).

Often the cutoffs or decision rules used to classify cigarette smokers are based on a single item (e.g., light smokers defined as those smoking ≤ 5 cpd). Disadvantages of using univariate cutoffs include ignoring both measurement error and multivariate associations that exist in the data. Inclusion of cases in an analysis based on a single item response assumes the item in question is perfectly reliable (i.e., measures the behavior in question without error). Using several such univariate cutoff rules for different items may compound the effects of misclassification errors. Additionally, forming groups on the basis of a single indicator (e.g., lumping individuals together based on past month cpd), assumes there are no informative higher order or interactive effects between that item and other items. Important (and informative) associations among variables may be ignored or appear altered when portions of a sample are included on the basis of a single cutoff score.

Furthermore, the approach described previously with univariate cut-points on a single item assumes variability in an individual's cigarette smoking is not important to the formation of groups. That is, if a cutoff of ≤ 5 cpd in the past month defines light smokers, then one assumes those who smoked 6 or 7 cpd in the past month do not belong in the same category with certainty. Perhaps some of these same people might just as well have smoked 5 cpd. The important issue may not be whether the person smoked 4 or 5 or 6 cpd in the past month, but rather, is it correct to group all these smokers together, perhaps labeling them as light smokers, "typically" consuming 5 cpd monthly? Given these limitations, it may be desirable to model subgroups of smokers in a manner that allows for measurement error, multivariate associations, and within-group variability. The LC model meets these criteria.

Given a set of cigarette smoking items, exploratory LCA will identify classes in the data. That is what the estimation procedure does. These results, however, must then be considered in light of substantive tobacco research. Do the derived classes make sense broadly? Might one expect other cigarette smoking patterns? Are items functioning as one would expect? Do existing items have good psychometrics? Are all the important characteristics assumed to distinguish cigarette smoking patterns included? Beyond these basic issues, how do these items perform in other populations? What is comparable and what is not (i.e., measurement invariance analysis)? In addition to serving as a realistic LCA case study, the work presented in this chapter begins this measurement development process.

Data Characteristics

This sample used for this illustration is from the 2004 National Survey of Drug Use and Health (NSDUH; U.S. Department of Health and Human Services, 2004), a national survey of U.S. households focused on substance use, abuse, and associated risk factors. The present work focuses on the subsamples of adult, non-Hispanic, White men and women. Therefore, unless otherwise specified, for the rest of the chapter, the terms *men* and *women* will be used to refer to the adult non-Hispanic, White men and women in this sample. Furthermore, the 2004 NSDUH oversampled younger respondents, yielding more respondents between 18 and

25 years old, than over 25 years old. Analyses were conducted within these two age groups to allow differences in smoking patterns to emerge as necessary. A more refined age group was not possible with the public use data. The sample was further limited to include only those respondents indicating some cigarette smoking in the past 30 days. With these restrictions, the sample consisted of 9,182 respondents: 2,639 men 18 to 25 years old; 1,947 men 26 years or older; 2,678 women 18 to 25 years old; and 1,918 women 26 years or older.

Four items measured current and past cigarette smoking. The first item was "Have you smoked at least 100 cigarettes in your entire life?" and the second item was "Has there ever been a period in your life when you smoked cigarettes every day for at least 30 days?" Both items were coded as 1 = *no* and 2 = *yes*. A third item asked, "During the past 30 days, on how many days did you smoke part or all of a cigarette?" Respondents provided a number between 1 and 30. For the current analysis, these responses were grouped as 1 = *1–9 days;* 2 = *10–19;* 3 = *20–29;* and 4 = *30 days;* daily smoking was reserved as its own category. A fourth item assessed the amount smoked: "On the days you smoked, how many cigarettes did you smoke per day, on average?" This item was coded as 1 = ≤ 1 cpd; 2 = 2–5; 3 = 6–15; and 4 = ≥ 16 cpd.

Demographic items and measures of nicotine dependence were used to predict class membership. Demographic variables included age, education, the subjects' poverty status, and government program participation. For the 18- to 25-year-olds, levels of the age variable were 18, 19, 20, 21, 22 or 23, and 24 or 25. Among those 26 or older, the levels of the age variable were 26–29, 30–34, 35–49, 50–64, and 65 or higher. Education was coded as 1 = *high school or less;* 2 = *some college or more.* The poverty item was coded as 1 = *less than 100% of the federal poverty threshold;* 2 = *between 100 and 199% of the federal poverty threshold;* and 3 = *higher than 200%.* The government program use variable was coded such that a value of 1 denoted some program use and a value of 2 denoted no program use.

Scores on the subscales of the Nicotine Dependence Syndrome Scale (NDSS; Shiffman, Waters, & Hickcox, 2004) and the time to first cigarette after waking are measures of nicotine dependence. The NDSS is a multidimensional measure of nicotine dependence following from Edwards' multidimensional model of alcohol dependence (Edwards & Gross, 1976). The scale is composed of five subscales: drive (craving or urge to smoke), priority (choose smoking over other activities), continuity (regularity of smoking over time), stereotypy (rigidity of behavior), and tolerance (more nicotine needed to feel pleasurable effects). The version of the NDSS in the NSDUH is somewhat different from the version discussed in Shiffman et al. (2004). The present analyses used scale scores as similar to the original scores as possible.

Analytic Approach

The unconditional LCAs were estimated with a Linux version of latent transition analysis (Collins, Flaherty, Hyatt, & Schafer, 1999) and covariate models with PROC LCA for SAS[1] (Lanza, Collins, Lemmon, & Schafer, 2007). All analyses were replicated within four demographic groups formed by crossing gender and age group: 18- to 25-year-old women, 26-year-old or older women, and the same age groups for men. Cases with partial missing data were retained in the analysis, although overall there were relatively few missing data. Sample weights were not included in the analysis because the sampling design of the 2004 NSDUH was largely based upon age, race or ethnicity, and gender. As these analyses are being conducted within those demographics subgroups, the effects of oversampling are largely statistically controlled. Furthermore, incorporating them by reweighting the response frequencies adversely affects the fit statistics (Vermunt & Magidson, 2007). Between two and six class models were fit in the younger groups and between two and five class models were fit to the data from those 26 years of age and older. The final number of classes was chosen based on model fit as reflected by the likelihood ratio statistic (G^2), the interpretability of the results, and AIC and BIC.

Upon choosing the number of classes, the measurement structure of the classes was examined and parameter restrictions (Formann, 1985, 1989) were

[1] PROC LCA is available from Penn State's Methodology Center at http://methodology.psu.edu/

imposed where reasonable. Reasonable constraints could be that two classes of smokers characterized by relatively heavy smoking have equal probabilities of replying yes to the question about ever smoking 100 or more cigarettes. If estimated response probabilities were near random, constraining those estimates to random levels (e.g., 50/50 for binary items) also was considered. These are both examples of reasonable equality restrictions. Constraints across both items and classes were not considered at this initial stage of measurement development, although such patterns of restrictions could be considered subsequently. Sets of equality restrictions were compared with the unrestricted model, and those deemed acceptable based on nested model comparisons were used in the final constrained model.

Membership in the final constrained classes was then predicted with multinomial logistic regression (Bandeen-Roche, Miglioretti, Zeger, & Rathouz, 1997; Dayton & Macready, 1988). In each analysis, the reference class was the heaviest smoking class. Predictors of class membership were examined for two reasons. First, to demonstrate construct validity, it is useful to show that expected class relations with theoretically important covariates hold. Univariate multinomial regression analysis was used for this purpose. The second reason emphasizes the need to begin examining theoretically interesting factors that may help understand differences in cigarette smoking pattern class memberships. Multivariate analyses highlight these independent covariate effects.

TABLE 24.2

Latent Class Model Fit Assessment for 18- to 25-Year-Old Age Group by Gender

	Women (n = 2,678)				
Number of classes	**G^2**	***df***	***p*-value**	**AIC**	**BIC**
2	660.44	46	≈ 0	694.44	788.94
3	144.37	37	≈ 0	196.37	349.58
4	62.64	28	.0002	132.64	338.89
5	28.45	19	.075	116.45	375.73
6	11.67	10	.307	117.67	429.99
Final 5 class	30.64	25	.903	106.64	330.57
	Men (n = 2,639)				
Number of classes	**G^2**	***df***	***p*-value**	**AIC**	**BIC**
2	749.08	46	≈ 0	783.08	877.58
3	145.63	37	≈ 0	197.63	350.46
4	54.11	28	.002	124.11	329.84
5	19.84	19	.404	107.84	366.48
6	7.31	10	.696	113.31	424.85
Final 5 class	20.81	25	≈ 1.0	96.81	320.18

Note. Underlined values indicate the preferred model for G^2, AIC, and BIC. The last line of the section for each gender includes the fit information for the final constrained model. *df* = degrees of freedom; *p*-value is the probability of the G^2 statistic under the null model; AIC = Akaike's Information Criterion; BIC = Bayesian Information Criterion.

Unconditional Model Selection and Measurement Constraints

Tables 24.2 and 24.3 summarize the model fit criteria for unrestricted LC models for the four age–gender groups. Among the younger men and women, five LCs were necessary to fit the data. Among the older groups, four classes fit both genders. G^2 and AIC nearly always indicated the same solution, whereas BIC always indicated one fewer class. Given this difference and the fact that these are exploratory analysis, the best-fitting and most reasonably descriptive models were chosen. For example, the five-class model for the younger women fit statistically (at a 0.05 α cutoff; $G^2 = 28.45$, $df = 19$, $p = .075$), included no hard-to-interpret classes, and included no extremely small classes. Agreement between G^2 and AIC was considered further support. In contrast, for the older female sample, the four-class model fit statistically ($G^2 = 26.34$, $df = 28$, $p = .554$), but AIC indicated preference for the five-class model. The *p*-value for the five-class model in this sample was .999, which was considered too good and likely overfitting the data. The five-class model also did not have a clear best solution (i.e., was not statistically identified; for an introductory discussion, see Collins & Lanza, 2010, section 4.4). Therefore, the four-class model was selected for the older female sample.

Examination of measurement restrictions followed the selection of the number of classes. (Tables of unrestricted estimates are available from the author.) There were several reasonable and theoretically appealing possible parameter restrictions,

TABLE 24.3

Latent Class Model Fit Assessment for 26 Years and Older Age Group by Gender

Number of classes	G^2	*df*	*p*-value	AIC	BIC
Women (n = 1,918)					
2	228.09	46	≈ 0	262.09	356.59
3	75.48	37	.0002	127.48	272.01
4	26.34	28	.554	96.34	290.91
5	3.584	19	.999	91.58	336.18
Final 4 class	26.86	31	.969	90.86	278.96
Men (n = 1,947)					
2	228.87	46	≈ 0	262.87	357.37
3	66.57	37	.002	118.57	263.49
4	19.56	28	.880	89.56	284.65
5	3.58	19	≈ 1.0	91.58	336.84
Final 4 class	19.56	31	≈ 1.0	83.56	271.64

Note. Underlined values indicate the preferred model for G^2, AIC, and BIC. The last line of the section for each gender includes the fit information for the final constrained model. *df* = degrees of freedom; *p*-value is the probability of the G^2 statistic under the null model; AIC = Akaike's Information Criterion; BIC = Bayesian Information Criterion.

although several of these turned out to be boundary estimates (i.e., probability estimates at 0.0 or 1.0 exactly). In the tobacco literature, both binary items (i.e., ever smoked 100 and ever smoked every day for a month) have been treated as indicators of past regular smoking. However, they did not perform in a parallel fashion in these analyses. Response probabilities for the ever smoked 100 item were most often on the boundary. That is, members of the identified classes seldom had nonzero error rates on the smoked 100 item. In contrast, the ever smoked daily for a month item was much more likely to have response probabilities connoting response variability. In a couple of cases, response probabilities for this item were random or nearly so. The last lines in each section of Tables 24.2 and 24.3 contain the fit information for the final restricted model. (Tables summarizing the equality restriction tests are also available from the author.)

Examination of Cigarette Smoking Classes

There was substantial variability in smoking patterns, although three common classes emerged across the four gender and age subgroups: heaviest daily smokers, new smokers, and very light or very intermittent smokers. Furthermore, each subgroup included light smokers, but recent and lifetime smoking differed for these classes across age and gender subgroups. Figures 24.1 through 24.4 show the LC response profiles for the age and gender subgroups. Equality constraints also are noted. (Model estimates are available from the author.)

The largest class of smokers across all subgroups was the heaviest daily smokers, corresponding to the first rows of Figures 24.1 through 24.4. These are the stereotypical smokers. Members of these four classes were all over 90% likely to report smoking every day in the past 30 days. With the exception of the 18- to 25-year-old women, members of these classes were also most likely to report smoking ≥16 cpd (ranging from 48% for the 18–25 men to 69% for the 26 and older men). Among 18- to 25-year-old women, 6–15 cpd was most likely (55%). Members of all four heaviest smoking classes definitely reported "Yes" to both cigarette smoking history items.

Very light and intermittent smokers consisted of 8% to 15% of each age and gender group (Row 3 in Figures 24.1 and 24.3; Row 2 in Figures 24.2 and 24.4). These smokers most likely reported smoking between 1 and 9 days in the past 30 days and ≤1 cpd on those days. Members of this class were certain (or nearly so) to report ever smoking 100 or more cigarettes. Women in these classes were more likely to have ever smoked every day for a month, whereas men were equally split or nearly so.

New smoker classes also emerged in all age and gender subgroups, accounting for from 2% to 14% of the samples (Row 4 in Figures 24.1, 24.3, and 24.4 and Row 3 in Figure 24.2). Among the 18- to 25-year-old subgroups, respondents in the new smoker class were overwhelmingly likely to indicate smoking 1–9 days of the past 30 days and smoking ≤1 cpd. Members of the new smoker classes were not likely to report either ever having smoked every day for a month or ever smoking 100 or more cigarettes.

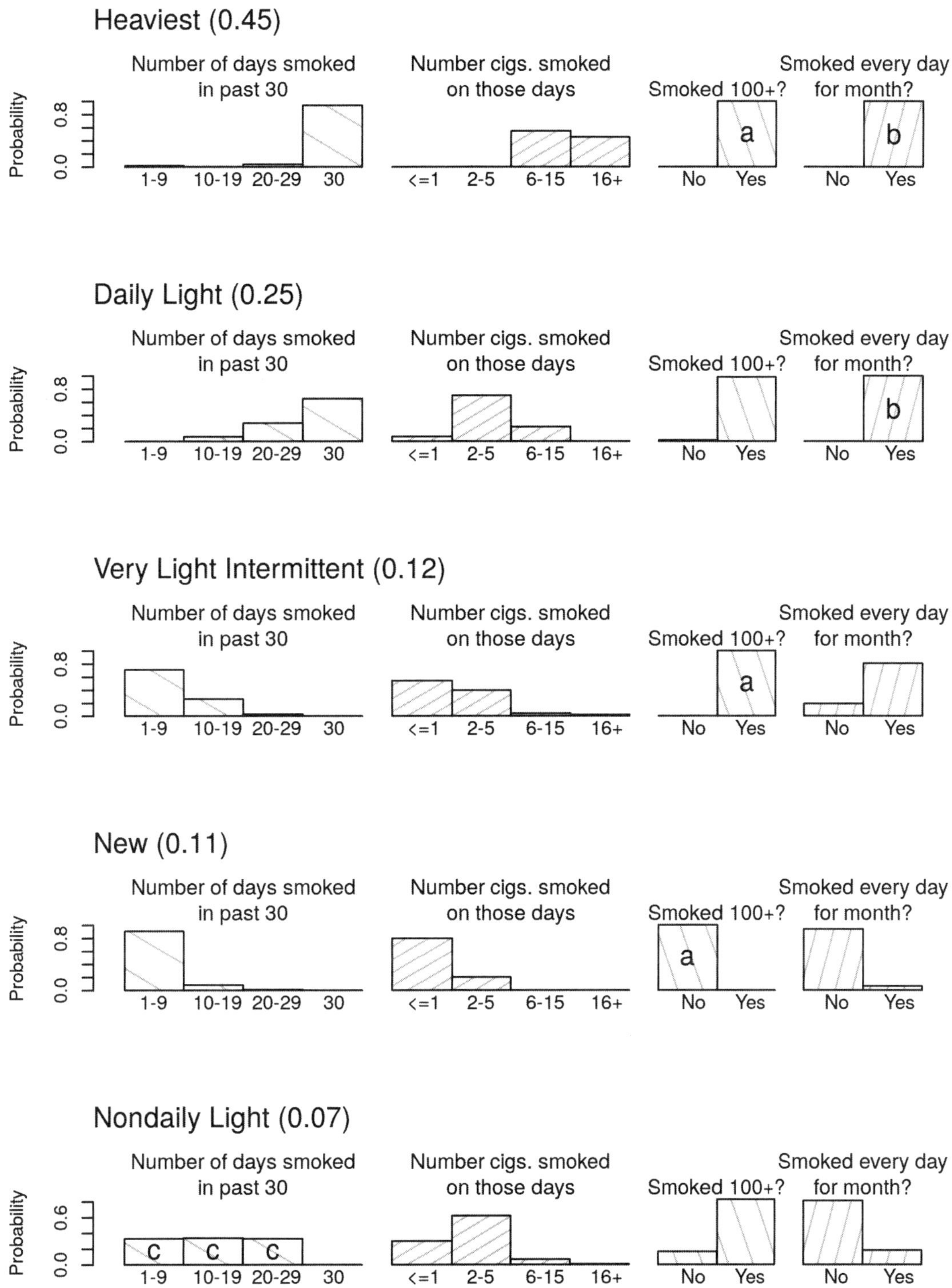

FIGURE 24.1. LC profiles for five cigarette smoking classes among 18- to 25-year-old White U.S. women. LC labels and proportions given in upper left of each plot. Lowercase letters are used to denote equality restrictions in response probabilities.

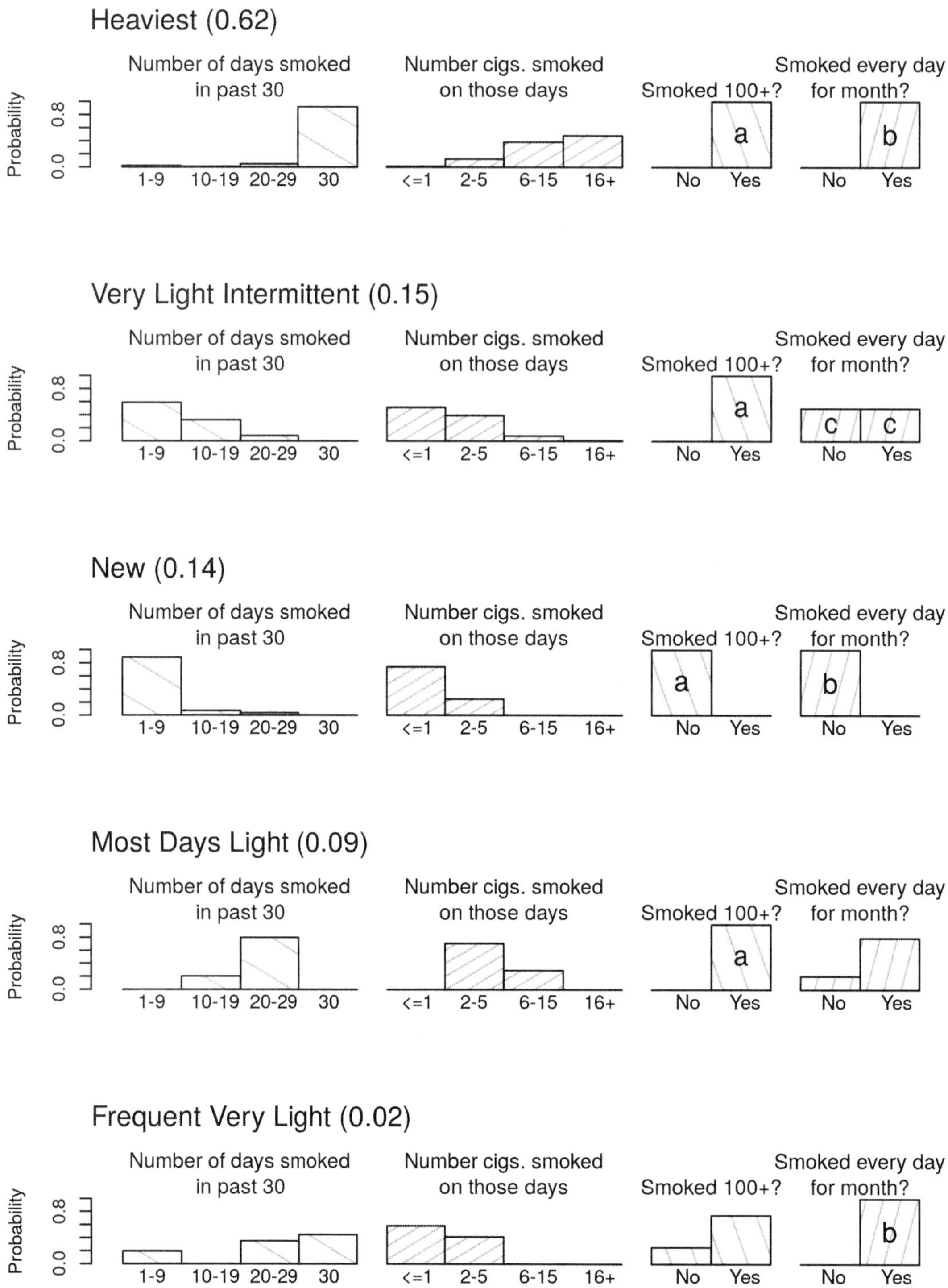

FIGURE 24.2. LC profiles for five cigarette smoking classes among 18- to 25-year-old White U.S. men. LC labels and proportions given in upper left of each plot. Lowercase letters are used to denote equality restrictions in response probabilities.

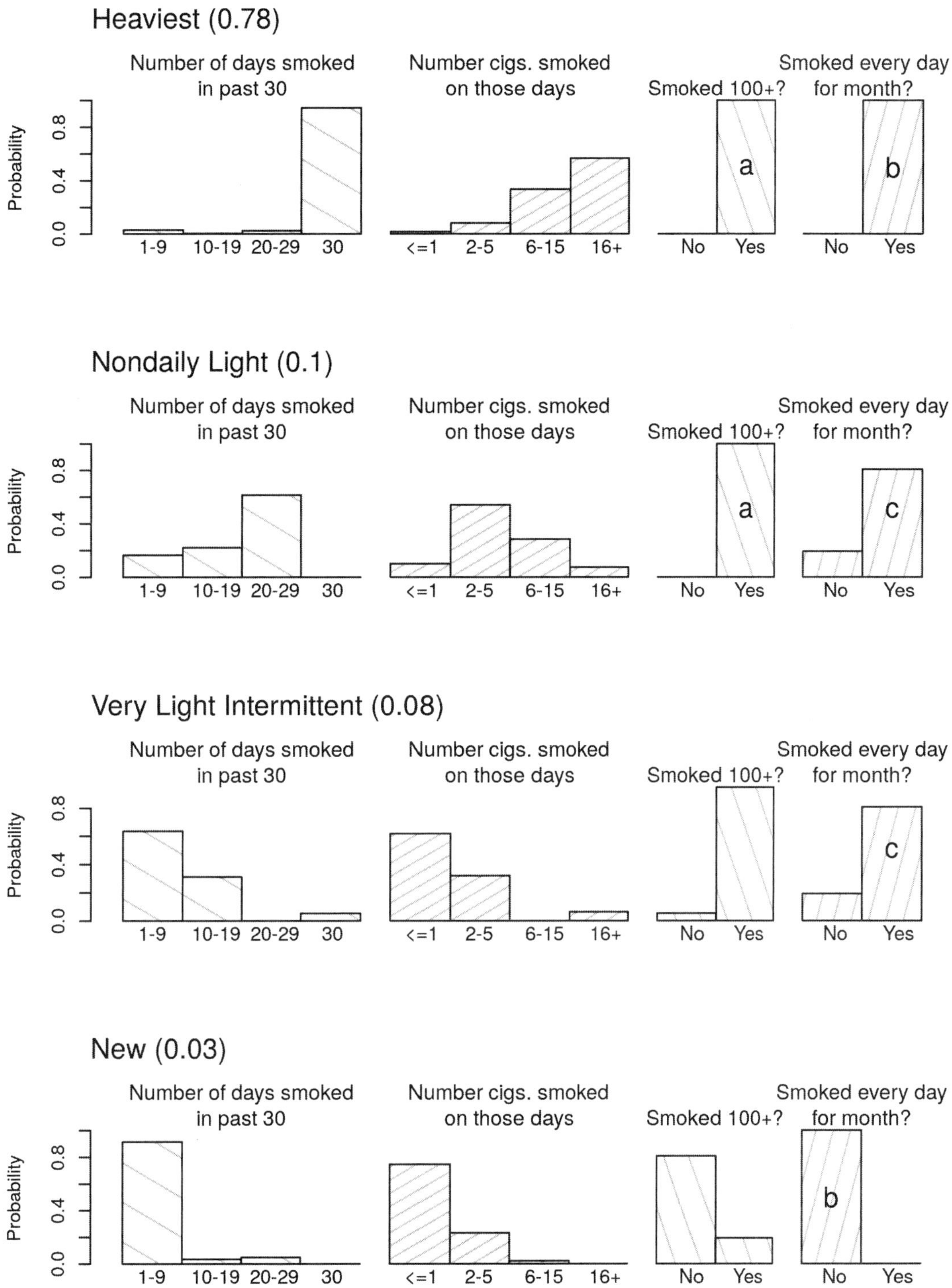

FIGURE 24.3. LC profiles for five cigarette smoking classes among 26 years and older White U.S. women. LC labels and proportions given in upper left of each plot. Lowercase letters are used to denote equality restrictions in response probabilities.

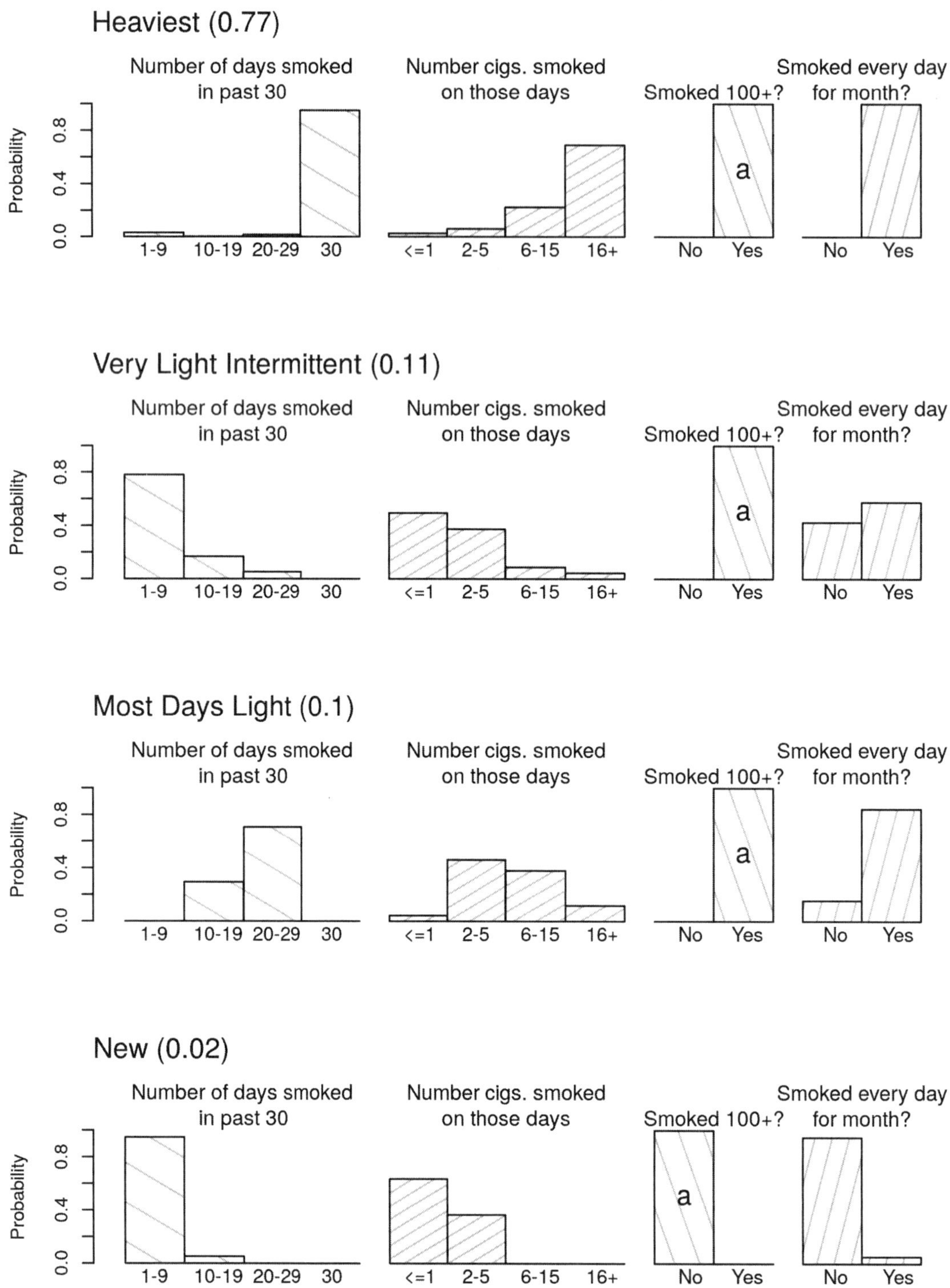

FIGURE 24.4. LC profiles for five cigarette smoking classes among 26 years and older White U.S. men. LC labels and proportions given in upper left of each plot. Lowercase letters are used to denote equality restrictions in response probabilities.

Remaining classes involved variations on light and intermittent smoking. The largest of these classes (25%) was a daily (or nearly so) light smoking class in the 18- to 25-year-old female subgroup (Row 2 in Figure 24.1). Of these respondents, 65% reported smoking all 30 of the past 30 days and most of the rest indicated smoking on 20–29 days. On those days, these individuals were 70% likely to report smoking 2–5 cpd, with only 23% reporting 6–10 cpd. Members of this class of responses to the two history items nearly paralleled the heaviest smokers, but the ever smoked 100 or more cigarettes item could not be constrained to be equal to the heaviest smoker class (denoted with a *b* in Figure 24.1). This is likely due to the other estimates lying on the boundary.

There was no similar daily light smoking class among the other three demographic groups. The smallest class (2%) among the 18- to 25-year-old men is perhaps closest (Row 5 in Figure 24.2; frequent very light). Members of this class were characterized by typically frequent and very light smoking. Possibly also some of these smokers had recently started, but they had smoked quite frequently in that past month. New smokers with this pattern would not fit in the new smoker class.

The smallest class among the 18- to 25-year-old women (6%; Row 5 in Figure 24.1; nondaily light) also had an unusual pattern of days smoked in the past 30 days. The probability of endorsing any of the categories, other than daily, was equal (0.333). That is, no members of this class reported smoking daily, but they could have smoked any number of days less than 30 in the past 30 days. Members of this class were also most likely to report 2–5 cpd on those days smoked. With respect to smoking history, most of the people in the class reported smoking 100 or more cigarettes but not ever having smoked every day for a month.

The remaining three classes reflect primarily nondaily light smokers, and their profiles are similar across both genders in the 26 years and older age group and for 18- to 25-year-old men (Row 4 in Figure 24.2, Row 2 in Figure 24.3, and Row 3 in Figure 24.4). In each case, these smokers indicated frequent, but not daily, smoking. Members of these classes did not smoke all 30 days of the past 30, but they were most likely to smoke 20–29 days in the past 30 days. On days smoked, 2–5 cpd was most common, although individuals in the 26 years and older male most-days-light smoker class were nearly as likely to report 6–10 cpd. As with the very light, intermittent smokers, these smokers were certain to indicate ever smoking 100 cigarettes, but they were less certain to have ever smoked every day for a month.

Associations With Class Membership: Univariate Summary

Univariate associations (not shown, but available from the author) generally bore out expectations that LCs with higher levels of cigarette smoking were associated with higher nicotine dependence scores, were older, and were indicators of lower socioeconomic status. Formal education was one of the strongest predictors. Across groups, with the exception of one of the smallest classes, individuals reporting some college were more likely to be members of any of the lighter cigarette consumption classes compared with the heaviest smoker class. These odds ratios (ORs) ranged from 1.8 to 5.0. The other demographic variables tended to have relatively smaller effect sizes.

Univariate effects among the nicotine dependence measures also generally turned out as expected. Higher NDSS subscale scores on drive, continuity, and tolerance were all associated with increased probability of membership in the heaviest smoker classes across gender and age groups. Time to first cigarette was also associated as expected: A greater lag between waking and smoking the first cigarette was associated with lower odds of being in the heaviest smoker class. NDSS priority subscale scores largely had small effect sizes and did not help distinguish among the classes. However, stereotypy was the reverse of the direction expected. Across each age and gender group, higher stereotypy scores were associated with higher odds of membership in the very light and intermittent or new smoker classes (ORs ranging from 1.6 to 5.5). With the exception of the priority and stereotypy NDSS subscales, the univariate covariate analysis lends support to the construct validity of the LCs.

Associations With Class Membership: Multivariate Analysis

Tables 24.4 and 24.5 contain the partial ORs from models with all the demographic predictors separately for each age and gender group. Age and education

TABLE 24.4

Effect Sizes for Demographics Predicting Class Membership Among 18- to 25-Year-Olds

White women	Daily light	Nondaily light	Very light intermittent	New	Δ in 2 × log-likelihood	*df*	*p*-value
Age	0.83	0.88	0.92	0.64	98.20	4	<.001
Education	2.09	3.58	3.57	6.77	191.94	4	<.001
Poverty	0.93	0.93	1.00	0.78	8.06	4	.09
Government program	1.42	3.01	0.69	2.51	34.71	4	<.001
White men	**Most days light**	**Frequent very light**	**Very light intermittent**	**New**	**Δ in 2 × log-likelihood**	***df***	***p*-value**
Age	0.80	0.89	0.83	0.59	179.01	4	<.001
Education	3.07	0.32	4.53	5.72	245.80	4	<.001
Poverty	0.82	1.35	0.92	0.74	19.04	4	<.001
Government program	1.84	0.76	1.30	2.01	13.37	4	.010

Note. Odds ratios are from multivariate models; heaviest smokers are the reference class. Δ = change; *df* = degrees of freedom.

have the same pattern of associations with class membership as observed with the univariate case. Poverty status and government program participation had no effects among those 26 years or older and small, mixed effects in the 18- to 25-year-old age group.

Tables 24.6 and 24.7 contain the ORs for the NDSS subscales and time to first cigarette. The ORs in these tables are from models including all nicotine dependence predictors. The columns of the tables have been reordered to facilitate comparison across the tables. The classes were sorted on the basis of the authors' assessment of the similarity to the heaviest smoker class, primarily based on typical within-class past 30-day cigarette consumption.

The most important feature of Tables 24.6 and 24.7 is the largely monotonic decreasing pattern of the ORs for the drive, continuity, and tolerance subscales of the NDSS. In each case, higher drive scores (higher drive to smoke) are associated with lower odds of membership in every other class compared

TABLE 24.5

Effect Sizes for Demographics Predicting Class Membership Among 26-Year-Olds and Older

White women	Nondaily light	Very light intermittent	New	Δ in 2 × log-likelihood	*df*	*p*-value
Age	0.65	0.93	0.51	39.42	3	<.001
Education	2.52	1.98	4.24	52.41	3	<.001
Poverty	1.35	1.04	1.57	5.72	3	.13
Government program	1.12	0.88	1.51	0.83	3	.84
White men	**Most days light**	**Very light intermittent**	**New**	**Δ in 2 × log-likelihood**	***df***	***p*-value**
Age	0.79	0.71	0.59	37.64	3	<.001
Education	1.64	2.50	3.00	46.15	3	<.001
Poverty	1.42	0.96	1.73	5.71	3	.13
Government program	0.98	1.90	0.68	5.30	3	.15

Note. Odds are ratios from multivariate models; heaviest smokers are the reference class. Δ = change; *df* = degrees of freedom.

TABLE 24.6

Effect Sizes for Nicotine Dependence Measures Predicting Class Membership Among 18- to 25-Year-Olds

White women	Daily light	Nondaily light	Very light intermittent	New	Δ in 2 × log-likelihood	*df*	*p*-value
Drive	0.51	0.19	0.12	0.03	267.11	4	<.001
Priority	0.65	1.45	1.07	2.07	28.50	4	<.001
Continuity	0.48	0.21	0.01	0.08	344.93	4	<.001
Stereotypy	0.89	0.72	1.55	2.02	47.91	4	<.001
Tolerance	0.75	0.52	0.26	0.22	45.82	4	<.001
Time to first cigarette	2.06	3.26	2.74	2.84	99.00	4	<.001
White men	**Most days light**	**Frequent very light**	**Very light intermittent**	**New**	**Δ in 2 × log-likelihood**	***df***	***p*-value**
Drive	0.52	0.73	0.26	0.13	176.37	4	<.001
Priority	1.14	1.11	1.31	1.29	1.73	4	.79
Continuity	0.33	0.49	0.15	0.20	375.00	4	<.001
Stereotypy	0.65	1.01	1.24	1.95	91.25	4	<.001
Tolerance	0.75	0.78	0.50	0.28	63.19	4	<.001
Time to first cigarette	2.16	1.67	3.15	3.09	136.24	4	<.001

Note. Odds are ratios from multivariate models; heaviest smokers are the reference class. Δ = change; *df* = degrees of freedom.

TABLE 24.7

Effect Sizes for Nicotine Dependence Measures Predicting Class Membership Among 26-Year-Olds and Older

White women	Nondaily light	Very light intermittent	New	Δ in 2 × log-likelihood	*df*	*p*-value
Drive	0.37	0.15	0.03	178.29	3	<.001
Priority	1.17	1.58	0.47	5.62	3	<.001
Continuity	0.31	0.17	0.16	209.53	3	.13
Stereotypy	0.66	1.34	1.80	32.98	3	<.001
Tolerance	0.62	0.41	0.50	18.96	3	<.001
Time to first cigarette			Estimation problems			
White men	**Most days light**	**Very light intermittent**	**New**	**Δ in 2 × log-likelihood**	***df***	***p*-value**
Drive	1.00	0.24	0.08	102.15	3	<.001
Priority	1.16	1.16	1.44	1.30	3	.73
Continuity	0.33	0.26	0.08	195.54	3	<.001
Stereotypy	0.60	1.19	1.39	25.94	3	<.001
Tolerance	0.67	0.52	0.55	16.64	3	<.001
Time to first cigarette	2.14	2.17	1.65	60.20	3	<.001

Note. Odds ratios are from multivariate models; heaviest smokers are the reference class. Δ = change; *df* = degrees of freedom.

with the heaviest smoker class. The pattern also holds for continuity and tolerance. Furthermore, looking across rows (e.g., the top row in Table 24.6, Drive), odds of membership in the comparison class as drive scores increase are smaller as we move from next heaviest smoker (left) to least heaviest smoker (right). For example, among women 18 to 25 years old, the odds of being a daily light smoker compared with the heaviest class are reduced by one half as drive scores increase. But the odds of being in the nondaily light smoking class compared with the heaviest are cut by 80% for a unit increase in drive score. Similar relative patterns hold across all the other groups. The only exception is the frequent and very light class in the 18- to 25-year-old male group. Their profile on all the nicotine dependence measures is most similar to the heaviest smoker class.

The NDSS priority scale did not reliably differentiate the classes in these multiple predictor models. This measure was a significant predictor among the 18- to 25-year-old women only and the pattern of differentiation observed was mixed. Higher priority scores were associated with higher odds of membership in the new and nondaily light classes compared with the heaviest smokers. But higher priority scores were associated with lower odds of membership in the daily light smoker class compared with the heaviest smokers.

Stereotypy has a more complex pattern of association with class membership. In each table, the OR differentiating the second heaviest class of smokers (first column of each table) from the heaviest smoker classes is less than 1.0, as we would expect. That is, for each of these comparisons, higher stereotypy scores are associated with lower odds of membership in the lighter smoker class. In comparisons of the very light and intermittent or new smoker classes with the heaviest smoker class, however, higher stereotypy scores are associated with higher odds of membership in the very light and intermittent or new smoker classes. This is reflected in the fact that those ORs are all more than 1.0.

Time to first cigarette was consistently associated with class memberships across groups.[2] Compared with the heaviest smoking classes, later time to first cigarette predicted higher membership odds in the other classes. The pattern of coefficients for time to first cigarette was not monotonic as it was for NDSS drive, continuity, and tolerance subscales.

CONCLUSION

Questions

This chapter presents the results of an exploratory LCA of cigarette smoking history and current use within four age–gender groups of White U.S. smokers. Other demographic groups will be examined separately to provide a similar targeted view of cigarette smoking patterns therein. One goal of this work is to begin development of a cigarette smoking pattern scale based on the LC model. A further goal of this work is to highlight issues in model selection and validation during measure development with LCA. The goal of these exploratory analyses is not to declare three or four behavioral phenotypes but rather to begin thoughtful consideration of class and mixture structure and measurement design starting with commonly used cigarette smoking items.

The data used for the analyses presented in this chapter contained substantial variability and multiple classes were required to account for differential patterns of association among and across the four subgroups. Model selection was based on statistical fit indices and interpretability. Measurement restrictions were applied to conditional response probabilities in a theoretically meaningful manner. These restrictions serve to highlight similarities and differences across classes as well as highlight items that are completely unassociated with a particular class membership (i.e., random response probabilities). Association structure of the data was more complex in the younger age groups, requiring more complex final models than the older age groups. Some similar classes were identified across the age and gender groups, such as heaviest, very light and intermittent, and new smokers. New smokers accounted for only 2% to 3% in the 26 years and older groups. Remaining classes reflected variations of light and intermittent smoking. Notably, the 18- to 25-year-old women had two classes primarily composed of daily smokers: one heavy and one relatively light.

[2] Estimation errors occurred among the 26-year-old and older women with time to first cigarette.

Importantly, the differentiations among smokers identified are not possible with one or a series of univariate cutoffs. Furthermore, the fact that there were many parallel classes across the groups (which provides a modest test of replication) suggests that these results are likely to be tapping real "behavioral" structure. Replication or refinement of the smaller classes in the younger age group represents an important goal of future work.

Following final model specification, construct validity was examined by looking at how other demographic and nicotine dependence measures distinguished the smoking patterns. Largely, results were consistent with current models of nicotine addiction (Rose, 2006) and documented associations between demographics and cigarette smoking (Lawrence, Fagan, Backinger, Gibson, & Hartman, 2007). As with the overall class structure, largely similar covariate patterns held across the four demographic groups, including the unexpected pattern of association between stereotypy and class membership.

Construct validity of the identified classes was largely supported, in that other demographics and key indicators of nicotine dependence distinguished members of the classes in an expected fashion. Largely, membership in classes characterized by more intense smoking was associated with higher drive to smoke, tolerance, and continuity of smoking. Interestingly, the stereotypy subscale of the NDSS did not reveal this same pattern. The newest and lightest smokers had the strongest association with high stereotypy scores. Overall, the pattern of association between stereotypy and class membership appears U-shaped with new and very light smokers endorsing the highest stereotypy and heaviest smokers next highest. This implies at least two possibilities: either subscale items did not perform as expected, or the underlying construct is more complex than presumed. The former seems most plausible, in that the question wording appears to allow very light and heavy smokers to each honestly make similar responses. For example, one of the items is "The number of cigarettes you smoke per day is often influenced by other things—how you're feeling, or what you're doing, for example." Presumably, addicted cigarette smokers should reply that this is not at all like them. They are addicted and need to smoke across contexts to stave off withdrawal discomfort. On the other hand, a very light smoker (e.g., someone who only smokes at parties) also could reply honestly that this item does not describe him or her. This person's smoking is not variable across contexts either. Responses of this sort could cause the U-shaped pattern found here between stereotypy and class membership.

Items selected for class indicators reflected cigarette smoking history and current consumption information. Nicotine dependence, while a relevant construct, served as a validity check for the identified classes. Similarly, distal demographic variables served as predictors of class membership. Not all previous LCA of cigarette smoking has maintained such important conceptual distinctions. Flaherty (2002) presented an LCA of a U.S. sample of adolescent smokers in the context of assessing psychometric reliability. Likewise, Chen et al. (2004), Furberg et al. (2005), and Rose et al. (2007) all presented descriptive analyses of cigarette smoking in combination with other items. Chen et al. included quit attempts. Furberg et al. included nicotine dependence and smoking cessation items. Rose et al. analyzed smoking, demographics, and attitudinal items together. LC and mixture analyses of item sets composed of different types of variables may be useful at elucidating interesting item response patterning and tendencies; however, it is difficult to distill information from these different studies on types of cigarette smokers because the solutions are driven by many extraneous item associations and not item associations solely assessing cigarette smoking. To develop a psychometrically sound measure of cigarette smoking patterns, key characteristics of class members must first be identified and then measurement must be evaluated.

Distinguishing latent variable indicators and covariates and outcomes also highlights important substantive questions of construct association and prediction. For example, what is the connection between cigarette smoking pattern and nicotine dependence? Are nicotine dependence measures indicators of smoking patterns, or is it best conceptualized as a covariate or even an outcome? Here these questions were treated as concurrent predictors, simply to determine whether classes were differentiated in the manner expected. Another important scientific question is how are multiple constructs structured and related? Should we identify cigarette smoking patterns and examine nicotine dependence as an outcome, or are there nicotine dependence subtypes with cigarette smoking as the outcome (e.g., Xian et al., 2007)? The present analyses followed from the literature discussing cigarette smoking patterns. The choice of how to measure cigarette smoking patterns is largely a scientific one, although usefully informed by statistical models. This issue is likely to be encountered in many substantive domains involving multiple complex constructs (i.e., alcohol use could follow the same pattern using abuse and dependence to establish criterion-related validity).

These analyses were conducted within gender and age groups of White smokers to allow group differences to emerge, paralleling measurement invariance assessment in factor analysis. Ultimately, estimating these differences has tremendous scientific value. One concern is whether the different classes within demographic groups suggest the need for different intervention or prevention strategies. Had gender and age been treated as covariates predicting class membership only, measurement invariance would have been assumed and the gender differences in the younger age group would not have surfaced.

Methodologically, this work raises several considerations. First, this work highlights the difficulty of relying on a single fit index (e.g., BIC). Even though BIC performs well in simulations (Lubke & Neale, 2006; Nylund, Asparouhov, & Muthén, 2007), this work conclusively demonstrates that it may ignore scientifically important and plausible data features. Model selection must rely on credible scientific evaluation and not merely a statistical question. The small new smoker classes in the 26 years and older groups are interpretable, substantively important, and qualitatively quite different from the other classes. It seems quite likely that approaches to intervene with adolescent new smokers may not work with new smokers over 25 years old. Furthermore, omitting this class would have included these smokers in the other two lighter smoking classes, essentially adding noise to any subsequent analysis. The smallest class among 18- to 25-year-old men, frequent and very light smokers, also is interesting because of their opposite pattern of covariate associations compared with other light consumption classes. So, although relatively small in sheer numbers, individuals assigned to these classes could represent an interesting group of smokers. But most important, these results are not being advanced as the final story in cigarette smoking patterns, but rather they represent the start of serious consideration regarding measurement of these patterns. If this small class of male smokers replicated in other data sets or their subgroup classification were predicted by a particular relevant theory, their scientific value would increase. If not, the hypothesized taxonomic structure rightfully will fall off the radar.

Second, this work focuses on differential item-class associations and theoretically motivated use of parameter restrictions to clarify differences and similarities across classes. As mentioned earlier, item function is more complex in LC models, than when measuring a hypothesized dimension across a population. That is, some items may be good for some classes but not others; or for some classes, items could be redundant indicators, but not for others. In factor or item response models (not mixture versions of these models), items work well or not, are redundant or not, for the entire population. Additionally, because many typological theories are not well specified, but rather, one suspects there may be meaningful subgroups, good measurement is likely to be an evolving process, as the class structure is clarified. As a further consideration, in the present illustration, parameter restrictions were used only within items and across classes. At this exploratory stage, it was felt that this was more reasonable than specifying some redundant indicators within class. From the estimates, however, it appears that there are a handful of places where redundant indicators seem plausible and will be investigated in future work.

The items used here represent common public health surveillance items, but they might not be the best or only items we should use to build a cigarette smoking pattern scale. Perhaps other items are necessary to accurately distinguish classes. The fundamental question of how we best differentiate theoretically meaningful classes of people is primarily a substantive question, with statistics playing a supporting role in helping to evaluate subsequent success. Conceivably, because the four items used here were not designed for a latent variable measurement model, they may need to be slightly altered or even replaced. Again, these are important questions for tobacco and measurement research to address.

More generally, at this early stage of development, beginning with exploratory analysis of existing measures is probably the best start. The next steps, however, are driven by ultimate goals. If LC models are being used as data-partitioning tools, then next steps will tend to focus on predictors and outcomes of class memberships. If, however, measure development is deemed important, then the next steps involve looking at item performance by class and examining what classes are measured well and which are not (Flaherty, 2002). Perhaps, previously omitted features or characteristics of some classes need to be included to better distinguish members of a class. Beyond iterative construct validity assessment, serious substantive attention to predictors and outcomes should not happen until an investigator is confident that the important existing classes are being distinguished reliably.

Third, and consistent with the underlying exploratory nature of this LCA study, the obtained classes represent a first pass at creating a meaningful partitioning of the data. However, the differential performance of the NDSS subscales may be regarded as bidirectional construct validity assessment. The NDSS's performance has been studied (Costello et al., 2007; Shiffman et al., 2004) but not in empirically derived subgroups. The fact that three of the subscales (drive, continuity, and tolerance) all worked as expected lends support to meaningful class structure. As mentioned earlier, however, the U-shaped pattern of association between class membership and the stereotypy subscale indicates potential measurement and construct-level questions.

Fourth, as mentioned earlier, these empirical analyses are likely to represent a best case scenario for applied LCA, especially in psychological studies in which sample sizes tend to be less than the approximately 1,500 to 2,000 per group in this study. A clear implication of this is reduced power to identify smaller classes. This finding, however, also argues for the value of serious consideration of measurement. Rather than treating parameter restrictions as an ad hoc device to get an algorithm to work in problematic data, a priori measurement models and measurement restrictions could go a long way toward leveraging the limited information in smaller samples for expected substantively important differences.

Limitations

This chapter presented an exploratory LCA to illustrate several important points about the methodology and use of LCA. Despite these intentions, several limitations are worth noting. First, the data are entirely cross-sectional, yet the substantive issues regarding cigarette smoking demand developmental analysis. One concern is that the age-related difference in the number of classes may reflect development, secular change, or both. A reduction of smoking variability between 18- to 25-year-olds and those 26 years and older is reasonable; however, given recent policy changes that address smoking cigarettes in public places, it is conceivable that secular shifts also could explain some of these observed differences. As is usual, longitudinal work on this issue will be invaluable to teasing apart secular and developmental trends from noise.

A further challenge when using many large-scale public use federal data sets is that national behavioral monitoring questionnaires often include skip patterns and data cleaning or logic checks that can cause problems for latent variable models. For example, in these data, no one who indicated smoking all 30 days in the past month also said no to the question about ever smoking every day for a month. Of course that is logical, but in raw survey data, one would expect some measurement error. The absence of variability leads very low or zero error rates for some items. Presumably, if these items were included in a community survey of adults, there would not be as many boundary estimates, and error rate estimates (or within-class variability) likely would be greater.

Also related to the use of large national data, the available response categories somewhat hampered the ability to examine more nuanced slices of the data. Only the two age groups presented were reasonable, given the available sample size, but pooling everyone 26 years old or older is less than ideal. Furthermore, the response categories for the number of cigarettes consumed on the days smoked item limited the examination of how different cutoffs might influence class identification (e.g., less than 10, instead of less than 5).

Although not a limitation in this author's view, readers may want to incorporate findings from alternative models, including, for example, item response or factor mixture models. An overriding reason for sticking with the standard LC model for a case study of this sort is that it is among the simplest mixture models. There are few assumptions, and the methodology has been around a long time. If there are still challenging applied issues for the LC model, there can only be more of these issues encountered in newer, less studied models, such as factor mixture models. This is not to say, for example, that factor mixture models should not be considered, but rather, that it is perhaps more prudent to begin with a simpler model and see how far it goes toward addressing important scientific concerns. Furthermore, with the emphasis on measurement, it is important to point out that as researchers we choose the items that we include in surveys to ask specific questions of interest. We also design the measurement scales. If we are serious about a typological view of smoking patterns, why not start with a simple statistical representation and design the items accordingly? As argued initially, use of LC models as measurement models has not been given much attention. A good approach might be to think through some psychometric issues in a simple case and then move up to more complex and assumption-laden models as necessary. The LC model and categorical measures of smoking patterns are both approaches, although that does not necessarily reduce their scientific value.

This work highlights important considerations in the use of LC models as measurement models, provides substantively valuable results, and begins serious consideration of measuring smoking patterns. Next steps involve iteratively refining the scale, assessing reliability and validity, and examining scale performance across groups of interest (e.g., racially classified and other social groups) and developmentally.

References

Agresti, A., & Yang, M. C. (1987). An empirical investigation of some effects of sparseness in contingency tables. *Computational Statistics and Data Analysis, 5,* 9–21. doi:10.1016/0167-9473(87)90003-X

Akaike, H. (1987). Factor analysis and AIC. *Psychometrika, 52,* 317–332. doi:10.1007/BF02294359

Bandeen-Roche, K., Miglioretti, D. L., Zeger, S. L., & Rathouz, P. J. (1997). Latent variable regression for multiple discrete outcomes. *Journal of the American Statistical Association, 92,* 1375–1386. doi:10.1080/01621459.1997.10473658

Bartholomew, D. J., Knott, M., & Moustaki, I. (2011). *Latent variable models and factor analysis: A unified approach.* Hoboken, NJ: Wiley. doi:10.1002/9781119970583

Browne, M. W., & Cudeck, R. (1993). Alternative ways of assessing model fit. In K. A. Bollen & J. S. Long (Eds.), *Testing structural equation models* (pp. 136–162). Newbury Park, CA: Sage.

Centers for Disease Control and Prevention. (2010). *Tobacco use: Targeting the nation's leading killer (No. 12).* Washington, DC: U.S. Department of Health and Human Services. Retrieved from http://www.cdc.gov/nccdphp/publications/aag/osh.htm

Chen, X. G., Li, X. M., Stanton, B., Mao, R., Sun, Z. F., Zhang, H. S., & Thomas, R. (2004). Patterns of cigarette smoking among students from 19 colleges and universities in Jiangsu province, China: A latent class analysis. *Drug and Alcohol Dependence, 76,* 153–163. doi:10.1016/j.drugalcdep.2004.04.013

Clogg, C. C. (1995). Latent class models. In G. Arminger, C. C. Clogg, & M. E. Sobel (Eds.), *Handbook of statistical modeling for the social and behavioral sciences* (pp. 311–359). New York, NY: Plenum Press. doi:10.1007/978-1-4899-1292-3_6

Collins, L. M., Flaherty, B. P., Hyatt, S. L., & Schafer, J. L. (1999). *WinLTA user's guide 2.0.* University Park: Pennsylvania State University.

Collins, L. M., & Lanza, S. (2010). *Latent class and latent transition analysis with applications in the social, behavioral, and health sciences.* Hoboken, NJ: Wiley.

Costello, D., Dierker, L., Sledjeski, E., Flaherty, B., Flay, B., Shiffman, S., & the Tobacco Etiology Research Network. (2007). Confirmatory factor analysis of the nicotine dependence syndrome scale in an American college sample of light smokers. *Nicotine & Tobacco Research, 9,* 811–819. doi:10.1080/14622200701484979

Dayton, C. M., & Macready, G. B. (1988). Concomitant-variable latent-class models. *Journal of the American Statistical Association, 83,* 173–178. doi:10.1080/01621459.1988.10478584

Edwards, G., & Gross, M. M. (1976). Alcohol dependence: Provisional description of a clinical syndrome. *British Medical Journal*, *1*, 1058–1061. doi:10.1136/bmj.1.6017.1058

Embretson, S. E., & Reise, S. P. (2000). *Item response theory for psychologists*. Mahwah, NJ: Erlbaum.

Fagan, P., & Rigotti, N. A. (2009). Light and intermittent smoking: The road less traveled. *Nicotine and Tobacco Research*, *11*, 107–110. doi:10.1093/ntr/ntn015

Flaherty, B. P. (2002). Assessing reliability of categorical substance use measures with latent class analysis. *Drug and Alcohol Dependence*, *68*, S7–S20. doi:10.1016/S0376-8716(02)00210-7

Formann, A. K. (1985). Constrained latent class models: Theory and applications. *British Journal of Mathematical and Statistical Psychology*, *38*, 87–111. doi:10.1111/j.2044-8317.1985.tb00818.x

Formann, A. K. (1989). Constrained latent class models: Some further applications. *British Journal of Mathematical and Statistical Psychology*, *42*, 37–54. doi:10.1111/j.2044-8317.1989.tb01113.x

Furberg, H., Sullivan, P. F., Bulik, C., Maes, H., Prescott, C. A., Kendler, K. S., & Lerman, C. (2005). The types of regular cigarette smokers: A latent class analysis. *Nicotine & Tobacco Research*, *7*, 351–360. doi:10.1080/14622200500124917

Gibson, W. A. (1959). Three multivariate models: Factor analysis, latent structure analysis and latent profile analysis. *Psychometrika*, *24*, 229–252. doi:10.1007/BF02289845

Goodman, L. A. (1974). Exploratory latent structure analysis using both identifiable and unidentifiable models. *Biometrika*, *61*, 215–231. doi:10.1093/biomet/61.2.215

Gorsuch, R. L. (1983). *Factor analysis*. Hillsdale, NJ: Erlbaum.

Hu, L., & Bentler, P. M. (1999). Cutoff criteria for fit indexes in covariance structure analysis: Conventional criteria versus new alternatives. *Structural Equation Modeling*, *6*(1), 1–55. doi:10.1080/10705519909540118

Husten, C. G. (2009). How should we define light or intermittent smoking? Does it matter? *Nicotine & Tobacco Research*, *11*, 111–121. doi:10.1093/ntr/ntp010

Husten, C. G., McCarty, M. C., Giovino, G. A., Chrismon, J. H., & Zhu, B. (1998). Intermittent smokers: A descriptive analysis of persons who have never smoked daily. *American Journal of Public Health*, *88*, 86–89. doi:10.2105/AJPH.88.1.86

Lanza, S. T., Collins, L. M., Lemmon, D. R., & Schafer, J. L. (2007). PROC LCA: A SAS procedure for latent class analysis. *Structural Equation Modeling*, *14*, 671–694. doi:10.1080/10705510701575602

Lawrence, D., Fagan, P., Backinger, C. L., Gibson, J. T., & Hartman, A. (2007). Cigarette smoking patterns among young adults aged 18–24 years in the United States. *Nicotine and Tobacco Research*, *9*, 687–697. doi:10.1080/14622200701365319

Lo, Y., Mendell, N. R., & Rubin, D. B. (2001). Testing the number of components in a normal mixture. *Biometrika*, *88*, 767–778. doi:10.1093/biomet/88.3.767

Lubke, G., & Muthén, B. O. (2005). Investigating population heterogeneity with factor mixture models. *Psychological Methods*, *10*, 21–39. doi:10.1037/1082-989X.10.1.21

Lubke, G., & Neale, M. C. (2006). Distinguishing between latent classes and continuous factors: Resolution by maximum likelihood? *Multivariate Behavioral Research*, *41*, 499–532. doi:10.1207/s15327906mbr4104_4

MacKay, J., & Eriksen, M. (2002). *The tobacco atlas*. Geneva, Switzerland: World Health Organization. Retrieved October 2, 2009, from http://www.who.int/tobacco/publications/surveillance/tobacco_atlas/en/

McCutcheon, A. L. (1987). *Latent class analysis*. Thousand Oaks, CA: Sage.

McLachlan, G. J. (1987). On bootstrapping the likelihood ratio test statistic for the number of components in a normal mixture. *Applied Statistics*, *36*, 318–324. doi:10.2307/2347790

Muthén, B., & Shedden, K. (1999). Finite mixture modeling with mixture outcomes using the EM algorithm. *Biometrics*, *55*, 463–469. doi:10.1111/j.0006-341X.1999.00463.x

Nylund, K. L., Asparouhov, T., & Muthén, B. O. (2007). Deciding on the number of classes in latent class analysis and growth mixture modeling: A Monte Carlo simulation study. *Structural Equation Modeling*, *14*, 535–569. doi:10.1080/10705510701575396

Owen, N., Kent, P., Wakefield, M., & Roberts, L. (1995). Low-rate smokers. *Preventive Medicine*, *24*, 80–84. doi:10.1006/pmed.1995.1011

Rose, J. E. (2006). Nicotine and nonnicotine factors in cigarette addiction. *Psychopharmacology*, *184*, 274–285. doi:10.1007/s00213-005-0250-x

Rose, J. S., Chassin, L., Presson, C., Sherman, S. J., Stein, M. D., & Col, N. (2007). A latent class typology of young women smokers. *Addiction*, *102*, 1310–1319. doi:10.1111/j.1360-0443.2007.01889.x

Rubin, D. B., & Stern, H. S. (1994). Testing in latent class models using a posterior predictive check distribution. In A. von Eye & C. C. Clogg (Eds.), *Latent variables analysis: Applications for developmental research* (pp. 420–438). Thousand Oaks, CA: Sage.

Schwarz, G. (1978). Estimating the dimension of a model. *Annals of Statistics*, *6*, 461–464. doi:10.1214/aos/1176344136

Shiffman, S. (1989). Tobacco "chippers"–Individual differences in tobacco dependence. *Psychopharmacology*, *97*, 539–547. doi:10.1007/BF00439561

Shiffman, S., Waters, A., & Hickcox, M. (2004). The nicotine dependence syndrome scale: A multidimensional measure of nicotine dependence. *Nicotine & Tobacco Research, 6*, 327–348. doi:10.1080/1462220042000202481

Tanaka, J. S. (1993). Multifaceted conceptions of fit in structural equation models. In K. A. Bollen & J. S. Long (Eds.), *Testing structural equation models* (pp. 10–39). Newbury Park, CA: Sage.

Titterington, D. M., Smith, A. F. M., & Makov, U. E. (1985). *Statistical analysis of finite mixture distributions.* New York, NY: Wiley.

Upton, G. J. G. (1978). *The analysis of cross-tabulated data.* New York, NY: Wiley.

U.S. Department of Health and Human Services, Substance Abuse & Mental Health Services Administration. (2004). *National survey on drug use and health, 2004* [computer file]. (Vol. ICPSR04373-v1). Ann Arbor, MI: Interuniversity Consortium for Political and Social Research

Vermunt, J. K., & Magidson, J. (2007). Latent class analysis with sampling weights—A maximum-likelihood approach. *Sociological Methods and Research, 36*, 87–111. doi:10.1177/0049124107301965

Xian, H., Scherrer, J. F., Eisen, S. A., Lyons, M. J., Tsuang, M., True, W. R., & Bucholz, K. K. (2007). Nicotine dependence subtypes: Association with smoking history, diagnostic criteria and psychiatric disorders in 5440 regular smokers from the Vietnam era twin registry. *Addictive Behaviors, 32*, 137–147. doi:10.1016/j.addbeh.2006.03.031

Zhu, S.-H., Pulvers, K., Zhuang, Y., & Báezconde-Garbanati, L. (2007). Most Latino smokers in California are low-frequency smokers. *Addiction, 102*, 104–111. doi:10.1111/j.1360-0443.2007.01961.x

Chapter 25

STATISTICAL MODELS OF MEDIATION FOR DRUG PROGRAM EVALUATION

Yasemin Kisbu-Sakarya, David P. MacKinnon, and Holly P. O'Rourke

Mediation analysis is the statistical method used to investigate how a prevention program changes mediating constructs that are hypothesized to influence designated outcomes. Mediation analysis contribute to program evaluation and improvement by identifying the causal intervening mechanism, determining effective and ineffective program components, checking manipulation, and refining the program accordingly. This chapter describes examples of mediation that form the backbone of drug prevention theory and quantitative mediation analysis in drug prevention research. The following areas are described: estimation of the mediated effect, assumptions and effect size measures, multiple mediator models, multilevel mediation, longitudinal mediation models, person-centered approaches, and categorical outcomes. Finally, recent promising quantitative methods and experimental design approaches to address causal inference in mediation models are described. Several of these approaches include estimation methods based on the potential outcomes approach, in which counterfactual data for each participant is estimated, to improve causal conclusions from mediation analysis. Also, sensitivity analyses that can test how robust the mediated effect is to violations of assumptions underlying causal inferences are presented. Future directions for mediation analysis are discussed.

Prevention programs are designed to target intervening variables (known as *mediators*) to prevent health problems. As many chapters in this volume reinforce, preventive interventions involve multiple "modalities" and as a result frequently target more than one social and cognitive process. The focus on multiple target risk mechanisms requires positing multiple mediators to maximize the intended effects of a program on consistent program outcomes. Mediation analysis is the statistical method used to investigate how a prevention program changes mediators (i.e., alters behaviors, skills, and cognitions) and the precise way mediators influence outcomes. A mediator differs from other third variables, such as confounders or moderators, in that the mediator is logically positioned as an "intervening" mechanism on the path from the program assignment measure to the designated outcome. In this respect, mediation analysis is also called *process analysis* because it is used to investigate the process through which an intervention exerts its effects (Judd & Kenny, 1981; MacKinnon, 2008). Moreover, mediation analysis is also known as *effect decomposition* in which the total effect of a program is separated into direct and indirect effects reflecting the different manner in which the program influences the outcome. This chapter describes examples of mediation that form the backbone of

Preparation for this chapter was supported by a grant from the National Institute on Drug Abuse (R01DA009757). The content of this chapter is solely the responsibility of the authors and does not necessarily represent the official views of the National Institute on Drug Abuse.

http://dx.doi.org/10.1037/14550-026
Handbook of Adolescent Drug Use Prevention: Research, Intervention Strategies, and Practice, L. M. Scheier (Editor)

drug prevention theory and describe quantitative mediation analysis in drug prevention research.

The literature articulates three broad categories of reasons for using mediators in prevention studies (Judd & Kenny, 1981; MacKinnon, 1994; MacKinnon et al., 1991; McCaul & Glasgow, 1985). These reasons touch on theoretical, program improvement, and practical aspects of evaluating prevention programs.

One of the most important reasons for including mediators in prevention studies is their ability to confirm or refute prevention theory. Prevention programs are developed on the basis of theory articulating how components affect targeted outcomes (Sussman, 2001). Two critical aspects in developing prevention programs are conceptual theory and action theory (Chen, 1990). Figure 25.1 graphically illustrates the sequence used to assess mediation in a drug prevention program. The path designated by *a* informs action theory, or in other words, the effect of a prevention program on the targeted mediator; and the path indicated by *b* informs conceptual theory, that is, the effect of the mediator on the outcome. The action theory is based on the intervention theory relating the prevention program (the education strategies) to the targeted mediator, whereas the conceptual theory is based on the developmental or etiology theory relating the mediating variable to the outcome variable (Chen, 1990; Lipsey, 1993; MacKinnon, Taborga, & Morgan-Lopez, 2002). Conceptual theory justifies the mediators targeted by the prevention program.

Mediating variables in drug prevention research can be identified on the basis of a wide variety of information. Usually, this includes knowledge of epidemiology and etiology supported by empirical data, social learning theory, developmental theory, and even biological theories. After an in-depth study of action and conceptual theories, researchers decide which mediators will be measured based on research aims and practical considerations. Action theory guides the selection of program components to affect the targeted mediators. The success of drug prevention programs usually is measured with outcome variables assessing a wide range of behaviors, including alcohol misuse or marijuana use as well as intentions to use or quit using a particular drug. One advantage of mediation studies is that if the program has no effect on the designated outcome, researchers can identify which part of the program (action theory or conceptual theory) may have failed. Action and conceptual theories illustrate that mediation is linked closely with a developmental and theoretical framework connecting risk and behavior. Martino (2011) stated that "mediation analyses are not meaningful without theory, and theory cannot be tested without mediation analyses" (p. S2). Furthermore, according to the law of maximum expected potential effect, the magnitude of the relation between the mediator and the outcome influences the potential effect size of a program (Hansen & McNeal, 1996). This statistical limitation arises because axiomatically speaking the focus of a drug prevention program is to influence

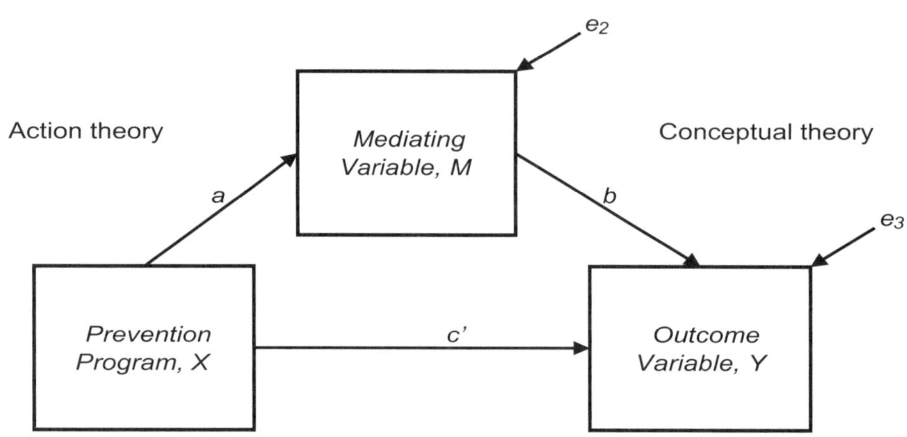

FIGURE 25.1. Single mediator model.

the mediator (i.e., reduce vulnerability by altering skills, beliefs, or attitudes), assuming that the relation between the mediator and the outcome has been established in prior research. Strictly speaking, the relation between the mediator and behavior is "unaffected" by the program. Because the relation between the mediator and the outcome already is expected based on theory and prior literature, the goal of the implemented program is to establish the link between the program and the mediator. Thus, the success of a program, from a mediation point of view, is primarily the degree to which the program changes the mediator, not the degree to which the mediator changes the behavior. The appeal of mediation analysis is evident in program improvement:

> This kind of research is important because it can identify the "*active ingredients*" in existing prevention programs, guide future refinements to existing prevention approaches, and provide important information that may lead to the development of new prevention approaches. Examining the way in which effective prevention programs work can also lead to further refinements of the theories upon which current prevention approaches are based. (Botvin, 2000, p. 893)

Consider a drug prevention program that targets decision-making skills. If the program does little to change decision-making skills, program developers will need to reconsider whether their intervention strategies effectively boost skills. There are many reasons for program failure, foremost among them the intervention model may not be developmentally sound, the implementation design may be flawed, and the measures of active ingredients may not be sensitive to change. Corrective action for each of these problems requires reconsideration of the program delivery methods as well as construction of the hypothesized mediation chain. Also, if a program does not cross-validate well with other populations, this may indicate that the program component needs to be further refined for lack of external validity.

A practical reason to conduct mediation analysis is that process evaluation provides a manipulation check for the prevention program. In other words, mediation provides a means for program developer to assess whether their intervention strategies change skills, beliefs, and attitudes, which then produces behavioral change. McCaul and Glasgow (1985) also called this *treatment construct validity*, suggesting that mediation provides the necessary information to evaluate whether the program worked in the manner hypothesized. For example, a prevention program aimed at reducing intentions to use drugs by increasing knowledge about the negative effects of drug use should have a significant effect on measures of drug consequence knowledge. Furthermore, mediation analysis can reduce program costs by identifying ineffective program components, which can be discarded in the interest of a more cost-effective and streamlined program.

EXAMPLES OF MEDIATION IN DRUG USE PREVENTION RESEARCH

Many different types of possible mediators can be applied in prevention research. Drug prevention programs typically target psychological measures as mediators (e.g., future intentions to use or expectancies that take shape as beliefs about the perceived effects drugs will have when used) or behavioral indicators as mediators (e.g., drug refusal or resistance behaviors). Certain psychological characteristics referred to as risk or protective factors (Hansen, 2002) often are targeted by prevention programs to modify outcomes. Table 25.1 provides examples of studies that have used mediation analysis as well as the target mediators, outcomes, and corresponding statistical methods used to evaluate program efficacy.

Social influence components constitute an important set of mediators for drug prevention programs (Cuijpers, 2002). Social influence programs examine mediators such as social norms, perceived peer approval of drug use, and perceived acceptability of drug use (Donaldson et al., 1996). Other programs found that social norms among friends were a significant mediator for drug prevention programs in school settings, whereas refusal skills were

TABLE 25.1

Examples of Mediation Studies in Drug Prevention Research

Reference	Mediators	Outcomes	Analysis
Ellickson, McCaffrey, & Klein, 2009	Alcohol misuse Drug misuse	Unprotected sex because of drug use Sex with multiple partners Inconsistent condom use	Sobel test
Buhler, Schroder, & Silbereisen, 2008	Knowledge about life skills	Alcohol use Nicotine use	Sobel test
DeGarmo, Eddy, Reid, & Fetrow, 2009	Youth aggression Youth social and problem-solving skills Family problem solving	Tobacco use Alcohol use Illicit drug use	Latent growth curve analysis
Henry, 2008	Association with friends who use drugs	Alcohol use Marijuana use Tobacco use	Structural equation modeling
Longshore, Ellickson, McCaffrey, & St. Clair, 2007	Resistance self-efficacy Intentions to use Positive and negative beliefs about drinking and smoking consequences Perceived-peer influence	Marijuana use Alcohol use/Consequences High-risk alcohol use	Causal steps and also Sobel test
Orlando, Ellickson, McCaffrey, & Longshore, 2005	Resistance self-efficacy Positive and negative beliefs about drinking and Smoking consequences Perceived peer influence	Cigarette and alcohol use Alcohol misuse Intentions to use	Longitudinal structural equation modeling
Spoth, Trudeau, Guyll, Shin, & Redmond, 2009	Substance initiation in adolescence	Alcohol, cigarette, and illicit drug use Polysubstance use	Latent growth curve analysis
Stephens et al., 2009	Intention to use (alcohol) Intention to use (cigarettes) Intention to use (marijuana)	Alcohol use Cigarette use Marijuana use	Structural equation modeling with categorical outcomes, also adjusting for cluster effects
Wang, Simons-Morton, Farhart, & Luk, 2009	Maternal knowledge Paternal knowledge Peer substance use	Alcohol use Cigarette use Marijuana use	Structural equation modeling
Epstein & Botvin, 2008	Drug skill refusal techniques	Adolescent drinking	Longitudinal structural equation modeling
Wenzel, Weichold, & Silbereisen, 2009	School bonding	Alcohol use	Multiple regression with residual change scores
Woodford, Krentzman, & Gattis, 2012	Experiencing/witnessing incivility Experiencing/witnessing hostility	Alcohol use/abuse Substance use/abuse	Logistic regression Sobel test Bootstrapping

not (Donaldson, Graham, & Hansen, 1994; Hansen & Graham, 1991; MacKinnon et al., 1991; Wynn, Schulenberg, Maggs, & Zucker, 2000). Likewise, Project Northland (Komro et al., 2001) found that peer influence to use alcohol significantly mediated program effects on behavior, whereas reducing access to alcohol did not mediate program effects.

Programs targeting similar outcomes (i.e., drug use) may focus on different mediators and use different statistical methods to assess mediation. Following conventions proposed by Hansen (1992), MacKinnon, Taborga, and Morgan-Lopez (2002) suggested grouping mediators into categories, including attitudes toward drug use, prevalence estimation, perceived benefits of drug use, availability, social norms, and refusal skills. Researchers may target different mediators to achieve similar program outcomes. For example, Bühler, Schröder, and Silbereisen (2008) examined whether knowledge of life skills mediated program effects on nicotine and alcohol use. DeGarmo, Eddy, Reid, and Fetrow (2009) investigated the effects of the Linking the Interest of Families and Teachers (LIFT) on tobacco, alcohol, and drug use outcomes for students from fifth to 12th grade. The program was designed to influence aggressive behavior on the playground and affect family problem-solving skills. Project ALERT modeled resistance self-efficacy and positive beliefs about use as significant mediators of program effects on drug use (Orlando et al., 2005). The Midwestern Prevention Project found that perceived peer reactions and intentions to use significantly mediated program effects on drug use in sixth- and seventh-grade students (MacKinnon et al., 1991).

The Single Mediator Model

To describe the quantitative methods used to estimate mediated effects, we use a school-based prevention program (i.e., indicated by the convention *X*) targeting the use of gateway drugs (e.g., alcohol, cigarettes, and marijuana, or outcome variables represented by *Y*) as an example throughout the remainder of the chapter. To continue with this example, discussion of mediation entails the role of social norms (indicated by the convention *M*). Social norms, for argument sake, entail the perception of how many peers or adults are using drugs (i.e., whether drug use is socially normative or acceptable). A potential covariate (i.e., using *W*) that possibly can affect the mediation paths is gender of the students (e.g., the program may have a stronger effect for girls than boys). Additional mediators and design elements will be added to the example in the following sections. In our example, individual students are assigned randomly to treatment and control groups, although mediation analysis also can be performed with nonrandomized *X* variables with corresponding analyses to address potential confounders of an observed effect in a nonrandomized intervention.

The following regression equations are used to assess mediation in a single mediator model:

$$Y = i_1 + cX + dW + e_1 \tag{25.1}$$

$$Y = i_2 + c'X + bM + eW + e_2 \tag{25.2}$$

$$M = i_3 + aX + fW + e_3 \tag{25.3}$$

where *Y* is the dependent (outcome) variable; *X* is the independent variable; *M* is the mediator; *W* is the covariate i_1, i_2, and i_3 are intercepts (i.e., the value of the dependent variable when the independent variables are set to zero); and e_1, e_2, and e_3 are residuals (i.e., unexplained variability). Using the example outlined earlier emphasizing social norms as the mediator and drug use as the outcome variable, the coefficient *c* in Equation 25.1 represents the total effect of the prevention program on drug use adjusted for the effect of participants' gender. The coefficient c' in Equation 25.2 is the effect of the prevention program adjusted for the effects of social norms and participants' gender (i.e., this notation indicates the *direct* effect). The coefficient *b* in this same equation is the effect of social norms on drug use adjusted for the program effect and the effect of participants' gender. The coefficient *a* in Equation 25.3 represents the relation between the prevention program and social norms adjusted for the effect of participants' gender.

Estimating the Mediated Effect

Mediation traditionally has been evaluated using three different approaches: the causal steps approach, the difference in coefficients approach, and the product of coefficients approach (MacKinnon, Lockwood, Hoffman, West, & Sheets, 2002). The causal steps approach also is known as the Baron and Kenny method (Baron & Kenny, 1986; Hyman, 1955; Judd & Kenny, 1981). This approach requires the following four steps are conducted in sequence: (a) The effect of *X* on *Y* in the first equation must be significant (i.e., the *c* path); (b) the effect of *X* on *M* in Equation 25.3 must be significant (i.e., the *a* path); (c) the effect of *M* on *Y* adjusted for *X* must be significant (i.e., the *b* path); and (d) the relation between *X* and *Y* should be weaker (or even approach zero) when the mediator is added to the model. In other words, c-c' should be greater than zero. Although the causal steps approach commonly has been used by researchers, it has important limitations. First, the magnitude and significance of the mediated effect is not estimated. Second, the method requires a significant total effect, whereas a prevention program's effect on the outcome variable may be mediated even when the total effect is not statistically significant. Third, the requirement of a significant total effect means that the method also requires larger sample sizes compared with other methods (Fritz & MacKinnon, 2007).

A second approach to estimating the mediated effect is the difference in coefficients method. This method quantifies the mediated effect as *c-c′* and allows for the computation of the standard error of the mediated effect, confidence intervals, and significance testing. An important limitation of this method, however, is that it does not allow computing individual mediated effects in a multiple mediator model.

A third approach, termed the product of coefficients method, computes the mediated effect as the product of the path coefficients *a* and *b*. The standard *z* method for testing significance of the mediated effect uses the point estimate of the effect, *ab*, divided by its standard error and compares it with the normal distribution. The standard error of the product of coefficients is based on the multivariate delta method (Sobel, 1982).

$$SE(ab) = \sqrt{a^2 SE(b)^2 + b^2 SE(a)^2}$$

$$CI(ab) = ab \pm SE(ab) * z_{Type\ I\ error}$$

This method constructs confidence intervals for the mediated effect assuming that the product term *ab* is distributed normally. The product of two normally distributed coefficients, however, may not follow a normal distribution (Aroian, 1947). This results in low statistical power for the test of the mediated effect, especially for small to moderate sample sizes (MacKinnon, Fritz, Williams, & Lockwood, 2007; MacKinnon, Lockwood, & Williams, 2004) Currently, the program PRODCLIN (MacKinnon et al., 2007), also available in the R software package RMediation (Tofighi & MacKinnon, 2011), computes the confidence limits for the mediated effect using the distribution of the product term.

An alternative method to adjust for the nonnormality of the product of coefficients is the resampling approach. Resampling methods, such as bootstrapping, obtain repeated samples from the data set (with replacement or without replacement depending on the method used). The mediated effects for each sample then are calculated to form an empirical distribution of the mediated effect to be used in confidence interval construction (Bollen & Stine, 1990; MacKinnon et al., 2004). A main advantage of the resampling approach to mediation is that it is not limited to two-path mediated effect (as PRODCLIN is) and so it can be used in multiple path models. Also, studies on resampling methods in mediation showed that the bias-corrected bootstrap had more statistical power than the percentile bootstrap or PRODCLIN methods, but the methods may have high Type I error rates in small sample sizes (Fritz & MacKinnon, 2007; Fritz, Taylor, & MacKinnon, 2012). Several bootstrapping software options are now available in Mplus (L. K. Muthén & Muthén, 1998–2010), Amos (Arbuckle & Wothke, 1999), EQS (Bentler, 1997), and in SAS and SPSS (Lockwood & MacKinnon, 1998; Preacher & Hayes, 2004).

Assumptions

To accurately estimate the mediated effect in single mediator models, several statistical assumptions need to be met. First, it is assumed that the variables in the model are reliable and valid measures of the study variables. The second assumption, the additivity assumption, holds that *X* and *M* do not interact (Collins, Graham, & Flaherty, 1998; Judd & Kenny, 1981). An interaction between *X* and *M* in the single mediator model means that the effect of *M* on *Y* differs across levels of *X*. In other words, the effect of social norms on drug use would differ for the treatment and control group before the intervention. This interaction can be tested and added to the model to control for any pretest differences between experimental conditions. It also is assumed that the variables are continuous and normally distributed; however, models with nonnormally distributed variables may be estimated accurately using transformations (Cohen, Cohen, West, & Aiken, 2003; MacKinnon, 2008).

There are several assumptions regarding the causal nature of the mediation model to identify the mediated effect. It is assumed that the causal paths between *X*, *M*, and *Y* are correctly specified without bidirectional effects. Additionally, there are no omitted variables affecting the causal paths in the model, an assumption that will be discussed in more detail in the section on causal inference (Holland, 1988; Pearl, 2001, 2012; Robins & Greenland, 1992).

Effect Size Measures

In addition to testing the significance of the mediated effect, researchers usually want to know the magnitude of the mediated effect to practically evaluate the achievements of a prevention program (see previous discussion about statistical limitations to this effect). Although the standardized regression coefficients are also measures of effect size, several ratio measures can be used to determine the effect size of the mediated effect. A common method is the *proportion mediated*, which is the ratio of the mediated effect to the total effect [$ab/(ab+c')$]. For example, a proportion-mediated measure of 0.20 would mean that 20% of the total effect of the drug prevention program may be due to the mediated effect through social norms. Another measure is the *ratio mediated*, which is the ratio of the mediated effect to the direct effect (ab/c'). According to prior research, large sample sizes are required to have stable measures of these effect size measures (Freedman, 2001; MacKinnon, Warsi, & Dwyer, 1995). The *standardized effect* is also a ratio measure, which yields the size of the mediated effect in terms of the standard deviation of the outcome variable for a one unit change in *X* such as program versus control (ab/s_y; MacKinnon, 2008). Additionally, researchers may use R^2 effect size measures to determine the observed variance in the outcome variable that is attributable to the mediated effect or direct effect. R^2 effect size measures are shown to perform well for smaller sample sizes (Fairchild, MacKinnon, Taborga, & Taylor, 2009).

Multiple Mediator Models

Up until this point, discussion of mediation has focused on a single mediator. This is a simplified view of drug prevention, which normally entails multiple mediators corresponding to multiple program modalities. To illustrate, in the example used throughout this chapter, a multimodal drug prevention program may target additional mediators, such as knowledge about the consequences of drug use and attitudes about drugs (in addition to social norms). Given this is the current Zeitgeist for most prevention programs, it is important for the researchers to investigate the potential multiple causal mechanisms of the prevention program. Multiple mediators can be added easily to Equations 25.2 and 25.3. For instance, the equations for a two mediator model can be as follows:

$$Y = i_1 + cX + dW + e_1 \tag{25.4}$$

$$Y = i_2 + c'X + b_1M_1 + b_2M_2 + eW + e_2 \tag{25.5}$$

$$M_1 = i_3 + a_1X + fW + e_3 \tag{25.6}$$

$$M_2 = i_4 + a_2X + gW + e_4 \tag{25.7}$$

where M_1 and M_2 are the two mediators (i.e., social norms and attitudes toward drugs), *X* is the independent variable (program assignment), *W* is the covariate (i.e., gender of the participant), and *Y* is the outcome variable (drug use). The specific mediated effects for the two mediators M_1 and M_2 are then equal to the product of coefficients a_1b_1 and a_2b_2, respectively. The standard errors for the mediated effects to compute the confidence intervals are given in MacKinnon (2008). Also, the equality of multiple mediated effects can be tested (formulas provided in MacKinnon, 2000). The sum of the two mediated effects is called the *total mediated effect* of *X* on *Y*.

When all the mediated and direct effects in a mediation model have the same sign, then it is termed a *consistent mediation model*. If one of the mediated effects has a different sign, however, it is an *inconsistent mediation model* (Blalock, 1969; Davis, 1985; MacKinnon, Krull, & Lockwood, 2000). For example, participants in the treatment group may report an increased interest in marijuana use, which leads to an increase in marijuana use, at the same time that the program reduces intentions to use marijuana, which reduces marijuana use. In such a case, researchers may not detect the program effect if they do not investigate pathways corresponding to multiple mediators.

Multiple mediator models also may specify mediators in a sequential "chain." For instance, a model specifying three mediation paths could hypothesize the following sequence: $X \rightarrow$ Mediator 1 $\rightarrow$ Mediator 2 $\rightarrow$ Outcome. Taylor, MacKinnon, and Tein (2008) found that joint significance tests or resampling methods produced more accurate results for testing three path models. For models with multiple *X*, *M*, and *Y* variables, structural equation modeling is needed to correctly estimate the individual paths and indirect effects (Bollen, 1987).

Multilevel Mediation

Multilevel mediation models take into account the clustering effects determined by sampling such characteristics as school, family, or hospital. Individuals in the same group (i.e., cluster) have correlated observations because they have shared characteristics. These shared characteristics often occur with intact social groups that share unique environmental contexts (neighborhoods or workplace units). Failure to acknowledge the magnitude of clustering violates the independence of observations assumption and leads to elevated Type I error rates (i.e., false positives). Multilevel analysis corrects for the standard errors of clustered data and achieves better Type I error rates and statistical power (Raudenbush & Sampson, 1999). Clustering also can occur when multiple observations are obtained from the same individual. Multilevel mediation analysis provides a framework to incorporate longitudinal measures in which the individual is the second level and repeated observations within each individual constitute the first level. Also, programs that incorporate treatment for dyads (e.g., husband and wife, parent and child) may require multilevel analysis. Methods for multilevel mediation models have been developed and studied in simulation studies (Dagne, Brown, & Howe, 2007; Krull & MacKinnon, 1999, 2001; Pituch, Stapleton, & Kang, 2006).

An important feature of multilevel mediation analysis is that this approach estimates program effects at more than one level. Clustering of individuals in contexts means that contextual-level factors may influence the results. Failure to take contextual effects into consideration may lead to asserting stronger effects for individual-level variables than are appropriate. For example, continuing with the drug prevention example outlined earlier, a school-based program may influence the school environment (creating more conservative social norms schoolwide) as well as the individuals (altering resistance skills; MacKinnon, Kisbu-Sakarya, & Gottschall, 2013). In addition, in modeling mediation, path coefficients can be modeled as fixed (i.e., constant across clusters) or random (i.e., varying across clusters). For instance, in the case of repeated observations within each individual, program effects can be tested for each individual (i.e., do individuals change across time) and also across the mean of individuals aggregated by school membership, the latter representing program effects for which school is the unit of observation.

Longitudinal Mediation Models

Temporal precedence is an essential assumption in mediation analysis (Gollob & Reichardt, 1991; Judd & Kenny, 1981). The general framework for mediation suggests that *X* should precede *M*, and *M* should precede *Y* to provide an appropriate amount of time for program effects to occur. Cross-sectional data typically do not contain sufficient information to address longitudinal relations (Cheong, MacKinnon, & Khoo, 2003; Cole & Maxwell, 2003; MacKinnon, 2008). Importantly, longitudinal designs allow researchers to detect potential delayed effects, increase the statistical power to find an effect through reduction in error variance, and investigate developmental phenomena across time (Fritz & MacKinnon, 2012; Venter & Maxwell, 1999). This framework requires the mediator and outcome to be measured on at least two measurement occasions separated by sufficient time to allow program effects to surface. Adding more measurement waves provides additional information that can reveal the underlying developmental process linking the prevention program with change in the target outcomes. The need for temporal sequencing, however, also introduces a challenge in determining the measurement timing of each variable, which needs to rely on theory and prior research. Furthermore, the tendency to measure follow-up at 1-year intervals may lead to missing effects among measurements, especially processes occurring soon after program delivery and bursts of activity that occur during the onset of drug use, for example. Additionally, researchers need to be careful not to omit potential variables or paths to avoid misspecification error. In the following sections, several common methods for two- and three-wave (or more) models are outlined.

Two-Wave Models

Many longitudinal studies have two waves of data, including a baseline pre- and single posttest or follow-up assessment. There are three commonly used approaches to the analysis of two-wave data: analysis of covariance (ANCOVA), difference score analysis, and residualized change score analysis (Bonate, 2000; Kisbu-Sakarya, MacKinnon, & Aiken, 2013). The ANCOVA approach treats the baseline measures of the variables as covariates in mediation equations to adjust for baseline differences. Following the drug prevention example used thus far, a program developer can assess social norms and self-reported drug use at baseline. These variables can be assessed again at follow-up staged a few months after delivery of the program. The difference score approach computes the difference between the change in social norms from baseline to posttest, and likewise it computes the same score for self-reported drug use as the change from baseline to posttest. These difference scores then are used to test mediation.

Residualized change scores first regress a posttest score on its corresponding pretest score. Then the residualized change scores are computed by subtracting the predicted posttest scores from the observed posttest scores. The residualized change scores then are modeled in the mediation equations. If a researcher wants to reduce the two waves of measurement into single scores in modeling mediation, then residualized change scores can be used as an alternative to difference score analysis because difference score analysis may encounter reliability problems with floor and ceiling effects (Cronbach & Furby, 1970). Theoretically, the residualized change score approach is similar to ANCOVA because both analyses adjust for baseline measurement. The statistical adjustments used in both methods, however, differ (Bonate, 2000).

Autoregressive Models

Autoregressive mediation models for the analysis of three or more wave models specify adjacent longitudinal relations consistent with longitudinal mediation. Figure 25.2 shows the basic autoregressive model consistent with two follow-up waves of data collection following program implementation. The autoregressive model shown in Figure 25.2 tests a lagged measurement configuration separating the program (X) from the mediator (M) and the outcome (Y) by temporally spacing the assessment waves ($X_{T1} \rightarrow M_{T2} \rightarrow Y_{T3}$). Furthermore, contemporary mediation relations (e.g., $X_{T1} \rightarrow M_{T2}$, $M_{T2} \rightarrow Y_{T2}$) can be added to the longitudinal autoregressive mediation model to estimate the cross-sectional mediated effect within each wave, except for the first wave, in which the relations among X, M, and Y usually are specified as correlated (or fixed at zero owing to randomization of X, which should lead to nonsignificant correlations between X_{T1} and M_{T1} and X_{T1} and Y_{T1}).

Autoregressive models allow researchers to test for specific mediated effects and to compare them with other specific mediated effects within the same model, especially for many repeated measurements. The significance of specific mediated effects then can be tested by using the point estimate of the mediated effect and its standard error. The sum of all specific mediated effects between the prevention program and drug use is equal to the total mediated effect that also can be tested for significance. The total mediated effect represents the effect of the prevention program measured at Time 1 on the drug use outcome measured at the last wave of measurement, as mediated by social norms (specified as an intervening mechanism). A possible limitation of autoregressive models is that the model is fixed for

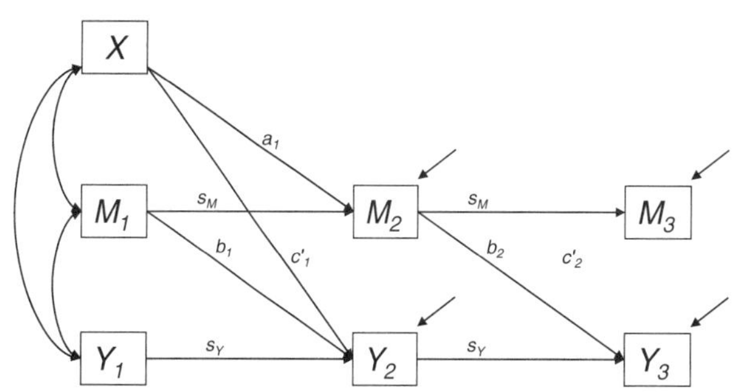

FIGURE 25.2. An autoregressive mediation model.

each individual in the study rather than allowing change to differ across individuals (Rogosa, 1988). As a different longitudinal approach, latent growth models (described in the next section as well as in Chapter 26, this handbook) may be preferred over autoregressive models if researchers are interested in the mediation of change across time, such as the relation between change in social norms and change in drug use.

Latent Growth Curve Models

Latent growth curve modeling (LGM) incorporates growth (change) in measures over time and individual differences in growth (B. O. Muthén & Curran, 1997). LGM computes continuous variable change (i.e., slopes) and intercepts as latent variables. Three growth trajectories are estimated for X, M, and Y to investigate whether the change in X is related to the change in M and if the change in M is related to the change in Y. Other model configurations also can be estimated, including positing a relation between an intervention and change in social norms and a change in drug use, or the effect of change in social norms on change in drug use at some later point in time. Cheong et al. (2003) used a piecewise parallel process model to estimate program effects on mediators at one point in time and then estimated effects of the mediator on growth of drug use at a later point in time. Piecewise modeling allows the investigator to dissect the curve into segments that may correspond to program effects at one point in time (junior high school) from effects that may surface at later points in time (high school).

Higher order cubic or quadratic trends can be estimated in addition to linear growth, positing that drug use reduces rapidly immediately after program delivery, but it then remains stable after a certain time period or starts to increase again. The LGM approach has been used in prevention program evaluation many times (Cheong, MacKinnon, & Khoo, 2001, 2003; Cheong, MacKinnon, & Pentz, 2002; Trim et al., 2007). When conducting LGM analysis, researchers should apply measurement invariance constraints over time because the change in measurement properties for developmental constructs may lead to confounded estimates. Furthermore, large sample sizes are needed to obtain adequate statistical power and a correctly hypothesized growth trajectory is required to obtain accurate estimates of program effects (Cheong, 2011).

Latent Change Score Models

In a latent change score (LCS) model, change scores are latent variables with error-free difference between the scores measured at two different time points (Ferrer & McArdle, 2010; MacKinnon, 2008; McArdle, 2001). LCS models allow researchers to estimate dynamic change in terms of the difference between assessment waves. The LCS model can be especially beneficial when testing a model in which the program affects the change in the outcome variable at earlier times but not at later times. For example, a smoking prevention program can have a favorable influence on cigarette use between Time 1 and Time 2, but it may have little effect on the same behavior between Time 3 and Time 4. LCS models also can estimate the rate of acceleration or deceleration between waves (i.e., second derivatives; Malone, Lansford, Castellino, Berlin, & Dodge, 2004). MacKinnon (2008) has provided additional information on estimation of LCS models with mediation.

Person-Centered Approaches

Up until this point in the discussion, the focus has been on variable-centered methods. Variable-centered methods estimate the influence of one set of variables on another set of variables using primarily correlation-based techniques. This methodology uses rank ordering and distributional overlap to discern statistical relations. Person-centered analyses, on the other hand, emphasize individuals' response patterns and statistical profiles based on their marginal distributions. That is, in person-centered analyses, whether individuals aggregate into discrete or homogeneous subgroups based on their response profiles is of greater interest than how one variable influences another. Tests of person-centered models can be used to examine whether a model is consistent or inconsistent with hypothesized mediation. The person-centered approaches include finite mixture models estimating trajectory classes (B. O. Muthén & Muthén, 2000), staged response across trials (Collins, Graham, & Flaherty, 1998), and configural frequency analysis (von Eye, Mun, & Mair, 2009).

All of these different approaches provide researchers a means to understand the mediational mechanisms at the individual level as well as at the group level. In the trajectory classes and staged response across trials methods, categorical latent variables usually are created to identify whether the individuals' responses are consistent with the mediation pattern. Configural frequency analysis, on the other hand, specifies the frequencies of responses to independent, mediating, and dependent variables that are consistent with the mediation pattern (von Eye et al., 2009).

Collins et al. (1998) also proposed a person-centered approach for categorical measures of *X*, *M*, and *Y* (where responses are coded as yes or no). The latent transition analysis (LTA) approach identifies mediation using an individual's probability of attaining the expected level of the mediator (e.g., negative attitudes toward cigarette use) and likewise estimates the probability of membership in a binary outcome variable (e.g., cigarette use or not). To illustrate the LTA approach, there should be a greater probability of transitioning from higher to lower status of risk (i.e., attitudes toward cigarette use) in the treatment group than the comparison control group. Also, individuals who transition into a lower level of risk also should have lower risk for the outcome variable (e.g., cigarette smoking). The transitional probabilities corresponding to the risk and consumption status groups are used to indicate program efficacy. Mediation is determined by estimating program effects on movement from a higher to lower risk status and movement from a higher to lower consumption status (or even from use to nonuse).

There are several assumptions to using the LTA approach. For one thing, classification methods like LTA assume there is a homogeneous group of individuals that belong within a discrete status group, for instance, a cluster of youth who report very strong antitobacco attitudes at baseline. This may not be realistic given that a very heterogeneous mixture of youth usually have both favorable and unfavorable attitudes toward tobacco use. This prevents there from being a clear demarcation of individuals based on their respective attitudes (or beliefs) toward tobacco use and its consequences. LTA, however, assigns youth based on a posteriori probabilities to membership in discrete status groups (those who responded favorably to anti-drug attitudes versus those who endorsed prodrug attitudes), an approach that may overlook making finer distinctions (Lockhart, MacKinnon, & Olrich, 2011). Additionally, the method is applicable only to categorical measures of *X*, *M*, and *Y*, which reduces statistical power to detect an effect. A test of significance for mediation using a person-centered approach has been proposed by Fairchild and MacKinnon (2009).

Categorical Outcomes

Categorical outcomes that capture discrete consumption patterns (e.g., tobacco use or no use) or drug use diagnostic categories (abuse/dependence) are fairly common in drug prevention research. In the case of categorical outcomes, Equations 25.1 and 25.2 can be estimated using logistic regression. Researchers, however, need to be careful when computing the mediated effect. The coefficient c' depends on both the mediated effect and the scaling of *Y* in Equation 25.2, and so the c-c' estimate of the mediated effect can be inaccurate (MacKinnon & Dwyer, 1993). The c-c' estimate is also no longer equivalent to the *ab* estimate, although researchers can convert the c-c' estimate into the *ab* estimate metric by simultaneously standardizing the regression coefficients to be used in estimating the mediated effect (MacKinnon & Dwyer, 1993; MacKinnon, Taylor, Yoon, & Lockwood, 2010; Winship & Mare, 1983). Pearl (2012) proposed a new formulation of the mediated effect that accommodates the nonlinear relations involved in categorical outcomes.

Causal Inference in Mediation

New methods have been proposed recently to improve causal inference in mediation analysis (Frangakis & Rubin, 2002; Holland, 1988; Jo, 2008; Pearl, 2009, 2010; Robins & Greenland, 1992; Rubin, 2004; Sobel, 2008). Several of these approaches include estimation methods to improve causal conclusions from mediation analysis, and they also offer sensitivity analyses that can test how robust the mediated effect is to violations of assumptions underlying causal inferences. Most of the approaches to causal inference in the mediation literature use the counterfactual approach, in which counterfactual data for each participant is estimated (Rubin, 1974). To understand the counterfactual method, consider a drug prevention program in which participants are assigned randomly to treatment and control conditions. Counterfactual scores for participants in the treatment condition would be the participants' potential responses if they had been assigned to the control condition, as is described in more detail in the later sections.

The main concern in causal inference for mediation is the effects of potential omitted variables (confounders) on the estimated paths. Omitted variables can introduce bias by reinforcing potential explanations for the relations estimated in the hypothesized mediation model (MacKinnon, 2008). For example, with randomization to experimental condition, the relation between program assignment (treatment vs. control) and the mediator (i.e., social norms) can be assumed to be causal because randomization balances the influence of omitted variables. In a single mediator model, randomization allows the path designating the "intervention effect" (*a*) to be interpreted as causal. Furthermore, randomization also allows the total effect (corresponding to the *c* path) of the drug prevention program on drug use outcomes to be causal. The effect, however, of social norms on drug use (the relation between the mediator and the outcome) cannot be interpreted as causal because social norms are not randomized; thus, omitted variables may contribute bias to the *b* path. Similarly, the direct effect of the program on drug use adjusted for the effect of social norms (the c' path) cannot be interpreted as causal.

The omitted variables (confounder) bias is described more formally by the *sequential ignorability* assumption (Imai, Keele, & Tingley, 2010; Lynch, Cary, Gallop, & Ten Have, 2008; Ten Have et al., 2007). The sequential ignorability assumption contains two parts. According to the *sequential ignorability I* assumption, there is no unmeasured confounder for the relation between *X* and *M*. Typically, this assumption is ensured by the randomization of participants to levels of *X* because randomization makes all other variables equivalent between the levels of *X*. According to the *sequential ignorability II* assumption, there is no unmeasured confounder for the relation between *M* and *Y*. In other words, there are no potential omitted variables that can lead to a potential explanation for the relation between the mediator and the outcome variable. Because the score on the mediator is not assigned randomly to participants but is self-selected by participants, this assumption is difficult to satisfy. Therefore, several methods have been proposed to address this important issue.

Sensitivity Analysis

Given the potential challenge to causal inference with studies that rely on mediation analysis, a researcher may want to assess how robust his or her results are to the effect of unmeasured third variables. The following discussion assumes randomization of *X*. Sensitivity analysis assesses how large a confounder effect (i.e., sequential ignorability II) corresponding to the M→Y relation must be to invalidate conclusions about mediation (Frank, 2000; Y. Li, Bienias, & Bennett, 2007; Rosenbaum, 2002). Current approaches that investigate sensitivity to confounder bias display the confounder values that would reduce the observed mediated effect to zero using plots (Imai, Keele, & Tingley, 2010; VanderWeele, 2010). The approach by Imai et al. (2010) presents confounder bias as correlated error terms between the error in the mediator model and the error in the outcome model (i.e., the error terms e_2 and e_3 in the single mediator model equations). If the sequential ignorability II assumption holds, then e_2 and e_3 must be uncorrelated. The plots by Imai et al. (2010) illustrate how much the mediated effect changes as a function of the magnitude of correlation between e_2 and e_3. Another sensitivity analysis approach by VanderWeele (2010) is based on the relation of the confounder to *Y* and the difference in the proportion of people with the confounder at the same value of mediator between groups. In addition to assessing the sensitivity of results to potential violations of the sequential ignorability assumption, several quantitative methods (described in the following sections) are proposed to improve causal interpretation of coefficients in mediation.

Inverse Probability Weighting

The potential outcomes framework (Holland, 1988; Rubin, 1974) makes a distinction between an individual's observed and counterfactual outcomes. Suppose an individual is assigned to the treatment group in a drug prevention program and as a result obtains an observed outcome value. Then the counterfactual outcome for that individual is the value she or he would have obtained on the outcome variable if she or he had been assigned to the control condition. According to Rubin (1974), the causal effect of the program on the outcome is then equal to the difference between the observed outcome for that individual and her counterfactual outcome. Because it is often not possible for the same person to appear in both groups (referred to as the "fundamental problem of causal inference" by Holland, 1988), the average causal effect then is computed as the mean difference between the observed outcomes of individuals under the treatment and control groups.

The potential outcomes framework allows for new definitions of direct and mediated effects using marginal structural models. Marginal structural models are different from linear regression models because they focus on potential outcomes, whereas linear regression models examine observed outcomes. Marginal structural models usually are estimated with inverse probability weighting (IPW), which creates a pseudo-population as a randomized cohort (Robins, Hernan, & Brumback, 2000). The IPW method creates weights that correspond to the inverse probability of receiving the treatment that the participant actually received, conditional on the measured confounder variables. IPW assumes that all confounders are measured and so allows for the estimation of causal effects. In a mediation context, the mediation equations are weighted using the derived weights. This procedure adjusts for possible confounders of the mediator-outcome relation. To illustrate, several potential confounder variables including gender and attitudes about drugs can be used to estimate a propensity score by regressing the mediator on a set of confounders. Then, the mediation Equation 25.2 can be weighted by using the IPW method based on those propensity scores. The IPW method has been used thus far in drug prevention research in a nonmediation context (Bray et al., 2006; L. Li, Evans, & Hser, 2010). Further details and data analysis syntax on conducting the IPW method in the presence of mediators and moderators can be found in Coffman and Zhong (2012).

Instrumental Variable Method

The instrumental variable (IV) method mimics randomization by introducing an instrument to the estimation process (Angrist, Imbens, & Rubin, 1996; Angrist & Krueger, 2001; Shadish, Cook, & Campbell, 2002). In the mediation context, for example, the random treatment assignment X can be used as an instrument to improve the causal interpretation of social norms on drug use. The instrumental variables approach uses the two-stage least squares method in which two equations are jointly modeled. In the first stage of estimation, the mediator M is predicted from the instrumental variable. In the second stage, the outcome variable Y is regressed on the predicted M scores. Then, the statistical significance of the coefficient relating predicted values of M to Y is the causal test of the b path for the mediated effect.

The IV approach has several required assumptions, four of which are described briefly here. First, the treatment assignment (i.e., instrumental variable) is random, implying that the treatment assignment is uncorrelated with unobserved pretreatment characteristics of the participants. A second assumption is that the random assignment affects the outcome only through the mediator (i.e., the exclusion restriction assumption). Third, the treatment assignment has a significant effect on the mediator (i.e., a significant a path). The instrument needs to be related strongly to the mediator to allow the predicted M to reflect randomization. Fourth, no participants act in the opposite direction of their treatment assignment. In the instrumental variables literature, this assumption is called *monotonicity*, suggesting that participants assigned to the intervention condition receive the treatment, and participants who are assigned to the control (untreated) condition do not receive any treatment (i.e., there is no "contamination" in the assignment procedure). These assumptions usually limit the applicability of the IV approach. Yet, more applications of IV mediation methods are needed to uncover the potential benefits of this approach.

Principal Stratification

The principal stratification method is based on the classification of different response patterns for the relations among X, M, and Y. Subgroups of study participants are identified based on how the relation between M and Y could change in response to the treatment, as will be described (Jo, 2008). For instance, in a drug prevention program with control and treatment groups, four subsets of people can be specified: (a) never-improvers, people whose mediator would not improve if they were in either treatment condition; (b) forward-improvers, people who would benefit from the intervention only if they received the treatment; (c) backward-improvers, people who would improve only if they were in the control group; and (d) always-improvers, people whose mediator would improve if they were in either treatment group. Covariates usually are used to determine stratification so that the classification is independent of individual treatment assignment (Jo, Stuart, MacKinnon, & Vinokur, 2011; Stuart, Perry, Le, & Ialongo, 2008). The mediated effect then is estimated within and between these stratifications (Angrist, Imbens, & Rubin, 1996; Frangakis & Rubin, 2002; Jo, 2008).

Experimental Design Approaches

Mediation analysis provides important information on a prevention program by exploring the underlying "psychological" processes affecting the outcome. The typical experimental design to test mediation involves an experimental manipulation hypothesized to change an outcome through the mediator, a process that is measured in each treatment group. Because the assignment to treatment conditions is usually random, the effect of the treatment X on the mediator M can be interpreted as causal. Because the mediator is not manipulated directly, the effect of the mediator M on the outcome Y does not represent a causal relation, nor does the mediated effect (as described in the earlier section discussing causal inference). This violation of the sequential ignorability assumption can be addressed by several research designs (MacKinnon, 2008) in addition to the quantitative methods described in the previous section.

The enhancement design is one experimental design that can strengthen causal inference with mediation. In this design, exposure to the mediator is manipulated by enhancing the dose of the mediator (e.g., Klesges, Vasey, & Glasgow, 1986). If M is a true mediator, then the $X \rightarrow Y$ relation will occur in greater magnitude in the enhanced mediator condition. Consider again the example of a prevention program that targets reducing intentions to use drugs by changing social norms. The program essentially teaches youth that drug use is not socially acceptable or normative (prevalence themes) and demonstrate to youth the anticipated effects of drugs are not beneficial. Participants in the treatment condition can be assigned randomly to enhanced social norm versus standard social norm conditions. The enhanced social norm condition then can manipulate normative education with the intention of deterring youth from using drugs based on altering perceived social acceptability of drug use. If social norms significantly mediate program effects, then the treatment group with the enhanced social norm condition should show a greater reduction in intentions to use drugs than the low social norm or control group. This type of stratification approach, which experimentally manipulates the mediator, is much needed to discern the relative importance of program dose.

A second approach involves strategies to "block" or stratify the mediator as a means of examining whether the mediated relation is observed in the usual treatment condition but not in the blocked condition (Robins & Greenland, 1992). Here, the mediator is blocked in one condition to provide evidence that the relation from $X \rightarrow Y$ depends on the mediator. For instance, using the social norm example provided previously, participants in the treatment condition would be assigned to a condition using the usual social activities (e.g., role-playing, small group consensus building) that change social norms, whereas a blocking condition would not have any of the social activities designed to change group norms. The idea is that blocking the activities that change social norms would not allow the social norm mediator to change, thereby blocking the program effect. If the $X \rightarrow Y$ relation no longer exists in the blocked mediator condition, then there is evidence that social norms mediate program effects.

Blocking and enhancement designs have several advantages and disadvantages. For one thing, these designs provide experimental evidence for causality, temporal precedence, and specificity (i.e., *Y* only occurs under certain conditions of *X* and *M*) of the mediated relation (MacKinnon & Pirlott, 2010; Spencer, Zanna, & Fong, 2005). Furthermore, the enhancement design reinforces the convergent validity of the mediating relation by testing its consistency across different representations of the same construct. On the other hand, these designs can strategically be difficult to employ. Although the use of experimental design to test for mediation is not new, only recently has this approach received more attention in the literature (Imai, Tingley, & Yamamoto, 2013; MacKinnon, 2008; Spencer et al., 2005). New developments in modern causal methods can be combined with experimental designs to achieve more evidence for mediated effects.

CONCLUSION

Mediation analysis is used widely across a range of areas, but it is of particular interest in drug prevention research where it can be used for design planning, analysis, and theory development. Taken as a whole, mediation analyses provide a means for investigators to test (and even contrast) multiple theories regarding how and for whom a drug prevention program works. Testing for mediation can extend to complex models with multiple mediators or can be applied (and help resolve) inconsistent models that contain opposing effect signs. More complex models also include nested mediation models and longitudinal mediation models, which can be tested using multilevel modeling, LGM, and LCS modeling. In addition to assessing mediation by looking at relations among variables, person-oriented approaches to mediation, which evaluate the patterns underlying individual response styles, can be used as well. Person-centered approaches to mediation are a new way to elucidate mediating mechanisms and provide a good contrast to the traditional variable-centered approaches that have formed the bulk of studies assessing mediation. A combination of person-centered and variable-centered approaches potentially could be beneficial as well.

Causal inference in mediation is an area of research that is now being studied in greater depth and continues to be an important area for advancements. Research in causal inference in mediation analysis has led to recent advancements in analyses designed to address causal assumptions of mediation models. Methods for handling causal inference assumptions in mediation, as well as tests of robustness to violations of those assumptions, are an important subject for future exploration. Enhancing mediation models through experimental designs is another new way to address causal inference issues in mediation and requires further examination as well. Developments in these areas will continue to broaden our knowledge of the mediation process and will increase our understanding of how prevention programs work.

References

Angrist, J. D., Imbens, G. W., & Rubin, D. B. (1996). Identification of causal effects using instrumental variables (with discussion). *Journal of the American Statistical Association, 91*, 444–455. doi:10.1080/01621459.1996.10476902

Angrist, J. D., & Krueger, A. B. (2001). Instrumental variables and the search for identification: From supply and demand to natural experiments. *Journal of Economic Perspectives, 15*, 69–85. doi:10.1257/jep.15.4.69

Arbuckle, J. L., & Wothke, W. (1999). *Amos users' 4.0 (Version 3.6)*. Chicago, IL: Smallwaters.

Aroian, L. A. (1947). The probability function of the product of two normally distributed variables. *Annals of Mathematical Statistics, 18*, 265–271. doi:10.1214/aoms/1177730442

Baron, R. M., & Kenny, D. A. (1986). The moderator-mediator variable distinction in social psychological research: Conceptual, strategic, and statistical considerations. *Journal of Personality and Social Psychology, 51*, 1173–1182. doi:10.1037/0022-3514.51.6.1173

Bentler, P. M. (1997). *EQS for Windows (version 5.6)* [Computer program]. Encino, CA: Multivariate Software.

Blalock, H. M. (1969). *Theory construction: From verbal to mathematical formulations*. Englewood Cliffs, NJ: Prentice Hall.

Bollen, K. A. (1987). Total, direct, and indirect effects in structural equation models. In C. Clogg (Ed.), *Sociological methodology* (pp. 37–69). Washington, DC: American Sociological Association. doi:10.2307/271028

Bollen, K. A., & Stine, R. (1990). Direct and indirect effects: Classical and bootstrap estimates of variability. *Sociological Methodology*, *20*, 115–140. doi:10.2307/271084

Bonate, P. L. (2000). *Analysis of pretest-posttest designs*. Boca Raton, FL: Chapman & Hall. doi:10.1201/9781420035926

Botvin, G. J. (2000). Preventing drug abuse in schools: Social and competence enhancement approaches targeting individual-level etiologic factors. *Addictive Behaviors*, *25*, 887–897. doi:10.1016/S0306-4603(00)00119-2

Bray, B. C., Almirall, D., Zimmerman, R. S., Lynam, D., & Murphy, S. A. (2006). Assessing the total effect of time-varying predictors in prevention research. *Prevention Science*, *7*, 1–17. doi:10.1007/s11121-005-0023-0

Bühler, A., Schröder, E., & Silbereisen, R. K. (2008). The role of life skills promotion in substance abuse prevention: A mediation analysis. *Health Education Research*, *23*, 621–632. doi:10.1093/her/cym039

Chen, H. T. (1990). *Theory-driven evaluations*. Newbury Park, CA: Sage.

Cheong, J. (2011). Accuracy of estimates and statistical power for testing mediation in latent growth modeling. *Structural Equation Modeling*, *18*, 195–211. doi:10.1080/10705511.2011.557334

Cheong, J., MacKinnon, D. P., & Khoo, S. T. (2001). A latent growth modeling approach to mediation analysis. [Abstract.] In L. M. Collins & A. Sayer (Eds.), *New methods for the analysis of change* (pp. 390–392). Washington, DC: American Psychological Association.

Cheong, J., MacKinnon, D. P., & Khoo, S. T. (2003). Investigation of mediational processes using parallel process latent growth curve modeling. *Structural Equation Modeling*, *10*, 238–262. doi:10.1207/S15328007SEM1002_5

Cheong, J., MacKinnon, D. P., & Pentz, M. A. (2002, June). *Evaluation of the mediating mechanisms of a drug prevention program to reduce adolescent DUI*. Poster presented at the annual meeting of the Research Society on Alcoholism, San Francisco, CA.

Coffman, D. L., & Zhong, W. (2012). Assessing mediation using marginal structural models in the presence of confounding and moderation. *Psychological Methods*, *17*, 642–664. doi:10.1037/a0029311

Cohen, J., Cohen, P., West, S. G., & Aiken, L. S. (2003). *Applied Multiple Regression / Correlation Analysis for the Behavioral Sciences* (3rd ed.). Mahwah, NJ: Erlbaum.

Cole, D. A., & Maxwell, S. E. (2003). Testing mediational models with longitudinal data: Questions and tips in the use of structural equation modeling. *Journal of Abnormal Psychology*, *112*, 558–577. doi:10.1037/0021-843X.112.4.558

Collins, L. M., Graham, J. W., & Flaherty, B. P. (1998). An alternative framework for defining mediation. *Multivariate Behavioral Research*, *33*, 295–312. doi:10.1207/s15327906mbr3302_5

Cronbach, L. J., & Furby, L. (1970). How should we measure "change" or should we? *Psychological Bulletin*, *74*, 68–80. doi:10.1037/h0029382

Cuijpers, P. (2002). Effective ingredients of school-based drug prevention programs: A systematic review. *Addictive Behaviors*, *27*, 1009–1023. doi:10.1016/S0306-4603(02)00295-2

Dagne, G. A., Brown, C. H., & Howe, G. W. (2007). Hierarchical modeling of sequential behavioral data: Examining complex association patterns in mediation models. *Psychological Methods*, *12*, 298–316. doi:10.1037/1082-989X.12.3.298

Davis, J. A. (1985). *The logic of causal order.* Beverly Hills, CA: Sage. doi:10.4135/9781412986212

DeGarmo, D. S., Eddy, J. M., Reid, J. B., & Fetrow, R. A. (2009). Evaluating mediators of the impact of the Linking the Interests of Families and Teachers (LIFT) multimodal preventive intervention on substance use initiation and growth across adolescence. *Prevention Science*, *10*, 208–220. doi:10.1007/s11121-009-0126-0

Donaldson, S. I., Graham, J. W., & Hansen, W. B. (1994). Testing the generalizability of intervening mechanism theories: Understanding the effects of adolescent drug use prevention interventions. *Journal of Behavioral Medicine*, *17*, 195–216. doi:10.1007/BF01858105

Donaldson, S. I., Sussman, S., MacKinnon, D. P., Severson, H. H., Glynn, T., Murray, D. M., & Stone, E. J. (1996). Drug abuse prevention programming. Do we know what content works? *American Behavioral Scientist*, *39*, 868–883. doi:10.1177/0002764296039007008

Ellickson, P. L., McCaffrey, D. F., & Klein, D. J. (2009). Long-term effects of drug prevention on risky sexual behavior among young adults. *Journal of Adolescent Health*, *45*, 111–117. doi:10.1016/j.jadohealth.2008.12.022

Epstein, J. A., & Botvin, G. J. (2008). Media resistance skills and drug skill refusal techniques: What is their relationship with alcohol use among inner-city adolescents? *Addictive Behaviors*, *33*, 528–537. doi:10.1016/j.addbeh.2007.11.001

Fairchild, A. J., & MacKinnon, D. P. (2009). A general model for testing mediation and moderation effects. *Prevention Science*, *10*, 87–99. doi:10.1007/s11121-008-0109-6

Fairchild, A. J., MacKinnon, D. P., Taborga, M., & Taylor, A. B. (2009). R^2 effect-size: Measures for mediation analysis. *Behavior Research Methods, 41*, 486–498. doi:10.3758/BRM.41.2.486

Ferrer, E., & McArdle, J. J. (2010). Longitudinal modeling of developmental changes in psychological research. *Current Directions in Psychological Science, 19*, 149–154. doi:10.1177/0963721410370300

Frangakis, C. E., & Rubin, D. B. (2002). Principal stratification in causal inference. *Biometrics, 58*, 21–29. doi:10.1111/j.0006-341X.2002.00021.x

Frank, K. A. (2000). Impact of a confounding variable on a regression coefficient. *Sociological Methods and Research, 29*, 147–194. doi:10.1177/0049124100029002001

Freedman, L. S. (2001). Confidence intervals and statistical power of the 'validation' ratio for surrogate or intermediate endpoints. *Journal of Statistical Planning and Inference, 96*, 143–153. doi:10.1016/S0378-3758(00)00330-X

Fritz, M. S., & MacKinnon, D. P. (2007). Required sample size to detect the mediated effect. *Psychological Science, 18*, 233–239. doi:10.1111/j.1467-9280.2007.01882.x

Fritz, M. S., & MacKinnon, D. P. (2012). Mediation models for developmental data. In B. Laursen, T. Little, & N. Card (Eds.), *Handbook of developmental research methods* (pp. 291–310). New York, NY: Guilford.

Fritz, M. S., Taylor, A. B., & MacKinnon, D. P. (2012). Explanation of two anomalous results in statistical mediation analysis. *Multivariate Behavioral Research, 47*, 61–87. doi:10.1080/00273171.2012.640596

Gollob, H. F., & Reichardt, C. S. (1991). Interpreting and estimating indirect effects assuming time lags really matter. In L. M. Collins & J. L. Horn (Eds.), *Best methods for the analysis of change: Recent advances, unanswered questions, future directions* (pp. 243–259). Washington, DC: American Psychological Association. doi:10.1037/10099-015

Hansen, W. B. (1992). School-based substance abuse prevention: A review of the state of the art in curriculum, 1980–1990. *Health Education Research, 7*, 403–430. doi:10.1093/her/7.3.403

Hansen, W. B. (2002). Program evaluation strategies for substance abuse prevention. *Journal of Primary Prevention, 22*, 409–436. doi:10.1023/A:1015231724053

Hansen, W. B., & Graham, J. W. (1991). Preventing alcohol, marijuana, and cigarette use among adolescents: Peer pressure resistance training versus establishing conservative norms. *Preventive Medicine, 20*, 414–430. doi:10.1016/0091-7435(91)90039-7

Hansen, W. B., & McNeal, R. B. (1996). The law of maximum expected potential effect: Constraints placed on program effectiveness by mediator relationships. *Health Education Research, 11*, 501–507. doi:10.1093/her/11.4.501

Henry, K. L. (2008). Low prosocial attachment, involvement with drug-using peers, and adolescent drug use: A longitudinal examination of mediational mechanisms. *Psychology of Addictive Behaviors, 22*, 302–308. doi:10.1037/0893-164X.22.2.302

Holland, P. W. (1988). Causal inference, path analysis, and recursive structural equation models. *Sociological Methodology, 18*, 449–484. doi:10.2307/271055

Hyman, H. H. (1955). *Survey design and analysis: Principles, cases, and procedures.* Glencoe, IL: Free Press.

Imai, K., Keele, L., & Tingley, D. (2010). A general approach to causal mediation analysis. *Psychological Methods, 15*, 309–334. doi:10.1037/a0020761

Imai, K., Tingley, D., & Yamamoto, T. (2013). Experimental designs for identifying causal mechanisms. *Journal of the Royal Statistical Society: Series A (Statistics in Society), 176*, 5–51. doi:10.1111/j.1467-985X.2012.01032.x

Jo, B. (2008). Causal inference in randomized experiments with mediational processes. *Psychological Methods, 13*, 314–336. doi:10.1037/a0014207

Jo, B., Stuart, L., MacKinnon, D. P., & Vinokur, A. (2011). The use of propensity scores in mediation. *Multivariate Behavioral Research, 46*, 425–452. doi:10.1080/00273171.2011.576624

Judd, C. M., & Kenny, D. A. (1981). *Estimating the effects of social interventions.* New York, NY: Cambridge University Press.

Kisbu-Sakarya, Y., MacKinnon, D. P., & Aiken, L. S. (2013). A Monte Carlo comparison study of the power of the analysis of covariance, simple difference, and residual change scores in testing two-wave data. *Educational and Psychological Measurement, 73*, 47–62. doi:10.1177/0013164412450574

Klesges, R. C., Vasey, M. M., & Glasgow, R. E. (1986). A worksite smoking modification competition: Potential for public health impact. *American Journal of Public Health, 76*, 198–200. doi:10.2105/AJPH.76.2.198

Komro, K. A., Perry, C. L., Williams, C. L., Stigler, M. H., Farbakhsh, K., & Veblen-Mortenson, S. (2001). How did Project Northland reduce alcohol use among young adolescents? Analysis of mediating variables. *Health Education Research, 16*, 59–70. doi:10.1093/her/16.1.59

Krull, J. L., & MacKinnon, D. P. (1999). Multilevel mediation modeling in group-based intervention studies. *Evaluation Review, 23*, 418–444. doi:10.1177/0193841X9902300404

Krull, J. L., & MacKinnon, D. P. (2001). Multilevel modeling of individual and group level mediated effects.

Multivariate Behavioral Research, 36, 249–277. doi:10.1207/S15327906MBR3602_06

Li, L., Evans, E., & Hser, Y. (2010). A marginal structural modeling approach to assess the cumulative effect of treatment on later drug use abstinence. *Journal of Drug Issues, 40,* 221–240. doi:10.1177/002204261004000112

Li, Y., Bienias, J., & Bennett, D. (2007). Confounding in the estimation of mediation effects. *Computational Statistics and Data Analysis, 51,* 3173–3186. doi:10.1016/j.csda.2006.10.016

Lipsey, M. W. (1993). Theory as method: Small theories of treatments. In L. B. Sechrest & H. G. Scott (Eds.), *Understanding causes and generalizing about them* (pp. 5–38). San Francisco, CA: Jossey-Bass. doi:10.1002/ev.1637

Lockhart, G., MacKinnon, D. P., & Olrich, V. (2011). Mediation analysis in psychosomatic medicine research. *Psychosomatic Medicine, 73,* 29–43. doi:10.1097/PSY.0b013e318200a54b

Lockwood, C. M., & MacKinnon, D. P. (1998). Bootstrapping the standard error of the mediated effect. *Proceedings of the 23rd Annual Meeting of SAS Users Group International* (pp. 997–1002). Cary, NC: SAS Institute, Inc.

Longshore, D., Ellickson, P. L., McCaffrey, D. F., & St. Clair, P. A. (2007). School-based drug prevention among at-risk adolescents: Effects of ALERT. *Health Education and Behavior, 34,* 651–668. doi:10.1177/1090198106294895

Lynch, K. G., Cary, M., Gallop, R., & Ten Have, T. R. (2008). Causal mediation analyses for randomized trials. *Health Services and Outcome Methodology, 8,* 57–76. doi:10.1007/s10742-008-0028-9

MacKinnon, D. P. (1994). Analysis of mediating variables in prevention intervention studies. In A. Cazares & L. A. Beatty (Eds.), *Scientific methods for prevention intervention research. NIDA research monograph 139* (DHHS Pub. No. 94-3631, pp. 127–153). Washington, DC: U. S. Government Printing Office.

MacKinnon, D. P. (2000). Contrasts in multiple mediator models. In J. Rose, L. Chassin, C. C. Presson, & S. J. Sherman (Eds.), *Multivariate applications in substance use research: New methods for new questions* (pp. 141–160). Mahwah, NJ: Lawrence Erlbaum Assoc.

MacKinnon, D. P. (2008). *Introduction to statistical mediation analysis.* Mahwah, NJ: Erlbaum.

MacKinnon, D. P., & Dwyer, J. H. (1993). Estimating mediated effects in prevention studies. *Evaluation Review, 17,* 144–158. doi:10.1177/0193841X9301700202

MacKinnon, D. P., Fritz, M. S., Williams, J., & Lockwood, C. M. (2007). Distribution of the product confidence limits for the indirect effect: Program PRODCLIN. *Behavior Research Methods, 39,* 384–389. doi:10.3758/BF03193007

MacKinnon, D. P., Johnson, C. A., Pentz, M. A., Dwyer, J. H., Hansen, W. B., Flay, B. R., & Wang, E. Y. I. (1991). Mediating mechanisms in a school-based drug prevention program: One year effects of the Midwestern Prevention Project. *Health Psychology, 10,* 164–172. doi:10.1037/0278-6133.10.3.164

MacKinnon, D. P., Kisbu-Sakarya, Y., & Gottschall, A. (2013). Developments in mediation analysis. In T. D. Little (Ed.), *Oxford handbook of quantitative methods* (pp. 338–360). New York, NY: Oxford University Press.

MacKinnon, D. P., Krull, J. L., & Lockwood, C. M. (2000). Equivalence of the mediation, confounding, and suppression effect. *Prevention Science, 1,* 173–181. doi:10.1023/A:1026595011371

MacKinnon, D. P., Lockwood, C. M., Hoffman, J. M., West, S. G., & Sheets, V. (2002). Comparison of methods to test mediation and other intervening variable effects. *Psychological Methods, 7,* 83–104. doi:10.1037/1082-989X.7.1.83

MacKinnon, D. P., Lockwood, C. M., & Williams, J. (2004). Confidence limits for the indirect effect: Distribution of the product and resampling methods. *Multivariate Behavioral Research, 39,* 99–128. doi:10.1207/s15327906mbr3901_4

MacKinnon, D. P., & Pirlott, A. (2010). *The unbearable lightness of b.* Paper presented at the Annual Meeting of the Society for Personality and Social Psychology, Las Vegas, NV.

MacKinnon, D. P., Taborga, M. P., & Morgan-Lopez, A. A. (2002). Mediation designs for tobacco prevention research. *Drug and Alcohol Dependence, 68,* 69–83. doi:10.1016/S0376-8716(02)00216-8

MacKinnon, D. P., Taylor, A. B., Yoon, M., & Lockwood, C. M. (2010). *A comparison of methods to test mediation and other intervening variable effects in logistic regression.* Unpublished manuscript.

MacKinnon, D. P., Warsi, G., & Dwyer, J. H. (1995). A simulation study of mediated effect measures. *Multivariate Behavioral Research, 30,* 41–62. doi:10.1207/s15327906mbr3001_3

Malone, P. S., Lansford, J. E., Castellino, D. R., Berlin, L. J., & Dodge, K. A. (2004). Divorce and child behavior problems: Applying latent change score models to life event data. *Structural Equation Modeling, 11,* 401–423. doi:10.1207/s15328007sem1103_6

Martino, S. (2011). Oral health behavioral and social intervention research concepts and methods. *Journal of Public Health Dentistry, 71,* S2–S6. doi:10.1111/j.1752-7325.2011.00217.x

McArdle, J. J. (2001). A latent difference score approach to longitudinal dynamic structural analysis. In R. Cudeck, S. du Toit, & D. Sörbom (Eds.), *Structural equation modeling: Present and future. A festschrift in honor of Karl Jöreskog* (pp. 341–380). Lincolnwood, IL: Scientific Software International.

McCaul, K. D., & Glasgow, R. E. (1985). Preventing adolescent smoking: What have we learned about treatment construct validity? *Health Psychology*, *4*, 361–387. doi:10.1037/0278-6133.4.4.361

Muthén, B. O., & Curran, P. J. (1997). General longitudinal modeling of individual differences in experimental designs: A latent variable framework for analysis and power estimation. *Psychological Methods*, *2*, 371–402. doi:10.1037/1082-989X.2.4.371

Muthén, B. O., & Muthén, L. K. (2000). Integrating person-centered and variable-centered analyses: Growth mixture modeling with latent trajectory classes. *Alcoholism: Clinical and Experimental Research*, *24*, 882–891. doi:10.1111/j.1530-0277.2000.tb02070.x

Muthén, L. K., & Muthén, B. (1998–2010). *Mplus user's guide, 6th*. Los Angeles, CA: Muthén & Muthén.

Orlando, M., Ellickson, P. L., McCaffrey, D. F., & Longshore, D. L. (2005). Mediation analysis of a school-based drug prevention program: Effects of project ALERT. *Prevention Science*, *6*, 35–46. doi:10.1007/s11121-005-1251-z

Pearl, J. (2001). Direct and indirect effects. *Proceedings of the 17th conference on uncertainty in artificial intelligence* (pp. 411–420). San Francisco, CA: Morgan Kaufmann.

Pearl, J. (2009). *Causality: Models, reasoning, and inference*. Cambridge, England: Cambridge University Press. doi:10.1017/CBO9780511803161

Pearl, J. (2010). The foundations of causal inference. *Sociological Methodology*, *40*, 75–149. doi:10.1111/j.1467-9531.2010.01228.x

Pearl, J. (2012). The causal mediation formula: A guide to the assessment of pathways and mechanisms. *Prevention Science*, *13*, 426–436. doi:10.1007/s11121-011-0270-1

Pituch, K., Stapleton, L. M., & Kang, J. Y. (2006). A comparison of single sample and bootstrap methods to assess mediation in cluster randomized trials. *Multivariate Behavioral Research*, *41*, 367–400. doi:10.1207/s15327906mbr4103_5

Preacher, K. J., & Hayes, A. F. (2004). SPSS and SAS procedures for estimating indirect effects in simple mediation models. *Behavior Research Methods, Instruments, and Computers*, *36*, 717–731. doi:10.3758/BF03206553

Raudenbush, S. W., & Sampson, R. (1999). Assessing direct and indirect effects in multilevel designs with latent variables. *Sociological Methods and Research*, *28*, 123–153. doi:10.1177/0049124199028002001

Robins, J. M., & Greenland, S. (1992). Identifiability and exchangeability for direct and indirect effects. *Epidemiology*, *3*, 143–155. doi:10.1097/00001648-199203000-00013

Robins, J. M., Hernan, M., & Brumback, B. (2000). Marginal structural models and causal inference in epidemiology. *Epidemiology*, *11*, 550–560. doi:10.1097/00001648-200009000-00011

Rogosa, D. R. (1988). Myths about longitudinal research. In K. W. Schaie, R. T. Campbell, W. M. Meredith, & S. C. Rawlings (Eds.), *Methodological issues in aging research* (pp. 171–209). New York, NY: Springer.

Rosenbaum, P. R. (2002). *Observational studies*. New York, NY: Springer. doi:10.1007/978-1-4757-3692-2

Rubin, D. B. (1974). Estimating causal effects of treatments in randomized and nonrandomized studies. *Journal of Educational Psychology*, *66*, 688–701. doi:10.1037/h0037350

Rubin, D. B. (2004). Direct and indirect causal effects via potential outcomes. *Scandinavian Journal of Statistics*, *31*, 161–170. doi:10.1111/j.1467-9469.2004.02-123.x

Shadish, W. R., Cook, T. D., & Campbell, D. T. (2002). *Experimental and quasi-experimental designs for generalized causal inference*. Boston, MA: Houghton Mifflin.

Sobel, M. E. (1982). Asymptotic confidence intervals for indirect effects in structural equation models. In S. Leinhardt (Ed.), *Sociological methodology 1982* (pp. 290–312). Washington, DC: American Sociological Association. doi:10.2307/270723

Sobel, M. E. (2008). Identification of causal parameters in randomized studies with mediating variables. *Journal of Educational and Behavioral Statistics*, *33*, 230–251. doi:10.3102/1076998607307239

Spencer, S. J., Zanna, M. P., & Fong, G. T. (2005). Establishing a causal chain: Why experiments are often more effective than meditational analyses in examining psychological processes. *Journal of Personality and Social Psychology*, *89*, 845–851. doi:10.1037/0022-3514.89.6.845

Spoth, R., Trudeau, L., Guyll, M., Shin, C., & Redmond, C. (2009). Universal intervention effects on substance use among young adults mediated by delayed adolescent substance initiation. *Journal of Consulting and Clinical Psychology*, *77*, 620–632. doi:10.1037/a0016029

Stephens, P. C., Sloboda, Z., Stephens, R. C., Teasdale, B., Grey, S. F., Hawthorne, R. D., & Williams, J. (2009). Universal school-based substance abuse prevention programs: Modeling targeted mediators and outcomes for adolescent cigarette, alcohol, and marijuana use. *Drug and Alcohol Dependence*, *102*, 19–29. doi:10.1016/j.drugalcdep.2008.12.016

Stuart, E. A., Perry, D. F., Le, H., & Ialongo, N. S. (2008). Estimating intervention effects of prevention programs: Accounting for noncompliance. *Prevention Science*, *9*, 288–298. doi:10.1007/s11121-008-0104-y

Sussman, S. (Ed.). (2001). *Handbook of program development for health behavior research and practice*. Thousand Oaks, CA: Sage. doi:10.4135/9781412991445

Taylor, A. B., MacKinnon, D., & Tein, J. Y. (2008). Test of the three-path mediated effect. *Organizational Research Methods*, *11*, 241–269. doi:10.1177/1094428107300344

Ten Have, T. R., Joffe, M. M., Lynch, K. G., Brown, G. K., Maisto, S. A., & Beck, A. T. (2007). Causal mediation analysis with rank preserving models. *Biometrics*, *63*, 926–934. doi:10.1111/j.1541-0420.2007.00766.x

Tofighi, D., & MacKinnon, D. P. (2011). RMediation: An R package for mediation analysis confidence intervals. *Behavior Research Methods*, *43*, 692–700. doi:10.3758/s13428-011-0076-x

Trim, R. S., Meehan, B. T., King, K. M., & Chassin, L. (2007). The relation between adolescent substance use and young adult internalizing symptoms: Findings from a high-risk longitudinal sample. *Psychology of Addictive Behaviors*, *21*, 97–107. doi:10.1037/0893-164X.21.1.97

VanderWeele, T. J. (2010). Bias formulas for sensitivity analysis for direct and indirect effects. *Epidemiology*, *21*, 540–551. doi:10.1097/EDE.0b013e3181df191c

Venter, A., & Maxwell, S. E. (1999). Maximizing power in randomized designs when N is small. In R. H. Hoyle (Ed.), *Statistical strategies for small sample research* (pp. 31–58). Thousand Oaks, CA: Sage.

von Eye, A., Mun, E. Y., & Mair, P. (2009). What carries a mediation process? Configural analysis of mediation. *Integrative Psychological and Behavioral Science*, *43*, 228–247. doi:10.1007/s12124-009-9088-9

Wang, J., Simons-Morton, B. G., Farhart, T., & Luk, J. W. (2009). Socio-demographic variability in adolescent substance use: Mediation by parents and peers. *Prevention Science*, *10*, 387–396. doi:10.1007/s11121-009-0141-1

Wenzel, V., Weichold, K., & Silbereisen, R. K. (2009). The life skills program IPSY: Positive influences on school bonding and prevention of substance misuse. *Journal of Adolescence*, *32*, 1391–1401. doi:10.1016/j.adolescence.2009.05.008

Winship, C., & Mare, R. D. (1983). Structural equations and path analysis for discrete data. *American Journal of Sociology*, *89*, 54–110. doi:10.1086/227834

Woodford, M. R., Krentzman, A. R., & Gattis, M. N. (2012). Alcohol and drug use among sexual minority college students and their heterosexual counterparts: The effects of experiencing and witnessing incivility and hostility on campus. *Substance Abuse and Rehabilitation*, *3*, 11–23. doi:10.2147/SAR.S26347

Wynn, S. R., Schulenberg, J., Maggs, J. L., & Zucker, R. A. (2000). Preventing alcohol misuse: The impact of refusal skills and norms. *Psychology of Addictive Behaviors*, *14*, 36–47. doi:10.1037/0893-164X.14.1.36

CHAPTER 26

GROWTH REDEFINED IN TERMS OF PREVENTING DRUG USE AND DELINQUENCY

W. Alex Mason, Eric C. Brown, Charles B. Fleming, and Kevin P. Haggerty

This chapter examines latent growth curve modeling (LGM) as a flexible tool for testing the effects of drug use and delinquency preventive interventions. The chapter reviews basic LGM and describes extensions of the model, such as parallel process and two-part LGMs, that can be used to examine nuanced research questions of interest to prevention science (e.g., mediation). Caveats are noted, and the chapter concludes by encouraging drug use and delinquency prevention researchers to increase their use of LGM to test theory-driven hypotheses about intervention effects. It is our hope that this chapter, which is conceptual and illustrative in nature, will help expand the ways in which researchers examine hypothesized processes of change relevant to the fields of drug use and also delinquency prevention.

We begin the chapter with a general overview of basic LGM, including unconditional and conditional latent growth curve models. Next, we illustrate how basic LGM can be used to test randomized preventive interventions. Then, we discuss extensions of LGM that can be used to examine specific questions about hypothesized program effects. We address LGM for testing hypothesized intervention-induced mediating processes and discuss two-part models for examining differential prevention effects on the multiple dimensions of complex, time-varying outcome variables. Recent advancements in models for testing preventive intervention effects across latent or unobserved trajectory groups also are reviewed briefly, as are developments in so-called shared-parameters models, which combine LGM with other longitudinal data analytic techniques, such as survival analysis. Concluding the chapter are some cautionary notes and a discussion of future research directions.

LATENT GROWTH MODELING IN PREVENTION

The field of drug use and delinquency prevention concerns the science and practice of behavioral change. Accordingly, theories developed within the discipline have been designed with the principal goal to understand and facilitate change over time. This focus has led to the creation of numerous drug use and delinquency prevention, as well as health promotion, interventions (Foxcroft, Ireland, Lister-Sharp, Breen, & Lowe, 2003; Piquero, Farrington, Welsh, Tremblay, & Jennings, 2009; Tobler et al., 2000). Testing interventions and their underlying theories has required the use of longitudinal research designs and data analysis techniques to maximize use of the available data. Recent years have witnessed a rapid increase in the development of advanced techniques for the analysis of longitudinal data. Here, we focus attention on LGM conducted within the general structural equation modeling (SEM) framework,

The authors would like to thank Mary B. Chmelka for her assistance with the chapter.

http://dx.doi.org/10.1037/14550-027
Handbook of Adolescent Drug Use Prevention: Research, Intervention Strategies, and Practice, L. M. Scheier (Editor)

a potent analytic tool for use within prevention science and related disciplines (Bollen & Curran, 2006; Duncan, Duncan, & Strycker, 2006; Preacher, Wichman, MacCallum, & Briggs, 2008).

To begin with, we adopt the definition of *prevention* suggested by Gillham, Shatté, and Freres (2000), and reiterated by Horowitz and Garber (2006), which refers to program activities that result in a "diminished expected increase" (Horowitz & Garber, 2006, p. 402) in targeted problem outcomes (e.g., delaying the initiation of alcohol use or reducing the normative increase in delinquency over early adolescence). LGM is well suited for testing the effects of prevention programs under this definition and has been used to evaluate family (Brody et al., 2006; Park et al., 2000), school (Taylor, Graham, Cumsille, & Hansen, 2000), and community interventions (Scheier & Grenard, 2010).

Questions About Trajectories of Change Over Time: Unconditional LGM

The behaviors targeted by drug use and delinquency prevention efforts change systematically during development. Juvenile delinquency, which typically refers to illegal behaviors (e.g., property offenses, violence) committed by minors, peaks in mid-adolescence and declines gradually thereafter; adolescent drug use, which also is an illegal behavior (e.g., underage alcohol and cigarette use, marijuana and other drug use) tends to increase throughout the teen years and into early adulthood (Johnston, O'Malley, Bachman, & Schulenberg, 2013; Kessler et al., 2005; Loeber et al., 2003). Delinquency and drug use are distinct but correlated behaviors that have many common risk factors and represent, in part, indicators of an underlying propensity for general deviance (Donovan & Jessor, 1985; Durlak, 1998). Initial questions in the study of these behaviors concern describing the patterns of change for a population. We might be interested in the rate at which the average frequency of drug use increases across adolescence, whether this rate of change accelerates or decelerates, and whether frequency of use in early adolescence is related to subsequent increases in use. Furthermore, we might be interested in the degree to which patterns of change differ between individuals.

Modeling linear change. LGM conventionally begins by testing "unconditional" models in which level and change in a behavior are not conditioned on predictor variables. Figure 26.1 shows hypothetical individual trajectories of linear growth in an outcome, such as drug use, based on four time points of data representing, perhaps, annual assessments from early (age 12) to middle (age 15) adolescence. The bold line in the center of this figure represents the average trajectory of growth. Figure 26.1 illustrates that individuals vary both in their initial levels of drug use and in their rates of change across time points. The unconditional LGM can be used to describe both the average trajectory and estimate variability around this average.

LGM accomplishes this by modeling repeated measures data in a latent variable framework (McArdle & Epstein, 1987; Meredith & Tisak, 1990). The latent growth factors capture the level and change in repeated measures of a given phenomenon across time. Figure 26.2 shows a two-factor linear growth curve model for four time points of repeated measures data-spaced 1 year apart. Taking delinquency as an example, the two growth factors include an intercept factor (*I*), which typically describes the initial level of delinquency or starting point of the "curve," and a slope factor (*S*), which describes the linear rate of change in delinquency per unit of time. Although annual data collection is common in prevention trials that assess drug use and delinquency across adolescence and change is often expressed per year, for some research questions, change across shorter time intervals may be of interest and data may be collected more frequently. For example, growth may be more appropriately modeled in terms of change per month, week, or day (Collins & Graham, 2002).

Each growth factor has two parameters of interest: a mean and a variance (i.e., *M* and *V*, respectively, in Figure 26.2). In an unconditional model, the estimated means represent the average for the population (e.g., dark bold line in Figure 26.1, representing average level at the starting point and average rate of linear change). Tests of statistical significance reveal whether means for these two parameters differ from zero more than we would expect by chance. For the slope factor in Figure 26.2, the

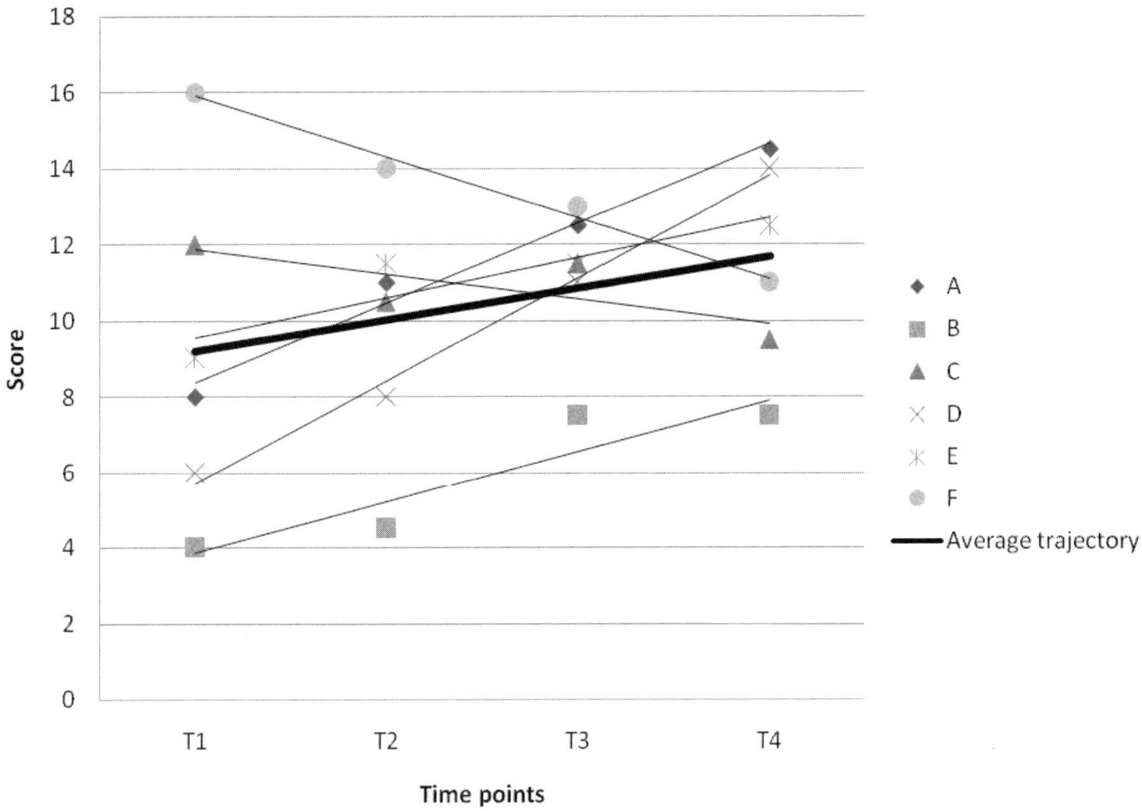

FIGURE 26.1. A sample of individual trajectories of linear growth in an outcome based on four time points of data. The bold line represents the average trajectory for the sample.

estimated mean can tell us whether the population, on average, increases (positive value) or decreases (negative value) in delinquency across the repeated measures. Variance estimates represent between-individual variability in level and change; significance tests for variance parameters tell us whether this between-individual variance is greater than we would expect by chance. Statistically significant variance for the slope factor is evidence of heterogeneity in systematic change in delinquency with respect to time. The variance in the repeated measures at particular time points usually is not entirely explained by the growth factors. Therefore, there is residual variance in growth factor indicators (i.e., e1–e4 in Figure 26.2). Unconditional latent growth curve models can accommodate different structures for the error variances of the repeated measures (e.g., constraining them to equality across time).

Choice of growth factor loadings. The meaning of growth factors is set by specifying factor loadings with reference to the time intervals between repeated measurements (Stoolmiller, 1995). A simple model of the average level of a given variable across time would have one growth factor (i.e., an intercept factor) with loadings of 1 on all repeated measures indicators. A two-factor model of linear change, as illustrated in Figure 26.2, also includes a slope factor, representing rate of change with loadings set to model change in delinquency, for our example, per unit of time (e.g., years, months). In a two-factor linear latent growth curve model, the intercept or level factor is anchored to a particular time point, representing the expected value at the time point on which the slope factor has a loading of zero. In Figure 26.2, given the fixed intercept [1,1,1,1] and slope [0,1,2,3] factor loadings, the intercept factor (*I*) represents the expected value of delinquent offending at the first time point, while the change factor (*S*) represents linear change in delinquency (with equally spaced intervals).

A covariance typically is estimated between the slope and the intercept growth factors. This added

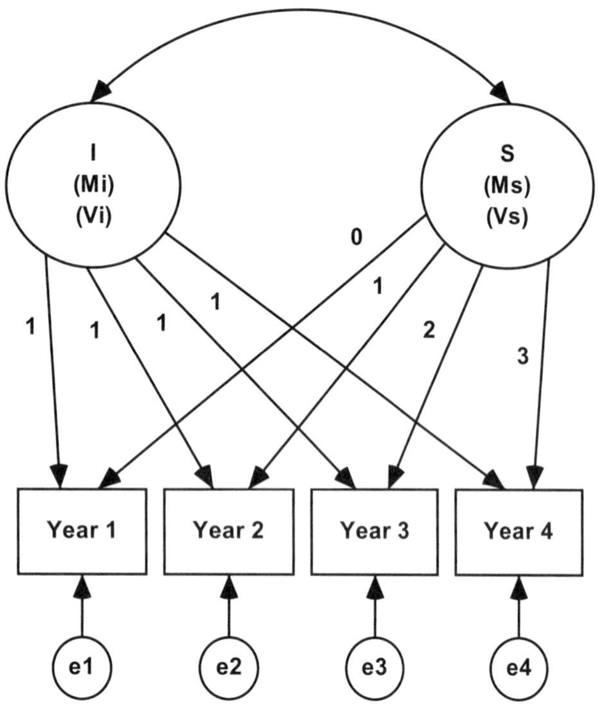

FIGURE 26.2. Unconditional two-factor latent growth curve model with intercept (*I*) representing expected level at the first time point and slope (*S*) representing rate of linear change over time. Growth factor means (*M*) and variances (*V*) are estimated, as are residual variances of the growth factor indicators (i.e., e1–e4).

parameter can be important to the interpretation of relations between the growth factors. For example, when an intercept factor is specified as representing level at the first time point, the covariance between intercept and slope is often negative because of regression to the mean, ceiling, or floor effects. Individuals who start at relatively high levels of delinquency, for example, are likely to have less subsequent increase in delinquent offending than those who start relatively lower.

Varying the factor loadings for the slope factor produces a different interpretation of the intercept (Stoolmiller, 1995). For instance, a slope factor coding of −3, −2, −1, and 0 results in the intercept taking on the meaning of the expected level at the last time point and a coding of −1.5, −.5, .5, and 1.5 results in the intercept taking on the meaning of the expected level at the middle of the time points. The interpretation of the covariance between the intercept and slope factor also changes accordingly. Of course, these choices should be guided by the research question at hand and the anticipated pattern of change.

Modeling nonlinear change. With more time points of data, additional dimensions of level and change can be modeled to capture nonlinear growth trajectories. Commonly, in addition to linear change, acceleration or deceleration in growth is modeled with factor loadings on a quadratic growth factor fixed as a function of time squared (e.g., 0, 1, 4, 9 across four time points). For example, adolescent delinquency typically displays a pattern of change characterized as the age-crime curve—with steady increases from early to middle adolescence and gradual declines thereafter—requiring the specification of a three-factor latent growth curve model, including intercept, slope, and quadratic growth factors (Windle, 2000). Piecewise latent growth curve models that specify an inflection point in a continuous pattern of change in an outcome also can be used (Raudenbush & Bryk, 2002), representing another type of three-factor model of nonlinear change. Modeling change in linear patterns of growth between the third and fourth time points in a six-wave study, for example, can be conducted using slope factor loadings of 0, 1, 2, 2, 2, 2 (first slope factor) and 0, 0, 0, 1, 2, 3 (second slope factor). Furthermore, deviations from linear and nonlinear patterns of continuous growth can be modeled by adding additional growth factors that capture seasonal- or date-specific increases in the behavior in question (e.g., excessive alcohol use during holidays; Del Boca, Darkes, Greenbaum, & Goldman, 2004).

Model fit. The process of testing unconditional models is usually an iterative one of comparing the fit of different models to the data. The researcher must balance considerations of finding models that fit a given data set and using a model that is parsimonious and will allow for addressing the primary research questions. A χ^2 difference test can be used to test the statistical significance of differences in fit resulting from adding additional parameters to a latent growth curve model, such as would be entailed by adding another growth factor (e.g., quadratic factor to capture acceleration or deceleration). Also, fit indices such as the comparative fit index,

Tucker Lewis index, and root mean square error of approximation can be examined to assess the fit of models. Although benchmarks of adequate fit often are used for these indices (Hu & Bentler, 1999), recent advancements in the assessment of fit indicate that analysts should exercise care in using these benchmarks for latent growth curve models because of the time-ordered nature of the data (Wu, West, & Taylor, 2009).

Questions About Predictors and Consequences of Change Over Time: Conditional LGM

Predictors of growth processes. Primary research questions commonly focus on how variations (i.e., individual differences) in different dimensions of growth trajectories are related to other variables. These questions generally concern whether independent variables predict variation in level and change in a phenomenon, such as drug use, over time. Probative questions might entail addressing whether group assignment in a prevention trial influences the rate of growth in drug use, or likewise, whether level of some risk factor influences both the intercept and slope growth terms, which can be answered by regressing both the intercept and slope growth factors on covariates in a conditional LGM. A model such as the one shown in Figure 26.3 tests whether a risk factor predicts initial level of and rate of linear increase in a behavior across the time period. An example of this type of model can be found in a study by Cortes, Fleming, Mason, and Catalano (2009), who

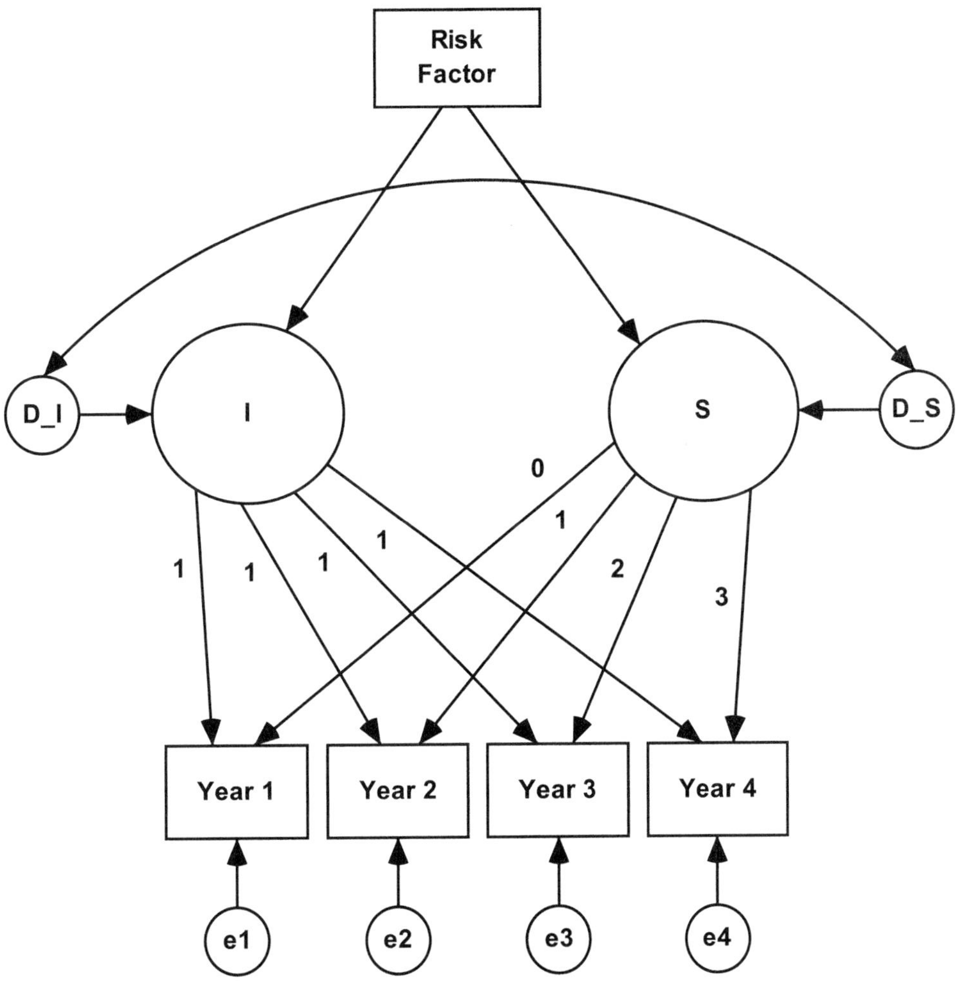

FIGURE 26.3. Conditional two-factor latent growth curve model examining a risk factor in relation to level (intercept, *I*) and linear change (slope, *S*) in an outcome over time. A covariance between growth factor disturbances (*D_I* and *D_S*) is estimated.

examined predictors of level and change in different types of drug use across adolescence. They found, for instance, that a teacher report of child antisocial behavior taken in late childhood predicted higher levels of late childhood alcohol and marijuana use as well as higher rates of increase in use of these drugs between early and late adolescence.

Consequences of growth processes. Growth factors capturing variation in level and change also can be explanatory variables, predicting variation in outcomes. For example, one might be interested in whether level and change in a risk factor, such as peer delinquency, across a defined period predict later problem behaviors, such as adolescent delinquency. In this case, a measure of adolescent delinquency would be regressed on the slope and intercept factors of a peer delinquency latent growth curve model. Such a model could indicate whether any predictive value can be obtained from knowing rates of change in peer delinquency over and above what is explained by the level of that risk factor at a particular period. This finding would support the logic of theories that hypothesize links between rates of change in risk factors and levels of specific outcomes. Fleming, Harachi, Cortes, Abbott, and Catalano (2004) tested this hypothesis with latent growth curve models of attention problems and reading scores between Grades 3 and 6 and problem behaviors (covert antisocial behavior, physical aggression, and drug use) in Grade 7. For both attention problems and reading scores, rates of change between Grades 3 and 6 predicted problem behaviors over and above what was predicted by initial levels of these variables, suggesting that affecting change in these variables may have valuable prevention effects.

Questions About Preventive Intervention Impact: LGM for Tests of Intervention Effects

Questions about intervention efficacy within the context of a randomized controlled trial (RCT) are important for determining evidence-based programs. Researchers increasingly are incorporating multiple waves of repeated measures data into the design of their prevention trials. As mentioned, such data often are collected annually; however, LGM can be used to model change during shorter or longer periods of time. The decision of how frequently to conduct repeated assessments should be made carefully and mapped onto the hypothesized timing of intervention effects. Whatever the spacing may be, repeated measures are necessary because preventive interventions typically are administered before the onset of targeted behaviors; therefore, intervention participants must be followed into (and even beyond) the period of peak risk for the emergence of such behaviors to test for a "diminished expected increase" (i.e., a prevention effect) relative to control participants. For example, prevention trials often target early adolescents before the period when they initiate or begin rapidly increasing their drug use and delinquent behavior and follow study participants at regular intervals throughout the teen years and into young adulthood, developmental periods characterized by peak risk for these problem behaviors (Johnston et al., 2013; Kessler et al., 2005; Loeber et al., 2003).

LGM tests of prevention effects: Covariate strategy. Two general strategies can be used to test for preventive intervention effects within the LGM framework: the *covariate* strategy and the multiple group strategy. The covariate strategy is a conditional latent growth curve model in which growth factors are regressed on a dichotomous program variable (or set of dichotomous program variables, if the study incorporates more than two experimental conditions) that delineates the experimental or intervention conditions. A statistically significant regression coefficient associated with a program variable suggests the presence of an intervention effect, the direction of which is determined by the sign of the coefficient.

To illustrate, Mason, Kosterman, Hawkins, Haggerty, and Spoth (2003) tested the effect of Preparing for the Drug Free Years (PDFY; now called Guiding Good Choices), a family-focused drug use preventive intervention, on growth in polydrug use (measured as a count of the number of different substances used, e.g., alcohol, cigarettes, marijuana) modeling five waves of data extending from early (Grade 6) to middle (Grade 10) adolescence.

Analyses specified a conditional two-factor latent growth curve model positing a linear increase in polydrug use (see Figure 26.4), in which the polydrug use slope factor was regressed on the polydrug use intercept factor (defined as pretest level of polydrug use), covariates (age and gender; not shown), and a dichotomous program variable indexing random assignment to either the PDFY condition (coded 1) or the control condition (coded 0).

Results revealed a negative effect of PDFY on the polydrug use slope factor ($\beta = -.22$, $p < .01$). This finding demonstrated that "compared with control group assignment, assignment to the PDFY condition was associated with a slower rate of increase in polydrug use over time, adjusting for pretest level of polydrug use, age, and gender" (Mason et al., 2003, p. 208). Further analyses in this study used this same strategy

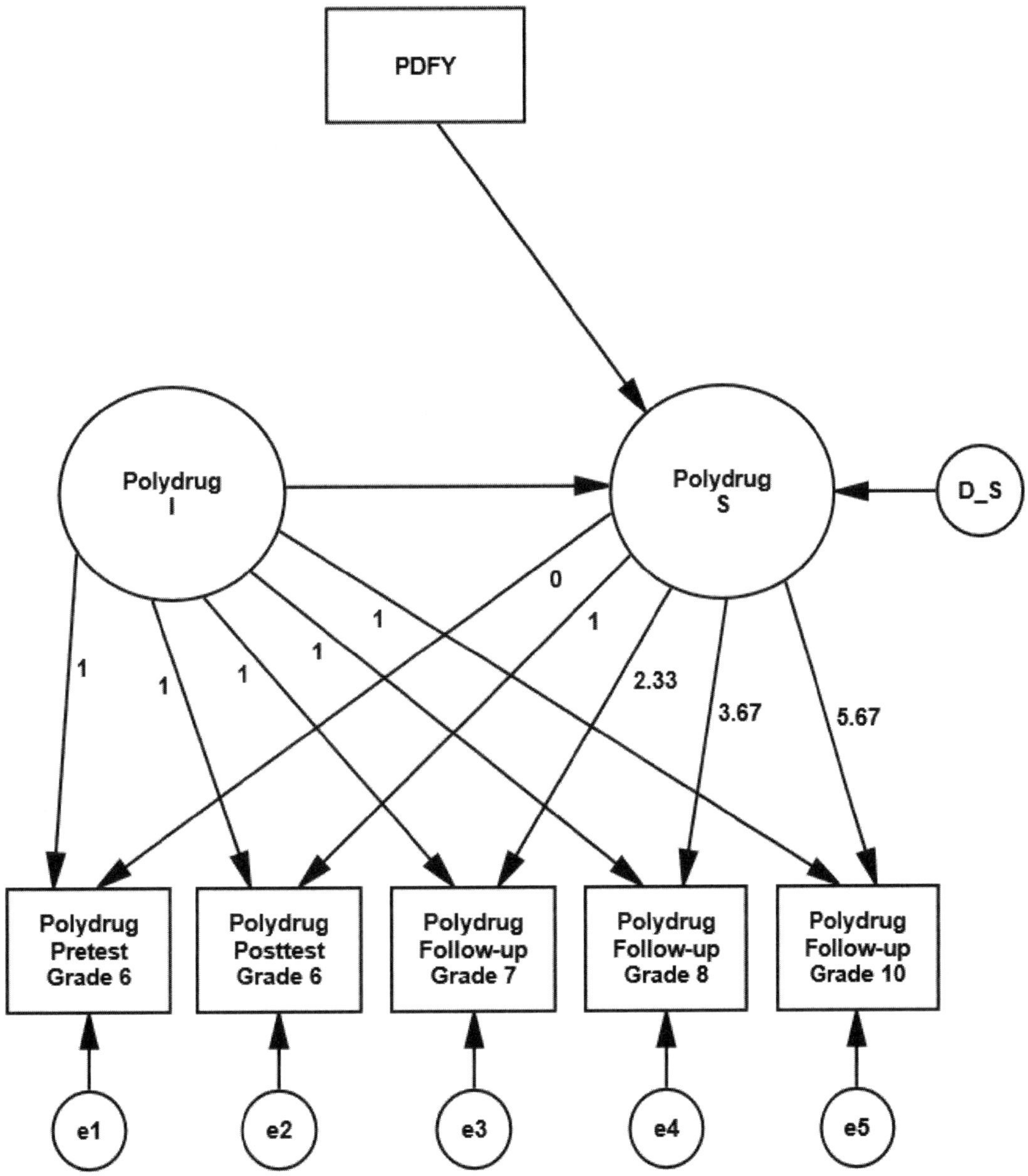

FIGURE 26.4. Conditional two-factor latent growth curve modeling examining the effect of PDFY on the Polydrug use slope factor (Polydrug *S*) representing rate of linear increase in polydrug use over time, controlling for the Polydrug use intercept factor (Polydrug *I*) representing pretest level of polydrug use as well as gender and age (not shown). Factor loadings represent linear growth over nonequidistant time points. PDFY = Preparing for the Drug Free Years.

to examine intervention effects on a measure of nondrug delinquency. Results showed that PDFY also slowed the rate of increase in delinquency over time (e.g., $\beta = -.22$, $p < .01$ < for the PDFY → Delinquency Slope).

Even the relatively straightforward growth model described above implies critical modeling decisions that must be made, preferably guided by the specific research questions under investigation. In the Mason et al. (2003) example, the polydrug use and delinquency slope factors were regressed on the polydrug use and delinquency intercept factors, respectively, which adjusted for possible pretest differences in these behaviors across conditions, similar to adding the pretest measure as a covariate in an analysis of covariance model (Park et al., 2000). In these latent growth curve model examples, the observed pretest measures of polydrug use and delinquency are additional indicators of the growth factors. Alternatively, if the focus is on modeling growth in an outcome exclusively postintervention, then the pretest measure of the outcome can be incorporated into the model by regressing growth factors, which are indicated by the posttest and follow-up measures, on the pretest measure as an observed covariate (Taylor et al., 2000). As an additional consideration, different factor loadings could be used to alter the meaning of the intercept, as described previously. For instance, in the Mason et al. (2003) example, the intercept factors could have been defined as the average levels of polydrug use and delinquency at the last follow-up and regressed on the program variable to provide a test of point-in-time differences between PDFY and control adolescents in polydrug use and delinquency at Grade 10 (Raudenbush & Bryk, 2002) as well as in the rate of change over time (Taylor et al., 2000). This technique represents an important model specification for prevention studies, for which the goal is to test differences at a distal time point in which diverging trajectories of problem behavior for control and intervention participants are expected to be at their maximum. Thus, alternative model specifications provide a way to test precise questions about intervention effects on both the level and rate of change in the targeted outcome variable, according to theory-guided expectations.

LGM tests of prevention effects: Multiple group strategy. A second strategy, *multiple group analysis*, can provide results for intervention tests that are very similar, and under certain conditions identical, to those provided by the covariate strategy. The multiple group strategy involves a latent growth curve model conducted separately but simultaneously across groups. For the case of randomized prevention trials, the groups represent the experimental conditions to which participants were assigned. Tests of intervention effects in multiple group latent growth curve models are conducted using constraints on the parameters of interest, along with associated χ^2 difference tests to determine the degree to which estimated parameters are significantly different across groups. For example, Park and her colleagues (2000) conducted tests of PDFY effects on targeted parenting, family interaction, and youth skills outcomes, as well as on youth alcohol use, using a series of multiple group latent growth curve models. To illustrate, the researchers conducted a latent growth curve model of the average increase in parental norms against adolescents' substance use, first, in an unconstrained model that allowed the mean of the parental norms slope to differ for PDFY versus control participants and, then, in a constrained model that tested an equivalent slope factor mean across experimental conditions. Results showed a significant χ^2 difference test between these two nested models, indicating that the constraint on the parental norms slope factor mean was untenable and that significant group differences exist; a higher positive mean value in the PDFY compared with the control group was consistent with the hypothesis that PDFY participants demonstrated a faster rate of increase in parental norms against alcohol use following intervention than control participants during the study.

LGM tests of prevention effects: Summary. The covariate and multiple-group strategies have advantages and disadvantages. The multiple-group strategy provides the ability to test group differences in any estimated parameter of interest, depending on the research question. For example, a researcher might test group differences in the growth factor variances, in the covariance between the intercept and slope factors, or in the residual variances of the growth factor indicators. In general, however, the covariate strategy provides greater flexibility in testing intervention effects in more complex models that incorporate a consideration of additional variables, such as covariates, interaction terms, and mediators. Because of the increased flexibility of the covariate strategy, the following sections restrict their focus to latent growth curve models that represent experimental conditions using a program variable or variables.

Questions About the Mechanisms of Intervention Effects: LGM for Testing Mediation

A critical consideration for prevention science involves understanding the precise mechanisms through which evidence-based preventive interventions obtain their effects on targeted outcomes (e.g., drug use, delinquency). The general approach for examining intervention mechanisms uses mediation analysis (MacKinnon, 2008). LGM is well suited for conducting mediation tests in randomized prevention trials. A mediator, itself, may be conceptualized as a growth process, linking program assignment to a long-term, point-in-time outcome. Such a test represents a conditional latent growth curve model that includes both predictors (e.g., a program variable, covariates) and a consequence (i.e., a targeted outcome behavior) of growth factors, which are conceptualized as hypothesized mechanisms of effects. To illustrate, Spoth, Trudeau, Guyll, Shin, and Redmond (2009) used LGM to test mediation of the effects of universal family-focused substance use preventive interventions, including PDFY and the Iowa Strengthening Families Program (ISFP; now called the Strengthening Families Program 10–14), on problem substance use at age 21 years. They posited mediation via the average level (intercept) and average rate of change (slope) in adolescent substance use initiation and involvement. As expected, the family interventions reduced both the overall level and the rate of increase in substance use initiation and involvement over the teen years, a time in which substance initiation and use increase normatively. Such reductions were associated, in turn, with lower levels of selected problem substance use indicators in young adulthood, particularly for the more intensive ISFP.

Often, preventive interventions are expected to affect systematic changes in both targeted mechanisms and outcomes, requiring the concurrent modeling of multiple growth processes. Such modeling can be conducted via parallel process LGM (Willett & Sayer, 1996), which examines simultaneously changes in two or more outcomes over time. Parallel process LGM is a multivariate analytic technique that has been used to examine interrelationships among various developmental outcomes, including co-occurring drug use and delinquency, in adolescents and young adults (Curran, Stice, & Chassin, 1997; Farrell, Sullivan, Esposito, Meyer, & Valois, 2005; Fleming, Mason, Mazza, Abbott, & Catalano, 2008; Simons-Morton, Chen, Abroms, & Haynie, 2004). This technique can be used to test intervention effects on multiple correlated outcomes simultaneously, rather than conducting tests on separate outcomes, limited only by practical constraints of model complexity and sample size. Cheong, MacKinnon, and Khoo (2003) described a parallel process growth model for testing the mechanisms of preventive intervention effects. Mason et al. (2007) applied this technique to examine the spillover impact of PDFY on depressive symptoms among adolescents. They expected a previously established PDFY effect on a reduced linear increase in adolescent polydrug use (Mason et al., 2003) to mediate the effect of the intervention on adolescent depressive symptoms.

The parallel process mediational LGM is depicted in Figure 26.5. Preliminary unconditional LGM analyses supported the tenability of a two-factor latent growth curve model of polydrug use: (a) an intercept factor (Polydrug *I*) capturing a pretest level and (b) a slope factor (Polydrug *S*) capturing a linear increase in polydrug use over all six (nonequidistant) waves of adolescent data. Preliminary unconditional latent growth curve analyses further supported the tenability of a three-factor model of depressive symptoms: (a) a time-averaged intercept factor (*DEP I*) capturing the overall level, (b) a slope factor (*DEP S*) capturing linear increase, and (c) a quadratic factor (*DEP Q*) capturing a leveling off in depressive symptoms over the five waves of postintervention data.

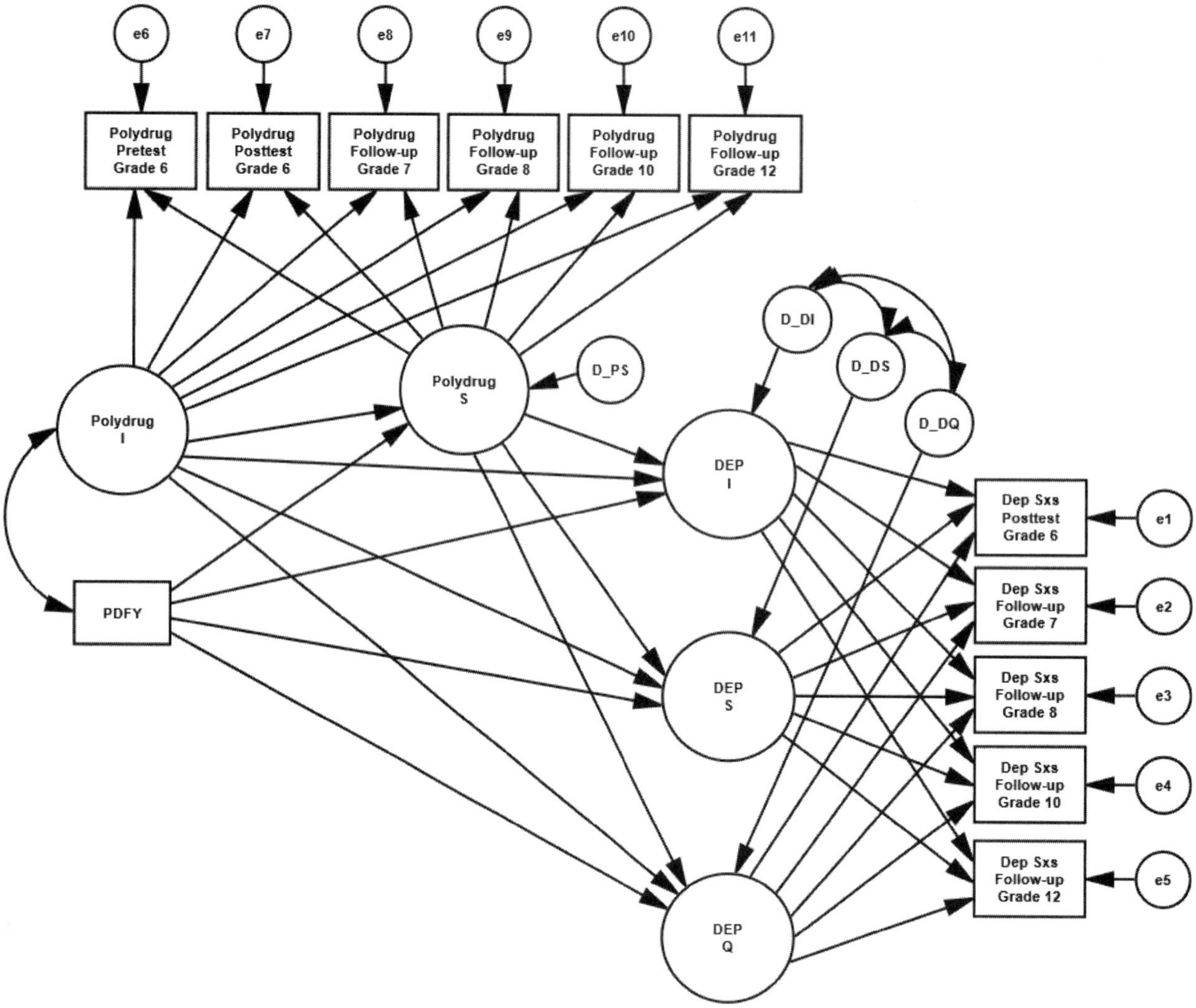

FIGURE 26.5. Latent growth curve model examining mediation of the PDFY effect on change in depressive symptoms through change in polydrug use. Fixed factor loadings were as follows: Polydrug use intercept factor (Polydrug *I*) = [1, 1, 1, 1, 1, 1]. Polydrug use slope factor (Polydrug *S*) = [0, 1, 2.33, 3.67, 5.67, 8.33]. Depressive symptoms intercept factor (*DEP I*) = [1, 1, 1, 1, 1]. Depressive symptoms slope factor (*Dep S*) = [−2.4, −1.4, −.4, 1.1, 3.1]. Depressive symptoms quadratic factor (*Dep Q*) = [5.76, 1.96, .16, 1.21, 9.61]. PDFY = Preparing for the Drug Free Years.

The model included the pretest level of depressive symptoms and other covariates as control variables. Mason et al. (2007) hypothesized that PDFY would slow the rate of increase in polydrug use (tested via the PDFY → Polydrug *S* path), which, in turn, would be associated with a lower overall level of depressive symptoms (tested via the PDFY → *DEP I* path), a slower rate of increase in depressive symptomatology (tested via the PDFY → *DEP S* path), and a faster rate of leveling off in this outcome (tested via the PDFY → *DEP Q* path). Results showed a negative path from PDFY to the polydrug use slope factor ($\beta = -.22$, $p < .05$). Furthermore, the polydrug use slope factor had a positive association with the depressive symptoms slope factor ($\beta = .19$, $p < .05$), suggesting that the PDFY-induced reduction in the rate of increase in polydrug use was associated, in turn, with a reduction in the natural rate of increase in depressive symptoms (Kessler et al., 2012).

The model depicted in Figure 26.5 has several limitations. Whereas intervention theories typically specify multiple mechanisms by which prevention programs are expected to have their effects, Mason et al. (2007) tested only one plausible mediator of the link between PDFY and adolescent depressive symptoms. Parallel process latent growth curve models can be used to test multiple mediating processes, again limited only by the feasibility of estimating a large number of parameters in increasingly complex models. The model depicted in Figure 26.5 also is limited because of the substantial overlap in the timing of both the mediator and the outcome. Cole and Maxwell (2003) noted the importance of conducting mediation tests in cases in which there is temporal ordering for the predictor, mediator, and outcome variables.

Questions About Differential Effects on Multidimensional Outcomes: Two-Part LGM

Complexity of drug use and delinquency outcomes. Drug use and delinquency are complex outcomes that are multidetermined, time-varying, and, often, multidimensional in nature. For example, adolescent and young adult alcohol involvement is composed of multiple dimensions, including onset, quantity and frequency of use, problem drinking, and alcohol use disorders (Auerbach & Collins, 2006; Mason & Spoth, 2012). These dimensions are not independent but are correlated both within and across time. This complexity suggests a range of relevant intervention targets for multicomponent drug use and delinquency preventive interventions. For example, alcohol use prevention programs may seek to encourage adolescents to delay alcohol initiation or to abstain from heavy drinking in social settings. The nature of drug use and delinquency outcomes also results in measured variables with complex and often nonnormal distributions. A challenge is to address the full potential of relevant intervention-related research questions while handling practical data complexities in applied drug use and delinquency prevention trials. LGM provides a way to meet this challenge.

Distributional assumptions in LGM. An assumption of LGM is that the distribution of errors for each indicator of the outcome in question is normally (Gaussian) distributed. Failure to meet this assumption can compromise regression coefficient estimation and result in biased confidence intervals. Various strategies are available to appropriately model continuous but nonnormally distributed as well as categorical variables in LGM (Lu, Poon, & Tsang, 2011). The assumption of normality often is not met in an examination of intervention effects on adolescent behaviors, such as alcohol use, that are being initiated or experimented with during this developmental period. This unique pattern of development suggests a "pile up" of zeros in the frequency distributions of alcohol use during adolescence, representing alcohol nonuse. If the duration of the study is sufficiently long to capture the onset of alcohol use for a relatively large portion of the sample, methods such as discrete-time survival analysis (Singer & Willett, 1993) may be appropriate to capture the "right censoring" in the outcome. This strategy is consistent with a research question that tests whether an intervention delayed onset of use, rather than testing whether an intervention changed a normative pattern of use over time. If the duration of the study is for a limited period in which many adolescents do not engage in this behavior, then other methods (e.g., zero-inflated and censored-normal models; Atkins, Baldwin, Zheng, Gallop, & Neighbors, 2013) may be needed. Longitudinal growth analyses that attempt to model change in these behaviors need to address the semicontinuous nature of these data.

Two-part LGM. One technique to examine longitudinal outcomes that have a large number of right-censored cases is the two-part latent growth curve model (Brown, Catalano, Fleming, Haggerty, & Abbott, 2005; Capaldi, Stoolmiller, Kim, & Yoerger, 2009). This model decomposes the distribution of the dependent variable into two separate, but correlated, parts (Manning, 1997; Olsen & Schafer, 2001). Part 1 represents a dichotomous indicator reflecting the occurrence or absence of a behavior (e.g., alcohol use vs. nonuse). Part 2 represents a Gaussian-distributed frequency of occurrence variable that is conditional upon a positive response to the behavior in question in Part 1 (e.g., frequency of alcohol use). Nonoccurrence of the outcome is represented as missing frequency data in model Part 2. This decomposition of the outcome variable allows for fitting different growth functions and for testing an intervention's impact on each of the two parts of the model. This is shown in Figure 26.6, in which adolescent alcohol use from Grades 6 to 10 is modeled by separate growth functions: one for annual alcohol use versus nonuse (Part 1) and one for the frequency of use conditional upon having used alcohol during that interval (Part 2).

The previous example is taken from an analysis of the efficacy of the Raising Healthy Children (RHC) intervention (Brown et al., 2005), which contains

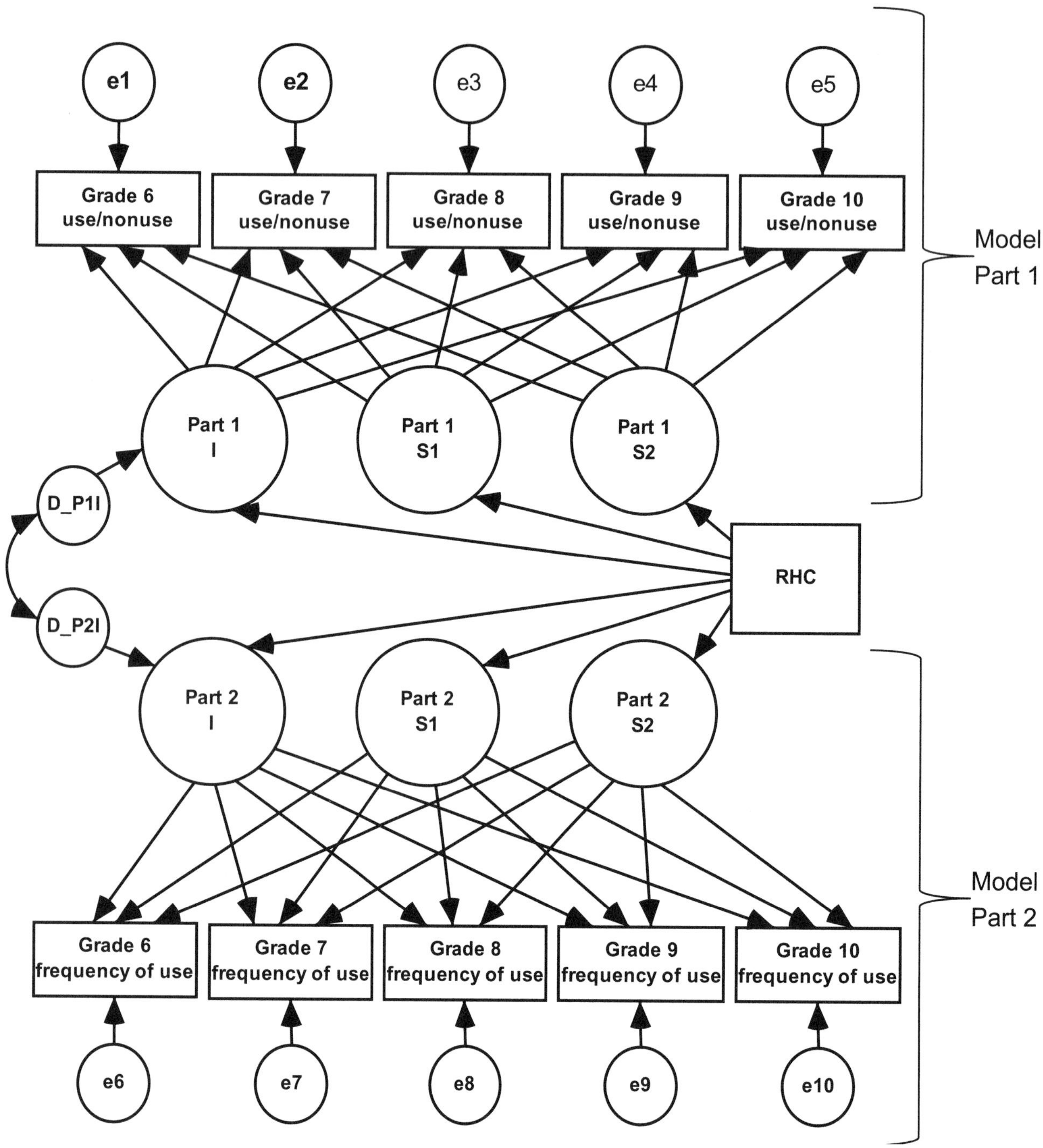

FIGURE 26.6. Path diagram for two-part latent growth curve model. Top portion of diagram depicts Part 1 of the model (i.e., alcohol use vs. nonuse); bottom portion depicts Part 2 of the model (i.e., frequency of alcohol use). Slope factors 1 (*S1*) and 2 (*S2*) correspond to piecewise linear growth factors (correlations between slope factors within each model part are omitted for clarity). I = intercept; RHC = Raising Healthy Children.

program components that target both drug use abstinence and harm reduction. Thus, use of the two-part modeling strategy for this intervention was both developmentally and conceptually appropriate. The choice to posit a two-part model was also practical and met the modeling assumptions for a semicontinuously distributed outcome. The two research questions underlying this analysis were (a) Has the intervention been efficacious in reducing adolescents' likelihood to use alcohol? and (b) Has the intervention been efficacious in reducing the frequency with which adolescent drinkers use alcohol?

Results of an unconditional two-part latent growth curve model of adolescent alcohol use indicated that the data were best modeled using a piecewise specification with an inflection in the linear patterns of growth in the frequency of alcohol use at Grade 8. The piecewise specification was used to model use versus nonuse as well. Intercept factors for model Parts 1 and 2 were centered at Grade 8, which corresponded to the time point at which participants thereafter would transition to high school. Although slope factors may or may not be correlated between model Parts 1 and 2, intercept factors for each part were correlated to model the potential conditionality of model Part 2 (frequency) upon model Part 1 (use). For the RHC alcohol use data, intercept factors were correlated at $r = .69$, indicating the positive conditionality of the higher frequency of alcohol use on the propensity to engage in alcohol use. Regressing growth factors on intervention status in the conditional two-part model indicated that the RHC intervention affected the rate of decline in the frequency of alcohol use from Grades 8 to 10 ($\beta = -.199$, $p < .05$), but the intervention was not efficacious in reducing the likelihood of engaging in alcohol use during this period. No significant intervention effect was found to reduce alcohol use or frequency of use during the earlier portion of the intervention from Grades 6 through 8.

The two-part latent growth curve model provides a novel approach to disentangle discontinuity in the distribution of outcomes that are being initiated or experimented with during adolescence. Aside from the practical benefit of meeting the statistical assumption of normality in error terms for indicator variables, the two-part latent growth curve model also has the advantage of addressing different research questions accentuating the two parts of the distribution. Caution, however, is advised because these research questions should be governed by theoretical considerations (e.g., abstinence vs. harm reduction foci of an intervention program) as opposed to a post hoc exploration of intervention effects in outcome data.

Review of Recent Advancements in LGM

Growth mixture modeling. The effects of preventive interventions may vary across different classes or groups of individuals. For example, evidence from several drug use and delinquency prevention trials suggests that individuals who are high risk at baseline tend to benefit more from intervention than their low-risk counterparts (Conduct Problems Prevention Research Group, 1999; Dolan, Kellam, Brown, & Werthamer-Larsson, 1993). A key assumption of LGM is that individual trajectories are drawn from a single population of growth curves; heterogeneity in the population is represented by the estimated variances of the growth factors (e.g., heterogeneity in initial starting points or rates of linear change; Figure 26.1). It is possible, however, that there are discrete subgroups of individuals, each with a different pattern of change in problem behavior. When the subgroups are known and measured, traditional multiple group LGM techniques can be used to test for group differences in patterns, predictors, and consequences of change. Often, however, developmental subgroups are unknown or are unobservable, in which case growth mixture modeling (GMM) may be appropriate. GMM is a person-centered, rather than variable-centered, approach that treats heterogeneity in growth patterns as resulting from underlying, unobserved classes or subpopulations characterized by different trajectories. For example, GMM could be used to identify a latent class of individuals that do not engage in substance use during the study period (i.e., "structural zeroes"), which can be helpful in modeling semicontinuous or right-censored distributions.

GMMs and related techniques have been implemented in studies of the developmental etiology of drug use and delinquency (Colder et al., 2001; Wiesner & Windle, 2004). Muthén et al. (2002)

described and illustrated general GMMs for randomized preventive interventions. These models are concerned primarily with the question of whether or not there are differential intervention effects across latent trajectory classes, but these models also can be used to determine the degree to which interventions generate changes in trajectory class membership. Increasingly, GMMs are being applied to data from drug use and delinquency prevention trials (Connell, Dishion, & Deater-Deckard, 2006; Liu, Hedeker, Segawa, & Flay, 2010; Petras et al., 2008). For example, Liu et al. (2010) used GMM within the context of the Aban Aya Youth Project to examine differential intervention effects of social development and community empowerment health promotion programs on drug use for urban minority youth. Results showed that the program had a favorable effect on a class of rapidly increasing users but not on a class of slowly increasing uses who started with initially high levels of drug use. This illustrates the potential for differential intervention effects across latent trajectory groups.

Further extensions of GMM include models for examining latent trajectory class membership as a mediator of intervention effects on distal outcomes and models for considering nonparticipation in intervention studies (Connell, Dishion, Yasui, & Kavanagh, 2007; Jo & Muthén, 2003). Clearly, GMM provides a useful analytic tool for addressing critical questions resulting from longitudinal randomized prevention trials; however, as a more data-driven (vs. confirmatory) technique, care is required in its use (Bauer, 2007; Bauer & Curran, 2003).

Shared-parameters models. To this point, LGM has been shown to provide an approach for addressing research questions related to an examination of individual differences in rates of change over time, such as in tests of diverging trajectories for intervention versus control participants in RCTs. Although critically important for the field, these are not the only questions of interest to drug use and delinquency prevention researchers. Additional questions, such as those related to duration of a state or condition, are relevant. For example, a primary goal of most drug use preventive interventions is to delay the onset of drug use (e.g., initiation of alcohol use). The ability to test these questions calls for alternative longitudinal data analytic techniques, such as survival analysis mentioned earlier. The underlying logic models of many preventive interventions suggest a host of research questions about interrelationships among multiple outcomes, where each outcome can manifest itself in a different form of change over time, such as continuous growth (e.g., in parental rules about drug use) or duration to onset (e.g., in adolescent drug involvement). Traditionally, these questions have been addressed independently in separate analyses, but recent developments in a new class of "shared-parameters" models (Guo & Carlin, 2004; McArdle, Small, Bäckman, & Fratiglioni, 2005) that blend growth and survival analytic techniques permit a more comprehensive examination of linked hypotheses and help deal with the problem of separately examining correlated outcomes.

McArdle et al. (2005) described a class of shared-parameters models applied to an examination of early predictors of the onset of Alzheimer's disease in a longitudinal study of aging. In one primary analysis, LGM and the survival model were estimated jointly, specifying latent growth factors capturing level and change in a measure of cognitive capacity as predictors of the age of onset of Alzheimer's disease. Although we are unaware of existing substantive applications to preventive interventions, the growth-to-onset model used by McArdle et al. has relevance for drug use and delinquency prevention researchers. For example, the model might be extended to test hypothesized mediating pathways leading from family-focused drug use prevention to higher levels of and faster rates of increases in parental rules about drug use postintervention and, in turn, to delayed onset of adolescent drug use.

CONCLUSION

LGM is a useful tool for drug use and delinquency researchers to conceptualize and evaluate the effects of randomized preventive interventions. Indeed, the definition of a prevention effect suggests the need for a statistical model that describes and explains individual differences in patterns of change in risk and protective factors as well as problem and prosocial behaviors. The expectation is that prevention programming will alter the natural trajectory of change in targeted intervention outcomes. LGM permits an examination of nuanced questions about prevention effects (e.g., mediation, differential impact) because it can accommodate both predictors and consequences of growth processes as well as model multiple growth processes and multidimensional outcomes simultaneously. Generalizations of LGM that model unobserved trajectory subgroups and permit an examination of growth in relation to alternative types of change, such as time to onset, further extend the potential for addressing emerging questions of interest to prevention science.

Other generalizations of the LGM approach fall beyond the scope of this chapter. For example, this chapter did not discuss second-order latent growth curve models (Chan, 1998; Hancock, Kuo, & Lawrence, 2001; Sayer & Cumsille, 2001), in which growth factor indicators are represented as time-specific, multiple-indicator latent variables to correct for measurement error in the repeated measures and to model hypothesized relationships among multiple correlated measures simultaneously. Also, the chapter did not discuss multilevel LGM for situations in which there are higher order levels of nesting in the data (e.g., time nested within students nested within schools; Curran & Bauer, 2011). Often, larger contextual effects have not been considered or incorporated into the LGM. The extension of the LGM to a multilevel framework provides a way to address this gap, accounting for contextual effects by explicitly modeling the hierarchical structure of the data. Finally, we did not review recent developments in the specification of advanced growth curve models, such as latent difference score modeling (McArdle, 2001) and autoregressive latent trajectory analysis (Bollen & Curran, 2004), which are being used to examine lead-lag and reciprocal relations in multiple outcomes, such as co-occurring adolescent drug use and delinquency, over time.

The many generalizations of LGM further illustrate that researchers can be well equipped to conduct tests of the underlying theories of their preventive interventions. Moreover, LGM brings additional, more practical benefits, such as enhanced statistical power compared with traditional methods used to analyze longitudinal data (Fan, 2003; Muthén & Curran, 1997). LGM also can easily accommodate advanced missing data estimation techniques, such as full information maximum likelihood estimation.

Cautionary Notes

Like any flexible analytic technique, LGM must be used with careful consideration. We have emphasized the importance of choosing LGM based on theory-driven hypotheses and have encouraged thinking carefully about how specific types of questions can be addressed with precise model specifications (Ferrer & McArdle, 2010). LGM often is applied without taking steps to define a clear theory of change. Giving sufficient attention to these critical initial steps places the analyst on the way to appropriate application of LGM to questions that can advance the field of drug use and delinquency prevention research.

Once LGM is selected as an analytic technique, it is important to proceed in a systematic model-building process that begins with descriptive statistics and basic analyses, such as unconditional latent growth curve models, and then proceeds to more complex model specifications. During this process, a tension can emerge between staying true to the model that best matches the guiding theory versus making modifications that, although not hypothesized, are logical and result in the best fitting model. Giving sole priority to fitting a growth model to the data can result in a model that estimates parameters that are irrelevant to the research questions. For example, many tests of interventions are concerned with whether an intervention affected a linear increase or decrease in targeted outcomes (i.e., intervention effects on a slope factor) and may have no clear hypotheses about acceleration or deceleration (i.e., intervention effects on a quadratic factor). Thus, a three-factor model of quadratic growth should be used cautiously, given that it will lead to tests of relations that are exploratory, even though the specified model might provide the best fit to the data.

There are no simple solutions to this modeling tension. In some circumstances, it may be important to settle on a model that fits less well than alternatives but that provides the precise test of interest. In other circumstances, unanticipated model modifications might improve fit and point toward necessary theoretical revisions. When this is the case, it remains vital to proceed from a well-articulated theory of change and to document model-building decisions that diverge from theory, thereby making it evident which analyses are confirmatory and which are exploratory.

Future Directions

Advancements in LGM are progressing rapidly. What are needed now are more substantive applications, including advanced generalizations of latent growth curve models, in the drug use and delinquency prevention research literature. As noted, one goal of this chapter was to illustrate to researchers the potential of LGM to address research questions regarding change over time. The tension between theory-guided model specification and model modification indicates that advancements in developmental and prevention theories also are needed. Such theories can now be articulated with a high degree of specificity, with the knowledge that analytic tools exist to provide precise tests of the interrelationships among variables of interest. Current knowledge and practice in LGM, combined with anticipated future advancements, make for an exciting time in drug use and delinquency prevention research. We hope it is evident that findings from LGM analyses can advance the field by providing a powerful and flexible tool to inform both intervention theory and prevention practice.

References

Atkins, D. C., Baldwin, S. A., Zheng, C., Gallop, R. J., & Neighbors, C. (2013). A tutorial on count regression and zero-altered count models for longitudinal substance use data. *Psychology of Addictive Behaviors*, *27*, 166–177. doi:10.1037/a0029508

Auerbach, K. J., & Collins, L. M. (2006). A multidimensional developmental model of alcohol use during emerging adulthood. *Journal of Studies on Alcohol*, *67*, 917–925.

Bauer, D. J. (2007). 2004 Cattel award address: Observations on the use of growth mixture models in psychological research. *Multivariate Behavioral Research*, *42*, 757–786. doi:10.1080/00273170701710338

Bauer, D. J., & Curran, P. J. (2003). Distributional assumptions of growth mixture models: Implications for overextraction of latent trajectory classes. *Psychological Methods*, *8*, 338–363. doi:10.1037/1082-989X.8.3.338

Bollen, K. A., & Curran, P. J. (2004). Autoregressive latent trajectory (ALT) models: A synthesis of two traditions. *Sociological Methods and Research*, *32*, 336–383. doi:10.1177/0049124103260222

Bollen, K. A., & Curran, P. J. (2006). *Latent curve models: A structural equation perspective*. Hoboken, NJ: Wiley.

Brody, G. H., Murry, V. M., Gerrard, M., Gibbons, F. X., McNair, L., Brown, A. C., . . . Chen, Y. F. (2006). The strong African American families program: Prevention of youths' high-risk behavior and a test of a model of change. *Journal of Family Psychology*, *20*, 1–11. doi:10.1037/0893-3200.20.1.1

Brown, E. C., Catalano, R. F., Fleming, C. B., Haggerty, K. P., & Abbott, R. D. (2005). Adolescent substance use outcomes in the Raising Healthy Children Project: A two-part latent growth curve analysis. *Journal of Consulting and Clinical Psychology*, *73*, 699–710. doi:10.1037/0022-006X.73.4.699

Capaldi, D. M., Stoolmiller, M., Kim, H. K., & Yoerger, K. (2009). Growth in alcohol use in at-risk adolescent boys: Two-part random effects prediction models. *Drug and Alcohol Dependence*, *105*, 109–117. doi:10.1016/j.drugalcdep.2009.06.013

Chan, D. (1998). The conceptualization and analysis of change over time: An integrative approach incorporating longitudinal mean and covariance structures analysis (LMACS) and multiple indicator latent growth modeling (MLGM). *Organizational Research Methods*, *1*, 421–483. doi:10.1177/109442819814004

Cheong, J., MacKinnon, D. P., & Khoo, S. T. (2003). Investigation of mediational processes using parallel process latent growth curve modeling. *Structural Equation Modeling*, *10*, 238–262. doi:10.1207/S15328007SEM1002_5

Colder, C. R., Mehta, P., Balanda, K., Campbell, R. T., Mayhew, K., Stanton, W. R., . . . Flay, B. R. (2001). Identifying trajectories of adolescent smoking: An application of latent growth mixture modeling. *Health Psychology*, *20*, 127–135. doi:10.1037/0278-6133.20.2.127

Cole, D. A., & Maxwell, S. E. (2003). Testing mediational models with longitudinal data: Questions and tips in the use of structural equation modeling. *Journal of Abnormal Psychology*, *112*, 558–577. doi:10.1037/0021-843X.112.4.558

Collins, L. M., & Graham, J. W. (2002). The effect of the timing and spacing of observations in longitudinal studies of tobacco and other drug use: Temporal design considerations. *Drug and Alcohol Dependence*, *68*, 85–96. doi:10.1016/S0376-8716(02)00217-X

Conduct Problems Prevention Research Group. (1999). Initial impact of the Fast Track prevention trial for conduct problems: I. The high-risk sample. *Journal of Consulting and Clinical Psychology*, *67*, 631–647. doi:10.1037/0022-006X.67.5.631

Connell, A. M., Dishion, T. J., & Deater-Deckard, K. (2006). Variable- and person-centered approaches to the analysis of early adolescent substance use: Linking peer, family, and intervention effects with developmental trajectories. *Merrill-Palmer Quarterly*, *52*, 421–448. doi:10.1353/mpq.2006.0025

Connell, A. M., Dishion, T. J., Yasui, M., & Kavanagh, K. (2007). An adaptive approach to family intervention: Linking engagement in family-centered intervention to reductions in adolescent problem behavior. *Journal of Consulting and Clinical Psychology*, *75*, 568–579. doi:10.1037/0022-006X.75.4.568

Cortes, R. C., Fleming, C. B., Mason, W. A., & Catalano, R. F. (2009). Risk factors linking maternal depressed mood to growth in adolescent substance use. *Journal of Emotional and Behavioral Disorders*, *17*, 49–64. doi:10.1177/1063426608321690

Curran, P. J., & Bauer, D. J. (2011). The disaggregation of within-person and between-person effects in longitudinal models of change. *Annual Review of Psychology*, *62*, 583–619. doi:10.1146/annurev.psych.093008.100356

Curran, P. J., Stice, E., & Chassin, L. (1997). The relation between adolescent alcohol use and peer alcohol use: A longitudinal random coefficients model. *Journal of Consulting and Clinical Psychology*, *65*, 130–140. doi:10.1037/0022-006X.65.1.130

Del Boca, F. K., Darkes, J., Greenbaum, P. E., & Goldman, M. S. (2004). Up close and personal: Temporal variability in the drinking of individual college students during their first year. *Journal of Consulting and Clinical Psychology*, *72*, 155–164. doi:10.1037/0022-006X.72.2.155

Dolan, L. J., Kellam, S. G., Brown, C. H., & Werthamer-Larsson, L. (1993). The short-term impact of two classroom-based preventive interventions on aggressive and shy behaviors and poor achievement. *Journal of Applied Developmental Psychology*, *14*, 317–345. doi:10.1016/0193-3973(93)90013-L

Donovan, J. E., & Jessor, R. (1985). Structure of problem behavior in adolescence and young adulthood. *Journal of Consulting and Clinical Psychology*, *53*, 890–904. doi:10.1037/0022-006X.53.6.890

Duncan, T. E., Duncan, S. C., & Strycker, L. A. (2006). *An introduction to latent variable growth curve modeling: Concepts, issues, and applications* (2nd ed.). Mahwah, NJ: Erlbaum.

Durlak, J. A. (1998). Common risk and protective factors in successful prevention programs. *American Journal of Orthopsychiatry*, *68*, 512–520. doi:10.1037/h0080360

Fan, X. (2003). Power of latent growth modeling for detecting group differences in linear growth trajectory parameters. *Structural Equation Modeling*, *10*, 380–400. doi:10.1207/S15328007SEM1003_3

Farrell, A. D., Sullivan, T. N., Esposito, L. E., Meyer, A. L., & Valois, R. F. (2005). A latent growth curve analysis of the structure of aggression, drug use, and delinquent behaviors and their interrelations over time in urban and rural adolescents. *Journal of Research on Adolescence*, *15*, 179–204. doi:10.1111/j.1532-7795.2005.00091.x

Ferrer, E., & McArdle, J. J. (2010). Longitudinal modeling of developmental changes in psychological research. *Current Directions in Psychological Science*, *19*, 149–154. doi:10.1177/0963721410370300

Fleming, C. B., Harachi, T. W., Cortes, R. C., Abbott, R. D., & Catalano, R. F. (2004). Level and change in reading scores and attention problems during elementary school as predictors of problem behavior in middle school. *Journal of Emotional and Behavioral Disorders*, *12*, 130–144. doi:10.1177/10634266040120030101

Fleming, C. B., Mason, W. A., Mazza, J. J., Abbott, R. D., & Catalano, R. F. (2008). Latent growth modeling of the relationship between depressive symptoms and substance use during adolescence. *Psychology of Addictive Behaviors*, *22*, 186–197. doi:10.1037/0893-164X.22.2.186

Foxcroft, D. R., Ireland, D., Lister-Sharp, D. J., Breen, R., & Lowe, G. (2003). Longer-term primary prevention for alcohol misuse in young people: A systematic review. *Addiction*, *98*, 397–411. doi:10.1046/j.1360-0443.2003.00355.x

Gillham, J. E., Shatté, A. J., & Freres, D. R. (2000). Preventing depression: A review of cognitive-behavioral and family interventions. *Applied and Preventive Psychology*, *9*, 63–88. doi:10.1016/S0962-1849(00)80007-4

Guo, X., & Carlin, B. P. (2004). Separate and joint modeling of longitudinal and event time data using standard computer packages. *American Statistician*, *58*, 16–24. doi:10.1198/0003130042854

Hancock, G. R., Kuo, W. L., & Lawrence, F. R. (2001). An illustration of second-order latent growth models. *Structural Equation Modeling*, *8*, 470–489. doi:10.1207/S15328007SEM0803_7

Horowitz, J. L., & Garber, J. (2006). The prevention of depressive symptoms in children and adolescents: A meta-analytic review. *Journal of Consulting and Clinical Psychology*, *74*, 401–415. doi:10.1037/0022-006X.74.3.401

Hu, L., & Bentler, P. M. (1999). Cutoff criteria for fit indexes in covariance structure analysis: Conventional criteria versus new alternatives. *Structural Equation Modeling, 6*, 1–55. doi:10.1080/10705519909540118

Jo, B., & Muthén, B. O. (2003). Longitudinal studies with intervention and noncompliance: Estimation of causal effects in growth mixture modeling. In S. P. Reise & N. Duan (Eds.), *Multilevel modeling: Methodological advances, issues, and applications* (pp. 112–139). Mahwah, NJ: Erlbaum.

Johnston, L. D., O'Malley, P. M., Bachman, J. G., & Schulenberg, J. E. (2013). *Monitoring the Future national survey results on drug use, 1975–2012: Vol. 2. College students and adults ages 19–50.* Ann Arbor: University of Michigan.

Kessler, R. C., Avenevoli, S., Costello, E. J., Georgiades, K., Green, J. G., Gruber, M. J., . . . Merikangas, K. R. (2012). Prevalence, persistence, and sociodemographic correlates of DSM-IV disorders in the National Comorbidity Survey Replication Adolescent Supplement. *Archives of General Psychiatry, 69*, 372–380. doi:10.1001/archgenpsychiatry.2011.160

Kessler, R. C., Berglund, P., Demler, O., Jin, R., Merikangas, K. R., & Walters, E. E. (2005). Lifetime prevalence and age-of-onset distributions of DSM-IV disorders in the National Comorbidity Survey Replication. *Archives of General Psychiatry, 62*, 593–602. doi:10.1001/archpsyc.62.6.593

Liu, L. C., Hedeker, D., Segawa, E., & Flay, B. R. (2010). Evaluation of longitudinal intervention effects: An example of latent growth mixture models for ordinal drug-use outcomes. *Journal of Drug Issues, 40*, 27–43. doi:10.1177/002204261004000103

Loeber, R., Farrington, D. P., Stouthamer-Loeber, M., Moffitt, T. E., Caspi, A., White, H. R., Wei, E. H., & Beyers, J. M. (2003). The development of male offending: Key findings from fourteen years of the Pittsburgh Youth Study. In T. P. Thornberry & M. D. Krohn (Eds.), *Taking stock of delinquency: An overview of findings from contemporary longitudinal studies* (pp. 93–136). New York, NY: Kluwer Academic/Plenum.

Lu, T. Y., Poon, W. Y., & Tsang, Y. F. (2011). Latent growth curve modeling for longitudinal ordinal responses with applications. *Computational Statistics and Data Analysis, 55*, 1488–1497. doi:10.1016/j.csda.2010.10.014

MacKinnon, D. P. (2008). *Introduction to statistical mediation analysis.* New York, NY: Taylor & Francis.

Manning, W. G. (1997). Alternative econometric models of alcohol demand. In K. J. Bryant, M. Windle, & S. G. West (Eds.), *The science of prevention: Methodological advances from alcohol and substance abuse research* (pp. 101–121). Washington, DC: American Psychological Association.

Mason, W. A., Kosterman, R., Hawkins, J. D., Haggerty, K. P., & Spoth, R. L. (2003). Reducing adolescents' growth in substance use and delinquency: Randomized trial effects of a parent-training prevention intervention. *Prevention Science, 4*, 203–212. doi:10.1023/A:1024653923780

Mason, W. A., Kosterman, R., Hawkins, J. D., Haggerty, K. P., Spoth, R. L., & Redmond, C. (2007). Influence of a family-focused substance use preventive intervention on growth in adolescent depressive symptoms. *Journal of Research on Adolescence, 17*, 541–564. doi:10.1111/j.1532-7795.2007.00534.x

Mason, W. A., & Spoth, R. L. (2012). Sequence of alcohol involvement from early onset to young adult alcohol abuse: Differential prediction and moderation by family-focused preventive intervention. *Addiction, 107*, 2137–2148. doi:10.1111/j.1360-0443.2012.03987.x

McArdle, J. J. (2001). A latent difference score approach to longitudinal dynamic structural analyses. In R. Cudeck, S. du Toit, & D. Sorbom (Eds.), *Structural equation modeling: Present and future* (pp. 342–380). Lincolnwood, IL: Scientific Software International.

McArdle, J. J., & Epstein, D. (1987). Latent growth curves within developmental structural equation models. *Child Development, 58*, 110–133. doi:10.2307/1130295

McArdle, J. J., Small, B. J., Bäckman, L., & Fratiglioni, L. (2005). Longitudinal models of growth and survival applied to the early detection of Alzheimer's disease. *Journal of Geriatric Psychiatry and Neurology, 18*, 234–241. doi:10.1177/0891988705281879

Meredith, W., & Tisak, J. (1990). Latent curve analysis. *Psychometrika, 55*, 107–122. doi:10.1007/BF02294746

Muthén, B., Brown, C. H., Masyn, K., Jo, B., Khoo, S. T., Yang, C. C., . . . Liao, J. (2002). General growth mixture modeling for randomized preventive interventions. *Biostatistics, 3*, 459–475. doi:10.1093/biostatistics/3.4.459

Muthén, B. O., & Curran, P. J. (1997). General longitudinal modeling of individual differences in experimental designs: A latent variable framework for analysis and power estimation. *Psychological Methods, 2*, 371–402. doi:10.1037/1082-989X.2.4.371

Olsen, M. K., & Schafer, J. L. (2001). A two-part random-effects model for semicontinuous longitudinal data. *Journal of the American Statistical Association, 96*, 730–745. doi:10.1198/016214501753168389

Park, J., Kosterman, R., Hawkins, J. D., Haggerty, K. P., Duncan, T. E., Duncan, S. C., & Spoth, R. (2000). Effects of the "Preparing for the Drug Free Years" curriculum on growth in alcohol use and risk for alcohol use in early adolescence. *Prevention Science, 1*, 125–138. doi:10.1023/A:1010021205638

Petras, H., Kellam, S. G., Brown, C. H., Muthén, B. O., Ialongo, N. S., & Poduska, J. M. (2008).

Developmental epidemiological courses leading to antisocial personality disorder and violent and criminal behavior: Effects by young adulthood of a universal preventive intervention in first- and second-grade classrooms. *Drug and Alcohol Dependence, 95*, S45–S59. doi:10.1016/j.drugalcdep.2007.10.015

Piquero, A. R., Farrington, D. P., Welsh, B. C., Tremblay, R., & Jennings, W. G. (2009). Effects of early family/parent training programs on antisocial behavior and delinquency. *Journal of Experimental Criminology, 5*, 83–120. doi:10.1007/s11292-009-9072-x

Preacher, K. J., Wichman, A. L., MacCallum, R. C., & Briggs, N. E. (2008). *Latent growth curve modeling.* Thousand Oaks, CA: Sage.

Raudenbush, S. W., & Bryk, A. S. (2002). *Hierarchical linear models: Applications and data analysis methods* (2nd ed.). Thousand Oaks, CA: Sage.

Sayer, A. G., & Cumsille, P. E. (2001). Second-order latent growth models. In L. M. Collins & A. G. Sayer (Eds.), *New methods for the analysis of change* (pp. 179–200). Washington, DC: American Psychological Association. doi:10.1037/10409-006

Scheier, L. M., & Grenard, J. L. (2010). Influence of a nationwide social marketing campaign on adolescent drug use. *Journal of Health Communication, 15*, 240–271. doi:10.1080/10810731003686580

Simons-Morton, B., Chen, R., Abroms, L., & Haynie, D. L. (2004). Latent growth curve analyses of peer and parent influences on smoking progression among early adolescents. *Health Psychology, 23*, 612–621. doi:10.1037/0278-6133.23.6.612

Singer, J. D., & Willett, J. B. (1993). It's about time: Using discrete-time survival analysis to study duration and the timing of events. *Journal of Educational Statistics, 18*, 155–195. doi:10.2307/1165085

Spoth, R., Trudeau, L., Guyll, M., Shin, C., & Redmond, C. (2009). Universal intervention effects on substance use among young adults mediated by delayed adolescent substance initiation. *Journal of Consulting and Clinical Psychology, 77*, 620–632. doi:10.1037/a0016029

Stoolmiller, M. (1995). Using latent growth curve models to study developmental processes. In J. M. Gottman (Ed.), *The analysis of change* (pp. 103–138). Mahwah, NJ: Erlbaum.

Taylor, B. J., Graham, J. W., Cumsille, P., & Hansen, W. B. (2000). Modeling prevention program effects on growth in substance use: Analysis of five years of data from the Adolescent Alcohol Prevention Trial. *Prevention Science, 1*, 183–197. doi:10.1023/A:1026547128209

Tobler, N. S., Roona, M. R., Ochshorn, P., Marshall, D. G., Streke, A. V., & Stackpole, K. M. (2000). School-based adolescent drug prevention programs: 1998 meta-analysis. *Journal of Primary Prevention, 20*, 275–336. doi:10.1023/A:1021314704811

Wiesner, M., & Windle, M. (2004). Assessing covariates of adolescent delinquency trajectories: A latent growth mixture modeling approach. *Journal of Youth and Adolescence, 33*, 431–442. doi:10.1023/B:JOYO.0000037635.06937.13

Willett, J. B., & Sayer, A. G. (1996). Cross-domain analysis of change overtime: Combining growth modeling and covariance structure analysis. In G. A. Marcoulides & R. E. Schumacker (Eds.), *Advanced structural equation modeling. Issues and techniques* (pp. 125–157). Mahwah, NJ: Erlbaum.

Windle, M. (2000). A latent growth curve model of delinquent activity among adolescents. *Applied Developmental Science, 4*, 193–207. doi:10.1207/S1532480XADS0404_2

Wu, W., West, S. G., & Taylor, A. B. (2009). Evaluating model fit for growth curve models: Integration of fit indices from SEM and MLM frameworks. *Psychological Methods, 14*, 183–201. doi:10.1037/a0015858

Part IX

DISSEMINATION OF BEST PRACTICES

CHAPTER 27

PROMOTING THE POSTFUNDING SUSTAINABILITY OF EVIDENCE-BASED SUBSTANCE ABUSE INTERVENTIONS THROUGH RESEARCH AND PRACTICE

Melissa K. Tibbits

This chapter presents information about the factors at each stage of the Rogers (2003) diffusion of innovations theory that affect the postfunding sustainability of evidence-based substance abuse interventions. As a whole, the extant literature suggests that having an effective dissemination system, allowing adequate time for planning and enhancing community readiness, implementing interventions with fidelity, and engaging in ongoing sustainability planning are important predictors of postfunding sustainability. Topics for future research relevant to the diffusion and long-term sustainability of evidence-based also are discussed. Prevention science has provided strong evidence that substance abuse is preventable and treatable. Numerous substance abuse interventions have been developed, proven to be effective through rigorous research trials, and deemed to be evidence based by organizations such as the Substance Abuse and Mental Health Services Administration. As a result, evidence-based substance abuse interventions are available for numerous populations and settings.

Despite the effectiveness and availability of substance abuse interventions, substance abuse continues to be a significant problem in the United States. Approximately 17.7 million Americans age 12 or older (7% of the population) were alcohol dependent or alcohol abusers in 2012, and an additional 4.3 million Americans were marijuana dependent or marijuana abusers (National Institute on Drug Abuse, 2014). Although many factors contribute to the persistence of substance abuse in the United States, one known issue is that evidence-based interventions (EBIs) focused on substance abuse prevention and treatment are not commonly adopted by communities. Furthermore, when EBIs are adopted, many communities face challenges in implementing and sustaining them in the long term under real-world conditions (e.g., without ongoing technical assistance and training; Hallfors & Godette, 2002; Rohrbach, Grana, Sussman, & Valente, 2006). For the purpose of this chapter, *sustainability* is defined as the long-term continuation of intervention activities (Pluye, Potvin, & Denis, 2004).

I would like to thank Brian Bumbarger, Dr. Linda Caldwell, Dr. Mark Greenberg, and Dr. Edward Smith for providing mentorship and training that has greatly enhanced my understanding of the issues that emerge when communities adopt, implement, and attempt to sustain evidence-based interventions.

http://dx.doi.org/10.1037/14550-028
Handbook of Adolescent Drug Use Prevention: Research, Intervention Strategies, and Practice, L. M. Scheier (Editor)

Given that EBIs require financial resources for staff time, training, and intervention materials, many communities are not able to implement an EBI unless they initially receive funding from federal or local agencies. This has led some researchers to speculate that funding is one of the most important factors influencing the long-term sustainability of EBIs and to advocate for the formulation of long-term funding plans during the early stages of intervention adoption (Elias, Zins, Graczyk, & Weissburg, 2003; Swisher, 2000).

The sustainability of EBIs after the conclusion of the original funding period (i.e., postfunding) has been examined in a few large EBI diffusion trials (Elliott & Mihalic, 2004; Fagan, Hanson, Briney, & Hawkins, 2012; Tibbits, Bumbarger, Kyler, & Perkins, 2010). The findings from these studies suggest that postfunding sustainability is possible under the right circumstances. For example, Tibbits and colleagues (2010) found that 44% of communities were still implementing EBIs 5 years postfunding. Additionally, many communities were able to secure additional funding to support their chosen EBIs.

The purpose of this chapter is to further discuss a wide range of factors known to support and hinder postfunding sustainability. The discussion is framed within the four stages of the Rogers (2003) diffusion of innovations theory: dissemination, adoption, implementation, and maintenance/sustainability. I comment on the rationale for using Rogers's theory, its applicability to theories of substance abuse prevention, and its utility as a broad overarching theoretical framework to examine the sustainability of substance abuse prevention.

DIFFUSION OF INNOVATIONS

Substance abuse researchers have developed and utilized several theories to describe and better understand the diffusion and subsequent sustainability of EBIs (Rohrbach et al., 2006). The most commonly cited framework is diffusion of innovations (Rogers, 2003). This framework suggests that diffusion of an EBI is a four-stage process: (a) dissemination (public availability and marketing of the EBI); (b) adoption (agreement to use the EBI); (c) implementation (actual use of the EBI), and (d) maintenance/sustainability (continued use of the EBI over time).

DISSEMINATION

As previously noted, *dissemination* refers to the process of making EBI publicly available and marketing EBI to communities. The EBI dissemination process generally includes several steps. First, standardized, professionally designed materials such as lesson plans, scripts, and activities must be created. Second, a distribution method must be developed to market and allow other communities to purchase the EBI. Third, a system for training and technical assistance must be established to ensure that communities receive the resources necessary to achieve a high level of implementation fidelity. *Implementation fidelity* is defined as delivering an EBI the way it was designed by the developer (i.e., replicating the lesson plans and activities presented in the standardized materials).

Currently, there is a dearth of research on characteristics of the dissemination process that may contribute to the sustainability of EBIs. At a minimum, developer capacity to provide high-quality, standardized materials and to coordinate ongoing training and technical assistance should be examined (Botvin & Griffin, 2010). This is particularly important given that many EBIs were developed and tested by academicians who had little experience with distributing the interventions on a wide scale and that testing and commercialization of prevention programs are two dramatically different areas of expertise.

Many different methods of disseminating EBIs have been developed. Most often, EBI developers initially distribute their interventions and offer their training and technical assistance services directly through their home institutions. One example is Project Towards No Drug Abuse (Sussman, Dent, & Stacy, 2002), which is distributed through the University of Southern California.

In other cases, EBI materials are refined and distributed by professional curricula companies, but training and technical assistance are provided directly by EBI developers. Examples include Life Skills Training (Botvin & Griffin, 2004), which is distributed through National Health Promotion Associates, and Project Towards No Tobacco Use (Dent et al., 1995), which is distributed by ETR.

Less commonly, EBI developers form organizations with numerous staff devoted to dissemination. Examples include the Nurse-Family Partnership (Eckenrode et al., 2010) National Service Office, The Incredible Years (Webster-Stratton & Reid, 2008) organization, and the Center for Communities That Care (Fagan et al., 2012; also see Chapter 19, this handbook) at the University of Washington. These organizations all focus on providing training and technical assistance to support the adoption and high-quality implementation of their EBI.

These different dissemination methods highlight the fact that there are many inconsistencies in the dissemination process between different EBI. The Substance Abuse and Mental Health Administration's National Registry of Evidence-Based Programs and Practices (http://www.nrepp.samhsa.gov) quantifies the differences in dissemination with Readiness for Dissemination scores ranging from 0 (*low readiness*) to 4 (*high readiness*). Consequently, the ability of potential EBI adopters to acquire standardized intervention materials, training, and technical assistance varies substantially for different EBIs.

These inconsistencies in the dissemination process have several implications for communities' ability to adopt, implement, and ultimately sustain EBIs. Some communities, particularly those without access to a prevention scientist, may have limited knowledge of the full range of EBIs available and may experience difficulty in adopting and implementing their chosen EBIs with fidelity. These implementation difficulties may be exacerbated postfunding, given fewer resources to coordinate and pay for continued technical assistance and training needed to resolve issues such as staff turnover. Given the potential long-term effects of the dissemination stage of the diffusion of innovations model, more attention should be focused on the dissemination processes that promote EBI adoption, implementation, and sustainability.

ADOPTION

Unlike the case for dissemination, there is substantial literature about the role of the adoption phase in the sustainability of EBIs. A discussion of research on motivation for adopting EBI and community readiness for adoption follows.

Motivation for Adopting EBI

Given that a large percentage of communities do not implement EBIs, it is important to consider the factors that motivate the adoption of EBI. Some communities have well-functioning substance abuse coalitions that include partners from a variety of sectors and fields, including prevention science. In these cases, formal needs assessments often are used to analyze and interpret data to determine community needs, then to adopt and implement appropriate EBIs to address those needs. Examples of this model for EBI adoption include Communities That Care (Hawkins, Catalano, & Arthur, 2002) and PROSPER (Spoth, Greenberg, Bierman, & Redmond, 2004; see also Chapter 15, this handbook), both of which are covered in considerable detail in this handbook. Communities that implement these models can often sustain EBI postfunding, thanks to extensive planning, conducted during the adoption and implementation phases, that has focused on ensuring integration with existing organizations, securing ongoing funding, and fostering community buy-in (Fagan et al., 2012; Spoth, Guyll, Redmond, Greenberg, & Feinberg, 2011).

In contrast to communities that employ coalitions, planning, and extensive preparation to adopt, implement, and sustain EBIs, some communities and school district curriculum coordinators may feel pressure to adopt EBIs from funding regulations that require them (Bumbarger & Campbell, 2012; Hallfors & Godette, 2002). For example, Safe and Drug Free Schools and Communities Act State Grant applicants were required to undertake only those interventions supported by scientific evidence. In other cases, resources may be sought from funding agencies requiring the use of EBI in order to maintain jobs for current staff (e.g., within community organizations such as after-school programs).

Agencies that choose to implement EBIs purely for political or financial reasons may be less likely to sustain them for many reasons. First and foremost, political and/or financial motivations for implementing interventions may affect the planning phase of the intervention, which should include securing strong agency support, providing appropriate training, and planning for sustainability (Dusenbury, Brannigan, Falco, & Hansen, 2003; Elias et al.,

2003; Elliott & Mihalic, 2004). On average, it is estimated that thorough planning requires at least 6 to 9 months (Elliott & Mihalic, 2004). Inadequate planning could lead to low implementation fidelity, and in turn less than optimal outcomes, thus decreasing motivations for sustaining the EBI postfunding. Therefore, one might conclude that community readiness is a likely mediator of motivations for implementing EBI and postfunding sustainability.

Community Readiness

Community readiness is commonly cited in the literature as an important predictor of sustainability (Edwards, Jumper-Thurman, Plested, Oetting, & Swanson, 2000). Common themes include motivation for change, organizational capacity to implement change, and buy-in of influential leaders (Adelman & Taylor, 2000; Elliott & Mihalic, 2004; Johnson, Hays, Center, & Daley, 2004).

Motivation for change occurs at the individual and community levels. Rohrbach et al. (2006) noted that it is worthwhile to consider several individual-level theories of behavior in order to better understand motivation for change relevant to community-level EBI adoption. These include social cognitive theory (Bandura, 1986), the theory of planned behavior (Ajzen, 1985), and the transtheoretical model (Prochaska, Johnson, & Lee, 2009). Taken together, these theories suggest that, at a minimum, key leaders within a community have to (a) perceive that there is a problem in need of intervention and (b) perceive that this problem is modifiable in order to be motivated to change. Additionally, key leaders must have a substantial level of influence in order to translate their individual-level motivation for change into community action. When EBI adoption is motivated by political and/or financial factors, these conditions may not be met.

Organizational capacity to adopt EBI is an additional component of community readiness. *Organizational capacity* includes maintaining trained and appropriate staffing levels (e.g., implementers and support staff), effectively managing funding, and working toward shared goals (Elliott & Mihalic, 2004; Johnson et al., 2004; Rohrbach et al., 2006; Swisher, 2000). Arguably the most detailed explanation of the organizational demands of implementing EBI in the literature is provided by Fox, Gottfredson, Kumpfer, and Beatty (2004) in their description of the Washington, DC, replication of the Strengthening Families Program. Similar to real-world replications of EBI, for this project a government agency subcontracted funds to established city and community agencies with diverse characteristics that then were responsible for all aspects of EBI implementation. In this study, organizational capacity of the agencies to implement the intervention varied in several important domains that often are overlooked in the literature, such as the amount of agency administrator time dedicated to the project, response to staff turnover, how the needs of target populations influence agency administration, and accounting practices that impact budgeting and payroll. Although few studies have empirically examined the relationship between organizational capacity and sustainability, the practice literature makes it clear that the factors listed above likely play a critical role in postfunding sustainability.

Organizational capacity often is tied to buy-in, another aspect of community readiness. *Buy-in* encompasses belief in and support of EBI. Several researchers have noted the importance of garnering the buy-in of agency administrators and community leaders to the long-term sustainability of EBIs (Adelman & Taylor, 2000; Johnson et al., 2004; Payne, Gottfredson, & Gottfredson, 2006). In the school context, the importance of principal buy-in has been well established, but more research is needed to understand how buy-in from district-level curriculum coordinators impacts community readiness to implement and sustain EBIs.

Additionally, buy-in of frontline implementers also plays an important role in sustainability (Altman, 1995; Chilenski, Greenberg, & Feinberg, 2007; Scheirer, 2005). Fox and colleagues (2004) found that facilitator buy-in in the Strengthening Families Program replication was limited for a variety of reasons, including the absence of administrator buy-in, being denied the opportunity to adapt the program to increase relevance to the targeted population, and challenges with receiving payment for services provided. The limited buy-in of the facilitators contributed to poor implementation fidelity, and in turn, smaller program effects.

One strategy for increasing buy-in is aligning interventions with the goals and needs of the sponsoring agency and community (Adelman & Taylor, 2000; Altman, 1995; Johnson et al., 2004). In a study of long-term postfunding sustainability, alignment of the EBI with the goals of the implementing agency was a significant predictor of postfunding sustainability (Tibbits et al., 2010). Although buy-in and alignment appear to increase postfunding sustainability, it is important to note that these characteristics may not be sufficient to overcome challenges related to insufficient organizational capacity.

Another important, but often overlooked, aspect of community readiness is willingness to stop implementing interventions that have little evidence of impact. Some communities are hesitant to implement EBIs, which often have substantial start-up costs, when they already have familiar, potentially cheaper, community-developed and/or community-supported interventions. In communities that are forced to implement EBI (because of policy or financial imperatives), existing programs could serve as a significant barrier to EBI sustainability. This barrier may be even more pronounced when the community-supported interventions have anecdotal evidence of effectiveness. As a result, after funding for an EBI ends, agencies may choose to revert back to the original intervention that is not evidence based but is either more cost-effective or more familiar. Alternately, communities may choose to pursue novel interventions that are perceived to have more current information or to better employ available technology. These facts highlight the need to better understand the role of competing interventions in the postfunding sustainability of EBI.

Often communities have some aspects of readiness to implement EBI but not others. For instance, a community may have motivation to change but insufficient organizational capacity. Another community may have organizational capacity but insufficient motivation to change. As a whole, one can conclude that EBIs that are aligned with the implementing agency and community's broader objectives and goals are more likely to have the buy-in of key administrators and leaders. In turn, when funding periods end, these administrators and leaders likely will be stronger advocates for the EBI and more likely to seek out additional funding for it, particularly when the community is motivated to change, there is sufficient organizational capacity to implement the intervention, and there are no competing interventions.

IMPLEMENTATION

After an EBI has been adopted, factors affecting its implementation become of paramount importance to sustainability. This section discusses the role of implementation fidelity, training, and technical assistance in postfunding sustainability.

Implementation Fidelity

Community readiness likely impacts sustainability through its effect on implementation fidelity. In a large EBI diffusion study, Elliott and Mihalic (2004) found that administrative support and staffing, commitment of resources, community acceptance of the intervention, and support of a local champion predicted implementation fidelity. Similarly, Payne and colleagues (2006) found that school principal support predicted overall level of EBI use in schools. These findings suggest that, at minimum, communities should be open to change, have the support of an influential leader, and have an adequate organizational/administrative structure before implementation is attempted. In cases in which communities are ready for change but do not have the organizational resources to successfully implement interventions, extensive planning may allow them to build the necessary capacity.

Implementation fidelity is important to consider in regard to postfunding sustainability for several reasons. First, agencies or communities that have difficulty implementing EBI are unlikely to have the resources and capacity to do so in the long term. Another factor that often is overlooked is that agencies with limited resources are not included in prevention trials as a result of being insufficiently organized (Elliott & Mihalic, 2004), but they may be more likely to receive funding to implement such interventions (Gager & Elias, 1997). The discrepancy between the contexts in which prevention research is conducted and the contexts in which EBIs are adopted is a serious threat to implementation fidelity. For instance, schools with limited resources that receive funding may encounter barriers to implementation fidelity (e.g., higher teacher turnover, fewer funds for administrative support, trouble meeting the demands of No Child Left Behind; Elias et al., 2003) not present or as prominent in schools with greater resources. As a result, they may not have the desire or ability to implement the EBI and/or may not have the capacity to apply for additional funding to support the EBI past the original funding period.

Additionally, EBIs that are not implemented with fidelity may have decreased effectiveness (Domitrovich & Greenberg, 2000; Durlak & DuPre, 2008). In turn, decreased effectiveness may lead to loss of the support for the intervention, particularly when difficult choices about the utilization of time and resources are necessary. In conclusion, many factors influence implementation fidelity, and these same factors may also affect agencies' acquisition of additional funds to support EBI after the initial funding period.

Training and Technical Assistance

Community readiness, implementation fidelity, and, in turn, postfunding sustainability can be increased through the provision of training and technical assistance (Dusenbury et al., 2003; Gottfredson & Gottfredson, 2002). School-based studies that have examined the relationship between teacher training and implementation fidelity have shown a positive association (Dusenbury et al., 2003; Dusenbury, Brannigan, Hansen, Walsh, & Falco, 2005; Ennett et al., 2003; Gager & Elias, 1997), but this relationship is weaker than might be expected. For example, Gottfredson and Gottfredson (2002) found only small correlations among various measures of training quality and fidelity ($r = .10–.15$).

These findings correspond to research suggesting that even when teachers consider training to be of high quality, they often feel unprepared to effectively implement EBIs (Elliott & Mihalic, 2004). Ennett et al. (2003) found that teachers who had been recently trained and were more comfortable with intervention material were significantly more likely to implement interventions with fidelity. Further, teachers exhibiting these characteristics were more likely to use an interactive teaching style, which has been associated with greater effectiveness in substance abuse preventive interventions (Tobler, 2000).

Studies of community-based preventive interventions also highlight the importance of thorough training. In their examination of 20 CTC sites, Greenberg, Feinberg, Brendan, Gomez, and Osgood (2005) found that school board members' knowledge of key prevention concepts that were emphasized in training, such as risk and protective factors, predicted adherence to the CTC model.

An important barrier to adequate training, however, is staff turnover. Nearly 50% of teachers leave the profession within their first three years; the average term for superintendents is two years (Elias et al., 2003). Community coalitions and agencies also often have high staff turnover (Greenberg et al., 2005). As a result, even when EBIs are initially supported and training is provided, implementation quality may decline over time. One avenue for preventing turnover-related decline may be the provision of ongoing training and technical assistance (Greenberg et al., 2005). Research is needed to understand how to best work with school staff (e.g., district-level curriculum coordinators and principals) and community leaders early in the EBI adoption process to ensure that ongoing training is prioritized and available to facilitators. Further, these findings suggest that ongoing training and technical assistance should be included when communities purchase EBI.

In sum, high-quality, ongoing training and technical assistance are essential to promote implementation fidelity. In addition to simply covering all required material, however, trainers should make efforts to ensure that facilitators truly understand and feel comfortable with the content of the EBI. For example, open conversations should be promoted between the trainer and facilitators about the developmental appropriateness of the EBI, the congruence of the underlying message of the EBI with local values, and the applicability of the material to the local context and population. These conversations may increase implementation fidelity, thus resulting in stronger effects and greater desire for continued EBI implementation postfunding.

SUSTAINABILITY

Having an effective EBI dissemination system, adoption with adequate time for planning and enhancing community readiness, and high-quality implementation clearly play important roles in postfunding sustainability. Even in the presence of these factors, however, it is unlikely that an EBI will be sustained postfunding without explicit sustainability planning (Tibbits et al., 2010). Two interconnected types of sustainability planning are important: alignment and financial planning.

As noted, ensuring that the benefits of an EBI are aligned with the needs of the community and implementing agency is an important first step toward promoting postfunding sustainability. Several researchers have offered suggestions about the characteristics and facilitators of alignment (Adelman & Taylor, 2000; Altman, 1995; Bumbarger & Campbell, 2012; Greenberg, 2004; Johnson et al., 2004; Payne et al., 2006). Prevention scientists are in agreement that alignment requires acquiring and maintaining a thorough understanding of the priorities and responsibilities of the implementing agency, and respecting those priorities when adopting and implementing EBIs and discussing how to sustain them. Practicing these strategies can increase the agencies' perceived need for the EBI (Adelman & Taylor, 2000; Johnson et al., 2004).

Another common suggestion is to ensure that the intervention can become a line item on an agency's budget so that it inherently is included in future financial planning for the agency rather than being considered a temporary initiative. This highlights the fact that alignment and financial sustainability planning often are interconnected. Ideally, one should plan for both alignment and financial sustainability early in the process of EBI adoption and implementation in order to promote postfunding sustainability.

FUTURE DIRECTIONS FOR RESEARCH

The discussion presented in this chapter about the postfunding sustainability of evidence-based substance abuse interventions suggests many directions for future research on this topic. First and foremost, although dissemination and adoption are the initial stages of the diffusion of innovations, one might argue that they also are the areas that currently need the most attention in terms of research and practice relevant to the diffusion of substance abuse EBIs.

A common concern of community members is that EBIs will not be applicable and relevant for their particular community. Assuming it is possible to overcome that initial challenge and a community decides to adopt EBIs, as a field, prevention science should provide sufficient information and assistance to help them select appropriate interventions, even if the community does not have a prevention scientist on its team. Currently, one could argue that that is not happening. For example, although databases of EBI provide helpful descriptions and contact information, the EBIs are listed in overwhelming numbers. It is probable that EBIs that are packaged and marketed most effectively may have the higher adoption rates, even if other EBIs may be more appropriate.

Therefore, the field of prevention science would benefit from taking a step back to better understand how characteristics of the dissemination process impact adoption, implementation, and ultimately postfunding sustainability. Specifically, there is a dearth of information about the process communities use to decide between competing EBIs (e.g., prior familiarity with a specific EBI, availability of information about the EBI, alignment with community needs, cost) when they are adopting EBIs outside of the context of organized research trials. This information is vital to the success of prevention scientists who invest time and energy over many years developing and testing interventions that are problem and population specific. Further, the knowledge gained from this type of inquiry can lead to the development of dissemination strategies that are useful not only to prevention scientists and highly functioning coalitions, but also to smaller communities with fewer resources, thus increasing the public health impact of EBIs.

Implementation is the phase of the diffusion of innovation theory that has received the most research attention. It is clear that achieving implementation is challenging to communities, particularly when community readiness is less than ideal. Because implementation fidelity directly affects program effectiveness and, potentially, postfunding sustainability, additional research is needed to understand how to promote implementation fidelity through the delivery of effective training and technical assistance. Additionally, the field of prevention science should strengthen the availability and quality of diverse training and technical assistance options (e.g., web-based training) to meet the needs of communities with limited financial and organizational resources.

Planning for sustainability, particularly alignment and financial planning, clearly is critical for promoting postfunding sustainability. Although alignment and financial planning nearly always are mentioned in the sustainability literature, there is little research about how to encourage communities to incorporate sustainability planning into standard practice. For example, the literature about alignment largely is written by and for prevention scientists within academic institutions. As previously noted, the premise often is that they have a specialized product (the EBI) and they must align with community needs. An equally plausible scenario, however, is that a grassroots substance abuse coalition implements an EBI without the involvement of a prevention scientist. Substance abuse coalitions often consist of members from diverse backgrounds who are passionate about the topic for a variety of reasons. Given that not everyone in a given community will share that passion, research is needed about how grassroots coalitions can align with broader community and agency needs to encourage broad support and the sustainable implementation of EBIs.

Furthermore, additional attention should be paid to Altman's (1995) assertion that not all interventions should be sustained. Sometimes communities would like to sustain an EBI but genuinely do not have and cannot find the resources to do so. In other instances, however, they make the decision not to seek funding or try to sustain the intervention. Although the factors mentioned in this chapter likely contribute to these decisions, research should explore whether or not other important factors should be considered to promote postfunding sustainability.

The field of prevention science continues to offer information and interventions that have the potential to improve the public's health by preventing and treating substance abuse. To realize that potential, it is critical that EBIs be adopted, implemented with fidelity, and sustained in a variety of communities and by a variety of partners. Considering postfunding sustainability throughout the process of diffusing an EBI and developing EBI materials with the assumption that communities will not have access to a prevention scientist will help increase the public health impact of EBIs and decrease the burden of substance abuse on individuals and society.

References

Adelman, H. S., & Taylor, L. (2000). Moving prevention from the fringes into the fabric of school improvement. *Journal of Educational & Psychological Consultation, 11*, 7–36. doi:10.1207/S1532768XJEPC1101_3

Ajzen, I. (1985). From decisions to actions: A theory of planned behavior. In J. Kuhl & J. Beckmann (Eds.), *Action-control: From cognition to behavior* (pp. 11–39). New York, NY: Springer. doi:10.1007/978-3-642-69746-3_2

Altman, D. G. (1995). Sustaining interventions in community systems: On the relationship between researchers and communities. *Health Psychology, 14*, 526–536. doi:10.1037/0278-6133.14.6.526

Bandura, A. (1986). *Social foundations of thought and action: A social cognitive theory.* Englewood Cliffs, NJ: Prentice Hall.

Botvin, G. J., & Griffin, K. W. (2004). Life Skills Training: Empirical findings and future directions. *The Journal of Primary Prevention, 25*, 211–232. doi:10.1023/B:JOPP.0000042391.58573.5b

Botvin, G. J., & Griffin, K. W. (2010). Advances in the science and practice of prevention: Targeting individual-level etiologic factors and the challenge of going to scale. In L. M. Scheier (Ed.), *Handbook of drug abuse etiology: Theory, methods, and empirical findings* (pp. 631–650). Washington, DC: American Psychological Association.

Bumbarger, B. K., & Campbell, E. M. (2012). A state agency–university partnership for translational research and the dissemination of evidence-based prevention and intervention. *Administration and Policy in Mental Health and Mental Health Services Research, 39*, 268–277. doi:10.1007/s10488-011-0372-x

Chilenski, S. M., Greenberg, M. T., & Feinberg, M. E. (2007). Community readiness as a multidimensional construct. *Journal of Community Psychology, 35*, 347–365. doi:10.1002/jcop.20152

Dent, C. W., Sussman, S., Stacy, A. W., Craig, S., Burton, D., & Flay, B. R. (1995). Two year behavior outcomes of Project Towards No Tobacco Use. *Journal of Consulting and Clinical Psychology, 63*, 676–677. doi:10.1037/0022-006X.63.4.676

Domitrovich, C. E., & Greenberg, M. T. (2000). The study of implementation: Current findings from effective programs that prevent mental disorders in school-aged children. *Journal of Educational &*

Psychological Consultation, 11, 193–221. doi:10.1207/S1532768XJEPC1102_04

Durlak, J. A., & DuPre, E. P. (2008). Implementation matters: A review of research on the influence of implementation on program outcomes and the factors affecting implementation. *American Journal of Community Psychology, 41*, 327–350. doi:10.1007/s10464-008-9165-0

Dusenbury, L., Brannigan, R., Falco, M., & Hansen, W. B. (2003). A review of research on fidelity of implementation: Implications for drug abuse prevention in school settings. *Health Education Research, 18*, 237–256. doi:10.1093/her/18.2.237

Dusenbury, L., Brannigan, R., Hansen, W. B., Walsh, J., & Falco, M. (2005). Quality of implementation: Developing measures crucial to understanding the diffusion of preventive interventions. *Health Education Research, 20*, 308–313. doi:10.1093/her/cyg134

Eckenrode, J., Campa, M., Luckey, D. W., Henderson, C. R., Cole, R., Kitzman, H., . . . Olds, D. (2010). Long-term effects of prenatal and infancy nurse home visitation on the life course of youths: 19-year follow-up of a randomized trial. *JAMA Pediatrics, 164*, 9–15.

Edwards, R. W., Jumper-Thurman, P., Plested, B. A., Oetting, E. R., & Swanson, L. (2000). Community readiness: Research to practice. *Journal of Community Psychology, 28*, 291–307. doi:10.1002/(SICI)1520-6629(200005)28:3<291::AID-JCOP5>3.0.CO;2-9

Elias, M. J., Zins, J. E., Graczyk, P. A., & Weissburg, R. P. (2003). Implementation, sustainability, and scaling up of social-emotional and academic innovations in public schools. *School Psychology Review, 32*, 303–319.

Elliott, D. S., & Mihalic, S. (2004). Issues in disseminating and replicating effective prevention programs. *Prevention Science, 5*, 47–53. doi:10.1023/B:PREV.0000013981.28071.52

Ennett, S. T., Ringwalt, C. L., Thorne, J., Rohrbach, L. A., Vincus, A., Simons-Rudolph, A., & Jones, S. (2003). A comparison of current practice in school-based substance use prevention programs with meta-analysis findings. *Prevention Science, 4*, 1–14.

Fagan, A. A., Hanson, K., Briney, J. S., & Hawkins, J. D. (2012). Sustaining the utilization and high quality implementation of tested and effective prevention programs using the Communities That Care prevention system. *American Journal of Community Psychology, 49*, 365–377. doi:10.1007/s10464-011-9463-9

Fox, D. P., Gottfredson, D. C., Kumpfer, K. K., & Beatty, P. D. (2004). Challenges in disseminating model programs: A qualitative analysis of the Strengthening Washington DC Families program. *Clinical Child and Family Psychology Review, 7*, 165–176. doi:10.1023/B:CCFP.0000045125.68018.61

Gager, P. J., & Elias, M. J. (1997). Implementing prevention programs in high-risk environments: Application of the resiliency paradigm. *American Journal of Orthopsychiatry, 67*, 363–373. doi:10.1037/h0080239

Gottfredson, D. C., & Gottfredson, G. D. (2002). Quality of school-based prevention programs: Results from a national survey. *Journal of Research in Crime and Delinquency, 39*, 3–35. doi:10.1177/002242780203900101

Greenberg, M. T. (2004). Current and future challenges in school-based prevention: The researcher perspective. *Prevention Science, 5*, 5–13. doi:10.1023/B:PREV.0000013976.84939.55

Greenberg, M. T., Feinberg, M. E., Brendan, J., Gomez, B. J., & Osgood, D. W. (2005). Testing a community prevention focused model of coalition functioning and sustainability: A comprehensive study of communities that care in Pennsylvania. In T. Stockwell, P. Gruenewald, J. W. Toumbourou, & W. Loxley (Eds.), *Preventing harmful substance use: The evidence base for policy and practice* (pp. 129–142). London, England: Wiley.

Hallfors, D., & Godette, D. (2002). Will the "principles of effectiveness" improve prevention practice? Early findings from a diffusion study. *Health Education Research, 17*, 461–470. doi:10.1093/her/17.4.461

Hawkins, J. D., Catalano, R. F., & Arthur, M. W. (2002). Promoting science-based prevention in communities. *Addictive Behaviors, 27*, 951–976. doi:10.1016/S0306-4603(02)00298-8

Johnson, K., Hays, C., Center, H., & Daley, C. (2004). Building capacity and sustainable prevention innovations: A sustainability planning model. *Evaluation and Program Planning, 27*, 135–149. doi:10.1016/j.evalprogplan.2004.01.002

National Institute on Drug Abuse. (2014). *DrugFacts: Nationwide trends.* Retrieved from http://www.drugabuse.gov/publications/drugfacts/nationwide-trends

Payne, A. A., Gottfredson, D. C., & Gottfredson, G. D. (2006). School predictors of intensity of implementation of school-based prevention programs: Results from a national study. *Prevention Science, 7*, 225–237.

Pluye, P., Potvin, L., & Denis, J. (2004). Making public health programs last: Conceptualizing sustainability. *Evaluation and Program Planning, 27*, 121–133. doi:10.1016/j.evalprogplan.2004.01.001

Prochaska, J. O., Johnson, S., & Lee, P. (2009). The transtheoretical model of behavior change. In S. A. Shumaker, J. K. Ockene, & K. A. Riekert (Eds.), *The handbook of health behavior change* (3rd ed., pp. 59–83). New York, NY: Springer.

Rogers, E. M. (2003). *Diffusion of innovations* (5th ed.). New York, NY: Free Press.

Rohrbach, L. A., Grana, R., Sussman, S., & Valente, T. W. (2006). Type II translation: Transporting prevention interventions from research to real-world settings.

Evaluation & the Health Professions, *29*, 302–333. doi:10.1177/0163278706290408

Scheirer, M. (2005). Is sustainability possible? A review and commentary on empirical studies of program sustainability. *American Journal of Evaluation*, *26*, 320–347. doi:10.1177/1098214005278752

Spoth, R., Greenberg, M., Bierman, K., & Redmond, C. (2004). PROSPER community-university partnership model for public education systems: Capacity-building for evidence-based, competence-building prevention. *Prevention Science*, *5*, 31–39. doi:10.1023/B:PREV.0000013979.52796.8b

Spoth, R., Guyll, M., Redmond, C., Greenberg, M., & Feinberg, M. (2011). Six-year sustainability of evidence-based intervention implementation quality by community-university partnerships: The prosper study. *American Journal of Community Psychology*, *48*, 412–425. doi:10.1007/s10464-011-9430-5

Sussman, S., Dent, C. W., & Stacy, A. W. (2002). Project Towards No Drug Abuse: A review of the findings and future directions. *American Journal of Health Behavior*, *26*, 354–365. doi:10.5993/AJHB.26.5.4

Swisher, J. D. (2000). Sustainability of prevention. *Addictive Behaviors*, *25*, 965–973. doi:10.1016/S0306-4603(00)00124-6

Tibbits, M. K., Bumbarger, B. K., Kyler, S. J., & Perkins, D. F. (2010). Sustaining evidence-based interventions under real-world conditions: Results from a large-scale diffusion project. *Prevention Science*, *11*, 252–262. doi:10.1007/s11121-010-0170-9

Tobler, N. S. (2000). Lessons learned. *The Journal of Primary Prevention*, *20*, 261–274. doi:10.1023/A:1021362620740

Webster-Stratton, C., & Reid, M. J. (2008). Preventing conduct problems and improving school readiness: Evaluation of The Incredible Years Teacher and Child Training Programs in high-risk schools. *Journal of Child Psychology and Psychiatry*, *49*, 471–488. doi:10.1111/j.1469-7610.2007.01861.x

CHAPTER 28

THE DISSEMINATION AND (LACK OF) ADOPTION OF EVIDENCE-BASED PRACTICES

James H. Derzon

This chapter documents the modest rate of schools' adoption of evidence-based practices (EBPs) for the prevention of substance abuse. Here I use the five intrinsic characteristics of an innovation suggested by Rogers's (2003) theory of diffusion as sensitizing concepts to organize evidence and ideas that may explain, in part, why many schools fail to adopt such EBPs. First, it is proposed that the relative advantage of EBPs may be overshadowed by the time commitment necessary to fully implement them. Then, although the goals of EBPs are likely shared by teachers and school administrators, relatively few EBPs have content compatible with the primary values and practices of teachers. The complexity of evaluating evidence establishing an EBP precludes even researchers from agreeing what programs are evidence based, and different standards of evidence may exist for different users of evidence. Also, many EBPs are expensive to implement and may lack Rogers's "trialability." And finally, the results of effective substance use prevention may not be observable in the school settings in which they are implemented. After reviewing these aspects of the acceptance, or not, of EBPs in schools, the chapter closes by identifying several strategies that might be leveraged to increase the adoption and dissemination of EBPs.

In all areas of public health, medicine, and education, science-based evidence is increasingly warranted for programs that claim to improve the human condition. For school-based drug and violence prevention, incorporation of research-validated prevention programs was formally established in the No Child Left Behind Act (NCLB) of 2001 (No Child Left Behind, 2002). This important legislation mandated that drug and violence prevention programs and activities funded through the federal government's Office of Safe and Drug Free Schools and Communities would "be based on scientifically based research that provides evidence that the program to be used will reduce violence and illegal drug use" (§4115(a)(1)(c)). Eleven years have passed since NCLB took effect, and the national prevalence of youth drug use has continued to remain relatively high (Johnston, O'Malley, Bachman, & Schulenberg, 2013a, 2013b). Now is perhaps the time to examine the extent to which schools have in fact incorporated evidence-based prevention programs into their classrooms and to consider possible reasons for the relative success or failure of their effort.

PREVALENCE OF RESEARCH-BASED PROGRAMS

Although estimates of the percentage of schools and districts adopting EBPs vary greatly, none of the estimates approaches 100% (see Table 28.1). The

Preparation for this chapter was supported by a grant from the National Institute on Drug Abuse (1R43DA026219-01A1) with cofunding from the Battelle Memorial Institute. The content of this chapter is solely the responsibility of the author and does not necessarily represent the official views of the National Institute on Drug Abuse or the Battelle Memorial Institute.

Thanks are given to Lawrence M. Scheier, who invited and encouraged me to think and write on this topic. Correspondence concerning this chapter should be directed to James Derzon at derzonj@battelle.org.

http://dx.doi.org/10.1037/14550-029
Handbook of Adolescent Drug Use Prevention: Research, Intervention Strategies, and Practice, L. M. Scheier (Editor)

TABLE 28.1

Evidence of Schools' Adoption of Evidence-Based Practices for Reducing Youth Substance Use

Study	Method	Outcome measure	Prevalence estimate	Other observations
Hallfors & Godette (2002)	Purposive sample of 104 school districts in 12 states	District adopted at least one of six research-based programs that appeared on a list developed by Drug Strategies.	59.0 %	Districts were more likely to adopt non-research-based programs (e.g., D.A.R.E.) than research-based programs.
Pankratz & Hallfors (2004)	Based on a survey of all school districts in North Carolina in 2001	District implemented promising or effective program included on one of the following lists: (1) National Institute on Drug Abuse, (2) Drug Strategies, (3) Centers for Disease Control and Prevention, (4) Center for Substance Abuse Prevention, or (5) Safe and Drug-Free Schools Program.	72.0 %	Middle schools were more likely to use such curricula. Other factors associated with the adoption of research-based curricula were district urbanicity, prevention coordinator time available, and coordinator experience.
Hantman & Crosse (2000)	National probability sample survey of 600 districts in 1998	District was using a substance abuse prevention program that was consistent with existing research (e.g., curricula and instruction directed at social competencies).	9.0%	
Rohrbach, Ringwalt, Ennett, & Vincus (2005)	National probability sample of 1,593 districts conducted in 1999	Implemented at least one of 10 specified research-based programs (same lists used by Pankratz and Hallfors, 2004) in at least one middle school within the district.	47.5%	The factors associated with use of these programs included district enrollment, urbanicity, and prevention coordinator time available.
Ringwalt, Ennett, Vincus, Thorne, et al. (2002)	1,905 public and private middle schools (in the same districts included in the Rohrbach et al., 2005 study)	Implemented one or more research-based programs (same lists used by Pankratz and Hallfors, 2004).	34.6%	The factors associated with adoption of one of those programs included urbanicity, geographical region, school enrollment, and lead prevention teacher experience.
Ringwalt et al. (2008)	2005 from a nationally representative sample of 1,392 school districts including high school grades	Implemented at least one of six curricula rated as effective by the Substance Abuse and Mental Health Services Administration's National Registry of Effective Programs and Practices or Blueprints for Violence Prevention.	10.3% of districts that included high school grades reported administering at least one evidence-based curriculum. 5.7% reported that they used one of these curricula the most.	56.5% of the nation's districts with high school grades administered any substance use prevention programming in at least one of their constituent high schools.

TABLE 28.1 (*cont.*)

Study	Method	Outcome measure	Prevalence estimate	Other observations
Ringwalt, Ennett, Vincus, Thorne, et al. (2002)	A nationally representative sample of 1,905 of the nation's public and private schools that include middle school grades	Three federally sponsored registries were used to specify 10 effective curricula which were considered evidence based.	26.8% of all schools, 34.6% of public schools, 12.6% of private schools used at least one of the evidence-based programs.	Few school or respondent characteristics were related to program implementation; 2/3 of schools used > one curriculum, almost half reported using three or more.
Hanley et al. (2010)	A nationally representative survey of 1,563 public school districts in the U.S. that include grades 1–5 in 2005	Nine programs identified by NREPP, Blueprints for Violence Prevention, or by the U.S. Department of Education.	35% are using one that is evidence-based; 14% are using an evidence-based curriculum more than any other prevention curriculum.	72% of districts administer a substance use prevention curriculum to their elementary students.
Gottfredson et al. (2000) Crosse, Burr, Cantor, Hagen, & Hantman (2002)	3,691 program providers in a national probability sample of public and private schools during the 1997–98 school year	The quality of prevention programs and the extent to which program characteristics met criteria derived from a review of the literature.	Of the programs, 61% met criteria for use of best practices on content; 33% met criteria on best practices for methods.	
U.S. Department of Education (2011)	Nationally representative survey of 2,500 public school districts and 5,847 public schools of prevention programs during the 2004–2005 school year, response rate was 86%	Nineteen programs were identified by Mihalic (2002) with two independent trials, each of which met minimal methodological criteria for documented effectiveness.	In 2004–2005 school year, 7.8% of the prevention programs in operation were research based; 40.7% of schools implemented at least one research-based program; 44.3% of the research-based curriculum programs provided in schools met minimum standards for overall fidelity of implementation (3.5% of programs overall).	

highest estimate comes from a survey of all school districts in North Carolina in 2001 (Pankratz & Hallfors, 2004), and the lowest estimate comes from a nationally representative sample of schools (U.S. Department of Education, 2011). Consistent with all scientific inquiry, scientists only know what they examine. Studies that queried whether a school district had implemented at least one EBP (in at least one school or classroom) showed the highest rates of implementing EBPs; studies that estimated the ratio of EBPs to all programs being implemented returned the lowest rates. Also strongly affecting reported adoption rates was how the researchers defined the term *research-based program*. For five of the seven studies shown in Table 28.1, a program was considered research-based if it was included on one or more specific lists of promising or effective EBPs. In these studies, estimates of the percentage of schools or districts implementing an EBP ranged from 34.6% to 72%, with the larger percentages coming from studies using multiple lists to identify evidence-based programs.

The most recent studies examined EBPs implemented during the 2004–2005 school year. The study that estimated prevalence of EBPs using an "any school in the district" approach and limited the scope of EBPs to programs appearing in three nationally sponsored registries found that 10.3% of districts with high schools and 35% of districts with elementary schools implemented at least one EBP (Hanley et al., 2010; Ringwalt et al., 2008). The second study (U.S. Department of Education, 2011) used a national probability sample of nearly 6,000 schools and conducted an extensive review of over 400 programs included in an inventory of 12 EBP lists compiled at the Center for the Study and Prevention of Violence (CSPV; 2012) by Sharon Mihalec. This study also examined the original research conducted to establish the evidence base for each program included on the lists that met the following criteria.

Criteria for Evidence Based

To be considered evidence based for preventing substance abuse or violence, the U.S. Department of Education study required findings from two independent trials (i.e., the program was implemented and tested in two or more settings with different subjects), each of which met appropriate minimal quality standards (e.g., the intervention tested was similar to the program model, minimal differential attrition, sample represented English-speaking North American school-age youths). Other requirements were that the program was school based, the trials reported significant favorable results for substance abuse or violence (i.e., the programs were not just effective on risk factors for these outcomes), and the program was available for dissemination (i.e., manualized). Of the over 400 programs in CSPV's inventory, only 19 met these standards. The U.S. Department of Education added two additional programs that were not in the inventory, resulting in 21 EBPs with proven efficacy in reducing substance abuse or violence. The study results indicated that although approximately 40.7% of schools had implemented at least one of these research-based prevention programs during the school year, only 7.8% of all prevention programs in operation during the 2004–2005 year were research based.

The Innovation Curve

In fields ranging from medicine (Institute of Medicine, 2001) to refrigeration, adoption of EBPs show startling lags between when an EBP is documented and when it is widely adopted (Glasgow, Lichtenstein, & Marcus, 2003). Moreover, these lags are not unique to EBPs. An oft-cited graph by Nicholas Felton displays the past 100-year history of the adoption of many now common household items (Cox & Alm, 2008). It shows, for example, how recently home refrigeration became ubiquitous even though the importance of cooling food to retard bacterial growth had long been recognized and artificial refrigeration was first introduced in 1748. The first electric refrigerators for home use weren't developed until 1927 (Freidberg, 2010), and not until circa 1963 did home refrigeration become fairly common and cost-effective in the United States. Adoption of innovations tends to follow a classic S-curve, with slow initial growth, a period of accelerated growth, and a leveling off, often with less than 100% adoption.

UNDERSTANDING DIFFUSION

Much of what is understood about the diffusion of innovations comes from Rogers's (2003) review of 508 diffusion studies. Rogers posited that there are five intrinsic characteristics of an innovation that explain between 49% and 87% of the variation in the speed of adoption and, indeed, whether a new product, innovation, or practice is ever adopted. These characteristics include:

1. relative advantage—the perceived improvement over what is being replaced in areas that matter to users;
2. compatibility with existing values and practices—the extent to which an innovation is perceived

by end users as being consistent with the values, past experiences, and needs of potential adopters;
3. complexity—the degree to which an innovation is perceived as difficult to understand and use;
4. trialability—the degree to which an innovation can be experimented with on a limited basis; and
5. observability—the degree to which innovation results are visible to other potential end users who may benefit from the change; the easier it is for individuals to see the results of an innovation, the more likely they are to adopt it.

Despite the rational appeal of Rogers's (2003) model, it is unlikely that assimilation of EBPs by schools follows such a predictable pattern. As Rogers noted, organizations are not people, and there is limited support for the notion that organizational assimilation of innovations mimics individual adoption strategies. It may be, given a high-ranking champion for a particular innovation, that assimilation is more predictable in rigid, tightly coupled, mature hierarchical organizations, such as the military, or when decisions can be made in isolation, such as a school system in which a single substance abuse coordinator selects a program. However, few schools or districts operate in such a manner. Schools are complex multidimensional systems that exist to meet the needs of multiple stakeholders, including students, parents, staff, faculty, and administration, and, further, they meet those needs within broader community, cultural, and legislative contexts that can influence decision making (Rohrbach, D'Onofrio, Backer, & Montgomery, 1996). Each stakeholder group has multiple representatives with different personalities, priorities, and opinions about what causes—and what would prevent—substance use. Moreover, these stakeholders interact within formal and informal power structures, all of which influence the decision whether or not to adopt an EBP.

Thus, whereas several of the determinants of school decision-making may be described using Rogers's (2003) framework, in the real world of schools, his intrinsic characteristics of diffusion can be thought of as sensitizing rather than definitive concepts. According to Blumer (1954), sensitizing concepts "provide a general sense of reference and guidance in approaching empirical instances" (p. 7) rather than a clear set of attributes and fixed benchmarks by which to describe a rigid process. According to Greenhalgh, Robert, MacFarlane, Bate, and Kyriakidou (2004), with limited exceptions "the determinants of organizational innovativeness interact in a complex, unpredictable, and nongeneralizable way with one another" (p. 606), and organizational assimilation of any innovation is "punctuated by shocks, setbacks, and surprises" (p. 601). It is assumed in this discussion that the process of assimilating EBPs is no different and that, although measurement models of adoption and implementation are emerging (Damschroder et al., 2009), Rogers's intrinsic characteristics of diffusion provide a useful framework for organizing evidence for why EBPs may not be more widely adopted.

DIFFUSION THEORY APPLIED TO EVIDENCE-BASED PROGRAMS

The following discussion explores the five Rogers (2003) characteristics of innovation as concepts for examining what does and does not achieve acceptance and success with EPBs.

Relative Advantage

Despite the apparent lack of any systematic research contrasting whether EBPs require more time to implement than non-EBPs, it is well known that the time requirements of EBPs are not trivial. An analysis by Hansen et al. (2010) of the programs contained in the National Registry of Evidence-Based Programs and Practices (NREPP; 2013) identified 25 programs that had both manuals and information on the effectiveness of the program in reducing youth substance abuse. According to their manuals, full implementation of these 25 EBP programs required an average of 61 sessions. Programs targeting elementary-school-aged participants generally required the most sessions ($M = 121.3$, $SD = 239.4$), with progressively fewer sessions necessary for middle school ($M = 31.7$, $SD = 44.4$), and high school participants ($M = 15.7$, $SD = 15.2$). Although there is considerable variation in the required number of sessions for full implementation, Hansen et al. (2010) observed no significant correlations between the total number of sessions, the average numbers of sessions per year, or the number of developmental years spanned by the program with the reported effectiveness of the program.

If EBPs require multiple sessions and significantly displace the time available for required learning activities relative to non-EBPs, they are unlikely to be seen as representing a relative advantage over non-EBPs in school settings. Similarly, if EBPs are more expensive than non-EBPs, then their relative advantage is diminished (costs of EBPs are discussed under Trialability). If non-EBPs are perceived as filling the need for substance use prevention programming—and involve significantly less burden—schools may opt to adopt the shorter, cheaper, less intrusive program, even if evidence of its effectiveness is not recognized by scientists as credible.

Compatibility With Existing Values and Practices

It is likely that substance abuse prevention is an ideal consistent with the values, past experiences, and needs of potential school adopters. This assumption is probably reflected in the observation that 85.2% of schools implement some sort of substance use and/or school violence prevention program, with the average school implementing nine different prevention programs and 11.1% implementing more than 20 unique programs (U.S. Department of Education, 2011).

Since the passage of NCLB (2002), schools have been under intense pressure to improve student performance on NCLB performance metrics, and teachers are increasingly evaluated on the basis of student performance on various standardized metrics (Hamilton et al., 2007). On nearly equal footing with student academic skills is the ability of both teachers and administrators to effectively manage classrooms. If we consider that the school day represents a zero-sum environment, in which devoting time to EBPs reduces exactly the time available for other topics, an EBP may not be seen as an improvement over the learning curriculum it replaces—especially if it requires more time than an alternative non-EBP.

Hansen, Dusenbury, Bishop, and Derzon (2007) conducted a systematic review and meta-analysis of substance abuse prevention programs listed on NREPP as of 2003. Of the 96 EBPs listed, one half (48 programs) had manuals to guide implementation and were thus available for dissemination. Of those 48 programs, 12 programs (25%) devoted either "some" or "a lot" of content to academic skills, whereas only nine (18.8%) devoted either "some" or "a lot" of content to classroom management. If improving students' academic skills is the principal goal of schools, and if effective classroom management is necessary to achieve that goal, then the majority of EBPs are not likely to be compatible with the primary values and practices of teachers.

Complexity

In applying the concept of complexity to the decision to adopt an EBP, it may be useful to focus on what is meant by *evidence of effectiveness* and how its meaning may differ between social scientists and school administrators. Scientists evaluate evidence of effectiveness on the basis of the logical (objective) methods used to generate the evidence and, in the case of experimental design, on whether the probability of the outcome in a comparison group exceeds the probability of the outcome in the treatment group, given sampling error and an infinite number of trials. They may further consider evidence of efficacy (i.e., that an intervention achieves its results under optimal conditions) as evidence of the effectiveness that an intervention would achieve a similar result if implemented with fidelity under real-world conditions (Flay et al., 2005).

It is likely that what is recognized as credible evidence among social scientists may not garner the same recognition in a nonscientific community. Evidence is a complex idea that among scientists is often reduced to a "probability calculus" (S. I. Miller & Safer, 1993), which ranks randomized controlled trials as the gold standard and testimonials at the bottom of the evidentiary pyramid (see, e.g., Burns, Rohrich, & Chung, 2011). Scientists are expected to judge evidence based on the choice of research design (see, e.g., the Oxford Centre for Evidence-Based Medicine's [OCEBM], 2011, Levels of Evidence), the quality of the methods used to produce the findings (e.g., Altman et al., 2001), and the statistical significance of the result. There is little evidence that the applied logic of evaluating evidence is a normal practice of humans not engaged in science. For example, Kahneman's (2011) Nobel Prize–winning research on PROSPECT theory shows that people are prey to making miscalculations about perceived "harm" and that by nature we are "risk avoidant." In fact, the occurrence of a single salient event, for instance, a local teen's drunk-driving death, may be enough for a community or school to condemn a program as not effective even though scientific evidence may validate its overall success.

Who's the expert? More to the point, perhaps, is the fact that when researchers are talking about EBPs, they are talking about evidence of causality, their confidence that the difference observed in post-trial substance use can be attributed to the intervention. Among researchers, acceptance of the findings is conditioned by acceptance of the methods used to generate the findings. For most of the human experience, causality has been inferred from covariation, temporal order, contiguity in time and space, and similarity of cause and effect (Einhorn & Hogarth, 1986). It is likely that without training in research design and experience in evaluating evidence, many teachers and school administrators use the idea of evidence more broadly and consider testimonials and change over time in one-group pre–post trials as evidence for effectiveness. Given the proliferation of user and consumer reviews, the utility of testimonials for purchaser decision making is not trivial.

Evaluating research-based evidence. As a proxy for the expertise necessary to evaluate causal evidence and to aid schools and communities in identifying EBPs, several federal and private agencies conduct systematic reviews of the research literature and produce lists and common language summaries of evidence- or science-based programs. Seven of those lists (Coalition for Evidence-Based Policy, Blueprints for Violence Prevention, NREPP–Substance Abuse and Mental Health Services Administration [SAMHSA], Communities That Care, Office of Juvenile Justice and Delinquency Prevention Model Programs Guide, Office of Justice Programs, Crimesolutions.gov, and Child Trends/LINKS) are summarized by the CSPV (Center for the Study and Prevention of Violence, 2012). Each of the lists uses different criteria to determine whether the programs are effective or promising, and a scan of this matrix suggests that these criteria differences matter; many programs appear on one list, but not others, or the same program is endorsed at different levels across the lists.

For example, in 2007–2008, the CSPV matrix indexed 491 programs across 12 lists. A systematic review and meta-analysis of the evidence in support of the listed programs identified 46 of these 491 programs that were school based, had implementation materials (so they could be disseminated), had been tested in two or more trials (replication is a tenet of science), met minimum methodological criteria (e.g., experimental design or equivalent, integrity of implementation, limited attrition, lack of historical confounding), and reported one or more substance use or antisocial behavior outcomes (Alford & Derzon, 2012). Eligible outcomes included all measures of alcohol, tobacco, marijuana, or other drug use, as well as all measures capturing aggressive/disruptive behavior, antisocial behavior, delinquent behavior, or physical aggression.

Using standard meta-analytic techniques, these programs tended to be effective in improving youth outcomes, that is, for each outcome the overall grand mean was significant and positive. These programs, on average, are effective in preventing or reducing substance use and antisocial behavior. However, looking at the evidence at the study by program level, of 46 programs meeting the stated criteria, 21 showed consistent positive and significant evidence of effectiveness within a single outcome for substance use or antisocial behavior. An additional 25 programs reported null, negative, or mixed effects across independent trials. In other words, for programs that had been tested in multiple trials, findings of effectiveness for a single substance or antisocial behavior did not replicate for slightly more than one half of the programs. Moreover, although most of the programs are marketed as effective for substance use, antisocial behavior, or both, most of the programs did not provide evidence of effectiveness for multiple substance use or antisocial behavior outcomes. Of the 21 programs that did report multiple outcomes, eight reported significant and positive effects for each of the substance use or antisocial behavior outcomes reported; the remaining 13 were effective for only one of the reported outcomes. Finally, of the five programs that reported findings in both the substance use and antisocial behavior domains, three reported positive and significant effects in reducing both substance use and antisocial behavior. It can also be observed that although most of these trials collected evidence of effectiveness using multiple measures or scales in assessing substance use and/or antisocial behavior, the evidence of effectiveness was often presented using a single outcome measure.

Deciding whether a program is evidence based is a complex process that varies even among experienced researchers and evaluation experts (Atkins et al., 2004). What counts as "evidence" is often a consequence of the scientific standards adopted, with more restrictive standards returning smaller amounts of credible evidence (see, e.g., Gandhi, Murphy-Graham, Petrosino, Chrismer, & Weiss, 2007; Gorman, 2005). For example, for the majority of lists summarized in the CSPV matrix, a program can be judged promising, model, or even exemplary if it documents improvement in a risk factor associated with the designated substance abuse or problem behavior outcome. Demonstrating consistent positive results in reducing the actual problem behaviors that these programs are designed to affect is not typically a requirement, even though the relation between the putative risk factors and later substance abuse or problem behavior is often modest at best (Derzon, 2007). In fact, as noted on the NREPP website, "NREPP rates the quality of the research supporting intervention outcomes and the quality and availability of training and implementation materials. NREPP ratings do not reflect an intervention's effectiveness" (NREPP, 2013).

Trialability

Most EBPs are proprietary and originated out of research and development through a commercial product-testing phase (Flay et al., 2005). The extent to which local schools can "try it before they buy it" is likely limited, and EBPs are often expensive to purchase and costly to implement (Griffith & Scheier, 2013). Using information supplied by the developers and listed on SAMHSA's NREPP website, Shamblen and Derzon (2009) estimated the median per setting costs of implementing model universal and selected or indicated prevention programs targeting alcohol or marijuana or both. Universal programs, which are applied to everyone in a population regardless of risk, were estimated to cost $12,347 to implement, whereas selected and indicated programs, programs designed to be applied to those at risk or already engaged in substance use, were nearly twice as expensive ($23,269) to implement. T. R. Miller and Hendrie (2009) reported that the average per-student cost of implementing a school-based life skills program is $220 (range $100–$400) per student. Detailed cost-to-implement information on many individual programs is available through NREPP.

Despite these costs, Caulkins, Rydell, Everingham, Chiesa, and Bushway (1999) and T. R. Miller and Hendrie (2009) suggested that the cost of implementing EBPs is justified from a societal perspective. That is, because of the high cost of substance abuse (estimated to be $510.8 billion in 1999—two thirds of which is attributable to the indirect cost of productivity lost due to illness [alcohol], incarceration [illicit drugs], and premature death [tobacco]), the benefit of even expensive EBPs is justified. Whether existing school budgets should or can accommodate the cost of implementing these EBPs is not, however, well addressed by these authors, although T. R. Miller and Hendrie (2009) claimed that "the out-of-pocket expenses would be repaid by savings to the education system alone in less than 2 years" (p. 34).

Observability

Whether the effectiveness of EBPs in reducing substance use is likely to be observed depends, in part, on whether the EBP being implemented is interactive or noninteractive (didactic). In a meta-analysis of school-based adolescent substance use prevention programs, Tobler et al. (2000) observed that evaluations of 69 interactive programs yielded a mean weighted effect size of approximately $d = 0.16$ across small and large programs. In contrast, the 24 noninteractive programs yielded a mean weighted effect size of approximately $d = 0.03$. Tobler et al. converted these estimates to success rates of 8% and 1%, respectively, using the Rosnow, Rosenthal, and Rubin (2000) binomial effect size display (BESD). This simple conversion assumes a 50% substance abuse rate for both the experimental and control groups and then differences the success rate (substance use or no substance use) for each condition assuming an underlying normal distribution. It is worth noting that simulations by T. R. Miller, Hendrie, and Derzon (2011) revealed that BESD only approximates the reduction in the outcome an intervention might well achieve when the problem outcome occurs in 35% to 65% of cases. For less common outcomes (e.g., most serious substance use and abuse), BESD substantially overestimates the impact of an intervention.

Although these results are statistically significant and positive, there are no objective criteria for estimating whether the effects can be considered large or small or socially meaningful, particularly when applied to prevention. For example, if the reduction in substance use observed in Tobler et al.'s (2000) meta-analysis were attributable to those youth who were destined to become problem users, even a 1% reduction might be celebrated because the costs of implementing the programs would have been far outweighed by the social benefits obtained. According to T. R. Miller and Hendrie (2009), the cost–benefit ratio of school-based life skills programs range from $0 (D.A.R.E.–Original program) to $34 (All Stars). If, on the other hand, experimental users simply desist earlier, delay initiation, or elect not to experiment at all, then even an 8% reduction in use might have little observable personal or social consequence. Until researchers have reliable means of predicting, with high sensitivity and specificity, who will and who will not become a problem user, interpreting the impact of effective prevention programming remains, at best, an inexact science.

A pertinent question is whether teachers would observe these effects. According to drug surveillance information, alcohol is the most commonly abused drug among high school seniors, with 63.5% reporting using alcohol in the past year and 28.1% reporting getting drunk in the past month (Monitoring the Future Study; Johnston et al., 2013a). Of those high school seniors who reported using alcohol in 2010, fully 93.2% reported that they never used alcohol at school (Bachman, Johnston, & O'Malley, 2011). If use is not occurring at school, or if the program is administered in younger grades when use is less likely, teachers may not be in a position to observe the effectiveness of EBPs and would not be able to contrast the results of EBPs and non-EBPs.

In sum, if the five intrinsic characteristics of diffusion of innovation are able to explain much of the variability regarding speed of adoption, then there is little reason to believe that adoption of EBPs will spontaneously increase. Regulatory changes that are enforced and that require schools to adopt EBPs would likely produce rapid change in adoption rates, but this sort of change seems unlikely. There are, however, two other factors associated with adoption that may be leveraged. These are discussed next.

SOCIAL PROCESSES IN THE THEORY OF DIFFUSION

Each of the five intrinsic characteristics of innovation described in the previous discussion of the Rogers (2003) diffusion theory influences the speed with which a drug prevention program is adopted. There are two social factors, communication and leadership, associated with adoption of EBPs. Below we discuss how social processes and EBP communication may impede or improve the adoption of EBPs.

Communication

The actual decision to adopt an innovation (i.e., drug prevention program) involves several steps. Rogers (2003) explained that this process is moderated by whether one is an early adopter, a laggard, or somewhere in between. Central to Rogers's theory is the importance of social processes in the communication of innovations. Before an innovation can be adopted, it must be communicated to potential adopters in ways that influence behavior. What Rogers and others have observed is that, although knowledge may be gained through one-way communication, for innovations of high risk or uncertainty, two-way communication with peers who share the same values and language, an opinion leader within the target's social system, and local champions to act as change agents are typically necessary.

Although program developers use multiple channels to disseminate their programs, publication in a peer-reviewed journal is the distinguishing benchmark for EBPs. If effective communication of innovations requires two-way communication and a common language, there is little reason to expect that the data in such publications will trickle down to teachers and school administrators. Publications are, by necessity, full of field-specific jargon (necessary for effective and accurate communication of complex ideas within any specialized field) and are written primarily to convey theory, method, findings, and/or conclusions to other researchers. Report summaries and lists provide a partial solution (by simplifying and providing searchable access to EBPs), but they are still primarily one-way communications that are unlikely to significantly enhance the adoption of EBPs.

Opinion Leaders

The process of conveying information about EBPs is to some degree based on social influence. The question arises then, who are the effective influencers? Opinion leaders are thought to be particularly important in promoting innovation. Often these individuals exist outside the local chain of authority (Collins, Hawks, & Davis, 2000; Katz & Lazarsfeld, 2005), which may have an interest, acknowledged or otherwise, in maintaining the status quo (Perrow, 1978). Opinion leaders are thought to have higher social status within a group (those of equal class status), greater exposure to relevant mass media, and greater interest and knowledge in the area of influence; they also tend to be more gregarious and more familiar with and loyal to group standards and values than are nonleaders (Loudon & Della Britta, 1992).

Transformational Leaders

In a study of the nonprofit organization Community in Schools, Jaskyte (2011) observed that the implementation of new services, programs, or products is related to the number of job classifications of personnel in an organization (but not size) and the presence of transformational leadership. Transformational leaders are those who motivate employees to pursue goals they may not otherwise have attempted, encourage innovation, and provide the means to achieve change.

Opinion and transformational leaders may promote EBPs, but there is nothing inherent in this leadership that ensures EBPs will be promoted. Leaders may have the capacity to influence an adoption decision, but if research-based evidence is not appreciated by these innovators relative to other considerations, they can just as easily influence the decision to adopt substance abuse programs with less empirical support.

PROMOTION OF EBPs REDEFINED

Despite the best efforts of researchers and agencies in promoting EBPs, it should be clear for multiple reasons that EBPs are not being effectively disseminated to and adopted by schools. Here, we describe two approaches that may increase the adoption of, and appreciation for, EBPs. The first describes a new role, termed *school substance abuse facilitator*, which is based on an idea that has been promoted within evidence-based medicine (practice facilitation). The second approach describes an approach to both building the evidence base and making schools partners in evidence-based substance abuse prevention.

Practice Facilitators

Greater efforts to create local champions who understand both the value and availability of EBPs, have expertise and training in organizational change, and can help local schools and administrators identify and adopt EBPs might provide the two-way communication and expert opinion necessary to influence their adoption. Evidence-based medicine has created the role of practice facilitator to fill this niche and promote the use of evidence-based treatments among primary care physicians.

Practice facilitation is a supportive service by a trained individual or team of individuals to help physicians develop the skills they need to adapt evidence-based medicine to the specific circumstance of a local practice environment. Facilitation supports a broad range of quality improvement activities and usually involves both a long-term relationship and a close connection to the local practice. Facilitators focus on assessing initial conditions, creating a tailored approach based on specific local needs, and developing feedback mechanisms to capture improvement over time. In doing this, they help promote a culture of learning and quality improvement within practices, thus setting the stage for meaningful, sustainable practice redesign (Knox et al., 2011). In many respects, the role of a practice facilitator merges the roles of a local evaluator with those of an organizational change specialist, building support for quality improvement by providing local practices with data, coaching, and objective feedback in support of improved care.

A recent meta-analysis found that primary care practices were 2.76 times as likely to adopt evidence-based guidelines if they used a practice facilitator (95% CI [2.18–3.43]; Baskerville, Liddy, & Hogg, 2012). Moreover, variation among the 23 studies included in the synthesis could be explained by sampling error. This suggests that the effect is consistent and robust across settings. Although substance abuse coordinators are tasked with filling this role, the evidence suggests that there are significant differences in the impact these professionals are having.

Practice Facilitators for EBPs in Schools

School-based practice facilitators provide expertise and support for substance abuse prevention and help to formulate effective school responses to the problem of youth substance use. As such, their value may be discounted as representing just one of the many competing services schools provide students. As conceptualized here, if their role were expanded to make them advocates for the adoption of EBPs across all school tasks and disciplines, these practice facilitators would be instrumental in creating a school culture that understands and values evidence-based programs and practices, not just for substance abuse prevention but for all school activities.

If practice facilitation provides an appropriate model for creating the change necessary to increase the adoption of EBPs, then the training and requirements for school substance abuse coordinators should be expanded to include the additional organizational change and evaluation skills of facilitators. "Practice facilitators are generalists trained in primary care improvement and have competencies in many areas, including quality improvement methods, project management, and team facilitation" (Knox et al., 2011, p. 1). This represents a new role for school-based substance abuse professionals, one that emphasizes organizational development, project management, quality improvement, and, ultimately, practice improvement. In addition to providing local expertise, evidence-based practice facilitators could provide a mechanism for two-way communication, a link between the published evidence and local practice, as well as the skills needed to promote the organizational change necessary for EBP adoption.

Synthetic Comparison

The current world of evidence-based substance abuse prevention is based on a model where experimental research is conducted on limited samples to produce (hopefully) generalizable evidence of effectiveness. The principal channel for disseminating those results is peer-reviewed journal articles. An alternative to this approach, which uses crowd-sourced evidence provided by schools and classrooms, is currently under development at Tanglewood Research in Greensboro, North Carolina. Using a synthetic difference-in-differences design (S-DID) discussed in Derzon (2014), In this model, local pre- and posttest evidence documenting the change in outcomes is collected and combined in a meta-analytic database that can be used to contrast the results of similar interventions with alternative interventions. The schools can contrast their performance with that of other schools that have implemented the same program to assess their effectiveness and perhaps identify areas for program improvement.

The idea behind the Tanglewood effort is simple. Borrowing from a research design known as differences-in-differences, the approach exploits the many natural experiments offered by the ubiquity of substance abuse interventions in schools. It is likely that many schools are using the same program or activity in an effort to reduce youth substance use. By pooling evidence from similar interventions, the synthetic comparison approach looks at the consistency of effect across multiple similar interventions and compares them with the consistency of effect from multiple implementations of an alternative intervention. The approach is associational, not causal, and documents only whether the program, as disseminated, is associated with improved outcomes relative to alternatives. Instead of a single carefully controlled trial to estimate a program's central tendency and dispersion of expected impact, the distribution and consistency of evidence across multiple program implementations is used to document an intervention's value relative to alternatives.

In this model, students provide data on risk and protective factors and substance use behaviors, which are summarized to the classroom level, while instructional staff complete a short web-based survey identifying which program and what activities were implemented, classroom demographics, and information on the school and setting in which the program was implemented. Once the data are entered, staff can access their results, compare them against other schools' implementations of the same intervention, and select how similar those comparison schools are on student or other programmatic characteristics (Hansen, Derzon, & Reese, 2012). These results can then be used to evaluate local performance and contrast the current programs' results across multiple implementations with those returned by alternative programs.

There are several reasons to believe that the synthetic comparator approach will encourage adoption of EBPs. Programs are amalgams of activities, and there is limited understanding of which activities are the core components for effectiveness (Hansen et al., 2010). Using synthetic comparators, the core components included in these programs or tested in communities can be identified and the amount of time devoted to EBPs reduced by implementing only those core activities. Because the synthetic comparators approach is primarily descriptive, for users untrained in statistical theory and research methodology, the evidence returned by the tool is likely to be more accessible (and more informative) than the statistical evidence that dominates the published literature. Because schools directly participate in creating evidence, they are more likely to trust the findings summarized by the tool. Finally, by allowing teachers to access evidence on student populations similar to theirs, they are more likely to find the evidence returned by the tool relevant to their students. In sum, the synthetic comparators approach provides a forum for testing and observing the effects of drug prevention efforts relative to alternatives, and it supports the American Association of School Administrators (2002) call for the use of data for innovation and adoption of effective practices.

On the other hand, the proposed system is only as good as the crowd-sourced data that populate the system. If local implementers and evaluators do not contribute valid and reliable data, the tool will have little value. If only a few schools participate, the findings will have little meaning. Moreover, there is the potential for misattribution; the tool assumes that all the observed change, or lack thereof, in substance abuse is attributable to the intervention entered. Since intervention selection is not random or assigned, there may be unmeasured factors correlated with intervention selection that are responsible for the result. Nonetheless, as interventions are tested across multiple settings and samples, the evidence generated in this system is self-correcting. If the majority of schools provide valid data, exceptions will appear as outliers; if third factors bias the results, their impact will become apparent over time and through follow-on implementations.

SUMMARY

In summary, although EBPs can be expected to reduce substance abuse, Rogers's (2003) theory of diffusion suggests that there may be structural, social, and evidence-based reasons that have limited their adoption in schools. To encourage the adoption of EBPs, two approaches have been proposed: use of schools' substance abuse prevention facilitators and a synthetic comparators approach to evidence generation and program evaluation. Effective adoption of EBPs requires trust in and engagement with systematic inquiry and the scientific method. Evidence-based substance abuse prevention is best understood as a quality improvement effort and not a commitment to solutions. The evidence suggests that only when decision makers understand the value of research-based evidence—and observe these programs working in their school—will they fully embrace evidence-based prevention programming.

References

Alford, A. A., & Derzon, J. (2012). Meta-analysis and systematic review of the effectiveness of school-based programs to reduce multiple violent and antisocial behavioral outcomes. In S. Jimerson, A. Nickerson,

M. Mayer, & M. Furlong (Eds.), *Handbook of school violence and school safety: International research and practice* (2nd ed., pp. 593–606). New York, NY: Routledge.

Altman, D. G., Schulz, K. F., Moher, D., Egger, M., Davidoff, F., Elbourne, D., . . . Lang, T. (2001). The revised CONSORT statement for reporting randomized trials: Explanation and elaboration. *Annals of Internal Medicine, 134*, 663–694. doi:10.7326/0003-4819-134-8-200104170-00012

American Association of School Administrators. (2002). *Using data to improve schools: What's working*. Arlington, VA: Author.

Atkins, D., Eccles, M., Flottorp, S., Guyatt, G. H., Henry, D., Hill, S., . . . The GRADE Working Group. (2004). Systems for grading the quality of evidence and the strength of recommendations I: Critical appraisal of existing approaches. The GRADE Working Group. *BMC Health Services Research, 4*, 38. doi:10.1186/1472-6963-4-38

Bachman, J. G., Johnston, L. D., & O'Malley, P. M. (2011). *Monitoring the Future: Questionnaire responses from the nation's high school seniors, 2010*. Ann Arbor, MI: Institute for Social Research.

Baskerville, N. B., Liddy, C., & Hogg, W. (2012). Systematic review and meta-analysis of practice facilitation within primary care settings. *Annals of Family Medicine, 10*, 63–74. doi:10.1370/afm.1312

Blumer, H. (1954). What is wrong with social theory? *American Sociological Review, 19*, 3–10. doi:10.2307/2088165

Burns, P. B., Rohrich, R. J., & Chung, K. C. (2011). The levels of evidence and their role in evidence-based medicine. *Plastic and Reconstructive Surgery, 128*, 305–310. doi:10.1097/PRS.0b013e318219c171

Caulkins, J. P., Rydell, C. P., Everingham, S. S., Chiesa, J., & Bushway, S. (1999). *An ounce of prevention, a pound of uncertainty: The cost-effectiveness of school-based drug prevention programs*. Santa Monica, CA: RAND Corporation.

Center for the Study and Prevention of Violence (CSPV). (2012). *Blueprints for violence prevention*. Retrieved from http://www.colorado.edu/cspv/blueprints/index.html

Collins, B. A., Hawks, J. W., & Davis, R. (2000). From theory to practice: Identifying authentic opinion leaders to improve care. *Managed Care, 9*, 56–58, 61–52.

Cox, W. M., & Alm, R. (February 10, 2008). You are what you spend. *The New York Times*. Retrieved from http://www.nytimes.com/2008/02/10/opinion/10cox.html?_r=0 http://www.nytimes.com/imagepages/2008/02/10/opinion/10op.graphic.ready.html

Crosse, S., Burr, M., Cantor, D., Hagen, C. A., & Hantman, I. (2002). *Wide scope, questionable quality: Drug and violence prevention efforts in American schools. (DOC #2001-35)*. Washington, DC: U.S. Department of Education.

Damschroder, L. J., Aron, D. C., Keith, R. E., Kirsh, S. R., Alexander, J. A., & Lowery, J. C. (2009). Fostering implementation of health services research findings into practice: A consolidated framework for advancing implementation science. *Implementation Science, 4*, 50. doi:10.1186/1748-5908-4-50

Derzon, J. H. (2007). Using correlational evidence to select youth for prevention programming. *The Journal of Primary Prevention, 28*, 421–447. doi:10.1007/s10935-007-0107-7

Derzon, J. H. (2014). Differences-indifferences in approaches. In G. J. N. Bruinsma & D. L. Weisburd (Eds.), *Encyclopedia of criminology and criminal justice* (pp. 1054–1064). New York, NY: Springer Science+Business Media.

Einhorn, H. J., & Hogarth, R. M. (1986). Judging probable cause. *Psychological Bulletin, 99*, 3. doi:10.1037/0033-2909.99.1.3–19.

Flay, B. R., Biglan, A., Boruch, R. F., Castro, F. G., Gottfredson, D., Kellam, S., . . . Ji, P. (2005). Standards of evidence: Criteria for efficacy, effectiveness and dissemination. *Prevention Science, 6*, 151–175. doi:10.1007/s11121-005-5553-y

Freidberg, S. (2010). *Fresh: A perishable history*. Cambridge, MA: Harvard University Press.

Gandhi, A. G., Murphy-Graham, E., Petrosino, A., Chrismer, S. S., & Weiss, C. H. (2007). The devil is in the details: Examining the evidence for "proven" school-based drug abuse prevention programs. *Evaluation Review, 31*, 43–74. doi:10.1177/0193841X06287188

Glasgow, R. E., Lichtenstein, E., & Marcus, A. C. (2003). Why don't we see more translation of health promotion research to practice? Rethinking the efficacy-to-effectiveness transition. *American Journal of Public Health, 93*, 1261–1267. doi:10.2105/AJPH.93.8.1261

Gorman, D. M. (2005). Drug and violence prevention: Rediscovering the critical rational dimension of evaluation research. *Journal of Experimental Criminology, 1*, 39–62. doi:10.1007/s11292-004-6461-z

Gottfredson, G. D., Gottfredson, D. C., Czeh, E. R., Cantor, D., Crosse, S. B., & Hantman, I. (2000). *National Study of Delinquency Prevention in Schools: Final report*. Ellicott City, MD: Gottfredson Associates. doi:10.1017/CBO9780511720246

Greenhalgh, T., Robert, G., MacFarlane, F., Bate, P., & Kyriakidou, O. (2004). Diffusion of innovations in service organizations: Systematic review and recommendations. *Milbank Quarterly*, *82*, 581–629. doi:10.1111/j.0887-378X.2004.00325.x

Griffith, K. N., & Scheier, L. M. (2013). Did we get our money's worth? Bridging economic and behavioral measures of program success in adolescent drug prevention. *International Journal of Environmental Research and Public Health*, *10*, 5908–5935. doi:10.3390/ijerph10115908

Hallfors, D., & Godette, D. (2002). Will the "Principles of Effectiveness" improve prevention practice? Early findings from a diffusion study. *Health Education Research*, *17*, 461–470. doi:10.1093/her/17.4.461

Hamilton, L. S., Stecher, B. M., Marsh, J. A., McCombs, J. S., Robyn, A., Russell, J., & Barney, H. (2007). *Standards-based accountability under No Child Left Behind: Experiences of teachers and administrators in three states.* Santa Monica, CA: RAND Corporation.

Hanley, S. M., Ringwalt, C. L., Ennett, S. T., Vincus, A. A., Bowling, J. M., Haws, S. W., & Rohrbach, L. A. (2010). The prevalence of evidence-based substance use prevention curricula in the nation's elementary schools. *Journal of Drug Education*, *40*, 51–60. doi:10.2190/DE.40.1.d

Hansen, W. B., Derzon, J. H., Dusenbury, L., Bishop, D., Campbell, K., & Alford, A. A. (2010). Operating characteristics of prevention programs: Connections to drug etiology. In L. M. Scheier (Ed.), *Handbook of drug use etiology: Theory, methods, and empirical findings* (pp. 597–616). Washington, DC: American Psychological Association.

Hansen, W. B., Derzon, J. H., & Reese, E. L. (2012). A synthetic comparator approach to local evaluation of school-based substance use prevention programming. *Evaluation & the Health Professions*, *37*, 258–282.

Hansen, W. B., Dusenbury, L., Bishop, D., & Derzon, J. H. (2007). Substance abuse prevention program content: Systematizing the classification of what programs target for change. *Health Education Research*, *22*, 351–360.

Hantman, I., & Crosse, S. (2000). *Progress in prevention: Report on the National Study of Local Education Agency Activities under the Safe and Drug-Free Schools and Communities Act.* Washington, DC: U.S. Department of Education.

Institute of Medicine. (2001). *Crossing the quality chasm: A new health system for the 21st Century.* Washington, DC: The National Academies Press. Retrieved from http://www.nap.edu/catalog.php?record_id=10027

Jaskyte, K. (2011). Predictors of administrative and technological innovations in nonprofit organizations. *Public Administration Review*, *71*, 77–86. doi:10.1111/j.1540-6210.2010.02308.x

Johnston, L. D., O'Malley, P. M., Bachman, J. G., & Schulenberg, J. E. (2013a). *Monitoring the Future: National survey results on drug use, 1975–2012. Vol. I. Secondary school students.* Ann Arbor: Institute for Social Research, The University of Michigan.

Johnston, L. D., O'Malley, P. M., Bachman, J. G., & Schulenberg, J. E. (2013b). *Monitoring the Future: National results on drug use, 2012 overview: Key findings on adolescent drug use.* Ann Arbor: Institute for Social Research, The University of Michigan. Retrieved from http://monitoringthefuture.org/pubs/monographs/mtf-overview2012.pdf

Kahneman, D. (2011). *Thinking, fast and slow.* New York, NY: Farrar, Straus, & Giroux.

Katz, E., & Lazarsfeld, P. (2005). *Personal influence: The part played by people in the flow of mass communications.* Piscataway, NJ: Transaction.

Knox, L., Taylor, E. F., Geonnotti, K., Machta, R., Kim, J., Nysenbaum, J., & Parchman, M. (2011). *Developing and running a primary care practice facilitation program: A how-to guide.* Prepared by Mathematica Policy Research under Contract No. HHSA290200900019I TO 5 (AHRQ Publication No. 12-0011). Rockville, MD: Agency for Healthcare Research and Quality.

Loudon, D. L., & Della Britta, A. J. (1992). *Consumer behavior: Concepts and applications* (4th ed.). New York, NY: McGraw-Hill.

Mihalic, S. (2002). *Matrix of programs as identified by various federal and private agencies.* Retrieved from http://blueprintsprograms.com/resources/Matrix_Criteria.pdf

Miller, S. I., & Safer, L. A. (1993). Evidence, ethics and social policy dilemmas. *Education Policy Analysis Archives*, *1*, 1–15.

Miller, T. R., & Hendrie, D. (2009). *Substance abuse prevention dollars and cents: A cost-benefit analysis* (DHHS Pub. No. [SMA] 07-4298). U.S. Department of Health and Human Services. Substance Abuse and Mental Health Services Administration. Rockville, MD: Center for Substance Abuse Prevention.

Miller, T. R., Hendrie, D., & Derzon, J. (2011). Exact method for computing absolute percent change in a dichotomous outcome from meta-analytic effect size: Improving impact and cost-outcome estimates. *Value in Health*, *14*, 144–151. doi:10.1016/j.jval.2010.10.013

National Registry of Evidence-Based Practices and Programs. (2013). *SAMHSA's National Registry of Evidence-Based Practices and Programs: About NREPP.* Retrieved from http://www.nrepp.samhsa.gov/AboutNREPP.aspx

No Child Left Behind Act of 2001, Pub. L. No. 107-110, § 115 (2002).

Oxford Centre for Evidence-Based Medicine. (2011). *The Oxford 2011 Levels of Evidence.* Retrieved from http://www.cebm.net/index.aspx?o=5653

Pankratz, M. M., & Hallfors, D. D. (2004). Implementing evidence-based substance use prevention curricula in North Carolina public school districts. *The Journal of School Health, 74*, 353–358. doi:10.1111/j.1746-1561.2004.tb06628.x

Perrow, C. (1978). Demystifying organizations. In R. C. Sarri & Y. Hasenfeld (Eds.), *The Management of human services* (pp. 105–122). New York, NY: Columbia University Press.

Ringwalt, C., Hanley, S., Vincus, A., Ennett, S., Rohrbach, L., & Bowling, J. (2008). The prevalence of effective substance use prevention curricula in the nation's high schools. *The Journal of Primary Prevention, 29*, 479–488. doi:10.1007/s10935-008-0158-4

Ringwalt, C. L., Ennett, S., Vincus, A., Thorne, J., Rohrbach, L. A., & Simons-Rudolph, A. (2002). The prevalence of effective substance use prevention curricula in U.S. middle schools. *Prevention Science, 3*, 257–265. doi:10.1023/A:1020872424136

Rogers, E. M. (2003). *Diffusion of innovations* (5th ed.). New York, NY: Free Press.

Rohrbach, L. A., D'Onofrio, C. N., Backer, T. E., & Montgomery, S. B. (1996). Diffusion of school-based substance abuse prevention programs. *American Behavioral Scientist, 39*, 919–934. doi:10.1177/0002764296039007012

Rohrbach, L. A., Ringwalt, C. L., Ennett, S. T., & Vincus, A. A. (2005). Factors associated with adoption of evidence-based substance use prevention curricula in U.S. school districts. *Health Education Research, 20*, 514–526. doi:10.1093/her/cyh008

Rosnow, R. L., Rosenthal, R., & Rubin, D. B. (2000). Contrasts and correlations in effect-size estimation. *Psychological Science, 11*, 446–453. doi:10.1111/1467-9280.00287

Shamblen, S. R., & Derzon, J. H. (2009). A preliminary study of the population-adjusted effectiveness of substance abuse prevention programming: Towards making IOM program types comparable. *The Journal of Primary Prevention, 30*, 89–107. doi:10.1007/s10935-009-0168-x

Tobler, N. S., Roona, M. R., Ochshorn, P., Marshall, D. G., Streke, A. V., & Stackpole, K. M. (2000). School-based adolescent drug prevention programs: 1998 meta-analysis. *The Journal of Primary Prevention, 20*, 275–336. doi:10.1023/A:1021314704811

U.S. Department of Education. (2011). *Prevalence and implementation fidelity of research-based prevention programs in public schools: Final report.* Office of Planning, Evaluation and Policy Development, Policy and Program Studies Service. Washington, DC: U.S. Department of Education.

CHAPTER 29

DISSEMINATION OF EVIDENCE-BASED PREVENTION PROGRAMS: THE BROAD PICTURE

Elise T. Pas and Catherine P. Bradshaw

This chapter summarizes promising approaches for overcoming common obstacles encountered in the dissemination of evidence-based substance abuse prevention programs. We start by defining the many facets and prevailing theories of dissemination that inform these definitions, as the lack of clarity in terms has limited our ability to draw inferences from the extant dissemination research. Next, we discuss how the research process can further enhance understanding, and therefore dissemination, of prevention interventions. We then highlight the current mechanisms for diffusing information on effective programs and identify areas to consider in the development of programs to enhance dissemination. We conclude with recommendations for research and the practice of dissemination.

We adopt a Type 2 translational research perspective (Spoth et al., 2013; Woolf, 2008) throughout this chapter and emphasize the importance of future work in the area of dissemination and implementation science. Unlike Type 1 translational research, which uses clinical trials to establish the efficacy of interventions, Type 2 research examines the effectiveness of these proven practices, interventions, or treatments when they are disseminated and implemented in real-world settings (Woolf, 2008). This framework provides an overarching theme for our exploration of factors influencing and facilitating the program dissemination process (Fishbein & Ridenour, 2013; Pentz, 2010).

A primary goal of prevention science is to achieve population-level effects for scientifically based and rationally sound interventions that target important public health concerns (Flay et al., 2005). Large-scale dissemination of effective practices is required to achieve this laudable goal. In the case of substance use prevention, a long tradition of rigorously conducted, theory-driven experimental trials demonstrate the efficacy and effectiveness of a variety of interventions that can be implemented across multiple settings, involving schools, after-care settings, health clinics, or even whole communities. Despite repeated efforts demonstrating the possibility of developing efficacious drug-use prevention programs, a remaining concern is how to disseminate these interventions broadly enough that they can be used to promote the public health agenda. Currently, the dissemination of evidence-based prevention programs lacks significant and consistent progress. Recent studies document, for example, that fewer than 10% of the programs implemented in schools to prevent drug use and crime are research based and less than half of all schools implement even one research-based program (Ringwalt et al., 2011; U.S.

Preparation of this chapter was supported by grants for the U.S. Department of Education (R305A090307 and R324A07118). The content of this chapter is solely the responsibility of the authors and does not necessarily represent the official views of the U.S. Department of Education.

The authors would like to thank Dr. Nicholas Ialongo for contributions to this chapter.

http://dx.doi.org/10.1037/14550-030
Handbook of Adolescent Drug Use Prevention: Research, Intervention Strategies, and Practice, L. M. Scheier (Editor)

Department of Education, 2012a). These recent findings support earlier research showing consistently poor dissemination and implementation of evidence-based programs (Gottfredson & Gottfredson, 2002; Ringwalt et al., 2009).

PREVAILING THEORIES OF DISSEMINATION

A number of models have been proposed to describe the process of dissemination of interventions. Much of the research in this area has characterized dissemination as a nonlinear process. Whereas some theories focus on the stages involved in implementing new programs (Adelman & Taylor, 1997), other theories emphasize the processes needed to ensure that interventions are spread and implemented (Domitrovich et al., 2008; Rogers, 2002; Wandersman et al., 2008). The prevailing theories of dissemination recognize that for an intervention to reach the target population, a number of conditions must be met. For example, in aiming to disseminate their intervention (Wandersman et al., 2008), researchers must provide information to the public, specifically to local agencies such as schools, community and rehabilitative centers, and the like, which would utilize the program or *diffuse* the model (Rogers, 2002). Rogers (2002) described the process of diffusion as the communication of information about an innovation such as a new idea or program "through certain channels over time" (p. 990), providing insights into different ways to ensure that innovations gain acceptance and are adopted. This includes obtaining stakeholder buy-in, garnering the enthusiasm of "local champions," and facilitating the diffusion of the intervention through social and peer networks (Dearing, 2009). Rogers outlined a series of stages of the diffusion process that can be easily applied to the terms *adoption, implementation, dissemination*, and *maintenance* (Rohrbach, Grana, Sussman, & Valente, 2006), each of which is described in the following sections.

Theory suggests that when an organization (e.g., a school) is trying to engage in programmatic change, it must first create *readiness for change*. This requires garnering stakeholder buy-in (i.e., community support) and preparation with regard to the time, staff, resources, and materials needed for the successful adoption of a program (Adelman & Taylor, 1997). Next, the organization can engage in an *initial implementation*, which focuses on providing support and guidance to staff for the actual implementation. Wandersman and colleagues (2008) referred to these preparation and initial implementation phases as the *prevention support systems*, within their interactive systems framework (ISF) for dissemination and implementation. Following initial implementation is *institutionalization*, in which an agency accepts responsibility for ensuring that the intervention is pursued in the long term (i.e., maintenance), including devising ways (e.g., ongoing supports and training) to counteract opposing forces that may diminish implementation fidelity over time. Finally, the fourth stage is *ongoing evolution and renewal*, which refers to the continued feedback on the agency's progress and obstacles faced, allowing for the *maintenance* of a program. With the accumulation of evaluation knowledge, it is expected that the program or intervention may undergo some refining. When a program is widely disseminated within a jurisdiction (e.g., a county, city, state), or scaled up, there are additional considerations (Bradshaw & Pas, 2011; Bradshaw et al., 2012; Dearing, 2009; Pas & Bradshaw, 2012).

Wandersman et al. (2008) identified three systems (prevention delivery, prevention support, and prevention synthesis and translation systems) that are involved in the translation of research to practice in the ISF for dissemination and implementation. This framework suggests that a system needs to be in place to deliver interventions, to facilitate implementation, and to prepare interventions to be received and used. Research evidence, and thus the preparation for intervention *diffusion*, is provided by the prevention synthesis and translation system. The prevention delivery system refers to the infrastructure needed (e.g., time, funding) by the implementing organization (Wandersman et al., 2008); the development of the prevention delivery system is what takes place when *creating readiness* (Adelman & Taylor, 1997). The issue of putting facilitating supports in place for schools was discussed by Domitrovich and colleagues (2008); they also presented macro-, school-, and individual-level factors and the appropriate supports that will "reduce variability in the quality of program implementation by providing the means and establishing the context for the delivery of interventions" (p. 7). Like Wandersman et al. (2008), Domitrovich et al. discussed the intervention and support systems as two layers to be considered in the implementation model.

DEFINING THE MULTIPLE FACETS OF DISSEMINATION

In summarizing the research on the dissemination of preventive intervention programs for substance use and abuse, one should first define the term *dissemination* and acknowledge the numerous terms used in relation to dissemination theory and research. Dissemination within prevention science is typically considered the dispersal of research-based practices, programs, or interventions that target prevention of negative outcomes such as substance use or abuse, delinquency, smoking, obesity, physical diseases, and so on. Defining dissemination is complicated because, to disseminate programs effectively, a number of conditions must be met and nonlinear steps must be taken, as outlined above. These steps introduce additional terms, some of which are used interchangeably with one another and with the term *dissemination*. In addition, within different fields (e.g., physical health, mental health, education, sociology), different terms are used or emphasized, further confusing the issue. The stages of adoption, implementation, dissemination, and maintenance are described more fully, and overlap and commonalities are highlighted, in the discussion that follows.

Adoption

The construct of *adoption* entails multiple steps. First, any agency (e.g., a school) must gain knowledge of the existence of a program and make a decision that they are interested in using it (Rogers, 2002). This may occur (a) because an agency recognizes a need for intervention and seeks out a specific program (i.e., a user-based approach; Wandersman et al., 2008); (b) as part of a top-down process whereby an agency (e.g., a school) is told to implement a program by a higher authority (e.g., the district or state); (c) through a partnership between researchers (e.g., university faculty) and the agency, whereby a university is looking to examine the effects of a program or study the dissemination process; or (d) through a marketing process undertaken by a program developer. The latter two situations are "source-based dissemination" (Wandersman et al., 2008, p. 173) and can be credited with much of the research on evidence-based programs (Botvin, Baker, Dusenbury, Tortu, & Botvin, 1990; Sussman, Dent, & Stacy, 2002).

Once an agency acquires information about a program, personnel must decide to adopt it (Dearing, 2009; Rogers, 2002); adoption may involve engaging in some agreement to participate (i.e., by requesting or purchasing instructional materials and distributing these among personnel). Following the decision to adopt a program, an agency will often also need to receive some training (e.g., by a program developer, an agency-based trainer, a community- or district-based trainer). The construct of adoption is subsumed under *creating readiness* and the *initial implementation* stages (Adelman & Taylor, 1997) and involves the *diffusion* stage discussed by Rogers (2002).

Implementation

Defining when an agency is actively *implementing* a program or the *quality* with which an intervention is implemented is the most complex of the steps involved in the dissemination process. There are many terms associated with implementation and little consensus and specificity as to their definition. In addition, the line between *adoption* and *implementation* is somewhat blurry. Rogers (2002) suggested that an agency "adopts" a program when they have agreed to use it. However, it is conceivable that adoption should include evidence that the program was actually implemented and not just purchased (e.g., Bradshaw & Pas, 2011). Implementation is one of the most important areas to consider when thinking about dissemination, as implementation quality has implications for the outcomes attained. Current studies indicate that implementation of drug abuse prevention programs is poor (i.e., fewer than half of programs are implemented with minimal fidelity; Ringwalt et al., 2011; U.S. Department of Education, 2012a), highlighting that the need is not just about disseminating programs but rather disseminating programs that are then implemented with high fidelity.

In the literature regarding implementation, common terms used are *implementation quality*, *fidelity*, *fidelity of implementation (FOI)*, and *program integrity* (e.g., see Dane & Schneider, 1998; Domitrovich & Greenberg, 2000; Gresham, Gansle, Noell, Cohen, & Rosenblum, 1993). These terms can all be used quite broadly, where *quality* refers to how well a program is implemented and *fidelity* and *integrity* capture the extent to which the practice of the intervention mirrors the planned, and often prescribed, practice (Dusenbury, Brannigan, Falco, & Hansen, 2003). There is an implicit expectation that determining when fidelity has occurred can be measured by the implementation of the *critical components* of the intervention (Century, Rudnick, & Freeman, 2010). Notwithstanding, assessing fidelity is difficult, given the lack of empirical evidence regarding critical components of interventions—an issue that is further discussed later in this chapter.

The terms *quality, fidelity*, and *integrity* are also used interchangeably with a number of other terms. For example, *implementation quality* has been used to describe how well the implementer delivers the message of the program specifically (e.g., content and affect, implementer enthusiasm for the intervention; Domitrovich & Greenberg, 2000). In some cases, *fidelity* and simply *implementation* have been used interchangeably with *adherence* (e.g., Blakely et al., 1987; Domitrovich & Greenberg, 2000; Glasgow, Vogt, & Boles, 1999), which has been defined as the extent to which an intervention is implemented as indicated (i.e., the same definition as fidelity; Century et al., 2010) or the extent to which the implementer abides by the implementation parameters detailed in a treatment manual or curriculum and/or uses the treatment materials, respectively (Beets et al., 2008; Domitrovich & Greenberg, 2000). *Dosage* has been described similarly to adherence, as the amount of treatment someone receives (e.g., frequency and duration; Dusenbury et al., 2003).

Three other terms, *exposure*, *program differentiation*, and *participant responsiveness* have also been identified as components of implementation (Bloomquist, August, Horowitz, Lee, & Jensen, 2008; Dane & Schneider, 1998; Domitrovich & Greenberg, 2000) but are less well defined or clearly related to implementation. *Exposure* has been measured a number of different ways, including Likert-type items asking how frequently parts of a curriculum are used (e.g., Beets et al., 2008) and, more like dosage, as the number of sessions conducted (Bloomquist et al., 2008). *Program differentiation* is the extent to which a program is measurably different from other interventions being implemented. The concept of differentiation is useful in determining that a treatment and comparison condition do in fact experimentally differ with regard to level of manipulation. This distinction is particularly useful in the context of research trials examining evidence-based interventions (Dane & Schneider, 1998) and can contribute to the study of intervention components (Dusenbury et al., 2003), but it is not a component of implementation in practice (Century et al., 2010). *Participant responsiveness* can also be discussed and measured as engagement, participation, and enthusiasm for the intervention (Century et al., 2010; Dane & Schneider, 1998).

Collectively, *implementation science* refers to the ongoing, empirically based research program that assesses the elements mentioned above. In order to contribute knowledge to implementation science, researchers must measure multiple facets of implementation and include factors at multiple levels (Domitrovich et al., 2008), both to determine whether null effects could be due to less than optimal implementation and to highlight associations between desired outcomes and the implementation of intervention components (Dane & Schneider, 1998; Domitrovich & Greenberg, 2000; Gresham et al., 1993). Currently, the assessment of implementation fidelity is often lacking or completely absent (Dane & Schneider, 1998; Durlak & Wells, 1998) in studies conducted across many fields, although this is less problematic in the drug abuse prevention literature (Domitrovich & Greenberg, 2000).

Maintenance, Sustainability, and Institutionalization

Along with the multiple facets of implementation and dissemination, many facilitators and obstacles to these processes have been theoretically, and in some cases empirically, identified. Examples include

(a) the attitudes and beliefs about the program on the part of the designated implementers (Beets et al., 2008); (b) climate of the setting where a program will be implemented (Beets et al., 2008); (c) training and coaching provided to implementers (Dane & Schneider, 1998; Dusenbury et al., 2003); (d) structure of the intervention (Domitrovich et al., 2009; Domitrovich & Greenberg, 2000; Pas, Bradshaw, & Cash, 2013); (e) the user-friendly nature of instructional materials (Rohrbach et al., 2006); (f) buy-in and commitment from high-ranking officials, such as principals in schools (Kam, Greenberg, & Walls, 2003); (g) time elapsed since training (Bradshaw & Pas, 2011); and (h) contextual aspects of the environment where the program is being implemented (e.g., leadership, organization; Domitrovich et al., 2009; Glisson & Green, 2006).

These facilitators and detractors for implementation directly relate to the issue of *maintenance* or *institutionalization*, whereby an organization is able to utilize a program or intervention for the long term and has put in place supports (e.g., personnel, budgetary, policy) to ensure continued implementation. *Sustainability* refers to the extent to which a program lends itself to becoming part of the agency's greater mission in the long term. If a program cannot be implemented in the short term because of insurmountable (real or perceived) obstacles, then it certainly will not be sustainable over the long term. When barriers to implementation are removed, it is possible that effect sizes for programs will be greater and therefore programs will be more desirable to the public (Ginexi & Hilton, 2006). Finally, the widespread *dissemination* of interventions across multiple agencies is referred to in the literature as *diffusion* (Rogers, 2002), *replication* (Adelman & Taylor, 1997), *scaling up* (Bradshaw & Pas, 2011), or *rolling out* (Adelman & Taylor, 1997) of interventions (Botvin & Griffin, 2010).

HOW RESEARCH INFORMS THE DISSEMINATION PROCESS

There is increasing interest among federal agencies, researchers, and policymaker sin moving research findings into real-world settings, often referred to as *translational research* or *Type 2 research* (Fishbein & Ridenour, 2013; Pentz, 2010; Spoth et al., 2013). Type 2 research explores the translation of programs or the processes by which they are disseminated and for whom and under what circumstances the programs best work. The effectiveness of a program (vs. its efficacy) can be thought of as the interplay between efficacy in clinical trials and implementation in the real world (Glasgow et al., 1999) and is an essential part of demonstrating that an intervention is replicable (Collins, Murphy, & Bierman, 2004).

Unfortunately, effectiveness trials conducted in the real world often have supplemental supports (e.g., external funding, training) to promote implementation fidelity that may not be present in real-world, non–trial-based implementation (Glasgow et al., 1999) the infusion of such support and funding also limits the external validity of effectiveness study findings. In addition, because cooperation and buy-in are important elements of implementation, as they are for involvement in research trials, current research is often conducted in samples that are highly motivated. This compounds concerns regarding generalizability and external validity because the trial samples do not necessarily represent the true target population (Glasgow et al., 1999; Humphreys, Harris, & Weingardt, 2008). Within the framework of efficacy, concerns about external validity are to be expected, given that efficacy trials are supposed to determine effects under *ideal circumstances*.

Although there is an established literature supporting the efficacy and effectiveness of a variety of intervention approaches or programs targeting drug use (e.g., Derzon, Sale, Springer, & Brounstein, 2005; O'Connell, Boat, & Warner, 2009; Tobler & Stratton, 1997; Wilson, Gottfredson, & Najaka, 2001), as well as ongoing developmental work, the missing key to successfully addressing substance use and addiction at a population level is the translation of evidence-based interventions (Domitrovich & Greenberg, 2000; Rohrbach et al., 2006; Woolf, 2008). More specifically, Type 2 translational research "that investigates the complex processes and systems through which evidence-based interventions are adopted, implemented, and sustained on a large scale" (Spoth et al., 2013, p. 319) is lacking. There is a dearth of knowledge on how efficacious programs are chosen by communities and schools, the factors that influence their adoption, whether these programs are adequately implemented when communities independently implement them, the conditions under which programs are successfully disseminated, and the effects of programs outside of the context of research trials. The lacking knowledge about the aforementioned issues illustrates a clear need for additional research on the process of dissemination (or planned diffusion; Schoenwald & Hoagwood, 2001) of evidence-based programs.

THE EVIDENCE BEHIND EVIDENCE-BASED PROGRAMS

The federal government has taken an instrumental role in promoting the examination of interventions, as well as in publicizing information regarding interventions that are deemed effective. These efforts are present in policy emphasizing the funding of research into the efficacy of drug abuse prevention programs and in the requirement that agencies use federal funds to implement such programs (Office of National Drug Control Policy, 1999). In response to these requirements, many studies have evaluated the effectiveness of a wide range of interventions, and government agencies have produced and publicly shared documentation of this process (e.g., Center for Substance Abuse Prevention, 2001). Following on the heels of this work, numerous repositories now list programs that are effective or exemplary (i.e., "model"), promising, or in need of further validation and empirical scrutiny (e.g., the Blueprints for Healthy Youth Development [Blueprints], Center for the Study and Prevention of Violence, 2014; National Registry for Evidence-Based Programs and Practices [NREPP], The What Works Clearinghouse, U.S. Department of Education, 2012b; U.S. Department of Health and Human Services, 2012).

Generally speaking, the compilation of exemplary, effective, or evidence-based programs depends on an external and objective determination (i.e., by an expert panel assigned by a government-funded contractor) of the research to ensure that the program has been rigorously tested and demonstrated clinically significant effects. The rigor with which these reviews are conducted and repositories created is critical, given that in past years the majority of states receiving funds from the Safe and Drug-Free Schools and Communities Act (established within an amendment to the Elementary and Secondary Education Act of 1965; now referred to as the Safe and Supportive Schools Initiative) select their evidence-based programs from such federal registries (Hallfors, Pankratz, & Hartman, 2007). Thus, federal registries such as NREPP or the Blueprints serve as a main vehicle for providing information to the public about what has passed scientific scrutiny and is considered evidence based.

A criticism of existing repositories is that the standard chosen to determine that a program is "exemplary" or "evidence based" varies across lists. For example, Blueprints (Center for the Study and Prevention of Violence, 2014) has evaluation criteria that require studies to undertake a randomized controlled trial or employ matched-comparison groups and demonstrate implementation fidelity. In addition, to be labeled a "model program," replication studies of effectiveness must be available (Center for the Study and Prevention of Violence, 2014). The requirement for replication is required only by the Blueprints criteria and not by other federally organized repositories such as NREPP (U.S. Department of Health and Human Services, 2012). Thus, other repositories may categorize programs as exemplary or evidence based solely on the basis of the results of developer-conducted research. In some cases, developers and nondevelopers have conducted research regarding the effectiveness of programs when replication was not possible, so using developer-conducted research can be problematic. To further exacerbate the issue around replication, null findings often fail to be published but, rather, are relegated to a file drawer of nonpublishable results. Therefore, when a replication study fails to demonstrate the same (significant) findings as a developer-led study, the results may never reach the public. Therefore, it is most desirable that programs be determined to be evidence based only when there is replication of findings and that, ideally, such activity be conducted by a team that has no financial ties to the intervention or developer (Flay et al., 2005; Gorman, 1998, 2005).

BRINGING PROGRAMS TO THE PUBLIC THAT GAIN ACCEPTANCE AND ARE ADOPTED

Development and Packaging Considerations

Kreuter and Bernhardt (2009) asserted that the "near-total absence of systems and infrastructure to carry out marketing and distribution" (p.1) of prevention programs is to blame for the absence of dissemination of these programs (see also Fixsen, Naoom, Blase, Friedman, & Wallace, 2005). The proper market research (Adelman & Taylor, 1997, p. 203) should be conducted as a means for creating readiness for programmatic change. The market research would include (a) assessing what potential adopting agencies want or need; (b) packaging the intervention for ready use and application; (c) promoting the intervention; (d) distributing the intervention; (e) communicating before, during, and after adoption; (f) providing proper training, technical assistance, and rapid response to needs; (g) coordinating the services; and (h) collecting and analyzing data (Kreuter & Bernhardt, 2009; Rohrbach et al., 2006). In other words, a program needs to be tailored to the needs of its "audience" so that it is perceived as compatible with the agency's goals (Rogers, 2002). It is also critical that support (e.g., coaching, training) be provided to ensure proper implementation. The disconnect in the former may occur because marketing is very business oriented, whereas many of the prevention programs found to be effective are developed by researchers with expertise in behavioral sciences and less experience in product commercialization. To assist in overcoming these impediments to marketing, the federal government offers funding to commercialize programs developed and tested with federal funds, through the Small Business Innovation Research mechanism.[1]

In addition, prevention scientists can, and have, outlined dissemination processes to ensure that the preventive interventions reach communities that would most likely benefit from them. One example of these dissemination processes is the Communities That Care model (CTC; Developmental Research and Programs, 1997; Hawkins & Catalano, 2004). CTC (see Chapter 19, this handbook) supports the collection and systematic use of community-level data for a needs assessment, which then guides the selection and implementation of preventive strategies, including those targeting substance use (Hawkins, Catalano, & Arthur, 2002). The community-prevention partnership collaborative model uses a five-phase, data-driven, analytic problem-solving approach to form an action plan, select evidence-based interventions, and implement them. This type of dissemination approach has also been referred to as a *user-based model* (Wandersman et al., 2008). CTC often incorporates schools into the prevention activities, thereby targeting school-age children and adolescents. CTC aims to create prosocial norms and community bonds by providing opportunities for communication among community members and guiding community mobilization and by providing training through a central organization (Hawkins et al., 2002). Ultimately, it is expected that the involved community will take ownership of the process. Studies of CTC in four states (Pennsylvania [Feinberg, Bontempo, & Greenberg, 2008]; Oregon [Harachi, Ayers, Hawkins, & Catalano, 1996]; Washington [Manger, Hawkins, Haggerty, & Catalano, 1992]; Indiana [Myers & Arter, 2005]) and a randomized, controlled trial (Fagan, Arthur, Hanson, Briney, & Hawkins, 2011; Fagan, Hanson, Hawkins, & Arthur, 2008) consistently have documented that, even with limited funding, communities can implement the CTC process, and, furthermore, CTC sites are more likely to select evidence-based programs than are non-CTC sites.

Similarly, programs that are easy to implement (Dearing, 2009; Dusenbury et al., 2003; Rogers, 2002), that are familiar and user friendly (Rohrbach et al., 2006), and that can be integrated with existing work conducted by the agency (Dearing, 2009; Domitrovich et al., 2010) are likely to be the most well received and, one hopes, implemented with fidelity. To ensure these elements are present, a program must have a clear theory of behavior change with identified core elements that are explicitly stated (Dusenbury et al., 2003). This crucial issue is discussed further in the following paragraphs and in the Recommendations section.

[1] Available from http://www.drugabuse.gov/funding/funding-opportunities/science-education-grants-contracts/sbirsttr

Adaptability and Portability of Programs

The issue of marketing prevention programs is further complicated by the extent to which the program is adaptable and portable. To reach a broad audience (i.e., to be disseminated widely), a program needs to meet the needs of many individuals and organizations. This is quite onerous for a single, highly structured program that emphasizes primary prevention (Dusenbury et al., 2003). To address this, interventions should be flexible enough to allow implementers to make changes without dramatically altering the essential elements of the intervention (Han & Weiss, 2005). Such flexibility would address the fact that practitioners in the real world desire programs that are adaptable to fit the perceived needs of their institution (e.g., treatment centers, schools) and target audience (Dane & Schneider, 1998). Moreover, the agency wants to know that they can institute desired adaptations whether or not the intervention is designed to be adapted (Dusenbury et al., 2003). In fact, research for decades has shown that agencies will make adaptations by modifying existing components, adding components, or even excluding components they feel are unnecessary or irrelevant (Dusenbury, Brannigan, Hansen, Walsh, & Falco, 2005; Rohrbach et al., 2006). These types of ad hoc modifications present an important issue, as the empirical basis for evidence-based interventions almost never provides support for dropping, modifying, or adding components. In the meantime, one recommendation is that local implementers be encouraged to add, rather than change or delete, elements of an intervention (Dearing, 2009). The deletion of elements is not recommended, as implementers may inadvertently dilute effects by eliminating a core component.

The issue of adaptation is important for many reasons. First, interventions are not always studied within the samples of people who need them most (e.g., within diverse samples in terms of race/ethnicity, socioeconomic status, geographic location; Glasgow et al., 1999). If an intervention is deemed culturally misaligned with a target population, practitioners may adapt it despite lacking formal science to guide this process. Adaptations can also benefit an agency; by making the intervention a better fit for the agency, ownership of the program is enhanced (Blakely et al., 1987). Adaptations that ensure that the cultural needs of the population are met should promote maintenance and sustainability of the programs. Without scientific evidence about the extent to which a program can be altered and achieve desired outcomes, however, practitioners and researchers cannot know where to draw the line in the argument for or against adaptation. Researchers and program developers need to find the fine balance between an essential set of core components and the flexibility for implementation across a variety of settings (Dusenbury et al., 2003).

Funding of Programs

Funding of intervention programs can have a measurable, if not large, impact on all parts of the dissemination process. Without adequate funding, agencies are unlikely to adopt an intervention, even if it is evidence based and would replace non–evidence-based programs. When considering whether to adopt an intervention, agencies will inevitably look at the relative advantage of implementing a new program (Dearing, 2009; Rogers, 2002), and both present and future costs are likely to play into this decision. This raises the issue of less expensive programs that have small effects in the present and larger, more beneficial effects in the future, versus more costly programs in the present that may net immediate effects but have less influence on future behavior. Both scenarios can encourage or dissuade agencies from adopting an intervention. When interventions are funded by a special program or are set into motion as part of a research trial, particularly in the case of expensive interventions, agencies are unlikely to continue their work with the program if there are additional costs to continue once the financial stimulus from the research trial ends (e.g., in schools; Adelman & Taylor, 1997). The problem of continued funding is further exacerbated when an agency agrees to implement an intervention only as part of a special project, to attain additional resources, but has no real commitment to using the program. This disjoint can detract from both implementation and sustainability (Adelman & Taylor, 1997).

Positive Behavioral Interventions and Supports (PBIS; Horner, Sugai, Todd, & Lewis-Palmer, 2005; Sugai & Horner, 2006) is an example of how widely disseminated a low-cost and adaptable framework can be. PBIS is a noncurricular prevention framework that helps school personnel alter the school environment in order to promote positive student behaviors. The intervention is implemented in over 20,000 schools in the United States, partly because it is free of cost and materials are available via the Internet. In addition, given that PBIS is a framework rather than a manualized intervention, it is flexible and adaptable to the organizational level. In addition, the development of partnerships and infrastructure to train schools across states has enabled large-scale school and even district-wide trainings (Barrett, Bradshaw, & Lewis-Palmer, 2008; Bradshaw & Pas, 2011; Bradshaw et al., 2012).

RECOMMENDATIONS FOR IMPROVING THE DISSEMINATION OF PREVENTION PROGRAMS

To improve the dissemination of prevention programs, improvements upon research, interventions, and the message surrounding the programs will be needed. Here we expand on each of these areas.

Improving Research

The scope of research on prevention programs needs to be expanded in order to enhance our understanding of dissemination and our ability to achieve the population-level effects sought. In doing so, first, the language used in reference to implementation and dissemination needs clarification. As this chapter highlights, there is a large lexicon of terms used when discussing dissemination and implementation; often these words are used interchangeably and yet have different conceptual anchors. The absence of consistency in the use of terms makes the conversation about dissemination more difficult. In addition, the range of terms is symptomatic of and also likely the cause of an inconsistency in the measurement of areas of implementation, maintenance, and dissemination. It is impossible to expect that there can be a shared approach to measuring these constructs when there is no shared conceptual framework to describe them. Although researchers may vary in their use of terminology, the field as a whole should be cognizant of the language used to capture key constructs and clarify these terms in peer-reviewed publications. Focal constructs that fall under this discussion have included adoption, fidelity, dissemination, implementation, diffusion, and evidence-based, to name a few. Beyond the clarification of language in the literature, two specific lines of research are needed, and are summarized in the following sections.

Improving understanding of implementation in the real world. One way to specifically improve research is to include measures that are broader in nature to help create a more cohesive dissemination and implementation science (Century et al., 2010). Though many researchers are thinking and writing about these important issues, and in some cases even analyzing implementation and dissemination data, measures are too often "based on their particular contexts and programs of interest, leaving the field with a collection of disparate measures and ad hoc theories" (Century et al., 2010, p. 200). Faced with a large variety of measures serving different purposes, capturing different constructs, and achieving varying levels of reliability and validity, researchers find it difficult to compare preventive efforts across settings; to determine how widely implemented certain evidence-based practices or approaches are; to compare treatment and comparison or control conditions to determine the extent of differentiation in the two settings; or to compare the findings from evaluations of different programs (Century et al., 2010). In addition, Dusenbury et al. (2003) suggested that the reliability and validity of implementation measures is often assumed, rather than empirically examined. These issues are explicitly talked about within *implementation science* but should be part of the conversation in all effectiveness research.

Explicitly studying the dissemination process. Second, research should explicitly examine the dissemination process following a comprehensive framework for Type 2 translational research, including (a) Translation stage-setting, (b) Institutional or individual adoption, (c) Effective implementation, and (d) Sustainability (TIES; SPR MAPS II Task Force, 2008). These four elements of research comprehensively address the dissemination issues related to prevention and intervention programs targeting a number of public health outcomes, including the prevention of drug use. More specifically, studies that explore the acceptability and feasibility of interventions (translation stage-setting) are needed, including the diffusion of knowledge to agencies regarding the intervention and garnering their interest. Institutional or individual adoption of an evidence-based intervention should be studied through the examination of factors relating to the decision to adopt an intervention and assessing ways to transmit the intervention to the larger community (e.g., schools, clinics, hospitals, after-care programs). Finally, implementation studies that incorporate comprehensive assessments, as well as those that assess the long-term use of interventions, are scarce in the extant literature (Spoth et al., 2013).

Improving Interventions

The purpose of improving research regarding dissemination and implementation is to improve interventions, making them more feasible, acceptable, and accessible, and therefore more widely used. This process occurs through a feedback loop whereby refined research occurs regarding components of interventions, interventions are disseminated, and research continues. Research regarding the *essential elements* (also referred to as core components, critical components, and active ingredients) of drug use prevention is currently lacking (see also Century et al., 2010). Below, we focus on approaches that will provide empirical evidence for the adaptation of interventions, mainly by isolating core components and optimizing interventions.

Explicitly study evidence-based practices, not just interventions. Prevention programs have often been built with multiple components in order to ensure effects can be caused and detected; this is a goal that has been reached in many instances. In the future, greater testing for and inclusion of the necessary elements to achieve change or outcomes is also desired.

The key to meeting this need is to focus more on the effects of individual program components, for example, isolating specific modalities such as social skills training and normative education. This distinction would result in the study of interventions with fewer components and comparing components incrementally with one another (i.e., componential analysis); this requires clear theoretical models for interventions as well as an explicit measurement of program differentiation (Collins et al., 2011; Dusenbury et al., 2003). Once research supports the individual impacts of components, the synergistic effects of multimodal programs will also be better understood. Framed somewhat differently, a focus on components rather than whole interventions may be the distinction between evidence-based *practices* versus evidence-based *interventions* or *programs* or what has also been referred to as "kernels" (Embry & Biglan, 2008).

The issue of essential elements also relates to the issue of adaptation. With a better understanding of the essential elements of interventions, it will be easier to decipher what can and cannot be modified or excluded from practitioners' implementation. Programs that fit with a particular context are more likely to be implemented (Hogan et al., 2003). The explicit study of interventions in different target populations and the effectiveness of adaptations is also required to provide greater external validity of interventions and promote their widespread dissemination. Currently, anyone trying to understand which parts of an intervention are essential or whether the intervention truly needs to be implemented as prescribed to have the desired effects will find that the knowledge base is incomplete (Domitrovich & Greenberg, 2000).

Optimize interventions. Taken a step further, by understanding the effects of individual components, prevention researchers can *optimize* prevention interventions. Collins et al. (2011) provided an overview of the multiphase optimization strategy (or MOST), a process that uses factorial experiments to test varying core components of an intervention. This process ensures incremental benefits of each component while meeting consumer constraint criteria (e.g., cost, time). The MOST approach focuses on determining the most efficient components to achieve outcomes, while taking into account the constraints of the consumers. The MOST approach may also lead to interventions that include only essential elements, rather than providing a collection of components, some of which may or may not work (Collins et al., 2011). Methodologically, the factorial design approach in the MOST maximizes statistical power because, although there are multiple conditions, the main effects estimates are based on the full sample (Collins et al., 2011). Furthermore, causal conclusions can be drawn because the factorial design utilizes randomization to test a priori hypotheses; this is in juxtaposition to post hoc implementation analyses in randomized trials, which simply compare one treatment and one control condition (Collins et al., 2011).

Improving and Diffusing the Message

Prevention researchers also need to enhance how information about evidence-based interventions is diffused. In order to do so, a two-pronged approach should be taken whereby a large audience is first informed about the interventions (e.g., through mass media) to spread the word broadly (Rogers, 2002). This effort needs to be balanced with promoting the formation of positive attitudes regarding the intervention, which is best achieved by peers, rather than experts (Rogers, 2002). As discussed above, market research may be an important aspect of this process (Adelman & Taylor, 1997; Kreuter & Bernhardt, 2009). Taken a step further, interventions that engage mass media and technology are more likely to be widely disseminated and potentially perceived favorably. Mass media and technology fit well within the prevention framework, as a means for providing universal prevention through awareness (see Chapters 20–22, this volume). This technique has also been used successfully in the past (e.g., in the 1980s and 1990s to disseminate antismoking messages; see Wakefield et al., 2008).

Currently, the Internet is a dominant source of published information regarding available effective programs. Understandably, the rigor with which interventions are evaluated varies, and therefore so do program ratings. Though the majority of states refer schools to federal registries for the selection of programs paid for by the Safe and Drug Free Schools and Communities Act, there is little information regarding how well utilized these lists are and whether they satisfy the needs of agencies, especially schools. We do, however, know that utilization of research-based programs is poor enough to warrant concern (U.S. Department of Education, 2012a). It also happens that states refer schools to websites that no longer exist (Hallfors et al., 2007). Improvements could be made to the consistency of these registries, perhaps by aligning them with the Society for Prevention Research Standards of Evidence (Flay et al., 2005; also see Hallfors et al., 2007). These registries could also be more dynamic, reflecting the most recent knowledge about a program, in terms of a program's being more or less effective (Hallfors et al., 2007).

CONCLUSION

This chapter defined and summarized the multiple concepts associated with the dissemination of evidence-based substance abuse prevention programs. A foundation that outlines the essential ingredients of effective dissemination is crucial for obtaining clarity as the field begins to explore factors that both inhibit and accelerate "going to scale." This chapter also identified various mechanisms for providing agencies with information regarding the effectiveness of existing programs. Although there remains much work to be done in the area of dissemination science, the increasing emphasis on Type 2 translational research provides a framework for guiding future research in this area.

References

Adelman, H. S., & Taylor, L. (1997). Toward a scale-up model for replicating new approaches to schooling. *Journal of Educational & Psychological Consultation*, *8*, 197–230. doi:10.1207/s1532768xjepc0802_6

Barrett, S. B., Bradshaw, C. P., & Lewis-Palmer, T. (2008). Maryland statewide PBIS initiative: Systems, evaluation, and next steps. *Journal of Positive Behavior Interventions*, *10*, 105–114. doi:10.1177/1098300707312541

Beets, M. W., Flay, B. R., Vuchinich, S., Acock, A. C., Li, K.-K., & Allred, C. (2008). School climate and teachers? Beliefs and attitudes associated with implementation of the positive action program: A diffusion of innovations model. *Prevention Science*, *9*, 264–275. doi:10.1007/s11121-008-0100-2

Blakely, C. H., Mayer, J. P., Gottschalk, R. G., Schmitt, N., Davidson, W. S., Roitman, D. B., & Emshoff, J. G. (1987). The fidelity-adaptation debate: Implications for the implementation of public sector social programs. *American Journal of Community Psychology*, *15*, 253–268. doi:10.1007/BF00922697

Bloomquist, M. L., August, G. J., Horowitz, J. L., Lee, S. S., & Jensen, C. (2008). Moving from science to service: Transposing and sustaining the Early Risers prevention program in a community service system. *The Journal of Primary Prevention*, *29*, 307–321. doi:10.1007/s10935-008-0142-z

Botvin, G. J., Baker, E., Dusenbury, L., Tortu, S., & Botvin, E. M. (1990). Preventing adolescent drug abuse through a multimodal cognitive-behavioral approach: Results of a 3-year study. *Journal of Consulting and Clinical Psychology, 58*, 437–446. doi:10.1037/0022-006X.58.4.437

Botvin, G. J., & Griffin, K. W. (2010). Advances in the science and practice of prevention: Targeting individual-level etiologic factors and the challenge of going to scale. In L. Scheier (Ed.), *Handbook of drug use etiology: Theory, methods, and empirical findings* (pp. 631–650). Washington, DC: American Psychological Association.

Bradshaw, C. P., & Pas, E. T. (2011). A state-wide scale-up of Positive Behavioral Interventions and Supports (PBIS): A description of the development of systems of support and analysis of adoption and implementation. *School Psychology Review, 40*, 530–548.

Bradshaw, C. P., Pas, E. T., Barrett, S., Bloom, J., Hershfeldt, P., Alexander, A., . . . Leaf, P. (2012). A state-wide partnership to promote safe and supportive schools: The PBIS Maryland Initiative. *Administration and Policy in Mental Health and Mental Health Services Research, 39*, 225–237. doi:10.1007/s10488-011-0384-6

Center for Substance Abuse Prevention. (2001). *Science-based substance abuse prevention: A guide* (DHHS Publication No. SMA 01-3505). Rockville, MD: Department of Health and Human Services.

Center for the Study and Prevention of Violence. (2014). *Blueprints for Healthy Youth Development*. Retrieved from http://www.colorado.edu/cspv/blueprints/criteria.html

Century, J., Rudnick, M., & Freeman, C. (2010). A framework for measuring fidelity of implementation: A foundation for shared language and accumulation of knowledge. *The American Journal of Evaluation, 31*, 199–218. doi:10.1177/1098214010366173

Collins, L. M., Baker, T. B., Mermelstein, R. J., Piper, M. E., Jorenby, D. E., Smith, S. S., . . . Fiore, M. C. (2011). The Multiphase Optimization Strategy for engineering effective tobacco use interventions. *Annals of Behavioral Medicine, 41*, 208–226. doi:10.1007/s12160-010-9253-x

Collins, L. M., Murphy, S. A., & Bierman, K. L. (2004). A conceptual framework for adaptive preventive interventions. *Prevention Science, 5*, 185–196. doi:10.1023/B:PREV.0000037641.26017.00

Dane, A. V., & Schneider, B. H. (1998). Program integrity in primary and early secondary prevention: Are implementation effects out of control? *Clinical Psychology Review, 18*, 23–45. doi:10.1016/S0272-7358(97)00043-3

Dearing, J. W. (2009). Applying diffusion of innovation theory to intervention development. *Research on Social Work Practice, 19*, 503–518. doi:10.1177/1049731509335569

Derzon, J. H., Sale, E., Springer, J. F., & Brounstein, P. (2005). Estimating intervention effectiveness: Synthetic projection of field evaluation results. *The Journal of Primary Prevention, 26*, 321–343. doi:10.1007/s10935-005-5391-5

Developmental Research and Programs. (1997). *Communities That Care: A comprehensive prevention program*. Seattle, WA: Author.

Domitrovich, C. E., Bradshaw, C. P., Greenberg, M. T., Embry, D., Poduska, J. M., & Ialongo, N. S. (2010). Integrated models of school-based prevention: Logic and theory. *Psychology in the Schools, 47*, 71–88.

Domitrovich, C. E., Bradshaw, C. P., Poduska, J. M., Hoagwood, K. E., Buckley, J. A., Olin, S., . . . Ialongo, N. S. (2008). Maximizing the implementation quality of evidence-based preventive interventions in schools: A conceptual framework. *Advances in School Mental Health Promotion, 1*, 6–28. doi:10.1080/1754730X.2008.9715730

Domitrovich, C. E., Gest, S. D., Gill, S., Bierman, K. L., Welsh, J. A., & Jones, D. (2009). Fostering high-quality teaching with an enriched curriculum and professional development support: The Head Start REDI Program. *American Educational Research Journal, 46*, 567–597. doi:10.3102/0002831208328089

Domitrovich, C. E., & Greenberg, M. T. (2000). The study of implementation: Current findings from effective programs that prevent mental disorders in school-age children. *Journal of Educational & Psychological Consultation, 11*, 193–221. doi:10.1207/S1532768XJEPC1102_04

Durlak, J. A., & Wells, A. W. (1998). Evaluation of indicated preventive intervention (secondary prevention) mental health programs. *American Journal of Community Psychology, 26*, 775–802. doi:10.1023/A:1022162015815

Dusenbury, L., Brannigan, R., Falco, M., & Hansen, W. B. (2003). A review of research on fidelity of implementation: Implications for drug abuse prevention in school settings. *Health Education Research, 18*, 237–256. doi:10.1093/her/18.2.237

Dusenbury, L., Brannigan, R., Hansen, W. B., Walsh, J., & Falco, M. (2005). Quality of implementation: Developing measures crucial to understanding the diffusion of preventive interventions. *Health Education Research, 20*, 308–313. doi:10.1093/her/cyg134

Elementary and Secondary Education Act of 1965 (ESEA), as amended, Title IV, Part A, Subpart 1, Secs. 4111–4117; 20 U.S.C. § 7111–7117.

Embry, D. D., & Biglan, A. (2008). Evidence-based kernels: Fundamental units of behavioral influence. *Clinical Child and Family Psychology Review, 11*, 75–113. doi:10.1007/s10567-008-0036-x

Fagan, A. A., Arthur, M. W., Hanson, K., Briney, J. S., & Hawkins, J. D. (2011). Effects of Communities That

Care on the adoption and implementation fidelity of evidence-based prevention programs in communities: Results from a randomized controlled trial. *Prevention Science, 12*, 223–234. doi:10.1007/s11121-011-0226-5

Fagan, A. A., Hanson, K., Hawkins, J. D., & Arthur, M. W. (2008). Bridging science to practice: Achieving prevention program implementation fidelity in the Community Youth Development Study. *Journal of Community Psychology, 41*, 235–249. doi:10.1007/s10464-008-9176-x

Feinberg, M. E., Bontempo, D. E., & Greenberg, M. T. (2008). Predictors and level of sustainability of community prevention coalitions. *American Journal of Preventive Medicine, 34*, 495–501. doi:10.1016/j.amepre.2008.01.030

Fishbein, D. H., & Ridenour, T. A. (2013). Advancing transdisciplinary translation for prevention of high-risk behaviors: Introduction to the special issue. *Prevention Science, 14*, 201–205. doi:10.1007/s11121-013-0394-6

Fixsen, D. L., Naoom, S. F., Blase, K. A., Friedman, R. M., & Wallace, F. (2005). *Implementation research: A synthesis of the literature.* Tampa: University of South Florida, Louis de la Parte Florida Mental Health Institute, The National Implementation Research Network.

Flay, B. R., Biglan, A., Boruch, R. F., Castro, F. G., Gottfredson, D., Kellam, S., . . . Ji, P. (2005). Standards of evidence: Criteria for efficacy, effectiveness and dissemination. *Prevention Science, 6*, 151–175. doi:10.1007/s11121-005-5553-y

Ginexi, E. M., & Hilton, T. F. (2006). What's next for translation research? *Evaluation & the Health Professions, 29*, 334–347. doi:10.1177/0163278706290409

Glasgow, R. E., Vogt, T. M., & Boles, S. M. (1999). Evaluating the public health impact of health promotion interventions: The REAIM framework. *American Journal of Public Health, 89*, 1322–1327. doi:10.2105/AJPH.89.9.1322

Glisson, C., & Green, P. (2006). The effects of organizational culture and climate on the access to mental health care in child welfare and juvenile justice systems. *Administration and Policy in Mental Health and Mental Health Services Research, 33*, 433–448. doi:10.1007/s10488-005-0016-0

Gorman, D. M. (1998). The irrelevance of evidence in the development of school-based drug prevention policy, 1986–1996. *Evaluation Review, 22*, 118–146. doi:10.1177/0193841X9802200106

Gorman, D. M. (2005). Drug and violence prevention: Rediscovering the critical rational dimension of evaluation research. *Journal of Experimental Criminology, 1*, 39–62. doi:10.1007/s11292-004-6461-z

Gottfredson, G. D., & Gottfredson, D. C. (2002). Quality of school-based prevention programs: Results from a national survey. *Journal of Research in Crime and Delinquency, 39*, 3–35. doi:10.1177/002242780203900101

Gresham, F. M., Gansle, K. A., Noell, G. H., Cohen, S., & Rosenblum, S. (1993). Treatment integrity of school-based behavioral intervention studies: 1980–1990. *School Psychology Review, 22*, 254–272.

Hallfors, D. D., Pankratz, M., & Hartman, S. (2007). Does federal policy support the use of scientific evidence in school-based prevention programs? *Prevention Science, 8*, 75–81. doi:10.1007/s11121-006-0058-x

Han, S. S., & Weiss, B. (2005). Sustainability of teacher implementation of school-based mental health programs. *Journal of Abnormal Child Psychology, 33*, 665–679. doi:10.1007/s10802-005-7646-2

Harachi, T. W., Ayers, C. D., Hawkins, J. D., & Catalano, R. F. (1996). Empowering communities to prevent adolescent substance abuse: Process evaluation results from a risk- and protection-focused community mobilization effort. *The Journal of Primary Prevention, 16*, 233–254. doi:10.1007/BF02407424

Hawkins, J. D., & Catalano, R. F. (2004). *Communities That Care: Prevention strategies guide.* South Deerfield, MA: Channing Bete.

Hawkins, J. D., Catalano, R. F., & Arthur, M. W. (2002). Promoting science-based prevention in communities. *Addictive Behaviors, 27*, 951–976. doi:10.1016/S0306-4603(02)00298-8

Hogan, J. A., Baca, I., Daley, C., Garcia, T., Jaker, J., Lowther, M., & Klitzner, M. (2003). Disseminating science-based prevention: Lessons learned from CSAP's CAPTs. *Journal of Drug Education, 33*, 233–243. doi:10.2190/DWMW-0T6T-61N1-GB7X

Horner, R. H., Sugai, G., Todd, A. W., & Lewis-Palmer, T. (2005). School-wide positive behavior support. In L. Bambara & L. Kern (Eds.), *Individualized supports for students with problem behaviors: Designing positive behavior plans* (pp. 359–390). New York, NY: Guilford Press.

Humphreys, K., Harris, A. H. S., & Weingardt, K. R. (2008). Subject eligibility criteria can substantially influence the results of alcohol-treatment outcome research. *Journal of Studies on Alcohol and Drugs, 69*, 757–764.

Kam, C. M., Greenberg, M. T., & Walls, C. T. (2003). Examining the role of implementation quality in school-based prevention using the PATHS curriculum. *Prevention Science, 4*, 55–63. doi:10.1023/A:1021786811186

Kreuter, M. W., & Bernhardt, J. M. (2009). Reframing the dissemination challenge: A marketing and distribution perspective. *American Journal of Public Health, 99*, 2123–2127. doi:10.2105/AJPH.2008.155218

Manger, T. H., Hawkins, J. D., Haggerty, K. P., & Catalano, R. F. (1992). Mobilizing communities to reduce risks for drug abuse: Lessons on using research to guide prevention practice. *The Journal of Primary Prevention*, *13*, 3–22. doi:10.1007/BF01341778

Myers, D. L., & Arter, M. (2005). Evaluating the implementation of Indiana area Communities That Care. *Crime Prevention and Community Safety*, *7*, 43–52. doi:10.1057/palgrave.cpcs.8140208

O'Connell, M. E., Boat, T., & Warner, K. E. (2009). *Preventing mental, emotional, and behavioral disorders among young people: Progress and possibilities*. Washington, DC: National Academies Press.

Office of National Drug Control Policy. (1999). *National drug control strategy: Performance measures of effectiveness: Implementation and findings*. Washington, DC: Executive Office of the President.

Pas, E. T., & Bradshaw, C. P. (2012). Examining the association between implementation and outcomes: State-wide scale-up of School-Wide Positive Behavior Intervention and Supports. *The Journal of Behavioral Health Services & Research*, *39*, 417–433. doi:10.1007/s11414-012-9290-2

Pas, E. T., Bradshaw, C. P., & Cash, A. (2013). Coaching classroom-based preventive interventions. In M. Weist, N. Lever, C. P. Bradshaw, & J. Owens (Eds.), *Handbook of School Mental Health* (2nd ed., pp. 255–268). New York, NY: Springer.

Pentz, M. A. (2010). Translating research into practice and practice into research for drug use prevention. In L. Scheier (Ed.), *Handbook of drug use etiology: Theory, methods, and empirical findings* (pp. 581–596). Washington, DC: American Psychological Association.

Ringwalt, C., Vincus, A. A., Hanley, S., Ennett, S. T., Bowling, J. M., & Rohrbach, L. A. (2009). The prevalence of evidence-based drug use prevention curricula in U.S. middle schools in 2005. *Prevention Science*, *10*, 33–40. doi:10.1007/s11121-008-0112-y

Ringwalt, C. L., Vincus, A. A., Hanley, S., Ennett, S. T., Bowling, J. M., & Haws, S. (2011). The prevalence of evidence-based drug use prevention curricula in U.S. middle schools in 2008. *Prevention Science*, *12*, 63–69. doi:10.1007/s11121-010-0184-3

Rogers, E. M. (2002). Diffusion of preventive innovations. *Addictive Behaviors*, *27*, 989–993. doi:10.1016/S0306-4603(02)00300-3

Rohrbach, L. A., Grana, R., Sussman, S., & Valente, T. W. (2006). Type II Translation: Transporting prevention interventions from research to real-world settings. *Evaluation & the Health Professions*, *29*, 302–333. doi:10.1177/0163278706290408

Schoenwald, S. K., & Hoagwood, K. (2001). Effectiveness, transportability, and dissemination of interventions: What matters when? *Psychiatric Services*, *52*, 1190–1197. doi:10.1176/appi.ps.52.9.1190

Spoth, R., Rohrbach, L. A., Greenberg, M., Leaf, P., Brown, C. H., Fagan, A., . . . Hawkins, J. D. (2013). Addressing core challenges for the next generation of Type 2 translation research and systems: The Translation Science to Population Impact (TSci Impact) Framework. *Prevention Science*, *14*, 319–351. doi:10.1007/s11121-012-0362-6

SPR MAPS II Task Force. (2008). *Type 2 translational research: Overview and definitions*. Retrieved from http://www.preventionscience.org/SPR_Type%202%20Translation%20Research_Overview%20and%20Definition.pdf

Sugai, G., & Horner, R. H. (2006). A promising approach for expanding and sustaining School-Wide Positive Behavior Support. *School Psychology Review*, *35*, 245–259.

Sussman, S., Dent, C. W., & Stacy, A. W. (2002). Project Towards No Drug Abuse: A review of the findings and future directions. *American Journal of Health Behavior*, *26*, 354–365. doi:10.5993/AJHB.26.5.4

Tobler, N. S., & Stratton, H. H. (1997). Effectiveness of school-based drug prevention programs: A meta-analysis of the research. *The Journal of Primary Prevention*, *18*, 71–128. doi:10.1023/A:1024630205999

U.S. Department of Education. (2012a). *Prevalence and implementation fidelity of research-based prevention programs in public schools: Final report*. Washington, DC: Author. Retrieved from http://www2.ed.gov/rschstat/eval/other/research-based-prevention.pdf

U.S. Department of Education. (2012b). *What Works Clearinghouse*. Retrieved from http://ies.ed.gov/ncee/wwc/findwhatworks.aspx

U.S. Department of Health and Human Services. (2012). *SAMHSA's National Registry of Evidence-Based Programs and Practices*. Retrieved from http://www.nrepp.samhsa.gov/

Wakefield, M. A., Durkin, S., Spittal, M. J., Siahpush, M., Scollo, M., Simpson, J. A., . . . Hill, D. (2008). Impact of tobacco control policies and mass media campaigns on monthly adult smoking prevalence. *American Journal of Public Health*, *98*, 1443–1450. doi:10.2105/AJPH.2007.128991

Wandersman, A., Duffy, J., Flaspohler, P., Noonan, R., Lubell, K., Stillman, L., . . . Saul, J. (2008). Bridging the gap between prevention research and practice: The Interactive Systems Framework for Dissemination and Implementation. *American Journal of Community Psychology*, *41*, 171–181. doi:10.1007/s10464-008-9174-z

Wilson, D. B., Gottfredson, D. C., & Najaka, S. S. (2001). School-based prevention of problem behaviors: A meta-analysis. *Journal of Quantitative Criminology*, *17*, 247–272. doi:10.1023/A:1011050217296

Woolf, S. H. (2008). The meaning of translational research and why it matters. *JAMA*, *299*, 211–213. doi:10.1001/jama.2007.26

CHAPTER 30

CONCLUDING REMARKS: THE FUTURE IS HERE NOW

Lawrence M. Scheier

> We are not students of some subject matter but students of problems. (Popper, 1963, p. 88)

I had quite simple intentions when I initially outlined the chapters for this handbook. The first was to offer a forum for the exchange of ideas about what makes prevention so valuable to our society. I surmise that readers now have a much clearer picture of the social importance of our work, the benefits of prevention to youths as well as to society, and also the tremendous economic windfall that arises from promoting healthy, socially minded, law-abiding youths. My second intention involved a bit of guile and sheer provocation. Here, I asked, or quite frankly goaded, certain chapter authors to undress their programs, many of which are multimodal, and discuss how they work (as opposed to spending time rehashing that they work). My sole intention in this activity was to have luminaries in the field of prevention science ruminate about the action theories that drive their program content. I coupled this with a specific request to embed this discussion of intervening mechanisms in a theoretical context. I felt this put a nice touch on the handbook, whose contents are driven mostly by theory, some by application, and all by great problems weighing on society. Honestly speaking, the contributing authors have exceeded my expectations in every way imaginable. This leads me to believe that the handbook should have tremendous utility for readers and provide a microscopic view of what we all yearn to know.

My third intention was to ensure that the handbook serves a broader pedagogic function. Here, my aspirations can be summarized quite succinctly by stating that I wanted readers from all walks of life, coming from different academic disciplines, and occupying varying points in their career to realize that success in prevention science comes from blending theory with methods, not choosing one over the other (an excellent illustration of this point can be found in Bentler & Speckart, 1979). If we carefully follow the lead provided by the basic tenets of prevention science, we can use the powerful tool of theory as a way to clarify how something as complex as the human mind actually works. The effort of combining theory and methods brings us one step closer to resolving the critical black-box issues that define important goals for the science of prevention.

Practically speaking, the handbook had one additional focus, which was to stimulate the necessary social dialogue that places science within the realm of practice. Kuhn (1970) argued that the ingredients of this dialogue are essential for the success of science overall. The dialogue (persuasive argumentation) is so vital because it provides the means for science as a whole to reveal any faults in our thinking and find ways to refine the errors that plague our models. In defending the basic approach of science, Kuhn wrote that the "process of learning a theory depends upon the study of applications, including practice problem-

http://dx.doi.org/10.1037/14550-031
Handbook of Adolescent Drug Use Prevention: Research, Intervention Strategies, and Practice, L. M. Scheier (Editor)

solving both with a pencil and paper and with instruments in the laboratory" (p. 47). He also indicated that science provides a means to confirm or dispute theories of human behavior, and in the current context, this effort, manifested through well-conceived interventions, is an attempt to clarify our hunches about the world (i.e., this is the maturity and refinement that science provides).

Many of the handbook's chapters emphasized application so that readers could gain an appreciation of the day-to-day labors required to bring science into the classroom or the community at large. Cowen (1980) called this effort the "wooing of primary prevention," underscoring that program developers are essentially agents of change. Regardless of perspective, education, or professional training, the contributors to this handbook collectively focused on discovering the kernels, or seeds, that represent reliable ways to change human behavior (Embry & Biglan, 2008). Kernels, according to Embry and Biglan (2008), "provide prescriptions for how the social environment can show more support of human development" (p. 79). In the context of drug prevention, kernels can be as simple as verbal praise, using public commitments to prevent youth cigarette smoking, discussing descriptive norms to encourage antidrug attitudes, or teaching techniques for relaxed breathing and progressive relaxation to reduce anxiety. On a grander scale, kernels can be associations built through exposure to statewide or national media campaigns—associations that resonate to the point they suppress youths' desire to smoke marijuana. In any of these examples, kernels have the power to change behavior. This clarifies that the task of prevention science is to elaborate action theory on the basis of kernels that effectively alter behavior. The handbook provides a roadmap to study these kernels, close up, from the point of conception to delivery in real-world contexts.

EDUCATING PREVENTION SCIENTISTS

When I entered graduate school in the early 1980s, the academic community showed no indication of formally recognizing prevention science. I found my way to this field indirectly through counseling psychology and stimulated by the necessity of finding gainful employment to support my graduate education. This is not the case today because individuals can find their way to formal education in prevention science (e.g., Eddy, Smith, Brown, & Reid, 2005). Members of the older "vintage" generation might find this quite odd, given that formal training in health promotion initially had very little traction in academic circles. The propitious beginnings of prevention science took hold across various disciplines but largely relied on evaluation science (e.g., Lipsey & Cordray, 2000; Mark, 2003). To my recollection, back in the 1980s there was no prevention department to speak of and little university backing for degree certification in this field. More important, there was little in the way of specific curriculum instruction dedicated to prevention science.

How quickly things have changed. Today, one can obtain advanced graduate training in prevention science with exposure to diverse curricula. The Society for Prevention Research lists several degree-oriented programs (http://www.preventionresearch.org/conferences/training/), and several National Institutes of Health T32 training centers focused on advanced prevention science training offer both pre- and postdoctoral fellowship opportunities (e.g., the Prevention Methodology and Training Program at Pennsylvania State University, which can be found at http://methodology.psu.edu/pamt/; the Center for Prevention Implementation Methodology at the University of Miami, which can be found at http://cepim.med.miami.edu; and the Prevention Research Center at the University of California, Berkeley, in conjunction with the Pacific Institute for Research and Evaluation, which can be found at http://www.prev.org/preventiontraining/). These are only a handful of funded centers that teach prevention science, and many chapters in this handbook are written by contributors from various government-funded prevention research centers.

Almost 30 years ago, Price (1986; see also Price, Cowen, Lorion, & Ramos-McKay, 1989) suggested that education of prevention scientists was a "haphazard affair" (p. 293) and that, with few exceptions, prevention science was traditionally run as an apprenticeship model rather than as part of some formal education. Price also pointed out that "the design of preventive innovations still relies more heavily on the individual skills of a few adventurous researchers than it does on a set of standard scientific principles and criteria for the development of effective innovations" (p. 290). In making these claims, Price also discussed the concept of "boundary spanning" (p. 301), suggesting that the complexity of prevention science necessitated a broad but systematic education. Even today, 3 decades later, scholarly publications routinely suggest that prevention science is nothing less than complex (Lich, Ginexi, Osgood, & Mabry, 2013).

Quite frankly, Price (1986) forecasted a bit of where we are today in several ways. First, he suggested that prevention scientists require several layers of requisite knowledge. This knowledge includes etiology and risk factor research (problem analysis), program development (innovation design and technology), intervention (implementation and evaluation of field trials), and innovation diffusion (modification followed by standardization). Today, a modest refinement would include integrating research with practice and detailing whether this process contributes to policy formulation (Biglan & Fishbein, 2011; Hallfors, Pankratz, & Hartman, 2007; Pentz, 2000). This latter emphasis reminds us that program evaluation is not just about methodology and logic models but also concerns establishing the benefits to society from applying rigorous scientific practices to study behavior change in a way that can influence positive youth adaptation.

Price (1983) also felt that it was near impossible that "any single role is capable of encompassing the enormous complexity and diversity of the research to be undertaken in the name of prevention" (p. 291). It is interesting, notwithstanding the passage of time, that Price's views dovetail nicely with the emphasis of modern prevention science. In more than one way, for Price and others, the future of prevention is now. The education of prevention scientists is now front and center with a vastly greater amount of resources placed by the federal government to create the next generation of prevention scientists. The educational focus now blends developmental life-span psychology with population-based epidemiology (Kellam, Koretz, & Mościcki, 1999). A heavy dose of statistical knowledge is also required to support program evaluation (e.g., MacKinnon, Lockwood, Hoffman, West, & Sheets, 2002). This effort can entail, for example, use of novel classification techniques to examine treatment specificity (e.g., Lanza & Rhoades, 2013). There is also greater emphasis on cross-fertilization of ideas from different facets of neuroscience, genetics, medicine, economics, and behavioral studies. To wit, Collins, Murphy, and Bierman (2004) proposed concepts borrowed from engineering to structure a framework of adaptive interventions. Any number of programs have used the adaptive strategies concept (i.e., stepped-up graded intervention practices), including the very successful Fast Track program, which targets, among other things, preventing conduct disorders (Conduct Problems Prevention Research Group, 2000).

Perhaps the greatest change in the education of prevention scientists is recognizing that the petri dish in which evaluation studies take place is actually a thriving community of sorts. Regardless of their intrinsic size or whether they encompass after-school settings in boys and girls clubs, entire school districts, or whole communities, it is necessary to understand the needs, wishes, and desires of the prevention allies before implementation (Arthur & Blitz, 2000). This effort has created a new wave of community–research partnerships (Feinberg, Chilenski, Greenberg, Spoth, & Redmond, 2007; Spoth, Greenberg, Bierman, & Redmond, 2004) effectively designed around building capacity (Johnson, Hays, Center, & Daley, 2004). Here, I am reminded of Joe Durlak's introduction to this handbook, in which he addressed the bundle of activities surrounding program adoption and the essential factors that fuel implementation science, including among other mainstays fidelity, capacity, diffusion, and sustainability.[1] As Joe pointed out, all of this effort makes prevention real and, when addressed systematically, can make prevention effective.

[1] I have noticeably left out mention of cultural appropriateness or the suitability of programs for different sociocultural contexts. Culture is one of several tailoring variables (e.g., Barrera & Castro, 2006; Marek, Brock, & Sullivan, 2006), and the evidence has suggested this social construction is more than just skin deep (Rowe, Vazsonyi, & Flannery, 1994). At the very least, a program intended for broad dissemination cannot sustain itself if it is not culturally appropriate. Several recent publications have suggested that culture is part of the process of implementation and is also vital to construction of program content (e.g., Barrera, Castro, & Holleran Steiker, 2011). Culturally grounded interventions (e.g., Kulis et al., 2005) have suggested that community-initiated modifications to curriculum development and building capacity from the ground up will more readily bring programs to scale (Castro, Barrera, & Martinez, 2004). Nevertheless, these issues are adequately covered under capacity and sustainability without distinguishing cultural sensitivity as a unique feature of program development.

Consideration of Joe's comments regarding program adoption produces three overarching concerns: fostering community members' belief that (a) program benefits would improve the community's prevention goals (practices); (b) the community would be provided sufficient resources to execute the program (money, materials, and personnel); and (c) there would be an appreciation of the human dynamics of change, involving rewards, incentives, and encouragement, all leading to user involvement and ownership. This is the crux of what makes a community motivated to adopt a program and also provides a basis for continued implementation long after the researcher has left town (e.g., Chaskin, 2001; Swisher, 2000).

The general framework of capacity building has been discussed in terms of behavioral science technology transfer, involving efforts to build sufficient resources, motivation, desire, and capability in the community in which the program will be fully vested (Backer, Davis, & Soucy, 1995; Simpson, 2002). According to Backer et al. (1995), the ability to engage communities in capacity building depends on the recognition of current organizational climate factors. How ready and how willing are members of the institution to change their mores (work or otherwise)? Also, how willing are they to subject themselves to the type of scrutiny that accompanies research and implementation of novel training methods? Building capacity really means that schools, communities, and even larger organizations that could potentially benefit from a prevention program are given the proper toolkit to implement, adopt, and evaluate the program on the basis of their own resources and skill set. Today, with hindsight (i.e., wisdom), there is much greater emphasis on implementation science helping prevention researchers avoid any "voltage drop" that occurs because of poor fidelity in the real world (Kilbourne, Neumann, Pincus, Bauer, & Stall, 2007).

SEARCHING FOR SYNTHESIS

The story that unfolded in this handbook also raises several other points that may require scrutiny. As a field invoking the moniker *science*, we still have a difficult time addressing certain very compelling questions. One in particular that really piques my interest is this: When faced with similar life circumstances, what really prompts one youth to become deviant while another succeeds in unimaginable ways? Consider two youths who come from the same poverty-stricken side of town and who both reside in emotionally turbulent homes and experience less-than-optimal forms of parenting. Both youths walk to their middle school, traversing a physically rundown neighborhood lacking community resources and replete with nefarious activity, including drug merchandising. Why does one youth find the road to an Ivy League education, and the other ends up incarcerated in prison? The take-home message from several chapters appearing early in the handbook is that these two individuals may differ in resilience, highlighting the need to further elaborate the basic psychological processes that foster vulnerability.[2]

When push comes to shove, drawing a distinction between the individual and his or her environment is probably unnecessary, however.[3] The truth

[2] Rutter (1990) framed the same concern when he discussed the possible "spin of the roulette wheel of life" (p. 182) that differentiates one individual who maintains high self-esteem when faced by adversity and another who gives up and loses hope despite facing the same adversity. Kaplan (1999) also addressed this very point and presented a cogent argument suggesting a lack of clarity in what is termed *risk*, which can be adversity faced in the environment, and what is considered individual vulnerability. In his thought-provoking literature review, he outlined the difficulties of separating risk from vulnerability and the fuzzy nature of these conceptualizations. For instance, by itself, poor attention skills or novelty seeking may not be a risk factor; however, when coupled with punitive responses from parents, poor school performance, or peer reinforcement of risky decisions, these conditions supply the proper etiologic surface to promote drug use. What is required to advance any of these notions is a theoretically informed and parsimonious definition of vulnerability, one that incorporates causal or temporal order and adequately addresses mechanisms appropriate for intervention. My own view suggests that a systems or transactional view may be the appropriate holistic way to think about the interface of environment and individual that encourages developmental vulnerability (e.g., Lerner, 1982; Lerner & Spanier, 1978; von Bertalanffy, 1968).

[3] Drawing the distinction between the environment and the individual is perhaps moot in the study of prevention science. The difference between relying on environmental interventions versus strategies that influence individual behavior change directly is merely a matter of focus and level of consideration. At the end of the day, whether we measure community-sponsored interdiction efforts through the use of sobriety checks, quantify the influence of identification checks for underage tobacco sales, enforce underage drinking laws, or implement any of the plausible environmental strategies discussed in this handbook, our principal goal is to reduce tobacco, alcohol, or other drug use by minors. The active ingredients or causal agents of change in population-based, environmental strategies involve higher level constructs, including changing school alcohol norms, improving neighborhood antidrug resources, drafting legislation to promote drug-free school zones, and applying health persuasion social marketing strategies through media campaigns, to name a few. The end game for the wide panoply of harm reduction, community intervention, policy-related, and regulatory strategies still remains reducing youth drug use.

is that we should probably set our sights on the confluence of both processes as they merge seamlessly into the individual's sense of reality. I believe that the strength of this handbook is the even-handed treatment of all the different theoretical perspectives, intervention approaches, implementation strategies, and evaluative techniques required to advance prevention science. Indeed, as many of the chapters in the handbook note, no one approach will provide the answers to the vexing questions we ask. Only when we heed the advice given by Price (1986) and cross boundaries, blending our ideology with a cohesive prevention framework, will we approach the science for which we so arduously strive.

A good example of the forged ties that provide the foundation for this discussion involves the use of developmental cascade models to track the life course of resilient children (e.g., Bonds McClain, Wolchik, Winslow, Tein, Sandler, & Milsap, 2010; Burt, Obradovic, Long, & Masten, 2008). The cascade model derives from a long line of empirical research examining developmental outcomes from early resilience (e.g., Masten, Desjardins, McCormick, Kuo, & Long, 2010). This approach to studying resilience contains explicit theoretical statements regarding how different markers of resilience (i.e., competence and conventional behaviors) that have roots in childhood family socialization practices influence a wide range of behavioral and psychosocial outcomes over the life course (Cicchetti, 1993).

Conceivably, we can draw on the strengths of this model to account for how certain age-salient developmental tasks, many of which overlap with research in drug prevention (i.e., social and personal skills) and relate to later features of adult role socialization (e.g., work-related functioning, life and relationship satisfaction). Theoretically speaking, the axiomatic connections underlying cascade models are based on the simple premise that "competence begets competence as the skills formed in one period of development become the tools for achieving success in the future" (Masten et al., 2010, p. 680). This approach is consonant with a probabilistic epigenesis model suggesting that timely resolution of age-salient tasks organizes the individual's life course and stimulates further skill refinement that enhances developmental opportunities (Cicchetti & Rogosch, 1999). Although there are any number of theoretically relevant ways to account for consistent trajectories over the life span, one way to bridge these different approaches is to examine whether favorable intervention effects on competence cascade into or promote positive youth adaptation in other areas of life functioning (e.g., Catalano, Hawkins, Berglund, Pollard, & Arthur, 2002).

Gottlieb's (1991, 1997) model of experiential canalization provides another perspective from which to understand how early developmental experiences carve pathways to later functioning. There are in fact clear parallels between his model of genetic assault and its effects on embryonic development and current drug prevention efforts. Consider that the strict interpretation of canalization suggests that quite diffuse behaviors become more distinct or organized with increasing maturity (i.e., experience). Gottlieb (1991) suggested that "the developing organism's usual or typical experience can play a canalizing role that not only brings about species-specific behavior but also prevents the developing organism from being susceptible to non-species-typical forms of stimulation" (p. 6). His animal model for canalization relied on mallard and wood duckling hatchlings and examined the environmental and genetic contingencies that stimulated the hatchlings to differentiate their mother's call from those of other species, essentially protecting them from the threat of danger.

It should be apparent that youths are not wood duck hatchlings with built-in imprinting systems that involve progressively orienting their heads toward the mother duck's acoustic calls (as opposed to heeding maternal calls from other duck species). Nevertheless, the analogy suggests that early exposure to competence has the same lure, a species-specific behavior reinforced over and over that canalizes youths toward a life of enduring protection. In the context of drug prevention, canalization takes place as a form of progressive selection or experiential channeling in which individuals benefit from exposure to competence-enhancing environments. Channeling has the potential to encourage intervention-exposed youths to adopt new skills and behaviors (i.e., according to a self-efficacy formulation experience, testing these skills will enhance their application through mastery). This may occur through a process of selective optimization (Blair & Raver, 2012)—a winnowing of behaviors that will place them on a uniquely protective developmental trajectory that sustains them through adult role socialization.

PREVENTION AND LIFE COURSE CONTINUITY MODELS

Building from this general framework of canalization, continuity models (e.g., Caspi, Bem, & Elder, 1989; Roberts & Caspi, 2003) would argue that youths track differently after treatment exposure (i.e., they have different experiences than nonintervention youths, which effectively molds their behavior). In a cumulative continuity model, tracking arises because individuals select environments that play to their personality strengths. Tracking takes place in the form of social selection, in which youths pick optimal environments (and people according to interactional continuity models) that reinforce their strengths, which are usually positively valued personality characteristics (i.e., agreeableness or cooperativeness). The cumulative continuity model also suggests that after selection, the environment then perpetuates behavior as a matter of fit. The argument here would suggest that youths benefiting from interventions targeting improved competence would search out more conventional, law-abiding friends, and this selection process protects them from drug use.

Participation in prosocial environments perpetuates competent behaviors, which are richly rewarded through reinforcement (by peers, parents, and school authorities). The type of environments that reinforce cumulative continuity can include small peer-group experiences in which differential association theory, among others, can be used to account for how youths choose friends, deviant or otherwise, and then acquire new behavioral standards and norms that are either pro- or antisocial (e.g., Burgess & Akers, 1966; Sutherland, 1947). The channeling that underlies continuity can take place within larger contexts involving educational environments (higher educational aspirations among competent youths are reinforced by peers and parents), employment (competent youths are rewarded through higher paying jobs), and interpersonal situations (competent youths receive supportive feedback from stable, prosocial interpersonal relations). The channeling effects of an intervention can also flourish through assortative mating, promoting selection of spouses or significant others that reinforces a young adult's competence (e.g., Caspi & Herbener, 1990). In all of these cases, youths are rewarded for the positive features of their behavior, all of which was jump-started, in theory, by exposure to a competence enhancement intervention.

EVIDENCE SUPPORTING CASCADE AND CONTINUITY EFFECTS

Developmental cascade, canalization, and cumulative continuity approaches to development are based on complex theoretical models that explain how behavior unfolds. More than one chapter in this handbook either referenced these different approaches or used them to frame intervention effects. Nonetheless, documenting empirical evidence about any one of these developmental models is difficult and requires a longitudinal design that spans significant portions of the life cycle. To date, only a handful of longitudinal studies have followed youths who participated in drug prevention trials well beyond their initial years of exposure. Naturally, this effort requires longevity on the part of the investigator as well as ample funding to address these pressing questions. Although not representing precise tests of any of the three models discussed, a few studies have illustrated how canalization, continuity, or cascade might work.

Griffin, Botvin, and Nichols (2006) conducted a 10-year follow-up of students participating in a group-randomized, school-based drug prevention program. They reported that intervention youths were at lower risk for sexual behaviors and HIV infection as young adults than control students. Treated youths were exposed to a 3-year, 30-session competence enhancement intervention (Life Skills training) in junior high school targeting a wide range of generic social and personal competence skills (see Chapter 10, this handbook). The program also included normative education and provided students with information about the consequences of drug use. Additional analyses of a high-fidelity sample (using a threshold of 60% or higher exposure to curriculum materials based on classroom observations) indicated the intervention diminished the growth trajectory of alcohol and marijuana use for treated youths compared with untreated controls.

In a different prevention setting, Spoth and colleagues have shown sustained long-term effects from a seven-session family-based intervention (Iowa Strengthening Families Program) that is delivered alone or in combination with Life Skills training. Overall, their findings have shown that youths exposed to the SFP 11-14 family-based drug prevention program report fewer psychological symptoms, less methamphetamine use (Spoth, Clair, Shin, & Redmond, 2006), less high-risk drinking (Spoth, Randall, Shin, & Redmond, 2005), and lower delinquency (Mason, Kosterman, Hawkins, Haggerty, & Spoth, 2003).

As a third example, Hawkins, Kosterman, Catalano, Hill, and Abbott (2008) showed that a cognitive and social skills training program (the Seattle Social Development Project) delivered in an elementary school setting produced a wide range of favorable effects on later young adult functioning. Effects at age 21 involved reductions in several major cost drivers, including mental health, crime, sexual risk behavior, early pregnancy, and favorable effects on educational attainment among treated compared with control youths. Parents also received intervention exposure including either five or seven sessions involving training in child management, academic development support, and skills training to attenuate their child's problem behaviors. The beneficial program effects persisted 3 to 6 years later into young adulthood, including higher educational attainment, significantly fewer symptoms of mental health disorders (using criteria of the *Diagnostic and Statistical Manual of Mental Disorders, Fourth Edition*; American Psychiatric Association, 1994), and lower prevalence of ever having a sexually transmitted disease. Most of these effects were for the group receiving the full intervention delivered across multiple years in elementary school (reinforcing a dose–response relationship).

Overall, these and related studies have reinforced the importance of extending time frames well beyond the critical intervention years to assess the durability of program effects (see Catalano, Hill, Haggerty, Fleming, & Hawkins, 2010, for an excellent discussion of detecting longitudinal effects in randomized trials). They have also provided evidence that programs targeting one or more behaviors in adolescence can channel youths toward a life of positive adaptation, marked by greater law abidance, fewer high-risk behaviors that can be injurious to themselves and significant others (i.e., sexually transmitted disease or driving while under the influence), and more conservative and positive transactions with the environment (i.e., civic mindedness and educational pursuits). Equipped with these types of findings, it is conceivable that the field is ready for a theoretical expansion to account for the multiplicity and durability of favorable program effects and match this enthusiasm with a unified model to account for unintended spillover effects.

A PLACE FOR POSITIVE PSYCHOLOGY

Given the mounting evidence supporting resilience initiatives in youth development, I would be remiss if I failed to consider the emerging role of positive psychology in drug use prevention. Briefly, positive psychology gained traction in the late 1990s when its major proponent, Martin Seligman (1999; Seligman & Csikszentmihalyi, 2000), began to voice concern over psychology's preoccupation with what is wrong with people and its relentless focus on the roots of human pathology. Indeed, a hundred or so years of abnormal psychology had routinely scrutinized the sources of human emotional pain to characterize factors that detract from full and complete living. In his inaugural presidential address to the American Psychological Association, Seligman (1999) encouraged the field (and society) to consider a new paradigm emphasizing psychological strengths and assets, specifically positive emotions that enable people to flourish even in the face of adversity (e.g., Peterson, Park, & Seligman, 2005). Two popular psychology books, *Authentic Happiness: Using the New Positive Psychology to Realize Your Potential for Lasting Fulfillment* (Seligman, 2002) and *Flourish: A Visionary New Understanding of Happiness and Well-Being* (Seligman, 2011), both addressed the fundamental notion of learned helplessness and the pivotal role of optimism in protecting individuals from depression. Much of his own experimental work developing learned helplessness theory helped Seligman formulate a clinically relevant model positing how negative rumination and catastrophic thinking contribute to depression and impede normal functioning (e.g., Abramson, Seligman, & Teasdale, 1978; Maier & Seligman, 1976; Peterson & Seligman, 1984).

Since its inception, positive psychology has gained significant ground as a subdiscipline of psychology (e.g., Linley, Joseph, Harrington, & Wood, 2006; Mills, Fleck, & Kozikowski, 2013), sharing more than several traditions with research on resilience (Masten, 2001). Indeed, considerable evidence has reinforced any number of resilience-based protective influences that help steward children and youths away from the vicissitudes of life and prepare them to persevere even in the face of adversity (Rutter, 1999, 2000). It is this concerted emphasis on protection and compensatory resources that have finally found credence and support in the educational system (Park & Peterson, 2009). Studies have shown the benefits of mindfulness curricula (e.g., Broderick & Metz, 2009; Huppert & Johnson, 2010) and coursework focusing on resilience and character strengths training that improve student outcomes (e.g., Clonan, Chafoulea, McDougal, & Riley-Tillman, 2004; Seligman, Ernst, Gillham, Reivich, & Linkin, 2009). Relevant positive psychology resilience training efforts have successfully used school counseling outlets (Park & Peterson, 2008) and primary care settings (Gillham, Hamilton, Freres, Patton, & Gallop, 2006) to improve student outcomes. All of this training bears on the importance of providing youths with psychological capital to offset stress.

Seligman's (2011) emphasis on teaching youths learned optimism suggests that the focus of schooling should involve attention to positive emotions, engagement, relationships, meaning, and accomplishment as a means of establishing well-being (Gillham et al., 2011). Resilience training, or what Seligman termed *psychological immunization*, will instill youths with optimism (hope), meaning (satisfaction), and a sense of well-being (mastery) that presents a natural cognitive barrier to negative rumination and catastrophic thinking (e.g., "I am always failing, it is my fault, this is part of me, and it will be the same for everything I do"). The internal, stable, and pervasive features of negative and pessimistic thinking (what Seligman called *explanatory style*) are what foster depression and other mental health problems.

The extension here is that youths trapped by negative explanatory style (what was traditionally but erroneously termed *low self-esteem*) feel hopeless, and it is this despair that underscores their pessimistic *Weltanschauung*. Chronically despairing youths make awkward if not difficult friendships, leading to social marginalization. Parker and Asher's (1987, 1993) classic studies provide an early glimpse of the deficits that accompany peer rejection. Such an early assault on so important a human endeavor as social relations must cast a pall on emotional development. As youths transition through adolescence, drugs serve two functions in resolving this predicament. On the one hand, they can reduce central nervous system activity and help youths relax and feel better. This is a shortcut to positive emotions that has no productive end. Added to this, in their darkest hour, many youths find that social lubricants such as alcohol provide therapeutic value because they chip away at mental barriers that inhibit self-actualization. Lonely, pessimistic, brooding individuals who possess a negative view of life find solace in drinking or getting high as a form of mental retreat. This is the basis of disconnect that drives youths away from conventional institutions (school, family, church, and community), the lifeline that keeps them tethered to a productive and fulfilling life.

Knowing this, building strengths and assets, teaching resilience, and creating opportunities to live a full life represent a worthy institutional goal not only for psychologists but also for society as a whole (Peterson, Ruch, Beerman, Park, & Seligman, 2007). As the favorable evidence mounts for programs such as the Penn Resiliency Program (Brunwasser, Gillham, & Kim, 2009), greater attention will be paid to activities that emphasize increasing optimism and reducing hopelessness, two integral components of adolescent drug use (e.g., Galaif, Sussman, Newcomb, & Locke, 2007; Harlow, Newcomb, & Bentler, 1986; Minehan, Newcomb, & Galaif, 2000). These efforts are in addition to the usual emphasis on providing assertiveness, self-control, social, and decision-making skills that we encounter in current drug prevention. As Seligman first pointed out in his 1999 APA presidential address, there needs to be a culture change for this transition to occur, and slowly but surely as the evidence rolls in, the groundswell will begin to give a new face to prevention.

A CLARION CALL

If anything, this handbook relays a very important story about the inner workings of prevention science. It is told through a lifelong journey that has involved both success and failure. Perhaps amid all of these very important and hard-fought lessons is a surge of activity that will affect the next generation of prevention scientists. Their mission, if you will, is to absorb the history behind the contents of this handbook and then look for ways to improve on our efforts. True, any number of unsolved problems await future generations of prevention scientists. Commenting on this very subject, Kubie (1953) wrote,

> I suppose that it is not inaccurate to say that of the many unsolved problems of human life two which are of major importance are how to enable successive generations to learn from the mistakes of their predecessors without repeating them, and how to make it possible for young people to anticipate the future realistically. (p. 599)

Not only do we wish the next generation of prevention scientists much success, but we also hope that the capable individuals who choose to advance this cause represent our work in a way that showcases the strengths of our field. Admittedly, this is a herculean task, which is why Price (1986) had his finger on the pulse of things when he suggested an integrated holistic framework for educating prevention scientists. The education of the next generation of prevention scientists should be our prime focus as we confront the new challenges that will accompany us into the future.

References

Abramson, L. Y., Seligman, M. E. P., & Teasdale, I. (1978). Learned helplessness in humans: Critique and reformulation. *Journal of Abnormal Psychology, 87*, 49–74. doi:10.1037/0021-843X.87.1.49

American Psychiatric Association. (1994). *Diagnostic and statistical manual of mental disorders* (4th ed.). Arlington, VA: Author.

Arthur, M. W., & Blitz, C. (2000). Bridging the gap between science and practice in drug abuse prevention through needs assessment and strategic community planning. *Journal of Community Psychology, 28*, 241–255. doi:10.1002/(SICI)1520-6629(200005)28:3<241::AID-JCOP2>3.0.CO;2-X

Backer, T. E., Davis, S. L., & Soucy, G. (1995). The challenge of technology transfer. In T. E. Backer, S. L. Davis, & G. Soucy (Eds.), *Reviewing the behavioral science knowledge base on technology transfer* (NIDA Research Monograph 155, NIH Publication No. 95-4035, pp. 1–19). Rockville, MD: National Institute on Drug Abuse.

Barrera, M., & Castro, F. G. (2006). A heuristic framework for the cultural adaptation of interventions. *Clinical Psychology: Science and Practice, 13*, 311–316. doi:10.1111/j.1468-2850.2006.00043.x

Barrera, M., Castro, F. G., & Holleran Steiker, L. K. (2011). A critical analysis of approaches to the development of preventive interventions for subcultural groups. *American Journal of Community Psychology, 48*, 439–454. doi:10.1007/s10464-010-9422-x

Bentler, P. M., & Speckart, G. (1979). Models of attitude-behavior relations. *Psychological Review, 86*, 452–464. doi:10.1037/0033-295X.86.5.452

Biglan, A., & Fishbein, D. H. (2011). Implications for translational prevention research: Science, policy, and advocacy. In M. T. Bardo, D. H. Fishbein, & R. S. Milich (Eds.), *Inhibitory control and drug abuse prevention: From research to translation* (pp. 305–316). New York, NY: Springer. doi:10.1007/978-1-4419-1268-8_16

Blair, C., & Raver, C. C. (2012). Child development in the context of adversity: Experiential canalization of brain and behavior. *American Psychologist, 67*, 309–318. doi:10.1037/a0027493

Bonds McClain, D., Wolchik, S. A., Winslow, E., Tein, J.-Y., Sandler, I. N., & Milsap, R. E. (2010). Developmental cascade effects of the New Beginnings Program on adolescent adaptation outcomes. *Development and Psychopathology, 22*, 771–784. doi:10.1017/S0954579410000453

Broderick, P., & Metz, S. (2009). Learning to BREATHE: A pilot trial of a mindfulness curriculum for adolescents. *Advances in School Mental Health Promotion, 2*, 35–46. doi:10.1080/1754730X.2009.9715696

Brunwasser, S. M., Gillham, J. E., & Kim, E. S. (2009). A meta-analytic review of the Penn Resiliency Program's effect on depressive symptoms. *Journal of Consulting and Clinical Psychology, 77*, 1042–1054. doi:10.1037/a0017671

Burgess, R. L., & Akers, R. L. (1966). A differential association-reinforcement theory of criminal behavior. *Social Problems, 14*, 128–147. doi:10.2307/798612

Burt, K. B., Obradovic, J., Long, J. D., & Masten, A. S. (2008). The interplay of social competence and psychopathology over 20 years: Testing transactional and cascade models. *Child Development, 79*, 359–374. doi:10.1111/j.1467-8624.2007.01130.x

Caspi, A., Bem, D. J., & Elder, G. H. (1989). Continuities and consequences of interactional styles across the life span. *Journal of Personality, 57*, 375–406. doi:10.1111/j.1467-6494.1989.tb00487.x

Caspi, A., & Herbener, E. S. (1990). Continuity and change: Assortative marriage and the consistency of personality in adulthood. *Journal of Personality and Social Psychology, 58*, 250–258.

Castro, F. G., Barrera, M., & Martinez, C. R. (2004). The cultural adaptation of prevention interventions: Resolving tensions between fidelity and fit. *Prevention Science, 5*, 41–45. doi:10.1023/B:PREV.0000013980.12412.cd

Catalano, R. F., Hawkins, J. D., Berglund, L., Pollard, J. A., & Arthur, M. (2002). Prevention science and positive youth development: Competitive or cooperative frameworks? *Journal of Adolescent Health, 31*, 230–239. doi:10.1016/S1054-139X(02)00496-2

Catalano, R. F., Hill, K. G., Haggerty, K. P., Fleming, C. B., & Hawkins, J. D. (2010). Social development interventions have extensive, long-lasting effects. In A. E. Fortune, P. McCallion, & K. Briar-Lawson (Eds.), *Social work practice research for the 21st century* (pp. 72–80). New York, NY: Columbia University Press.

Chaskin, R. J. (2001). Building community capacity: A definitional framework and case studies from a comprehensive community initiative. *Urban Affairs Review, 36*, 291–323. doi:10.1177/10780870122184876

Cicchetti, D. (1993). Developmental psychopathology: Reactions, reflections, projections. *Developmental Review, 13*, 471–502. doi:10.1006/drev.1993.1021

Cicchetti, D., & Rogosch, F. A. (1999). Psychopathology as risk for adolescent substance use disorders: A developmental psychopathology perspective. *Journal of Clinical Child Psychology, 28*, 355–365. doi:10.1207/S15374424jccp280308

Clonan, S., Chafoulea, S., McDougal, J., & Riley-Tillman, T. (2004). Positive psychology goes to school: Are we there yet? *Psychology in the Schools, 41*, 101–110. doi:10.1002/pits.10142

Collins, L. M., Murphy, S. A., & Bierman, K. L. (2004). A conceptual framework for adaptive preventive interventions. *Prevention Science, 5*, 185–196. doi:10.1023/B:PREV.0000037641.26017.00

Conduct Problems Prevention Research Group. (2000). Merging universal and indicated prevention programs: The Fast Track model. *Addictive Behaviors, 25*, 913–927. doi:10.1016/S0306-4603(00)00120-9

Cowen, E. L. (1980). The wooing of primary prevention. *American Journal of Community Psychology, 8*, 258–284.

Eddy, J. M., Smith, P., Brown, C. H., & Reid, J. B. (2005). A survey of prevention science training: Implications for educating the next generation. *Prevention Science, 6*, 59–71. doi:10.1007/s11121-005-1253-x

Embry, D. D., & Biglan, A. (2008). Evidence-based kernels: Fundamental units of behavioral influence. *Clinical Child and Family Psychology Review, 11*, 75–113. doi:10.1007/s10567-008-0036-x

Feinberg, M. E., Chilenski, S. M., Greenberg, M. T., Spoth, R. L., & Redmond, C. (2007). Community and team member factors that influence the operations phase of local prevention teams: The PROSPER Project. *Prevention Science, 8*, 214–226. doi:10.1007/s11121-007-0069-2

Galaif, E. R., Sussman, S., Newcomb, M. D., & Locke, T. F. (2007). Suicidality, depression, and alcohol use among adolescents: A review of empirical findings. *International Journal of Adolescent Medicine and Health, 19*, 27–35.

Gillham, J. E., Adams-Deutsch, Z., Werner, J., Reivich, K., Coulter-Heindl, V., Linkins, M., . . . Seligman, M. E. P. (2011). Character strengths predict subjective well-being during adolescence. *Journal of Positive Psychology, 6*, 31–44. doi:10.1080/17439760.2010.536773

Gillham, J. E., Hamilton, J., Freres, D. R., Patton, K., & Gallop, R. (2006). Preventing depression among early adolescents in the primary care setting: A randomized controlled study of the Penn Resiliency Program. *Journal of Abnormal Child Psychology, 34*, 195–211. doi:10.1007/s10802-005-9014-7

Gottlieb, G. (1991). Experiential canalization of behavioral development: Theory. *Developmental Psychology, 27*, 4–13. doi:10.1037/0012-1649.27.1.4

Gottlieb, G. (1997). *Synthesizing nature-nurture: Prenatal roots of instinctive behavior.* Mahwah, NJ: Erlbaum.

Griffin, K. W., Botvin, G. J., & Nichols, T. R. (2006). Effects of a school-based drug abuse prevention program for adolescents on HIV risk behavior in young adulthood. *Prevention Science, 7*, 103–112. doi:10.1007/s11121-006-0025-6

Hallfors, D. D., Pankratz, M., & Hartman, S. (2007). Does federal policy support the use of scientific evidence in school-based prevention programs? *Prevention Science, 8*, 75–81. doi:10.1007/s11121-006-0058-x

Harlow, L. L., Newcomb, M. D., & Bentler, P. M. (1986). Depression, self-derogation, substance use, and suicide ideation: Lack of purpose in life as a mediational factor. *Journal of Clinical Psychology, 42*, 5–21. doi:10.1002/1097-4679(198601)42:1<5::AID-JCLP2270420102>3.0.CO;2-9

Hawkins, J. D., Kosterman, R., Catalano, R. F., Hill, K. G., & Abbott, R. D. (2008). Effects of social development intervention in childhood fifteen years later. *Archives of Pediatrics & Adolescent Medicine, 162*, 1133–1141. doi:10.1001/archpedi.162.12.1133

Huppert, F., & Johnson, D. (2010). A controlled trial of mindfulness training in schools: The importance of practice for an impact on well-being. *Journal of Positive Psychology, 5*, 264–274. doi:10.1080/17439761003794148

Johnson, K., Hays, C., Center, H., & Daley, C. (2004). Building capacity and sustainable prevention innovations: A sustainability planning model. *Evaluation and Program Planning, 27*, 135–149. doi:10.1016/j.evalprogplan.2004.01.002

Kaplan, H. B. (1999). Toward an understanding of resilience: A critical review of definitions and models. In M. D. Glantz & J. L. Johnson (Eds.), *Resilience and development: Positive life adaptations* (pp. 17–83). New York, NY: Kluwer Academic.

Kellam, S. G., Koretz, D., & Mościcki, E. K. (1999). Core elements of developmental epidemiologically based prevention research. *American Journal of Community Psychology, 27*, 463–482. doi:10.1023/A:1022129127298

Kilbourne, A. M., Neumann, M. S., Pincus, H. A., Bauer, M. S., & Stall, R. (2007). Implementing evidence-based interventions in health care: Application of the replicating effective programs framework. *Implementation Science, 2*. doi:10.1186/1748-5908-2-42

Kubie, L. S. (1953). Some unsolved problems of the scientific career. *American Scientist, 41*, 596–613.

Kuhn, T. S. (1970). *The structure of scientific revolutions*. Chicago, IL: University of Chicago Press.

Kulis, S., Marsiglia, F. F., Elek, E., Dustman, P., Wagstaff, D. A., & Hecht, M. L. (2005). Mexican/Mexican American adolescents and keepin' it REAL: An evidence-based substance use prevention program. *Children & Schools, 27*, 133–145. doi:10.1093/cs/27.3.133

Lanza, S. T., & Rhoades, B. L. (2013). Latent class analysis: An alternative perspective on subgroups analysis in prevention and treatment. *Prevention Science, 14*, 157–168. doi:10.1007/s11121-011-0201-1

Lerner, R. M. (1982). Children and adolescents as producers of their own development. *Developmental Review, 2*, 342–370. doi:10.1016/0273-2297(82)90018-1

Lerner, R. M., & Spanier, G. B. (1978). A dynamic interactional view of child and family development. In R. M. Lerner & G. B. Spanier (Eds.), *Child influences on marital and family interaction: A life-span perspective* (pp. 1–22). San Francisco, CA: Academic Press. doi:10.1016/B978-0-12-444450-8.50007-9

Lich, K. H., Ginexi, E. M., Osgood, N. D., & Mabry, P. L. (2013). A call to address complexity in prevention science research. *Prevention Science, 14*, 279–289. doi:10.1007/s11121-012-0285-2

Linley, P. A., Joseph, S., Harrington, S., & Wood, A. M. (2006). Positive psychology: Past, present, and (possible) future. *Journal of Positive Psychology, 1*, 3–16. doi:10.1080/17439760500372796

Lipsey, M. W., & Cordray, D. S. (2000). Evaluation methods for social intervention. *Annual Review of Psychology, 51*, 345–375. doi:10.1146/annurev.psych.51.1.345

MacKinnon, D. P., Lockwood, C. M., Hoffman, J. M., West, S. G., & Sheets, V. (2002). A comparison of methods to test mediation and other intervening variable effects. *Psychological Methods, 7*, 83–104. doi:10.1037/1082-989X.7.1.83

Maier, S. F., & Seligman, M. E. P. (1976). Learned helplessness: Theory and evidence. *Journal of Experimental Psychology: General, 105*, 3–46. doi:10.1037/0096-3445.105.1.3

Marek, L. I., Brock, D.-J. P., & Sullivan, R. (2006). Cultural adaptations to a family life skills program: Implementation in rural Appalachia. *Journal of Primary Prevention, 27*, 113–133. doi:10.1007/s10935-005-0017-5

Mark, M. M. (2003). Program evaluation. In J. A. Schinka & W. F. Velicer (Eds.), *Handbook of psychology: Vol. 2. Research methods in psychology* (pp. 323–347). Hoboken, NJ: Wiley.

Mason, W. A., Kosterman, R., Hawkins, J. D., Haggerty, K. P., & Spoth, R. L. (2003). Reducing adolescents' growth in substance use and delinquency: Randomized trial effects of a parent-training prevention intervention. *Prevention Science, 4*, 203–212. doi:10.1023/A:1024653923780

Masten, A. S. (2001). Ordinary magic: Resilience processes in development. *American Psychologist, 56*, 227–238. doi:10.1037/0003-066X.56.3.227

Masten, A. S., Desjardins, C. D., McCormick, C. M., Kuo, S. I.-C., & Long, J. D. (2010). The significance of childhood competence and problems for adult success in work: A developmental cascade analysis. *Development and Psychopathology, 22*, 679–694. doi:10.1017/S0954579410000362

Mills, M. J., Fleck, C. R., & Kozikowski, A. (2013). Positive psychology at work: A conceptual review, state-of-practice assessment, and a look ahead. *Journal of Positive Psychology, 8*, 153–164. doi:10.1080/17439760.2013.776622

Minehan, J. A., Newcomb, M. D., & Galaif, E. R. (2000). Predictors of adolescent drug use: Cognitive abilities, coping strategies, and purpose in life. *Journal of Child & Adolescent Substance Abuse, 10*, 33–52. doi:10.1300/J029v10n02_04

Park, N., & Peterson, C. (2008). Positive psychology and character strengths: Application to strengths-based school counseling. *Professional School Counseling, 12*, 85–92. doi:10.5330/PSC.n.2010-12.85

Park, N., & Peterson, C. (2009). Strengths of character in school. In R. Gilman, E. S. Huebner, & M. J. Furlong (Eds.), *Handbook of positive psychology in schools* (pp. 77–88). New York, NY: Routledge.

Parker, J. G., & Asher, S. R. (1987). Peer relations and later personal adjustment: Are low accepted children at risk? *Psychological Bulletin, 102*, 357–389. doi:10.1037/0033-2909.102.3.357

Parker, J. G., & Asher, S. R. (1993). Friendship and friendship quality in middle childhood: Links with peer group acceptance and feelings of loneliness and social dissatisfaction. *Developmental Psychology, 29*, 611–621. doi:10.1037/0012-1649.29.4.611

Pentz, M. A. (2000). Institutionalizing community-based prevention through policy change. *Journal of Community Psychology, 28*, 257–270. doi:10.1002/(SICI)1520-6629(200005)28:3<257::AID-JCOP3>3.0.CO;2-L

Peterson, C., Park, N., & Seligman, M. E. P. (2005). Orientations to happiness and life satisfaction: The full life versus the empty life. *Journal of Happiness Studies, 6*, 25–41.

Peterson, C., Ruch, W., Beerman, U., Park, N., & Seligman, M. E. P. (2007). Strengths of character, orientations to happiness, and life satisfaction. *Journal of Positive Psychology, 2*, 149–156. doi:10.1080/17439760701228938

Peterson, C., & Seligman, M. E. P. (1984). Causal explanation as a risk factor for depression: Theory and evidence. *Psychological Review, 91*, 347–374. doi:10.1037/0033-295X.91.3.347

Popper, K. R. (1963). *Conjectures and refutations: The growth of scientific knowledge*. London, England: Routledge & Kegan Paul.

Price, R. H. (1983). The education of a prevention psychologist. In R. D. Felner, L. Jason, J. Moritsugu, & S. S. Farber (Eds.), *Preventive psychology: Theory, research and practice in community intervention* (pp. 290–296). Elmsford, NY: Pergamon Press.

Price, R. H. (1986). Education for prevention. In M. Kessler & S. E. Goldston (Eds.), *A decade of progress in primary prevention* (pp. 288–306). Lebanon, NH: New England Universities Press.

Price, R. H., Cowen, E. L., Lorion, R. P., & Ramos-McKay, J. (1989). The search for effective prevention programs: What we learned along the way. *American Journal of Orthopsychiatry, 59*, 49–58. doi:10.1111/j.1939-0025.1989.tb01634.x

Roberts, B. W., & Caspi, A. (2003). The cumulative continuity model of personality development: Striking a balance between continuity and change in personality traits across the life course. In U. M. Staudinger & U. Lindenberger (Eds.), *Understanding human development: Dialogues with lifespan psychology* (pp. 183–214). Norwell, MA: Kluwer Academic. doi:10.1007/978-1-4615-0357-6_9

Rowe, D. C., Vazsonyi, A. T., & Flannery, D. J. (1994). No more than skin deep: Ethnic and racial similarity in developmental process. *Psychological Review, 101*, 396–413. doi:10.1037/0033-295X.101.3.396

Rutter, M. (1990). Psychosocial resilience and protective mechanisms. In J. Rolf, A. S. Masten, D. Cicchetti, K. H. Nuechterlein, & S. Weintraub (Eds.), *Risk and protective factors in the development of psychopathology* (pp. 181–214). New York, NY: Cambridge University Press.

Rutter, M. (2000). Resilience reconsidered: Conceptual considerations, empirical findings, and policy implications. In J. P. Shonkoff & S. J. Meisels (Eds.), *Handbook of early childhood intervention* (2nd ed., pp. 651–682). New York, NY: Cambridge University Press. doi:10.1017/CBO9780511529320.030

Rutter, M. L. (1999). Psychosocial adversity and child psychopathology. *British Journal of Psychiatry, 174*, 480–493. doi:10.1192/bjp.174.6.480

Seligman, M. E. P. (1999). The president's address. *American Psychologist, 54*, 559–562.

Seligman, M. E. P. (2002). *Authentic happiness: Using the new positive psychology to realize your potential for lasting fulfillment*. New York, NY: Free Press.

Seligman, M. E. P. (2011). *Flourish: A visionary new understanding of happiness and well-being*. New York, NY: Free Press.

Seligman, M. E. P., & Csikszentmihalyi, M. (2000). Positive psychology: An introduction. *American Psychologist, 55*, 5–14. doi:10.1037/0003-066X.55.1.5

Seligman, M. E. P., Ernst, R., Gillham, J., Reivich, K., & Linkin, M. (2009). Positive education: Positive psychology and classroom interventions. *Oxford Review of Education, 35*, 293–311. doi:10.1080/03054980902934563

Simpson, D. D. (2002). A conceptual framework for transferring research to practice. *Journal of Substance Abuse Treatment, 22*, 171–182. doi:10.1016/S0740-5472(02)00231-3

Spoth, R., Greenberg, M., Bierman, K., & Redmond, C. (2004). PROSPER community-university partnership model for public education systems: Capacity-building for evidence-based, competence-building prevention. *Prevention Science, 5*, 31–39. doi:10.1023/B:PREV.0000013979.52796.8b

Spoth, R., Randall, G. K., Shin, C., & Redmond, C. (2005). Randomized study of combined universal family and school prevention interventions: Patterns of long-term effects on initiation, regular use, and weekly drunkenness. *Psychology of Addictive Behaviors, 19*, 372–381. doi:10.1037/0893-164X.19.4.372

Spoth, R. L., Clair, S., Shin, C., & Redmond, C. (2006). Long-term effects of universal preventive interventions on methamphetamine use among adolescents. *Archives of Pediatrics & Adolescent Medicine, 160*, 876–882. doi:10.1001/archpedi.160.9.876

Sutherland, E. H. (1947). *Principles of criminology* (4th ed.). Philadelphia, PA: J. B. Lippincott.

Swisher, J. D. (2000). Sustainability of prevention. *Addictive Behaviors, 25*, 965–973. doi:10.1016/S0306-4603(00)00124-6

von Bertalanffy, K. L. (1968). *General system theory: Foundations, development, applications* (Rev. ed.). New York, NY: Braziller.

Index

Page numbers followed by f *and* t *refer to figures and tables, respectively.*

About the Editor

Lawrence M. Scheier, PhD, is senior fellow at the Positive Psychology Center, University of Pennsylvania. He is also Chief of Science, Research Facilitation Team, Army Analytics Group, Office of the Deputy Under Secretary of the Army. Dr. Scheier is author of more than 100 articles and essays looking at studies of youth development, resilience, and factors that spur positive youth adaptation. He has also edited four books on grant writing, parenting, drug etiology, and drug prevention. His current research program emphasizes the role of psychological strengths and assets in health outcomes and health care utilization among U.S. Army soldiers. Dr. Scheier is a nationally and internationally renowned scholar who blends theory and methodological tools with longitudinal data mining to examine psychosocial factors that influence growth and change in normal development. He has also examined programmatic-based change with many different school- and community-based drug prevention approaches. His work has been funded by the National Institutes of Health, and he has engaged the private business sector in research on youth development and health. Dr. Scheier has been a member of several national government panels, including the Media Campaign Advisory Team for the National Youth Anti-Drug Media Campaign and assisted the U.S. Department of Education in a large-scale program evaluation of school-based mandatory school drug testing. He has provided expert consulting to the federal government on matters related to youth drug treatment and school-based drug prevention programs.